PRAYER TIME

A Guide For Personal Worship

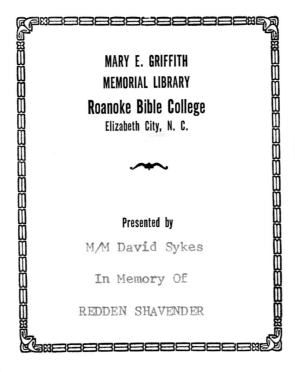
College Press Publishing Company, Joplin, Missouri

INTERCESSION FOR THE LOST WORLD is reprinted with
permission from OPERATION WORLD by Patrick Johnstone,
published by Send The Light, P.O. Box 28, Waynesboro,
Georgia 30830.

Library of Congress Catalog Card Number: 81-82986
International Standard Book Number: 0-89900-146-7

ANSWERING THE NEED FOR PERSONAL WORSHIP

In the Sermon on the Mount our Lord did not ask us to pray. He *assumed we would.*

He said: "When you pray" (not *if* you pray). He then gave us the method. "Enter your closet — or inner chamber — or secret place — or quiet place, and close the door!" We close all else out and are closed in with Him.

The question of our Lord to His disciples probes our conscience: "Could you not watch with me one hour?" In the closet of prayer we can answer with a confident "Yes, Lord." But how shall we do it?

For some long time we struggled with attempts to establish our personal worship. On some days we were successful, on others we were a miserable failure.

After much searching and trying we came upon an arrangement we have found to be a joy in developing our time of devotion.

We know it can help you!

Don De Welt

The key that opens the closet of prayer is to divide the time into twelve segments. Each segment could be five minutes each and your time would be an hour of worship. You could spend 2½ minutes per segment and have 30 minutes of worship. Simply read what we have written for 15 minutes of worship.

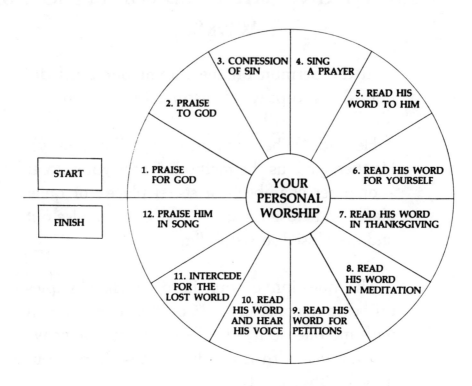

1. **Praise for God.** You just adore God for Himself.

2. **Praise to God** for all He has done and is doing for you. We give you 365 qualities of God to help you here. We show you by example what to say. We leave an area open for your own expression of praise.

3. **Confession of Sin,** first, as it relates to the quality of God you have just considered — and then for your personal sins. We again help you by example.

4. **Sing a prayer.** We suggest a prayer song you can sing as your prayer.

5. **Read His word to Him.** This is a form of praise — thanksgiving or confession as you tell God what His word means to you.

6. **Read His word for yourself** to find personal manna for strength for the day. We offer an example to help you.

7. **Read His word in thanksgiving.** Find as many reasons in the text for thanking Him as you can. Once again we show you by example.

8. **Read His word in meditation.** In our book we will show you how.

9. **Read the word for daily petitions.** Each passage of scripture opens up areas for your requests. We leave a space for your own personal petitions and answers.

10. **Listen** to His voice from the five previous uses of His word. It is totally remarkable what direction you can get for your life in this period. We demonstrate by example.

11. **Intercession.** Intercession is a ministry of prayer by itself. The larger area of personal intercession is left open for your development. We offer you help in intercession for the lost world. We make extensive use of *Operation World, A Handbook for Intercession.* This is a 272 page book listing the 220 countries of the world with prayer points for each country.

12. **Sing a prayer of praise.** We offer praise songs you can use or you can sing from your own hymn book.

A MORE COMPLETE EXPLANATION OF
THE TWELVE TIMES OF PERSONAL WORSHIP

1. PRAISE GOD FOR WHO HE IS.

We must say real often that if you do not express your praise audibly or write it out you will not do it at all. We must lift our voices or our words up in adoration. We "hallow" his name—his very person—*himself!* We list a quality of God for each day of the year. As an example here are thirty-one attributes of our great God. We shall use these in the first month.

Thirty-one Qualities of God For Which I Praise Him!

1. Love	12. Justice-Judge	22. Sanctifier
2. Power	13. Sovereign	23. Redeemer
3. Wisdom	14. Creator	24. Savior
4. Grace	15. Ruler	25. Forgiver
5. Mercy	16. Complete	26. Cleanser
6. Kindness	17. Spirit	27. Christ-like
7. Patience	18. Joy	28. Owner
8. Presence	19. Intelligence	29. Filler
9. Father	20. Lonesome	30. Satisfying
10. Eternal	21. Shepherd	31. Writer-Author
11. Unchangeable		

2. PRAISE GOD FOR WHAT HE MEANS TO ME!

For all he has done and is doing for you praise him! Please, please, make personal application of the qualities of his nature. *The same quality you related to God himself you now relate to your own life.* We shall show you by example. We will also leave an area open for your own either written or spoken expression of personal praise for what he means to you.

3. CONFESSION OF SIN.

We first ask you to relate your sin to the quality of God you have just considered. If you have just praised God for being total LOVE, how adequately or inadequately have you related to LOVE? Be open and honest with your sin. Audibly name it—label it. We list biblical sins to which we can all relate. We leave an area open for the listing of your needs. Remember: we *must* name our sins —we *must* get them out or they will become rottenness within us. Here are 31 sins God has listed in his word. Consider these in this first month.

1. Lying	17. Fits of rage
2. Stealing	18. Selfish ambition
3. Gossip	19. Dissensions
4. Lewd thoughts	20. Factions
5. Profanity	21. Envy
6. Hatred	22. Drunkenness
7. Anger	23. Orgies
8. Wrath	24. Hardening of heart
9. Railing	25. Continual lust
10. Shameful speaking	26. Deceit
11. Passion	27. Bitterness
12. Covetousness	28. Greed
13. Sexual immorality	29. Foolish talk
14. Idolatry	30. Coarse joking
15. Witchcraft	31. Empty words
16. Jealousy	

Please be as ready to accept God's forgiveness as you are now ready to confess your sin. After confession you are just as if you had never sinned!

4. SING A PRAYER.

This is a beautiful satisfying time of prayer. After a full confession of sin you are ready to express your prayer in the words of the song writer. We offer you one verse and a chorus of a prayer song. If you do not wish to sing audibly, read these meaningful words very slowly. Keep your hymn book with you and open it to the prayer song section. Here are the 31 songs we have used in this month.

1. Sweet Hour of Prayer	17. Jesus, Saviour, Pilot Me
2. Tell It to Jesus	18. There Shall Be Showers of Blessings
3. In the Secret of His Presence	19. Did You Think to Pray?
4. 'Tis the Blessed Hour of Prayer	20. Love Divine
5. What a Friend We Have in Jesus	21. More Holiness Give Me
6. Abide With Me	22. More Love to Thee
7. Break Thou the Bread of Life	23. My Faith Looks Up to Thee
8. Dear Lord and Father of Mankind	24. My Jesus, I Love Thee
9. Draw Me Nearer	25. Near the Cross
10. Guide Me, O Thou Great Jehovah	26. O Jesus, I Have Promised
11. I Am Praying For You	27. O Master Let Me Walk With Thee
12. I Am Coming, Lord	28. Open My Eyes That I May See
13. Stand Up, Stand Up for Jesus	29. Nearer, Still Nearer
14. I Must Tell Jesus	30. Savior, Like a Shepherd Lead Us
15. I Need Thee Every Hour	31. There's a Stranger at the Door
16. Jesus, Lover of My Soul	

5. READ HIS WORD TO HIM!

Is there anything you like to hear more than the appreciation of someone who has been blessed or helped by what you said? Do you think God is any different? This is a wonderful form of praise—confession or thanksgiving. Tell God in detail what every verse means to you. We are reading through the harmony of the four gospels.

6. READ HIS WORD FOR YOURSELF.

You will be reading the same passage of scripture *six* times before we finish our personal worship. This is the second time. Open up your heart—let every word speak to your need. Look into this mirror of God's word to see what you are and what you could be. We present an example for you of our own response to His word—but we want you to express your own heart response to what He says.

7. READ HIS WORD IN THANKSGIVING.

We have found it altogether possible to express seven times of thanksgiving from each daily portion of scripture. Look for the application of his word to your life and express your gratitude to him. This can be, and should be, one of the most meaningful of your expressions of personal prayer. How could we better pray than to say "thank you" seven times to our Lord for the meaning of his word in our lives?

8. READ HIS WORD IN MEDITATION.

Please find one verse and develop the theme or thought of that verse. This should not be difficult to do since you have already prayed about these verses three times. Meditation is a form of careful analysis. In this period you are thinking as deeply as possible God's thoughts after Him. There will be praise—confession—and thanksgiving in your meditation. Use your own words. We offer you examples which are only our meditations each day. We leave an area open for your personal worship in meditation.

9. READ THE WORD FOR YOUR DAILY PETITIONS.

It is amazing how personal the requests are that arise right out of the words of the text. We have given you an example of this practice for each day in this year. We strongly encourage you to make your own list. We want to also leave room for your own requests and God's answers.

10. READ HIS WORD AND WAIT—LISTEN—GOD SPEAKS!

His word is living and active. His word is "spirit and life." Each day God can and will apply his word to your personal needs. There is a particular appropriation he wants to make to your life for this day. I have only listed three of the messages he has given to me for each day. There are many more. Each of them is full of meaning and direction for your life.

11. MAKE INTERCESSION FOR THE LOST WORLD.

We use by permission the book *Operation World—A Handbook for World Intercession* by P. J. Johnstone. We will quote two or three prayer points each day (some days only one). These are prayer suggestions for some country of our world. We shall begin with *The Western World* and then to the more than two hundred countries in *North America, Europe—Eastern Europe, Asia* (Communist) and *Asia* (Free), *Middle East, Africa, Caribbean Area, Latin America, Pacific*. We shall have not less than 600 prayer points for the lost of our world.

12. SING A PRAYER OF PRAISE.

This closes our time of personal worship. Here are thirty-one praise songs, one for each day of this month. Get your hymnal out and sing them in worship to our wonderful Heavenly Father. We print a verse or a chorus to get you started.

1. Blessed Be the Name
2. Christ Is King
3. Crown Him with Many Crowns
4. Face to Face
5. Fairest Lord Jesus
6. Glory to His Name
7. He Is So Precious to Me
8. I Will Sing the Wondrous Story
9. It's Just Like His Great Love
10. Jesus Is All the World to Me
11. Hallelujah! What a Savior
12. I Will Sing of My Redeemer
13. O for a Thousand Tongues
14. Oh, How I Love Jesus
15. Praise Him, Praise Him
16. Revive Us Again
17. The Great Physician
18. The Lily of the Valley
19. The Name of Jesus
20. What a Wonderful Savior
21. Standing on the Promises
22. Golden Harps Are Sounding
23. Blessed Assurance
24. The Church's One Foundation
25. O Worship the King
26. We Gather Together
27. More Love to Thee
28. My Jesus I Love Thee
29. Since I Have Been Redeemed
30. Holy, Holy, Holy
31. All Glory Laud and Honor

We now share with our readers a day-by-day experience—our own expression of personal worship. We have hesitated to do this but we believe the help to others in developing their personal prayer life is more important than our privacy.

Dear Reader:

In the first year of *Prayer Time* we will be praying through the book of Acts and a harmony of all four gospels. We use *Acts in The Pictorial New Testament*; this book is available from College Press Publishing Company, Box 1132, Joplin, Mo. 64801. The present price is $7.95 each, plus postage.

A PERSONAL WORD WITH THE READER

There three thoughts I want to share with you before you begin this book:

1. What you read here was not at first written to be read. I have discovered, out of much painful experience, that if I do not express my prayers audibly or write them out word-for-word I simply fail to be consistent in my personal devotions. After I had been writing my prayers for several months of this past year the idea of this book formed in my mind. If what you read sounds personal and somewhat disconnected it is because it is. *I am doing for myself what I hope you will do for yourself.* Indeed, what you *must do* for yourself. If you do not express yourself audibly or in written form you *will not* sustain your personal worship. I am delighted to tell you that after 21 days you would not miss it for the world.

2. What you are reading here was written under very trying—sometimes almost impossible—circumstances. When some of you read that I am a teacher in Bible College you could have a very unreal image of what is involved in keeping a seven-day-a-week schedule of worship. I travel almost every weekend; so the past year of devotions were written in somebody's home—and sometimes in a motel room in the following places:

1. Griffith, Indiana
2. LaCrosse, Wisconsin
3. Eden, North Carolina
4. Fletcher, Oklahoma
5. Covington, Indiana
6. Wayne, Nebraska
7. Unionville, Missouri
8. St. Louis, Missouri
9. Cincinnati, Ohio
10. Pasco, Washington
11. Fort Wayne, Indiana
12. Bartlesville, Oklahoma
13. Cashion, Oklahoma
14. Eldon, Missouri
15. Meadsville, Pennsylvania
16. Knoxville, Iowa
17. Springfield, Missouri
18. Louisville, Kentucky
19. Charleston, Indiana
20. Rolla, Missouri
21. Wheelersburg, Ohio
22. Peoria, Illinois
23. Morton, Illinois
24. Morristown, Illinois
25. Sterling, Illinois
26. Indianapolis, Indiana
27. Mooresville, Indiana
28. Engelwood, Kansas
29. Johnson City, Tennessee
30. Kansas City, Missouri
31. Jefferson City, Missouri
32. Hutsonville, Indiana
33. Rose Hill, Kansas
34. New Palestine, Indiana
35. Farwell, Michigan
36. Norfolk, Virginia
37. Paradise, California
38. Big Cabin, Oklahoma
39. Chickasha, Oklahoma
40. Joplin, Missouri

I am "a morning person," so all of my prayer time is kept between 4 and 6:30 a.m. I teach a full load at the college and work as editor to College Press Publishing Company. I said all of the above for just *one* reason: *if an old man past 60 years old can do it, you can do it!*

Once again: you must make your own prayer journal.

This example *is not your prayer diary*, it is mine. Make your own—what an incalculable blessing it will be.

It can change your whole life—please, please do it!

3. What you are reading here would never have been written if some few years ago my wife and I had not been introduced to "The World Literature School of Prayer." I am glad to give credit to Dick Eastman of WLC for the concept of dividing the time of prayer into segments. If *The School of Prayer* is sponsored in your area, by all means go to it. You can write to Box 1313, Studio City, California 91604 for more information.

WEEK ONE — SUNDAY

1. PRAISE GOD FOR WHO HE IS.

Love: Could I ever, ever say enough to express my heart to YOU? *Long* is your love: forever and forever — never ending — your love, it endureth. *Overcoming* is your love — nothing can stop your affection — yea, much more. *Victorious* love, not only triumphant, but building trophies of conquest. *Enduring* is your love. Praise your name, which is LOVE!

Express yourself in adoration for this quality of God.
Speak it audibly or write out your praise in your own devotional journal.

2. PRAISE GOD FOR WHAT HE MEANS TO ME.

But your love for *me* is the best — nay, I cannot say the *best* because such is selfish, but oh how I need your love; how I *seek* your love; how I want your love. Yea, I love you. The *fact* of your love is such a comfort to me — such a strength in weakness — such an encouragement in weariness. I love *you* because you loved me — the prior claim to love is yourself!

How do you personally relate to the love of God, and God who is love?
Speak it out or write it out. It is *so important* that you establish *your own* devotional journal.

3. CONFESSION OF SIN

My sin is forever before me — I cannot hide it — I cannot ignore it — I cannot confess it (as I should and want to). I rejoice in my position of justification, but confession is essential to cleansing and I want so much to be *clean!* Bless your name. "O, now I see the cleansing wave, I plunge and O, it cleanseth me!" I freely, fully, confess, admit and renounce my sin and relax in my forgiveness. Any form of lying is a sin. Forgive me!

What personal sins do you want to confess? We *must* speak them to remove them.
Do it! *Now.* There is no one else you have sinned against more than God. Tell him so!

4. SING A PRAYER TO GOD.

Sweet hour of prayer, sweet hour of prayer,
That calls me from a world of care
And bids me, at my Father's throne,
Make all my wants and wishes known!

In seasons of distress and grief,
My soul has often found relief
And oft escaped the temper's snare
By thy return, sweet hour of prayer.

Open your hymn book and sing the rest of the verses — or even sing another prayer song.

5. READ HIS WORD TO HIM!

This is a preface to your own petitions. By reading God's word to him, you not only further glorify him, but you also see what his will is. This will allow you to pray with confidence.

His Word

[16]Then the eleven disciples went to Galilee, to the mountain where Jesus had told them to go. [17]When they saw him, they worshiped him; but some doubted. [18]Then Jesus came to them and said, "All authority in heaven and on earth has been given to me. [19]Therefore go and make disciples of all nations, baptizing them in the name of the Father and of the Son and of the Holy Spirit, [20]and teaching them to obey everything I have commanded you. And surely I will be with you always, to the very end of the age."   *Matthew 28:18-20, NIV.*

Read His Word to Him.

That you would give such a command indicates your personal interest in *every man* in *every nation.* How I praise you for such a concern! You have made provision for *every* man's salvation — none need be lost. Backed with all authority, we stand in wonder and amazement at what now is an historical fact. Oh, dear Savior, we hear you — we fall at your feet with the disciples in worship!

Please express your response to this beautiful text. Put your expression in your own prayer diary.

6. READ HIS WORD FOR YOURSELF.

I want to go and stand amid the eleven in Galilee—Can I see him there? do I doubt? or do I worship? Perhaps my doubt is of myself not of him. How eagerly and gladly do I acknowledge that all authority is his—in the celestial world of the spirit and in the physical world of all nations. Dear God, making disciples is the *one* thing you want me to do. Oh, how I need grace—forgiveness—power—help me!

It is so important that you pause in his presence and either audibly or in written form tell him all his word means to you.

7. READ HIS WORD IN THANKSGIVING.

How can I thank you enough? I *can* baptize them, I *can* teach them. Thank you, wonderful Savior for the privilege of doing this. Thank you for being Father, Son and Holy Spirit. And oh, oh, how I thank you for the promise that you will be with me to the very end of the age.

Give yourself to your own expression of gratitude—write it or speak it!

8. READ HIS WORD IN MEDITATION.

Let us go again to the mountain in Galilee where Jesus has told us to go. We all need an elevated place where we can get things in their proper perspective. What will be our response? The very same as that of Peter and John; James and Andrew; Philip and Thomas; Bartholomew and Matthew; James the son of Alphaeus; Simon the Zealot and Judas the son of James. How is it possible that some could doubt? We are glad Matthew does not tell us what they doubted—perhaps they doubted themselves —we do—I do. Perhaps the word "doubt" means "amazement" or total wonder as if they were in a trance. It was too good to be true—there are times like that for us, for me. But they overcame their doubts and obeyed him and went. In forty years "The gospel . . . was preached in all creation under heaven" (Colossians 1:23; 1:6; Romans 1:8).

Pause—wait—think—then express yourself in thoughtful praise or thanks.

9. READ HIS WORD FOR PETITIONS.

Let him speak to you and tell you what he wants. Pause before him and *ask*! (1) I want you to speak the great commission to me. (2) I want to yield all of me to your absolute authority. (3) I want to obey just like the angels of heaven. (4) Dear Lord, disciple me that I might disciple others. (5) Dear Father, give me someone to baptize—at least one—someone this year. (6) I want to understand the equality of the Godhead. (7) I want you to remind me of your presence today!

Right here add your personal requests—and his answers.

10. READ HIS WORD AND WAIT—LISTEN—GOD SPEAKS!

Pause before his throne of grace—what has he said to you in these few minutes? (1) "My commission is still in force." (2) "I have not lost my authority." (3) "There is no reason to doubt—there is every reason to believe and worship."

11. INTERCESSION FOR THE LOST WORLD

Canada — Population: 23,100,000. Growth 1.3% (nearly half growth through immigration). Two thirds of population within 150 km. of the 7,000 km. U.S. border. Two people per sq. km.

Points for prayer: (1) *Unreached peoples are many.* The many immigrant peoples have tended to settle in communities that retain their customs and languages. Many of these groups must be evangelized—especially the Greeks and Italians in the east, and the Chinese and East Indians in the west. (2) *The French Canadians* are almost entirely Roman Catholic, and there have not been many who have come to a living faith. Persecution of preachers and converts was severe in the past. The last 10 years has seen many new attempts by evangelical groups to witness to them, yet there are now still more than 30,000 French Canadians for every evangelical worker. Pray for the planting of many live churches.

12. SING PRAISES TO OUR LORD.

All praise to Him who reigns above
In majesty supreme,
Who gave His Son for man to die,
That He might man redeem!

Blessed be the name, blessed be the name,
Blessed be the name of the Lord;
Blessed be the name, blessed be the name,
Blessed be the name of the Lord.

WEEK ONE — MONDAY

1. PRAISE GOD FOR WHO HE IS.

Power: It will not be difficult to praise your wonderful self for your stupendous *power* in the physical world. The ten million galaxies testify to your infinite *power*—the smallest flower—and every molecule of matter has an eloquent voice. Pervasive — omnipotent — wonderful — eternal — reoccurring is your power. Bless your total beautiful person.

Express yourself in adoration for this quality of God.
Speak it audibly or write out your praise in your own devotional journal.

2. PRAISE GOD FOR WHAT HE MEANS TO ME.

Power. For *me*! How I need this quality for myself! According to your everlasting power and divinity—according to the power that worketh in me, both to will and to do! Oh, to know your powerful presence in and through and above. *Power* to live as well as do—to be all you want me to be.

How do you personally relate to the power of God, and God who is Power?
Speak it out or write it out. It is *so important* that you establish *your own* devotional journal.

3. CONFESSION OF SIN

How easy it is to lie! Dear God, I am guilty—forgive—cleanse—remove! To misrepresent in any way is a lie! To claim more than is really a fact—to mix desire with truth is a lie. Dear, dear God, wonderful Savior. I claim thy cleansing blood! Oh, to always match words and deeds with reality! "Thou desirest truth in the inwards parts." This is where lying begins—forgive and set a guard on my lips.

What personal sins do you want to confess? We *must* speak them to remove them.
Do it! *Now.* There is no one else you have sinned against more than God. Tell him so!

4. SING A PRAYER TO GOD.

Are you weary, are you heavy-hearted?
Tell it to Jesus, Tell it to Jesus;
Are you grieving over joys departed?
Tell it to Jesus alone.

Tell it to Jesus, tell it to Jesus,
He is a friend that's well known;
You've no other such a friend or brother,
Tell it to Jesus alone.

Open your hymn book and sing the rest of the verses—or even sing another prayer song.

5. READ HIS WORD TO HIM!

His Word

1 In my former book Theophilus, I wrote about all that Jesus began to do and to teach ²until the day he was taken up to heaven, after giving instructions through the Holy Spirit to the apostles he had chosen. ³After his suffering, he showed himself to these men and gave many convincing proofs that he was alive. He appeared to them over a period of forty days and spoke about the kingdom of God. ⁴On one occasion, while he was eating with them, he gave them this command: "Do not leave Jerusalem, but wait for the gift my Father promised, which you have heard me speak about. ⁵For John baptized with water, but in a few days you will be baptized with the Holy Spirit."

⁶So when they met together, they asked him, "Lord, are you at this time going to restore the kingdom to Israel?"

⁷He said to them: "It is not for you to know the times or dates the Father has set by his own authority. ⁸But you will receive power when the Holy Spirit comes on you; and you will be my witnesses in Jerusalem, and in all Judea and Samaria, and to the ends of the earth."

—Acts 1:1-8, NIV

Read His Word to Him.

I want to praise you for making your appearances so convincing—not only to those present, but for all who would come after them. I gladly read the record of Luke—praise you for such a beautiful treatise. I am convinced you are alive—you do live to love me and plead my case with our Father. Dear Savior, speak to me about your rule in the hearts of men. What would it be to eat with One who was alive from the dead? Wonder of wonders!

Please express your response to this beautiful text. Put your expression in your own prayer diary.

6. READ HIS WORD FOR YOURSELF.

I want to read this text all over again. Here are his words to his apostles about their soon-coming baptism in the Holy Spirit — as they waited in Jerusalem. What a wonder must have filled their hearts. I am not greatly surprised at the question of the apostles — perhaps I would have asked it too. Is our Savior saying the Holy Spirit is the motivation for talking about Him? Wasn't it the resurrection that opened their mouths? The Holy Spirit gave them the power of speaking just the words God wanted (our Lord wanted), but his being alive after his suffering gave them (and me) the reason to speak. Dear God, I will witness of my living Lord today.

It is so important that you pause in his presence
and either audibly or in written form tell him all his word means to you.

7. READ HIS WORD IN THANKSGIVING.

Thank you: (1) I can be a "Theophilus" or a lover of God. (2) The gospel of Luke and the book of Acts is written to me today. (3) My Lord is alive and sees and hears *right now*. (4) For the wonderfully convincing proofs of his resurrection. (5) That he so thoughtfully made appearances: at night, in the morning, with 500, with one, in many, many varied circumstances. (6) He ate with them — a ghost does not eat. (7) The patience of my Lord with my ignorance and mistakes as with the disciples.

Give yourself to your own expression of gratitude — write it or speak it!

8. READ HIS WORD IN MEDITATION.

My Lord chose me and you even as he did the twelve. Jesus spent all night in prayer before he chose the twelve. If we were examining their lives and backgrounds we might be tempted to think his prayer did him no more good than some of ours. But we know we are wrong — we are limited — we are faithless (about his prayer and ours). He looked at the whole person — the twelve men were all available. It wasn't their ability — it was their willingness. Dear Lord, I am willing, and I know you will make me more and more willing as I am willing to be willing. When I am thus yielded, you will work through me — and even in spite of me.

Pause — wait — think — then express yourself in thoughtful praise or thanks.

9. READ HIS WORD FOR PETITIONS.

Let him speak to you and tell you what he wants. Pause before him and *ask*! (1) I do want to know everything my Lord did and said. (2) I want to learn all you taught your apostles. (3) I want to accept totally the evidence of your resurrection. (4) Dear God, may your kingdom — your rule, be in me. (5) I want to understand more fully the baptism in the Holy Spirit. (6) I want to be as patient with ignorant misunderstanding people as you were. (7) Dear God, I want to accept your "times and seasons" in my life. (8) I want the power to witness.

Please, please remember these are prayers — speak them — reword them!

10. READ HIS WORD AND WAIT — LISTEN — GOD SPEAKS!

Pause with me before his throne of grace. What has he said to you in the last few minutes? (1) You are "God's lover" (Theophilus) today. (2) You are his chosen one — his "sent one" for today in your world. (3) You can be and should be convinced of his being alive now.

11. INTERCESSION FOR THE LOST WORLD.

Canada — Point for prayer: *Bible preaching groups are growing.* Pray that it may become a mighty voice for God and righteousness in the land — this is much needed in this materialistic society.

12. SING PRAISES TO OUR LORD.

Come, friends sing, of the faith that's so dear to me,
Revealed thro' God's Son, in Galilee;
He brought peace on earth and good will to the sons
   of men,
Go tell it to the world, her King reigns again.
I am so happy in Jesus,
Captivity's Captor is He;

Angels rejoice when a soul's saved,
Some day we like Him shall be,
Sorrow and joy have the same Lord,
Valley of shadows shall sing;
Death has its life, its door opens in heaven eternally,
Christ is King.

WEEK ONE — TUESDAY

1. PRAISE GOD FOR WHO HE IS.

Wisdom: How well does this word describe your very person. Wisdom is the best use of knowledge. You have put things together in every realm of life. How appropriate are all your ways!

Express yourself in adoration for this quality of God.
Speak it audibly or write out your praise in your own devotional journal.

2. PRAISE GOD FOR WHAT HE MEANS TO ME.

You have been so very wise with me in all the years — yea, each day of my life. Whereas I cannot understand all the reasons yet it is a great source of comfort and strength to know you are working it out for my best interests. Praise your wonderful self, you are love — LOVE and total WISDOM — what a combination!

How do you personally relate to the wisdom of God, and God who is Wisdom?
Speak it out or write it out. It is *so important* that you establish *your own* devotional journal.

3. CONFESSION OF SIN

I freely and even gladly confess my need of cleansing. As often as my physical being needs soap and water for refreshment so does my spirit need confession and the blood of my Dear Lord to cleanse my conscience from dead works that I might rejoice in the Living God! I hide nothing — I am ashamed — but I am also forgiven. Praise his name! Rebuilding without repeating is the power of deep forgiveness.

What personal sins do you want to confess? We *must* speak them to remove them.
Do it! *Now.* There is no one else you have sinned against more than God. Tell him so!

4. SING A PRAYER TO GOD.

In the secret of His presence
  how my soul delights to hide!
Oh, how precious are the lessons
  which I learn at Jesus' side!

Earthly cares can never vex me,
  neither trials lay me low;
For when Satan comes to tempt me,
  to the secret place I go, to the secret place I go.

Open your hymn book and sing the rest of the verses — or even sing another prayer song.

5. READ HIS WORD TO HIM!

His Word

⁹After he said this, he was taken up before their very eyes, and a cloud hid him from their sight. ¹⁰They were looking intently up into the sky as he was going, when suddenly two men dressed in white stood beside them. ¹¹"Men of Galilee," they said, "why do you stand here looking into the sky? This same Jesus, who has been taken from you into heaven will come back in the same way you have seen him go into heaven."

— *Acts 1:9-11, NIV*

Read His Word to Him.

Oh, how beautiful to stand with the eleven and watch your son be lifted into the air — to try to feel as they felt and see as they saw. I want to enter into every thought and reaction. To *know right now* there are ministering spirits called angels; right in this room they are helping me. I accept their message to the eleven. He (your son, my Lord) *is* coming back — praise your name!

Please express your response to this beautiful text. Put your expression in your own prayer diary.

6. READ HIS WORD FOR YOURSELF.

Am I looking intently into the sky? I can and should — he will return as he went and I want to be found looking for him! O, Maranatha! "Even so *come* Lord Jesus!" I must be about my Lord's business — but all the while I am asking if perhaps today He will come! Perhaps today! The same Jesus in the same way — what a wonder!

It is so important that you pause in his presence
and either audibly or in written form tell him all his word means to you.

7. READ HIS WORD IN THANKSGIVING.

Delight, delight thyself in the Lord! Indeed I do. To thank him: (1) for being so visible—tangible—real and leaving no doubt that you were here and that you left. (2) A cloud came to add beauty and perspective. (3) The white clothes of the angels—beautiful purity—so attractive and uplifting. (4) They know my name—who I am—where I am —oh, thank you! (5) He will come suddenly—visibly —bodily—to his own. Wonder of thanksgivings.

Give yourself to your own expression of gratitude—write it or speak it!

8. READ HIS WORD IN MEDITATION.

Notice how specific and personal all this account is: (1) "Their *very* eyes"—angels, our Lord and our Father are all interested in our very eyes, very ears and very brain—and very hands and your very feet—and mine. (2) They were looking *intently*—the focus of amazement and total interest—how good to give that same kind of interest to my Lord in prayer and the reading of His word. Dear Lord, help me never, never to lose the focus of amazement! (3) ". . . two men dressed in white stood *beside* them"—not just there—nor in heaven—but close to them —because they needed such close attention and proximity. He is "with me"—"beside me"—*right now*! and "in me"— and beneath me—and above me—and ahead of me—and behind me. I am comforted and secure!

Pause—wait—think—then express yourself in thoughtful praise or thanks.

9. READ HIS WORD FOR PETITIONS.

What requests arise out of this text? Make these as personal as possible. Such as: (1) May I lift my eyes often to heaven in expectation of his return. (2) I want to look at clouds with a new meaning—he will return on them. (3) May I see him with the eyes of my heart even as he is alive and full of power. (4) May I not hinder your angel's ministry to me. (5) Help me to be busy in what you have given me to do for today. (6) I believe the angel's message —help my unbelief. (7) Maranatha—come Lord Jesus!

Right here add your personal requests—and his answers.

10. READ HIS WORD AND WAIT—LISTEN—GOD SPEAKS!

Allow these words to penetrate your deepest consciousness. He says to me through this text: (1) "I am alive and personally interested in you." (2) "Do not wait when I have clearly commanded you." (3) "I could come back today."

11. INTERCESSION FOR THE LOST WORLD

Canada — Point for prayer: *The Eskimos in the Arctic* are mostly Anglicans, but the impact of the worst of Western civilization has greatly harmed their way of life, and a work of preaching the gospel among them is greatly needed.

United States of America — Population: 215,300,000. Growth 0.8% per year. People per sq. km.—23. Points for prayer: (1) *The economic and political stability of the U.S.A. is of vital importance* to the whole world. Pray for the President, Congress and all in authority in these difficult times. Pray that there may be many men in high positions who have moral integrity and Christian principles. (2) *The U.S.A. is a divided and troubled nation.* The impact of television on American life is incalculable and has brought violence into every home—racial hatred and programs of pornography and bloodshed. Violence seems to have become an accepted part of life to many. The nation is divided over civil rights, the gap between the rich and poor, the gap between the young and the old, and there is a revolt against all forms of authority. There are many evil people who desire to exploit these differences for their own ends and delight to help in the destruction of this great nation. Pray that the forces of evil at work may be bound in the name of the Lord Jesus. (3) *The very freedom that made the U.S.A. great* is being used by some to destroy that greatness. In the name of freedom every form of sinful perversion, drug abuse and filth is being more and more condoned. In the name of the freedom of the press the open betrayal of state secrets, and destruction of national security is made a virtue. In the name of freedom of religion the Christian heritage is destroyed. Such freedom only leads to bondage—drugs, immorality and alcohol, and possibly to the enslavement of the whole people under a terrible tyranny. Pray for the true liberty that comes only from the Spirit of God. Pray for revival. Pray that these things may drive the people of God to their knees before Him.

12. SING PRAISES TO OUR LORD.

Crown Him with many crowns,
The Lamb upon His throne;
Hark! how the heav'nly anthem drowns
All music but its own!

Awake, my soul, and sing
Of Him who died for thee;
And hail Him as thy matchless King
Thro' all eternity.

WEEK ONE — WEDNESDAY

1. PRAISE GOD FOR WHO HE IS.

Grace: Oh, wonder of wonders! God is full of un-earned favor! All the earth and the heaven of the heavens is his handiwork — and they owe him all they have and are. He has freely given us all things — this is his very nature and how I praise him that such is true. We do not deserve it but he is love and that love is expressed in giv-ing — all is undeserved — grace upon grace.

Express yourself in adoration for this quality of God.
Speak it audibly or write out your praise in your own devotional journal.

2. PRAISE GOD FOR WHAT HE MEANS TO ME.

Grace to me! for me — in me — of me — oh, the beauty of it all! How I love him. I can surely confess my own un-worthiness. I am the object and example of his nature in eternal goodness undeserved! I want to respond adequately to all he is in this the grandest of his qualities. We are saved by grace — kept by grace and debtors of grace. Bless and worship him forever!

How do you personally relate to the grace of God, and God who is Grace?
Speak it out or write it out. It is *so important* that you establish *your own* devotional journal.

3. CONFESSION OF SIN

Oh, how I need a guard upon my lips. Why, oh, why do I speak when I should be silent? It is because of what is in man — out of my heart comes the words — cleanse my heart — deeply cleanse and purify. "Stealing" — I have not been tempted to take possessions — but taking that which belongs to another of praise or credit — or recognition — Dear Lord, make me pure within!

What personal sins do you want to confess? We *must* speak them to remove them.
Do it! *Now.* There is no one else you have sinned against more than God. Tell him so!

4. SING A PRAYER TO GOD.

'Tis the blessed hour of prayer,
   when our hearts lowly bend,
And we gather to Jesus,
   our Saviour and Friend;
If we come to Him in faith,
His protection to share,

What a balm for the weary!
O how sweet to be there!
Blessed hour of prayer,
Blessed hour of prayer;
What a balm for the weary!
O how sweet to be there!

Open your hymn book and sing the rest of the verses — or even sing another prayer song.

5. READ HIS WORD TO HIM!

His Word

[12]Then they returned to Jerusalem from the hill called the Mount of Olives, a Sabbath day's walk from the city.
— *Acts 1:12, NIV*

[30]Jesus did many other miraculous signs in the presence of his disciples, which are not recorded in this book. [31]But these are written that you may believe that Jesus is the Christ, the Son of God, and that by believing you may have life in his name.
— *John 20:30, 31, NIV*

Read His Word to Him.

Oh, how expectant they were as they returned from Olivet to Jerusalem. Dear God, I want to be just that open to your coming again as I move toward the New Jerusalem. How far is it to the New Jerusalem? Only you know — but I am excited — humbled — full of wonder. Such humble men you used to establish the church — the "called out ones" — of your Son. I take courage that you could and can and will use me.

Please express your response to this beautiful text. Put your expression in your own prayer diary.

WEEK ONE — WEDNESDAY

6. READ HIS WORD FOR YOURSELF.

The marvelous signs Jesus did have convinced me—I am saved. I have nothing but amazement when I read the whole record of the gospel of John. I do believe Jesus is the Christ, the Son of your very self! I claim the new life of heaven he has given me. In the presence of his learners he did all the signs or miracles recorded by John—may I again and again stand with them and behold and wonder and believe and live!

It is so important that you pause in his presence
and either audibly or in written form tell him all his word means to you.

7. READ HIS WORD IN THANKSGIVING.

It would seem I can never thank you enough—I know such is true: (1) I thank you for Jerusalem and all it has meant and does mean through all these centuries to millions of people. (2) That there is yet a little chain of hills one of which is Olivet where our Lord ascended—there is a real physical, geographical place from which he left for your house. (3) It is really not very far at all to the New Jerusalem when we consider time in the light of eternity. (4) There are hundreds of other miracles I can ask John about when I get to see him in heaven.

Give yourself to your own expression of gratitude—write it or speak it!

8. READ HIS WORD IN MEDITATION.

Gather around the family circle and answer five questions. We will only give a brief answer—you read the questions: (1) Our Lord asked them to meet him in Galilee. He has asked us to meet him at his table of remembrance. (2) Teach them—baptize them—teach them again—accept by faith his presence. (3) To be baptized or clothed in the Holy Spirit. (4) He ascended into the sky—what a wonder and amazement—even now he is alive praying for us before God. (5) That we might believe and live eternally in heaven.

Pause—wait—think—then express yourself in thoughtful praise or thanks.

9. READ HIS WORD FOR PETITIONS.

We let these requests arise from the text itself! (1) I want to journey to the new Jerusalem with the apostles' eager anticipation. (2) From where I am today I want to move toward you conscious of your presence. (3) Dear Lord, help me to read again the advertisement of your deity. (4) Help me to be a real learner. (5) Do I appreciate what it means to read a book 2,000 years old? I *want* to. (6) I want to make Jesus king in my home and school. (7) Help me to understand "eternal life."

Please, please remember these are prayers—speak them—reword them!

10. READ HIS WORD AND WAIT—LISTEN—GOD SPEAKS!

Out of these two texts he says to me: (1) "Return to your job with joy and hope!" (2) "Reread the gospel of John." (3) "Believing produces life or death. Which will it be?"

11. INTERCESSION FOR THE LOST WORLD

United States of America — Point for prayer: (1) *Most of the modern missionary sects originated in this land.* The Watchtower, Mormons, Seventh Day Adventists, Christian Scientists, and now Scientology aggressively propagate their errors all over the world. The Mormons have 20,000 short-term missionaries all over the world. There are probably about 7,000,000 adherents of these various groups in the U.S.A. Pray that believers may show the love of Christ to such, and bring them to the salvation offered by the Lord Jesus in His Word.

12. SING PRAISES TO OUR LORD.

Face to face with Christ, my Savior,
Face to face—what will it be?
When with rapture I behold Him,
Jesus Christ who died for me.

Face to face I shall behold Him,
Far beyond the starry sky;
Face to face in all His glory,
I shall see Him by and by!

WEEK ONE — THURSDAY

1. PRAISE GOD FOR WHO HE IS.

Mercy: Mercy is unearned, unmerited personal kindness—how often has such described your dealing with me? 10,000 times 10,000! Mercy is a quality constant—with all the world and all creatures below it will finally be shown that mercy was given in every case. When all the facts are in for proper evaluation, it will be mercy we see and for which we will praise you throughout an endless eternity—not of constraint but gladly.

Express yourself in adoration for this quality of God.
Speak it audibly or write out your praise in your own devotional journal.

2. PRAISE GOD FOR WHAT HE MEANS TO ME.

Mercy for me, to me, how infallibly true this is. I have been so unworthy of your goodness and love to me—I have earned wrath and received mercy—by thy goodness lead me to a change of mind. To not respond in deep joy would be a sad admission of need—but even there wrath would be mixed with mercy. Dear God, how I love you for this quality. How often we do need mercy!

How do you personally relate to the mercy of God, and God who is Mercy?
Speak it out or write it out. It is *so important* that you establish *your own* devotional journal.

3. CONFESSION OF SIN

Gossip: Confession is an attitude as well as an act. In specific, I have a temptation here and sin here. I need forgiveness—and claim it—praise your name for freedom and cleanness. What a wonder and joy through being washed—I can be moved to stop it by a knowledge of how far reaching is the effect of such a sin.

What personal sins do you want to confess? We *must* speak them to remove them.
Do it! *Now.* There is no one else you have sinned against more than God. Tell him so!

4. SING A PRAYER TO GOD.

What a Friend we have in Jesus,
All our sins and griefs to bear!
What a privilege to carry
Ev'rything to God in prayer!

O what peace we often forfeit;
O what needless pain we bear,
All because we do not carry
Ev'rything to God in prayer!

Open your hymn book and sing the rest of the verses—or even sing another prayer song.

5. READ HIS WORD TO HIM!

His Word

[12]Then they returned to Jerusalem from the hill called the Mount of Olives, a Sabbath day's walk from the city. [13]When they arrived, they went upstairs to the room where they were staying.   — *Acts 1:12, 13a, NIV*

Read His Word to Him.

How thoughtful it was for our Lord to appear for forty days after his resurrection. I wish I could have been present in every one of the appearances—and in a sense I can be! I have the clear imperishable record of each appearance. I can look and look at the ascension of my Lord as represented by the artist—and this helps—but only your presence in person in heaven will answer all my questions.

Please express your response to this beautiful text. Put your expression in your own prayer diary.

6. READ HIS WORD FOR YOURSELF.

I wonder what the eleven talked about as they walked through the gate of the city? What is John saying to Peter—James to Andrew? They must have shared again and again the wonder and expectation found in the promise of the soon-coming baptism in the Holy Spirit. Up the familiar stairs into the room—was it the same room of the last supper? Is that John Mark and Mary on the porch? Oh, dear Savior, I love you and want to serve you.

It is so important that you pause in his presence
and either audibly or in written form tell him all his word means to you.

7. READ THE WORD IN THANKSGIVING.

It will be easy to read these two verses with thanksgiving: (1) Thank you dear Lord that you kept your word about your death, resurrection and ascension — every word came to pass even as you said. (2) Thank you for the very humanness of this whole account — wonder — doubt — personal exchange — walking — visiting — and yet in the very presence of deity! (3) For the upper room — so full of memories — the house of Mary, the mother of John Mark — the place of the last supper — the place for prayer.

Give yourself to your own expression of gratitude — write it or speak it!

8. READ HIS WORD IN MEDITATION.

Has the Lord ever appeared to me over a period of forty days; one month and nine or ten days? Why not set an appointment with him every four days during forty days? Review his appearances and write out your expression of worship on each of those days. Let's see what could happen in renewed love and faith. Start on a Lord's day early in the morning — go with the women to the tomb — prepared to anoint his body only to be startled and overjoyed that the tomb is open and empty — there is an angel there! Read Mark 16:9-14; Luke 24:11-31 and John 20:1-11 and 21:4-23 and meet him all over again!

Pause — wait — think — then express yourself in thoughtful praise or thanks.

9. READ HIS WORD FOR PETITIONS.

If my requests come directly from your word and reflect its intent I *know* you will answer. I do want to so ask of you. (1) Help me just for today to walk conscious you are "with me always." (2) Make me aware of my limitations and your provisions. I am so much like the twelve. (3) May I find an "upper room" where I can often go to wait before you. (4) Help me to be like Peter: quick to repent. (5) May I be like John: full of love. (6) I want to be like James: faithful till death. (7) Oh, to be like Andrew and bring someone to Jesus.

Right here add your personal requests — and his answers.

10. READ HIS WORD AND WAIT — LISTEN — GOD SPEAKS!

You are speaking to me now through these verses: (1) "My word is so detailed and accurate you can accept it for just what it says." (2) "You must accept all the limitations of men today as I did with the twelve." (3) "Sometimes waiting is a command."

11. INTERCESSION FOR THE LOST WORLD

United States of America — Points for prayer: (1) *The young people* have immense problems in modern American society. The bitter fruits of humanistic philosophies are now being harvested in the immoral, drug-addicted and rebellious youth of today. Yet in the midst of all this degradation God worked a few years ago in what later became known as the Jesus Revolution. Many thousands were converted across the country. This movement is now largely a thing of the past. Many of these converts went into established churches through the influence of such as Campus Crusade and the Billy Graham Association, others formed their own charismatic house churches. Some sadly sank into grievous doctrinal error. Pray that the present tendency to emphasize experience and feelings may be replaced by a greater willingness to personal discipline and a study of the Word of God. One great result of the Jesus Revolution was the upsurge in missionary interest among young people. (2) *The Blacks* number 24,000,000; many living in the centers of the great cities. The 12 largest cities are more than one half black. They are generally poorer than their white counterparts despite the achievements of the civil rights movement. There yet remains a legacy of bitterness and division. Pray for the healing of the wounds of the past, and a fair society for all sections of the community. Pray for the restoring of the many lifeless Protestant churches among them. Pray that the rising interest in foreign missions may be properly fostered and directed.

12. SING PRAISES TO OUR LORD.

Fairest Lord Jesus! Ruler of all nature!
O Thou of God and man the Son!

Thee will I cherish, Thee will I honor,
Thou, my soul's glory, joy, and crown!

WEEK ONE — FRIDAY

1. PRAISE GOD FOR WHO HE IS.

Kindness: To contemplate yourself as total kindness is such a beautiful thought! Kindness is much like mercy: it is meeting human need wherever you find it. How fully does this describe what you do every day for everyone! Your thoughtful kindness is giving rain — fruitful seasons — the beauty of flowers, birds and insects; the compassion of a mother — the warmth of the sunshine; then when the kindess of God our Savior appeared in the person of your son we all knew the ultimate of thoughtful mercy.

Express yourself in adoration for this quality of God.
Speak it audibly or write out your praise in your own devotional journal.

2. PRAISE GOD FOR WHAT HE MEANS TO ME.

Kindness to me — such a surprise and delight is your kindness. When I deserve justice you offer me kindness. Praise your glorious name — your goodness is to give me opportunity to recognize the source of all those good gifts and so begin to live soberly, righteously and in the presence of yourself. Dear God, I do so respond. May I be as kind to others as you are to me.

How do you personally relate to the kindness of God, and God who is Kindness?
Speak it out or write it out. It is *so important* that you establish *your own* devotional journal.

3. CONFESSION OF SIN

Of all my sins the sin of unkindness is at the same time both the easiest and the most difficult to confess. It is easy to admit I have been thoughtlessly, selfishly unkind — it is more than difficult to tell why. My life has been cast in the midst of those who love me — in the center of an abundance of good things — why, oh why, should I ever be selfish and mean? Forgive me — but open my eyes to a deeper need: to stay humble-minded.

What personal sins do you want to confess? We *must* speak them to remove them.
Do it! *Now.* There is no one else you have sinned against more than God. Tell him so!

4. SING A PRAYER TO GOD.

Abide with me, fast falls the even tide,
The darkness deepens, Lord, with me abide.

When other helpers fail and comforts flee,
Help of the helpless, O abide with me.

Open your hymn book and sing the rest of the verses — or even sing another prayer song.

5. READ HIS WORD TO HIM!

His Word

Those present were Peter, John, James and Andrew; Philip and Thomas, Bartholomew and Matthew; James son of Alphaeus and Simon the Zealot, and Judas son of James. ¹⁴They all joined together constantly in prayer, along with the women and Mary the mother of Jesus, and his brothers.
¹⁵In those days Peter stood up among the believers (a group numbering about a hundred and twenty)
— *Acts 1:13b-15*

Read His Word to Him.

Oh, to look into the faces of these eleven men and to know you were able to use them in spite of all their imperfections (sins). Each of them was precious and important to you. These men gave themselves to prayer, continued steadfastly in prayer — what does this mean? Prayer was such an important part of their life. Dear God, dear God, I want it to be so with me!

Please express your response to this beautiful text. Put your expression in your own personal diary.

6. READ HIS WORD FOR YOURSELF.

In prayer and worship I come to read these words — ignite them, let them burn into my heart. All of these persons were steadfast in prayer, i.e. time after time, i.e. with energy and purpose. May I so pray — I do commit myself to so pray! How much Mary had to pray about! How much our Lord's brothers (whether in the flesh or Spirit) had to pray about! How much I have about which to pray.

It is so important that you pause in his presence
and either audibly or in written form tell him all his word means to you.

7. READ HIS WORD IN THANKSGIVING.

How easy this is to do: (1) For Peter and John—*action* and *thought*; (2) James and Andrew—*judgment* and *evangelism*; (3) Philip and Thomas—*sincerity* and *caution*; (4) Matthew and Bartholomew—*Jewishness* and *the unknown*; (5) James the son of Alphaeus and Simon the Zealot—the *fisherman* and the *patriot*; (6) Judas the son of James—not all men named Judas were Iscariot. Thank you for blessed Mary, our Lord's brothers, thank you for the unnamed one he added.

Give yourself to your own expression of gratitude—write it or speak it!

8. READ HIS WORD IN MEDITATION

Has the Lord ever appeared to me over a period of forty days? One month and nine or ten days? Why not set an appointment with him every four days during the forty days? Review his appearances and write out your expression of worship on each of those days? Let's see what could happen in renewed love and faith. Start on a Lord's day early in the morning—go with the women to the tomb—prepared to anoint his body only to be startled and overjoyed that the tomb is open and empty—there is an angel there! Read Mark 16:9-14; Luke 24:11-31 and John 20:1-11 and 21:4-23 and meet him all over again! Bless His Name!

Pause—wait—think—then express yourself in thoughtful praise or thanks.

9. READ HIS WORD FOR PETITIONS.

How I do *want* to make my requests the fulfillment of your desire for me: (1) Make me as bold as Peter. (2) Make me as deeply repentant as Peter. (3) Give me the holy wonder and love for you that filled the heart of John. (4) James, our Lord's brother (not the James of the text), became a believer who worked—who produced—I want to be like him. (5) Andrew an unselfish, sharing man—oh, to be like him! (6) Philip saw God in Jesus—so may I. (7) All of these men learned from your son—I am his disciple—teach me Lord!

Please, please remember these are prayers—speak them—reword them!

10. READ HIS WORD AND WAIT—LISTEN—GOD SPEAKS!

Just as if he had pronounced the words, I listen from the text—speak Lord, thy servant heareth: (1) "If these men could believe and give their lives—and they did! for what are you waiting?" (2) "Accept gladly the service and work of women—our Lord did!" (3) "Learn all you can from Mary the mother of Jesus."

11. INTERCESSION FOR THE LOST WORLD

United States of America — Points for prayer: (1) *The American Indians* number 900,000 in about 150 different tribes (11 in Alaska), but many of these people (possibly 50%) now live in the cities. Only 42 of their languages are still commonly used. Pray for those living on the reservations—often in great need, and hardened to the Gospel. Pray for outreach to them. Especially needy are the Navajos (137,000), Lakota (20,000), Zuni (6,000), Paiute (5,000), Towa (1,800) and Jemez Pueblo (1,800). (2) *The Jews* (6,500,000) are influential in every part of U.S. life. One third of the Jews of the world live in the States. Witness among them is not easy. Pray for the various societies working among them. Pray for the Jews for Jesus—converted Jews who retain their Jewish links as Christians. They report 7,000 conversions a year.

Austria — Population: 7,500,000. Annual growth 0.1%. People per sq. km.—90. Points for prayer: (1) *Austria is a mission field with only a small evangelical witness.* No more than 20% of the people are estimated to have ever had contact with the Gospel. Many have had dealings with the occult, and the illegitimacy and suicide rates are among the highest in Europe. (2) *Many areas are without a permanent witness.* It is reckoned that there are only about 160 of the 4,000 towns and villages with a group of believers that regularly meets together. There are still about 70 towns of over 5,000 people with no permanent witness. Most of the believers are found in the cities. Pray for the reaping of a great harvest of souls. (3) *The land is nominally Roman Catholic*, but there is a marked drift away from the church in the cities. Nevertheless, people still fear to have too much contact with Bible believers, thinking them to be a sect. Pray that the barriers to the entry of the Gospel into their hearts may be broken down.

12. SING PRAISES TO OUR LORD.

Down at the cross where my Savior died,
Down where for cleansing from sin I cried;
There to my heart was the blood applied;
Glory to His name.

Glory to His name,
Glory to His name;
There to my heart was the blood applied;
Glory to His name.

WEEK ONE — SATURDAY

1. PRAISE GOD FOR WHO HE IS.

Patience or longsuffering. I was in camp yesterday and *my* longsuffering patience was tested as to time and place for devotion. I praise your name I was able to meet with you—not as I wished—but during the day I praised you and indeed, in you I live and move and have my very being. Your patience with me is a wonder to behold. Your longsuffering with all mankind calls forth praise.

Express yourself in adoration for this quality of God.
Speak it audibly or write out your praise in your own devotional journal.

2. PRAISE GOD FOR WHAT HE MEANS TO ME.

Patience for myself and your love to me for all the most poor ways—sinful—selfish ways I have insulted your goodness—indeed—I am saved by your patience. Blessed be your name!

How do you personally relate to the patience of God, and God who is Patience?
Speak it out or write it out. It is *so important* that you establish *your own* devotional journal.

3. CONFESSION OF SIN

To be truly, honestly, deeply *humble* in spirit—"poor in Spirit" is my goal in life. I do want to open up to you in sincere gut-level admission of my need—to be washed—cleansed—made whiter than snow! to be clean from the *inside*. Blessed be your name. I claim your newness.

What personal sins do you want to confess? We *must* speak them to remove them.
Do it! *Now.* There is no one else you have sinned against more than God. Tell him so!

4. SING A PRAYER TO GOD.

Break Thou the bread of life,
Dear Lord, to me,
As Thou didst break the loaves
Beside the sea;

Beyond the sacred page
I seek Thee Lord;
My spirit pants for Thee,
O living Word.

Open your hymn book and sing the rest of the verses—or even sing another prayer song.

5. READ HIS WORD TO HIM!

His Word

[16]and said, "Brothers, the Scripture had to be fulfilled which the Holy Spirit spoke long ago through the mouth of David concerning Judas, who served as guide for those who arrested Jesus—[17]he was one of our number and shared in this ministry." [18](With the reward he got for his wickedness, Judas bought a field; there he fell headlong, his body burst open and all his intestines spilled out. [19]Everyone in Jerusalem heard about this, so they called that field in their language Akeldama, that is, Field of Blood.)
[20]"For," said Peter, "it is written in the book of Psalms,

"'May his place be deserted;
let there be no one to dwell in it,'
and,
"'May another take his place of leadership.'
[21]Therefore it is necessary to choose one of the men who have been with us the whole time the Lord Jesus went in and out among us, [22]beginning from John's baptism to the time when Jesus was taken up from us. For one of these must become a witness with us of his resurrection."
— *Acts 1:16-22, NIV*

Read His Word to Him.

The Holy Spirit spoke through the Scriptures as David wrote them. I do take great courage and strength from this thought! Judas was described long before he was born. Dear Lord, how could he do it? i.e. betray your son? He was and is much like all of us. Our Lord called him and taught him and loved him. Judas prepared for his own death and burial. He sold your dear son so cheaply — but for no less than we have sold him—time and again.

Please express your response to this beautiful text. Put your expression in your own prayer diary.

6. READ HIS WORD FOR YOURSELF.

Judas fell headlong and opened up himself for all to see—a tragic, pathetic, unsightly spectacle. When I betray and sell out my Lord I am preparing the same kind of end for myself. What shall they call the record of my life? What shall men remember about me? Much more important, what will you say? Of Judas it was said—"May his place be deserted; let no one dwell in it—may another take his place of leadership"—may it never, never be so said of me.

It is so important that you pause in his presence
and either audibly or in written form tell him all his word means to you.

7. READ HIS WORD IN THANKSGIVING

Ten expressions of thanksgiving from this text: (1) For the wonderful Scriptures; (2) For David; (3) For the Holy Spirit; (4) For our Lord's patience and love with those who betrayed him; (5) For the law of sowing and reaping; (6) For the wonderful detail of fulfilled prophecy; (7) For outstanding sinners who warn us all; (8) That there are others to carry on when others betray and die; (9) For the preparation of every apostle; (10) That the apostles were all eye-witnesses of what they preached.

Give yourself to your own expression of gratitude—write it or speak it!

8. READ HIS WORD IN MEDITATION.

The wonderful march of servants who remain faithful in spite of those who desert and leave. Notice: (1) The record from Genesis to Revelation is that God carries on if man does fail. Many have failed but neither the gates of death nor man's failure prevails against his "called out ones"; (2) We can hear and not hear, learn and not be taught, be loved and not return the love; (3) Gain at the expense of truth and suffer a terrible loss; (4) There *are* others who can take your place.

Pause—wait—think—then express yourself in thoughtful praise or thanks.

9. READ HIS WORD FOR PETITIONS.

These requests arise from your word: (1) I want your word to find fulfillment in my life. (2) I want my life to find fulfillment in your scriptures. (3) Dear Lord, deliver me from any form of betraying my Savior. (4) May I receive with joy the portion you have given me in your service. (5) Keep me aware that others will use what I leave when I die—for good or evil. (6) Keep me humble like a child. (7) Make me your witness today.

Right here add your personal requests—and his answers.

10. READ HIS WORD AND WAIT—LISTEN—GOD SPEAKS!

I open my heart—speak to me through your word; (1) "Another can and will take your place if you are faithless." (2) "I have infinite patience—but there is an end." (3) "I could have changed Judas any time he was willing"—so it is with me!

11. INTERCESSION FOR THE LOST WORLD.

Austria — Points for prayer: (1) *There is much formality and lifelessness in the established Protestant Churches.* There are a number of Bible believing pastors, and their number is now being increased by graduates of the Free Evangelical Seminary in Basel, Switzerland. Pray for a move of the Spirit of God in these churches that will make them a force for the evangelization of the land. (2) *The Bible believing witness is small, but now growing.* There are now about 200 Bible study or church groups meeting regularly—most being very young. There are now possibly 10,000-15,000 born again believers in the country. Pray for the growth of the church planting ministry.

12. SING PRAISES TO OUR LORD.

So precious is Jesus, my Savior, my King,
His praise all the day long with rapture I sing;
To Him in my weakness for strength I can cling,
For He is so precious to me.
For He is so precious to me,

For He is so precious to me;
'Tis Heaven below
My Redeemer to know,
For He is so precious to me.

WEEK TWO — SUNDAY

1. PRAISE GOD FOR WHO HE IS.

Presence. What an amazing quality to discuss! How much I want to enter fully into this attribute of yourself and appreciate more than ever before the fact that you are now present with me—in me—above me—before me—behind me—ahead of me—and what is true for me is true for all men. What a startling awesome fact! I want you to permeate all the atmosphere—all my being. As an invisible person you could be present and no one would know it—only those who sense, or are sensitive—are made aware of this reality. Only a few appreciate your presence.

Express yourself in adoration for this quality of God.
Speak it audibly or write out your praise in your own devotional journal.

2. PRAISE GOD FOR WHAT HE MEANS TO ME.

Present for me. Dear God, this is one mind-staggering concept! That you as the almighty God are *here present!* I fall down before you like John of old. That you can see and hear and know totally all about me and be at the same time in me is such information I cannot assimilate. Will you make your presence known? Yes, yes, I could not write these words if you had not already told me you were present. I read it in your book. At the same time I want to practice your presence—I want to ask you to share my thoughts—every minute of the day—it can be done—I have thought that often about other things or people. Oh, present one, I love you!

How do you personally relate to the presence of God, and God who is present?
Speak it out or write it out. It is *so important* that you establish *your own* devotional journal.

3. CONFESSION OF SIN

One of the sins of all sins! to ignore your presence—to live and talk and think just as if you were not always there. To not include you in my conversation—to not look your way to gain your nod of approval or frown of disapproval. To talk on and on to others and fail to talk with you or about you. I know, I know you are interested in all I say and do and want to help (in areas I so much need your help) but I fail to ask or seek your face. Dear God, forgive me, forgive me! *Deceit* is sin. This sin strikes so close to my heart. Dear God, I want to be open and transparent before men. (I know I am always open and known to you.) I fear men and their frown more than yours—forgive me—penetrate my conscience deeply.

What personal sins do you want to confess? We *must* speak them to remove them.
Do it! *Now.* There is no one else you have sinned against more than God. Tell him so!

4. SING A PRAYER TO GOD.

Dear Lord and Father of mankind,
Forgive our foolish ways!
Reclothe us in our rightful mind;

In purer lives Thy service find,
In deep rev'rence, praise.

Open your hymn book and sing the rest of the verses—or even sing another prayer song.

5. READ HIS WORD TO HIM!

His Word

[23]So they proposed two men: Joseph called Barsabbas (also known as Justus) and Matthias. [24]Then they prayed, "Lord, you know everyone's heart. Show us which of these two you have chosen [25]to take over this apostolic ministry, which Judas left to go where he belongs." [26]Then they drew lots, and the lot fell to Matthias; so he was added to the eleven apostles. — *Acts 1:23-26, NIV*

Read His Word to Him.

How I praise you for your interest in "Joseph called Barsabbas"—also known as "Justus." I will one day meet him and talk with him and he with me. How could he be selected from among so many? How could each one yet be just as important?—but they were and are. Dear God, it is a sobering and penetrating thought that "You know every one's heart," and yet I know you do!

Please express your response to this beautiful text. Put your expression in your own prayer diary.

6. READ HIS WORD FOR YOURSELF.

How I need to pray about the hearts of men today. I commit these to you. I can not and do not know man on the inside. The lot will fall upon someone. The particular job you have for me has fallen from your hold upon me. Dear God, may I as confidently as Matthias take up the tasks you have given for just this day!

It is so important that you pause in his presence and either audibly or in written form tell him all his word means to you.

7. READ HIS WORD IN THANKSGIVING.

I thank you for: (1) The ability to evaluate and decide; (2) For the friends and loved ones we can and do have in your service; (3) That it is *not* necessary to become jealous of others — your will is good for everyone. If we do not have this job we have a better one; (4) We can and should pray about the one the Lord wants for a job; (5) We can be confident God is at work in every changing circumstance of daily life.

Give yourself to your own expression of gratitude — write it or speak it!

8. READ HIS WORD IN MEDITATION.

(1) The apostles felt a need and an opportunity to be continuously in the temple adoring and praising you. I feel the same need and opportunity; (2) Mary and our Lord's brothers — the women were praying — I identify with the brothers — who had doubts and fears about our Lord — but they came to commit their whole lives to Him. (3) The words of the Psalm so graphically fulfilled in Judas — how awesome to see detailed, fulfilled prophecy! (4) We are responsible — (both positively and negatively) for the reactions of our decisions. Judas bought the field through the priests.

Pause — wait — think — then express yourself in thoughtful praise or thanks.

9. READ HIS WORD FOR PETITIONS.

I have my own personal and family petitions — but these are from your desire for me: (1) May I not look down on Barsabbas because he was not chosen — there are many such men. (2) Help me to pray about all decisions. (3) Open my understanding to your knowledge of all men's hearts. (4) I want to believe your work will always be done — help me! (5) May I believe there are men going to hell every minute! (6) Direct me in my understanding of just how you work in human actions. (7) May I add to my acceptance everyone you add to your church.

Please, please remember these are prayers — speak them — reword them!

10. READ HIS WORD AND WAIT — LISTEN — GOD SPEAKS!

You are saying to me: (1) "There *are* qualifications for service." (2) "I hear prayer and know men." (3) "Men die — but God and his church lives!"

11. INTERCESSION FOR THE LOST WORLD

Austria — Points for prayer: (1) *The cults are aggressive and growing.* There are now about 13,000 "Jehovah's Witnesses" and 2,000 Mormons. Their work does untold harm to the efforts of Bible believers to evangelize this needy land. (2) *The witness among students* is one of the most fruitful in the land today. There are strong groups in 5 of the 17 universities, and the groups are growing in depth and outreach. Pray that these young Christians may really have an impact on the land and its churches.

12. SING PRAISES TO OUR LORD.

I will sing the wondrous story
Of the Christ who died for me,
How He left His home in glory
For the cross of Calvary.

Yes, I'll sing the wondrous story
Of the Christ who died for me,
Sing it with the saints in glory,
Gathered by the crystal sea.

WEEK TWO — MONDAY

1. PRAISE GOD FOR WHAT HE MEANS TO ME.

Father. You are the father of all mankind. Not one person has ever been born on this earth until first you sent that person (spirit) into the genetic combination of the mother and father. What an awesome thought! All of us share your likeness. Praise your wonderful name — all of us, each of us in your image.

Express yourself in adoration for this quality of God.
Speak it audibly or write out your praise in your own devotional journal.

2. PRAISE GOD FOR WHAT HE MEANS TO ME.

Father — to me! I am so glad to read of your qualities — to accept you and admit and welcome you into my house — i.e. my body. You have arrived in the person of the Holy Spirit! My Father who is not only in heaven but very much on earth and in myself — a father on a level and in qualities I so much need! Oh, bless your name.

How do you personally relate to the fatherliness of God, and God who is Father?
Speak it out or write it out. It is *so important* that you establish *your own* devotional journal.

3. CONFESSION OF SIN

Why do I fail? Why do I so obviously fail? Why do I allow pride and desire to direct my words and actions? Dear God, forgive. Through the wonderful intercessor at your right hand you do forgive. I am so glad to claim your cleansing; to be made whole; to be released. Oh, dear God, accept my praise.

What personal sins do you want to confess? We *must* speak them to remove them.
Do it! *Now.* There is no one else you have sinned against more than God. Tell him so!

4. SING A PRAYER TO GOD.

I am Thine, O Lord,
I have heard Thy voice,
And it told Thy love to me;
But I long to rise in the arms of faith,
And be closer drawn to Thee.

Draw me nearer, nearer, blessed Lord,
To the cross where Thou hast died;
Draw me nearer, nearer, blessed Lord,
To Thy precious, bleeding side.

Open your hymn book and sing the rest of the verses — or even sing another prayer song.

5. READ HIS WORD TO HIM!

His Word

[26]On the day of firstfruits, when you present to the Lord an offering of new grain during the Feast of Weeks, hold a sacred assembly and do no regular work. [27]Present a burnt offering of two young bulls, one ram and seven male lambs a year old as an aroma pleasing to the Lord. [28]With each bull there is to be a grain offering of three-tenths of an ephah of fine flour mixed with oil; with the ram, two-tenths; [29]and with each of the seven lambs, one-tenth. [30]Include one male goat to make atonement for you.   — *Numbers 28:26-30, NIV*
Refer to Leviticus 23:15-22; Acts 2:1-21.

Read His Word to Him.

The day of thanksgiving is the day of Pentecost. How very thoughtful it was for you to set aside this day for this purpose. How meaningful are the objects for thanksgiving: harvest, i.e. your blessing and provision for man's physical needs — and the law the provision for man's spiritual needs.

Please express your response to this beautiful text. Put your expression in your own prayer diary.

6. READ HIS WORD FOR YOURSELF.

What a large offering was made—bulls—sheep—rams—goats—grain—fruit—oil—bread. It all belongs to you. This is only a representative expression of our gratitude and a clear recognition of your ownership. How I thank you for the more than adequate provision made for our food—both for the body and the spirit.

It is so important that you pause in his presence
and either audibly or in written form tell him all his word means to you.

7. READ HIS WORD IN THANKSGIVING.

Surely this will be easy to do: (1) Thank you for the special days you have set aside to remind us. (2) The tangible items that we can touch and taste to reach our senses with your message. (3) For the fire of sacrifice that shows us the temporary nature of all physical blessings. (4) For the laws of harvest that constantly remind us just who provides for us. (5) For your law telling us just how wonderfully interested you are in every part of our life.

Give yourself to your own expression of gratitude—write it or speak it.

8. READ HIS WORD IN MEDITATION.

Pentecost means 50—or "fifty days"—marking the time lapse from the Passover. Tradition has it that it was also fifty days from the exodus from Egypt at the first Passover till the giving of the law at Mt. Sinai. Be that as it may, it was but fifty days from the sacrifice of God's Lamb to the coming of the Other Comforter. As the first fruit of the harvest was given in gratitude and in an acknowledgment of the source of all the harvest, so the day of Pentecost was and is the first fruit of God's eternal harvest of the lives of men and women. Also a clear acknowledgment that all who are gathered into His eternal garner will be of the same source and kind.

Pause—wait—think—then express yourself in thoughtful praise or thanks.

9. READ HIS WORD FOR PETITIONS.

What shall I ask as you speak to me about the day of Pentecost? (1) May I be willing to give those gifts which cost me much—even as the expensive animals were given. (2) I want to thank you with my substance. (3) Open my eyes to truly recognize all you have given me. (4) I want to be obedient to the law of the Spirit of life. (5) Break my heart that I might want to follow you. (6) Even rams and goats are given to you—I know their is hope for me. (7) Give me deep gratitude for all food as your gift.

Right here add your personal requests—and his answers.

10. READ HIS WORD AND WAIT—LISTEN—GOD SPEAKS!

What do you say to me in the purpose of Pentecost? (i.e., in the Old Testament). (1) "I want to be thanked for my gifts." (2) "All you are and have comes from me." (3) "Your place is to obey—not excuse yourself."

11. INTERCESSION FOR THE LOST WORLD.

Austria — Point for prayer: *Migrant laborers* — little has yet been done for the Muslim Turks. There is one small Yugoslav church in Vienna, but most of this large community has yet to be evangelized. This community is very strategic for the evangelizing of Yugoslavia as that land becomes increasingly difficult for Christian work.

12. SING PRAISES TO OUR LORD.

A Friend I have, called Jesus,
Whose love is strong and true,
And never fails howe'er 'tis tried,
No matter what I do;
I've sinned against this love of His,
But when I knelt to pray,
Confessing all my guilt to Him,
The sin-clouds rolled away.
It's just like Jesus to roll the clouds away.
It's just like Jesus to keep me day by day,
It's just like Jesus all along the way,
It's just like His great love.

WEEK TWO — TUESDAY

1. PRAISE GOD FOR WHO HE IS.

Eternal. You shall never change. There will never be a time when you do not live. This is a source of great strength and encouragement to me. Blessed be your name! There is no way I can truly encompass such a thought.

Express yourself in adoration for this quality of God.
Speak it audibly or write out your praise in your own devotional journal.

2. PRAISE GOD FOR WHAT HE MEANS TO ME.

For me He ever liveth to make intercession. He is alive as an example of what will happen to me when I slip out of this house of clay. I am so glad to share His nature — "from everlasting to everlasting thou art God." There will never be a time when I do not live and know and feel and rejoice in him! Wonder of all wonders. "He that believeth in me shall never die." How I need this reality spelled out real often!

How do you personally relate to the eternality of God, and God who is Eternal?
Speak it out or write it out. It is *so important* that you establish *your own* devotional journal.

3. CONFESSION OF SIN.

Dear God, I am truly sorry I have sinned. I am a sinner — I do harbor rebellion — I do not want to sin, but when I would do good, evil is present. The good (oh, so much of it) that I would, I do not get done — the evil that I would not — and there are so many and various ways that I do evil; some are more evident than others. Dear Lord, cleanse me! Wash me clean and I shall be whiter than snow!

What personal sins do you want to confess? We *must* speak them to remove them.
Do it! *Now.* There is no one else you have sinned against more than God. Tell him so!

4. SING A PRAYER TO GOD.

Guide me, O Thou great Jehovah,
Pilgrim thro' this barren land;
I am weak, but Thou art mighty,
Hold me with Thy pow'rful hand:

Bread of Heaven,
Feed me till I want no more;
Bread of Heaven,
Feed me till I want no more.

Open your hymn book and sing the rest of the verses — or even sing another prayer song.

5. READ HIS WORD TO HIM!

His Word

2 When the day of Pentecost came, they were all together in one place. ²Suddenly a sound like the blowing of a violent wind came from heaven and filled the whole house where they were sitting. ³They saw what seemed to be tongues of fire that separated and came to rest on each of them. ⁴All of them were filled with the Holy Spirit and began to speak in other tongues as the Spirit enabled them.
— Acts 2:1-4, NIV

Read His Word to Him.

What an amazing experience! How intently the twelve are listening to "the sound as of a violent wind from heaven." Such a sound is filling the room where they are seated. Dear Lord, you surely act in unusual ways — in most dramatic sensational ways. Tongues of fire! Fire sitting on everyone! Speaking in languages no one has ever learned! Amazing, I too am confounded and bewildered! I, like those who first saw this, am overcome!

Please express your response to this beautiful text. Put your expression in your own prayer diary.

6. READ HIS WORD FOR YOURSELF.

I know these apostles are being immersed in the Holy Spirit — I am totally impressed. I have a difficult time understanding all the implications of what is happening — the supernatural equipment needed to establish His "called out ones." To suddenly be enabled to speak in a language before not known, to see fire, hear a wind, to be overwhelmed with a divine person — this is perplexing!

It is so important that you pause in his presence
and either audibly or in written form tell him all his word means to you.

WEEK TWO — TUESDAY

7. READ HIS WORD IN THANKSGIVING

Gladly do I do this: (1) The day was promised and the promise was kept. (2) The apostles were prepared through prayer for what happened. (3) The suddenness of all your important acts such as: creation, regeneration, immortalization. (4) The appeal to the senses of man do convince him of your presence and power. (5) That the Holy Spirit can work in and with and for and through men.

Give yourself to your own expression of gratitude—write it or speak it!

8. READ HIS WORD IN MEDITATION.

I want to pause to think deeply upon the wonder of it all! (1) That Jesus would spend all night in prayer for leadership and come up with these twelve men. (2) That they would indeed "leave all" and follow him—no one was working or involved with "other things." (3) The Holy Spirit filled or baptized all, but not all responded in exactly the same way, i.e., Peter spoke with a different word choice than John. (4) That I can respond to the Holy Spirit in me.

Pause—wait—think—then express yourself in thoughtful praise or thanks.

9. READ HIS WORD FOR PETITIONS.

Here is the purpose of Pentecost for the Apostles. How glad I am to see a number of requests here for me: (1) I want to accept the fact that you work through groups as well as individuals. (2) Help me to see you sometimes use very unusual approaches to speak to men. (3) You *do* communicate on a sensate level—I believe—help my unbelief. (4) Open my mind as to the real significance of the sound and fire. (5) May I have a clear indelible definition of "tongues" as used here. (6) I want to truly know *why* the apostles needed these "tongues." (7) Why does anyone think this experience could or should be repeated?

Please, please remember these are prayers—speak them—reword them!

10. READ HIS WORD AND WAIT—LISTEN—GOD SPEAKS!

My ears are open to your voice: (1) "I keep my promises to those for whom I made them." (2) "I can unite the diverse group of the twelve by my Spirit." (3) "I want to show my splendor to the unbeliever through men."

11. INTERCESSION FOR THE LOST WORLD

Belgium — Population: 9,800,000. Annual growth 0.3%. Densely populated - 320 people/sq. km.

Points for prayer: (1)*Belgium is one of the less evangelized lands of the world.* Only 60 km. from the coast of England is a land that is as much a mission field as India, for the proportion of Bible believers to the population is about the same. The former colony, the Belgian Congo (now Zaire), has nearly 200 times as many Bible believers as Belgium itself. There are few Christians in the Ardennes region, and there are over 140 towns of over 10,000 people without a witness to the Lord Jesus. Pray for the evangelization of Belgium. (2) *The majority of the people are* *Roman Catholic*, though few are ardent. The Roman Catholic Church is fast losing influence—dramatically illustrated when a protestant group recently acquired one of the largest Jesuit colleges in Europe as a new and larger base for the Belgian Bible Institute. Vatican II and the theological turmoil within the R.C. Church has brought a new spirit of enquiry to the people. (3) *The Protestant witness is very small*, but growing slowly. Opportunities for evangelization have never been greater. Pray for the believers that there might be more effective use of the opportunities and a greater boldness in outreach.

12. SING PRAISES TO OUR LORD.

Jesus is all the world to me,
My life, my joy, my all;
He is my strength from day to day,
Without Him I would fall.

When I am sad, to Him I go,
No other one can cheer me so;
When I am sad He makes me glad,
He's my Friend.

21

WEEK TWO — WEDNESDAY

1. PRAISE GOD FOR WHO HE IS.

Unchangeable. It is a comfort to know someone, SOMEONE who will never, never deviate in any way relating to character. How impressive to leave a record of yesterday — how complete is the history of your character and what a strength to me — to all men. Your love, kindness and interest is always the same.

Express yourself in adoration for this quality of God.
Speak it audibly or write out your praise in your own devotional journal.

2. PRAISE GOD FOR WHAT HE MEANS TO ME.

Changeable for me! I can expect you to be forever what you have forever been. Praise your holy (pure) name — or person. How satisfied I am in you — how full and fulfilled. It is all because I know you love me without change. The cosmos will dissolve but thou abidest the same!

How do you personally relate to the unchangeableness of God, and God who is Unchangeable?
Speak it out or write it out. It is *so important* that you establish *your own* devotional journal.

3. CONFESSION OF SIN

I have a strong tendency to rationalize my sins — to justify my disobedience. In this hour I drop such pretense! Dear God, help me to leave it dropped. I freely admit my wrong, my sin. I name it before thee. I at the same time claim your cleansing. I gladly, eagerly leap into the fountain for sin and uncleanness. Bless your dear person — how good to be clean.

What personal sins do you want to confess? We *must* speak them to remove them.
Do it! *Now.* There is no one else you have sinned against more than God. Tell him so!

4. SING A PRAYER TO GOD.

I have a Father; to me He has given
A hope for eternity, blessed and true;
And soon He will call me to meet Him in heaven,
But oh, that He'd let me bring you with me, too!

For you I am praying,
For you I am praying,
For you I am praying,
I'm praying for you.

Open your hymn book and sing the rest of the verses — or even sing another prayer song.

5. READ HIS WORD TO HIM!

His Word

[6]When they heard this sound, a crowd came together in bewilderment, because each one heard them speaking in his own language. [7]Utterly amazed, they asked: "Are not all these men who are speaking Galileans? [8]Then how is it that each of us hears them in his own native language? [9]Parthians, Medes and Elamites; residents of Mesopotamia, Judea and Cappadocia, Pontus and Asia, [10]Phrygia and Pamphylia, Egypt and the parts of Libya near Cyrene; visitors from Rome [11](both Jews and converts to Judaism); Cretans and Arabs — we hear them declaring the wonders of God in our own tongues!" [12]Amazed and perplexed, they asked one another, "What does this mean?"

[13]Some, however, made fun of them and said, "They have had too much wine."

[14]Then Peter stood up with the Eleven, raised his voice and addressed the crowd: "Fellow Jews and all of you who are in Jerusalem, let me explain this to you; listen carefully to what I say. [15]These men are not drunk, as you suppose. It's only nine in the morning!   — *Acts 2:6-15, NIV*

Read His Word to Him.

How amazing are your actions! Past tracing out are your purposes. You told your apostles to go into all the world and preach, then you brought men from every nation so they would hear what you wanted preached. I now consider the incredible fact that all present heard in their own languages the mighty works of your own self.

Please express your response to this beautiful text. Put your expression in your own prayer diary.

6. READ HIS WORD FOR YOURSELF.

I want to read these words—dear Lord, just as if I had never read them before. I have a difficult time assimilating all that is happening here: (1) Twelve Galileans speaking in more than a dozen languages they have never heard before or surely they had never spoken. (2) Some (seemingly) intentionally misunderstand. But then I know many do this today—even myself. Peter is so patient with them—help me to be the same way.

It is so important that you pause in his presence
and either audibly or in written form tell him all his word means to you.

7. READ HIS WORD IN THANKSGIVING.

This is the area where I most keenly enjoy the expression of worship. To thank you for: (1) God-fearing men of all nations of all time that made it possible for me—or anyone else to fear and love you. (2) For Jerusalem and all of its tremendous associations—over so long, with so many people and incidents. (3) The tremendous supernatural ability to speak in a language never learned for the purpose of communicating. This is the very antithesis of the tower of Babel. (4) Again and again you do choose the humble to accomplish your work.

Give yourself to your own expression of gratitude—write it or speak it!

8. READ HIS WORD IN MEDITATION.

Oh, dear God, holy and present Spirit, beautiful Savior. Peter said to listen carefully, and I want to do just that! (1) Can I hear the sound? i.e., of the mighty, rushing wind? of the blowing of a violent wind from heaven? The *lost* heard the *wind*. It wasn't for the saved that the wind sound came. (2) They were all called together—in Jerusalem and in the Temple in Jerusalem. Is there a pattern here for evangelism? (3) The religious folk were the first to hear and become Christians—they were bewildered—utterly amazed—perplexed. So it is today: we must seek a work in our day to do the same thing—call attention to yourself, not ourselves! (4) We will need someone like Peter to explain, but he needs to be *like Peter*.

Pause—wait—think—then express yourself in thoughtful praise or thanks.

9. READ HIS WORD FOR PETITIONS.

What inquiries shall I make from these precious verses? (1) Are there God-fearing people (even one) for every nation of the world? How sad to say "no." (2) What can I do, what can you do through me—to call a crowd to hear? (3) Has anyone heard his own language spoken by one who did not know it? i.e., since Pentecost? (4) I am asking questions for I expect an answer. Help me. (5) I want to identify the languages spoken today in the provinces mentioned. (6) I want to know the full meaning of this experience. (7) How does drunkenness and nine in the morning relate?

Right here add your personal requests—and his answers.

10. READ HIS WORD AND WAIT—LISTEN—GOD SPEAKS!

Communication is the point of this text—communicate with me! (1) "I want every man to hear my word in his own language." (2) "Humble station is no reason for not speaking my word." (3) "There will always be those who do not understand and will mock."

11. INTERCESSION FOR THE LOST WORLD

Belgium — Points for prayer: (1) *Immigrant workers need to be evangelized* — North Africans (55,000) and Turks (5,000) present a unique and urgent challenge for prayer and evangelism. *Yugoslavs* — there are several small churches among them. *The many diplomats, businessmen, etc.* from other European lands are neglected and are not able to be reached by normal evangelism.

Cyprus — Population 670,000. Point for prayer: (1) *Pray that this suffering land may have a fair chance to hear the Gospel.* Bible believing Christians are very few and there is only a handful of full time workers.

12. SING PRAISES TO OUR LORD.

Bearing shame and scoffing rude,
In my place condemned He stood;

Sealed my pardon with His blood;
Hallelujah! what a Savior!

WEEK TWO — THURSDAY

1. PRAISE GOD FOR WHO HE IS.

Justice-Judge. He will and is judging me! But he is also love and mercy and grace so whereas his judgment will be justice, it will also be kind and patient.

Express yourself in adoration for this quality of God.
Speak it audibly or write out your praise in your own devotional journal.

2. PRAISE GOD FOR WHAT HE MEANS TO ME.

He will indeed judge the whole world and all men who have ever lived or are now alive. Blessed be his name, and yet I know I stand condemned before him! Only by grace will I ever—am I now saved!

How do you personally relate to the justice-judgment of God, and God who is Justice-Judge?
Speak it out or write it out. It is *so important* that you establish *your own* devotional journal.

3. CONFESSION OF SIN

Confession of my guilt and sin and weakness and selfishness of my misplaced love. How could I so love myself? Dear God, forgive! I accept your forgivenss, but I wonder if you accept my poor repentance? My sin is an embarrassment and a weight and a hindrance and a stake in my flesh—make me whole!

What personal sins do you want to confess? We *must* speak them to remove them.
Do it! *Now.* There is no one else you have sinned against more than God. Tell him so!

4. SING A PRAYER TO GOD.

I hear Thy welcome voice,
That calls me, Lord, to Thee
For cleansing in Thy precious blood
That flowed on Calvary.

I am coming, Lord!
Coming now to Thee!
Wash me, cleanse me in the blood
That flowed on Calvary!

Open your hymn book and sing the rest of the verses—or even sing another prayer song.

5. READ HIS WORD TO HIM.

His Word

[22]"Men of Israel, listen to this: Jesus of Nazareth was a man accredited by God to you by miracles, wonders and signs, which God did among you through him, as you yourselves know. [23]This man was handed over to you by God's set purpose and foreknowledge; and you, with the help of wicked men, put him to death by nailing him to the cross. [24]But God raised him from the dead, freeing him from the agony of death, because it was impossible for death to keep its hold on him. [25]David said about him:
"'I saw the Lord always before me.
  Because he is at my right hand,
  I will not be shaken.
[26]Therefore my heart is glad and my tongue rejoices;
  my body also will live in hope,
[27]because you will not abandon me to the grave,
  nor will you let your Holy One see decay.
[28]You have made known to me the paths of life;
  you will fill me with joy in your presence.'
[29]"Brothers, I can tell you confidently that the patriarch David died and was buried, and his tomb is here to this day. [30]But he was a prophet and knew that God had promised him on oath that he would place one of his descendants on his throne. [31]Seeing what was ahead, he spoke of the resurrection of the Christ, that he was not abandoned to the grave, nor did his body see decay. [32]God has raised this Jesus to life, and we are all witnesses of the fact.
— *Acts 2:22-32, NIV*

Read His Word to Him.

How concise and complete are the words of Dr. Luke, but at the same time the words of yourself. Jesus your dear son was accredited—among men—as they well knew. What confidence we have in Him and in you!—"handed over to you by God's set purpose and foreknowledge." —what a mind-staggering thought! What man did was not only foretold but planned by God.

Please express your response to this beautiful text. Put your expression in your own prayer diary.

WEEK TWO – THURSDAY

6. READ HIS WORD FOR YOURSELF.

You raised him from the dead — praise God — one day you will raise me from death. It is just as impossible for death to keep me as to keep him. What David said I do want to say — "I saw the Lord always before me!" — how beautifully did the prophecy find fulfillment in my Lord — each detail complete and in place! Jesus, my king, is on David's throne and reigning for me and interceding for me.

It is so important that you pause in his presence
and either audibly or in written form tell him all his word means to you.

7. READ HIS WORD IN THANKSGIVING.

(1) How glad I am I *can* and do *listen* to what you say. (2) Thank you, thank you for the more than adequate accredited Lord! (3) Thank you he died for my sins as well as for the sins of the whole world. (4) That my Lord lives today — sees me — reads every one of these words I pray — reads also, every one of the intents and purposes of my heart. (5) For men's tombs and my Lord's empty tomb!

Give yourself to your own expression of gratitude — write it or speak it!

8. READ HIS WORD IN MEDITATION.

David as a prophet: (1) Surely a good man, but surely not a perfect man — surely then, God can use you and me. (2) Was glad to be a servant as well as a king — we are all kings and priests unto God, (Rev. 1:5, 5:10; I Peter 2:8, 9), but our primary purpose is to serve as priests — intercede — and as kings to rule over Satan. (3) David took great courage and comfort in the presence and promises of God — most especially about his Son. How I do want to do the same thing!

Pause — wait — think — then express yourself in thoughtful praise or thanks.

9. READ HIS WORD FOR PETITIONS.

What shall I ask as I consider this text? (1) I want all the words Joel spoke that relate to me to be fulfilled. (2) Am I living in the "last days"? I believe we have been since Pentecost. (3) How can I best appreciate the gift of your Spirit? (4) How can I best use the Spirit's gifts? (5) Open my mind as to how to accept fulfilled prophecy. (6) When will the sun turn to darkness and the moon into blood? (7) If in the next twinkling of the eye he should come, would I welcome him?

Please, please remember these are prayers — speak them — reword them!

10. READ HIS WORD AND WAIT — LISTEN — GOD SPEAKS!

As you spoke through Peter to those on Pentecost, speak to me through the same man: (1) "You have what Joel promised." (2) "Salvation for all men is available now!" (3) "In another sense — every day is a day of the Lord — live it for me!"

11. INTERCESSION FOR THE LOST WORLD

Cyprus — Points for prayer: (1) *The Turkish part of the island has no active Christian witness,* though several Turkish Christians have recently moved there from the mainland. Pray that it may be possible for some to enter the area to tell these Muslims of the Savior. Pray for the entry of Christian literature from Turkey. (2) *Over one third of the Greeks are refugees.* Many still live in tents and much work of resettlement remains to be done. Christians helped much, and through their witnessing some outsiders have been saved. Pray that this disaster may open many hearts to the Gospel.

12. SING PRAISES TO OUR LORD.

I will sing of my Redeemer,
And His wondrous love to me;
On the cruel cross He suffered,
From the curse to set me free.

Sing, oh, sing . . . of my Redeemer,
With His blood . . . He purchased me, . . .
On the cross . . . He sealed my pardon,
Paid the debt, . . . and made me free.

WEEK TWO — FRIDAY

1. PRAISE GOD FOR WHO HE IS.

Sovereign. How wonderful to *know* someone is in control! Praise your eternal, unchangeable, nature!

Express yourself in adoration for this quality of God.
Speak it audibly or write out your praise in your own devotional journal.

2. PRAISE GOD FOR WHAT HE MEANS TO ME.

It is sobering to realize I have turned the management over to this ONE who is at work directing all things under his sovereign will. To me it is a great source of encouragement. He is *at work* in my life, and I want to open my heart (all of it) to him! I want to cooperate in all ways with him. He *knows all about everything.*

How do you personally relate to the sovereignty of God, and God who is Sovereign?
Speak it out or write it out. It is *so important* that you establish *your own* devotional journal.

3. CONFESSION OF SIN

Dear Lord, dear Lord, forgive my sins that I here now confess to you. Each one hurts you and myself. Cleanse me! forgive me! Remove from your record, clear my record. How eternally good it is to be able to pray this prayer. Oh, to claim, to *know* the removal of guilt! Wonder and joy and standing in grace!

What personal sins do you want to confess? We *must* speak them to remove them.
Do it! *Now.* There is no one else you have sinned against more than God. Tell him so!

4. SING A PRAYER TO GOD.

Stand up, stand up for Jesus,
Ye soldiers of the cross;
Lift high His royal banner,
It must not suffer loss:

From vict'ry unto vict'ry
His army shall He lead,
Till ev'ry foe is vanquished,
And Christ is Lord indeed.

Open your hymn book and sing the rest of the verses — or even sing another prayer song.

5. READ HIS WORD TO HIM!

His Word

[17]"'In the last days, God says,
  I will pour out my Spirit on all people.
Your sons and daughters will prophesy,
  your young men will see visions,
  your old men will dream dreams.
[18]Even on my servants, both men and women,
  I will pour out my Spirit in those days,
  and they will prophesy.

and signs on the earth below,
  blood and fire and billows of smoke.
[20]The sun will be turned to darkness
  and the moon to blood
  before the coming of the great and
  glorious day of the Lord.
[21]And everyone who calls
  on the name of the Lord will be saved.'

— *Acts 2:17-21, NIV*

Read His Word to Him.

You have said, you are saying and you always will say, "In the last days — which began on Pentecost and end when Jesus comes — you will pour out your Spirit upon all flesh — prophecy — visions and dreams will be given — have been given. I am simply affirming what you said — to stand in wonder and amazement at grace extended to such unworthy people!

Please express your response to this beautiful text. Put your expression in your own prayer diary.

6. READ HIS WORD FOR YOURSELF.

Dear God, I'm so glad you have given *me* your Spirit. In days gone by I have had some visions—not for anyone else, but my little area of work—and the people who work with me—now that I am old I have had some dreams. I have spoken your word to some who received it for what it was; many who didn't. I have seen and beheld the wonder of heaven above—even your dear Son and your precious self!

It is so important that you pause in his presence
and either audibly or in written form tell him all his word means to you.

7. READ HIS WORD IN THANKSGIVING

Thank you dear, dear Lord for: (1) The last days—we are living in them. Of all the thousands and thousands of years *we* live in the last days—praise you! (2) That your Spirit, even the Holy Spirit the Other Comforter, has come! Oh, grace upon grace! (3) We have the prophecy of some of those young men like John Mark in his beautiful gospel. (4) There are yet servants and handmaidens with the presence of the Holy Spirit—your teachers all with us today. (5) Maranatha—oh, day of the Lord—even so come *today* Lord Jesus!

Give yourself to your own expression of gratitude—write it or speak it!

8. READ HIS WORD IN MEDITATION.

Gather around these three thoughts and let the Lord speak to you: (1) *The sound of a violent wind* filled the house—what fills my house today? Does the sound of his name and his word fill it? (2) *Tongues of fire*—representative of the supernaturalness of the abilities given. Oh, just to add splendor and attract attention. Dear God, you have my attention. (3) They all spoke in other languages. Until we get the mighty words of God known in the languages of the world, the world will remain lost! As you know dear God, I'm trying to do this.

Pause—wait—think—then express yourself in thoughtful praise or thanks.

9. READ HIS WORD FOR PETITIONS.

What desires arise from you as I read your word? (1) I want to see my Lord as the most creditable person I know. (2) Let me examine his signs all over again! (3) Let me know your set purpose for me today. (4) Do I appreciate the resurrection as I should? (5) Thank you for every word of King David. (6) Open my mind to understand the prophecies of David. (7) Give me a deep appreciation of my resurrection body.

Right here add your personal requests—and his answers.

10. READ HIS WORD AND WAIT—LISTEN—GOD SPEAKS!

You want to say something very special to me from this text: (1) "My son is your Lord—accept him!" (2) "Death has no hold at all on you." (3) "Jesus is alive now!"

11. INTERCESSION FOR THE LOST WORLD

Cyprus — Points for prayer: (1) *The national believers* were much strengthened through the 1974 crisis. Pray for their growth in grace and for a continuing increase in their outreach to the lost. The believers are strongest in Limassol and Nicosia. Pray for the planting of new churches in other areas. (2) *Literature* is distributed through the Christian book store in Limassol, and also by British servicemen who love the Lord; the latter coming from the NATO military bases on the island. Pray also for the occasional Gospel advertisements placed in national newspapers.

12. SING PRAISES TO OUR LORD.

O for a thousand tongues to sing
My great Redeemer's praise,

The glories of my God and King,
The triumphs of His grace.

WEEK TWO — SATURDAY

1. PRAISE GOD FOR WHO HE IS.

Creator. How wonderfully and beautifully you created the world in which we live. To look and consider the smallest of your handiwork is to be full of delight, full of praise for such a one. Blessed be your powerful wise ability! You are yet in the creation business. You have not only created the world, you have recreated man!

Express yourself in adoration for this quality of God.
Speak it audibly or write out your praise in your own devotional journal.

2. PRAISE GOD FOR WHAT HE MEANS TO ME.

Each day there are a myriad of flowers, plants, chemicals that change and reform and manifest your continuing interest in creation—and man. Oh, the amazing thought: It was all done that I might enjoy it!

How do you personally relate to the creations of God, and God who is Creator?
Speak it out or write it out. It is *so important* that you establish *your own* devotional journal.

3. CONFESSION OF SIN

I do believe the programming of my subconscious mind has much to do with sin. If I program into it a blunt refusal for a period of three weeks it will be then much easier to obey than to disobey. Dear God, help me to so decide; but just now I accept your cleansing forgiveness. How good to know I have no record of wrong!

What personal sins do you want to confess? We *must* speak them to remove them.
Do it! *Now.* There is no one else you have sinned against more than God. Tell him so!

4. SING A PRAYER TO GOD.

I must tell Jesus all of my trials;
I cannot bear these burdens alone;
In my distress He kindly will help me;
He ever loves and cares for His own.

I must tell Jesus! I must tell Jesus!
I cannot bear my burdens alone;
I must tell Jesus! I must tell Jesus!
Jesus can help me, Jesus alone.

Open your hymn book and sing the rest of the verses—or even sing another prayer song.

5. READ HIS WORD TO HIM!
His Word

[33]Exalted to the right hand of God, he has received from the Father the promised Holy Spirit and has poured out what you now see and hear. [34]For David did not ascend to heaven, and yet he said,
"'The Lord said to my Lord:
"Sit at my right hand
[35]until I make your enemies
a footstool for your feet."'

[36]"Therefore let all Israel be assured of this: God has made this Jesus, whom you crucified, both Lord and Christ."
[37]When the people heard this, they were cut to the heart and said to Peter and the other apostles, "Brothers, what shall we do?" [38]Peter replied, "Repent and be baptized, every one of you, in the name of Jesus Christ so that your sins may be forgiven. And you will receive the gift of the Holy Spirit.   — *Acts 2:33-38, NIV*

Read His Word to Him.

How could I ever say what it means to you to have your son? He who was and is and is to come now back in your presence? These are but poor stammering ignorant, meaningless words. Jesus sent the Holy Spirit! He is exalted at your right hand. You have made him both Lord and Christ. The Savior is now King, or the Anointed One!

Please express your response to this beautiful text. Put your expression in your own prayer diary.

6. READ HIS WORD FOR YOURSELF.

As if I had never read it before—there are words and thoughts that have escaped my notice—such as "the Father"—only *one* Father—"ascend to heaven"—there is an "up" and a "down" in the expressions of this text. Have I ever been truly "cut to the heart"? The wonder, the enormity of the transactions of Calvary has not yet been fully probed!

It is so important that you pause in his presence
and either audibly or in written form tell him all his word means to you.

7. READ HIS WORD IN THANKSGIVING

Thank you for: (1) My exalted Lord. (2) He is ever active in intercession for me. (3) The promised Holy Spirit—he was seen and heard through men—as he is today! (4) Jesus is indeed "my Lord"—how glad I am to claim him as such. (5) He is my sin bearer—my sin for me—my Lord and King. (6) I am cut to the heart all over again when I see him there dying for me! (7) Dear God, I do repent—I am so glad I was baptized to stop my sin and receive the blessed Holy Spirit.

Give yourself to your own expression of gratitude—write it or speak it!

8. READ HIS WORD IN MEDITATION.

If I do what they did I will become what they were. Oh, that I might single out one of the multitude and put myself in his place. I want to hear unlearned, ignorant men from the hills of Galilee speak in my own native dialect. This would be by itself an amazement to me. I want to be convinced by evidence that Jesus of Nazareth was indeed my long promised and looked for Messiah. I want to understand not in a small way but in an overwhelming way that he, Jesus, was God's lamb slain for my sins and all sins of all men for all time. My mind, my whole being is changed! The wonderful Holy Spirit is present to accompany and accomplish this change. My baptism like theirs made me a Christian—together with all others who share with me I became a member of his church—or part of the "called out ones."

Pause—wait—think—then express yourself in thoughtful praise or thanks.

9. READ HIS WORD FOR PETITIONS.

How I want to ask that I might receive: (1) Give me a fresh sense of my Lord's exalted position. (2) May I believe I now have the Holy Spirit. (3) Make your enemies your footstool in my life today. (4) May your son be both Lord and Christ in me. (5) Cut me to the heart with your love for the lost world. (6) Help me to change my mind about all sin. (7) May I appreciate more than ever my baptism.

Please, please remember these are prayers—speak them—reword them!

10. READ HIS WORD AND WAIT—LISTEN—GOD SPEAKS!

Speak to me deeply, personally through Peter: (1) "You are a member of the same body as those on Pentecost." (2) "The Holy Spirit wants you." (3) "Acknowledge my Son as Lord and King in your whole life!"

11. INTERCESSION FOR THE LOST WORLD

Denmark — Population: 5,100,000 *Danes.* Growth rate 0.4% p.a. People per sq. km.—120.

Points for prayer: (1) *Denmark is reputed to be the pornographic capital of the world.* Liberal laws have legalized many social sins and there is no longer any censorship of literature, films, etc. The moral degradation of a permissive society has brought no peace or happiness to the people. Pray for this needy land. (2) *The Lutheran Church is largely formal.* There is a general belief in baptism as the only way to be saved. Pray for this Protestant nation that is so far from God. (3) *Bible believers seem unconcerned about the unsaved around them.* Pray for revival to stir the believers into a vital witness.

12. SING PRAISES TO OUR LORD.

There is a name I love to hear,
I love to sing its worth;
It sounds like music to mine ear,
The sweetest name on earth.

Oh, how I love Jesus,
Oh, how I love Jesus,
Oh, how I love Jesus,
Because He first loved me!

WEEK THREE — SUNDAY

1. PRAISE GOD FOR WHO HE IS.

Ruler. I want to be ruled by you! I rejoice in your law. I gladly accept your Lordship. You are ruler over all and are in all. Praise your essential Being. To rule is your nature; this is your normal expression. How complete and fulfilling is this quality of your character.

Express yourself in adoration for this quality of God.
Speak it audibly or write out your praise in your own devotional journal.

2. PRAISE GOD FOR WHAT HE MEANS TO ME.

Oh, how I need and want someone to take over the reins of my heart. Take my mind, my will, my emotions and my conscience. Gladly do I turn them over to you. I know my choice and personal commitment are involved in your rulership. But as to choice, I with delight choose you and your dear Son and the present Holy Spirit.

How do you personally relate to the rule of God, and God who is Ruler?
Speak it out or write it out. It is *so important* that you establish *your own* devotional journal.

3. CONFESSION OF SIN

My inability to rule my own life the way you want me to relates directly to my desire for you to rule! I want to please you. I want you to forgive me. I know, I feel, I accept the fact that you do. It is a beautiful experience to be freely, totally forgiven. I am full of wonder before you. Blessed is he whose transgression is forgiven, whose sin is covered. Blessed is the man to whom the Lord imputes *no iniquity*, and in whose spirit *there is no deceit!* Read verse 5 of Psalm 32. Oh, the joy of forgiveness.

What personal sins do you want to confess? We *must* speak them to remove them.
Do it! *Now.* There is no one else you have sinned against more than God. Tell him so!

4. SING A PRAYER TO GOD.

I need Thee every hour,
Most gracious Lord;
No tender voice like Thine
Can peace afford.

I need Thee, O I need Thee;
Ev'ry hour I need Thee!
O bless me now, my Savior,
I come to Thee!

Open your hymn book and sing the rest of the verses—or even sing another prayer song.

5. READ HIS WORD TO HIM!

His Word

[39]The promise is for you and your children and for all who are far off—for all whom the Lord our God will call." [40]With many other words he warned them; and he pleaded with them, "Save yourselves from this corrupt generation." [41]Those who accepted his message were baptized, and about three thousand were added to their number that day. [42]They devoted themselves to the apostles' teaching and to the fellowship, to the breaking of bread and to prayer.
— *Acts 2:39-42, NIV*

Read His Word to Him.

My wonderful Father, how gladly I read these words of your book back to you to tell you how very much I appreciate them. I do claim the promise of salvation and the Holy Spirit! I include myself in those "afar off." I am a Gentile but I can and do now "save myself" by accepting your Son and his salvation. I want also to escape the corruption that is in this world (generation) through lust. How gladly I count myself among the baptized. Oh, oh, that I might obtain the motivation of devotion. I want to each day meditate on your word—to help others—to remember your Son's death—and most of all to pray.

Please express your response to this beautiful text. Put your expression in your own prayer diary.

6. READ HIS WORD FOR YOURSELF.

Dear Lord, I see Peter pointing at me. I hear through his words; it is *your call.* I want to be warned. I give myself in response—I enter into salvation. I accept your message—deepen my willingness to live it out in daily life today. Praise your wonderful grace that there are thousands and thousands of others who share the same salvation with me. Together we can continue our worship as the body of your Son on this earth.

It is so important that you pause in his presence
and either audibly or in written form tell him all his word means to you.

WEEK THREE — SUNDAY

7. READ HIS WORD IN THANKSGIVING.

Yes, yes, thank you: (1) Your promise has been kept — salvation is here. (2) You do call men through the gospel today as on Pentecost. (3) That you plead and warn us — this is out of your mercy — we do not deserve such. (4) The joy of others feeds my happiness. (5) There is a way to sustain our joy. (6) For the teachings of the apostles and prophets in the New Testament. (7) For the blessed supper of my Lord.

Give yourself to your own expression of gratitude — write it or speak it!

8. READ HIS WORD IN MEDITATION.

There *is*, there *is* something I *must* do to be saved. I can and do save myself. I *must* within my own heart respond to Him. I am reluctant, I need someone to plead and warn me. I can respond to the good news but I do not want to until someone like Peter pleads with me and warns me of hell and what being lost really means. Can we see today what we see here on Pentecost? Can 3,000 be won today? Indeed they can and are when we have preachers like Peter. God is ready to call to save through his preachers and his Spirit — through the acceptance of those who hear and believe and repent and are baptized.

Pause — wait — think — then express yourself in thoughtful praise or thanks.

9. READ HIS WORD FOR PETITIONS.

Let me request what I know you will give: (1) Help me to enjoy the promised salvation. (2) Make me a messenger to those who have never heard. (3) Break my heart that I might plead with men. (4) I want to be saved from my lost generation. (5) Are there 3,000 somewhere today who would accept your son? (6) If I do what they did will I not become what they were? (7) Dear Lord, help me to devote myself to all they did.

Right here add your personal requests — and his answers.

10. READ HIS WORD AND WAIT — LISTEN — GOD SPEAKS!

In a special way speak to me through these beautiful words: (1) "You need the fellowship I have for you with me and other Christians." (2) "You have not yet found the depth of meaning there is in my supper." (3) "You really do not know the joy you could have in prayer."

11. INTERCESSION FOR THE LOST WORLD

Denmark — Points for prayer: (1) *Higher unemployment* has forced many young people to go as "guest workers" to Sweden. Pray that some of these may have contact with Swedish believers. (2) *Although Protestant, Denmark is really a pioneer mission field today.* Few Danes have really heard the Gospel. Evangelistic and church planting ministries are needed. There are some denominational and non-denominational missionaries serving in the land, but reinforcements are needed. (3) *There are no Bible believing Bible Schools or Seminaries in the country.* There is a great need for a good Bible teaching ministry and training in evangelism and church planting.

12. SING PRAISES TO OUR LORD.

Praise Him! praise Him! Jesus, our blessed Redeemer!
Sing, O Earth, His wonderful love proclaim!
Hail Him! hail Him! highest archangels in glory:
Strength and honor give to His holy name!
Like a shepherd, Jesus will guard His children,
In His arms He carries them all day long:
Praise Him! praise Him! tell of His excellent greatness;
Praise Him! praise Him! ever in joyful song!

31

WEEK THREE — MONDAY

1. PRAISE GOD FOR WHO HE IS.

Complete. How could we better describe your self! There is nothing you lack. Your are whole in every sense. It would help me to worship you if I listed just two areas where all men can find you *complete.* (1) *Complete in knowledge.* There is no branch of science in which you do not have absolute and total information. It will be a part of the joy of heaven to investigate your resource of information. (2) *Complete in sympathetic understanding love.* My love and the love of all men is so inadequate — alloyed with our own selfishness. How glorious to worship and praise and know you — to commit myself — and for all men to do likewise. It is no effort — it is a privilege!

Express yourself in adoration for this quality of God.
Speak it audibly or write out your praise in your own devotional journal.

2. PRAISE GOD FOR WHAT HE MEANS TO ME.

What all men find generally in you I now find personally and intimately. I want to enter into a secret pact. In you I am whole for you are wholeness itself! I can pause anytime of the day and cast myself upon you. I *know* you care for me. (Peter said so.) You love me — forgive me — chasten me — have specific plans for me — bless your wonderful name! I find *no* help — *no* hope — *no* fulfillment in anyone or anything else! You have made my life so full — so meaningful. I want to reaffirm my wholeness in you. I am real eager to enter into the larger part of my life right on the other side of my last heart beat!

How do you personally relate to the completeness of God, and God who is complete?
Speak it out or write it out. It is *so important* that you establish *your own* devotional journal.

3. CONFESSION OF SIN

If you are so complete for every area of life, how is it I seek fulfillment outside yourself? It could be easy to say with Paul "It is not I who do it, but sin which lives in me." — or "So then it is no longer I that do it, but sin which dwells within me" (Rom. 7:17, RSV). Jesus *can* and *does* deliver me from this bondage of separation. I live by my response to my environment. My largest need then is to so condition my reflexes that I will always (by habit) respond to your sweet will and not that of Satan who is the deceiver. I have lived so long in Satan's world (with all that is in his (the) world) that I am like the Israelites who didn't recognize the Deliverer. Oh, dear God, dear Savior, I do want out! *Bitterness* is a sin. I have been (am I now?) bitter about some things. Have I ever been bitter against my dear wife? Dear Lord, why? I repent — change my mind — I was wrong, wrong, wrong! forgive me. Bless your name I'm whole!

What personal sin do you want to confess? We *must* speak them to remove them.
Do it! *Now.* There is no one else you have sinned against more than God. Tell him so!

4. SING A PRAYER TO GOD.

Jesus, Lover of my soul,
Let me to Thy bosom fly,
While the nearer waters roll,
While the tempest still is high;

Hide me, O my Savior, hide,
Till the storm of life is past;
Safe into the haven guide,
O receive my soul at last.

Open your hymn book and sing the rest of the verses — or even sing another prayer song.

5. READ HIS WORD TO HIM!
His Word

[43]Everyone was filled with awe, and many wonders and miraculous signs were done by the apostles. [44]All the believers were together and had everything in common. [45]Selling their possessions and goods, they gave to anyone as he had need. [46]Every day they continued to meet together in the temple courts. They broke bread in their homes and ate together with glad and sincere hearts, [47]praising God and enjoying the favor of all the people. And the Lord added to their number daily those who were being saved. — *Acts 2:43-47, NIV*

Read His Word to Him.

I want to be constantly filled with awe and wonder! There is more than enough all about me to make such a response very possible. Dear Lord, just to consider the beauty of the variety of birds, the color and delicate form of the flowers, to look down at my own hand. When I consider the millions and millions of stars and planets all held in place by your word. Physical healing is a source of wonder and awe and by the hands of your "sent ones" they were done. You are healing today in answer to prayer and I praise you — most of all for the awesome wonder of Calvary and the open tomb!

Please express your response to this beautiful text. Put your expression in your own prayer diary.

6. READ HIS WORD FOR YOURSELF.

Dear Lord, I *do*. I want to stand in the Temple court and feel the thrill of the risen Lord! I want to be consumed with the love for those in need. I want to be moved by the example and spirit of my Lord, to give what I have to help others. What a possession: *a glad, sincere heart*! The Lord will add to our number today when we have the same total involvement with you. In only thirty years the whole Roman world knew of your dear Son and his salvation (Col. 1:6, 23; Rom. 1:8).

It is so important that you pause in his presence
and either audibly or in written form tell him all his word means to you.

7. READ HIS WORD IN THANKSGIVING.

I always approach this time with exuberant expectation: (1) Thank you that I am not blind — that I can see. (2) Thank you that I can see through the eyes of Jesus — through the eyes of yourself — you have given me an inward eye transplant (the eyes of my heart)! (3) Thank you for the capacity of awe and wonder, and for objects and acts that produce such a reaction. (4) Oh, that all believers — *all* believers were together and had *all* things in common. I thank you for those who do — and for their example to show us we could if we would. (5) Thank you that you have given us favor with many, many people over a *long* period of time.

Give yourself to your own expression of gratitude — write it or speak it!

8. READ HIS WORD IN MEDITATION.

Let's meditate over three thoughts: (1) Jesus' miracles were his divine credentials. You placed your approval and acceptance upon him and his life and words by these acts of power. (2) God's set purpose was to take away the sin of the world — he did it — you did it! by your Lamb — even our Lord Jesus. He was "the Lamb slain before the earth was created." I do not understand it, but I know it is true. (3) The men of his own generation killed Jesus. His death was a violation of their own law. Men now do the same thing in their rejection of him. Praise your name *we can* change.

Pause — wait — think — then express yourself in thoughtful praise or thanks.

9. READ HIS WORD FOR PETITIONS.

What are you saying to me? What should I ask of you? (1) How can I find a deeper reverence? (2) Lord, I believe, help my unbelief! (3) Am I willing to sell what I have to help others? Open my heart! (4) How can I have the joy and unity with others I see in the Jerusalem church? (5) Help me to make every meal an act of worship. (6) Give me an attitude of love for all. (7) How can people be saved every day in my town?

Please, please remember these are prayers — speak them — reword them!

10. READ HIS WORD AND WAIT — LISTEN — GOD SPEAKS!

I hear you say to me: (1) "The Apostles are my voice." (2) "It is more blessed to help others than to be helped." (3) "Every Christian is a member of my church."

11. INTERCESSION FOR THE LOST WORLD

Denmark — Points for prayer: (1) *The Faroe Islands* between Britain and Iceland are a part of Denmark. There is a much higher proportion of true believers among the 40,000 people than in Denmark itself. The Brethren are strong — pray that these believers may have a greater burden for the evangelization of the Mainland. (2) *The large island of Greenland* in the Arctic, N.E. of Canada, is also Danish. Greenland is 51 times larger than Denmark, yet only has a population of 50,000. The island is largely ice covered and inhospitable. The majority of the people are Eskimos. Some of these are true believers, but many little communities are without a witness. Most of the Christian work being done is by Pentecostals.

12. SING PRAISES TO OUR LORD.

We praise Thee, O God! for the Son of Thy love,
For Jesus who died, and is now gone above.
Hallelujah! Thine the glory;

Hallelujah! Amen!
Hallelujah! Thine the glory;
Revive us again.

WEEK THREE — TUESDAY

1. PRAISE GOD FOR WHO HE IS.

Spirit. Indeed you are! Not mysterious but at the same time, who can trace out your ways? You are an all pervading intelligent Person. Invisible but clearly seen in the face of our Savior. Praise his holy, wonderful name!

Express yourself in adoration for this quality of God.
Speak it audibly or write out your praise in your own devotional journal.

2. PRAISE GOD FOR WHAT HE MEANS TO ME.

You are present in me in the person of the Holy Spirit. But it is also your capability to dwell everywhere at the same time. You are presently aware of all that I say and think and do. What a comforting fact! God as Spirit *de-sires* me to worship him, is actually "seeking men to worship him" (John 4:24, 25). You have surely found one who will!

How do you personally relate to the Spirit of God, and God who is Spirit?
Speak it out or write it out. It is *so important* that you establish *your own* devotional journal.

3. CONFESSION OF SIN

I guess I am more troubled by "why" I sin than that I sin. I should suspect Satan is at work in my subconsciousness. If I can convince my subconscious I am in earnest about bringing every thought into captivity, it would be done! Dear God, please help me! Forgive and wash me clean! — but help me to stay clean.

What personal sins do you want to confess? We *must* speak them to remove them.
Do it! *Now.* There is no one else you have sinned against more than God. Tell him so!

4. SING A PRAYER TO GOD.

Jesus, Savior, pilot me
Over life's tempestuous sea;
Unknown waves before me roll,
Hiding rock and treacherous shoal;
Chart and compass came from Thee:
Jesus, Savior, pilot me.

Open your hymn book and sing the rest of the verses — or even sing another prayer song.

5. READ HIS WORD TO HIM!

His Word

3 One day Peter and John were going up to the temple at the time of prayer — at three in the afternoon. ²Now a man crippled from birth was being carried to the temple gate called Beautiful, where he was put every day to beg from those going into the temple courts. ³When he saw Peter and John about to enter, he asked them for money. ⁴Peter looked straight at him, as did John. Then Peter said, "Look at us!" ⁵So the man gave them his attention, expecting to get something from them.

⁶Then Peter said, "Silver or gold I do not have, but what I have I give you. In the name of Jesus Christ of Nazareth, walk."
— Acts 3:1-6, NIV

Read His Word to Him.

How good to talk about persons who are with you now. To discuss the glad day when Peter and John moved to the place of prayer — at the hour of prayer. I am glad you directed Luke to record this. In 2,000 years the record has not been lost. The preciousness of that record is just as real today as when it happened. All of this is a true source of wonder and praise for me. There is someone else in heaven — the unnamed beggar. I know he has a name and you know him. I want to meet him. I do praise and thank you for this beautiful story.

Please express your response to this beautiful text. Put your expression in your own prayer diary.

6. READ HIS WORD FOR YOURSELF.

These are those who carried him. These people took a personal, unselfish interest in the beggar. I want to meet these people too. To have never walked, to see others walking and not be able — I can only try to imagine it. Dear Lord, thank you for the right use of every member of my body. I want to identify with the day-by-day weariness, the day-by-day limitation — begging from others. To beg even from you hardly seems natural. We ask as a son not as a stranger, but to be a beggar among men! There are yet multitudes of such persons in our world. I have forgotten. Dear Lord, forgive!

7. READ HIS WORD IN THANKSGIVING.

This is a veritable cornucopia of thanksgiving: (1) Thank you for the hours of prayer—how is it I can only find one hour? (2) Thank you for our many public places of worship. (3) Thank you that our bodies are even *now* your Temple indwelt by your Spirit. (4) Thank you for the types of miracles you have chosen—cases with no doubt of their condition—"crippled from birth, carried daily"—more than "40 years old." (5) That Peter and John had mercy upon him—or were moved by your Spirit to express concern (perhaps they saw him often). (6) That Peter and John were poor men—like most men—but they did have a wonderful gift for the beggar. (7) For the joy and confidence seen in the attitude and actions of all three.

Give yourself to your own expression of gratitude—write it or speak it!

8. READ HIS WORD IN MEDITATION.

There are two billion beggars outside God's Temple gate. If this beggar ever heard of Jesus we do not know it. We can *know* there are two billion people who have never, never heard the name of our Lord. I believe many, many of them would be just as responsive as the man before us. But some of us must see them. Dear God, move me to prayer, but *more*, move me to speak to them, touch them, raise them, heal them! How is it we are so willing to do nothing?

Pause—wait—think—then express yourself in thoughtful praise or thanks.

9. READ HIS WORD FOR PETITIONS.

How I want to pray according to your word: (1) If Peter and John found time for prayer three times a day, why can't I? (2) Are there beggars at my gate? (3) Open my heart to the poor! (4) Make me kind toward those who disagree with me. (5) Lead me to those with felt needs. (6) Help me to look until I really see. (7) I can only give what I have—is it salvation?

Right here add your personal requests—and his answers.

10. READ HIS WORD AND WAIT—LISTEN—GOD SPEAKS!

I open my inner ear: (1) "There are many crippled people among the religious." (2) "Speak straight to the heart of those in need." (3) "Your faith can 'do greater works.'"

11. INTERCESSION FOR THE LOST WORLD

Finland — Population: 4,700,000. Annual growth 0.4%. People per sq. km. — 14. Points for prayer: (1) *The threat of a Russian takeover is always there* (Russia attacked Finland seeking territorial gain in 1939). Finland has a 1,300 km. frontier with Russia, and is bound rather tightly to Russia and there is a powerful Communist party. (2) *The people are more religious than most Scandinavians*, and very open to the Word of God. There is need for more open evangelism and soul winning. There is also a need for a deep national revival—the groundwork having already been laid by many smaller waves of revival affecting mainly the Lutherans over the past century. (3) *The missionary vision* of the Finnish believers has grown considerably in recent years as a result of many young people coming to the Lord and seeking God's will concerning service overseas.

12. SING PRAISES TO OUR LORD.

The great Physician now is near,
The sympathizing Jesus;
He speaks the drooping heart to cheer,
Oh, hear the voice of Jesus.

Sweetest note in seraph song,
Sweetest name on mortal tongue;
Sweetest carol ever sung,
Jesus, blessed Jesus.

WEEK THREE — WEDNESDAY

1. PRAISE GOD FOR WHO HE IS.

Joy. You are joy itself, the source of all joy, the reason for all happiness, the ultimate of spontaneity! Brightness —all this and 10,000 things more that all say, "praise and wonder" to me but only express a part of your total person. Joy unspeakable and full of your whole self!

Express yourself in adoration for this quality of God.
Speak it audibly or write out your praise in your own devotional journal.

2. PRAISE GOD FOR WHAT HE MEANS TO ME.

Joy for me—to me—through me. Oh, praise and peace and joy—this is mine! Jesus said, "I have come that your joy may be perfected!" My joy is in him my dear, wonderful Lord. My happiness is full and complete in him. Apart from him there is no life at all.

How do you personally relate to joy of God, and God who is Joy?
Speak it out or write it out. It is *so important* that you establish *your own* devotional journal.

3. CONFESSION OF SIN

Oh, how I want to admit to sin. I want to tell everyone against whom I have sinned. He alone knows why I do this or that against him—so he can help me—not only with forgiveness but with understanding and inward strength how to overcome. Dear Savior, forgive and illumine my mind as I read your word.

What personal sins do you want to confess? We *must* speak them to remove them.
Do it! *Now.* There is no one else you have sinned against more than God. Tell him so!

4. SING A PRAYER TO GOD.

"There shall be showers of blessing":
This is the promise of love;
There shall be seasons refreshing,
Sent from the Saviour above.

Showers of blessing,
Showers of blessing we need:
Mercy-drops round us are falling,
But for the showers we plead.

Open your hymn book and sing the rest of the verses—or even sing another prayer song.

5. READ HIS WORD TO HIM!

His Word

[7]Taking him by the right hand, he helped him up, and instantly the man's feet and ankles became strong. [8]He jumped to his feet and began to walk. Then he went with them into the temple courts, walking and jumping, and praising God. [9]When all the people saw him walking and praising God, [10]they recognized him as the same man who used to sit begging at the temple gate called Beautiful, and they were filled with wonder and amazement at what had happened to him.
[11]While the beggar held on to Peter and John, all the people were astonished and came running to them in the place called Solomon's Colonnade.   — *Acts 3:7-11, NIV*

Read His Word to Him.

Dear God, take me by the right hand and raise me up. I need to be healed! Your word is so precious to me! How I do appreciate the careful detail in this account: "right hand," "feet and ankles," "walking," and "jumping," and "praising," "wonder" and "amazement." Each word carries more and different meaning to the whole beautiful record. "Instant" is another word I like—"all" the people saw him —*no* question about your miracles! I too am filled with wonder and amazement. Dear God, help me to come running to you and your healing power.

Please express your response to this beautiful text. Put your expression in your own prayer diary.

6. READ HIS WORD FOR YOURSELF.

I have read these words several hundred times, but I read them all over again because I *love* your word. I love the *One* they describe! Dear Lord, I now come with the excitement of the one resurrected from "death in trespasses and sins" to walk and jump and praise before you! I want to share with others—most especially with those who understand *my joy!* The healing was no end in itself, i.e., a primary end, so I am not just saved primarily to enjoy it, but to share it.

It is so important that you pause in his presence
and either audibly or in written form tell him all his word means to you.

7. READ HIS WORD IN THANKSGIVING.

So easy to do: (1) For Peter and John who stopped and touched and raised. (2) For the total supernatural quality of the healing. (3) For the first steps of a new man! what wonder! (4) For the first time in the Temple—he could now see what was on the inside. (5) For all the people in the Temple—one day I shall see them and ask them about what they saw. (6) For the unnamed beggar himself—I want one day to know him and his name. (7) For Paula Nash who spent time and talent to give us a lovely painting to help us see and relate!

Give yourself to your own expression of gratitude—write it or speak it!

8. READ HIS WORD IN MEDITATION.

A Meditation on Acts 1:13-15

[13]When they arrived, they went upstairs to the room where they were staying. Those present were Peter, John, James and Andrew; Philip and Thomas, Bartholomew and Matthew; James son of Alphaeus and Simon the Zealot, and Judas son of James. [14]They all joined together constantly in prayer, along with the women and Mary the mother of Jesus, and his brothers.

[15]In those days Peter stood up among the believers (a group numbering about a hundred and twenty). . . .

Two thoughts stand out in this text for meditation: (1) All can and should continue steadfastly in prayer. Our requests, indeed our total praying should be very much like theirs. In light of the momentous event about to take place, what thoughts ascended in prayer? Tender gratitude that our Lord was going to meet their need in sending "The Other Comforter." How could our needs be better met than with the "Other Jesus"? Eager anticipation of an experience they had not before known—but it would all be good and full of meaning and purpose. Is not this possible for me today? As I ask, as I knock, as I seek, he has already promised "good things" for me and you. (2) Business transactions—i.e., the mundane affairs of this life (such as filling the office of Judus) is also a part of serving God. *"Whatsoever you do* in word or in deed do all in the name (or with the authority) of the Lord Jesus—giving thanks to God our Father" (Col. 3:17).

Pause—wait—think—then express yourself in thoughtful praise or thanks.

9. READ HIS WORD FOR PETITIONS.

In your word you speak to me—but it also moves me to speak to you: (1) Lead me to someone today I can help. (2) May I see those in need as you do. (3) Help me to remember that joy and delight can express true worship. (4) Does anyone register wonder or amazement at my spiritual healing? (5) Open my mind and will to your joy! (6) What can I use today to attract people to your Son? (7) How close should new converts relate to me?

Please, please remember these are prayers—speak them—reword them!

10. READ HIS WORD AND WAIT—LISTEN—GOD SPEAKS

There are some definite messages here for me: (1) "Do something for me and I'll do something for you." (2) "The physical does lead to the eternal." (3) "Misplaced praise is to be expected—but not encouraged."

11. INTERCESSION FOR THE LOST WORLD

France — Population: 53,100,000. Growth 0.8% (nearly one half through immigration). 551,000 sq. km. The largest country in Western Europe. People to sq. km. — 99.

Points for prayer: (1) *France is one of the world's more important mission fields today.* It is reckoned that over 40 million French people have no real understanding of the true Gospel, and no connection with a church, though most are baptized Roman Catholics. The powerful influence of the Communist Party and also the dabbling of many in occult practices are symptomatic of the need. Pray that the present freedom to evangelize may be used to the full to bring many to a saving knowledge of the Lord Jesus Christ. (2) *There are many unreached peoples and areas in France.* Only about 1,500 of France's 38,000 communes (towns, villages, etc.) have a permanent Bible believing witness. There is only a handful of believers to be found in many parts of North and Central France, and also Brittany and the Island of Corsica just to name a few areas. The many minority groups also must be evangelized.

12. SING PRAISES TO OUR LORD.

I have found a friend in Jesus,
He's everything to me,
He's the fairest of ten thousand to my soul;
The Lily of the Valley, in Him alone I see
All I need to cleanse and make me fully whole.

In sorrow He's my comfort, in trouble He's my stay,
He tells me every care on Him to roll:
He's the Lily of the Valley, the Bright and Morning Star,
He's the fairest of ten thousand to my soul.

WEEK THREE — THURSDAY

1. PRAISE GOD FOR WHO HE IS.

Intelligence. Total understanding—what an amazing quality! and yet to think less would be to worship One who was less than God himself. How wonderfully encouraging it is to be the son, yet the slave of a Father who knows *all*.

Express yourself in adoration for this quality of God.
Speak it audibly or write out your praise in your own devotional journal.

2. PRAISE GOD FOR WHAT HE MEANS TO ME.

Intelligence is the one quality of man that separates him from animals. To be able to reason, to know my needs because he shares them. He totally understands them. This by itself is almost beyond my grasp. How I truly praise him, praise you for yourself!

How do you personally relate to the intelligence of God, and God who is intelligence?
Speak it out or write it out. It is *so important* that you establish *your own* devotional journal.

3. CONFESSION OF SIN

To consider the awesome fact that God is absolute intelligence could be intimidating, except that he is total love as well as intelligence. So I am actually greatly encouraged. I openly confess because there is no hiding. I totally confess because there is nothing overlooked. But I am just as totally forgiven! Bless his holy, glorious, name! In no way could I adequately express my joy.

What personal sins do you want to confess? We *must* speak them to remove them.
Do it! *Now.* There is no one else you have sinned against more than God. Tell him so!

4. SING A PRAYER TO GOD.

Ere you left your room this morning,
Did you think to pray?
In the name of Christ our Savior,
Did you sue for loving favor,
As a shield today?

Oh, how praying rests the weary!
Prayer will change the night to day;
So in sorrow and in gladness,
Don't forget to pray.

Open your hymn book and sing the rest of the verses—or even sing another prayer song.

5. READ HIS WORD TO HIM.

His Word

[12]When Peter saw this, he said to them: "Men of Israel, why does this surprise you? Why do you stare at us as if by our own power or godliness we had made this man walk? [13]The God of Abraham, Isaac and Jacob, the God of our fathers, has glorified his servant Jesus. You handed him over to be killed, and you disowned him before Pilate, though he had decided to let him go. [14]You disowned the Holy and Righteous One and asked that a murderer be released to you. [15]You killed the author of life, but God raised him from the dead. We are witnesses of this.

— Acts 3:12-15, NIV

Read His Word to Him.

How good to see your action in human affairs. You are interested in men walking. But you are much more interested in their purpose for walking. Your power—oh, your power enables each of us to walk. In you we live and move and have our being. Your nature, manifest in your works of healing and helping is such an encouragement to all of us. How we want to accept and appreciate the glory (character or estimate) you give of your holy servant Jesus—even your dear son. Oh dear God, may I never, never repeat the tragic choice of those who cried for Barabbas.

Please express your response to this beautiful text. Put your expression in your own prayer diary.

6. READ HIS WORD FOR YOURSELF.

There I am in the crowd. I'm listening to Peter preach. I share the privilege of living in the generation when my Savior came to earth. There I am again! Can it be? It is so! I'm crying for His death. If we had no sin he would not have died. It was my sin that nailed him there. But I stand in the crowd at the cross and apply the words of my dear Lord to my heart. "You do (they) not know what you are doing." Bless the Lord, I'm also in the company who saw him "after his passion"—alive forevermore!

It is so important that you pause in his presence
and either audibly or in written form tell him all his word means to you.

7. READ HIS WORD IN THANKSGIVING.

Thanksgiving seems so appropriate: (1) For the super-human change in Peter—confident and humble. The living Lord did it. (2) John is there too—thoughtful and strong—thank you for the complement he is to Peter and Peter to him. (3) Thank you that this grafted branch can be a part of the heritage of Abraham, Isaac and Jacob. (4) How could I ever say thank you for "the Servant" of Isaiah—fulfilled in Jesus of Nazareth? (5) I cannot—I hesitate—I am full of amazement—but I share the prison cell of Barabbas—my Lord died for me and in my place! "Thank you" is not at all enough.

Give yourself to your own expression of gratitude—write it or speak it!

8. READ HIS WORD IN MEDITATION.

Let us think deeply on three observations: (1) Peter and John were going into the Temple at the hour of prayer. What a blessed sweet hour of prayer it can be. But sweet or not, we can go to it—we are the better for it. (2) He was lame from birth—so are we—since the birth of sin in our hearts. He was carried daily by his friends—our friends do us a favor by carrying us where they go—i.e., if they are Christians. If not, it is only a beggar's place. He was laid daily at such a place. "Life is so daily" but in the midst of it Jesus comes! (3) They looked intently at him. Oh, may we do the same for those outside God's Temple of worship today. Look at them with deep understanding and compassion.

Pause—wait—think—then express yourself in thoughtful praise or thanks.

9. READ HIS WORD FOR PETITIONS.

I want to ask from close contact with your word: (1) How can I point men away from me to you? (2) Help me to appreciate more fully your power. (3) Do I really know of what godliness consists? (4) What particular quality of our Lord is seen in this healing? (5) Please keep me reminded that evil men hate the light. (6) Deepen my appreciation of just how holy and how righteous is my Lord. (7) Make him the author of my life today.

Right here add your personal requests—and his answers.

10. READ HIS WORD AND WAIT—LISTEN—GOD SPEAKS!

Speak Lord—thy servant heareth: (1) "There is nothing as important as telling the good news." (2) "Follow the example of Peter." (3) "Jesus sees you *now!*"

11. INTERCESSION FOR THE LOST WORLD

France — Points for prayer: (1) *The influential Roman Catholic Church is in turmoil* with many tensions between the conservative traditionalists, liberals, modernists, radicals and now the growing charismatic movement. The latter has opened the hearts of many to the truths of God's Word and the acceptance of the need to be born again. Pray that there may be many won to the Lord through these pressures and influences.

12. SING PRAISES TO OUR LORD.

The name of Jesus is so sweet,
I love its music to repeat;
It makes my joys full and complete,
The precious name of Jesus.

"Jesus," oh, how sweet the name!
"Jesus," ev'ry day the same;
"Jesus," let all saints proclaim
Its worthy praise forever.

WEEK THREE — FRIDAY

1. PRAISE GOD FOR WHO HE IS.

Lonesome. How encouraging to know that God *wants* me. You have created *me* in your own image and I share your nature. You have put me here to commune with you. You long after me with an everlasting love. Love that is not expressed is really not love.

Express yourself in adoration for this quality of God.
Speak it audibly or write out your praise in your own devotional journal.

2. PRAISE GOD FOR WHAT HE MEANS TO ME.

I am delighted to be the object of your love. Your love is expressed by all your bounties. It is difficult to separate the two thoughts of your lonesomeness for me and my lonesomeness for you. I love you in return. I *want* you, *need* you, *desire* you, *embrace* you to my heart (mind, emotions, conscience). I am so, so lonesome without you! I worship before you in praise.

How do you personally relate to the lonesomeness of God, and God who is lonesome?
Speak it out or write it out. It is *so important* that you establish *your own* devotional journal.

3. CONFESSION OF SIN

I *am* a sinner. I do now need forgiveness. There is no day, no hour, no minute when I do not need your cleansing blood! But there must be a progress in conduct. How I long to be whole in my in-depth attitude! Oh, dear Savior, I love you and seek your forgiveness!

What personal sins do you want to confess? We *must* speak them to remove them.
Do it! *Now.* There is no one else you have sinned against more than God. Tell him so!

4. SING A PRAYER TO GOD.

Love divine, all loves excelling,
Joy of heav'n to earth come down;
Fix in us Thy humble dwelling;
All Thy faithful mercies crown.

Jesus, Thou art all compassion,
Pure, unbounded love Thou art;
Visit us with Thy salvation;
Enter ev'ry trembling heart.

Open your hymn book and sing the rest of the verses—or even sing another prayer song.

5. READ HIS WORD TO HIM!

His Word

saying that his Christ would suffer. [19]Repent, then, and turn to God, so that your sins may be wiped out, that times of refreshing may come from the Lord, [20]and that he may send the Christ, who has been appointed for you— even Jesus. [21]He must remain in heaven until the time comes for God to restore everything, as he promised long ago through his holy prophets. [22]For Moses said, 'The Lord your God will raise up for you a prophet like me from among your own people; you must listen to everything he tells you. [23]Anyone who does not listen to him will be completely cut off from among his people.'

[24]"Indeed, all the prophets from Samuel on, as many as have spoken, have foretold these days. [25]And you are heirs of the prophets and of the covenant God made with your fathers. He said to Abraham, 'Through your off-spring all peoples on earth will be blessed.' [26]When God raised up his servant, he sent him first to you to bless you by turning each of you from your wicked ways."

— *Acts 3:18b-26, NIV*

Read His Word to Him.

Oh, dear God! How I want to tell you what your word means to me. By faith the man was healed and made strong—the faith of Peter and John in your interest and involvement in needs of the religious but lost. I know you have the same interest today. The same faith will also fulfill your interest today. To act in ignorance and at the same time in fulfillment of prophecy is an amazement. But so is the wonder of your word and power.

Please express your response to this beautiful text. Put your expression in your own prayer diary.

6. READ HIS WORD FOR YOURSELF.

Times of refreshing can and will come—and even now come from your presence. As I turn from my sins and change the outer fringes and the inner center of my mind, I am refreshed. Oh, dear God, I do indeed change my mind.

He must stay in heaven until a certain time. You know the time of his coming. I do not. But I even now cry from my heart "Maranatha!" What is the word in the presence of the angels of light?

It is so important that you pause in his presence
and either audibly or in written form tell him all his word means to you.

7. READ HIS WORD IN THANKSGIVING.

How open is your word here for this exercise: (1) That our ignorance does not hinder or prevent your word from finding fulfillment. (2) That your goodness is such a strong incentive for repentance. (3) That times of refreshing can and do come from your presence. (4) That you will send my Lord the second time as surely as you sent him the first time. (5) How beautifully like Moses is my Lord! (6) That I can and do hear and harken to your prophet and my Lord. (7) Thank you for your present blessing.

Give yourself to your own expression of gratitude—write it or speak it.

8. READ HIS WORD IN MEDITATION.

Meditation on Luke 1:37: "For nothing is impossible with God."

For no word from God shall be void of power. (1) Thank you, that you have spoken. (2) In written, permanent form. (3) All your words are equal in source and fulfillment. (4) You can and do speak. (5) No emptiness or failure in yourself or your word. (6) Your power through yourself and your word is invincible. (7) The total encouragement I feel from this verse.

Pause—wait—think—then express yourself in thoughtful praise or thanks.

9. READ HIS WORD FOR PETITIONS.

How I want my petitions to be your petitions: (1) Did the lame man have any faith? (2) Wasn't it the gift of faith exercised by Peter that healed him? (3) Let Jesus work through me for "greater works" today. (4) How can I act in ignorance and yet be responsible? (5) Help me to repent all over again. (6) Give me the seasons of refreshing. (7) I want the blessing of turning from my sins.

Please, please remember these are prayers—speak them—reword them!

10. READ HIS WORD AND WAIT—LISTEN—GOD SPEAKS!

In these verses what do you say to me? (1) "Find out how Jesus is like Moses and teach it." (2) "I want all the peoples of the earth to be blessed." (3) "If you do not listen you will be cut off."

11. INTERCESSION FOR THE LOST WORLD

France — Point for prayer: (1) *The Protestants have had a long and glorious history* of zeal and persecution. Later the Reformed Church had a great missionary vision with many missionaries going out all over the world with the old Paris Evangelical Missionary Society. Most of the pastors of the Reformed Church are liberal in theology and many radical in politics, so numbers have been declining for many years. Most of the Protestants are very nominal and never attend church, yet there are staunch believers in many congregations. The Bible believing voice, muted for many years, is now becoming stronger.

12. SING PRAISES TO OUR LORD.

Christ has for sin atonement made,
What a wonderful Savior!
We are redeemed! the price is paid!

What a wonderful Savior!
What a wonderful Savior is Jesus, my Jesus!
What a wonderful Savior is Jesus my Lord!

WEEK THREE — SATURDAY

1. PRAISE GOD FOR WHO HE IS.

Shepherd. How easy it is to praise you for being a shepherd — shepherd of love — of total care and concern for me. How I need — how I accept your love and care in my life!

Express yourself in adoration for this quality of God.
Speak it audibly or write out your praise in your own devotional journal.

2. PRAISE GOD FOR WHAT HE MEANS TO ME.

Your pastures are green and your waters are still and your food is nourishing. I gladly accept your love and oversight. I sit at the table prepared in the presence of my enemies. I long to enter your eternal fold.

How do you personally relate to the shepherding of God, and God who is our shepherd.
Speak it out or write it out. It is *so important* that you establish *your own* devotional journal.

3. CONFESSION OF SIN

Oh, dear shepherd, how often does this sheep go astray — how welcome is your voice that calls me back to your care and love! I want to be healed of my self-inflicted wounds. Dear Lord, forgive — cleanse me of my sin — but purify within.

What personal sins do you want to confess? We *must* speak them to remove them.
Do it! *Now.* There is no one else you have sinned against more than God. Tell him so!

4. SING A PRAYER TO GOD.

More holiness give me,
More striving within;
More patience in suff'ring,
More sorrow for sin;

More faith in my Savior,
More sense of His care;
More joy in His service,
More purpose in prayer.

Open your hymn book and sing the rest of the verses — or even sing another prayer song.

5. READ HIS WORD TO HIM!

His Word

4 The priests and the captain of the temple guard and the Sadducees came up to Peter and John while they were speaking to the people. ²They were greatly disturbed because the apostles were teaching the people and proclaiming in Jesus the resurrection of the dead. ³They seized Peter and John, and because it was evening, they put them in jail until the next day. ⁴But many who heard the message believed, and the number of men grew to about five thousand.
⁵The next day the rulers, elders and teachers of the law met in Jerusalem. ⁶Annas the high priest was there, and so were Caiaphas, John, Alexander and the other men of the high priest's family. ⁷They had Peter and John brought before them and began to question them: "By what power or what name did you do this?"
— *Acts 4:1-7, NIV*

Read His Word to Him.

How gladly do I read again these words. Honor and thanks to you for causing them to be written. They are and have been such a source of blessing to so many for so long — too bad — oh, sad beyond words, that this word is not known to more. Dear God, give me the courage and wisdom to do what I can to tell those religious persons of our day of the resurrection of your Son.

Please express your response to this beautiful text. Put your expression in your own prayer diary.

6. READ HIS WORD FOR YOURSELF.

Teaching and preaching are linked with the same action. Dear God, give me the power and privilege to do the same thing today! Jesus will raise *me* from the dead — indeed all that sleep in the dust shall arise! (i.e., the bodies). "As in Christ all shall be made alive." Praise your wonderful name! Many that heard the word believed — I believe if more heard, more would believe. Oh, dear Lord, move me, enable me to make such possible!

It is so important that you pause in his presence
and either audibly or in written form tell him all his word means to you.

WEEK THREE — SATURDAY

7. READ HIS WORD IN THANKSGIVING.

How I thank you for: (1) Religious people who have a disposition to listen. (2) The power to think and speak your thoughts and words. (3) In Jesus we will be raised to live forever in heaven. (4) Jail is no disgrace if it is for him—it is an open door not a closed one. (5) For 5,000 who could hear and accept today if we would tell them. (6) For the historical accuracy of the account—names, places, etc. (7) "By what power or by what authority" do we do anything and everything?

It is so important that you pause in his presence
and either audibly or in written form tell him all his word means to you.

8. READ HIS WORD IN MEDITATION.

By what power have you done this? (1) Not the power of education for they were unlearned and ignorant. (2) Not by the power of personal moral courage because they fled and denied him but a few days earlier. (3) Not by the power of personal ambition, for they had everything to lose and nothing to gain by their actions. (4) Not by the power of money—silver and gold; they had none.

It was by the power of: (1) The resurrected Christ—he was alive and this news was so exciting and important it *must* be told. (2) It was by the power and person of the Holy Spirit of God. He enabled them when they trusted him. (3) It was by the power of love and concern that men would hear. (4) It was by the power of the spoken word.

Pause—wait—think—then express yourself in thoughtful praise or thanks.

9. READ THE WORD IN MEDITATION.

I am asking you out of your word—I claim your promises: (1) Reveal to me if I am in any way like these religious bigots. (2) How I want to proclaim the same message today—help me! (3) Open my mind as to the prominence of the resurrection in preaching. (4) Help me with the boldness I lack and want. (5) I do pray for my brothers in jail now for their faith. (6) How I want to make my intercession intelligent—help me! (7) How can I reach men today?

Right here add your personal requests—and his answers.

10. READ HIS WORD AND WAIT—LISTEN—GOD SPEAKS!

Speak to me in these words: (1) "You are not as willing to suffer as you should be!" (2) "Belief comes by hearing—speak out." (3) "Go to religious people first."

11. INTERCESSION FOR THE LOST WORLD

France — Points for prayer: (1) *The Bible believing churches* are relatively few, but growing. There is generally not much real growth among the churches linked with the missionary groups. Pray for the mobilization of believers for evangelism and church growth. Many believers find it very hard to witness to others due to the national reluctance to intrude into the private lives of others and also to the common indifference, materialism and even hostility to the things of God. Pray for revival among the believers. (2) *There is a great need for Christian workers.* There are estimated to be 1,360 full time Bible believing Christian workers in the country, i.e., one worker for every 40,000 people. Pray for the rising up of spiritual men of God for the ministry. (3) *Young people are probably the most receptive group to the Gospel.* Many groups and missions have specialized in this ministry. Pray for many young people to be saved and integrated into good Bible believing churches—the latter step usually being much harder than the former!

12. SING PRAISES TO OUR LORD.

Standing on the promises of Christ my King,
Thro' eternal ages let His praises ring;
Glory in the highest, I will shout and sing,
Standing on the promises of God.

Standing, standing,
Standing on the promises of God my Saviour;
Standing, standing,
I'm standing on the promises of God.

43

WEEK FOUR — SUNDAY

1. PRAISE GOD FOR WHO HE IS.

Sanctification. Dear God, how you do set people aside for your work. All that you do is sanctified—blessed be your name—what a wonder you are. You are much more a sanctification than anything else. All you have done is holy and pure and right and unique.

Express yourself in adoration for this quality of God.
Speak it audibly or write out your praise in your own devotional journal.

2. PRAISE GOD FOR WHAT HE MEANS TO ME.

Sanctification of myself. How I need you and want you to set me aside as a servant of yours. I want to be a vessel for use—whatever honor comes from this, let it be in the good works as a praise to you—even as my Lord has said.

How do you personally relate to the sanctification of God, and God who is Sanctifier.
Speak it out or write it out. It is *so important* that you establish *your own* devotional journal.

3. CONFESSION OF SIN

How easy it is to confess to you my sin. I do so in plain words. I am deeply sorry for my sin—not only so, I honestly purpose to forsake them! Dear Lord, help me! Cleanse me! I accept your forgiveness.

What personal sins do you want to confess? We *must* speak them to remove them.
Do it! *Now.* There is no one else you have sinned against more than God. Tell him so!

4. SING A PRAYER TO GOD.

More love to Thee, O Christ,
More love to Thee!
Hear Thou the prayer I make
On bended knee;

This is my earnest plea:
More love, O Christ to Thee,
More love to Thee!
More love to Thee!

Open your hymn book and sing the rest of the verses—or even sing another prayer song.

5. READ HIS WORD TO HIM!

His Word

[7]They had Peter and John brought before them and began to question them: "By what power or what name did you do this?"

[8]Then Peter, filled with the Holy Spirit, said to them: "Rulers and elders of the people! [9]If we are being called to account today for an act of kindness shown to a cripple and are asked how he was healed, [10]then know this, you and everyone else in Israel: It is by the name of Jesus Christ of Nazareth, whom you crucified but whom God raised from the dead, that this man stands before you completely healed. [11]He is

"'The stone you builders rejected, which has become the capstone.'

[12]Salvation is found in no one else, for there is no other name under heaven given to men by which we must be saved."

[13]When they saw the courage of Peter and John and realized that they were unschooled, ordinary men, they were astonished and they took note that these men had been with Jesus. [14]But since they could see the man who had been healed standing there with them, there was nothing they could say. [15]So they ordered them to withdraw from the Sanhedrin and then conferred together.

— Acts 4:7-15, NIV

Read His Word to Him.

How interesting it will be dear Lord when I can inquire personally about so many men who have crossed the canvas of time. What ever happened to Annas, and Caiaphas and John and Alexander, and all the other men of the high priest's family? I know you know and this is enough. Peter and John I expect to meet and talk with.

Please express your response to this beautiful text. Put your expression in your own prayer diary.

6. READ HIS WORD FOR YOURSELF.

Dear God, I want to *see my* salvation fulfilled in Him — even in your dear Son. He is my capstone — my hope — my door — my peace — my courage and boldness. Bless and adore his dear name! Oh, how I want to be so often personally with you that men will see reflected your presence in me.

It is so important that you pause in his presence
and either audibly or in written form tell him all his word means to you.

7. READ HIS WORD IN THANKSGIVING.

Thank you: (1) for every day as a judgment day. We will decide issues today that will not appear again. (2) The power in the name of our Lord — to save and forgive and bring joy. (3) Acts of kindness — in all the past (but for today is there one act for me?). (4) Jesus is alive, and even now sees me and knows me, loves me. (5) The capstone of all history. (6) What unschooled and ordinary men can do. (7) That I can this very day, right now be with Jesus.

Give yourself to your own expression of gratitude — write it or speak it!

8. READ HIS WORD IN MEDITATION.

Dear Lord, you know and I know these thoughts are fleeting and sometimes not at all profound. I want to wonder and praise in the thought of *trials before men* — we all have them every day. We threaten one another's interests and are brought into conflict. How shall we react? Perhaps Peter and John are saying something to us such as: (1) They were first of all and most of all "filled with the Holy Spirit" — filled with the power and name (authority) of the "Other Jesus." (2) They emphasized the good or the kindness done. (3) Gave all credit for all good to the One to whom it is due. (4) Did not ignore the problem — were ready to lay their lives on the line.

Pause — wait — think — then express yourself in thoughtful praise or thanks.

9. READ HIS WORD FOR PETITIONS.

How good it is to relate my requests to your unchanging word: (1) Am I to expect any better treatment from religious leaders today? (2) Perhaps all those who accept my Lord are my brothers — is this true? (3) What trophies of your triumph can I show to all men? (4) How can I convince men of the reality of my Lord's salvation? (5) I want Jesus to be the capstone of my life — help me! (6) Give this ordinary man extraordinary courage from yourself. (7) How can I establish a closer fellowship with my Lord?

Please, please remember these are prayers — speak them — reword them!

10. READ HIS WORD AND WAIT — LISTEN — GOD SPEAKS!

You are speaking — am I listening? (1) "I will be just as near to you as you are to me." (2) "Men will have nothing to say against you if you do good." (3) "Men are plotting now how to silence my witness."

11. INTERCESSION FOR THE LOST WORLD

France — Points for prayer: (1) *Foreign missions in France.* There are now about 43 different groups ministering with about 519 missionaries. There are 46 working among young people, 48 in technical ministries and the rest in evangelism, church planting and Bible teaching. There is plenty of work for new missionaries prepared to work under French leadership and French ways. There is a great need for missionaries to humbly adapt to the French culture. 38 of the 95 departments have no resident missionaries. (2) *There are 68 university type institutions,* but the Bible believing witness is still very small. Much more remains to be done to establish Bible believing groups in every faculty and to build up the believers for more effective witnessing among this rather receptive student population. There are about 100,000 foreign students in Paris alone. There are over 800,000 university students in France.

12. SING PRAISES TO OUR LORD.

Golden harps are sounding,
Angels voices ring,
Pearly gates are opened,
Opened for the King;
Christ, the King of glory,
Jesus, King of love,
Is gone up in triumph
To His throne above.
All His work is ended,
Joyful we sing;
Jesus hath ascended:
Glory to our King!

WEEK FOUR – MONDAY

1. PRAISE GOD FOR WHO HE IS.

Redeemer. "O blessed Redeemer, how precious Thou art." This is more than a song; it is the eternal truth. The amazing fact is you have paid the ransom price and bought us back to yourself. Blessed be your name forever – my redeemer – but also the world's redeemer. What a price you have paid! How I do appreciate it!

Express yourself in adoration for this quality of God.
Speak it audibly or write out your praise in your own devotional journal.

2. PRAISE GOD FOR WHAT HE MEANS TO ME.

You are *my* redeemer – my ransom from sin and bondage. I am deeply moved with the cost involved! O holy Redeemer, how precious you are to me! It is the wonder of ten million galaxies that you should take the form of man and pour out your blood for my redemption.

How do you personally relate to the redemption of God, and God who is Redeemer.
Speak it out or write it out. It is *so important* that you establish *your own* devotional journal.

3. CONFESSION OF SIN

Surely my deepest need is redemption and to be forgiven. I need to freely confess all my need and to be made clean. I do confess to One who knows and loves and heals. Dear God, forgive! To be open and free with you – I name and label my sin and accept the remission.

What personal sins do you want to confess? We *must* speak them to remove them.
Do it! *Now.* There is no one else you have sinned against more than God. Tell him so!

4. SING A PRAYER TO GOD.

My faith looks up to Thee,
Thou Lamb of Calvary,
Savior divine!
Now hear me while I pray,

Take all my guilt away,
O let me from this day
Be wholly Thine!

Open your hymn book and sing the rest of the verses – or even sing another prayer song.

5. READ HIS WORD TO HIM!

His Word

[16]"What are we going to do with these men?" they asked. "Everybody living in Jerusalem knows they have done an outstanding miracle, and we cannot deny it. [17]But to stop this thing from spreading any further among the people, we must warn these men to speak no longer to anyone in this name." [18]Then they called them in again and commanded them not to speak or teach at all in the name of Jesus. [19]But Peter and John replied, "judge for yourselves whether it is right in God's sight to obey you rather than God. [20]For we cannot help speaking about what we have seen and heard."

[21]After further threats they let them go. They could not decide how to punish them, because all the people were praising God for what had happened. [22]For the man who was miraculously healed was over forty years old.

– Acts 4:16-22, NIV

Read His Word to Him.

"What are we going to do with these men?" You surely must have been pleased when Peter and John caught the fire of love and zeal. What deep humility it took for these ordinary men to become such extra-ordinary slaves of King Jesus! Dear God, how I love the record of evangelism in this account. Oh! oh! that it might be repeated right here in our town. To speak to men and women in the name of Jesus is my desire – my commitment – my job. Is it right in the sight of God? in the sight of men? What have I seen and heard? Oh, speak and reveal yourself as I read your word.

Please express your response to this beautiful text. Put your expression in your own prayer diary,

6. READ HIS WORD FOR YOURSELF.

There is an open door in our town. I *want* to get your word in every home in *every* heart, in every life, in this town. If these men and women could fill Jerusalem, we surely can fill the place where I live. There *are* people here who will praise God for what is done. I have less reason than they did for not doing this. No one has commanded me not to do it. More want it than oppose it, what am I waiting for?

It is so important that you pause in his presence
and either audibly or in written form tell him all his word means to you.

7. READ HIS WORD IN THANKSGIVING.

Thank you, thank you for: (1) The honesty (though forced) of the men in authority — it could easily be the same today. (2) For the power of *his name*, his authority, his presence, his word, his total person. (3) For the directness and clarity of the words of Peter and John. (4) That they were willing to back up their words with their lives. (5) That people have the capacity of praise and wonder now as then.

Give yourself to your own expression of gratitude — write it or speak it!

8. READ HIS WORD IN MEDITATION.

The little leaven. Just two men, just two lives, just a poor beggar, just verbal expression — but leaven is total — all the leaven is leaven. Whenever Peter and John touched the lives of anyone they affected them. There was no time, no place, no one who touched Peter and John that was not infected with the leaven of joy and happiness. People were touched by the wonderous news that the Messiah had come! The lame man had a strong infection — he was incurably affected by the leaven of deliverance from sickness, boredom, meaninglessness, despondency.

Pause — wait — think — then express yourself in thoughtful praise or thanks.

9. READ HIS WORD FOR PETITIONS.

Indeed I do want to ask everything according to your word: (1) How can I let everyone in my town know of your son? (2) Am I in any way intimidated by my fear of men? (3) Do the laws of men today in any way oppose the laws of yourself? (4) I want to see more and hear more of your son — help me! (5) How can such an act of your power happen today? (6) I am the man who was healed — increase my witness. (7) How would it feel to beg for years and years?

Right here add your personal requests — and his answers.

10. READ HIS WORD AND WAIT — LISTEN — GOD SPEAKS!

Speak to me, Lord: (1) "Men will not always be convinced even by the best evidence." (2) "Most men will be convinced — keep on telling the story." (3) "There are men just waiting for your word of healing."

11. INTERCESSION FOR THE LOST WORLD

France — Points for prayer: (1) *Literature has been used of God.* Much evangelistic literature has been written over the last few years, and used for intensive literature campaigns. Pray for the production of good, relevant, French written tracts, etc. There is a lack of good devotional, teaching and missiological books in French. (2) *Minority groups: North Africans* number 1,300,000 and are Arabs and Berbers from Algeria, Tunisia and Morocco. There are only about 100 Christians among them; the majority being Muslims. There is one little assembly of believers among them and others have joined French Bible believing churches — one being pastored by a Berber. It is hard to bridge the gap of culture and resentment against "Christians." Pray that God may raise up believers from among these people who will return with the Gospel to North Africa.

12. SING PRAISES TO OUR LORD.

Blessed assurance, Jesus is mine!
Oh, what a foretaste of glory divine!
Heir of salvation, purchase of God,
Born of His Spirit, washed in His blood.

This is my story, this is my song,
Praising my Saviour all the day long;
This is my story, this is my song,
Praising my Saviour all the day long.

WEEK FOUR – TUESDAY

1. PRAISE GOD FOR WHO HE IS.

Savior. How good to call you by this name. Angels so described you. All that is valuable and has any meaning in this whole world is the object or trophy of your salvation. You have saved us all—most have just never heard of your offer.

Express yourself in adoration for this quality of God.
Speak it audibly or write out your praise in your own devotional journal.

2. PRAISE GOD FOR WHAT HE MEANS TO ME.

How easy it is to relate to your work in men. I have been saved from a life of frustration and emptiness to *one* of true joy and peace and eternal purpose. These are much more than mere words on paper. Joy in your presence and person—peace with you and all others—eternal purpose in what I do: Teaching, writing, speaking—without you there would be nothing. Indeed you have saved me!

How do you personally relate to the salvation of God, and God who is Savior.
Speak it out or write it out. It is *so important* that you establish *your own* devotional journal.

3. CONFESSION OF SIN

This is an admission—a tragic admission that at times I do not want to be saved! Most of the time it is because I do not know how lost I am. But there are other sad days when I am unwilling to change my mind in a way that will alter my conduct. Dear God, save me from this selfishness! Your salvation is *from* my sins—but is also *to* your happiness!

What personal sins do you want to confess? We *must* speak them to remove them.
Do it! *No.* There is no one else you have sinned against more than God. Tell him so!

4. SING A PRAYER TO GOD.

My Jesus I love Thee,
I know Thou art mine,
For Thee all the follies of sin I resign;

My gracious Redeemer, my Savior art Thou;
If ever I loved Thee, my Jesus 'tis now.

Open your hymn book and sing the rest of the verses—or even sing another prayer song.

5. READ HIS WORD TO HIM!

His Word

[23]On their release, Peter and John went back to their own people and reported all that the chief priests and elders had said to them. [24]When they heard this, they raised their voices together in prayer to God. "Sovereign Lord," they said, "you made the heaven and the earth and the sea, and everything in them. [25]You spoke by the Holy Spirit through the mouth of your servant, our father David:

'Why do the nations rage and the peoples plot in vain? [26]The kings of the earth take their stand and the rulers gather together against the Lord and against his Anointed One.'

[27]Indeed Herod and Pontius Pilate met together with the Gentiles and the people of Israel in this city to conspire against your holy servant Jesus, whom you anointed. [28]They did what your power and will had decided beforehand should happen. [29]Now, Lord, consider their threats and enable your servants to speak your word with great boldness. [30]Stretch out your hand to heal and perform miraculous signs and wonders through the name of your holy servant Jesus." — *Acts 4:23-30, NIV*

Read His Word to Him.

How easy it will be to praise you and wonder before you from this passage! I stand in the crowd to hear the exciting words of Peter and John. How encouraging and at the same time they are a cause of deep concern. How beautiful to find just the appropriate text for the situation. Men do only nothing without your knowledge. Men do not always do what you want, but they do nothing without your knowing it.

Please express your response to this beautiful text. Put your expression in your own prayer diary.

WEEK FOUR — TUESDAY

6. READ HIS WORD FOR YOURSELF.

I want to be a real part of "their company." I acknowledge not only your sovereignty but your intimacy and your personal interest in the affairs of men. For today with the president and congress and with our local officials — in all the occurrences of our town. Dear God, in my own life "stretch out your hand to heal." If you consider whatever threats there are, I have no fear. You know my needs and have much good prepared for me.

It is so important that you pause in his presence
and either audibly or in written form tell him all his word means to you.

7. READ HIS WORD IN THANKSGIVING.

(1) For all the varied lives that have made up your company — over the centuries. (2) That I can acknowledge your sovereignty now — creator of the heavens (fantastic!) and the earth and the sea and all in both — wow! (3) You inspired the Old Testament. David wrote and spoke through the Holy Spirit. (4) Jesus was and is your anointed One — the Messiah! (5) Men cannot successfully oppose you. (6) We can, by the Holy Spirit, speak the word with boldness.

Give yourself to your own expression of gratitude — write it or speak it!

8. READ HIS WORD IN MEDITATION.

Let's consider carefully these two thoughts: (1) Isn't it strange that the very men who should be glad were mad? The priests should have been the leaders in telling of their Messiah. The captain of the Temple never had better worshipers in his building. The Sadducees have now before them the most profound event in human history, but they were blind. (2) Many that heard the glad, good, life-giving word believed — 5,000 men plus many others. Belief *does* come by hearing the word. This progress was planned by God, not man.

Pause — wait — think — then express yourself in thoughtful praise or thanks.

9. READ HIS WORD FOR PETITIONS.

There are so many requests in this text — I make them mine: (1) Open my heart and mouth in a word to my friends for you. (2) Direct me to those who will pray with me. (3) I believe you did indeed create the heaven, the earth, the sea and all in each. (4) Help me to find the fulfillment of your word in my daily life. (5) Lord, I want to pray for the governor of our state — for lesser officials — help me! (6) Consider the threats in my life. (7) Grant me the same boldness I see in this text.

Please, please remember these are prayers — speak them — reword them!

10. READ HIS WORD AND WAIT — LISTEN — GOD SPEAKS!

Please visit me and let me open my heart to your word! (1) "I grant boldness in the speaking of my word." (2) "I am looking upon all threats to your life." (3) "Honor my holy Servant Jesus."

11. INTERCESSION FOR THE LOST WORLD

France — Points for prayer: (1) *Minority groups: Africans* 150,000 from former colonies in Central and West Africa. Missionaries witnessing to these people have many opportunities among these receptive people, many being Muslims. (2) *Portuguese* — these people are very open to the Gospel, but more must be done for them in Portuguese, for they do not adapt well to French ways of life. (3) *Gypsies* — over one third of these people have come to the Lord over the last few years and there is now a community of believers of about 60,000. They have their own churches and methods, and aggressively reach out to their fellow Gypsies in other lands.

12. SING PRAISES TO OUR LORD.

The Church's one foundation
Is Jesus Christ her Lord;
She is His new creation
By water and the word:

From Heav'n He came and sought her
To be His holy bride;
With His own blood He bought her,
And for her life He died.

WEEK FOUR — WEDNESDAY

1. PRAISE GOD FOR WHO HE IS.

Forgiver. This is your major work and characteristic. How I praise you that this is so! How many people have you forgiven? There are billions of people upon the earth —no two just alike and not even one that does not need forgiveness.

Express yourself in adoration for this quality of God.
Speak it audibly or write out your praise in your own devotional journal.

2. PRAISE GOD FOR WHAT HE MEANS TO ME.

Forgiver of myself! of my sins and basic selfishness. How I want to be clean and pure before your presence. How gladly do I confess my sins to obtain your cleansing. I must forgive as I have been forgiven.

How do you personally relate to the forgiveness of God, and God who is Forgiver?
Speak it out or write it out. It is *so important* that you establish *your own* devotional journal.

3. CONFESSION OF SIN

Oh, dear Lord, why should I want to hide my sins? I want to confess them and rid myself of them. Cleanse and remove and restore. Dear Lord, I do rejoice in forgive-ness, but I do not hesitate to freely, openly confess my sin and need! Thank you for accepting me!

What personal sins do you want to confess? We *must* speak them to remove them.
Do it! *Now.* There is no one you have sinned against more than God. Tell him so!

4. SING A PRAYER TO GOD.

Jesus, keep me near the cross,
There a precious fountain
Free to all—a healing stream,
Flows from Calv'ry's mountain.

In the cross, in the cross,
Be my glory ever;
Till my raptured soul shall find
Rest beyond the river.

Open your hymn book and sing the rest of the verses—or even sing another prayer song.

5. READ THE WORD TO HIM.

His Word

[32] All the believers were one in heart and mind. No one claimed that any of his possessions was his own, but they shared everything they had. [33] With great power the apostles continued to testify to the resurrection of the Lord Jesus, and much grace was with them all. [34] There were no needy persons among them. For from time to time those who owned lands or houses sold them, brought the money from the sales [35] and put it at the apostles' feet, and it was distributed to anyone as he had need.   — *Acts 4:32-35, NIV*

Read His Word to Him.

How glorious to read of your involvement with your children! To read that "all believers were one in heart and mind" is a total amazement. We have terrible trouble in this very area. We need today the same motivation—it is the risen Lord—it is the power Person of the Holy Spirit— it is the wonder of the Messiah concept. Has our King come? Has our Deliverer arrived? Has he spoken to us? Dear God, you know I am telling you just *how* much these verses say to me.

Please express your response to this beautiful text. Put your expression in your own prayer diary.

6. READ HIS WORD FOR YOURSELF.

I mix the direction of my worship. Dear Lord, I want it all to be of you. How can I truly say that nothing I possess is mine, but I have all things common with my fellow believers? What an all-consuming, all-powerful love swept across the hearts of the Christians in Jerusalem! What about my town? Telling and sharing truly *does* impress people—nay, it demonstrates our love and faith in you!

It is so important that you pause in his presence
and either audibly or in written form tell him all his word means to you.

7. READ HIS WORD IN THANKSGIVING.

Thank you, thank you for: (1) The desire to be one in heart (emotions) and mind (intellect). (2) The possibility of unity among believers. (3) For my risen, living Lord. (4) Every possession I have and can share. (5) For men who can administer means. (6) For the joy and blessedness of giving.

Give yourself to your own expression of gratitude—write it or speak it!

8. READ HIS WORD IN MEDITATION.

How I want to deeply meditate on these verses. *Much power in testifying—much grace in lives and giving.* Peter and John, James and Andrew and all of the other eight could say they saw the Lord after His passion. No wonder there was so much *power* behind their words! Have I seen the Lord today? Have you? Jesus is alive whether we can see him or not. He *is* speaking to me—not only through his word, the New Testament, but in all it means to my life and yours. The *power* is twofold: (1) What we say, but more powerfully, (2) what it means to us that is reflected in our total demeanor. Much unearned favor of the Lord was with them and worked through them! Dear God, may it be so today!

Pause—wait—think—then express yourself in thoughtful praise or thanks.

9. READ HIS WORD FOR PETITIONS.

What a beautiful area for requests: (1) Let me give my heart and mind to you. (2) Let me give my heart and mind to others. (3) Release my hold on my possessions when others are in need. (4) Open my heart to receive the full impact of my Lord's resurrection. (5) I want to continue steadfastly in the apostles' teaching—grant me wisdom. (6) How can I meet the needs of the hungry of the world today? (7) How can I relate physical and spiritual needs?

Right here att your personal requests—and his answers.

10. READ HIS WORD AND WAIT—LISTEN—GOD SPEAKS!

Surely I need to hear your voice in this text: (1) "Believers can be of one heart and one mind today." (2) "I want the unity of believers." (3) "The world will never care how much you believe until they see how much you care."

11. INTERCESSION FOR THE LOST WORLD

France — Points for prayer: (1) *Minority groups:* Many *Vietnamese* and *Cambodians* have fled to France since the fall of their lands to the Communists. Many have been seeking the Lord. Pray especially for the ministry of missionaries and pastors to their bodily and spiritual needs. (2) *Jews* number 570,000 but there are very few Christians among them. Pray for the missionaries who witness to them.

Germany (West) — Population 62,100,000. Annual growth 0.2%. 246,000 sq. km.

Points for prayer: (1) *Germany's spiritual restoration.* Her spiritual decline has been one of the tragedies of history. The rise of humanism and destructive criticism of the Bible enfeebled the churches, and opened the door to militarism and Hitler's Nazi tyranny with its wars and massacres. Post-war materialism and the permissive society have further helped to erode the place of the Church in society. (2) *The need of Germany* is highlighted by the growing interest in the occult, the rise of the New Left, and the rapid growth of the sects such as the New Apostles, Mormons and Watchtower. There are many areas where the Bible believing witness is very small or even unknown. (3) *The Roman Catholics* are predominant in parts of south and central Germany. Many are very confused by the tensions and divisions within the Roman Catholic Church, and are more open towards the Gospel and the witness of Bible believers than ever before. Pray for many Roman Catholics to come to a personal and Biblical faith.

12. SING PRAISES TO OUR LORD.

O worship the King, all glorious above,
And gratefully sing His wonderful love;

Our Shield and Defender, the Ancient of days,
Pavilioned in splendor, and girded with praise.

WEEK FOUR — THURSDAY

1. PRAISE GOD FOR WHO HE IS.

Cleanser. You do keep a balance in this total universe — to keep man clean is one immense task.

Express yourself in adoration for this quality of God.
Speak it audibly or write out your praise in your own devotional journal.

2. PRAISE GOD FOR WHAT HE MEANS TO ME.

My cleanser — praise your name! I am glad to claim your cleansing. How good to be clean! To know inward forgiveness is a great gift! Wash me and I shall be whiter than snow!

How do you personally relate to the cleansing of God, and God who is clean?
Speak it out or write it out. It is *so important* that you establish *your own* devotional journal.

3. CONFESSION OF SIN

How I do want to be honest and candid! To be open and clean before you! As I look over the list of sins in your word I am impressed with how many do have at least partial application to me. Dear God, forgive.

What personal sins do you want to confess? We *must* speak them to remove them.
Do it! *Now.* There is no one else you have sinned against more than God. Tell him so!

4. SING A PRAYER TO GOD.

O Jesus, I have promised
To serve Thee to the end;
Be Thou forever near me,
My Master and my Friend:

I shall not fear the battle
If Thou art by my side,
Nor wander from the pathway
If Thou wilt be my guide.

Open your hymn book and sing the rest of the verses — or even sing another prayer song.

5. READ HIS WORD TO HIM!

His Word

[36]Joseph, a Levite from Cyprus, whom the apostles called Barnabas (which means Son of Encouragement), [37]sold a field he owned and brought the money and put it at the apostles' feet.

5 Now a man named Ananias, together with his wife Sapphira, also sold a piece of property. [2]With his wife's full knowledge he kept back part of the money for himself, but brought the rest and put it at the apostles' feet.

[3]Then Peter said, "Ananias, how is it that Satan has so filled your heart that you have lied to the Holy Spirit and have kept for yourself some of the money you received for the land? [4]Didn't it belong to you before it was sold? And after it was sold, wasn't the money at your disposal? What made you think of doing such a thing? You have not lied to men but to God." — *Acts 4:36 — 5:4, NIV*

Read His Word to Him.

What a good man is Barnabas! To sell a field with no other thought than the good it could do for someone else is indeed a wonderful example. How I thank you for the preservation down through all these ages (2,000 years) of the lovely record. I am just as glad you have so care-fully kept the account of Ananias and Sapphira. I need and want to read and believe it all over again. Dear Lord, how good to have your estimate of the seriousness of a lie. Forgive me!

Please express your response to this beautiful text. Put your expression in your own prayer diary.

6. READ HIS WORD FOR YOURSELF.

To read this record and alternately take the place of each of these persons is an awesome experience — for I can (and do) stand in the sandals of Barnabas, Peter, Ananias, Sapphira, the rest of the apostles, and any other persons present. Dear Lord, may I examine before you all thoughts that bid for action — it could be that Satan is talking to me — but I have *your* written word — I want to inscribe every word of it on my mind and will and conscience.

It is so important that you pause in his presence
and either audibly or in written form tell him all his word means to you.

7. READ HIS WORD IN THANKSGIVING.

How shall I thank you through this text? (1) For Joseph the encourager—may I today be like him. (2) For money and what it can mean for your work in this world. (3) For hypocrites—or hypocrisy—as they and it display the contrast between truth and error. (4) For the marvelous power of choice—oh, how awesome it is. (5) For the living, real Holy Spirit. (6) That what we have of material means is indeed ours and at our disposal. (7) That you are right this moment listening and seeing and knowing—in all I do you *are* present.

Give yourself to your own expression of gratitude—write it or speak it!

8. READ HIS WORD IN MEDITATION.

What meditation shall we have on this meaningful text? How to distinguish the thoughts of God from the thoughts of Satan. (1) When *anything* we think is contrary to the Bible it is from the evil one. (2) When a thought is selfish—when a thought is prideful—when a thought exalts me and mine—it is from beneath. (3) When we must conceal and hide and become devious it is of Satan. (4) When we hesitate to do the obvious right and good thing to meet a human need we could be listening to the devil. (5) When the praise comes to us and not to God Satan is behind it.

Pause—wait—think—then express yourself in thoughtful praise or thanks.

9. READ HIS WORD FOR PETITIONS.

It is so easy to pretend—give me the courage to be candid. (1) Give me a godly fear that leads to repentance. (2) Guard me from the love of money. (3) Show me over again that no one deceives the Holy Spirit. (4) Help me to include you as a silent listener in all my conversation. (5) Open my heart to the real world of the Spirit. (6) I am glad I want to tell the truth—increase my desire. (7) May I have a clear, clean conscience if this is my last day.

Please, please remember these are prayers—speak them—reword them!

10. READ HIS WORD AND WAIT—LISTEN—GOD SPEAKS!

May I hear what the Spirit through his Word is saying to me: (1) "Your appointment with death has already been made." (2) "There is another very real world right on the other side of your last heartbeat." (3) "Try yourself, not the Holy Spirit."

11. INTERCESSION FOR THE LOST WORLD

Germany (West) — Points for prayer: (1) *The vision for mission work has grown* as a result of the Bible believing upsurge. There is a marked increase in the number of young people going out to the mission fields. Pray that many more churches and believers may see their responsibility for the winning of the world for the Lord. (2) *Christian Radio* — The German branch of Trans World Radio Evangeliums Rundfunk has made an immense impact on both Germanies and the German speaking world. Now programs are being produced for the Italian, Spanish, Yugoslav and Turkish immigrant workers. Pray for the staff and their ministry. (3) *Immigrant laborers* number over 2,000,000. Pray for the strategic work by a number of German and international groups among the Turks—there are now more Turkish believers in Germany than in Turkey itself. Others seek to witness to the 20,000 Albanian speaking Yugoslavs in Munich (the only sizable Albanian speaking community in the world that is open to the Gospel). Pray for those engaged in this demanding ministry to these Muslim people.

12. SING PRAISES TO OUR LORD.

We gather together to ask the Lord's blessing,
He chastens and hastens His will to make known;
The wicked oppressing cease them from distressing,
Sing praises to His name, He forgets not His own.

WEEK FOUR — FRIDAY

1. PRAISE GOD FOR WHO HE IS.

Christ-like. How attractive is this quality! What great assurance—what personalness—what hope. All that attracts me or "all men" to my Lord, attracts to you. Wonder of all wonders! God became man! To praise you is a joy and delight since you are just like the one who is all in all to me!

Express yourself in adoration for this quality of God.
Speak it audibly or write out your praise in your own devotional journal.

2. PRAISE GOD FOR WHAT HE MEANS TO ME.

Christ-like to me! I cannot—or do not—separate these qualities. Oh, dear God! You are full of wisdom—love—tenderness—peace—purpose—all because you are just like Jesus! Just like my dear, wonderful Savior! Praise your eternal self!

How do you personally relate to the Christ-likeness of God, and God who is Christ-like?
Speak it out or write it out. It is *so important* that you establish *your own* devotional journal.

3. CONFESSION OF SIN

How unworthy I am to be your son, but since I have nothing to hide, nothing to gain but cleanness—forgive. If you only forgave on the basis of performance there would be little hope for anyone. Bless your name, you forgive, cleanse and forget—just because we need it!

What personal sins do you want to confess? We *must* speak them to remove them.
Do it! *Now.* There is no one else you have sinned against more than God. Tell him so!

4. SING A PRAYER TO GOD.

O Master, let me walk with Thee
In lowly paths of service free;

Tell me Thy secret; help me bear
The strain of toil, the fret of care.

Open your hymn book and sing the rest of the verses—or even sing another prayer song.

5. READ HIS WORD TO HIM!

His Word

[5]When Ananias heard this, he fell down and died. And great fear seized all who heard what had happened. [6]Then the young men came forward, wrapped up his body, and carried him out and buried him.

[7]About three hours later his wife came in, not knowing what had happened. [8]Peter asked her, "Tell me, is this the price you and Ananias got for the land?"

"Yes," she said, "that is the price."

[9]Peter said to her, "How could you agree to test the Spirit of the Lord? Look! The feet of the men who buried your husband are at the door, and they will carry you out also."

[10]At that moment she fell down at his feet and died. Then the young men came in and, finding her dead, carried her out and buried her beside her husband.

— Acts 5:5-10, NIV

Read His Word to Him.

How glad I am that our lying is not so punished today! May great awe and reverence grip me and hold me as I see your estimate of the seriousness of a lie! I want to stand in that crowd and look for a long time at what happened that day in Jerusalem. You have given such graphic details of this incident that I'm sure we are to lay it to heart. I feel like Sapphira—i.e., I really do not know what happened—I can read it and see it, but the reality occurred in the spirit world.

Please express your response to this beautiful text. Put your expression in your own prayer diary.

6. READ HIS WORD FOR YOURSELF.

What do Ananias and Sapphira know now? They have been in the world of the unseen for almost two thousand years — in torment and anguish and remorse! Oh, oh, terrible, terrible thought! and yet according to Luke 16:19-31 it is true! My Lord, my Lord, keep me clean and ready, but full of joy and peace. Dear Lord, help me, help me to guard my lips — may they only speak what is true and faithful to you. Dear God, you need no test to prove your faithfulness to me!

It is so important that you pause in his presence
and either audibly or in written form tell him all his word means to you.

7. READ HIS WORD IN THANKSGIVING.

Thank you for: (1) Peter's holy courage and wisdom — really from you — but not without Peter's willingness. (2) The group effort in worship and learning — the pallbearers probably never forgot! (3) The clear record to produce wonder and belief in my heart. (4) For Peter's words to Sapphria — the last words she ever heard. (5) For the example of the seriousness of lying. (6) For your personal interest in truth. (7) For the fact that I can die to sin not in it.

Give yourself to your own expression of gratitude — write it or speak it!

8. READ HIS WORD IN MEDITATION.

"How could you agree to test the Spirit of the Lord?" Of course we would never do such a thing — or would we? Every time we question one word of the Spirit's word, i.e. the Bible, we are tempted in this same area. If we do not decide this side of death that God has said what he meant and meant what he said we will find it out too late. Every time we decide that God has not heard our prayers we tread dangerously in the same area. How much better to trust him completely.

Pause — wait — think — then express yourself in thoughtful praise or thanks.

9. READ HIS WORD FOR PETITIONS.

I want to ask as you would ask: (1) May I be ready for your great day of equity? (2) How can great fear seize the church today? (3) Am I right in believing only the apostles performed miraculous signs up till this time? (4) Dear Lord, I want to know the whole and true purpose of healings. (5) Why not be healed by someone else but Peter? (6) How could "all" be healed? (7) In what way were people "tormented" by demons?

Right here add your personal requests — and his answers.

10. READ HIS WORD AND WAIT — LISTEN — GOD SPEAKS!

Speak to me from these few verses: (1) "If men will not believe the apostles and prophets, there is no other message." (2) "Discipline can help the church." (3) "It is possible to have the same salvation today they had in Jerusalem."

11. INTERCESSION FOR THE LOST WORLD

Great Britain — Population: 56,200,000. Growth rate 0.1%. 242,000 sq. km. People per sq. km. — 232.

Points for prayer: (1) *Britain has a great spiritual need.* The nation has lost the sense of mission that made it one of the greatest moral and spiritual forces in modern history. The decline of true Christianity and the rise of the permissive society are characteristic of the age. There are now laws that permit homosexuality, witchcraft and abortion. The rise in the crime rate, immorality and the use of drugs is alarming. Pray for a national repentance and return to God. Pray that believers may be more concerned about the state of the country, and be more earnest in prayer. (2) *There is need for another revival.* The political and economic tensions have become so great that the disintegration of the whole country is not impossible. In similar national crises in the past, God has graciously sent revival, as in the time of Wesley. There has been a national revival every century for the past 800 years, but the revival for this century is overdue. Pray for it.

12. SING PRAISES TO OUR LORD.

More love to Thee, O Christ,
More love to Thee!
Hear Thou the prayer I make
On bended knee;

This is my earnest plea:
More love, O Christ, to Thee,
More love to Thee,
More love to Thee!

WEEK FOUR — SATURDAY

1. PRAISE GOD FOR WHO HE IS.

Owner. You are the original owner of all that is or ever will be! You own everything because you created it, and in man's case you bought him—all twice belong to you.

How I enjoy talking to such a Prominent Person! To think *you* want *me* to commune with you!

Express yourself in adoration for this quality of God.
Speak it audibly or write out your praise in your own devotional journal.

2. PRAISE GOD FOR WHAT HE MEANS TO ME.

Naught have I gotten but what I received—grace has bestowed it since I believed! Blessed be your eternal power —wisdom—knowledge—purpose—and to know I *belong* *to you!* This is a most comforting thought. Dear God, help me to let you manage your property.

How do you personally relate to the ownership of God, and God who is owner?
Speak it out or write it out. It is *so important* that you establish *your own* devotional journal.

3. CONFESSION OF SIN

I guess all sin is but a basic denial of the right of ownership—or at least an ignoring of it. Dear God, I *know* you can do so much better than I can, but I am just unwilling to let you have your way. Forgive me! Help me! Purify me, clear my record!

What personal sins do you want to confess? We *must* speak them to remove them.
Do it! *Now.* There is no one else you have sinned against more than God. Tell him so!

4. SING A PRAYER TO GOD.

Open my eyes, that I may see
Glimpses of truth Thou hast for me;
Place in my hands the wonderful key
That shall unclasp, and set me free.

Silently now I wait for Thee,
Ready, my God, Thy will to see;
Open my eyes, illumine me,
Spirit divine!

Open your hymn book and sing the rest of the verses—or even sing another prayer song.

5. READ HIS WORD TO HIM!

His Word

Then the young men came in and, finding her dead, carried her out and buried her beside her husband. [11]Great fear seized the whole church and all who heard about these events.

[12]The apostles performed many miraculous signs and wonders among the people. And all the believers used to meet together in Solomon's Colonnade. [13]No one else dared join them, even though they were highly regarded by the people. [14]Nevertheless, more and more men and women believed in the Lord and were added to their number. [15]As a result, people brought the sick into the streets and laid them on beds and mats so that at least Peter's shadow might fall on some of them as he passed by. [16]Crowds gathered also from the towns around Jerusalem, bringing their sick and those tormented by evil spirits, and all of them were healed.   — *Acts 5:10b-16, NIV*

Read His Word to Him.

How exciting and full of life are these words. How amazed and awe struck are the people of the city of Jerusalem. How I want to be "seized" by joy and fear—what a procession of healing is taking place! What wonderful respect and high regard is accorded the believers. How rapidly did the body of your dear Son grow! The little phrase "they were healed every one" or "all of them were healed" strikes me. How good that you helped in such a marvelous manner!

Please express your response to this beautiful text. Put your expression in your own prayer diary.

6. READ HIS WORD FOR YOURSELF.

I want to be just as reverent and full of wonder as those in the city on that day—both types of fear are seen here— reverent and judgmental. I am glad to say I come as a penitent child. How I long for the same kind of turning to the Lord as witnessed in Jerusalem. It does seem significant that miracles were done "by the hands of the apostles."— but the purpose was accomplished.

It is so important that you pause in his presence
and either audibly or in written form tell him all his word means to you.

7. READ HIS WORD IN THANKSGIVING.

Thank you, dear Lord, for: (1) Power and direction you give to all of life. (2) That you are interested in my body as well as my heart. (3) For the respect you can develop in the hearts of unbelievers for the good news. (4) That multitudes today can be and should be "added to the Lord." (5) That we together make up "the Lord" (his body) on this earth. (6) The deep respect people have for men who love you. (7) That evil spirits are subject to you.

Give yourself to your own expression of gratitude — write it or speak it!

8. READ HIS WORD IN MEDITATION.

Gather around his word and let him speak: (1) Dear Lord, we do not have a larger need than unity for today — one heart and one soul and one in material needs to help others — one in belief. (2) Needs can be met in any group anywhere — this is a startling statement, but it is true. (3) Joseph, a man of means, gave his means to you. (4) That I am not the body, but only a temporary resident — my house is not here and surely not in torment! (5) That there are laws by which we can live. (6) That such action happens today only spiritually and not physically.

What meditation will we do on this text? "The feet of the young men are at the door." It may be several years from now — it may be today — but someone will come and carry out your body and mine. May I believe it as deeply and personally as did Sapphira! It is appointed unto me — the appointment has already been made — I simply do not know the date — help me to so live this day as if the hour was in it for my departure — indeed I have a strong desire to depart this body and be at home with the Lord, which will be very far better!

Pause — wait — think — then express yourself in thoughtful praise or thanks.

9. READ HIS WORD FOR PETITIONS.

We are indeed moved to prayer requests in the face of this text: (1) Give me such young men who will serve in difficult situations. (2) Help me to remember that all that is buried is the body. (3) Lead our local body of believers into "great fear" (reverence). (4) May we so live and work that unbelievers will respect us. (5) Stop people from joining a religious club. (6) Dear Lord, add to our number through our witness for you. (7) May all our preachers be as humble as Peter.

Please, please remember these are prayers — speak them — reword them!

10. READ HIS WORD AND WAIT — LISTEN — GOD SPEAKS!

Dear Lord, if ever our ears were open it is now — speak to us through these verses: (1) "I want your whole attention all the time." (2) "I can — and do — work through all types of circumstances. (3) "There is no limit to what I can do when men love me and worship me."

11. INTERCESSION FOR THE LOST WORLD

Great Britain — Points for prayer: (1) *Few nations have produced such a galaxy of great men of God* — such as Wycliffe, Tyndale, Latimer, the Puritans, Whitfield, Wesley, Carey, Hudson Taylor, George Muller, etc. Pray that Britain may continue to give such men to the world. (2) *Despite growth, there are serious weaknesses found among Bible believers:* a) Lack of Bible teaching and personal study of the Scriptures have made the average believer hazy on doctrine, shallow in evangelism and undiscerning of error among those who claim to base their teachings on God's Word. b) A sad increase in worldliness and therefore, little real concern for world evangelism or the support of the missionary enterprise in prayer and giving. c) Divisions — denominational loyalty, ecumenism, neo-Pentecostalism, action on social issues and the bitter Calvinist-Arminian dispute — these all damage the unity of believers and hinder their witness to the world outside. (3) *Young people* have been turning to the Lord in fairly large numbers, but relatively few find a real home in Bible believing churches. Pray for the bridging of the very large generation gap — for many young people either never really become involved in the life of a church fellowship, or go off to form their own (often introspective) house groups.

12. SING PRAISES TO OUR LORD.

My Jesus, I love Thee, I know Thou art mine,
For Thee all the follies of sin I resign;

My gracious Redeemer, my Savior art Thou;
If ever I loved Thee, my Jesus, 'tis now.

WEEK FIVE — SUNDAY

1. PRAISE GOD FOR WHO HE IS.

Filler. He is the fulness of all things and he himself fills all things—for of his fulness we have all received—grace for grace—or grace upon grace. How I praise you, dear Lord, that this word so adequately describes you. In you were all filled and you are our fulness!

Express yourself in adoration for this quality of God.
Speak it audibly or write out your praise in your own devotional journal.

2. PRAISE GOD FOR WHAT HE MEANS TO ME.

Filler for me! I truly, truly find my fulness in him! He is before all things and in him all things hold together—in him is the fulness of the Godhead in bodily form. How beautiful he is to me—praise his glorious person!

How do you personally relate to the fulness of God, and God who fills all?
Speak it out or write it out. It is *so important* that you establish *your own* devotional journal.

3. CONFESSION OF SIN

To confess to such a one is no chore—nor need I hesitate—but opening my heart—all my mind—my total will, the depth of my affection, I give myself to you dear, wonderful Savior! Clean me up, wash me and I shall be whole!

What personal sins do you want to confess? We *must* speak them to remove them.
Do it! *Now.* There is no one else you have sinned against more than God. Tell him so!

4. SING A PRAYER TO GOD.

Nearer, still nearer, close to Thy heart,
Draw me, my Savior, so precious Thou art;
Fold me, O fold me close to Thy breast,
Shelter me safe in that "Haven of Rest,"
Shelter me safe in that "Haven of Rest."

Open your hymn book and sing the rest of the verses—or even sing another prayer song.

5. READ HIS WORD TO HIM!

His Word

[17]Then the high priest and all his associates, who were members of the party of the Sadducees, were filled with jealousy. [18]They arrested the apostles and put them in the public jail. [19]But during the night an angel of the Lord opened the doors to the jail and brought them out. [20]"Go, stand in the temple courts," he said, "and tell the people the full message of this new life."
[21]At daybreak they entered the temple courts, as they had been told.
— *Acts 5:17-21a, NIV*

Read His Word to Him.

How gladly I take up your word to tell you what it means to me and how much I appreciate what you have said and are saying to me. The opposition of your Son's body is most serious—all twelve apostles in prison—what beauty and surprise in the sudden appearance of the angel! Oh, dear Father, how I do want to tell the people of this town "the full message of this new life." How I admire and respect those men who laid their lives on the line for you.

Please express your response to this beautiful text. Put your expression in your own prayer diary.

6. READ HIS WORD FOR YOURSELF.

Let's not be surprised today if jealousy becomes a large part of the opposition we face. Greed and covetousness and jealousy all form a very real part of the opposition to your cause today. Wonder—praise—adoration for the ministry of your angels. I know they have not died since that day when one of them appeared in the prison cell in Jerusalem. The "full message" of the new life and hope in our Lord is *so* much needed today.

It is so important that you pause in his presence
and either audibly or in written form tell him all his word means to you.

7. READ HIS WORD IN THANKSGIVING.

Thank you for: (1) Disbelievers who can be answered—and some become believers. (2) That no prison can hold the light and love of our Lord. (3) For the new daybreak of every day—a prototype of the eternal daybreak of heaven. (4) That we can teach the people the same wonderful message. (5) For a place, oh, so many places for teaching people today. We need, dear God, we *need* to be reminded that the people taught were interested unbelievers.

Give yourself to your own expression of gratitude—write it or speak it!

8. READ HIS WORD IN MEDITATION.

"An angel (messenger) of the Lord" — (1) Night has no hindrance for him—the angels that minister to me can do it at night as well as the bright daytime—praise and thanksgiving—this is a real assurance to me. (2) He can open doors shut and barred by man—no physical, mental or psychological door can stand in his way. If he wants to open the doors, they will be opened! (3) We can stand in the very place where we were defeated and win! (4) How good—so good—to begin each day with you. Today I can do the same thing they did: teach. Oh, that I could teach unbelievers as well as believers!

Pause—wait—think—then express yourself in thoughtful praise or thanks.

9. READ HIS WORD FOR PETITIONS.

What requests come from this jail experience of the apostles? (1) Forgive me, Lord, for complaining when I have freedom. (2) May I check my motives today—am I jealous? (3) How can I be more and more aware of the presence of angels? (4) Open my heart to catch the full meaning of the expression: "new life." (5) Can I ever catch the full impact of meeting in Herod's temple? I want to try. (6) Give me wisdom to teach what the apostles taught. (7) I am glad to use daybreak each day to worship you—help me to guard it for you.

Right here add your personal requests—and his answers.

10. READ HIS WORD AND WAIT—LISTEN—GOD SPEAKS!

Here is what you say to me through your word: (1) "Do not expect present-day Sadducees to change." (2) "Angels are still opening prison doors." (3) "Go and stand in my presence and teach the people all the words of this new life."

11. INTERCESSION FOR THE LOST WORLD

Great Britain — Points for prayer: (1) *Students.* Pray for the work among young people and also among the college and university students. The proportion of Christian students in the universities is far higher than the national average. Pray for student leadership that they may have maturity. Pray for outreach to the unconverted students—often through evangelistic Bible studies. The believers are generally making a great impact on the spiritually fairly receptive student body. (2) *Overseas students* are a fertile field for missionary work by students. About 11.5% of the students in universities and colleges are from other lands (i.e., about 80,000—of which 15,000 are Muslim, and from lands closed to the Gospel). Pray for all programs to welcome and befriend overseas students, and pray that these may lead to the conversion of many—there have been some dramatic cases of conversions among these people. (3) *The West Indians* have immigrated from the poor islands of the Caribbean since World War II, and are now a very large minority in some cities. Too little has been done to make these nominally Christian people welcome in churches. There is increasing racial hatred which is made worse by Britain's economic plight. Pray for these frustrated people. (4) *The Chinese* number 100,000 and are mostly nurses and restaurant workers. Pray for several Chinese groups seeking to witness to these people, and win them for the Lord. Pray that such converts may become missionaries to Asia.

12. SING PRAISES TO OUR LORD.

I have a song I love to sing,
Since I have been redeemed,
Of my Redeemer, Savior, King,
Since I have been redeemed.
Since I . . . have been redeemed,

Since I have been redeemed,
I will glory in His name;
Since I . . . have been redeemed,
I will glory in my Savior's name.

WEEK FIVE — MONDAY

1. PRAISE GOD FOR WHO HE IS.

Satisfying. How could I more adequately describe your total character? The completion of all the material universe —the fulfillment of every need is due to your creative power. All of life is a result of your meeting our needs.

You satisfy in the realm of the spirit—the heart—the emotions—the body. Praise to you, you do indeed, in every way, for every thing—satisfy!

Express yourself in adoration for this quality of God.
Speak it audibly or write out your praise in your own devotional journal.

2. PRAISE GOD FOR WHAT HE MEANS TO ME.

To me you are total satisfaction. I can not even imagine a need you could not meet! For my purpose—hope—peace —strength—for my home—wife—children—you are the source for satisfaction in every situation. Wholeness is the

result of trusting you to satisfy! How I want to *increase* my trust. A deep awareness that all things fit together is my response to your satisfying nature. Praise your name!

How do you personally relate to the satisfaction of God, and God who satisfies?
Speak it out or write it out. It is *so important* that you establish *your own* devotional journal.

3. CONFESSION OF SIN

Could I be guilty of lying? This is no question—I am guilty of lying—to misrepresent the facts is a lie! No one wants to admit to lying—but I do—I want to be clean, forgiven. Dear God, behind most (if not all) the lies I have

told is pride—dear Lord, forgive me! Lift this burden from my heart. I confess other sins to you also—wash me and I shall be whiter than snow!

What personal sins do you want to confess? We *must* speak them to remove them.
Do it! *Now.* There is no one else you have sinned against more than God. Tell him so!

4. SING A PRAYER TO GOD.

Savior, like a shepherd lead us,
Much we need Thy tender care;
In Thy pleasant pastures feed us,
For our use Thy folds prepare:

Blessed Jesus, Blessed Jesus,
Thou hast bought us, Thine we are;
Blessed Jesus, Blessed Jesus,
Thou hast bought us, Thine we are.

Open your hymn book and sing the rest of the verses—or even sing another prayer song.

5. READ HIS WORD TO HIM!

His Word

[21] At daybreak they entered the temple courts, as they had been told, and began to teach the people.

When the high priest and his associates arrived, they called together the Sanhedrin—the full assembly of the elders of Israel—and sent to the jail for the apostles. [22] But on arriving at the jail, the officers did not find them there. So they went back and reported, [23] "We found the jail securely locked, with the guards standing at the doors; but when we opened them, we found no one inside." [24] On

hearing this report, the captain of the temple guard and the chief priests were puzzled, wondering what would come of this.

[25] Then someone came and said, "Look! The men you put in jail are standing in the temple courts teaching the people." [26] At that, the captain went with his officers and brought the apostles. They did not use force, because they feared that the people would stone them.

— Acts 5:21-26, NIV

Read His Word to Him.

That your leaders could be mistreated and thrown in jail is indeed an amazement! They were thrown in jail, but they were not kept there! How exciting it is to never know what you have ready next—different! We puzzle and

wonder, but have no explanation ever for the most elementary actions of yourself. I want to remain full of wonder and expectant amazement.

Please express your response to this beautiful text. Put your expression in your own prayer diary.

6. READ HIS WORD FOR YOURSELF.

How I rejoice at the devotion of the twelve—at the troubled authorities—at the angel's service. Dear God, I want to believe that there is *no* circumstance of life out of which you cannot bring some good. I am confined and

hindered so many times by Satan and circumstances. The purpose you have for me is to teach the lost. Dear God, help me to fulfill that purpose. I am today in my world— your "sent one."

It is so important that you pause in his presence
and either audibly or in written form tell him all his word means to you.

7. READ HIS WORD IN THANKSGIVING.

There is much here for which we can thank you: (1) For the accurate record preserved through centuries and centuries of time. (2) For the capacity and opportunity of visualizing these events in a most believable manner. (3) For freedom as compared with confinement — to be in jail is a miserable experience — how to appreciate fully what it means to come and go at choice. (4) You can deliver from any jail — indeed — our spirits cannot be bound. (5) The gospel would and does meet the needs of the average man.

Give yourself to your own expression of gratitude — write it or speak it!

8. READ HIS WORD IN MEDITATION.

The prison they found empty! What Satan thought would be a place or a way to confine and inhibit only proved to be an open door to new freedom. Such can be and is true of: (1) A financial crisis — God either delivers us out of it by supplying the means or through it by teaching us lessons we could not learn in any other way. (2) Lingering sickness — some confined people are the freest spirits we have on this earth — we are *not* the body — I repeat for clarity and emphasis, we are *not* the body. (3) Those in jail today — I have read their words of joy and praise and liberty of the human spirit — through the blessed Holy Spirit.

Pause — wait — think — then express yourself in thoughtful praise or thanks.

9. READ HIS WORD FOR PETITIONS.

My prayer requests are surely provided by your word: (1) Help me to pray for the heads of religious bodies today. (2) I now ask your grace to truly love those who hate me. (3) Thank you for the surprises you hand out so often. (4) Opposition is nothing when your power is present — I claim this promise. (5) The apostles did not run from opposition. Teach me! (6) May I remember that people usually know more than we think they do. (7) May I remember what a powerful force fear is.

Please, please remember these are prayers — speak them — reword them!

10. READ HIS WORD AND WAIT — LISTEN — GOD SPEAKS!

Speak Lord, thy servant heareth: (1) "Men's opposition is an opportunity for my power." (2) "I teach better when I have men's attention." (3) "Support can come from the strangest places."

11. INTERCESSION FOR THE LOST WORLD

Great Britain — Points for prayer: (1) *The Muslims* now number about 500,000 and the number of mosques in Britain has grown from 1 to 300 in 30 years. Most of the Muslims are Pakistanis and Indians, but some English have been converted to Islam. A concerted attempt is now being made by Muslims to win Britain for Islam. Pray for these Muslim people. Pray that believers will seek out opportunities to befriend and win them for Jesus. Pray for churches to initiate an active program aimed at teaching their members how to win Muslims and bring them into a Christian fellowship. A number of missionary societies have now appointed missionaries who have worked in Asia to witness to the Muslims and Hindus. Pray for the right strategy for the discipling of these people. (2) *The missionary vision* has grown dim through pessimism and lack of enthusiasm, and few young people show much interest. There are still about 7,000 British missionaries serving in lands all over the world. There are also many missionary societies operating from Britain. Pray for the return of a sacrificial concern to British Churches for the evangelization of the world, for much yet remains to be done. Pray that more young people may be inspired to serve the Lord through evangelization in Europe, and beyond, every summer. Pray that British believers may have a greater concern for other countries such as Belgium, Luxembourg, Italy, France, etc.

12. SING PRAISES TO OUR LORD.

Holy, Holy, Holy, Lord God Almighty!
Early in the morning our song shall rise to Thee;

Holy, Holy, Holy! Merciful and Mighty!
God in Three Persons, blessed Trinity!

WEEK FIVE — TUESDAY

1. PRAISE GOD FOR WHO HE IS.

Writer-Author. How glad I am you are just what this name indicates—the author and writer with 40 or more penmen) of the Bible, your word, your book! What an awesome thought! We have in our hands the book of which the great eternal God is the writer-author.

Express yourself in adoration for this quality of God.
Speak it audibly or write out your praise in your own devotional journal.

2. PRAISE GOD FOR WHAT HE MEANS TO ME.

Writer-Author—to me it means I should learn—read and reread every word you have written—nothing, utterly nothing is more important than the Bible—it becomes *the* book for my understanding—my mind should be occupied with nothing else. When ever I have a moment I need to be meditating upon it. I need to take many moments and give them gladly to a meditative reading of what the Eternal Creator has written!

How do you personally relate to the writership-authorship of God, and God who is writer-author?
Speak it out or write it out. It is *so important* that you establish *your own* devotional journal.

3. CONFESSION OF SIN

Confession must include the sad sinful fact that I have neglected a study of his word to the extent I should. Never, never could I read or learn enough from your book. Stealing could be taking that which rightfully belongs to God and selfishly using it for myself—such as time with his word, or honor and praise from him to me! God forgive! Dear God, look into my deepest consciousness and cleanse me!

What personal sins do you want to confess? We *must* speak them to remove them.
Do it! *Now.* There is no one else you have sinned against more than God. Tell him so!

4. SING A PRAYER TO GOD.

There's a Stranger at the door,
Let Him in;
He has been there oft before,
Let Him in;

Let Him in, ere He is gone,
Let Him in, the Holy One,
Jesus Christ, the Father's Son,
Let Him in.

Open your hymn book and sing the rest of the verses—or even sing another prayer song.

5. READ HIS WORD TO HIM!

His Word

²⁷Having brought the apostles, they made them appear before the Sanhedrin to be questioned by the high priest. ²⁸"We gave you strict orders, not to teach in this name," he said. "Yet you have filled Jerusalem with your teaching and are determined to make us guilty of this man's blood."

²⁹Peter and the other apostles replied: "We must obey God rather than men! ³⁰The God of our fathers raised Jesus from the dead—whom you had killed by hanging him on a tree. ³¹God exalted him to his own right hand as Prince and Savior that he might give repentance and forgiveness of sins to Israel. ³²We are witnesses of these things, and so is the Holy Spirit, whom God has given to those who obey him."

³³When they heard this, they were furious and wanted to put them to death. ³⁴But a Pharisee named Gamaliel, a teacher of the law, who was honored by all the people, stood up in the Sanhedrin and ordered that the men be put outside for a little while. ³⁵Then he addressed them: "Men of Israel, consider carefully what you intend to do to these men. ³⁶Some time ago Theudas appeared, claiming to be somebody, and about four hundred men rallied to him. He was killed, all his followers were dispersed, and it all came to nothing. ³⁷After him, Judas the Galilean appeared in the days of the census and led a band of people in revolt. He too was killed, and all his followers were scattered. ³⁸Therefore, in the present case I advise you: Leave these men alone! Let them go! For if their purpose or activity is of human origin, it will fail. ³⁹But if it is from God, you you will not be able to stop these men; you will only find yourselves fighting against God." — *Acts 5:27-39, NIV*

Read His Word to Him.

How exciting to identify with you in what you are saying in this text. How almost humorous must be the serious way men assume authority and position. How good it must have been—yea, still is, to see the city of Jerusalem filled with the teaching of the resurrection and salvation! How good to hear Peter do what he was not at all willing or even able to do a few days before—the resurrection of your Son, the reality of his power over *all* opposition, human or spiritual, gave Peter such courage. What was true of Peter was true of them all!

Please express your response to this beautiful text. Put your expression in your own prayer diary.

6. READ HIS WORD FOR YOURSELF.

Has my Lord asked me (and others) to fill Joplin with the same message? Indeed he has! Are you going to do it? Yes, yes, to call on every home — to reach by word of mouth — in person — one on one — everyone. In the whole area there are 20,000 houses. A witnessing survey could take about 40 days. Dear God, we *will* do it. Nothing prevents us from calling *right now* on those I see every day.

It is so important that you pause in his presence
and either audibly or in written form tell him all his word means to you.

7. READ HIS WORD IN THANKSGIVING.

Thank you for: (1) The Prince and Savior at God's right-hand. (2) For the forgiveness of sins. (3) For God induced repentance. (4) The Holy Spirit who has been given to us. (5) The ignorance of sinful men — as in Gamaliel's case it works to the advantage of the cause. (6) That the wrath of man has never, never worked the righteousness of God. (7) The cause of my Lord cannot and will not be defeated.

Give yourself to your own expression of gratitude — write it or speak it!

8. READ HIS WORD IN MEDITATION.

Fighting against God! How can we do this today? How can I possibly do it and not even know it? (1) To oppose in any way any spread of the word of God (if we waited until all Bible publishers or evangelists agreed with us we would have a long wait). (2) To resist anyone who preaches repentance and the forgiveness of sins through our blessed Lord! (3) Acting hastily in any circumstance — especially when related to the denial of the spread of the good news.

Pause — wait — think — then express yourself in thoughtful praise or thanks.

9. READ HIS WORD AND WAIT — LISTEN — GOD SPEAKS!

I want to ask in the light of your word: (1) Give me wisdom to know the difference between what you want and what I want. (2) Dear Lord, I am asking for grace to obey you in all things. (3) I do want to speak your word even if men do not want to hear — help me! (4) I accept my Prince and Savior — increase my willingness. (5) I do want to be able to identify false prophets — help me. (6) Are there wise men like Gamaliel today? Who? (7) Was Gamaliel's advice good? Does it apply today?

Right here add your personal requests — and his answers.

10. READ HIS WORD AND WAIT — LISTEN — GOD SPEAKS!

Speak to me from this text: (1) "You *must* obey me first." (2) "There is no forgiveness without repentance." (3) "Be careful you do not fight against me."

11. INTERCESSION FOR THE LOST WORLD

Greece — Population: 9,000,000. 132,000 sq. km.
Points for prayer: (1) *The Orthodox Church dominates the religious life of the country.* Much superstition and tradition with little knowledge of the Scriptures is found everywhere. Pray that the people may be liberated by the preaching of the Gospel. (2) *Formerly there was much persecution of the Protestants*, but the influence of the Orthodox Church has been weakened since the restoration of democracy in 1974. The Protestants are now more likely to be harassed or suffer discrimination. Pray that the believers may be delivered from fear. They are all too often unwilling to use the many opportunities to witness because they are a despised minority.

12. SING PRAISES TO OUR LORD.

All glory, laud and honor
To Thee, Redeemer, King,
To Whom the lips of children
Made sweet hosannas ring!

The people of the Hebrews
With palms before Thee went;
Our praise and prayer and anthems
Before Thee we present.

WEEK FIVE — WEDNESDAY

1. PRAISE GOD FOR WHO HE IS.

Listener. What a description of the very essence of your total being! To be sensitive of every move of every leaf — to be aware of every hurt of every man — to know the song of every bird. Oh, dear God, you listen! As compared with the best of men you so exceed them, there is only a contrast — men dull of hearing — your ears are always open. Thank you, praise you — oh, hear the deepest cry of my heart!

Express yourself in adoration for this quality of God.
Speak it audibly or write out your praise in your own devotional journal.

2. PRAISE GOD FOR WHAT HE MEANS TO ME.

Listen to me — I could never talk too much or say too little. You hear without time, are concerned without interruption — and give total attention to all I say as long as I want to say it. This is one of the greatest qualities (if not the greatest) I have ever considered. Oh, bless and hallow your name! To hear me at the lowest and highest level — to hear me all the time — Oh, it is almost more than I can assimilate!

How do you personally relate to the listening of God, and God who is listener?
Speak it out or write it out. It is *so important* that you establish *your own* devotional journal.

3. CONFESSION OF SIN

You *know* — as no one else ever could — *my sin — my sins,* I hide them not for I cannot hide them. I am ashamed of them — I am confused and chagrined and overcome — and humbled and embarrassed — but I am not hidden. Do not only forgive but grant the inward healing that I sin no more. I want to consider carefully one specific sin each day and ask myself if such has stained my record: *Gossip:* a form of slander and lying. Oh, dear God, *guilty!* Forgive me! Oh, may I set your guard upon my lips!

What personal sins do you want to confess? We *must* speak them to remove them.
Do it! *Now.* There is no one else you have sinned against more than God. Tell him so!

4. SING A PRAYER TO GOD.

Far away in the depths of my spirit tonight
Rolls a melody sweeter than psalm;
In celetial-like strains it unceasingly falls
O'er my soul like an infinite calm.

Peace! peace! wonderful peace,
Coming down from the Father above;
Sweep over my spirit forever, I pray,
In fathomless billows of love.

Open your hymn book and sing the rest of the verses — or even sing another prayer song.

5. READ HIS WORD TO HIM!

His Word

[40]His speech persuaded them. They called the apostles in and had them flogged. Then they ordered them not to speak in the name of Jesus, and let them go.
[41]The apostles left the Sanhedrin, rejoicing because they had been counted worthy of suffering disgrace for the Name. [42]Day after day, in the temple courts and from house to house, they never stopped teaching and proclaiming the good news that Jesus is the Christ.

— *Acts 5:40-42, NIV*

Read His Word to Him.

How I want to express my wonder at what you had recorded in this text — "not to speak at all in the name of Jesus" — Oh, I want to remember how oppressive persecution could be right here in our own country. We are never worthy of *the Name* — but when we suffer for him we are so glad — because we are like him — who suffered for us — "Jesus is the Christ." Dear God, give me an audience to whom I can tell the same glad tidings. "For his name's sake" — what a lovely expression!

Please express your response to this beautiful text. Put your expression in your own prayer diary.

6. READ HIS WORD FOR YOURSELF.

I do with joy and boldness enter into every word. Dear God, may I take the verbal flogging—or the financial flogging—or the social flogging—with the same resigned joy, your joy—the unlettered fishermen did. May the day-by-day experiences of life show the same devotion. How beautiful to know there were many who wanted to hear. More than this, the experience of Jesus our Lord—my Savior—made it possible. Bleeding backs are an eloquent testimony!

It is so important that you pause in his presence and either audibly or in written form tell him all his word means to you.

7. READ HIS WORD IN THANKSGIVING.

(1) That we can and must speak in the name of Jesus. (2) That there were (and are) men who count the reproach of our Lord a joy and privilege. Dear God, help me to be a part of that company. (3) That boldness in the face of opposition is a reality. (4) That houses were used as a place of testimony and teaching. (5) That both proclaiming and teaching are a part of the text—an example for us. (6) The same kind of people are here today to teach and be taught—to proclaim and to hear.

Give yourself to your own expression of gratitude—write it or speak it!

8. READ HIS WORD IN MEDITATION.

Let's gather around the questions and pray and think: (1) Jealousy is the cause of so much arrest in God's work—in our own lives. Dear Lord, help me to *always* rejoice in the success and weep in the failures of another. (2) An angel—Dear God, to consider that there is an angel of the Lord even now ministering to me is a beautiful thought. (3) His message to them and his (their) message to me is "to speak all the words of *this* life." (4) The people—the silent "moral majority" were a real threat—they *are* today—praise the Lord! (5) What a wonderful accusation—of filling Jerusalem with the teaching of our Lord. Oh, that man might accept the blood guilt of the crucifixion—and the joy of forgiveness!

Pause—wait—think—then express yourself in thoughtful praise or thanks.

9. READ HIS WORD FOR PETITIONS.

I truly enjoy making my petitions an extension of your word: (1) Dear Lord, how would I react to a beating? (2) Dear Father, I want to be worthy to suffer and rejoice in it. (3) How can I better understand the fulness of joy found in your name? (4) Just where can I speak your name today? (5) I want to be your teacher—help me! (6) How can I communicate that what I preach is "good news"? (7) Is Jesus truly Lord in every part of my life—I want him to be!

Please, please remember these are prayers—speak them—reword them!

10. READ HIS WORD AND WAIT—LISTEN—GOD SPEAKS!

Speak to me in these verses: (1) "You will speak only what 'has your heart.'" (2) "I want you to speak for me every day." (3) "It is an honor to suffer for me."

11. INTERCESSION FOR THE LOST WORLD

Greece — Points for prayer: (1) *Much of the country is without a Bible believing witness.* Pray for the evangelization of the country areas, the Aegean Islands and also the Muslim Turkish minority. (2) *The Protestant Church* is very small and is only growing at about the same rate as the population. Pray for the 60 or so Greek full time preachers and Christian workers. Pray for the mobilization of the believers for the winning of those in their local communities and also to reach out to the many areas without a witness. Pray that all legal means may be fully used to win the lost. (3) *There is a great need for Christian workers to be trained locally.* Many young Christians, who seek Bible training elsewhere, do not return to their spiritually hard homeland.

12. SING PRAISES TO OUR LORD.

Blessed assurance, Jesus is mine!
Oh, what a foretaste of glory divine!
Heir of salvation, purchase of God,
Born of His Spirit, washed in His blood.

This is my story, this is my song,
Praising my Saviour all the day long;
This is my story, this is my song,
Praising my Saviour all the day long.

WEEK FIVE — THURSDAY

1. PRAISE GOD FOR WHO HE IS.

Music-maker. How well does this describe one of the most meaningful qualities of your self. You have made music since in the cool of the day your lovely presence was heard and felt in the garden of perfection. You inspired the first man (Tubal-Cain?) to prepare a musical instrument. The capacity to enjoy music is a part of your very likeness. Indeed, the enjoyment of all the aesthetic is a further expression of your image. Praise your magnificent name or nature.

Express yourself in adoration for this quality of God.
Speak it audibly or write out your praise in your own devotional journal.

2. PRAISE GOD FOR WHAT HE MEANS TO ME.

Music-maker for my life. My life would have no music at all without you. With you and in you I hear and revel in a harmony only you can produce. Dear Lord, it isn't that I haven't had a thousand days when I had nothing to sing about — it is rather that you were (and are, and do) work all of those days into the total score of harmony to show me and Satan and all angels and men that you can produce a symphony of joy out of all our poor efforts and mistakes. Praise your name!

How do you personally relate to the music-making of God, and God who is music-maker?
Speak it out or write it out. It is *so important* that you establish *your own* devotional journal.

3. CONFESSION OF SIN

There is but little need to confess that I have sinned — we both know that — am I ever guilty of "lewd thoughts"? Why frame the sentence as a question? Only to hide my shame! Dear God, I do so need help here. I freely, openly, confess my sin — overcoming and stopping is what I need. I know — and claim the fact that habits are formed by repeating one act — one act here is to break the circumstances where lewd thoughts begin — TV — movies — magazines, etc. To think on him who is love and light even my blessed Lord — as found in the gospels. Forgive me and deepen my decisions.

What personal sins do you want to confess? We *must* speak them to remove them.
Do it! *Now.* There is no one else you have sinned against more than God. Tell him so!

4. SING A PRAYER TO GOD.

I'm pressing on the upward way,
New heights I'm gaining ev'ry day;
Still praying as I'm onward bound,
"Lord, plant my feet on higher ground."

Lord, lift me up and let me stand,
By faith, on Heaven's tableland,
A higher plane than I have found;
Lord, plant my feet on higher ground.

Open your hymn book and sing the rest of the verses — or even sing another prayer song.

5. READ HIS WORD TO HIM!

His Word

6 In those days when the number of disciples was increasing, the Grecian Jews among them complained against those of the Aramaic-speaking community because their widows were being overlooked in the daily distribution of food. [2]So the Twelve gathered all the disciples together and said, "It would not be right for us to neglect the ministry of the word of God in order to wait on tables. [3]Brothers, choose seven men from among you who are known to be full of the Spirit and wisdom. We will turn this responsibility over to them [4]and will give our attention to prayer and the ministry of the word."

[5]This proposal pleased the whole group. They chose Stephen, a man full of faith and of the Holy Spirit; also Philip, Prochorus, Nicanor, Timon, Parmenas, and Nicolas from Antioch, a convert to Judaism. [6]They presented these men to the apostles, who prayed and laid their hands on them.

[7]So the word of God spread. The number of disciples in Jerusalem increased rapidly, and a large number of priests became obedient to the faith.

[8]Now Stephen, a man full of God's grace and power, did great wonders and miraculous signs among the people. [9]Opposition arose, however, from members of the Synagogue of the Freedmen (as it was called). — *Acts 6:1-9a, NIV*

Read His Word to Him.

How gladly I relate this text to its ultimate author. How could you take an interest in such a mundane, incidental, personal subject as the feeding of widows? It is because *my* priority of interests are mixed. You are always concerned with human need. Your concern and compassion was caught and reflected in the lives of the men your Son chose — and yet these men had their priorities straight — prayer and "the ministry of the word" were the most important.

Please express your response to this beautiful text. Put your expression in your own prayer diary.

6. READ HIS WORD FOR YOURSELF.

How good to see the cooperation (and organization) of the body of our Lord in Jerusalem. I wish I knew each of the seven men—each of those twelve men—one day I shall know them—one day I shall see them—and then there will be also millions who have followed in their train—all those who have since that day "given themselves to prayer and the ministry of the word." The ministry of the word was practically tantamount to the increase—the spread of the word—what I would call evangelism!

It is so important that you pause in his presence
and either audibly or in written form tell him all his word means to you.

7. READ HIS WORD IN THANKSGIVING.

Praise you, thank you for: (1) The constant potential of the increasing of the members of your body. Disciple-making can and does occur today! (2) That everyone can be, and should be, interested in human needs. (3) That there were and are men who are known to be "full of the Spirit and wisdom." Stephen has his disciples—men who are "full of faith and the Holy Spirit." (4) For Stephen—*God's full man:* (a) full of the Holy Spirit, (b) full of wisdom, (c) full of faith, (d) full of grace, (e) full of power. (5) For honest-hearted priests who were willing to risk all to accept our Lord.

Give yourself to your own expression of gratitude—write it or speak it!

8. READ HIS WORD IN MEDITATION.

Even God's full man faces opposition—why? Here are some possible reasons: (1) In a certain sense we are either full of the Holy Spirit or we are resisting him—there were those religious people who were afraid or jealous—or both and resisted the Spirit. (2) We either evaluate the facts of life in the light of heaven or by the flickering candle of this world—i.e., we either have heavenly wisdom or the wisdom of this world. These are set in opposition to each other. (3) We either believe God's word (against all odds) or we reject it and accept rational, humanistic "explanations."

Pause—wait—think—then express yourself in thoughtful praise or thanks.

9. READ HIS WORD FOR PETITIONS.

How glad I am to relate all my requests to your word: (1) How easy it is to misunderstand. Help me to listen long enough to hear the whole story. (2) Should the church feed the poor among them? (3) Help me to identify today's "waiting on tables." (4) How could I identify those who are "full of the Spirit"? (5) Give me the heaven-sent motivation to give myself to prayer. (6) What is obedience to the faith in becoming a Christian? (7) Why did Stephen perform miraculous signs among the people?

Right here add your personal requests—and his answers.

10. READ HIS WORD AND WAIT—LISTEN—GOD SPEAKS!

Speak to me Lord! (1) "Let other people solve your problems." (2) "Give yourself to prayer." (3) "Give yourself to the ministry of the word."

11. INTERCESSION FOR THE LOST WORLD

Greece — Points for prayer: (1) *The small missionary force* of 25 or so has a majority of workers who are of Greek parentage or birth, but who were converted in North America or Australia and were led to return to witness in their native land. They need no residence visas, non-Greeks needing permits. Most of the missionaries are involved in pastoral, literature or Bible training ministries. Pray for more workers to be called to this land. (2) *University students* need to be reached with the Gospel. There is no permanent witness among them. Pray for such to be raised up. (3) *The printing of all forms of Christian literature is free*, but must, by law, be marked "evangelical," which is a derogatory term to most Greeks. Pray for the witness of the several Christian bookshops and the very active Greek Bible Society. The latter distributes Bibles in the Army, some schools and some other places. Advertisements of the Gospel placed in several national newspapers have proved fruitful—pray for this.

12. SING PRAISES TO OUR LORD.

Fairest Lord Jesus!
Ruler of all nature!
O Thou of God and man the Son!

Thee will I cherish,
Thee will I honor,
Thou, my soul's glory, joy, and crown!

WEEK FIVE — FRIDAY

1. PRAISE GOD FOR WHO HE IS.

Source of variety. How well does this describe our Heavenly Father—and how much variety you have created! All the complex beauty about us is but an extension of your own dear self. How I wonder and stand mute before such creative genius! And then to consider the variety in the men and women you have made—how many animals are there? how many butterflies? birds? fish?

Express yourself in adoration for this quality of God.
Speak it audibly or write out your praise in your own devotional journal.

2. PRAISE GOD FOR WHAT HE MEANS TO ME.

If I am but willing and open I could see variety in a blade of grass! Consider how the light strikes it, how the dew condenses upon it, the several shades of green in it, how it compares with other blades near it. I am overwhelmed at your essential Being, i.e., Spirit—spirit is the nature of man—how does man's spirit operate through his brain? How marvelously complex is man's eye, his ear, his hand. To think that you are my Father is amazement beyond my expression.

How do you personally relate to the creative genius of God, and God who is the source of such creation?
Speak it out or write it out. It is *so important* that you establish *your own* devotional journal.

3. CONFESSION OF SIN

Dear God, Creator, Father, only through my Savior can I approach you. How shall I confess my sins in a way I have not yet done? I have not yet committed a sin in the way I did yesterday, i.e., each sin needs to be confessed for itself—and forgiven for itself. I do fully, freely, confess, admit and accept responsibility for my sin, my latest sin. *Profanity* is such a ridiculous sin. Why? why? Pride and irritation. What should have taught me has been rejected —forgive me!

What personal sins do you want to confess? We *must* speak them to remove them.
Do it! *Now.* There is no one else you have sinned against more than God. Tell him so!

4. SING A PRAYER TO GOD.

Jesus, Lover of my soul,
Let me to Thy bosom fly,
While the nearer waters roll,
While the tempest still is high;

Hide me, O my Savior, hide,
Till the storm of life is past;
Safe into the haven guide,
O receive my soul at last.

Open your hymn book and sing the rest of the verses—or even sing another prayer song.

5. READ HIS WORD TO HIM!

His Word

Jews of Cyrene and Alexandria as well as the provinces of Cilicia and Asia. These men began to argue with Stephen, [10]but they could not stand up against his wisdom or the Spirit by which he spoke.
[11]Then they secretly persuaded some men to say, "We have heard Stephen speak words of blasphemy against Moses and against God."
[12]So they stirred up the people and the elders and the teachers of the law. They seized Stephen and brought him before the Sanhedrin. [13]They produced false witnesses, who testified, "This fellow never stops speaking against the holy place and against the law. [14]For we have heard him say that this Jesus of Nazareth will destroy this place and change the customs Moses handed down to us."
[15]All who were sitting in the Sanhedrin looked intently at Stephen, and they saw that his face was like the face of an angel.

7 Then the high priest asked him, "Are these charges true?" [2]To this he replied: "Brothers and fathers, listen to me! The God of glory appeared to our father Abraham while he was still in Mesopotamia, before he lived in Haran. [3]'Leave your country and your people,' God said, 'and go to the land I will show you.'   — Acts 6:9b — 7:3, NIV

Read His Word to Him.

How I do admire your wonderful man Stephen. How eloquent and wise he is! I thank you for giving me (and generation upon generation before me) this beautiful word. How evil and hateful man can be (we can be). Oh, may I right now respond as did your holy servant, Jesus. Stephen stood before the same men on the same charge and returned the same attitude. Thank you, thank you for your presence in him. Dear God, I want an angelic countenance!

Please express your response to this beautiful text. Put your expression in your own prayer diary.

6. READ HIS WORD FOR YOURSELF.

The response of Stephen was angelic, Christ-like, unanswerable, true, humble, bold, full of scripture, loving, urgent. Oh, dear God, that I might so react to opposition, particularly the kind of persecution Stephen faced. The "God of glory," the God of total virtue, of beauty and honor, of power beyond words, of personal communication—"Leave your people and your country and go! I will show you where."

It is so important that you pause in his presence
and either audibly or in written form tell him all his word means to you.

7. READ HIS WORD IN THANKSGIVING.

Thank you for: (1) Spirit and wisdom from yourself. (2) For opposition that sharply defines the issue. (3) That I know leaders who should know better can be stirred up against my Lord. (4) That the presence of my Lord and truth can be reflected physically. (5) That I know religious change is always opposed. (6) That a knowledge of your word will always be a help in persecution or temptation. (7) That I should be full of love and consideration—even if no one else is.

Give yourself to your own expression of gratitude—write it or speak it!

8. READ HIS WORD IN MEDITATION.

"They saw his face"—our total personality is reflected in our face, subtly, but visibly. The fundamental attitude of a person is seen in his facial expression. Has he decided he will oppose everyone and everything that opposes him? It shows. Has he within his spirit submitted and been beaten down? It can be seen. Has he looked beyond men and their words and what they can do to the One who can do all things? Such "other world" radiance will reflect through his eyes and in all his expression.

Pause—wait—think—then express yourself in thoughtful praise or thanks.

9. READ HIS WORD FOR PETITIONS.

There were no doubt Christians praying for Stephen. What requests can I find? (1) Help me to more fully appreciate the benefits of freedom. (2) Open my eyes to present day persecution of your followers. (3) Would I recognize someone with a face like an angel? (4) I want to understand this good man Stephen much better than I do. (5) Would I have spoken on the same subject if I had been Stephen? (6) Why did Stephen call these men "brothers"? (7) I want to understand more fully the meaning of the expression: "the God of glory."

Please, please remember these are prayers—speak them—reword them!

10. READ HIS WORD AND WAIT — LISTEN — GOD SPEAKS!

What word is there from the Lord? (1) "I work through men whose hearts are pure." (2) "You cannot oppose religious tradition without persecution." (3) "There are men like Stephen today—find them and help them."

11. INTERCESSION FOR THE LOST WORLD

Greece — Points for prayer: (1) *Radio*. Both Trans World Radio and IBRA have many Greek broadcasts weekly, and there has been some response to this. Pray for this ministry. (2) *Expatriate Greek communities* are large in Germany (250,000), Australia (approx. 260,000) and the U.S.A. (around 2 million). These people have been much more systematically evangelized, and there are now assemblies of believers among them in all these and several other lands. Pray for these believers and their missionary vision—especially for their homeland. Pray for the considerable amount of literature that is handed out to Greeks in these lands.

12. SING PRAISES TO OUR LORD.

So precious is Jesus, my Savior, my King,
His praise all the day long with rapture I sing;
To Him in my weakness for strength I can cling,
For He is so precious to me.
For He is so precious to me,

For He is so precious to me; . . .
'Tis Heaven below
My Redeemer to know,
For He is so precious to me.

WEEK FIVE — SATURDAY

1. PRAISE GOD FOR WHO HE IS.

Source of faith. How totally true this is. You have invaded the planet earth and we owe our faith to what you have said and done in the Person of your Son. You have spoken through the writers of your book the Bible. Faith comes by hearing, reading and believing your word. What an abundant source of faith, an abundant person you are, abundance is an essential part of your character. Praise, thanksgiving, wonder, deep satisfaction, are all mine because of my trust in you through your word.

Express yourself in adoration for this quality of God.
Speak it audibly or write out your praise in your own devotional journal.

2. PRAISE GOD FOR WHAT HE MEANS TO ME.

I know you are the ultimate source of faith, but your word is the immediate source. I want to thank you for my confidence in your providence. You are leading me in ways some people would call coincidences, but I see them as the expression of your concern in the little every day events of my life. You led me to a splendid book to confirm my faith. You led me to a medicine that will help my blood condition. Praise you for speaking in both your word and your daily care.

How do you personally relate to faith, and God who is the source of faith?
Speak it out or write it out. It is so important that you establish your own devotional journal.

3. CONFESSION OF SIN

That I have had hatred of one form or another in my heart toward men and women is true, but I want to be forgiven. I want real genuine love (described in I Cor. 13:3-8) in my mind, will and emotions. Please forgive me for any form of hatred. I have hated certain circumstances into which I put myself or others did — but ultimately it was hatred against you — and for this I am even more sorrowful. Oh, dear God, forgive me!

What personal sins do you want to confess? We must speak them to remove them.
Do it! Now. There is no one else you have sinned against more than God. Tell him so!

4. SING A PRAYER TO GOD.

O worship the King, all glorious above,
And gratefully sing His wonderful love;
Our Shield and Defender, the Ancient of days,
Pavilioned in splendor, and girded with praise.

Open your hymn book and sing the rest of the verses — or even sing another prayer song.

5. READ HIS WORD TO HIM!

His Word

[4]"So he left the land of the Chaldeans and settled in Haran. After the death of his father, God sent him to this land where you are now living. [5]He gave him no inheritance here, not even a foot of ground. But God promised him that he and his descendants after him would possess the land, even though at that time Abraham had no child. [6]God spoke to him in this way: 'Your descendants will be strangers in a country not their own, and they will be enslaved and mistreated four hundred years. [7]But I will punish the nation they serve as slaves,' God said, 'and afterward they will come out of that country and worship me in this place.' [8]Then he gave Abraham the covenant of circumcision. And Abraham became the father of Isaac and circumcised him eight days after his birth. Later Isaac became the father of Jacob, and Jacob became the father of the twelve patriarchs.

[9]"Because the patriarchs were jealous of Joseph, they sold him as a slave into Egypt. But God was with him [10]and rescued him from all his troubles. He gave Joseph wisdom and enabled him to gain the good will of Pharaoh king of Egypt; so he made him ruler over Egypt and all his palace.
— *Acts 7:4-10, NIV*

Read His Word to Him.

How good to read again of the people — the family with whom you worked in days gone by — but every one of these people are now alive with you — for you are the God of the living — Abraham — Isaac and Jacob and Joseph! Praise your name. What a strong encouragement it is to me to read your promises and to see them fulfilled. But there must be someone like Stephen to tell and retell these beautiful words if they are going to mean anything to succeeding generations.

Please express your response to this beautiful text. Put your expression in your own prayer diary.

6. READ HIS WORD FOR YOURSELF.

Dear God, some of your promises will be fulfilled in second and third generations—help me to be patient. The mistreatment, or even enslavement of your people does not mean you have forsaken them or forgotten them (even if it lasts twice as long as America is old). Circumcision always seemed such a strange act and interest on the part of yourself, but sex is so fundamental to man—such a deep part of man. God wants recognition and acceptance in *every* area of life. From *one son* a tribe can arise, a whole nation can come.

It is so important that you pause in his presence
and either audibly or in written form tell him all his word means to you.

7. READ HIS WORD IN THANKSGIVING.

(1) That every place I live can be a place where God lives. (2) That God is sending me and calling me whether I can see or hear or not. He is more interested in my needs than I could ever be! (3) That God's convenants are all kept—but they have two sides—I do purpose to keep mine. I know he will keep his. (4) I want to worship him in every place I go. I thank you that I can. (5) For family, who become so near and dear to us. (6) That you are a part of our family and work even through family quarrels. (7) Your plans will not and cannot be thwarted.

Give yourself to your own expression of gratitude—write or speak it!

8. READ HIS WORD IN MEDITATION.

"But God was with him, and rescued him from all his troubles." If we would attribute every good thing that happened to us to yourself (as we indeed should) and every evil thing to the evil one (as we should) then we could say really often that you have rescued me from all my troubles. I and my brothers brought on all the troubles we are in. There are various ways of exalting man—indeed you have ways that seem the very opposite, but viewed from your perspective become a compliment not a complaint—man means it for evil but God means it for good!

Pause—wait—think—then express yourself in thoughtful praise or thanks.

9. READ HIS WORD FOR PETITIONS.

History is a good teacher—if we are willing to learn—I am: (1) Help me to never become so attached to this country that I could not leave it. (2) I want to accept the full impact of fulfilled prophecy. (3) I want to appreciate the Hebrew fathers, such as: Abraham, Isaac and Jacob. (4) Such a good example I find in Joseph—I want to be like him. (5) In all of my life God is working something for my good. (6) Dear Lord, rescue me from my trouble. (7) What an outstanding example of devotion I see in Joseph—I want to know more by way of application.

Please, please remember these are prayers—speak them—reword them!

10. READ HIS WORD AND WAIT—LISTEN—GOD SPEAKS!

Speak to me through this text: (1) "I am serious about my covenants." (2) "My ways are not your ways, but I love you." (3) "Use whatever I give you to bring honor to me."

11. INTERCESSION FOR THE LOST WORLD

Iceland – Population: 221,000. Annual growth 1.3%. People per sq. km.—1.

Points for prayer: (1) *The Icelanders are nominally Christian*, but prosperity is causing a drift away from the churches and a growing interest in occultism, promiscuity and leftist ideology. Evangelistic work has been discouraging in this spiritual climate with much indifference shown to the things of God. (2) *Immigrant laborers* — there are a number of Yugoslavs and others working on development projects. Pray that these people may be evangelized in their work camps.

12. SING PRAISES TO OUR LORD.

How sweet the name of Jesus sounds
In a believer's ear!
It soothes his sorrows, heals his wound,
And drives away his fear.

WEEK SIX — SUNDAY

1. PRAISE GOD FOR WHO HE IS.

Revealer. My dear Father, you do indeed reveal all that man has ever known from the world of eternity. How much you have given us—"all things that relate to this life and the life to come" (II Pet. 1:3). Bless and adore your wonderful name. You also give wisdom (the best use of knowledge) which is a form of revelation. You have also revealed the secrets of men in times past and even now you do the same.

Express yourself in adoration for this quality of God.
Speak it audibly or write out your praise in your own devotional journal.

2. PRAISE GOD FOR WHAT HE MEANS TO ME.

Revealer to me. I am so glad to know someone who knows all things—to you I can come for any and all answers. You have given me a book in which I have the sum total of your revelation and yet you uncover new concepts to me of the application of your word and for this form of revelation (wisdom) I thank and praise you. You show me the hidden secrets of my heart and how much I need your forgiveness.

How do you personally relate to the revelations of God, and God who is revealer?
Speak it out or write it out. It is *so important* that you establish *your own* devotional journal.

3. CONFESSION OF SIN

How often I have been angry out of frustrated selfishness! Dear Lord, please forgive. Dear God, let my anger be directed toward the evil one. At times my anger comes from a lack of rest—for one reason or another I have not kept my priorities straight. Dear Lord, forgive and cleanse. How strong and helpful to have the total washing away of all guilt and sin. Wonderful!

What personal sins do you want to confess? We *must* speak them to remove them.
Do it! *Now.* There is no one else you have sinned against more than God. Tell him so!

4. SING A PRAYER TO GOD.

Dear Lord and Father of mankind.
Forgive our foolish ways!
Reclothe us in our rightful mind;

In purer lives Thy service find,
In deeper rev'rence, praise.

Open your hymn book and sing the rest of the verses—or even sing another prayer song.

5. READ HIS WORD TO HIM!

His Word

[11]"Then a famine struck all Egypt and Canaan, bringing great suffering, and our fathers could not find food. [12]When Jacob heard that there was grain in Egypt, he sent our fathers on their first visit. [13]On their second visit, Joseph told his brothers who he was, and Pharaoh learned about Joseph's family. [14]After this, Joseph sent for his father Jacob and his whole family, seventy-five in all. [15]Then Jacob went down to Egypt, where he and our fathers died. [16]Their bodies were brought back to Shechem and placed in the tomb that Abraham had bought from the sons of Hamor at Shechem for a certain sum of money.

[17]"As the time drew near for God to fulfill his promise to Abraham, the number of our people in Egypt greatly increased. [18]Then another king, who knew nothing about Joseph, became ruler of Egypt. [19]He dealt treacherously with our people and oppressed our forefathers by forcing them to throw out their newborn babies so that they would die.
— *Acts 7:11-19, NIV*

Read His Word to Him.

That a famine would strike anytime, anywhere is itself a tragic fact, but when you are in it, i.e., able to work through it and actually use it for your own advantage it is a source of wonder. The record of your thoughts, purposes and actions in the life of Joseph is typical of your interest in every man's life, i.e., if every man would be as responsive as your servant Joseph. Dear God, I want to be that man! You have and will and are fulfilling your promises today! Praise your faithfulness.

Please express your response to this beautiful text. Put your expression in your own prayer diary.

6. READ HIS WORD FOR YOURSELF.

A famine has often struck my emotional nature, but you always have grain somewhere and you will lead me to it if I am only willing. What seems a cause of need becomes an occasion for blessing. There will always be rulers "who know not what gain in faith previous rulers have made," but at the same time there is being born someone who is "no ordinary child"—he will deliver!

It is so important that you pause in his presence
and either audibly or in written form tell him all his word means to you.

7. READ HIS WORD IN THANKSGIVING.

Thank you: (1) For the wonderful way you are able to work through every circumstance of life for our good. (2) For the beautiful story of Joseph—such a good man—one who has helped me often. (3) That I am not the body—the bodies were carried over to Shechem, but the men had been with you. (4) Your cause can and does increase—just the law of averages takes care of some of it. (5) While someone dies—at the same time someone is born—both are an essential part of life. (6) Treacherous rulers are no threat to you, but are a trial to your people. (7) Courage and boldness are always possible.

Give yourself to your own expression of gratitude—write it or speak it!

8. READ HIS WORD IN MEDITATION.

Let us gather around your word and pray and think: The Grecian Jews were complaining about the Aramaic-speaking Jews. There is no disagreement quite so heated as that between brothers, but love can solve it—let the Grecian Jews take the lead in a solution. Prayer—and the ministry of the word—"to give myself" to prayer means much—myself, my total being. Dear God, forgive that I fail here—time and thought and energy. There are five men here about whom we know nothing, but this is typical of all your work—each is known to you and a record can be written in heaven for all of them.

Pause—wait—think—then express yourself in thoughtful praise or thanks.

9. READ HIS WORD FOR PETITIONS.

Stephen is speaking to me—I want to hear him: (1) Help me to go to the right man for food—a one like Joseph, even your Son. (2) Give me the humble forgiving spirit of Joseph. (3) Help me to remember the commandment to "honor your father and mother" has not been repealed. (4) May I remember that one day all that physically identifies me will return to the Lord. (5) May I also remember there will be millions to follow me who never heard of my God. (6) Whatever I am going to do for you must be done now. (7) Give me a sensitive heart that I might see something special in every child born.

Right here add your personal requests—and his answers.

10. READ HIS WORD AND WAIT—LISTEN—GOD SPEAKS!

What are you saying especially to me? (1) "People are starving without the water of life and the bread from heaven." (2) "Forgive freely from the heart as you have been forgiven." (3) "There are evil men to whom human life means nothing."

11. INTERCESSION FOR THE LOST WORLD

Ireland — Population: Eire 3,100,000; N. Ireland 1,500,000. People per sq. km.—107.

Points for prayer: (1) *Eire is the only Roman Catholic country in the English speaking world.* Although not the State Church, Rome controls, or has a say in every aspect of the life of the country. There are 4,500 priests in Eire, and many thousands of Roman Catholic missionaries have gone out all over the world. Since the Vatican II Council, the Roman Catholic hierarchy has lost a good deal of its influence, persecution of Protestants has diminished, and there is a new spirit of openness and freedom to study the Scriptures and to consider the claims of the Gospel. More and more Roman Catholics are turning to the Lord and forming their own little groups for prayer and Bible study (few join the Protestant denominations).

12. SING PRAISES TO OUR LORD.

When I saw the cleansing fountain
Open wide for all my sin,
I obeyed the Spirit's wooing,
When He said, Wilt thou be clean?

I will praise Him! I will praise Him!
Praise the Lamb for sinners slain;
Give Him glory, all ye people,
For His blood can wash away each stain.

WEEK SIX — MONDAY

1. PRAISE GOD FOR WHO IS.

Personally interested. To believe you are personally interested in every living human being upon the surface of this planet is one awesome thought! Most especially when I consider the thousand upon hundreds of thousands I have seen in India, or Korea, or the Philippines — yet, this I do believe and I'm glad I do! You know every thought and deed and at the same time the failures of each and all.

Express yourself in adoration for this quality of God.
Speak it audibly or write out your praise in your own devotional journal.

2. PRAISE GOD FOR WHAT HE MEANS TO ME.

Personally interested in me. I represent all others, i.e., who are your children. I know you want *all* men to be your family, but I take great courage in this thought. I raise my prayer up as a true expression of wonder and praise. I do need so much your help in so many areas — indeed I want to give my whole self to you. That you think of me as an individual is such a strength.

How do you personally relate to the personal interest of God, and God who is personally interested?
Speak it out or write it out. It is *so important* that you establish *your own* devotional journal.

3. CONFESSION OF SIN

I have sinned and do sin — I do not want to continue in sin! Do I have "wrath" as a sin? Yes, yes, but I have noticed lately a calming condition — I praise you for this. I want to show love which suffers long, with kindness — not impatient wrath which strikes out at any hindrance. Most of all I want to be clean within! Praise your name I accept such from you!

What personal sins do you want to confess? We *must* speak them to remove them.
Do it! *Now.* There is no one else you have sinned against more than God. Tell him so!

4. SING A PRAYER TO GOD.

Fairest Lord Jesus!
Ruler of all nature!
O Thou of God and man the Son!

Thee will I cherish,
Thee will I honor,
Thou, my soul's glory, joy, and crown!

Open your hymn book and sing the rest of the verses — or even sing another prayer song.

5. READ HIS WORD TO HIM!

His Word

[20]"At that time Moses was born, and he was no ordinary child. For three months he was cared for in his father's house. [21]When he was placed outside, Pharaoh's daughter took him and brought him up as her own son. [22]Moses was educated in all the wisdom of the Egyptians and was powerful in speech and action.

[23]"When Moses was forty years old, he decided to visit his fellow Israelites. [24]He saw one of them being mistreated by an Egyptian, so he went to his defense and avenged him by killing the Egyptian. [25]Moses thought that his own people would realize that God was using him to rescue them, but they did not. — *Acts 7:20-25, NIV*

Read His Word to Him.

You have set yourself among families — so very, very often you are involved with someone's son, father, mother, child or with many families. And always there is some really fine purpose behind your presence. Here we are in the house of Jocabed and her husband, but most of all with Moses. Indeed "he was no ordinary child" born anywhere — everyone is someone special — thanks to your presence in the family.

Please express your response to this beautiful text. Put your expression in your own prayer diary.

6. READ HIS WORD FOR YOURSELF.

To see Moses "educated in all the wisdom of the Egyptians — powerful in speech and action" — and yet devoted to you (or was he?) is a remarkable circumstance. He retained his racial identity, but trusted too much in himself. Dear God, may I see myself in this man Moses. I cannot do your work or carry out your will by human wisdom, speech or action, or by espousing a righteous cause. Without you and through yourself I can do nothing, utterly, totally, nothing!

It is so important that you pause in his presence
and either audibly or in written form tell him all his word means to you.

7. READ HIS WORD IN THANKSGIVING.

How I thank you for: (1) The family unit of which you are the best part. (2) For men like Stephen who know your word and its meaning. (3) For brave and humble Jocabed and all those who shared her devotion for the little one — who became such a great one. (4) For your presence at the Nile River on that most eventful day. (5) For Moses' compassion — backed with action — even when it was misplaced. (6) Your ways of humbling us. (7) That vengeance is your job.

Give yourself to your own expression of gratitude — write it or speak it!

8. READ HIS WORD IN MEDITATION.

Powerful in speech and action. Powerful by whose definition? Does God (through Stephen) say Moses was so gifted? We believe the answer is "yes," but because of selfish pride it was short-circuited — so with me — so with all who speak and act for God. However well trained and gifted we might be, without the inward, personal involvement with yourself, without the inward communion and Spirit's education, we say and do nothing that accomplishes your purpose. Your glory is eclipsed by our pride. Dear Lord, forgive!

Pause — wait — think — then express yourself in thoughtful praise or thanks.

9. READ HIS WORD FOR PETITIONS.

Here are needs of mine that arise from this text: (1) How can I care for the new ones of your family? (2) What risks can I take today that will indicate my trust in you? (3) Lead me to someone with a tender heart who will hear your word. (4) Prepare me to live an entirely different lifestyle for you — if such is to be. (5) Where can I get more power in speech and action? — from you I know — but how? (6) Moses' life was divided into periods — what are the periods of my life — maybe there aren't any. (7) Help me to bear patiently with the misunderstanding of men.

Please, please remember these are prayers — speak them — reword them!

10. READ HIS WORD AND WAIT — LISTEN — GOD SPEAKS!

Speak to me through these verses: (1) "I risked all on one man Moses." (2) "I work through unbelievers for my purposes." (3) "The wrath of man *never* works my righteousness."

11. INTERCESSION FOR THE LOST WORLD

Ireland — Points for prayer: (1) *The Protestants in the north* are more Bible believing than their counterparts in England. The true believers are the only bridge of sanity between the nominal Protestants and the Catholics, yet some extremist sections of the Church have sadly provoked intransigence and also brought division to the Bible believers on the difficult political issues. There are deepening divisions over the ecumenical movement and also the charismatic movement. Pray for real Bible based unity among believers, and also for their witness in these troubled times, that many may be saved through their Christ-like lives. The missionary vision of the believers is far greater than that found in England today. (2) *The evangelistic outreach in Eire* by many denominations and evangelistic missions continues unabated despite the tragic shadow of violence of the I.R.A. that hangs like a pall over all Ireland. There are a number of intrepid evangelists and colporteurs who witness through evangelistic meetings, open air meetings, personal witness and through Christian bookshops and literature displays in shows, fairs, etc. They face some opposition and converts are liable to suffer for their faith, yet the seed is sown and produces fruit in some lives.

12. SING PRAISES TO OUR LORD.

A Friend I have, called Jesus,
Whose love is strong and true,
And never fails howe'er 'tis tried,
No matter what I do;
I've sinned against this love of His,
But when I knelt to pray,

Confessing all my guilt to Him,
The sin-clouds rolled away.
It's just like Jesus to roll the clouds away,
It's just like Jesus to keep me day by day,
It's just like Jesus all along the way,
It's just like His great love.

WEEK SIX — TUESDAY

1. PRAISE GOD FOR WHO HE IS.

Hate. I know you have an abhorrence of evil—that you hate sin because of what it does to man. Not that you are hate per se, but directed toward what hurts and hinders us. I'm so glad you do hate sin and all that makes us less than we could be. No variance in your love, this is but the other side of the same quality. Praise your name that you protect us from what would destroy us.

Express yourself in adoration for this quality of God.
Speak it audibly or write out your praise in your own devotional journal.

2. PRAISE GOD FOR WHAT HE MEANS TO ME.

You hate the evil in my life, not me. You purpose to develop all the qualities of eternal purpose and oppose all those which only hinder and defeat. I'm delighted you have decided in your word just what is and is not to be opposed. I want to develop the same abhorrence for evil. I want to truly *hate* sin and *love* righteousness.

How do you personally relate to this quality of God, and God who hates evil?
Speak it out or write it out. It is *so important* that you establish *your own* devotional journal.

3. CONFESSION OF SIN

It is curious that I should now here relate to the reverse of righteous hatred and talk about, pray about, and confess to my righteous Father my need to be forgiven of "railing." It would seem that one form or another of this sin appears so very often—we rail at one another and at you. Cutting one another down in a false form of humor is one expression of this sin. Dear Lord, give me the deep love I want for all and most of all for you.

What personal sins do you want to confess? We *must* speak them to remove them.
Do it! *Now.* There is no one else you have sinned against more than God. Tell him so!

4. SING A PRAYER TO GOD.

A mighty fortress is our God.
A bulwark never failing;
Our helper He, amid the flood
Of mortal ills prevailing.
For still our ancient foe

Doth seek to work us woe;
His craft and pow'r are great,
And, armed with cruel hate,
On earth is not his equal.

Open your hymn book and sing the rest of the verses—or even sing another prayer song.

5. READ HIS WORD TO HIM!

His Word

²⁶The next day Moses came upon two Israelites who were fighting. He tried to reconcile them by saying, 'Men, you are brothers; why do you want to hurt each other?' ²⁷But the man who was mistreating the other pushed Moses aside and said, 'Who made you ruler and judge over us? ²⁸Do you want to kill me as you killed the Egyptian yesterday?' ²⁹When Moses heard this, he fled to Midian, where he settled as a foreigner and had two sons. ³⁰After forty years had passed, an angel appeared to Moses in the flames of a burning bush in the desert near Mount Sinai. ³¹When he saw this, he was amazed at the sight. As he went over to look more closely, he heard the Lord's voice: ³²'I am the God of your fathers, the God of Abraham, Isaac and Jacob.' Moses trembled with fear and did not dare to look.

³³"Then the Lord said to him, 'Take off your sandals; the place where you are standing is holy ground. ³⁴I have indeed seen the oppression of my people in Egypt. I have heard their groaning and have come down to set them free. Now come, I will send you back to Egypt.'

³⁵"This is the same Moses whom they had rejected with the words, 'Who made you ruler and judge?' He was sent to be their ruler and deliverer by God himself, through the angel who appeared to him in the bush. ³⁶He led them out of Egypt and did wonders and miraculous signs in Egypt, at the Red Sea and for forty years in the desert.

— Acts 7:26-36, NIV

Read His Word to Him.

The hatred and frustration and impatience of man—the abuse and misuse of time and body—no worship and total selfish interest—how odious all this must be to you, and yet you are at work. There is a message in all of this for us. There is a pattern in all man's mistreatment of himself and his fellowman. Did you decide Moses must flee and leave instead of staying and opposing? "After forty years had passed"—I'm sure you know how many days and weeks and months are in forty years, but not one word about one day of the 15,600 days in the 40 years.

Please express your response to this beautiful text. Put your expression in your own prayer diary.

6. READ HIS WORD FOR YOURSELF.

I see myself a good deal like Moses — a late starter — how late to start we all are in so many areas. I have preached and taught 40 years from June 1939 to June 1979. There are so many lessons to learn, and so many I did, but many more I did not. After 40 years an angel of God appeared to him in the flames of a burning bush. Dear God, please appear to me in the mundane of this day. May some common thing I have seen a thousand times suddenly ignite and burn with your power and beauty and warmth. Dear God, may I have eyes to see and ears to hear!

It is so important that you pause in his presence
and either audibly or in written form tell him all his word means to you.

7. READ HIS WORD IN THANKSGIVING.

Indeed, indeed, I do! For: (1) Perception for evaluation of what I should decide — you decide, through me. (2) All men *are* brothers. Oh, oh, that we might claim this blessed truth! (3) What is done in secret will be proclaimed in public. (4) Time is not at all a part of eternity — and yet so precious to man. (5) That you and your communication is a flame in a bush — so like me — and all us preachers. (6) Dear God, you are not dead. You see and hear our groanings! (7) He who men rejects can be accepted and used of God.

Give yourself to your own expression of gratitude — write it or speak it!

8. READ HIS WORD IN MEDITATION.

"Who made you a ruler and judge?" Man resents deeply any man anytime assuming rights not given — yet God *has* set and sent men over other men as rulers and *deliverers* — (not *judges* in the sense of condemnation). And who does God use? Look — (1) A tongue-tied old man. (2) A misfit from Egypt. (3) A Jew who lived like the Gentiles. (4) A man with a story no one would believe. (5) One who established a deep, deep reverence for God. (6) One who lost all confidence in himself and gained it all back a thousandfold as he placed his confidence in God. (7) One who obeyed God's words in spite of everything and everyone.

Pause — wait — think — then express yourself in thoughtful praise or thanks.

9. READ HIS WORD FOR PETITIONS.

Requests from Hebrew history: (1) May I wait upon your timing. (2) Give me the humility to recognize your negative answers. (3) Help me to see that inactivity can be productive. (4) Speak to me today in the ordinary circumstances of my life. (5) Give me a compassionate heart for those who suffer. (6) Where is the "Red Sea" in my life? (7) Open my eyes to follow our prophet, my Lord.

Right here add your personal requests — and his answers.

10. READ HIS WORD AND WAIT — LISTEN — GOD SPEAKS!

What does the record of Moses say to me? (1) "Stand still and see the salvation of your God." (2) "I speak today in my holy word." (3) "Men still await a deliverer."

11. INTERCESSION FOR THE LOST WORLD

Italy — Population: 56,300,000. Growth 0.8% annually. People per sq. km. — 187.

Points for prayer: (1) *Italy remains largely unreached by Bible believers.* Possibly only 1,000 of Italy's 31,000 communities have a Bible believing witness. There are many towns and cities without an effective group of believers. There are even whole provinces without a resident witness to the Lord. Most of Sardinia and Lecce in the S.E. have few Bible believers. (2) *Vatican City* is the last vestige of the Roman Catholic Pope's temporal empire in central Italy. It is an independent city-state with a population of 1,000. From here the Pope rules the world's 765,000,000 Roman Catholics. The Roman Church is in turmoil because of the conflict between the traditional and reforming factions, the impact of the ecumenical movement, the growing charismatic movement and the increasing use of the Bible by Roman Catholics. Pray that all these factors may be used of God to bring many into the light of the Gospel.

12. SING PRAISES TO OUR LORD.

Jesus is all the world to me,
My life, my joy, my all;
He is my strength from day to day,
Without Him I would fall.

When I am sad, to Him I go,
No other one can cheer me so;
When I am sad He makes me glad,
He's my Friend.

WEEK SIX — WEDNESDAY

1. PRAISE GOD FOR WHO HE IS.

Wrath. This would be hate expressed. I would soon lose heart if I only emphasized this aspect of your character, but I *must* face the fact and it is that you hate sin and do express your hate in wrath or punishment — no sin escapes — I do not say *sinner*, because many of us have cast ourselves upon your mercy — for you are not totally wrath. Great, wonderful, dear God, I am full of amazement!

Express yourself in adoration for this quality of God.
Speak it audibly or write out your praise in your own devotional journal.

2. PRAISE GOD FOR WHAT HE MEANS TO ME.

Wrath against my sin, because it hurts me as much as it offends your character. Dear God, I *must not* allow your mercy and grace to outweigh other qualities. You do hate my sin and express your wrath against it. Not only my sin but the sin of the whole world. Oh great God, Creator and Ruler of all, who can stand before your wrath? no one, nothing!

How do you personally relate to the wrath of God, and God who is wrath?
Speak it out or write it out. It is *so important* that you establish *your own* devotional journal.

3. CONFESSION OF SIN

How I waste the precious time you give me looking at TV — do you want me to rid myself of the set or looking at it? Dear Lord, forgive me, forgive all my rationalizations for my sin, deepen my love for you. "Shameful speaking" — dear Lord, forgive me, cleanse me.

What personal sins do you want to confess? We *must* speak them to remove them.
Do it! *Now.* There is no one else you have sinned against more than God. Tell him so!

4. SING A PRAYER TO GOD.

Are you weary, are you heavy-hearted?
Tell it to Jesus,
Tell it to Jesus;
Are you grieving over joys departed?
Tell it to Jesus alone.

Tell it to Jesus, tell it to Jesus,
He is a friend that's well-known;
You've no other such a friend or brother,
Tell it to Jesus alone.

Open your hymn book and sing the rest of the verses — or even sing another prayer song.

5. READ HIS WORD TO HIM.

His Word

[37]"This is that Moses who told the Israelites, 'God will send you a prophet like me from your own people.' [38]He was in the congregation in the desert, with our fathers and with the angel who spoke to him on Mount Sinai; and he received living words to pass on to us.

[39]"But our fathers refused to obey him. Instead, they rejected him and in their hearts turned back to Egypt. [40]They told Aaron, 'Make us gods who will go before us. As for this fellow Moses who led us out of Egypt — we don't know what has happened to him!' [41]That was the time they made an idol in the form of a calf. They brought sacrifices to it and held a celebration in honor of what their hands had made. [42]But God turned away and gave them over to the worship of the heavenly bodies. This agrees with what is written in the book of the prophets:
'Did you bring me sacrifices and offerings forty years in the desert, O house of Israel?
[43]You have lifted up the shrine of Moloch and the star of your god Rephan, the idols you made to worship. Therefore I will send you into exile beyond Babylon.'

[44]"Our forefathers had the tabernacle of Testimony with them in the desert. It had been made as God directed Moses, according to the pattern he had seen. [45]Having received the tabernacle, our fathers under Joshua brought it with them when they took the land from the nations God drove out before them. It remained in the land until the time of David, [46]who enjoyed God's favor and asked that he might provide a dwelling place for the God of Jacob. [47]But it was Solomon who built the house for him.

[48]"However, the Most High does not live in houses made by men. As the prophet says:
[49]'Heaven is my throne, and the earth is my footstool. What kind of house will you build for me?
says the Lord.
Or where will my resting place be?
[50]Has not my hand made all these things?'

[51]"You stiff-necked people, with uncircumcised hearts and ears! You are just like your fathers: You always resist the Holy Spirit! [52]Was there ever a prophet your fathers did not persecute? They even killed those who predicted the coming of the Righteous One. And now you have betrayed and murdered him — [53]you who have received the law that was put into effect through angels but have not obeyed it."
— *Acts 7:37-53, NIV*

WEEK SIX — WEDNESDAY

Read His Word to Him.

How wonderful is your promise of "a prophet like Moses" —how gloriously did you keep that promise: (1) Born under tyrants. (2) Persecuted in infancy. (3) Hid by loved ones. (4) Rejected by their own. (5) Prepared in seclusion. (6) Given divine credentials of miraculous signs. (7) Delivered people through death. Oh, wonder of wonders! Moses and our Lord were in the congregation (of men) in the wilderness with the fathers of Israel and with holy angels. Oh, oh, how solicitous angels must have been with our Lord!

Please express your response to this beautiful text. Put your expression in your own prayer diary.

6. READ HIS WORD FOR YOURSELF.

Oh, speak to me dear Lord—bless your name—you already have! As Moses received the "living words" so have I. Let them burn and warm and come alive in my total being! Dear Lord, that we might not repeat the sin of idolatry today—of apostasy—of sensualism—of admiration for the works of man's hands. Dear Lord, the most beautiful house you have on earth today is the body of man—together making up the body of your dear Son. Dear Father, deliver me from "stubbornness"—unclean mind—will—emotions conscience—unclean hearing and seeing and speaking. Oh, oh, may I not resist the blessed Holy Spirit—in every way let me be submissive.

It is so important that you pause in his presence
and either audibly or in written form tell him all his word means to you.

7. READ HIS WORD IN THANKSGIVING.

Thanksgiving from this word: (1) That Jesus even my present living Lord is my prophet, i.e., teacher. (2) He is with me now, inside in the person of the Holy Comforter. (3) In this desert wilderness he is my cloud by day and fire by night. (4) Dear Lord, I thank you for every time I have been willing to heed your word—and ask forgiveness for all the times I have resisted you. (5) Thank you, thank you, thank you that I am out of Egypt and hate the very thought of returning. (6) Thank you that I envision Jesus, oh, blessed Savior, on the throne of my heart. (7) Thank you for the mind-boggling display in the galaxies of planets and stars testifying of your everlasting power and super-human qualities.

Give yourself to your own expression of gratitude—write it or speak it!

8. READ HIS WORD IN MEDITATION.

"The Tabernacle of Testimony"—what an intriguing name! A dwelling place for God—note: (1) Covered with skin like your body and mine. (2) Totally dark inside except for the golden lampstand which had to be replenished each day, morning and evening. Oh, oh, how I want to let the light of your word permeate each day every dark recess of my heart and life. (3) Inside was the table of the Lord—where he could share a meal with us. Dear blessed Jesus sup with me as I do with you. (4) Oh, how I want to spend time with you "ministering in the Holy Place," and you with me.

Pause—wait—think—then express yourself in thoughtful praise or thanks.

9. READ HIS WORD FOR PETITIONS.

Petitions from Stephen's defense: (1) Dear Lord, may I hear your prophet Jesus. (2) May your word relate to all of life—all of my life. (3) Help me not to try your patience in my repentance. (4) May I treat your tabernacle—even my body—in a way that brings honor to you. (5) Lift my eyes above the ordinary to see your eternal purpose at work. (6) May I in no way resist the Holy Spirit. (7) Give me the courage to rebuke sin when it will help.

Please, please remember these are prayers—speak them—reword them!

10. READ HIS WORD AND WAIT—LISTEN—GOD SPEAKS!

Speak to me: (1) "Keep your heart out of Egypt." (2) "Burn up all your idols." (3) "The Most High does not live in houses made by men."

11. INTERCESSION FOR THE LOST WORLD

Italy — Point for prayer: (1) *The Roman Catholic Church is increasingly despised and ignored by Italians* because of its interference in politics and efforts to preserve the privileges of the powerful. This is especially true of the youth. Sadly, few of these disillusioned people have had the chance to hear the Gospel clearly, and it is the false promises of Communism that are winning their minds.

12. SING PRAISES TO OUR LORD.

My Jesus, I love Thee, I know Thou art mine,
For Thee all the follies of sin I resign;
My gracious Redeemer, my Savior art Thou;
If ever I loved Thee, my Jesus, 'tis now.

WEEK SIX — THURSDAY

1. PRAISE GOD FOR WHO HE IS.

Fire. A fire is not only destructive. But you *do* destroy as well as build up. A fire—even yourself—can and does warm those who are cold. How cold life is without you, and there are two billion people who have never heard of yourself or your Son! A fire offers light and you do indeed supply such light!

Express yourself in adoration for this quality of God.
Speak it audibly or write out your praise in your own devotional journal.

2. PRAISE GOD FOR WHAT HE MEANS TO ME.

Fire for me! Burn out all my dross! Warm the very depths of my total inward being, enlighten me in every area of need. Dear God, become fire for me, to me. How I want you to accomplish in me all of yourself, all of your personal qualities. Consume the chaff of this life in me.

How do you personally relate to the light and warmth of God, and God who is fire?
Speak it out or write it out. It is *so important* that you establish *your own* devotional journal.

3. CONFESSION OF SIN

How many unnecessary besetting sins I have—I know you hate them, your wrath is against them—only because they *hurt me.* Dear God, I do, I do want to lay them aside. I openly, fully, candidly, name my personal sins— "shameful speaking"—get it out of my mouth and clear my record—"passion"—immoral thoughts expressed in some form of "passion." Oh, God, deliver me!

What personal sins do you want to confess? We *must* speak them to remove them.
Do it! *Now.* There is no one else you have sinned against more than God. Tell him so!

4. SING A PRAYER TO GOD.

I must tell Jesus all of my trials;
I cannot bear these burdens alone;
In my distress He kindly will help me;
He ever loves and cares for His own.

I must tell Jesus! I must tell Jesus!
I cannot bear my burdens alone;
I must tell Jesus! I must tell Jesus!
Jesus can help me, Jesus alone.

Open your hymn book and sing the rest of the verses—or even sing another prayer song.

5. READ HIS WORD TO HIM!

His Word

[54]When they heard this, they were furious and gnashed their teeth at him. [55]But Stephen, full of the Holy Spirit, looked up to heaven and saw the glory of God, and Jesus standing at the right hand of God. [56]"Look," he said, "I see heaven open and the Son of Man standing at the right hand of God."

[57]At this they covered their ears and, yelling at the top of their voices, they all rushed at him, [58]dragged him out of the city and began to stone him. Meanwhile, the witnesses laid their clothes at the feet of a young man named Saul.

[59]While they were stoning him, Stephen prayed, "Lord Jesus, receive my spirit." [60]Then he fell on his knees and cried out, "Lord, do not hold this sin against them." When he had said this, he fell asleep.

8 And Saul was there, giving approval to his death. On that day a great persecution broke out against the church at Jerusalem, and all except the apostles were scattered throughout Judea and Samaria. [2]Godly men buried Stephen and mourned deeply for him.

— Acts 7:54—8:2, NIV

Read His Word to Him.

When your servant Stephen looked up into your presence what did he see? He saw because he was full of the Holy Spirit—he saw a revelation of a part of your very person, your character, your total being. But oh, oh, he saw Jesus standing at your right hand!! I do not know if there was any materialization of yourself. Whatever it was, it was a great source of strength for Stephen. He did not fear the face of man when he had looked into *your* face.

Please express your response to this beautiful text. Put your expression in your own prayer diary.

WEEK SIX — THURSDAY

6. READ HIS WORD FOR YOURSELF.

Dear Lord, help me to believe that in every death there is a purpose we cannot see—in the streets of Calcutta, or the homes of Kanpur, or an apartment in Tokyo, someone, several someones have died—one every two seconds die—most all of them with no knowledge of you whatsoever! Dear God, is there any purpose in their death? While my Lord lived 18 years in Joseph's home and worked in the carpenter's shop, men and women and boys and girls died and went to torment or comfort for what purpose? It was for a reasonable, all together good purpose, which you will explain as soon as I die.

It is so important that you pause in his presence
and either audibly or in written form tell him all his word means to you.

7. READ HIS WORD IN THANKSGIVING.

Thank you for: (1) A heaven into which I can look. (2) For another real world (of the Spirit) which is much more real than the one I am in. (3) No one can challenge Jesus' claim of Lordship. (4) Death is an open door, not a blind alley. (5) For someone who died like my Lord, i.e., in the same frame of mind. (6) That Saul saw beyond the stones and carnage. (7) That I can commit myself to the same Lord and faith for today.

Give yourself to your own expression of gratitude—write it or speak it!

8. READ HIS WORD IN MEDITATION.

Let's gather around his word and think and pray: Moses was taken care of for three months by someone else—even great Moses was once a helpless babe—so also was my Lord, and, so was I. Pharaoh's daughter had a mother's heart of love and concern—there are some today among the rich and powerful. A secular education does not need to corrupt you if you are taught by your mother. A visit to some people will not turn out like you think it will—some will love you—many will listen—some will hate you. But deliverance in the name and attitude of our Lord is yet our purpose in life.

Pause—wait—think—then express yourself in thoughtful praise or thanks.

9. READ HIS WORD FOR PETITIONS.

Stephen speaks to my heart: (1) Give me a new, fresh look at the character of God. (2) How I need to more freely understand the authority of my Lord. (3) Keep me more aware of your presence than the presence of men. (4) Remind me again and again that: "no word of God is void of power." (5) Give me the unselfish love of my Lord and Stephen for those who hated them. (6) May I be more aware of the world beyond. (7) Thank you for godly men, wherever I find them.

Right here add your personal requests—and his answers.

10. READ HIS WORD AND WAIT—LISTEN—GOD SPEAKS!

I hear you say: (1) "Love me in life—meet me in death." (2) "I give a hope both sure and steadfast." (3) "Persecution is not all bad."

11. INTERCESSION FOR THE LOST WORLD

Italy — Points for prayer: (1) *Pray for this land to remain open for the Gospel.* The gaining strength of Communism is most marked in the industrial north, and many have been hardened to the Gospel. A Communist takeover is likely, humanly speaking. Pray that the present opportunities for the Christians may not be lost. (2) *The Protestant witness is small and often not effective in outreach.* The centuries of Roman Catholic persecution and discrimination, though now largely a thing of the past, has left its mark and made the Protestants feel inferior and reluctant to witness to the oppressively large Roman Catholic majority. Several denominations are liberal in theology, and most denominations show little growth. Pray for revival to stir up these churches to the huge task of winning Italy for Jesus.

12. SING PRAISES TO OUR LORD.

Wounded for me, wounded for me,
There on the cross He was wounded for me;
Gone my transgressions, and now I am free,
All because Jesus was wounded for me.

WEEK SIX — FRIDAY

1. PRAISE GOD FOR WHO HE IS.

Holy-Pure. Dear Lord, holiness is a foreboding word, but this is one of the most attractive qualities of yourself! That you can be morally perfect as well as intellectually perfect is a wonderful quality — to know and worship Some-one who has never made a mistake (intellectually or morally) and never will is a thought of solid comfort! Eternal security is your very nature.

Express yourself in adoration for this quality of God.
Speak it audibly or write out your praise in your own devotional journal.

2. PRAISE GOD FOR WHAT HE MEANS TO ME.

Holy and pure for *me.* I could be terribly intimidated by such a thought, but the other qualities of yourself prevent this. I am instead full of admiration and wonder. You can and do impute this holiness and purity to me. Praise your holiness and purity.

How do you personally relate to the holiness and purity of God, and God who is holy and pure?
Speak it out or write it out. It is *so important* that you establish *your own* devotional journal.

3. CONFESSION OF SIN

When I consider my sin and ignorance and your holiness and purity I am overwhelmed, but I am also cleansed because you are total forgiveness and mercy. It is indeed not only good but needed. Dear God, I want to learn more fully how to repent and how to adequately confess my sins.

What personal sins do you want to confess? We *must* speak them to remove them.
Do it! *Now.* There is no one else you have sinned against more than God. Tell him so!

4. SING A PRAYER TO GOD.

'Tis the blessed hour of prayer,
  when our hearts lowly bend,
And we gather to Jesus,
  our Saviour and Friend;
If we come to Him in faith,
  His protection to share,

What a balm for the weary!
  O how sweet to be there!
Blessed hour of prayer,
Blessed hour of prayer;
What a balm for the weary!
O how sweet to be there!

Open your hymn book and sing the rest of the verses — or even sing another prayer song.

5. READ HIS WORD TO HIM!

His Word

[3]But Saul began to destroy the church. Going from house to house, he dragged off men and women and put them in prison.
[4]Those who had been scattered preached the word wherever they went. [5]Philip went down to a city in Samaria and proclaimed the Christ there. [6]When the crowds heard Philip and saw the miraculous signs he did, they all paid close attention to what he said. [7]With shrieks, evil spirits came out of many, and many paralytics and cripples were healed.
— Acts 8:3-7, NIV

Read His Word to Him.

How delighted I am to share your word — to contemplate the activities of your servant Saul. I know of the personal interest you had in his life (and every man — but as a servant of yours for a particular task). Dear God, how the example of those who were scattered blesses my life. To think that everywhere they went they were moved to tell of your love. Thank you, thank you for moving Dr. Luke to tell of Philip — he was only one among a multitude who told — but his bold, glad witness is such a help. Was it because the apostles laid their hands upon his head that he was able to do the miraculous signs?

Please express your response to this beautiful text. Put your expression in your own prayer diary.

6. READ HIS WORD FOR YOURSELF.

It was through the Holy Spirit that such signs were done — it was to confirm his word. The great joy in the city of Samaria was due to the good news as well as the healings and exorcism. Dear God, do you want us to do this today? Is not your word already confirmed by the complete record before us? Is the attention and interest of persons today to be secured by the supernatural? "Many paralytics and cripples were healed." Why? — as signs — to cause wonder and interest — would not such interest and wonder be caused by the same signs now? Is your word adequate today? How many signs will convince people? What did our Lord mean by his words: *a wicked and adulterous generation seeketh after a sign*?

It is so important that you pause in his presence
and either audibly or in written form tell him all his word means to you.

7. READ HIS WORD IN THANKSGIVING.

(1) Thank you, that when persecution comes you offer special help in signs and wonders — in the midst of ignorance and unbelief attention is polarized by the miraculous. (2) Thank you that the good news was so deeply implemented that those under stress were not discouraged, i.e., about the good news. (3) Thank you that there were those who so trusted your power and interest they were willing to accept difficulty as a purpose of your direction. (4) That the Samaritans were no longer despised. (5) That evil spirits can be overcome. (6) The joy of salvation and your interest in our lives is yet with us. (7) That Jesus is right now ready and listening even as I write these words.

Give yourself to your own expression of gratitude — write it or speak it!

8. READ HIS WORD IN MEDITATION.

"Philip proclaimed the Christ" — the power of *desire must* be present first. Why did Philip feel he *must* do this? (1) Our Lord told the apostles and they told Philip (and others) to do it. (2) It was too good to keep to himself. (3) He loved the people and wanted to meet their needs. A person to a person is God's way of communicating the good news. *"Great joy"* is an awesome thought!

Pause — wait — think — then express yourself in thoughtful praise or thanks.

9. READ HIS WORD FOR PETITIONS.

Requests amid opposition: (1) I need the zeal for truth Saul had for error. (2) I need the lifestyle evangelism of those in Jerusalem. (3) I want to be an evangelist like deacon Philip. (4) Make me ready to accept without qualification the evidence of Philip's signs. (5) How can I overcome evil with good? (6) Lead me to "the greater works" promised by my Lord. (7) Give me the joy of my salvation.

Please, please remember these are prayers — speak them — reword them!

10. READ HIS WORD AND WAIT — LISTEN — GOD SPEAKS!

I want to hear from you: (1) "Preach the word wherever you go." (2) "You have the product advertized by Philip's signs." (3) "Great joy only awaits great preaching."

11. INTERCESSION FOR THE LOST WORLD

Italy — Points for prayer: (1) *There are encouraging signs for the Gospel.* There is a new and genuine interest in the Gospel in nearly all levels of society and parts of the country. Some believers and denominations are very active and are seeing people converted. (2) *The need for foreign missionaries is very great.* There are now about 270 missionaries working in the land, but this number could be greatly increased. Believers from the U.S.A. and Australia of Italian descent and also Brazilians would probably be more easily able to adapt to the Italian way of life. There are many open doors for those willing to do a humble work of befriending people, overcoming their prejudices, and discipling them for the Lord and, above all, of working together with Italians to plant churches. Pray for the calling of such. (3) *The need for dedicated Italian full-time workers has never been greater.* There are no more than 50 Italians studying for the Lord's work in Italy. (4) *Literature distribution has borne fruit.* Pray for this valuable work.

12. SING PRAISES TO OUR LORD.

Come, we that love the Lord,
And let our joys be known;

Join in a song with sweet accord,
And thus surround the throne.

WEEK SIX — SATURDAY

1. PRAISE GOD FOR WHO HE IS.

Speaker. That you have spoken in times past is the record of your word — that you can speak is a part of your nature — that you are speaking to us through your word — and through nature is gloriously true! But do you speak to us in any other way? To listen to the multitude of conflicting reports will do us no good! I am very much content to open up your word and hear your voice. Dear God, speak, your servant is listening. Dear Father, I want to open my inner ear!

Express yourself in adoration for this quality of God.
Speak it audibly or write out your praise in your own devotional journal.

2. PRAISE GOD FOR WHAT HE MEANS TO ME.

Speaking is accomplished through words. How precious and eternally important is every word you have said — and written. Your words are full of yourself, for they are indeed the expression of your heart. A speaker is of no value without a listener, and one who truly has ears to hear. I propose to be that listener. Dear God, in the inwardness of my being I want to hear your voice as I read your word.

How do you personally relate to the speaking of God, and God who is speaker?
Speak it out or write it out. It is *so important* that you establish *your own* devotional journal.

3. CONFESSION OF SIN

Dear interested, listening Father, forgive my foolish, willful, ignorant, sins. *Covetousness* — have I wanted that which belongs to another? Dear Lord, forgive! It becomes a bore to confess over and over again the same sin, i.e., unless there is true repentance also present — 70 x 7 with true repentance is acceptable — if for men, it must be increasingly true for God. I do repent, I do confess. I am forgiven! Praise your name and blood!

What personal sins do you want to confess? We *must* speak them to remove them.
Do it! *Now.* There is no one else you have sinned against more than God. Tell him so!

4. SING A PRAYER TO GOD.

"Man of Sorrows," what a name
For the Son of God who came

Ruined sinners to reclaim!
Hallelujah! what a Savior!

Open your hymn book and sing the rest of the verses — or even sing another prayer song.

5. READ HIS WORD TO HIM!

His Word

[9]Now for some time a man named Simon had practiced sorcery in the city and amazed all the people of Samaria. He boasted that he was someone great,[10]and all the people, both high and low, gave him their attention and exclaimed, "This man is the divine power known as the Great Power." [11]They followed him because he had amazed them for a long time with his magic. [12]But when they believed Philip as he preached the good news of the kingdom of God and the name of Jesus Christ, they were baptized, both men and women. [13]Simon himself believed and was baptized. And he followed Philip everywhere, astonished by the great signs and miracles he saw.   — *Acts 8:9-13, NIV*

Read His Word to Him.

Praise you for the conquest of Simon the sorcerer — a trophy for yourself and your Son. Dear, dear Lord, deliver me from repeating his sin — we are not, have not seen and never will be any great one! You are the great One — just by your very nature as creator and sustainer, you are the true and only source of greatness — all others are but a poor reflection — sometimes on and sometimes of yourself. People are gullible and are like sheep — and do follow. But they will also believe Philip — if Philip is around to tell them.

Please express your response to this beautiful text. Put your expression in your own prayer diary.

6. READ HIS WORD FOR YOURSELF.

Do you see the words here on the page? The most unlikely persons can and do follow our Lord, but there *must* be a preacher. Will you be that preacher or will you train others that they might be the ones to bring the good news concerning the Kingdom of God and the name of the Lord Jesus? Philip must have preached something about baptism here (even as they did later to the eunuch) or men and women would not have been baptized. I am also astonished at the great signs and miracles he did. I know they confirmed the truthfulness of what he preached—my question is: "Do we need such confirmation today?" What would be confirmed that needs confirmation?

It is so important that you pause in his presence and either audibly or in written form tell him all his word means to you.

7. READ HIS WORD IN THANKSGIVING.

Thank you for: (1) That sorcery is so far inferior to the power of God. (2) That people will heed and listen and believe and follow. (3) That there is in man (*all men*) an innate desire to worship, to be amazed. (4) Praise your omnipotent name that you totally satisfy and never disappoint this desire to worship. (5) Belief comes by hearing— not through some other means. (6) It is good news for God to rule—it is good news that we can submit to the Lordship of Jesus. (7) Even Simon believed and was baptized and was saved—and continued in his Christian life for a period of time.

Give yourself to your own expression of gratitude—write it or speak it!

8. READ HIS WORD IN MEDITATION.

The conquest of Simon. Note he: (1) Had a deep attachment to a position of recognition. (2) Had established himself for years and years. (3) Must have been in league with Satan and manifest lying wonders. (4) Had some disdain for the dupes who followed him. (5) Could be impressed with the real thing! (6) Did believe that Jesus was the Messiah and Savior—and that Philip was God's spokesman (and not himself). (7) Went under the water to wash away his sins in the blood of Jesus. (8) Took a back seat and followed instead of leading.

Pause—wait—think—then express yourself in thoughtful praise or thanks.

9. READ HIS WORD AND WAIT—LISTEN—GOD SPEAKS!

Asking and receiving: (1) Give me the boldness of our Lord and his servants. (2) Deliver me from thinking of myself as "some great one." (3) May men hear the same message from me they heard from Philip. (4) Give me those who will believe and be baptized and be saved. (5) Give me heaven's confidence that delivers me from fear. (6) Even men like the sorcerer can be saved—help me to believe. (7) Thank you for the prejudice overcome by the Jews with the Samaritans.

Right here add your personal requests—and his answers.

10. READ HIS WORD AND WAIT—LISTEN—GOD SPEAKS!

Speak Lord, thy servant is listening: (1) "The power called great is my great power." (2) "The Samaritans were saved as an example for all men." (3) "Being with God's servants does not make you a servant of God."

11. INTERCESSION FOR THE LOST WORLD

Italy — Points for prayer: (1) *The follow-up of contacts* of mass evangelism presents real problems with the lack of spiritually qualified workers, and also the reluctance of new believers to associate with the despised Protestants. Pray for the increasing use of homes as neutral meeting places for Bible studies. (2) *Areas of special need:* a) *Sardinia,* an island with 1,600,000 people. There are only about 400 believers. b) *Sicily,* 5,000,000 people living in poverty. The Mafia gangster society affects much of the life of the island. There are small, but growing groups of believers. (3) *The 700,000 strong university student population* in 44 universities is more open to the Gospel than ever before, but has been largely ignored by Bible believers. There are tiny groups of Christians totalling 80 believers only, in a handful of universities.

12. SING PRAISES TO OUR LORD.

Praise Him! praise Him! Jesus, our blessed Redeemer!
Sing, O Earth, His wonderful love proclaim!
Hail Him! hail Him! highest archangels in glory;
Strength and honor give to His holy name!

Like a shepherd, Jesus will guard His children,
In His arms He carries them all day long:
Praise Him! praise Him! tell of His excellent greatness;
Praise Him! praise Him! ever in joyful song!

WEEK SEVEN — SUNDAY

1. PRAISE GOD FOR WHO HE IS.

Designer. Oh, bless your Holy Name. How delighted I am to acknowledge and praise you for all the tremendous designs I see all about me. The designs in the flowers, in the rocks, in the trees, in all of physical creation—your own handiwork. How I do worship before you. The intricate design in the human body is a total amazement, but the designing of human lives and destinies is your greatest work!

Express yourself in adoration for this quality of God.
Speak it audibly or write out your praise in your own devotional journal.

2. PRAISE GOD FOR WHAT HE MEANS TO ME.

Designer for me—Oh, dear God, wonderful heavenly Father! The ways you plan my life are beyond my understanding—the detail and interest you have in every area of my life is deeply appreciated—and acknowledged! Oh, that today I might cooperate with your design for just today. Bless your name that you have a plan for today. Oh, dear Lord, all your plans are good, and therefore it is relaxing to place one's self in the hands of One who does all things well.

How do you personally relate to the designing of God, and God who is designer?
Speak it out or write it out. It is *so important* that you establish *your own* devotional journal.

3. CONFESSION OF SIN

To confess is one thing; to forsake is quite another. As you know, I want to do both. Since we are in the presence of absolutes it is difficult to know how to do more than admit I am but a poor, weak, ignorant, willful sinner! I am most willful or I would not repeat my sin. But I do confess and I *do want* to forsake my sin. I do indeed claim the forgiveness, the freedom, the wholeness of forgiveness.

What personal sins do you want to confess? We *must* speak them to remove them.
Do it! *Now.* There is no one else you have sinned against more than God. Tell him so!

4. SING A PRAYER TO GOD.

I've found a Friend, oh, such a Friend!
He loved me ere I knew Him;
He drew me with the cords of love,
And thus He bound me to Him.

And round my heart still closely twine
Those ties which naught can sever,
For I am His, and He is mine,
Forever and forever.

Open your hymn book and sing the rest of the verses—or even sing another prayer song.

5. READ HIS WORD TO HIM!

His Word

[14]When the apostles in Jerusalem heard that Samaria had accepted the word of God, they sent Peter and John to them. [15]When they arrived, they prayed for them that they might receive the Holy Spirit, [16]because the Holy Spirit had not yet come upon any of them; they had simply been baptized into the name of the Lord Jesus. [17]Then Peter and John placed their hands on them, and they received the Holy Spirit.

[18]When Simon saw that the Spirit was given at the laying on of the apostles' hands, he offered them money and said, [19]"Give me also this ability so that everyone on whom I lay my hands may receive the Holy Spirit."

[20]Peter answered: "May your money perish with you, because you thought you could buy the gift of God with money!
— *Acts 8:14-20, NIV*

Read His Word to Him.

Oh, there are ten thousand Samarias that would receive the word today if we would go and tell them—perhaps you will need to scatter us—arrange for our persecution so we will be ready to share—but on second thought those who were scattered were filling Jerusalem with their teaching words before they went to Samaria—and it really was only *one* man, i.e., Philip who did it—but perhaps he was only representative. How I delight in the devotion of your servants!

Please express your response to this beautiful text. Put your expression in your own prayer diary.

WEEK SEVEN — SUNDAY

6. READ HIS WORD FOR YOURSELF.

It was no easier then than now — we can — and will share the word for the Lord today. Right now, I recommit myself to the spread of your good news. If the Samaritans were baptized believers (and they were), then they received the Holy Spirit — the new birth includes the gift of the Holy Spirit. We can't begin in the Christian life without Him (Holy Spirit) but His supernatural powers had not been given. Simon *saw* something supernatural and wanted it! I say all this because I need to think carefully here lest tradition become truth.

It is so important that you pause in his presence
and either audibly or in written form tell him all his word means to you.

7. READ HIS WORD IN THANKSGIVING.

Thank you for: (1) The willingness of Peter and John to be those who were sent rather than the senders. (2) Your power through humble men. (3) That all knew it was your power and not man's that moved men and women. (4) The "coming on" of the Holy Spirit — was it relegated to only the hands of the apostles? (5) Simon wanted an ability illegitimately. I want to learn of its true source: "the gift of God." (6) The courage of Peter — his direct application of truth to life. (7) That Simon was given a chance to be saved — i.e., to repent.

Give yourself to your own expression of gratitude — write it or speak it!

8. READ HIS WORD IN MEDITATION.

Prayer and the laying on of hands: In what sense did Peter and John pray that the Samaritans should receive the Holy Spirit? Can there be anyone anywhere who was saved or "born again" *without* the Holy Spirit? Weren't *all* the Corinthian Christians the temples or sanctuaries of the Holy Spirit (I Cor. 6:19, 20)? Didn't *all* the Christians (saints) at Rome have the Holy Spirit (Rom. 8:9)? Didn't *all* the Galatian Christians receive the Holy Spirit at the preaching of the faith (Gal. 3:1-5)? The answer is obvious. Since the Samaritans (including Simon) had believed and had been baptized they all had the Holy Spirit, but he had not "come upon" them. We must say this is a reference to the spiritual gifts for equipping the Samaritans to carry on the work of the Lord in the soon coming absence of Philip.

Pause — wait — think — then express yourself in thoughtful praise or thanks.

9. READ HIS WORD FOR PETITIONS.

Petitions from Samaria: (1) May I be as responsive to needs as Peter and John. (2) Open my mind as to the meaning of the little phrase, "the Holy Spirit had not yet come upon any of them." (3) Doesn't the Holy Spirit come with the baptism Jesus commanded? (4) Can one be saved without the Holy Spirit? (5) What did Simon see? (6) Give me the same holy honesty shown by Peter. (7) Keep me free from bribery.

Please, please remember these are prayers — speak them — reword them!

10. READ HIS WORD AND WAIT — LISTEN — GOD SPEAKS!

Speak Lord: (1) "The 'coming upon' of the Holy Spirit is different from the Holy Spirit as a gift." (2) "Money will never buy the gifts of God." (3) "Men do go to hell."

11. INTERCESSION FOR THE LOST WORLD

Andorra — A tiny independent principality of 465 sq. km. in the Pyrenee Mountains between Spain and France with a population of only 26,000. Only one third of the population is truly Andorran. The state depends on tourism and tax free concessions to banks and traders for its wealth. There are no known Bible believers; the entire population is Roman Catholic. Some Gospel literature has been distributed in the land. Pray for the evangelization of these people.

Monaco — A small independent principality on the south coast of France with an area of only 0.25 sq. km. and a population of 24,000. Points for prayer: (1) *This tiny land is almost entirely Roman Catholic.* No open evangelism is allowed. Pray that the Monagesque people may be evangelized. (2) *Trans World Radio has its home here.* This remarkable work of God has grown to a ministry that reaches out to the whole of Europe, the Communist lands and North Africa. Many of the lands in these areas are only able to be reached with the Gospel by means of radio.

12. SING PRAISES TO OUR LORD.

The name of Jesus is so sweet,
I love its music to repeat;
It makes my joys full and complete,
The precious name of Jesus.

"Jesus," oh, how sweet the name!
"Jesus," ev'ry day the same;
"Jesus," let all saints proclaim
Its worthy praise forever.

WEEK SEVEN — MONDAY

1. PRAISE GOD FOR WHO HE IS.

Sender. In times past you sent so many men (and women) to so many places—you are yet in the sending business. "Here am I, send me" should be the attitude of every man and woman on earth. In spite of reluctance, and downright refusal, you are still sending men to tell the glad tidings—our son is an example. Praise your wonderful name—I join the ranks—I did more than 40 years ago. You sent your Son as the first missionary—"the apostle and high-priest of our calling."

Express yourself in adoration for this quality of God.
Speak it audibly or write out your praise in your own devotional journal.

2. PRAISE GOD FOR WHAT HE MEANS TO ME.

Sender of me. Dear Lord, whereas I have been sent, and a good number of times I have responded to your call, there are many more times when I have refused, excused and rationalized until I did not go. I am so glad to read that when the church at Antioch sent Paul and Barnabas out amid prayer and fasting and laying on of hands, I yet read that it was by the Holy Spirit they were sent forth (Acts 13:1-4). I take courage in this inasmuch as the efforts of men can be the means of your sending today.

How do you personally relate to the sending of God, and God who is sender?
Speak it out or write it out. It is *so important* that you establish *your own* devotional journal.

3. CONFESSION OF SIN

My sin, my pride, my ignorance, my lies—forgive them. Deeply convict me, cleanse me wholly, move me to love, to joy, to acknowledgment of my cleanness. Oh, praise your name! Thank you for freedom, liberty! Open my inner heart to receive the blood and Spirit.

What personal sins do you want to confess? We *must* speak them to remove them.
Do it! *Now.* There is no one else you have sinned against more than God. Tell him so!

4. SING A PRAYER TO GOD.

Jesus is all the world to me,
My life, my joy, my all;
He is my strength from day to day,
Without Him I would fall.

When I am sad, to Him I go,
No other one can cheer me so;
When I am sad He makes me glad,
He's my Friend.

Open your hymn book and sing the rest of the verses—or even sing another prayer song.

5. READ HIS WORD TO HIM!

His Word

[21]"You have no part or share in this ministry, because your heart is not right before God. [22]Repent of this wickedness and pray to the Lord. Perhaps he will forgive you for having such a thought in your heart. [23]For I see that you are full of bitterness and captive to sin."

[24]Then Simon answered, "Pray to the Lord for me so that nothing you have said may happen to me."

[25]When they had testified and proclaimed the word of the Lord, Peter and John returned to Jerusalem, preaching the gospel in many Samaritan villages. — *Acts 8:21-25, NIV*

Read His Word to Him.

Could Simon have had a part in the ministry of healing and preaching? i.e., if his heart was right with you? Perhaps it is idle to ask—the answer is not there. Dear, dear God, I want, oh how I want, my heart to be right with you. No bitterness, no bondage. Is bitterness the root and bondage the fruit? I believe it is! But the real root cause is "thought." Am I bitter about *anything,* or *anyone*? Dear Lord, deliver me! forgive me! cleanse me, move me to the deepest repentance. That you should so clearly reveal what is needed for release and liberty and cleansing is so much appreciated.

Please express your response to this beautiful text. Put your expression in your own prayer diary.

6. READ HIS WORD FOR YOURSELF.

How often I kneel with Simon to piously prattle the empty words, "Pray to the Lord for me." Dear God, I want to pray, repent, yield for myself to you! That Peter and John proclaimed the word of the Lord is a wonderful evidence of your power and love, of the transformation you can perform in the lives of your servants. Peter and John were commercial fishermen of years and years of experience. They had no formal training, but oh, oh, they had been with our Lord—what a difference being with him makes! He captured the depths of the hearts—they *must* tell of him! The suffering Servant of Isaiah—the worship of the eunuch was not left in the Temple of Jerusalem. Dear God, while I travel today may I read from memory your word and worship your Son and yourself!

It is so important that you pause in his presence
and either audibly or in written form tell him all his word means to you.

7. READ HIS WORD IN THANKSGIVING.

Thank you for: (1) Each serving angel who speeds on errands for each Christian. (2) For obedient Philip—it must have been quite a shock to hear these instructions—no hesitancy, no arguments, no rationalizations, just "So he started out." (3) Thank you for humble-minded people in high places. (4) For the fact that eunuchs can be true servants and totally accepted by you—even if sometimes rejected of men. (5) That there is really nowhere convenient and no place inconvenient for the message of salvation. (6) That we have the same book of Isaiah to read today. (7) That angels are not commissioned to preach the glad tidings of great joy—we are!

Give yourself to your own expression of gratitude—write it or speak it!

8. READ HIS WORD IN MEDITATION.

An Ethiopian eunuch—the most unlikely candidate for salvation, i.e., by men's standards. Consider: (1) Wrong race—since they are not *our race*, you know they are of the wrong race. Praise God, he has no race that is right or wrong. (2) Wrong color—he had more pigment in his skin and therefore was wrong. Oh, oh, how shortsighted, how ignorant and bigoted. Praise your wonderful name, you are color-blind, i.e., see no skin color but only heart condition. (3) Wrong sexually—he was either born this way, made this way by man, or chose to be this way himself (i.e., according to our Lord in Matt. 19:10-12).

Pause—wait—think—then express yourself in thoughtful praise or thanks.

9. READ HIS WORDS FOR PETITIONS.

Out of these verses arise the following requests: (1) Keep my heart ever right before you. (2) Teach me true repentance. (3) Give me a tender heart free of bitterness. (4) Make me a captive of yourself. (5) Open my mouth to testify and proclaim your word. (6) Break down all race prejudice in my heart. (7) Keep me excited about the "good news."

Right here add your personal requests—and his answers.

10. READ HIS WORD AND WAIT—LISTEN—GOD SPEAKS!

What do you say to me from these verses? (1) "You cannot serve God and money." (2) "You can be totally ineffective through bitterness." (3) "Sin is a terrible master."

11. INTERCESSION FOR THE LOST WORLD

San Marino — A small 61 sq. km. republic with a population of 20,000 people. The state is an enclave in north central Italy. As far as is known all the people are Roman Catholic. There is no known Protestant witness in this little territory.

Luxembourg — Population: 360,000. Area: 2,600 sq. km. Points for prayer: (1) *The dominant position of the Roman Catholic Church* remains unchanged. The revolutionary changes within the Roman Catholic Church elsewhere have not really made the Luxembourgers more open to the Gospel. Pray for the spiritual liberation of this dark land. (2) *The Bible believing witness is very weak.* The believers are rather scattered and lack the fellowship they need. Pray for the planting of a vigorous Church in the land. Pray for the believers and their growth in grace. Pray that they may have a vision for the winning of the lost.

12. SING PRAISES TO OUR LORD.

O worship the King, all glorious above,
And gratefully sing His wonderful love;

Our Shield and Defender, the Ancient of days,
Pavilioned in splendor, and girded with praise.

WEEK SEVEN — TUESDAY

1. PRAISE GOD FOR WHO HE IS.

Historian. Historian seems an unusual designation, but in a wonderful way you are the greatest of historians for you have a record of *everyone's* life—no life is unimportant—it will be possible in the world to come to ask you for the record of anyone and learn all about them—*some* bright morning such *will* happen. You have given us a book predominantly full of history as an indication of your interest in the subject.

Express yourself in adoration for this quality of God.
Speak it audibly or write out your praise in your own devotional journal.

2. PRAISE GOD FOR WHAT HE MEANS TO ME.

Historian for me. I am glad you are keeping a record for I have forgotten most of what has happened with me. But nothing, utterly *nothing*, is unimportant with you—all has been kept and one glad day I will be able to relive those things that have eternal meaning from my life. It is because of the elusive transitory nature of all we do that I began writing—and encouraged others to do so—but if nothing is preserved here, *all* is preserved in the new world.

How do you personally relate to a God who keeps records, and God who is a historian?
Speak it out or write it out. It is *so important* that you establish *your own* devotional journal.

3. CONFESSION OF SIN

Idolatry—am I guilty? Of course I am! Whatever gets my attention—time, energy, talent—that ought to go to you is idolatry. In the area of evangelism I feel like a miserable sinner. Dear God, move into my mind and will and emotions and memory and let me see myself as you do—selfish and willful—please change me! Forgive me—open my heart to you, to the lost world.

What personal sins do you want to confess? We *must* speak them to remove them.
Do it! *Now.* There is no one else you have sinned against more than God. Tell him so!

4. SING A PRAYER TO GOD.

I gave My life for thee,
My precious blood I shed,
That thou might'st ransomed be,
And quickened from the dead;

I gave, I gave My life for thee,
What hast thou giv'n for Me?
I gave, I gave My life for thee,
What has thou giv'n for Me?

Open your hymn book and sing the rest of the verses—or even sing another prayer song.

5. READ HIS WORD TO HIM!

His Word

[26]Now an angel of the Lord said to Philip, "Go south to the road—the desert road—that goes down from Jerusalem to Gaza." [27]So he started out, and on his way he met an Ethiopian eunuch, an important official in charge of all the treasury of Candace, queen of the Ethiopians. This man had gone to Jerusalem to worship, [28]and on his way home was sitting in his chariot reading the book of Isaiah the prophet.
— *Acts 8:26-28, NIV*

Read His Word to Him.

That you would send an angel to instruct one of your servants is wondrously encouraging since I know they minister to me—and all others who shall inherit salvation (Heb. 1:14). You gave directions, and such strange directions they were. But you have ways and people not known to us, but so well known to you! You are interested in people not geography—only as it relates to people—and your purpose for them. Your purpose is to save the eunuch (and his queen through him). Dear, dear God, may I somehow capture your concern and establish your priorities as mine!

Please express your response to this beautiful text. Put your expression in your own prayer diary.

6. READ HIS WORD FOR YOURSELF.

I do expect to meet this man in the world and life to come, and he will speak to me and tell me of the joy he found in finding the Messiah. There are many more men just like him that I want to meet today.

It is so important that you pause in his presence
and either audibly or in written form tell him all his word means to you.

WEEK SEVEN — TUESDAY

7. READ HIS WORD IN THANKSGIVING.

Dear Lord I could really never thank you enough for: (1) The tremendous change in the "sons of thunder" that they are now ready to speak to the villages—to tell the good news that Jesus saves—not destroys. The "good Samaritan" was there to hear as well as some prejudiced people. (2) For the total honesty of Peter in defining the sin of Simon to his face. (3) That my heart—that anyone's heart—*can* be right with you. (4) That repentance is possible and for the renewal of repentance. (5) His forgiveness is *not* automatic, it is conditioned on sincere sorrow that leads to a real change of mind. (6) That peace and acceptance instead of bitterness and bondage can be mine. (7) That I want to repent and pray for myself (not that I do not appreciate the prayers of others).

Give yourself to your own expression of gratitude—write it or speak it!

8. READ HIS WORD IN MEDITATION.

Shall we (you and I) gather around the word and think and pray and praise together. Saul went from house to house dragging and committing to prison—what a reverse example for me in evangelism—if Saul had such zeal for opposition who am I to have less for saving men and women? Dear Lord, I am *not* like Philip (or like the others who were scattered). Do I speak the word wherever I go? i.e., spontaneously? I do if it is expected, or assigned— yes, but otherwise? No! God forgive. Thank you for speaking to me. Simon was a real convert! Bless your name! Wonderful Jesus accepted a man who was a eunuch and did not consider him anyone else.

Pause—wait—think—then express yourself in thoughtful praise or thanks.

9. READ HIS WORD FOR PETITIONS.

Requests from the experience of Philip: (1) May I be as responsive to your word as was Philip. (2) May I see opportunity in desert places of my life. (3) Break down my hesitancy in speaking to important people. (4) I want to believe there are some men in high places who are as open to the gospel as the eunuch. (5) Use me to reach just those people you want to reach. (6) May I use travel as a way to reach the lost. (7) Let me see men as you see them.

Please, please remember these are prayers—speak them—reword them!

10. READ HIS WORD AND WAIT—LISTEN—GOD SPEAKS!

Speak to me from these verses: (1) "I can appeal to all men." (2) "Eunuchs are prospects for salvation the same as all men." (3) "I am interested in religious people today."

11. INTERCESSION FOR THE LOST WORLD

Luxembourg — Points for prayer: (1) *There are only about 7 full time workers for the Lord* in the land, i.e., one for every 50,000 people. Pray for others to be called.

Malta — Population: 322,000 Maltese. Growth 0.4%. People per sq. km.—1,018. Points for prayer: (1) *Malta is Europe's least evangelized land.* The very dominant Roman Catholic Church opposed any Protestant missionary activity before independence in 1964. Pray for the Maltese people to come to a living faith in Jesus through the preaching of the Gospel. (2) *Pray for complete religious freedom.* There was no religious freedom before 1964, and all converts to the Lord had to leave the country. There are still many legal and social difficulties for the few Maltese believers, although the situation is improving. (3) *Much friendship has been shown by some in authority for the cause of the Gospel.* Pray that this may lead to the opening up of the land for the Lord Jesus. (4) *The Roman Catholics have shown more interest* in the study of the Bible and in the need of a personal faith. Pray for their salvation. (5) *Pray for new converts* who find it very difficult to identify with and integrate into the despised little groups of believers. Pray for the combined outreach of believers as they hold informal meetings in private homes seeking to win people in this tactful manner.

12. SING PRAISES TO OUR LORD.

We gather together to ask the Lord's blessing,
He chastens and hastens His will to make known;
The wicked oppressing cease them from distressing,
Sing praises to His name, He forgets not His own.

WEEK SEVEN — WEDNESDAY

1. PRAISE GOD FOR WHO HE IS.

Righteous. It is good to know Someone who is indeed always right. On any subject, at any time, you can and will always say the right thing. In every situation with anyone you will always do the right thing. Absolute and total knowledge and unlimited, never tiring energy to use it—an absolute love and compassion—not to mention grace and mercy to apply such knowledge and energy. Your righteousness then becomes such a tremendous blessing to all.

Express yourself in adoration for this quality of God.
Speak it audibly or write out your praise in your own devotional journal.

2. PRAISE GOD FOR WHAT HE MEANS TO ME.

Righteousness to me! To contemplate the giving or imputing of such righteousness to me is one awesome thought! That I can consider *my* standing as always right with you because I am in you and your Son—"He has become my righteousness." In the good news that Christ died for my sins and rose for my justification is the righteousness of God seen. His hatred for sin, his infinite love for the sinner—he has become at the same time both just and a justifier. Praise his name—which is his authority to declare me righteous.

How do you personally relate to the righteousness of God, and God who is righteous?
Speak it out or write it out. It is *so important* that you establish *your own* devotional journal.

3. CONFESSION OF SIN

I do, without hesitancy, name each and every sin of which I am guilty—not only admit them, but truly sorrow over them. I am hurt that you are hurt. I do wonder how demons relate to temptation, but I give Satan no more advantage than he already has. I resist him, reject him, hate him. I at the same time claim the cleansing blood and a totally clean record for this new beginning! Praise your wonderful name!

What personal sins do you want to confess? We *must* speak them to remove them.
Do it! *Now.* There is no one else you have sinned against more than God. Tell him so!

4. SING A PRAYER TO GOD.

When morning gilds the skies,
My heart awaking cries:
May Jesus Christ be praised;

Alike at work and prayer . . .
To Jesus I repair: . . .
May Jesus Christ be praised.

5. READ HIS WORD TO HIM!

His Word

[29] The Spirit told Philip, "Go to that chariot and stay near it."
[30] Then Philip ran up to the chariot and heard the man reading Isaiah the prophet. "Do you understand what you are reading?" Philip asked.
[31] "How can I," he said, "unless someone explains it to me?" So he invited Philip to come up and sit with him.
— *Acts 8:29-31, NIV*

Read His Word to Him.

Dear angel of God who appeared to Philip "the evangelist"—the servant at Jerusalem—appear to me. Perhaps someone more impressive than this angelic being has already spoken to me about every road in this town and every person in every house. When you asked Philip to "go to *that* chariot and stay near it," he acted and came running!

May I recognize your voice in the reading of your word. Dear God, sharpen my sense of hearing. May I see through your eyes those who would want to listen. Give me the wisdom to be able to say the very most appropriate thing to give you the greatest advantage.

Please express your response to this beautiful text. Put your expression in your own prayer diary.

6. READ HIS WORD FOR YOURSELF.

My blessed Lord was "like a sheep to the slaughter" — what a thought! Sheep are dumb animals. He truly emptied himself when he became flesh for me. He became a sheep — and what pain and suffering he endured for me. He was physically abused and mistreated, all for me. He was like a lamb to be shorn — standing meekly and silent awaiting the rough hands of man to cut for profit what belonged only to God. He was oppressed and given no fair trial. It was all for my sin. He was God's lamb to take away my sin.

It is so important that you pause in his presence
and either audibly or in written form tell him all his word means to you.

7. READ HIS WORD IN THANKSGIVING.

How gladly do I approach this section each day. Thank you for: (1) Philip who listened and heard, who ran and found, who heard and related. (2) For a rich man who read the scriptures. (3) That you expect us to tell others what you mean in your word. (4) For the limitless possibilities of where we can tell the story of our Lord. (5) For transportation to move us from place to place that we might carry the word of life. (6) For a desert place where we can meditate and understand your word. (7) That we want to be that "someone" who can and will explain what the prophet meant.

Give yourself to your own expression of gratitude — write it or speak it!

8. READ HIS WORD IN MEDITATION.

Going down from Jerusalem to Gaza. Let us think and pray in wonder and praise. (1) God sees possibilities where others see nothing. (2) Jerusalem must be left — not entered — to meet the Ethiopian. (3) God has a particular chariot as well as a road for us to "stay near." (4) Questions in the mind and heart of Philip were answered by obedience. (5) It is right sometimes to interrupt and insist on an audience. (6) Kindness and unselfish interest are always rewarded (at least by our Lord). (7) Religious people are lost too — and some are the best prospects for salvation.

Pause — wait — think — then express yourself in thoughtful praise or thanks.

9. READ HIS WORD AND WAIT — LISTEN — GOD SPEAKS!

How shall I ask from these verses? (1) Dear Lord, make me as sensitive to the Spirit's words in his book as was Philip when he spoke to him. (2) Let me run to do your will today — whatever it is. (3) Teach me to be silent when you want me to. (4) May I see or make opportunities to speak for you today. (5) Make me a good teacher of your word. (6) Teach me from the gospel prophet, Isaiah. (7) Bring an open hearted sinner into my experience.

Right here add your personal requests — and his answers.

10. READ HIS WORD AND WAIT — LISTEN — GOD SPEAKS!

I am listening — what do you say? (1) "Go, and I will go with you." (2) "Faith comes from hearing my word." (3) "There are many who will believe if they hear."

11. INTERCESSION FOR THE LOST WORLD

Malta — Points for prayer: (1) *Several missionaries visit the country on tourist visas.* Pray that some may be able to obtain residence visas. (2) *Literature.* Pray for the 500 copies of the Maltese New Testament now in circulation, and also that the problems hindering the completion of the Old Testament may be removed. Several thousand Maltese have written in for Bible correspondence courses. The believers aim to start a second coverage of every home in the land with Christian literature.

Netherlands — Population: 13,800,000. Growth 0.9%. People per sq. km. — 405. Points for prayer: (1) This land has a great history of revival and suffering for the sake of the Word of God. The Protestant Church has seen great decline with much deadness and formalism evident. The younger generation is generally leftist, free-thinking and churchless, and increasing in political power. Holland has gained a reputation for open immorality in Europe. *Revival is the land's greatest need.* (2) *The Roman Catholic Church* has been growing at the expense of the Protestants for decades, but now is also declining in numbers. The Roman Catholic Church is possibly more vital and rebellious of the Pope's authority than in most countries in Europe. In the growing declension, few are being won to a living faith in the Lord Jesus.

12. SING PRAISES TO OUR LORD.

I will sing the wondrous story
Of the Christ who died for me,
How He left His home in glory
For the cross of Calvary.

Yes, I will sing . . . the wondrous story
Of the Christ . . . who died for me, . . .
Sing it with . . . the saints in glory.
Gathered by . . . the crystal sea. . . .

WEEK SEVEN — THURSDAY

1. PRAISE GOD FOR WHO HE IS.

Majestic. Oh, dear, wonderful Father, how good it is to worship before you this morning! Majestic and mighty is your name throughout all the earth. I like this term in description of you. It suggests exaltation, wonder, beauty, and you are the sum total of all this and more! We expand our thinking way, way beyond the limitation of this little, very little planet upon which we live to the infinitely wide expanse of the total of all galaxies—beyond that, you are! Total power and immensity is your name. Majestic!

Express yourself in adoration for this quality of God.
Speak it audibly or write out your praise in your own devotional journal.

2. PRAISE GOD FOR WHAT HE MEANS TO ME.

How everlastingly good it is to be related to such a One, to know that I am your son, that you have made me, indeed all men, in your image! Not physically or outwardly but inwardly—and according to my spirit. I shall one day be liberated from this humiliating house and enter into an appreciation of your true Self. Man is majestic in his capacities and identity. But to me your majesty is exciting and mind expanding! Praise you!

How do you personally relate to the majesty of God, and God who is majestic?
Speak it out or write it out. It is *so important* that you establish *your own* devotional journal.

3. CONFESSION OF SIN

I want to admit and yield up all my limitations to you. Therefore, I shall confess all the particular sins I can bring to memory, but also review the ones you have listed in your word and relate them to myself. *"Jealousy"*—Dear God, I do not want to be jealous—it is such an unhappy quality! such a negative attitude! It is a competitive word. I do not like it and do not even want to think about it. Is this because I am guilty of it? If so, please forgive!

What personal sins do you want to confess? We *must* speak them to remove them.
Do it! *Now.* There is no one else you have sinned against more than God. Tell him so!

4. SING A PRAYER TO GOD.

The great Physician now is near,
The sympathizing Jesus;
He speaks the drooping heart to cheer,
Oh, hear the voice of Jesus.

Sweetest note in seraph song,
Sweetest name on mortal tongue;
Sweetest carol ever sung,
Jesus, blessed Jesus.

Open your hymn book and sing the rest of the verses—or even sing another prayer song.

5. READ HIS WORD TO HIM!

His Word

[31]"How can I," he said, "unless someone explains it to me?" So he invited Philip to come up and sit with him. [32]The eunuch was reading this passage of Scripture:
"He was led like a sheep to the slaughter,
and as a lamb before the shearer is silent,
so he did not open his mouth.
[33]In his humiliation he was deprived of justice.
Who can speak of his descendants?
For his life was taken from the earth."

[34]The eunuch asked Philip, "Tell me, please, who is the prophet talking about, himself or someone else?" [35]Then Philip began with that very passage of Scripture and told him the good news about Jesus.
[36]As they traveled along the road, they came to some water and the eunuch said, "Look, here is water. Why shouldn't I be baptized?" [38]And he ordered the chariot to stop. Then both Philip and the eunuch went down into the water and Philip baptized him. — *Acts 8:31-38, NIV*

Read His Word to Him.

The arrangements you have made to tell your message of glad tidings to all the world is seen right here—one-on-one—if at anytime we could sustain this desire into action 16 or 18 generations of it would convert the world in 30-33 years. How profoundly simple are all your plans for success. "The good news about Jesus" is just that, "good news," but man is so very hesitant to express the joys of heaven. Dear Lord, deliver us from our earth-bound perspective. Why did the eunuch want to be baptized? Because preaching Jesus as God's Lamb includes the need to be baptized to receive him. It is no accident, and I praise you for showing me that the convert rejoiced *after* he was baptized.

Please express your response to this beautiful text. Put your expression in your own prayer diary.

6. READ HIS WORD FOR YOURSELF.

Can I ask Philip to step aside and let me take his place? Dear Lord, would I be as immediately responsive? Would I think of my wife and daughters? Would I worry about my job? Would I question the choice of the Spirit for a candidate for conversion? Would I wonder why we were out here in this uninhabited territory? To all these questions I am much afraid I would answer, "yes." Dear God, I want to learn better—Philip is teaching me—or you are through Philip. Would I be as well prepared to tell the story of the death and resurrection of God's Lamb? I believe I would, but I ask for an increase in my desire and faith.

It is so important that you pause in his presence and either audibly or in written form tell him all his word means to you.

7. READ HIS WORD IN THANKSGIVING.

Gratitude—real, personal, thanksgiving is such an attractive quality! How I do thank you for: (1) Those who would invite us to teach if we would ask them. How many are there who will never be taught because we have never asked them? (2) For the Holy Spirit who knows just whom we should ask. (3) For the privilege of interpreting or explaining your word to men who want to know. It is up to us to tell "of whom the prophet spoke." (4) For the full, wonderful meaning of baptizing anyone—going down into the water to be "buried with Christ in baptism, to be raised to walk in a new life." (5) The meaning baptism has for the preacher as well as the baptized—it helps him in a way he needs so much. (6) Thank you for the great universal church of which Philip and the eunuch were members. (7) The very same joy of the eunuch is mine!

Give yourself to your own expression of gratitude—write it or speak it!

8. READ HIS WORD IN MEDITATION.

"He ordered the chariot to stop." How often have I wanted this chariot of life to stop, to stop long enough to fully appreciate the joy of telling the good news, to think as deeply as I could and should about my Lord, the Lamb of whom Isaiah spoke.

How much do I want the chariot of the daily routine to stop—stop—wait—change. If we stop, perhaps we will see a lovely expanse of water and it will become a grave for our old and a resurrection for the new—or we will at least see the ordinary in a new light with a new meaning, if we will only "order the chariot to stop."

Dear God, I want the chariot in which ride all the relationships I have with other people to stop—wait—let me change them—let me baptize them into the love of God—into the compassion of my Lord—into the reality of the value of our soul. Oh, chariot, stop! stop!

Pause—wait—think—then express yourself in thoughtful praise or thanks.

9. READ HIS WORD FOR PETITIONS.

It is so good to ask from your word: (1) Where are the open-hearted students of the word today? (2) Humble my spirit as I consider your Lamb! (3) May I never again complain about mistreatment in your service. (4) Should I include baptism in the preaching of the cross? (5) I want to baptize people in the same way and for the same reason as Philip—help me! (6) Why not baptize the chariot driver? Was it because he was not discipled? (7) How did Philip know the eunuch was to be taught baptism? Did he learn it from the apostles?

Please, please remember these are prayers—speak them—reword them!

10. READ HIS WORD AND WAIT—LISTEN—GOD SPEAKS!

What do you say to me in these verses? (1) "preach the death, burial and resurrection of my Son." (2) "Please tell people what Philip did to be saved." (3) "Remember the words of my Son: 'He that believes and is baptized shall be saved'" (Mark 16:16).

11. INTERCESSION FOR THE LOST WORLD

Netherlands — Point for prayer: (1) *The Protestant churches are generally dead,* formal, legalistic and losing people. Sadly, many preachers are more Marxist than Christian in their thinking. The churches need prayer that they return to a warm Bible believing faith, separation from the world, good Bible teaching and a burden to evangelize the many Dutch and immigrant peoples in their own land.

12. SING PRAISES TO OUR LORD.

When I saw the cleansing fountain
Open wide for all my sin,
I obeyed the Spirit's wooing,
When He said, Wilt thou be clean?

I will praise Him! I will praise Him!
Praise the Lamb for sinners slain;
Give Him glory, all ye people,
For His blood can wash away each stain.

WEEK SEVEN — FRIDAY

1. PRAISE GOD FOR WHO HE IS.

Social Being. How wonderful it is dear Father to know you *want* me to come to you — you have created me, and all men, for your own self — for mutual sharing! Society — all of it, should be a theocracy — an absolute theocracy. At the same time there is a marvelous interaction of an equal level. I want to be like you and you want me to. How good it is to talk with you and know you hear and care — to come into the oneness of spirit — into an awareness of your personal interest in all I do and in all I am. Praise your name.

Express yourself in adoration for this quality of God.
Speak it audibly or write out your praise in your own devotional journal.

2. PRAISE GOD FOR WHAT HE MEANS TO ME.

To be the Creator who made me for youself — what a lovely thought! Today in my conversations with others I do not want to forget to include you in it. In riding from place to place I want you in the car. When we sit down to the meal we not only thank you for it, we want to share it with you. In our task of teaching and preaching, may we do it before you and be constantly conscious of your presence with us and in us.

How do you personally relate to the socialableness of God, and God who is a social Being?
Speak it out or write it out. It is *so important* that you establish *your own* devotional journal.

3. CONFESSION OF SIN

To imagine or believe the end justifies the means is a constant temptation and source of sin (occasion). Dear God, purify my motives, guard my mouth, forgive my sin. I'm glad to say that "fits of rage" do not occur too often, but I am not immune. Dear Lord, "lead me not into temptation." The tenderness and kindness of my Lord — how I want it! It is good to come away from this time of prayer clean and pure and whole — thank you!

What personal sins do you want to confess? We *must* speak them to remove them.
Do it! *Now.* There is no one else you have sinned against more than God. Tell him so!

4. SING A PRAYER TO GOD.

The name of Jesus is so sweet,
I love its music to repeat;
It makes my joys full and complete,
The precious name of Jesus.

"Jesus," oh, how sweet the name!
"Jesus," ev'ry day the same;
"Jesus," let all saints proclaim
Its worthy praise forever.

Open your hymn book and sing the rest of the verses — or even sing another prayer song.

5. READ HIS WORD TO HIM!

His Word

[39]When they came up out of the water, the Spirit of the Lord suddenly took Philip away, and the eunuch did not see him again, but went on his way rejoicing. [40]Philip, however, appeared at Azotus and traveled about, preaching the gospel in all the towns until he reached Caesarea.
— *Acts 8:39, 40, NIV*

Read His Word to Him.

What unusual action for the Holy Spirit! Are we right in assuming the person of Philip was suddenly gone, i.e., in the supernatural sense? Or were some sudden instructions given which directed him to Azotus? In whatever circumstance (and your ways are past tracing out) the eunuch was so very, very glad and I am too. What a testimony of devotion that Philip continued to preach and work among the despised Samaritans — perhaps they were more prepared to hear than the house of Israel.

Please express your response to this beautiful text. Put your expression in your own prayer diary.

6. READ HIS WORD FOR YOURSELF.

I do, I do want to feed my soul on these two verses — when we all come out of the water we need to rejoice like the eunuch. After all we do have a similar experience. We are traveling through life — someone preaches Jesus to us. We learn of our need to be baptized. Since the suffering Savior was what was preached to us, salvation must also be involved in the purpose of our baptism, but what do we feel and know as we come out of the water? — a great, deep cause of joy begins in our innermost being — the blessed Holy Spirit takes up residence in us — we have found the cause and purpose of life indeed! Salvation!

It is important that you pause in his presence
and either audibly or in written form tell him all his word means to you.

WEEK SEVEN — FRIDAY

7. READ HIS WORD IN THANKSGIVING.

Thank you, thank you for: (1) The confidence you place on the self-sufficiency of the eunuch and his spiritual development or the supernatural work of the Holy Spirit in his life. (2) Your exciting and unaccountable actions of yourself—we will know why one day—it is enough now to thank you that we must trust. (3) That Philip didn't miss any towns of the Samaritans. (4) That he seems to establish a base for service in Caesarea (since he and his family were here twenty years later—(Acts 21:5-7). (5) The eunuch was also a preacher in Ethiopia. (6) That it is easier to preach and teach in every village, town and city of our state than it was in Philip's day. (7) That you left this permanent record for our following.

Give yourself to your own expression of gratitude—write it or speak it!

8. READ HIS WORD IN MEDITATION.

"When they came up out of the water . . ." How significant—the Spirit of God worked when they both came up out of the water. He works today in entering the lives of his servants when we baptize the lost. He went on his way rejoicing when they both came up out of the water—there is no joy at all like that of the lifesaver or the freshly saved—they both continued in the service of God.

Pause—wait—think—then express yourself in thoughtful praise or thanks.

9. READ HIS WORD FOR PETITIONS.

There is so much for which I can ask you from this text: (1) May your Spirit be very much a part of my work for you today. (2) I want to rejoice in my salvation for the same reasons the eunuch did. (3) As I move from place to place may I deliver the good news. (4) Help me to remember your work continues long after I have left the place of preaching. (5) Who labors for you in Ethiopia today? Surround them with your love. (6) May a door be opened for the preaching of the word in Samaria. (7) Break me out of the mold of American churchianity!

Right here add your personal requests—and his answers.

10. READ HIS WORD AND WAIT—LISTEN—GOD SPEAKS!

What are you saying to me here? (1) "I can act suddenly as well as slowly." (2) "Man can only truly rejoice in me." (3) "Ethiopia is still stretching out her hands to me."

11. INTERCESSION FOR THE LOST WORLD

Netherlands — Points for prayer: (1) *There is a growing shortage of full-time workers in the churches.* Most seminaries have few students. Only the few Bible believing Bible schools continue to maintain their numbers. (2) *The Bible believing witness is growing in effectiveness* and there are some encouraging signs of the Lord's working. There are many prayer and Bible study groups springing up all over the country. These house meetings are where most of the real Bible teaching and conversions occur. Pray that this movement may continue to grow, and be kept free from error and byways of doctrine. (3) *Foreign missions are few*, and workers from other lands number no more than 30, yet their influence is out of all proportion to their numbers. (4) *Missionary interest* is not very great and could be much increased. There are now about 120 missionaries in the denominational societies, and a further 250 in the interdenominational missions serving round the world. (5) *Young people need much prayer.* Christian youth groups are generally weak, worldly, lacking in discipline and possibly more dangerous than useful. Yet God has been working among young people in the last few years, but quite apart from the churches. Pray that such converts may make a useful contribution to the churches, and not be led into error.

12. SING PRAISES TO OUR LORD.

We praise Thee, O God! for the Son of Thy love,
For Jesus who died, and is now gone above.
Hallelujah! Thine the glory;

Hallelujah! Amen!
Hallelujah! Thine the glory;
Revive us again.

WEEK SEVEN — SATURDAY

1. PRAISE GOD FOR WHO HE IS.

Chastener. Dear Lord, how very, very effective you are as a chastener! I can speak from experience — and I know I am typical of all your children — at least in the basic areas. How tender, kind and persistent you are — how you have pursued me and found me — not to my hurt — but for my correction, for my maturing. So do you chasten all your children. All the lovely qualities of a mother are in you. All the strong qualities of an infinitely wise father are yours. With tender, constant attention you consider us — and we are corrected on our course — we are turned into a way of profit and peace.

Express yourself in adoration for this quality of God.
Speak it audibly or write out your praise in your own devotional journal.

2. PRAISE GOD FOR WHAT HE MEANS TO ME.

I can say from much experience that *no* chastening for the moment seems joyous — but grievous — but I surely do not wish to regard it lightly and call it "tough luck" — when all the while you are trying to get my attention, trying to reach my conscience. Dear God, you know I love you and respect your interest, your deep interest in my total life. Neither do I want "to faint" when I am reproved by you. I want to learn by this experience. I do so want to love you from the heart — the compass of all my being. Chasten me today as seems good to you.

How do you personally relate to the chastening of God, and God who is Chastener?
Speak it out or write it out. It is *so important* that you establish *your own* devotional journal.

3. CONFESSION OF SIN

Confession of my sin — of my need. "Selfish ambition" is such a besetting sin of mine! Dear Lord, I hesitate to say this — for fear I will be prevented from pursuing my own ambition — Oh, Lord, purify my motives but increase the drive, energy, eagerness within my total being — but humble my purpose, my direction. Oh, dear Lord, how I want help here. My goals and projects need your hand upon them. Forgive me, cleanse me — Amen!

What personal sins do you want to confess? We *must* speak them to remove them.
Do it! *Now.* There is no one else you have sinned against more than God. Tell him so!

4. SING A PRAYER TO GOD.

Jesus, Savior, pilot me
Over life's tempestuous sea;
Unknown waves before me roll,
Hiding rock and treacherous shoal;
Chart and compass came from Thee:
Jesus, Savior, pilot me.

Open your hymn book and sing the rest of the verses — or even sing another prayer song.

5. READ HIS WORD TO HIM!

His Word

9 Meanwhile, Saul was still breathing out murderous threats against the Lord's disciples. He went to the high priest ²and asked him for letters to the synagogues in Damascus, so that if he found any there who belonged to the Way, whether men or women, he might take them as prisoners to Jerusalem. — *Acts 9:1, 2, NIV*

Read His Word to Him.

Saul of Tarsus — what a man! How I look forward — when my mind is totally enlightened, when I have no other interest, when I have lost all selfishness, to talking with him, but much more his talking with me — of being so much enlightened by his words, by his presence. It will be so wonderful to have omnipresence and be able to talk and relate to multitudes all at the same time. How else would we be able to talk to Saul? "Letters to the synagogue in Damascus" — someone's name and the names of their loved ones would be in those letters — this means arrest, imprisonment, removal from all that was dear to them — but God had another plan for Saul. How much are we saved from of which we will never know? Praise your name!

Please express your response to this beautiful text. Put your expression in your own prayer diary.

6. READ HIS WORD FOR YOURSELF.

How wrong can one sincere man be? How moved I am to know God's hand is not shortened—nor his power limited by man's inability. It is very, very possible to be religiously wrong. Dear God, open my eyes, but you must first make me blind. How beautiful to be called "one who belongs to the Way." I gladly admit this position, this direction, this happy fact. I have found the way of gladness. I have found the way of joy, the way who is a person, even my Lord!

It is so important that you pause in his presence
and either audibly or in written form tell him all his word means to you.

7. READ HIS WORD IN THANKSGIVING.

Thank you, dear Lord for: (1) The high-priest who could be personally introduced to the power of God—did it make any difference in his life—no matter—it does make a difference in mine. He was given the opportunity to see and know. So have I—am I responding? adequately? commensurately? (2) For the letters—God's roll of the faithful. No doubt some of these very people became the dearest friends of the one who came to take them prisoners. (3) For every one who journeyed with Saul—how many became Christians? (4) For the same road today—everyone has his own road to Damascus.

Give yourself to your own expression of gratitude—write it or speak it!

8. READ HIS WORD IN MEDITATION.

My road to Damascus for today—consider: (1) We are either persecuting him or serving him; we are never neutral. If we are not aggressively for him we are positively against him—to hurt his body through neglect is to hurt him. (2) God reads the names on every church roll—not only here but in the prison camps and cells of suffering in places we will never know. God knows every one. (3) We never travel alone. He sees us and wants us to see him.

Pause—wait—think—then express yourself in thoughtful praise or thanks.

9. READ HIS WORD FOR PETITIONS.

Here are my requests from Acts 9:1, 2: (1) Give me the zeal of love—the fervency of concern. (2) I want to make more and more learners of you—help me. (3) Send me to the religiously confused—today! (4) How can I let men see "the way" in my experience? (5) May I in no way minimize the place of women in your work. (6) Send preachers to Damascus today. (7) Why has the good news been lost to Syria?

Please, please remember these are prayers—speak them—reword them!

10. READ HIS WORD AND WAIT—LISTEN—GOD SPEAKS!

Open my ears to hear: (1) "Threats and plots can be overcome." (2) "The ones who oppose the most are sometimes kicking against the goad of God." (3) "There are those as prisoners for me today—love them."

11. INTERCESSION FOR THE LOST WORLD

Netherlands — Point for prayer: (1) *The immigrant population needs to be evangelized.* A little work is done among Chinese, Portuguese and Yugoslavs, but the Turks, Moroccans and Spanish have little opportunity to hear the Gospel. Pray also for the Ambonese and Surinamese communities which do not really fit into the national life, and need specialized attention to win them.

Norway — Population: 4,000,000. Growth 0.7%. People per sq. km.—12. Points for prayer: (1) *Almost the entire population is Protestant*, but there are very many who do not understand about the new birth. The believers long for revival. (2) *The dissenting, or free, churches* are stagnant and need to come out of their isolation to evangelize. Pray that the leadership may continue to be Bible believing in theology and Biblically grounded. (3) *Norway has made a great contribution to world evangelization.* This little land has probably more missionaries than any other nation on earth for the size of its population. There are 23 Norwegian missionary societies, and about 1,500 Norwegians in these and international missions have gone to serve the Lord in other lands.

12. SING PRAISES TO OUR LORD.

Praise ye the Lord, the Almighty, the King of creation!
O my soul, praise Him, for He is thy health and salvation!
All ye who hear,

Now to His temple draw near;
Join me in glad adoration!

WEEK EIGHT — SUNDAY

1. PRAISE GOD FOR WHO HE IS.

Strong. How infinitely strong you are! Beyond all that we could say or think! What a comfort for mankind to have One who is never tired or unable! Praise your strong name. Praise to the One who is strength itself! Nothing is too large or small, too complex or simple for your strength and interest. How amazing. I am glad to express my joy and privilege before your power.

Express yourself in adoration for this quality of God.
Speak it audibly or write out your praise in your own devotional journal.

2. PRAISE GOD FOR WHAT HE MEANS TO ME.

Strength for me: "My strength indeed is small," as the poet said. I find in me not even the desire to do. My strength is in you. I refer to moral, spiritual and mental strength. I am strong enough physically to do what needs to be done, but even in this without you I would not even live or move or have my being. Praise and adoration ascends to your presence! The essence of strength! How good!

How do you personally relate to the strength of God, and God who is strong?
Speak it out or write it out. It is *so important* that you establish *your own* devotional journal.

3. CONFESSION OF SIN

It is an encouragement to be able to come to One who is Strength Itself. *You* can forgive and help. I do not want to be a part of *dissentions,* but at times I am drawn into them—forgive me. Oh, dear God, you see the depths of my heart and know I am indeed a sinner and need and seek forgiveness and cleansing. Purify me and I shall be whiter than snow!

What personal sins do you want to confess? We *must* speak them to remove them.
Do it! *Now.* There is no one else you have sinned against more than God. Tell him so!

4. SING A PRAYER TO GOD.

Take the name of Jesus with you,
Child of sorrow and of woe;
It will joy and comfort give you,
Take it, then, where'er you go.

Precious name, O how sweet!
Hope of earth and joy of Heav'n;
Precious name, O how sweet!
Hope of earth and joy of Heav'n.

Open your hymn book and sing the rest of the verses—or even sing another prayer song.

5. READ HIS WORD TO HIM!

His Word

[3]As he neared Damascus on his journey, suddenly a light from heaven flashed around him. [4]He fell to the ground and heard a voice say to him, "Saul, Saul, why do you persecute me?"

[5]"Who are you, Lord?" Saul asked.

"I am Jesus, whom you are persecuting," he replied.

[6]"Now get up and go into the city, and you will be told what you must do."

[7]The men traveling with Saul stood there speechless; they heard the sound but did not see anyone. [8]Saul got up from the ground, but when he opened his eyes he could see nothing. So they led him by the hand into Damascus.

— Acts 9:3-8, NIV

Read His Word to Him.

Damascus was and is a very real place. There must yet be the very place near the city where you (through your Son) appeared to this very real person called "Saul of Tarsus." Perhaps he was riding on a horse or walking. We do not know, but we do know a light above the brightness of the Syrian sun at noonday shown on him. A voice spoke to him, even your voice. He saw your dear Son, i.e., before his eyes failed him. The penetrating accusation never left his conscience: "I am Jesus whom you are persecuting." Dear God, I want to read and reread these words as if I had never seen them before!

Please express your response to this beautiful text. Put your expression in your own prayer diary.

6. READ HIS WORD FOR YOURSELF.

There is indeed a sense in which this experience is a norm or pattern for each of us in our conversion to you. But there is also a sense in which this is but the record of one man's experience with you. As example, I could hardly ask or expect everyone to imitate the details of my own conversion experience, but what are the principles in Saul's experience that speak to my heart? They are in part: (1) Jesus is alive—who sees and hears and knows all about me. (2) He can and does speak to me through his word. (3) My service to his body is a service to him—what hurts his people, hurts him. What helps his body helps him.

It is so important that you pause in his presence and either audibly or in written form tell him all his word means to you.

7. READ HIS WORD IN THANKSGIVING.

Praise your wonderful name, how easy it is to do this. Thank you for: (1) Your knowledge of every town where every man lives. (2) That you are light and in you is no darkness at all. (3) That you are speaking in words I understand—to me *now* from this word. (4) I can and do affect you in my actions and words. (5) You are Lord, my Lord—keep me down before you in worship. (6) Man must and does tell poor sinners what to do to be saved. (7) There are those who even if they do not hear or know you are kind and helpful to me.

Give yourself to your expression of gratitude—write it or speak it!

8. READ HIS WORD IN MEDITATION.

How to be saved like Saul. (1) Find out you are so very, very wrong—perhaps religious, but lost. (2) Develop or accept God's goad in your conscience. (3) See our Lord in all his exalted majesty and authority. (4) Let the light blind you to all others—remember Saul never saw the light but a person in the light—it wasn't the light that held his attention until he was blind, but Jesus in the light. (5) See him personally, hear him personally, relate to him personally. (6) Wait for a time until the reality takes a hold of your inner being. (7) Let others lead you as directed by the Lord.

Pause—wait—think—then express yourself in thoughtful praise or thanks.

9. READ HIS WORD FOR PETITIONS.

You move me to ask: (1) Am I near a major decision for you? (2) Shine your new light on my way now. (3) Am I in any way persecuting your body today? (4) Show me your Lordship in my personal life. (5) I want to know more and more of your rule in my life. (6) Am I listening when you tell me what to do? (7) Shut my eyes to other things that I might see you.

Right here add your personal requests—and his answers.

10. READ HIS WORD AND WAIT—LISTEN—GOD SPEAKS!

Having ears, let me hear: (1) "I can and do speak to your personal needs." (2) "You either hurt me or help me." (3) "Those around you will not see me or hear me."

11. INTERCESSION FOR THE LOST WORLD

Portugal — Population: 9,500,000. Growth—0.4%. Area: 91,631 sq. km.

Points for prayer: (1) *Pray for peace and stability* as well as freedom for the Portuguese people. The Communists still have much power despite their recent setbacks. The new political freedom has generated much division and bitterness. Pray for the conversion of many who now claim to be atheists. (2) *The terrible sufferings of many Portuguese* over the last few years have made them more open to the Gospel. Pray for a mighty harvest of souls in these days. (3) *The refugees from the former colonies* came to Portugal in 1975 possessing nothing, and with little prospect for many of making a living in Portugal. They are bitter, frustrated and angry. Pray for the evangelization of these people, for few have ever heard the Gospel.

12. SING PRAISES TO OUR LORD.

Holy, Holy, Holy, Lord God Almighty!
Early in the morning our song shall rise to Thee;

Holy, Holy, Holy! Merciful and Mighty!
God in Three Persons, blessed Trinity!

WEEK EIGHT — MONDAY

1. PRAISE GOD FOR WHO HE IS.

Female-like. To consider you in the image of woman is a reverse, but nonetheless a true concept! All the dear, beautiful qualities of the best mother and wife as seen in Proverbs 31 can be multiplied a millionfold and yet could not approximate *your* true, real self. Soft and kind and full of concern is altogether true of yourself. How I love you for all you are — a Father *and* a Mother to me and to all the peoples of the earth if they *only, only* knew it.

Express yourself in adoration for this quality of God.
Speak it audibly or write out your praise in your own devotional journal.

2. PRAISE GOD FOR WHAT HE MEANS TO ME.

Female-like to me. Oh, dear Person, not only heavenly Father but heavenly Mother and all that means to me. All the care when I did not even know it, all the thoughtfulness not understood and or appreciated, days of concern and prayer, nights of vigil and work, total interest and dedication is what my dear mother and wife have given — are you like that? Yea, and a million times more!

How do you personally relate to the female-likeness of God, and God who is female-like?
Speak it out or write it out. It is *so important* that you establish *your own* devotional journal.

3. CONFESSION OF SIN

The first thing to confess would be my unworthiness, my terrible lack of gratitude, of strong desires that are fulfilled outside your will, status, sex, food, things. Dear God, dear God, forgive me. I pronounce the particular sins before you — accept inwardly the cleansing and feel free, free! Praise you!

What personal sins do you want to confess? We *must* speak them to remove them.
Do it! *Now.* There is no one else you have sinned against more than God. Tell him so!

4. SING A PRAYER TO GOD.

Will your anchor hold in the storms of life,
When the clouds unfold their wings of strife?
When the strong tides lift, and the cables strain,
Will your anchor drift, or firm remain?

We have an anchor that keeps the soul
Steadfast and sure while the billows roll,
Fastened to the Rock which cannot move,
Grounded firm and deep in the Savior's love.

Open your hymn book and sing the rest of the verses — or even sing another prayer song.

5. READ HIS WORD TO HIM!

His Word

8Saul got up from the ground, but when he opened his eyes he could see nothing. So they led him by the hand into Damascus. 9For three days he was blind, and did not eat or drink anything.
10In Damascus there was a disciple named Ananias. The Lord called to him in a vision, "Ananias!"

"Yes, Lord," he answered.
11The Lord told him, "Go to the house of Judas on Straight Street and ask for a man from Tarsus named Saul, for he is praying. 12In a vision he has seen a man named Ananias come and place his hands on him to restore his sight."
— Acts 9:8-12, NIV

Read His Word to Him.

How better can I read this word to you my wonderful Savior and Father than to visualize the actual scene? I know it is imaginary, but I want to make it true to each word you have given us. There is Saul, blind, confused, overcome, full of wonder, led and not leading. For three days in darkness, i.e., physically, inwardly he was seeing as he had never seen before. Were not the eyes of his heart enlightened as they had never been before? You spoke to your children in words, words from you and in marvelous specific detail. Help me to read your word with the same interest.

Please express your response to this beautiful text. Put your expression in your own prayer diary.

6. READ HIS WORD FOR YOURSELF.

Oh, yes, yes, I want to hear it, read it and see it again and again. In so many ways I am like Saul (all men are like Saul). Stubborn and self-willed, hurting the One who loves you most, kicking against your own conscience — God can and does knock you down, shuts out and stops all your plans — you are rendered impotent! You lose appetite for all that seemed so important. All your plans are dead! Then a vision! a strange inexplicable vision! A man comes to you with God's will and deliverance — God's sight! Oh, to see now with God's vision, to look through his eyes! Praise him!

It is so important that you pause in his presence
and either audibly or in written form tell him what his word means to you.

7. READ HIS WORD IN THANKSGIVING.

Yes, oh yes, thank you: (1) Someone thinks enough of me to lead me by the hand — man or yourself. (2) The voluntary loss of appetite, in grief or joy, or wonder. (3) Three days — three days in the tomb — enough time to truly decide. (4) For unknown disciples who are far more ready to hear and do than some who are well known. (5) That you know all our names and our very selves — better than we know ourselves. (6) For Judas who offered his hospitality to Saul, for the unusual name for the street — straight is the way — and all life. (7) The *"touching"* interest God and Ananias had in Saul, and in me and in all.

Give yourself to your own expression of gratitude — write it or speak it!

8. READ HIS WORD IN MEDITATION.

"For he is praying." Indeed he is! (1) Saul is praying in deep personal repentance! This happened because he saw and heard the Lord in full reality. It will and can produce the same effect in me! (2) He prayed in total brokenness of his plans and life style and purpose. It was now: "What will you have me to do?" Unless prayer carries this element it is not true prayer. (3) He prayed *not knowing* what God would have him to do — not to figure it out for himself — but to wait and hear — he knew God knew and would tell him, so he waited. "Wait upon the Lord." "Hope in the Lord."

Pause — wait — think — then express yourself in thoughtful praise or thanks.

9. READ HIS WORD FOR PETITIONS.

Petitions arise from Acts 9:8-12: (1) Help me to make fasting a way of life. (2) Give me grace to repent after the example of Saul. (3) How I want to be like Ananias — give me wisdom to know how. (4) May I be as specific in meeting needs as you were with Saul. (5) What were the prayer requests of Saul? "God be merciful to me a sinner." — Amen! (6) Give me a vision of those who can open my eyes. (7) Help me to be your man to touch someone with the *eye-opening* good news.

Please, please remember these are prayers — speak them — reword them!

10. READ HIS WORD AND WAIT — LISTEN — GOD SPEAKS!

What are you saying to me here? (1) "It is not weakness to sometimes be led." (2) "My will for you can be more important than food." (3) "I want to lead you from darkness to light."

11. INTERCESSION FOR THE LOST WORLD

Portugal — Points for prayer: (1) *Unreached peoples in Portugal* — in both the far north and south there are many areas with no real Bible believing witness. The many new city dwellers and the middle and upper classes have largely been passed by and need to be evangelized. Pray that the believers may get a vision for winning these people. (2) *The extraordinary freedom since 1974* has given the Bible believers an amazing opportunity to evangelize openly by all means — open air meetings, house visitation, literature and extensive use of Christian and commercial broadcasting. Pray that the believers and missionaries may be bold to use these means now. (3) *The churches are growing rapidly.* Pray for the effective discipling of the many young believers in the churches. The great need is for mature leaders and Bible teachers.

12. SING PRAISES TO OUR LORD.

All glory, laud and honor
To Thee, Redeemer, King,
To Whom the lips of children
Made sweet hosannas ring!

The people of the Hebrews
With palms before Thee went;
Our praise and prayer and anthems
Before Thee we present.

WEEK EIGHT — TUESDAY

1. PRAISE GOD FOR WHO HE IS.

Intimate. What a wonderful word this is for you. You want to be (and are) dearer and nearer than anyone else. How I love you and praise you for this quality! That you want to share a part and be a part of all I say, think or do is a real marvelous fact. I do so want you to be that involved with all I am and do and think. I *know* you have a deep interest and concern with all of my life all the time. Praise you, welcome to all that I have and am.

Express yourself in adoration for this quality of God.
Speak it audibly or write out your praise in your own devotional journal.

2. PRAISE GOD FOR WHAT HE MEANS TO ME.

What I say for myself I know can be said for all your children. How totally interested you are with *all men*, every man, every woman, to thus commune with you is a wonder and beauty beyond description. How I *do, do* want you to counsel me on so many things. How I do want your help and strength. Into my subconsciousness and in my every self-conscious moment, welcome dear Father, wonderful Savior.

How do you personally relate to the intimacy of God, and God who is intimate?
Speak it out or write it out. It is *so important* that you establish *your own* devotional journal.

3. CONFESSION OF SIN

I come each day in a deep sense of my own need and freely admit my violation of your will for my life, and truly seek and claim forgiveness, removal, freedom, cleansing. Have I been envious of someone? Am I envious now? Dear Lord, open my mind and memory, deliver me, forgive me — may I be totally satisfied with what you give me now — what I presently have! I rejoice in you!

What personal sins do you want to confess? We *must* speak them to remove them.
Do it! *Now.* There is no one else you have sinned against more than God. Tell him so!

4. SING A PRAYER TO GOD.

Christ has for sin atonement made,
What a wonderful Savior!
We are redeemed! price is paid!

What a wonderful Savior!
What a wonderful Savior is Jesus, my Jesus!
What a wonderful Savior is Jesus, my Lord!

Open your hymn book and sing the rest of the verses — or even sing another prayer song.

5. READ HIS WORD TO HIM!

His Word

[13]"Lord," Ananias answered, "I have heard many reports about this man and all the harm he has done to your saints in Jerusalem. [14]And he has come here with authority from the chief priests to arrest all who call on your name."
[15]But the Lord said to Ananias, "Go! This man is my chosen instrument to carry my name before the Gentiles and their kings and before the people of Israel. [16]I will show him how much he must suffer for my name."
[17]Then Ananias went to the house and entered it. Placing his hands on Saul, he said, "Brother Saul, the Lord — Jesus, who appeared to you on the road as you were coming here — has sent me so that you may see again and be filled with the Holy Spirit." [18]Immediately, something like scales fell from Saul's eyes, and he could see again. He got up and was baptized, [19]and after taking some food, he regained his strength.
Saul spent several days with the disciples in Damascus.
— *Acts 9:13-19, NIV*

Read His Word to Him.

How good to see and read of your tremendous interest in the life of one unworthy man — even Saul of Tarsus — How carefully have you characterized him: "my chosen instrument" — to carry my name — I will show him. You gave him a vision of Ananias before Ananias ever came.

One blind man was led — you turned his darkness to light. Praise to your love and power and mercy — the man was the same (in personality or basic inward being), but his goals and purposes were totally changed.

Please express your response to this beautiful text. Put your expression in your own prayer diary.

WEEK EIGHT — TUESDAY

6. READ HIS WORD FOR YOURSELF.

As you changed Saul you have changed me (and all others who are also your "chosen instruments"). It is wonderful to know that every Christian is just this! Saul was changed by the One he saw—when once the eyes of his heart were enlightened he could never forget *who* he saw, but more importantly, the glory and majesty and power present in the One he saw. I have come to see him in the same light—King of kings and Lord of lords. He heard his name, "Saul, Saul" (even in the Hebrew language). Dear Lord, I know you know me by name and call me, even me by name. I gladly, humbly, answer "Lord, what will you have me to do?"

It is so important that you pause in his presence
and either audibly or in written form tell him all his word means to you.

7. READ HIS WORD IN THANKSGIVING.

Gladly do I do this: (1) Thank you for a multitude of humble men like Ananias who are ready anytime to obey you—not without reason. (2) That we are to carry your name—which represents all you are—angels or prophets would gladly carry it, but *we* are given the priceless privilege. (3) The kings and those who are in high places can be influenced for our Lord—you want them to be—you sent Saul to them for that very purpose. (4) We *must* suffer for yourself for your "name's sake"—because we are yours, we suffer as you did—or for you. Help me to rejoice that I am counted worthy to do this. (5) That we can be and want to be "filled with the Holy Spirit." (6) Saul was baptized—what a trophy for King Jesus! (7) The same joyous fellowship Saul had with the disciples at Damascus can be ours today.

Give yourself to your own expression of gratitude—write it or speak it!

8. READ HIS WORD IN MEDITATION.

Let us gather around your word: (1) Saul went to the high priest for letters of condemnation and he himself became God's great letter of salvation to the same people. (2) As he drew near to the city the light fell upon him—as we draw near to the great cities of our world is our Lord trying to enlighten our hearts with a message for them? (3) "Saul, Saul, why persecutest thou me?" To in any way hurt the body of Christ is to hurt my Lord. Dear God, may I remember this today! (4) Some small man told Saul what to do to be saved. Dear God, help me to do that today! (5) Help me to see the light and hear the voice!

Pause—wait—think—then express yourself in thoughtful praise or thanks.

9. READ HIS WORD FOR PETITIONS.

How I do want to ask according to your will revealed in Acts 9:13-19: (1) May I be as candid with you as was Ananias. (2) I want to refer to Christians as saints as used here and mean the same thing. (3) Dear Lord, I call upon your name, i.e., your authority—how glad I am to claim it in so many areas of my life. (4) Do you have a few "chosen instruments" or is everyone such as a Christian? (5) How much do I need to suffer for your name? (6) I claim the beautiful promise of Isaiah 42:16. (7) May I so decrease that he may increase in me and through me.

Right here add your personal requests—and his answers.

10. READ HIS WORD AND WAIT—LISTEN—GOD SPEAKS!

What are you saying through these beautiful verses? (1) "I accept no excuses when I command." (2) "I can appear to you every time you read my word." (3) "Your baptism gave you the potential of being filled with the Holy Spirit."

11. INTERCESSION FOR THE LOST WORLD

Portugal — Points for prayer: (1) *Bible training assumes new importance in today's Portugal.* There are a number of good denominational Seminaries and Bible Schools, but little on an interdenominational basis. (2) *Missionaries are now much needed* after the years of restriction on their activities. There is a growing number of Brazilian missionaries entering the land. Pray for reinforcements to seize the present opportunities.

12. SING PRAISES TO OUR LORD.

There is never a day so dreary,
There is never a night so long,
But the soul that is trusting in Jesus
Will somewhere find a song.

Wonderful, wonderful Jesus,
In the heart He implanteth a song: . . .
A song of deliv'rance, of courage, of strength,
In the heart He implanteth a song.

WEEK EIGHT — WEDNESDAY

1. PRAISE GOD FOR HE IS.

Employer. How very good it is to be your employee. I gladly claim my place in your task force, in your grand enterprize. Oh, dear Lord, it is *good, good,* to be in your presence today. I want to follow your directions, but most of all to get well acquainted with the One for whom I work. Please, please help me as I start to work for you. The eternal value of the job we have to do, the beauty and blessedness of our work itself, to say nothing of the incalculable value of the precious eternal persons who are the end product—all are overwhelming in thought.

Express yourself in adoration for this quality of God.
Speak it audibly or write out your praise in your own devotional journal.

2. PRAISE GOD FOR WHAT HE MEANS TO ME.

I hesitate to relate myself to you as an employee. As you well know I struggle with my own selfish ambition— my own ideas and projects. I want every one of them to be yours. I would like to back right out of the whole effort if the effort would proceed on its own, but then you know my need and I am delighted to work for you. I will repent just as often as I need to, but you can not save the world nor educate your children with good intentions, nor can you with selfish introspection.

How do you personally relate to the employment of God, and God who is employer?
Speak it out or write it out. It is *so important* that you establish *your own* devotional journal.

3. CONFESSION OF SIN

The above has much repentance and confession in it and I want to reinforce all my decisions, and confessions. I want to hide *nothing, nothing*—as a plain matter of fact, I know I cannot and do not. If you can work through me, do so—I am open—ready—and in the process, cleanse me of (hidden to man) sins and the obvious ones. Oh, dear Lord, forgive. How you know I need it and how I do claim your cleansing and freedom and cleanness.

What personal sins do you want to confess? We *must* speak them to remove them.
Do it! *Now.* There is no one you have sinned against more than God. Tell him so!

4. SING A PRAYER TO GOD.

I have found a friend in Jesus,
He's everything to me,
He's the fairest of ten thousand to my soul;
The Lily of the Valley, in Him alone I see
All I need to cleanse and make me fully whole.

In sorrow He's my comfort, in trouble He's my stay,
He tells me every care on Him to roll:
He's the Lily of the Valley, the Bright and Morning Star,
He's the fairest of ten thousand to my soul.

Open your hymn book and sing the rest of the verses—or even sing another prayer song.

5. READ HIS WORD TO HIM!

[19]and after taking some food, he regained his strength. Saul spent several days with the disciples in Damascus. [20]At once he began to preach in the synagogues that Jesus is the Son of God. [21]All those who heard him were astonished and asked, "Isn't he the man who raised havoc in Jerusalem among those who call on this name? And hasn't he come here to take them as prisoners to the chief priests?"
— *Acts 9:19-21, NIV.*

[15]But when God, who set me apart from birth and called me by his grace, was pleased [16]to reveal his Son in me so that I might preach him among the Gentiles, I did not consult any man, [17]nor did I go up to Jerusalem to see those who were apostles before I was, but I went immediately into Arabia and later returned to Damascus.
— *Galatians 1:15-17, NIV.*

Read His Word to Him.

How could you do it? Set a man apart from birth? What power! What purpose, what love! I believe I was set apart from birth—I believe *all* men have been! All men have been called by your grace too, but most men are like those with Saul on the road—hear a noise, but hear no voice or see no One! Only one who is sensitive and responsive and willing could or would hear or see. Only one who was "kicking against the goad"—i.e., resisting your work in his conscience could be or will be open to hear or see.

Please express your response to this beautiful text. Put your expression in your own prayer diary.

6. READ HIS WORD FOR YOURSELF.

Why did Saul go to Arabia? I do not know—no one else knows either—but we can all relate this to ourselves and tell why we would go to Arabia. I would go there (if I were Saul) to pray and preach—to develop the capacity of receiving revelation from yourself—at the same time to tell the glad, exquisite, good news to all who would listen— to all who would pause and hear that God so loved that he gave. I would want to be above—unhurried and uncluttered with the One who loves and lives and is in and through and around and behind and before all things. Before he left he found the usual response of those who have ears and do not hear, eyes and do not see.

It is so important that you pause in his presence
and either audibly or in written form tell him all his word means to you.

7. READ HIS WORD IN THANKSGIVING.

How good it is to thank you for: (1) The overcoming love that sent Jesus, God in human form. Lord, I believe, but I can never know the depth of love, the eternal meaning of all you meant when you sent him. (2) That you can reveal your Son—not only in history—but in man, in even me! (3) He is revealed to be preached—if he is not preached the purpose of his revelation is defeated. Oh, God forbid. (4) We need not consult with man about what you have already said—man's counsel is not to obtain your revelation, or to affirm it, or to deny it, or to modify it. Those who loved him before we did can give us much, but there is nothing to be added to what you have already said or to what you already are! (6) Men seldom understand—You always understand. (7) Love—true love— Christ's love, must be present to do anything anywhere with anyone.

Give yourself to your own expression of gratitude—write it or speak it!

8. READ HIS WORD IN MEDITATION.

I did not consult any man. This needs to be understood— I want to understand it! It means: (1) Man cannot interpret my personal relationship with you—only yourself as revealed in your Son and your word can do this. (2) Even those who have had a similar experience have not had your experience and can add nothing but confusion to your inquiry. (3) Our Lord, my Lord set me apart—not man—I am answerable first, last and always to you. I am indeed answerable to man—our Lord was to his parents —to Moses and the law—to the apostles as he served and taught them—but the first and final court of appeal was you—is you—always will be you.

Pause—wait—think—then express yourself in thoughtful praise or thanks.

9. READ HIS WORD FOR PETITIONS.

The requests from Galatians 1:15-17 and Acts 9:19-21 are full of meaning: (1) Keep me "set apart," always aware of my new birth. (2) Reveal your son in me. (3) Dear God, make my preaching effective! (4) Help me to first consult your word before I consult *any* man about *anything.* (5) Those who have been preachers for a long time can help me, but not like you can. (6) May I be enabled to so preach Jesus as your Son that men will hear and heed.

Please, please remember these are prayers—speak them—reword them!

10. READ HIS WORD AND WAIT—LISTEN—GOD SPEAKS!

As I speak to you in prayer may I hear you through your word: (1) "Remember, you are called, saved and serve through grace." (2) "Do not be so impressed with men—they are not your masters." (3) "Speak boldly regardless of the response."

11. INTERCESSION FOR THE LOST WORLD

Portugal — Points for prayer: (1) *Student work is yet in its infancy.* Pray for the work in universities where Communism and anti-religious feeling is strong. Pray also for the work among school children.

12. SING PRAISES TO OUR LORD.

A Friend I have, called Jesus,
Whose love is strong and true,
And never fails howe'er tried,
No matter what I do;
I've sinned against this love of His,
But when I knelt to pray,
Confessing all my guilt to Him,
The sin-clouds rolled away.
It's just like Jesus to roll the clouds away,
It's just like Jesus to keep me day by day,
It's just like Jesus all along the way,
It's just like His great love.

WEEK EIGHT — THURSDAY

1. PRAISE GOD FOR WHO HE IS.

Cannot fail. I can, but he *can't.* Praise your wonderful and holy name. How more than encouraging it is to know you cannot and will not fail in any area of life—all your promises are "yea and amen"—all your plans will and do find fulfillment—all your judgments are right. How comforting when I know of your essential being! How strong and confident you are—how *all knowing*—when I confide in you no word you have given shall fall to the ground— Bless and praise and wonder!

Express yourself in adoration for this quality of God.
Speak it audibly or write out your praise in your own devotional journal.

2. PRAISE GOD FOR WHAT HE MEANS TO ME.

Cannot fail for me. Let me stand back and shout "glory, and honor, and power." When I consider even one of your promises to me—that I will be released from this body and share in the excitement and beauty of your presence— and such a promise *cannot* fail. That no temptation has ever taken me—or will ever come my way without the way of escape—that I *can* endure it if I will *only, only* trust you. I am most humbly aware of your total provision for my life, here and hereafter.

How do you personally relate to the faithfulness of God, and God who cannot fail?
Speak it out or write it out. It is *so important* that you establish *your own* devotional journal.

3. CONFESSION OF SIN

Dear Lord, dear Lord! Receive my frank and candid confession that I need to be washed and made clean within. To come to the Lamb who can and does take away the sins of the world is a joy and privilege. Dear Lord, deliver me from any hardening of my heart, keep me always sensitive and responsive. I am glad to die and have my whole life hid with you in my Lord, and hid with my Lord in you.

What personal sins do you want to confess? We *must* speak them to remove them.
Do it! *Now.* There is no one else you sinned against more than God. Tell him so!

4. SING A PRAYER TO GOD.

There is a name I love to hear,
I love to sing its worth;
It sounds like music in mine ear,
The sweetest name on earth.

Oh, how I love Jesus,
Oh, how I love Jesus,
Oh, how I love Jesus,
Because He first loved me!

Open your hymn book and sing the rest of the verses—or even sing another prayer song.

5. READ HIS WORD TO HIM!

His Word

[22]Yet Saul grew more and more powerful and baffled the Jews living in Damascus by proving that Jesus is the Christ.
[23]After many days had gone by, the Jews conspired to kill him, [24]but Saul learned of their plan. Day and night they kept close watch on the city gates in order to kill him.
— *Acts 9:22-24, NIV*

Read His Word to Him.

The reasoning process by which Saul proved the deity of your Son offers such an example to me and to all Christians. Religious people can be confused—illinformed—or misinformed—but these religious people can be and will be convinced (Praise the Lord for this assurance.). How I appreciate this encouragement, but it is a warning as well —there are those—there always have been those who will not (or cannot) understand—and in the name of religion will conspire—if not to kill at least to oppose. Praise your name, you are always present. If we are not delivered from it we can be delivered while in the midst of it.

Please express your response to this beautiful text. Put your expression in your own prayer diary.

WEEK EIGHT — THURSDAY

6. READ HIS WORD FOR YOURSELF.

Read this word for myself—indeed I can and to some extent I do each time I read the text. Dear Lord, how is it that my zeal is not so intense? The constituents of my day would not look with favor on my challenging the Baptist, Methodist, Presbyterians, Lutherans, to say nothing of the Catholics or Episcopalians. The issue is not the deity of Jesus, but it is serious—such as liberalism or salvation—such as division or One Body. Dear God, give me desire and boldness. Help me to grow more and more powerful (in your strength, not mine). I do not want only to baffle people, I want to win them to your dear son.

It is so important that you pause in his presence
and either audibly or in written form tell him all his word means to you.

7. READ HIS WORD IN THANKSGIVING.

Thank you for: (1) Your word—a sword, a mirror, a fire, a hammer, a light. May I use it use for all these purposes in teaching others. (2) Jesus *is* the Messiah—oh, the beauty of the thought! (3) There is an Arabia to which each of us can go to teach and prepare. (4) That you can frustrate the hatred of men. (5) That there is someone who loves us and watches on our behalf—both man and yourself. (6) I can learn of men's plans to defeat your work and take appropriate action. (7) It *is* sometimes right to run from the problem—when bodily harm is a real threat.

Give yourself to your own expression of gratitude—write it or speak it!

8. READ HIS WORD IN MEDITATION.

Then Saul went to Arabia. We learn from Galatians 1:15-18 that it was three years before he left Damascus for Jerusalem, we would assume he spent over two years in Arabia. What did he do there? There are some things I do not believe he did: (1) He did not get a new or special revelation or inspiration he did not have at Damascus. He was filled (I believe baptized) with the Holy Spirit at Damascus. (2) He did not attend some school of eastern scholars to obtain new understanding. What *did* he do? 1) He preached and taught all he found there, and it was populated with several large cities in the country. 2) He did find much time and a good place to meditate and re-orient his life.

Pause—wait—think—then express yourself in thoughtful praise or thanks.

9. READ HIS WORD FOR PETITIONS.

How good to ask from your word and know we shall receive: (1) Give me wisdom as I study the Old Testament evidence of the Messiah. (2) Teach me patience with men who will not believe. (3) Give me the same grace our Lord had with men who hated him. (4) What did Paul do in Arabia? (I expect you to help me find out.) (5) Thank you for all blessed accidents—your providence! (6) How can I help those who are persecuted today? (7) Keep me aware that you guard me and all your children—day and night.

Right here add your personal requests—and his answers.

10. READ HIS WORD AND WAIT—LISTEN—GOD SPEAKS!

What do you say to me in these words? (1) "Baffling people does not necessarily win them." (2) "The devil conspires to kill the zeal of Christians today." (3) "Greater is he who is in you than he who is in the world" (I John 4:4).

11. INTERCESSION FOR THE LOST WORLD

Portugal — Point for prayer: (1) *Pray for the evangelization of the very receptive Portuguese* in other European countries. Many live in barracks and hostels, and only a few with their families. Many have been converted, but the need is for more workers to bring the Gospel to them and plant churches among them.
Spain — Population: 36,000,000. Growth 1.1%. People per sq. km.—71.
Points for prayer: (1) *The ending of the dominance of the Roman Catholic Church* and the new spirit of freedom in Spain is bringing an openness to disillusioned Roman Catholics to new ideas. Sadly, many are attracted by Communism, for few have had the opportunity to hear the true Gospel. Pray that there may now be a great harvest for the Kingdom of God. (2) *Spain is now one of the countries most open to the Gospel* after centuries of ruthless persecution of non-Catholics. This is an answer to prayer. Pray that there may now be a period of freedom for the Gospel. There is a real threat of a Communist revolution or takeover.

12. SING PRAISES TO OUR LORD.

Jesus has loved me—wonderful Savior!
Jesus has loved me, I cannot tell why;
Came He to rescue sinners all worthless,
My heart He conquered—for Him I would die.

Glory to Jesus—wonderful Savior!
Glory to Jesus, the One I adore;
Glory to Jesus—wonderful Savior!
Glory to Jesus, and praise evermore.

WEEK EIGHT — FRIDAY

1. PRAISE GOD FOR WHO HE IS.

Always interested. Oh, wonder of all wonders! This must surely be the ultimate of your beautiful qualities! That you will always listen to every man, everywhere, in every language, that you will always be attentive and never tired. What a wonder of all your qualities! I do not have the adequate words, but I surely do have the joy and praise and exuberance to tell you again and again how I, and all your children appreciate your constant interest.

Express yourself in adoration for this quality of God.
Speak it audibly or write out your praise in your own devotional journal.

2. PRAISE GOD FOR WHAT HE MEANS TO ME.

That you take an interest in me is a great source of amazement, but that you are always interested is much more of an amazement. An interest and concern about my character is, I am sure, your first concern, although all I am and do are integrated. I love you and want to so live and think that we can share in all I do. I know how very ignorant my efforts and thoughts appear, but then, there is no "put down" in your nature! Bless your holy name!

How do you personally relate to the interest of God, and God who is always interested?
Speak it out or write it out. It is *so important* that you establish *your own* devotional journal.

3. CONFESSION OF SIN

I am just as glad to confess my sin. I have no rationale for it (or them). I simply lay them before you and ask that you cast them in your sea of forgetfulness. I could worry and fret over my repeated sins — I am truly sorry — and I do not want such, but I confess with Paul that "the evil I would not that I practice," but such being so "it is Satan who dwells within." Free me! Let me loose! Cleanse and forget! Praise and glory — I accept your forgivenesss!

What personal sins do you want to confess? We *must* speak them to remove them.
Do it! *Now.* There is no one else you have sinned against more than God. Tell him so!

4. SING A PRAYER TO GOD.

More about Jesus would I know,
More of His grace to others show;
More of His saving fullness see,
More of His love who died for me.

More, more about Jesus,
More, more about Jesus;
More of His saving fullness see,
More of His love who died for me.

Open your hymn book and sing the rest of the verses — or even sing another prayer song.

5. READ HIS WORD TO HIM.

His Word

²⁵But his followers took him by night and lowered him in a basket through an opening in the wall.
²⁶When he came to Jerusalem, he tried to join the disciples, but they were all afraid of him, not believing that he really was a disciple. ²⁷But Barnabas took him and brought him to the apostles. He told them how Saul on his journey had seen the Lord and that the Lord had spoken to him, and how in Damascus he had preached fearlessly in the name of Jesus.   — *Acts 9:25-27, NIV*

Read His Word to Him.

I wonder if you have a sense of humor? Surely the incongruity of Saul's coming and leaving has occurred to you. I feel almost irreverent to thus express it, but he did come in as a lion and left as a lamb! Here begins the lessons on "how many things he must suffer for my name's sake." Saul had "followers" even in these early days of his service to you. What a price he had to pay for the pearl of great price, but it was more than worth it all. How I do appreciate each word of your revelation.

Please express your response to this beautiful text. Put your expression in your own prayer diary.

6. READ HIS WORD FOR YOURSELF.

I want to travel with Saul. I want to feel as he felt — to pray with him. What mixed emotions filled Saul's heart! Great discovery! of both the mind of God and of man: of how infinitely merciful God was and how merciless man could be. Thank God for Barnabas. Oh, how I want to be like him! full of concern and love — when others doubted, he trusted, when others were afraid he was trusting. When and where had Saul and Barnabas first met? In Jerusalem? Barnabas knew the apostles — they probably had the gift of discernment hence they would trust Saul, or did they trust the words of Barnabas?

It is so important that you pause in his presence
and either audibly or in written form tell him all his word means to you.

7. READ HIS WORD IN THANKSGIVING.

Thank you, thank you for: (1) Daring friends who will risk their own lives to help. (2) For a basket and a rope to be used for such a precious cargo. God supplies the little things as well as what we consider big things. (3) For disciples in Jerusalem who act like disciples everywhere. It gives us all identity with others to see their human qualities. (4) For Saul who had seen the Lord. How I believe I can see Him through his words and the words of many others, and through the eyes of my heart. (5) For fearless preaching in the name (authority) of Jesus. (6) For every one of the twelve apostles. Oh, where shall we find 12 "sent ones" for today? (7) For a place for Saul to stay and talk and pray and love and thank you.

Give yourself to your own expression of gratitude — write it or speak it!

8. READ HIS WORD IN MEDITATION.

"But they were all afraid of him." How the fear of man does work a snare: (1) A snare to fellowship — we could have such a wider, sweeter fellowship if we loved and trusted one another. (2) A snare to the work of God in our lives — God could have overcome this problem if someone had only asked him (thank God for Barnabas). (3) A snare to what God is doing through someone else — we will really never know if we do not trust. (4) A snare to the mercy God has in the lives of others — we will never know until perfect love casts out this fear.

Pause — wait — think — then express yourself in thoughtful praise or thanks.

9. READ HIS WORD FOR PETITIONS.

There are requests I would never have considered if I had not found them in this text: (1) Give me the courage and humility I see in Saul. (2) Grant me the willingness to suffer as found in Paul. (3) Help me to be as creative in overcoming Satan. (4) If I should be misunderstood give me persistence. (5) Lead me to some friend like Barnabas. (6) Thank you for the gift of discernment found in the apostles. (7) May my change from serving self to serving my Lord be as complete as Saul's.

Please, please remember these are prayers — speak them — reword them!

10. READ HIS WORD AND WAIT — LISTEN — GOD SPEAKS!

There are several things you want to say to me from this text — give me ears to hear. (1) "I give grace to the humble." (2) "Even good men make mistakes." (3) "There is always someone who will trust you and understand."

11. INTERCESSION FOR THE LOST WORLD

Spain — Point for prayer: (1) *The Protestant Church is very small*, but growing fairly rapidly and spreading into new areas. Only Greece, Cyprus and Malta in Free Europe have a proportionately smaller number of believers.

12. SING PRAISES TO OUR LORD.

Come, friends sing, of the faith that's so dear to me, . . .
Revealed thro' God's Son, in Galilee;
He brought peace on earth and good will to the sons of men,
Go tell it to the world, her King reigns again.
I am so happy in Jesus,
Captivity's Captor is He; . . .

Angels rejoice when a soul's saved,
Some day we like Him shall be, . . .
Sorrow and joy have the same Lord,
Valley of shadows shall sing; . . .
Death has its life, its door opens in heaven eternally,
Christ is King. . . .

WEEK EIGHT — SATURDAY

1. PRAISE GOD FOR WHO HE IS.

Wants you and me. How glad to be wanted—most especially by the great God of the whole cosmos. I realize you want every man, woman and child who has been born or will be born on this earth. You want them be-cause they were brought into being for yourself. How I do praise you for your plan for every life. None escape unnoticed or unwanted.

Express yourself in adoration for this quality of God.
Speak it audibly or write out your praise in your own devotional journal.

2. PRAISE GOD FOR WHAT HE MEANS TO ME.

Wants me—Since I twice belong to you I am most glad to give myself to you. Use me, cleanse me, direct and fill my life. I do so want you. I love you and worship you in deep humility and wonder. Dear God, move in my life. I am trying to be sensitive to your desires.

How do you personally relate to the love of God, and God who wants you and me?
Speak it out or write it out. It is *so important* that you establish *your own* devotional journal.

3. CONFESSION OF SIN

Deceit and bitterness—I have sinned, I am a sinner in both areas. Please change me, forgive me! Dear God, I do want to change. I have changed and I am being changed—an openness to your presence and love is doing more for me than anything else. Praise you—I accept my cleanness. I want to be deeply moved to repentance.

What personal sins do you want to confess? We *must* speak them to remove them.
Do it! *Now.* There is no one else you have sinned against more than God. Tell him so!

4. SING A PRAYER TO GOD.

My hope is built on nothing less
Than Jesus' blood and righteousness;
I dare not trust the sweetest frame,
But wholly lean on Jesus' name.

On Christ, the solid Rock, I stand;
All other ground is sinking sand,
All other ground is sinking sand.

Open your hymn book and sing the rest of the verses—or even sing another prayer song.

5. READ HIS WORD TO HIM.

His Word

[28]So Saul stayed with them and moved about freely in Jerusalem, speaking boldly in the name of the Lord. [29]He talked and debated with the Grecian Jews, but they tried to kill him. [30]When the brothers learned of this, they took him down to Caesarea and sent him off to Tarsus. [31]Then the church throughout Judea, Galilee and Samaria enjoyed a time of peace. It was strengthened; and encouraged by the Holy Spirit, it grew in numbers, living in the fear of the Lord. — *Acts 9:28-31, NIV*

Read His Word to Him.

Dear God, I want to look at these words as if I had never before seen them—as if I was a brand new convert! How generous and thoughtful it was for the apostles to offer Saul a place to stay in Jerusalem. Was it in the house of John Mark? How vastly familiar and yet unfamiliar every place in the city looked to Saul! Boldness is a by-product of reality. When something or someone is as important as was salvation and our Lord, it *must* be, he *will* be shared. The apostles had to hear of the attempts to kill Saul from someone else other than Saul. Did it mean so little to him that he would not even mention it? Surely the love, devotion, total surrender of Saul is a beautiful example for me.

Please express your response to this beautiful text. Put your expression in your own prayer diary.

6. READ HIS WORD FOR YOURSELF.

I have read this word for myself too much — I want you in it — in all of it. I have pondered a long time as to the meaning of the little phrase, "the church . . . was strengthened; and *encouraged by the Holy Spirit, it grew in numbers, living in the fear of the Lord.*" Just what is involved here? How can I — and others — "be encouraged by the Holy Spirit"? Is this a direct operation of the Holy Spirit on the human spirit? or is this indirect in the sense of using words? We are encouraged in two ways (perhaps more): (1) Through what we sometimes call a "fortuitous set of circumstances." The Holy Spirit could be the Person behind the arrangement of these circumstances. (2) *Through words* of promise — or information to direct and explain — such is the ministry of the Spirit in the word he has given us. Before his words were written they were spoken — and no doubt repeated orally.

It is so important that you pause in his presence
and either audibly or in written form tell him all his word means to you.

7. READ HIS WORD IN THANKSGIVING.

I thoroughly enjoy expressing this time of prayer and worship! Thank you — (1) That Saul and the twelve could get together in Jerusalem and talk and pray into the hours of the days and nights of two weeks. (2) That Saul was willing to be a true witness (martyr) in Jerusalem — that he probably went back to the Grecian synagogues to undo what he did with Stephen. (3) That surprise of a pleasant kind is always possible in your work. (4) That men can praise you because of each other. (5) That brothers can care for our lives more than we do. (6) That Saul could receive counsel and act upon it. (7) That church growth is a byproduct of the encouragement of the Holy Spirit and walking in the fear of yourself!

Give yourself to your own expression of gratitude — write it or speak it!

8. READ HIS WORD IN MEDITATION.

Let's gather around your word and think together: Saul had a need that Barnabas met. He became such a good friend to Saul and Saul became more than a friend to Barnabas — so it can be with friends today. Saul stayed in Jerusalem just 15 days — it only took this long to stir up a riot — and a revival! Praise our Lord for the devotion of your bondservant Saul. The Grecian Jews of the synagogue of "the freed men" became a place of bondage to Saul, but then he understood it — a few brief years before he had led such an opposition against Stephen.

Pause — wait — think — then express yourself in thoughtful praise or thanks.

9. READ HIS WORD FOR PETITIONS.

Paul always obtained a response — in the reaction here there are several requests: (1) May I be as generous to those I do not know in your service as the apostles were with Saul. (2) Give me the holy boldness I need. (3) Give me fearless courage necessary for debate. (4) May I learn more and more how to effectively "preach the faith." (5) Help me to praise you instead of men. (6) May I be ready to heed the advice of my Christian brothers who know you and love me. (7) How I want to see the church today strengthened and encouraged by the Holy Spirit!

Right here add your personal requests — and his answers.

10. READ HIS WORD AND WAIT — LISTEN — GOD SPEAKS!

What are you saying to me through these verses? (1) "Speak out boldly for me." (2) "It is not necessary that all men agree with you." (3) "Please live in the fear of myself."

11. INTERCESSION FOR THE LOST WORLD

Spain — Points for prayer: (1) *There are serious weaknesses among believers* which hinder the churches from taking full advantage of the many opportunities: a) The feelings of inferiority after years of being a despised, oppressed minority that was officially rejected by society. b) The lack of both education and Bible teaching among believers which makes it very hard for most to give a reasonable account of the faith that is in them. Pray for their spiritual liberation and empowering so that they may become a mighty force for the evangelization of Spain.

12. SING PRAISES TO OUR LORD.

Crown Him with many crowns,
The Lamb upon His throne;
Hark! how the heav'nly anthem drowns
All music but its own!

Awake, my soul, and sing
Of Him who died for thee;
And hail Him as thy matchless King
Thro' all eternity.

WEEK NINE — SUNDAY

1. PRAISE GOD FOR WHO HE IS.

Light-giver. Dear Lord, when you said "Let there be light" we received the physical light we presently have. When you sent "the light of the world" we were given light all about us—within us and above us, behind us, ahead of us. How beautiful is light! Sparkling, scintillating, diffusing and spreading everywhere—so may your dear Son be in my heart and mind.

Express yourself in adoration for this quality of God.
Speak it audibly or write out your praise in your own devotional journal.

2. PRAISE GOD FOR WHAT HE MEANS TO ME.

Light-giver for me! All the light I have or want on any subject I get from you—either directly from your word, or indirectly from your children who have used the intelligence you gave them. Praise your name! I am *so, so* glad for the light that constantly comes into my life through my study of your word—but more—by him, my Lord, who is the Light of my life.

How do you personally relate to the light of God, and God who is the light-giver?
Speak it out or write it out. It is *so important* that you establish *your own* devotional journal.

3. CONFESSION OF SIN

Why, oh, why, do I want to walk in darkness—in any form? Forgive me. I am so strongly drawn to the light— bless the Lord. Cleanse me, forgive me, help me. Move in my conscience to a deeper repentance. Let *all* bitterness be totally rooted out! Give me the sweet, deep peace I need and want.

What personal sins do you want to confess? We *must* speak them to remove them.
Do it! *Now.* There is no one else you have sinned against more than God. Tell him so!

4. SING A PRAYER TO GOD.

Sweetly, Lord, have we heard Thee calling,
"Come, follow Me!"
And we see where Thy footprints falling

Lead us to Thee.
Footprints of Jesus, that make the pathway glow!
We will follow the steps of Jesus where'er they go.

Open your hymn book and sing the rest of the verses—or even sing another prayer song.

5. READ HIS WORD TO HIM!

His Word

[32] As Peter traveled about the country, he went to visit the saints in Lydda. [33] There he found a man named Aeneas, a paralytic who had been bedridden for eight years. [34] "Aeneas," Peter said to him, "Jesus Christ heals you. Get up and take care of your mat." Immediately Aeneas got up. [35] All those who lived in Lydda and Sharon saw him and turned to the Lord.

[36] In Joppa there was a disciple named Tabitha (which, when translated, is Dorcas), who was always doing good and helping the poor.
— *Acts 9:32-36, NIV*

Read His Word to Him.

How I would like to have been one of the saints in Lydda when Peter paid a visit! I know you were present at that time—and yet *now* you are present—indeed, you live in the *Eternal Present*—so you were present here and there all at the same time (for there is no time with you). What an amazing thought! To have been in bed for eight years and then all at once to "immediately" obey the command "get up"—is beyond my comprehension! As wonderful as this was to Aeneas it was not for his sake alone that the command was given, but for all those who lived in the city of Lydda and the plain of Sharon. Dear God, I do believe.

Please express your response to this beautiful text. Put your expression in your own prayer diary.

6. READ HIS WORD FOR YOURSELF.

How shall I relate to this miracle and to the many others in this Acts account? There are several questions I ask myself. Dear God, help me, help me with the answers. (1) Since I have the same message and people here in Joplin have the same need, why do we not have the same credentials to confirm our message? *Answers:* a) Peter was an apostle, but Philip wasn't and he did the same.

b) But the apostles laid their hands upon Philip—so they did, and by the apostles hands such miraculous signs were given (Acts 8 & 19). But simply because the hands of the apostles were laid on Philip are we to be totally sure that this is how he obtained this power? We are assuming at best. Is it an assumption beyond question? Give me wisdom to answer aright.

It is so important that you pause in his presence
and either audibly or in written form tell him all his word means to you.

7. READ HIS WORD IN THANKSGIVING.

Thank you, thank you for: (1) Peter's visit to me on this day so far removed from Lydda and the first century. (2) Aeneas—whom I will one day see (will it be soon?) and ask him just what he thought and felt and said and did—and because there will be no restriction, it will be easy to do, i.e., of time, space, etc. (3) That men and women turned to the Lord—turned from the vain things of their

lives and associations. (4) That you are helping me to project myself back to that time and place and become a participator with them. (5) That total surrender is possible!—the Lordship of Jesus can be and must be and will be a reality with me. (6) For dear saints who love you better than life. (7) That helping the poor is "doing good" by your standards.

Give yourself to your own expression of gratitude—write it or speak it!

8. READ HIS WORD IN MEDITATION.

"All who saw him turned to the Lord." Why? Because they saw obvious evidence of the power of God—at least they believed Peter when he told them the source of this miracle. Because they had an Old Testament background that prepared them for such signs associated with God's

men. Because they knew Aeneas and his condition—they knew him before the miracle and they knew him afterwards. Because they wanted to believe, they wanted to worship an all powerful, all caring, all knowing God—and they did.

Pause—wait—think—then express yourself in thoughtful praise or thanks.

9. READ HIS WORD FOR PETITIONS.

Aeneas and Dorcas are saying much to me—what should I ask of you? (1) Give me the love necessary to see people as "your holy ones." (2) I need to do much more visiting—help me. (3) Help me to see the potential of wholeness in every man. (4) May I learn the lesson of

faith in the healing of Aeneas. (5) Turn me more and more to yourself. (6) Send women like Dorcas into our fellowship. (7) You see the importance of deeds of physical help—open my eyes, change my values!

Please, please remember these are prayers—speak them—reword them!

10. READ HIS WORD AND WAIT—LISTEN—GOD SPEAKS!

There are surely several things you say to me here. What are they? (1) "Healing was a means—the end was

teaching." (2) "Help people in every way you can." (3) "The poor are still with you—help them."

11. INTERCESSION FOR THE LOST WORLD

Spain — Points for prayer: (1) *The leadership in the churches.* Pray that they may be able to both teach and inspire their fellowships to action as they plan the strategy to win their country for the Lord Jesus. (2) *There is an acute need for more and better trained national preachers.* Many of the 350 preachers have had little formal Bible

training. There are now about 8 Bible Schools and Seminaries (some part time). Pray for these that a growing stream of mature men of God may go out to serve the Lord. Pray that Spanish believers may give more liberally for their support, for too many are supported entirely by funds from other lands.

12. SING PRAISES TO OUR LORD.

Face to face with Christ, my Savior,
Face to face—what will it be?
When with rapture I behold Him,
Jesus Christ who died for me.

Face to face I shall behold Him,
Far beyond the starry sky;
Face to face in all His glory,
I shall see Him by and by!

WEEK NINE — MONDAY

1. PRAISE GOD FOR WHO HE IS.

Honey giver. This is such an attractive quality of your character! Honey is sweet — i.e., to the taste — you are sweet and pleasant to all the senses of man. Honey is nourishing — how very nourishing you are to all, and for all our needs! Dear God, you do indeed and in truth know and meet every need. Honey is made from the body of the bee — your goodness and sweetness and strength has been given to us through the body of your dear Son. Honey produces energy. How I praise you for your life-giving qualities!

Express yourself in adoration for this quality of God.
Speak it audibly or write out your praise in your own devotional journal.

2. PRAISE GOD FOR WHAT HE MEANS TO ME.

Honey-giver to me. How much more sweet — indeed *all* sweetness comes to me because of you. If my nature has qualities of endearment — you are the source. How full of energy and nourishment I have found you. I surely praise you for this quality. I owe my very life to you. When I think and contemplate the fact that all I have comes through the body of your Son, I am full of sorrow and joy. Praise your dear self!

How do you personally relate to the sweetness of God, and God who is divine energy?
Speak it out or write it out. It is *so important* that you establish *your own* devotional journal.

3. CONFESSION OF SIN

I come to your throne to receive grace and help, to be made clean, to lose all guilt. How foolish is foolish talk! Forgive me! Praise you for the desire to open up and pour out all my guilt and sins. Dear God, I want to be clean! pure! whole! I know you in the Person of your Son as seen in the beautiful record of your word.

What personal sins do you want to confess? We *must* speak them to remove them.
Do it! *Now.* There is no one you have sinned against more than God. Tell him so!

4. SING A PRAYER TO GOD.

What a Friend we have in Jesus,
All our sins and griefs to bear!
What a privilege to carry
Ev'rything to God in prayer!

O what peace we often forfeit,
O what needless pain we bear,
All because we do not carry
Ev'rything to God in prayer!

Open your hymn book and sing the rest of the verses — or even sing another prayer song.

5. READ HIS WORD TO HIM!

His Word

[37] About that time she became sick and died, and her body was washed and placed in an upstairs room. [38] Lydda was near Joppa; so when the disciples heard that Peter was in Lydda, they sent two men to him and urged him, "Please come at once!"   — *Acts 9:37, 38, NIV*

Read His Word to Him.

Oh, yes, yes, Dorcas did what all of us will do — died! After she had left her body (which is the real definition of death) her body, not Dorcas, was washed and laid out for burial. Thank you that I will never be buried. How clearly does this text say what you want all men to hear and see. Only you can help in the time of death. I wonder what Dorcas saw and heard before Peter arrived, i.e., in the brief time she was apart from her body? It is idle and *wrong* to speculate! It was very far better than being in the body — it was to be in your home — it was in the Paradise of the Unseen World (Hades), but as to personal response we will ask you all about it when we get there. What we need to know is before us in your word.

Please express your response to this beautiful text. Put your expression in your own prayer diary.

6. READ HIS WORD FOR YOURSELF.

One day someone will wash my dead body — one day I will be out of this clay tabernacle — one day there will be no more days for me! Praise your name. I have a great desire to even now depart this house, since I know how very far better it will be! God's man has the only help available at the time of death. How important the preacher feels when he is called to assist at the funeral — he knows he has the sole source of comfort and strength. Preacher, "come at once."

It is so important that you pause in his presence
and either audibly or in written form tell him all his word means to you.

7. READ HIS WORD IN THANKSGIVING.

How easy it is to thank you at such a time: (1) For dear ones who truly love us and will miss us. (2) For the lasting value of good works in the lives of others who will live longer than we will. (3) For God's value system that says: robes and other clothes are important. (4) That you are at work all the time — arranging the proximity of Lydda and Joppa — it was no accident that Peter was nearby — you knew it before he left Jerusalem. (5) That Peter had nothing more important to do than to help those who grieved. (6) That Peter had left all to follow him — even when our Lord was with you. (7) That you told Peter what to do and when to do it (how else could he have acted "by faith"?).

Give yourself to your own expression of gratitude — write it or speak it!

8. READ HIS WORD IN MEDITATION.

Does God raise the dead today? It is not because he lacks the power to do so. It is not because he has changed his mind that "it is appointed unto man once to die." Let's say God does raise the dead today, we then must ask why would he do it? Here are some possible answers: (1) He wants to demonstrate his power and love and personal interest in man — how many people will he need to raise and under what circumstances? Will all men draw the same conclusion from the miracle? How will this prove more than the records of Dorcas, or the widow of Nain's son, or Lazarus? (2) That he wants to prove his word through his messengers is true. Hasn't this already been done? Is there another word from him other than that in his word, the Bible? Aren't the *credentials* given *with* the word? The word was spoken (and later written) and the signs accompanied this word. What will raising the dead prove about his word that has not already been proven? Please do not side-step the issue, *answer the questions!*

Pause — wait — think — then express yourself in thoughtful praise or thanks.

9. READ HIS WORD FOR PETITIONS.

Death prompts many requests: (1) Remind me all over again that I am not the body. (2) Help me to accept your will in sickness and death. (3) Help me to bring your own comfort to those who have lost loved ones. (4) May I be prepared to be interrupted today as pleases you. (5) Give me grace to know what is urgent and what is not. (6) I want to see death as overcome by our Lord — help me. (7) May I appreciate much more fully my good health.

Right here add your personal requests — and his answers.

10. READ HIS WORD AND WAIT — LISTEN — GOD SPEAKS!

Speak to me: (1) "Life is brief — live and work today." (2) "The best of people die — for reasons best known to me." (3) "Do not wait for a better time — serve me today."

11. INTERCESSION FOR THE LOST WORLD

Spain — Point for prayer: (1) *Areas of greatest need.* The Bible believing churches are more concentrated in certain areas — Catalonia in N.E., Andalusia in the S.W., Valencia on the east coast and Madrid. The rest of the country is under-evangelized. Especially needy are the central provinces south of Madrid, Galicia in the N.W. and the Basque provinces in the north. Pray that the whole country may soon be covered with live and powerful churches.

12. SING PRAISES TO OUR LORD.

Down at the cross where my Savior died,
Down where for cleansing from sin I cried,
There to my heart was the blood applied;
Glory to His name.

Glory to His name, . . .
Glory to His name; . . .
There to my heart was the blood applied;
Glory to His name.

WEEK NINE — TUESDAY

1. PRAISE GOD FOR WHO HE IS.

Protector. Amen! You are in truth my only protection from the evil one—and from myself and from my enemies and my friends. What is true of me is true of all men upon this little sphere. Praise your name, we will never know the terrible things that could have happened to us, and didn't because you guarded and protected us. Bless your name, which is power and love, the essence of mercy.

Express yourself in adoration for this quality of God.
Speak it audibly or write out your praise in your own devotional journal.

2. PRAISE GOD FOR WHAT HE MEANS TO ME.

Protector of myself. I know you have stretched forth your hand and said to Satan—"This far and no further." You have led me into the ways of pleasantness, i.e., in which I presently walk and protected me from so many unhappy incidents and events. You have kept me from the tongues of those who would lie and cheat and deceive. Bless your wonderful name. How you have hidden me in the shelter of my dear, wonderful Lord—the Rock in a weary land!

How do you personally relate to the protection of God, and God who is protector?
Speak it out or write it out. It is *so important* that you establish *your own* devotional journal.

3. CONFESSION OF SIN

As I look over the list of sins in your word I am convinced I am implicitly guilty of most of them and explicitly guilty of several. I confess indeed my specific sins, but "foolish talking," "empty words"—they too need to be examined and repented of. Dear God, how good to be whole and clean and free! A liberty wherein the blood of your Son has set me free!

What personal sins do you want to confess? We *must* speak them to remove them.
Do it! *Now.* There is no one you have sinned against more than God. Tell him so!

4. SING A PRAYER TO GOD.

Abide with me: fast falls the eventide;
The darkness deepens; Lord with me abide:
When other helpers fail, and comforts flee,
Help of the helpless, O abide with me!

Open your hymn book and sing the rest of the verses—or even sing another prayer song.

5. READ HIS WORD TO HIM!

His Word

[39] Peter went with them, and when he arrived he was taken upstairs to the room. All the widows stood around him, crying and showing him the robes and other clothing that Dorcas had made while she was still with them. [40] Peter sent them all out of the room; then he got down on his knees and prayed. Turning toward the dead woman, he said, "Tabitha, get up." She opened her eyes, and seeing Peter she sat up.

— *Acts 9:39, 40, NIV*

Read His Word to Him.

How often (millions of times) have men traveled with Peter from Joppa to Lydda and walked up the steps and entered the upper room into the presence of the dead body of Dorcas? But on this day I want to share your presence in that room. How every eye focuses on the still form of the body, on the unusual, but how different is your view of this scene! Your devoted servant is already enjoying the wonder of your presence—to return her spirit to her body would be no advantage. But because it would prepare many to enter life rather than eternal death, you grant (and even prompt) the prayer of Peter.

Please express your response to this beautiful text. Put your expression in your own prayer diary.

6. READ HIS WORD FOR YOURSELF.

How good were the good works of this good woman, but how temporary—how soon forgotten—or were they? We and two millenniums of readers have not forgotten them! Somehow I want to believe that no good deed done in the spirit of the One who did the menial tasks of the carpenter's shop will ever be forgotten. You have already indicated you have the ability of instantaneous recall in returning to the mind of the apostles all that Jesus taught them—via the Holy Spirit. For those to whom it could mean appreciation or understanding, I want to believe every thoughtful deed and word will be returned in the world to come.

It is so important that you pause in his presence
and either audibly or in written form tell him all his word means to you.

7. READ HIS WORD IN THANKSGIVING.

Amen! Thank you for: (1) The widows who would never cease talking of the resurrection of Dorcas (oh, that the resurrection from trespasses and sins might mean as much to everyone). (2) That someday we too will be able to talk to Dorcas and the widows and Peter and smile and rejoice. (3) That Peter did not want to obtain the praise of men (women)—the miracle happened while he was alone in the room. (4) That prayer is associated with the miracle since it identifies and focuses the source. (5) That true dependence and humility is seen in the words and posture of Peter. (6) That Dorcas never said anything about what she saw and heard while her body was dead and she was in the spirit world. (7) That I have been raised from a worse death and greater loss.

Give yourself to your own expression of gratitude—write it or speak it!

8. READ HIS WORD IN MEDITATION.

Shall we raise the dead today? Oh, how I want to project myself back to the time and place of the writing of these words. I notice no "ordinary Christians" did this; it was an apostle. There was no wide scale, wholesale raising from the dead—only the leaders of the body did it: Stephen, Philip, Peter and John, the apostles. Why? Why? Because they were speaking the word of the Lord and these signs were their credentials. The miracles proved or confirmed their word. All Christians went everywhere preaching the word, but no miracles are associated with them. Why? Why? Because they were giving a testimony and not a body of teaching that needed confirmation.

Pause—wait—think—then express yourself in thoughtful praise or thanks.

9. READ HIS WORD FOR PETITIONS.

Going to a funeral moves all of us to ask questions—and offer petitions: (1) Give me patience and love to answer calls for help. (2) Open my eyes to see that investment in lives is what lasts. (3) May I have as tender a heart as Peter. (4) Break my heart over the heart-break of others. (5) Let me know again just how final death is. (6) Move me to prayer in the presence of need. (7) Thank you for your interest in the sad scene.

Please, please remember these are prayers—speak them—reword them!

10. READ HIS WORD AND WAIT—LISTEN—GOD SPEAKS!

What do you say in the presence of death? (1) "Dorcas was with me, not the widows or Peter." (2) "I sent her back to help people believe there is no death." (3) "Prayer is the most powerful force in the universe."

11. INTERCESSION FOR THE LOST WORLD

Spain — Points for prayer: (1) *There are now about 300 missionaries* in 54 different organizations, but what are so few when faced with the great need? Pray that the Lord may raise up many more willing to pour out their lives for the salvation of Spain. This could be a very fruitful field for believers in Spanish speaking America. Pray for the right relationships between the national believers and missionaries, and that the latter may have the right strategy for the planting of strong churches. There are now a number of different ministries open to missionaries —evangelism, church planting, Bible teaching, literature, etc. (2) *Literature has proved to be the most potent weapon* for the conversion of Spanish people. There is now freedom to print and sell literature in the country. Pray for the publishing and colportage ministries. There are, as yet, few Christian bookshops in the country.

12. SING PRAISES TO OUR LORD.

I will sing the wondrous story
Of the Christ who died for me,
How He left His home in glory
For the cross of Calvary.

Yes, I'll sing . . . the wondrous story
Of the Christ . . . who died for me, . . .
Sing it with . . . the saints in glory,
Gathered by . . . the crystal sea.

WEEK NINE — WEDNESDAY

1. PRAISE GOD FOR WHO HE IS.

Opportunity-maker. It is a joy for me to relate to this quality of yourself! All the good open doors for a knowledge of yourself—all the opportunities to teach and preach your word for others are arranged by you. Every copy of the scriptures is a marvelous opportunity for someone to know you. Oh, praise your beautiful name. How *good* to know you are the One who opens every door that leads to life!

Express yourself in adoration for this quality of God.
Speak it audibly or write out your praise in your own devotional journal.

2. PRAISE GOD FOR WHAT HE MEANS TO ME.

Opportunity for me—you are opportunity itself for me. I attribute every project to you. If they failed it was a lack of either faith or wisdom, both I could have had from you. If the projects succeed, I want to offer every ounce of credit to you! There have been *so* many opportunities for me! I have had some response in teaching and preaching and writing and publishing and in it all I want to let everyone glorify you (I am *so* sad and sorry that my terrible pride and ignorance have hindered this.), but I do wonder and worship in praise before you!

How do you personally relate to the opportunities of God, and God who is opportunity-maker?
Speak it out or write it out. It is *so important* that you establish *your own* devotional journal.

3. CONFESSION OF SIN

Dear Opportunity-maker, I want to be forgiven for every time I forced a situation and made my own opportunity—although I must confess just as freely I that have not always known the difference. Dear One, cleanse me of *all* my hidden faults.

What personal sins do you want to confess? We *must* speak them to remove them.
Do it! *Now.* There is no one else you have sinned against more than God. Tell him so!

4. SING A PRAYER TO GOD.

There's a Stranger at the door,
Let Him in;
He has been there oft before,
Let Him in;

Let Him in, ere He is gone,
Let Him in, the Holy One,
Jesus Christ, the Father's Son,
Let Him in.

Open your hymn book and sing the rest of the verses—or even sing another prayer song.

5. READ HIS WORD TO HIM!

His Word

[40]Peter sent them all out of the room; then he got down on his knees and prayed. Turning toward the dead woman, he said, "Tabitha, get up." She opened her eyes, and seeing Peter she sat up. [41]He took her by the hand and helped her to her feet. Then he called the believers and the widows and presented her to them alive. [42]This became known all over Joppa, and many people believed in the Lord. [43]Peter stayed in Joppa for some time with a tanner named Simon.
— *Acts 9:40-43, NIV*

Read His Word to Him.

What shall I say to you about raising the dead? Wow! I'm nonplused, I am speechless, I really have no words to register my response! I do want to be one of those "believers" who saw Dorcas after her resurrection—the primary purpose was not her resurrection but to cause many to believe in your dear Son. Jesus is the great miracle—his resurrection is far more important—he was raised to die no more.

Did Peter teach these eager, open-hearted people? Of course he did. This was the real power and purpose behind the raising of this dear woman. I want to hear every word he said (says). I can read Peter's epistles and receive some of the same teaching he must have given to these disciples.

Please express your response to this beautiful text. Put your expression in your own prayer diary.

6. READ HIS WORD FOR YOURSELF.

"Tabitha, get up." Such a word will one day (oh, that glad last day) be heard—every man and woman's name will be called and we all shall "get up." My Lord, are you saying to me right now, "get up," "arise you who are asleep" and I will shine upon you like the light of the bright morning sun. It does seem to me that if this were a pattern to be repeated it would have happened in at least one more "Joppa"—or Joplin—since that day. Bless the Lord, "a greater work," a truly greater work has happened. Someone has been raised from an eternal death in trespasses and sins. Raised to walk in the fresh new sunlight of your love!

It is so important that you pause in his presence
and either audibly or in written form tell him all his word means to you.

7. READ HIS WORD IN THANKSGIVING.

I always look forward to this expression. Thanks seems so inadequate. (1) For your definition of death—"the body apart from the Spirit is dead"—her body had been washed and laid out on the bed—and it was to that body Peter turned and spoke. (2) For your definition of seeing—or sight—we see with our spirits—through our eyes—when the Spirit is absent so is sight. (3) For the courtesy of Peter—thoughtful, kind man—like our Lord. (4) For the circumstances of your miracle—open, public, no question of the reality. (5) To be alive twice—once alive in the old life, now alive in a new life—the same old friends and surroundings, but something beautiful has been added. (6) That Peter was "at home" or comfortable with "a tanner" (an unlikely man with whom to stay). (7) For the commonness of all the record, the common name of "Simon"—like Bill or Henry today. Thank you for this lovely, lovely account.

Give yourself to your own expression of gratitude—write it or speak it!

8. READ HIS WORD IN MEDITATION.

We can gather around your word with absorbed and absorbing interest: Why did Peter visit Lydda? He was on a journey for *some* reason—perhaps what he did when he got there would indicate why he came. He came to see and confirm the faith of the saints—in the process he healed Aeneas. The facts about Aeneas: a) He was a paralytic in advanced stages of paralysis. b) He had been in bed for eight years. c) He was instantaneously healed. We could add that all who lived in the town and the country saw him, knew him and turned to the Lord. How careful and complete is the confirmation of our faith.

Pause—wait—think—then express yourself in thoughtful praise or thanks.

9. READ HIS WORD FOR PETITIONS.

What a glad amazing time is a resurrection. I am moved to ask: (1) How can I better speak to those dead in sin? (2) Give me the same purpose in preaching and serving that filled the heart of Peter. (3) May I remember that I have been raised from a death worse than physical. (4) Dear Lord, where is the "new life" and wonder of forgiveness? (5) Teach me the real indepth meaning of: "repentance unto life"? (6) How can I better rejoice over those who are raised from the dead? (7) What kind of "personal evangelism" did Peter do in Joppa?

Right here add your personal requests—and his answers.

10. READ HIS WORD AND WAIT—LISTEN—GOD SPEAKS!

I truly want to hear what you will say from these verses: (1) "There is something worse than death—it is hell!" (2) "You believe—now do something about it!" (3) "Most men do not care if people are dead in sin—do you?"

11. INTERCESSION FOR THE LOST WORLD

Spain — Points for prayer: (1) *Radio ministry.* The short wave Trans World Radio transmissions from Monaco can only be received by a minority of Spanish radio sets. Pray that there may be complete freedom to use the state and commercial medium wave stations in Spain for broadcasting the Gospel. (2) *Student ministry.* There are 10 universities with no Bible believing group. The 180,000 university students are now open for the Gospel as never before.

12. SING PRAISES TO OUR LORD.

My Jesus, I love Thee, I know Thou art mine,
For Thee all the follies of sin I resign;

My gracious Redeemer, my Savior art Thou;
If ever I loved Thee, my Jesus, 'tis now.

WEEK NINE — THURSDAY

1. PRAISE GOD FOR WHO HE IS.

You are truth. What a solid thought. What a strong, satisfying quality of character. On any subject you can give me the facts — the truth on that subject. About any man or woman you can give us the total truth about them, the whole story. You indeed, are the source of all truth and then in the Person of your Son you came into this world as "the way, the truth and the life"!

Express yourself in adoration for this quality of God.
Speak it audibly or write out your praise in your own devotional journal.

2. PRAISE GOD FOR WHAT HE MEANS TO ME.

To me you are the truth — how I wander, and hesitate, i.e., in any area, but with you I can be sure. I can be calm. I am on firm ground. I have found *the truth*! No word of yours will fall short of fulfillment. When you tell me I am justified, reconciled, forgiven, I can and do believe it! When you tell me of a place and purpose in heaven, I believe it, and eagerly look forward to it. How personally assuring to cast myself into the arms of TRUTH.

How do you personally relate to the truth of God, and God who is truth?
Speak it out or write it out. It is *so important* that you establish *your own* devotional journal.

3. CONFESSION OF SIN

To admit falling short, of missing the mark, of transgression of your law is easy in fact, but unless I link it with your love and a total confidence in your forgiveness, I would be discouraged, but I am not at all. I am washed and made clean. Praise for your love and mercy — I have named my sin, but just as freely claimed your cleansing. Amen!

What personal sins do you want to confess? We *must* speak them to remove them.
Do it! *Now*. There is no one else you have sinned against more than God. Tell him so!

4. SING A PRAYER TO GOD.

"Give me thy heart," says the Father above,
No gift so precious to Him as our love,
Softly He whispers wherever thou art,
"Gratefully trust me, and give me thy heart."

"Give my thy heart, Give me thy heart,"
Hear the soft whisper, wherever thou art;
From this dark world He would draw thee apart,
Speaking so tenderly, "Give me thy heart."

Open your hymn book and sing the rest of the verses — or even sing another prayer song.

5. READ HIS WORD TO HIM!

His Word

10 At Caesarea there was a man named Cornelius, a centurion in what was known as the Italian Regiment. ²He and all his family were devout and God-fearing; he gave generously to those in need and prayed to God regularly. ³One day at about three in the afternoon he had a vision. He distinctly saw an angel of God, who came to him and said, "Cornelius!" — *Acts 10:1-3, NIV*

Read His Word to Him.

You had such a good man in Cornelius — an Italian — I'm sure there have been ten million or more just like him in the land of Italy as well as equal number in so many other countries around the world. He was attracted by his need to the scriptures, and to the lives of some of the Jews in Caesarea. It is only through the word of God we obtain faith (Rom. 10:17), but it is as much by a felt need that we reach for the scriptures and help from others. How gloriously have you made man and how perfectly you have provided for his every, deepest need. Cornelius set the pace, not only for his Regiment but for his family. Even as this man, dear God, I know you see our prayers and our giving!

Please express your response to this beautiful text. Put your expression in your own prayer diary.

WEEK NINE — THURSDAY

6. READ HIS WORD FOR YOURSELF.

Dear Lord, how can I be both "devout and God-fearing"? I take the first thought to refer to acts of devotion such as the hours of prayer — and giving of alms — the second to refer to a total attitude of humility and respect before yourself. How I *do want this*! Will I ever see an angel? If I do or do not I can indeed believe they are even now in this room where I pray. Whether I hear my name called by one of them I yet know they are here to assist me in ways I do not know. How full of meaning it is for me to look upon the very first Gentile (someone like me) to ever hear the good news. At Jesus' birth the good news was for "all men" but God knows we are hard of hearing.

It is so important that you pause in his presence
and either audibly or in written form tell him all his word means to you.

7. READ HIS WORD IN THANKSGIVING.

Oh, thank you: (1) For your interesting choice of the first Gentile nation to hear the good news — Italians — I find this provocative (not because I am Italian). (2) That you chose a leader and an important one to lead in the spread of your word — only heaven will tell us how widespread it became. (3) That you chose a family to model the type of people you want — after whom you "seek to worship you" (John 4:23). (4) That *regular* prayer is commended. (5) That an Italian army captain could arrange his schedule to include an hour of prayer three times a day. (6) That angels talk our language and know our names. (7) That our alms and prayers affect others as well as God and ourselves.

Give yourself to your own expression of gratitude — write it or speak it!

8. READ HIS WORD IN MEDITATION.

Angels today: "The angel of the Lord encampeth round them that fear him, and delivereth them" (Psa. 34:7). Here is some general information to make us aware and sensitive to the ministry of angels: (1) God created angels (Psa. 148:2-5; Neh. 9:6; Col. 1:16ff.; Job 38:7). They were created before this world. (2) Angels are both holy (except those who chose to be evil) and happy (Mark 8:38; I Tim. 5:21; Isa. 6:1-8; Rev. 5:11, 12). Happiness is a by-product of holiness. (3) There are innumerable such intelligent beings (Matt. 26:53; Heb. 12:22; Rev. 5:11). (4) You will see in the above references that they are ranked: a) Archangels; b) seraphim; c) cherubim. They have: a) thrones; b) dominions; c) might; d) powers; e) principalities. Angels are distinct, neither God, human nor animal (Psa. 8:4, 5; Heb. 1:3ff.; 2:9, 10, 16-18).

Pause — wait — think — then express yourself in thoughtful praise or thanks.

9. READ HIS WORD FOR PETITIONS.

We are introduced to a good man who prayed. He prompts requests from our own hearts: (1) Send me to men like Cornelius. (2) Teach me that regardless of their job there are men who can be reached. (3) Teach me the concern you have for devout God-fearing people. (4) Rebuke my heart — if those who are not Christians can give generously and pray regularly, what is my excuse? (5) Should I not pray at least three times per day? (6) If angels served Cornelius I know you serve me — thank you! (7) Keep my heart tender that you might reach me with your word.

Please, please remember these are prayers — speak them — reword them!

10. READ HIS WORD AND WAIT — LISTEN — GOD SPEAKS!

I, like Cornelius, wait before you: (1) "Being good is not enough for salvation." (2) "You are not saved if you do not give and pray." (3) "There are other men who would listen like Cornelius if I had someone like Peter."

11. INTERCESSION FOR THE LOST WORLD

Spain — Point for prayer: (1) *The Gypsy people movement* is as noticeable here as in France, Germany and Rumania. Many thousands of these people are turning to the Lord and little Gypsy churches are springing up all over Spain. Pray for the continuation of this work of God. Pray also that these enthusiastic believers may be able to play a part in evangelizing Spain.

12. SING PRAISES TO OUR LORD.

Christ has for sin atonement made,
What a wonderful Savior!
We are redeemed! the price is paid!

What a wonderful Savior!
What a wonderful Savior is Jesus, my Jesus!
What a wonderful Savior is Jesus, my Lord!

WEEK NINE — FRIDAY

1. PRAISE GOD FOR WHO HE IS.

Peace. You *are* my peace and the peace of the whole world. Peace is not just the absence of hostility, but a deep sense of oneness and wholeness. A total rest of the being of man. You have made a peace we are to accept.

Praise your wonderful name! I am so glad my life and the lives of all men of the earth can be a tranquil day of peace. All nature is at peace with you — all the billions of constellations in the heavens are at peace.

Express yourself in adoration for this quality of God.
Speak it audibly or write out your praise in your own devotional journal.

2. PRAISE GOD FOR WHAT HE MEANS TO ME.

The greatest area of peace is my own heart! In my thoughts: do I rest all intellectual activity finally in your word? Am I perfectly willing to let your peace that passeth my understanding garrison my thoughts? Dear God, I am willing — make me more willing. Am I at peace in my will?

— i.e., am I willing to do your will? Sometimes I have great difficulty deciding just what your will is. I think I know, but it does seem so impossible! Dear God, I need trust, not knowledge. Right now, I commit, I submit, I wait, I will!

How do you personally relate to the peace of God, and to God who is peace?
Speak it out or write it out. It is *so important* that you establish *your own* devotional journal.

3. CONFESSION OF SIN

"Their god is their stomach." This is a sad, sinful description of our (my) generation and society. I am influenced by such a permeating, pervasive influence. Dear God, help

me! Help me to beat, bruise, control my body — lest it control me. Forgive me, dear God! Move me into total interest in the "things of the Spirit."

What personal sins do you want to confess? We *must* speak them to remove them.
Do it! *Now.* There is no one else you have sinned against more than God. Tell him so!

4. SING A PRAYER TO GOD.

I stand amazed in the presence
Of Jesus the Nazarene,
And wonder how He could love me,
A sinner, condemned, unclean.

How marvelous! how wonderful!
And my song shall ever be:
How marvelous! how wonderful
Is my Savior's love for me!

Open your hymn book and sing the rest of the verses — or even sing another prayer song.

5. READ HIS WORD TO HIM!

His Word

[4]Cornelius stared at him in fear. "What is it, Lord?" he asked.

The angel answered, "Your prayers and gifts to the poor have come up as a remembrance before God. [5]Now send men to Joppa to bring back a man named Simon who is called Peter. [6]He is staying with Simon the tanner, whose house is by the sea."

[7]When the angel who spoke to him had gone, Cornelius called two of his servants and one of his soldiers who was a devout man. [8]He told them everything that had happened and sent them to Joppa.

[9]About noon the following day as they were approaching the city, Peter went up on the roof to pray.

— *Acts 10:4-9, NIV*

Read His Word to Him.

What a delight to share with you what you have shared with me (and all men). I want to think deeply upon the words of the angel you sent to the Italian army captain: "your prayers and gifts to the poor" — not only what was said but the habit of prayer was noticed; not only the gifts but the condition of the ones receiving them. The poor-

ness of the poor was seen by you. The occupation, address and name of all men are known to you and your messengers. Cornelius was heard and known, not as one who was saved (cf. 11:15), but as one much loved. He had help in every way possible — men, means and an angel.

Please express your response to this beautiful text. Put your expression in your own prayer diary.

6. READ HIS WORD FOR YOURSELF.

Just as if I had never seen it before—the three men—I wonder what they thought? strange man, strange orders, but a trip to Joppa probably was not unwelcome. "He told them everything that had happened" and such a strange story he had to tell them! What a shock to learn of a God who cared and sent a messenger to men—and to their master in particular. Could I become that "devout military aide"? I have no reason to doubt the reality of what is said. I do want to follow the incident to its conclusion. I am most curious as to *why* all this has happened.

It is so important that you pause in his presence and either audibly or in written form tell him all his word means to you.

7. READ HIS WORD IN THANKSGIVING.

Indeed I shall read the word in thanksgiving. Thank you for: (1) Cornelius—devout and God-fearing, generous, prayerful, obedient, and careful—what a good man! (2) The angel—direct, real, precise, supernatural. (3) The messengers—informed, obedient, dedicated to their task. (4) For yourself—fully aware, interested in each person, patient, dramatic. (5) A real time and place—Caesarea, Joppa, 1st century, sand and sea. (6) The tanner Simon—for his hospitality which made all this a reality. (7) For preserving this record for 2,000 years! Praise you!

Give yourself to your own expression of gratitude—write it or speak it!

8. READ HIS WORD IN MEDITATION.

"As a remembrance before God"—Everyone wants to be remembered. We would all like to think that something we did or said had value beyond the moment. Most of all we want God to remember us. Here is how: There are two things of lasting value to God—of lasting value within themselves—these two things have intrinsic value—they are: (1) *Your prayers*—not just that you prayed, but your devoted habit of prayer—in his case it was 9, 12 and 3 each day. (2) *Your use of money to help the poor*—we remember our Lord "sat over by the treasury" and marked the amounts cast in. Communion or fellowship or joint sharing with God and man is what will be remembered throughout all eternity.

Pause—wait—think—then express yourself in thoughtful praise or thanks.

9. READ HIS WORD FOR PETITIONS.

Surely there are several requests that come from Acts 9:5-9. (1) Move my heart that the sense of sacred awe may never leave me! (2) Make me keenly aware that money and prayer declare the genuineness of my worship. (3) Open my heart to know you know everything I do and everywhere I go. (4) Make me as responsive to what you are saying in your word as Cornelius was to the angel. (5) Am I at all race prejudiced? Show me. (6) Teach me how to arrange my schedule to include prayer at noon. (7) Work out your timing for the salvation of the lost through me—help me to be ready to respond.

Right here add your personal requests—and his answers.

10. READ HIS WORD AND WAIT—LISTEN—GOD SPEAKS!

Dear Lord, I want to understand you when you speak: (1) "Giving and praying are tangible evidence of faith." (2) "I have sent the witness to request the salvation of the lost: Myself, my Son and the Holy Spirit." (3) "I still speak to people when they pray."

11. INTERCESSION FOR THE LOST WORLD

Ceuta and Melilla — Population: 170,000. Point for prayer: (1) Small Spanish-ruled enclaves on the north coast of Morocco. Ten percent of the population is Muslim. It is not known if there is any Bible believing witness in this potentially strategic bridgehead for the Gospel in North Africa.

Canary Islands — Population: 1,200,000. A barren group of islands off the N.W. coast of Africa that form two provinces of Spain. Point for prayer: (1) There are only about 500 scattered Protestants and several small church fellowships. Pray for the many lonely believers on islands without an established Bible believing group, and for efforts to teach them through visitation and cassettes. Pray for a greater concern among the believers to reach out in evangelism. Pray for missionary reinforcements.

12. SING PRAISES TO OUR LORD.

My Jesus, I love Thee, I know Thou art mine;
For Thee all the follies of sin I resign;
My gracious Redeemer, my Saviour art Thou;
If ever I loved Thee, my Jesus 'tis now.

Jesus, Jesus, Name that I love,
Blest Name of my Saviour,
Who came from above.

WEEK NINE — SATURDAY

1. PRAISE GOD FOR WHO HE IS.

Goodness. There could never be enough said about this quality of yourself! Your goodness should lead all mankind to repentance, i.e., the daily, hourly, provision for our life; the balance in the creation about us; the delay in your wrath — all should suggest to us that Someone, even yourself, is standing behind this scene with an infinite interest of deep love. Of course, if man does not read your word, such an understanding will never be his.

Express yourself in adoration for this quality of God.
Speak it audibly or write out your praise in your own devotional journal.

2. PRAISE GOD FOR WHAT HE MEANS TO ME.

Good to me! Praise your name, it is not difficult to express this praise to you! It would seem my life has been one long example of your goodness. You gave me good parents — such a dear mother and father; you were good to me in my early childhood — food, shelter and friends; and then led me to salvation and service. Ever since that day in 1936 my feet have been directed in pleasant paths. What a tremendous blessing you gave me in my dear wife! Your daily, continual goodness move me to praise and wonder.

How do you personally relate to the goodness of God, and God who is goodness?
Speak it out or write it out. It is *so important* that you establish *your own* devotional journal.

3. CONFESSION OF SIN

Dear God, it is not difficult to confess my sins when they are framed by your goodness! Black shows up clearest on white. I am at a loss to know how best to word my prayer — shall I itemize the errors within error? Shall I admit I have not overcome what I have often confessed before? Shall I lose heart and hide my sins? None of these will clear my record! Dear God, all of them together are no answer. I just do *want* to be obedient, humble, forgiving, kind — forgive me, cleanse me!

What personal sins do you want to confess? We *must* speak them to remove them.
Do it! *Now.* There is no one else you have sinned against more than God. Tell him so!

4. SING A PRAYER TO GOD.

What a Friend we have in Jesus,
All our sins and griefs to bear!
What a privilege to carry
Ev'rything to God in prayer!

O what peace we often forfeit,
O what needless pain we bear,
All because we do not carry
Ev'rything to God in prayer!

Open your hymn book and sing the rest of the verses — or even sing another prayer song.

5. READ HIS WORD TO HIM!

His Word

[10]He became hungry and wanted something to eat, and while the meal was being prepared, he fell into a trance. [11]He saw heaven opened and something like a large sheet being let down to earth by its four corners. [12]It contained all kinds of four-footed animals, as well as reptiles of the earth and birds of the air. [13]Then a voice told him, "Get up, Peter. Kill and eat."

[14]"Surely not, Lord!" Peter replied. "I have never eaten anything impure or unclean."

[15]The voice spoke to him a second time, "Do not call anything impure that God has made clean."

[16]This happened three times, and immediately the sheet was taken back to heaven.   —*Acts 10:10-16, NIV*

Read His Word to Him.

What a wonder and amazement is this! My appreciation and praise is my response to what you are saying here not only to Peter, but to me and to all men. The circumstances you chose for revealing this information is by itself an amazement. You gave Peter a revelation, a vision, a message, at noon, in the broad daylight, by himself, on the second story or roof of a house, while he was hungry and his interest was on food. Animals on the sheet are also a wonder. The detailed identification and variety is of real interest. Your voice, your command! — a positive and a negative word — wonderful!

Please express your response to this beautiful text. Put your expression in your own prayer diary.

6. READ HIS WORD FOR YOURSELF.

What a jarring word! Take unto yourself others who do not understand you or appreciate you — indeed whom you do not understand or appreciate. What a shock to find out I have been calling any thing unclean or impure you have cleansed or consider clean! The artificial, provincial barriers I have built up, break them down, remove them. Oh, that I might think as deeply as Peter did that day!

It is so important that you pause in his presence
and either audibly or in written form tell him all his word means to you.

7. READ HIS WORD IN THANKSGIVING.

Thank you, *so* much for: (1) You reveal yourself in the ordinary pursuits of life, like eating. (2) That Peter was open to a vision from you — help me to be open to hear your voice in the circumstances of today. (3) That I can make comparisons in the physical world with the Spiritual world and learn much. (4) For the thoroughness of your words — all these categories: animals, birds and snakes are represented. (5) For Peter's knowledge of your word — even if it was misunderstood — no answer to you with desire to know is lost. (6) There is a moral as well as physical cleanness. (7) You repeat yourself for all of us who are dull of hearing.

Give yourself to your own expression of gratitude — write it or speak it!

8. READ HIS WORD IN MEDITATION.

GOD HAS MADE CLEAN! What a happy thought, what a beautiful fact, what a glorious acceptance! God has made me clean, pure, whole, without spot or wrinkle or any such thing. I refer to imputed pureness. I am clean in our Lord, or I am not clean at all in your sight. I might be clean by men's estimates, but my own conscience is a better judge. When you say clean, pure, whole, bless your name I believe it, I accept it, I claim it, I need it, I want it. Amen! and Amen!

Pause — wait — think — then express yourself in thoughtful praise or thanks.

9. READ HIS WORD FOR PETITIONS.

There is much for which we can ask our Lord from this text: Dear Lord, there are several parallels between eating physically and eating spiritually. I need help here: (1) Give me a consuming appetite for the bread from heaven. (2) Teach me regular habits in spiritual nourishment. (3) May I be as thoughtful with your menu as I am with dinner. (4) Help me to vary my diet of your word. (5) Give me friends with whom I can share this food. (6) I want to eat only your living bread — not any of Satan's substitute. (7) Let me chew adequately lest I suffer indigestion.

Please, please remember these are prayers — speak them — reword them!

10. READ HIS WORD AND WAIT — LISTEN — GOD SPEAKS!

As you spoke to Peter from heaven so I listen to your word: (1) "Break out of your apathy — eat and live." (2) "There is indeed a word from heaven — hear it." (3) "Never doubt my word — even when it contradicts your desires."

11. INTERCESSION FOR THE LOST WORLD

Gibraltar — Population: 27,000. Points for prayer: (1) *The Protestant witness.* There are three churches for the English speaking people — Methodist, Presbyterian and Church of England, and two for the Spanish speaking — Pentecostal and Evangelical. The last two maintain a lively witness to the Gibraltans. (2) *The witness to the Muslim Moroccans.* There are about 7,000 migrant laborers from Morocco. Pray that some of these may be won for the Lord. There is now a small group of Arab believers who meet regularly. (3) *Christian Literature Crusade has a small bookshop* with several workers who seek to witness to both Arabs and Gibraltans. (4) *Pray about the political future of Gibraltar* — that the best for the Gospel may be done.

12. SING PRAISES TO OUR LORD.

So precious is Jesus, my Savior, my King,
His praise all the day long with rapture I sing;
To Him in my weakness for strength I can cling,
For He is so precious to me.
For He is so precious to me, . . .

For He is so precious to me; . . .
'Tis Heaven below
My Redeemer to know,
For He is so precious to me.

WEEK TEN — SUNDAY

1. PRAISE GOD FOR WHO HE IS.

Preacher-maker. Praise your name! It is not my job to make preachers. I am glad to cooperate in any way I can. I am glad to offer myself. But over the centuries you have produced the preachers. I am glad to acknowledge your infinite ability in this crucial area of life. Dear God, we need nothing more and at the same time nothing less than preachers for this world. There are thirty young men in my two classes who want to learn how to preach. I know you will do it or it will not be done. I'm so glad you are not through with making me a preacher.

Express yourself in adoration for this quality of God.
Speak it audibly or write out your praise in your own devotional journal.

2. PRAISE GOD FOR WHAT HE MEANS TO ME.

Making preachers—the complicated procedure is only done by you. I want to lift my heart in wonder for all that is done. Some marvelous work of grace and power has found fulfillment here. Praise your name for whatever has been done with me! Dear God, how deeply I need help in this area—preachers have such a large ego problem—they are constantly in the light of the public and under the criticism of those they try to teach and reach. Oh, help every young man who asks you to make him a fisher of men!

How do you personally relate to the preacher-making of God, and God who is a preacher-maker?
Speak it out or write it out. It is *so important* that you establish *your own* devotional journal.

3. CONFESSION OF SIN

Dear Lord, for each and every sin, I confess them—emotion is totally minus—just the fact that I sin and identify it—label it with your label. I feel defeated and overcome—I need *your* strength, but also your joy! I claim your presence and help! I want, need and enter into your forgiveness—and even now contemplate the robe of your righteousness which covers and envelopes me! Praise your name and grace.

What personal sins do you want to confess? We *must* speak them to remove them.
Do it! *Now.* There is no one you have sinned against more than God. Tell him so!

4. SING A PRAYER TO GOD.

Jesus, Lover of my soul,
Let me to Thy bosom fly,
While the nearer waters roll,
While the tempest still is high;

Hide me, O my Savior, hide,
Till the storm of life is past;
Safe into the haven guide,
O receive my soul at last.

Open your hymn book and sing the rest of the verses—or even sing another prayer song.

5. READ HIS WORD TO HIM!

His Word

[17]While Peter was wondering about the meaning of the vision, the men sent by Cornelius found out where Simon's house was and stopped at the gate. [18]They called out, asking if Simon who was known as Peter was staying there.

[19]While Peter was still thinking about the vision, the Spirit said to him, "Simon, three men are looking for you. [20]So get up and go downstairs. Do not hesitate to go with them, for I have sent them."

[21]Peter went down and said to the men, "I'm the one you're looking for. Why have you come?"

[22]The men replied, "We have come from Cornelius the centurion. He is a righteous and God-fearing man, who is respected by all the Jewish people. A holy angel told him to have you come to his house so that he could hear what you have to say." [23]Then Peter invited the men into the house to be his guests.

The next day Peter started out with them, and some of the brothers from Joppa went along.   — *Acts 10:17-23, NIV*

Read His Word to Him.

Gladly, gladly do I read to you what you have written to me in deepest appreciation for every word. Peter, like me and millions of others, "was wondering about the meaning . . ." of your communication to him. Oh, how we all wonder, and misunderstand, and ignore and reject your word—but your answer is never far behind—while we are still thinking about it you are sending the meaning to us. I believe we have missed, overlooked or rejected your messengers full many a time. It has not been your lack of interest that has left me confused, but my insensitivity and preoccupation with other things.

Please express your response to this beautiful text. Put your expression in your own prayer diary.

6. READ HIS WORD FOR YOURSELF.

Read this word to myself—in praise, adoration, thanksgiving, petition—I eagerly approach what you are saying to me. Are you sending men to speak to me concerning your will for my life? Indeed you are! In every message from your word I hear you speaking to me, i.e., if I have ears to hear. Dear God, may I today be ready to welcome your messengers. "I am the one you are looking for," so said Peter and so say I! Dear Lord, I believe you will be looking for someone to stand in the gap for you in so many areas. I want to be that man. I know I must first invite you to be my house-guest before I can be used of you. Come in and sup with me, dear Savior!

It is so important that you pause in his presence
and either audibly or in written form tell him all his word means to you.

7. READ HIS WORD IN THANKSGIVING.

This always seems to be the most spontaneous time of prayer. Thanksgiving seems to be the most obvious natural expression of our relationship with you. Thank you for: (1) The quality of persistence in fulfilling your word. If Peter was not found, your work could not be done. (2) The Holy Spirit is an intelligent Being who speaks. He speaks in easily understood words, about very mundane, but important matters. (3) For men today like Cornelius—dear God, help me to be as willing as Peter to help them. (4) For the three unnamed men—I'll find out their names and ask them all about the trip, i.e., when I see them in your presence. (5) For the beautiful sea beside which Peter stayed for a few days. (6) That there are "holy" angels—some have chosen not to be. Thank you for all who chose to be holy—may I do likewise. (7) That only poor, weak, ignorant, sinful man can tell anyone what to do to be saved. Not even *holy* angels can do that.

Give yourself to your own expression of gratitude—write it or speak it!

8. READ HIS WORD IN MEDITATION.

Let's gather around your word and see what the Lord is saying to us: (1) I too can be: a) *devout*—an attitude of the heart—I *chose* to be humble, singleminded, meek, willing; b) *God-fearing*—it is a fool who doesn't fear God. My Lord told me to fear you not abjectly, but in reality and truth; c) *gave generously*—Oh, how good it is to testify that we are so blessed when we give generously to those who have a need. The percentage of giving surprises me and humbles me! d) *Prayed to you regularly*—this I want and will *do*! and I so, so enjoy it! Some days it is not any easier for me than it was for the Italian army captain. (2) Just who was the heavenly visitor? No name is given—perhaps Gabriel or Michael—but not named so we could relate him to the angels encamped around our lives.

Pause—wait—think—then express yourself in thoughtful praise or thanks.

9. READ HIS WORD AND WAIT—LISTEN—GOD SPEAKS!

It is so good to ask directly from your word: (1) Give me goals from yourself in reaching the lost in my community. (2) I want to know the proper combination of human and divine in reaching the lost. (3) Are there men even today who are seeking me to hear what to do to be saved? (4) Give me insight in using my home as a place to introduce men and women to you. (5) Who today are like the three men from Cornelius? (6) Open my mind to the tremendous power of words. (7) I am not as concerned as I should be with the righteous, God-fearing, but lost men—help me!

Right here add your personal requests—and his answers.

10. READ HIS WORD AND WAIT—LISTEN—GOD SPEAKS!

Open my inner ears to hear what the Spirit is saying through his word: (1) "My word will always give meaning to your visions." (2) "When I send, do not hesitate." (3) "Welcome all I send to you."

11. INTERCESSION FOR THE LOST WORLD

Sweden — Population: 8,200,000. Growth 0.4%.
Point for prayer: (1) *National revival is Sweden's greatest need.* Great revivals have swept over the land in past years. Yet now the country is well known for its welfare state, wealth, materialism, very permissive society, suicides, immorality and drunkenness (42% increase in the latter in 10 years). Yet there are signs of a new interest in spiritual things among young people during the last 7 years.

12. SING PRAISES TO OUR LORD.

All glory, laud and honor
To Thee, Redeemer, King,
To Whom the lips of children
Made sweet hosannas ring!

The people of the Hebrews
With palms before Thee went;
Our praise and prayer and anthems
Before Thee we present.

WEEK TEN — MONDAY

1. PRAISE GOD FOR WHO HE IS.

City-builder. You are indeed the builder of the city-foursquare—the One who builds the city for which Abraham looked. What a good thought: all the excitement and interest of a city, minus all the lust of the flesh, eyes and pride of life. How intrinsically beautiful the city would be if you were the architect and builder. The abiding places or apartments would be something to behold! I am not thinking of wealth or physical luxury in the same sense as we have it today. A million times better.

Express yourself in adoration for this quality of God.
Speak it audibly or write out your praise in your own devotional journal.

2. PRAISE GOD FOR WHAT HE MEANS TO ME.

City-builder for me. You are just as concerned about all men as you are any one man—but to build a city just to please me, or anyone, I really do not have a large consuming interest in a city. I am quite interested in things of beauty—in form, color and usefulness—the combination of all the beauty and color you have placed in a new world would be a wonder to behold. I praise you for the interest you have in providing for those who deserve nothing.

How do you personally relate to the city-building of God, and God who is city-builder?
Speak it out or write it out. It is *so important* that you establish *your own* devotional journal.

3. CONFESSION OF SIN

It is monotonous to confess the same sin every day, not because I do not want to repent, I do!—but because I see such little improvement. I will continue to name, by label, my sins and sincerely repent of them, but I want to open your word and examine my heart in the light of the sins you have named: 1. *Lying:* How easy, so incredibly easy, it is to misrepresent. I believe pride is behind most of my lies. The fear of man is also a very real cause. I want to work on the reason, the source and hopefully I can change the result. Dear God, forgive!

What personal sins do you want to confess? We *must* speak them to remove them.
Do it! *Now.* There is no one else you have sinned against more than God. Tell him so!

4. SING A PRAYER TO GOD.

I am Thine, O Lord, I have heard Thy voice,
And it told Thy love to me;
But I long to rise in the arms of faith,
And be closer drawn to Thee.

Draw me nearer, nearer, blessed Lord,
To the cross where Thou hast died;
Draw me nearer, nearer, nearer, blessed Lord,
To Thy precious bleeding side.

Open your hymn book and sing the rest of the verses—or even sing another prayer song.

5. READ HIS WORD TO HIM!

His Word

[23]Then Peter invited the men into the house to be his guests.

The next day Peter started out with them, and some of the brothers from Joppa went along. [24]The following day he arrived in Caesarea. Cornelius was expecting them and had called together his relatives and close friends. [25]As Peter entered the house, Cornelius met him and fell at his feet in reverence. [26]But Peter made him get up. "Stand up," he said, "I am only a man myself."

[27]Talking with him, Peter went inside and found a large gathering of people. [28]He said to them: "You are well aware that it is against our law for a Jew to associate with a Gentile or visit him. But God has shown me that I should not call any man impure or unclean. [29]So when I was sent for, I came without raising any objection. May I ask why you sent for me?"

[30]Cornelius answered: "Four days ago I was in my house praying at this hour, at three in the afternoon. Suddenly a man in shining clothes stood before me [31]and said, 'Cornelius, God has heard your prayer and remembered your gifts to the poor. [32]Send to Joppa for Simon who is called Peter. He is a guest in the home of Simon the tanner, who lives by the sea.' [33]So I sent for you immediately, and it was good of you to come. Now we are all here in the presence of God to listen to everything the Lord has commanded you to tell us."
—Acts 10:23-33, NIV

WEEK TEN — MONDAY

Read His Word to Him.

What an interesting conversation must have passed between Peter and the three from Caesarea along with the six Jewish Christians from Joppa. The details of the vision of Peter and Cornelius must have been repeated several times. I know you could repeat every word spoken by all ten men. It was a somewhat leisurely walk, judging the distance and the time. Just who were the relatives and friends of Cornelius? I should like to meet them—every one—when there is no time and we have supernatural powers of communication, I shall indeed do it! What a good man is this first Gentile convert! What a humble man is Peter!

Please express your response to this beautiful text. Put your expression in your own prayer diary.

6. READ HIS WORD FOR YOURSELF.

Dear Lord, there is so much for me to learn and accept from these verses: (1) Association with others—a joint sharing—I have such a tendency to be by myself. (2) To respect other people, to honor them, to prefer them to myself. (3) When God speaks through a man and it is evident, people *will* come out to hear and see. (4) I should not, in any sense, call any man impure or unclean—i.e., fail to associate with and share the good news with them. (5) The first sermon to Jews was at a prayer time—9 a.m. —the first sermon to Gentiles was at a prayer time—3 p.m. Doesn't this say something to me about prayer time?

Pause in his presence and either audibly or in written form tell him all his word means to you.

7. READ HIS WORD IN THANKSGIVING.

Thank you for: (1) For the well established word, i.e., that there were not two or three but *six* Jewish Christians to confirm what was done and said—so is all of your word so very clearly, openly established! (2) That Peter refused to be worshipped—for whatever reason—"only a man" says so well what all of us are. (3) That the law of exclusiveness has been abrogated. (4) That God is in the "show and tell" business for us children. (5) That God has a way of removing man's objections. (6) That even a busy army captain can keep the hours of prayer. (7) That we can be in your presence at anytime, anywhere, but most especially for the preaching of the word!

Give yourself to your own expression of gratitude—write it or speak it!

8. READ HIS WORD IN MEDITATION.

"It was good of you to come." (A) It was good of God to come in the Person of his Son—to give himself for us who lived in darkness. (B) It was good of the angels to come to certain poor shepherds and brighten up their night with "joy to the world." (C) It was good of the Holy Spirit to come and clothe himself with the minds of the apostles and tell the good news to the nations, beginning at Jerusalem. (D) It was good of God to come in a vision to Peter on Simon's housetop. (E) It was good of Peter to come to the "unclean" service man in Caesarea.

Pause—wait—think—then express yourself in thoughtful praise or thanks.

9. READ HIS WORD FOR PETITIONS.

As you spoke to Peter, so speak to me as to my needed requests: (1) All of this record is so believable—help me to remember the truths I learn. (2) Dear Lord, help me in my sometimes inordinate admiration of men. (3) Break down the barriers I have built between myself and other men. (4) Forgive me for calling men stupid or ignorant. May I share your value system. (5) Give me courage and direction that one day I might be given the "shining clothes" of heaven. (6) Am I willing to make unexpected moves?—i.e., if you direct them, I want to be. (7) Give me a deep appreciation for other servants of yourself.

Please, please remember these are prayers—speak them—reword them!

10. READ HIS WORD AND WAIT—LISTEN—GOD SPEAKS!

You are indeed speaking to me from these verses: (1) "Accept all I say—it is established by many witnesses." (2) "In no way worship any man." (3) "Respect all those who speak for me."

11. INTERCESSION FOR THE LOST WORLD

Sweden — Point for prayer: (1) *The new government needs prayer*, for the damage of years of permissive legislation and erosion of respect for the things of God by those in high authority must be rectified.

12. SING PRAISES TO OUR LORD.

Wounded for me, wounded for me,
There on the cross He was wounded for me;
Gone my transgressions, and now I am free,
All because Jesus was wounded for me.

WEEK TEN — TUESDAY

1. PRAISE GOD FOR WHO HE IS.

Life-planner. Dear Lord, you are surely in this business if any at all. I know all things are planned by you. Every life is the object of your interest. Praise your name! You do have a plan for every life. Whether your plan is accepted or not is man's choice, but is not because of any lack of interest on your part. How wondrously good it is to know our lives are in your heart. Dear Lord, I am glad you have an interest in my life.

Express yourself in adoration for this quality of God.
Speak it audibly or write out your praise in your own devotional journal.

2. PRAISE GOD FOR WHAT HE MEANS TO ME.

Please work on my life for today—just for today—I know if this is my prayer each day that my whole life will have been planned of you. I do want to submit my stubborn will to your lovingness, to you kindness, to your cheerfulness, to your willingness. However grandiose my ideas of your plan for my life might be, if I do not allow you to plan my character, there is no real fulfillment of any plan—i.e., you are more interested in me than what I do or fail to do.

How do you personally relate to the life-planning of God, and God who is life-planner?
Speak it out or write it out. It is *so important* that you establish *your own* devotional journal.

3. CONFESSION OF SIN

Dear Lord, I freely confess stealing time that should have been given to the saving of the lost, to attempting to edify or educate those who do not want to be edified or educated—or at least so it would seem. I have stolen the devotion that should have been yours and squandered it on myself. Dear Lord, forgive. I have stolen money from the poor and starving and have given it to myself and for my "things." Dear Lord, forgive.

What personal sins do you want to confess? We *must* speak them to remove them.
Do it! *Now.* There is no one else you have sinned against more than God. Tell him so!

4. SING A PRAYER TO GOD.

He leadeth me, O blessed tho't!
O words with heav'nly comfort fraught-
Whate'er I do, where'er I be,
Still 'tis God's hand that leadeth me.

He leadeth me, He leadeth me!
By His own hand He leadeth me!
His faithful foll'wer I would be,
For by His hand He leadeth me.

Open your hymn book and sing the rest of the verses—or even sing another prayer song.

5. READ HIS WORD TO HIM!

His Word

[34]Then Peter began to speak: "I now realize how true it is that God does not show favoritism [35]but accepts men from every nation who fear him and do what is right. [36]This is the message God sent to the people of Israel, telling the good news of peace through Jesus Christ, who is Lord of all. [37]You know what has happened throughout Judea, beginning in Galilee after the baptism that John preached—[38]how God anointed Jesus of Nazareth with the Holy Spirit and power, and how he went around doing good and healing all who were under the power of the devil, because God was with him. [39]"We are witnesses of everything he did in the country of the Jews and in Jerusalem. They killed him by hanging him on a tree, [40]but God raised him from the dead on the third day and caused him to be seen. [41]He was not seen by all the people, but by witnesses whom God had already chosen—by us who ate and drank with him after he rose from the dead. [42]He commanded us to preach to the people and to testify that he is the one whom God appointed as judge of the living and the dead. [43]All the prophets testify about him that everyone who believes in him receives forgiveness of sins through his name."
— *Acts 10:34-43, NIV*

Read His Word to Him.

How I do want to agree with and confirm in my own heart every word you have given me through Peter. I will list the qualities of yourself I see here in this text and embrace them to my heart: (1) No favoritism. (2) Accepts men from every nation who fear you. (3) Accepts those who do what is right, i.e., accept your dear Son. (4) You sent good news of peace (What good news *peace* is!). (5) That *Jesus is Lord of all*! (6) You anointed Jesus with the Holy Spirit and power. (7) Your dear Son went around doing good. He went around healing all who were under the power of the devil. (8) He went around doing all of this because you were with him. Oh, so much more—for all the above I fall at your feet in wonder and praise!

Please express yourself to this beautiful text. Put your expression in your own prayer diary.

6. READ HIS WORD FOR YOURSELF.

To continue my praise: (9) You provided eyewitnesses and gave them the Holy Spirit to enable them to speak with total accuracy and tell us of all that was done to your dear Son in his suffering and death. (10) You raised him from the dead (by the Holy Spirit) on a specific day— the third day. (11) You *caused him* to be seen, i.e., his appearances were set in such circumstances as to be undeniable—not just by chance but by plan; to witnesses who could well establish what they had seen, chosen by you for this very task. Wonderful. Praise your name!

It is so important that you pause in his presence
and either audibly or in written form tell him all his word means to you.

7. READ HIS WORD IN THANKSGIVING.

Indeed I shall! Thank you: (1) For those "who ate and drank with my blessed Lord after he rose from the dead." I want to savor every swallow and every bite, and talk to everyone. (Oh God, give me the questions to ask them.) (2) That you have "commanded us to preach"—it is not just a good idea—it is an imperial edict! (3) You have also commanded us (through the example of the apostles) to give our personal testimony of all you have done for us!

(4) You are the judge of the living—every living person upon the face of this earth, and all who have lived, or will live upon this little speck called "earth." (5) Jeremiah, Isaiah, Daniel, Micah and all the prophets who have told us so much about our Lord. (6) Oh, what a word! "EVERYONE"! Whosoever and everyone means *me*! receives forgiveness of sins. (7) That I can believe—it is all because of what is included in *his name*!

Give yourself to your own expression of gratitude—write it or speak it!

8. READ HIS WORD IN MEDITATION.

This is such a blessed passage; I am overwhelmed. Upon what shall we meditate? Here it is! *"We are witnesses of everything he did in the country of the Jews and in Jerusalem."* Please, please turn to the four gospels and absorb every word of those eyewitnesses of his majesty! The description of Israel as "the country of the Jews" is most intriguing. What did he do there? He lived and worked for 30 years in a little town called Nazareth. When he was tired from much work he did not grouse or com-plain. When he saw others with much more than he had he remembered the place where all has eternal value. When he saw the terrible inequities of life He knew there will be a day when all shall find equity. He went to a wedding feast and turned the water—the necessary, but tasteless water, the routine of life—into the refreshing red fruit of the vine. This he was to do for all of life for all men, for all time.

Pause—wait—think—then express yourself in thoughtful praise or thanks.

9. READ HIS WORD FOR PETITIONS.

This is such a blessed section of scripture that I rejoice in the privilege of considering petitions from the text: (1) Help me to accept every one God accepts. (2) Give me the peace the great prince has purchased for me. (3) How I do want Jesus to be Lord of all in my life. (4) Just what "good" did Jesus do? Help me to do the same. (5) Deliver me day by day from the power of the evil one. (6) What confidence I can have in the risen Lord. How can I share this confidence? (7) Oh, dear Lord, that your son will judge the living and the dead is indeed an awesome thought! What can I do to prepare men for this event?

Right here add your personal requests—and his answers.

10. READ HIS WORD AND WAIT—LISTEN—GOD SPEAKS!

You spoke so eloquently through your son—through him speak to me: (1) "I show no favoritism—do you?" (2) "My good news contains peace." (3) "There will be a judgment for all men."

11. INTERCESSION FOR THE LOST WORLD

Sweden — Points for prayer: (1) *Needy areas* — past revivals were often very localized, and some areas have many believers, yet others virtually none. Many of the newer urban areas have no churches, and their people have never been effectively evangelized. (2) *Young people* *have been very adversely affected* by the permissive society, and a recent survey indicates that 41% do not believe there is a God. Pray that there may be an effective outreach to them.

12. SING PRAISES TO OUR LORD.

Jesus shall reign where'er the sun
Does his successive journeys run;

His kingdom spread from shore to shore,
Till moon shall wax and wane no more.

WEEK TEN — WEDNESDAY

1. PRAISE GOD FOR WHO HE IS.

Harvester. Indeed you are! All the harvest and reports of all us preachers is but a reflection of (and somtimes on) your work. You *are* "the Lord of the harvest." The physical harvest all about us testifies to your power, to your provision, to your personal interest in man! I love you for all you are but most of all for every precious person you have brought to yourself through what feeble efforts I have given. How wonderful, beyond adjectives, to be a workman together with you! I shall never, never be able to say an adequate "thank you."

Express yourself in adoration for this quality of God.
Speak it audibly or write out your praise in your own devotional journal.

2. PRAISE GOD FOR WHAT HE MEANS TO ME.

Harvester for me. In my life if there is to be a harvest in character, or in any project, it will be because I have cooperated in "the law of the harvest." Plant—yes, yes, I must plant the seed of the word of God, and he that soweth bountifully shall reap bountifully. I want to plant the seed of your word in *millions* of hearts. Water the seed—I want to have whatever part I can in this, but I also want to be an encourager for others to do this. Cultivate—dear God, I am somewhat unwillingly engaged in this, but please forgive. You will give the increase and we shall reap if we do not lose heart.

How do you personally relate to the harvesting of God, and God who is harvester?
Speak it out or write it out. It is *so important* that you establish *your own* devotional journal.

3. CONFESSION OF SIN

Gossip—a hard word to say because we know to some extent how guilty we are (I am). Why repeat an evil report? Why tell of someone's failure? Why embellish a report of success? Why must we tell what we hear of someone else? Dear God, help me to turn gossip into praise and thanksgiving and if the report is not good, help me to not repeat it. You did say, you do *now* say, "speak not evil one of another." I believe; forgive me for not believing more totally. Pride and prejudice—what odious sins. Forgive me!

What personal sins do you want to confess? We *must* speak them to remove them.
Do it! *Now.* There is no one else you have sinned against more than God. Tell him so!

4. SING A PRAYER TO GOD.

I am resolved no longer to linger,
Charmed by the world's delight;
Things that are higher, things that are nobler,
These have allured my sight.

I will hasten to Him,
Hasten so glad and free;
Jesus, Greatest, Highest,
I will come to Thee.

Open your hymn book and sing the rest of the verses—or even sing another prayer song.

5. READ HIS WORD TO HIM!

His Word

[44]While Peter was still speaking these words, the Holy Spirit came on all who heard the message. [45]The circumcised believers who had come with Peter were astonished that the gift of the Holy Spirit had been poured out even on the Gentiles. [46]For they heard them speaking in tongues and praising God.

Then Peter said, [47]"Can anyone keep these people from being baptized with water? They have received the Holy Spirit just as we have." [48]So he ordered that they be baptized in the name of Jesus Christ. Then they asked Peter to stay with them for a few days.

The apostles and the brothers throughout Judea heard that the Gentiles also had received the word of God. [2]So when Peter went up to Jerusalem, the circumcised believers criticized him [3]and said, "You went into the house of uncircumcised men and ate with them."

[4]Peter began and explained everything to them precisely as it had happened:
— *Acts 10:44 — 11:4, NIV*

Read His Word to Him.

Indeed, indeed I want to read this word to you. I have such concern that I fully, or more fully understand the supernatural manifestation of the Holy Spirit. Such an unusual thing! What a surprise to all, what a surprise to all of us. Just what are you saying to me? I do want to appreciate *all* you say. The Holy Spirit was "poured out" on the whole household—the "gift of the Holy Spirit" or the "Holy Spirit as a gift." The major emphasis is in that they were Gentiles and as such received the baptism of the Holy Spirit. Talk about instant initiation, here it is! It will take man years to accept what God did in a moment! Praise your beautiful love and acceptance of all men.

Please express your response to this beautiful text. Put your expression in your own prayer diary.

6. READ HIS WORD FOR YOURSELF.

So many questions I have asked for such a long time (40 plus years): (1) Was this just a one-time event for a one-time purpose? It would seem to be, i.e., the Gentiles were being inducted into the family of God by this means. (2) Were there several languages represented in the household? There could have been since Caesarea was an international seaport and on the caravan route. Or there weren't and the supernaturalness of the event is what you want emphasized. (3) Why command them to be baptized "in water"? Was it not for the same purpose our Lord indicated in Mark 16:16 and Peter repeated in Acts 2:38 and in his letter I Peter 3:23? If so, then the Gentiles were lost when they had this supernatural experience and its primary purpose was for the Jews present, and all subsequent Jews.

It is so important that you pause in his presence
and either audibly or in written form tell him all his word means to you.

7. READ HIS WORD IN THANKSGIVING.

How do I raise my heart and voice in gratitude for: (1) You interrupt what you yourself commanded to be done to show you have a dual purpose, (or is it a single purpose?) that could only be accomplished here in this unusual manner. (2) That the Holy Spirit is a gift—if he comes in this manifestation or another, he is always a gift—oh, blessed beautiful gift! (3) That Peter and the six were ready to receive your conclusion and choice. (4) The "name" or authority of the Lord Jesus is behind all actions and words. (5) That good news can spread so rapidly even without present day communication media. (6) At the dinner table is where we can share our faith. (7) That Peter was willing to patiently explain.

Give yourself to your own expression of gratitude—write it or speak it!

8. READ HIS WORD IN MEDITATION.

Everything precisely as it happened! How encouraging it is to know that everything our Lord did to and through Peter was recorded, not only by the honesty and faithfulness of the apostle but under the immediate direction of the Holy Spirit. All these 2,000 years later we yet have the precision account of the salvation of the very first Gentiles. If we are as precise in our commitment to him as was Peter in his record we can become precisely what they were, i.e., Christians. Dear Lord, I do believe you sent your Son to be the anointed Savior of myself and all those who will trust him. A piece of precision machinery would fade into a clumsy anachronism when coupled to the multiplicity of prophecies and plans that mesh in the coming of yourself in the person of Jesus.

Pause—wait—think—then express yourself in thoughtful praise or thanks.

9. READ HIS WORD FOR PETITIONS.

With real zest I relate my requests to the text of Acts 10:44—11:4: (1) May I never, never refuse the gospel to any man. (2) Keep me sensitive enough to be astonished at your work. (3) I want to appreciate more fully than ever the presence of the Holy Spirit in my body. (4) I do want to understand every word about the baptism of these Gentiles with the Holy Spirit. (5) Open my mind as to the purpose of speaking in tongues and praising God. (6) Had Peter changed his mind as to the purpose of water baptism, i.e., since Pentecost? (7) When these Gentiles were baptized in the name of Jesus Christ what did they become? Dear God, I ask these questions in the full assurance you will answer me in the study of your word!

Please, please remember these are prayers—speak them—reword them!

10. READ HIS WORD AND WAIT—LISTEN—GOD SPEAKS!

Speak to me through this text: "To have the Holy Spirit is to have my approval." (2) "Do not be as slow as Peter was in hearing my message for the whole lost world." (3) "Don't be surprised if some of your brothers do not understand."

11. INTERCESSION FOR THE LOST WORLD

Sweden — Points for prayer: (1) *Bible Schools* are not common in Scandinavia and much more must be done to provide good Bible teaching for believers. (2) *Missionary outreach* has been exceptional. There are now about 1,700 Swedish missionaries serving all over the world. Pray for a quickening of this vision, for Sweden's unusual stand in world politics makes her strategic for bringing help to the believers in Communist lands and also evangelizing many other areas of the world closed to most western missionaries. (3) *Pray for the evangelization of migrant laborers* — especially for the Greeks and Yugoslavs — a little is now being done to reach them.

12. SING PRAISES TO OUR LORD.

Amazing grace! how sweet the sound,
That saved a wretch like me!

I once was lost, but now am found,
Was blind, but now I see.

WEEK TEN — THURSDAY

1. PRAISE GOD FOR WHO HE IS.

Lord. How glad I am to claim your lordship in my life, but you are Lord if I claim you or if I do not claim you. You are Lord of all the world and ten billion worlds (physical planets) like ours. What a total wonder to know you are all you are independently of my response or anyone else's response. Dear, dear God, to know you is peace and joy and hope. To love you is the fulfillment of all that is right and true. To own your Lordship is only to acknowledge what is obvious. But, oh, how much there is in that little word "Lord." Ruler, despot, king, and 10 million more qualities.

Express yourself in adoration for this quality of God.
Speak it audibly or write out your praise in your own devotional journal.

2. PRAISE GOD FOR WHAT HE MEANS TO ME.

Lord in *my* life. I want you to take control in the innermost area of my life. I have *such* a problem yielding my inner-self to you. I want you to dominate, but I find a passivity about yourself, i.e., you cannot and will not violate your decision to leave me totally free to choose, to invite and initiate the action. Only when I truly think your thoughts will your thoughts be mine, and I must think them (those found in your word) in such a manner that I love them. I am eager to *do* them, to will to *do* what you have šaid. When (and only when) I act upon what you have said will your Lordship become a reality to me.

How do you personally relate to the lordship of God, and God who is Lord?
Speak it out or write it out. It is *so important* that you establish *your own* devotional journal.

3. CONFESSION OF SIN

"Lewd thoughts" is a sin mentioned in your word. I am not either emphasizing my sin here or rationalizing so as to deny it. I also know the evil one is present even now and is seeking to defeat my love and devotion to you. I live in the middle of an environment that promotes lewd thoughts. Illicit sex has become a way of life with millions of people. I want to treat the cause not the effect. "To the pure all things are pure." Dear God, I am a sinner and I sin in this area. Forgive me, cleanse me, wash me! Praise your holy self!

What personal sins do you want to confess? We *must* speak them to remove them.
Do it! *Now.* There is no one else you have sinned against more than God. Tell him so!

4. SING A PRAYER TO GOD.

The great Physician now is near,
The sympathizing Jesus;
He speaks the drooping heart to cheer,
Oh, hear the voice of Jesus.

Sweetest note in seraph song,
Sweetest name on mortal tongue;
Sweetest carol ever sung,
Jesus, blessed Jesus.

Open your hymn book and sing the rest of the verses — or even sing another prayer song.

5. READ HIS WORD TO HIM!

His Word

[5]"I was in the city of Joppa praying, and in a trance I saw a vision. I saw something like a large sheet being let down from heaven by its four corners, and it came down to where I was. [6]I looked into it and saw four-footed animals of the earth, wild beasts, reptiles, and birds of the air. [7]Then I heard a voice telling me, 'Get up, Peter. Kill and eat.'

[8]"I replied, 'Surely not, Lord! Nothing impure or unclean has ever entered my mouth.'

[9]"The voice spoke from heaven a second time, 'Do not call anything impure that God has made clean.'[10]This happened three times, and then it was all pulled up to heaven again.

[11]"Right then three men who had been sent to me from Caesarea stopped at the house where I was staying. [12]The Spirit told me to have no hesitation about going with them. These six brothers also went with me, and we entered the man's house. [13]He told us how he had seen an angel appear in his house to say, 'Send to Joppa for Simon who is called Peter. [14]He will bring you a message through which you and all your household will be saved.'

[15]"As I began to speak, the Holy Spirit came on them as he had come on us at the beginning. [16]Then I remembered what the Lord had said, 'John baptized with water, but you will be baptized with the Holy Spirit.' [17]So if God gave them the same gift as he gave us, who believed in the Lord Jesus Christ, who was I to think that I could oppose God!"

[18]When they heard this, they had no further objections and praised God, saying, "So then, God has even granted the Gentiles repentance unto life." — *Acts 11:5-18, NIV*

Read His Word to Him.

How I appreciate the care in repeating in clear terms all you did for Peter. You came down to where Peter was and in a form or manner he could—and could not understand—and so you have from that day to this. More than I'll ever say adequately I want to say "thank you" for appearing to me in so very many ways and times. Many I could not understand and many I rejected "out of hand." Later you rebuked me, sometimes bluntly and sometimes gently, but I heard your voice and know your meaning.

Please express your response to this beautiful text. Put your expression in your own prayer diary.

6. READ HIS WORD FOR YOURSELF.

I can surely take the place of some of the ones who criticized Peter. Dear Lord, I am too critical of too many people and things. I want to hear with open ears. I want you to open my eyes to see all you want me and others to see. Peter was most careful in his recounting. He applied the promise our Lord made to himself and the other apostles (Acts 1:2-5) to the household of Cornelius. Peter said the household was baptized in the Holy Spirit. This fact convinced those Jews the Gentiles were to be granted "repentance unto life." The whole household was "saved" through the message Peter gave them and their response to it (11:15) not through the baptism in the Holy Spirit.

Pause in his presence and either audibly or in written form tell him all his word means to you.

7. READ HIS WORD IN THANKSGIVING.

Yes, yes, let me hasten to do so. Thank you for: (1) The open, spontaneous acceptance of the Lordship of the One speaking to Peter. (2) Peter's immediate application of what you said to the circumstance—he gave your answer to this question of morality. (3) That there is progression in revelation. (4) That you repeat what you want several times—you don't have to—out of your mercy you do. (5) You synchronize your actions so we can get the whole lesson. (6) That Peter identifies Pentecost as "the beginning" —what a beginning! (7) That the apostles received because they believed and so is the equasion of reception from that day till now.

Give yourself to your own expression of gratitude—write it or speak it!

8. READ HIS WORD IN MEDITATION.

Six Jewish Christians went as witnesses. How I want to add my name and presence to theirs. Cornelius was expecting Peter, and in a most expectant, eager manner he had made preparations—all his relatives and close friends were in his house waiting. The deepest respect was expressed to Peter in falling at his feet. It was out of politeness and thoughtfulness that Peter responded as he did. God told Peter three times each time he requested information. The careful time reference of the army captain was additional confirmation to the hesitant Jewish apostle.

Pause—wait—think—then express yourself in thoughtful praise or thanks.

9. READ HIS WORD FOR PETITIONS.

Shall I ever lose my eagerness to absorb every word you have said? I pray I shall not. (1) Give me the careful patience in repeating what should have been understood the first time. (2) Remind me all over again that you love everyone! (3) Move me to see that evaluations must be made in the light of your word. (4) If you had to say things three times before they were heard I too must do the same. (5) Keep me aware of your timing. (6) Give me six brothers to help me in my witness for you. (7) Impress upon me deeply that men are saved by the message I bring.

Right here add your personal requests—and his answers.

10. READ HIS WORD AND WAIT—LISTEN—GOD SPEAKS!

I hear you Lord! (1) "I am counting on you to tell men for me about my Son." (2) "The Holy Spirit is speaking to you today through his word—hear him!" (3) "The baptism of the Holy Spirit has never been for salvation at anytime with anyone."

11. INTERCESSION FOR THE LOST WORLD

Switzerland — Population: 6,333,000.
Point for prayer: (1) *There is a marked drift away from the churches.* There is little active evangelism so this means that the majority of Swiss people have little knowledge as to what the true Gospel is. Pray for the revival for which Switzerland awaits.

12. SING PRAISES TO OUR LORD.

Blessed assurance, Jesus is mine!
Oh, what a foretaste of glory divine!
Heir of salvation, purchase of God,
Born of His Spirit, washed in His blood.

This is my story, this is my song,
Praising my Saviour all the day long;
This is my story, this is my song,
Praising my Saviour all the day long.

WEEK TEN — FRIDAY

1. PRAISE GOD FOR WHO HE IS.

End-maker. I'm sure you already know when my end, i.e., on this earth will be. Indeed, you know the end of all things, the consummation of the whole plan of this little planet. To now talk with the one who has such knowledge and such power is indeed an awesome thought.

But I praise you for such grace and mercy extended to me. How unbearably sad it is that the end of those not your children will be just that for this world, and the beginning of torment in the world to come. I look forward to the new heaven and the new earth.

Express yourself in adoration for this quality of God.
Speak it audibly or write out your praise in your own devotional journal.

2. PRAISE GOD FOR WHAT HE MEANS TO ME.

The end of my life, i.e., as a certainty, is best left to you. I am not hastening the day, nor do I dread it. Indeed, I welcome it and rejoice at the prospect. What a wonder that it is given to man to know that the entrance into the next world has already been prepared — "the abiding places,"

the rejoicing angels, the spirits of just men made perfect. I simply rest my whole case with you through the One who said, "I am the resurrection and the life — he that liveth and believeth in me shall never die."

How do you personally relate to the end-making of God, and God who is end-maker?
Speak it out or write it out. It is *so important* that you establish *your own* devotional journal.

3. CONFESSION OF SIN

Am I ever profane? Dear God, forgive me for taking what you have given and treating it lightly and as if I did not know you had made it. I refer to other people, to your physical universe, to my own body, and then to put such an attitude into words of profanity! Awful! And yet I

have done this. Forgive me! All of life is sacred, holy and should be so considered. I want to increasingly develop the sense of wonder and awe in all I do and say. Only when my outlook and basic attitude is pure can I escape profanity.

What personal sins do you want to confess? We *must* speak them to remove them.
Do it! *Now.* There is no one else you have sinned against more than God. Tell him so!

4. SING A PRAYER TO GOD.

Break Thou the bread of life,
Dear Lord, to me,
As Thou didst break the loaves
Beside the sea;

Beyond the sacred page
I seek Thee, Lord;
My Spirit pants for Thee,
O living Word.

Open your hymn book and sing the rest of the verses — or even sing another prayer song.

5. READ HIS WORD TO HIM!

His Word

[19]Now those who had been scattered by the persecution in connection with Stephen traveled as far as Phoenicia, Cyprus and Antioch, telling the message only to Jews. [20]Some of them, however, men from Cyprus and Cyrene, went to Antioch and began to speak to Greeks also, telling them the good news about the Lord Jesus. [21]The Lord's hand was with them, and a great number of people believed and turned to the Lord.

[22]News of this reached the ears of the church at Jerusalem, and they sent Barnabas to Antioch.

— *Acts 11:19-22, NIV*

Read His Word to Him.

How is it that the first disciples were infected with a desire to share and so many since are not? The answer is in the word "disciple" — many since that glad day did not "so learn Christ." Dear Father, how shall I accept this fact? The point you are making in this text is that only Jews heard — but they *did* hear. We have Jews and

Gentiles and neither one of them hear! How I would like to be in Antioch for a few days to see and hear and know the very first persons who were called Christians. To hear the men from Cyprus and northern Africa tell of my Lord and his love — the good news about the Lord Jesus. What a privilege that would be!

Please express your response to this beautiful text. Put your expression in your own prayer diary.

6. READ HIS WORD FOR YOURSELF.

Read this word to or for myself in praise and thanksgiving, in confession and adoration. What a great city Antioch must have been when these men first came — "the hand of the Lord was with them." Just what is involved? — probably miracles, the divine credentials. Did the apostles lay their hands upon them? They could have, but it does not say such happened and just how do we know such powers were given to others to pass on to others because of the hands of the apostles? Simon the sorcerer wanted such from the apostles — he didn't get it — did anyone else? Philip and Stephen did miracles to confirm their words and the hands of the apostles were laid upon them (Acts 6:1ff.) but for what purpose? Was it not to set them aside with others to serve the widows? What happened to the other five? Here are "men" — just "men" — from Cyprus and Cyrene. Dear Lord, I'm listening.

It is so important that you pause in his presence
and either audibly or in written form tell him all his word means to you.

7. READ HIS WORD IN THANKSGIVING.

I do indeed! Thank you: (1) For the encouragement that there were no doubt many like Philip who went to Samaria. What he did there others did in Phoenicia and others in Cyprus and still others at Antioch. (2) If Philip needed to confirm his word with signs didn't also these people? Thank you for this insight. (3) Telling "the message," the "good news about the Lord Jesus" is what saves. Oh, oh, tell it! (4) That we can turn *from* our sin and turn *to* the Lord. (5) News about the good news is also news. (6) For Barnabas that *good man.* (7) "The church at Jerusalem" — the one right, true, loyal, faithful church.

Give yourself to your own expression of gratitude — write it or speak it!

8. READ HIS WORD IN MEDITATION.

Telling the message — this seems to dominate all this passage. These are transitional verses to introduce us to the record of the spread of this good news in the Gentile center of Antioch. How is it I am so content to tell the message by indirect means of the printed page? Of course the printed page becomes a direct means when used by others. This is no substitute for a one-on-one encounter. I put myself in the place of Barnabas — he was an encourager of others. Through his exhortation many people were brought to the Lord.

Pause — wait — think — then express yourself in thoughtful praise or thanks.

9. READ HIS WORD FOR PETITIONS.

In the midst of evangelism there are so many requests. (1) How can we today move believers to tell the message? (2) Break down our religious prejudice. (3) When will the "good news" live up to its name in the lives of those who have it to tell? (4) May your hand be with me today in my efforts to evangelize. (5) Turn me more and more to the authority and direction of my Lord. (6) Motivate me, like Barnabas to encourage people. (7) I want to be a member of the same church as Barnabas and others in Jerusalem.

Please, please remember these are prayers — speak them — reword them!

10. READ HIS WORD AND WAIT — LISTEN — GOD SPEAKS!

I am listening: (1) "All who are saved are members of my eternal universal church." (2) "My goodness is like leaven — put it into the lump." (3) "I cannot, and will not work without you and others like you."

11. INTERCESSION FOR THE LOST WORLD.

Switzerland — Points for prayer: (1) *The small Bible believing witness is becoming stronger.* Pray for a greater unity and desire for the evangelizing of the Roman Catholic areas and the many foreign workers as well as the many unconverted and nominal Protestants. There is a growing hunger for spiritual reality among the believers. (2) *The immigrant labor force* is mostly Roman Catholic, Orthodox or Muslim. Pray for them — especially the 21,000 Greeks and the 17,000 Muslim Turks. (3) *Liechtenstein* is an independent principality of 18,000 people between Austria and Switzerland. It is now virtually a 23rd Canton of Switzerland. The people are almost entirely Roman Catholic, and the legal position of the very few Protestants is difficult. There is one small group of Bible believers in this mini-state. Pray for these wealthy but unreached people.

12. SING PRAISES TO OUR LORD.

In loving-kindness Jesus came
My soul in mercy to reclaim,
And from the depth of sin and shame
Thro' grace He lifted me. . . .

From sinking sand He lifted me,
With tender hand He lifted me,
From shades of night to plains of light,
Oh, praise His name, He lifted me!

WEEK TEN — SATURDAY

1. PRAISE GOD FOR WHO HE IS.

Slave-maker. Surely this is a voluntary bondage, since all of us will indeed serve someone. All men should gladly choose you as their master. Servitude on a glad choice should be the response of all men. *Every* knee shall bow and *every* tongue confess that your Son is Lord to bring a revelation of your true character. This is a promise yet to be fulfilled, but nonetheless a definite reality. Praise your name for the joy of bondage and yet I need to be reminded that service and yielding and obeying is not in word but in *deed* and *truth.*

Express yourself in adoration for this quality of God.
Speak it audibly or write out your praise in your own devotional journal.

2. PRAISE GOD FOR WHAT HE MEANS TO ME.

My master—I am your bond servant. Bless your name, I do yield my whole self, i.e., as much as I am able to understand. I do want to deepen my desire. I gladly own your Lordship. I have made such a mess out of my efforts to rule. How can I develop a deeper commitment? Bless your omnipotent name. I ask to receive in this area of character development. Move within through your Spirit, direct from without through your word, prepare ahead through your providence. "Behold the bond servant of the Lord." Can I say this? Not as I want to.

How do you personally relate to the slave-making of God, and God who is slave-maker?
Speak it out or write it out. It is *so important* that you establish *your own* devotional journal.

3. CONFESSION OF SIN

Dear Master, forgive me for my pretense. Forgive me for hatred toward those I see who reject your will when they do not know it, and I am so many times unwilling to tell them. Move in my heart—to truly submit, to give myself away to others that I might serve you. I know in service I find fulfillment—forgive me for resenting the energy loss and tiredness. I know from much experience I will feel fine again. One day I will feel fine forever. Dear God, give me a gentle and quiet spirit.

What personal sins do you want to confess? We *must* speak them to remove them.
Do it! *Now.* There is no one else you have sinned against more than God. Tell him so!

4. SING A PRAYER TO GOD.

Jesus, Savior, pilot me
Over life's tempestuous sea;
Unknown waves before me roll,

Hiding rock and treacherous shoal;
Chart and compass came from Thee:
Jesus, Savior, pilot me.

Open your hymn book and sing the rest of the verses—or even sing another prayer song.

5. READ HIS WORD TO HIM!

His Word

[23]When he arrived and saw the evidence of the grace of God, he was glad and encouraged them all to remain true to the Lord with all their hearts. [24]He was a good man, full of the Holy Spirit and faith, and a great number of people were brought to the Lord.

[25]Then Barnabas went to Tarsus to look for Saul, [26]and when he found him, he brought him to Antioch. So for a whole year Barnabas and Saul met with the church and taught great numbers of people. The disciples were first called Christians in Antioch.   — *Acts 11:23-26, NIV*

Read His Word to Him.

What a wonderful man you have in Joseph called Barnabas! Although he was a Jew he could see evidence of your favor and goodness among non-Jewish people— *all* non-Jewish people—he did not begrudgingly admit it, but was glad, happy, delighted and he looked upon it as a continuing condition. What a meaningful expression— "to remain true to the Lord—with all their hearts"—to adhere, or be glued to you with all my mind, will, emotions and conscience. This I want to do, this I gladly embrace. What you through Luke say of Barnabas—oh, how I want it to be said of me: (1) "He was a good man." (2)"He was full of the Holy Spirit." (3) "He was full of faith."

Please express your response to this beautiful text. Put your expression in your own prayer diary.

6. READ HIS WORD FOR YOURSELF.

Just what was the *"evidence of the grace of God"*? Was it the joy, the exuberance of the believers? It could well have been. Was it the miraculous signs that accompanied the preaching? This is far more likely. After all, the miraculous was the *evidence* of his presence and power. Signs were to credential the word spoken. Do we need evidence today for the same word? Do not the signs already accompany the word, i.e., in the same book where we read the word, do we not also read of the signs? But some will say, "Reading the word is not tantamount to hearing the word" — "signs accompanied the *spoken* word, not the *written* word." John said he *wrote* signs that we might believe (John 20:30, 31). I read this word to probe my own heart and help me to love you more and serve you better.

It is so important that you pause in his presence and either audibly or in written form tell him all his word means to you.

7. READ HIS WORD IN THANKSGIVING.

Amen, and amen! Thank you for: (1) For every one of the first Gentile Christians or disciples who were first called Christians in Antioch. I shall speak to each of them in total leisure and interest. How interesting a time that will be! (2) For Saul who had been now several years at home in Tarsus — I'll ask him what he did there when I see him. I wish I could today! (3) For all the conversation that was shared by the old friends — Barnabas and Saul — what did they say? Sometime (where there is no time) I'll know. (4) That there are ten thousand Antiochs today — just waiting for Barnabas and Saul. (5) The church is simply the collective group of Christians anywhere — in Jerusalem or Antioch. (6) That teaching as well as preaching was the primary job of evangelism and confirmation. (7) Thank you for all the ensuing years and generations in thousands of places who did what they did in Antioch and became what they were.

Give yourself to your own expression of gratitude — write it or speak it!

8. READ HIS WORD IN MEDITATION.

"He was a good man." This is such a generic description today that it means anything anyone wants it to. In the text before us it means that a good man is one who not only has a large generous spirit or attitude toward those who are different than we are, but a man who is "filled with the Holy Spirit and faith." The Holy Spirit through our response to his presence produces the qualities of our Lord in our character — also called "the fruit of the Spirit." Faith will move us to do what our Lord commanded — no wonder "a great number of people were brought to the Lord." Dear God, I want to be like him.

Pause — wait — think — then express yourself in thoughtful praise or thanks.

9. READ HIS WORD FOR PETITIONS.

As you see my needs move me to make appropriate requests: (1) Help me to see your grace in the lives of saved men and women. (2) How I want to be true to you from my heart. (3) I want to be emptied of self and filled with the Holy Spirit. (4) Dear Lord, how I need to be filled with faith! (5) Are men brought to you only when we are filled with the Holy Spirit and faith? (6) I need to realize you want others to work with me. (7) May I be able to rejoice in the success of others as much as in your blessing upon my efforts.

Right here add your personal requests — and his answers.

10. READ HIS WORD FOR PETITIONS.

What do you want me to hear from this text? (1) "Your faithfulness is your responsibility." (2) "If you will, I will." (3) "You need help — from me and from men."

11. INTERCESSION FOR THE LOST WORLD

Albania — Population: 2,500,000. Growth 2.4%. People per sq. km. — 87.

Points for prayer: (1) *Albania is Europe's most closed and least evangelized land.* Pray for the miraculous opening of this needy land for the Word of God. (2) *Pray that the spiritual vacuum in the hearts of the people may be filled* — Communism can never do this. Most of the people know no religion but Islam.

12. SING PRAISES TO OUR LORD.

Jesus is all the world to me,
My life, my joy, my all;
He is my strength from day to day,
Without Him I would fall.

When I am sad, to Him I go,
No other one can cheer me so;
When I am sad He makes me glad,
He's my Friend.

WEEK ELEVEN — SUNDAY

1. PRAISE GOD FOR WHO HE IS.

Liberty-maker. Bless your name you are just that to me! But to all men everywhere you are the true source of freedom! Openness is the attitude you produce in life—this gives freedom. Oh, to love to do what you choose to do! and this is exactly what you produce in life. When we establish a deep love for you and your Son, then we are so excited and happy about you, we establish goals of eternal value and you move us to reach for them. The very nature of yourself and your works sets us free—we are glad to do what we choose to do. There could be no One or no enterprise that offers such excitement, adventure and value. Praise your very self!

Express yourself in adoration for this quality of God.
Speak it audibly or write out your praise in your own devotional journal.

2. PRAISE GOD FOR WHAT HE MEANS TO ME.

Liberty-maker for me! How set free I feel! I have been led into a task I love to do, and I'm paid for it! I have found that thinking of you and your work all the time is the best way to establish goals that last, beauty with meaning, hope for eternity. The only limitations I have are self-imposed, or demon directed. The truth of life and its meaning has set me free. The truth about life's true goals has broken me loose from the bondage of boredom! Praise your dear beautiful self in the person of your Son. His life was one of total liberty—I want to follow him in the deepest areas of my mind.

How do you personally relate to the liberty-making of God, and God who is liberty-maker?
Speak it out or write it out. It is *so important* that you establish *your own* devotional journal.

3. CONFESSION OF SIN

Dear, dear Lord, deliver me from the terrible sin of substituting tradition for truth. Just because we have always done it a certain way does not make it true or right. In evangelizing how tragically I have capitulated to tradition! Dear Lord, deliver me! It is not right, it is not true that asking people to "come to the meeting" is evangelism. Evangelism is going and sharing. Truth in the realm of personal purity is not compromise but commitment! We have much to learn!

What personal sins do you want to confess? We *must* speak them to remove them.
Do it! *Now.* There is no one else you have sinned against more than God. Tell him so!

4. SING A PRAYER TO GOD.

More love to Thee, O Christ,
More love to Thee!
Hear Thou the prayer I make
On bended knee;

This is my earnest plea:
More love, O Christ to Thee,
More love to Thee,
More love to Thee!

Open your hymn book and sing the rest of the verses—or even sing another prayer song.

5. READ HIS WORD TO HIM!

His Word

[26]and when he found him, he brought him to Antioch. So for a whole year Barnabas and Saul met with the church and taught great numbers of people. The disciples were first called Christians at Antioch.
[27]During this time some prophets came down from Jerusalem to Antioch. [28]One of them, named Agabus, stood up and through the Spirit predicted that a severe famine would spread over the entire Roman world. (This happened during the reign of Claudius.) [29]The disciples, each according to his ability, decided to provide help for the brothers living in Judea. [30]This they did, sending their gift to the elders by Barnabas and Saul.

— *Acts 11:26-30, NIV*

Read His Word to Him.

"For a whole year (what year was it? 39? 40?) Barnabas and Saul met with "the called out ones" and taught great numbers of people. I know you were also present then and there as you are present here and now. How many disciples were there? What was taught to them? If the same disciples were there all year, what were they taught all year? There must have been much direct revelation given to Barnabas and Saul. Did you call them Christians? Was this your choice of a name? "The ones who belong to the Anointed One"—is this a good meaning? Dear Lord, I want it to describe me.

Please express your response to this beautiful text. Put your expression in your own prayer diary.

6. READ HIS WORD FOR YOURSELF.

The church, "the called out ones" of my Lord, was built upon the teaching of the apostles and prophets. Here is one of them — Agabus is his name — you have anticipated the need and are here making provision for it. The Holy Spirit really did the speaking through the prophet. What an act of unselfish generosity — to help those they had never seen, who actually did not like them! The Jews hated the Gentiles. Those living in the province occupied by the Holy City would be especially prejudiced, but were not these learners called by the name of the One (even yourself) who gave himself to those who hated him? May I also so learn of you!

It is so important that you pause in his presence
and either audibly or in written form tell him all his word means to you.

7. READ HIS WORD IN THANKSGIVING.

Yes, yes, thank you for: (1) The church in Antioch that could listen and learn. (2) For the honorable, blessed name of those who belong to the "Anointed One." (3) For Agabus who would make the long journey and would plainly, boldly predict a famine. (4) That all your promises find fulfillment. (5) Each disciple gave not as his neighbor did, but as he was moved by the need and yourself according to his ability. (6) Barnabas and Saul were willing to be "errand boys." (7) That money is a very spiritual commodity given by Apostles to elders.

Give yourself to your own expression of gratitude — write it or speak it!

8. READ HIS WORD IN MEDITATION.

Is ability here equated with income? It would seem to be so — at least in the amount given — but all ability comes from God, therefore all income is from God. The surprising fact of this generosity is not its amount but rather that everyone had a part in it. "Each (one)" was involved. Ability relates to several areas of life such as: (1) Intelligence quotient. (2) Art — in music or painting or drama. (3) The gifts of the Spirit — God needs each of these to help those who are starving for the bread of life.

Pause — wait — think — then express yourself in thoughtful praise or thanks.

9. READ HIS WORD FOR PETITIONS.

In life saving, spiritual and physical, there are petitions: (1) How can I learn to teach from the example of Barnabas and Saul? (2) What was the great attraction for the people of Antioch? In these two requests I am asking for help in the deep needs of my own life. (3) Please help me to appreciate more fully the gift of prophecy. (4) I want the unselfish love these Gentiles had for the Jews. (5) Am I giving according to my ability? (6) Open my eyes that I might see that money is a spiritual commodity. (7) How do elders relate to the use of money?

Please, please remember these are prayers — speak them — reword them!

10. READ HIS WORD AND WAIT — LISTEN — GOD SPEAKS!

There is much I should hear from these verses: (1) "All disciples (learners) are Christians." (2) "All Christians are disciples." (3) "All Christians are brothers."

11. INTERCESSION FOR THE LOST WORLD

Albania — Points for prayer: (1) *There are still believers meeting together in secret* — despite the claim that all religious superstitions have been eradicated. The Albanian press complained in 1975 that there was a remarkable increase in the public and secret practice of religion! Pray for these isolated and persecuted believers and their continued secret witnessing. (2) *There is a growing concern in Western countries* for the evangelization of the Albanian people. There are about 1,000,000 Albanians who live in southern Yugoslavia where there has been a limited freedom to preach the Gospel, and there are now several groups of Albanian believers there. Many of these Albanians go to Western European lands temporarily for work. Pray that some may be converted there. There are Christian workers seeking to reach the large community of Albanians working in Munich, West Germany where several have come to the Lord.

12. SING PRAISES TO OUR LORD.

Walking in sunlight, all of my journey;
Over the mountains, thro' the deep vale;
Jesus has said "I'll never forsake thee,"
Promise divine that never can fail.

Heavenly sunlight, heavenly sunlight,
Flooding my soul with glory divine:
Hallelujah, I am rejoicing,
Singing His praises, Jesus is mine.

WEEK ELEVEN — MONDAY

1. PRAISE GOD FOR WHO HE IS.

The Seeing One. Oh, oh bless your name you *see* me! Blessed wonder of wonders! You see all men at one time, *all* events, all the sequence of all things. There is no past-present-future with you, neither is there anything happening that is a surprise to you. Dear God, my heavenly Father, to try to contemplate your omniscience and omnipresence is beyond my wildest imagination, but I want to try. It stretches my mind and gives me more cause for adoration and holy amazement. How limited is the likeness of man to yourself — at least in this realm.

Express yourself in adoration for this quality of God.
Speak it audibly or write out your praise in your own devotional journal.

2. PRAISE GOD FOR WHAT HE MEANS TO ME.

The Seeing One — "Thou Lord seest me," but not as man seeth but you look into my mind — you know the true and real *purpose* of my life. You contemplate the emotions or affections that sweep my life. You can see the total meaning of the approval or disapproval I give to any one circumstance of life. You see me now but you see me in the total perspective of the ever-present now! How beyond all human understanding and yet a thrill of excitement pulsates through such contemplation.

How do you personally relate to the seeing of God, and God who is the seeing-one?
Speak it out or write it out. It is *so important* that you establish *your own* devotional journal.

3. CONFESSION OF SIN

Anger is a sin of mine. I am angry at the wrong thing, at the wrong persons — my anger is most easily released when I am tired and have concentrated on something for a long time. I really can not and do not rationalize and excuse such bursts of rage or resentment. Dear God, please forgive — right now I wonder how I could have done it, but I did and I apologized to those involved — and to you. Our Lord was angry — "he looked about on them with anger because of the hardness of their hearts" at the healing of the man with the withered hand. His anger was deep compassion expressed in the hot surge of desire to help. Dear God, may I be like him!

What personal sins do you want to confess? We *must* speak them to remove them.
Do it! *Now.* There is no one you have sinned against more than God. Tell him so!

4. SING A PRAYER TO GOD.

I gave My life for thee,
My precious blood I shed,
That thou might'st ransomed be,
And quickened from the dead;

I gave, I gave My life for thee,
What hast thou giv'n for Me?
I gave, I gave My life for thee,
What hast thou giv'n for Me?

Open your hymn book and sing the rest of the verses — or even sing another prayer song.

5. READ HIS WORD TO HIM!

His Word

[9]James, Peter and John, those reputed to be pillars, gave me and Barnabas the right hand of fellowship when they recognized the grace given to me. They agreed that we should go to the Gentiles, and they to the Jews. [10]All they asked was that we should continue to remember the poor, the very thing I was eager to do. — *Gal. 2:9, 10, NIV*

Read His Word to Him.

How good it is to read of the meeting of two of your most devoted servants, Peter and Paul. Peter, James and John had the reputation of being "pillars." How did you see them? How far from fact is reputation? But they were given divine perception — perhaps the gift of discernment — you know and I do not — but I am trying to think your thoughts. What is "the right hand of fellowship"? It probably was the shaking of hands — and using the right hand it signified the strength of the agreement. Can you give me such a hand? I know you want to. Dear God, I want to so agree with all you want done that we can hold on to one another as we get it done. Wouldn't angels do a better job? *No,* they are not an extension of yourself like I am.

Please express your response to this beautiful text. Put your expression in your own prayer diary.

6. READ HIS WORD FOR YOURSELF.

It is so comforting to know that even in the earliest of days, in the pristine purity of the apostolic church, there were those who wondered about the reaction of others. It is easy enough to say that what others think makes no difference—it doesn't to our essential relationship with you—but in the extension of your rule in the hearts of men it can make a very large difference—it can also be the difference between eating or not eating, of working here or there, or not working at all. It was with these areas Paul was concerned. In all these relationships, dear God, wonderful Lord, help me to remember to "see" the *grace*, the unearned favor you give to me, and to others. Help me to operate and let others do likewise out of the sense of *need* as well as grace. "Remember the poor" —remember the wide field.

Pause in his presence and either audibly or in written form tell him all his word means to you.

7. READ HIS WORD IN THANKSGIVING.

Thank you for: (1) The unselfish generosity of the Gentiles meeting the needs of the Jews. (2) That grain and fruit and meat are just as "spiritual" as prayer and Bible reading and singing. (3) That God does expect someone to lead in this work, i.e., he wants to lead *through* someone. (4) Regardless of what we preach, human need, physical human need has a priority. (5) We can and should work with those who approach service from a very different background. (6) An emotional, warm friendship can exist in his work, indeed *should* exist. (7) That Peter, James and John could serve together for several years and still be the closest of friends.

Give yourself to your own expression of gratitude—write it or speak it!

8. READ HIS WORD IN MEDITATION.

There were so many who left Jerusalem at the stoning of Stephen. They went "everywhere" and all of them as they went spoke or told or proclaimed the good news. Some went to Phoenicia, others to Antioch and yet others to Cyprus. Some even went to northern Africa. It is most difficult for us to understand just how prejudiced some people can be (or we are). For 2,000 years God had been working with and through the Jews. There was nothing in common in the Jewish mind or life with Gentiles. God changed their minds through the marvelous miracle at the house of Cornelius. It is most interesting that *the church sent Barnabas*. Why didn't the apostles send him? Why wasn't one of the apostles sent? Most especially is this true if only by the hands of the apostles could the supernatural gifts of the Spirit be given—perhaps that is why Barnabas went to find Paul. But the report of his work and many turning to the Lord occurs *before* Paul arrived. How long was he there before Paul arrived? These are moot questions, but they need to be asked.

Pause—wait—think—then express yourself in thoughtful praise or thanks.

9. READ HIS WORD FOR PETITIONS.

In the meeting of leaders of your Son's body there are several petitions: (1) I want to be like James who said, "Faith without works is dead." (2) I want to be like Peter who said, "We become partakers of the divine nature." (3) I want to be just like John who said, "God is love." (4) I want to be like Barnabas who sold his own possessions to give to others. (5) I want to be like Paul who said, "For me to live is Christ." (6) I want to recognize God's grace in the lives of others. (7) I want to give to the poor, not because they will thank me, but because I love them.

Right here add your personal requests—and his answers.

10. READ HIS WORD AND WAIT—LISTEN—GOD SPEAKS!

Speak to me dear Lord: (1) "Give and it shall be given unto you." (2) "People have physical as well as spiritual needs." (3) "Let others serve without being suspicious of their efforts."

11. INTERCESSION FOR THE LOST WORLD

Albania — Point for prayer: (1) *Christian literature in Albania* has been almost totally lacking since World War II. The New Testament was reprinted in 1972, and a number of books and booklets have been produced since then. Pray for fruit among the relatively few Albanians in the Free World, and for the Albanians in Yugoslavia. Pray that some of this literature may find its way over virtually sealed borders into Albania itself from Greece and Yugoslavia. It is almost impossible for the few well-guarded tourists to distribute any literature inside the country as in other Communist lands. Pray that the slight thaw in relations with the West may result in more openings.

12. SING PRAISES TO OUR LORD.

I love Thy Kingdom, Lord,
The house of Thine abode,

The Church our blest Redeemer saved
With His own precious blood.

WEEK ELEVEN — TUESDAY

1. PRAISE GOD FOR WHO HE IS.

Hearing. You hear the prayers of all men, but much more: You hear all the conversations of all tongues of all men at the same time—it is, to me, a total impossibility and redundancy. Why would you *want* to do this? But it is an essential part of your very nature. You are not frustrated since there is nothing you do not know. You are never impatient for the same reason. To hear all words as well as to know all thoughts is one awesome concept! To imagine less than this for yourself is to attribute less than omniscience to your nature. Praise and wonder are my response.

Express yourself in adoration for this quality of God.
Speak it audibly or write out your praise in your own devotional journal.

2. PRAISE GOD FOR WHAT HE MEANS TO ME.

Hearing me. To hear everyone and everything is one thing, to hear me and my prayers (as well as all other words) is something else! How wonderfully good it is—comforting and solidly reassuring to *know* you hear every word and give thoughtful consideration to each one. Even now you know I am trying to express my deep appreciation for your true nature. You read these words and know their meaning (or lack of it). Dear Father, give me traveling direction—a mercy today as I travel over treacherous highways. One day (perhaps soon—or not soon) I will be delivered from this clay house to enter into a full realization of the One who heard me—even when I wasn't listening to him. Bless your merciful Person.

How do you relate to the hearing of God, and God who hears all?
Speak it out or write it out. It is *so important* that you establish *your own* devotional journal.

3. CONFESSION OF SIN

Wrath—that I should express intense anger at anything but sin itself is sad. It is a reflection upon your creation and providence. Forgive me! I can blame my fits of wrath on my nerves but who is responsible for the health of these nerves? Who aggravates them? Am I not the sinner here too? Forgive me! How I want your peace to guard my emotions and my mind. How I seek your powerful penetrating cleansing for my sin. How eagerly I draw to myself your promise of wholeness! Bless the Lord oh my total self!

What personal sins do you want to confess? We *must* speak them to remove them.
Do it! *Now.* There is no one else you have sinned against more than God. Tell him so!

4. SING A PRAYER TO GOD.

I would be true, for there are those who trust me;
I would be pure, for there are those who care;
I would be strong, for there is much to suffer;

I would be brave, for there is much to dare;
I would be brave, for there is much to dare.

Open your hymn book and sing the rest of the verses—or even sing another prayer song.

5. READ HIS WORD TO HIM!

His Word

12 It was about this time that King Herod arrested some who belonged to the church, intending to persecute them. ²He had James, the brother of John, put to death with the sword. ³When he saw that this pleased the Jews, he proceeded to seize Peter also. This happened during the Feast of Unleavened Bread. ⁴After arresting him, he put him in prison, handing him over to be guarded by four squads of four soldiers each. Herod intended to bring him out for public trial after the Passover.

⁵So Peter was kept in prison.   — *Acts 12:1-5a, NIV*

Read His Word To Him.

It really meant something to "belong to the church" in the year 44! Did James have a wife and children? What were their feelings of terror and loss as they saw their loved one led away? I'm sure you can answer these questions with full detail and accuracy. I would like to know someday (when there are no more days) just what kind of a man was Herod? How cheap was the price of human life! How precious to you—how meaningless to Herod. What were the thoughts of James as he laid his head down for the last time? How delighted I am to know someone who knows perfectly every answer—and several more questions I have not even considered. Praise your name!

Please express your response to this beautiful text. Put your expression in your own prayer diary.

6. READ HIS WORD FOR YOURSELF.

I want to take Peter's place, or the place of one of those at the feast of unleavened bread. What questions could have been asked of you and of one another? (1) How could God permit an arrest during the sacred feast? (2) What will we do if Peter is beheaded like James? (3) How can God let our enemies, and his enemies, overcome us? (4) Why doesn't God strike Herod dead? (5) What have we done to deserve this? All these questions, and others I would have asked or thought. I'm so, so glad to have all the answers in this historical record. May I remember when it happens again!

Pause in his presence and either audibly or in written form tell him all his word means to you.

7. READ HIS WORD IN THANKSGIVING.

Yes, yes, thank you for: (1) King Jesus, who was truly and is truly and will be truly GREAT. (2) The called out ones (the church) became a clearly defined community in 44 A.D. (3) For the others who were arrested and persecuted that we do not know—but you do—and one day we shall meet and know and appreciate. (4) For death that is but a door into your presence and the wonderful world and life to come. (5) That we can only and finally please you—man is never pleased with anyone or anything. (6) For our Passover who is ever alive to intercede for us. (7) That 16 soldiers cannot keep God's servant in prison when you want him out!

Give yourself to your own expression of gratitude—write it or speak it!

8. READ HIS WORD IN MEDITATION.

"Some who belonged to the church." Let's ask and answer several questions about these unnamed persons: (1) To what church did they belong? (2) Can I belong to it today? (3) In what sense did they belong? (4) Why were they persecuted? (5) What happened to that church to which they belonged? *Answers:* (1) There was only one "called out" body of Christ—if we do and believe what they did we can become what they were—Christians who together formed the church of our Lord. (2) Indeed we can! The church is composed of all Christians—the same thing (or One) who saved me made me a member of his church. (3) They had been bought with a price and belonged to him, but in another sense they belonged to each other. (4) They respresented a threat to the vested interests of the religious leaders. (5) The church is alive—not as well as it might be—but whenever persons became Christians his church lived through them.

Pause—wait—think—then express yourself in thoughtful praise or thanks.

9. READ HIS WORD FOR PETITIONS.

Out of persecution we can find much for which we must have your answers: (1) "Why do the Gentiles rage, and the people imagine vain things"? You have an answer—my need is trust! (2) Give me the same courage in the face of prosperity that your children had in persecution. (3) Keep me aware that with some people nothing is sacred—with me all of life is sacred. (4) Keep me aware of the temporariness of this life. (5) I want to affirm my confidence in your power to deliver out of any trouble—(help thou my unbelief). (6) Keep me tender-hearted toward those who are slaves to their jobs. (7) May I live today as if it were the last day!

Please, please remember these are prayers—speak them—reword them!

10. READ HIS WORD AND WAIT—LISTEN—GOD SPEAKS!

What do you say to me out of these verses? (1) "Do not fear what man can do to you." (2) "In this life right does not always win." (3) "Eternal life is right on the other side of your last heartbeat."

11. INTERCESSION FOR THE LOST WORLD

Albania — Point for prayer: (1) *Christian Radio broadcasts* are the only way, at present, to get the Gospel into the land. Pray for the raising up of more believers in the West who are fluent in Albanian who can help the brother who prepares programs for Trans World Radio for transmission from Monaco. There are now five programs beamed on Albania every week. Pray that the news of these broadcasts may reach those who need the message of the Gospel.

Bulgaria — Population: 8,800,000. Growth 0.7%. People per sq. km. —79.

Point for prayer: (1) *Many Bulgarians have never had a chance to hear the true* Gospel; their land is one of the more needy of Eastern Europe. Pray that they may hear of the Savior.

12. SING PRAISES TO OUR LORD.

Face to face with Christ, my Savior,
Face to face—what will it be?
When with rapture I behold Him,
Jesus Christ who died for me.

Face to face I shall behold Him,
Far beyond the starry sky;
Face to face in all His glory,
I shall see Him by and by!

WEEK ELEVEN — WEDNESDAY

1. PRAISE GOD FOR WHO HE IS.

King of all the earth. Bless your beautiful name! You are much more than king of all the earth, the creator and sustainer of ten trillion galaxies—but for this little speck called "earth" you are indeed ruler and Lord, but a loving, non-interfering ruler, i.e., if we do not want your rule in our lives then your rule will only include the physical universe and the creatures (great and small). One of our days (when days shall cease to be) all mankind will know of your kingship—every knee shall acknowledge and every tongue will pronounce the words of wonder either in horror or honor. Right now I am most happy to own you as my king.

Express yourself in adoration for this quality of God.
Speak it audibly or write out your praise in your own devotional journal.

2. PRAISE GOD FOR WHAT HE MEANS TO ME.

King of all the earth for me. To stand back and contemplate the globe and relate yourself with the land surface—nay—all the peoples who live and move upon the land mass—and if there be other worlds with other peoples, you are the king, creator and owner of each of them. But in a particularly personal manner you are king of my life and my world. Dear King, how strange it seems to describe your rule in such large dimensions and then circumscribe and hinder your rule in my own daily living—forgive me! How I do *want* you to reign. Long live the King! in my own heart, home, job—total life!

How do you personally relate to the kingship of God, and God who is king?
Speak it out or write it out. It is *so important* that you establish *your own* devotional journal.

3. CONFESSION OF SIN

To confess my sins becomes totally monotonous and useless unless I truly repent. Dear God, move me to repentance. I know this is a dangerous prayer, but I do pray it because I sincerely want to repent and change. Sins named in your book form the basis of my confession in the general area of my sin, then my particular sins will be confessed along with them. "Railing"—I am blood guilty of this sin. I have railed at my students and have asked their forgiveness, and yours; at my wife and no one deserves less such treatment. Forgive, forgive. I have railed at circumstances when they are under your control. Open my eyes, humble my heart, forgive my sin.

What personal sins do you want to confess? We *must* speak them to remove them.
Do it! *Now.* There is no one else you have sinned aginst more than God. Tell him so!

4. SING A PRAYER TO GOD.

All for Jesus, all for Jesus!
All my being's ransomed pow'rs:
All my tho'ts and words and doings,
All my days and all my hours.

All for Jesus! all for Jesus!
All my days and all my hours;
All for Jesus! all for Jesus!
All my days and all my hours.

Open your hymn book and sing the rest of the verses—or even sing another prayer song.

5. READ HIS WORD TO HIM!

His Word

⁵So Peter was kept in prison, but the church was earnestly praying to God for him.
⁶The night before Herod was to bring him to trial, Peter was sleeping between two soldiers, bound with two chains, and sentries stood guard at the entrance. ⁷Suddenly an angel of the Lord appeared and a light shone in the cell. He struck Peter on the side and woke him up. "Quick, get up!" he said, and the chains fell off Peter's wrists.
— *Acts 12:5-7, NIV*

Read His Word to Him.

What a thought! You know by name and experience every member of that church in Jerusalem. You could repeat *every* prayer. How I would like to have been there! What commitment! Peter was sound asleep the night before his execution! What was in his mind? How did he so view yourself that he was able to accept the restful, peaceful sleep? Sentries at the entrance and soldiers, between which slept Peter the Apostle. These men, all of them, needed you. All of them were soon to be abruptly ushered into your eternal presence. Who were they? Were any of them saved from hell? Who was the angel? I know you know and one day I believe I will!

Please express your response to this beautiful text. Put your expression in your own prayer diary.

WEEK ELEVEN — WEDNESDAY

6. READ HIS WORD FOR YOURSELF.

Is there a connection between the prayers of the church and the appearance of the angel? This strikes at a very, very basic issue. I think it altogether wonderful how you are able to answer prayer and then leave it up to man to interpret it as a coincidence or happenstance or "good luck." What you want and I want to give is real trust and confidence in your interest and answer in my life. Yes, I believe the angel came in answer to prayer—would he have been there if there had been no prayer? Why ask such a question? It is of little or no profit.

It is so important that you pause in his presence
and either audibly or in written form tell him all his word means to you.

7. READ HIS WORD IN THANKSGIVING.

Amen—so be it. Thank you for: (1) *Earnest* prayer—it effects and affects much in its working. (2) For the inclusive word "church"—no doubt there were present there, as today, some who were immature in their prayer life. (3) For the wonder of sleep—how much a boon it is to man—the power of the peaceful heart to bring peaceful rest! (4) The very real physical efforts of man to thwart (defeat) your plans. How puny they are when you are ready to deliver! (5) The suddenness of some of your acts—all are sudden when not expected—a delightful surprise is the name of your game with me! (6) The light that shone into the cell—you didn't have to use a light, but you did. It surely brightened up the whole picture. (7) The materialization of the angel—or is this the explanation?—at least Peter could see him. Perhaps it was giving Peter capacities of sight into a dimension that exists all the time—the Spirit world.

Give yourself to your own expression of gratitude—write it or speak it!

8. READ HIS WORD IN MEDITATION.

Suddenly an angel of the Lord appeared. Since the meaning of the name "angel" is messenger, it would be easy to say that any humble servant of the Lord who carries a message from the Lord is God's angel. Of course this is an accommodated use of the word, but the lowest of a servant of our Lord, like Ananias of Damascus, can do what an arch-angel like Gabriel could not do: tell the good news to Saul of Tarsus and baptize him that his sins might be washed away and he could be filled with the Holy Spirit. "Suddenly" somewhere, sometime a messenger of the Lord appeared and told us the good news or we would not be here to record it. It would be *oh, so good* to have an angel materialize in the midst of the busy activities of life, but it would be better to go where you know no one has ever come with the glad tidings of great joy—after all it was given "for all the people."

Pause—wait—think—then express yourself in thoughtful praise or thanks.

9. READ HIS WORD FOR PETITIONS.

How many requests I can find in the example of Peter: (1) I want to be an example of "earnest prayer"—help me. (2) Give me the settled peace that guarded the heart of Peter. (3) I am aware of angels, but not as much as I should be—help me! (4) I want to affirm that there are no doors you cannot open! (5) Shine the light of your word upon my own bondage and set me free! (6) Keep me alert. Sometimes you act suddenly. I do not want to miss your direction. (7) I praise you that as I go about life today you are aware of it all. Sensitize my heart.

Right here add your personal requests—and his answers.

10. READ HIS WORD AND WAIT—LISTEN—GOD SPEAKS!

Through your word, visit me! What do you say? (1) "I am listening to those who pray—even if they have but little faith." (2) "The word of God is not bound." (3) "I am interested in all the details of life."

11. INTERCESSION FOR THE LOST WORLD

Bulgaria — Points for prayer: (1) *Propaganda against believers is extreme.* Pray that this continual assault on believers and the Bible may cause the many disillusioned Communists to seek for the Truth. (2) *The persecution of believers* has been very severe. Many Christian leaders suffered long terms of imprisonment and death in the early years of Communist rule. Since 1972 the level of persecution has again been stepped up, and many believers are suffering in prison for their faith. Pray for Christian prisoners and their families.

12. SING PRAISES TO OUR LORD.

Crown Him with many crowns,
The Lamb upon His throne;
Hark! how the heavenly anthem drowns
All music but its own!

Awake, my soul, and sing
Of Him who died for thee;
And hail Him as thy matchless King
Thro' all eternity.

149

WEEK ELEVEN — THURSDAY

1. PRAISE GOD FOR WHO HE IS.

Reigning. The fact is you *are* reigning *now* and always have been, and always will be, over the entire physical inanimate world, over all the animal kingdom you are king, and in the hearts of all men who want your Lordship you reign. Dear Lord, count me as one who wants your rule because I need it so desperately. To attribute all power, all authority in heaven and on earth is to but repeat the words of your dear Son. One day, when there are no more days, you will claim your reign and all that has not yielded, gladly, to your reign will be removed. Right now I am most happy to acknowledge your supreme Lordship and try, help my trying, to yield my whole being to you.

Express yourself in adoration for this quality of God.
Speak it audibly or write out your praise in your own devotional journal.

2. PRAISE GOD FOR WHAT HE MEANS TO ME.

"Let not therefore sin (Satan) reign in your mortal body that you should fulfill the lusts thereof" (Rom. 6:12). It is possible for me to "let" either you my great, loving Father-Creator to reign or sin through Satan, or Satan through sin. I can *let* either one—the choice is mine—but is there really a choice considering the results? As much as we choose Satan and sin one would imagine there was some benefit, at least beyond the momentary pleasure of the moment, or season. What I need to do is to be creative about the means of entering into the joys, delights and satisfactions of the Lord!

How do you personally relate to the reign of God, and God who reigns?
Speak it out or write it out. It is *so important* that you establish *your own* devotional journal.

3. CONFESSION OF SIN

Selfish ambition—how can I eliminate this? By being sure the purpose or goal of my ambition is unselfish. But there are other sins for which I should be and I am heartily sorry and want to repent. At the bottom line is selfishness—perhaps the largest is "self-deception,"i.e., pretending I am something I am not. It must appear positively humorous to you, or infinitely sad. All that I deceive is myself. Dear God, cleanse me in the blood of your Son, clothe me in the best robe in your house—the red robe of righteousness. Comfort me and deepen my dependence on you.

What personal sins do you want to confess? We *must* speak them to remove them.
Do it! *Now.* There is no one else you have sinned against more than God. Tell him so!

4. SING A PRAYER TO GOD.

I have found a friend in Jesus,
He's everything to me,
He's the fairest of ten thousand to my soul;
The Lily of the Valley, in Him alone I see
All I need to cleanse and make me fully whole.

In sorrow He's my comfort, in trouble He's my stay,
He tells me every care on Him to roll:
He's the Lily of the Valley, the Bright and Morning Star,
He's the fairest of ten thousand to my soul.

Open your hymn book and sing the rest of the verses—or even sing another prayer song.

5. READ HIS WORD TO HIM!

[7]Suddenly an angel of the Lord appeared and a light shone in the cell. He struck Peter on the side and woke him up. "Quick, get up!" he said, and the chains fell off Peter's wrists.
[8]Then the angel said to him, "Put on your clothes and sandals." And Peter did so. "Wrap your cloak around you and follow me," the angel told him. [9]Peter followed him out of the prison, but he had no idea that what the angel was doing was really happening; he thought he was seeing a vision. [10]They passed the first and second guards and came to the iron gate leading to the city. It opened for them by itself, and they went through it. When they had walked the length of one street, suddenly the angel left him.
— *Acts 12:7-10, NIV*

Read His Word to Him.

What amazement filled the face and heart of Peter when he opened his eyes and saw the angel! Even after he saw the angel and heard him and obeyed him he yet could not believe it. How good it is that we can live this incident all over again. What must it be to live in the "eternal present" —it is just as clear and real today with you as it was two thousand years ago! How precise and thoughtful is the angel. Angels seem to have a habit of waking people up— the shepherds, Cornelius and now Peter. How I do want to awake with the apostle—chains and iron gates mean nothing when you are ready to deliver! You can and do direct the thinking and actions of people, i.e., when it suits your purpose—the first and second guards did not know Peter left!

Please express your response to this beautiful text. Put your expression in your own prayer diary.

WEEK ELEVEN — THURSDAY

6. READ HIS WORD FOR YOURSELF.

Your angels are here in this room, I just cannot see them. Are they saying much the same thing to me? "Quick, get up," it is late and the world is going to hell! All chains of hesitancy and bondage can and do fall off! "Put on the whole armor of God." — righteousness, truth, good news of peace, faith, etc. Fasten this armor on tightly, i.e., be personally knowledgeable that you have it on. "Follow me," God's angel — *the* angel of God says this to me. I can follow him out of prison. Oh, the amazement of it all! Oh, the total freedom!

It is so important that you pause in his presence
and either audibly or in written form tell him all his word means to you.

7. READ HIS WORD IN THANKSGIVING.

How I love to do this. (1) Thank you for your servants who needed to be awakened. I do too! (2) That personal contact can and is made to wake us up — of one type or another. (3) When my hands are set free I can serve. (4) He wants me dressed to serve him. (5) The angel compensates for Peter's dullness or lack of belief. (6) There were visions in which you communicated. (7) The poor soldiers were left behind.

Give yourself to your own expression of gratitude — write it or speak it!

8. READ HIS WORD IN MEDITATION.

He had no idea it was really happening! This could well characterize most of life. In a dozen ways I have been delivered and I really did not know it. (1) I had no idea what was happening when our three children were born. (2) I had no idea what was involved when our children were married — I thought I did, but I didn't. (3) Grandchildren are full of surprises! (4) I had no idea what was really happening when I baptized the very first convert — a little boy about 10 or 11. (5) I knew not that the humble meeting I held of 10 or 15 saints was "the house of God and the gate of heaven." (6) I had no idea what really happened when a totally sincere girl gave her heart to me and pledged her life with mine. How could I ever know the ten thousand blessings she would bring?

Pause — wait — think — then express yourself in thoughtful praise or thanks.

9. READ HIS WORD FOR PETITIONS.

Wake me up to the requests I should make as related to these verses. (1) Show me just what is urgent and what is not in your work. (2) Release me from the bondage of useless routine. (3) Strike from my hands all desire to do my own will. (4) Show me the reality of what appears as but a dream of spiritual conquest. (5) Clothe me for the battle of following your leading. (6) Lead me past all the barricades of Satan. (7) Open doors for me I really never knew could be opened.

Please, please remember these are prayers — speak them — reword them!

10. READ HIS WORD AND WAIT — LISTEN — GOD SPEAKS!

What living word do you speak to me from this text? (1) "Get up and tell of your deliverance." (2) "Leave all and follow me." (3) "I can deliver from every prison."

11. INTERCESSION FOR THE LOST WORLD

Bulgaria — Points for prayer: (1) *Pray for the leaders of the churches* who face constant harassment from the authorities and betrayal at the hands of informers who have been infiltrated into both official and underground groups. There are ministers who live a hunted life ministering to the secret groups. Pray for their ministry. It is impossible to obtain an adequate Bible training for those who would enter the ministry. (2) *The churches* are not restricted by law from holding meetings, but the long working hours and lack of Sunday rest greatly limit their activities. The limitation on registration of new churches forces many groups to meet illegally. Pray for these believers that their faith may be strong, and that their witness may win many to the Lord. (3) *Young people* are now more receptive to the Gospel despite the years of indoctrination in Marxism, but there is a strict restriction on their attendance of church services (except in the tourist season!). There is also a problem of a generation gap between the enthusiastic young believers and the older people in the churches.

12. SING PRAISES TO OUR LORD.

A wonderful Savior is Jesus my Lord,
A wonderful Savior to me,
He hideth my soul in the cleft of the rock,
Where rivers of pleasure I see.
He hideth my soul in the cleft of the rock

That shadows a dry, thirsty land;
He hideth my life in the depths of His love,
And covers me there with His hand,
And covers me there with His hand.

WEEK ELEVEN — FRIDAY

1. PRAISE GOD FOR WHO HE IS.

For us. Wonderful Lord, great God, I know you love me and every man, every woman. You have planned and provided the very best for each of us. It is a wonderful source of strength to know of your infinite interest. How carefully you have given us "all things to enjoy." In the smallest of detail you have indicated your interest and concern that we have all we need. In you we are full and have all things. If you are for us — and we know you are — then who could be against us? i.e., successfully oppose us?

Express yourself in adoration for this quality of God.
Speak it audibly or write out your praise in your own devotional journal.

2. PRAISE GOD FOR WHAT HE MEANS TO ME.

For me. In so many little areas of life I have found evidence of your interest! How I praise you this is true. For today and its needs and opportunities I know you will be there to help me, to indicate your involvement in all human affairs. Man may not see it or appreciate it, or acknowledge it, to say nothing of thanking you for it, nonetheless, you are there behind what man can see, or interpret, to provide. How is it we have an atmosphere on this small piece of matter that is especially suited to our needs?

How do you personally relate to the love of God, and God who is for you?
Speak it out or write it out. It is *so important* that you establish *your own* devotional journal.

3. CONFESSION OF SIN

Hardening of the heart. This is a sin and I want to be rid of it. I want to hold an open, tender heart toward yourself. How shall I learn of your heart and your interest if I am not sensitive toward your will in my life? Dear God, I do want you to penetrate my inmost being and have control of my thoughts. Most of all, just now, cleanse and forgive me of all and each of my sins. I confess them all to you!

What sins do you want to confess? We *must* speak them to remove them.
Do it! *Now.* There is no one else you have sinned against more than God. Tell him so!

4. SING A PRAYER TO GOD.

"Are ye able," said the Master,
"To be crucified with Me?"
"Yea," the conquering Christians answered,
"To the death we follow Thee."
Lord, we are able,

Our spirits are Thine,
Remold them, make us like Thee, divine:
Thy guiding radiance above us shall be
A beacon to God,
To love and loyalty.

Open your hymn book and sing the rest of the verses — or even sing another prayer song.

5. READ HIS WORD TO HIM!

His Word

[10] They passed the first and second guards and came to the iron gate leading to the city. It opened for them by itself, and they went through it. When they had walked the length of one street, suddenly the angel left him.
— *Acts 12:10, NIV*

Read His Word to Him.

On Peter's strange journey — I want to think of it as you do, and as Peter did, for you do know how he felt! Here again we walk with Simon — you are as interested as he is. There is no aloof detachment with you — you are involved in all human affairs — they are your affairs too. How does it feel to follow an angel in the middle of the night — or better, in the wee hours of the early morning? How do the stones feel on your feet? Did the iron gate make a noise when it opened? How many houses did they pass before they had walked the length of the street? Did Peter get a really good look at the angel just before he left? What expression was on the angel's face? I'm sure you can answer all these foolish questions, but I wish I could.

Please express your response to this beautiful text. Put your expression in your own prayer diary.

WEEK ELEVEN — FRIDAY

6. READ HIS WORD FOR YOURSELF.

Dear Lord, I would much rather follow an angel than to have an angel follow me. Could you arrange that for today? I do not say this or pray this in an altogether facetious manner. Can you through your angels open closed doors to cities today? Oh, indeed, indeed. More than sixty years of my life have gone by, but even now I know you can deliver me from all that binds me, limits me, confines me. You can lead me into the "wide place." You can find for me my own "Rehoboth" (Gen. 26:22). Dear God, open the gate to the city!

*It is so important that you pause in his presence
and either audibly or in written form tell him all his word means to you.*

7. READ HIS WORD IN THANKSGIVING.

With enthusiasm I do! Thank you for: (1) For all barricades put up by men — for how else could we know your power except through overcoming? (2) For some gates — hindrances that seem to solve themselves — now I know who is really doing it. (3) That we "never walk alone" — your servants of heaven are with us, you are with us, the Holy Spirit is *in* us. (4) We can go "through" all hindrances to your way. (5) Your personal, powerful, sensate presence need be with us but for "the length of one street." (6) Night is no hindrance or problem with you. (7) The angel did — and did not — leave him.

Give yourself to your own expression of gratitude — write it or speak it!

8. READ HIS WORD IN MEDITATION.

"The iron gate leading to the city opened for them by itself." Why did Luke include this little insight? Why mention the *iron* gate? Because to men such seems unmovable, impregnable, but with God in the fulfillment of God's purpose it becomes animated, no longer cold, unmoved metal, but a living thing responsive to the will of God. Nothing is indifferent when God speaks. Dear Lord, great God, moving Holy Spirit, ministering angels — this is the *real* world. When God moves into the sphere of man there are no barriers.

Pause — wait — think — then express yourself in thoughtful praise or thanks.

9. READ HIS WORD FOR PETITIONS.

Into the excitement of that memorable night I want to go for petitions: (1) Keep me aware that even when I do not know it you are leading me. (2) Teach me over again that so many things that "work out" are of your own doing. (3) Impress upon me that if I do not move you cannot. (4) I need a lesson in patience retaught to me each day. (5) Let me know how far it is from where I am to where you want me to go. (6) Teach me how to separate what I should do from what you are doing. (7) Thank you for the simple, trusting faith of Peter.

Right here add your personal requests — and his answers.

10. READ HIS WORD AND WAIT — LISTEN — GOD SPEAKS!

What are you saying in this verse? (1) "Iron gates are no problem for me." (2) "Some problems will solve themselves." (3) "It takes time to lead even in a miraculous manner."

11. INTERCESSION FOR THE LOST WORLD

Bulgaria — Points for prayer: (1) *Literature.* No literature for believers is allowed to be printed or distributed in the country. The famine of literature is so great there is much hand copying of the Scriptures and good Christian books. Pray for those who seek to bring literature from the West to these believers. (2) *Christian Radio* — pray for the broadcasts to the country from Trans World Radio Monaco and others, and also for those who prepare the programs.
Czechoslovakia — Population: 14,900,000. Growth rate 0.8%. People per sq. km. — 116.
Point for prayer: (1) *The Czech Protestants* have been persecuted for nearly 6 centuries (since the martyrdom of the great early Reformer Huss in 1415). The Communist regime has followed a carefully stepped up program for the erosion of the influence and ultimate liquidation of the Church since 1973. Pray for our suffering brethren that they may stand firm and continue to win people for the Lord.

12. SING PRAISES TO OUR LORD.

Holy, Holy, Holy,
Lord God Almighty!
Early in the morning our songs shall rise to Thee;

Holy, Holy, Holy!
Merciful and Mighty!
God in Three Persons, blessed Trinity!

WEEK ELEVEN — SATURDAY

1. PRAISE GOD FOR WHO HE IS.

Faithful. How beautifully this word does describe your very self. This quality means so *very* much — consistency is a habit we all need to cultivate — you need not; you are consistent in *every* relationship. Faithfulness means you keep every promise. How glad we are to acknowledge this. Not one promise has fallen short in any regard, for anyone. Faithfulness presupposes an interest. I am so glad you have an interest in all men all the time.

Express yourself in adoration for this quality of God.
Speak it audibly or write out your praise in your own devotional journal.

2. PRAISE GOD FOR WHAT HE MEANS TO ME.

Faithful to me. It is for my need and my weakness you express your faithfulness. You have given me every good and perfect thing, or event, or relationship that I have — for this I praise you. I love you for being just the same yesterday, today and tomorrow — as spelled out in man's perspective — but remaining only what you have always been. Glory and honor, adoration and amazement are all words to say how deeply grateful I am to you.

How do you personally relate to the faithfulness of God, and God who is faithful?
Speak it out or write it out. It is *so important* that you establish *your own* devotional journal.

3. CONFESSION OF SIN

Deceit. Dear God, when it would be better to tell the truth, i.e., for our own advantage, we tell a lie. When it would be better to love we hate. When it would be so much better to admit we evade. Dear God, forgive me (not them). Cleanse me, free me, love me. I love you!

What personal sins do you want to confess? We *must* speak them to remove them.
Do it! *Now.* There is no one else you have sinned against more than God. Tell him so!

4. SING A PRAYER TO GOD.

I've found a Friend, oh, such a Friend!
He loved me ere I knew Him;
He drew me with the cords of love,
And thus He bound me to Him.

And round my heart still closely twine
Those ties which naught can sever,
For I am His, and He is mine,
Forever and forever.

Open your hymn book and sing the rest of the verses — or even sing another prayer song.

5. READ HIS WORD TO HIM!

His Word

[11]Then Peter came to himself and said, "Now I know without a doubt that the Lord sent his angel and rescued me from Herod's clutches and from everything the Jewish people were anticipating."

[12]When this had dawned on him, he went to the house of Mary the mother of John, also called Mark, where many people had gathered and were praying. [13]Peter knocked at the outer entrance, and a servant girl named Rhoda came to answer the door. [14]When she recognized Peter's voice, she was so overjoyed she ran back without opening it and exclaimed, "Peter is at the door!"

[15]"You're out of your mind," they told her. When she kept insisting it was so, they said, "It must be his angel."

— Acts 12:11-15, NIV

Read His Word to Him.

How good it must have been to hear Peter express the very thoughts you intended by your action in his life! "To know without a doubt!" Ah, fond desire! But this we can and do have in our confidence in your character as revealed in your word and the life of your Son. Peter knew of the plans of Herod and the Jews. He knew also where the prayer meeting was held. How do you view the actions of Rhoda? It must be your delight to surprise with joy all such young women and all such faithless disciples. Thank you, thank you that you desire to so speak to man.

Please express your response to this beautiful text. Put your expression in your own prayer diary.

6. READ HIS WORD FOR YOURSELF.

Just whose place shall I take? Could I be as confident as Peter in the face of soon coming death? I am sure I would be as surprised as he in the deliverance. Can I approximate the overjoyed wonder of Rhoda? Dear Lord, I *want* to. Peter was not only knocking but speaking. I wonder what he said. One day I shall ask Rhoda—and know. Until then I would like to hear in my imagination a few of his shouts of joy. Has anyone accused me lately of losing my mind because of my testimony concerning the living Savior? or my telling of a supernatural deliverance of one of his servants? I wonder what someone meant by saying "It must be his angel"? Did Peter have a single angel assigned to him? Do all of us have such?

Pause in his presence and either audibly or in written form tell him all his word means to you.

7. READ HIS WORD IN THANKSGIVING.

Of many texts this should be a source of gratitude: (1) For the fact that you are in the "resource business." (2) That you do not ignore or minimize the opposition of man. (3) That your revelation, even to Peter, was progressive. (4) That the largest part of praying is adoration and thanksgiving. (5) That even a lowly servant girl was known of you and knew Peter in a personal way, i.e., she knew his voice. (6) Excitement is a part of your work with men. (7) Sharing God's blessings is natural and compatible with your plan.

Give yourself to your own expression of gratitude—write it or speak it!

8. READ HIS WORD IN MEDITATION.

"It must be his angel." The term angel means "messenger" so it seems strange to relate this expression to the death of Peter—as if this person is saying he died and his spirit has returned. We have not known the spirit of man and the term angel being used interchangeably. Are we to learn here that each person has an angel assigned to them? If so, why would the angel knock at the gate? Perhaps it was but the outpouring of amazed confusion. There is one static lesson: angels are very real, intelligent beings who have a great interest in men. They are deathless beings alive in the world today.

Pause—wait—think—then express yourself in thoughtful praise or thanks.

9. READ HIS WORD FOR PETITIONS.

How like the disciples in Mary's house are all of us! (1) Shock me into the reality of the spirit world! (2) Deliver me today from Satan's clutches and all he has anticipated. (3) I do knock on the doors of opportunity today, confident that you will open. (4) Help me to be patient with those who act out of impulse and not thought. (5) If the door does not open right away keep me persistent in knocking. (6) Give me the joy of Rhoda as related to my Lord knocking on the door of my heart. (7) In spite of all who doubt or deny move me to affirm that he is indeed knocking for admission into all of my life.

Please, please remember these are prayers—speak them—reword them!

10. READ HIS WORD AND WAIT—LISTEN—GOD SPEAKS!

What do you say just here? (1) "My answers to prayer are not always what people expect." (2) "Joy need not always make sense." (3) "Believe me first, last and always."

11. INTERCESSION FOR THE LOST WORLD

Czechoslovakia — Points for prayer: (1) *The religious freedom of 1966-68 was a gift of God.* The rather discouraged Christian witness was revived by a move of the Spirit right across the country. The churches were filled, many were converted and new chuches built. The move was especially marked among the young people. There has been a great deepening of spiritual life since the Russian invasion and the subsequent sufferings. (2) *Communism has been completely discredited* in the country by the Russian occupation of the land. Pray that this will lead to a great turning to the Lord in spite of the high cost of following the Savior.

12. SING PRAISES TO OUR LORD.

To God be the glory, great things He hath done,
So loved He the world that He gave us His Son,
Who yielded His life an atonement for sin,
And opened the Lifegate that all may go in.
Praise the Lord, praise the Lord,

Let the earth hear His voice!
Praise the Lord, praise the Lord,
Let the people rejoice!
O come to the Father, thro' Jesus the Son,
And give Him the glory, great things He hath done.

WEEK TWELVE — SUNDAY

1. PRAISE GOD FOR WHO HE IS.

Covenant-maker. How remarkable that you want to make an agreement with man. You want man to enter your mind and heart and agree with you concerning this matter or that. We have such a full record of your faithfulness in covenant agreements — of land, of a great nation, of your dear Son. But of all the agreements you have made and kept, none are more important, indeed all seem to be but the preparation for your final agreement in the blood and righteousness of your dear Son. That you would want to transact business with me is a total amazement. Praise your faithful name! How glad I am for your goodness.

Express yourself in adoration for this quality of God.
Speak it audibly or write out your praise in your own devotional journal.

2. PRAISE GOD FOR WHAT HE MEANS TO ME.

Covenant-maker with me. To claim my part of this testament is so important and yet so very humbling. How glad I am to claim the remission (the stopping of sin) in my life and record. I want to enter the fullness of fulfillment as related to your covenant with me. Trusting reliance upon your faithfulness is my part — which I gladly give — but to stop sinning is accomplished in fact in only a relative manner; to stop all sinning I would have to know all things, i.e., where I am imperfect and I would need a power I do not now have "to will is present, but to perform is not." I can see and claim the guilt of sin stopped — the record of sin removed — but the practice?? Dear God, I surely, sorely *want* to!

How do you personally relate to the covenant-making of God, and God who is covenant-maker?
Speak it out or write it out. It is *so important* that you establish *your own* devotional journal.

3. CONFESSION OF SIN

Which indeed leads me to openly admit my need, deep, deep need. I am a sinner — one who violates your law, misses your mark, falls far, far short of your glory (character). I could (and do) specify several categories, and specific sins. I cast myself daily and momentarily upon your mercy and love. Wash me and I shall be whiter than snow! I claim by faith, not by work, my freedom and joy of acceptance. I am such a poor example of obedience if obedience is performance. I have failed if obedience is an attitude and desire. Dear God, I agree! I want to obey. I see no reason at all of myself not to obey, but there is another law in my members bringing me into bondage. Thanks be to yourself! There is therefore now no condemnation to those who are hidden in him.

What personal sins do you want to confess? We *must* speak them to remove them.
Do it! *Now.* There is no one else you have sinned against more than God. Tell him so!

4. SING A PRAYER TO GOD.

Thou, my everlasting portion,
More than friend or life to me;
All along my pilgrim journey,

Savior, let me walk with Thee.
All along my pilgrim journey,
Savior, let me walk with Thee.

Open your hymn book and sing the rest of the verses — or even sing another prayer song.

5. READ HIS WORD TO HIM!

His Word

[16]But Peter kept on knocking, and when they opened the door and saw him, they were astonished. [17]Peter motioned for them to be quiet and described how the Lord had brought him out of prison. "Tell James and the brothers about this," he said, and then he left for another place.

[18]In the morning, there was a great commotion among the soldiers. "What could have happened to Peter?" they asked.
— *Acts 12:16-18, NIV*

Read His Word to Him.

It must please you to see men pleased, especially when the surprise is associated with your answer to prayer! How totally beyond belief was the deliverance of Peter, was the presence of Peter and the recounting of your action in his life. Who asked what? What were the comments in the house of Mary that day? I want to hear it all over again — you know James so much better than we do — what was his response? Leadership was a very real and needed activity in the church at Jerusalem. You know the names (and serial numbers) of every one of the soldiers in the empty cell of the prison. Was it your choice that they die? No. No. You have no pleasure in the death of wicked (or lost) — it was Herod's choice!

Please express your response to this beautiful text. Put your expression in your own prayer diary.

6. READ HIS WORD FOR YOURSELF.

I want to "be quiet" and hear, as for the first time, what Peter — what you are saying to me! The Lord brought him out of prison — even when angels are the means the cause is "the Lord" — yourself, or your Son. You are cognizant of physical wood and stone buildings. "Tell James and the brothers" — James the brother of my Lord, James the one who did not know his own brother, i.e., the One who lived with him in the same house — but now he did — now he leads others to know. My, how he could speak with help to me! It is so good to have spiritual brothers just like those in Jerusalem!

Pause in his presence and either audibly or in written form tell him all his word means to you.

7. READ HIS WORD IN THANKSGIVING.

Indeed I can: (1) Thank you for the persistence and boldness of Peter. (2) Thank you for the thrill of divine astonishment. (3) That in quietness we learn. (4) That it can still be told to the leaders and brothers and sisters how the Lord can and does deliver his servants! Amen! (5) That Peter never stayed around for congratulations — he cared more for the safety of the disciples. (6) He never told them where he was going — what wisdom he had from you! (7) That this incident could have caused some of these soldiers to become Christians before they saw you.

Give yourself to your own expression of gratitude — write it or speak it!

8. READ HIS WORD IN MEDITATION.

"What could have happened to Peter?" This was the question of the soldiers, but it can be a question for each of us. (1) What could have happened to Peter if Jesus had not made a personal resurrection appearance to him? He could have become discouraged and quit. (2) What could have happened to Peter if our Lord had not prayed for him that his faith fail not? (3) What could have happened to Peter if Jesus had given up on him the third time he went to sleep when he asked him to watch and pray? (4) What could have happened to Peter if he decided God was against him and therefore he was in prison? (5) What if the Christians had not prayed for him?

Pause — wait — think — then express yourself in thoughtful praise or thanks.

9. READ HIS WORD FOR PETITIONS.

In the midst of the excitement of these verses there arise requests: (1) I want to keep the capacity to be astonished at your goodness. (2) Help me to tell someone today what the Lord has done for me. (3) I want to respect and admire your work in others. (4) May I seek to protect others by what I do not say. (5) May I, like John Mark, drink in eagerly every word of this wonder of your grace. (6) It is good at times to leave — help me to know when. (7) Keep me alert to the beautiful accuracy of this text.

Right here add your personal requests — and his answers.

10. READ HIS WORD AND WAIT — LISTEN — GOD SPEAKS!

My ears are open — speak to me from these verses: (1) "Time is a very important factor in some of my work." (2) "People need to hear over and over again all I have done." (3) "There is no avoiding loss as well as gain in some of my work."

11. INTERCESSION FOR THE LOST WORLD

Czechoslovakia — Points for prayer: (1) *The pressures are especially great upon the preachers.* They are only allowed to preach if approved by the state and have taken an oath of loyalty. The number of legal meetings has been greatly cut, and some preachers are now in prison for exceeding that number. Preachers are not allowed to send out pastoral letters, own duplicating equipment or do visitation. Many are now in prison, forbidden to preach or subjected to harassment and intimidation. Pray for these leaders and their ministry in such trials. (2) *Pray for the larger and more formal churches* that have been dominated by non-Biblical theology and formalism. There are born-again believers among them — pray that their number may increase as the persecution increases.

12. SING PRAISES TO OUR LORD.

The Church's one foundation
Is Jesus Christ her Lord;
She is His new creation
By water and the word:

From Heav'n He came and sought her
To be His holy bride;
With His own blood He bought her,
And for her life He died.

WEEK TWELVE — MONDAY

1. PRAISE GOD FOR WHO HE IS.

Lord of hosts. The hosts of heaven are under your command. Indeed, all the hosts of men and angels will be (and now in the light of eternity are) under your control. Praise your powerful name! In all the battles of the Old Testament record you led forth in triumph — in whatever opposition to the hearts or lives of men there are ten million angels — all the strength of omnipotence ready for use. I doubt not your total ability — it is only that you do not choose to use such power.

Express yourself in adoration for this quality of God.
Speak it audibly or write out your praise in your own devotional journal.

2. PRAISE GOD FOR WHAT HE MEANS TO ME.

Lord of hosts for me. There are truly legions of angels at work on behalf of man's needs. I praise you for such interest and involvement in the passing show of man's little flutter of existence. Oh, dear God, keep me open and reaching out to you in praise and wonder — you merit all such praise, yea, much, much more. Lead on O King Eternal — the day of march has come!

How do you personally relate to the power of God, and God who is Lord of hosts?
Speak it out or write it out. It is *so important* that you establish *your own* devotional journal.

3. CONFESSION OF SIN

To simply and fully confess all my sin to you is no burden — it is a grand release! I have at times been bitter at you (at least indirectly) for the inequities of life — and even now I do not understand them any better than before, but bitterness is totally self-defeating, for which I ask forgiveness. It is a sin against myself, as well as yourself! against my dear wife who surely does not deserve any such treatment. Cleanse and relieve me of this! Calmness and peace are the fruit of forgiveness. Praise your name forever!

What personal sins do you want to confess? We *must* speak them to remove them.
Do it! *Now.* There is no one else you have sinned against more than God. Tell him so!

4. SING A PRAYER TO GOD.

Jesus is all the world to me,
My life, my joy, my all;
He is my strength from day to day,
Without Him I would fall.

When I am sad, to Him I go,
No other one can cheer me so;
When I am sad He makes me glad,
He's my Friend.

Open your hymn book and sing the rest of the verses — or even sing another prayer song.

5. READ HIS WORD TO HIM!

His Word

[19] After Herod had a thorough search made for him and did not find him, he cross-examined the guards and ordered that they be executed.

Then Herod went from Judea to Caesarea and stayed there for a while. [20] He had been quarreling with the people of Tyre and Sidon; they now joined together and sought an audience with him. Having secured the support of Blastus, a trusted personal servant of the king, they asked for peace, because they depended on the king's country for their food supply. — *Acts 12:19, 20, NIV*

Read His Word to Him.

How typical of all men are the soldiers of Herod. I'm sure that thought occurred to you. When you do not want someone or something to be found it will not be found. You have your own purposes for hiding all that is hidden. Such purposes are also past tracing out. Perhaps one day (when there is no day) you will open the treasure of your hidden secrets to our wondering view. At the same time, these soldiers represent all men who are in a search for you — at least implicitly this is true — some are truly reaching out, although you are not far from any one of us. These poor soldiers represent all of us — cross examined by your truth we have no defense — we, unlike them, are blood guilty and deserve to die. You, unlike the cruel, selfish, prideful king, are the king of mercy and love. Praise your name!

Please express your response to this beautiful text. Put your expression in your own prayer diary.

6. READ HIS WORD FOR YOURSELF.

As I have already said, it is not difficult to take my place in the frantic search of the soldiers. I am so glad that I have found you! I have deserved to die and you have forgiven me! I am more than glad I do not have to accept the judgments of men, but of yourself. I do accept all my mistakes among men and their consequences — some deserved and some undeserved — both good and bad — but only because I know my eternal judge and sentence is in your hands. Blessed, wonderful judge of all the earth! It is good to have the close record of a little despot long ago and far away to let us know that no one and not a thing is either long ago or far away with you!

Pause in his presence and either audibly or in written form tell him all his word means to you.

7. READ HIS WORD IN THANKSGIVING.

Oh, indeed! Thank you, thank you for: (1) For every Christian home in Jerusalem. (2) That none of the Christians knew where Peter was. (3) For your way of making the authorities aware of the number of Christians and the miraculous aspect of their faith. (4) A measure of justice, i.e., responsibility and guilt prevails in human society, even some pagan societies. (5) For death that will usher us into the larger life — awesome, awful thought for those unprepared. I have a hard time believing the soldiers did not accept our Lord and his hope of eternal life before they were executed. How many days were involved, etc., we do not know. (6) For the total accuracy of the Acts account, historical and geographical. (7) That we do not have such a ruler over us today.

Give yourself to your own expression of gratitude — write it or speak it!

8. READ HIS WORD IN MEDITATION.

A thorough search was made for him and did not find him. I am so glad that this in *no way* describes you, my blessed Lord — indeed, you have been in a thorough search for all men since before the beginning of time, and you have "found" those who have eyes to see and ears to hear and hearts to believe. Dear God, you have found me! The son of man came to "seek" — you "seek" those to worship you. You are the shepherd in search of the sheep — the Samaritan who found poor, robbed and beaten mankind on the roadside of life. You are the shepherd who calls and leads and carries his sheep. Bless your tender heart! In another figure you are "the hound of heaven" — the love that will not let me go! What a lovely captivity to be caught and held by you!

Pause — wait — think — then express yourself in thoughtful praise or thanks.

9. READ HIS WORDS FOR PETITIONS.

I love to think through every word of these two verses: (1) I want to be aware that any time you wish I can show up very inadequate in the presence of men. (2) May I not take out my punctured pride in the hurt of others. (3) May I remember if you do not want us to find something it is useless to look. (4) Forgive me dear Lord if I cause any innocent people to suffer because of my selfishness. (5) May I find set-backs a lesson in humility. (6) Dear Lord, help me to freely admit the miraculous in the record of your book. (7) Give me a clear memory of all you have done to prove your love and your power.

Please, please remember these are prayers — speak them — reword them!

10. READ HIS WORD AND WAIT — LISTEN — GOD SPEAKS!

What do you say to me from these two verses? (1) "Learn from Herod that your conscience can become dull." (2) "Sometimes innocent people suffer." (3) "You will find no peace in browbeating other people."

11. INTERCESSION FOR THE LOST WORLD

Czechoslovakia — Points for prayer: (1) *There are relatively fewer believers in Slovakia.* Pray for the evangelization of every part of the land. (2) *Very much literature was taken into the country* before the Russian invasion, but this could not meet the great and growing need. No literature is now permitted from the West — some Christians from the West have been imprisoned for seeking to bring Bibles to believers. Pray for all involved in this dangerous ministry. Over 120,000 Bibles were printed between 1969-1973 in the country, but now no more. There is now a severe lack of Bibles despite permission for a few small consignments of Bibles to enter the country recently. (3) *Radio ministry.* Pray for those producing and broadcasting Czech and Slovak programs in the West.

12. SING PRAISES TO OUR LORD.

Standing on the promises of Christ my King,
Thro' eternal ages let His praises ring;
Glory in the highest, I will shout and sing,
Standing on the promises of God.

Standing, standing,
Standing on the promises of God my Saviour;
Standing, standing,
I'm standing on the promises of God.

WEEK TWELVE — TUESDAY

1. PRAISE GOD FOR WHO HE IS.

Reverend. "Reverend and holy is his name." How interesting that a title so often applied to men is really your name—a quality of your character. Dear God, I accept this quality as perhaps the *one* quality I most relate to yourself. To me you are to be worshiped, hallowed, respected, and so indeed reverence is one of the first qualities that comes to mind. I want to bow before you, prostrate myself before you—holy, pure, separate, sanctified and reverend is your total person.

Express yourself in adoration for this quality of God.
Speak it audibly or write out your praise in your own devotional journal.

2. PRAISE GOD FOR WHAT HE MEANS TO ME.

Reverend for me—all men should and ultimately will reverence your name and I count myself as among them. "Sacred wonder" would be a good way to describe my attitude. How beautiful to lift up my inner being to you. To know you are altogether, yea and more, the source and full origin of all that is clean, right, good and holy. I love you, but it is a love full of amazement and shock! Dear God, I want to be speechless with true reverence before your face!

How do you personally relate to the reverence of God, and God who is reverend?
Speak it out or write it out. It is *so important* that you establish *your own* devotional journal.

3. CONFESSION OF SIN

In this frame of heart it is not at all difficult to bow in contrition before you. How shall my heart (entire inward being) be moved to change? I struggle each day with this problem—I do so need to change—I ask for a full view of your goodness that I might repent. "Love suffers long with kindness."—I do neither! How longsuffering you have been and now are with me! Dear God, Holy Father, forgive, but *change* me! May my fear of your judgment and condemnation in and endless suffering or punishment move me, shock me, startle me into a deep change of mind! Dear God, forgive—but change me.

What personal sins do you want to confess? We *must* speak them to remove them.
Do it! *Now.* There is no one else you have sinned against more than God. Tell him so!

4. SING A PRAYER TO GOD.

Take the name of Jesus with you,
Child of sorrow and of woe;
It will joy and comfort give you,
Take it, then, where'er you go.

Precious name, O how sweet!
Hope of earth and joy of Heav'n;
Precious name, O how sweet! . . .
Hope of earth and joy of Heav'n.

Open your hymn book and sing the rest of the verses—or even sing another prayer song.

5. READ HIS WORD TO HIM!

His Word

[20]He had been quarreling with the people of Tyre and Sidon; they now joined together and sought an audience with him. Having secured the support of Blastus, a trusted personal servant of the king, they asked for peace, because they depended on the king's country for their food supply. [21]On the appointed day Herod, wearing his royal robes, sat on his throne and delivered a public address to the people. [22]They shouted, "This is the voice of a god, not a man." [23]Immediately, because Herod did not give praise to God, an angel of the Lord struck him down, and he was eaten by worms and died.
[24]But the word of God continued to increase and spread.
— Acts 12:20-24, NIV

Read His Word to Him.

To read this account in the light of eternity surely gives a vastly different estimate of the actions of those involved. As Herod looked down upon the people so you looked down on the whole scene. What had Blastus told the people of Tyre and Sidon that helped them as they appeared before this poor puppet? Perhaps he said to flatter him as much as at all possible—did he tell them that Herod had an inexhaustible desire to be accepted by men—to be recognized as a man of power—and he would do *anything* to get it? Poor, poor man! You alone can satisfy the human ego—for the human ego is the human spirit created in *your* image and restless and unfulfilled until at rest and completed in you! But the options are no options at all—we either give you the praise or we are "eaten of worms."

Please express your response to this beautiful text. Put your expression in your own prayer diary.

WEEK TWELVE — TUESDAY

6. READ HIS WORD FOR YOURSELF.

What powerful words are in these verses! From what we are told by contemporary writers Herod *was* a good speaker—he did have real ability in oratory—but at the best his voice was not in any sense "the voice of a god," and what he said was blaspheming to the true One God. Dear Lord, help me to remember the source of all speak-ing ability—to know how fickle and fallible are the praises of men. To remember that you *are* listening to every word I speak (or write). It is a fearful, wonderful, awesome thing to speak in the sight of God and Christ Jesus and the holy angels.

Pause in his presence and either audibly or in written form tell him all his word means to you.

7. READ HIS WORD IN THANKSGIVING.

Thank you for: (1) Honesty and duplicity do exist in all human exchange. (2) That our country is not dependent upon a despot for food supply. (3) That we have peace and prosperity in our free land. (4) For clothes and shelter—Dear God, help us to be content. (5) The plain lesson on the results of pride a pomp. (6) The strong message that we should give you the praise for all we are and have. (7) That in spite of all, your word can and does spread.

Give yourself to your own expression of gratitude—write it or speak it!

8. READ HIS WORD IN MEDITATION.

Let's remember and learn from these questions: (1) From what was Peter delivered? From "Herod's clutches and everything the Jewish people were anticipating." It is interesting that the motives of Herod and the Jews are spelled out and in no uncertain terms. (2) Explain the strange actions of a servant girl. For all time her exuberant joy and surprise will be ours. Her overlooking the obvious is so characteristic of such surprise—the account becomes all the more authentic. (3) The appearance of Peter was either the imagination of a distraught mind or the super-natural appearance of an angel—of course, it was neither one—but such is the disbelief of men. Lord, have mercy.

Pause—wait—think—then express yourself in thoughtful praise or thanks.

9. READ HIS WORD FOR PETITIONS.

How powerfully do these verses move me to ask of you! (1) Dear Lord, I want to seek my importance in you—not men. (2) Keep me aware that there is always a way to deceive—guard me from it. (3) Teach me what a bless-ing is my daily bread from your hand. (4) May I remember that native talents can be given to you or prostituted. (5) Make me more aware how deadly is the praise of men. (6) Help me to brand as a lie that man has said anything of truth without you. (7) I want to remember that sooner or later the worms will eat us all.

Right here add your personal requests—and his answers.

10. READ HIS WORD AND WAIT—LISTEN—GOD SPEAKS!

Directly from heaven via your word—speak to me: (1) "I will not share my glory with another." (2) "Most men are liars." (3) "The word of God will continue long after all the world is gone."

11. INTERCESSION FOR THE LOST WORLD

East Germany — Population: 16,800,000. Growth 0.3%. People per sq. km.—157.

Points for prayer: (1) *Nominal Christianity is waning rapidly* under the pressures of vigorously propagated atheism, increasing materialism and discrimination against believers. Few of the Protestants go to church and the number of baptisms in the State Church is declining dramatically. Pray for a move of the Spirit among the many discouraged and nominal Christians. (2) *There are still many more freedoms* for German Christians to wor-ship and witness than is usual for a Communist state. Pray that the true believers may be courageous and strong to use the opportunities that they have to evangelize while it is still possible.

12. SING PRAISES TO OUR LORD.

I have a song I love to sing,
Since I have been redeemed,
Of my Redeemer, Savior, King,
Since I have been redeemed.
Since I . . . have been redeemed,

Since I have been redeemed,
I will glory in His name;
Since I . . . have been redeemed,
I will glory in my Savior's name.

WEEK TWELVE — WEDNESDAY

1. PRAISE GOD FOR WHO HE IS.

Rock. Praise your wonderful name! One of your names is "Rock." This gives all men the assurance of stability, of strength, of protection, of a shade from the heat of the sun. The immense bulk of a great rock is most impressive, as is the weight involved. All those qualities—and more—tell me and all men of your character. I can and all can hide in you from the storms of life. What a tremendous need is met in shelter, protection, shade, refreshment and peace. Praise your name I am delighted to be in you.

Express yourself in adoration for this quality of God.
Speak it audibly or write out your praise in your own devotional journal.

2. PRAISE GOD FOR WHAT HE MEANS TO ME.

My Rock, my fortress and high tower! The psalmist uses this figure to describe you, or his response to you. So do I. I want to get away, to leave, to hide from this life and all and everyone in it. I'm so glad you are "my escape"—not from reality but into reality—into the One who cares about every hurt of everyone. I stand before you as I would stand before a gigantic rock—larger than any rock I have ever seen, like the overwhelming bulk of the rock at Alice Springs in the outback of Australia. Oh, wonder upon wonder. Praise you.

How do you personally relate to the strength of God, and God who is a Rock?
Speak it out or write it out. It is *so important* that you establish *your own* devotional journal.

3. CONFESSION OF SIN

To confess my sin is not difficult—I am daily reminded, and always aware of my short comings, my missing the mark. I do not ever, ever want to become comfortable with this. I want always to be sincerely, deeply sorry and full of desire to do better, to lean upon you, to hide in you. To love—love you so deeply that my response (which is my lifestyle) will not include selfishness, pride, flesh. Dear God, forgive my insensitivity. Clean me up.

What personal sins do you want to confess? We *must* speak them to remove them.
Do it! *Now.* There is no one else you have sinned against more than God. Tell him so!

4. SING A PRAYER TO GOD.

There is a name I love to hear,
I love to sing its worth;
It sounds like music in mine ear,
The sweetest name on earth.

Oh, how I love Jesus,
Oh, how I love Jesus,
Oh, how I love Jesus,
Because He first loved me!

Open your hymn book and sing the rest of the verses—or even sing another prayer song.

5. READ HIS WORD TO HIM!

His Word

[11]When Peter came to Antioch, I opposed him to his face, because he was in the wrong. [12]Before certain men came from James, he used to eat with the Gentiles. But when they arrived, he began to draw back and separate himself from the Gentiles because he was afraid of those who belonged to the circumcision group. [13]The other Jews joined him in his hypocrisy, so that by their hypocrisy even Barnabas was led astray. — *Gal. 2:11-13, NIV*

Read His Word to Him.

Gladly, gladly! How fallible are your servants! even Peter (the rock) becomes shifting sand. How strong beyond belief is peer pressure! How marvelous is your check and balance in the problems and weaknesses of men. What a snare is the fear of men! Oh, dear God, how I do see myself in this group. I have vacillated in both roles. Some days I have been Peter and other times among those from James. Dear God, forgive! How more than patient you have been—yea, you *are* today! How we struggle for identity and acceptance with one another, when our identity is always in you! In you we are important and accepted!

Please express your response to this beautiful text. Put your expression in your own prayer diary.

6. READ HIS WORD FOR YOURSELF.

How easily and personally can I allow you to speak to me! Have I been listening when some dear, courageous brother (or sister) has opposed me to the face? and "even in the presence of them all"? No, no not all the time, but I *have* had second thoughts — and when the clamor of my emotions was stilled I could hear, sometimes — Oh, how I need to hear. Have I had the courage and boldness and real love of the apostle Paul to oppose some brother to the face when he stood condemned? Is this my place? If it isn't, who will do it?

Pause in his presence and either audibly or in written form tell him all his word means to you.

7. READ HIS WORD IN THANKSGIVING.

Yes, yes, thank you: (1) That Peter was willing to go to Antioch — it was a long journey. (2) For the fellowship or partnership that was shared around a dinner table. (3) For the lesson those from James could have learned from the words of Paul to Peter. (4) That such segregation was labeled for what it was, "hypocrisy." (5) That God has only one "group." (6) For the healing and liberating power of truth received. (7) For the overwhelming tender love that must have accompanied every sharp word from Paul to Peter — for Peter's tender heart and sensitive conscience that let him receive and respond to the rebuke.

Give yourself to your own expression of gratitude — write it or speak it!

8. READ HIS WORD IN MEDITATION.

"Even Barnabas was led astray." How could it be? We know how, by the hypocrisy of the "other Jews" at Antioch this dear good man was led. This speaks both well and ill of him: (1) *Well:* He was submissive, i.e., he could be led. He admired and respected other men and their opinions. He truly wanted to be careful in his relationship with God and men. (2) *Ill:* He did not look beyond the moment. He did not look at the whole picture. He allowed pride of position and party majority (which is usually wrong) to rule over what God had plainly said. Praise your wonderful love and Barnabas' grace, he repented! We can change our minds several times and be acceptable to God!

Pause — wait — think — then express yourself in thoughtful praise or thanks.

9. READ HIS WORD FOR PETITIONS.

In the mistakes of others I can find requests for my needs: (1) In the midst of unfamiliar surroundings keep me humble-minded. (2) Give me the wisdom to know the difference between culture and sin. (3) Give me a man as bold as Paul to speak to my inconsistencies. (4) May I be as humble-minded as Peter. (5) Teach me how pervasive is my influence, for good or evil! (6) Show me your face, O my Father, that I need not fear the face of man! (7) How subtle is hypocrisy — show me my sin!

Please, please remember these are prayers — speak them — reword them!

10. READ HIS WORD AND WAIT — LISTEN — GOD SPEAKS!

If ever I need to listen and hear it is now! (1) "I expect obedience under all conditions of life." (2) "You are always in need of instruction — listen!" (3) "Repentance means restitution — win Barnabas back."

11. INTERCESSION FOR THE LOST WORLD

East Germany — Points for prayer: (1) *Persecution is increasing.* More and more discrimination against believers and their children in job and education opportunities is being applied. It is now virtually impossible for a believer to obtain a university education. There is the ever present danger of compromise for the sake of their families. (2) *There seems to be a plan to force the Church* into the same situation as in Russia. This may mean loss of legal status for the Church, expropriation of all church owned land and institutions, and ultimately the destruction of the Church as a witnessing body. Pray that the devil's plans may be thwarted.

12. SING PRAISES TO OUR LORD.

I will sing the wondrous story
Of the Christ who died for me,
How He left His home in glory
For the cross of Calvary.

Yes, I'll sing . . . the wondrous story
Of the Christ . . . who died for me,
Sing it with . . . the saints in glory,
Gathered by . . . the crystal sea.

WEEK TWELVE — THURSDAY

1. PRAISE GOD FOR WHO HE IS.

One. There is one true God and his name is Jehovah— Lord—his name is many, but this is One—three persons— but one in nature. There are three separate, distinct, divine beings, but all are the same in Being. I praise you for the beauty and meaning of this important quality. To know the one true God is no small matter—indeed the most important fact of my life or the life of any man upon this earth. I try to contemplate the meaning of such a thought. Why would there be three beings? I do not know, but I see multiples of the triune all about me in the world in which I live—man is body, soul and spirit. Praise you for one more amazing characteristic.

Express yourself in adoration for this quality of God.
Speak it audibly or write out your praise in your own devotional journal.

2. PRAISE GOD FOR WHAT HE MEANS TO ME.

One to me. I believe the oneness of your purpose, accomplished by yourself, your son and the Holy Spirit, is one source of amazement to me. Just to consider two or three areas: (1) *Salvation.* You thought it—"God so loved that you gave"—Jesus effected it, and the Holy Spirit sealed it. (2) *Creation.* You conceived it, Jesus did it, the Holy Spirit coordinated it. (3) *Resurrection.* The thought originated in your mind, Jesus was the first fruit, the prototype, and the Holy Spirit was the power to accomplish it. Praise and wonder before the three in One!

How do you personally relate to the oneness of God, and God who is One?
Speak it out or write it out. It is *so important* that you establish *your own* devotional journal.

3. CONFESSION OF SIN

"Their god is their stomach—their glory is their shame." When I allow my body to run me it becomes my god. When I joke and laugh and ignore the problem, my glory is a shame, my characterization of the problem is a true shame —I mind earthly things. Dear God, forgive! The lust of the flesh is no joke. The desires of the body are only two— as near as I know: sex and food. They are closely associated, if not integrated. To sin in one area opens the door for sin in the other. Dear Lord, I want to beat my body—I do not at any time want it to beat me! Forgive, cleanse, renew and transform!

What personal sins do you want to confess? We *must* speak them to remove them.
Do it! *Now.* There is no one else you have sinned against more than God. Tell him so!

4. SING A PRAYER TO GOD.

I gave My life for thee,
My precious blood I shed,
That thou might'st ransomed be,
And quickened from the dead;

I gave, I gave My life for thee,
What has thou giv'n for Me?
I gave, I gave My life for thee,
What hast thou giv'n for Me?

Open your hymn book and sing the rest of the verses—or even sing another prayer song.

5. READ HIS WORD TO HIM!

His Word

13 In the church at Antioch there were prophets and teachers: Barnabas, Simeon called Niger, Lucius of Cyrene, Manaen (who had been brought up with Herod the tetrarch) and Saul. ²While they were worshiping the Lord and fasting, the Holy Spirit said, "Set apart for me Barnabas and Saul for the work to which I have called them." ³So after they had fasted and prayed, they placed their hands on them and sent them off. — *Acts 13:1-3, NIV*

Read His Word to Him.

How good is this word! We are back "in the church" at Antioch. How do you see us today? Are we *in* the same called out assembly today? Dear, dear God, we *do*, we do want to do just what they did to become what they were. We do want you to see in the earth today the same faith and faithful men that you saw in the church at Antioch.

Oh, dear God, if you want to make me or anyone else "a prophet," i.e., one with direct heavenly input of information, I am more than ready, but what shall I say in my forth telling that has not already been said? The content of the teaching—what shall it be? Dear Lord, how I struggle—help me! If I said more than your word it would be too much.

Please express your response to this beautiful text. Put your expression in your own prayer diary.

6. READ HIS WORD FOR YOURSELF.

How easily I can identify with these burning, living words! Whom did you call to lead the first Gentile church? "Simeon called Niger"—if he were here today there are those among us who would call him something else and reject him. Cyrene is northern Africa. Are we looking at "another one of them"? A man who had been educated and lived in the court of Herod? They were worshiping you. What were they doing? Surely in prayer, praise, adoration, and at the same time "they were fasting." Are you saying to me that you speak to men, most unlikely, unworthy men in a period of devotion and fasting? I can only answer in the affirmative! Dear God, I want so much to imitate their faith and love for you!

Pause in his presence and either audibly or in written form tell him all his word means to you.

7. READ HIS WORD IN THANKSGIVING.

Amen! Thank you for: (1) Barnabas, Simeon called Niger, Lucius, Manaen and Saul—I want to be much more specific, but I can't. I am deeply grateful for them. They say so much to me. (2) Thank you that you have teachers in the church today. We have no direct input of curriculum but we do teach *your word*. (3) You call men of experience to new experiences. (4) I can worship, I can fast today. (5) You want men "to work" not just or only to worship. (6) That others can and should send us forth to your work. (7) The laying on of hands for approval and separation and blessing is such a beautiful part of your church.

Give yourself to your own expression of gratitude—write it or speak it!

8. READ HIS WORD IN MEDITATION.

"After they had fasted and prayed." How *very* much more can be done *after* we fast and pray and *during* a fast and prayer! We clean out our ears so we can hear the voice of the Holy Spirit. He is speaking today just as clearly and personally through his word as he was in the church at Antioch. Indeed, he is speaking right here and right now as we read this Acts account. He is saying: All the areas of the world have not heard. As I sent Barnabas and Saul to Cyprus, I'm sending you to ____(fill it in)____. (You fill in the blank.) But we are too full of Christmas and New Years, etc., feasting to hear the gentle dove-like voice of the Holy Spirit. How clear would be our desire to share if we would fast and pray! We would find some sorcerers in our experiences but we would have the same resources as the first two missionaries. Dear God, when will we fast and pray?

Pause—wait—think—then express yourself in thoughtful praise or thanks.

9. READ HIS WORD FOR PETITIONS.

These three verses (Acts 13:1-3) have been precious to me for more than 40 years. I want to pray out of them for my needs: (1) Keep me aware that I a member of the same church that met in Antioch! (2) I am no prophet, but oh, how I want to be a teacher! Teach me! (3) Help me to be a true "son of encouragement." (4) I am glad there was a man called "black" in the first Gentile church. (5) There was even a man from the "third world" of northern Africa. This says something—open my ears! (6) A man reared in the immoral court of Herod the tetrarch would be so polluted there could be no hope—wrong, wrong! He was a leader in the body of Christ! I know several like him. Help me to be open to your power to change people. (7) And last of all was Saul. There was a time when all of us were last of all—that time is *now*!

Right here add your personal requests—and his answers.

10. READ HIS WORD AND WAIT—LISTEN—GOD SPEAKS!

As you spoke and separated and called so speak now through these verses: (1) "I can call better where men fast and pray." (2) "Men can hear better when they fast and pray." (3) "I will not separate men and send them out without fasting and prayer."

11. INTERCESSION FOR THE LOST WORLD

East Germany — Point for prayer: (1) *The preachers are coming under severe pressures.* There are now some Christians in prison. There is increased surveillance and interrogation of preachers—especially effective ones. Many younger preachers are now seeking to go to free West Germany —the Communists help them to leave. Pray for stability and faithfulness to the Lord and their flocks among the preachers.

12. SING PRAISES TO OUR LORD.

When morning gilds the skies,
My heart awakening cries:
May Jesus Christ be praised;

Alike at work and prayer . . .
To Jesus I repair: . . .
May Jesus Christ be praised.

WEEK TWELVE — FRIDAY

1. PRAISE GOD FOR WHO HE IS.

Triune. Praise your threefold self! The total cooperation of your three persons is a constant source of amazement! You are all in each area, i.e., absolute fulness — as God, as the Word, as the Holy Spirit. Help me and all other men to understand this quality better. Let me try to relate your triune nature to some other areas of your work. *Revela-tion.* (1) The thoughts originate in your mind. (2) The expression of them is from the One who became our Lord. (3) The power to carry this out was of the Spirit. *Judgment.* (1) The definition or balance between what is right or wrong from yourself. (2) The decisions stated by your Son. (3) The power to carry them out from the Spirit.

Express yourself in adoration for this quality of God.
Speak it audibly or write out your praise in your own devotional journal.

2. PRAISE GOD FOR WHAT HE MEANS TO ME.

Triune to me. All the above expession of praise does is enable me to praise you and enter into a time of wonder at your greatness. All three Divine Beings have the same nature, i.e., all of you are *eternal*, having no beginning and no end. Alpha and Omega can be as easily applied to all as One. All of you are *omnipotent*, i.e., total in power. This is more than I can grasp, but I thank you and try to worship adequately before you. All of you are *omniscient* i.e., absolute wisdom and knowledge — that each one could have all that the others had in knowledge and wisdom would assure Oneness in action and thought. How feeble do my words appear when related to your essential Being. Praise is too weak a word.

How do you personally relate to the threefold nature of God, and God who is triune?
Speak it out or write it out. It is *so important* that you establish *your own* devotional journal.

3. CONFESSION OF SIN

Truly, truly, *nothing* is hidden from you — my sin cannot be unknown — the hollow efforts of man to explain anything apart from your word is a total absurdity. There is no meaning without you and no explanation without your revelation. Forgive me of the sin of reading or expressing one thought apart from you. Dear God, speak into my being every word of your book. I love your word, for in it alone can I find answers to the deep questions of who? why? where? how? For other sins which essentially reflect upon my unwillingness to accept your total rule, I seek forgiveness.

What personal sins do you want to confess? We *must* speak them to remove them.
Do it! *Now.* There is no one else you have sinned against more than God. Tell him so!

4. SING A PRAYER TO GOD.

More about Jesus would I know,
More of His grace to others show;
More of His saving fulness see,
More of His love who died for me.

More, more about Jesus,
More, more about Jesus;
More of His saving fulness see,
More of His love who died for me.

Open your hymn book and sing the rest of the verses — or even sing another prayer song.

5. READ HIS WORD TO HIM!

His Word

[4]The two of them, sent on their way by the Holy Spirit, went down to Seleucia and sailed from there to Cyprus. [5]When they arrived at Salamis, they proclaimed the word of God in the Jewish synagogues. John was with them as their helper.
[6]They traveled through the whole island until they came to Paphos. There they met a Jewish sorcerer and false prophet named Bar-Jesus, [7]who was an attendant of the proconsul, Sergius Paulus. The proconsul, an intelligent man, sent for Barnabas and Saul because he wanted to hear the word of God.   — *Acts 13:4-7, NIV*

Read His Word to Him.

Dear, dear Lord, how is it that the Holy Spirit sent these two servants of yours? Was it only by the instructions you gave them in Antioch? I wish fervently that I *knew* the answer to this question. I do want to be sent by you — help me dear Lord, I am so, so glad to see you at work in the very ordinary activities of places on a map. You selected Seleucia and Cyprus — or did you? Perhaps Barnabas did since it was his early home (4:36) and you honored his choice, or worked through it. Dear Lord, I do wish I knew for certain what is meant here, in the expression "they proclaimed *the word of God*." They had no Bible. They did know your word from the Old Testament scriptures but this must then be intuitive information and they speak as your prophets. Is this correct? How many synagogues heard their word? Were there no converts? How did John help? I know you will answer all of these questions when I see you face to face. Amen!

Please express your response to this beautiful text. Put your expression in your own prayer diary.

WEEK TWELVE — FRIDAY

6. READ HIS WORD FOR YOURSELF.

I do so want to be with these two men. The actions and words of Barnabas and Saul are all so natural, i.e., unforced and spontaneous. Did they talk to the men who worked on the ship as it carried them to Cyprus? Did they call on any of the thousands or hundreds of homes in Salamis? Why didn't they stop at the many cities or villages on the way from Salamis to Paphos? Perhaps they did. Some commentators say the word "traveled" refers to a leisurely journey, but it is quite possible that I am reading into the text the cultural milieu of today's world. Help me, dear Lord, to walk in their sandals. How did they see Bar-Jesus? i.e., what was their attitude toward him? Are there today such evil men as Bar-Jesus? To ask the question is to answer it. Can we expect God to blind the eyes (understanding) so as to defeat their counsel? Will God use men like Barnabas and Saul to provide this blindness? All such questions are much more easily asked than answered.

Pause in his presence and either audibly or in written form tell him all his word means to you.

7. READ HIS WORD IN THANKSGIVING.

Yes, yes, I thank you for: (1) The sending power of the Holy Spirit. (2) That you did not tell us who decided to go to Cyprus. (3) That the pattern of working with the religiously oriented people is yet applicable for today. (4) That proclamation (or preaching) was a very real, large part of your work in the early church. (5) That there are helpers as well as leaders. (6) So much could be done with no mechanical transportation. (7) That your word recognizes intelligence and ability wherever it is found.

Give yourself to your own expression of gratitude—write it or speak it!

8. READ HIS WORD IN MEDITATION.

"A Jewish sorcerer and false prophet named Bar-Jesus." There are so many interesting things to consider here: (1) That a man who was a Jew could also be a sorcerer is more than too bad. How was he ensnared in the occult? What was the mixture of Jewish religion and the pagan influences? (2) Evidently he used his so-called power to represent himself to Sergius Paulus as a prophet of the gods. (3) It strikes us as more than strange that his name should be "son of Jesus," or Joshua. He appears to have a very aggressive temperament. This is sometimes an indication of insecurity. When his position and influence were threatened by Paul and Barnabas he became very adamant in his attempts to dissuade the governor. What shall we say of this one? Is he beyond redemption? He must be shocked out of his bondage. Were the eyes of his understanding opened while his physical sight was gone? We like to think so—we do not know.

Pause—wait—think—then express yourself in thoughtful praise or thanks.

9. READ HIS WORD FOR PETITIONS.

As Paul and Barnabas begin their journey there are naturally several requests: (1) May the journey of each day be under the direction of the Holy Spirit. (2) Help me to see finding passage on the ship at Seleucia was of the Holy Spirit. (3) Did Barnabas suggest work on the island of Cyprus because he once lived there? Is this also the leading of the Holy Spirit? (4) Luke reports no converts at Salamis. This does not mean there were none—give me a balance of values. (5) Luke reports nothing of the wonderful messages preached in several synagogues at Salamis—puncture my pride! (6) Luke does not tell us how John helped—am I ready for that kind of obscurity? (7) Although they walked 100 miles and could have spoken in several towns, Luke has a higher purpose than reporting preaching success—do I?

Please, please remember these are prayers—speak them—reword them!

10. READ HIS WORD AND WAIT—LISTEN—GOD SPEAKS!

You have already spoken to me—speak again: (1) "No man is impossible of influence for me." (2) "Intelligence is not the property of the saved." (3) "There are false prophets in the land today."

11. INTERCESSION FOR THE LOST WORLD

East Germany — Point for prayer: (1) *Youth.* It is extremely costly for a young person to follow the Lord Jesus —mocking in school, deprivation of education opportunities and poverty, yet there is a growing and enthusiastic response to the Gospel among young people.

12. SING PRAISES TO OUR LORD.

I will sing of my Redeemer,
And His wondrous love to me;
On the cruel cross He suffered,
From the curse to set me free.

Sing, oh, sing . . . of my Redeemer,
With His blood . . . He purchased me,
On the cross . . . He sealed my pardon,
Paid the debt . . . and made me free.

167

WEEK TWELVE — SATURDAY

1. PRAISE GOD FOR WHO HE IS.

Generous. What a happy choice of qualities for yourself. You are so much more generous than any man has ever been to any other man — some men who have emulated your grace have expressed this quality in lovely ways. You are so generous in so many realms, such as: (1) In the animal world you have created such a generous amount in every species — how many kinds of dogs are there? (2) With birds you have been so infinitely generous. I looked over a handbook for bird watchers and was once again I am amazed at your handiwork — hundreds of different birds, every one perfect, every one beautiful. (3) In the creation of trees — oh, how intricate, every leaf perfect.

Express yourself in adoration for this quality of God.
Speak it audibly or write out your praise in your own devotional journal.

2. PRAISE GOD FOR WHAT HE MEANS TO ME.

Generous to me. This is but another way of saying you are full of grace — indeed you are to me — you have placed me in the most prosperous country in the world, both financially, in productivity, in access to the Word of God — if we lose it all, I have enjoyed more than sixty years of abundance! Dear God, accept my gratitude for every second of every day you have placed me in the midst of a people who love you and each other and want to help me and I want to help them. Bless your heart of grace! You have supplied all our physical needs, and we have more than we need. How fully, yet poorly does this word describe you — amazing generosity!

How do you personally relate to the generosity of God, and God who is generous?
Speak it out or write it out. It is *so important* that you establish *your own* devotional journal.

3. CONFESSION OF SIN

I suppose the sin of ingratitude is the worst of all sins. It springs from some sins and produces others, but it is a terrible sin. I want to be forgiven, and open my eyes to see how uncaring I am in so many ways and times. I am afraid to care — is that true? I do not see, therefore I do not care? For whatever reason — surely best known to you — forgive! And yet for one more sin forgive, and that is false humility. Help me, move me, cleanse me — I claim your cleanness.

What personal sins do you want to confess? We *must* speak them to remove them.
Do it! *Now.* There is no one else you have sinned against more than God. Tell him so!

4. SING A PRAYER TO GOD.

Sing them over again to me,
Wonderful words of Life;
Let me more of their beauty see,
Wonderful words of Life.
Words of life and beauty,

Teach me faith and duty;
Beautiful words, wonderful words,
Wonderful words of Life.
Beautiful words, wonderful words,
Wonderful words of Life.

Open your hymn book and sing the rest of the verses — or even sing another prayer song.

5. READ HIS WORD TO HIM!

His Word

[7]who was an attendant of the proconsul, Sergius Paulus. The proconsul, an intelligent man, sent for Barnabas and Saul because he wanted to hear the word of God. [8]But Elymas the sorcerer (for that is what his name means) opposed them and tried to turn the proconsul from the faith. [9]Then Saul, who was also called Paul, filled with the Holy Spirit, looked straight at Elymas and said, [10]"You are a child of the devil and an enemy of everything that is right! You are full of all kinds of deceit and trickery. Will you never stop perverting the right ways of the Lord? [11]Now the hand of the Lord is against you. You are going to be blind, and for a time you will be unable to see the light of the sun."

Immediately mist and darkness came over him, and he groped about, seeking someone to lead him by the hand. [12]When the proconsul saw what had happened, he believed, for he was amazed at the teaching about the Lord.

— *Acts 13:7-12, NIV*

Read His Word to Him.

I truly, truly love to read this word — your words — to yourself! For someone to request an audience with yourself! What a beautiful desire and request. How was it produced? It all seems so natural, but you have your part and you have given man his part — did the news of the efforts of Barnabas and Saul to spread your word reach the ears of the governor? All of the thinking processes of Elymas and Paul and Barnabas and the proconsul — you can and do enter fully and understand perfectly. Praise your omniscience! You also know me in the same way.

Please express your response to this beautiful text. Put your expression in your own prayer diary.

168

6. READ HIS WORD FOR YOURSELF.

Yes, yes. Paul was "full of the Holy Spirit" when he read the mind and heart (i.e., motives) of the sorcerer. Does this mean that the Holy Spirit gave him such power? – the text seems to say this. Why was such power given? To prevent the defeat of "the word of the Lord" – your own defeat in the eyes of the governor, and all men of the island. Your word had not been recorded – the governor could not read it; he would know nothing more than what was said on this occasion. If your cause was to be sustained it must be here and now! Notice the qualities of this man: (1) "child of the devil" – what an awesome thought! (2) enemy of *everything* that is right – *everthing*? This seems so inclusive! but it is true. (3) Full of all kinds of deceit and trickery – all for selfish ends. (4) Perverter of the right ways of the Lord – probably a reference to his false prophecies and Jewish background.

Pause in his presence and either audibly or in written form tell him all his word means to you.

7. READ HIS WORD IN THANKSGIVING.

(1) Thank you that some men in leadership want to hear your word. (2) Thank you that some servants are so energetic and full of zeal and love that they develop such an interest in men of leadership. (3) Thank you there is "the faith" from which to turn or toward which we can turn. (4) Thank you that we can be filled with the Holy Spirit today and through him overcome opposition. (5) Thank you that I can become a promoter and friend of all that is right. (6) Thank you that I am your child. (7) Thank you that I can be open, honest, true and known and read of all men.

Give yourself to your own expression of gratitude – write it or speak it!

8. READ HIS WORD IN MEDITATION.

Shall we think and pray as we answer these questions? (1) Why did Paul oppose Peter – and that publicly? Because he stood self-condemned as a hypocrite – praise God for both Paul's courage and Peter's repentance. (2) Even the good man Barnabas was not at all immune from peer pressure and became confused and was led astray. He was no doubt led back by the same rebuke Paul gave to Peter. All of the disciples were in debt to Paul. (3) How is a man justified? By faith not by law. God *must give* us a standing before him or we could never stand at all. We are neither good enough nor smart enough to be saved by anything but grace. (4) The death of our Lord for our sins would be useless if we could be justified by obeying the law. (5) In the church at Antioch were three most unlikely prophets and teachers: Black Simon, Simeon of Africa and the half-brother of Herod – plus the illustrious Barnabas, and last of all Saul.

Pause – wait – think – then express yourself in thoughtful praise or thanks.

9. READ HIS WORD FOR PETITIONS.

In the midst of opposition so many questions arise which can be turned to petitions: (1) Lead me to men in high places who want to hear the word of God. (2) Give me the courage to speak in spite of all opposition. (3) There are many "wise ones" who need to be converted – give me grace and boldness. (4) May the Holy Spirit fill me to meet every crisis with His wisdom and power. (5) I ask by faith for the wisdom from above that I might answer Elymas. (6) Help my unbelief that you can defeat liars and tricksters today. (7) Send a mist and darkness over the eyes of those who oppose your work in my experience.

Right here add your personal requests – and his answers.

10. READ HIS WORD AND WAIT – LISTEN – GOD SPEAKS!

How dramatically did you speak to Paul, Barnabas, the proconsul and Elymas – speak to me through their experience: (1) "Expect opposition when someone wants to hear the word." (2) "You must face and answer opposition to overcome." (3) "Greater is He who is in you than he who is in Elymas."

11. INTERCESSION FOR THE LOST WORLD

East Germany – Point for prayer: (1) *Literature* is more freely available than in any other Communist land. Bibles and some Christian literature (censored) are sold in the shops, though there is a great lack of good, new literature. Pray that this freedom may continue – for there is real danger that this may be stopped.

12. SING PRAISES TO OUR LORD.

O for a thousand tongues to sing
My great Redeemer's praise,

The glories of my God and King,
The triumphs of His grace.

WEEK THIRTEEN — SUNDAY

1. PRAISE GOD FOR WHO HE IS.

Courageous. In so, so many ways you are courageous in the affairs of men. From man's perspective it took great courage to create the worlds, the ten million galaxies, as you have—but since nothing you do in the physical world can fail—it is only from our perspective that courage is present. But I want to say, and all your children will stand back aghast at the courage present in creating man and angels! That you would place your confidence in my willingness to do your will and leave me open to Satan's efforts is an act of courage beyond human words! At the same time I thank you that such is true!

Express yourself in adoration for this quality of God.
Speak it audibly or write out your praise in your own devotional journal.

2. PRAISE GOD FOR WHAT HE MEANS TO ME.

The courage in the promise of "the woman's seed"—what boldness and adventure it took for your Son to become flesh and live among men—courage to believe in me for me to believe in you—how is it that I lack this quality? Dear God, I repent—if you believe in me, then I *know* it shall be done. How I want your perfect will to find fulfillment! For your strength and character I thank you and glorify your very self!

How do you personally relate to the courage of God, and God who is courageous?
Speak it out or write it out. It is *so important* that you establish *your own* devotional journal.

3. CONFESSION OF SIN

"To be carnally minded is death," is separation from your presence, to be cut off by my own thoughts. To think on the things above, to meditate upon them *immediately* removes this sin. But it is the "set" of the mind that directs the life. "To be spiritually minded is life and peace," but only when it is the habit of thinking! Dear God, I do, I do want to repent—*"change my mind"* down deep in the depths of my being. I want to change my mind; to set my mind upon those things which are: (1) true, (2) noble, (3) right, (4) pure, (5) lovely, (6) admirable, (7) excellent, (8) praiseworthy. All these qualities could be seen in my Lord, and in his servant Paul. Dear Lord, if I meditate upon them they will be seen in me!

What personal sins do you want to confess? We *must* speak them to remove them.
Do it! *Now.* There is no one else you have sinned against more than God. Tell him so!

4. SING A PRAYER TO GOD.

O Jesus, I have promised
To serve Thee to the end;
Be Thou forever near me,
My Master and my Friend:

I shall not fear the battle
If Thou art by my side,
Nor wander from the pathway
If Thou wilt be my guide.

Open your hymn book and sing the rest of the verses—or even sing another prayer song.

5. READ HIS WORD TO HIM!

His Word

[13] From Paphos, Paul and his companions sailed to Perga in Pamphylia, where John left them to return to Jerusalem. [14] From Perga they went on to Pisidian Antioch. On the Sabbath they entered the synagogue and sat down.
— *Acts 13:13, 14, NIV*

Read His Word to Him.

Were you on board the ship that sailed from Cyprus to Perga? I'm sure—confident—you were. How very interesting that we are now following "Paul and his companions" instead of Barnabas and Paul. You have moved him to the front of the narrative, as you do in all of life in the experience of all men—someone *must* lead and others *must* follow. In a certain sense all of us are leaders and all of us are followers, but in the record of historians, like Luke, it is "Paul and company." Praise your name for your leadership which we all want to follow. I have not been to this part of Turkey, but I have been in the country. What time of the year was it? What type of weather faced them? What was the attitude of the people in Perga? All of these questions I know you can answer, but perhaps none of them influenced John Mark's decision to go back to Jerusalem. Thou knowest!

Please express your response to this beautiful text. Put your expression in your own prayer diary.

6. READ HIS WORD FOR YOURSELF.

I know it displeased Paul that John Mark "left them and *would not* go with them to the work" in Antioch of Pisidia. Paul felt he had been deserted by this young man — was Paul right? What were the feelings of John Mark? Some people feel it was when he returned to Jerusalem that he wrote what we now have as the gospel of Mark. If this is true he was not depressed or discouraged. I can indeed relate to all three men. I would be sorely concerned if a relative of mine made some inexplicable move that could reflect upon him and the work of our Lord, to say nothing of our family. So was the place of Barnabas — I would think — "Leave then if you do not want the work. You cannot be the servant we need and God wants." So, perhaps, were the thoughts of Paul. But most of all I relate to Mark — "What can I do with men so capable as these? I am of little or no help at all. I could do much more in Jerusalem."

Pause in his presence and either audibly or in written form tell him all his word means to you.

7. READ HIS WORD IN THANKSGIVING.

Yea and amen! (1) Thank you for transportation — then and now. (2) Thank you for the clear record preserved by your power to this very day. (3) Thank you for thoughtful Luke, and the Holy Spirit who never told us who was at fault in John's leaving. (4) For the shocking fact that no travel scenes are described by this historian. It was more than a hundred miles of rough territory from Perga to Antioch. Luke's value system was almost totally spiritual. (5) Thank you that Paul *used* the religious practices to his own advantage — such as the synagogue and the sabbath day. (6) It seems right to "sit" before you to learn and converse. (7) For all the unnamed people who sat there that day and heard for the first time the wonderful words of life. I shall be there too one day!

Give yourself to your own expression of gratitude — write it or speak it!

8. READ HIS WORD IN MEDITATION.

John Mark left them to return to Jerusalem. Evidently there is much more in this text than we read in the Acts account — the choice of Mark was not acceptable to Paul, neither the choice Mark made to leave them at Perga, nor the choice Barnabas made later to take Mark on the journey. What possible reasons did John Mark have? (1) He had an urgent message from his mother that he was sorely needed at home — perhaps his mother was sick and needed him, or had a financial crisis only Mark could meet. (2) He did not find the work he was doing with Paul and Barnabas what he expected. He was really not needed — as is shown subsequently, these two men were quite sufficient unto themselves and John Mark could do a better work elsewhere, like writing the third gospel in Jerusalem.

Pause — wait — think — then express yourself in thoughtful praise or thanks.

9. READ HIS WORD FOR PETITIONS.

In an incident so briefly mentioned here, so largely considered later, we have several requests: (1) "Paul and his companions" is vastly different than "Barnabas and Saul." Help me to learn *you* identify and select leaders. (2) Keep me from homesickness — except it be heaven. (3) Keep me from self-pity which encourages nothing but weakness. (4) Keep me from personality conflicts which hinder your work. (5) Keep me from judging the motives of others. (6) Keep me from unforgiven ill-will. (7) Keep me from bragging about difficulties as if others have not so suffered.

Please, please remember these are prayers — speak them — reword them!

10. READ HIS WORD AND WAIT — LISTEN — GOD SPEAKS!

Surely there is much you can say to me from these two verses: (1) "Every servant is important — John Mark included." (2) "Luke never gave a travelogue — he told of God's work in preaching." (3) "These men spoke to the religiously confused and uninformed."

11. INTERCESSION FOR THE LOST WORLD

East Germany — Points for prayer: (1) *The Churches are still able to give theological training* to potential preachers. The University Theological Faculties are increasingly dominated by Marxist staff, but the Seminaries are still free of state interference. There is now an independent theological faculty for Bible believers connected with Seeheim (q.v.) in West Germany. Pray for this freedom to continue. (2) *Christian Radio.* The large and effective German branch of Trans World Radio produces a number of daily programs for broadcasting to both Germanies. Pray for this ministry.

12. SING PRAISES TO OUR LORD.

O worship the King, all glorious above,
And gratefully sing His pow'r and His love;

Our Shield and Defender, the Ancient of Days,
Pavilioned in splendor, and girded with praise.

WEEK THIRTEEN — MONDAY

1. PRAISE GOD FOR WHO HE IS.

Healer. How strange to discuss this quality of yourself when I spent all of yesterday in class discussing the healing of Aeneas. You are the source of all healing, of all restoration of the imperfect function of all the human body. Why, why are we *so* interested in the function or malfunction of this machine? It is already doomed—the death sentence is upon it—to dust shall it return. The answer is as obvious as the question because while we live in this house we become very closely associated with it—indeed we struggle for independent identity. Praise your wonderful name—I am not, have never been and will not be this body.

Express yourself in adoration for this quality of God.
Speak it audibly or write out your praise in your own devotional journal.

2. PRAISE GOD FOR WHAT HE MEANS TO ME.

You can and do heal me! I have been very sick, i.e., my body has malfunctioned. I sought your help first—last and always—through doctors my back was healed. Through the same means (but you are the source) other parts of my body were made well. The only difference in these healings and any others was *time*. You did it! Praise you. It took longer, but you did it! Why shouldn't we praise you for all that doctors and nurses know about restoring my body? Because you have to work through men and women and it takes longer yet this does not deny your power. I'm right here to record my deepest praise for your healing!

How do you personally relate to the healing of God, and God who is healer?
Speak it out or write it out. It is *so important* that you establish *your own* devotional journal.

3. CONFESSION OF SIN

I have been greatly helped by understanding you as power only because of and through your power can I overcome sin. I do not hesitate in admitting my sin, indeed I want to—to you, not to men unless they are involved in it. What I need and claim is the power to overcome. I want not only to *know* the scriptures but the power of God. I do not—do not—want to be like the Parisees who were ignorant of both—many of them knew the scriptures but not the power of yourself. I want you to work in me, through me. Forgive me, cleanse me, wash me, purify me, but most of all, *enable* me!

What personal sins do you want to confess? We *must* speak them to remove them.
Do it! *Now.* There is no one else you have sinned against more than God. Tell him so!

4. SING A PRAYER TO GOD.

All to Jesus I surrender,
All to Him I freely give;
I will ever love and trust Him,
In His presence daily live.

I surrender all, I surrender all.
All to Thee, my blessed Savior,
I surrender all.

Open your hymn book and sing the rest of the verses—or even sing another prayer song.

5. READ HIS WORD TO HIM!

His Word

[15]After the reading from the Law and the Prophets, the synagogue rulers sent word to them, saying, "Brothers, if you have a message of encouragement for the people, please speak."

[16]Standing up, Paul motioned with his hand and said: "Men of Israel and you Gentiles who worship God, listen to me! [17]The God of the people of Israel chose our fathers and made the people prosper during their stay in Egypt. With mighty power he led them out of that country [18]and endured their conduct forty years in the desert. [19]He overthrew seven nations in Canaan and gave their land to his people as their inheritance. [20]All this took about 450 years.

"After this, God gave them judges until the time of Samuel the prophet. — *Acts 13:15-20, NIV*

Read His Word to Him.

Oh, dear Lord, you have always "a message of encouragement" for me—most of all it is you have come to heal me of all my diseases, inward plagues I have brought upon myself. The God of the people of Israel is my God. You are my God. I acknowledge, gladly, all your mighty works. Your choice of "the fathers" indicates there is hope and purpose for all men. Your endurance in the wilderness of the complainers and faithless indicates your kindness. Your war against the seven nations demonstrates your hatred against disobedience. Most of all what you promised you surely will fulfill. 450 years is one long time by our measure, but a brief time with you. Blessed be your name for your careful record of deliverance and love.

Please express your reponse to this beautiful text. Put your expression in your own prayer diary.

6. READ HIS WORD FOR YOURSELF.

How I would like to have been one of the Gentiles who worshiped in the Antioch synagogue on that Sabbath so long ago! What a verbal commentary Paul or Barnabas could have given me. But wonder of wonders, it would have been no different from the record I now have in your word. I can read, and I want to read, the books of Exodus, Numbers, Joshua, Judges and Ruth. How personally helpful are all the records which tell me over and over again of your power in the lives of men and women.

Pause in his presence and either audibly or in written form tell him all his word means to you.

7. READ HIS WORD IN THANKSGIVING.

Yea, and amen: (1) Thank you for the purpose of teaching and preaching to one another, i.e., encouragement! (2) Thank you we all as Christians can be "brothers" in an even more precious relationship than the Jewish brothers. (3) That verbal communication is just as effective, with its facial expression and hand gestures, as it was when Paul spoke. (4) Thank you that I can learn from Paul how to speak to religious people and reach them for your Son. (5) That you are the author or source of prosperity and adversity when it suits your purpose. (6) That you can (and do) lead me out of my own Egypt. (7) That you are more than patient with me. Dear God, I repent, please forgive me!

Give yourself to your own expression of gratitude—write it or speak it!

8. READ HIS WORD IN MEDITATION.

Overthrew the seven nations. It would sound upon hearing it or reading it that the whole initiative was with yourself, but it was Moses and his army, it was Joshua and his men, who did it. But you at the same time through them did it. Without you they could never have done it, but without them you would not have done it. You have bound yourself by your own laws—and one of them that you will accomplish your purposes through man. Blessed be your name, I believe you are even now at work overthrowing and raising up as you will. I want to be in the front lines being used of you for your will.

Pause—wait—think—then express yourself in thoughtful praise or thanks.

9. READ HIS WORD FOR PETITIONS.

As we attend one of the Jewish worship services there are several petitions that occur to us: (1) Teach me to preach from the example of Paul. (2) Give me wisdom as I study your word. (3) Help me to speak to everyone who attends my class. (4) Give me the same conviction of historical facts that Paul had as I preach your word. (5) If you endured the conduct of Israel 40 years surely I can endure some people with the same love you had. (6) Thank you that you are fighting for me today. (7) Give me a time perspective like yours. Events, not time, are important.

Right here add your personal requests—and his answers.

10. READ HIS WORD AND WAIT—LISTEN—GOD SPEAKS!

Please speak to me through this text: (1) "History is His story." (2) "Please learn from the example of others." (3) "I have always worked through men."

11. INTERCESSION FOR THE LOST WORLD

Hungary — Population: 10,600,000. Growth rate 0.6%. People per sq. km.—114.
Points for prayer: (1) *Persecution used to be more by threats,* harassments and discrimination. This is now changing with more preachers being interrogated, watched and dismissed. Some unofficial Christian workers are now in prison. Uncertainty and fear pervades the country. Pray for the believers in these difficult circumstances. (2) *Bible training for Bible believers is very hard to obtain.* Pray for the raising up of more laborers willing to pay the high price of serving the Lord full time.

12. SING PRAISES TO OUR LORD.

The name of Jesus is so sweet,
I love its music to repeat;
It makes my joys full and complete,
The precious name of Jesus.

"Jesus," O how sweet the name!
"Jesus," every day the same;
"Jesus," let all saints proclaim
Its worthy praise forever.

WEEK THIRTEEN — TUESDAY

1. PRAISE GOD FOR WHO HE IS.

Life-giver. You are the one who gives life and the one who decides when our sojourn here will end. A profound thought: that all life has its origin in yourself or of yourself. Man's life is a part of yourself, i.e., we are created in your image and share your nature—animals and all other life are created and are temporary. It is so good to know the life you have given to all men will never end. In the other world there will be a life beyond our very fondest dreams. How I do praise your name for life here and especially that my life is in America.

Express yourself in adoration for this quality of God.
Speak it audibly or write out your praise in your own devotional journal.

2. PRAISE GOD FOR WHAT HE MEANS TO ME.

Life-giver for me—my life came from you. I am more than grateful—I am overwhelmed with the thought—all I am, all I hope to be or do, the source of life energy and thought process comes from you. I shall not have life one more day than you choose. If this is my last day of life for this world it will be your giving. Blessed be your name! I came from you and to you I shall return. In giving life you must also sustain it—what an amazement! to maintain a life you have started! I shall never in ten lifetimes be able to thank you enough for all that is involved in life!

How do you personally relate to the life-giving of God, and God who is life-giver?
Speak it out or write it out. It is *so important* that you establish *your own* devotional journal.

2. CONFESSION OF SIN

I want forgiveness for the misuse and dissipation of life—such a precious commodity—and how easily, lightly we abuse it! Only one little minute, but eternity is in it. For harshness in word and attitude, dear Lord, dear, gentle Jesus, forgive me. I can blame it on nerves, but whose nerves are they? I can rest, I can relax, I can pray and I need not be harsh or unkind. For this sin, this selfish sin, forgive me. Each day, every day, I want to arise from the fountain of cleansing "just as if I had never sinned." Praise your name!

What personal sins do you want to confess? We *must* speak them to remove them.
Do it! *Now.* There is no one else you have sinned against more than God. Tell him so!

4. SING A PRAYER TO GOD.

Out of my bondage, sorrow and night,
Jesus, I come, Jesus, I come;
Into Thy freedom, gladness and light,
Jesus, I come to Thee.

Out of my sickness into Thy health,
Out of my want and into Thy wealth,
Out of my sin and into Thyself,
Jesus, I come to Thee.

Open your hymn book and sing the rest of the verses—or even sing another prayer song.

5. READ HIS WORD TO HIM!

His Word

21 Then the people asked for a king, and he gave them Saul son of Kish, of the tribe of Benjamin, who ruled forty years. 22 After removing Saul, he made David their king. He testified concerning him: 'I have found David son of Jesse a man after my own heart; he will do everything I want him to do.' 23 From this man's descendants God has brought to Israel the Savior Jesus, as he promised. 24 Before the coming of Jesus, John preached repentance and baptism to all the people of Israel. 25 As John was completing his work, he said: 'Who do you think I am? I am not that one. No, but he is coming after me, whose sandals I am not worthy to untie.'

26 "Brothers, children of Abraham, and you God-fearing Gentiles, it is to us that this message of salvation has been sent. 27 The people of Jerusalem and their rulers did not recognize Jesus, yet in condemning him they fulfilled the words of the prophets that are read every Sabbath. 28 Though they found no proper ground for a death sentence, they asked Pilate to have him executed.   — *Acts 13:21-28, NIV*

Read His Word to Him.

Dear, dear God! When you give people what they ask, it is seldom good! We are so full of pride and selfishness, but even in the midst of our ignorance you can work it out for our good if only we would have eyes to see! Such was the case with Saul the son of Kish. You would but the people wouldn't—how often this has been repeated!

How I wish I could fully appreciate David the son of Jesse. Dear God, I want to have the very same disposition—"after your own heart"—or full of desire to do and be all you would do and be if you were man—even the great son of David.

Please express your response to this beautiful text. Put your expression in your own prayer diary.

6. READ HIS WORD FOR YOURSELF.

May I stand with John and freely confess that "I am not worthy of the least of his favor" — nay — I fall prostrate at his feet in contrition and confession. How more than glad I am to be a child of Abraham by faith and to claim all the promises God made to Abraham: the forgiveness of all my sins and salvation in him! Shall I repeat the monstrous sin of finding no proper ground for a death sentence and yet refuse to allow him to be king of my life? Dear Lord, no, no! "Crown him, honor him, worship him," is the cry of my heart.

Pause in his presence and either audibly or in written form tell him all his word means to you.

7. READ HIS WORD IN THANKSGIVING.

(1) Thank you for the farm boy king — Saul the son of Kish — he could have been so much — he is so much like me. (2) Thank you for the sweet singer of Israel — David the shepherd boy — he was a farm boy too, but what a difference! (3) Doing as well as being, or being and therefore doing is the secret — thank you for David. (4) Thank you for the long, patient record of history — it is "His story." (5) Thank you that there had to be Mary and Joseph and angels and shepherds to bring your Son — for we see our part in your great plan. (6) Thank you, thank you that I *can* and *do* recognize Jesus for who he is! (7) Thank you that I was not Pilate — and yet help me today to release Jesus and let him be king.

Give yourself to your own expression of gratitude — write it or speak it!

8. READ HIS WORD IN MEDITATION.

"John preached repentance and baptism to all the people of Israel." There is surely no message more sorely needed today. Where has real genuine repentance gone? Who is being used of God to bring deep sorrow for sin that leads to a complete change of conduct? Repentance needs to be preached — we can't mention it as a viable option to present problems. It must be infused into the heads and hearts of the listeners as God's command. Preaching includes all the rhetorical devices possible to elicit an involvement with the message. Can you see John on the banks of the Jordan? His words were alive with the presence of the Spirit of God. He named their sins and told them they were guilty before God. If there is no godly sorrow there is no repentance. We *do* sin against God. We *will* have to give an account for the deeds done in the body. There *is* a judgment and there *is* a hell. Somebody needs to tell it like it is! John did.

Pause — wait — think — then express yourself in thoughtful praise or thanks.

9. READ HIS WORD FOR PETITIONS.

There are questions from history that can easily be requests: (1) Dear God, I am too much like Saul the son of Kish — forgive me. (2) David was the man "after your heart" — teach me all this means. (3) All you want done I do not always want to do — help me! (4) Thank you for the long promised Savior — I want him to save me from my own selfishness. (5) I have no greater need than a daily repentance — I claim your answer! (6) Help me to accept my sonship as a son of Abraham by faith. (7) I, like Pilate, find no fault in him, but do I, like Pilate, evade him? No, no, he is Lord!

Please, please remember these are prayers — speak them — reword them!

10. READ HIS WORD AND WAIT — LISTEN — GOD SPEAKS!

You have surely spoken to me in this text — I am still listening: (1) "I will remove those who will not obey me." (2) "I can use anyone who loves me from the heart." (3) "Salvation's message is the same today."

11. INTERCESSION FOR THE LOST WORLD

Hungary — Points for prayer: (1) *Young People are turning to the Lord all over the country.* They are compelled to meet illegally in most cases. There are some large and enthusiastic groups. Pray that these young believers may remain faithful under the many pressures to which they are subjected. To be a Christian endangers their future livelihood. (2) *There is an awakening among the Gypsies* in the east of the country. Pray that this movement may grow and spread to other areas. (3) *Christian literature* is sometimes available in limited quantities, but there is a great inadequacy of supplies. Some Bibles have been printed in the land, others have been legally imported; yet it is now virtually impossible to buy a Bible and now illegal to transport or receive literature from the West, so pray for those who seek to bring such greatly needed literature from the West to this land.

12. SING PRAISES TO OUR LORD.

Come, we that love the Lord,
And let our joys be known;

Join in a song with sweet accord,
And thus surround the throne.

WEEK THIRTEEN — WEDNESDAY

1. PRAISE GOD FOR WHO HE IS.

Hope. How shall we live without hope? We cannot! We *do* not. Hope is the beautiful quality that gives anticipation and relish to our efforts. You are the one who creates hope! Blessed and holy and wonderful is your name! You have been the source of hope for every man from the beginning of time—what a great thought! Hope in the face of the grave! "All men"—i.e., *"all men* will hear his voice and come forth" (John 5:23-29). As in Adam all die and surely they do, just so certainly in Christ shall *all* be made alive (I Cor. 15:22).

Express yourself in adoration for this quality of God.
Speak it audibly or write out your praise in your own devotional journal.

2. PRAISE GOD FOR WHAT HE MEANS TO ME.

My hope. Dear wonderful Lord, how delightfully good it is to write, to pray, to praise before you! Without my hold on your word full of your promises life would be worse than useless—for there would be no purpose or point. But because I have your very nature, your Holy Spirit, or (the Holy Spirit), I have all things that have meaning and purpose. You are my all and you are in all I want and do. You are my hope—the wonderful fact is: all that we hope in you happens. No hope is short of reality. No idle dreams, all living fact! Praise your name which is hope!

How do you personally relate to the hope of God, and God who is hope?
Speak it out or write it out. It is *so important* that you establish *your own* devotional journal.

3. CONFESSION OF SIN

To return wrong for wrong might seem to me to be "natural" but it is sin, and an indication I am living by self and selfishness and not by the Spirit of my Lord who when he was reviled, reviled *not* again. Dear Lord, deliver me from the need to have my own way. Forgive me for resentment and frustration at being interrupted. Our Lord was interrupted in the midst of a far more important work than I will ever do and he did not resent it.

What personal sins do you want to confess? We *must* speak them to remove them.
Do it! *Now.* There is no one else you have sinned against more than God. Tell him so!

4. SING A PRAYER TO GOD.

O happy day that fixed my choice
On Thee, my Savior and my God!
Well may this glowing heart rejoice,
And tell its raptures all abroad.
Happy day, happy day,

When Jesus washed my sins away!
He taught me how to watch and pray,
And live rejoicing ev'ry day;
Happy day, happy day,
When Jesus washed my sins away!

Open your hymn book and sing the rest of the verses—or even sing another prayer song.

5. READ HIS WORD TO HIM!
His Word

[29]When they had carried out all that was written about him, they took him down from the tree and laid him in a tomb. [30]But God raised him from the dead, [31]and for many days he was seen by those who had traveled with him from Galilee to Jerusalem. They are now his witnesses to our people.

[32]"We tell you the good news: What God promised our fathers [33]he has fulfilled for us, their children, by raising up Jesus. As it is written in the second Psalm:

"'You are my Son;
today I have become your Father.'

[34]The fact that God raised him from the dead, never to decay, is stated in these words:

"'I will give you the holy and sure
blessings promised to David.'

[35]So it is stated elsewhere:

"'You will not let your Holy One see decay.'

[36]"For when David had served God's purpose in his own generation, he fell asleep; he was buried with his fathers and his body decayed. [37]But the one whom God raised from the dead did not see decay. [38]Therefore, my brothers, I want you to know that through Jesus the forgiveness of sins is proclaimed to you. [39]Through him everyone who believes is justified from everything you could not be justified from by the law of Moses. [40]Take care that what the prophets have said does not happen to you:

[41]"'Look, you scoffers,
wonder and perish,
for I am going to do something in your days
that you would never believe,
even if someone told you.'"

[42]As Paul and Barnabas were leaving the synagogue, the people invited them to speak further about these things on the next Sabbath. [43]When the congregation was dismissed, many of the Jews and devout converts to Judaism followed Paul and Barnabas, who talked with them and urged them to continue in the grace of God.

— Acts 13:29-43, NIV

WEEK THIRTEEN — WEDNESDAY

Read His Word to Him.

How easy this is to relate this text to yourself! How interesting that *all* you had written was fulfilled before your dear Son was taken down from the cross! That one verse: "But God raised him from the dead!" Praise, adoration, wonder, joy, all such words are not enough to say all that is in my heart as I consider what happened when you raised him from the dead! You knew how slow and dull we are in relation to divine reality, so you appeared for many days. Dear, dear Lord, how kind and good you are, how patient with our willfulness.

Please express your response to this beautiful text. Put your expression in your own prayer diary.

6. READ HIS WORD FOR YOURSELF.

Indeed, indeed I have been doing that very thing! Those who came up with him from Galilee to Jerusalem were both men and women who had followed him. They were all eyewitnesses of his majesty. He was and is king over all! Death, life, hell, the grave, king over all! They saw him, talked with him, handled him, ate with him, feasted their eyes upon him. Oh what "good news" it is! He is alive today, right now!

Pause in his presence and either audibly or in written form tell him all his word means to you.

7. READ HIS WORD IN THANKSGIVING.

How could we do less? Thank you, thank you for: (1) Every single promise fulfilled in him. (2) That our Lord was truly dead and buried to show the power of his resurrection. (3) That the evidence for his resurrection is so overpowering. (4) The promises made to the fathers can be fulfilled in the lives of the children. (5) For the holy and sure blessings of David in the resurrection of Jesus. (6) Each man can serve his own generation — there is no other time to do it. (7) That right today we can proclaim from the housetops the forgiveness of sins!

Give yourself to your own expression of gratitude — write it or speak it!

8. READ HIS WORD IN MEDITATION.

"Urged them to continue in the grace of God." This is a word from Paul to the devout Gentiles of Antioch of Pisidia. They had not yet become Christians — at the same time they were urged to "continue in the grace of God," i.e., to continue in God's favor. Their interest in God's Son put them in the favor of God. Indeed, in one sense there are degrees of grace or favor: (1) God looks with grace upon the whole human race or we would all be destroyed long ago. Are Christians "the salt of the earth" that gives God's favor and preserves the population from destruction? (2) God looks with favor on those who have an interest — like the first Gentile Christian, Cornelius. Those who seek him will be found by him.

Pause — wait — think — then express yourself in thoughtful praise or thanks.

9. READ HIS WORD FOR PETITIONS.

Paul's sermons produce all manner of requests in prayer: (1) Impress upon my memory all the prophecies of his death that I might teach and preach them. (2) Thank you for the overwhelming evidence of his resurrection — move me to preach it! (3) Dear Lord, may I serve your purpose in my generation. (4) There is no greater need today than for men to know they can be forgiven — move me to tell it! (5) I believe, I am always seeking help in my unbelief. (6) In every way, help me to continue in your grace. (7) Open my heart and mouth to preach even to those who do not want to hear.

Right here add your personal requests — and his answers.

10. READ HIS WORD AND WAIT — LISTEN — GOD SPEAKS!

You were speaking through Paul to those in Antioch of Pisidia — speak to me through him today: (1) "Men who hear for the first time do not always understand." (2) "Detailed teaching can produce wonderful results if you keep it up." (3) "I am looking in favor upon all who are interested in my word."

11. INTERCESSION FOR THE LOST WORLD

Poland — Population: 34,400,000.
Point for prayer: (1) *This land is one of the least evangelized countries* in Communist Europe, yet it is the most open for Christian work. Many areas of the country are without a Bible believing witness. Pray for the evangelization of this land.

12. SING PRAISES TO OUR LORD.

All hail the pow'r of Jesus' name!
Let angels prostrate fall:
Bring forth the royal diadem,
And crown Him Lord of all,
Bring forth the royal diadem,
And crown Him Lord of all!

WEEK THIRTEEN — THURSDAY

1. PRAISE GOD FOR WHO HE IS.

Potter. This is a beautiful figure (metaphor) to describe yourself and your relationship to man. As the potter finds the clay—you have done even more—you have created the clay, and you remember that we are dust. You moisten this dust to make it pliable. In one way or another you must and do moisten us that we might be clay in your hands. How long will it take to beat all the air bubbles out of us? Air pockets in the furnace of the kiln will burst the purpose of the potter. Just what form do you have for me? (and ten billion like me?) I'm sure it is no problem since I raked ten billion leaves just last week and there wasn't one exactly like another—is not man of more value (or thought) than leaves? Indeed he is!

Express yourself in adoration for this quality of God.
Speak it audibly or write out your praise in your own devotional journal.

2. PRAISE GOD FOR WHAT HE MEANS TO ME.

I praise you about my pot—I am clay—of a most perishable substance and to the dust shall I return, but this is a discussion not only of the outward but the inward man. On the inside I feel my weakness, but it is with the inside you work. We have the bodies of flesh from our parents—it is with spirit that you work. I'm so, so glad that none of the comparisons here made are static (i.e., cannot be changed). You are *constantly* in the process of the work of the potter. You are always kneeding me, you are always shaping me, you are always firing me, etc. I am also glad that in a sense you have shaped me for a work and it has been done, and now you are at work shaping me for another task, but I want to remember the whole process is present all the time.

How do you personally relate to the interest of God, and God who is the potter?
Speak it out or write it out. It is *so important* that you establish *your own* devotional journal.

3. CONFESSION OF SIN

As I think of you as the potter, I want to fully confess I have been, nay, I am: (1) full of rocks to be removed. (2) mixed with soil that needs screening. (3) stupid in that I try to tell you how I should be made. In this connection I want to confess to often grieving the Holy Spirit. I do so in thought and word and deed. I think thoughts unworthy of his presence. I speak words he must reject. I have spent my energies on tasks of no benefit or pleasure to him. Dear Lord, forgive! In the specifics I openly admit and repent of sin, yea sins. I claim your cleansing!

What personal sins do you want to confess? We *must* speak them to remove them.
Do it! *Now.* There is no one else you have sinned against more than God. Tell him so!

4. SING A PRAYER TO GOD.

Come, Thou Almighty King,
Help us Thy name to sing,
Help us to praise:
Father, all glorious,
O'er all victorious,
Come, and reign over us,
Ancient of Days.

Open your hymn book and sing the rest of the verses—or even sing another prayer song.

5. READ HIS WORD TO HIM!

His Word

[44] On the next Sabbath almost the whole city gathered to hear the word of the Lord. [45] When the Jews saw the crowds, they were filled with jealousy and talked abusively against what Paul was saying. [46] Then Paul and Barnabas answered them boldly: "We had to speak the word of God to you first. Since you reject it and do not consider yourselves worthy of eternal life, we now turn to the Gentiles. [47] For this is what the Lord has commanded us:
"'I have made you a light for the Gentiles,
that you may bring salvation to the ends of the earth.'" — *Acts 13:44-47, NIV*

Read His Word to Him.

Dear Lord, do you see all men as we see a crowd? or do you see each one all at the same time? or is there another way of seeing that I could not even imagine? "Almost the whole city of Pisidian Antioch" came out to hear the word of yourself—how large a crowd was that? How could such interest in your word be aroused? What did you do? What did your servants do? What should *I do* today to arouse such interest in the city where I speak?

Please express your response to this beautiful text. Put your expression in your own prayer diary.

6. READ HIS WORD FOR YOURSELF.

Yes, yes I do want to mingle in that crowd. I am a *most* interested Gentile. I want to *right now* respond as did these men and women to the abusive language of religious leaders who argue among themselves. Help me, help me, to hear from the original source and find the same light, eternal light, salvation, that these Gentiles did in Antioch. That your salvation was to be "to the ends of the earth" is a fascinating thought! Only if those taught were to teach others could this happen. "To teach others also" would seem to be *the one most important task* we have to perform. How beautiful are the words: *eternal life, light, salvation.* This is what we enjoy and share, but until we have caused others to share with others we reject eternal life — shut off the light and condemn the world.

Pause in his presence and either audibly or in written form tell him all his word means to you.

7. READ HIS WORD IN THANKSGIVING.

Yea and amen: (1) Thank you for the Sabbath day of the Jewish calendar — typical of the eternal Sabbath called heaven. (2) That there *are* cities today who would give the same attention to your word — help me to find them. (3) Thank you for men who will get sad, mad or glad — if they do not, nothing can be done. (4) Thank you for the bold words of Paul and Barnabas — they help me. (5) Thank you that whereas we must obey, we need not repeat a profitless effort. (6) Thank you that we decide if we are worthy of eternal life. (7) Thank you for the command to go to the ends of the earth.

Give yourself to your own expression of gratitude — write it or speak it!

8. READ HIS WORD IN MEDITATION.

". . . We had to speak the word of God to you first." The urgency of Paul and so many of the first century speaks so eloquently to me today. Do I feel the compelling "must" in my preaching? Is necessity laid upon me? Our Lord said the good news must first be spoken to the Jews — and then to the Gentiles. Is there a priority in audience today? It seems obvious to me that our Lord is sending us first to the religious people — what about the Mormons? the Jehovah Witnesses? Are these persons any more steeped in their religious beliefs than the Jews were in theirs? There are religions in the world such as those in India or other parts of Asia, but what of Europe? Do we owe a debt *first* to the religious people of the world? Dear Lord, most of all we owe a debt to you — it is preaching the word that matters most.

Pause — wait — think — then express yourself in thoughtful praise or thanks.

9. READ HIS WORD FOR PETITIONS.

As men and women gather to hear your word I want you to hear my prayers: (1) Lead me to religious people who will have an interest in your word. (2) May I respect the beliefs of those who do not know you, even as did Paul and Barnabas. (3) Give me courage and wisdom to stir people as did your servants here. (4) Give me grace to receive the abuse of men even as your Son. (5) Lead me to the very ones who should hear. (6) Keep me aware that it is in men's response the decision is made as to the worthiness of the person. (7) Do I believe salvation is for "the ends of the earth"? I do — help my unbelief!

Please, please remember these are prayers — speak them — reword them!

10. READ HIS WORD AND WAIT — LISTEN — GOD SPEAKS!

What do you say to me here? (1) "Crowds do not mean there will be no opposition." (2) "There are some who are disbelievers." (3) "There are always multitudes who will hear."

11. INTERCESSION FOR THE LOST WORLD

Poland — Point for prayer: (1) *The Roman Catholic church is very powerful,* and has successfully blocked all attempts by the atheist government to deprive it of its independence and freedom to work through its churches and institutions. Many Communist Party members remain Roman Catholic. The Church is really the center of Polish nationalism and culture in the face of Russian imperialism. The Church is very conservative, not in favor of the use of the Bible. Pray for the salvation of many Polish people.

12. SING PRAISES TO OUR LORD.

Great God of wonders! all Thy ways
Are matchless, God-like, and divine;
But the fair glories of Thy grace
More God-like and unrivaled shine,

More God-like and unrivaled shine.
Who is a pard'ning God like Thee?
Or who has grace so rich and free?
Or who has grace so rich and free?

WEEK THIRTEEN — FRIDAY

1. PRAISE GOD FOR WHO HE IS.

Husband. The whole world is not at all married to you, but all Christians are! Together we do indeed make up the bride. How comforting and full of strength is this fact. How thoughtful and careful are you as a husband. I know you created all men to be married to you. As a husband loves and provides for his wife so do you for us. Indeed, you are the pattern — the model for all husbands — a very good description of your love and care for your bride is found in the Old Testament as Israel was your beloved. Oh, may I not repeat their unfaithfulness.

Express yourself in adoration for this quality of God.
Speak it audibly or write it out. It is *so important* that you establish *your own* devotional journal.

2. PRAISE GOD FOR WHAT HE MEANS TO ME.

A husband to me. You have provided in so many, many ways for me! What clothes! The robe of unearned righteousness! The sandals of peace — not to mention the armor of warfare — I feel like the prodigal (and indeed I am) who received "the best robe in the Father's house" — I wear the ring of recognition, the blessed Holy Spirit. Blessed be your marvelous name — which is my name since I am married to you. All that I have said about you reflects in my life for I share your intimacy — what an ideal marriage — never, never, will you in any way at any time disappoint me!

How do you personally relate your marriage to God, and God who is your husband?
Speak it out or write it out. It is *so important* that you establish *your own* devotional journal.

3. CONFESSION OF SIN

I feel like an unfaithful wife — (which is exactly what I am) returning to blurt out my sin, my adultery, my stupidity, my unworthiness. I do not sin in anticipation of forgiveness, or do I? Dear God, oh, wonderful Savior, sweet Holy Spirit, may my love so increase, my intimacy be so constant that I will have no place for anyone else. Could I be predisposed with self-interest to such an extent that the needs of the sad world about me do not even reach me? Dear God, forgive. The more I think of my sin the more helpless and hopeless I become. It is in the cleansing I find release and freedom. Praise your wonderful name! Clean! free! forgiven!

What personal sins do you want to confess? We *must* speak them to remove them.
Do it! *Now.* There is no one else you have sinned against more than God. Tell him so!

4. SING A PRAYER TO GOD.

More like the Master I would ever be,
More of His meekness, more humility;
More zeal to labor, more courage to be true,
More consecration for work He bids me do. . . .

Take Thou my heart, . . . I would be Thine alone;
Take Thou my heart . . . and make it all Thine own;
Purge me from sin, . . . O Lord, I now implore, . . .
Wash me and keep . . . me Thine forevermore.

Open your hymn book and sing the rest of the verses — or even sing another prayer song.

5. READ HIS WORD TO HIM!

His Word

[48]When the Gentiles heard this, they were glad and honored the word of the Lord; and all who were appointed for eternal life believed.
[49]The word of the Lord spread through the whole region. [50]But the Jews incited the God-fearing women of high standing and the leading men of the city. They stirred up persecution against Paul and Barnabas, and expelled them from their region. [51]So they shook the dust from their feet in protest against them and went to Iconium.

— *Acts 13:48-51, NIV*

Read His Word to Him.

In the midst of the crowd of Gentiles in Antioch were those who were disposed to believe and those who were not. How remarkable it is that I could ever contemplate your position on this circumstance, but such is not at all different than what happened to me yesterday. You were the silent observer of all that happened. You read the hearts of the listeners, as well as the heart of the speaker. How many were truly listening? How many listeners thought the same thoughts as the speaker? How many truly understood even the basic point of the lesson? You know, you know.

Please express your response to this beautiful text. Put your expression in your own prayer diary.

6. READ HIS WORD FOR YOURSELF.

It is such an encouragement to read of the spread of the word "through the whole region" — how did it happen? It seems so obvious that those who heard and accepted were too glad and delightfully motivated to keep quiet. Was there more freedom and openness then? Were there less restrictions in "the whole region"? Were people ready to listen? We could say "yes" to all these questions and contrast them with what we imagine are the opposite conditions of our day, but since we are using our imagination in both instances we must just confess we do not know. What we *do know* is that the joy of the salvation these persons experienced was a contagion in their heart that spread itself through their lips and lives.

Pause in his presence and either audibly or in written form tell him all his word means to you.

7. READ HIS WORD IN THANKSGIVING.

How easy this will be — thank you, thank you for: (1) Every man and woman in Antioch who "honored" the word of the Lord — respected, accepted, believed — and were given the confident hope of eternal life. (2) For all who were "disposed or inclined or moved in the direction" of eternal life. I take this to mean that holding out eternal life as an offer appealed to some, and did not appeal to others. (3) That your word moves men to act; it is never neutral. (4) Even when the preachers were expelled, your word continued to grow. (5) That protest is not offensive to you. (6) That one day I will know the whole story of the spread of your word in the region of Antioch of Pisidia. (7) That in spite of persecution the learners of Jesus "were filled with joy and with the Holy Spirit."

Give yourself to your own expression of gratitude — write it or speak it!

8. READ HIS WORD IN MEDITATION.

"...they shook the dust from their feet in protest against them." There are several lessons in this for me: (1) The protest was against those who hindered others — not against the persecutors per se. It was the hindrance of the truth in the hearts of potential converts that caused the decision of protest. (2) Dust of the feet was washed away by our Lord — what a contrast! And yet his act was also a form of protest. (3) What does this act say? "Sorry we came — you can have your dust back." Or, "You dirty people — good riddance!" Or, "You are not worthy of our efforts!" Or, "Your rejection of us is God's rejection of you."

Pause — wait — think — then express yourself in thoughtful praise or thanks.

9. READ HIS WORD FOR PETITIONS.

As your word spreads I have several requests: (1) I want to honor your word and be appointed for eternal life. (2) Who does the appointing? I want to know! (3) If faith comes by hearing your word and eternal life is promised through believing, I have my answer. (4) Keep me aware of the influence of women in all of life. (5) In the midst of persecution give me peace. (6) In the center of opposition keep me steadfast. (7) It is right to protest — show me how.

Right here add your personal requests — and his answers.

10. READ HIS WORD AND WAIT — LISTEN — GOD SPEAKS!

Surely there is much you can say to me from these verses: (1) "In spite of your poorest efforts some will believe." (2) "In spite of your best efforts some will not believe." (3) "In spite of all your efforts it is still my work."

11. INTERCESSION FOR THE LOST WORLD

Poland — Point for prayer: (1) *The many freedoms for both Roman Catholics and Protestants* could be taken away. Increasing government efforts to weaken the influence of religion are evident. There is little persecution of believers, but restrictions and difficulties are often placed in the way of their witness. Pray that there may be continued freedom for the propagation of the Gospel to this needy land.

12. SING PRAISES TO OUR LORD.

Jesus has loved me — wonderful Savior!
Jesus has loved me, I cannot tell why; . . .
Came He to rescue sinners all worthless,
My heart He conquered — for Him I would die.

Glory to Jesus — wonderful Savior!
Glory to Jesus, the One I adore;
Glory to Jesus — wonderful Savior!
Glory to Jesus, and praise evermore.

WEEK THIRTEEN — SATURDAY

1. PRAISE GOD FOR WHO HE IS.

High-tower. What an interesting expression! I am sure it was used of you by those who had such towers for protection and observation. I can surely relate to this. You are the eternal protection, or security for every man alive as well as every man who has ever lived! How secure and safe I feel in you! How strong is the position of your children! The height of this tower is beyond human comprehension — into infinity! From this perspective there is nothing hidden from you. How full of meaning and value is the thought — all men of all time and place can run into this high tower and escape the corruption that is in the world through lust.

Express yourself in adoration for this quality of God.
Speak it audibly or write out your praise in your own devotional journal.

2. PRAISE GOD FOR WHAT HE MEANS TO ME.

The thought that you are *my* high-tower is beautiful! How I want so much to enter in and feel the cool, refreshing shade of your presence! To look around and know I have been removed from the rush of the world — I can ascend the stairs — or perhaps no such effort is needed to ascend to see what you can see! How do you see the world today? It surely must sadden your heart to see your children with your light hidden under the basket of their own interests. Dear God, I believe we could take your light to all men any time we decided we would.

How do you personally relate to the perspective of God, and God who is high-tower?
Speak it out or write it out. It is *so important* that you establish *your own* devotional journal.

3. CONFESSION OF SIN

I want to be the first to stand before you in guilt! I have not even spoken to those to whom I could speak. Dear God, I am here to confess my blood guiltiness and at the same time I am so ashamed to even ask your forgiveness. I purpose in my heart, here and now, to visit the homes in Joplin, to enlist others to help. For other sins, not too numerous to mention, I ask your cleansing, release me! free me! I believe you are working in me both *to will* and *to do* your good pleasure. By your willingness and your energy I shall overcome!

What personal sins do you want to confess? We *must* speak them to remove them.
Do it! *Now*. There is no one else you have sinned against more than God. Tell him so!

4. SING A PRAYER TO GOD.

I have a song I love to sing,
Since I have been redeemed,
Of my Redeemer, Savior, King,
Since I have been redeemed.
Since I . . . have been redeemed,

Since I have been redeemed,
I will glory in His name;
Since I . . . have been redeemed,
I will glory in my Savior's name.

Open your hymn book and sing the rest of the verses — or even sing another prayer song.

5. READ HIS WORD TO HIM!

His Word

[52] And the disciples were filled with joy and with the Holy Spirit.
14 At Iconium Paul and Barnabas went as usual into the Jewish synagogue. There they spoke so effectively that a great number of Jews and Gentiles believed. [2] But the Jews who refused to believe stirred up the Gentiles and poisoned their minds against the brothers. [3] So Paul and Barnabas spent considerable time there, speaking boldly for the Lord, who confirmed the message of his grace by enabling them to do miraculous signs and wonders.
— *Acts 13:52 — 14:3, NIV*

Read His Word to Him.

To read that the learners were filled with joy and with the Holy Spirit is a moving, challenging word to me. What does it mean? Oh, that you would explain it all to me. I know you know every nuance of meaning in these expressions — the text seems to separate the two thoughts and say they are not necessarily the same, i.e., being filled with joy is one thing and being filled with the Holy Spirit, although associated, is not altogether the same thing. What gave them their joy? Remember: they were Gentiles with but little background in the Jewish religion. Theirs was: (1) the joy of total forgiveness, (2) the joy of the true meaning of life, and the world in which we live, (3) the joy of the presence and power of the Holy Spirit in their work.

Please express your response to this beautiful text. Put your expression in your own prayer diary.

WEEK THIRTEEN — SATURDAY

6. READ HIS WORD FOR YOURSELF.

Careful now, read this text just as if you have never read it before. It seems striking to me that whereas the Holy Spirit is very prominent in the first century church, or the church described in Luke's second treatise, we find no reference to "miraculous signs and wonders" being performed by the disciples. Paul and Barnabas, or Silas, or Peter and John, or the apostles—yes—but *not* the Christians. Why? Why? At the same time I will not ignore the plain statement of their "being filled with the Holy Spirit." Neither will I ignore the obvious purpose of the supernatural acts of the Holy Spirit, i.e., to "confirm the message of his grace" (of *your* grace). Hasn't the message been confirmed by the preservation of this blessed account called *Acts?*

Pause in his presence and either audibly or in written form tell him all his word means to you.

7. READ HIS WORD IN THANKSGIVING.

Thank you for: (1) The dear disciples who no doubt faced problems much greater than mine and yet were filled with joy. (2) That I as a disciple can be and should be and want to be "filled with the Holy Spirit." (3) For the power of good habits, such as is suggested in the little expression "as usual." (4) For the fact that effective speaking is mentioned—it would suggest that some speaking was not effective. (5) For the willingness of some to believe —which in a sense made the speaking effective. (6) That it was the majority who believed, both of the religious and irreligious—so it is today if we would only get there with the message. (7) For the use of the term "refused to believe"—it is not a matter of evidence, it is a moral choice.

Give yourself to your own expression of gratitude—write it or speak it!

8. READ HIS WORD IN MEDITATION.

"Paul and Barnabas spent considerable time there, speaking boldly for the Lord, . . ." Really now, this is what it is all about. To worship and not reach the lost or educate the religious is a very unbalanced, unsatisfactory relationship. To even perform signs and wonders and yet remain silent about our Lord is to miss the whole point of miracles. It is such a privilege to speak on his behalf. Does the Lord need our help? Couldn't he speak for himself? Of course he could and at times he has spoken directly to men, but never, never has he told men what to do to be saved. He has never sent an angel on this mission. The greatest of all tasks he has given to us!

Pause—wait—think—then express yourself in thoughtful praise or thanks.

9. READ HIS WORD FOR PETITIONS.

In Iconium you were at work. From this experience I have petitions: (1) Give me the joy of the learners in Antioch. (2) Fill me with the Holy Spirit. (3) Enable me to so speak that men may believe. (4) Keep me aware that there are always wolves in sheep's clothing. (5) Remind me that all of us who work for you are brothers. (6) Give me the same boldness in the face of opposition that filled Paul and Barnabas. (7) Thank you for your confirmed word—help me to preach it with your wisdom.

Please, please remember these are prayers—speak them—reword them!

10. READ HIS WORD AND WAIT—LISTEN—GOD SPEAKS!

Speak to me through these few verses: (1) *"Nothing can overcome my joy."* (2) *"Your greatest need is to be* filled with the Holy Spirit." (3) "You can spend considerable time in the midst of opposition if I am with you."

11. INTERCESSION FOR THE LOST WORLD

Poland — Points for prayer: (1) *Literature* — there is a well used Bible Society depot in Warsaw which sells many Bibles and some Christian literature. Pray that this ministry may be continued and expanded. Literature is also able to be sent to some other Communist lands from this depot. A new Polish translation of the Bible is now being printed in Poland—pray that many may be converted by this new version. The government allows one evangelical Christian book to be printed every year— pray for the wisdom from above for those who write and those who choose these books that must be printed. (2) *The Bible believing churches* are very small, but slowly growing. Pray for a greater evangelistic fervor among the believers and a more open mind among the Roman Catholics. Pray for the planting of many more churches in hitherto unreached areas. Pray for government building permits to be issued more readily to churches seeking to put up new meeting places.

12. SING PRAISES TO OUR LORD.

Jesus, the very thought of Thee
With sweetness fills my breast;

But sweeter far Thy face to see,
And in Thy presence rest.

183

WEEK FOURTEEN — SUNDAY

1. PRAISE GOD FOR WHO HE IS.

Shield. You said to Abraham, "I am your shield and great reward" and so you have been to all those who trust in you! Oh, bless your wonderful self. I need protection — all men need *personal*, close protection. All of us want to feel secure and safe. We are in a constant battle and therefore we need you in such a real way. I am glad to believe Satan is held in check, i.e., according to the experience of Job. Many, many more fiery darts would be thrown our way were it not for your interest in and protection of your children. How I thank you. How many do not even know of your care?

Express yourself in adoration for this quality of God.
Speak it audibly or write out your praise in your own devotional journal.

2. PRAISE GOD FOR WHAT HE MEANS TO ME.

It is most difficult to pray about your essential being without relating to myself! I am the one who knows the result of not calling for your protection. I am most delightedly happy to get behind you, to put you out front in the thick of the battle. I want only to hide, but I know this is not essentially my place. As you can see I am struggling with the two aspects of your nature and mine; you can and are my shield only when I claim your presence and protection in the midst of the fight. You are indeed my shield, but not for hiding, for winning on the front lines of the struggle.

How do you personally relate to the shielding of God, and God who is our shield?
Speak it out or write it out. It is *so important* that you establish *your own* devotional journal.

3. CONFESSION OF SIN

I need not detail my losses in the fight, or perhaps I should. I must, I need the reinforcement of forgiveness to arm me for today's effort. There really is no way to write down the intimacy I feel and know in a confession of my personal failures. I thank you that you are indeed, indeed at work in me to will. You create the willingness. You live in and for me, i.e., in my place and you are at work in me to do. You provide the divine energy to get it done. I am so full of self and self desire, but if that self is changed by the renewing of my mind, bless your name I can be transformed! I claim your promise and your forgiveness.

What personal sins do you want to confess? We *must* speak them to remove them.
Do it! *Now.* There is no one else you have sinned against more than God. Tell him so!

4. SING A PRAYER TO GOD.

I need Thee ev'ry hour,
Most gracious Lord;
No tender voice like Thine
Can peace afford.

I need Thee, O I need Thee;
Ev'ry hour I need Thee!
O bless me now, my Savior,
I come to Thee!

Open your hymn book and sing the rest of the verses — or even sing another prayer song.

5. READ HIS WORD TO HIM!

His Word

[4]The people of the city were divided; some sided with the Jews, others with the apostles. [5]There was a plot afoot among the Gentiles and Jews, together with their leaders, to mistreat them and stone them. [6]But they found out about it and fled to the Lycaonian cities of Lystra and Derbe and to the surrounding country, [7]where they continued to preach the good news.
[8]In Lystra there sat a man crippled in his feet, who was lame from birth and had never walked. — *Acts 14:4-8, NIV*

Read His Word to Him.

It is refreshing to see people to whom a message about their Messiah meant so much. Today most men would not care. Perhaps if money and prestige became an issue as it did in Iconium we would suffer the same opposition. At the same time we would need to be as bold and confident as the apostles. Dear Lord, you know of the whole circumstance and have left it for me to ponder and that I do.

Please express your response to this beautiful text. Put your expression in your own prayer diary.

6. READ HIS WORD FOR YOURSELF.

Yes, yes. How is it I am content to live in my little comfortable world where no one takes sides? How is it that we are not in the thick of the battle for truth and right? If our missionaries turned a report in of constant opposition amid many successes, but not a few failures, what would be the response? It appears to me we are represented by the Jews whose little world was torn up by the "sword" our Lord came to thrust into society. Dear God, have I misjudged the situation, or have you opened my sleepy eyes?

It is so important that you pause in his presence
and either audibly or in written form tell him all his word means to you.

7. READ HIS WORD IN THANKSGIVING.

Indeed I shall: (1) Thank you for the term "apostle" as applied to Barnabas. He was a "sent one" along with Paul. He felt the sense of call and commission. He went because he was sent. (2) Thank you that however carefully planned and well supported, no plan or plot will work if you oppose it — good or bad. (3) Thank you that had they stoned them at Iconium you would have raised them up as you did at Lystra. (4) Thank you for that precious unnamed man or woman who told the apostles of the plot for their lives. (5) Thank you that we can go today to this same country and walk where those men walked. The millions of Turks there now are as lost as the Lycaonians of long ago. (6) Thank you, thank you that Paul and Barnabas just kept on preaching the good news. (7) Thank you for the unusual outreach of these men not only in cities but in "the surrounding country."

Give yourself to your own expression of gratitude — write it or speak it!

8. READ HIS WORD IN MEDITATION.

Let's answer the following two questions with some real thought: (1) A very important decision was made as related to preaching in Antioch. What was it? The Jews had judged themselves unworthy of eternal life, therefore the apostles turn to the Gentiles. It was even a fulfillment of Isaiah's prophecy. To me it seems an incongruity as to how a human decision could be made from those totally free of influence and yet be a fulfillment of what was said centuries before and yet this is part of the wisdom of God. (2) There were two responses to the preaching of Paul in Iconium. What were they? A great number believed — those who refused to believe opposed them. Can we expect a different response today?

Pause — wait — think — then express yourself in thoughtful praise or thanks.

9. READ HIS WORD FOR PETITIONS.

When men plot to kill there is hope in a prayer: (1) Help me to make the message so clear that men cannot be neutral. (2) Give me friends like those of Paul. (3) Help me to leave a place of labor for the same reasons that prompted Paul. (4) Thank you for your divine leading through circumstances. (5) Keep my focus clear — preaching the good news is my work. (6) Is it easier or more difficult to preach today? — open my eyes! (7) May the "surrounding" country where I live hear the good news.

Right here add your personal requests — and his answers.

10. READ HIS WORD AND WAIT — LISTEN — GOD SPEAKS!

There is much you can say to me: (1) "Division is not necessarily a reason for leaving." (2) "I have those who will help you." (3) "Sometimes the only safe route is out of town."

11. INTERCESSION FOR THE LOST WORLD

Poland — Point for prayer: (1) *Radio programs are prepared* by the United Evangelical Church in Warsaw for broadcasting from Trans World Radio Monaco. The government has reluctantly given permission for this, but this privilege could easily be withdrawn. There is such a good response to these broadcasts that the Bible believing churches have difficulty in finding enough mature Christians to follow up the contacts.

Romania — Population 21,500,000. Growth rate 1%. People per sq. km. — 91.
Point for prayer: (1) *The Romanian people are very hungry for God.* Intense atheistic propaganda and severe persecution have only stimulated this interest and refined the church. Pray that many more, even Marxists, may be converted.

12. SING PRAISES TO OUR LORD.

All glory, laud and honor
To Thee, Redeemer, King,
To Whom the lips of children
Made sweet hosannas ring!

The people of the Hebrews
With palms before Thee went;
Our praise and prayer and anthems
Before Thee we present.

WEEK FOURTEEN — MONDAY

1. PRAISE GOD FOR WHO HE IS.

Reward. You yourself are the reward! For all men you are the sole object of desire. In the person of your Son, you are "the Desire of the Ages" or "the Nations." In you is the full accomplishment of mankind. Reward is such a strong incentive — to gain yourself — and be found in you — what a goal! So many rewards are far less than the anticipation — the unknown becomes more attractive than the reality — not so with you. I am sure that when I enter your eternal presence I will say of you as the queen of the south said of Solomon, "the half has never yet been told."

Express yourself in adoration for this quality of God.
Speak it audibly or write out your praise in your own devotional journal.

2. PRAISE GOD FOR WHAT HE MEANS TO ME.

Reward for me. Just what do I really want? Deep down in the strongest desires of my heart, what do I want? (1) To create or bring into existence something of long lasting value — through you and your dear son and the powerful Holy Spirit, I can — but if I do not have you, if I am not in you, nothing shall be done. You are the creator. I am only a faint reflection of your likeness. (2) To grasp and help others to know the value of life, i.e., as lived by mankind past, present and to come. To coordinate the various areas of living — you are the only and real answer to the reason for living. Truly in you is an exceeding great reward. Your book gives me the key to open all the mysteries of who I am. Why I am. Where I am going. Praise your wonderful name!

How do you personally relate to the reward of God, and God who is reward?
Speak it out or write it out. It is *so important* that you establish *your own* devotional journal.

3. CONFESSION OF SIN

Grumbling and fault-finding. I am so very prone to be this way when I am excessively tired. The weakness of my body becomes the weakness of my temperament. Why? I believe it is because I have not built up a reserve of resolve. It is also because I fail to pause and pray before I think and speak. Here in the cool of this garden let me sweat out the resolve to keep my heart sweet and kind and my mouth open only to your praise. If I can't (or won't) say something good, may I be like my savior who was truly excessively tired as he carried the cross for me. He said, "Forgive them, they know not what they do." — or *he said nothing.* Forgive and cleanse me.

What personal sins do you want to confess? We *must* speak them to remove them.
Do it! *Now.* There is no one else you have sinned against more than God. Tell him so!

4. SING A PRAYER TO GOD.

How firm a foundation, ye saints of the Lord,
Is laid for your faith in His excellent Word!

What more can He say than to you He hath said,
To you who for refuge to Jesus have fled?

Open your hymn book and sing the rest of the verses — or even sing another prayer song.

5. READ HIS WORD TO HIM!

His Word

[9]He listened to Paul as he was speaking. Paul looked directly at him, saw that he had faith to be healed [10]and called out, "Stand up on your feet!" At that, the man jumped up and began to walk.

[11]When the crowd saw what Paul had done, they shouted in the Lycaonian language, "The gods have come down to us in human form!"
— *Acts 14:9-11, NIV*

Read His Word to Him.

How many men and women who sit along the highway of life, or in the market place of living, have never walked? I'm sure you can see and identify every cripple in the whole wide world. It is sad, and in comparison to those who can walk in this life, but how many are there who will never walk the streets of gold? I take the latter to be the purpose for the healing. How is it that faith on the part of the lame man is here mentioned and was not mentioned in the case at Jerusalem? It would seem it was Peter and John's faith not the lame man's that made him whole. Dear Lord, I know you want all men to be whole, whether it is through my faith or theirs. If I do not preach they will never believe and be made well. Help me!

Please express your response to this beautiful text. Put your expression in your own prayer diary.

6. READ HIS WORD FOR YOURSELF.

That men could so widely misunderstand your purpose seems more than remarkable and yet they do! Men have and do and will misunderstand my purposes—at times will give to me far more credit than is due (since *none* is due). How zealous and creative was Paul! How enterprizing! Did he make a mistake in his evaluation of the possible response of the people? Did he expect the same response as Peter and John at the gate beautiful? We do not know — the candid report of Dr. Luke casts no blame, we are out of place doing so. How do we relate to the principle today? i.e., what are we doing to attract the interest and attention of our audience; with one, or a thousand?

It is so important that you pause in his presence
and either audibly or in written form tell him all his word means to you.

7. READ HIS WORD IN THANKSGIVING.

Thank you, thank you for: (1) That human need does become a catalyst for listening to the one who can help. (2) For the direct, personal interest of Paul. (3) For Paul's adventuresome willingness to do anything to get an interest in the good news. (4) For the record of work in totally heathen culture. (5) For the power to heal—used as a sign—not an end, but a means to an end. (6) That somebody understood the Lycaonian language—was it Paul—who "spoke in tongues more than anyone"? (7) For the wonderful power of public speaking.

Give yourself to your own expression of gratitude—write it or speak it!

8. READ HIS WORD IN MEDITATION.

Stand up on your feet! How could God better describe our permanent posture? We are not animals, so "stand up on your feet!" We need not grovel to any man—"stand up on your feet!" We have strength and health—and in him all things—so "stand up on your feet"! I have a journey ready for you—a real important, urgent task for you to do. "Stand up on your feet." At the same time how better could we describe the man outside of salvation than "crippled in his feet, who had never walked from birth." At one time sin crippled us, but Jesus healed us and we have been made to walk in the presence of men and God with the assurance of freedom and strength. In him, indeed we are whole—"stand up on your feet"!

Pause—wait—think—then express yourself in thoughtful praise or thanks.

9. READ HIS WORD FOR PETITIONS.

In the midst of those who do not believe I need prayer: (1) Thank you for the miracles of Paul (of you through Paul). Teach me all their meaning. (2) When do men need faith and when do men not need faith to be healed? (I expect to get an answer from your word.) (3) Why did Paul heal the lame man? (4) What response did Paul expect from the healing? (How I do want to meditate on these questions.) (5) Which was the most important to the man healed—his healing or his salvation? (6) Some one understood the Lycaonian language—who was it? (7) Dear Lord, I labor among people who misunderstand motives. Help me.

Please, please remember these are prayers—speak them—reword them!

10. READ HIS WORD AND WAIT—LISTEN—GOD SPEAKS!

Through this experience you spoke to Barnabas and Paul—speak to me: (1) "Men will interpret your actions in different ways than you intended." (2) "Healing the lives and homes of people is a greater work." (3) "Men are hero worshipers—turn them from yourself to me."

11. INTERCESSION FOR THE LOST WORLD

Romania — Points for prayer: (1) *Persecution in the 1950s was very severe.* Many believers were martyred and imprisoned. Presently persecution has been more in the line of frequent house searches, interrogations, very heavy fines, dismissal from work and imprisonment. The intensity of persecution has markedly increased since 1974. Pray for Christian prisoners and their suffering families. (2) *New laws have made the life of believers much harder.* All people in responsible positions must now take an oath of loyalty to the furtherance of Communism, which is, in effect, for Christians, a denial of their faith. Refusal to take the oath leads to dismissal from work. Pray for the believers when faced with this agonizing decision. It is easy to compromise.

12. SING PRAISES TO OUR LORD.

All praise to Him who reigns above
In majesty supreme,
Who gave His Son for man to die,
That He might man redeem!

Blessed be the name, blessed the name,
Blessed be the name of the Lord;
Blessed be the name, blessed be the name,
Blessed be the name of the Lord.

WEEK FOURTEEN — TUESDAY

1. PRAISE GOD FOR WHO HE IS.

Light. Such a beautiful representation of yourself! There are several qualities of light that tell me and all the world of yourself. To illumine is the first quality of light. How truly do you open and uncover and make plain all things. There is nothing in the dark that cannot be set in the light. How beyond human thought it is for you to live in eternal light—in you and of you there is no darkness at all. You are the light, the Father of lights, and when we walk in you we find warmth—and comfort.

Express yourself in adoration for this quality of God.
Speak it audibly or write out your praise in your own devotional journal.

2. PRAISE GOD FOR WHAT HE MEANS TO ME.

Light for me! How very, very much do I need light in so many areas of life. I am glad to acknowledge you can and will and do give me light—or I have none. Your word is a lamp for my daily path and a light at the end of the road; and illumination all along the way. I need and want light on how best to teach the students who sit in my classes. Dear God, you do open my mind with your light as to how best to present what you have said in your word. Another name for this would be what James 1:5 calls "wisdom," i.e., the best use of knowledge. Praise you, how I depend on you and ask in total confidence, and receive!

How do you personally relate to the light of God, and God who is light?
Speak it out or write it out. It is *so important* that you establish *your own* devotional journal.

3. CONFESSION OF SIN

I have so often become frustrated in one area or another because I did not ask for your light. I walked and stumbled in the darkness. When I trust in my own wisdom it becomes darkness. How mean and hard we can become when we know not where to turn for light! How relaxing and softening is the illumination of the whole picture. Dear, dear God, forgive me. Such a circumstance is no excuse for perverseness and unkindness—it is a plain indication of a lack of trust in the one who can see the end from the beginning and who dwells in everlasting light. I claim your cleansing!

What personal sins do you want to confess? We *must* speak them to remove them.
Do it! *Now.* There is no one else you have sinned against more than God. Tell him so!

4. SING A PRAYER TO GOD.

Sing them over again to me,
Wonderful words of Life;
Let me more of their beauty see,
Wonderful words of Life.
Words of life and beauty,

Teach me faith and duty:
Beautiful words, wonderful words,
Wonderful words of Life.
Beautiful words, wonderful words,
Wonderful words of Life.

Open your hymn book and sing the rest of the verses—or even sing another prayer song.

5. READ HIS WORD TO HIM!

His Word

[13]The priest of Zeus, whose temple was just outside the city, brought bulls and wreaths to the city gates because he and the crowd wanted to offer sacrifices to them.

[14]But when the apostles Barnabas and Paul heard of this, they tore their clothes and rushed into the crowd, shouting: [15]"Men, why are you doing this? We too are only men, human like you. We are bringing you good news, telling you to turn from these worthless things to the living God, who made heaven and earth and sea and everything in them. [16]In the past, he let all nations go their own way. [17]Yet he has not left himself without testimony: He has shown kindness by giving you rain from heaven and crops in their seasons; he provides you with plenty of food and fills your hearts with joy." [18]Even with these words, they had difficulty keeping the crowd from sacrificing to them. — *Acts 14:13-18, NIV*

Read His Word to Him.

How sad must have been your heart when you saw the procession of the followers of Zeus—animals to sacrifice to a god who is no god at all. But then, it has been repeated millions of times since—and even today you can see men sacrificing to dumb idols. Do we get as excited as Paul and Barnabas? Are we as jealous as you are about the homage that really belongs to you? Dear God, how apathetic I have been! How I long to let the whole world know of your greatness—the "one who made heaven and earth and sea and everything in them." Oh, open my ears and eyes to hear and see your testimony: rain, crops, food, good health. How good to acknowledge the creator who is a giver!

Please express your response to this beautiful text. Put your expression in your own prayer diary.

6. READ HIS WORD FOR YOURSELF.

Dear Lord, I want to identify with your two missionaries or apostles, your "sent ones." How, oh how, will I stop idol worship and turn the hearts of men to you? Dear Lord, I need motivation, not only information. I want to listen with my heart to the message I must speak to others. You are saying to me: (1) "You are only a weak human vessel but you are the only vessel I have for the little part of the world where you live." (2) I have "good news"—I will never, never hear it enough, i.e., that you have given me GOOD NEWS! GOOD NEWS! GOOD NEWS! Put a smile upon my heart! (3) I must preach repentance—"turn from" as well as "turn to." (4) I serve a living God, not a dead idol. (5) A powerful living God who created all! Impregnate my heart!

It is so important that you pause in his presence
and either audibly or in written form tell him all his word means to you.

7. READ HIS WORD IN THANKSGIVING.

How gladly I do this. Thank you for: (1) Flowers I can enjoy as the expression of your creative genius. (2) Animals as the means of food and service to man. (3) You want me to be very upset with idolatry. (4) That you want me to try to stop man's onward rush to hell. (5) That you have plainly said some activity in this life is worthless. (6) You have a permissive will—you "let" the nations go their own way, not that you wanted it. (7) That we should see the phsyical world about us as your "testimony."

Give yourself to your own expression of gratitude—write it or speak it!

8. READ HIS WORD IN MEDITATION.

"They had difficulty keeping the crowd from sacrificing to them." Once popularity is established a sore temptation assails the man of God. It can take various forms, i.e., he has several choices: (1) He can disclaim man's adoration and worship in such weak terms that it becomes but an invitation to continue. (2) He can interpret the worship as but the ignorant expression of the masses to the real God who is seen through him. (3) He can reject it in such a decisive manner that he even risks the wrath of those who worship him—very much like the example before us.

Pause—wait—think—then express yourself in thoughtful praise or thanks.

9. READ HIS WORD FOR PETITIONS.

How I do need your help in the midst of misunderstanding: (1) Keep me aware of who I am and whose I am. (2) Teach me how to relate to those who worship other gods. (3) How I need the power to turn men from the vain things of this world. (4) Keep me aware constantly that I have "good news." (5) Open my eyes to see the world as created by yourself. (6) The next time it rains may I see it as your testimony of goodness. (7) May I remember that all joy comes from you.

Right here add your personal requests—and his answers.

10. READ HIS WORD AND WAIT—LISTEN—GOD SPEAKS!

What do you say amidst all this confusion? (1) "I am not confused—only men." (2) "Men must be told many times before they hear." (3) "My goodness can and should lead to repentance."

11. INTERCESSION FOR THE LOST WORLD

Romania — Point for prayer: (1) *There has been a remarkable people movement among the Gypsies.* Many thousands of these little understood people have been converted since 1972. Pray for these new believers, and their fine leaders, some who have already suffered much for their faith. The Bible is now being translated into their language, Romany.

12. SING PRAISES TO OUR LORD.

Fairest Lord Jesus!
Ruler of all nature!
O Thou of God and man the Son!

Thee will I cherish,
Thee will I honor,
Thou, my soul's glory, joy, and crown!

WEEK FOURTEEN — WEDNESDAY

1. PRAISE GOD FOR WHO HE IS.

Understanding. How glad I am that someone understands everything and everyone — your understanding is total! Nothing escapes your notice. I worship before you in calm assurance that all is well — with you and your plans. All is not at all either calm or right here in the maelstrom of human affairs, but you are not confused or tired since you are *perfect understanding.* What an amazement. Won't it be an amazement when one day all is explained to all men? I can rest in you. I can trust the one who has never made a mistake. You who are the originator of all the complexities of this physical world have no problem with the social, emotional, mental, moral complexities of man. It is all clear and clean and right with you. Dear God, it is too much for me. I trust you.

Express yourself in adoration for this quality of God.
Speak it audibly or write out your praise in your own devotional journal.

2. PRAISE GOD FOR WHAT HE MEANS TO ME.

Understanding of myself — my amazement at the outer world is only matched by that of the inner world. "The heart (intellect, will, emotions, conscience) is desperately wicked and full of deceit — who can know it?" You can and do! It is *my* heart that you understand. I'm glad you do — I have given up the effort long ago. I am constantly surprised at my selfish willfulness. Dear God, forgive me! I do believe if I am ready to read and accept you are ready to reveal your will for my life. You understand me in a way (ways) that no man ever could, or that I could myself. How comforting it is to give myself to the one who not only understands, but is at work to help and bless and use my life.

How do you personally relate to the understanding of God, and God who understands?
Speak it out or write it out. It is *so important* that you establish *your own* devotional journal.

3. CONFESSION OF SIN

With no reservations I admit my willfulness, my stubbornness, my resistance to your love. It is kindness, meekness, gentleness, tenderness that I resist. Why? Why? Because there is someone lying to me who himself is the very antithesis of each of these virtues. He appeals to my selfish interests and says: "They (your interests) are being threatened, demand your rights — and such an expression becomes very unkind in attitude and word — and in all areas he lies to me but why do I believe his lies? It is the weakness of my flesh; it is because I have lived such a long time in this sick, sinful environment — but most of all — because I can't or won't or don't hear your voice. Forgive me!

What personal sins do you want to confess? We *must* speak them to remove them.
Do it! *Now.* There is no one else you have sinned against more than God. Tell him so!

4. SING A PRAYER TO GOD.

So precious is Jesus, my Savior, my King,
His praise all the day long with rapture I sing;
To Him in my weakness for strength I can cling,
For He is so precious to me.
For He is so precious to me, . . .

For He is so precious to me; . . .
'Tis Heaven below
My Redeemer to know,
For He is so precious to me.

Open your hymn book and sing the rest of the verses — or even sing another prayer song.

5. READ HIS WORD TO HIM!

His Word

[19]Then some Jews came from Antioch and Iconium and won the crowd over. They stoned Paul and dragged him outside the city, thinking he was dead. [20]But after the disciples had gathered around him, he got up and went back into the city. The next day he and Barnabas left for Derbe.
— *Acts 14:19, 20, NIV*

Read His Word to Him.

How very good it is to attempt (and how poorly I succeed only you can know) to relate to these two verses just as you would! Your own people opposing your own servants — how it must have broken your heart! How such an attitude today does grieve your heart! What words were used to persuade the multitude who but a little time before were ready to worship Paul and Barnabas. They are now ready to stone them. You heard them. They are recorded. Will they be rehearsed at judgment? Where was Barnabas? Perhaps there is much in this account we do not know — you know — and I do so want to hear it when I am in your presence. Was Paul dead? Did he come into the third heaven and "see you"? Did you encourage him?

Please express your response to this beautiful text. Put your expression in your own prayer diary.

WEEK FOURTEEN — WEDNESDAY

6. READ HIS WORD FOR YOURSELF.

I want to gather around the prostrate form of Paul. I see Timothy, Lois, Eunice and several others there. I see tears streaming down the face of Timothy—years later Paul was to write to him and say "remembering your tears" (II Tim. 1:4). If Paul left the next day—and he did—a heal-ing must have taken place. Dr. Luke's careful report does not mention it. What a wonderful man is Paul, but what a wonderful Savior, and divine Father! Oh, that I might remain in Lystra to think and meditate and pray over all I had heard and seen.

It is so important that you pause in his presence and either audibly or in written form tell him all his word means to you.

7. READ HIS WORD IN THANKSGIVING.

Oh, how gladly I do thank you for: (1) The plain fact that crowd approval is not based on truth—not on evidence but emotion—and is *never* dependable and should always be balanced with facts. (2) That Paul was ready, even glad, to suffer for his name's sake, to bear in his body the sufferings of our Lord. (3) What men think is often blessedly wrong! (4) For the love and concern and courage of the learners at Lystra. (5) That God raised Paul from whatever suffering he had to endure. (6) Paul was ready to go back to the very place where he suffered the most. (7) The vast understatement of Dr. Luke about Derbe—I would like to hear about each conversion—one day I shall. Praise him!

Give yourself to your own expression of gratitude—write it or speak it!

8. READ HIS WORD IN MEDITATION.

"They preached the good news in that city (Derbe) and won a large number of disciples." It is so unusual to read an understatement concerning evangelism. The whole book of Acts is such an understatement. The appearance of the country through which they journeyed is not mentioned. The conversion stories of the thousands who became Christians does not find a place here. The personal impact of the sermons is not a part of the record. Where did they preach? Since both Lystra and Derbe were Gentile cities it must have been in the market place. How could they proclaim the word in the winter? Just what constitutes "a large number"?

Pause—wait—think—then express yourself in thoughtful praise or thanks.

9. READ HIS WORD FOR PETITIONS.

If I were present at the stoning of Paul I would surely have had several requests and so I do now: (1) Help me never to underestimate either the ignorance of "the crowd" or the persuasiveness of Satan. (2) Prepare me to suffer physically and respond as did Paul. (3) May I use the freedom I have while I have it. (4) Thank you for your mercy in Paul's life. What an example! (5) Give me the same tender identity with those of Lystra. (6) May I remember the tears and prayers of those who have ministered to me. (7) I need the courage to carry me beyond the opposition of men.

Right here add your personal requests—and his answers.

10. READ HIS WORD AND WAIT—LISTEN—GOD SPEAKS!

As you spoke to Paul, speak through Paul to me: (1) "What men think is dead is often very much alive." (2) "Suffering binds people closer to each other than any other one thing." (3) "There is always a blessing in every suffering."

11. INTERCESSION FOR THE LOST WORLD

Romania — Point for prayer: (1) *There is a crucial lack of literature.* The much publicized 100,000 Bibles printed in Rumania in 1971 never reached the Protestants. The only source of Bibles and Christian literature is from the West, and much has been smuggled into the land. Now the government has passed a law forbidding the receiving, transporting, storing or distributing of literature from abroad. Heavy sentences have been meted out to those doing so. Yet the believers continue to plead for more literature from the West despite the risk. Pray for those who risk their lives in getting the Word of God out to to the believers. Pray for the preservation of Bibles already in the land. The police continue to arrest believers with Bibles and destroy all Bibles and literature that they find.

12. SING PRAISES TO OUR LORD.

Down at the cross where my Savior died,
Down where for cleansing from sin I cried,
There to my heart was the blood applied;
Glory to His name.

Glory to His name, . . .
Glory to His name; . . .
There to my heart was the blood applied;
Glory to His name.

WEEK FOURTEEN — THURSDAY

1. PRAISE GOD FOR WHO HE IS.

I am. Blessings and praise to yourself — the great Self, existent one — there never has been a time when you were not. In time past, in time present, in all time to come you are the "I am that I am" — your dear Son so described himself. What an encouragement to all men to know they worship one who is never surprised, or confused, or asks a question — all things are immediately known to you. All the qualities of love, mercy, power, wisdom, etc. are static. Praise and wonder is my totally inadequate response to such qualities.

Express yourself in adoration for this quality of God.
Speak it audibly or write out your praise in your own devotional journal.

2. PRAISE GOD FOR WHAT HE MEANS TO ME.

"I am" for me. How shall I possibly tell you all I see and feel in your divine permanence? "Change and decay in all around I see — oh, thou who changes not abide with me" — so sang the poet and so sings my heart. When I know of the fluctuations of my own heart and try to comprehend what it would be to be always and constant in character — I am like Moses, on holy ground, and an unholy man, unworthy, and full of need for fogiveness and your strength. It will be altogether glorious to one day enter into a static state where I shall not struggle with the changes otherwise known as wrong choices — when I have no option how glad I will be!

How do you personally relate to the "I am" of God, and God who is "I am"?
Speak it out or write it out. It is *so important* that you establish *your own* devotional journal.

3. CONFESSION OF SIN

Why should, why do I choose to accept Satan's offers? Is it because I have not developed the attractiveness of your choice? Perhaps. Is it because I have been such a long time repeating sin? To repeatedly accept is to make acceptance easier than rejection. If I knew that the next time I accepted Satan's suggestion I would never be forgiven, would I accept it? No! Am I not then sinning twice over in presuming on your mercy? Dear Lord, forgive!

What personal sins do you want to confess? We *must* speak them to remove them.
Do it! *Now.* There is no one else you have sinned against more than God. Tell him so!

4. SING A PRAYER TO GOD.

Give me a faithful heart,
Likeness to Thee,
That each departing day
Henceforth may see

Some work of love begun,
Some deed of kindness done,
Some wand'rer sought and won,
Something for Thee.

Open your hymn book and sing the rest of the verses — or even sing another prayer song.

5. READ HIS WORD TO HIM!

His Word

[21]They preached the good news in that city and won a large number of disciples. Then they returned to Lystra, Iconium and Antioch, [22]strengthening the disciples and encouraging them to remain true to the faith. "We must go through many hardships to enter the kingdom of God," they said. [23]Paul and Barnabas appointed elders for them in each church and, with prayer and fasting, committed them to the Lord in whom they had put their trust. [24]After going through Pisidia, they came into Pamphylia, [25]and when they had preached the word in Perga, they went down to Attalia.

[26]From Attalia they sailed back to Antioch, where they had been committed to the grace of God for the work they had now completed. [27]On arriving there, they gathered the church together and reported all that God had done through them and how he had opened the door of faith to the Gentiles. [28]And they stayed there a long time with the disciples.
— *Acts 14:21-28, NIV*

Read His Word to Him.

My heart always skips a beat when I try to truly enter this expression of prayer and devotion. How can I *really* and *truly* read the word as you would? I can't. It is an impossible task, but one I love to try each day!

How pleased you must have been to follow Paul and Barnabas back into the houses of your children in Lystra, Iconium and Antioch. Every one of them is a learner — were they good students? They were better students after Paul and Barnabas came. They were "strengthened and encouraged to remain true to the faith." Faith is something they had both subjectively and objectively.

How is it that Paul and Barnabas led in the appointing of the elders for them in each church — three sets of elders in three churches. The word "appoint" means "to stretch out the hand." I am embarrassed to mention this to you — how much, much more you know about this than I do.

Please express your response to this beautiful text. Put your expression in your own prayer diary.

6. READ HIS WORD FOR YOURSELF.

I have been unable to keep from reading for my own personal help before now, but let me now devour every word! Just how did these preachers "with prayer and fasting commit the church and its leadership to the Lord in whom they had put their trust"? There must have been a time set aside for fasting and prayer for the whole church and the elders — in each church — was it just one day? A three-day fast? or perhaps a seven-day period?

One day is the most common practice, but a three-day fast would not be unusual. Where is this practice today? Gone with the devotion and evangelism that accompanied it?

Perhaps the words of Paul and Barnabas are a key to our problem: "We must go through many hardships to enter the kingdom of God." We do not want and will not accept the hardships and therefore reject the rule of God in our lives.

It is so important that you pause in his presence
and either audibly or in written form tell him all his word means to you.

7. READ HIS WORD IN THANKSGIVING.

Thank you for: (1) The supernatural gifts or abilities of the Holy Spirit which kept the assemblies alive in the absence of the apostles. (2) For "the faith" to which they could be true — indeed that there was such a distinction made between truth and error. (3) For the sharp rebuke I feel in my own conscience when I read of the faith and devotion of these disciples. (4) For the "grace of God"

that accomplished all that was done. (5) For the fact that "the church" could be gathered — the people were "the church" not the building where they gathered. (6) For the credit given to your working through your servants. (7) For the "door of faith" opened to anyone, everyone, when there are men of faith like Paul and Barnabas.

Give yourself to your own expression of gratitude — write it or speak it!

8. READ HIS WORD IN MEDITATION.

"And they stayed there a long time with the disciples." What did they do? Wouldn't it be interesting to follow Paul and Barnabas through six months of day-by-day activity? They *did* spend six months or more in the large city of Antioch. Did they keep the Jewish hours of prayer? If so, then nine o'clock found them in prayer. At what time did they arise in the morning? Was the example of our

Lord in often finding a place of prayer a part of their daily routine? Was Paul supported by the Christians at Antioch so it was not necessary to make tents? What was the occupation of Barnabas? Most of all we would like to know how they won others to the Lord in this large metropolitan city. We can answer this last important question: They did it one at a time.

Pause — wait — think — then express yourself in thoughtful praise or thanks.

9. READ HIS WORD FOR PETITIONS.

What courage and love led Paul and Barnabas back to where they had been mistreated! Such action prompts requests: (1) May I love people and your word more than I fear trouble. (2) Help me to have the same goals in my ministry — of "strengthening the disciples." (3) How I want to encourage people — help me! (4) There *is* a faith to

which we must remain true. I want to know it and teach it. (5) The rule of God is always attended with hardships — help me to remember! (6) Dear Lord, give me wisdom in the appointment of elders. (7) Open my desire to fast — fulfill its purpose in me.

Please, please remember these are prayers — speak them — reword them!

10. READ HIS WORD AND WAIT — LISTEN — GOD SPEAKS!

From your word speak to me: (1) "People are eager to hear what I have done — tell them." (2) "I am in the 'door opening' business today, but I do not have enough Pauls

and Barnabases." (3) "Paul and Barnabas stayed a long time with the Antioch church — you can do the same where you are if your purpose is the same."

11. INTERCESSION FOR THE LOST WORLD

Romania — Point for prayer: (1) *Christian radio broadcasts* from Monaco are a source of immense comfort and

blessing to the believers and a means of evangelizing the lost.

12. SING PRAISES TO OUR LORD.

When I saw the cleansing fountain
Open wide for all my sin,
I obeyed the Spirit's wooing,
When He said, Wilt thou be clean?

I will praise Him! I will praise Him!
Praise the Lamb for sinners slain;
Give Him glory, all ye people,
For His blood can wash away each stain.

WEEK FOURTEEN — FRIDAY

1. PRAISE GOD FOR WHO HE IS.

Omnipotent. All powerful God! To put no limitations on your power in any area of expression—this is an awesome thought, but it is much more than a *thought*; it is a *fact*. Evidence of your "everlasting power" is all about us—being clearly seen—and has been available since the foundation of the world. The power of your intellect is what impresses me. My little feeble efforts at prayer and praise are known to you and are not counted as either little or feeble. But as compared with your knowledge and person, they do look but what they are: the expression of one of your billions of beings in your likeness. Power in the moral realm is the most impressive since it is where we are the weakest—to will and to do and to always do is indeed an awesome thought.

Express yourself in adoration for this quality of God.
Speak it audibly or write out your praise in your own devotional journal.

2. PRAISE GOD FOR WHAT HE MEANS TO ME.

Omnipotent for me. To be able to link myself with the one who has total power in the physical, mental and moral realm is a wonder of all wonders. It excites me more than I can say, or express, although I do indeed want to try. If I but yield myself, give myself away to you, integrate my being in you, surrender in faith—it can happen. How much I need and want the inward strength—shall I call it "grace" for that is what it truly is—to fulfill the desires of your heart—and my heart—"according to the *power* that worketh in us, both *to will and to do* his good pleasure"! Dear God, give me the grace to let go and let you fulfill your promise!

How do you personally relate to the omnipotence of God, and God who is omnipotent?
Speak it out or write it out. It is *so important* that you establish *your own* devotional journal.

3. CONFESSION OF SIN

Forgive—I have been selfish, prideful, afraid and just plain unwilling to let your power be manifest through or in me. It is easy to say, "I want to"—but do I? If I did you would! Forgive me! I am the poorer, weaker, for my sin. Dear, dear God, change me! I am a congenital liar—from the birth of sin in my heart (Jas. 1:13-17) I have lied when it would have been easier to tell the truth. I could say that most of the time—(there I go, lying again) at least *some* of the time I have been inhibited by fear—perfect love casts all such fear out. Cleanse me—oh, cleanse me!

What personal sins do you want to confess? We *must* speak them to remove them.
Do it! *Now.* There is no one else you have sinned against more than God. Tell him so!

4. SING A PRAYER TO GOD.

I am Thine, O Lord,
I have heard Thy voice,
And it told Thy love to me;
But I long to rise in the arms of faith,
And be closer drawn to Thee.

Draw me nearer, nearer, blessed Lord,
To the cross where Thou hast died;
Draw me nearer, nearer, nearer blessed Lord,
To Thy precious, bleeding side.

Open your hymn book and sing the rest of the verses—or even sing another prayer song.

5. READ HIS WORD TO HIM!

His Word

15 Some men came down from Judea to Antioch and were teaching the brothers: "Unless you are circumcised according to the custom taught by Moses, you cannot be saved." [2]This brought Paul and Barnabas into sharp dispute and debate with them. So Paul and Barnabas were appointed, along with some other believers, to go up to Jerusalem to see the apostles and elders about this question. — *Acts 15:1, 2, NIV*

Read His Word to Him.

First the folk in Antioch were called "disciples"—now they are "brothers." How good it is to be in your family! The record of the Antioch church is not ancient with you —all the incidents of all the people there are as well known to us as are all the events of our lives today. The legalists from Jerusalem were not the first, and by no means the last, who taught, "Unless you agree with us you cannot be saved." Why, why do men do this? I want you to speak your answer right into the depths of my heart! Because man has mistaken a gift for a possession he has somehow earned. Salvation will always be a gift. I have it but it is only mine as a gift. I have had it for such a long time. I have become so familiar with it that somehow I believe I deserve it. Once I do then I can ask others to adopt my attitudes or they cannot have the gift. How ridiculous!

Please express your response to this beautiful text. Put your expression in your own prayer diary.

6. READ HIS WORD FOR YOURSELF.

I want to listen with the "brothers" at Antioch for the first time to these jarring words: "Unless you are circumcised according to the law of Moses (the custom taught by Moses) you cannot be saved"! I do wonder just what form of expression the arguments took as the sharp dispute got under way. It was extended into a debate. Essentially it must have been a careful separation of the response of law such as circumcision or a thousand other acts of devotion and the nature of salvation which is grace or un-merited favor. Let me try to stand now with Paul and Barnabas. Would I have been willing to go to Jerusalem to settle this question? Hadn't it already been settled? Didn't I already know God's answer? Where is my humility and love?

It is so important that you pause in his presence
and either audibly or in written form tell him all his word means to you.

7. READ HIS WORD IN THANKSGIVING.

Thank you dear Lord for: (1) That even legalists are our brothers and I can treat them as such. (2) For teachers in the church like Paul who have the courage to correct. (3) That disputing and debating are not wrong in themselves. (4) That there was a body of men (elders) in the church at Antioch whom Paul respected and accepted. (5) That "other believers" were also responsible and respected. (6) That apostles *and* elders were the leaders at Jerusalem. (7) That supernatural powers of the Spirit do not eliminate free discussion.

Give yourself to your own expression of gratitude — write it or speak it!

8. READ HIS WORD IN MEDITATION.

"To see the apostles and elders about this question." How we *do* need to see the same people about any question we have as to who is a Christian, what a Christian should or should not do. Are we to understand that the elders of the Jerusalem church were on a par with the Apostles? If so (and so it would seem) they must have had supernatural aid in their oversight. How is it that an apostle had to ask apostles when both were supernaturally guided? Are there elements in the divine direction we do not know?

Pause — wait — think — then express yourself in thoughtful praise or thanks.

9. READ HIS WORD FOR PETITIONS.

Debate and questions can also lead to prayer. I want this to happen here: (1) I like the constant use of the term "brothers" — help me to use it. (2) May I know false teaching when I hear it. (3) Impress upon me all over again that we are saved by grace through faith. (4) Say it again to me! "*Nothing, nothing* we do earns salvation or the forgiveness of sins"! (5) Help me to be as well prepared in debate as were Paul and Barnabas. (6) If Paul and Barnabas were "appointed" with others by the elders of the chruch in Antioch who am I to resist elders' oversight? (7) May I always consult the apostles (as found in the New Testament) about every problem.

Right here add your personal requests — and his answers.

10. READ HIS WORD AND WAIT — LISTEN — GOD SPEAKS!

In the midst of many voices let me hear your voice: (1) "Without me all men are liars." (2) "Unless you know everything and do everything, you must be saved by grace." (3) "Be humble-minded; you can learn nothing if you are not."

11. INTERCESSION FOR THE WORLD

Romania — Point for prayer: (1) *The severe earthquake of March 1977* gave the believers closer contact with those from the free world, less persecution and unparallelled opportunities to witness.
Yugoslavia — Population: 21,500,000. Growth rate 0.9%. People per sq. km. — 84.

Point for prayer: (1) *The political future is dark* — the shadow of repressive Russian Communism falls over the land. The present relative freedom to preach the Gospel is ending. Pray for more freedom for the Gospel. Pray that believers may use the opportunities that there are.

12. SING PRAISES TO OUR GOD.

A Friend I have, called Jesus,
Whose love is strong and true,
And never fails howe'er 'tis tried,
No matter what I do;
I've sinned against this love of His,
But when I knelt to pray,

Confessing all my guilt to Him,
The sin-clouds rolled away.
It's just like Jesus to roll the clouds away,
It's just like Jesus to keep me day by day,
It's just like Jesus all along the way,
It's just like His great love.

WEEK FOURTEEN — SATURDAY

1. PRAISE GOD FOR WHO HE IS.

Omniscient. This refers to your total knowledge — you know *all things.* This does not refer to the fact that you will know all things, or that you have known all things, but that right now and always you do know all things about all things. What a source of amazement! When man's knowledge is increasing, when man's confidence is in his own efforts such a quality strikes straight across man's self-sufficiency. What we learn you have always known. I want to face before you and worship in silence. I have no words to respond to absolute omniscience — even the adjective is a redundancy. "Holy (set apart)" is all I can say.

Express yourself in adoration for this quality of God.
Speak it audibly or write out your praise in your own devotional journal.

2. PRAISE GOD FOR WHAT HE MEANS TO ME.

Omniscience — I shall try to personally respond as best (so poorly) as I can. It is one thing to consider that you know all things of the world around me; it is quite another matter to know you know all things that relate to the world within me. To even state this truth is to ask "why can't I have access to such knowledge?" The answer is that I do! Your word will furnish me wholly (thoroughly) for every effort of this life — my response to your omniscience is to meditate on your word day and night! You have given me access to your knowledge of my heart in answer to prayer. I come to you for character development and you do hear and I am being formed into the likeness of my dear Lord by your chastening and blessing which are but an extension of your omniscience.

How do you personally relate to the omniscience of God, and God who is omniscient?
Speak it out or write it out. It is *so important* that you establish *your own* devotional journal.

3. CONFESSION OF SIN

To lean upon my own understanding when such omniscience is available is more than folly, but I have often played the fool. Dear wonderful, all knowing Father, forgive me. "Stealing" — to take what belongs to another without their permission. I have taken out of pure selfishness what I wanted for myself — of so many things. Most of my stealing has been from you — the precious moments loaned to me by you and so many, many of them used up as if they were mine. Intellect — but an extension of yourself — how often have I used it for the Giver? Dear God, forgive. Let him that stole, steal no more! Amen!

What personal sins do you want to confess? We *must* speak them to remove them.
Do it! *Now.* There is no one else you have sinned against more than God. Tell him so!

4. SING A PRAYER TO GOD.

Break Thou the bread of life,
Dear Lord, to me,
As Thou didst break the loaves
Beside the sea;

Beyond the sacred page
I seek Thee, Lord;
My spirit pants for Thee,
O living Word.

Open your hymn book and sing the rest of the verses — or even sing another prayer song.

5. READ HIS WORD TO HIM!

His Word

[3]The church sent them on their way, and as they traveled through Phoenicia and Samaria, they told how the Gentiles had been converted. This news made all the brothers very glad. [4]When they came to Jerusalem, they were welcomed by the church and the apostles and elders, to whom they reported everything God had done through them.
— *Acts 15:3, 4, NIV*

Read His Word to Him.

How wonderfully good to read "the church" sent them, or gave them provisions and money for their journey — it is more than two hundred miles from Antioch to Jerusalem. Oh, oh what a day when there was only one church! There were even in that day several congregations, perhaps many more than I could imagine — but only *one* body — one called out assembly. Here were Jewish Christians talking to despised Gentiles about the good news of the success of their first evangelistic journey among non-Jewish people. It was the same church that welcomed them that sent them! Dear, dear Lord, how do you see us today?

Please express your response to this beautiful text. Put your expression in your own prayer diary.

WEEK FOURTEEN — SATURDAY

6. READ HIS WORD FOR YOURSELF.

Indeed I do! I want to be a member of that same church — it is the one that is right and cannot be wrong. I want to do exactly what they did to become a member, and be the same kind of person they were. The names used here are most interesting to me: (1) brothers, (2) apostles, (3) elders, (4) church. It would not seem to me that we could have successors to the eye witnesses of Jesus or the apostles — but for the others — how I want to be a true living, loving brother to every other Christian. How I do want to honor and respect the older men of the faith. How I long to see all men called out of the world into the one body! His church!

It is so important that you pause in his presence
and either audibly or in written form tell him all his word means to you.

7. READ HIS WORD IN THANKSGIVING.

Read this word with real thanksgiving — Amen! Thank you for: (1) A body of believers who placed confidence in and gave generously to their leaders. (2) Men who were willing to walk 300 miles to settle a matter that was already settled in their mind. (3) For men who were not so ego centered that they forgot the real meaning of the Christian life is the conversion of sinners. (4) That there were brothers in Phoenicia and Samaria — how did they get there? (5) For the mutual joy, happiness, delightful meaning we can all share in our salvation — even as then, so now! (6) The open acceptance by the apostles and elders. (7) The wonderful new creation in the old city of Jerusalem.

Give yourself to your own expression of gratitude — write it or speak it!

8. READ HIS WORD IN MEDITATION.

"This news made all the brothers very glad." Oh, that we might always rejoice over the success of others! It could seem that such would easily be always true as related to the salvation of the lost. Such is *not true* — for somehow we see what others are doing as a threat, or reflection on what we are (or are not) doing. We are so guilty of impuning motives that we just know "those ignorant Gentiles really never knew what they were doing" — or "they will not be Christians long." How we can learn from the ignorant brothers in Samaria and Phoenicia. We overcome this sin by faith in the power of God and unselfish love for the lost.

Pause — wait — think — then express yourself in thoughtful praise or thanks.

9. READ HIS WORD FOR PETITIONS.

There is a whole volume of instruction in these two verses: (1) The church sent Paul and Barnabas. I want to be sent by the same agency. (2) I believe this means the church at Antioch paid their way. Am I right? (3) May I have the same kind of unselfish joy in my heart as the Phoenicians and Samaritans. (4) Teach me that *conversion is what you want. (5) Open my heart to count all* Christians as my brothers. (6) How I need to see your work as you do — simple, clear, alive. (7) Give me joy in the midst of conflict.

Please, please remember these are prayers — speak them — reword them!

10. READ HIS WORD AND WAIT — LISTEN — GOD SPEAKS!

You can say so much in just two verses: (1) "My church is my sending agency." (2) "I want men converted today as they were in Antioch." (3) "Elders are not apostles but they are important."

11. INTERCESSION FOR THE LOST WORLD

Yugoslavia — Points for prayer: (1) *Unreached peoples* — many areas of the country are without a Bible believing witness. Pray especially for the reaching of the two and one half million Muslims, the million Albanians (many of whom are Muslim), the Montenegrins and Macedonians. The Dalmatian coast, so well known to tourists, is largely unevangelized. Pray for the believers witnessing to these groups — there have been a number of conversions of Albanians recently and there are now several little groups of believers among them. (2) *The Government is reversing the previous liberalizing trend* in the face of the dangerous political situation. There has been increasing pressure on all church groups since 1971. Much harsher laws against religious groups were introduced in 1976. Pray for the believers in this time of fear and increasing uncertainty.

12. SING PRAISES TO OUR LORD.

Jesus is all the world to me,
My life, my joy, my all;
He is my strength from day to day,
Without Him I would fall.

When I am sad, to Him I go,
No other one can cheer me so;
When I am sad He makes me glad,
He's my Friend.

WEEK FIFTEEN — SUNDAY

1. PRAISE GOD FOR WHO HE IS.

Alpha — the author, cause, establisher — "from everlasting to everlasting." How well does this word describe you, both in the form of your son and yourself! You are the author of not only the literature of the Bible but of this book of nature in which we live. What a careful, accurate, colorful, knowledgeable writer you are. You are the cause as well as the conclusion of all things. I try to stand back and appreciate fully the meaning of "establisher" — or "from everlasting to everlasting." The best I can do is to fall before you in wonder and praise.

Express yourself in adoration for this quality of God.
Speak it audibly or write out your praise in your own devotional journal.

2. PRAISE GOD FOR WHAT HE MEANS TO ME.

Alpha to me. Indeed, indeed, I want you to be first in all of my life — if I begin with you, you are indeed and in truth my author. Do I truly meditate on what you have written? How is it I have not memorized every word of your book, the Bible? Dear Lord, forgive me. I am delighted by reading the book of creation all about me! I thank you for the beauty, but more do I thank you for the purpose. You are indeed the establisher or it will never be established. Dear God, wonderful Savior, blessed present Holy Spirit, may every day — this one, all of them — begin (and end) with you. How I want you to be the first cause of all I think and do today!

How do you personally relate to the First Cause of God, and God who is Alpha?
Speak it out or write it out. It is *so important* that you establish *your own* devotional journal.

3. CONFESSION OF SIN

Self-interest and "what do I get out of it" has been too often the first cause in my choices — forgive me! "Before the mountains were brought forth, or even thou hadst formed the earth and the world, even from everlasting to everlasting thou art God" (Isa. 90:2). It does seem incongruous that I can live so independently of the one who "upholds all things by the word of his power." I am the poorer — what strength and help I refuse. Dear Lord, I renew my desire to "seek first your rule in my life and your order of living." Forgive and cleanse and remove. Praise your name — it is done!

What personal sins do you want to confess? We *must* speak them to remove them.
Do it! *Now.* There is no one else you have sinned against more than God. Tell him so!

4. SING A PRAYER TO GOD.

All to Jesus I surrender,
All to Him I freely give;
I will ever love and trust Him,
In His presence daily live.

I surrender all, I surrender all.
All to Thee, my blessed Savior,
I surrender all.

Open your hymn book and sing the rest of the verses — or even sing another prayer song.

5. READ HIS WORD TO HIM!

His Word

[4]When they came to Jerusalem, they were welcomed by the church and the apostles and elders, to whom they reported everything God had done through them.
[5]Then some of the believers who belonged to the party of the Pharisees stood up and said, "The Gentiles must be circumcised and required to obey the law of Moses."

[6]The apostles and elders met to consider this question. [7]After much discussion, Peter got up and addressed them: "Brothers, you know that some time ago God made a choice among you that the Gentiles might hear from my lips the message of the gospel and believe.

— *Acts 15:4-7, NIV*

Read His Word to Him.

I try to stand back and objectively read this passage as if you were reading it. I know I can not do this, but I want to read it to you with as much appreciation of your point of view as at all possible. As Paul and Barnabas report to the crowd in Jerusalem, "everything you had done through them" — did you protect them from any exaggeration or false interpretation? If I were telling it no doubt I would over emphasize some things and forget other matters that should have been said. How was it on that day? If there was any impatience with the bigotry of the Pharisees it was not mentioned (maybe it was not bigotry), but there was much discussion. What did they say? Thou knowest!

Please express your response to this beautiful text. Put your expression in your own prayer diary.

6. READ HIS WORD FOR YOURSELF.

I have unavoidably been doing this, but as an act and expression of praise and confession and adoration. I want to travel again with the apostles and see and hear all over again what happened at Salamis, Paphos, Perga, Antioch, Iconium, Lystra, Derbe. I want to rejoice and feel the wonder of your work through these men. I do want to be as generous and sympathetic as the apostles and elders who met to consider carefully and fully this emotion-packed subject. How do I relate to those who sharply disagree with me?

It is so important that you pause in his presence
and either audibly or in written form tell him all his word means to you.

7. READ HIS WORD IN THANKSGIVING.

Yes, yes, thank you for: (1) The willingness and responsibility of Paul and Barnabas in reporting all. (2) The humility and honesty of the apostles in recognizing your power working through them. (3) That we too can look back over their first journey and share their joy. (4) That the gospel does have an appeal to even those who misinterpret it. (5) That the apostles and elders were not all "easily offended." (6) That the question has been carefully considered and settled. (7) For the total beautiful example this whole incident is to us in the church of today.

Give yourself to your own expression of gratitude — write it or speak it!

8. READ HIS WORD IN MEDITATION.

"The party of the Pharisees." The record of the Pharisees is not all bad. This group of men believed in the inspiration of every word of the Old Testament. They accepted the supernatural occurrences of the Old Testament. They knew there would be a resurrection and judgment. They believed in purity of life. However, their fundamental flaw was in their trust — they trusted in law — it became a source of pride and failure. What a galling yoke trust in the law principle becomes! How easy to trace the record: we lie and cheat and deceive to hide our failure — open confession and humble confidence in our Lord did not occur to them.

Pause — wait — think — then express yourself in thoughtful praise or thanks.

9. READ HIS WORD FOR PETITIONS.

While some question, others pray: (1) May I always believe you are at work through my feeble efforts. (2) Give me the joy of sharing the good news of your work with others. (3) May I expect some to disagree. Help me not to respond in pride. (4) Open my mind to know one more time that nothing I do will provide merit for heaven. (5) May I listen to the apostles through their writings for your will on all matters. (6) Give me a working association with elders in your son's body today. (7) Shut my mouth that I might allow others to contribute.

Right here add your personal requests — and his answers.

10. READ HIS WORD AND WAIT — LISTEN — GOD SPEAKS!

As you worked through the body then speak to me now through your word: (1) "It is good to testify to others what I have done." (2) "There are Pharisees today." (3) "In the counsel of apostles (their word) and elders is the solution of all church problems."

11. INTERCESSION FOR THE LOST WORLD

Yugoslavia — Points for prayer: (1) The Bible believers are relatively few. Their witness is spoiled by disunity for there are several damaging splits among them. The churches are not growing as fast as in some other Communist lands although they have had a greater freedom to witness. Pray that these believers may be effective for God. (2) The training of preachers is legal. As a result of the 1974 Lausanne Congress Bible believing groups have started a theological faculty in Zagreb. Pray for these institutions and for the calling of many into the Lord's service. (3) Literature has been fairly freely sold in the country. Bibles are printed in Yugoslavia in the four main languages. Yet a recent law makes it difficult for literature to enter the country from other lands. Pray for the lifting of this restriction. There is a Bible Society depot in Belgrade.

12. SING PRAISES TO OUR LORD.

O Word of God incarnate,
O Wisdom from on high,
O Truth unchanged, unchanging,
O Light of our dark sky;

We praise Thee for the radiance
That forms the hallowed page,
A lantern to our footsteps
Shines on from age to age.

WEEK FIFTEEN — MONDAY

1. PRAISE GOD FOR WHO HE IS.

Amen—credible, true, finality, the God of truth or amen, faithfulness—our Lord is the final "amen." I think of your dear Son who was born in Bethlehem. Oh, oh, I love to pause and bow before you and tell you all (or a small part) of what you are. Life makes no sense at all without you. Life is nonsense without you—credible, true. In all you have said, or promised, you are *truth*. Truth I define as that which coincides with fact or "that which equals reality." Without you there is no point of reference. I do not know who I am, why I am or where I'm going without you. You are life's reality, life's truth.

Express yourself in adoration for this quality of God.
Speak it audibly or write out your praise in your own devotional journal.

2. PRAISE GOD FOR WHAT HE MEANS TO ME.

Amen to me! In him, even my Lord, is the **Amen**—the finality, the final and first word. To say that Jesus, even your dear Son and my Lord, is alpha and amen is to say the beginning and the end. I have nothing I want except him. I want, just now, to renew my worship before him and as much as I can to give myself again to him. Here is a lovely little poem that perfectly expresses my desire.

I'm but a slave!
I have no freedom of my own,
I cannot choose the smallest thing,
Nor e'en my way.
I'm a slave!
Kept to do the bidding of my Master!
He can call me, night or day.
Were I a servant, I could claim wages.
Freedom, sometimes, anyway.
But I was *bought!*
Blood was the price my Master paid for me.
And I am now His slave—
And ever more will be.
He takes me here, He takes me there,
He tells me what to do;
I just obey, that's all—
I TRUST Him too!

— M. Warburton Booth

How do you personally relate to the finality of God, and God who is Amen?
Speak it out or write it out. It is *so important* that you establish *your own* devotional journal.

3. CONFESSION OF SIN

So often do the words of the frantic father come to mind—"Lord, I believe; help thou my unbelief." I want you at the beginning of every day—and in everything. I want you in and through and among all I do or say or think. I want your conclusion to all I do. I do, I do *want* to be your slave, your clay, your wife, help thou my unwillingness. I am so insensitive, so dull of perception, so slow in hearing your voice, so unwilling. Is it my environment? No, no. Jesus lived in a worse, much worse place. Is it my nerves? How could it be when God made them? He is larger than nerves. Just deepen my desire to accept your ownership in every area of life. Forgive and cleanse.

What personal sins do you want to confess? We *must* speak them to remove them.
Do it! *Now.* There is no one else you have sinned against more than God. Tell him so!

4. SING A PRAYER TO GOD.

Come, ev'ry soul by sin oppressed,
There's mercy with the Lord,
And He will surely give you rest
By trusting in His word.

Only trust Him, only trust Him,
Only trust Him now.
He will save you, He will save you,
He will save you now.

Open your hymn book and sing the rest of the verses—or even sing another prayer song.

5. READ HIS WORD TO HIM!

His Word

[7]After much discussion, Peter got up and addressed them: "Brothers, you know that some time ago God made a choice among you that the Gentiles might hear from my lips the message of the gospel and believe. [8]God, who knows the heart, showed that he accepted them by giving the Holy Spirit to them, just as he did to us. [9]He made no distinction between us and them, for he purified their hearts by faith. [10]Now then, why do you try to test God by putting on the necks of the disciples a yoke that neither we nor our fathers have been able to bear? [11]No! We believe it is through the grace of our Lord Jesus that we are saved, just as they are."

[12]The whole assembly became silent as they listened to Barnabas and Paul telling about the miraculous signs and wonders God had done among the Gentiles through them.

— Acts 15:7-12, NIV

Read His Word to Him.

How good it is to try to take my place with you as I read these verses! From the lips of Peter the fisherman — your "called one," your "sent one" — I hear him tell of your call to him; it became your call to all of us, i.e., all of us Gentiles. It was through the hearing of the good news we obtained faith. Yes, yes, it was *your* gift, but through the lips of man and our acceptance of that message. I are more than delighted that you know my heart — no one else does, not even myself. You do!

Please express your response to this beautiful text. Put your expression in your own prayer diary.

6. READ HIS WORD FOR YOURSELF.

It is most difficult to separate the points of view — indeed, I couldn't — but I open my heart wide to receive each word! Your acceptance of me is indicated in the presence of the Holy Spirit in my body! But in the case of Cornelius your acceptance had to be seen and known by the Jews, so they would "make no distinction" between themselves and the Gentiles. I love that little phrase "purified their hearts by faith." My *mind* can be pure, whole, clean; my *will* can be pure, one, whole; my *emotions* can be pure, united, not divided, clean, whole. I believe in your marvelous provision for such purifying — it is done!

It is so important that you pause in his presence and tell him all his word means to you.

7. READ HIS WORD IN THANKSGIVING.

(1) Thank you I am free of the yoke and burden of the law. I am not saved by what I do, but by what my Lord did at Calvary and the open tomb! (2) Thank you that grace moved me to do much more for my Lord (not for merit) than law ever could. (3) Thank you for your great persistence and patience in moving Peter to tell the good news to us Gentiles. (4) Thank you, thank you for the blessed Holy Spirit. May I relate hourly to him. (5) Dear God, how thankful I am that I need not test you at all — I flunk the test; you know all the answers so you need not take it. (6) That "I am saved" just as are all Christians. (7) That I am being saved — and I will be saved.

Give yourself to your own experience of gratitude — write it or speak it!

8. READ HIS WORD IN MEDITATION.

"God made a choice among you." God has always made choices of men among men. We would surely question some of his choices, i.e., in our own fallible, human judgment. Peter seems a poor choice to us, but he is such an encouragement to the weakest, most limited among us. If God could change Peter, then he could change me.

Pause — wait — think — then express yourself in thoughtful praise or thanks.

9. READ HIS WORD FOR PETITIONS.

The apostle Peter always had a message worth hearing. In it and from it I want to make some requests: (1) May Gentiles hear the same message from my lips as fell from the lips of Peter. (2) Keep me aware if men do not hear they cannot believe. (3) Search my heart — forgive me. (4) Thank you for the Holy Spirit — may he fill my heart. (5) Thank you for a pure heart — keep it pure. I want to see you. (6) Break the yoke of works salvation, in my life, in my teaching. (7) Thank you for your amazing grace — may I offer it to others.

Please, please remember these are prayers — speak them — reword them!

10. READ HIS WORD AND WAIT — LISTEN — GOD SPEAKS!

What are you saying to me? (1) "I have chosen all men to be saved. Tell them for me." (2) "I know the sin in the lives of people — if you do not preach, I cannot forgive." (3) "Salvation is free but it must be accepted."

11. INTERCESSION FOR THE LOST WORLD

Yugoslavia — Point for prayer: (1) *There are nearly a million Yugoslavs working in Western Europe,* for longer and shorter periods. Many live in special barracks or hostels in Germany, Holland, Switzerland, etc. Pray for those seeking to win these people for the Lord there.

12. SING PRAISES TO OUR LORD.

Down at the cross where my Savior died,
Down where for cleansing from sin I cried,
There to my heart was the blood applied;
Glory to His name.

Glory to His name, . . . Glory to His name;
There to my heart was the blood applied;
Glory to His name.

WEEK FIFTEEN — TUESDAY

1. PRAISE GOD FOR WHO HE IS.

Ancient of days. This is a prophetic description of our Lord and refers to his eternality — like one who never dies. It is so beautifully descriptive of yourself! There has never been a day since Eden's garden that you have not been alive and well and awake and alert and interested in all that happens in every life upon this terrestrial ball. Praise your wonderful name — and of him who was The Word — and of the Eternal Spirit — no event in any day has escaped your notice, yea more, your intense interest! We all know men of age who have acquired deep wisdom and patience, kindness and the gentleness that comes with much experience. Such qualities are to be associated in our minds with yourself and your Son — there is so *much* more — but this is enough now.

Express yourself in adoration for this quality of God.
Speak it audibly or write out your praise in your own devotional journal.

2. PRAISE GOD FOR WHAT HE MEANS TO ME.

The ancient of days for me. I am comforted by the thought that there has never been a day, and there never will be one, when you, dear Lord, loving Father, are not a part of it. There have been many days of which I am ashamed, but you know; you are more unhappy about them than I am. You forgive because I want — indeed, I do want — to love you and serve you. Your are not a great, great grandfather — for all such lose capacities — you change not, but the kindliness and thoughtfulness and personal interest of my grandfather was a real source of strength to me. Multiply that by ten million for you and your Son!

How do you personally relate to the ancient of days of God, and God who is ancient of days?
Speak it out or write it out. It is *so important* that you establish *your own* devotional journal.

3. CONFESSION OF SIN

"Gossip." This is repeating what we have heard and have not confirmed. It is usually negative and critical of some person. Dear Lord, you know just how guilty I am in this area. I have tried to go to the ones I have offended in this way, but there are too many involved, and I am repulsed by this sin. It is the total antithesis of love. How could we lie about people, when we love them? We somehow become important when we know something no one else does, but we really do not know it — it is pure hearsay, gossip. Oh, dear Lord, would I want this said of me? Why *must* I find importance in such a poor, miserable manner? You have made me so very, very important as a Christian, and this is no gossip! Forgive, and put a hold on my tongue!

What personal sins do you want to confess? We *must* speak them to remove them.
Do it! *Now.* There is no one else you have sinned against more than God. Tell him so!

4. SING A PRAYER TO GOD.

Holy, Holy, Lord God Almighty!
Early in the morning our song shall rise to Thee;

Holy, Holy, Holy! Merciful and Mighty!
God in Three Persons, blessed Trinity!

Open your hymn book and sing the rest of the verses — or even sing another prayer song.

5. READ HIS WORD TO HIM!

His Word

[12]The whole assembly became silent as they listened to Barnabas and Paul telling about the miraculous signs and wonders God had done among the Gentiles through them. [13]When they finished, James spoke up: "Brothers, listen to me. [14]Simon has described to us how God at first showed his concern by taking from the Gentiles a people for himself. [15]The words of the prophets are in agreement with this, as it is written:
[16]"'After this I will return
  and rebuild David's fallen tent.

Its ruins I will rebuild,
  and I will restore it,
[17]that the remnant of men may seek
    the Lord,
  and all the Gentiles who bear my
    name,
  says the Lord, who does these
    things
[18] that have been known for ages.'

— *Acts 15:12-18, NIV*

Read His Word to Him.

Dear Lord, how many more signs and wonders were done that Dr. Luke did not record? Oh, how I want to appreciate fully each sign. I want to be filled with the same awe and amazement that filled those who first saw such signs. But more than this, I want to buy the product these signs advertize — even the deity of your own dear Son — the truthfulness of the message Paul and Barnabas spoke, their authority as apostles of yourself. The signs and wonders were only a means to an end. The words of my Lord speak to me, ". . . He that believeth on me, the works that I do shall he do also; *and* greater works than these shall he do; because I go unto my Father" (John 14:12).

Please express your response to this beautiful text. Put your expression in your own prayer diary.

6. READ HIS WORD FOR YOURSELF.

Indeed, indeed I do! God through miracles spoke in two instances: (1) Peter, and (2) Paul and Barnabas. He spoke again through the prophets. In all cases of miracles they were a means. The message was in the *words* of Peter and in the *words* of Paul and Barnabas, and in the *words* of the prophet. Your word is yet with me — do I hear and heed it? Do I read and memorize it? Yea, Lord — not as I could or should, but I do believe I *do* accept! I do hear! Open my inner ear! Do we need miracles to confirm your message today? Your word includes the evidence for its acceptance — the same writers who give us what you said, tell us what you did to credential what you said. Will the miracles today do a better job than what has already been done?

Pause in his presence and tell him all his word means to you.

7. READ HIS WORD IN THANKSGIVING.

How delighted I am to do this: (1) Thank you for your power to heal the sick and cast out demons, raise the dead, etc., as seen in the Acts account, but most of all for the product these signs advertized — even your wonderful Son, my Lord! (2) Thank you for James, my Lord's half-brother — he once did not believe, but now he is a leader of the believers in the very city where he disbelieved. (3) For the knowledge of the prophets on the part of Jesus. (4) That we Gentiles are "a people for God's own self"! (5) That we are the very "house or temple of David" rebuilt as the dwelling place of God in the Spirit. (6) Thank you, oh, thank you that you have made provisions for all mankind through us. (7) That there are no hasty plans with you.

Give yourself to your own expression of gratitude — write it or speak it!

8. READ HIS WORD IN MEDITATION.

"All the nations that bear my name" — The only nation we know who bore the name and accepted the authority of our God was Israel, and they were poor, poor examples. This is a prophecy of Amos fulfilled in the "new Israel." How encouraging to read this prophecy and anticipate its fulfillment. Will there be a day when the nations of the earth honor and respect the name of God? The spread of the good news in the first century made this prophecy a reality. We believe what Paul wrote to those living in what we now call Turkey is true: ". . . the gospel . . . which has been preached to every creature under heaven, . . ." (Col. 1:23). Has any other generation fulfilled this prophecy? Sad, sad admission of disobedience and failure! The gospel hasn't lost its power — it just hasn't been preached.

Pause — wait — think — then express yourself in thoughtful praise or thanks.

9. READ HIS WORD FOR PETITIONS.

How easy it is to see needed requests in these verses: (1) Miracles were a sign of your approval. may I accept what they approved: the apostle's word. (2) I thank you for the humility of Paul and Barnabas — they didn't need to defend their authority. (3) I am so glad to be a part of the people you have chosen for yourself. May I be grateful enough to tell others. (4) How good to be a part of the new temple of David — dwell in my heart and life. (5) Thank you for the words of Amos fulfilled in the Gentiles church — there are others not yet in it. (6) For the privilege of bearing your name, I thank you. (7) Thank you that I can live at the end of the age in which the promise of salvation is mine.

Right here add your personal requests — and his answers.

10. READ HIS WORD AND WAIT — LISTEN — GOD SPEAKS!

I want these men to speak from you to me. (1) *Paul and Barnabas:* "You have greater signs to do than God helped us to do." (2) *Peter:* "There are many more people I did not call." (3) *James:* "You have all the reality of which prophecy was but a shadow."

11. INTERCESSION FOR THE LOST WORLD

Russia — Population: 257,000,000. Growth rate 0.9%. Point for prayer: (1) *Praise God for the spread of the Gospel to* every corner of the land despite 60 years of possibly the most severe persecution of Christians that the world has ever seen. Sometimes the very persecution endured has spread the Gospel to unevangelized areas and among unreached peoples. One hundred years ago there were hardly any Bible believers.

12. SING PRAISES TO OUR LORD.

When my life-work is ended, and I cross the swelling tide,
When the bright and glorious morning I shall see;
I shall know my Redeemer when I reach the other side,
And His smile will be the first to welcome me.

I shall know . . . Him, I shall know Him,
And redeemed by His side I shall stand,
I shall know . . . Him, I shall know Him
By the print of the nails in His hand.

WEEK FIFTEEN — WEDNESDAY

1. PRAISE GOD FOR WHO HE IS.

Anointed. Messiah, Christ, Prophet, Priest, King. What was said of our Lord can surely be said of our heavenly Father—nowhere can I find a reference to you as anointed, so I'll worship my Lord who said, "He that hath seen me, hath seen the Father." To consider one who knows all the future as easily and as fully as I know the past or present is a source of wonder to me. Bless his holy name forever. You anointed him with the Holy Spirit and power. You gave him the Spirit with no limitations, i.e., in expression the Holy Spirit by reason of his nature has no limitations. To talk with such a prophet, priest and king is an awesome thought.

Express yourself in adoration for this quality of God.
Speak it audibly or write out your praise in your own devotional journal.

2. PRAISE GOD FOR WHAT HE MEANS TO ME.

Anointed for me. To consider this one as fulfilling his ministry through, or because of me is amazing. He was anointed as a prophet to teach me and all other men your will for our lives; to predict all the future of my life; to look all the way down the corridor of time and see every part of the changing scene. To be *my priest*, to listen patiently to my babblings and interrupt them to read the motive—to know the *real* need. Oh, oh, to be my king—you have a right twice over to the throne of my heart. Dear Lord, speak, intercede, reign. I gladly own you and worship you.

How do you personally relate to the anointed of God, and God who is anointer?
Speak it out or write it out. It is *so important* that you establish *your own* devotional journal.

3. CONFESSION OF SIN

How poorly have I expressed my love for you—forgive me! What a sin it is to accept you as my prophet and not heed what you say—to know you are my intercessor but leave you unemployed. To claim you as king but refuse your rule! In all these ways I am blood guilty and I ask you to not only forgive but give me grace to fulfill what those names mean in my life!

What personal sins do you want to confess? We *must* speak them to remove them.
Do it! *Now.* There is no one else you have sinned against more than God. Tell him so!

4. SING A PRAYER TO GOD.

Come, Thou Almighty King,
Help us Thy name to sing,
Help us to praise:
Father, all glorious,
O'er all victorious,
Come, and reign over us,
Ancient of Days.

Open your hymn book and sing the rest of the verses—or even sing another prayer song.

5. READ HIS WORD TO HIM!

His Word

[19]"It is my judgment, therefore, that we should not make it difficult for the Gentiles who are turning to God. [20]Instead we should write to them, telling them to abstain from food polluted by idols, from sexual immorality, from the meat of strangled animals and from blood. [21]For Moses has been preached in every city from the earliest times and is read in the synagogues on every Sabbath."

[22]Then the apostles and elders, with the whole church, decided to choose some of their own men and send them to Antioch with Paul and Barnabas. They chose Judas (called Barsabbas) and Silas, two men who were leaders among the brothers. [23]With them they sent the following letter:

The apostles and elders, your brothers,
To the Gentile believers in Antioch, Syria and Cilicia:

Greetings.

[24]We have heard that some went out from us without our authorization and disturbed you, troubling your minds by what they said. [25]So we all agreed to choose some men and send them to you with our dear friends Barnabas and Paul—[26]men who have risked their lives for the name of our Lord Jesus Christ. [27]Therefore we are sending Judas and Silas to confirm by word of mouth what we are writing. [28]It seemed good to the Holy Spirit and to us not to burden you with anything beyond the following requirements: [29]You are to abstain from food sacrificed to idols, from blood, from the meat of strangled animals and from sexual immorality. You will do well to avoid these things.
Farewell.

— *Acts 15:19-29, NIV*

WEEK FIFTEEN — WEDNESDAY

Read His Word to Him.

Dear God, what a penetratingly real text there is here for me to share with you — for you, indeed, to share with me! How very often I have made it difficult for men and women who have been turning to you. I have bound on them certain regulations of my own judgment. I want always to immediately relate them to your word, not mine — for-

give me! Are the four prohibitions of this letter for me today? (1) I want *nothing* to do with idols. (2) Blood is not appetizing to me — and I see in it your price for my redemption — I'll not eat it. (3) Eating the meat of strangled animals would be dangerous to my health. (4) I want nothing to do with any form of immorality!

Please express your response to this beautiful text. Put your expression in your own prayer diary.

6. READ HIS WORD FOR YOURSELF.

I have read to you, but I have applied to me — now I want to do so even more. Somehow I get the impression that such prohibitions were accommodations, or provisions for

the benefit of the Jewish believers. The law of Moses speaks out most clearly against such practices *under the penalty of death.*

Pause in his presence and tell him all his word means to you.

7. READ HIS WORD IN THANKSGIVING.

Somehow this always becomes the easiest time of worship — joy and peace! (1) Thank you for James' judgment which was accompanied by the Holy Spirit. (2) For the wonderful way the Gospel appeals to all men. (3) For the practical nitty-gritty interest you have in what we eat and feel. (4) For your involvement in social distinctions. (5)

That there were indeed elders (no mention of deacons or "the pastor") in the first century church. (6) The apostles, elders, and whole church could and did give "authorization" to men and decisions. (7) That our work is not unappreciated. It is not wrong to be complimented, or to compliment someone else.

Give yourself to your own expression of gratitude — write it or speak it!

8. READ HIS WORD IN MEDITATION.

"It seemed good to the Holy Spirit and to us." May this ever be the deciding factor in all my actions and attitudes. "What do you think about it?" must be asked of the Holy Spirit. His word has much to say. There are four ways I believe he will use in directing my steps: (1) His word — much of it is not read; we just talk about reading it. (2) His

teachers — God set teachers in the body for the purpose of direction — listen to them. (3) His providence — which is only perceived in retrospect. (4) Answer to prayer — Until I have searched out all these areas most carefully, I cannot say the Holy Spirit did not speak. He did, He is. I'm just not listening.

Pause — wait — think — then express yourself in thoughtful praise or thanks.

9. READ HIS WORD FOR PETITIONS.

There is so much for which to pray in these verses: (1) Help me not to make it difficult for anyone to accept you, i.e, through my own selfishness. (2) Deliver me from all idolatry. (3) From all forms of immorality, dear Lord,

deliver me. (4) May I respect those who have rules I do not know. (5) May I include "the whole church" in my decision making. (6) Somehow show me how the leadership and the whole body can agree on decisions.

Please, please remember these are prayers — speak them — reword them!

10. READ HIS WORD AND WAIT — LISTEN — GOD SPEAKS!

Speak to me through this letter: (1) "There are unauthorized men who trouble my people. Are you one of them?" (2) "The decisions of the apostolic church are

the decisions of the Holy Spirit." (3) "If the first Gentiles needed to abstain from these things, so do you."

11. INTERCESSION FOR THE LOST WORLD

Russia — Point for prayer: (1) *Pray for the suffering peoples of Russia* that many may see the barrenness and failure of Communism and turn to Christ. Pray that more of the leaders of the country may be saved. There have

been some very remarkable conversions to Christ in recent years — Stalin's daughter, Kosygin's wife, Solzhenitsyn and some of the most brilliant writers and scientists Russia has produced.

12. SING PRAISES TO OUR LORD.

We would see Jesus, for the shadows lengthen
Across this little landscape of our life;

We would see Jesus, our weak faith to strengthen
For the last weariness, the final strife.

WEEK FIFTEEN — THURSDAY

1. PRAISE GOD FOR WHO HE IS.

The Apostle and high priest of our calling. This is said of our Lord and he often said it of himself, i.e., that he was "sent" from heaven or your presence. Both the sent and the sender are involved. I could never thank you enough for sending your Son. I could never thank him enough for coming! I need to understand much more fully what happens when you come and what happens when you do not, i.e., in my own experience. It is one thing for my blessed Lord to leave the wonders of the eternal world and come to this earth; it is quite another to be as prepared as was the earth when he came. He came "in the fulness of time." He came when many, many prophecies were being fulfilled.

Express yourself in adoration for this quality of God.
Speak it audibly or write out your praise in your own devotional journal.

2. PRAISE GOD FOR WHAT HE MEANS TO ME.

The Apostle for me. Am I as prepared as the stable in Bethlehem? Surely there is an obvious comparison. What an unworthy, unholy, filthy place to be born. Am I to understand he is growing in me as he grew in Nazareth? I believe (Thank you, Lord!) this is the key to the change I want in my life—that you want more than I do! "Until Christ be formed within you." Dear God—the Sender—I want to open my mind, yield all of my will, totally identify with the One who lives inside! How shall I think his thoughts? Memorize the record of his life! Review those words until they become spirit and life! Pray into your will the words you memorize! Do this over and over and over again and Christ will become real to you! (I write this to you for me.)

How do you personally relate to God the Sender and God the Sent?
Speak it out or write it out. It is *so important* that you establish *your own* devotional journal.

3. CONFESSION OF SIN

How miserably I have failed in the highest, most joyous of experiences!—i.e., of emotionally identifying with the Living Presence within! You are the sender, he is the "Sent One." I am the recipient—my heart the manger! Could the tragedy of Bethlehem be repeated all over again? "He came to his own and they who were his own didn't receive him"—or know him.

Until the desires of the body and of the mind are satisfied repeatedly in you, there is no option but to seek satisfaction where there is none. Dear Lord, for today: let me discover all over again your coming into the world and into my heart. I freely, openly confess my sin, my violation of your law. Forgive me, cleanse me!

What personal sins do you want to confess? We *must* speak them to remove them.
Do it! *Now.* There is no one else you have sinned against more than God. Tell him so!

4. SING A PRAYER TO GOD.

There is a place of quiet rest,
Near to the heart of God,
A place where sin cannot molest,
Near to the heart of God.

O Jesus, blest Redeemer,
Sent from the heart of God,
Hold us, who wait before Thee,
Near to the heart of God.

Open your hymn book and sing the rest of the verses—or even sing another prayer song.

5. READ HIS WORD TO HIM!

[30]The men were sent off and went down to Antioch, where they gathered the church together and delivered the letter. [31]The people read it and were glad for its encouraging message. [32]Judas and Silas, who themselves were prophets, said much to encourage and strengthen the brothers. [33]After spending some time there, they were sent off by the brothers with the blessing of peace to return to those who had sent them.   — *Acts 15:30-33, NIV*

Read His Word to Him.

What an understatement is found in verse thirty! It is a 300-mile walk from Jerusalem to Antioch, but distance is no distance with you—or so it would seem with your historian, Dr. Luke. The purpose, not the distance, was important—help me to remember this. The church was not a building—it was people who needed to be gathered into a building. How I would like to have been there! The letter essentially said "how to get along with Jews": Respect them, accept them, love them, learn from them. Am I right about this? I love the little designation *"the brothers"* repeated twice in these three verses. Thank you for speaking to me of this. Prophets encouraged and strengthened—aside from the direct supernatural input of their message I have the same job. Praise you!

Please express your response to this beautiful text. Put your expression in your own prayer diary.

6. READ HIS WORD FOR YOURSELF.

This will not be difficult. I *want* to read each word into my conscience. Who paid for the expense of the trip? I travel almost every week and someone has to pay for the trip. Money never seemed to be mentioned—because it was no problem, any more than it was for our dear Lord who had to depend on others to cook his meals and wash his clothes and pay the inn keepers. Is a servant above his master? Who read the letter to the assembly? "The people" —or was it available for all to read? There was only *one* copy. Who were Judas and Silas? Praise God there were several men named Judas who did a good work—one of them our Lord's brother and another this wonderful prophet!

It is so important that you pause in his presence and either audibly or in written form tell him all his word means to you.

7. READ HIS WORD IN THANKSGIVING.

Indeed I shall: (1) Thank you for the beautiful dedication of Luke the writer of this record. (2) Thank you that we can be the same church today they were in Antioch. (3) For the education you permitted (or directed) in the first century that gave us your word. (4) Thank you that encouragement is such a large part of the life of the church in Antioch. (5) Thank you that words from you can produce such inward joy and strength. (6) For every precious day we can spend together worshipping and learning. (7) Thank you, thank you for "the blessing of peace."

Give yourself to your own expression of gratitude—write it or speak it!

8. READ HIS WORD IN MEDITATION.

"With the blessing of peace." Just what is involved in this little expression? When we consider carefully it becomes not a "little" expression at all. The term "blessing" can have the following meanings: (1) A bounty or benefit from God or man—such as the creatures of air and sea (Gen. 1:20). The benediction God placed on Adam and Eve (Gen. 11:28). (2) A recognition of God's favor in a thankful and adoring manner (Psa. 103:1; Matt. 26:26). (3) The invoking of God's favor on another—such as is indicated in the reference we are considering.

The meaning of peace is far more than the absence of hostility. Essentially peace is an attitude of the heart— this wish or prayer for Judas and Silas is for God to so arrange the circumstances and the attitude of their heart that they might confidently face every circumstance of life with total trust in God.

Pause—wait—think—then express yourself in thoughtful praise or thanks.

9. READ HIS WORD FOR PETITIONS.

It was a 300-mile walk from Jerusalem to Antioch. Dr. Luke was so anxious to tell us of the events in Antioch he totally ignored the distance. There is much in this to prompt praying: (1) Give me the same attitude toward the body of Christ as seen here. (2) Remind me again that there is just one church—the body of your Son. (3) How I long to meet in heaven some of the men and women who were first called Christians. (4) How I want to be an encouragement to others—enable me! (5) Lift up my heart that I might help others. (6) Open the eyes of my heart to see all Christians as my blood relatives. (7) I need the blessing of peace in my service for you.

Right here add your personal requests—and his answers.

10. READ HIS WORD AND WAIT—LISTEN—GOD SPEAKS!

In these three verses speak to me: (1) "Deliver my letters of joy to my body today." (2) "There is nothing men need more than encouragement." (3) "Spend enough time to get my task completed."

11. INTERCESSION FOR THE LOST WORLD

Russia — Point for prayer: (1) *Pray for the triumph of the Gospel over Communism.* The Bible provides the only viable alternative to the philosophy of Communism, and hence is bitterly opposed by the rulers of the land. The intellectual revolt daily gains in power, influence and sophistication; it derives much of its inspiration from Christianity.

12. SING PRAISES TO OUR LORD.

When morning gilds the skies,
My heart awakening cries:
May Jesus Christ be praised;

Alike at work and prayer . . .
To Jesus I repair: . . .
May Jesus Christ be praised.

WEEK FIFTEEN — FRIDAY

1. PRAISE GOD FOR WHO HE IS.

Beginning—the cause and author. Everlasting Father. I love the beginning—of the day, of a new project, of life, of most things I like the beginning best. It is wonderful to know someone who is the Everlasting Beginning—actually the first cause or origin, or head, or the One who stands as the ruler. In every life that has been a failure, you are the new beginning. There is a place (It is a Person.) of "beginning again." How marvelously thoughtful to know Some One like that! Today at the beginning you are there to make it the very best day I have had, or anyone anywhere has had. You are the freshness and strength of new energy. You indeed are the essence of energy and hence always Beginning.

Express yourself in adoration for this quality of God.
Speak it audibly or write out your praise in your own devotional journal.

2. PRAISE GOD FOR WHAT HE MEANS TO ME.

Beginning for me—how often I do need a fresh start! How gloriously good to only use those things of the past which help—all else is forgiven and forgotten, i.e., with you! I should like today to begin and develop a new thought—I need your help. Oh, bless your holy, pure, separate name, you are beginning! Dear Lord, I want to begin the outreach to your children—my brothers and sisters in encouraging them to pray. Only you can teach us to pray. You did so, best of all, by your example. Dear Beginning: Give me the wisdom (the best use of the knowledge I have) to approach and develop this concept in just the way you want it done!

How do you personally relate to the beginning of all, and God who is the Beginning?
Speak it out or write it out. It is *so important* that you establish *your own* devotional journal.

3. CONFESSION OF SIN

There have been beginnings when you were *not* in them! Dear God, if somehow I could be so aware, so *wise*, that I would pause—wait—consider—and then "in faith" or "trust" move, I believe you would be honored. I'm not at all sure I have pure connections so I can not say all my beginnings are right, but now they will surely be much better than many others. Forgive me for ignoring the most obvious need I have. In the sins mentioned in your word Satan offers an "easy way out"—a way with no responsibility—but a way that leaves guilt and unfulfilledness! Forgive and make me whole!

What personal sins do you want to confess? We *must* speak them to remove them.
Do it! *Now.* There is no one else you have sinned against more than God. Tell him so!

4. SING A PRAYER TO GOD.

I am Thine, O Lord,
I have heard Thy voice,
And it told Thy love to me;
But I long to rise in the arms of faith,
And be closer drawn to Thee.

Draw me nearer, nearer, blessed Lord,
To the cross where Thou hast died;
Draw me nearer, nearer, nearer, blessed Lord,
To Thy precious, bleeding side.

Open your hymn book and sing the rest of the verses—or even sing another prayer song.

5. READ HIS WORD TO HIM!

His Word

[35]But Paul and Barnabas remained in Antioch, where they and many others taught and preached the word of the Lord.
[36]Some time later Paul said to Barnabas, "Let us go back and visit the brothers in all the towns where we preached the word of the Lord and see how they are doing." [37]Barnabas wanted to take John, also called Mark, with them, [38]but Paul did not think it wise to take him, because he had deserted them in Pamphylia and had not continued with them in the work.
— Acts 15:35-38, NIV

Read His Word to Him.

Dear Lord, it is easy to see how Paul and Barnabas could teach and preach the "word of the Lord," but "many others" did it too—where did they get "the word of the Lord"? The most obvious answer is the only right answer: They were directly inspired or instructed by the Holy Spirit. The Holy Spirit programmed their minds and they, out of their mouths, gave the "read out" or "the word of the Lord." There *was no* New Testament to consult to prepare them to "teach and preach the word of the Lord." I write this in your presence O Lord—am I right?

Please express your response to this beautiful text. Put your expression in your own prayer diary.

WEEK FIFTEEN — FRIDAY

6. READ HIS WORD FOR YOURSELF.

Dear Lord! If inspired men have disagreements and cannot decide your will, i.e., who is right in a given circumstance, how can I possibly decide when I do not even have direct inspiration? The answer is in the purpose of inspiration—not to make a "better Christian"—that is move in my personal response to your will for life, but to give information from you that is not otherwise available.

It is so important that you pause in his presence
and either audibly or in written form tell him all his word means to you.

7. READ HIS WORD FOR THANKSGIVING.

There is *so much* for which I can thank you in this text: (1) Thank you for the combining of teaching and preaching in the same men (since this is what I do). (2) Thank you for the unnamed prophets in the church in Antioch (we have the names of three of them in 13:1), but for the "many" others we will wait until we see them and ask them all about it.(3) Thank you for the unselfish interest of Paul and Barnabas in their converts. (4) Thank you for the confidence Barnabas had in John Mark. (5) Thank you for Paul's concern for the work and the workers. (6) Thank you for human disagreements since it teaches us you can use us. (7) Thank you that there were two missionary journeys instead of one and both could fulfill the same original purpose.

Give yourself to your own expression of gratitude—write it or speak it!

8. READ HIS WORD IN MEDITATION.

Why rebuild the fallen house of David? James quotes the very words of the prophets in answer: "That the rest of mankind may seek the Lord, and all the Gentiles who bear my name, says the Lord. . . ." The allusion in this text is the beautiful Temple of Solomon. When we consider the church as the rebuilt Temple we stand back in wonder. Remember its beauty? Its value? Its impressive size? It should have been built of the living stones of the Jewish nation. The purpose was to evangelize the Gentiles. How sadly did that purpose fail of fulfillment.

Pause—wait—think—then express yourself in thoughtful praise or thanks.

9. READ HIS WORD FOR PETITIONS.

In the midst of personal disagreement there is a need for prayer: (1) How could "many others" or even Paul and Barnabas teach your word unless they had direct inspiration? (2) Give me such an earnest desire to spread your word today. (3) I want the same concern for those I have taught as filled the heart of Paul and Barnabas. (4) Could both be right in the disagreement over John Mark? (5) Was Paul applying his definition of love to John Mark? (Cf. I Cor. 13:3-9). (6) Thank you for the encouraging words of I Cor. 9:6; Col. 4:10; II Tim. 4:11 and Philemon 24.

Please, please remember these are prayers—speak them—reword them!

10. READ HIS WORD AND WAIT—LISTEN—GOD SPEAKS!

Speak to me for my service in your body today: (1) "The service of my Son's body requires many to teach." (2) "Disagreement does not necessarily mean anyone is right or wrong." (3) "Sometimes more is accomplished because of disagreement."

11. INTERCESSION FOR THE LOST WORLD

Russia — Point for prayer: (1) *The persecution of believers continues* to this day with increased ferocity. No one will ever know how many died for their faith under Communism through torture and ill treatment in prisons and labor camps—probably millions. Some estimate that there are now about 1,000,000 people in prison or exile in Siberia for their faith. Pray for these believers that they may remain strong in the Lord in the awful conditions under which they must live. Pray for the families of believers who are left behind—often in great hardship and poverty.

12. SING PRAISES TO OUR LORD.

Wounded for me, wounded for me,
There on the cross He was wounded for me;
Gone my transgressions, and now I am free,
All because Jesus was wounded for me.

WEEK FIFTEEN — SATURDAY

1. PRAISE GOD FOR WHO HE IS.

Beloved. This was said by God of his Son at his baptism and his transfiguration. It could well have been returned by the Son to the Father—"This is my beloved Father in whom I am well pleased." This is indeed true of all men as they relate to you. Of all men you are the sum total of their emotional, mental and physical need! All the qualities of your being enhance you to us. We find in you the perfect expression of love. For ten thousand reasons we can call you "Beloved." It is like some wonderful person whom to know is to love. If we do not know, we cannot and do not love. *Only* when we know you do we love you. Left to ourselves, we feel a great loneliness that only you can fulfill. The one essential ingredient is "communion, or union, or fellowship with you."

Express yourself in adoration for this quality of God.
Speak it audibly or write out your praise in your own devotional journal.

2. PRAISE GOD FOR WHAT HE MEANS TO ME.

Beloved for me. This is a delight to express. How very, very much I have found you "the Beloved One"! I am not ignoring the days—and nights—of struggle, nor my disappointing coldness toward you, but you have not changed! You are and always have been "the beloved." I surely agree with your estimate of Jesus—"your blessed Son"—our (my) beloved Savior and Lord—in him I also am very, very well pleased! I want to hear him and see him all over again—just for today—just right now! See him at the happy wedding feast; see him in the house of Levi around the banquet table; see him in Simon's house addressing the prostitute; hear him say, "My joy I give to you and no man shall take it away."

How do you personally relate to the belovedness of God, and God who is Beloved?
Speak it out or write it out. It is *so important* that you establish *your own* devotional journal.

3. CONFESSION OF SIN

I cannot say that I have even consciously thought of you as anything less than "beloved." I have failed, however, to make this objective fact as subjectively personal as I should have and could have. To feel estranged from my beloved is sad, and for which I do indeed seek forgiveness. I rush again into your open arms! One sin listed in your word is "profanity"—to lower the pure to the dirt, to treat lightly and of little account that which is so important and valuable! Dear, dear God, how I need, how I want to make all of life sacred, holy, true, beautiful; to not "put down" what you have lifted up. All men are precious to you. Help me to look up beyond their words and actions as you do.

What personal sins do you want to confess? We *must* speak them to remove them.
Do it! *Now.* There is no one else you have sinned against more than God. Tell him so!

4. SING A PRAYER TO GOD.

Anywhere with Jesus I can safely go;
Anywhere He leads me in this world below;
Anywhere without Him dearest joys would fade;

Anywhere with Jesus I am not afraid.
Anywhere! anywhere! Fear I cannot know;
Anywhere with Jesus I can safely go.

Open your hymn book and sing the rest of the verses—or even sing another prayer song.

5. READ HIS WORD TO HIM!

His Word

[40]but Paul chose Silas and left, commended by the brothers to the grace of the Lord. [41]He went through Syria and Cilicia, strengthening the churches.

16 He came to Derbe and then to Lystra, where a disciple named Timothy lived, whose mother was a Jewess and a believer, but whose father was a Greek.
— *Acts 15:40 — 16:1, NIV*

Read His Word to Him.

I never tire of attempting to adopt your point of view in reading this text. It is so, so good to thank you, adore you and seek forgiveness as you speak to me. I thought Silas left and returned to Jerusalem. Perhaps the time element is the answer—he did leave—time has gone by and he has returned, perhaps in answer to Paul's request to accompany him. Just how did "the brothers" at Antioch *commend* Paul and Silas to your grace? Did they pray? Did they fast? Were their hands laid on their heads? Thou knowest! What churches were in northern Syria? What churches were in Cilicia other than Tarsus? How I would like to know—one day I shall!

Please express your response to this beautiful text. Put your expression in your own prayer diary.

6. READ HIS WORD FOR YOURSELF.

Dear Lord, forgive my self-centeredness. I do want you to speak your word into my heart. Didn't Paul and Silas further evangelize in the areas of Syria and Cilicia? We cannot build a case on what is *not said*, but the strengthening of the love and devotion of those who were already Christians is what Luke deems important; so do I! There *were* several congregations in these two provinces. Did the prophets establish them? Was it better to have those who had direct inspiration rather than everyone with a copy of your revelation in their hand? Dear, dear Lord, it is not a matter of inspiration or revelation, it is a desperate need for motivation! Even in the primitive church of pure direction there were those who had a divided house.

It is so important that you pause in his presence
and either audibly or in written form tell him all his word means to you.

7. READ HIS WORD IN THANKSGIVING.

Yes, yes — (1) Thank you, thank you for your grace that will protect me and direct me as well as forgive me. (2) Thank you for those who were willing to be missionaries without a missionary organization—or were "the brothers" at Antioch their source of support? (3) Thank you for telling me all over again my task is to strengthen churches as well as establish them. (4) Thank you for telling me churches can grow from the seed planted by anyone. (5) Thank you so much for Timothy—as Paul said, "There is none like him." (6) Thank you for "fruit that remains." Eunice and Lois and Timothy were probably all converts from the first trip. (7) Thank you for the challenge of winning Timothy's father.

Give yourself to your own expression of gratitude—write it or speak it!

8. READ HIS WORD IN MEDITATION.

". . . whose father was a Greek." There are so many wonderful people in the Bible who have just one flaw in their character—just one exception in an otherwise flawless record. Was it Timothy's fault his father was a Greek? Of course not, but it is always mentioned when we discuss Timothy. What is the "chink" in your armor? What is the hole in your dike? All of us have one. And we do not have one flaw; we have a thousand. There isn't one opening in our armor, there are a hundred. The dike is all but swept away in the flood.

We have just described Timothy as man sees him, but as God sees him Paul's word could well describe him: "I have none like him."

Pause—wait—think—then express yourself in thoughtful praise or thanks.

9. READ HIS WORD FOR PETITIONS.

As we travel with Paul and Silas we pray: (1) Choose the very persons with whom I should work for you. (2) Thank you for those who pray for me today. I claim your grace. (3) Keep me aware that there are many more churches than those I have visited. (4) Lead me to men like Timothy. (5) Enable me to influence women like Eunice and Lois. (6) Give me the humility and honesty necessary to be like Timothy. (7) Thank you for the faith of mothers who share their treasure with their children.

Right here add your personal requests—and his answers.

10. READ HIS WORD AND WAIT—LISTEN—GOD SPEAKS!

Out of the experience of Timothy speak to me: (1) "There are jewels in the most unlikely places." (2) "I have a Timothy to take Mark's place in several of life's relationships." (3) "A Christian home is fine, but all my children are born again."

11. INTERCESSION FOR THE LOST WORLD

Russia — Point for prayer: (1) *The legal position of Christians* is now more difficult than ever before. The law is so ambiguously worded that Christians are easily sentenced as criminals. In 1975 new laws made it illegal to hold house meetings without permission. The authorities turn a blind eye to unlawful breakings-up and molestation of believers attending meetings. A vast organization is being built up to co-ordinate the destruction of the "underground" church. Pray that God may give both wisdom and strength to our brethren in these conditions. The registered churches are also coming under more and more harassment in spite of their legality.

12. SING PRAISES TO OUR LORD.

There is a name I love to hear,
I love to sing its worth;
It sounds like music in mine ear,
The sweetest name on earth.

Oh, how I love Jesus,
Oh, how I love Jesus,
Oh, how I love Jesus,
Because He first loved me!

WEEK SIXTEEN — SUNDAY

1. PRAISE GOD FOR WHO HE IS.

Blessed. This has primary reference to our Lord (Luke 1:42), but God is in the highest possible sense of the word "THE BLESSED ONE." Indeed, indeed! How exalted above man. In every way I can think of you, you are blessed, i.e., have all things, all the qualities of beauty and goodness or moral excellence. You have all the capacities of ruling in power and love — the accumulation of all the more than one hundred qualities of yourself accumulated and multiplied could not truly express how much you are "blessed" — and in the same context, a blessing to all men.

Express yourself in adoration for this quality of God.
Speak it audibly or write out your praise in your own devotional journal.

2. PRAISE GOD FOR WHAT HE MEANS TO ME.

Blessed for me. I want to praise or pronounce a blessing upon your name — to love you from my heart. I do so want to identify with you. "Bless the Lord O my inward being (soul) and forget not all his benefits." He has, he is, forgiving all my sins; healing all my diseases. Since this one word comes from the very heart of human-divine relationship I can only fall before you in speechless praise! Every blessing, or benefit in my life comes from the Blessed One — even yourself! Can I not pause now and review a thousand blessings given in the past year?

How do you personally relate to the blessing of God, and God who is Blessed?
Speak it out or write it out. It is *so important* that you establish *your own* devotional jounal.

3. CONFESSION OF SIN

The sin of ingratitude strikes so close to the cause of all sin — selfishness! Dear God, forgive me for at any time associating myself as the source of any good thing — every good and perfect gift comes from you — not just some of them. The sin of "hatred" — i.e., for any man or woman — hatred — abhorrence for my sin and for sin itself should increase. Dear God, I want it to! But the same attitude cannot, should not, will not be directed toward any man. Vengeance and revenge are too heavy for me; they belong to you. Dear Lord, you have heard from my heart my failures and disappointments — cleanse and forgive!

What personal sins do you want to confess? We *must* speak them to remove them.
Do it! *Now.* There is no one else you have sinned against more than God. Tell him so!

4. SING A PRAYER TO GOD.

My soul in sad exile was out on life's sea,
So burdened with sin and distrest,
Till I heard a sweet voice saying,
"Make me your choice";
And I entered the "Haven of Rest"!

I've anchored my soul in the "Haven of Rest,"
I'll sail the wide seas no more;
The tempest may sweep o'er the wild, stormy deep,
In Jesus I'm safe evermore.

Open your hymn book and sing the rest of the verses — or even sing another prayer song.

5. READ HIS WORD TO HIM!

His Word

[2]The brothers at Lystra and Iconium spoke well of him. [3]Paul wanted to take him along on the journey, so he circumcised him because of the Jews who lived in that area, for they all knew that his father was a Greek. [4]As they traveled from town to town, they delivered the decisions reached by the apostles and elders in Jerusalem for the people to obey. [5]So the churches were strengthened in the faith and grew daily in numbers.   *— Acts 16:2-5, NIV*

Read His Word to Him.

How gladly I take up the reading of your word with yourself! I try to take Timothy's place. I try to imagine how you saw Timothy. He must have asked many questions of the people from Antioch, Iconium and his own house of Lystra. Did he go to Derbe too? — i.e., to make inquiry? As he inquired of Paul, others were inquiring about him — it is always so. What others only heard — and poorly reported — you knew perfectly. *Why* did Paul want to take this young man? Did Paul have need of a cook? An apprentice? I appreciate what I do not know, as well as what I do know about this journey. I'm so glad to worship and to inquire about the blank spaces.

Please express your response to this beautiful text. Put your expression in your own prayer diary.

6. READ HIS WORD FOR YOURSELF.

How I want to imitate Timothy. I can learn so very much by following closely all that happened to him. I can and want to learn of his total devotion to carrying the good news—the number one priority in Paul's life was evangelism. Paul needed help and helpers—Paul was conscious of culture distinctions and problems. I must have, and even look for help in the work I do for my Lord. I can-

not and will not run rough-shod over the taboos of others. Dear Lord, help me to believe with Paul and Silas and all the disciples in each town that there are decisions reached by the apostles that *must* be obeyed. What was "the faith" in which the churches were strengthened? How could they grow so rapidly?

It is so important that you pause in his presence
and either audibly or in written form tell him all his word means to you.

7. READ HIS WORD IN THANKSGIVING.

Yea, Lord, gladly. (1) Thank you for the power to raise Paul from the stoning at Lystra. This story has blessed untold millions. (2) Thank you that brothers who are not of the same town can recognize quality of character when they see it. (3) Thank you that team work is our Lord's work and Paul's work. (4) Thank you that you let me know here that it is sometimes better to ignore a prob-

lem than to fight it. (5) Thank you for men who are willing to overcome heredity defects that could hinder the spread of the word. (6) Thank you for the Holy Spirit's ability to work through apostles and elders. He must do that today. (7) Thank you for the emphasis on evangelism in the first century church.

Give yourself to your own expression of gratitude—write it or speak it!

8. READ HIS WORD IN MEDITATION.

"So the churches . . . grew daily in numbers." With no Bible—no publishing company—no TV or radio—with none of our special programs; i.e., campaigns of any type—without even a preacher, for Paul soon left—the increase of disciples was large and daily! How could it be? What caused it to happen? Dear Lord, how I would like to be able to answer these questions! I cannot say, I will

not say, that these people were all so different and more easily persuaded than the people in my own town. Of course the direct input of inspired speaking must have been a telling factor, but we could speak the word of the Lord in such a clear, interesting manner today if we would. These people allowed their relationship with our Lord to break through all barriers of social resistance.

Pause—wait—think—then express yourself in thoughtful praise or thanks.

9. READ HIS WORD FOR PETITIONS.

Timothy's experience prompts us to pray: (1) Help me to follow again the experiences of Paul in these cities, to appreciate all that happened. (2) May I gather with Timothy, Eunice and Lois as we kneel before the broken body of Paul. When Paul opened his eyes he saw the tear stained faces of these loved ones (so we interpret II Tim. 1:4). (3) Give me such a consistent life that men might

speak well of me. (4) I want to be a help to all those who work for you. (5) May I submit to anything necessary to better open the hearts of those who hear me. (6) How I want to deliver from town to town the decisions reached by your inspired writers. (7) Somehow may I be used to strengthen the church where I worship.

Please, please remember these are prayers—speak them—reword them!

10. READ HIS WORD AND WAIT—LISTEN—GOD SPEAKS!

There are several messages to hear from your word: (1) "Keep on following closely all Paul did." (2) "So live that

men will see your good works and glorify me—not you." (3) "Churches can and should grow in numbers daily."

11. INTERCESSION FOR THE LOST WORLD

Russia — Point for prayer: (1) *The individual Christian* faces many terrible forms of persecution—pray for them. Constant propaganda and crude attempts at conversion to Communism at work and in the home. Discrimination in job opportunities and education, so believers are thus con-

demned to a life of poverty and deprivation even greater than average. Heavy fines are levied for attending "illegal" meetings. Imprisonment and deportation to Siberia. Many refined methods of torture and "treatment" in mental institutions for those who obstinately persist in believing.

12. SING PRAISES TO OUR LORD.

Amazing grace! how sweet the sound,
That saved a wretch like me!

I once was lost, but now am found,
Was blind, but now I see.

WEEK SIXTEEN — MONDAY

1. PRAISE GOD FOR WHO HE IS.

Builder. God is portrayed as a builder in Psa. 102:16; 127:1; Matt. 16:18; 26:61; 27:40; John 3:13-22; Amos 9:11, 12. It is wonderfully good to consider you as the builder and maker of all days! You are indeed "the builder" of everything, all the time, but it would be so much more meaningful if I would consider you as the builder of one life — representative of millions, even billions of lives: (1) You built the spirit which contains all powers of expression. I believe at this moment I am writing words because you built into my spirit or "programmed" my spirit with this capacity. (2) You also built the body in which man lives — it is wondrously made — out of the dust of the earth. The capacities and strength and durability of the organs you have built into the body are a constant source of amazement. Truly, truly on this day I want to praise you!

Express yourself in adoration for this quality of God.
Speak it audibly or write out your praise in your own devotional journal.

2. PRAISE GOD FOR WHAT HE MEANS TO ME.

Builder of myself. I have anticipated this quality of yourself, but it is here that you, the Builder, become real, powerful, personal! I want to watch your handiwork in building abilities into man. Let's meditate and praise around the ability to paint. To be able to put on canvas or paper — or some substitute — a representation of what you have put before us is a true gift from you and surely one of your higher forms of building. To copy or transfer from sight the surface is one thing, and it is truly a blessed thing to do, especially when we but try to express our appreciation of the physical world you have built — but to be able to see with the eye of the imagination and transfer that to a surface and then to see all the shades and shadows of the scene and express it. That is a true source of wonder and praise from my heart! What tremendous capacities you have built into man! Oh, praise and glory be to your name!

How do you personally relate to the building of God, and God who is Builder?
Speak it out or write it out. It is *so important* that you establish *your own* devotional journal.

3. CONFESSION OF SIN

To admit that I have not at all accepted your capacities for building in my own life is almost too obvious to be mentioned, but I do want to enter into the depth of confession and guilt and admit this very fundamental sin. I am far, far, far below what you could make me. I am speaking primarily of moral building. I believe you can (and will) enable me to "present my body a living sacrifice, holy and acceptable to you" — no longer as a vessel of selfish dishonor, but of honor for your service, by the renewing of my mind I can be transformed! Dear God, dear Lord, I this day do commit myself to a mind renewal; to a body giving. Forgive me for my unwillingness to receive your work in me!

What personal sins do you want to confess? We *must* speak them to remove them.
Do it! *Now.* There is no one else you have sinned against more than God. Tell him so!

4. SING A PRAYER TO GOD.

All the way my Savior leads me;
What have I to ask beside?
Can I doubt His tender mercy,
Who thro' life has been my Guide?
Heav'nly peace, divinest comfort,

Here by faith in Him to dwell!
For I know, whate'er befall me,
Jesus doeth all things well;
For I know, whate'er befall me,
Jesus doeth all things well.

Open your hymn book and sing the rest of the verses — or even sing another prayer song.

5. READ HIS WORD TO HIM!

His Word

[6]Paul and his companions traveled throughout the region of Phrygia and Galatia, having been kept by the Holy Spirit from preaching the word in the province of Asia. [7]When they came to the border of Mysia, they tried to enter Bithynia, but the Spirit of Jesus would not allow them to. [8]So they passed by Mysia and went down to Troas. [9]During the night Paul had a vision of a man of Macedonia standing and begging him, "Come over to Macedonia and help us." [10]After Paul had seen the vision, we got ready at once to leave for Macedonia, concluding that God had called us to preach the gospel to them.

[11]From Troas we put out to sea and sailed straight for Samothrace, and the next day on to Neapolis.

— *Acts 16:6-11, NIV*

WEEK SIXTEEN — MONDAY

Read His Word to Him.

Now it is "Paul and *his* companions"—it used to be "Paul and Barnabas" or even "Barnabas and Paul"—why the change in leadership? I am glad to acknowledge this change; it teaches me much for today—ability expressed and used and matured is your way of change. Praise your name! How did the Holy Spirit keep them from preaching the word in Asia? *Why* would the Holy Spirit want to hinder the preaching of the word at any time, any place? Once again they are held back—was it by a direct audible voice? Was it through a set of circumstances they attributed to you? Was it through mutual intuition that was defined as your voice?

Please express your response to this beautiful text. Put your expression in your own prayer diary.

6. READ HIS WORD FOR YOURSELF.

Yes, yes! Dear Lord, you *do* have priorities in places for preaching! Is this a one-time occurrence that has no principle for repetition? It would seem here that Europe would never have heard (at least at this time) if Paul had not been sensitive to the leading of the Spirit. Was there something in the hindrances of Asia and Bithynia that made them think about Macedonia? Am I to read into all the activities of my life the direction of your Spirit?

Pause in his presence and tell him all his word means to you.

7. READ HIS WORD IN THANKSGIVING.

(1) Thank you for your negative answers—without them we would all have much less. (2) Thank you that the one job of these men—and your men today—is preaching the Word. (3) Thank you that the Holy Spirit is called "the Spirit of Jesus." I know what type of person he is. (4) Thank you that you appeal to us through men. (5) Thank you that you are willing to beg us to do your work. (6) Thank you that even the man of Macedonia didn't expect Paul to do it all—"help *us*" was his request. (7) Thank you that Paul acted at once—no procrastination or rationalization.

Give yourself to your own expression of gratitude—write it or speak it!

8. READ HIS WORD IN MEDITATION.

". . . Concluding that God had called us to preach the gospel to them." Here is a good example of being called to preach. Notice the factors involved: (1) Complete trust by the preacher. (2) Total desire to preach anywhere to anyone. (3) Paul and his companions were already serving in whatever way they could. (4) The need of the people to be evangelized was communicated to Paul. (5) He had a vision of what could and should be done.

Pause—wait—think—then express yourself in thoughtful praise or thanks.

9. READ HIS WORD FOR PETITIONS.

While Paul was seeking direction for his service we can seek answers to our prayers: (1) Why am I sometimes prevented by the Holy Spirit from preaching the word? Give me wisdom to know. (2) Help me not to mistake my unwillingness for the hindrance of the Holy Spirit. (3) May the "Spirit of Jesus" give me definite help in my efforts to reach men with your word. (4) I do want to be responsive to any Macedonian call I might hear today. (5) Give me as good helpers as Paul had in Silas, Timothy and Luke. (6) I am glad to rest my travels in your hands.

Right here add your personal requests—and his answers.

10. READ HIS WORD AND WAIT—LISTEN—GOD SPEAKS!

In ways past my understanding, speak to me from these verses: (1) "There are many calls for help if you only had your ears open." (2) "Passing by a place where lost people live does not necessarily mean you are insensitive." (3) "Without your response to my message people will perish."

11. INTERCESSION FOR THE LOST WORLD

Russia — Point for prayer: (1) *The children of believers are singled out for persecution if they follow their parents in believing and refuse to join the Communist Youth groups.* It is illegal for parents to teach the children about their faith, and the state often removes children from their families and deprives the mothers and fathers of their parental rights for this. Pray for the Christian families and their preservation. Pray for those parents weeping for their children, and children suffering in harsh atheist orphanages.

12. SING PRAISES TO OUR LORD.

Blessed assurance, Jesus is mine!
Oh, what a foretaste of glory divine!
Heir of salvation, purchase of God,
Born of His Spirit, washed in His blood.

This is my story, this is my song,
Praising my Saviour all the day long;
This is my story, this is my song,
Praising my Saviour all the day long.

WEEK SIXTEEN — TUESDAY

1. PRAISE GOD FOR WHO HE IS.

Chosen. In response to our Lord, but also related to the One who does the choosing (Isa. 28:16; 42:1-4; Haggai 2:23). In a sense we of ourselves could never know my Lord is *your Chosen One.* You are the One to make the choices. In the mundane matters of daily life it is good to know "our lives are ordered" or chosen by you. You have prepared our minds in the study of your word and in this way you direct our conduct, or exercise influence. In the larger arena of history you have been so very active in the choices of kings and rulers. I like to believe that at the final judgment we will all be able to see and understand your choices in the nations and peoples of the world. Most of all you have set aside your dear Son as *the Chosen One,* chosen to be given as Personified Love for us that we through him might live with you. Bless your wonderful name!

Express yourself in adoration for this quality of God.
Speak it audibly or write out your praise in your own devotional journal.

2. PRAISE GOD FOR WHAT HE MEANS TO ME.

Chosen for me. As you chose your Son, so in every life you have chosen us. Because I have chosen you, you have chosen me! Why? "To bring forth fruit" in my own life the fruit of Spirit-sponsored character—your kind of love, joy, peace, kindness. Dear God, may your purpose in choosing be fulfilled! Why have you chosen me?—not only to be, but to do. If your purposes of the salvation of the world is accomplished it will be through poor, weak people like myself. Dear Lord, I know you didn't make a mistake in choosing me. May I not disappoint you, or myself! Why did you choose me? That I might be conformed to the image of your Son. He was the prototype for all who were chosen. Dear Lord, be formed in me! May I yield myself to him.

How do you personally relate to the choosing of God, and God who is the Chosen?
Speak it out or write it out. It is *so important* that you establish *your own* devotional journal.

3. CONFESSION OF SIN

Dear Lord, forgive me for choosing my own way—choices *were* made each time I sinned! Dear Lord, how clearly do I see that *discipline* is the *first* quality for development—*all the time!* I hear you speak to me: "If any man (this is me) would be my disciple (learner), let him (first) deny himself—take up his cross (a public declaration of the death sentence) and follow me"—does this mean that without this disciplined denial I cannot, or will not, follow you? What else *could* it mean? It no doubt means more but it will never mean less. Thank you for opening my mind. Forgive me for my selfish, undisciplined indulgence. Dear God, I want to choose your way that I might be chosen by you, i.e., in the area of overcoming sin. Thank you for cleansing.

What personal sins do you want to confess? We *must* speak them to remove them.
Do it! *Now.* There is no one else you have sinned against more than God. Tell him so!

4. SING A PRAYER TO GOD.

More about Jesus would I know,
More of His grace to others show;
More of His saving fullness see,
More of His love who died for me.

More, more about Jesus,
More, more about Jesus;
More of His saving fullness see,
More of His love who died for me.

Open your hymn book and sing the rest of the verses—or even sing another prayer song.

5. READ HIS WORD TO HIM!

His Word

[12]From there we traveled to Philippi, a Roman colony and the leading city of that district of Macedonia. And we stayed there several days.

[13]On the Sabbath we went outside the city gate to the river, where we expected to find a place of prayer. We sat down and began to speak to the women who had gathered there. [14]One of those listening was a woman named Lydia, a dealer in purple cloth from the city of Thyatira, who was a worshiper of God. The Lord opened her heart to respond to Paul's message. [15]When she and the members of her household were baptized, she invited us to her home. "If you consider me a believer in the Lord," she said, "come and stay at my house." And she persauded us.
— *Acts 16:12-15, NIV*

Read His Word to Him.

How I do want to go from Neapolis to Philippi! I know it is no problem for you to go every day. (For there are no days—you live in the everlasting now—so all past, present and future are open to you. What an amazing thought!) Could we walk in the streets and look into the shops? What did the river look like? How many women were present for the prayer meeting? What were they praying before Paul arrived?

Please express your response to this beautiful text. Put your expression in your own prayer diary.

6. READ HIS WORD FOR YOURSELF.

Why not preach on the streets? Why not call in the homes? Why go to a place of prayer for women?—and on the Sabbath besides! Paul is my example in evangelism. I must search out those who have a felt need that relates to you. Not all religious people are saved. I can almost hear the message Paul preached to these sincere women—the Old Testament prophecies of the Messiah fulfilled in Jesus. Do I know the scriptures well enough to do this?

Pause in his presence and tell him all his word means to you.

7. READ HIS WORD IN THANKSGIVING.

I am glad to do this: (1) Thank you for the adventurous spirit of Paul and Silas and Timothy. (2) Thank you for religious associations we can use for telling the good news. (3) Thank you for all the beauties of your outdoors—it makes it easy to pray. (4) Thank you for the Sabbath rest for the people of God toward which we all press. (5) Thank you for the strange fact that the first convert in Europe was from Asia. (6) Thank you that there are business people who love you more than money. (7) Thank you for the clear example of how to become a Christian.

Give yourself to your own expression of gratitude—write it or speak it!

8. READ HIS WORD IN MEDITATION.

". . . who was a worshiper of God. The Lord opened her heart to respond to Paul's message." Just who is a good prospect? How do we know who is "not far from the Kingdom of God"? Lydia is a really good example. Those who choose God are chosen by God. The sincere openness on her part to worship God was a marvelous preparation for Paul's preaching. The arguments from the Old Testament fell upon receptive ears. Here was "the good and honest heart" that produced a harvest unto eternal life. We are glad to acknowledge the presence of God in all that happened, but we cannot ignore Lydia's attitude. She herself referred to her attitude—"If you consider me a believer in the Lord." Our Lord said, "He that believeth and is baptized shall be saved, and he that believeth not shall be condemned." Lydia believed and was baptized and was saved.

Pause—wait—think—then express yourself in thoughtful praise or thanks.

9. READ HIS WORD FOR PETITIONS.

Upon arrival at Philippi there are many things for which we can pray: (1) Is there a pattern for the choice of places of evangelism as seen in these verses? Grant me wisdom. (2) Did Paul keep up his personal devotional life in the midst of his travels? Help me to learn how. (3) How precious was the Sabbath to the Jewish people—do we have a *day* of worship? (4) Lead me to a group who will meet regularly with me in prayer. (5) Help me to share with women in the same concerned manner as Paul. (6) Open the hearts of those to whom I speak your word. (7) Open my mind and heart to always baptize converts for the same reason as Paul did.

Please, please remember these are prayers—speak them—reword them!

10. READ HIS WORD FOR MEDITATION.

Speak to me dear Lord: (1) "Accept hospitality; it helps those who offer it." (2) "Business people can sometimes be the very best prospects for salvation." (3) "Find those who have a felt need and meet it."

11. INTERCESSION FOR THE LOST WORLD

Russia — Point for prayer: (1) *The training of preachers* is virtually impossible by normal means. Pray for the raising up of mature leaders well acquainted with the Scriptures to replace those now being imprisoned.

12. SING PRAISES TO OUR LORD.

Glorious things of thee are spoken,
Zion, city of our God;
He, whose word cannot be broken,
Formed thee for His own abode:

On the Rock of Ages founded,
What can shake thy sure repose?
With salvation's walls surrounded,
Thou mayst smile at all thy foes.

WEEK SIXTEEN — WEDNESDAY

1. PRAISE GOD FOR WHO HE IS.

Counsellor. Isa. 9:6 — applied to our Lord — Isa. 11:2; 25:1; 40:13-28; 46:10; Jer. 23:18; 22:32. One who has absolute knowledge and wisdom — what a beautiful expression to describe yourself! Counselling is such a large part of the preacher's work today. How do you view some of our efforts? With your capacities our efforts must indeed seem feeble! How you long to be the confidant of all men on all levels with all problems. What a careful listening ear you would (and do) give to all men! What marvelous advice, what penetrating counsel you have for those who have ears. It was the habit of your dear Son to walk and talk and counsel men. Dear Father! May I hear him today!

Express yourself in adoration for this quality of God.
Speak it audibly or write out your praise in your own devotional journal.

2. PRAISE GOD FOR WHAT HE MEANS TO ME.

Counsellor for me! Oh, this is indeed how I view yourself. I am such a child, such a poor student. I do need so sorely your words of light and life. Dear Lord, how I long to sit like Mary at your feet and eagerly grasp each word. At the same time I lose interest when my energy lags. Dear Lord, you know my limitations. Forgive my negligence, strengthen my weakness. How good it would be to read and absorb every word you have spoken on 100 subjects! Such can be done in searching your word. It is so much easier to think of you as a counsellor in some subjective manner that requires no effort on my part, but listening (and full many a time I do not want even to do this), but to suggest a careful research project! Do I have a greater need or a more important task?

How do you personally relate to the counselling of God, and God who is Counsellor?
Speak it out or write it out. It is *so important* that you establish *your own* devotional journal.

3. CONFESSION OF SIN

How slow and dull I am in listening with the inner ear! Forgive me. It is more than rude not to listen when someone has an important word he wants to share. It is more than impolite to be occupied with my own interests when you are speaking to my deepest needs. It is a sin! Forgive me. Oh, stop me! Unstop my ears! Shut my mouth! Make me to lie down in your green pastures to be healed by your words! It is in quietness I learn more than in the rush of many words! Forgive me, speak deep peace and calm to my whole life! For other sins that are only a result of this lack of attention, forgive! Cleanse, release!

What personal sins do you want to confess? We *must* speak them to remove them.
Do it! *Now.* There is no one else you have sinned against more than God. Tell him so!

4. SING A PRAYER TO GOD.

My hope is built on nothing less
Than Jesus' blood and righteousness;
I dare not trust the sweetest frame,
But wholly lean on Jesus' name.

On Christ, the solid Rock, I stand;
All other ground is sinking sand,
All other ground is sinking sand.

Open your hymn book and sing the rest of the verses — or even sing another prayer song.

5. READ HIS WORD TO HIM!

His Word

[16]Once when we were going to the place of prayer, we were met by a slave girl who had a spirit by which she predicted the future. She earned a great deal of money for her owners by fortune-telling. [17]This girl followed Paul and the rest of us, shouting, "These men are servants of the Most High God, who are telling you the way to be saved." [18]She kept this up for many days. Finally Paul became so troubled that he turned around and said to the spirit, "In the name of Jesus Christ I command you to come out of her!" At that moment the spirit left her. [19]When the owners of the slave girl realized that their hope of making money was gone, they seized Paul and Silas and dragged them into the marketplace to face the authorities. [20]They brought them before the magistrates and said, "These men are Jews, and are throwing our city into an uproar [21]by advocating customs unlawful for us Romans to accept or practice."

[22]The crowd joined in the attack against Paul and Silas, and the magistrates ordered them to be stripped and beaten.

— *Acts 16:16-22, NIV*

WEEK SIXTEEN — WEDNESDAY

Read His Word to Him.

I perceive that Dr. Luke joined "Paul and his companions" (Timothy and Silas) at Troas. How did Paul find Luke? Or how did Luke find Paul? Why did Luke join the work? Was Luke a Christian at the time Paul first met him?

How often did they go to "the place of prayer"? Was it every day at 9, 12 and 3? Could Lydia interrupt her business so often? We do for coffee! Our hours are 10, 12 and 3, but we do pause for refreshment.

Please express your response to this beautiful text. Put your response in your own prayer diary.

6. READ HIS WORD FOR YOURSELF.

Demons could and did predict the future. Slavery was a very real part of first century society! I am so delighted to be the slave of the only one who knows unerringly all about the future. How often can the lost find me on the way to the place of prayer? Paul did have the capacity to discern spirits or identify the presence of a demon in this poor girl. However, Dr. Luke seems to indicate in his historical record that the presence of an evil spirit was evident to all: the actions and attitudes of the girl clearly indicated this. What strange words came from her mouth. But no different from those from demons who acknowledged the deity of my Lord.

Pause in his presence and tell him all his word means to you.

7. READ HIS WORD IN THANKSGIVING.

How anxious I am to do this: (1) Thank you for the slave girl. What was her name? Surely she later became a slave to King Jesus. (2) Thank you that I am told again and again of the regular schedule of prayer time. (3) Thank you for the persistence in Paul's prayer and preaching pattern — he did it "for many days." (4) Thank you that it is *not* necessary to correct a problem as soon as you know of its existence. (5) Thank you that Paul was ready to pay the price of misunderstanding and judgment to help a possessed slave girl and to exonerate the name of our Lord. (6) Thank you I can be warned that whenever money is involved danger is present.

Give yourself to your own expression of gratitude — write it or speak it!

8. READ HIS WORD IN MEDITATION.

"These men are Jews, and are throwing our city in an uproar." The contrast here is a little different than we face today, but what a change it would be if Christians had the same testimony today! How many total cities have been affected with the good news? In Paul's day the real issue was ignored — the trumped up charge was money and politics, not the facts of salvation or miraculous powers. Dear Lord, somehow we are afraid of the consequences of challenging Satan's power in the lives of people.

Pause — wait — think — then express yourself in thoughtful praise or thanks.

9. READ HIS WORD FOR PETITIONS.

As we read of the occult, we all need prayer: (1) Give me a place of prayer — with others and for myself. (2) May I always link prayer and evangelism. (3) Keep me, guard me from the evil one. (4) Deliver me from those who would distract hearers of your word. (5) Give me the courage to rebuke Satan in the lives of those who would be helped. (6) Overcome the prejudice of men in my efforts to teach the lost.

Right here add your personal requests — and his answers.

10. READ HIS WORD AND WAIT — LISTEN — GOD SPEAKS!

There are so many things you could say to me in these verses: (1) "Never minimize the power of the love of money." (2) "Truth from an inconsistent life does not say anything to anyone."

11. INTERCESSION FOR THE LOST WORLD

Russia — Point for prayer: (1) *There appears to be revival* spreading across the country. Young people are turning to the Lord in large numbers. Many villages with 2-3 believers three years ago now have large groups of 50-100. Pray for the deepening and widening of this revival. The authorities are said to be very alarmed by this.

12. SING PRAISES TO OUR LORD.

Jesus has loved me — wonderful Savior!
Jesus has loved me, I cannot tell why; . . .
Came He to rescue sinners all worthless,
My heart He conquered — for Him I would die.

Glory to Jesus — wonderful Savior!
Glory to Jesus, the One I adore; . . .
Glory to Jesus — wonderful Savior!
Glory to Jesus, and praise evermore.

WEEK SIXTEEN — THURSDAY

1. PRAISE GOD FOR WHO HE IS.

Dayspring. Luke 1:78; Isa. 11:1; Zech 3:8; 6:12; Isa. 61:11. The uprising—the rising of the sun or a star. How lovely—and so much to be desired is the sunrise—to relate you to the sunrise, to the spring of the day, the fresh new beginning—there could be no more beautiful figure of speech. The charming pastel colors I see in the sunrise do indeed remind me of you. There are so many ways you are the *Dayspring!*—as is your dear Son: (1) A fresh, new beginning—the very source of this is yourself! How good to find we can start all over again! Bless your wonder-ful self! (2) Cool and still and calm, more than placid the silentness of all your movements, this is emphasized in a beautiful way at sunrise! (3) The colors of the morning—how soft and mysterious they are! Unknown except to the observer—soft and magnificent in shading—so is your total being, beyond human understanding, but soft and lovely. We can look and look and look at sunrise and wish it were always this time of day—so we do with you dear, beautiful, heavenly Father. The Dayspring on high! How full of amazement you are to us!

Express yourself in adoration for this quality of God.
Speak it audibly or write out your praise in your own devotional journal.

2. PRAISE GOD FOR WHAT HE MEANS TO ME.

Dayspring to me. To continue the qualities of sunrise I have seen in you, and to relate them to myself! Oh, praise your name! (4) The promise of a new day—each day is new, has never been here before, is different and distinct. So is yourself—I shall never find enough days to reveal all the phases of your Being. Bless the Source of infinite variety! (5) The source of light is reminding us again that without him we would have no light.

How do you personally relate to the dayspring of God, and God who is Dayspring?
Speak it out or write it out. It is *so important* that you establish *your own* devotional journal.

3. CONFESSION OF SIN

Oh, to confess that I have been so unappreciative of the newness of life you give to all of life. Indeed, I do so confess! Forgive me! Lest I become only generic in my admission of sin, let me say specifically that from sins listed in your word, "anger" is my sin. I do become angry with those I should love the most—my dear family. Oh, dear God, keep my heart soft and open, and like you. I know you can empower me to overcome this sin of the temperament. It is a pure form of sin for it comes as a direct extension of my own selfishness. Do, do forgive and cleanse me! Help me to relax and let you work out the problems of life.

What personal sins do you want to confess? We *must* speak them to remove them.
Do it! *Now.* There is no one else you have sinned against more than God. Tell him so!

4. SING A PRAYER TO GOD.

Sweet hour of prayer! sweet hour of prayer!
That calls me from a world of care,
And bids me at my Father's throne
Make all my wants and wishes known;

In seasons of distress and grief,
My soul has often found relief,
And oft escaped the temper's snare
By thy return, sweet hour of prayer.

Open your hymn book and sing the rest of the verses—or even sing another prayer song.

5. READ HIS WORD TO HIM!

His Word

[23] After they had been severely flogged, they were thrown into prison, and the jailer was commanded to guard them carefully. [24] Upon receiving such orders, he put them in the inner cell and fastened their feet in the stocks.
[25] About midnight Paul and Silas were praying and singing hymns to God, and the other prisoners were listening to them. [26] Suddenly there was such a violent earthquake that the foundations of the prison were shaken. At once all the prison doors flew open, and everybody's chains came loose. [27] The jailer woke up, and when he saw the prison doors open, he drew his sword and was about to kill himself because he thought the prisoners had escaped. [28] But Paul shouted, "Don't harm yourself! We are all here!"   — *Acts 16:23-28, NIV*

Read His Word to Him.

Dear Lord, how can I relate these verses to yourself? Our high-priest was so beaten, so misrepresented, if he hurt I know you did. I am sure in a way I cannot fully appreciate, you do suffer when any one of your children hurt. This is a capacity I just do not know how to express, but it is a great source of strength and identity for me, and all men with you. The first night in a strange place—with antagonistic strangers—there have been thousands (millions?) since who wondered if you knew or felt the deep hurt of a beating! Dear Lord, I believe you do—help my poor, limited understanding!

Please express your response to this beautiful text. Put your expression in your own prayer diary.

6. READ HIS WORD FOR YOURSELF.

I truly have a difficult time relating personally with this circumstance. I have never been so beaten. Never, under such conditions have I sung hymns. I am so glad to acknowledge the liberating power of song, i.e., to the human spirit. We are somehow lifted right out of our environment into the meaning of what we are singing. I wonder what Psalm or hymn or spiritual song Paul and Silas were singing? Whatever it was, it was loud enough to be heard by the other prisoners. Why is it that so many of your actions in human affairs are so sudden, so shocking? It must be that we poor mortals do not pay attention to your daily silent messages of your world about us.

In either audible or written form tell him all his word means to you.

7. READ HIS WORD IN THANKSGIVING.

(1) Thank you for the clear record of total commitment of these men. We would have never known of their beating if Luke had not recorded it. (2) Thank you for the example of the jailer who became one of the first trophies for King Jesus in the church at Philippi. (3) Thank you for the comfort of song. (4) Thank you for your answer to prayer in the form of an earthquake. This is not the first time (Read Acts 4:31.). (5) Thank you for the insight this incident gives us into Roman law—the jailer's life was held forfeit—we appreciate our law system more. (6) Thank you for Paul's immediate reaction of concern for others. (7) Thank you for the unnamed prisoners who shared the jail with Paul and Silas. Were some of them converted? I plan on asking Paul one day.

Give yourself to your own expression of gratitude—write it or speak it!

8. READ HIS WORD IN MEDITATION.

"Do yourself no harm for we are all here!" What a good phrase to use for the church in the midst of a world bent on self-destruction. The injuries of most of the world are self-inflicted. Man seems determined to commit suicide regardless of his bounties. It is a strange but true fact that all men have within them the capacity for self-destruction. Such is a part of the wages of sin. How this old sad world needs more men like Paul, ready to lift up their voice like a trumpet and assure men that life *does* have meaning—all is *not* lost; there *is* hope.

Pause—wait—think—then express yourself in thoughtful praise or thanks.

9. READ HIS WORD FOR PETITIONS.

An earthquake moves many to pray: (1) Lord, prepare my heart to suffer for you. Forgive my lax, even luxurious living as compared with those who even now are suffering for you. (2) How can I truly understand the conditions of "the inner cell"? Speak to my conscience. (3) Oh, for a song to sing in every situation—teach me. (4) I want wisdom to be able to teach "prisoners" today the song of deliverance. (5) May I be reminded of my Lord's words about those in prison today. (6) Give me the spontaneous courage to call out to the lost. (7) Lead me to someone who is even this day about to end his life. Open my heart to stop him to teach him.

Please, please remember these are prayers—speak them—reword them!

10. READ HIS WORD AND WAIT—LISTEN—GOD SPEAKS!

There are several messages from you to me in this text: (1) "No prison can hold my message prisoner." (2) "Find someone who hurts—he will hear my word." (3) "I have no pleasure in the death of the wicked."

11. INTERCESSION FOR THE LOST WORLD

Russia — Point for prayer: (1) *There is a famine of Bibles* in the country. Despite official claims to the contrary, no Bible have been printed in the U.S.S.R. recently for distribution to the public. Pray for the many worthy organizations and individuals from non-Communist lands who use many strange ways to get Bibles into the hands of the believers—this is a dangerous ministry: pray for it! Pray also for the underground presses now producing hymn books and Bibles with growing efficiency despite the seizure of the underground press in Latvia in 1974 (which produced 220,000 Bibles and portions in 8 languages in 1973). There is reckoned to be, on average, only 1 Bible for every 25 believers. Many will go to extreme lengths in order to obtain a copy.

12. SING PRAISES TO OUR LORD.

A wonderful Savior is Jesus my Lord,
A wonderful Savior to me,
He hideth my soul in the cleft of the rock,
Where rivers of pleasure I see.
He hideth my soul in the cleft of the rock

That shadows a dry, thirsty land;
He hideth my life in the depths of His love,
And covers me there with His hand,
And covers me there with His hand.

WEEK SIXTEEN — FRIDAY

1. PRAISE GOD FOR WHO HE IS.

Deliverer. (Isa. 59:20; Rom. 11:26; Isa. 61:1, 2; Psa. 14:7.) I truly emphathize with this name. It seems to me you have been in the delivery business for a very long time with a great number of your people. Let's start at the beginning. Most of the deliverance was subjective, i.e., delivering man from himself as he yielded to Satan. Adam was delivered in the blood sacrifice from his own nakedness and guilt. Noah was delivered through water in an ark you helped him prepare. You delivered Abram from the pagan worship of idols. You delivered Lot from Sodom, but you had real problems in delivering Sodom from Lot and his daughters. You delivered Jacob from Laban and Jacob's own selfishness. Then there were those who would not be delivered! What a wonderful deliverer you are — in history and my own experience!

Express yourself in adoration for this quality of God.
Speak it audibly or write out your praise in your own devotional journal.

2. PRAISE GOD FOR WHAT HE MEANS TO ME.

A deliverer for me! How many thousands of times you have delivered me! Oh, praise your wonderful name! How often have you delivered me from an accident that could have happened, but didn't? From how many bouts of sickness have I found blessed escape? From encounters with unreasonable men or circumstances, how often have I been delivered? Dear, dear Lord, you have made my way one of pleasantness and peace! How often, how many ten thousand times ten thousand have I been delivered from overbearing temptations? I have prayed so, so often, "Lead me not into temptation" and you have delivered me! Bless your marvelous hidden name! What other men call a coincidence I *know* is your deliverance! As a father pitieth his children and gets up before they awake and provides in many ways for them, even removing some of their toys so they will not stumble, so you have done for me.

How do you personally relate to the deliverance of God, and God who is Deliverer?
Speak it out or write it out. It is *so important* that you establish *your own* devotional journal.

3. CONFESSION OF SIN

Dear, dear Lord, I have been so very negligent in seeing your deliverance. I have been so lacking in perception and faith. Please forgive me! It seems to me this is one of the most serious sins I have. It is such a sad reflection on my insensitiveness and selfishness — do forgive me and open my eyes! "Railing" is a sin mentioned in your word. At times I have done this — at my dear wife, or children, or myself — and in all such sin I am only railing at you. I was mad because I could not have or do or be something I thought was right. Oh, oh, the sin of it all! Forgive me! This is Satan's substitute for praise.

What personal sins do you want to confess? We *must* speak them to remove them.
Do it! *Now.* There is no one else you have sinned against more than God. Tell him so!

4. SING A PRAYER TO GOD.

I need Thee every hour,
Most precious Lord;
No tender voice like Thine
Can peace afford.

I need Thee, O I need Thee;
Every hour I need Thee!
O bless me now, my Saviour,
I come to Thee!

Open your hymn book and sing the rest of the verses — or even sing another prayer song.

5. READ HIS WORD TO HIM!

His Word

[29]The jailer called for lights, rushed in and fell trembling before Paul and Silas. [30]He then brought them out and asked, "Men, what must I do to be saved?"

[31]They replied, "Believe in the Lord Jesus, and you will be saved — you and your household." [32]Then they spoke the word of the Lord to him and to all the others in his house. [33]At that hour of the night the jailer took them and washed their wounds; then immediately he and all his family were baptized. [34]The jailer brought them into his house and set a meal before them, and the whole family was filled with joy, because they had come to believe in God.

[35]When it was daylight, the magistrates sent their officers to the jailer with the order: "Release those men."

— Acts 16:29-35, NIV

Read His Word to Him.

Oh, holy Father! How I do want to see these verses as you do! How very near to death and loss was the jailer! You know him as an individual—you know his family. How I would like to know his name and ask him how he transformed his interest from saving his life so quickly to saving his relationship with you. Somehow he associated the earthquake and safety of the men in his prison with Paul and Silas. How did he do this? Why did he? Dear Lord, I have so many questions you alone can answer. It would seem that physical safety and teaching about yourself and your Son were all a part of the same subject. Is this right? Why was everyone so concerned about baptism—even in the middle of the night? A meal was eaten in the early hours of the morning—how unusual!

Please express your response to this beautiful text. Put your expression in your own prayer diary.

6. READ HIS WORD FOR YOURSELF.

Here I am a part of the jailer's household! What do I know about you before I meet Paul and Silas? Did I hear Paul or Silas speak in the synagogue? Perhaps my willingness or deep desire to believe is what led me to open my heart to the word of the Lord. All was accepted at face value as soon as it was spoken. How wonderfully good it is to embrace and cherish each blessed thought! I never tasted a meal that had such flavor and nourishment. There is no joy like that of the first opening of the eyes of my heart to the meaning of life from your perspective.

It is so important that you pause in his presence and either audibly or in written form tell him all his word means to you.

7. READ HIS WORD IN THANKSGIVING.

(1) Thank you for "the lights" that illumined the evidence of your destruction, but also the opportunity to hear your word. (2) Thank you for Paul—always ready to turn events to your advantage. (3) Thank you for the sincere evidence of repentance on the part of the jailer in washing the wounds of Paul and Silas. (4) Thank you for the preaching of baptism as a part of "the word of the Lord." (5) Thank you that this Gentile jailer could learn enough in a few hours to become a sincere Christian—yea, with all his house. (6) Thank you for the influence this father had over the members of his family. (7) Thank you for this clear model of evangelism and salvation.

Give yourself to your own expression of gratitude—write it or speak it!

8. READ HIS WORD IN MEDITATION.

"The whole family was filled with joy, because they had come to believe in God." Here is surely one of the first Gentile families. There are several things to say about these wonderful people: (1) The father and mother had some really strong influence upon the children and in this case for good. How many members were there? (2) We must be discussing persons of an age of reasoning because they are "filled with joy" because of what they believed. (3) Their baptism must have been a part of their faith for it just preceded their expressions of happiness.

Pause—wait—think—then express yourself in thoughtful praise or thanks.

9. READ HIS WORD FOR PETITIONS.

The jailer's needs call forth requests in our own lives: (1) May I often fall down before you with a request for deliverance. (2) Keep me as aware of my need for a Savior as was the jailer. (3) Open my heart to know all that is included in believing in my Lord. (4) Dear Lord, save my whole household! (5) May I show my repentance as clearly as the jailer. (6) Help me to supply the same source for belief as given by Paul and Silas to the jailer. (7) Give me the joy of salvation—may it be based on the same foundation as that of the jailer and his household.

Right here add your personal requests—and his answers.

10. READ HIS WORD AND WAIT—LISTEN—GOD SPEAKS!

How clearly you can speak to me out of this text: (1) "It will take a moral earthquake to save some people today." (2) "Men are saved today by the same word spoken to the jailer." (3) "Please notice *when* the jailer rejoiced."

11. INTERCESSION FOR THE LOST WORLD

Russia — Point for prayer: (1) *Bible translation.* It is reckoned that 60,000,000 people do not have anything of the Word of God in their language. Pray for the work of those working in surrounding lands on new translations.

12. SING PRAISES TO OUR LORD.

I love Thy Kingdom Lord,
The house of Thine abode,

The Church our blest Redeemer saved
With His own precious blood.

WEEK SIXTEEN — SATURDAY

1. PRAISE GOD FOR WHO HE IS.

Desire(s) of all nations (Haggai 2:7). Precious, pleasant. "Whom you delight in" — "desirable." Of our Lord, but of God also. Surely all nations — all men of all time desire him (you) not in a definable form. The deep disatisfaction and yearning is but a reaching out to you. You give all men life and breath and everything else. You determined the times set for them and the exact places where they should live. Since you have such an investment in man, it is only part of your design that men would once they found you, or better, you found them, would find you precious or most desirable. How wonderful it would be to have universal worship and love for you. Indeed you are my desire — my desires are fulfilled in you.

Express yourself in adoration for this quality of God.
Speak it audibly or write out your praise in your own devotional journal.

2. PRAISE GOD FOR WHAT HE MEANS TO ME.

Desire of all nations for me. What a high and exalted Person I worship, i.e., as man would look at him — the focus of interest and desire of all the nations of the world! All 220 nations reaching out to find fulfillment in you. Surely I should be mightily encouraged in this fact. At the same time I should stand aghast that more than half of the world's population does not know you. Dear Lord, forgive me and help me to fulfill your intention that the knowledge of yourself should cover the earth like the waters cover the sea. Dear Lord, may this same kind of knowledge at least cover the "world" where I live! You are sending me out into it that it might be true.

How do you personally relate to the desirability of God, and God who is the Desire of all nations?
Speak it out or write it out. It is *so important* that you establish *your own* devotional journal.

3. CONFESSION OF SIN

When I think of "blood guiltiness" I think of the lack of world evangelism. We now live in the year of 1982, almost 2,000 years since our Lord gave the command — and yet, nations wait, full of desire not satisfied! What a reproach! Forgive me — I cannot ask for others. "Railing" (a sin I need to mention again) — yes, I'm guilty — I do not now think of a specific time or place, but I have railed at others, at circumstances, at an act poorly performed at least by my standards, and what good came of all these angry words? None! Sin came of it. Dear Lord, dear Lord as near as I can remember I have not railed at you. I am not immune, but I do want to be. Forgive my lack of love and faith.

What personal sins do you want to confess? We *must* speak them to remove them.
Do it! *Now.* There is no one else you have sinned against more than God. Tell him so!

4. SING A PRAYER TO GOD.

I must tell Jesus all of my trials;
I cannot bear these burdens alone;
In my distress He kindly will help me;
He ever loves and cares for His own.

I must tell Jesus! I must tell Jesus!
I cannot bear my burdens alone;
I must tell Jesus! I must tell Jesus!
Jesus can help me, Jesus alone.

Open your hymn book and sing the rest of the verses — or even sing another prayer song.

5. READ HIS WORD TO HIM!

[36]The jailer told Paul, "The magistrates have ordered that you and Silas be released. Now you can leave. Go in peace."
[37]But Paul said to the officers: "They beat us publicly without a trial, even though we are Roman citizens, and threw us into prison. And now do they want to get rid of us quietly? No! Let them come themselves and escort us out."

[38]The officers reported this to the magistrates, and when they heard that Paul and Silas were Roman citizens, they were alarmed. [39]They came to appease them and escorted them from the prison, requesting them to leave the city. [40]After Paul and Silas came out of the prison, they went to Lydia's house, where they met with the brothers and encouraged them. Then they left. — *Acts 16:36-40, NIV*

Read His Word to Him.

It seems each day is a new beginning in the worship and praise to you through your word — and indeed it is! Can you hear the words of the messengers who came to report the decision to release Paul and Silas? I am sure you can! These words were spoken 2,000 years ago, but time is no hindrance with you. "Instant play back" on any event of any life is no problem at all! How surprised and pleased the jailer must have been to hear the words of Paul. Evidently the rights of a Roman citizen were a proper claim when they would help the cause of yourself. How I would like to have been a spectator at the meeting of Paul and the magistrates. What happened to the good work at Philippi?

Please express your response to this beautiful text. Put your expression in your own prayer diary.

6. READ THE WORD FOR YOURSELF.

How can I use the privileges of my American citizenship to the advantage of my Lord? The magistrates and officers, indeed the whole colony-right of Philippi, was put on trial by Paul's words. No wonder they were alarmed. Dear Lord, am I as ready to stand up and be counted as were these, intrepid servants of yourself?

May I learn that the essential facts of many a case have never been considered. How many millions have lost their very lives — to say nothing of freedom — because of their love for you and your Son? How is it with my courage and boldness?

It is so important that you pause in his presence
and either audibly or in written form tell him all his word means to you.

7. READ HIS WORD IN THANKSGIVING.

(1) Thank you for the jailer who was so full of joy and gratitude. (2) Thank you for Paul who spoke up and stood up for your place in the community. (3) Thank you for Silas who was glad to sing the second verse — to back up all Paul did — all you did through Paul. (4) For Timothy and Luke who began the experience in Philippi with Paul and Silas. What happened to them? (5) Thank you for the shock-wave that was sent through the Roman Colony. (6) Thank you for the maid who was "free indeed." (7) Thank you for Lydia and "the brothers" whom I confidently hope to meet in your home.

Give yourself to your own expression of gratitude — write it or speak it!

8. READ HIS WORD IN MEDITATION.

Shall we consider three thoughts on the work at Philippi? (1) The blessed facts about the slave-girl: (a) She found the greatest treasure — she obtained it from her owner. (b) She transferred masters — she was a glad, willing slave. (c) She found what she proclaimed: "The way to be saved." (2) Three helpful facts about Timothy: (a) He, like us, was a witness to all that happened at Philippi. (b) He somehow escaped the imprisonment. (c) He no doubt taught many people in the city. (3) How did the jailer come to have saving faith? He was moved by the earthquake and freeing of the prisoners to ask for salvation. Paul spoke the word of the Lord to him. He felt his lostness and welcomed God's answer through Paul. His saving faith included repentance, indicated in washing the wounds of Paul and Silas — it included baptism as indicated in the same hour.

Pause — wait — think — then express yourself in thoughtful praise or thanks.

9. READ HIS WORD FOR PETITIONS.

Paul's actions and attitudes are the basis for many requests: (1) Give me the wisdom to answer those in power so you can have the advantage. (2) Keep me aware of my privileges as an American citizen — and to thank you for it. (3) May I right now review the privileges of my citizenship of heaven. (4) Help me to be able to separate what is an action of selfishness and pride — and what is not. (5) Thank you for the candid honesty of the Acts account. (6) May I have words of encouragement for "the brothers." (7) Thank you for those who continued the work in Philippi after Paul left.

Please, please remember these are prayers — speak them — reword them!

10. READ HIS WORD AND WAIT — LISTEN — GOD SPEAKS!

In the fleeting hours of change speak to me: (1) "You need not always heed the words of officials." (2) "The most surprising actions for the advantage of the gospel are possible if you have courage." (3) "My church will be well and strong long after you leave."

11. INTERCESSION FOR THE LOST WORLD

Russia — Point for prayer: (1) *Unreached peoples* — it is almost impossible to obtain facts about peoples that have not intelligently heard the Gospel. Pray for the following: *The Jews* have been severely persecuted over the last few years, yet there are many finding the Lord Jesus in Moscow and other places. Pray that their hardships may bring them to Christ. Pray for the evangelizing of those who have emigrated to Israel. *The Muslims.* Some estimate them to even number up to 50,000,000, speaking a great variety of languages, never having been adequately evangelized.

12. SING PRAISES TO OUR LORD.

We praise Thee, O God! for the Son of Thy love,
For Jesus who died, and is now gone above.
Hallelujah! Thine the glory,

Hallelujah! amen;
Hallelujah! Thine the glory, revive us again.

WEEK SEVENTEEN — SUNDAY

1. PRAISE GOD FOR WHO HE IS.

"And he said, I will make all my *goodness* pass before thee, and I will proclaim the name of the Lord before thee" (Exodus 33:19). Indeed this is just what you have done throughout all my life. I wish to acknowledge this quality of yourself. How you did fulfill the promise to Moses: (1) He was an unusual child when he was born (is not every baby so considered by the parents)? Thanks be to you, such was indeed true of this son of Jocebed. (2) He was born into a loving, caring family. How good it was to find a mother and father with such courage. (3) What unusual goodness came his way when he was "found" by the Pharaoh's daughter — he could have been discovered and destroyed by any one of many others. (4) What a good education you gave him! (5) What you did in the past life of Moses was only typical of what was to come. Praise your wonderful name!

Express yourself in adoration for this quality of God.
Speak it audibly or write out your praise in your own devotional journal.

2. PRAISE GOD FOR WHAT HE MEANS TO ME.

Your goodness has been more than evident in my life. Oh, bless and adore your very essential Being — which is altogether *good*! If I believe you are good — and I do — then I will look for expressions of this in my life. They are not hard to find: (1) I was born into a loving home. I believe my father almost worshiped my mother in his love for her. He was born into a very humble circumstance — commercial fisherman and logger. His mother died when he was born; his father raised him. A good deal of raising me was done by him; my mother was sick a good deal of the time, but I'm sure I was very much wanted and loved when I came. I thank you for this. (2) The care and provision of food and clothing and a home was a very big concern of my parents — thanks to you through them. (3) A trust and love for my parents was easily transferred to you. Praise your name! And praise you for Marie and Charles, my dear mother and father.

How do you personally relate to the goodness of God, and God who is Goodness?
Speak it out or write it out. It is *so important* that you establish *your own* devotional journal.

3. CONFESSION OF SIN

Surely your goodness has led me to repentance — and more than once has this happened. I want to change my mind again and again as I rethink your word in the two books of nature and the Bible, to say nothing of the record of your blessing and direction in my daily living. How totally selfish and thoughtless I have been. Forgive me! I would have long been in hell had you given me what I have so richly deserved. "Shameful speaking" is a sin mentioned in your word. Dear Lord, if you could play back examples of this sin in my life — and I know you could — what ones of the many would you choose? I know I would bow my head and heart in shame as I do now, and no doubt I would be as surprised as much in what you included as what you left out. Dear God, forgive me!

What personal sins do you want to confess? We *must* speak them to remove them.
Do it! *Now.* There is no one else you have sinned against more than God. Tell him so!

4. SING A PRAYER TO GOD.

Open my eyes, that I may see
Glimpses of truth Thou hast for me;
Place in my hands the wonderful key
That shall unclasp, and set me free.

Silently now I wait for Thee,
Ready, my God, Thy will to see;
Open my eyes, illumine me, Spirit divine!

Open your hymn book and sing the rest of the verses — or even sing another prayer song.

5. READ HIS WORD TO HIM!

His Word

17 When they had passed through Amphipolis and Apollonia, they came to Thessalonica, where there was a Jewish synagogue. [2] As his custom was, Paul went into the synagogue, and on three Sabbath days he reasoned with them from the Scriptures, [3] explaining and proving that the Christ had to suffer and rise from the dead. "This Jesus I am proclaiming to you is the Christ," he said. [4] Some of the Jews were persuaded and joined Paul and Silas, as did a large number of God-fearing Greeks and not a few prominent women. — *Acts 17:1-4, NIV*
Read also II Thess. 3:7, 8, NIV.

Read His Word to Him.

Gladly, gladly do I approach this time of worship with you. How I would like to go into the Jewish synagogue of Thessalonica. Can I hear the conversations of several groups gathered? Is it dark or light inside the building?

What were the fragrances? Paul was in the custom of attending, i.e., from his childhood. He had a new, delightful message in a very old setting. Dear Lord, I want to hear it.

Please express your response to this beautiful text. Put your expression in your own prayer diary.

6. READ HIS WORD FOR YOURSELF.

What did Paul and Silas do during the three weeks? i.e., between the Sabbath days? "Out of the heart proceed the issues (or actions and motivations) of life." They spoke personally and door to door about our Lord (i.e., if Ephesus is an example). I want to listen ever so closely to what Paul is saying: "He reasoned with them from the Scrip-

tures." His reasoning was in the form of explaining and "proving." This says so much to me. The Holy Spirit supplements and implements all that Paul says, i.e., the Holy Spirit gave the Old Testament scriptures. The Holy Spirit gave Paul wisdom (the best use of the knowledge he obtained by his study of the Old Testament).

It is so important that you pause in his presence
and either audibly or in written form tell him all his word means to you.

7. READ HIS WORD IN THANKSGIVING.

(1) Thank you, dear Lord, for the example of the apostles who were selective in where they preached the word. (2) Thank you for good habits — such as regular attendance of public worship. (3) Thank you for your wonderful Scriptures — the same ones Paul used. (4) Thank you I can reason — explain and prove in the use of your

word. (5) Thank you that I am convinced Jesus is your Son and my anointed King. (6) Oh, for the meaning of his suffering and resurrection — how could I ever thank you enough? (7) Thank you for the power of the gospel in all social strata of mankind.

Give yourself to your own expression of gratitude — write it or speak it!

8. READ HIS WORD IN MEDITATION.

"We worked night and day, laboring and toiling so that we would not be a burden to any of you" (II Thess. 3:7, 8). What an example Paul and Silas were to the

Thessalonians — and to all of us. Would he be classified as a workaholic? As compared with whom? Our Lord?

Pause — wait — think — then express yourself in thoughtful praise or thanks.

9. READ HIS WORD FOR PETITIONS.

While working for you in Thessalonica there was much reason for prayer: (1) Give me "customs" or habits that lead me to places of worship. (2) I need your wisdom to be able to reason from your word. (3) I do want the same approach to religious people today as seen in the life of

Paul. (4) Open the eyes of my heart to see again your suffering Servant put to death for my sins. (5) Show me again the open tomb. (6) What an example of energy under your control is seen in the life of Paul and Silas. I want to be like them!

Right here add your personal requests — and his answers.

10. READ HIS WORD AND WAIT — LISTEN — GOD SPEAKS!

I am glad to hear you speak to me from these verses: (1) "Paul passed by some large cities to find one where he would have the ears of the people." (2) "Men are fickle

and inconsistent, but so are you." (3) "I am always the same and I love you and will use you."

11. INTERCESSION FOR THE LOST WORLD

Russia — Point for prayer: (1) Help from the West. Much can be done by believers in the Free World to alleviate the suffering of the believers. Practical aid for families of prisoners and preachers (through publicizing of the

needs) — pray for the organizations and couriers who arrange this. The publicizing of the persecution of believers in the U.S.S.R. has made the Communists afraid to go too far.

12. SING PRAISES TO OUR LORD.

I will sing of my Redeemer
And His wondrous love to me;
On the cruel cross He suffered,
From the curse to set me free.

Sing, oh, sing . . . of My Redeemer,
With His blood . . . He purchased me,
On the cross . . . He sealed my pardon,
Paid the debt . . . and made me free.

WEEK SEVENTEEN — MONDAY

1. PRAISE GOD FOR WHO HE IS.

"... *unto a land that I will show you*" (Gen. 12:1b). *You are our guide!* Bless and praise your name. As he guided the wise men to Bethlehem by the finger of light, so He makes so plain the path of duty that "the wayfaring man, though a fool, shall not err therein" (Isa. 35:8). How reassuring to know our way is under *your* direction. We can place ourselves confidently in your hands. Just for today (I have no other.) I give myself to you to show me the path I should take. "And the Lord went before them by day in a pillar of a cloud, to lead them the way; and by night in a pillar of fire, to give them light; to go by day and night: He took not away the pillar of the cloud by day, nor the pillar of fire by night, from before the people." Dear Lord, let me learn the lessons in this for me: (1) It is your very self manifested in the circumstances of my life today — you are *in* the phone calls, letters, people, etc., of today's activities. (2) You are present to guide at night — I can choose to stay in my tent and not look for the fire!

Express yourself in adoration for this quality of God.
Speak it audibly or write out your praise in your own devotional journal.

2. PRAISE GOD FOR WHAT HE MEANS TO ME.

Guide for me. I apologize for the personalness of the above — what I said of myself, I say for all — "as thou very well knowest"! Dear Lord, how glad I am to acknowledge your direction for my life. (3) The cloud was high in the sky to give general direction. It was up to the people to step over the stones and avoid the snakes. So it is with the plain principles in your word — my pillar of cloud and fire. You said "to prefer one another." It is up to me to make application. You said "love one another fervently from the heart" — even those who are not at all lovable. (4) God expects us to move — we *are* moving whether we know it or not.

How do you personally relate to the guidance of God, and God who is our Guide?
Speak it out or write it out. It is *so important* that you establish *your own* devotional journal.

3. CONFESSION OF SIN

How easy and "natural" it is to make up my own mind and ignore your presence or interest in the "affairs of this life." Dear God, this must be the ultimate sin — forgive, forgive me! Kindly, patiently, let me walk through this day!

A sin listed in your word is "passion." This is a synonym for illicit sex, i.e., arousing the desire of sex with someone other than your wife. Dear God, forgive me! The sex desire is generic — like the desire for food is genereic — we make the choice of where and when and how these desires will be fulfilled. If we decide that your choice of food is not adequate or attractive, we look elsewhere. We are essentially saying, "You do not know what you are doing — I know how better to satisfy these desires than you do." Oh, oh, what a sin! Forgive me!

What personal sins do you want to confess? We *must* speak them to remove them.
Do it! *Now*. There is no one else you have sinned against more than God. Tell him so!

4. SING A PRAYER TO GOD.

Are you weary, are you heavy-hearted?
Tell it to Jesus,
Tell it to Jesus;
Are you grieving over joys departed?
Tell it to Jesus alone.

Tell it to Jesus, tell it to Jesus,
He is a friend that's well known;
You've no other such a friend or brother,
Tell it to Jesus alone.

Open your hymn book and sing the rest of the verses — or even sing another prayer song.

5. READ HIS WORD TO HIM!

His Word

⁵But the Jews were jealous; so they rounded up some bad characters from the marketplace, formed a mob and started a riot in the city. They rushed to Jason's house in search of Paul and Silas in order to bring them out to the crowd.   — *Acts 17:5, NIV*
¹⁶for even when I was in Thessalonica, you sent me aid again and again when I was in need.   — *Phil. 4:16, NIV*

Read His Word to Him.

Dear Father, how I do want to stand back from the text and attempt to see it through your eyes — at the same time to praise you for what I see. Paul was truly in need in Thessalonica. Again and again he was hungry and had no certain dwelling place. Even with his working night and day, he was overjoyed with the gifts from Philippi. Am I right in this estimate? There must have been some exchange between the two cities. These people were truly interested in each other — they cared! So much like you! I know you care for me, for you have sent me aid again and again when I was in need.

Please express your response to this beautiful text. Put your expression in your own prayer diary.

6. READ HIS WORD FOR YOURSELF.

There are always some "bad characters" around. They frequent the "market places" of the whole wide world. It is only because someone did not get to their parents or grandparents with the "good news" of regeneration. What terrible things jealousy will cause men to do, will cause *me* to do! What a lesson there is in these few words. Paul stayed in the most difficult town in spite of all opposition — up until his life was threatened — then he left, but not until then. How did Jason react to this circumstance? We believe he gladly paid the bond. Even in the distortion of the truth there is an element of truth. There is another king and *his name is Jesus!*

It is so important that you pause in his presence
and either audibly or in written form tell him all his word means to you.

7. READ HIS WORD IN THANKSGIVING.

Thank you for the dear friendship of those who care — and "put their money where their mouth is." (2) Thank you for those who do not care once and forget until next Christmas, but come again and again to help. (3) Thank you for the aggressiveness of Paul and Silas that caused a real threat to someone's status. (4) Thank you for the "ring of truth" in all this account. (5) Thank you for Jason who helped an unpopular cause and leader. (6) Thank you for yourself as the silent observer of all that happened. (7) Thank you for Dr. Luke who researched so carefully the facts of this incident.

Give yourself to your own expression of gratitude — write it or speak it!

8. READ HIS WORD IN MEDITATION.

"Bad characters from the marketplace." There never seems to be a lack of such persons. How many millions are there today in the marketplaces of the world? Why are they "bad"? Only because their purpose in life was bad. When there is no reason for living beyond the daily routine of today and tomorrow, frustration sets in and anger and meanness become a way of life. Such a lifestyle prevents responsible work — a "quick dollar" is a welcome offer to such persons. Dear Lord, shall we ever break out of our little mold of middle class respectability and go to the marketplace?

Pause — wait — think — then express yourself in thoughtful praise or thanks.

9. READ HIS WORD FOR PETITIONS.

The opposition in Thessalonica moved Paul to pray, and it does the same for me: (1) Thank you for those dear people who remember with gifts those who labor for you. (2) Keep me aware that jealousy is a very common sin. (3) Guard my heart with your peace that I might not envy others. (4) Thank you for every person with whom I have stayed in my many travels. (4) Keep me aware that there are men in today's marketplace who will do anything for money. (5) Dear Lord, deliver me from the deadness of a *"religious club"* with a social emphasis. (6) Give me the excitement of suffering for your name's sake. (7) Guard me from seeking sensationalism.

Please, please remember these are prayers — speak them — reword them!

10. READ HIS WORD AND WAIT — LISTEN — GOD SPEAKS!

There is much you can say to me in your word: (1) "There are those who work for me today who are in need — you could send them a gift." (2) "Jealousy is self-destructive." (3) "Violence is still possible today."

11. INTERCESSION FOR THE LOST WORLD

Russia — Point for prayer: (1) *The Radio ministry* has grown phenomenally. There are 10 missionary stations that ring Russia. There are now about 243 hours of broadcasting time a week from these stations to the U.S.S.R. One out of every two people in the U.S.S.R. has a radio, and millions listen in. Some believe that there have been over one million people converted through these broadcasts, and many new churches planted as a result in hitherto unevangelized places. Pray for the production of the right programs that are relevant to the needs of believers and atheist-indoctrinated unbelievers.

12. SING PRAISES TO OUR LORD.

When I saw the cleansing fountain
Open wide for all my sin,
I obeyed the Spirit's wooing,
When He said, Wilt thou be clean?

I will praise Him! I will praise Him!
Praise the Lamb for sinners slain;
Give Him glory, all ye people,
For His blood can wash away each stain.

WEEK SEVENTEEN — TUESDAY

1. PRAISE GOD FOR WHO HE IS.

Faithful who promised. Dear Lord, this does so fully describe you. In so many promises you have demonstrated your concern and your faithful interest in the affairs of men. Bless your name for this wonderful quality. It is awesome to consider your promises of wrath were just as real and true as your fulfillment of blessings. The promise of a flood, the promise of destruction for Sodom, the promise of the death of the first born — all these are now historical facts that were once only words. The promise of a great nation — of the land of Canaan — your presence in the sanctuary and Temple as well as in the bodies of your children are also eloquent testimonies that you are faithful to your promises. How I rest upon your promises for this day.

Express yourself in adoration for this quality of God.
Speak it audibly or write out your praise in your own devotional journal.

2. PRAISE GOD FOR WHAT HE MEANS TO ME.

Faithful to me who promised. You promised to me release from all the weight of my sin. Bless your name — you *are* faithful. You promised my name in the eternal roll book of heaven — it is there even now! Dear God, I purpose to remain faithful, not perfect (in the sense of sinless), but mature and in this sense perfect. You have promised to treat me as a needy son and supply my lack. In a wonderful way you have done this physically, and I would not minimize this, but in so many other precious ways you have, and are meeting my heart needs. You are so good to me!

How do you personally relate to the faithfulness of God, and God who is Faithful?
Speak it out or write it out. It is *so important* that you establish *your own* devotional journal.

3. CONFESSION OF SIN

That I have not always relied upon your promises — dear Lord, I have not even known them — forgive me! I have so often wandered as an orphan when all the while you were a searching Father. Dear Father, forgive me and receive me!

Another sin listed in your word is "covetousness." This is essentially wanting that which belongs to someone else — another form of stealing, but it refers not so much to the act as the desire to act. What have I wanted, yearned after, that belonged to my neighbor or relative? Right here and right now I cannot think of anything, but I'm sure I have done so — reveal to me the deceitfulness of my heart, the frailty and pride of my memory. The desire to be accepted among men is a form of covetousness. Dear Lord, open my mind and humble my spirit. Forgive.

What personal sins do you want to confess? We *must* speak them to remove them.
Do it! *Now.* There is no one else you have sinned against more than God. Tell him so!

4. SING A PRAYER TO GOD.

Thou, my everlasting portion,
More than friend or life to me;
All along my pilgrim journey,

Savior, let me walk with Thee.
All along my pilgrim journey,
Savior, let me walk with Thee.

Open your hymn book and sing the rest of the verses — or even sing another prayer song.

5. READ HIS WORD TO HIM.

His Word

[6]But when they did not find them, they dragged Jason and some other brothers before the city officials, shouting: "These men who have caused trouble all over the world have now come here, [7]and Jason has welcomed them into his house. They are all defying Caesar's decrees, saying that there is another king, one called Jesus." [8]When they heard this, the crowd and the city officials were thrown into turmoil. [9]Then they made Jason and the others post bond and let them go.

[10]As soon as it was night, the brothers sent Paul and Silas away to Berea. On arriving there, they went to the Jewish synagogue. [11]Now the Bereans were of more noble character than the Thessalonians, for they received the message with great eagerness and examined the Scriptures every day to see if what Paul said was true.

— Acts 17:6-11, NIV

Read His Word to Him.

The cry of alarm still rings in your ears. I am sure however we represent the gathering before the city officials it is less than complete. But I do want to identify with you and each person at the trial. Who expressed the charge? It *was true* that men like Jason had affected the "whole world." (Read again Col. 1:23.) It *was true* that there is another king than Caesar and his name is Jesus! It *was true* that these men defied the laws of the government when they contradicted your laws! What excitement! What turmoil! But it was all so clear and obvious to you.

Please express your response to this beautiful text. Put your expression in your own prayer diary.

6. READ HIS WORD FOR YOURSELF.

How can I sit passively by and not reason and persuade men? I refer to men who have not heard what you have said. Dear Lord, I purpose to reach every man and woman, every boy and girl, in the city where I live. I cannot be personally responsible for people in Africa or India, but I am going to be held for those right next door or in the next block. I believe there are many faithful, trusting men like Jason, but they will never be discovered without men like Paul and Silas. Dear God, at least I can be Jason.

It is so important that you pause in his presence
and either audibly or in written form tell him all his word means to you.

7. READ HIS WORD IN THANKSGIVING.

(1) Thank you for the unnamed brothers who shared the unjust trial with Jason. (2) Thank you we can affect and effect society. (3) Thank you some are ready to invest their money in the cause. (4) Thank you for the example of leaving as well as staying. (5) Thank you for the noble Bereans. (6) Thank you that we do not have to travel far to find an entirely new environment. (7) Thank you we have your wonderful scriptures today we can search and believe just like those of Berea!

Give yourself to your own expression of gratitude — write it or speak it!

8. READ HIS WORD IN MEDITATION.

Meditate on this word: ". . . *They received the message with great eagerness.*" Does not your message merit eagerness? They were eager to hear of the fulfillment of prophecy in Jesus of Nazareth — their Messiah. We Gentiles can never appreciate the long hopes of the Jewish nation. They were eager to hear how they could "escape the corruption that is in the world through lust." Oh, to find "the Way," to be the overcomer instead of the overcome, to be the victor instead of the victim. To not just drag along and live somehow, but triumphantly! Our blessed Savior fulfills his name! They were eager to find the relief of forgiveness, which could never be found in the law.

Pause — wait — think — then express yourself in thoughtful praise or thanks.

9. READ HIS WORD FOR PETITIONS.

In Acts 17:6-11 several reasons for prayer arise: (1) Dear Lord, help me to so live and work for you that at least men will do more than yawn. (2) In several areas of my life I need Jesus to be king. (3) Give me friends like Jason who will risk life and money for you. (4) May I have the courage of Paul to leave when your work is helped by my doing so. (5) Thank you for those I meet who have the same attitude as those of Berea. (6) Keep me always aware that just nearby is a much better response to your word. (7) Give me wisdom as I read again the two letters Paul wrote to the Thessalonians.

Right here add your personal requests — and his answers.

10. READ HIS WORD AND WAIT — LISTEN — GOD SPEAKS!

I am sure Paul prayed often and sought your direction while working in Thessalonica. What do you say to me from this text? (1) "There is another king — his name is Jesus." (2) "Appreciate those who suffer unjustly — sometimes because of you." (3) "I have a nobility in the world — they are all who are like the Bereans."

11. INTERCESSION FOR THE LOST WORLD

Cambodia — Population: 7,735,000. Points for prayer: (1) *Pray for the tragic people of Cambodia.* The vast majority have never had a chance to hear the Gospel. Nearly all the little mountain tribes are unevangelized but for those reached in refugee camps in Pnomh Penh or in neighboring lands. (2) *Pray for the conversion of the Communist rulers* — men who have been more savagely cruel and vengeful than possibly any in modern history. (3) *The persecuted believers* have now been scattered all over the country, and probably all the leaders and older Christians have been martyred but for the few who managed to escape to Thailand. Nearly all the Christian literature in the country has been destroyed. The believers are few, very young in the faith and most without the comfort of the Word or fellowship.

12. SING PRAISES TO OUR LORD.

To God be the glory, — great things He hath done,
So loved He the world that He gave us His Son,
Who yielded His life an atonement for sin,
And opened the Lifegate that all may go in.
Praise the Lord, praise the Lord,

Let the earth hear His voice!
Praise the Lord, praise the Lord,
Let the people rejoice!
O come to the Father, thro' Jesus the Son,
And give Him the glory, — great things He hath done.

WEEK SEVENTEEN — WEDNESDAY

1. PRAISE GOD FOR WHO HE IS.

Ensign—"The Lord our banner" (Ex. 17:15; Ps. 60:4). I love this beautiful figure of speech—"Hold up the banner and call the troops to move forward"! Dear God, you have been my banner, my Ensign for more than 40 years. The real standard held up before me has been your own dear Son. He has always been and is today so attractive and compelling and he has always led the way—I have wanted to follow him. How wonderfully good it is to have a standard, a goal, a mountain to climb. You have put within us such a desire and you yourself are the top of the mountain. You are the ultimate goal of all of life and of every day in it. I see you now beckoning me on!

Express yourself in adoration for this quality of God.
Speak it audibly or write out your praise in your own devotional journal.

2. PRAISE GOD FOR WHAT HE MEANS TO ME.

Ensign for me. Of course what has just been said applies to all men as well as myself but just here I have the privilege of personal relationship to you as *my ensign*, my flag of triumph! There have been days when I did not have the commensurate emotion, but this is not one of them. I am full of joy and praise and eagerness and I am delighted to expend it before you. I gladly exclaim over the conquests you have already given and those ahead: "Lead on oh King Eternal—the day of march has come! henceforth in fields of conquest our tents (bodies) shall be thy home."

How do you personally relate to the leadership of God, and God who is Ensign?
Speak it out or write it out. It is *so important* that you establish *your own* devotional journal.

3. CONFESSION OF SIN

You have led and we have not followed is many times sadly true. Dear Lord, forgive. Oh, Father, why are we so reluctant? It is the fear of the unknown and the untried. Fear of our own weakness and inability. All of this is indicative of the sin of unbelief. We are "more than conquerors through him who loved us and gave himself up for us." Dear Commander, forgive me!

Another sin mentioned in your word is "sexual immorality." I have been intrigued of late in the use of the expression, ". . . we have divine power to destroy *strongholds*" (II Cor. 10:4). I take this to mean that any area of sin repeated often can become a "stronghold" of Satan. Sexual immorality is one such sin, one such stronghold. How shall we tear it down? By his divine power—it is his strength, not ours. Exodus 23:29 says, "I will not drive them out in a single year." Little by little take possession and be faithful in the territory conquered. Dear God, forgive and lead me!

What personal sins do you want to confess? We *must* speak them to remove them.
Do it! *Now.* There is no one else you have sinned against more than God. Tell him so!

4. SING A PRAYER TO GOD.

What a fellowship, what a joy divine,
Leaning on the everlasting arms;
What a blessedness, what a peace is mine,
Leaning on the everlasting arms.

Leaning, leaning,
Safe and secure from all alarms;
Leaning, leaning,
Leaning on the everlasting arms.

Open your hymn book and sing the rest of the verses—or even sing another prayer song.

5. READ HIS WORD TO HIM!

His Word

[11]Now the Bereans were of more noble character than the Thessalonians, for they received the message with great eagerness and examined the Scriptures every day to see if what Paul said was true. [12]Many of the Jews believed, as did also a number of prominent Greek women and many Greek men.

[13]When the Jews in Thessalonica learned that Paul was preaching the word of God at Berea, they went there too, agitating the crowds and stirring them up. [14]The brothers immediately sent Paul to the coast, but Silas and Timothy stayed at Berea. [15]The men who accompanied Paul brought him to Athens and then left with instructions for Silas and Timothy to join him as soon as possible.
— *Acts 17:11-15, NIV*

Read His Word to Him.

How grand an example the Bereans offer to all of us. Were the work hours less in this town than in our own? We can see how the men and women with means would have time, but what of the slaves and the "common people" who are always the ones to hear the message with gladness? Evidently there were enough copies of the Old Testament scriptures for such a daily general examination. There are three groups identified in Berea: (1) Many Jews believed. (2) A number of prominent Greek women. (3) Many Greek men believed. How helpful to me to know your message appeals to everyone.

Please express your response to this beautiful text. Put your expression in your own prayer diary.

WEEK SEVENTEEN — WEDNESDAY

6. READ HIS WORD FOR YOURSELF.

How persistent is hatred! The Jews in Thessalonica just would not give up! Why did they feel so very negative about Paul? Perhaps a re-reading of Paul's letters to the Christians in Thessalonica would help us. Dear Lord, I want to be as open as the Bereans, not closed like the Thessalonians. I know my source of liberty is the same as theirs — your word. I want to examine it all over again today! It is good to read that Silas and Timothy were with Paul in Berea — no doubt they came from Philippi and Thessalonica. The term "brothers" says so much!

It is so important that you pause in his presence
and either audibly or in written form tell him all his word means to you.

7. READ HIS WORD IN THANKSGIVING.

(1) Thank you that there is a norm called "truth" — it is your word. (2) Thank you, you expect us to be able to make evaluations you will accept. (3) Thank you for the intensity of investigation — a good example I want to follow. (4) Thank you that the lines of truth and error can be drawn so sharply. (5) Thank you for those who care enough to leave their jobs for the help of a brother, i.e., to accompany Paul. (6) Thank you for the second mile (miles) they went with Paul all the way to Athens. (7) Thank you for the example of Paul — he wanted and sought the company and help of others.

Give yourself to your own expression of gratitude — write it or speak it!

8. READ HIS WORD FOR MEDITATION.

We shall look at three principles in this record: (1) Paul reasoned and explained but one fact; it became the source of all his trouble — a real "stumbling block" to the Jews, the fact was: "that the Christ had to suffer and rise again from the dead." This gave Paul no end of persecution and misunderstanding. (2) The text gives us the reason for the opposition: "But the Jews were jealous." Can it be that men would go to such extremes as those of Thessalonica just for envy or jealousy? Of course the Jews would not so define their motive, but the Holy Spirit has already done so. (3) It is interesting to notice that three groups believed in both Thessalonica and Berea: (1) Jews; (2) Greeks; (3) prominent women; and in Berea: (1) Jews; (2) Greeks; (3) prominent Greek women. What does this say to me?

Pause — wait — think — then express yourself in thoughtful praise or thanks.

9. READ HIS WORD FOR PETITIONS.

While some opposed and others believed, Paul prayed — and so do we: (1) Give me a great consuming hunger and thirst for your word. (2) Open my mind to see your Son in all the scriptures. (3) How can I influence the influential? (4) Keep me aware that there are men who will do almost anything to oppose your work. (5) May I be willing to trust others with your work. (6) Lead me to the very place where I can work most effectively for you. (7) Teach me the patience, and yet strong zeal I see in Paul.

Please, please remember these are prayers — speak them — reword them!

10. READ HIS WORD AND WAIT — LISTEN — GOD SPEAKS!

Speak to me from Acts 17:11-15: (1) "The ratio of converts is proportionate to Bible study." (2) "Disbelievers are much different from unbelievers." (3) "I still want Athens evangelized."

11. INTERCESSION FOR A LOST WORLD

Cambodia — Points for prayer: (1) *The Muslim Cham people* were beginning to show interest in the Gospel in 1975, and a few had sought the Lord. (2) *The Khmer people* in Vietnam number 2,000,000 and through missionary work and the Khmer Church in Cambodia, 700 believed in the last few months before Vietnam fell to the Communists. Pray for these believers. (3) *By the end of 1976 about 60,000 Cambodians had managed to flee* from their land. The great majority of escapees died or were killed before reaching Thailand. Most of these refugees are going to live in France, U.S.A., etc. There are 10,000 refugees in poverty stricken conditions and in a state of traumatic shock in 5 refugee camps at any one time in Thailand. Pray for missionaries seeking to minister to the bodily and spiritual needs of these poor people. Pray for the ministry of literature, cassette messages and personal work. Over 2,000 Khmer have sought the Lord in these camps.

12. SING PRAISES TO OUR LORD.

Christ has for sin atonement made,
What a wonderful Savior!
We are redeemed! the price is paid!

What a wonderful Savior!
What a wonderful Savior is Jesus, my Jesus!
What a wonderful Savior is Jesus, my Lord!

233

WEEK SEVENTEEN — THURSDAY

1. PRAISE GOD FOR WHO HE IS.

Foundation (Isa. 28:16). How good it is to contemplate God as the foundation of all things—surely of all life. This whole visable cosmos and billions like it have their foundation in yourself! You are the original source—the planner and builder of all we see, and all we do not see. What incredible power and wisdom is yours! Blessing and praise, wonder and amazement is mine and all the men and women of this little speck of your creation called earth! When the foundation is faulty, the whole structure is in danger. But when the foundation of life is: absolute knowledge, total wisdom, unending love, infinite mercy, unquestionable justice, how permanent is the life of the superstructure. Dear God, once again I am shocked into silence and wonder! You have not only laid the foundation of all things, you yourself are the foundation. Thank you, thank you!

Express yourself in adoration for this quality of God.
Speak it audibly or write out your praise in your own devotional journal.

2. PRAISE GOD FOR WHAT HE MEANS TO ME.

Foundation for me. Let me explore the various areas of my life which need and have found a strong foundation in yourself: (1) My home life—my marriage—Dear Lord, without you and our mutual love for you we would have long ago been living our own selfish lives apart from each other. We are in love with each other because we are both in love with you. (2) My job—what a wonder and amazement it is that I can spend my whole time meditating on and teaching and preaching your word. But if I do not keep a close, personal foundation contact with you even this task can be a bore. But when I build my task directly on you in personal devotion it is a joy no man can express!

How do you personally relate to the permanence of God, and God who is our Foundation?
Speak it out or write it out. It is *so important* that you establish *your own* devotional journal.

3. CONFESSION OF SIN

Dear, dear Father, that I should ever start the day or plan a project without first building the foundation for it in yourself is surely the greatest of all my sins. This is my daily original sin. Please forgive me! Deepen my awareness of my need!

Idolatry is a sin mentioned in your word. An idol is any thing or any one who gets our heart, thought, will, emotions. More than this an idol is whatever gets our worship, adoration, supplication, dependence. What is it in my life that gets my total, constant attention and upon which I depend? Dear Lord, if it is anyone, or anything but you I have an idol and I am an idolater. Some of the projects in which I have been (and am presently) involved could come dangerously near to this definition. Dear God, open my eyes! Forgive me!

What personal sins do you want to confess? We *must* speak them to remove them.
Do it! *Now.* There is no one else you have sinned against more than God. Tell him so!

4. SING A PRAYER TO GOD.

Christ the Lord is ris'n today, Alleluia!
Sons of men and angels say: Alleluia!

Raise your joys and triumphs high, Alleluia!
Sing, ye heav'ns, and earth reply. Alleluia!

Open your hymn book and sing the rest of the verses—or even sing another prayer song.

5. READ HIS WORD TO HIM!

His Word

[15]The men who accompanied Paul brought him to Athens and then left with instructions for Silas and Timothy to join him as soon as possible.

[16]While Paul was waiting for them in Athens, he was greatly distressed to see that the city was full of idols.

[17]So he reasoned in the synagogue with the Jews and the God-fearing Greeks, as well as in the marketplace day by day with those who happened to be there.

— *Acts 17:15-17, NIV*

Read His Word to Him.

Blessed experience: to travel again to Athens! Here is Paul about to leave his friends and go into the streets of Athens all alone, but not without you. At the same time Paul felt your presence he felt the real lack and loss of human companionship. Paul was gregarious and needed and wanted companionship in preaching and teaching.

Even while Paul was by himself he was thinking of others. "So when we could stand it no longer, we thought it best to be left alone at Athens (left by ourselves in Athens). We sent Timothy, who is our fellow worker in spreading the gospel of Christ (to Thessalonica).

Please express your response to this beautiful text. Put your expression in your own prayer diary.

6. READ HIS WORD FOR YOURSELF.

Am I as greatly distressed as Paul? Or am I distressed at all as compared with him? "A city full of idols." Dear God, what did he do about it? "So he reasoned in the synagogue with the Jews and the God-fearing Greeks." He didn't smash the statuary! Someone else could do that, someone else would do that, someone else *did* do that.

I have been to Athens—the statues are all gone, but the idols are still there. It is *only* in reasoning, teaching, motivating, challenging, awakening, that idols will fall and Christ will be Lord! Paul did it, but the ground gained has been lost again.

It is so important that you pause in his presence
and either audibly or in written form tell him all his word means to you.

7. READ HIS WORD IN THANKSGIVING.

(1) Thank you for Paul's attitude of confidence, and even dependence upon those who worked with him. (2) Thank you for the wonderful insight that says: his we are whom we serve (worship) slaves to God—or "no gods." (3) Thank you for Timothy who is an example for all of us—"our brother," God's fellow worker. (4) Thank you for the work Timothy had to do: (a) spread the good news,

(b) *strengthen* the Christians, (c) *encourage* the Christians. (5) Thank you there is "a faith" and "the faith" in which we can be strengthened and encouraged. (6) Thank you for the same Scriptures out of which we can reason today. (7) Thank you that Paul was shocked, but not overcome by the idolatry of Athens.

Give yourself to your own expression of gratitude—write it or speak it!

8. READ HIS WORD IN MEDITATION.

"Slaves to the *things* that are no gods" (Gal. 4:8). Why serve something or someone who will not respond to your service? Fear of the unknown and a misinterpretation of the calamities and blessings of life is the explanation. Man is indeed incurably religious. If he is not introduced to the

One True God, he will invent gods of his own to fill the void he feels within himself. How restless we are until we find rest in the bosom of our heavenly Father! Such a comment by Paul shows us the proper relationship. We are glad for willing slaves of our Master who is Love.

Pause—wait—think—then express yourself in thoughtful praise or thanks.

9. READ HIS WORD FOR PETITIONS.

Paul's spirit was moved to concern as he considered the needs of Athens—so we are moved to pray: (1) Send me helpers in the gigantic task of evangelizing thousands of people. (2) Open my eyes to see idols as idols. (3) Keep me constantly aware of the futility of self-service. (4) There

are men like Timothy and Silas today—may I learn from them. (5) I need the wisdom to know how to relate men to tasks—or tasks to men—help me. (6) May I remain steadfast amid trials. (7) I need your wisdom to add depth to my reasoning.

Right here add your personal requests—and his answers.

10. READ HIS WORD AND WAIT—LISTEN—GOD SPEAKS!

I open my ears to hear what you have for me in these verses: (1) "You always work better with others." (2) "Keep your eyes open to life as I see it." (3) "Reasoning precedes converting."

11. INTERCESSION FOR THE LOST WORLD

Cambodia — Points for prayer: (1) *The majority of the Khmer are going to France and U.S.A.* There are some Khmer preachers and also former missionaries to Cambodia seeking to help the believers to form fellowship groups and witness to the uprooted unconverted in both these lands. Others are constantly being converted. There is

a critical lack of Khmer speaking Christian workers to do this work. Pray for the efforts made to train young Khmer believers for leadership. (2) *There are now daily broadcasts* prepared by Khmer preachers and transmitted from Manila. Pray that believers may be strengthened and the lost and the Communists converted thereby.

12. SING PRAISES TO OUR LORD.

Praise Him! praise Him!
Jesus, our blessed Redeemer!
Sing, O Earth, His wonderful love proclaim!
Hail Him! hail Him! highest archangels in glory;
Strength and honor give to His holy name!

Like a shepherd, Jesus will guard His children,
In His arms He carries them all day long:
Praise Him! praise Him! tell of His excellent greatness:
Praise Him! praise Him! ever in joyful song!

WEEK SEVENTEEN — FRIDAY

1. PRAISE GOD FOR WHO HE IS.

Fountain. (Ps. 87:8; Jer. 2:13; 17:13; Ezek. 47:3-10) How refreshing to appear before you this day and relate you to the bubbling, sparkling water of a great fountain! How I would love to jump in! Bless your wonderful self, I can easily see the comparison — a fountain opened for sin and poor, weary, dirty sinners. How sore and old I feel — I represent ten million more — how delightful to be well and young again! I have found the fountain of youth — come to the fountain, stand by my side — come to the waters — you won't be denied — jump in, quench your thirst, wash your body, relax in the strength and unfathomed depth of the clear, warm water — suddenly you can swim, no fear, what excitement. But most of all you are as clean and renewed on the inside as you are on the outside. Bless your name!

Express yourself in adoration for this quality of God.
Speak it audibly or write out your praise in your own devotional journal.

2. PRAISE GOD FOR WHAT HE MEANS TO ME.

Fountain for me! I have so closely related to this lovely figure of speech and Person that what I intended for this whole world had much personal involvement. But just now let me think and praise as I stand before the fountain: (1) the fountain is both blue and green in color. Because blue is royal and blue is the sky, it seems so very appropriate, but this blue color is alive, moving, changing blue! Green — as green as the growing, luxurious vegetation all about me. So is your clear, beautiful self — the King of ten trillion galaxies — alive in the eternal strength of an endless life. (2) This fountain is never the same, and yet always the same. In you I find infinite variety and unchanging character. Oh, how I love you!

How do you personally relate to the refreshment of God, and God who is the Fountain?
Speak it out or write it out. It is *so important* that you establish *your own* devotional journal.

3. CONFESSION OF SIN

Dear, dear Lord, I have not always felt this way, nor have I always even made the mental, emotional effort to do so. I am the poorer, but you have not been honored as you should in my life — forgive me! A sin mentioned in your word is *witchcraft.* At first thought I can see but little relationship to me, but on second thought, I had better reconsider. Satan is not dead; witchcraft is a real thing. I am so glad I can "bind Satan" not only by the simple verbal rejection of his influence, but by the aggressive refusal to consider even his name, I thus remove his thoughts from my mind. The positive, active presence of my Lord does more than anything else — after all, it is Jesus who binds the strong man.

What personal sins do you want to confess? We *must* speak them to remove them.
Do it! *Now.* There is no one else you have sinned against more than God. Tell him so!

4. SING A PRAYER TO GOD.

The Lord is my Shepherd, no want shall I know;
I feed in green pastures, safefolded I rest;
He leadeth my soul where thy still waters flow,
Restores me when wand'ring, redeems when oppressed;
Restores me when wand'ring, redeems when oppressed.

Open your hymn book and sing the rest of the verses — or even sing another prayer song.

5. READ HIS WORD TO HIM!

His Word

[17]So he reasoned in the synagogue with the Jews and the God-fearing Greeks, as well as in the marketplace day by day with those who happened to be there. [18]A group of Epicurean and Stoic philosophers began to dispute with him. Some of them asked, "What is this babbler trying to say?" Others remarked, "He seems to be advocating foreign gods." They said this because Paul was preaching the good news about Jesus and the resurrection. [19]Then they took him and brought him to a meeting of the Areopagus, where they said to him, "May we know what this new teaching is that you are presenting? [20]You are bringing some strange ideas to our ears, and we want to know what they mean."
— Acts 17:17-20, NIV

Read His Word to Him.

Oh, dear Father, it is a rare privilege I have to each day pause before your word and think with you your thoughts. Your man, Paul, is in the marketplace of Athens. Wasn't it frustrating for him to address those who had almost no knowledge of you? The ones who did listen called him "a babbler." Bless your holy name, there is always something attractive and captivating in the message of the resurrection of your dear Son. It sounded strange and foreign but the call of "deep to deep" was there. They had to hear more, and so do I.

Please express your response to this beautiful text. Put your expression in your own prayer diary.

6. READ HIS WORD FOR YOURSELF.

Among the general populace I surely do not have the reputation of "a babbler" — they have never heard from me. Paul was not forever and always known as "a babbler," but for awhile in Athens this was his reputation. Could it not be so for me for at least a little while? Would I receive rebuff or interest? I will never know till I try. Would I ever face men of the same syndrome as the Athenians who "spent their time doing nothing but talking about and listening to the latest ideas"? How sad that the ideas from heaven are still "strange." I am more than delighted to commit myself to making such ideas very understandable and popular.

It is so important that you pause in his presence
and either audibly or in written form tell him all his word means to you.

7. READ HIS WORD IN THANKSGIVING.

(1) Thank you for the unqualified courage of Paul. (2) Thank you that the gospel meets the needs of both the Stoics and the Epicureans. (3) Thank you for the determination of Paul against great odds. (4) Thank you that I need not preach any more or less than "Jesus and the resurrection" to accomplish God's purpose in this world. (5) Thank you that Paul was willing to speak anytime, anywhere to anyone about His Lord. (6) Thank you that Paul's preaching as also "a teaching." (7) Thank you for every Athenian who heard Paul and that there are probably more in Athens today who have never heard than in the time of the Apostle (what a field!).

Give yourself to your own expression of gratitude — write it or speak it!

8. READ HIS WORD IN MEDITATION.

May we know what this new teaching is? The teaching of John 3:16 is brand new to millions and millions of people upon this earth. How could it be that we have so miserably failed to do the one thing above all others our Lord wants done? Such was not true in the first century. By 130 A.D. all men had heard, and the teaching was no longer strange or new. Perhaps it is because the gospel has lost its freshness that we have not fulfilled the commission. But this is only a symtom — the real cause is our failure in a personal relationship with our Lord. Commercial fisherman from the Sea of Galilee, a tax collector and a super-patriot are not the kind of people to lead in world conquest, but they did! Peter and John gave the secret: "We can not but speak the things which we have seen and heard."

Pause — wait — think — then express yourself in thoughtful praise or thanks.

9. READ HIS WORD FOR PETITIONS.

Surely Paul on Mars Hill can prompt prayer requests: (1) Evangelism with Paul was not so much what he did as what he was. I want to be like him. (2) Give me wisdom to answer the Stoics of my day. (3) Our nation is overrun with Epicurian disciples — I need your help in communicating your Son to them. (4) May I learn how to relate my Lord to the life of all. (5) Give me an audience with important and influential people. (I really do not know how you will answer, but I have not because I ask not.) (6) May I have wisdom in relating to the life-style of my generation your message. (7) Open my heart to see the total depth of meaning in the resurrection.

Please, please remember these are prayers — speak them — reword them!

10. READ HIS WORD AND WAIT — LISTEN — GOD SPEAKS!

May I hear your voice in the words of Paul: (1) "There are yet many marketplaces where I need to be heard." (2) "People will still mock — but some will believe." (3) "Philosophy will never satisfy until I am the philosopher."

11. INTERCESSION FOR THE LOST WORLD

China — Population: 857,000,000. Growth rate 1.7%. Average number of people per sq. km. — 88.

Point for prayer: (1) *Praise God for the purified and growing church in China,* despite severe persecution and isolation from believers in other lands and also the death and imprisonment of nearly every outstanding Christian leader. The number of Bible believing Christians may have increased more than six fold since the Communist seizure of power. There is now hardly a town or village without a Christian group.

12. SING PRAISES TO OUR LORD.

O worship the King, all glorious above,
And greatfully sing His pow'r and His love;

Our Shield and Defender, the Ancient of Days,
Pavilioned in splendor, and girded with praise.

WEEK SEVENTEEN — SATURDAY

1. PRAISE GOD FOR WHO HE IS.

Heir—possessor of heaven and earth (Gen. 14:19). How beautifully poignant is this word. You are the heir of all things—our Lord an heir with you and you have made us joint-heirs with him. How gloriously good and encouraging this thought is to me! You have right to all the physical world by creation—the right or ownership of all men—every man twice over, by creation and redemption.

Blessed be your name! When time shall be no more and all men are called to the judgment, as well as the innumerable hosts of angels, all intelligent beings will then know who is the real heir of this whole universe—and all others like it or unlike it! This is a mind boggling concept, but it really does not express totally your wealth or inheritance—or essential Being. I pause before you in amazement!

Express yourself in adoration for this quality of God.
Speak it audibly or write out your praise in your own devotional journal.

2. PRAISE GOD FOR WHAT HE MEANS TO ME.

Heir to me! It would make but little more than curious interest to contemplate how much I have if it were not for two facts: (1) You are my Father and Savior and God. (2) I am a joint-heir with your only begotten Son! This changes all my thinking and surprises me with joy! I am rich beyond the wildest dreams of any man. The treasure I now have in a clay pot called a body is the total content

of the sixty-six books called the Holy Book. It is *holy* in the sense of being separate or different than all other books. The precious scintillating jewels in this volume are beautiful beyond all words to describe them. Oh, how I revel in their eternal value! Your daily guidance in my life is such a wonderful part of my inheritance. And then there is a whole wide, wonderful life to come!

How do you personally relate to the inheritance of God, and God who is Heir?
Speak it out or write it out. It is *so important* that you establish *your own* devotional journal.

3. CONFESSION OF SIN

Dear, dear Lord, for living and thinking like a pauper when I am a billionaire—please, forgive. How sad to walk in the dark when we can open the door to the light. How pathetic to lie in bed sick when the Great Physician can raise us to radiant health anytime we reach out for him. Oh, dear Father, forgive this blind, ungrateful son.

When we are willfully blind, we even wonder about forgiveness. Dear Lord, I repent of my terrible ingrown selfishness, deception. Another sin mentioned in your word is jealousy, which somehow seems to fit. I have been envious of the poor when I was rich and didn't know it.

What personal sins do you want to confess? We *must* speak them to remove them.
Do it! *Now.* There is no one else you have sinned against more than God. Tell him so!

4. SING A PRAYER TO GOD.

I need Thee ev'ry hour,
Most gracious Lord;
No tender voice like Thine
Can peace afford.

I need Thee, O I need Thee;
Ev'ry hour I need Thee!
O bless me now, my Savior,
I come to Thee!

Open your hymn book and sing the rest of the verses—or even sing another prayer song.

5. READ HIS WORD TO HIM!

His Word

[21](All the Athenians and the foreigners who lived there spent their time doing nothing but talking about and listening to the latest ideas.)

[22]Paul then stood up in the meeting of the Areopagus and said: "Men of Athens! I see that in every way you are very religious. [23]For as I walked around and observed your objects of worship, I even found an altar with this inscription: TO AN UNKNOWN GOD. Now what you worship as something unknown I am going to proclaim to you.

[24]"The God who made the world and everything in it is the Lord of heaven and earth and does not live in temples built by hands. [25]And he is not served by human hands, as if he needed anything, because he himself gives all men

life and breath and everything else. [26]From one man he made every nation of men, that they should inhabit the whole earth; and he determined the times set for them and the exact places where they should live. [27]God did this so that men would seek him and perhaps reach out for him and find him, though he is not far from each one of us. [28]'For in him we live and move and have our being.' As some of your own poets have said, 'We are his offspring.'

[29]"Therefore since we are God's offspring, we should not think that the divine being is like gold or silver or stone—an image made by man's design and skill.

— Acts 17:21-29, NIV

Read His Word to Him.

I realize it is almost impossible to separate my point of view from yours, i.e., to truly look at this text through your eyes, but I never tire of trying. It was good that Paul could speak to the men of "the Areopagus"—but in your sight they are of no more value than the men or women in the marketplace. These men had more influence, but no more worth. Paul really addressed himself to the whole city, and all men in it£ How did these men indicate their "religion"? By "worship" or that which gets our attention and admiration? Did not the idols and altars only represent the gods who were worshipped?

Please express your response to this beautiful text. Put your expression in your own prayer diary.

6. READ HIS WORD FOR YOURSELF.

I am so glad I need not reach out into the dark to find you. You have reached down in the Person of your Son to find me. Dear God, right now I want to worship you, acknowledge, yield, bow, honor you as: (1) The creator of all—the heaven and earth. (2) You are not in buildings we mistakenly call your house—our own bodies are your house! (3) My service is not because you need it—I do! Others do! You could get everything I do done in a better way by a better means. (4) I owe my life (soul, existence) to you. I owe my breath (life, spirit) to you, as do all men.

Either audibly or in written form tell him all his word means to you.

7. READ HIS WORD IN THANKSGIVING.

(1) Thank you that Paul plainly puts his stamp of acceptance on the Genesis account of creation. (2) Thank you that my time on earth is set by you—as is the time for all men. (3) Thank you that because of what happened in centuries gone by I now live in America. (4) Thank you that your goodness was given to lead us to you. (5) Thank you that right now you are not far away. You are in me in the person of the "Other Comforter." (6) Thank you that Paul said all men are by right of creation "your children." (7) Thank you that our nature is our accurate reflection of your nature.

Give yourself to your own expression of gratitude—write it or speak it!

8. READ HIS WORD IN MEDITATION.

"He is not far from each one of us." How beautifully true this statement is. God is just a prayer away. We can see his character in his Son. We can see his power in his creation. We can see his children in our friends. We can see his very self in the Person of the Holy Spirit—who lives in our bodies. From God's perspective he is even closer to us. He sees each of us all the time. He knows the thoughts and the intents of our hearts. How could he be any closer than he is? Dear God, may we practice your presence in us and with us.

Pause—wait—think—then expreess yourself in thoughtful praise or thanks.

9. READ HIS WORD FOR PETITIONS.

Paul's sermon moved me to ask of you: (1) Give me faith to believe that all men everywhere can and will become your children. (2) Grant me wisdom in seeing beyond the external into the eternal needs of man. (3) Deepen my appreciation of your creative power. (4) Speak your word about a place of worship into my heart. (5) Dear Lord, I look up to you in thanksgiving as the giver of every good and perfect gift. (6) Keep me keenly aware of the plain statement of creation made here by Paul. (7) Thank you that of you, in you, from you, I live and move and have my being.

Right here add your personal requests—and his answers.

10. READ HIS WORD AND WAIT—LISTEN—GOD SPEAKS!

As some of the Athenians heard you speak through Paul, may I also: (1) "God made the world and everything in it." (2) "God lives in the bodies of people not in buildings." (3) "I have decided the exact places men should live."

11. INTERCESSION FOR THE LOST WORLD

China — Point for prayer: (1) *Pray for the leaders of the new post-Mao China* that they may grant more freedom for Christians to meet together. Pray that this land may be freed from tyranny and fear. Pray that the Gospel may be freely preached.

12. SING PRAISES TO OUR LORD.

We praise Thee, O God, our Redeemer, Creator,
In grateful devotion our tribute we bring.
We lay it before Thee, we kneel and adore Thee,
We bless Thy holy Name, glad praises we sing.

WEEK EIGHTEEN — SUNDAY

1. PRAISE GOD FOR WHO HE IS.

Jehovah — the "Self-Existent One" — the "Absolute." Dear Lord, in a very real sense this is the greatest of your names. I wanted and longed so many, many times, before I became a Christian, for an explanation of all things, i.e., for an original Source or Cause. So many times since I accepted you I have rejoiced in the wholeness of life and the world in which we live when you are related to it. "The Self-Existent One" — what a marvelous designation. Blessing and praise and adoration are not at all adequate to describe my wonder — or the amazement of all mankind before you.

Express yourself in adoration for this quality of God.
Speak it audibly or write out your praise in your own devotional journal.

2. PRAISE GOD FOR WHAT HE MEANS TO ME.

The Absolute, the Cause, the Source. Dear Father! I enter your presence with abject confoundment — I want to be silent in the effulgent brightness of your presence! As your children feared to even pronounce your name and substituted other designations such as Adoni — or Lord so I am speechless before your majesty. At the same time I am full of eager longing to praise your name. To know that I share your nature is a thought to lift us up and move us to cry with the psalmist "Thou has dealt well with thy servant, O Lord, according to thy word."

How do you personally relate to the self-existence of God, and God who is Jehovah?
Speak it out or write it out. It is *so important* that you establish *your own* devotional journal.

3. CONFESSION OF SIN

What a confession of sin it is to admit you have neglected to praise or even recognize the greatness of yourself — disrespect or sacrilege is behind this sin. At times, too many times, I have been guilty. Dear Lord, forgive me! "Fits of rage" is a sin mentioned in your word. Yes, I have sinned here — how juvenile is such action and attitude! Just what prompted such an outburst? Fortunately, I cannot remember; but I know you could replay the whole sordid incident if you chose. You have cleared the record and it is there no more! Thank you for wholeness and that clean feeling *inside*!

What personal sins do you want to confess? We *must* speak them to remove them.
Do it! *Now.* There is no one else you have sinned against more than God. Tell him so!

4. SING A PRAYER TO GOD.

'Tis the blessed hour of prayer, when our hearts lowly bend,
And we gather to Jesus, our Saviour and Friend;
If we come to Him in faith, His protection to share,
What a balm for the weary! O how sweet to be there!

Blessed hour of prayer,
Blessed hour of prayer,
What a balm for the weary!
O how sweet to be there!

Open your hymn book and sing the rest of the verses — or even sing another prayer song.

5. READ HIS WORD TO HIM!

His Word

[30]In the past God overlooked such ignorance, but now he commands all people everywhere to repent. [31]For he has set a day when he will judge the world with justice by the man he has appointed. He has given proof of this to all men by raising him from the dead."
[32]When they heard about the resurrection of the dead, some of them sneered, but others said, "We want to hear you again on this subject." [33]At that, Paul left the Council. [34]A few men became followers of Paul and disbelieved. Among them was Dionysius, a member of the Areopagus, also a woman named Damaris, and a number of others.

— *Acts 17:30-34, NIV*

Read His Word to Him.

In what sense did you "overlook such ignorance"? Are you saying you look beyond such ignorance of yourself to the coming of your dear Son? I am so glad you judge men by their motives and not by their record — their motives become their record with you. Dear God, when you judge me "with justice" I am so glad it will be "by my Lord" — because he is also my advocate, my intercessor with you. The one proof for all men of all time is the resurrection. Oh, my Father! I want to make it as important in my mind as it is in yours.

Please express your response to this beautiful text. Put your expression in your own prayer diary.

WEEK EIGHTEEN — SUNDAY

6. READ HIS WORD FOR YOURSELF.

When I hear of the judgment and the resurrection, what do I do? I want to hear about it again and again. I want to never tire of hearing of the end of time and the resurrection! One day I shall see him as he is. One day I shall be judged—not for my sins; they are already judged and forgiven—for the deeds done in the body: the bad, forgiven; the good? Dear God, to escape hell will be enough! How I want to follow Paul and believe. I accept his words as indeed they are: the word of the living God.

*It is so important that you pause in his presence
and either audibly or in written form tell him all his word means to you.*

7. READ HIS WORD IN THANKSGIVING.

(1) Thank you for your love and mercy in overlooking men's ignorance, but judging them in absolute justice. (2) Thank you for the strong, solid assurance the resurrection gives me, for all you have said and are. (3) Thank you for the day already set when all the inequities of life will be made straight. (4) Thank you that I can constantly repent (change my mind) in light of the judgment. (5) Thank you there is something wonderfully fascinating about the gospel—even to those who have never heard. (6) Thank you that I can hear more and more about him who is raised from the dead. (7) Thank you for the prominent converts at Athens—and for "a number of others."

Give yourself to your own expression of gratitude—write it or speak it!

8. READ HIS WORD IN MEDITATION.

"After this Paul left Athens." We want to answer three questions about Athens: (1) Did Paul fail in Athens? Luke does not say he did, hence we can see no reason to say so ourselves. Luke *does* say he won Dionysius, a prominent man, along with a prominent woman named Damaris, along with a number of others. How large was the number—no matter, he did not fail if success is winning people to our Lord. (2) How did Paul describe God? (a) Creator of all. (b) Within reach of all. (c) Judge of all. The Old Testament prophecies were not used with these Gentiles. (3) Did Paul preach the death of our Lord in Athens? He preached "Jesus and the resurrection"—this would necessarily include the crucifixion. We believe Paul was an outstanding success by God's standard—"he was faithful."

Pause—wait—think—then express yourself in thoughtful praise or thanks.

9. READ HIS WORD FOR PETITIONS.

It would seem Paul had a difficult time in Athens—from this experience there are a number of requests: (1) Teach me how to communicate repentance. (2) Give me the sorrow from yourself that I might repent. (3) Help me to prepare men for the judgment. (4) Open my heart to the reality of your Son's resurrection. (5) Give me the humility to receive the sneers of men as Paul did. (6) How can I reach those of position and influence with your good news? (7) How did Paul decide it was time to leave Athens?

Please, please remember these are prayers—speak them—reword them!

10. READ HIS WORD AND WAIT—LISTEN—GOD SPEAKS!

You spoke through Paul to a number of people in Athens. Speak to me through his message: (1) "I still command all men everywhere to repent." (2) "My living Son will judge all men." (3) "The mocking of men does not alter the truth."

11. INTERCESSION FOR THE LOST WORLD

China — Points for prayer: (1) *Christians in other lands ought to be more concerned* for the spiritual need of China. Pray for the evangelization of China. (2) *Nearly 600 million Chinese* have never known anything but Communistic atheism. For nearly all, life is a drab and purposeless struggle, constant revolution with much fear and insecurity and no hope for the future. More and more young people are looking for a deeper meaning to life than Communism offers. Pray that many may turn to the Lord Jesus. Pray that the believers may be alert to seek out such.

12. SING PRAISES TO OUR LORD.

There is never a day so dreary,
There is never a night so long,
But the soul that is trusting Jesus
Will somewhere find a song.

Wonderful, wonderful Jesus,
In the heart He implanteth a song:
A song of deliv'rance, of courage, of strength,
In the heart He implanteth a song.

WEEK EIGHTEEN — MONDAY

1. PRAISE GOD FOR WHO HE IS.

Mighty — or the Mighty One. (Isa. 1:24; 49:26) Bless your wonderful name you are indeed just that to all men everywhere, to all the angels of heaven and to every need of the human heart. You are mighty in your works: (1) *Creation;* (2) *Preservation;* (3) *Resurrection;* (4) *Judgment.* To try to appreciate what you have made, I have looked at a book with pictures of some of the species of birds — what an array of beauty and variety! I am a "bird watcher" only so I can better appreciate the One who created them all. What would a book in which were drawn all the insects look like? Or all the trees? Or even all the weeds? At the same time you also "uphold all things by the word of your power." All who have ever died will by your might be recreated! All men — billions and billions of them — will stand to be individually judged for the deeds done in their bodies. *Mighty* is too weak a word!

Express yourself in adoration for this quality of God in your own devotional journal.

2. PRAISE GOD FOR WHAT HE MEANS TO ME.

Mighty for me! Dear Lord, you have shown yourself more than able — yea, abundantly able, to handle all my needs — "according to your riches in glory": (1) My daily bread; (2) my protection or preservation; (3) my resurrection. I could never thank you enough for all these past many years of supplying food, shelter and raiment. How it is that I have these things in abundance and there are 30,000,000 who starve every year, I do not know! Over how many miles have you given me safe travel? From how many overbearing temptations have you kept me? I do stand in awe of the promise that the very Holy Spirit who lives in this body of mine will recreate it at the resurrection!

How do you personally relate to the mightiness of God, and God who is the Mighty One?
Speak it out or write it out. It is *so important* that you establish *your own* devotional journal.

3. CONFESSION OF SIN

I fall at your feet in praise and pause to know I am unclean and need the coal from your altar to cleanse me! The blood from Calvary, the water of your fountain. How wonderfully good it is to be clean! If ever I felt unworthy it is in the face of your greatness!

A sin mentioned in your word is "selfish ambition." Dear God, if ever I had an ambition in which you were not the sole object of glory, strike it from my heart!

What personal sins do you want to confess? We *must* speak them to God to remove them.

4. SING A PRAYER TO GOD.

Redeemed — how I love to proclaim it!
Redeemed by the blood of the Lamb;
Redeemed thro' His infinite mercy,
His child, and forever, I am.

Redeemed, . . . redeemed, . . .
Redeemed by the blood of the Lamb;
Redeemed, . . . redeemed, . . .
His child, and forever, I am.

Open your hymn book and sing the rest of the verses — or even sing another prayer song.

5. READ HIS WORD TO HIM!

His Word

18 After this, Paul left Athens and went to Corinth. ²There he met a Jew named Aquila, a native of Pontus, who had recently come from Italy with his wife, Priscilla, because Claudius had ordered all the Jews to leave Rome. Paul went to see them, ³and because he was a tentmaker as they were, he stayed and worked with them. ⁴Every Sabbath he reasoned in the synagogue, trying to persuade Jews and Greeks.

⁵When Silas and Timothy came from Macedonia, Paul devoted himself exclusively to preaching, testifying to the Jews that Jesus was the Christ. — *Acts 18:1-5, NIV*

Read His Word to Him.

It is so good to get acquainted all over again with these two wonderful people. I wonder how and where Paul met Aquila? Was Aquila a Christian when Paul met him? I always have questions only you can answer. One day you can tell me all about the blanks that are necessarily left in Luke's narrative. Right now I want to praise you for several things about Aquila and Priscilla: (1) Praise you for showing me that men and women in the time-consuming task of tentmaking can love you and serve you in the midst of their work. (2) Praise you for opening my eyes to Paul's attitude toward support. He did not complain or wait — he went to work.

Please express your response to this beautiful text. Put your expression in your prayer diary.

6. READ HIS WORD FOR YOURSELF.

Dear Father, I want each word of these five verses to take on meaning for me. Luke was specific about the time of this record — no fiction writer would do this. Jews got something done, had influence, therefore were not at all popular with some people. Paul knew a trade and did not have to beg. Paul did not shun controversy — it made some people very unhappy — that was not wrong. Paul used persuasion by argument. Perhaps Silas and Timothy brought financial help from Philippi or Thessalonica or Berea so Paul could spend full time with preaching.

It is important that you pause in his presence
and either audibly or in written form tell him all his word means to you.

7. READ HIS WORD IN THANKSGIVING.

(1) Thank you for Paul's boldness and willingness to go to Corinth. (2) Thank you that political actions can be used to your advantage. (3) Thank you that Paul was ready to adapt himself to living in someone else's home. (4) Thank you for the dedication of three tentmakers. (5) Thank you that Paul was able to "work within the system" of the Sabbath synagogue service. (6) Thank you for "self-starters" like Silas and Timothy — they worked with Paul — but they worked on their own also. (7) Thank you for the strong emphasis Paul placed on preaching.

Give yourself to your own expression of gratitude — write it or speak it!

8. READ HIS WORD IN MEDITATION.

"Paul devoted himself exclusively to preaching." I wonder how much of his content was from his study of the Old Testament Scriptures at the feet of Gamaliel and how much was by divine, direct input of the Holy Spirit? We are sure that he preached in Corinth "Jesus and him crucified." The record of his preaching is right here in Acts and we can gain much by reading the two letters addressed to this church. Paul spoke to many Gentiles, but most converts among them were in the general context of their interest in the Jewish religion. They are described as "devout Greeks." Paul's preaching was powerful in his effect on the lives of these sensual people. Dear Lord, help me to expect reaction only when people have been confronted with the message. We have no similar results because we will not "devote ourselves exclusively to preaching."

Pause — wait — think — then express yourself in thoughtful praise or thanks.

9. READ HIS WORD FOR PETITIONS.

There is so much to pray about in your work in Corinth: (1) Give me the adventuresome courage of Paul. (2) It will be so good to hear from Paul just how he met Aquila — lead me to a servant of yours like Aquila. (3) Help me to more deeply appreciate my wife who works with me for you. (4) How I need heaven's wisdom to speak persuasively. (5) Thank you for the priceless privilege of devoting myself exclusively to preaching and teaching. (6) Thank you for fellow laborers who encourage me in your work. (7) Thank you for Paul's efforts in a difficult city — may his example move me to the same attitude.

Right here add your personal requests — and his answers.

10. READ HIS WORD AND WAIT — LISTEN — GOD SPEAKS!

Speak to me from these few verses in Acts 18: (1) "You can serve me in several ways." (2) "Argument is good if I am in it." (3) "I work best through a team effort."

11. INTERCESSION FOR THE LOST WORLD

China — Point for prayer: (1) *The Church in China* is completely "underground." Believers meet whenever they can in homes or outside in little groups — sometimes only in twos and threes, and in some areas in larger groups. The believers have been purified by great suffering. Their high spiritual standards shame the believers in the free world. Pray that they may be protected from betrayal by informers and from giving way to compromise when under pressure. Pray that God may give them courage and the openings to testify to others and win them for the Lord. Pray for the children of believers that they may not be hindered from believing in a society where family ties are deliberately weakened or even broken due to the regimentation of the life of the people.

12. SING PRAISES TO OUR LORD.

I've a message from the Lord, Hallelujah!
The message unto you I'll give;
'Tis recorded in His word, Hallelujah!
It is only that you "look and live."

"Look and live," . . . my brother, live,
Look to Jesus now and live;
'Tis recorded in His word, Hallelujah!
It is only that you "look and live."

WEEK EIGHTEEN — TUESDAY

1. PRAISE GOD FOR WHO HE IS.

Preacher (Psa. 19:1ff.; Isa. 61:1, 2). It is unusual to think of yourself—your almighty self as a preacher—yet your voice has gone out to the ends of the earth, i.e., in the form of the creation above us, beneath us and all around us. How eloquently do you speak to all who have ears to hear! The Bible is another expression of your communication to man—your written sermons—I want to give you a triple A+ in my Homiletics grade book. You have spoken to me and to all other preachers as a model of all we would like to be. How total is your preparation—your living sermon preached in the Person of your Son was prepared several centuries before you spoke to us through him.

Express yourself in adoration for this quality of God.
Speak it audibly or write out your praise in your own devotional journal.

2. PRAISE GOD FOR WHAT HE MEANS TO ME.

Preacher to me. Dear Lord, wonderful Father, Eternal Spirit—I hear you! Your word is clear and constant! Dear Lord, I rejoice and revel in the reading of your message to me. I want to memorize every word and not only so but to assimilate its full meaning; to listen and learn is my highest joy and I shall never, never hear or know fully; but I do purpose to know as fully as I can. Today, just for today, speak to me in the world you have made and in the book you have authored!

How do you personally relate to the preaching of God, and God who is *Preacher*?
Speak it out or write it out. It is *so important* that you establish *your own* devotional journal.

3. CONFESSION OF SIN

I fully admit that there are times when I am not listening—when I will not hear your voice through my own conscience—when I follow the ground instead of the sky and hear no more than the creatures who creep upon it. There are times when the faculties you have given me are focused on the mad and ignorant—to say nothing of the evil and false. What a sad admission of sin. Forgive me! The sin of *dissensions*—how could I better describe the conflicting voices heard in our lives today? If you said it; and I believe it; that settles it! Give me inner ears to hear and heed what you say!

What personal sins do you want to confess? We *must* speak them to remove them.
Do it! *Now.* There is no one else you have sinned against more than God. Tell him so!

4. SING A PRAYER TO GOD.

Give of your best to the Master;
Give of the strength of your youth;
Throw your soul's fresh, glowing ardor
Into the battle for truth.
Jesus has set the example;
Dauntless was He, young and brave; . . .

Give Him your loyal devotion,
Give Him the best that you have. . . .
Give of your best to the Master;
Give of the strength of your youth;
Clad in salvation's full armor,
Join in the battle for truth.

Open your hymn book and sing the rest of the verses—or even sing another prayer song.

5. READ HIS WORD TO HIM!

His Word

[5]When Silas and Timothy came from Macedonia, Paul devoted himself exclusively to preaching, testifying to the Jews that Jesus was the Christ. [6]But when the Jews opposed Paul and became abusive, he shook out his clothes in protest and said to them, "Your blood be on your own heads! I am clear of my responsibility. From now on I will go to the Gentiles."

[7]Then Paul left the synagogue and went next door to the house of Titius Justus, a worshiper of God. [8]Crispus, the synagogue ruler, and his entire household believed in the Lord; and many of the Corinthians who heard him believed and were baptized.

[9]One night the Lord spoke to Paul in a vision: "Do not be afraid; keep on speaking, do not be silent. [10]For I am with you, and no one is going to attack and harm you, because I have many people in this city."

— *Acts 18:5-10, NIV*

WEEK EIGHTEEN — TUESDAY

Read His Word to Him.

How gladly I take up your word. I want to join the crowd in the synagogue of Corinth—not to oppose but to understand. How I would like to hear the word of Paul as he testified and argued that Jesus was your anointed One.

Why did these Jews object? Was it out of pride and hurt? Was it because their king could not be a lowly Nazarene? How did Paul say the words: "Your blood be on your own heads. I am clear of my responsibility"?

Please express your response to this beautiful text. Put your expression in your own prayer diary.

6. READ HIS WORD FOR YOURSELF.

How many members in the household of the former (or present) synagogue ruler? All included were old enough to understand because they "believed." Such faith came by hearing with understanding. What did the Corinthians hear? What did they believe? This seems such an obvious

fulfillment of Mark 16:16. These dear people heard the same good news that I want to hear all over again—"The Anointed One—my King—died for my sins, was buried in a rich man's borrowed grave, and was raised from the dead by your Holy Spirit on the third day."

Either audibly or in written form tell him all his word means to you.

7. READ HIS WORD IN THANKSGIVING.

(1) Thank you for the personalness of Paul's preaching —it was a testimony as well as an argument. (2) Thank you for the overwhelming evidence in the Old Testament and the record of His life that Jesus was the Messiah. (3) Thank you for opposition—it is evidence the message

is alive. (4) Thank you for Paul's protest—dramatic and personal—clear. (5) Thank you for the possible transfer of responsibility when we have done what we could. (6) Thank you for Paul's unusual boldness in speaking just next door to those who abused him.

Give yourself to your own expression of gratitude—write it or speak it!

8. READ HIS WORD IN MEDITATION.

"I have many people in this city." It is more than provocative to read here that God knew the potential responsiveness of every member of the body of Christ in Corinth. God said something very, very important in this connection. Notice: (1) Because I have many people in this city, i.e., many who will accept if they hear the good news, *"Do not be afraid."* Dear Lord, how I need to hear this word from you. Paul had more reasons to be afraid

than I do. What raw hatred and physical violence faced Paul—what malicious jealousy and envy daily looked him in the face! (2) Because I have many people who will go to heaven and not hell if you speak — *"keep on speaking—do not be silent."* God used both the positive and negative for emphasis. It is always easier to stay where you are—or to close your mouth—or to talk about something else.

Pause—wait—think—then express yourself in thoughtful praise or thanks.

9. READ HIS WORD FOR PETITIONS.

In the wild city of Corinth there was much of both acceptance and rejection—petitions arise spontaneously: (1) May I know how to testify in such a manner that men will accept your Anointed One. (2) How I need the grace to know when to register a rejection of those who oppose. (3) Thank you again for the holy boldness of Paul. (4) How

could Paul escape the abusive treatment of the synagogue if he met just next door? (I need wisdom here.) (5) Help me to preach as Paul did—and obtain the same results— those who hear will believe and be baptized and be saved. (6) Deliver me from all fear of men. (7) Help me to call out of the city where I live a people for your name.

Please, please remember these are prayers—speak them—reword them!

10. READ HIS WORD AND WAIT—LISTEN—GOD SPEAKS!

Open my eyes and ears to your messages in these verses: (1) "Clear yourself of the blood of those in your city."

(2) "I have those who will respond—keep on speaking." (3) "Lo, I am with you even till the end of the world."

11. INTERCESSION FOR THE LOST WOLRD

China — Point for prayer: (1) *Revivals* have occurred all over China since 1930. These prepared the believers for the suffering that was to come. Local revivals burst out

in answer to the earnest prayers of some believers. Pray for a greater work of the Holy Spirit that will demonstrate the power of our Lord over atheistic Communism.

12. SING PRAISES TO OUR LORD.

All glory, laud and honor
To Thee, Redeemer, King,
To Whom the lips of chidren
Made sweet hosannas ring!

The people of the Hebrews
With palms before Thee went;
Our praise and prayer and anthems
Before Thee we present.

WEEK EIGHTEEN — WEDNESDAY

1. PRAISE GOD FOR WHO HE IS.

Everlasting Strength (Isa. 26:4). (So many of these terms are applied to our Lord Jesus, but I like to remember the oneness of the nature of my Lord and our Father—as well as the blessed Holy Spirit.) It is one thing to be strong some of the time—it is quite another to be strong all the time. To contemplate One who is described as "Everlasting Strength" is quite beyond our grasp, but nonetheless just what I want, what all men want for our God! Bless your name! There has never been a time when you were not strong. There has never been a circumstance in which you were anything less than Everlasting Strength. There never lived a man who has ever found you less than Everlasting in Strength.

Express yourself in adoration for this quality of God.
Speak it audibly or write out your praise in your own devotional journal.

2. PRAISE GOD FOR WHAT HE MEANS TO ME!

Everlasting Strength for me! Dear, dear God! How more than encouraging this is to me! My strength is multiplied infinitely when I recognize by faith that my strength is your strength—"according to the power that worketh in me—both to will and to work your good pleasure" (Phil. 2:13). My strength is not "like that of ten thousand"—nay —but like the strength of the Creator of all. I have often blocked the channel of both receiving and communicating this Divine energy, but it is not because it is not there or I could not or should not have it. For the tasks of today— for the temptations of today—for the opportunities of today—Oh, Thou my Everlasting Strength!

How do you personally relate to the everlasting strength of God, and God who is Everlasting Strength?
Speak it out or write it out. It is *so important* that you establish *your own* devotional journal.

3. CONFESSION OF SIN

What a commentary on sin! I am weak when I could be strong! This is the fundamental sin: "Don't bother me, I'll do it myself"! "For while we were without strength Christ died for the ungodly"—it is because we left you out that we were without strength. Dear God, forgive me for the sin of all sins—living, thinking, willing, without you!
"Factions"—When some poor weak man has gathered a little group about him and separates from others, and somehow feels he has "found the truth" a faction is formed.

There is no one else you have sinned against more than God. Tell him so!

4. SING A PRAYER TO GOD.

Sing them over again to me,
Wonderful words of life;
Let me more of their beauty see,
Wonderful words of Life.
Words of life and beauty,

Teach me faith and duty:
Beautiful words, wonderful words,
Wonderful words of Life.
Beautiful words, wonderful words,
Wonderful words of Life.

Open your hymn book and sing the rest of the verses—or even sing another prayer song.

5. READ HIS WORD TO HIM!

His Word

[11]So Paul stayed for a year and a half, teaching them the word of God.
[12]While Gallio was proconsul of Achaia, the Jews made a united attack on Paul and brought him into court. [13]"This man," they charged, "is persuading the people to worship God in ways contrary to the law."
[14]Just as Paul was about to speak, Gallio said to the Jews, "If you Jews were making a complaint about some misdemeanor or serious crime, it would be reasonable for me to listen to you. [15]But since it involves questions about words and names and your own law—settle the matter yourselves. I will not be a judge of such things." [16]So he had them ejected from the court. [17]Then they all turned on Sosthenes the synagogue ruler and beat him in front of the court. But Gallio showed no concern whatever.
[18]Paul stayed on in Corinth for some time. Then he left the brothers and sailed for Syria, accompanied by Priscilla and Aquila.
— *Acts 18:11-18a, NIV*

Read His Word to Him.

Paul stayed eighteen months in Corinth after you spoke to him in a vision. I am glad for the heavenly vision of your Son through whom you speak to me today. How long was Paul in Corinth before you spoke to him? Six months? Was he two years in Corinth? So good to read here that Paul's primary task in Corinth was "teaching them the word of God." Who was taught? The potential people of God—the very ones our Lord commanded us to teach. After he taught them be baptized them and then taught them again.

Please express your response to this beautiful text. Put your expression in your own prayer diary.

6. READ HIS WORD FOR YOURSELF.

You promised that "no one is going to attack and harm you" — yet here is a united attack made on Paul in the very place where the promise was made. When did it occur? Eighteen months later — after many people were taught and became Christians. What came of the efforts? Harm came to the attackers not to the attacked. The judge's sympathies were be with Paul, not those who opposed him. How encouraging it is to see you at work in the affairs of men. You work through opposition — politicians and any or all misunderstandings. It turned out to Paul's good and your glory. Dear God, I know you are at work today in ever changing circumstances of my life.

It is so important that you pause in his presence
and either audibly or in written form tell him all his word means to you.

7. READ HIS WORD IN THANKSGIVING.

(1) Thank you for Paul's letters — full of meaning and help to us. (2) Thank you for Paul's sentimental attachment to those with whom he worked. (3) Thank you that Paul was a "persuader" — what an example! (4) Thank you for Roman law which helped Paul and others to respect orderly, fair procedure (at least at times). (5) Thank you for Gallio — perhaps he was one of "your people" in Corinth — at least he seems to be able to evaluate. (6) Thank you that sometimes the law of planting and sowing produces a harvest in this life, i.e., as in the case of Sosthenes. (7) Thank you for all the many converts made in Corinth. I hope to meet each one and hear of all the circumstances of their conversion. In heaven there will be no time or thought limitations. Amen!

Give yourself to your own expression of gratitude — write it or speak it!

8. READ HIS WORD IN MEDITATION.

"Paul stayed on in Corinth for some time." This statement appears after all the opposition. What caused such a decision? Perhaps it was the words of the Lord in the vision: "I have many people in this city." Paul wanted to find a few more of God's family. Perhaps it was his attachment to the people he had already found. How near and dear these new Christians became to Paul. The encouragement of the people themselves — i.e., their words of gratitude and love could have been a large factor. By reading again the two letters Paul wrote to this assembly we see the strong attachment Paul had with them. Establishing new believers in the faith was a very large part of Paul's work. May such dedication and purpose ever be with us.

Pause — wait — think — then express yourself in thoughtful praise or thanks.

9. READ HIS WORD FOR PETITIONS.

This was the time and place for Paul's first of many letters to the churches he established. There are a number of requests suggested: (1) May I have the perseverance necessary to continue amid opposition. (2) Thank you for the wonderful capacity of memory. (3) Give me the grace to write a letter of encouragement — even this day. (4) Help me to appreciate the law and order that makes all our preaching and teaching so much easier. (5) Deliver me from unreasonable and wicked men. (6) Give me wisdom as I read the letters Paul wrote to the church at Corinth. (7) Thank you for the family concept so evident in all Paul's work — help me to imitate him.

Right here add your personal requests — and his answers?

10. READ HIS WORD AND WAIT — LISTEN — GOD SPEAKS!

Speak to me from these few verses: (1) "Find your fulfillment in the joy of others." (2) "I can bring the wisdom of this world to nothing." (3) "There are men who will not listen — find some who will."

11. INTERCESSION FOR THE LOST WORLD

China — Point for prayer: (1) *Persecution of believers is severe.* No one will ever know how many Christians were martyred for their faith. It is estimated that 50,000,000 people were liquidated by the Communists after they took power — many of the Christians would be in this number. Many other believers were deported to inhospitable regions as slave labor, thus spreading the Gospel to hitherto unevangelized regions. Pray for Christians in prison today, and also for their families who remain behind. Pray for the believers that their faith may remain strong under seemingly heavy pressures.

12. SING PRAISES TO OUR LORD.

All praise to Him who reigns above
In majesty supreme,
Who gave His Son for man to die,
That He might man redeem!

Blessed be the name, blessed be the name,
Blessed be the name of the Lord;
Blessed be the name, blessed be the name,
Blessed be the name of the Lord.

WEEK EIGHTEEN — THURSDAY

1. PRAISE GOD FOR WHO HE IS.

Shepherd (Psa. 80:1-17; Isa. 40:11; Jer. 28:4). We think of our Lord as the "good shepherd"' and he is indeed. But we need also to worship you as the Great shepherd of all men. How beautifully good it is to hallow your name as "Shepherd." (1) You know every man who has ever lived or will live—by name and by every need. There are no sheep caught in the dark and cold that you do not want to bring light and warmth. (2) For every sheep you have for food just the greenest of pastures and the quietest of waters for restoration of heart. (3) There are many in high places who do not know the families or interest of those who work for them. This is not at all true with you.

Express yourself in adoration for this quality of God.
Speak it audibly or write out your praise in your own devotional journal.

2. PRAISE GOD FOR WHAT HE MEANS TO ME.

Shepherd for me. It is one thing to worship you as the universal shepherd; it is quite another thing to consider your personal interest in every part of my life. The dark valley of death is not the only valley through which you have led me—and will lead me. (1) The valley of decision—how often have I come into this place. I want to pause and read your directions and look up, and wait and then walk for you are "with me." (2) The valley of disappointment—how dark this place can be! But this could well describe the total response you received in the visit of yourself in the Person of your Son. You have been there—you can lead and comfort me. I pause to read again and again and pray again and again to you the Great Shepherd.

How do you personally relate to the shepherding of God, and God who is Shepherd?
Speak it out or write it out. It is *so important* that you establish *your own* devotional journal.

3. CONFESSION OF SIN

Oh, oh, how basic is my sin! To be a dumb (stupid) sheep—and I am—and to imagine (somehow) that I could "direct my own feet" is so fundamental a sin as to be the parent of all other sins. Dear Father and Shepherd, forgive me! I do love you. I know by sad experience I cannot find my way without you. I come again into your care and acknowledge gladly your interest and direction in all of my life.

Envy—do I envy those who do more or have more in the same area of my interests? A super-critical attitude toward them would indicate I am indeed envious. When you have given me abilities and possessions to say nothing of a particular position that no one else has—for the simple but profound fact that no one else is me! Why should I be envious? Forgive me!

What personal sins do you want to confess? We *must* speak them to remove them.
Do it! *Now.* There is no one else you have sinned against more than God. Tell him so!

4. SING A PRAYER TO GOD.

Sowing in the morning, sowing seeds of kindness,
Sowing in the noontide and the dewy eve;
Waiting for the harvest, and the time of reaping,
We shall come rejoicing, bringing in the sheaves.

Bringing in the sheaves, bringing in the sheaves,
We shall come rejoicing, bringing in the sheaves;
Bringing in the sheaves, bringing in the sheaves,
We shall come rejoicing, bringing in the sheaves.

Open your hymn book and sing the rest of the verses—or even sing another prayer song.

5. READ HIS WORD TO HIM!

His Word

Before he sailed, he had his hair cut off at Cenchrea because of a vow he had taken. [19]They arrived at Ephesus, where Paul left Priscilla and Aquila. He himself went into the synagogue and reasoned with the Jews. [20]When they asked him to spend more time with them, he declined. [21]But as he left, he promised, "I will come back if it is God's will." Then he set sail from Ephesus. [22]When he landed at Caesarea, he went up and greeted the church and then went down to Antioch.
— *Acts 18:18b-22, NIV*

Read His Word to Him.

How I do wonder what vow Paul had. It has taken the form of the Nazarite, but what was the content of the agreement? It could very well have related to the work at Corinth. I wonder why Luke included this comment if he does not tell us what it means. Thou Lord knowest! Am I to take a vow today? Priscilla and Aquila could tell me. I want only to thank you and praise you for all you are saying to me in these verses. Why is it the wife is here mentioned first? How good to see your will being worked out in the every day activities of Paul.

Please express your response to this beautiful text. Put your expression in your own prayer diary.

6. READ HIS WORD FOR YOURSELF.

If I were to take a vow to lose weight, or to overcome a habit, or to fulfill a project, how would I do it? Perhaps more important: should I see Paul's practice as an example? He *was* a Jew, and a Pharisee—vows *were* a part of the Old Testament economy, but was this why Luke included this comment, i.e., to teach us something for today? Paul let his hair grow until a certain time—he took the hair he cut and put it on the altar in Jerusalem, as a part of the ceremony of the Nazarite vow. Are vows necessary if we have made the all-time, one-time commitment to our Lord. Because I do not have answers and so want to *know*! —help me!

Either audibly or in written form tell him all his word means to you.

7. READ HIS WORD IN THANKSGIVING.

(1) Thank you for mind-stretching incidents and questions. (2) Thank you that I can choose; that no one is forcing me into a choice not my own. (3) Thank you for the great city of Ephesus and all the associations we shall have later with this place. (4) Thank you that your will is found in the daily activities of life—Jesus said his Father was always at work. (5) Thank you for Paul's careful thoughtfulness. He left someone to serve when he himself could not. He brought greetings to the church to whom he really never owed anything. (6) Thank you for the wonderful renewal of friendships that must have occurred at Antioch.

Give yourself to your own expression of gratitude—write it or speak it!

8. READ HIS WORD IN MEDITATION.

Three facts about Aquila: (1) He and his wife were both tentmakers and therefore shared in the source of livelihood. (2) They worked together in hospitality for Paul. Perhaps they shared together in their acceptance of Jesus as their Messiah and Savior. (3) They shared together in accompanying Paul to Ephesus and in the work of our Lord there. What did Paul do every Sabbath? He attended the synagogue services—with the purpose of sharing his faith with the Jewish people there. Why did Paul separate himself from the Jews at Corinth? In each case the Jews separated from Paul—they judged themselves unworthy of eternal life.

Pause—wait—think—then express yourself in thoughtful praise or thanks.

9. READ HIS WORD FOR PETITIONS.

The record of the second journey is completed in these verses. It is a good time to seek your will in prayer: (1) Although we do not know the purpose of Paul's vow, give me the same dedication for your purposes. (2) Thank you for Priscilla and Aquila—give me fellow workers of similar attitudes. (3) Dear Lord, I need reasoning powers from yourself. (4) Help me to know when to stay and when to go in every situation. (5) Thank you for the confidence I can have that your will is being worked out through circumstances. (6) Thank you for every safe journey.

Please, please remember these are prayers—speak them—reword them!

10. READ HIS WORD AND WAIT—LISTEN—GOD SPEAKS!

Speak to me from 18:18-22: (1) "Vows made and kept can help your discipline." (2) "Even Paul did not accept all speaking opportunities." (3) "Follow Paul's example in selfless dedication."

11. INTERCESSION FOR THE LOST WORLD

China — Point for prayer: (1) *There are very few Bibles* left in China. Many Bibles were destroyed by the Red Guards in the cultural revolution. Pray that these precious Bibles may be preserved. The believers are now beginning to print Bibles and Christian literature on primitive presses in secret—pray for this dangerous ministry. It is very difficult to get Bibles into the land from Hong Kong and other lands. Pray for the several Chinese and Western groups seeking to prepare, print and introduce the new script New Testaments into China and also pray that the Lord may show these brethren ways of getting the Bibles to those who need them so much. Pray for the radio programs in which Bible passages are read at dictation speed for believers to write down by hand.

12. SING PRAISES TO OUR LORD.

Come, friends sing, of the faith that's so dear to me, . . .
Revealed thro- God's Son, in Galilee;
He brought peace on earth and good will to the sons of men,
Go tell it to the world, her King reigns again.
I am so happy in Jesus,
Captivity's Captor is He; . . .

Angels rejoice when a soul's saved,
Some day we like Him shall be, . . .
Sorrow and joy have the same Lord,
Valley of shadows shall sing; . . .
Death has its life, its door opens in heaven eternally,
Christ is King.

WEEK EIGHTEEN — FRIDAY

1. PRAISE GOD FOR WHO HE IS.

Redeemer (Isa. 59:20, 21; Hosea 13:14; Gen. 3:15). The last few names have had a dual meaning, i.e., our Lord as well as our Father. You surely are a redeemer through the person of your Son. All the work of your Son is a joint-work with yourself—blessed and wonderful is your name. All mankind has sold himself to Satan—the ransom price was paid out of your love for us. How tragic to be taken captive and held for ransom—and yet this is just what has happened to the whole world. Why would you want to ransom someone who has chosen of his own free will to be a captive? What an enormous price must be paid! What could possibly be of equal value to the eternal spirits of all men of all time? Billions of dollars would not be an adequate price. The ramson is for something of moral worth—it can not be in animal blood, or in silver or gold. Spirit must pay for spirit—man must pay for man—but in this transaction it was through the Son of Man. You considered the death of your Son of equal value to the eternal death of all men. We are redeemed!

Express yourself in adoration for this quality of God.
Speak it audibly or write out your praise in your own devotional journal.

2. PRAISE GOD FOR WHAT HE MEANS TO ME.

I am redeemed! Dear Lord, I do, I do want to enter fully into this relationship! That you would consider me so valuable that if I was the *only one* to be taken captive you would have left heaven to pay the price for me. Is God obligated to Satan? Of course not! I am! It was my debt he paid. He paid the wages of sin for me.

If I have not heard that the price has been paid or I have not accepted it Satan yet has possession of me. But once I have accepted the incredible fact of my redemption I am now free! The beautiful thought is that the price that freed me bound me to my redeemer with golden cords of love. I am free to serve you—this is the only true freedom!

How do you personally relate to the redemption from God, and God who is Redeemer?
Speak it out or write it out. It is *so important* that you establish *your own* devotional journal.

3. CONFESSION OF SIN

How sad to return to the bondage from which I have been liberated. "For freedom did Christ set me free." Oh, dear God, that I should want to return to slavery! I am so constituted that I must—I will serve someone, or something, and his I am whom I serve—if sin, then death, separation, frustration—if I serve my Lord, then I have all that is in him. Dear, dear God, I do not want to return to bondage; I do love you, I do gladly accept the freedom of service in my Lord.

Drunkenness is a sin described in your word. What a terrible price is paid for intoxication! Battered wives and children are part of the price. Horrible self-loathing is more of the same price. But there is intoxication in more than the bottle of liquor. I have been drunk on pride more times than I like to think. God, forgive me—oh, humble me—I hear you say "humble yourselves." I have been drunk on self-pity—my values have been so, so distorted. Forgive, forgive, heal me!

What personal sins do you want to confess? We *must* speak them to remove them.
Do it! *Now.* There is no one else you have sinned against more than God. Tell him so!

4. SING A PRAYER TO GOD.

I am Thine, O Lord, I have heard Thy voice,
And it told Thy love to me;
But I long to rise in the arms of faith,
And be closer drawn to Thee.

Draw me nearer, nearer, blessed Lord,
To the cross where Thou hast died;
Draw me nearer, nearer, nearer, blessed Lord,
To Thy precious, bleeding side.

Open your hymn book and sing the rest of the verses—or even sing another prayer song.

5. READ HIS WORD TO HIM!

His Word

[23] After spending some time in Antioch, Paul set out from there and traveled from place to place throughout the region of Galatia and Phrygia, strengthening all the disciples.
[24] Meanwhile a Jew named Apollos, a native of Alexandria, came to Ephesus. He was a learned man, with a thorough knowledge of the Scriptures. [25] He had been instructed in the way of the Lord, and he spoke with great fervor and taught about Jesus accurately, though he knew only the baptism of John. [26] He began to speak boldly in the synagogue. When Priscilla and Aquila heard him, they invited him to their home and explained to him the way of God more adequately. — *Acts 18:23-26, NIV*

6. READ HIS WORD FOR YOURSELF.

Paul's task is my task — if he was ready to revisit some places several times so as to teach and encourage I am sure I can and should do likewise. What a pleasant name is "disciple" — or learner. My blessed Lord is still at work through his learners making more disciples. We can all become stronger in our understanding, and dear Lord I purpose to do so, and help others to become strong!

I like this man Apollos — I want to be just like him! (1) A "learned man" — probably meaning he had a good formal education from the schools in Alexandria. There are fine Christian secular schools where one's mind could be disciplined. (2) "With a thorough knowledge of the Scriptures." Dear God, this means a knowledge of *every word* you have written — if you will give me strength and time I will pray through every word you have given in your book. (3) He was instructed in the way of the Lord — someone had taught him. I want to be taught every day, everyday by someone.

It is so important that you pause in his presence
and either audibly or in written form tell him all his word means to you.

7. READ HIS WORD IN THANKSGIVING.

(1) Thank you for men who speak with fervor — it sets your fire in us. (2) Thank you for accuracy, i.e., concerning our Lord. I want to be most accurate on every word and thought of my blessed Savior. (3) Thank you for the capacity and desire to change, to learn more. (4) Thank you once again for the marvelous example of the greatest born of woman. (5) Thank you for many, many men and women who spoke out boldly for you in the face of severe misunderstanding. (6) Thank you for the loving concern of Priscilla and Aquila. (7) Thank you for a humble heart in an eloquent man — a rare combination only our Lord could produce.

Give yourself to your own expression of gratitude — write it or speak it!

8. READ HIS WORD IN MEDITATION.

"Explained to him the way of God more adequately." How good to find a preacher who will listen to two "laymen" explain the scriptures to him. Most especially when they are pointing out his difficiencies. But perhaps we are assuming something that didn't exist, i.e., the distinction between "the clergy" and "the laity." Perhaps Priscilla and Aquila were on the same level as Apollos as a brother and sister in the Lord. Perhaps it was the scriptures themselves that became the authority for right and wrong.

Pause — wait — think — then express yourself in thoughtful praise or thanks.

9. READ HIS WORD FOR PETITIONS.

The record of Apollos is a cause for prayer. (There are so many like him today.) (1) I do not know what prompted Paul's third journey — give me the courage to strengthen whatever disciples I can. (2) Thank you for men like Apollos who have become true students of the scriptures — I want to be one of them. (3) Thank you for whoever it was that instructed Apollos — may I be patient with those who disagree with me. (4) Give me the fervor of Apollos. (5) I need more boldness. (6) Send men and women like Priscilla and Aquila into my acquaintance. (7) Help me to find the time and thought to speak one-on-one with those whom I consider limited in their understanding.

Right here add your personal requests — and his answers.

10. READ HIS WORD AND WAIT — LISTEN — GOD SPEAKS!

From 18:23-26 I want to hear your messages to me: (1) "There are yet some who would make human merit a part of salvation." (2) "Knowledge of the scriptures does not always mean a man cannot be taught more." (3) "There are humble disciples like Priscilla and Aquila who could teach you much if you would listen."

11. INTERCESSION FOR THE LOST WORLD

China — Point for prayer: (1) *The opening of China for missionary work again* is not impossible but pray that the Lord may give the right strategy for the evangelization of the land; the old methods cannot be used again. Believers in other lands must be ready to stand behind the Chinese believers on whom the great burden will fall.

12. SING PRAISES TO OUR LORD.

Crown Him with many crowns,
The Lamb upon His throne;
Hark! how the heav'nly anthem drowns
All music but its own!

Awake, my soul, and sing
Of Him who died for thee;
And hail Him as thy matchless King
Thro' all eternity.

WEEK EIGHTEEN — SATURDAY

1. PRAISE GOD FOR WHO HE IS.

Immortal (II Tim. 1:10). How good to find Someone over whom death holds no sway. The whole source of a deathless existence is found in you! Wonder and praise and joy and hope! All these and much more are in yourself! Man was not created to die, but to live—death is a result of failure—and itself is the ultimate failure. Would not all men be delighted to discover there is a Being—the Being over whom death has no influence at all? Created in your image, i.e., sharing your nature, death does not affect us any more than yourself—only our bodies—it is the body that is mortal. We will be given an immortal body and live in the land of endless day! Amen! Amen!

Express yourself in adoration for this quality of God.
Speak it audibly or write out your praise in your own devotional journal.

2. PRAISE GOD FOR WHAT HE MEANS TO ME.

Immortal to me. Endless life—a deathless body—what astounding thoughts are these! My body gives me no end of problems: two operations on organs that do not function as they should; repair of a major kind—all testify that this body is wearing out. I'm so, so glad I am not the body—as fearfully and wonderfully as I am made it is still made out of dust and to dust shall it return. What a joy— what tingling anticipation is mine for the new body! Not only for myself, but for my dear father whom I miss greatly—and one day we shall live in the New Jerusalem in the new body. It is all because of Calvary "all who are in the grave (the only thing that comes out of the grave is what went into it—the body) will come out."

How do you personally relate to the immortality of God, and God who is Immortal?
Speak it out or write it out. It is *so important* that you establish *your own* devotional journal.

3. CONFESSION OF SIN

If the body is doomed to death—and we know it is—how is it we spend so much time with it? It is the only tool or instrument we have until the resurrection! Yet it should be buffeted, brought into subjection, made a servant. Dear God, this is my sin! If I do not beat my body it will beat me. I do not, I will not be a body slave. You do not want me to; your Son was no such slave—forgive me for pampering the flesh.

The sin of *orgies* seems particularly appropriate in light of a discussion of the proper and improper use of the house you have given us. Any excessive, selfish, indulgent use of the senses is an orgy—particularly in self. Dear God, from such bondage deliver me!

What personal sins do you want to confess? We *must* speak them to remove them.
Do it! *Now.* There is no one else you have sinned against more than God. Tell him so!

4. SING A PRAYER TO GOD.

I need Thee ev'ry hour,
Most gracious Lord;
No tender voice like Thine
Can peace afford.

I need Thee, O I need Thee;
Ev'ry hour I need Thee!
O bless me now, my Savior,
I come to Thee!

Open your hymn book and sing the rest of the verses—or even sing another prayer song.

5. READ HIS WORD TO HIM!

His Word

[27]When Apollos wanted to go to Achaia, the brothers encouraged him and wrote to the disciples there to welcome him. On arriving, he was a great help to those who by grace had believed. [28]For he vigorously refuted the Jews in public debate, proving from the Scriptures that Jesus was the Christ. — *Acts 18:27, 28, NIV*

Read His Word to Him.

Why did Apollos want to go to Achaia? (to Corinth?) Was it because Priscilla and Aquila had just come from there and had shared the joys and needs of Corinth with him? Was it because he felt some embarrassment at returning to the synagogue in Ephesus to tell of his new found faith? What did "the brothers" at Ephesus say to him as words of encouragement in his desire to go to Achaia? What was written in the letter to the disciples in Achaia? I ask these questions because I know you know the answers and I will too one day. What a charming expression: "those who by grace had believed"! Paul or someone else had told them of how the grace of God appeared in the person of his Son (Titus 2:11). From this hearing and grace came belief!

Please express your response to this beautiful text. Put your expression in your own prayer diary.

6. READ HIS WORD FOR YOURSELF.

It does bother me greatly that I am so complacent about the religious people around me who are inadequate in some areas of their belief. I have not "vigorously refuted" them in public debate. Some say today that no good can come of this. If Apollos would have asked those who believed in Corinth, he might have received the same discouraging response. This could have been true in days gone by when public debate became a great source of education. Are the scriptures given as a riddle or a revelation? Would public debate help clarify this? Dear God, speak to my heart!

It is so important that you pause in his presence
and either audibly or in written form tell him all his word means to you.

7. READ HIS WORD IN THANKSGIVING.

(1) Thank you for the desire of Apollos to speak in an area he did not know—and where he was not known. (2) Thank you for brothers who encourage us—without them we might never go. (3) Thank you for the example here of what we might call "a church letter," i.e., a letter of recommendation from one congregation to another. (4) Thank you for the vigorous manner of Apollos— wherever and with whomsoever he was. (5) Thank you for those who listened to the debate and were helped—the participants perhaps were not convinced, but others were. (6) Thank you that it is possible to prove from the Old Testament scriptures that Jesus is the Anointed One. (7) Thank you for the wide acceptance this man found in Corinth. Cf. I Cor. 1:12.

Give yourself in your own expression of gratitude—write it or speak it!

8. READ HIS WORD IN MEDITATION.

"The brothers wrote to the disciples to welcome him." It would seem "the brothers" were running the church in Ephesus. The elders were not yet a part of the church here. Literacy was assumed in the congregations of those days. The term disciples was used with more frequency than "Christians." Hospitality was a large part of the life of the body. All of these facts speak to us right now. We need to feel that every member is a vital working part of the body of Christ. Genuine hospitality can be a blessed part of our mutual life for each other.

Pause—wait—think—then express yourself in thoughtful praise or thanks.

9. READ HIS WORD FOR PETITIONS.

What a good man was Apollos—he moves us all to prayer: (1) Help me to remember how very much we all influence each other for good or bad. (2) There are so many letters I could write to encourage—help me to write one today. (3) Give me the openness to be an ecouragement to others. (4) May I always remember that it is by grace I have believed. (5) I want to be known as a helper of my brothers. (6) What kind of debate can I use today to help men to believe? (7) Thank you for the overwhelming evidence that Jesus was the Christ.

Please, please remember these are prayers—speak them—reword them!

10. READ HIS WORD AND WAIT—LISTEN—GOD SPEAKS!

Speak to me from these verses: (1) "Others depend on you to help them in my service." (2) "You depend on others for your service to me." (3) "Argument can be very helpful or harmful—it depends on the attitude of those involved."

11. INTERCESSION FOR THE LOST WORLD

China — Point for prayer: (1) *Praise God for the missionary work* done before the door closed to missionaries in 1951. The 100 years of missionary work in a time of great unrest and hatred for all foreign influences was a miracle. The Gospel was preached in nearly every part of the land, and many churches were planted. At one time there were about 8,500 Protestant missionaries serving in China. There were failings in this work—too many non-Bible believing missionaries, too much emphasis of Chinese Christian leaders and teaching of believers. As a result the Church was ill prepared for the Communist holocaust. Pray that the warnings of China may be heeded by missionaries in other lands.

12. SING PRAISES TO OUR LORD.

Face to face with Christ, my Savior,
Face to face—what will it be?
When with rapture I behold Him,
Jesus Christ who died for me.

Face to face I shall behold Him,
Far beyond the starry sky;
Face to face in all His glory,
I shall see Him by and by!

WEEK NINETEEN — SUNDAY

1. PRAISE GOD FOR WHO HE IS.

Precious or held in honor, reverence (Psa. 8:5; Isa. 28:16). There could be no more appropriate title or name. You are precious to all men—the sad fact is they do not even know. How can I pray this prayer, express this thought before you and not do more about it? The whole world could know today like no other time in human history. If somehow the preciousness of yourself could be broadcast on all TV networks and held before the world for just 24 hours thousands would believe—thousands would not believe and many more thousands would not understand. Personal teaching as done by your Son is the way to tell of your preciousness.

Express yourself in adoration for this quality of God.
Speak it audibly or write out your praise in your own devotional journal.

2. PRAISE GOD FOR WHAT HE MEANS TO ME.

Precious to me. Dear, dear Lord, you *are* precious to me. I want to hold you up before me in honor, majesty, power, beauty, holiness—all this and ten thousand times more. I purpose to so honor you today before men that others will want to share your honor with all they meet. This is no substitute for my personal witness and teaching—but you do receive the recognition that you so richly deserve—I love you! To pause before your throne and accumulate all the names of yourself and but read them overwhelms my mind and heart!

How do you personally relate to the preciousness of God, and God who is Precious?
Speak it out or write it out. It is *so important* that you establish *your own* devotional journal.

3. CONFESSION OF SIN

I have read that you will not share your honor with another. This disturbs me greatly because I have accepted praise that truly, truly belongs to you. Forgive me, rebuke me even more deeply than I presently feel the conviction of your Spirit. Surely this is a basic sin. When we are so ready and anxious to spend time and money and so much energy to promote anything but the beauty of yourself we are sinners! Forgive me!

"Hardening of the heart." This seems to be my occupation! Dear God, how often I have repressed or resisted or hesitated to open my mouth or compassion and the end result was hardening, or shutting up of my heart. I hardly know what to do but confess it and ask for forgiveness. I truly want to repent, but I know not how.

What personal sins do you want to confess? We *must* speak them to remove them.
Do it! *Now.* There is no one else you have sinned against more than God. Tell him so!

4. SING A PRAYER TO GOD.

Holy, Holy, Holy,
Lord God Almighty!
Early in the morning our song shall rise to Thee;

Holy, Holy, Holy!
Merciful and Mighty!
God in Three Persons, blessed Trinity!

Open your hymn book and sing the rest of the verses—or even sing another prayer song.

5. READ HIS WORD TO HIM!

His Word

19 While Apollos was at Corinth, Paul took the road through the interior and arrived at Ephesus. There he found some disciples ²and asked them, "Did you receive the Holy Spirit when you believed?"

They answered, "No, we have not even heard that there is a Holy Spirit."

³So Paul asked, "Then what baptism did you receive?"
"John's baptism," they replied.
⁴Paul said, "John's baptism was a baptism of repentance. He told the people to believe in the one coming after him, that is in Jesus."
— Acts 19:1-4, NIV

Read His Word to Him.

The term *Achaia* now becomes a synonym for *Corinth*. Was it because of the time of the year, i.e., when the mountain passes were open that Paul makes this long trek to Ephesus? It is easy enough for Luke to cover hundreds of miles and days and days of weary walking in only one verse. But then, I know you were with him and shared every step. Dear Lord, I do want to know if the disciples Paul met in Ephesus were converts of Apollos? Their knowledge had the same limitations. It would seem as clear as words can make it that the Holy Spirit was expected when they became Christians. Was it because of some lack in their attitudes that Paul asked the question: "Did you receive the Holy Spirit when you believed?" I believe it was. But you know and I only surmise. Christian baptism gives us the Holy Spirit seems to be the point of Paul's question: "Then what baptism did you receive?"

Please express your response to this beautiful text. Put your expression in your own prayer diary.

WEEK NINETEEN — SUNDAY

6. READ HIS WORD FOR YOURSELF.

Read this word for *myself*! Indeed I shall! Did I receive the Holy Spirit when I became a Christian? Yea, and amen! He came as a gift at my new birth—indeed he was involved in my new birth. I "came out of" the water and the Spirit at the time I became a Christian. He is present as an unseen guest in my body now. My physical home is his holy tabernacle. Sad to say, at times I am so un-responsive to his presence, to his word that my attitudes belie his presence in me. I want to repent, from the inside out, to change my mind. Is there some way I can consciously identify the Holy Spirit's presence in my body, i.e., apart from the plain statement of the text that it is so? If there were, of what help would this be?

It is so important that you pause in his presence
and either audibly or in written form tell him all his word means to you.

7. READ HIS WORD IN THANKSGIVING.

(1) Thank you for the tremendous amount of energy Paul gave in walking from place to place in your service. (2) Thank you for the twelve disciples of John—they were so transparently sincere, ready to learn and grow. (3) Thank you for the blessed Holy Spirit all of us receive when we become Christians. (4) Thank you for the various designations for becoming a Christian—here it is "when you believed." (5) Thank you for the clear examples in the Acts accounts of men and women becoming Christians. (6) Thank you again for the good man, John the Baptist. (7) Thank you so much for repentance—how often I need it—I want to grow!

Give yourself to your own expression of gratitude—write it or speak it!

8. READ HIS WORD IN MEDITATION.

"A baptism of repentance"! Was baptism the important emphasis or repentance? John let us know as he spoke to some who came to be baptized. "Bring forth fruit worthy of repentance." He actually refused to baptize some people. Actions and attitudes would be the fruit of repentance. Deep, genuine, personal sorrow for sin was the prepara-tion for repentance. The volitional choice to do what is right is repentance. In such a frame of mind men and women were prepared for John's baptism and the reign of the Messiah in their lives. We need to be told again and again that repentance was an essential prerequisite to Christian baptism.

Pause—wait—think—then express yourself in thoughtful praise or thanks.

9. READ HIS WORD FOR PETITIONS.

What a *long* walk it is from Antioch to Ephesus. Paul must have prayed much on this journey. We too can find petitions in the text: (1) Keep me aware that others work for you each day in their field as I do in my field. (2) Keep me sensitive to the task of making disciples. (3) Why did Paul ask about the Holy Spirit? (4) Dear Lord, give me wisdom as I seek your answers to questions raised in this text. (5) What relation does baptism have with the Holy Spirit? (6) Give me courage to repent. (7) Dear Lord, may I baptize people today for the same reason Paul did in Ephesus.

Right here add your personal requests—and his answers.

10. READ HIS WORD AND WAIT—LISTEN—GOD SPEAKS!

In these four verses you can speak to me: (1) "All disciples have not learned the same lesson." (2) "The Holy Spirit is your birthright." (3) "The baptism of Christ gives you the Holy Spirit."

11. INTERCESSION FOR THE LOST WORLD

China — Points for prayer: (1) *The training of new leaders* for the Church is almost impossible. There are hardly any preachers or leaders left who have had any formal Bible training. Pray that the present leaders may be taught the deep things of God by the Spirit, and be able to minister to the real needs of the believers. Pray for those who live the dangerous life of an underground preacher. Pray for the opening of the way for more be-lievers to be able to obtain training in Hong Kong and return to China; there was one such in 1977. (2) *The unreached peoples of China.* Many of the minority groups in China have been only very slightly influenced by the Gospel due to their inaccessibility or resistance to the Gospel. It is unknown what the present situation is, but all these groups now must use Mandarin Chinese, and are thus more open to the witness of Chinese believers.

12. SING PRAISES TO OUR LORD.

Fairest Lord Jesus!
Ruler of all nature!
O Thou of God and man the Son!

Thee will I cherish,
Thee will I honor,
Thou, my soul's glory, joy, and crown!

255

WEEK NINETEEN — MONDAY

1. PRAISE GOD FOR WHO HE IS.

Kindness. To contemplate yourself as total kindness is such a beautiful thought! Kindness is much like mercy — it is meeting human need wherever you find it. How fully does this describe what you do everyday for everyone! Your thoughtful kindness is giving rain, fruitful seasons, the beauty of flowers, birds and butterflies, the compassion of a mother, the warmth of the sunshine. Then when the kindness of God our Savior appeared in the person of your Son, we all knew the ultimate of thoughtful mercy.

Express yourself in adoration for this quality of God.
Speak it audibly or write out your praise in your own devotional journal.

2. PRAISE GOD FOR WHAT HE MEANS TO ME.

Kind to me — such a surprise and delight is your kindness. When I deserve justice, you offer me kindness. Praise your glorious name. Your goodness is to give me opportunity to recognize the source of all those good gifts and begin to live soberly, righteously, and in the presence of yourself. Dear God, I so respond. May I be as kind to others as you are to me.

How do you personally relate to the kindness of God, and God who is Kindness?
Speak it out or write it out. It is *so important* that you establish *your own* devotional journal.

3. CONFESSION OF SIN

Of all my sins, the sin of unkindness is at the same time both the easiest and the most difficult to confess. It is easy to admit I have been thoughtlessly, selfishly unkind; it is more than difficult to tell why. My life has been cast in the midst of those who love me — in the center of an abundance of good things — why, oh why, should I ever be selfish and mean? Forgive me, but open my eyes to a deeper need — to stay humble-minded.

"Continual lust" is a sin — not only for sex — although this is true — but of "status" and "things." Break this bondage by my happy marriage, by my understanding of how *you* see me in society, by "things" of eternal beauty and value.

What personal sins do you want to confess? We *must* speak them to remove them.
Do it! *Now.* There is no one else you have sinned against more than God. Tell him so!

4. SING A PRAYER TO GOD.

Jesus, the very·thought of Thee
With sweetness fills my breast;

But sweeter far Thy face to see,
And in Thy presence rest.

Open your hymn book and sing the rest of the verses — or even sing another prayer song.

5. READ HIS WORD TO HIM!

His Word

[5]On hearing this, they were baptized into the name of the Lord Jesus. [6]When Paul placed his hands on them, the Holy Spirit came on them, and they spoke in tongues and prophesied. [7]There were about twelve men in all.

[8]Paul entered the synagogue and spoke boldly there for three months, arguing persuasively about the kingdom of God. [9]But some of them became obstinate; they refused to believe and publicly maligned the Way. So Paul left them. He took the disciples with him and had discussions daily in the lecture hall of Tyrannus. [10]This went on for two years, so that all the Jews and Greeks who lived in the province of Asia heard the word of the Lord.

— *Acts 19:5-10, NIV*

Read His Word to Him.

What unusual and moving words are these! These twelve men were baptized in the name (or by the authority) of your dear Son. Did they not at that time and in that act receive the Holy Spirit? Is not the expression: "the Holy Spirit came on them" to be associated with his supernatural coming? The very same words are used in reference to the hands of Peter and John in Acts 8:16, 17. Dear Lord, I want to be right in my understanding. But then I know you are right and I am sincere in my desire to know and this is enough! If I am to define the word "tongues" from the day of Pentecost (and where else will I look for a definition?) then these men are given the ability to speak in languages they never learned. In the multi-lingual city of Ephesus they would need this ability in their teaching and preaching.

Please express your response to this beautiful text. Put your expression in your own prayer diary.

6. READ HIS WORD FOR YOURSELF.

What an example for me! Speaking boldly in the synagogue is equal to what in my experience? Boldness is almost equated with confidence. I cannot avoid the fact that I think of several denominational bodies of people of several cults in the same category. What have I done about it? Almost nothing! Dear God, forgive me and move me!

It is so important that you pause in his presence
and either audibly or in written form tell him all his word means to you.

7. READ HIS WORD IN THANKSGIVING.

(1) Thank you that the text is so clear about believing — they could if they would. (2) Thank you for that beautiful description of "the Way." — Oh, I want to walk in it! (3) Thank you that even Paul could not stay with some people. (4) Thank you that Paul did not run away but stayed to work and win. (5) Thank you that Paul's discussions (was this preaching? teaching?) were with the disciples, and happened every day — when? how? (6) Thank you for daily discussions for two years that produced self-starters that shared their faith with thousands of others. (7) Thank you for the "one body" — neither Jew nor Greek — and through it you reached out to the many cities of Asia (Turkey today). Dear God, where is our faith now?

Give yourself to your own expression of gratitude — write it or speak it!

8. READ HIS WORD IN MEDITATION.

"So that all the Jews and Greeks who lived in the province of Asia heard the word of the Lord." We do not believe it was possible for all the Jews and Greeks of Asia to gather in the lecture hall of Tyrannus. It was rather that those who heard the daily discussions fanned out into the whole province of Asia with the glad tidings. Was this the seven churches of Asia? There was something wonderfully solid about the life and witness of these early Christians. There are 43 million people living in the whole country of Turkey. How many thousands lived in the province of Asia? It can happen again, even in the same district where it happened before. In the Aegean region of Turkey today there are 4 million eight hundred thousand people. This is much of the same area where Paul worked. Dear God, I lift these people up to you!

Pause — wait — think — then express yourself in thoughtful praise or thanks.

9. READ HIS WORD FOR PETITIONS.

It is so good to pray directly from your word: (1) Help me to help disciples today who know nothing about the Holy Spirit. (2) How good it is to baptize people into the name of the Lord Jesus — help me to promise them all you have promised. (3) Why did Paul lay his hands on these men? (4) What were "the tongues" spoken by these men? (5) Why the gift of prophecy here? (6) I claim your wisdom as I search your word for the answers to these questions. (7) May I live as a citizen of the kingdom of heaven — right here and right now.

Please, please remember these are prayers — speak them — reword them!

10. READ HIS WORD AND WAIT — LISTEN — GOD SPEAKS!

How much you can say to me through these verses: (1) "Be as helpful and bold as Paul in meeting the needs of men." (2) "If Paul could succeed in Asia you can where you are." (3) "Ephesus offers an example in so many ways — read the letter to this church."

11. INTERCESSION FOR THE LOST WORLD

China — Point for prayer: (1) *The many peoples of Sinkiang* — the vast desert and semi-desert northwest where many different peoples live as nomads or in cities and oases. The main groups being the Muslim Uighurs, Buddhist Mongols, etc. Most of the smaller groups like the Uzbeks, Kazakhs, etc. are Muslim. The land was only partially open for the Gospel in the 1930's and some outstanding evangelistic work was done and a few churches planted.

12. SING PRAISES TO OUR LORD.

Down at the cross where my Savior died,
Down where for cleansing from sin I cried,
There to my heart was the blood applied;
Glory to His name.

Glory to His name, . . .
Glory to His name; . . .
There to my heart was the blood applied;
Glory to His name.

WEEK NINETEEN — TUESDAY

1. PRAISE GOD FOR WHO HE IS.

Presence. What an amazing quality to discuss! How much I want to enter fully into this attribute of yourself and appreciate more than ever before the fact that you are now present with me — in me, above me, before me, behind me, ahead of me — and what is true for me is true for all men. What a startling, awesome fact! I want you to permeate all the atmosphere, all my being. As an invisible Person you could be present and no one would know it — only those who sense, or are sensitive, who are made aware of this reality, appreciate your presence.

Express yourself in adoration for this quality of God.
Speak it audibly or write out your praise in your own devotional journal.

2. PRAISE GOD FOR WHAT HE MEANS TO ME.

Present for me. Dear God, this is one mind-staggering concept! That you as the almighty God are here present. I fall down like John of old — that you can see and hear and know totally all about me and be at the same time in me is such information I cannot assimilate. Will you make your presence known? Yes, yes, I could not write these words if you had not already told me you were present. I read it in your book. At the same time I want to practice your presence. I want to ask you to share my thoughts every minute of this day. It can be done. I have thought that often about other things or people. Oh, Present One, I love you!

How do you personally relate to the presence of God, and God who is present?
Speak it out or write it out. It is *so important* that you establish *your own* devotional journal.

3. CONFESSION OF SIN

The sin of all sins! To ignore your presence — to live and talk and think just as if you were not always present. To not include you in my conversation, to not look your way to gain your nod of approval or frown of disapproval. To talk on and on to others and fail to talk with you. I *know*, I *know* you are interested in all I say and do and want to help (in ways I so much need your help), but I fail to ask or seek your face. Dear God, forgive me, forgive me!

Deceit. This sin strikes so close to my heart. Dear God, I want to be open and transparent before men (I know I am always open and known to you.). I fear men and their frown more than yours. Forgive me. Penetrate my conscience deeply.

What sins do you want to confess? We *must* speak them to remove them.
Do it! *Now.* There is no one else you have sinned against more than God. Tell him so!

4. SING A PRAYER TO GOD.

Abide with me: fast falls the eventide;
The darkness deepens; Lord, with me abide:

When other helpers fail, and comforts flee,
Help of the helpless, O abide with me!

Open your hymn book and sing the rest of the verses — or even sing another prayer song.

5. READ HIS WORD TO HIM!

His Word

[11]God did extraordinary miracles through Paul. [12]Handkerchiefs and aprons that had touched him were taken to the sick, and their illnesses were cured and the evil spirits left them.
[13]Some Jews who went around driving out evil spirits tried to invoke the name of the Lord Jesus over those who were demon-possessed. They would say, "In the name of Jesus whom Paul preaches, I command you to come out." [14]Seven sons of Sceva, a Jewish chief priest, were doing this. [15]The evil spirit answered them, "Jesus I know and Paul I know about, but who are you?"

— *Acts 19:11-15, NIV*

Read His Word to Him.

Dear Lord, how unusual, how indeed "extraordinary" is the description I read here of your work through Paul. Was it because there were so many persons in Ephesus who needed such confirmation of your word before they would believe? From what we know of the religious background of these worshipers of Diana, and many other gods such seems to be the case. Are we to expect the same "extraordinary" miracles in a similar situation today? Surely we do as to people and their circumstance. But we also have today the record in written form of your confirming word. This those of Ephesus did not have. Does this make a large difference? Why was it written and preserved through two thousand years if it did not? Open my mind, dear Lord, I *want* to know.

Please express your response to this beautiful text. Put your expression in your own prayer diary.

6. READ HIS WORD FOR YOURSELF.

I know you can do such work today! I would be much closer to accepting the account here and elsewhere as normative if someone like myself instead of Paul, the apostle, did such signs. I know that such signs were to follow "believers" (Mk. 16:17), but the "believers" according to the Acts are the apostles and those upon whom they laid their hands. Since Paul spent at least two years in Corinth on one occasion and visited there at least twice afterward, it could have been that all the signs described in I Cor. 12:1ff. could be from this same source. I am sure there must have been hundreds of prophets spread over the Roman Empire (if not thousands). Could the twelve or Paul have laid their hands on each one of them? It is possible.

It is so important that you pause in his presence and either audibly or in written form tell him all his word means to you.

7. READ HIS WORD IN THANKSGIVING.

(1) Thank you for the miraculous works that galvanized the attention of the Ephesians so they could hear with their inner ear the message of salvation. (2) Thank you that as strong as Satan is Jesus is stronger. (3) Thank you that we are protected from pretenders, i.e., if we want to be. (4) Thank you that you cannot be deceived. (5) Thank you for the clear difference between religion and Christianity. (6) Thank you for the reminder that the spirit world is the real world. (7) Thank you for the poor possessed man from whom we can learn so many things.

Give yourself to your own expression of gratitude—write it or speak it!

8. READ HIS WORD IN MEDITATION.

"Jesus I know and Paul I know, but who are you?" These are the words of a demon through the lips of a man. This is a mind-challenging thought! There are yet demons in the world. Here are several questions I have asked myself and my Lord about them: (1) Are demons in me? Am I to associate my stubborn sins with demons?, i.e., am I to conclude because I cannot, or will not, stop this sin or that one that such is the work of a demon or demons? I would be glad to thus interpret my sinning if such were Biblical. The only reference to stubborn resistance of demons has reference to a son who had some physical, emotional, mental problem not a stubborn unyielding sin problem. The possessed was but a child—not a Christian because salvation through his blood was yet a promise.

(2) How do I recognize demons in myself or others? By discerning spirits. What a large claim to make! How was the presence of demons determined in the city of Ephesus? Paul and those upon whom he laid his hands had such powers. Perhaps the efforts of these seven sons were done on those who had no demons until they met one who did. If they identified demons someone had the gift of discernment.

Pause—wait—think—then express yourself in thoughtful praise or thanks.

9. READ HIS WORD FOR PETITIONS.

There is something wonderfully extraordinary about this whole text (19:11-15): (1) Why did you do the unusual things you did in Ephesus? (2) Why were the miracles performed in this city? (3) Dear Lord, I am expecting real wisdom in answering these questions as I search your word. (4) Deliver me from deciding truth from experience —good or bad. (5) Protect me from the attacks of demons today. (6) May I know your Son in such a personal manner that He will be Lord of all in my life.

Right here add your personal requests—and his answers.

10. READ HIS WORD AND WAIT — LISTEN — GOD SPEAKS!

What can I hear from this text especially for my life? (1) "Evil spirits are nothing to treat lightly." (2) "Evil spirits were not in Christians." (3) "Evil spirits know and respect Jesus as one of all authority."

11. INTERCESSION FOR THE LOST WORLD

China — Point for prayer: (1) *Inner Mongolia and the Mongolians.* These strong Buddhist people live along China's northern border with the U.S.S.R. and the U.S.S.R. puppet state of Mongolia (with a further 1,500,000 Mongolians). Only a few little churches were known to have been planted in Chinese Inner Mongolia. Most have never really heard the Gospel.

12. SING PRAISES TO OUR LORD.

"Man of Sorrows," what a name
For the Son of God who came

Ruined sinners to reclaim!
Hallelujah! what a Savior!

WEEK NINETEEN — WEDNESDAY

1. PRAISE GOD FOR WHO HE IS.

Complete. How could we better describe yourself! There is nothing you lack—you are whole in every sense. It would help me to worship you if I listed just two areas where all men can find you perfect: (1) Complete in knowledge—there is no branch of science in which you do not have absolute, complete information. It will be a part of the joy of heaven to investigate this total body of information. (2) Complete in sympathetic understanding love. My love and the love of all men is so inadequate—alloyed with our own selfishness. How glorious to worship and praise and know you; to commit myself, and for all men to do likewise is no effort, it is a privilege!

Express yourself in adoration for this quality of God.
Speak it audibly or write out your praise in your own devotional journal.

2. PRAISE GOD FOR WHAT HE MEANS TO ME.

Complete for me. What all men find in you I now find personally and intimately. I want to enter into a secret pact. In you I am whole for you are wholeness itself! I can pause any time of any day and cast myself upon you. I *know* you care for me, you love me, forgive me, chasten me, have specific plans for me—bless your wonderful name! I find *no* help, *no* hope, *no* fulfillment in any one or any thing else! You have made my life so full, so meaningful—I want to reaffirm my wholeness in you! I am really anxious to enter into the larger part of my life right on the other side of my last heart beat!

How do you personally relate to the completeness of God, and God who is Complete?
Speak it out or write it out. It is *so important* that you establish *your own* devotional journal.

3. CONFESSION OF SIN

If you are so complete for every area of life, how is it I seek fulfillment outside yourself? It would be easy to say with Paul, "It is not I who do it, but sin which lives in me."—or, "So then it is no longer I that do it, but sin which dwells within me" (Rom. 7:17, RSV). Jesus *can* and *does* deliver me from this bondage of separation. I live by my response to the environment. My largest need then is to so condition my reflexes that I will always (by habit) respond to your sweet will and not that of Satan, the deceiver. I have lived so long in Satan's world (with all that is in his [the] world), that I am like the Israelites who didn't recognize the deliverer. Oh, dear God, dear Savior, I do want out!

What sins do you want to confess? We *must* speak them to remove them.
Do it! *Now.* There is no one else you have sinned against more than God. Tell him so!

4. SING A PRAYER TO GOD.

Dear Lord and Father of mankind,
Forgive our foolish ways!
Reclothe us in our rightful mind;

In purer lives Thy service find,
In deeper rev'rence, praise.

Open your hymn book and sing the rest of the verses—or even sing another prayer song.

5. READ HIS WORD TO HIM!

His Word

[16]Then the man who had the evil spirit jumped on them and overpowered them all. He gave them such a beating that they ran out of the house naked and bleeding.
[17]When this became known to the Jews and Greeks living in Ephesus, they were all seized with fear, and the name of the Lord Jesus was held in high honor. [18]Many of those who believed now came and openly confessed their evil deeds. [19]A number who had practiced sorcery brought their scrolls together and burned them publicly. When they calculated the value of the scrolls, the total came to fifty thousand drachmas. [20]In this way the word of the Lord spread widely and grew in power.

— *Acts 19:16-20, NIV*

Read His Word to Him.

Dear Father, I am sure you must smile as I do when we find out who cast whom out! The seven men were all cast out of the house by the one poor demon-possessed man. I am impressed and warmed when I see what super human strength this man had. I do not underestimate the power or strength of the enemy. I am no more able to overcome than the sons of Sceva. This but points up negatively my need of you! Satan can and will hurt me. It is more than interesting that the devil leaves us naked and bleeding. Oh, oh, my Lord, when will I ever learn that I cannot do anything without you and with you I can do all things. Teach me—I am listening, I am waiting, I am yielding!

Please express your response to this beautiful text. Put your expression in your own prayer diary.

6. READ HIS WORD FOR YOURSELF.

Dear Lord, I want this text to penetrate the deepest recesses of my heart! When something truly divine — truly significant — happens, word of it spreads and it is known! How many Jews and Greeks were living in Ephesus at this time? Were there as many as 100,000 or even 200,000? This is not at all impossible. How I want to examine this phenomenon *carefully*: (1) It was so obviously supernatural that no one even thought of denying it. (2) The standard of truth was very clear — no question about morality — the source of right and wrong was very plain. — "Jesus, whom Paul preached" gave peace and deliverance.

It is so important that you pause in his presence
and either audibly or in written form tell him all his word means to you.

7. READ HIS WORD IN THANKSGIVING.

(1) Thank you for the clear definition of repentance. We cannot mix sin and righteousness; superstition and prayer. We cannot, we must not, we dare not serve God and mammon. (2) Thank you for the example of open confession of sin. (3) Thank you for the final full break with sin — it was burned up! (4) Thank you for the shocking (?) revelation that Christians in Ephesus were not at all as mature as we have at times imagined them to be. (5) Thank you for the public participation in the life of the church — everyone knew! (6) Thank you that Christians were willing to spend thousands and thousands of dollars to show their faith and commitment. (7) Thank you for a demonstration of how the faith can spread as widely today as then.

Give yourself to your own expression of gratitude — write it or speak it!

8. READ HIS WORD IN MEDITATION.

"In this way the word of the Lord spread widely and grew in power." In this day of emphasis on church growth we surely do want to know just how "the word of the Lord spread widely and grew in power." Notice: (1) It was through an open confession of personal sins. (2) It was through a public declaration of their break with sorcery and idolatry. (3) It was when men and women began to "put their money where their mouth was." As large as the congregation was in Ephesus, as influential as some of the people were, those actions and attitudes had a strong impact on the city.

Pause — wait — think — then express yourself in thoughtful praise or thanks.

9. READ HIS WORD FOR PETITIONS.

A good number of petitions must have been raised in the homes of the Ephesian Christians: (1) May Jesus be Lord of all in all my life. (2) Help me to fear him who can destroy both body and soul in hell. (3) Lord, I want to learn from the tragic experiences of those who have disobeyed you. (4) Somehow may I see just how exalted is the name of my Lord, even in the world of demons. (5) Give me the humility necessary to confess my sins to my brothers. (6) Keep me aware that the spirit world is the real world. (7) Burn up all that is false in my worship.

Please, please remember these are prayers — speak them — reword them!

10. READ HIS WORD AND WAIT — LISTEN — GOD SPEAKS!

In these verses you can reach my conscience: (1) "You are no match for Satan without me." (2) "Honor me in your thoughts." (3) "If I cannot rule your spirit I cannot rule you at all."

11. INTERCESSION FOR THE LOST WORLD

China — Point for prayer: (1) *Tibet* was an independent Buddhist nation until invaded by China in 1950. A systematic attempt to destroy the Tibetan people has reduced the population to 1,300,000, but 500,000 of these are now Chinese. A few missionaries were just beginning to penetrate this closed and unevangelized land when Communism came. Pray for this needy and tragic people. Pray for the 85,000 Tibetans who fled to India and other lands. Among these latter there are now groups of believers in Ladakh (Kashmir) and North India. Pray for the emerging of a strong Church, and also for the reaching of Tibetans in China through literature smuggled over the Himalaya passes and by radio from Manila.

12. SING PRAISES TO OUR LORD.

So precious is Jesus, my Savior, my King,
His praise all the day long with rapture I sing;
To Him in my weakness for strength I can cling,
For He is so precious to me.

For He is so precious to me, . . .
For He is so precious to me; . . .
'Tis Heaven below, My Redeemer to know,
For He is so precious to me.

WEEK NINETEEN — THURSDAY

1. PRAISE GOD FOR WHO HE IS.

Spirit — what a profound thought! You are an all powerful spirit being! Spirit is the real essence of being — for yourself or man. I am full of wonder as I try to contemplate just what this means. An all-pervasive intelligent divine being — as a spirit being you see, hear, speak, think. I know so much more about you in the Person of Jesus. Just now I want to pause before you in silent wonder, to praise and thank you for all you are, to sense — at least to some extent — your presence with me and in me. Out of my spirit — your own likeness, I bless your holy name!

Express yourself in adoration for this quality of God.
Speak it audibly or write out your praise in your own devotional journal.

2. PRAISE GOD FOR WHAT HE MEANS TO ME.

Spirit to me. What I have said so far could be, and should be, said by all men who love you, but I want to be very personal in my acceptance of you as Spirit. As Spirit you are seeking or looking, searching for my worship of you — so said your Son (John 4:23). To know you are more eager to have my praise and joy than I am to give it moves me to tears — to true humility. Oh, Divine One, how can I ever love you enough? Dear Lord, I want to cultivate the habit of practicing your presence. This is far more than quietness — it is that — but it is *work*: to wrench, subdue my mind until it takes the track of your thoughts. To focus my total attention on your blessed self, or on one or two qualities of your Being. Dear God, help me. May I not lose the sense I now have of your presence with me and in me!

How do you personally relate to the Spirit of God, and God who is Spirit?
Speak it out or write it out. It is *so important* that you establish *your own* devotional journal.

3. CONFESSION OF SIN

That I should ever forget you or neglect your presence, or ignore your promptings in my conscience to sin against your essential Being is to repeat surely the original sin of Adam. How can I forget you see me? How can I think and not think your thoughts? speak and not speak your words? work and ignore your work? Dear God, may I in you live and move and have my being. This seems but the illusive dream of the poet. Forgive me. It is the most gut-level reality. I am blind; open my eyes!

"Greed." This is but the misdirected natural desire. This is "the lust for other things" which does indeed choke out the word. Forgive me! May my insatiable desire be for you.

What personal sins do you want to confess? We *must* speak them to remove them.
Do it! *Now*. There is no one else you have sinned against more than God. Tell him so!

4. SING A PRAYER TO GOD.

Break Thou the bread of life,
Dear Lord, to me,
As Thou didst break the loaves,
Beside the sea;
Beyond the sacred page I seek Thee, Lord;
My spirit pants for Thee, O living Word.

Open your hymn book and sing the rest of the verses — or even sing another prayer song.

5. READ HIS WORD TO HIM!

His Word

[21]After all this had happened, Paul decided to go to Jerusalem, passing through Macedonia and Achaia. "After I have been there," he said, "I must visit Rome also." [22]He sent two of his helpers, Timothy and Erastus, to Macedonia, while he stayed in the province of Asia a little longer.
— *Acts 19:21, 22, NIV*

[5]After I go through Macedonia, I will come to you —
— *I Cor. 16:5a, NIV*

Read His Word to Him.

Just how was it that Paul made his decision to leave Ephesus? What caused him to delay his departure? No doubt the events just described related to his decision, but how? Why did Paul decide to go through Macedonia and Achaia? The love Paul had for each Christian is such a boon for me. I want to notice your wonderful influence in Paul's life: (1) He wanted to share again and again with those who had heard and those who had not. (2) The excitement of travel, new places and new people, was a part of Paul. (3) Paul had a dominate leadership motivation — others were "his helpers." (4) Paul was not at all hesitant to ask for help from those who knew him. (5) All of Paul's plans were subject to your change. (6) Paul took advantage of opportunities as they arose. (7) Paul was protective of the weak or inexperienced — such as Timothy with the Corinthians.

Please express your response to this beautiful text. Put your expression in your own prayer diary.

WEEK NINETEEN — THURSDAY

6. READ HIS WORD FOR YOURSELF.

Indeed, indeed! I do like the use of names in this text! The names of places: (1) Macedonia, (2) Jerusalem, (3) Achaia, (4) Rome, (5) Corinth, (6) Asia, (7) Ephesus. The names of people: (1) Timothy, (2) Erastus, (3) Apollos, (4) "the brothers." I want to think through and pray through each of these eleven names. Every one is saying something to me.

(1) Macedonia means Philippi, Thessalonica and Berea and all for which these churches stand. (2) Jerusalem — oh, how precious and beautiful where my Lord died, was buried and rose again! (3) Achaia — how many lessons can I learn from these Greeks? (4) Rome — the letter to these people has lifted me to heaven. (5) Corinth — I read the two letters as if they were mine! (6) Asia — the seven churches — Colossae, Ephesus — so full of memories. (7) Ephesus — the message of Paul to the elders — here is a message to me!

It is so important that you pause in his presence and either audibly or in written form tell him all his word means to you.

7. READ HIS WORD IN THANKSGIVING.

(1) Thank you for the trails out of which a door opened. (2) Thank you for the dear human interest Paul had with the saints of Macedonia and Achaia. (3) Thank you that Paul was fascinated or captivated with the thought of seeing the imperial city of Rome. (4) Thank you that Paul needed helpers and loved and accepted helpers. (5) Thank you that plans can be changed and still be in your will. (6) Thank you for long winters we can spend with friends in mutual interests. (7) Thank you for timid Timothy — he represents many of us.

Give yourself to your own expression of gratitude — write it or speak it!

8. READ HIS WORD IN MEDITATION.

(1) "Be on your guard; (2) stand firm in the faith; (3) be men of courage, (4) be strong, (5) do everything in love." What good words for all Christians everywhere! Our adversary is full of wily deceit, therefore, we must be on guard. When we know sin in clear definition, we are forearmed against him. When we know what to believe, we can stand firm in it. Paul does not ask us to argue about it, but to stand firm in it. All of us are characterized by some term. There are men of timidity, men of change, men of complaint. With our Lord as example, we can be and want to be, men of courage! It is a remarkable fact that our strength comes both from him and from ourselves! Can we be as inclusive as Paul? *Everything* in love? Yes, everything!

Pause — wait — think — then express yourself in thoughtful praise or thanks.

9. READ HIS WORD FOR PETITIONS.

As Paul plans his future we can see reasons for prayer: (1) Help me to decide and know it is your decision. (2) May I have the same purpose as Paul for my plans. (3) Keep me aware that your work depends on many servants. (4) Give me the time and interest to write to some of your servants. (5) Keep me aware that nothing happens apart from your permission. (6) I want to be on guard against Satan. (7) Give me firmness in the faith.

Right here add your personal requests — and his answers.

10. READ HIS WORD AND WAIT — LISTEN — GOD SPEAKS!

Surely there is much to hear from you in these verses: (1) "Be a man of courage." (2) "Be a man with my strength." (3) "Do everything in love."

11. INTERCESSION FOR THE LOST WORLD

China — Points for prayer: (2) *The many southern tribes* of Yunnan, Kweichow and Kwangsi were opening to the Gospel in a wonderful way between 1930-1950 and fine church groups were growing among the Meo, Lisu and other tribes. Many more were never evangelized, and have nothing of God's Word. Many of these tribes are also found in neighboring lands of Burma, Thailand, Laos and Vietnam where work was continued when China was closed to the Gospel. (2) *The Overseas Chinese* number nearly 40,000,000. Many have fled from Communism to other S.E. Asian lands. The large Chinese communities in Indonesia and Philippines as well as the Chinese lands of Taiwan, Hong Kong and Singapore are open to the Gospel, and a mighty harvest of souls is now being reaped, and strong churches developing. Pray for the growth of the missionary vision among these people both for Mainland China and the many needy Chinese communities all over the world where materialism and the old religions of China with their demonic powers are still keeping many from the Lord.

12. SING PRAISES TO OUR LORD.

How sweet the name of Jesus sounds
In a believer's ear!
It soothes his sorrows, heals his wounds,
And drives away his fear.

WEEK NINETEEN — FRIDAY

1. PRAISE GOD FOR WHO HE IS.

Sanctifier. This is surely one of the essential qualities of yourself. Indeed it would seem to me your primary work among men was to set this one aside — to set aside a nation, to set aside a half-tent half-house for worship called a tabernacle, and to set aside or sanctify all the utensils of the tabernacle for use in worship. *The Separator* would be a good description of yourself. Bless your name — sanctify, set apart, set aside your name, your person from all else. To consider in wonder and praise, in absolute adoration, the Great Sanctifier or The Sanctified would be so appropriate designation! It is so good to know someone who is totally distinct from everyone else, from everything else, even yourself!

Express yourself in adoration for this quality of God.
Speak it audibly or write out your praise in your own devotional journal.

2. PRAISE GOD FOR WHAT HE MEANS TO ME.

Sanctifier for me and of me. It is great to contemplate and adore you as such a "set apart One," but quite something else to realize I have been also "set apart" as a clearly distinct person to worship and serve you. "In any large house there are not only gold and silver dishes but also wooden and earthen ones, some for great occasions and some for ordinary uses. So if a man will cleanse himself from these things, he will be put to great uses, consecrated (sanctified) and used by the master of the house himself, and ready for any good use" (Goodspeed). How poignantly does this text speak to me of my part and your part in my sanctification. What a high honor and privilege to be used by the master of the house himself (even your blessed self).

How do you personally relate to the sanctification of God, and God who is Sanctifier?
Speak it out or write it out. It is *so important* that you establish *your own* devotional journal.

3. CONFESSION OF SIN

That I have been unwilling to set myself apart prevents the fulfillment of your intention to do so. It is so, so *good* to know that sanctification is like salvation: (1) I have been sanctified at Calvary. (2) I am being sanctified by my willingness and your power. (3) I will be eternally sanctified in heaven. Right now I want to cleanse myself and be cleansed. Dear God, dear God, forgive me and make me clean!

"Foolish talk." How very much of it I have heard and expressed — foolish in the sense that it has no sense and its ultimate purpose is empty and meaningless. Stop me, shock me, put a guard on my lips. Forgive me!

What personal sins do you want to confess? We *must* speak them to remove them.
Do it! *Now.* There is no one else you have sinned against more than God. Tell him so!

4. SING A PRAYER TO GOD.

Ere you left your room this morning,
Did you think to pray?
In the name of Christ our Savior,
Did you sue for loving favor,
As a shield today?

Oh, how praying rests the weary!
Prayer will change the night to day;
So in sorrow and in gladness,
Don't forget to pray.

Open your hymn book and sing the rest of the verses — or even sing another prayer song.

5. READ HIS WORD TO HIM!

His Word

[23] About that time there arose a great disturbance about the Way. [24] A silversmith named Demetrius, who made silver shrines of Artemis, brought in no little business for the craftsmen. [25] He called them together, along with the workmen in related trades, and said: "Men, you know we receive a good income from this business.
— *Acts 19:23-25, NIV*

Read His Word to Him.

How good to meet Demetrius again! Was he ever converted? Perhaps he was and I will meet him in heaven. You know, I do not. But I would like to think he reconsidered his motives and actions. I want to reconsider his motives and action with you as my co-reader and silent guide. It was "the Way" in Ephesus. Not "a way," but "the Way." If Paul had only offered one more god among the many already there, Demetrius would not have been so upset. I was in Ephesus, I stood in the streets, I visited the theater. How near was I to the house of Demetrius? Income for his business more important than anything else. Had Demetrius heard Paul preach? He only heard one thing out of all Paul said: "my business is threatened"! How easy it is to filter all we hear through the sieve of our personal interests.

Please express your response to this beautiful text. Put your expression in your own prayer diary.

6. READ HIS WORD FOR YOURSELF.

How soon is "a great disturbance" left behind. At the same time, how great was the disturbance? (1) Great in the number of people involved—somehow we can fit into the city of Diana and never cause a ripple. (2) Great in the issues involved—who is God? We are not willing to let the god of mammon go unchallenged. (3) Great in the results—many, many would never have seriously considered the one god if Paul had not challenged Diana or Artemis. We do not have these results because we do not offer a similar challenge.

It is so important that you pause in his presence
and either audibly or in written form tell him all his word means to you.

7. READ HIS WORD IN THANKSGIVING.

(1) Thank you for the adversaries who make us aware of the open door. (2) Thank you for the confirmation of archaeology in the city of Ephesus for the Acts record. (3) Thank you for the long record of the working principle for a gainful occupation. (4) Thank you for the ability of Paul to communicate to all men. What an example for me. (5) Thank you for the epistle to the Ephesians. It means so much more when I read it in the light of this account. (6) Thank you for the additional information of Phil. 2:19-24. (7) Thank you for your motivation within me to worship you amid every changing circumstance of my life.

Give yourself to your own expression of gratitude—write it or speak it!

8. READ HIS WORD IN MEDITATION.

"... we receive a good income from this business." How often in human history has this been *the* motive for either opposing or pursuing religion? When our god becomes a source of income, when we are using him we are not worshiping him. Whatever becomes the focus of our interest is our source of worship. Dear God, deliver me from using you in any way to promote my own welfare. Whenever service to God becomes a lucrative business, or our motive is to make it so, we need to be on guard—our friend Demetrius has come to life again!

Pause—wait—think—then express yourself in thoughtful praise or thanks.

9. READ HIS WORD FOR PETITIONS.

In opposition there is always a place for prayer: (1) In all my relationships today may I seek for "the Way." (2) Give me the same bold humility as Paul in the face of men like Demetrius. (3) Keep me aware that today there are men who plot the overthrow of your cause. May I use the freedom we have for you. (4) Deliver me from the love of money. (5) It is so easy to mistake greed for zeal—help me. (6) Help me to know more fully than ever all who live godly will suffer persecution. (7) Deliver me from provoking persecution in order to parade my righteousness.

Please, please remember these are prayers—speak them—reword them!

10. READ HIS WORD AND WAIT—LISTEN—GOD SPEAKS!

You can indeed speak to me through these verses: (1) "Never underestimate the power of the love of money." (2) "Never underestimate my power to overcome." (3) "The worship of Artemis is not dead."

11. INTERCESSION FOR THE LOST WORLD

China — Points for prayer: (1) *The Ministries of Help for China from the Free World: Prayer* — the most important, but this is not an easy ministry with the lack of information coming out of China. (2) *Literature* — pray that more and more Bibles and Christian literature may be printed and taken into China. Pray for the writing and printing of the right type of literature for the new Communist-indoctrinated China. There are a number of good Christian organizations working on this ministry in the strategically placed Hong Kong.

12. SING PRAISES TO OUR LORD.

When I saw the cleansing fountain
Open wide for all my sin,
I obeyed the Spirit's wooing,
When He said, Wilt thou be clean?

I will praise Him! I will praise Him!
Praise the Lamb for sinners slain;
Give Him glory, all ye people,
For His blood can wash away each stain.

WEEK NINETEEN — SATURDAY

1. PRAISE GOD FOR WHO HE IS.

Cleanser. Surely this describes your work for mankind. The parallels in nature and in revelation are most interesting. You must constantly cleanse this earth to keep it alive. We must wash away impurities or our daily life would be unbearable. A very large function of the human body is cleansing itself. How glad I am you are the grand original source for all that is clean. Man and your other creation truly is "fouled up" when cleansing does not happen. It is more than good to be clean—it is absolutely essential! Bless your name for being so adequate in every area of life.

Express yourself in adoration for this quality of God.
Speak it audibly or write out your praise in your own devotional journal.

2. PRAISE GOD FOR WHAT HE MEANS TO ME.

Cleanser for me. Dear God, I have a constant need of being renewed from within. I do not consider sin and failure inevitable, but I do know I must seek your forgiveness each day. I am neither intelligent enough nor morally strong enough to be saved any other way. I love to think of you as the Cleanser in the figures of speech (or literary devices) you have given in your word: (1) "A Fountain for sin and uncleanness" is my blessed Lord and his blood. (2) The laver of regeneration, or "the bath of the new birth" (Titus 3:5). (3) The burnt offering—fire is a great purifier—so all our sins are gone in the consuming fire of his love. Bless your name!

How do you personally relate to the cleansing of God, and God who is Cleanser?
Speak it out or write it out. It is *so important* that you establish *your own* devotional journal.

3. CONFESSION OF SIN

All my praise has been for the forgiveness I have from confession of sin. Dear God, help me to hold back nothing in naming my sin that I might be wholly forgiven. How sad to learn that the very expression of your self is to cleanse and then fail to recognize I am dirty. "There is a fountain filled with blood drawn from Immanuel's veins, and sinners plunged beneath that flood lose all their guilty stains." Oh, indeed, indeed I do!

"Course jokes." Sin is no joke. Satan wants us to believe it is. Sin has the potential of a joke since humor is based on incongruity, but the sad tragic fact is such is but a testimony of man's moral failure. His conduct is so far away from what God expected it appears ludicrous. Dear God, forgive.

What personal sins do you want to confess? We *must* speak them to remove them.
Do it! *Now.* There is no one else you have sinned against more than God. Tell him so!

4. SING A PRAYER TO GOD.

From ev'ry stormy wind that blows,
From ev'ry swelling tide of woes.

There is a calm, a sure retreat:
'Tis found beneath the mercy seat.

Open your hymn book and sing the rest of the verses—or even sing another prayer song.

5. READ HIS WORD TO HIM.

His Word

[26] And you see and hear how this fellow Paul has convinced and led astray large numbers of people here in Ephesus and in practically the whole province of Asia. He says that man-made gods are no gods at all. [27] There is danger not only that our trade will lose its good name, but also that the temple of the great goddess Artemis will be discredited, and the goddess herself, who is worshiped throughout the province of Asia and the world, will be robbed of her divine majesty."

[28] When they heard this, they were furious and began shouting: "Great is Artemis of the Ephesians!"

— Acts 19:26-28, NIV

Read His Word to Him.

How convincing was Paul! How very many people were taught and led by him! This incident at Ephesus could be only representative of what he did in so many places. Dear Lord, I want to express my wonder and praise for what I see and hear before you. When the world begins to testify as to the power and influence of the good news we have reason to rejoice.

I see here that Demetrius was worried not only about money, but status—"our trade will lose its good name." Perhaps money and a good name are the same thing here. Thank you for showing me what one man could do—rather what you could do through one man.

Please express your response to this beautiful text. Put your expression in your own prayer diary.

6. READ HIS WORD FOR YOURSELF.

Oh, how I want to hear these verses; burn them into my conscience: "large numbers of people here at Ephesus —practically the whole province of Asia"! "the temple of . . . Artemis will be discredited." When I consider the dimension of the work here described, I am just nonplused! How could it happen that one of the seven wonders of the ancient world would be threatened by one man? But then it was no wonder to you or to Paul.

Why am I impressed with the works and claims and standing of men? Dear God, deliver me from such! Show me where I can influence as many men and women for you!

It is so important that you pause in his presence
and either audibly or in written form tell him all his word means to you.

7. READ HIS WORD IN THANKSGIVING.

(1) Thank you for Paul's desire to convince all that there is just one God. (2) Thank you for the truth for to-day—we worship false gods if we worship anything but you. (3) Thank you for the lesson in the temporariness of earthly glory. (4) Thank you for the excitement of opposition—out of it can come eternal good. (5) Thank you for your divine majesty in stark contrast to Artemis. (6) Thank you that I can read a record two thousand years old and feel the conflict and heart-beat of those in it. (7) Thank you for the multiple applications I see in this incident for my life today.

Give yourself to your own expression of gratitude—write it or speak it!

8. READ HIS WORD IN MEDITATION.

"... robbed of her divine majesty." Just how was this done? (1) By challenging the claims of Diana—what possible evidence could be presented for the claim that she fell down out of heaven? (2) By offering a far more meaningful explanation of the world and all in it. (3) By credentialling or supporting the claims of Jesus with miracles. (4) By the example of confidence and happiness as seen in the lives of the followers of the Way.

Pause—wait—think—then express yourself in thoughtful praise or thanks.

9. READ HIS WORD FOR PETITIONS.

In the words of Demetrius there is much occasion for prayer: (1) May I remember the zeal of those against you is as great or greater than those who are for you. (2) Thank you for the wide influence of Paul. May I follow his example. (3) How I need to remember and teach that "man-made gods are no gods at all." (4) Keep me aware the temple of Artemis was one of the seven wonders of the ancient world—how empty is her glory! (5) Help me to discredit false gods of my day. (6) Impress upon me again that the wrath of man does not work the righteousness of God. (7) Give me the zeal and wisdom to know how to reach my generation as Paul reached his.

Right here add your personal requests—and his answers.

10. READ HIS WORD AND WAIT—LISTEN—GOD SPEAKS!

I know you can speak to me in these verses: (1) "You can lead many away from false gods today." (2) "Be careful when you touch men's pocketbooks." (3) "Great is Jesus, King of Glory."

11. INTERCESSION FOR THE LOST WORLD

China — Points for prayer: (1) *Radio* — many hours of programs are beamed into China each day from Cheju, Manila, Guam, etc. Direct contact with people by post is now impossible, so follow-up work, obtaining feed-back on the effectiveness of programs and publicizing the times of programs is very hard. Pray that God may over-rule in this to make these programs as effective as possible, despite these hindrances. Occasional reports do come from tourists and refugees as to the value of these broad-casts. (2) *Christian Tourists* — it is very hard for non-Chinese tourists to enter and meet people, yet Overseas Chinese are now given a very warm welcome, and are permitted to visit relatives. There have been wonderful accounts of such visitors being converted in China on finding their relatives now following the Lord. Other Christians have been used of God to bring encouragement and blessing to their people. Through these Christians a trickle of literature is now going all over China.

12. SING PRAISES TO OUR LORD.

I will sing the wondrous story
Of the Christ who died for me,
How He left His home in glory
For the cross of Calvary.

Yes, I'll sing . . . the wondrous story
Of the Christ . . . who died for me, . . .
Sing it with . . . the saints in glory,
Gathered by . . . the crystal sea.

WEEK TWENTY — SUNDAY

1. PRAISE GOD FOR WHO HE IS.

Beautiful. I'm so glad to have this word to describe yourself! In every way you are beautiful! How many ways shall I describe your beauty? (1) Beautiful in your creative genius. I think of the bud of a red rose—words fail to describe the color, the fragile design, the lovely fragrance. Yet this is only one example of ten thousand that could be produced. (2) Beautiful in your management of history. If beauty is seen in purpose and design, if beauty is seen in infinite patience and unending love, then you are yourself the essence of beauty. (3) Beautiful in your plans for the future—"the land that is fairer than day"—even the brighest of days. Most of us live on the promise of something better and are disappointed when it arrives—not so with you. What beauty I will find in the world to come! It will not be a comparison but a contrast with the anticipations of our wildest imaginations! Bless your name!

Express yourself in adoration for this quality of God.
Speak it audibly or write out your praise in your own devotional journal.

2. PRAISE GOD FOR WHAT HE MEANS TO ME.

Beautiful to me. Your greatest expression of beauty is in your development of your own image in man—in myself. "We all with unveiled face behold in a mirror the character (glory) of yourself (in the Person of your Son) are changed into the same image—or likeness from character to character. This happens from yourself in the Person of the Holy Spirit." (This is a paraphrase of II Cor. 3:18.) This is also a testimony of whatever change has happened in me. I believe the key or the power to this change is in the little word "behold." It is a word of amazement or shock or wonder. It is only when I clear the veils from my face to stand face to face with your Beauty that I am changed. I need to stand mind-to-mind, spirit-to-spirit. I shall always fall down and cry with Isaiah or Peter "depart from me I am an unclean man"—but *I will be changed!*

How do you personally relate to the beauty of God, and God who is Beautiful?
Speak it out or write it out. It is *so important* that you establish *your own* devotional journal.

3. CONFESSION OF SIN

To refuse to live in the presence of beauty—to prefer and choose to live in squalor and dirt. What a loss! Dear Lord, I have made such a tragic choice. But once I see your beautiful self, I shall never be the same. Forgive me for the sin of second best.

"Their glory is their shame." This seems to have sensual overtones, i.e., what we take pleasure in of sexual excesses should really be an embarrassment to us. It could refer to all the money we spent to own this trinket or that, this possession or that. We are proud of it when we should be ashamed of our lust for things. It could refer to where we are on the top of the status pile of people in our little mad scramble. Dear God, in all these areas I repent. I now change my mind and goals. Forgive me and change me.

What personal sins do you want to confess? We *must* speak them to remove them.
Do it! *Now.* There is no one else you have sinned against more than God. Tell him so!

4. SING A PRAYER TO GOD.

Jesus, Lover of my soul,
Let me to Thy bosom fly,
While the nearer waters roll,
While the tempest still is high;

Hide me, O my Savior, hide,
Till the storm of life is past;
Safe into the haven guide,
O receive my soul at last.

Open your hymn book and sing the rest of the verses—or even sing another prayer song.

5. READ HIS WORD TO HIM!

His Word

[29]Soon the whole city was in an uproar. The people seized Gaius and Aristarchus, Paul's traveling companions from Macedonia, and rushed as one man into the theater. [30]Paul wanted to appear before the crowd, but the disciples would not let him. [31]Even some of the officials of the province, friends of Paul, sent him a message begging him not to venture into the theater. — *Acts 19:29-31, NIV*

Read His Word to Him.

What a record of man's vain efforts to defeat your work! I want to share the violence of the crowd with Gaius and Aristarchus. Can I hear them shout the name of Paul? What else are they shouting? I'm sure this incident did not happen in the past on your time table. There is no time with you. This incident is still clear and every man is indentified—all of them are long gone from the earthly scene, but not from your mind or record. Dear Lord, I do gladly share the abuse of men if that will advance your cause. I say this with apprehension—for I know you hear it.

Please express your response to this beautiful text. Put your expression in your own prayer diary.

6. READ HIS WORD FOR YOURSELF.

Paul was ready to give his life if necessary. He was not afraid of the mob. Paul wanted to defend the name of the body of your Son. Paul knew the officials of the province would stand behind his words. Paul had endeared himself to these important men. How? By life and words. Undoubtedly Paul had shared with them in conversation. He had captivated the minds and hearts of these Greeks. Dear Lord, I do want to follow his example. Whom can I influence for my Lord today? Lead me to some life where your light can shine through me! At the same time, help me to remember that sometimes it is not wise to address those who do not want to hear. In Paul's case it is was not even safe.

Pause in his presence and either audibly or in written form tell him all his word means to you.

7. READ HIS WORD IN THANKSGIVING.

(1) Thank you for Gaius and Aristarchus. I confidently expect to meet them and appreciate more fully all they did for our Lord. (2) Thank you for every Christian in Ephesus. What a jarring experience Paul's persecution must have been to them. (3) Thank you for the beautiful letter of Ephesians written to these people. (4) Thank you for the officials of the province who possibly saved Paul's life. (5) Thank you for your wonderful superintending providence that works something good out of this strange circumstance. (6) Thank you for the wonderful archaeological research done in Ephesus which serves to confirm this account by Dr. Luke. (7) Thank you for the confident joy of salvation which no persecution could stop.

Give yourself to your own experience of gratitude—write it or speak it!

8. READ HIS WORD IN MEDITATION.

They "begged him not to venture into the theater." We can almost hear their voices as they pled with the apostle. We can, in our imagination, see them taking hold of Paul and gesturing wildly as they repeated their entreaties. Why did they do this? (1) Paul was a valuable man. His voice must not be silenced by a senseless mob. (2) They had not heard all they wanted to about the Way. Paul must be kept alive long enough to tell them. (3) These men knew the men who opposed Paul, there was no reasoning or meaning to their actions. There was but one motive —money. The people were but pawns of these powerful leaders.

Pause—wait—think—then express yourself in thoughtful praise or thanks.

9. READ HIS WORD FOR PETITIONS.

Two men were seized because they were friends of Paul. Did Paul and others pray for them? We are sure they did. We can find petitions in this incident: (1) How can I arouse the whole city in which I live? (2) May I remember when people are aroused all of them will not be friendly. (3) Keep me aware that men will do almost anything to keep their money. (4) Remind me again that public sentiment is usually wrong. (5) Speak to me in these words—even Paul was not always right in his personal decisions, or is this saying there are several *right* options? (6) Help me to make friends of those with influence. (7) May I remember that one leader is worth many followers.

Please, please remember these are prayers—speak them—reword them!

10. READ HIS WORD AND WAIT—LISTEN—GOD SPEAKS!

You were speaking in various ways in the middle of this confusion: (1) "The whole city can be wrong." (2) "To travel with me will produce a real adventure." (3) "Listen to your friends—they are sometimes right."

11. INTERCESSION FOR THE LOST WORLD

Korea (North) — Population: 16,300,000. Growth rate —2.7%. People per sq. km.—134.

Points for prayer: (1) *The remaining believers* are forced to worship in great secrecy. There are occasional reports of the discovery of a group of believers and their subsequent martyrdom or imprisonment. Pray for these few remaining believers and their witness. (2) *Pray for a change in the attitude of the government* towards believers.

12. SING PRAISES TO OUR LORD.

A Friend I have, called Jesus,
Whose love is strong and true,
And never fails howe'er 'tis tried,
No matter what I do;
I've sinned against this love of His,
But when I knelt to pray,

Confessing all my guilt to Him,
The sin-clouds rolled away.
It's just like Jesus to roll the clouds away,
It's just like Jesus to keep me day by day,
It's just like Jesus all along the way,
It's just like His great love.

WEEK TWENTY — MONDAY

1. PRAISE GOD FOR WHO HE IS.

Teacher. I wonder why I did not think of this name earlier? It is the name often used of your dear Son. All that all men know is from you as their teacher. Oh, how well you do instruct us. Not all who sit in class learn the lesson. Not all who have passed through the classroom called life learn the sweet, dear, beautiful lessons you have to teach them. It is not that you are not teaching; it is but that they are so dull of hearing. What powerful visual aids you use. What an inhaustible textbook you have given us in your word. In it are *all things* that relate to the conduct of this life and the life to come. How long lasting are your lessons! Dear Lord, how I want to learn from you!

Express yourself in adoration for this quality of God.
Speak it audibly or write out your praise in your own devotional journal.

2. PRAISE GOD FOR WHAT HE MEANS TO ME.

Teacher to me! Speak into my deepest consciousness: "Take my yoke upon you and *learn* from me." Only when my head is bowed, and I willingly receive your total Lordship can I really learn anything. Dear God, I am such a slow learner! But you are such a great teacher! I simply revel at the variety and depth of your instruction! Bless your name! I love to trace every word of your book. I see and absorb something new and fresh every day! I confidently expect to keep right on learning from you in the world (classroom?) to come. I am sure there are lessons to learn our poor minds could not even begin to appreciate. Glory, Hallelujah! I am eager to enroll!

How do you personally relate to the teaching of God, and God who is Teacher?
Speak it out or write it out. It is *so important* that you establish *your own* devotional journal.

3. CONFESSION OF SIN

At the same time, I am eager to admit my unwillingness to learn. I know the meaning, but I do not want it! Some of your lessons are in discipline. I "*learn* obedience by the things that I suffer." Am I then different or above my Master "who with *strong cries and tears*" so learned from you? Dear Lord, forgive me! How often do you need to repeat some lessons? Just until you see the truth reproduced in my character. What an infinitely patient teacher you are!

"Hollow philosophy." How could we better chose a sin that relates to you as a teacher? The words of men are empty without nourishment, clouds without water. Forgive me, that I should at any time be impressed with their philosophy of empty pretense.

What personal sins do you want to confess? We *must* speak them to remove them.
Do it! *Now.* There is no one else you have sinned against more than God. Tell him so!

4. SING A PRAYER TO GOD.

'Tis the blessed hour of prayer, when our hearts lowly bend,
And we gather to Jesus, our Saviour and Friend;
If we come to Him in faith, His protection to share,
What a balm for the weary!
O how sweet to be there!

Blessed hour of prayer,
Blessed hour of prayer;
What a balm for the weary!
O how sweet to be there!

Open your hymn book and sing the rest of the verses — or even sing another prayer song.

5. READ HIS WORD TO HIM!
His Word

[32]The assembly was in confusion: Some were shouting one thing, some another. Most of the people did not even know why they were there. [33]The Jews pushed Alexander to the front, and some of the crowd shouted instructions to him. He motioned for silence in order to make a defense before the people. [34]But when they realized he was a Jew, they all shouted in unison for about two hours: "Great is Artemis of the Ephesians!"
— *Acts 19:32-34, NIV*

Read His Word to Him.

How the mob in the theater of Ephesus typifies all mankind in the theater of life. "The assembly was in confusion: some were shouting one thing, some another. Most of the people did not even know why they were there." It is more than interesting that the term "*ecclesia*" is used of this crowd. We are either in your "assembly" or church or we are in the "assembly" or "church" of Demetrius. How true it is that the world is "in confusion." Why? Because one shouts and insists and supports and enforces "one thing" and someone else, something else. Most poor people are like sheep with no shepherd, or truth; with many shepherds who do not themselves know why they are here! Have I represented things as they are? Dear Lord, I want to!

Please express your response to this beautiful text. Put your expression in your own prayer diary.

WEEK TWENTY — MONDAY

6. READ HIS WORD FOR YOURSELF.

We all have at times felt like poor Alexander. He could have said something significant if he had ever been heard! How many men and women have been just like this man? How we would like to have heard them, but because he or she was this or that they were never heard. How more than sad that a confused mob can drown out the voice of one who can make sense out of confusion if he were only given a chance. Alexander only wanted to defend the Jews and exonerate them in the light of the opposition to Paul who was a Jew, but even in this he was never heard. Praise you, oh, praise you that some people are being heard today!

It is so important that you pause in his presence
and either audibly or in written form tell him all his word means to you.

7. READ HIS WORD IN THANKSGIVING.

(1) Thank you for the use of the term "assembly" — translated many times "church" — it lets me know that the church is your "called out ones." (2) Thank you that we need not be in confusion — we *know* why we are here. (3) Thank you for the courage of Alexander. (4) Thank you for the "called out ones" of Ephesus and all they mean to you. (5) Thank you for the cry of the human heart that can never be satisfied with anything but yourself. (6) Thank you for the record which we can follow today. (7) Thank you for the desire to learn and know.

Give yourself to your own expression of gratitude — write it or speak it!

8. READ HIS WORD IN MEDITATION.

"The assembly was in confusion: Some were shouting one thing some another." Isn't this typical of a religious meeting? How sad it is that the followers of Paul have become more like Demetrius than the apostle. Even someone who could offer an explanation is shouted down by the babble of confusion. Is there no answer? Perhaps the answer we want is not what we will get. It could be God has a town clerk ready in the form of international terrorism ready to tell us to settle it in the court of God with His word or prepare for destruction.

Pause — wait — think — then express yourself in thoughtful praise or thanks.

9. READ HIS WORD FOR PETITIONS.

The confusion of the assembly at Ephesus reminds me of some other times and places — at the same time there are areas for prayer: (1) Help me to be used of you to bring meaning out of confusion for a number of assemblies. (2) How tragic that upon this earth there are so many people who do not know why they are here. Help me to help them. (3) How sad are the efforts of men to explain the chaos in which man finds himself — help me to send the light! (4) May I appreciate the difficulties of other people to the extent of being patient with them. (5) Show me more than ever the greatness of my Lord. (6) Open my heart to the deeds of the darkened world in which I live. (7) Deliver me from the blindness of religious form.

Right here add your personal requests — and his answers.

10. READ HIS WORD AND WAIT — LISTEN — GOD SPEAKS!

I am glad to receive messages from Someone who knows the end from the beginning. (1) "The confused assembly represents the needs of men." (2) "There are times when men will not listen." (3) "Let everyone know of my greatness."

11. INTERCESSION FOR THE LOST WORLD

Korea (North) — Points for prayer: (1) *A little literature still enters the land* — these methods are often ingenious: floating little packets in the sea, balloons, the post, etc. Pray that more of the written word may enter this closed land by some means. (2) *Radio* is the only direct way to reach people. Pray for the broadcasts in Korean from stations in South Korea. Pray that people may hear of these programs and start listening in.

12. SING PRAISES TO OUR LORD.

Jesus is all the world to me,
My life, my joy, my all;
He is my strength from day to day,
Without Him I would fall.

When I am sad, to Him I go,
No other one can cheer me so;
When I am sad He makes me glad,
He's my Friend.

WEEK TWENTY — TUESDAY

1. PRAISE GOD FOR WHO HE IS.

Abba (Mk. 14:36; Rom. 8:15; Gal. 4:16). What a lovely, poignant, personal name this is! It is the name used by the Son and the Holy Spirit as they became intimate and very personal in their conversation with you. It is indeed the designation you would like all men to use when addressing you. The household term such as what we mean when we call our father "papa or daddy." How humbling it is to think that you the Almighty Ruler wish to establish a very personal relationship with all men. And when I say "all men" I think of some who would be very poor close-up members of the family. Perhaps an appreciation of yourself would be essential to this expression. Surely a love for you would be an essential prerequisite to calling you "Abba."

Express yourself in adoration for this quality of God.
Speak it audibly or write out your praise in your own devotional journal.

2. PRAISE GOD FOR WHAT HE MEANS TO ME.

"Abba" for me. As I follow your dear Son and my Savior into the garden and see him there prostrate before you and hear him cry "Abba, Father," I am overcome with amazement that you have sent forth the Holy Spirit into my heart to prompt the same cry from me! Oh, I do want to say this word, but I want to mean it. It must come from the warm depths of emotion, but it must come from the knowledgable grasp of your total Being—most of all, it must come (and *does* come) from a spontaneous willingness to establish and hold this intimacy with you! I know you, I want you, I love you—"Abba," Father!

How do you personally relate to the intimate fatherhood of God, and God who is "Abba"?
Speak it out or write it out. It is *so important* that you establish *your own* devotional journal.

3. CONFESSION OF SIN

Whereas the above expression is an open, happy expression of praise and adoration—there are times (too many of them) when I am too involved with other things to sustain or maintain this nearness. Forgive me! I am the loser. I can think of times when I was totally immersed in a project and my earthly father dropped in all unexpected—I looked into his dear face—and all my childhood attachments flooded back and in a surprised and delighted tone, I said: "Daddy"! or "Dad"! Dear God, break through to-day—surprise me often!

"Tradition for truth." Tradition is good and precious but when it contradicts truth it must be changed! A tradition is a habit repeated so often in a meaningful environment that it becomes a part of our emotional nature. We all have them—is our Savior a part of them? Does God have a place in them? Is the Holy Spirit welcome? Dear Lord, help me to establish new traditions for myself and my children.

What personal sins do you want to confess? We *must* speak them to remove them.
Do it! *Now.* There is no one else you have sinned against more than God. Tell him so!

4. SING A PRAYER TO GOD.

I am trusting Thee, Lord Jesus!
Trusting only Thee!

Trusting Thee for full salvation,
Great and free.

Open your hymn book and sing the rest of the verses—or even sing another prayer song.

5. READ HIS WORD TO HIM!

His Word

[35]The city clerk quieted the crowd and said: "Men of Ephesus, doesn't all the world know that the city of Ephesus is the guardian of the temple of the great Artemis and of her image, which fell from heaven? [36]Therefore, since these facts are undeniable, you ought to be quiet and not do anything rash. [37]You have brought these men here, though they have neither robbed temples nor blasphemed our goddess. [38]If, then, Demetrius and his fellow craftsmen have a grievance against anybody, the courts are open and there are proconsuls. They can press charges. [39]If there is anything further you want to bring up, it must be settled in a legal assembly. [40]As it is, we are in danger of being charged with rioting because of today's events. In that case we would not be able to account for this commotion, since there is no reason for it." [41]After he had said this, he dismissed the assembly.

20 When the uproar had ended, Paul sent for the disciples and, after encouraging them, said good-by and set out for Macedonia. [2]He traveled through that area, speaking many words of encouragement to the people.

— Acts 19:35 — 20:2a, NIV

Read His Word to Him.

How gladly do I enter into this experience! We can hear the word of the city clerk all over again! Did he really believe what he said? Wasn't he only repeating what he knew men expected and wanted to hear? Do we do the same today with no more power with you than he had? The temple of Diana was indeed one of the wonders of the world of that day. How absurd that claim must have sounded to you!

Please express your response to this beautiful text. Put your expression in your own prayer diary.

6. READ HIS WORD FOR YOURSELF.

"The courts are open." Indeed they are! The courts of this world, as recorded in human history, are open. I want to be one of the "proconsuls" for the case of Paul and his friends. Let the record show that the "goodness from heaven" is in every way far superior to Artemis who supposedly fell from heaven. Indeed the myth of Artemis is but a distortion of the truth. Someone *did* come from heaven of his own choice—but it wasn't Artemis.

Either audibly or in written form tell him all his word means to you.

7. READ HIS WORD IN THANKSGIVING.

There is indeed so much in this text for which we can thank you. (1) Thank you for "law and order," i.e., the ministers of yourself in government. (2) Thank you for the strong desire of man to worship. (3) Thank you for the wisdom you gave to the city clerk. (4) Thank you for Gaius and Aristachus—the released hostages. (5) Thank you for the honesty of this man—there really were no charges against Paul. (6) Thank you for the dedication of Paul who let nothing stop him from his purpose of preaching.

Give yourself to your own expression of gratitude—write it or speak it!

8. READ HIS WORD IN MEDITATION.

". . . speaking many words of encouragement to the people." I wonder just what thoughts were in these words. We can surely find an answer in Paul's letters to some of these very churches. He could have spoken as he wrote: "Therefore, my dear friends, as you have always obeyed —not only in my presence, but now much more in my absence—continue to work out your salvation with fear and trembling, for it is God who works in you to will and to act according to his good purpose" (Philippians 2:12, 13). Or he could have said, "Be joyful always; pray continually, give thanks in all circumstances, for this is God's will for you in Christ Jesus" (I Thessalonians 5:16ff.).

Pause—wait—think—then express yourself in thoughtful praise or thanks.

9. READ HIS WORD FOR PETITIONS.

In the words of the city clerk, there are areas for prayer: (1) Move me to make it true that all the world knows who Jesus is—at least to do my part. (2) Grant me the wisdom I need to quiet the chaos in the hearts of those to whom I speak. (3) Keep me responsible as your spokes-man. (4) May I be ready if today you call me to give an account before your judgment seat. (5) Protect me from the wrath of unreasonable men. (6) Dear Lord, help me to have words of encouragement—men need this so much. (7) Move me to Paul's kind of compassionate concern.

Please, please remember these are prayers—speak them—reword them!

10. READ HIS WORD AND WAIT—LISTEN—GOD SPEAKS!

What a great work Paul did in Ephesus! Speak to me from it: (1) "I have persons through whom I work that you could not even imagine." (2) "There is a time to leave a field of service." (3) "Even Paul was so burdened he could not speak—read II Corinthians 2:11, 12."

11. INTERCESSION FOR THE LOST WORLD

Mongolia — Population: 1,500,000. Growth rate 3.0%. People per sq. km.—one.

Points for prayer: (1) *There has never been permanent missionary work in the land.* Pray that this land may somehow be opened for the Gospel. (2) *There are no copies of the old translation of Mongolian Bible* still circulating. It is almost impossible to get new Bibles into the land from the free world.

12. SING PRAISES TO OUR LORD.

I will sing of my Redeemer,
And His wondrous love to me;
On the cruel cross He suffered,
From the curse to set me free.

Sing, oh, sing . . . of my Redeemer,
With His blood . . . He purchased me, . . .
On the cross . . . He sealed my pardon,
Paid the debt, . . . and made me free.

WEEK TWENTY — WEDNESDAY

1. PRAISE GOD FOR WHO HE IS.

Holy Father (John 17:11). I have worshiped you as both Holy and Father. But now I want as much as at all possible to approach you as your Son did (how presumptuous of me). For all men you want to be the heavenly Parent. Dear God, how can this be? It *could* happen in any generation. It could have happened in any past generation. The simple mathematics of each-one-win-one soon reaches every person on earth. It has been shown to me that in the same length of time your dear Son lived upon this earth all men could be told of your love for them.

You are not "holy" in the sense of being unapproachable — "holy" only in the sense of being gloriously different — but full of love and personal concern for every man.

Express yourself in adoration for this quality of God.
Speak it audibly or write out your praise in your own devotional journal.

2. PRAISE GOD FOR WHAT HE MEANS TO ME.

"Holy Father" for me. Jesus, my wonderful Lord, had such a concern for his "sent ones" and for all men through the twelve. He must have brought each of the apostles by name and need before you — each one was so important to him. I am not an apostle, but I am important to you. I believe if I were the sole resident of this earth, you would send your Son to save me! Dear Father, Holy Father, I cannot say with your Son, "I have accomplished the work you have sent me to do" — or can I? As much as my poor ignorance and weakness will permit I am trying to fulfill your work for me. Dear Lord, as much as in me is I want to set you apart in my heart as worthy of all praise and love.

How do you personally relate to the holiness of God, and God who is our Holy Father?
Speak it out or write it out. It is *so important* that you establish *your own* devotional journal.

3. CONFESSION OF SIN

Dear Lord, I have mixed up your two wonderful qualities — at times I have been drawn to you as my Father — at other times I am ashamed to speak because you are holy. I never thought before of embarrassing you as "Holy Father" — what a soul-purifying experience! I feel so very often like the prodigal from the pig sty, full of the smell of the hog waller. "I am not worthy to be called your son," but I come for I do need you and love you.

"False humility." I need to read this sin every day. I honestly do not know when I am false or true. When I want to be humble I express it in pride of one form or another. I pause just now to get a good look at my own heart. I'm surely glad for the "best robe" in your house. The red robe of the righteousness of your Son! Praise your name!

What personal sins do you want to confess? We *must* speak them to remove them.
Do it! *Now.* There is no one else you have sinned against more than God. Tell him so!

4. SING A PRAYER TO GOD.

Jesus, Savior, pilot me
Over life's tempestuous sea;
Unknown waves before me roll,
Hiding rock and treacherous shoal;
Chart and compass come from Thee:
Jesus, Savior, pilot me.

Open your hymn book and sing the rest of the verses — or even sing another prayer song.

5. READ HIS WORD TO HIM!

His Word

[2]He traveled through that area, speaking many words of encouragement to the people, and finally arrived in Greece, [3]where he stayed three months. Because the Jews made a plot against him just as he was about to sail for Syria, he decided to go back through Macedonia.

— *Acts 20:2-3, NIV*

Read also II Cor. 7:5-7; Rom. 1:7-11,15; Gal. 1:1-5.

Read His Word to Him.

How wonderfully good it is to worship you through your word! How glad I am to read that Paul's body was not Paul. He said, ". . . this body of ours" as if it were an eternal possession — which indeed it is! Paul was not the body — it was his possession. You did not protect Paul from harassment. Indeed he had *much* harassment! I wonder who gave Paul so much trouble, so much conflict? We know it was those of Macedonia — i.e., those of Thessalonica, Philippi and Berea. These are the cities of Macedonia mentioned by Luke. There could have been others. How is it that Paul had "fears" on the inside? Are we right in thinking that Paul was downcast? I thought he rejoiced all the time! I am so glad to be able to put these two factors together. Thank you. It was like this: The substrata of Paul's heart was "joy in the Lord" — on the upper levels of life he did indeed have fears, harassment — he was indeed downcast but underneath were the everlasting arms of an all-knowing and all-powerful God.

Please express your response to this beautiful text. Put your expression in your own prayer diary.

6. READ HIS WORD FOR YOURSELF.

I read this word for my own heart! You can and do comfort me by other servants of yourself! In this case it was Titus—in my case it has been so many dear people. Titus had been to Corinth. What news he had to give to Paul: (1) "Your affection," i.e., the deep emotional involvement of Paul had good results. (2) "Your deep sorrow," i.e., over the sins Paul had rebuked in person and in his letter to the Corinthians was being received. (3) "Your ardent concern for me," is not unnoticed. Why are we so afraid of emotional involvement with other people? The Corinthians (and they were people with names and faces) were weeping and praying and talking about Paul. In return Paul expressed great joy!

It is so important that you pause in his presence
and either audibly or in written form tell him all his word means to you.

7. READ HIS WORD IN THANKSGIVING.

(1) Thank you for Paul's three-month stay in Corinth — which was in the country of Greece. How sad that we have so little work among the Greeks today. (2) Thank you for the beautiful letter Paul wrote to the Romans — what a wonderful reputation the saints in Rome had. (3) Thank you for Paul's personal concern over people he had never seen. (4) Thank you for Paul's powerful example of prayer. (5) Thank you for my rescue from this present evil age. (6) Thank you for the One who gave himself for my sins. (7) Thank you for the eagerness of Paul to preach the gospel.

Give yourself to your own expression of gratitude—write it or speak it!

8. READ HIS WORD IN MEDITATION.

". . . speaking many words of encouragement to the people. . . ." It should be noticed that this was the common practice of Paul. Paul knew as we need to remember that words of encouragement are what we look for more than any other expression. No wonder Luke says he spoke many words of encouragement. It is easy to find fault—it takes real love and creativity to find something good to say. In the hour of his great trial, just before our Lord went out to face Gethsemane, he said, "Be of good cheer, I have overcome the world. . . ."

Pause—wait—think—then express yourself in thoughtful praise or thanks.

9. READ HIS WORD FOR PETITIONS.

Reading the record of Paul's troubles and travels is a real help to me. (1) Thank you for the example of someone who gave himself for your cause. (2) Teach me that being a Christian does not deliver me from harassment. (3) If Paul had conflicts and fears and overcame them—I can too. (4) Give me a fellow servant like Titus. (5) Help me to appreciate all over again the power of your word. (6) May I remember my relationship to you: (a) beloved; (b) called "a holy one"; (c) "an anointed one." (7) Rescue me from this present evil age.

Right here add your personal requests—and his answers.

10. READ HIS WORD AND WAIT—LISTEN—GOD SPEAKS!

I know there is much you can say to me from these verses: (1) "I am the One who comforts the downcast." (2) "Talk to others, I can comfort you through them." (3) "You can be my comfort to someone today."

11. INTERCESSION FOR THE LOST WORLD

Korea (North) — Point for prayer: (1) There are two small groups of Mongolian believers in the free world—in Hong Kong and Taiwan—and they are the only source for new programs broadcast by TEAM from Korea and FEBC, Manila. Pray for this valuable radio ministry—one of the few means at present of reaching this unevangelized nation.

12. SING PRAISES TO OUR LORD.

When my lifework is ended, and I cross the swelling tide,
When the bright and glorious morning I shall see;
I shall know my Redeemer when I reach the other side,
And His smile will be the first to welcome me.

I shall know . . . Him, I shall know Him,
And redeemed by His side I shall stand,
I shall know . . . Him, I shall know Him
By the print of the nails in His hand.

WEEK TWENTY — THURSDAY

1. PRAISE GOD FOR WHO HE IS.

King of Glory (Psa. 24:7, 10). A name for my Lord, but one applied also to yourself! I am so much drawn to this beautiful description of your very self! That you are king of all—the ruler of absolute dimension is without question, but to associate such a quality with the word "glory" is more than interesting. "Glory" refers to *"character"* or essential being, so this is tantamount to saying,

"King of Character." "Glory" does refer to brightness or light, but such is only the reflection of your essential being. You are the sum and substance of all beautiful, fulfilling character qualities. *The King of Love, The King of Mercy, The King of Grace, The King of Peace*—How delightful to worship and bow as a glad slave of the King of Glory! Hallowed be your name!

Express yourself in adoration for this quality of God.
Speak it audibly or write out your praise in your own devotional journal.

2. PRAISE GOD FOR WHAT HE MEANS TO ME.

King of Glory to me! What I have just said could and should be said by all men—and I offer it up to you as representative of what I so fervently hope will one day be the expression of every man here on earth. Now, just now, I want to attempt to express some of the deep amazement I feel when I try to say with true meaning "King of Glory"!

That you are the absolute of *kindness*—thoughtful consideration on a grand scale! I see this so often in the life of Your Dear Self in the Person of your Son. He took little children upon his lap to lay his hands upon them and to pray for them. He made them feel so important because to him they were! How kind!

How do you personally relate to the glory of God, and God who is King of Glory?
Speak it out or write it out. It is *so important* that you establish *your own* devotional journal.

3. CONFESSION OF SIN

How could it be? We occupy the throne with Him! We are co-regent kings of glory ourselves. This fact brings a confession of sad failure! I am hardly the example of patience or compassion. Dear Lord, I *want* to be! I can be! I want to lay down my poor broken tools. Dear God, forgive. Grant grace to use the set of new ones. Blessed Lord, I do want to be a ruler in the realm of love and glory.

"Worship of angels." I do not relate to this except when I think of angels or "messengers" and I have been guilty of giving far more credit to some of your messengers than they deserved. All adoration and adulation goes to you. "Why fasten you your eyes on us? as though we through our godliness or power had made him to walk"? Look to God not to us.

What personal sins do you want to confess? We *must* speak them to remove them.
Do it! *Now.* There is no one else you have sinned against more than God. Tell him so!

4. SING A PRAYER TO GOD.

Lead, kindly Light, amid th' encircling gloom,
Lead Thou me on!
The night is dark, and I am far from home;

Lead Thou me on!
Keep Thou my feet; I do not ask to see . . .
The distant scene; one step enough for me.

Open your hymn book and sing the rest of the verses—or even sing another prayer song.

5. READ HIS WORD TO HIM!

His Word

[4]He was accompanied by Sopater son of Pyrrhus from Berea, Aristarchus and Secundus from Thessalonica, Gaius from Derbe, Timothy also, and from the province of Asia Tychicus and Trophimus. [5]These men went on ahead and waited for us at Troas. [6]But we sailed from Philippi after the Feast of Unleavened Bread, and five days later joined the others at Troas, where we stayed seven days.

[7]On the first day of the week we came together to break bread. Paul spoke to the people and, because he intended to leave the next day, kept on talking until midnight.
— *Acts 20:4-9a, NIV*

Read His Word to Him.

Gladly I do this! Why are there seven men with Paul? We learn from Romans 15:22-32 that the men were representatives from the churches who gave to the poverty stricken Christians in Judea. Perhaps the dear men were carrying the money so as to protect Paul from robbers and disgruntled church members. Is this true, dear Father? I am probably wrong in even thinking it. Forgive me.

How I do want to meet these seven men. I can add Luke, for he joins the group in Macedonia. Why does Luke mention the number of days involved? Perhaps to help us to appreciate his reference to "the first day of the week." Was the "breaking of the bread" just the supper of your Son? Or did it include a larger meal along with the supper?

Please express your response to this beautiful text. Put your expression in your own prayer diary.

WEEK TWENTY — THURSDAY

6. READ HIS WORD FOR YOURSELF.

There is much for me to learn here: Speak to me! (1) Paul wanted companionship and joint effort in his work. Do I want to "do it myself"? Why? There are: Sopater, Aristarchus, Secundus, Gaius, Timothy, Tychicus, Trophimus and Luke who are eager to help — will I deny them this privilege? (2) Paul traveled much or "was in journeys often" because men live in many parts of this world — do I begrudge travel to reach men? (3) Paul "preached" to whom? Was this room full of people all non-Christians? Not if they met for the Lord's supper; but he *is* preaching. Is then preaching to sinners and teaching to Christians? *Answer!* (4) The "lamps" evidently had something to do with the drowsiness of Eutychus — also the long sermon of Paul! Even Paul did not hold everyone's attention forever.

It is so important that you pause in his presence
and either audibly or in written form tell him all his word means to you.

7. READ HIS WORD IN THANKSGIVING.

(1) Thank you for the first day of the week when we can come together to break bread — but help me to remember that this was in a home and could have included more than the Lord's (my Lord's) Supper. (2) Thank you for Paul's preaching — a grand example for me. (3) Thank you for "Lucky" or "Fortunate" or "Eutychus" — his "luck" was your blessing. (4) Thank you for the humanness of this record — real people in a real circumstance. (5) Thank you so much for the "ring of truth" in the account — it reads like what it is: an account of an eyewitness. (6) Thank you for everyone who gathered on that memorable day. I want to meet each one of them. (7) Thank you for the dedication of Paul in putting real importance on the spoken word.

Give yourself to your own expression of gratitude — write it or speak it!

8. READ HIS WORD IN MEDITATION.

"Paul talked on and on." Indeed he did — how long was it? Perhaps it was supper time when they met. It would seem an appropriate time of the day to have the Lord's supper. Did they have a love feast with the table of the Lord? The honest answer is: *"We do not know."* Even if they did perhaps Paul could begin speaking at 8 p.m. — if so he had now been speaking for four hours. I'm sure there was much more to hear — and all of it very important, but then he was interrupted. Eutychus fell out of the window! Perhaps the stuffiness of the air and not the stuffiness of the preacher produced this response. Luke is careful to tell us of the many lamps in that upstairs room.

Pause — wait — think — then express yourself in thoughtful praise or thanks.

9. READ HIS WORD FOR PETITIONS.

In the journeys and words of Paul there is much to pray about. (1) From my reading of Romans 15:22-32 I see the need to protect the investment of other people in your work. (2) Thank you for Luke, Paul's biographer — may I be like him. (3) Open my mind as to the real meaning of meeting on the first day of the week. (4) I am so glad I can read many of the words of Paul today — no doubt much the same that he spoke that day in Troas. (5) Did they wait seven days for the special day of meeting? I want to follow their example. (6) The name "Eutychus" means "fortunate" — may I remember where all "good luck" comes from.

Please, please remember these are prayers — speak them — reword them!

10. READ HIS WORD AND WAIT — LISTEN — GOD SPEAKS!

No doubt Eutychus wanted to know what he missed in your message through Paul. (1) "Spiritual sleep is more dangerous than the sleep of 'Lucky.'" (2) "I still keep my promise to break the bread with you in my kingdom." (3) "Paul still speaks to us today — listen."

11. INTERCESSION FOR THE LOST WORLD

Laos — Population: 3,400,000. Growth rate 2.4%. People per sq. km. — 13.
Point for prayer: (1) *The Laotian people* are under the iron heel of Communism. The whole nation is being forcibly indoctrinated in Communism, with even Christians being compelled to lead indoctrination classes. Few of the people have believed in the Lord Jesus. Pray that somehow these people may be able to hear the Gospel.

12. SING PRAISES TO OUR LORD.

O could I speak the matchless worth,
O could I sound the glories forth
Which in my Savior shine,
I'd soar and touch the heav'nly string,
And vie with Gabriel while he sings
In notes almost divine,
In notes almost divine.

WEEK TWENTY — FRIDAY

1. PRAISE GOD FOR WHO HE IS.

Most high (Deut. 32:8). The words of Moses become my words, dear Father! In a thousands ways you are "most high" in this world that owes its total existence to you. You are exalted above the heaven of heavens in the physical world—"the third heaven" is associated with your presence or "dwelling place." Dear Lord, I believe that just on the other side of my last heart beat I will discover just how small this little planet is—just how removed from this infinitesimal speck you truly are. But when I consider the works of your fingers in this world, you are held up on high before me! How exalted is your knowledge! How great is your strength! How incalculable your planning!

Express yourself in adoration for this quality of God.
Speak it audibly or write out your praise in your own devotional journal.

2. PRAISE GOD FOR WHAT HE MEANS TO ME.

Most high for me! Blessed Lord, I will praise you in several areas of life: (1) You are the most-high in personal care. How very much does my dear wife care for me. How concerned are our children. I receive concerned care from Christian friends. But none of them could or would do anything without you. You supply the means and the motive for all such care. Beyond people is the fact that my body is healthy, my mind is functional, my clothes are adequate. Dear God, I gladly acknowledge that you are the exalted source for all these things. Indeed, I want to hold you up before my eyes as the One in whom I live and move and have my very being.

How do you personally relate to the exaltation of God, and God who is Most-High?
Speak it out or write it out. It is *so important* that you establish *your own* devotional journal.

3. CONFESSION OF SIN

That you should be any less than the most-high God, the Exalted-One, is in itself the epitome of sin. How I do want to see you in all I do—to worship you amid your creation, to commune with you within myself, to praise you in song with the rest of your children. That I should ever live as do the beasts of the field who cannot know you is the sin of all sins. Speak to me, awaken me that I might praise you!

"Carnality." How can it be that we will take the senses you gave us to express our worship to you and use them to mock and deny you? When the instrument becomes the end instead of the means we are terribly deceived. I am guilty; forgive and wash me clean!

What personal sins do you want to confess? We *must* speak them to remove them.
Do it! *Now*. There is no one else you have sinned against more than God. Tell him so!

4. SING A PRAYER TO GOD.

I gave My life for thee,
My precious blood I shed,
That thou might'st ransomed be,
And quickened from the dead;

I gave, I gave My life for thee,
What hast thou giv'n for Me?
I gave, I gave My life for thee,
What hast thou giv'n for Me?

Open your hymn book and sing the rest of the verses—or even sing another prayer song.

5. READ HIS WORD FOR HIM.

His Word

[9]Seated in a window was a young man named Eutychus, who was sinking into a deep sleep as Paul talked on and on. When he was sound alseep, he fell to the ground from the third story and was picked up dead. [10]Paul went down, threw himself on the young man and put his arms around him. "Don't be alarmed," he said. "He's alive!"
— *Acts 20:9, 10, NIV*

Read His Word to Him.

It does seem incongruous sometimes to read your word back to you. If, however, you caused this word to be written and I believe you did, then such a practice would be welcome however poorly done. Such is my persuasion. Dear Lord, I shall only ask you to help me as I comment on each phrase of these two verses. How clearly does Luke describe this incident! I can see the young man totally relaxed and in a deep sleep. How often I have dreamed of falling only to find I was sleeping too close to the edge of the bed. I imagine you are thinking that so many young and old will one day fall into the bottomless pit. It will be a terrible dream and reality with no end. *"He fell to the ground from the third story."* Did Eutychus awaken on the way down? I can't imagine he did not. What terror must have filled his total being! Is hell like falling forever? Is hell like the darkness of the darkest night? Is hell the second death? I know it is! Dear God, how can I be so casual about it?

Please express your response to this beautiful text. Put your expression in your own prayer diary.

6. READ HIS WORD FOR YOURSELF.

"... *and was picked up dead.*" Who picked him up? His mother and father? We do not know. Was he a Christian? If he wasn't we are sure he became one after this incident. Perhaps many others did too, although Luke says nothing about it. Paul interrupted his message to meet a real human need. Paul was very much involved — *"he threw himself on the young man."* This seems like a drastic way to act. But then the situation is drastic! What am I doing about those who have fallen to their death in trespasses and sins? Am I about to rush out and throw myself on these people? Oh, for the glad word! "Don't be alarmed." "He's alive." So many need first to awaken in the midst of their fall before they realize what is happening to them.

It is so important that you pause in his presence
and either audibly or in written form tell him all his word means to you.

7. READ HIS WORD IN THANKSGIVING.

(1) Thank you for sleep — it is such a blessing. (2) Thank you for awakening me to the desperate needs of men. (3) Thank you for the record of love in action as seen with Paul and Eutychus. (4) Thank you for the concern of others who shared the shock of Eutychus' fall. (5) Thank you for the comforting words of Paul, backed up with the power of God. (6) Thank you for the strong confirmation this miracle gave to Paul's work. (7) Thank you that young men who fall to their spiritual death can be raised today by the same One who raised Eutychus.

Give yourself to your own expression of gratitude — write it or speak it!

8. READ HIS WORD IN MEDITATION.

"Don't be alarmed, he's alive." I wonder what happened to Eutychus in the days and years that followed Paul's visit. Did he really appreciate his resurrection? We could answer this question in several possible ways. The more important question is what has happened to any one of us since we have been raised from death in trespasses and sins? (1) Did Eutychus explain away the miraculous element in his experience? No doubt someone in Troas told a similar story of someone else with no miracle connected. Any time we want to we can offer a humanistic explanation for the power of God. (2) Did Eutychus recognize the gift of life God gave him and use it for God's glory? We like to believe he did. We can know we should!

Pause — wait — think — then express yourself in thoughtful praise or thanks.

9. READ HIS WORD FOR PETITIONS.

Could there be two more dramatic verses than those in 20:9, 10? In them we can find prayer petitions: (1) Wake us up to the reality of the deadly danger of closing the eyes of our heart. (2) Move me away from a too-close-to-the-edge mentality on all issues of morality. (3) Help me to remember that hell is described as falling into a bottomless pit. (4) May I remember that all of us Christians should be named Eutychus or "Fortunate," i.e., considering our fall into sin and death. (5) Open my eyes on the way down that I might appreciate what power there is in my being raised from my own neglect. (6) Thank you for Paul's willingness to get involved in the lives of those who were hurting. (7) Thank you for the obvious supernatural power at work in the life of Paul.

Right here add your personal requests — and his answers.

10. READ HIS WORD AND WAIT — LISTEN — GOD SPEAKS!

This is a desperate situation — speak to me through it: (1) "Even Paul did not hold everyone's attention." (2) "Paul was concerned personally with everyone." (3) "There are several things worse than physical death."

11. INTERCESSION FOR THE LOST WORLD

Laos — Point for prayer: (1) *The Protestant Church* among the Lao has been weak, lacking in effective leadership and largely illiterate. The rate of backsliding has been high. Converts were generally from the socially rejected elements of society. Humanly speaking, this Church has little chance of surviving the onslaught of Communism. Pray that the fires of persecution may refine the small company of believers into an effective soul-winning force. Many of the strongest leaders have had to flee for their lives.

12. SING PRAISES TO OUR LORD.

O for a thousand tongues to sing
My great Redeemer's praise,

The glories of my God and King,
The triumphs of His grace.

WEEK TWENTY — SATURDAY

1. PRAISE GOD FOR WHO HE IS.

Heavenly Father (Matt. 6:26, 32). This is a delightful designation: "Our Father who is in heaven" is the beginning of my Lord's prayer to you—it surely means more than just a designation of where you are. You are "of heaven, heavenly," i.e., all of heaven in essence. Heaven must be a wonderful place or shall we say "state" or "condition,"—but your Son did say "I go to prepare a *place*" for you. He did call it your house or "abiding place." I do want to as much as at all possible appreciate heaven—for I plan on being with you there—as Jesus said "where I am (and you are) there you will be also." How can I possibly enter fully into a real awareness of where you are? It is not that you are removed in time and space near as much as that you are "other than" in every area of my thinking—this causes me to praise you even more!

Express yourself in adoration for this quality of God.
Speak it audibly or write out your praise in your own devotional journal.

2. PRAISE GOD FOR WHAT HE MEANS TO ME.

"Our Father who is in heaven" or "heavenly Father" for me. Perhaps you want me to apply all I know about heaven to my life today—yea, Lord, I gladly do this: (a) "He (you) have *prepared for them a city*" (Heb. 11:16) the new Jerusalem—you and your Son have been working on the preparation of this city for 2,000 years. Or is it even now all ready for me, and all the redeemed? (b) "I shall sit down at a banquet table—the marriage supper of your Lamb—with Abraham, Isaac and Jacob" (Matt. 8:11). (c) I shall share in "a great multitude no man can number of all the nations, tribes, peoples, and languages." I shall stand with them before your throne and before your Son. I shall have on a white robe and I shall carry a palm branch in my hand (Rev. 7:9).

How do you personally relate to the heavenly nature of God, and God who is Heavenly Father?
Speak it out or write it out. It is *so important* that you establish *your own* devotional journal.

3. CONFESSION OF SIN

How often was my mind and heart in heaven yesterday?—or will it be today? Since I believe there is a most glorious experience just on the other side of my last heart beat, should not this thought enter and re-enter my consciousness during this day? Since my real citizenship is in heaven shouldn't I have more than idle curiosity about this country? In all the above ways I have sinned! I have *not* thought about heaven—my mind has *not* been on "the things above where my blessed Lord is seated at your right hand." Dear God, forgive me—I am the loser.

"*Malice*." What an awful sin this is! The cause of the first murder—it blinds us to the light. The cause for the plot against many who loved our Lord: Daniel, Mordecai, John the Baptist and our Lord himself. Dear God, remind me to what ends hatred can lead!

What personal sins do you want to confess? We *must* speak them to remove them.
Do it! *Now.* There is no one else you have sinned against more than God. Tell him so!

4. SING A PRAYER TO GOD.

Will your anchor hold in the storms of life,
When the clouds unfold their wings of strife?
When the strong tides lift, and the cables strain,
Will your anchor drift, or firm remain?

We have an anchor that keeps the soul
Steadfast and sure while the billows roll,
Fastened to the Rock which cannot move,
Grounded firm and deep in the Savior's love.

Open your hymn book and sing the rest of the verses—or even sing another prayer song.

5. READ HIS WORD TO HIM.

His Word

[11] Then he went upstairs again and broke bread and ate. After talking until daylight, he left. [12] The people took the young man home alive and were greatly comforted.

[13] We went on ahead to the ship and sailed for Assos, where we were going to take Paul aboard. He had made this arrangement because he was going there on foot. [14] When he met us at Assos, we took him aboard and went on to Mitylene. [15] The next day we set sail from there and arrived off Chios. The day after that we crossed over to Samos, and on the following day arrived at Miletus. [16] Paul had decided to sail past Ephesus to avoid spending time in the province of Asia, for he was in a hurry to reach Jerusalem, if possible, by the day of Pentecost.
— *Acts 20:11-16, NIV*

WEEK TWENTY — SATURDAY

Read His Word to Him.

How good to share again with yourself and Paul. Paul took "a break" in the middle of the night, i.e., sometime after twelve o'clock. I wonder what went through his mind as he broke the bread and ate it? Was he thinking of "the young man"? From the fact that he walked the eight or ten miles from Troas to Assos after talking all night, we believe he must have had much on his mind. He was gathering an offering and perhaps he was concerned over this. It was eight to twelve hours of talking. I know how exhausted he was.

Please express your response to this beautiful text. Put your expression in your own prayer diary.

6. READ HIS WORD FOR YOURSELF.

How much of what Paul said in the all-night marathon of talking could be remembered by those gathered? Luke remembers that it happened. If it was not a help, it would not have been done. How greatly comforted were the friends of Eutychus! Are there friends and loved ones here in this town who would rejoice greatly if someone was raised up to live? Indeed they would! This record is all so accurate and believable!

Either audibly or in written form tell him all his word means to you.

7. READ HIS WORD IN THANKSGIVING.

(1) Thank you for the unselfish attitude of Paul in teaching others. (2) Thank you for the "new day" Eutychus faced because of Paul—because of yourself! (3) Thank you for the caring, sharing fellowship of believers in Troas. (4) Thank you for the example of Paul in meditation and prayer. (5) Thank you for Dr. Luke and his devotion to writing—we would have nothing of this record without him.

Give yourself to your own expression of gratitude—write it or speak it!

8. READ HIS WORD IN MEDITATION.

". . . he was in a hurry to reach Jerusalem, if possible, by the day of Pentecost." Why all this urgency? We learn from Romans 15:22-32 that he was intent on helping the poor Christians in Judea—and especially Jerusalem. Paul had been appointed—by the need and his love and ability to be a one-man committee (the best kind) to gather funds from the churches to help these people. He was very, very concerned that his generosity be received and accomplish its purpose. But perhaps the largest concern he had was with those who would misunderstand his motives. Most of the "bounty" or money came from Gentiles. Was there ever such an act of unselfish love? But there were areas of this circumstance that Paul did not know how to interpret.

Pause—wait—think—then express yourself in thoughtful praise or thanks.

9. READ HIS WORD FOR PETITIONS.

On Paul's journey he must have prayed often—we can share in some of those prayers: (1) Help me to say something when I speak for you. (2) Comfort is such a large part of the experience of your servants. I want to communicate this today. (3) Paul's emphasis was teaching—not healing—so make it mine. (4) Thank you for Dr. Luke —give me such a fellow servant. (5) Why did Paul walk from Troas to Assos? Was it meditation and prayer of the promises of suffering at Jerusalem? (6) Keep me aware that you are present in the very physical action of moving from one port to the next. (7) Give me the humble determination to spread your word that filled the life of Paul.

Please, please remember these are prayers—speak them—reword them!

10. READ HIS WORD AND WAIT—LISTEN—GOD SPEAKS!

In this moving scene of life speak to me: (1) "Paul worked with people who did not always agree with him." (2) "Please keep your priorities in order—it is sometimes better to sail past than to stop."

11. INTERCESSION FOR THE LOST WORLD

Laos — Point for prayer: (1) *Most of the Christians in the country* are among the Meo where there has been a great turning to the Lord. The New Testament in two dialects was ready just in time for distribution before the Communists came. Pray for this suffering people who have proved a hated thorn in the flesh to the Communists and are therefore in great danger now. Many Meo have fled to Thailand, where 10% of them are Christians.

12. SING PRAISES TO OUR LORD.

O Word of God incarnate,
O Wisdom from on high,
O Truth unchanged, unchanging,
O Light of our dark sky;

We praise Thee for the radiance
That from the hallowed page,
A lantern to our footsteps,
Shines on from age to age.

WEEK TWENTY-ONE — SUNDAY

1. PRAISE GOD FOR WHO HE IS.

True (John 3:33. "God is truthful."). How very good to approach you this day as the very essence of truth. Truth is that which is equal to reality — that which matches facts. How secure we can feel when we know we worship the original source of all truth — of all that is reality! All you say in the two books of which you are author, i.e., nature and the Bible — is totally equal to fact or it is truth. There are several obvious messages from the world all about us: (1) You have no problem with details — you produce millions, even trillions of them. (2) You speak in the same way at the same time under the same conditions each time. Uniformity is one constant message. (3) Check and balance — or plan and purpose are built into your handiwork.

Express yourself in adoration for this quality of God.
Speak it audibly or write out your praise in your own devotional journal.

2. PRAISE GOD FOR WHAT HE MEANS TO ME.

True for me! When you speak you speak truth — for *"Thy word is truth."* — indeed your name is *Truth.* How comforting and restful it is to open up and read a book with no error — "no shadow cast by turning," you speak to me and dear Lord I want to hear. I open your book to read: "Now these things occurred as examples (or types), and keep us from setting our hearts on evil things as they did" (I Cor. 10:6). The whole panorama of your message in the five books of Moses was to show us — teach us — speak to us — by models that what gets our thought, will, affection, gets our hearts. Whatever it is that receives much of my time in the above areas is my god. Dear God, I want to think your thoughts — will your will — feel your emotions and thus give you my heart.

How do you personally relate to the truth of God, and God who is True?
Speak it out or write it out. It is *so important* that you establish *your own* devotional journal.

3. CONFESSION OF SIN

You have been so true with me — you have always done what you said you would. How fickle I have been! Forgive me. I know you desire truth in the inward man. I want this also! My basic struggle is to match my conduct with what I know is right — true — fact. How easily I am deceived — forgive me — cleanse me — but renew my mind.

"Slander." This is lying about another with the intention of hurting them. Dear Lord, I have been tempted and I have sinned in this area — make me see how terrible this sin is! If you wanted to you could speak truth fully about the failures of my life — you forgive — may I love like you do and forgive as I have been forgiven.

What sins do you want to confess? We *must* speak them to remove them.
Do it! *Now.* There is no one else you have sinned against more than God. Tell him so!

4. SING A PRAYER TO GOD.

Lord, speak to me, that I may speak
In living echoes of Thy tone;

As Thou hast sought, so let me seek
Thy erring children lost and lone.

Open your hymn book and sing the rest of the verses — or even sing another prayer song.

5. READ HIS WORD TO HIM!

His Word

[17]From Miletus, Paul sent to Ephesus for the elders of the church. [18]When they arrived, he said to them: "You know how I lived the whole time I was with you, from the first day I came into the province of Asia. [19]I served the Lord with great humility and with tears, although I was severely tested by the plots of the Jews. [20]You know that I have not hesitated to preach anything that would be helpful to you but have taught you publicly and from house to house. [21]I have declared to both Jews and Greeks that they must turn to God in repentance and have faith in our Lord Jesus.

[22]"And now, compelled by the Spirit, I am going to Jerusalem, not knowing what will happen to me there.
— *Acts 20:17-22, NIV*

Read His Word to Him.

It is indeed with joy I approach an attempt to empathize with you on this text. Perhaps I could become one of the elders. (I am asking questions because I know you alone have the answers — perhaps somehow you will help me to know.) Do I have one or more of the supernatural gifts listed in Rom. 12:6-8 and I Cor. 12:9-11? I cannot see how I could function without them. If this is true why do I need instruction from Paul? There must be something I do not know about the operation of these gifts. Perhaps it is to learn from his example how best to use what I have. His example is one marvelous testimony: (1) He was the same every day. (2) He served with great humility — (How could he say it and still be humble?).

Please express your response to this beautiful text. Put your expression in your own prayer diary.

WEEK TWENTY-ONE — SUNDAY

6. READ HIS WORD FOR YOURSELF.

I am very much attracted by the little phrase "with tears." What made Paul cry? Here is a possible list: (a) The hard-hearted Jews. (b) The total ignorance of the Gentiles. (c) The misunderstanding of Christians. (d) His own weakness and sins. (e) The lack of spiritual-mindedness. What makes me cry? Or do I cry at all? Paul was severely tested by plots of the Jews. (What do I have to worry about compared with Paul?) It would seem there were two sets of Jews in the plotting business—the Jews who hated Paul and the Jews who loved Paul. The added element was yourself on the side of Paul.

Once again Paul is talking about preaching to Christians—the elders and others—his preaching consisted of helpful information for the Christian life—not the gospel of salvation. This is Paul the preacher—I'm glad to follow his example. When did Paul teach publicly and from house to house? Was this when he first came and declared to both Jews and Greeks that they must turn to God? Is Paul describing his work in Ephesus with both the saved and the lost? We believe he is.

It is so important that you pause in his presence and either audibly or in written form tell him all his word means to you.

7. READ HIS WORD IN THANKSGIVING.

(1) Thank you for the ability to constantly change my mind in relation to God and man. (2) Thank you for the faith, confidence, trust, I can have and do have in my Lord Jesus. (3) Thank you for the element of surprise found in the leading of the Holy Spirit. (4) Thank you for the bold humility of Paul's preaching. (5) Thank you for the example of house-to-house teaching. (6) Thank you for the example of public teaching. (7) Thank you for the ability to change my mind, to renew my mind, to cleanse my mind, to love with my mind.

Give yourself to your own expression of gratitude—write it or speak it!

8. READ HIS WORD IN MEDITATION.

". . . compelled by the Spirit, I am going to Jerusalem, not knowing what will happen to me there." Compelled by the Spirit is such an intriguing thought! Wouldn't we all like to have such a nearness and direction from the Spirit? There are several factors here to consider: (1) Paul was totally involved in the work of the Lord when the Spirit compelled him. The Holy Spirit worked amid the circumstances. (2) The Holy Spirit spoke through men to tell Paul some of the things that awaited him—the Holy Spirit did not move in a vacuum. (3) In spite of the fact that Paul had the direct operation of the Holy Spirit on his spirit he did not know everything that would befall him. He was given a sense of foreboding, but no details of just what the bonds and afflictions would be.

Pause—wait—think—then express yourself in thoughtful praise or thanks.

9. READ HIS WORD FOR PETITIONS.

How much there is about which we can pray in Paul's words to the Ephesian elders: (1) May I have as much concern for the elders with whom I work. (2) Give me the compassion for the flock that leads me to help the shepherds. (3) Dear Lord, how I need humility. (4) How can I serve you "with tears"? (5) Give me the same program of public and private teaching that characterized Paul. (6) Whom did Paul teach publicly and from house to house? I want to do the same. (7) Give me true repentance that I might share it with others.

Right here add your personal requests—and his answers.

10. READ HIS WORD AND WAIT—LISTEN—GOD SPEAKS!

Speak to me through the words of Paul: (1) "It is possible to live and work like Paul." (2) "You need more humility and many more tears." (3) "Even Paul did not know all the will of God all the time."

11. INTERCESSION FOR THE LOST WORLD

Laos — Point for prayer: (1) About half the believers and Christian leaders have fled to Thailand, and there are many large refugee camps in N.E. Thailand with a high proportion of believers. Pray for the preachers ministering to these uprooted people, and that this tragedy may lead to strong churches developing among the 50,000 Laotian refugees. Pray for the relief and spiritual work of missionaries among these people, and the resettlement of believers in areas useful for witness.

12. SING PRAISES TO OUR LORD.

There is a name I love to hear,
I love to sing its worth;
It sounds like music in mine ear,
The sweetest name on earth.

Oh, how I love Jesus,
Oh, how I love Jesus,
Oh, how I love Jesus,
Because He first loved me!

WEEK TWENTY-ONE — MONDAY

1. PRAISE GOD FOR WHO HE IS.

Ishi (salutary—Hosea 2:16, 17). This is a strange name for yourself, but you yourself chose it. As contrasted with Baal is this name Ishi. The new name means "husband," as compared with Baal which means "master." How wonderfully good it is to call you "husband"—indeed, indeed, I want to be married to you—all men should be, and could

be your bride. I want to be as attractive as possible to please such a marvelous groom—without spot or wrinkle or any such thing. How comforting to know I can live with you and you with me. I consider myself as but representative of all men.

Express yourself in adoration for this quality of God.
Speak it audibly or write out your praise in your own devotional journal.

2. PRAISE GOD FOR WHAT HE MEANS TO ME.

Ishi for me. I do not want to be allured by any other. Baal is but an ancient name for Satan—he operates in the three areas of man's needs: flesh, eyes, and pride or body, things and status. You tell me to control, not indulge the flesh; to use "things," not to be used by them;

to find my importance or status in you. Dear Lord, wonderful husband, I want to obey you. Because I have found your word to match with reality and your competitor a liar!

How do you personally relate to being married to God, and God who is Ishi?
Speak it out or write it out. It is *so important* that you establish *your own* devotional journal.

3. CONFESSION OF SIN

That I so often say one thing and do another is a mystery to me. There is something strange—ethereal (i.e., of the spirit world). At the same time, I feel totally responsible for my sin—my seeking fulfillment in "an affair" with Satan. No satisfaction beyond the moment in flesh—eyes or pride. Dear God, forgive me!

"Harshness." How well this does fit me! I am unhappy with myself and others suffer the harsh consequences—I am as hard and harsh with others as I feel toward myself. The answer is loving you—accepting your acceptance of me, and loving others. Forgive me, dear Lord!

What personal sins do you want to confess? We *must* speak them to remove them.
Do it! *Now.* There is no one else you have sinned against more than God. Tell him so!

4. SING A PRAYER TO GOD.

Sweetly, Lord, have we heard Thee calling,
"Come, follow Me!"
And we see where Thy footprints falling

Lead us to Thee.
Footprints of Jesus, that make the pathway glow!
We will follow the steps of Jesus where'er they go.

Open your hymn book and sing the rest of the verses—or even sing another prayer song.

5. READ HIS WORD TO HIM!

His Word

[23]I only know that in every city the Holy Spirit warns me that prison and hardships are facing me. [24]However, I consider my life worth nothing to me, if only I may finish the race and complete the task the Lord Jesus has given me—the task of testifying to the gospel of God's grace.

[25]"Now I know that none of you among whom I have gone about preaching the kingdom will ever see me again. [26]Therefore, I declare to you today that I am innocent of the blood of all men. [27]For I have not hesitated to proclaim to you the whole will of God. [28]Guard yourselves and all the flock of which the Holy Spirit has made you overseers. Be shepherds of the church of God, which he bought with his own blood. [29]I know that after I leave, savage wolves will come in among you and will not spare the flock. [30]Even from your own number men will arise

and distort the truth in order to draw away disciples after them. [31]So be on your guard! Remember that for three years I never stopped warning each of you night and day with tears.

[32]"Now I commit you to God and to the word of his grace, which can build you up and give you an inheritance among all those who are sanctified. [33]I have not coveted anyone's silver or gold or clothing. [34]You yourselves know that these hands of mine have supplied my own needs and the needs of my companions. [35]In everything I did, I showed you that by this kind of hard work we must help the weak, remembering the words the Lord Jesus himself said: 'It is more blessed to give than to receive.'"

— *Acts 20:23-35, NIV*

Please express your response to this beautiful text. Put your expression in your own prayer diary.

6. READ HIS WORD FOR YOURSELF.

How shall I rid myself of the blood of all men in Joplin? I must get to every house and tell them of your rule in the heart! Have I ever hesitated in telling to some people some things from your word? You know I have—forgive me. I do not need boldness near as much as deep compassion! How I need to guard myself, protect myself—my only real protection is in your word, in your love, in your presence. I am *not* a shepherd. He substituted as one until God could raise up, through Paul's teaching and preaching, true "pastors" of the flock. Paul's task is mine—to teach and preach the gospel of the Kingdom! Dear God, I hear it—speak it again—I have obstructions. "The church of God, which he purchased with his own blood."

Pause in his presence and either audibly or in written form tell him all his word means to you.

7. READ HIS WORD IN THANKSGIVING.

Oh, thank you—(1) For your warning that there *are* savage wolves who can hurt the flock. (2) For the warning that defection and distortion can happen anywhere. Jealousy and pride are such deceitful sins. (3) Men following me is a sin—thank you for saying it so plainly! (4) For the tremendous example of Paul—three years—night and day with tears—how could it be? I'm shocked! I'm rebuked! (5) Thank you that I never will know all the depth and power of your word—the word of your grace—but, oh, how it does build me up! (6) Thank you for my inheritance among the sanctified—what does that mean? Jesus is both my inheritance and my sanctification. (7) Thank you for the hand work in manual labor—it was commended and done by both my Lord and Paul.

Give yourself to your own expression of gratitude—write it or speak it!

8. READ HIS WORD IN MEDITATION.

"*. . . help the weak, remembering the words of the Lord Jesus: It is more blessed to give than to receive.*" I wonder who "the weak" were in Ephesus? Is this reference to those who did not have the means to support Paul and therefore were weak financially? Was Paul saying that those who were destitute were helped financially by his labor? i.e., he bought their meals and clothes? This seems to be close to the thought since he applies the words of our Lord to the circumstance. "It is more blessed to give than to receive." The facts are: Paul's companions did not have a gainful occupation they could use in Ephesus; they therefore lived from Paul's efforts. What an example Paul is to all of us! Paul did his work without complaining.

Pause—wait—think—then express yourself in thoughtful praise or thanks.

9. READ HIS WORD FOR PETITIONS.

How poignantly and personally do the words of Paul call me to prayer: (1) May I consider my life and its value by Paul's estimate. (2) Lord, may I finish the race of the Christian life. (3) May I complete the task of testifying to the gospel of God's grace. (4) Free me from the blood of those among whom I live—open my mouth to make it so. (5) Awaken me that I might guard myself. (6) Dear Lord, help me to communicate Paul's words to today's shepherds and overseers. (6) Impress deeply upon my heart these words: "*. . . the church of God, which he bought with his own blood.*" (7) May I in every way I can "be on guard."

Please, please remember these are prayers—speak them—reword them!

10. READ HIS WORD AND WAIT—LISTEN—GOD SPEAKS!

Speak to me in verses 31-35: (1) "Warn men night and day with tears." (2) "Supply your own needs if necessary to continue preaching." (3) "Remember, it *is* more blessed to give than to receive."

11. INTERCESSION FOR THE LOST WORLD

Laos — Point for prayer: (1) *The persecution of the believers in Laos* is building up in intensity. All land, buildings, crops and livestock have been nationalized, and there is starvation. A very close watch is kept on Christians, though services are still continuing in two churches, all others having been closed. Many young people have been drafted into the army and some pastors are in prison. Pray for these harassed believers. All evangelism is now strictly forbidden. The two Bible Schools are closed.

12. SING PRAISES TO OUR LORD.

Praise Him! praise Him! Jesus, our blessed Redeemer!
Sing, O Earth, His wonderful love proclaim!
Hail Him! hail Him! highest archangels in glory;
Strength and honor give to His holy name!

Like a shepherd, Jesus will guard His children,
In His arms He carries them all day long:
Praise Him! praise Him! tell of His excellent greatness;
Praise Him! praise Him! ever in joyful song!

1. PRAISE GOD FOR WHO HE IS.

Elohim—the plural form of "mighty." Used when you are contrasted with men or things. How exceedingly interesting to worship you in the plural. But plural in the form of might! I am now looking at a photograph of the *Trifid Nebula* in Sagittarius as taken by an Australian astronomer, D. F. Malin. Millions and millions—hundreds of millions of miles from the infinitesimal speck called "earth." What is all the opposition of man to an intelligent Spirit Being who has created the expanse of ten million galaxies? But there are three such Divine Beings—all sharing the same nature. I am indeed nonplused by the concept! I can only stand or fall in mute amazement!

Express yourself in adoration for this quality of God.
Speak it audibly or write out your praise in your own devotional journal.

2. PRAISE GOD FOR WHAT HE MEANS TO ME.

Elohim to me. Surely you are mighty beyond my poor human comprehension. At the same time, I am full of excitement in a desire to explore the ramifications of such worship. (1) Shall I think of you as three gigantic computers with equal infinite capacity? Of course the obvious question is: "Who is the programmer?" The simple answer is: You owe your programming to yourself. Man (myself) cannot understand such a concept. You would not be Elohim in intelligence if we could. (2) Shall I think of you as three great permeating, pervasive Spirit intelligences into which we can tune through faith and prayer? No, no. I shall think and worship you as three wonderful Persons found in your book, the Bible—Father, Son and Holy Spirit.

How do you personally relate to the mighty power of God, and God who is Elohim?
Speak it out or write it out. It is *so important* that you establish *your own* devotional journal.

3. CONFESSION OF SIN

Dear Lord, I have sinned against each of the three Divine Beings—the One true God. (1) I have sinned against my Savior for he has found me *in* my sin—but because I have been unwilling he has not saved me "from" my sin. (2) I have grieved, quenched, resisted and insulted the blessed Holy Spirit. (3) Dear God, dear Elohim, forgive me!

"Idleness"—this does not refer to inactivity, but to apathy toward worship and service. For this sin, forgive me!

What personal sins do you want to confess? We *must* speak them to remove them.
Do it! *Now.* There is no one else you have sinned against more than God. Tell him so!

4. SING A PRAYER TO GOD.

More about Jesus would I know,
More of His grace to others show;
More of His saving fullness see,
More of His love who died for me.

More, more about Jesus,
More, more about Jesus;
More of His saving fullness see,
More of His love who died for me.

Open your hymn book and sing the rest of the verses—or even sing another prayer song.

5. READ HIS WORD TO HIM!

His Word

[36]When he had said this, he knelt down with all of them and prayed. [37]They all wept as they embraced him and kissed him. [38]What grieved them most was his statement that they would never see his face again. Then they accompanied him to the ship.

21 After we had torn ourselves away from them, we put out to sea and sailed straight to Cos. The next day we went to Rhodes and from there to Patara. [2]We found a ship crossing over to Phoenicia, went on board and set sail. [3]After sighting Cyprus and passing to the south of it, we sailed on to Syria. We landed at Tyre, where our ship was to unload its cargo.

— *Acts 20:36—21:3, NIV*

Read His Word to Him.

Luke is an eyewitness to what is happening here. I want to be. I know you were and are! How did you see them as they knelt in prayer? As children in need of the Father's care and love? As sheep in the midst of wolves? How did you (how do you?) react to the tears and embraces? Your own dear Son shed tears—and many more than we know—one inspired writer says, "with many tears" (Heb. 5:7). How very close—how very emotionally identified were these men with Paul and he with them. How open and honest he was with them! Oh, speak this into my hard heart! How did Paul know he would never see these dear leaders again? Did you tell him? Didn't he expect to see them in heaven? Didn't he visit Ephesus after his first Roman imprisonment (I Tim. 1:3)? I ask because I do not know.

Please express your response to this beautiful text. Put your expression in your own prayer diary.

6. READ HIS WORD FOR YOURSELF.

How often do I kneel and pray with the leaders with whom I meet? There are surely times when I have no assurance that such men will see my face again or I theirs. The problem is (as far as comparison goes), I have not established with any set of elders such a close relationship that there would be such a spontaneous response of deep concern. Dear Lord, forgive me! There are elders with whom deep friendship exists, but not as deep as seen here! Let me not say that it is a cultural practice, or unnecessary. How will I learn if I do? It is so easy to use such rationalizing to eliminate anything that makes me uncomfortable because I judge others by my own motives. Forgive me and move me into the same tearful relationships my Lord had with his apostles.

It is so important that you pause in his presence
and either audibly or in written form tell him all his word means to you.

7. READ HIS WORD IN THANKSGIVING.

Indeed I shall! (1) Thank you for the loving fellowship Paul established with those with whom he worked. (2) Thank you for prayer—individually and collectively—what a boon to the weary! What solace and strength and direction we receive! (3) Thank you for all the various expressions of love and concern we have for each other. (4) Thank you for the *strong* tie of mutual effort in your service. (5) Thank you that those we do not see here we shall see over there. (6) Thank you for the beautiful example of Paul's commitment to the larger service—not only at Ephesus but also to Jerusalem and Rome. (7) Thank you for the completely accurate record of Luke's treatise.

Give yourself to your own expression of gratitude—write it or speak it!

8. READ HIS WORD IN MEDITATION.

"After we had torn ourselves away from them." What a tie of mutual interest and respect had developed between Paul and the elders from Ephesus! Indeed, such nearness and love was shared by Luke. We could think of the person or persons with whom we have developed a mutual interest and respect. Think of one who has gone out of his way to help you; who has stayed up nights when you were sick; who took a real interest in those things that were of interest to you. Have we ever established such nearness with someone that we could hardly think of their not being with us? Such was the love Paul had with them. Somehow such love and fellowship has been lost in our impersonal society.

Pause—wait—think—then express yourself in thoughtful praise or thanks.

9. READ HIS WORD FOR PETITIONS.

Paul's closing words to the elders move me to prayer: (1) I wonder just what the prayers were as they knelt upon the beach?—Perhaps: "Give Paul and his company your grace in travel." (2) Perhaps: "Guard our hearts that we fulfill your purpose in us." (3) Perhaps: "Keep us faithful that we might see Paul in the Father's house." (4) Perhaps: "Deliver Paul from unreasonable men." (5) Help me to have as much personal involvement with those with whom I work as Paul did. (6) Teach me to love others as my Lord loved me. (7) Give me the grace to believe you are at work in *all* circumstances of life.

Right here add your personal requests—and his answers.

10. READ HIS WORD AND WAIT—LISTEN—GOD SPEAKS!

Speak to me in these few verses: (1) "Prayer does help in every situation." (2) "Tears are the language of the heart." (3) "Close association is typical of my Son and his disciples—of Paul and his disciples."

11. INTERCESSION FOR THE LOST WORLD

Laos — Points for prayer: (1) *The many tribes* of the country are largely unevangelized. Missionaries were able to do a little evangelism between 1957 and 1961 before Communist incursions made it too dangerous. Some of these people were won for the Lord in refugee camps subsequently. Only among the Khamu (100,000), Ngeq (50,000) and Nyaheun (15,000) are there churches. Pray for the unreached tribes—only a few have anything of God's Word. These tribes alone total 700,000 people. Some may have escaped to Thailand. (2) *There were only about 10 believers* among the Vietnamese, and 150 among the Chinese in 1975. Pray that these people may be evangelized.

12. SING PRAISES TO OUR LORD.

We praise Thee, O God! for the Son of Thy love,
For Jesus who died, and is now gone above.
Hallelujah! Thine the Glory;

Hallelujah! Amen.
Hallelujah! Thine the glory;
Revive us again.

WEEK TWENTY-ONE — WEDNESDAY

1. PRAISE GOD FOR WHO HE IS.

From everlasting to everlasting (Gen. 21:33; Psa. 90:2). How beautiful a description this is of yourself! There never has been a time when you did not exist. The concept of infinity simply steps beyond the powers of our poor minds. In the eons of eternity, before this world existed, before there was an Adam and Eve, before there was one angel, you were even as you are now and even as you will ever be. Dear Father, this quality of yourself says several things to me. (1) You have the experience of millenniums of time to prepare you (Is that the right word?) for any and all experiences I will have.

Express yourself in adoration for this quality of God.
Speak it audibly or write out your praise in your own devotional journal.

2. PRAISE GOD FOR WHAT HE MEANS TO ME.

Everlasting to everlasting for me. (2) There never will be a time when you are not there. You will be present for every emergency — for every hard question — for every personal need, you are "always there" as perfect Person. (3) One day I will graduate from this school into the eternal realm where you have lived and are living and will live. I will live there with you and your dear Son and the blessed Holy Spirit. There I will understand so much more of what is only seen now dimly. (4) Praise somehow seems inadequate in your presence. But it is essentially all I have. I raise my whole heart to you!

How do you personally relate to the timelessness of God, and God who is from "Everlasting to Everlasting"?
Speak it out or write it out. It is *so important* that you establish *your own* devotional journal.

3. CONFESSION OF SIN

To fail to recognize your greatness is a sin of gigantic proportion. How sad it is for me to limit your eternal value to the time-frame of my own understanding. Dear everlasting Father: forgive me for not truly knowing you! Dear God, open my eyes. Cleanse my heart. Somehow I want to stand with Isaiah and see your total character fill the whole house of the world in which we live! *"Wrong for wrong."* Who gave us this concept? The law — the principle of equalness. Do you return wrong (i.e., punishment or hurt) for wrong? No, no, no, we would all be in torment this minute if you did. Can we not give to others what you have given to us?

What personal sins do you want to confess? We *must* speak them to remove them.
Do it! *Now.* There is no one else you have sinned against more than God. Tell him so!

4. SING A PRAYER TO GOD.

My hope is built on nothing less
Than Jesus' blood and righteousness;
I dare not trust the sweetest frame,
But wholly lean on Jesus' name.

On Christ, the solid Rock, I stand;
All other ground is sinking sand,
All other ground is sinking sand.

Open your hymn book and sing the rest of the verses — or even sing another prayer song.

5. READ HIS WORD TO HIM!

His Word

[4]Finding the disciples there, we stayed with them seven days. Through the Spirit they urged Paul not to go on to Jerusalem. [5]But when our time was up, we left and continued on our way. All the disciples and their wives and children accompanied us out of the city, and there on the beach we knelt to pray. [6]After saying good-by to each other, we went aboard the ship, and they returned home.
— *Acts 21:4-6, NIV*

Read His Word to Him.

How good to find learners at Tyre! Who were they? You know them — every one. How many other disciples have been at Tyre? Are there any there today? I ask these questions only to identify with the text. Seven days is enough time to know people rather well. How was it that "the disciples" "through the Spirit" urged Paul "not to go to Jerusalem" and the same spirit "compelled" him to go? Thank you — I know the answer: It was the disciples' reaction to the "bonds and afflictions" that awaited Paul in Jerusalem. Paul's reaction to "prison and hardships" was, "I consider my life worth nothing" as compared to the value of his work of teaching and preaching your rule among men. How wonderfully poignant is the scene on the beach! How I would like to hear the prayers! You have and do. Is not the record of all good kept? Perhaps I can one day hear them!

Please express your response to this beautiful text. Put your expression in your own prayer diary.

WEEK TWENTY-ONE — WEDNESDAY

6. READ HIS WORD FOR YOURSELF.

Yes, yes—where is the spontaneous personal interest in your Son and his work? How good to see the spread of your word over the length and breadth of the land of promise. How do I react to negative messages from the Holy Spirit? He has spoken very bluntly in his word: "Let *nothing* be done through envy or strife." "Count each one better than youself." "Speak not evil of one another." The reaction of Paul to personal harm needs to be my reaction to an assault on my ego! My life is of no value as compared to the value of your rule in the hearts of men beginning with my heart!

It is so important that you pause in his presence
and either audibly or in written form tell him all his word means to you.

7. READ HIS WORD IN THANKSGIVING.

(1) Thank you for the beautiful oneness described in the association of Paul and the Christians at Tyre. (2) Thank you for the whole families who are involved in Paul's visit—all Paul said related to the whole family. (3) Thank you for the kneeling in prayer—perhaps they learned this from our blessed Lord. (4) Thank you for the tearful parting—so encouraging to see such love. (5) Thank you for Luke's poignant words, ". . . and they returned home." (6) Thank you for the preservation of this record even until our day. (7) Thank you that I can find and have found people with the same unselfish love and interest.

Give yourself to your own expression of gratitude—write it or speak it!

8. READ HIS WORD IN MEDITATION.

"All the disciples and their wives and children accompanied us out of the city." The personalness of this record convinces us of its reality—especially when we know we are reading something nineteen hundred years old! The manuscripts of 350 A.D. give us a document over 1600 years old. What are the possibilities that men of the second or the third century fictionalized such an account? The details are too many and too accurate and too causal to be anything but the account of an eyewitness! There are other lines of evidence, but this needs to be said. I'm glad to say it! The whole family was reached for our Lord. How many disciples were there in Tyre? Perhaps we should ask, "How many family units were reached for our Lord?" The Holy Spirit lived in each member and spoke through some of them. The supernatural knowledge that Paul was to endure imprisonment and mistreatment at Jerusalem made them want to be with him as long as at all possible. I confidently expect to meet each one of these disciples and ask many more details than we have here.

Pause—wait—think—then express yourself in thoughtful praise or thanks.

9. READ HIS WORD FOR PETITIONS.

Paul's journey to Jerusalem was beset with warnings. He must have been often in prayer: (1) In the seven days at Tyre I wonder what was discussed? Perhaps: "Use Paul's witness to change hearts." (2) Grant me the same commitment to your will amid those who unwittingly wish to deter me. (3) May the tender love of family sharing be a part of my service. (4) Teach me how to share in personal public prayer. (5) Dr. Luke knew it was "through the Holy Spirit" that Paul was warned. How did Luke know this? (6) Help me to be willing to prefer traveling to "home" if others can know of my Lord. (7) May prayer mean more to me than ever before.

Please, please remember these are prayers—speak them—reword them!

10. READ HIS WORD AND WAIT—LISTEN—GOD SPEAKS!

In these three verses are three things you want to say to me: (1) "Disciples are 'learners'—are you a disciple?" (2) "The Holy Spirit is still directing the body of my Son." (3) "Pray with others—all of you will be blessed."

11. INTERCESSION FOR THE LOST WORLD

Laos — Point for prayer: (1) *There are now daily broadcasts* from Manila. There are few radios in the land and these are closely watched by the Communists. There is little electric power and batteries are almost unobtainable. Pray that despite this, many may hear the Word by this means.

12. SING PRAISES TO OUR LORD.

The great Physician now is near,
The sympathizing Jesus;
He speaks the drooping heart to cheer,
Oh, hear the voice of Jesus.

Sweetest note in seraph song,
Sweetest name on mortal tongue;
Sweetest carol ever sung,
Jesus, blessed Jesus.

WEEK TWENTY-ONE — THURSDAY

1. PRAISE GOD FOR WHO HE IS.

El - The Strong One. Our Lord used such a name on the cross when he said, "My God, my God," and Eloi, Eloi — *"My Strength, My Strength"* is a part of the same name. Dear Father, how glad I am to honor you as "the *strength* of my life." But you are "the strength" of the life of the whole world — and all that in it is. Is this the same as saying you are the sum source of "energy" or the "dynamic" of all life? I believe it is! Wonder of all wonders! Oh, *praise and amazement* does not at all adequately express my deep appreciation of your Person. How I need such inward reinforcements.

Express yourself in adoration for this quality of God.
Speak it audibly or write out your praise in your own devotional journal.

2. PRAISE GOD FOR WHAT HE MEANS TO ME.

The Strong One for me. Oh, that all the energy you have given to me for every task over all these many years might be attributed to the right source — it is not my strength or cleverness, not my inventive genius, but you, you are the true *Source* — the real power to will and to do. Praise your name forever! How profound is the thought that you are in truth the Intelligent Power or energy behind all that lives — indeed behind all that is animate or inanimate! Why should I *ever* doubt that *you are able to do* far abundantly *above anything* that I ask or think? *Not* for my glory — Dear God, deliver me from this, but for recognition of "El" — the Strong One!

How do you personally relate to the strength of God, and God who is "El" — the Strong One?
Speak it out or write it out. It is *so important* that you establish *your own* devotional journal.

3. CONFESSION OF SIN

How sad to say I have leaned upon the strength of "the flesh" which is so totally undependable. One day my body is rested and strong, the next weak and dull. Does this relate to you? Have you lost your strength? I act and speak and even think as if you have. Oh, it is sin, sin! Forgive me! Dear Lord, I need so very much to be able to pause in the midst of discouragement and identify the Source of my strength. Will you please help me to do it?

"Grieving the Holy Spirit." How unique! What greater sin against the blessed Holy One than to try to lift the weight of life in our own strength when *The Strength* of all the world awaits? He is grieved by my trusting in the arm of the flesh. Forgive me!

What personal sins do you want to confess? We *must* speak them to remove them.
Do it! *Now.* There is no one else you have sinned against more than God. Tell him so!

4. SING A PRAYER TO GOD.

A wonderful Savior is Jesus my Lord,
A wonderful Savior to me,
He hideth my soul in the cleft of the rock,
Where rivers of pleasure I see.
He hideth my soul in the cleft of the rock

That shadows a dry, thirsty land;
He hideth my life in the depths of His love,
And covers me there with His hand,
And covers me there with His hand.

Open your hymn book and sing the rest of the verses — or even sing another prayer song.

5. READ HIS WORD TO HIM!

His Word

[7]We continued our voyage from Tyre and landed at Ptolemais, where we greeted the brothers and stayed with them for a day. [8]Leaving the next day, we reached Caesarea and stayed at the house of Philip the evangelist, one of the Seven. [9]He had four unmarried daughters who had the gift of prophecy.
— *Acts 21:7-9, NIV*

Read His Word to Him.

What a beautiful visit! To stay a whole day at Ptolemais — on what day of the week was it? How many brothers were there? From whom did these men hear the good news? Once again, I'm only asking to get the flavor of the text as you already see the whole. I'm only looking into a very small part of the whole. What was discussed during the day with "the brothers" at Ptolemais? I can make up answers for each question, but I will await your full revelation. Oh, to be in Caesarea in 56 A.D.! How I long to accompany Luke and all the others as a visitor in the house of Philip the evangelist! Wouldn't it be wonderful to be introduced to Philip's gifted daughters? Indeed it would! Philip was one who heralded forth the glad tidings. But where did he get his information? Did he depend on "hearsay," i.e., what others could remember and told him? I think not! He shared the gift his daughters possessed. The Holy Spirit equipped him with information and miracles for accreditation. Have I read it right? Dear Lord, you know.

Please express your response to this beautiful text. Put your expression in your own prayer diary.

6. READ HIS WORD FOR YOURSELF.

How many people did Philip reach as he lived and labored in Caesarea? It has been a long time since we read in Acts 8:40 "Philip . . . preached the gospel in all the towns (of the plain of Sharon) until he reached Caesarea." It has been several years. How many? 10? 15? 20? 25? It has been at least 15 years. What has he been doing in this important seaport since he arrived? If his name is an indication of his work — and we believe it is — he has been preaching to the residents of this city and through Christians to others in the district. How did Philip, the evangelist, acquire a home? To whom did his daughters prophesy? Why were they unmarried? How intriguing are all these questions! How much I wish I knew the answers to them. We *can* say with confidence: (1) Philip did own a home — "the house of Philip." (2) His daughters did express their gift to those for whom it was intended.

It is so important that you pause in his presence
and either audibly or in written form tell him all his word means to you.

7. READ HIS WORD IN THANKSGIVING.

(1) Thank you for every unknown brother and sister who love you as I do. (2) Thank you for the accuracy of Luke's account that can be checked even today. (3) Thank you for Philip — such a faithful, consistent man. (4) Thank you for the warm, unqualified hospitality extended to Paul wherever he went. (5) Thank you for each of the daughters of Philip — I wish I knew their names — such a good testimony. (6) Thank you for Philip's unnamed wife — a real essential part of this team. (7) Thank you for the Spiritual gifts that equipped the church at Caesarea.

Give yourself to your own expression of gratitude — write it or speak it!

8. READ HIS WORD IN MEDITATION.

". . . four unmarried daughters who had the gift of prophecy." How we would like to know more about these girls. Here are some things we *can* know about them: (1) They were sorely needed inasmuch as there was no New Testament. The church was built upon "the apostles and prophets" (prophetess), Ephesians 2:20. The sum total of divine direction through teaching came from this source. (2) They were the literal fulfillment of prophecy. When Peter predicted through Joel "your sons and your daughters shall prophesy" (Acts 2:17-19), these are some of those who fulfilled the prophecy of these last days. (3) They were very likely not alone — in many congregations of the Roman empire there were other young women — or older women who had this ability.

Pause — wait — think — then express yourself in thoughtful praise or thanks.

9. READ HIS WORD FOR PETITIONS.

Tyre, Ptolemais and Caesarea are all such interesting places. Are there prayer requests in these verses? (1) May my first interest in any place be the salvation of the lost. (2) Teach me from the total lack of Christians in these places just how important it is to teach your word to every generation. (3) Dear Lord, help all who believe to be One. (4) How I would like to know just how Philip's daughters obtained the gift of prophecy. (5) Just whom did these daughters teach? (6) May I follow the example of Philip the evangelist — just where did he evangelize? (7) Why had Philip stayed in Caesarea for such a long time (cf. 8:40)? I confidently expect an answer to these requests in the study of your word.

Right here add your personal requests — and his answers.

10. READ HIS WORD AND WAIT — LISTEN — GOD SPEAKS!

Speak to me: (1) "If Paul could be friendly to those who were unfriendly, so can you." (2) "Many labor for me that you do not know or appreciate." (3) "Women have much to teach us in so many ways."

11. INTERCESSION FOR THE LOST WORLD

Vietnam — Population: 46,400,000. Growth rate 2.2%. Point for prayer: (1) *Missionary work in the land has ended.* There were 280 missionaries serving in 1974. Pray for these servants of God as they settle in other ministries and other lands.

12. SING PRAISES TO OUR LORD.

I have found a friend in Jesus,
He's everything to me,
He's the fairest of ten thousand to my soul;
The Lily of the Valley, in Him alone I see
All I need to cleanse and make me fully whole.

In sorrow He's my comfort, in trouble He's my stay,
He tells me every care on Him to roll:
He's the Lily of the Valley, the Bright and Morning Star,
He's the fairest of ten thousand to my soul.

WEEK TWENTY-ONE — FRIDAY

1. PRAISE GOD FOR WHO HE IS.

Elah or Eloah — The Adorable One (Ezra 4:24). You are not only the One God wholly worthy of our adoration, but you have such attractive attributes that adoring you is a spontaneous response of our hearts. Since all men and all women are but a faint reflection of yourself, we can find the most attractice person we could imagine and multiply their beauty ten thousand times and we would have but a hazy representation of your adorable self! If we would imagine a super generous benefactor who would give us gift after gift of both practical and divine value, and then enlarge immeasurably the generosity and thoughtfulness of such a Giver, it would be yourself! Surely you have merited all the love of all men!

Express yourself in adoration for this quality of God.
Speak it audibly or write out your praise in your own devotional journal.

2. PRAISE GOD FOR WHAT HE MEANS TO ME.

Elah or Eloah — "Adorable One" for me! Dear Father, I have indeed found you more than worthy of all my adoration. How can I say I love you? What I have told those I love I can express to you in total abandonment. There is nothing in my mind or experience in what I know of you that would in any way hinder me from absolute adoration! My wife never tires of hearing me say, "I love you" — surely I never tire of the same words from her. I try each time to demonstrate by action and thoughtfulness the truth of those precious words. So it is immeasurably more true in my worship at least in words, when I say "I love you." For today I do want to demonstrate in life just how true are those words.

How do you personally relate to the adorableness of God, and God who is Elah or Eloah?
Speak it out or write it out. It is *so important* that you establish *your own* devotional journal.

3. CONFESSION OF SIN

It is easier now to see why our blessed Lord spoke so often of loving God with all our hearts — of loving him, of loving one another — even of loving ourselves as we love our neighbor — for love is of yourself.

Sin in its essence is failing to return love. Dear Lord, that I should ever be so involved with the gifts that I forget the Giver! Forgive me!

"Quenching the Spirit" — how do I do this? Is the Holy Spirit a fire? He is so symbolized. A fire gives warmth — when I choose to be cold or cool I quench the Spirit. A fire gives light — when I choose to live in darkness, I quench him. A fire is fascinatingly interesting — when I am fascinated by someone else or something else, I quench him who lives in me. Dear God, on all these counts I plead guilty. Forgive me.

What personal sins do you want to confess? We *must* speak them to remove them.
Do it! *Now.* There is no one else you have sinned against more than God. Tell him so!

4. SING A PRAYER TO GOD.

There is a name I love to hear,
I love to sing its worth;
It sounds like music in mine ear,
The sweetest name on earth.

Oh, how I love Jesus,
Oh, how I love Jesus,
Oh, how I love Jesus,
Because He first loved me!

Open your hymn book and sing the rest of the verses — or even sing another prayer song.

5. READ HIS WORD TO HIM.

His Word

[10]After we had been there a number of days, a prophet named Agabus came down from Judea. [11]Coming over to us, he took Paul's belt, tied his own hands and feet with it and said, "The Holy Spirit says, 'In this way the Jews of Jerusalem will bind the owner of this belt and will hand him over to the Gentiles.'"

[12]When we heard this, we and the people there pleaded with Paul not to go up to Jerusalem. [13]Then Paul answered, "Why are you weeping and breaking my heart? I am ready not only to be bound, but also to die in Jerusalem for the name of the Lord Jesus." [14]When he would not be dissuaded, we gave up and said, "The Lord's will be done."

— *Acts 21:10-14, NIV*

WEEK TWENTY-ONE — FRIDAY

Read His Word to Him.

While in Caesarea a remarkable incident took place. How differently you look at it than I do. Agabus is so well known to you—so little do I know about him. He seems a strange man to me—indeed he is, but to you his mother, father, family and house are all known. Did you speak to him directly or did you communicate through someone else? Why this instance on the persecution of Paul? Were you trying to give Paul a choice or a test? I want to enter into this text in a deep appreciation of all you have said. Is Agabus saying anything Paul has not already heard? I am struggling over just why you sent this prophet with his dramatic warning. I am persuaded you are trying to show all of us just what real dedication to you and your Son means.

6. READ HIS WORD FOR YOURSELF.

Is there a pattern here for my imitation? We could say: "It was easy enough for Paul to endure hardships—he had the constant directions from the Holy Spirit. We do not know why things befall us—we do not hear the Holy Spirit speak to us today." Such is a pathetic expression of not only lack of faith, but of Biblical ignorance. Does the Holy Spirit now live in our bodies as his temple or not? Of course he does (Rom. 8:9-12; I Cor. 6:19)! Has the Holy Spirit given to us through his prophets and apostles "all things that relate to this life—and the life of faith" or not (II Pet. 1:3)? Of course he has!

7. READ HIS WORD IN THANKSGIVING.

(1) Thank you for the extended visit to Caesarea—even when Paul was in a hurry to get to Jerusalem he took time to visit and teach. (2) Thank you for the personal love and concern so many had in the life and welfare of Paul. (3) Thank you for the dramatic, exciting action the Holy Spirit took in communicating his message—nothing dull or stodgy here. (4) Thank you for your warnings— which are as much a part of your love as your blessings. (5) Thank you for tears and entreaties—all of which must be evaluated for meaning. (6) Thank you for your will which is indicated as much by man's choices as direction of circumstance. (7) Thank you for "the name (or authority) of the Lord Jesus"—by this Paul lived and was ready to die!

8. READ HIS WORD IN MEDITATION.

". . . we gave up and said, The Lord's will be done." How could we "give up" and still be in "the will of the Lord"? This is perhaps the one thing that indicates the presence of his will more than anything else. This indicates a real pattern for us. The disciples thought it reasonable to be concerned for Paul's safety. When they knew he was in danger, they thought it God's will to warn him—even to dissuade him from entering the place of danger.

9. READ HIS WORD FOR PETITIONS.

It will be easy to pray for Paul, and ourselves, from this text: (1) Dear Lord, may I know how to separate conflicting messages from those who know our Lord. (2) Give me wisdom in reading aright Paul's intention in this incident. (3) It is sometimes necessary to suffer for your name—let me know when and why. (4) If you do not choose to tell me when or why, may I be willing yet to suffer for you. (5) Why did Luke plead with Paul not to go to Jerusalem—wasn't Luke inspired? (6) Why wouldn't Paul be dissuaded? (7) What was "the Lord's will" in this circumstance? As always I confidently expect our answer to these questions.

10. READ HIS WORD AND WAIT—LISTEN—GOD SPEAKS!

There are so many messages for me in this text: (1) "Opposition does not necessarily mean you should change your plans." (2) "Sometimes all of your best friends are wrong." (3) "The only one who has all the answers is myself."

11. INTERCESSION FOR THE LOST WORLD

Vietnam — Point for prayer: (1) *The subjugation of the South* by the Communists was followed by a systematic looting in Saigon of all the vast military and consumer goods left by the U.S.A. Poverty and famine as well as the sending of over one million politically "unreliable" people to "re-education camps" has driven many to despair and suicide. There is the possibility of a massive massacre of a rumored two million people when all direct links with the outside world are severed. Pray that the ministry of many servants of God through the years may bear fruit in this hour of darkness.

12. SING PRAISES TO OUR LORD.

The name of Jesus is so sweet,
I love its music to repeat;
It makes my joys full and complete,
The precious name of Jesus.

"Jesus," oh, how sweet the name!
"Jesus," ev'ry day the same;
"Jesus," let all saints proclaim
Its worthy praise forever.

WEEK TWENTY-ONE — SATURDAY

1. PRAISE GOD FOR WHO HE IS.

God Most High (Gen. 14:18-22; Num. 24:16). Exalted — lifted up, ascended. Dear Father, you are all this to me, but it is your position before men — before all men with which I am concerned. One day — when all days will end — "Every tongue will offer you the praise and full recognition you now deserve." Every knee shall bow "and look up to see your exalted position — nay, more — your character. It is only because of a little salt you have not already destroyed this world. The unnamed poet has said it so well:

> Lord of all! enthroned afar,
> Thy glory flames from sun and star;
> Centre and Soul of my sphere,
> Yet to each loving heart how near.

We bow before you now and gladly acknowledge your greatness.

Express yourself in adoration for this quality of God.
Speak it audibly or write out your praise in your own devotional journal.

2. PRAISE GOD FOR WHAT HE MEANS TO ME.

God Most-High to me. I am a child — a citizen, a soldier — a slave of this God Most-High. Dear Lord, I want you to be "the most high God" in the nitty gritty relationships of life. Is your word exalted as the "most high" book I have in my library? Am I constantly searching every word you have said? Or am I more interested in what men have said you have said? Are you the most high God to me when I find a contradiction in my conduct or thought process? i.e., am I willing to change my mind or am I ready to accept a lower place for you? Dear God, I do want to mean just what these terms mean. You are above all — "before all."

How do you personally relate to the exaltation of God, and God who is Most-High?
Speak it out or write it out. It is *so important* that you establish *your own* devotional journal.

3. CONFESSION OF SIN

I have already begun to acknowledge my need — my sin. There is little need of seeing you "exalted" — "lifted up" before all men if you are not exalted in my life. I am seeking for more practical applications of this relationship. To exalt you is to exalt your character as seen in your Son. With my wife, will I exalt your kindness? With my students, will I exalt your patience? With other teachers, will I exalt your appreciation? Forgive me, Lord, I have sinned in all these areas. *"Shepherds who feed only themselves."* Could it be that they fail to exalt the Great Shepherd?

What personal sins do you want to confess? We *must* speak them to remove them.
Do it! *Now.* There is no one else you have sinned against more than God. Tell him so!

4. SING A PRAYER TO GOD.

True-hearted, whole-hearted, faithful and loyal,
King of our lives, by Thy grace we will be;
Under the standard exalted and royal,
Strong in Thy strength we will battle for Thee.

Peal out the watchword! silence it never!
Song of our spirits, rejoicing and free;
Peal out the watchword! loyal forever,
King of our lives, by Thy grace we will be.

Open your hymn book and sing the rest of the verses — or even sing another prayer song.

5. READ HIS WORD TO HIM.

His Word

[15]After this, we got ready and went up to Jerusalem. [16]Some of the disciples from Caesarea accompanied us and brought us to the home of Mnason, where we were to stay. He was a man from Cyprus and one of the early disciples. [17]When we arrived at Jerusalem, the brothers received us warmly. [18]The next day Paul and the rest of us went to see James, and all the elders were present. [19]Paul greeted them and reported in detail what God had done among the Gentiles through his ministry. [20]When they heard this, they praised God.

— *Acts 21:15-20a, NIV*

Read His Word to Him.

I want to get ready and go with the disciples up to Jerusalem. It could not have been without some real apprehension they approached the gates of the holy city. But there was a warm welcome and a spacious home awaiting them. *Mnason* is one more of the little known disciples. Only little known to me. Not with you. Did Mnason know Barnabas? Both were men of Cyprus, both were early disciples, both were open-hearted in sharing with others. Perhaps Mnason was just as generous with his words of love and encouragement as he was with room and board. What great expectations were present in this house! To hear of all God (yourself) had done through Paul's ministry — to anticipate the renewed meaning of the feast of Pentecost.

Please express your response to this beautiful text. Put your expression in your own prayer diary.

6. READ HIS WORD FOR YOURSELF.

How very good to look on others as your brothers! The dear close associations and remembrances of a family is what is involved here. To look into the faces of men you haven't before met and know that these are long unknown brothers—each of you want to hear what the mutual Father has been doing in your lives. How I would love to look into the face of James our Lord's brother! At the same time we ask, "Where is Judas, Simeon, and Joseph?—and what of our Lord's sisters?" (Matthew 13:54-56). We can assume that the letter of Jude was written by Judas, but what happened to the others? Were they "the brothers" in the upper room (Acts 1:20ff.)? We want to believe they were! How many elders were there to hear Paul?

It is so important that you pause in his presence
and either audibly or in written form tell him all his word means to you.

7. READ HIS WORD IN THANKSGIVING.

(1) Thank you for the generous hospitality of many in Jerusalem—Mnason in particular. (2) Thank you for the personal note of Luke about Mnason so we may appreciate his long time faithfulness. (3) Thank you for some Jews in Jerusalem who were not bigoted—who were willing to be open-minded and warm-hearted. (4) Thank you for James who came to accept and honor his divine brother. (5) Thank you for every elder—none of whom I know, but all are known to you. (6) Thank you for every detail of Paul's account, some of which we can read in this book of Acts. (7) Thank you for the willingness of the elders and apostles to praise God for the conversion of Gentiles.

Give yourself to your own expression of gratitude—write it or speak it!

8. READ HIS WORD IN MEDITATION.

"When they heard this they praised God." This is a statement of a tremendous breakthrough in human history. It is an amazing account! Jewish leaders in the holy city rejoicing over the conversion to a new religion a group of unclean Gentiles! We really cannot appreciate or approximate the kind of hatred and prejudice present in the hearts of the Jews. Surely two wonderful things had happened: (1) The authority and love our Lord and his message for all the world had penetrated their hearts. The example of the house of Cornelius no doubt helped. (2) The law-system of salvation had totally failed in their lives and was an obvious failure with the whole Jewish nation. We try to get the depth of the praise here lifted, but I'm sure we do not.

Pause—wait—think—then express yourself in thoughtful praise or thanks.

9. READ HIS WORD FOR PETITIONS.

Jerusalem at last! How Paul wanted to be there—and yet there was much about which to pray: (1) No mention is made here of the distribution of the money Paul collected on this journey (Cf. I Cor. 16:1-4). Read Romans 15:31 for Paul's prayer request. (2) Give me the unselfish, humble attitude that characterized Paul in this incident. (3) Thank you for the hospitality seen so often in the life of the apostolic church. (4) There seem to be "brothers" or "disciples" in almost every city—why? (5) I want to read the epistle of James to absorb his wisdom. (6) What were the elders in Jerusalem doing in the direction of the church there? (7) How could the elders rejoice at the conversion of the Gentiles when other Jews didn't?

Right here add your personal requests—and his answers.

10. READ HIS WORD AND WAIT—LISTEN—GOD SPEAKS!

In this prelude before the storm what do you say to me? (1) "There are many disciples today who would welcome you into their house—appreciate it!" (2) "I have placed elders in the body for a purpose." (3) "Tell others of my blessings upon your work—it will help them and you."

11. INTERCESSION FOR THE LOST WORLD

Vietnam — Point for prayer: (1) *The Protestant Church* has grown steadily and strongly. In recent years the growth has been dramatic among the mountain tribes, who now make up one third of the membership. This growth has been in a time of terror, intimidation, murder of preachers by Viet Cong terrorists and massive movements of population fleeing the war. There were about 800 Bible believing churches in the South when Communists took over.

12. SING PRAISES TO OUR LORD.

We would see Jesus, for the shadows lengthen
Across this little landscape of our life;

We would see Jesus, our weak faith to strengthen
For the last weariness, the final strife.

WEEK TWENTY-TWO — SUNDAY

1. PRAISE GOD FOR WHO HE IS.

El-Roi—The Lord That Seeth (Ge. 16:13, 14). Only once did you associate yourself with this quality, and at such an unexpected time. How I wish we knew more about Hagar. Dear Lord, I know you know all about her. You supplied her need for water for herself and her son. She even named her son after this incident, Ishmael—"the God who hears." Praise your many-faceted name! How wonderfully good to know Someone who sees with compassion and understanding like no one else. "Thou, Oh Lord, seest me." In the midst of family quarrels and sharp, deep misunderstanding, you see and understand like no one else.

Express yourself in adoration for this quality of God.
Speak it audibly or write out your praise in your own devotional journal.

2. PRAISE GOD FOR WHAT HE MEANS TO ME.

"The Lord that seeth me." You have not caught me as a spy, for nothing has been hidden from you. You see me as no one else ever could—for no one else can read and know my heart. Dear God, I do not even know my heart. I do know that a negative introspection becomes totally fruitless. I do want to repent of my sin, but I have found no help in lacerating my spirit; it has become a form of pride. I am glad to turn my deceitful heart over to the only One who truly knows it. Cleanse and heal and change me. Do you see a million lost persons saved through me? You saw a great nation in Hagar. Dear God, make it so!

How do you personally relate to the omnipresence of God, and God who is El-Roi?
Speak it out or write it out. It is *so important* that you establish *your own* devotional journal.

3. CONFESSION OF SIN

How often have I acted as if you did not see me! "Hidden sin" is only hidden from men. But bless your name! hidden virtue is only hidden from men. You see it, appreciate it, acknowledge it, reward it. I confess openly that I am far too interested in what men see and say than what you see and have said (and through this prayer time are now saying to me). Forgive me! I am afraid and try to hide myself—it is only a meaningless act of shame. Forgive me; lead me out into your light.

"Grumbling"—of all people who should not sin in this way, it is Americans. But as you hear the sound of grumbling when is it the most intense? I know you hear our groanings and cries—you said you do. Dear God, for one day you will not hear it from me!

What personal sins do you want to confess? We *must* speak them to remove them.
Do it! *Now.* There is no one else you have sinned against more than God. Tell him so!

4. SING A PRAYER TO GOD.

Jesus, keep me near the cross,
There a precious fountain
Free to all—a healing stream,
Flows from Calv'ry's mountain.

In the cross, in the cross,
Be my glory ever;
Till my raptured soul shall find
Rest beyond the river.

Open your hymn book and sing the rest of the verses—or even sing another prayer song.

5. READ HIS WORD TO HIM!

His Word

[20]When they heard this, they praised God. Then they said to Paul: "You see, brother, how many thousands of Jews have believed, and all of them are zealous for the law. [21]They have been informed that you teach all the Jews who live among the Gentiles to turn away from Moses, telling them not to circumcise their children or live according to our customs. [22]What shall we do? They will certainly hear that you have come, [23]so do what we tell you. There are four men with us who have made a vow. [24]Take these men, join in their purification rites and pay their expenses, so that they can have their heads shaved. Then everybody will know there is no truth in these reports about you, but that you yourself are living in obedience to the law. [25]As for the Gentile believers, we have written to them our decision that they should abstain from food sacrificed to idols, from blood, from the meat of strangled animals and from sexual immorality."

[26]The next day Paul took the men and purified himself along with them. Then he went to the temple to give notice of the date when the days of purification would end and the offering would be made for each of them.

— Acts 21:20-26, NIV

Read His Word to Him.

How sadly do I enter this portion of worship! I know you were present when this conversation first took place. There is always joy and sorrow mingled in the same cup. Thousands of Jews in Jerusalem have become Christians — what a testimony to the power of the good news. At the same time, these same persons are jealous of their supposed advantage over the Gentiles. It looks to me — correct me (and I *mean* it) if I am wrong — that these men are really asking all men to become as they are "Christian Jews" or Jewish Christians. To adopt all the traditional outlook of their background. How easy it is for me to do the same thing!

Please express your response to this beautiful text. Put your expression in your own prayer diary.

6. READ HIS WORD FOR YOURSELF.

Do I really know what others teach or am I willing to repeat "hearsay" or gossip! Do others really know what I teach? Does love prevail in either case? Just how much of the law and customs did Paul teach the Gentiles? Fortunately we have his letters to the Gentiles. We can answer this question best by reading Romans or Galatians.

Either audibly or in written form tell him all his word means to you.

7. READ HIS WORD IN THANKSGIVING.

(1) Thank you for thousands and thousands that could be converted today if we had the same zeal and love. (2) Thank you for the record of misunderstanding in the early church — it helps us in today's church. (3) Thank you for the example of the influence of one man — it helps me to appreciate the same thing today. (4) Thank you for efforts to reach out to those who violently disagree with us. (5) Thank you that we can hold very different views on matters of opinion and still both be Christians. (6) Thank you for the clear regulations for the Gentiles which obtain even today. (7) Thank you for Paul's humility, zeal, love, unselfishness, courage.

Give yourself to your own expression of gratitude — write it or speak it!

8. READ HIS WORD IN MEDITATION.

"You yourself are living in obedience to the law." Even such obedience would not provide salvation but it was hoped it would provide a bridge over which communication between the extreme right and Paul could flow. Several facts need to be noticed: (1) The Jews in Jerusalem were trying to do something about the problem. They did not hide from it or ignore it. (2) Paul was willing to allow the temple worship with all its ceremony if it was not made a test of fellowship. (3) The predictions of our Lord concerning the soon coming destruction of the temple could have been a factor in the hatred of some for the Christians.

Pause — wait — think — then express yourself in thoughtful praise or thanks.

9. READ HIS WORD FOR PETITIONS.

In the advice of the elders there is surely room for prayer: (1) Lead me into a circumstance where I could influence a whole ethnic group as Paul did with the Jews. (2) Open our hearts to love the Jewish people and tell them of their Messiah. (3) Give me grace to do all I can to accommodate and not compromise. (4) May I respect and keep the laws of the land that I might better be able to speak to all. (5) Thank you that it is possible to be purified by the sacrifice of Calvary. (6) Paul invested time, money and energy into a ritual that was not necessary to help those who hated him — I need your grace to be like him. (7) May I share some of the pathos of Romans 9:1, 2.

Please, please remember these are prayers — speak them — reword them!

10. READ HIS WORD AND WAIT — LISTEN — GOD SPEAKS!

As Paul hoped against hope, speak to me: (1) "Your very best intentions can be misinterpreted." (2) "It is not wrong to try to help even if you are rejected." (3) "I can work out something good from every circumstance."

11. INTERCESSION FOR THE LOST WORLD

Vietnam — Point for prayer: (1) *The believers in the North* are free to meet together, but preachers are strictly controlled in what they preach and are forced to report to the Communists on their activities and also on their members. The few Christians are under great pressure through the 7-day week and the use of Sundays for indoctrination classes. There is discrimination against believers in education and employment.

12. SING PRAISES TO OUR LORD.

Christ has for sin atonement made.
What a wonderful Savior!
We are redeemed! the price is paid!

What a wonderful Savior!
What a wonderful Savior is Jesus, my Jesus!
What a wonderful Savior is Jesus, my Lord!

WEEK TWENTY-TWO — MONDAY

1. PRAISE GOD FOR WHO HE IS.

The God of Israel (Gen. 33:18-20). You gave Jacob the new name—now he gives it back to you. As Jacob's claim to identity with you is in his new name, so is our identity in the new name you have given for all men: *"Christians"* —the new "Israel." Dear God, we have indeed struggled — or simply "hung on" to you—out of your grace you have given us this wonderful new name. We are so glad to be "the anointed ones." We reign with him a thousand years. How I do want to keep ever before me the astounding fact that you want *all* men to be Christians. The new Israel of yourself includes all men of all nations.

Express yourself in adoration for this quality of God.
Speak it audibly or write out your praise in your own devotional journal.

2. PRAISE GOD FOR WHAT HE MEANS TO ME.

I am the Israel of yourself! I surely can identify with Jacob—in so many ways his experiences parallel mine. What Jacob found in the physical land of Canaan I want to find in my sojourn here. There must be a day when I present my body as a living sacrifice and build a "Bethel" —or house of God—"gate to heaven." The wonder and beauty of that place (or commitment) must be so precious that I will simply not be influenced to conform to this world in which I live. I will be transformed by the daily renewal of my mind. Such renewal is largely a review of my relationship established at Bethel. I must "go back to Bethel" real often. When I do then I shall *know* your good and perfect and acceptable daily will for my life. Praise your holy name!

How do you personally relate to grace of God, and God who is the God of Israel?
Speak it out or write it out. It is *so important* that you establish *your own* devotional journal.

3. CONFESSION OF SIN

Dear Lord, you have been speaking to me most clearly through my praise to you, and for you. I do right now renew my mind—I see Jesus lifted up for my sins—I see him raised from the dead. I want to imagine the glory he has with you as intercessor for me at your right hand. I remember I am not my own; my whole body has already been given to you as a "thank offering." Dear Lord, forgive me for sacrilege, i.e., of using for myself what belongs to you. Dear God, deepen my commitment.

"Faultfinders"—since you find no fault in me, why should I be looking for fault in others?

What personal sins do you want to confess? We *must* speak them to remove them.
Do it! *Now.* There is no one else you have sinned against more than God. Tell him so!

4. SING A PRAYER TO GOD.

O for a thousand tongues to sing
My great Redeemer's praise,

The glories of my God and King,
The triumphs of His grace.

Open your hymn book and sing the rest of the verses—or even sing another prayer song.

5. READ HIS WORD TO HIM!

His Word

[27]When the seven days were nearly over, some Jews from the province of Asia saw Paul at the temple. They stirred up the whole crowd and seized him, [28]shouting, "Men of Israel, help us! This is the man who teaches all men everywhere against our people and our law and this place. And besides, he has brought Greeks into the temple area and defiled this holy place." [29](They had previously seen Trophimus the Ephesian in the city with Paul and assumed that Paul had brought him into the temple area.)
— Acts 21:27-29, NIV

Read His Word to Him.

(I am trying to get behind these words and see this record as you see it.) How silly and pointless must the action of some of your children seem to you. You are not defiled by the presence of Gentiles in a special building. Dear Lord, that we can be satisfied with the form and not the substance—what a loss when we settle for the shadow and not the substance. Why are men so willing to believe a lie? Satan is the answer—he is very much alive and very subtle too. Yea, even *now*. But I rebuke him in the name of my Lord! Out! Out! How much havoc among your people has been caused by gossip! When, oh, when will we check out what is said!

Please express your response to this beautiful text. Put your expression in your own prayer diary.

6. READ HIS WORD FOR YOURSELF.

I do not want to take Paul's place—at least to begin the meditation and worship through this text. Have I ever believed an evil report of a brother because of what I have seen or others have said without investigating the facts? Yes, yes. Dear God, help me to guard my eyes, to open my heart and to do to others what I want done to me. How impossible it is to break away from tradition without persecution! In the area of devotion and evangelism this is even more true. Am I ready to make a break when I see it is needed? Dear Lord, I say "yes," but how will I truly know until it happens with me as it happened with Paul?

It is so important that you pause in his presence
and either audibly or in written form tell him all his word means to you.

7. READ HIS WORD IN THANKSGIVING.

(1) Thank you for Paul's courage in not withdrawing from the Gentiles when he arrived in Jerusalem. (2) Thank you for the previous warnings that encouraged Paul in the knowledge that you were aware of all that happened. (3) Thank you for zeal that *can* be directed toward truth and love—as well as toward error and hatred. (4) Thank you that the former "holy place" has been replaced with our bodies as his temple. (5) Thank you that we really know what defiles "the holy place," anything that hinders the full capacity of our mind or body. (6) Thank you for Paul's wide influence—all done in just a few years. (7) Thank you for the new Jerusalem where nothing that defiles will enter.

Give yourself in your own expression of gratitude—write it or speak it!

8. READ HIS WORD IN MEDITATION.

"*. . . and assumed that Paul had brought him into the temple area.*" How very much both good and bad are built on assumption! We believe man is guilty until proven innocent. Such a sad assumption. Paul assumed certain Jews could be influenced to accept him as not opposed to the law of God, or the temple of God. How sad it is when we depend upon our fertile imagination for what we believe about men and about yourself. These Jews lived in the realm of the senses and not of truth. Paul was more than willing to discuss all the points of "speaking against the law, against the Jews and against the temple." But there was no way Paul could speak against the mob spirit of prejudiced hatred!

Pause—wait—think—then express yourself in thoughtful praise or thanks.

9. READ HIS WORD FOR PETITIONS.

In spite of the turmoil we believe Paul was often lifting his heart in prayer—so do we: (1) "When men lie about me, help me to be just as ready to give myself to them and you as was Paul. (2) Help me to resist in the same way as Paul. (3) Remind me again to see just how deep-seated is prejudice. (4) I want to always remember that lying is self-destructive as well as hurtful to others. (5) Help me to risk all as Paul did for friendship with someone other people despised. (6) Deliver me from religious bigots. (7) Guard me lest I become what I despise.

Right here add your personal requests—and his answers.

10. READ HIS WORD AND WAIT—LISTEN—GOD SPEAKS!

I wonder what messages Paul found in his experience of betrayal—speak to me through these words: (1) "There are men today who will lie for their cause." (2) "Aggressive teaching will produce enemies." (3) "Lo, I am with you always."

11. INTERCESSION FOR THE LOST WORLD

Vietnam — Point for prayer: (1) *The present situation* for the believers in the South is not yet one of severe persecution. Yet, about 50 preachers have been killed, many believers are in prison, and all suffer the economic hardships of the whole people. Yet churches are now free to meet, Christian workers to minister and Bibles are still openly sold. There are tensions within the churches, between the leftists and rightists. Pray that the believers may remain true to Jesus and not be beguiled into compromise. Pray that they may maintain their daily communion with the Lord and shine for Him, and be spared the ghastly slaughter seen in Cambodia.

12. SING PRAISES TO OUR LORD.

When morning gilds the skies,
My heart awaking cries:
May Jesus Christ be praised;

Alike at work and prayer . . .
To Jesus I repair: . . .
May Jesus Christ be praised.

WEEK TWENTY-TWO — TUESDAY

1. PRAISE GOD FOR WHO HE IS.

El Olam—God of Eternity or God the Everlasting. The older I become the more fleeting this life becomes. How soon most of life has come and gone. Perhaps I shall be given more than the three score and ten. The three score has already disappeared, only eight years on the ten are left. Will there be four score? Even if you in your mercy grant me these many days, my eightieth birthday will be the consumation of a vapor. I am so glad to worship before One who is "from everlasting to everlasting." It surely seems to me that all men are looking for the security—the stability of One who never changes. One who is always full of love and knowledge and care and personal concern—One who has not altered at all from yesterday—will be just the same Eternal, loving Father tomorrow! Blessed be thy eternal name!

Express yourself in adoration for this quality of God.
Speak it audibly or write out your praise in your own devotional journal.

2. PRAISE GOD FOR WHAT HE MEANS TO ME.

My Everlasting Father is also my eternal Savior. I honestly do not know how to relate to infinity. The limitations of time, the infirmities and physical presence of the body all tend to hinder my understanding or participation in this quality of your nature. I only want to pause here at your feet as a little child before his father. I am full of wonder and unknowing amazement! At the same time I am taken up in praise that I have found a rock—a solid rock—a solid everlasting dwelling place—a lodestar that never moves. Dear Father, I love you!

How do you personally relate to the eternity of God, and God who is El Olam?
Speak it out or write it out. It is *so important* that you establish *your own* devotional journal.

3. CONFESSION OF SIN

I am sure I could become more lucid if I were to open any number of books I have on my shelf, but this is another form of sin—pride. I am only opening my heart to you—not men. How is it that I know time is fleeting and death is sure and yet I live like there was no time and death but a word? I am glad for time and I do not fear death—I welcome it! But I want to live in the light of truth not sensual thoughtlessness. Forgive me. There are so many sins that have their roots in this attitude. Forgive me, I can and do name them.

"*Flattering*"—the most often and the most obvious expression of this sin in on myself. Oh, to see myself as you do! I then would not either think more nor less of myself than what is true. I could then also think the truth about others.

What personal sins do you want to confess? We *must* speak them to remove them.
Do it! *Now.* There is no one else you have sinned against more than God. Tell him so!

4. SING A PRAYER TO GOD.

Thou, my everlasting portion,
More than friend or life to me;
All along my pilgrim journey,
Savior, let me walk with Thee.

Close to Thee, close to Thee,
Close to Thee, close to Thee;
All along my pilgrim journey,
Savior, let me walk with Thee.

Open your hymn book and sing the rest of the verses—or even sing another prayer song.

5. READ HIS WORD TO HIM!

His Word

[30]The whole city was aroused, and the people came running from all directions. Seizing Paul, they dragged him from the temple, and immediately the gates were shut. [31]While they were trying to kill him, news reached the commander of the Roman troops that the whole city of Jerusalem was in an uproar. — *Acts 21:30, 31, NIV*

Read His Word to Him.

Dear Lord, how I do want to see these words from your perspective! This is what the Holy Spirit had said would happen. But in it you have your child. Are some of those who were beating and mistreating Paul also some of your children? How sad! How very sad! Most of those who ran and cried and joined in the beating really did not know what they were doing—and so it has been for centuries of time! Here is a repeat performance of the treatment of your Son. In the same place he suffered and for the same charge. How strange! to bring order out of chaos by those who do not believe. The Roman soldiers act with more meaning than your own children!

Please express your response to this beautiful text. Put your expression in your own prayer diary.

6. READ HIS WORD FOR YOURSELF.

What possible purpose did Paul have for doggedly determining that he would go to Jerusalem? Here is the fulfillment of the Spirit's words. What has Paul obtained to the advantage of our Lord? Here are some possible answers that at least speak to my heart. (1) Paul demonstrated for all who had eyes to see and hearts to believe that he was unselfishly interested in his own people. (2) Paul exemplified total trust in yourself—indeed he did not count his life as dear unto himself! (3) Paul called national attention to the cause of Jesus of Nazareth who was indeed the long sought for Messiah! (4) In all these ways and others Paul set before me an example of dedication.

It is so important that you pause in his presence
and either audibly or in written form tell him all his word means to you.

7. READ HIS WORD IN THANKSGIVING.

(1) Thank you so much for the stirring up of a general interest—no one was unmoved. (2) Thank you for the focus of interest—Paul was well able (by your help) to turn this to your advantage. (3) Thank you for the destruction of one temple so we can identify the real temple of the living God. (4) Thank you for "law and order" ordained of yourself! (5) Thank you for every Roman soldier who helped—no doubt some of them looked beyond the effect to the cause. (6) Thank you that this happened at Pentecost —no doubt some thought of another year and another Pentecost. (7) Thank you again that this record has been kept all these years.

Give yourself to your own expression of gratitude—write it or speak it!

8. READ HIS WORD IN MEDITATION.

". . . The whole city of Jerusalem was in an uproar." How wonderful that the cause of our Lord was given this same thought from the ministry of our Lord. Whatever else happened people were not going to be able to ignore our Lord. Why is it we do not have today the same effect upon our community? There are several reasons: (1) We do not get out into the mainstream of the community in which we live. We are not involved with those matters that touch the lives and pocketbooks of the people. (2) We somehow do not believe this is our arena of work. We are content to live and move among our own people where we feel comfortable. (3) We do not have a product that wears well, i.e., by the example of our lives. When people see what we have do they want it? In some cases and places the answer is a resounding "yes," but in many others it is greeted and answered by a cold shoulder.

Pause—wait—think—then express yourself in thoughtful praise or thanks.

9. READ HIS WORD FOR PETITIONS.

In just two verses so much happens about which we can pray: (1) There are various ways of polarizing interest —in my city how can I do it for you? (2) How did Paul relate what was happening to the prophecy of Agabus? (3) How did Paul relate this beating with the Holy Spirit's message to go to Jerusalem? (4) Dear Lord, give me wisdom in attempting an answer to the two previous requests. (5) Why drag Paul out of the temple?—open my heart to see just how wrong sincere people can be! (6) May I appreciate more than ever your ministries in the form of civil authorities. (7) Keep me aware that those to whom Paul was delivered, i.e., "the Gentiles" also saved Paul from the Jews. Thank you for your wonderful check and balance.

Please, please remember these are prayers—speak them—reword them!

10. READ HIS WORD IN MEDITATION.

Was Paul aware of your presence in the midst of this chaos?—we believe he was. (1) "I am never confused." (2) "Religious opposition does not mean I am against you." (3) "If I do not want a man to die, he will not die."

11. INTERCESSION FOR THE LOST WORLD

Vietnam — Points for prayer: (1) *The preachers and church leaders* need great wisdom in this dangerous situation. Pray that they may remain true to their calling whatever the cost. (2) *Several Bible Schools* are still open— pray for the staff and students in this tense time. Pray for the raising up of more spiritual men of God to lead the Church.

12. SING PRAISES TO OUR LORD.

There is never a day so dreary,
There is never a night so long,
But the soul that is trusting Jesus
Will somewhere find a song.

Wonderful, wonderful Jesus,
In the heart He implanteth a song: . . .
A song of deliv'rance, of courage, of strength,
In the heart He implanteth a song.

WEEK TWENTY-TWO — WEDNESDAY

1. PRAISE GOD FOR WHO HE IS.

El Shaddai — All-mighty, all-sufficient God (Ex. 3:15; 6:3). It is one thing to have and exercise total might; it is quite another thing to be absolute in sufficiency, i.e., to be able, to be willing to meet every need of every man. But this is just what this name implies. Praise and adoration surely arise from my heart to you for being the all-sufficient one for the entire world population. All men are in need in three areas: (1) The desires of the flesh. I believe there is more than enough food for all men if it were adequately distributed. I know thousands starve to death every day — possibly every hour — and I am shocked and frustrated. This is not your fault. Sex is another gigantic desire of the flesh. Marriage is your answer — it has a track record of success far ahead of anything else. Thank you!

Express yourself in adoration for this quality of God.
Speak it audibly or write out your praise in your own devotional journal.

2. PRAISE GOD FOR WHAT HE MEANS TO ME.

Praise you for myself, i.e., to you! (2) You are *all* sufficient in the area of "the strong desire for *things*." How many "things" did our Lord accumulate during his lifetime? How many houses did he have? How much land did he own? What kind of wardrobe did Jesus leave? Do I *really* believe his words? He said: "A man's *real* life, *real* happiness, *real* fulfillment, does not consist in the abundance of things"? How can I better make these words a part of my life? (3) You are the all-sufficient One in the area of the "pride of life," i.e., status and acceptance among men. Am I ready to accept your value system?

How do you personally relate to the all sufficiency of God, and God who is El Shaddai?
Speak it out or write it out. It is *so important* that you establish *your own* devotional journal.

3. CONFESSION OF SIN

How easy it is to admit my lack — my sin in this relationship. It seems I have always been too much self-sufficient. When will I truly learn my sufficiency is *not* in myself, but in you alone? Any accomplishments are not mine, but yours. Any possessions are your gifts — to be used to bring honor to you, not myself. Dear God, that men might see whatever good work you have helped me do and glorify you! Forgive me for the sin of pride.

"Scoffing" — I am guilty. Whatever seems to lack purpose, or quality, becomes a source of disdain to me. I have scoffed and lashed out at those involved. Dear God, how do my very best efforts look to you? You judge desire and motive not accomplishments. Oh, oh, may I leave such judgment with you! Forgive.

What personal sins do you want to confess? We *must* speak them to remove them.
Do it! *Now.* There is no one else you have sinned against more than God. Tell him so!

4. SING A PRAYER TO GOD.

How firm a foundation, ye saints of the Lord,
Is laid for your faith in His excellent Word!

What more can He say than to you He hath said,
To you who for refuge to Jesus have fled?

Open your hymn book and sing the rest of the verses — or even sing another prayer song.

5. READ HIS WORD TO HIM!

His Word

[32]He at once took some officers and soldiers and ran down to the crowd. When the rioters saw the commander and his soldiers, they stopped beating Paul. [33]The commander came up and arrested him and ordered him to be bound with two chains. Then he asked who he was and what he had done. [34]Some in the crowd shouted one thing and some another, and since the commander could not get at the truth because of the uproar, he ordered that Paul be taken into the barracks.   — *Acts 21:32-34, NIV*

Read His Word to Him.

We want to run with the commander to where Paul is being beaten by the crowd of Jews. Before he arrives you are there! What did you see? I'm sure it was much different than the troops or their leader. Yea, much different than we do now. Let me meditate upon what you could have seen: (1) You saw a reenactment of the mistreatment of your dear Son — the same men, the same hatred, the same wilfull ignorance. (2) You saw the wounds willingly received by Paul, who was completing or accepting in his body the suffering of our Lord — such an example of unselfish giving of his life. (3) You saw a group of Roman soldiers who knew not that there was a God in heaven. Any one of them and each one of them was the object of your love and concern. How unspeakably sad that the one thing that was intended to unite all men (your Son) has now divided them and prevented your expression of love for all.

Please express your response to this beautiful text. Put your expression in your own prayer diary.

WEEK TWENTY-TWO — WEDNESDAY

6. READ HIS WORD FOR YOURSELF.

I am much too glib and judgmental. How we have divided—how easily we fight and separate from each other! How confused is the lost world in which I live! The world in which I live knows about you less than the Roman soldiers. Dear Lord, we have less promise of the progress of your word, i.e., in some areas than Paul had in Jerusalem. On the other hand, there are your dear children being treated today as Paul was treated then. I think of Christians in China and many other places where persecution is a reality! I think also of the marvelous results Paul's living sacrifice produced in the city who crucified our Lord. Paul was catapulted by this experience to the ends of the earth in a proclamation of your word!

It is so important that you pause in his presence
and either audibly or in written form tell him all his word means to you.

7. READ HIS WORD IN THANKSGIVING.

Indeed, indeed! (1) Thank you for the immediate response of the commander—as we have said before: without this Paul would have been dead. (2) Thank you for the fear of reprisal that filled the hearts of the Jews. (3) Thank you for the strange and wonderful ways you have of protecting your children. (4) Thank you that Paul was never bound in his spirit—even if this was the beginning of a long imprisonment. (5) Thank you for the sense of justice prevailing in the handling of the prisoner. (6) Thank you for the fair reporting done by Dr. Luke. (7) Thank you that we are given liberty to speak your word openly today.

Give yourself to your expression of gratitude—write it or speak it!

8. READ HIS WORD IN MEDITATION.

"Some in the crowd shouted one thing and some another." How typical of some crowds I have been in! As you view the body of your dear Son is this the circumstance you see? What is the cause and cure for this confusion? (1) Most are led and not leaders. This is both good and bad. When the purpose of following is clearly communicated and that purpose is your purpose, it is good. But when hatred and excitement are the leading factors, it is very bad. (2) When men are unhappy with themselves they become easy prey for those who can show them who to blame. A scapegoat is gladly welcomed. All the griping and complaining in our present world is because we are unhappy with ourselves.

Pause—wait—think—then express yourself in thoughtful praise or thanks.

9. READ HIS WORD FOR PETITIONS.

What was Paul praying in the midst of his suffering? There are points for prayer: (1) Keep me aware of proper perspective—"This too will pass." (2) Help me to even rejoice inasmuch as my Lord was so persecuted. (3) May I remember that you are always at work. (4) Use the misguided zeal of the religious to attract the unbeliever to at least listen. (5) Give me the deep determination that filled the heart of Paul. (6) How precisely did the prophecy of Agabus come to pass! Keep me aware that you are always aware. (7) I want to remember: we are confused and do not know—you are never confused and know all.

Right here add your personal requests—and his answers.

10. READ HIS WORD AND WAIT—LISTEN—GOD SPEAKS!

Above the din of the voices of men speak to me in these verses: (1) "Paul was beaten often and did not die from the beatings." (2) "Where is your unselfishness when compared to Paul?" (3) "Paul balanced his part and my part in my will for his life—you can too."

11. INTERCESSION FOR THE LOST WORLD

Vietnam — Points for prayer: (1) The Church in many of the mountain tribes has grown fast through some remarkable people movements, often in refugee camps. The majority in some of these tribes would now call themselves Christian. Pray for these isolated believers; so many so ill-taught and without much of the Word of God, who must face the ruthless atheism of Communism. (2) The young people face acute trials in the new Vietnam—not the least being the permission granted to the Viet Cong soldiers to take any unmarried girl in marriage. Pray for the Christian girls that they may find a believing partner.

12. SING PRAISES TO OUR LORD.

Wounded for me, wounded for me,
There on the cross He was wounded for me;

Gone my transgressions, and now I am free,
All because Jesus was wounded for me.

WEEK TWENTY-TWO — THURSDAY

1. PRAISE GOD FOR WHO HE IS.

Adonai — Our Ruler, Master, Lord, Owner. (Heb. 3:19; Ezek. 8:1; Psa. 35:23; 38:15). How exceedingly good it is to worship before you this day! I gladly take my place as a servant ready to hear what my master wants to ask of me. I am here to acknowledge you as the ruler and Lord and owner of all men. More and more I am disturbed that so few know you! Dear Master, how can I help to spread the glory and beauty of your name over all the earth? Oh, oh, if we can publish your word in the Pictorial form in 10 languages, I can at least speak to 400,000 to 500,000 people. Thank you for speaking this into my heart.

Express yourself in adoration for this quality of God.
Speak it audibly or write out your praise in your own devotional journal.

2. PRAISE GOD FOR WHAT HE MEANS TO ME.

My ruler or owner. Oh, my Father, if I am owned by you, then I must express this relationship in fact, in truth, in deed. I am not my own; I belong to you. Dear Lord, I do want to express in a most practical sense my responsibility — open my mind to see just where this can be directed. I praise you for the amazing fact that your answers to my prayers take the form of what men would call coincidences, i.e., such things just "happen." Many, many answers are so subtle that they must be seen through the eyes of faith before they can be identified as your work in us both willing and doing your good pleasure! Bless your Holy name!

How do you personally relate to the rulership of God, and God who is Adonai?
Speak it out or write it out. It is *so important* that you establish *your own* devotional journal.

3. CONFESSION OF SIN

The words of my Savior and Lord surely take on new meaning as I begin to relate to you as Lord, or owner. The parable of the talents, of the vineyard, of the virgins — how often did my Lord speak of this relationship — indeed it seems to be the *one* basic expression of our living for you. Forgive me and move me into a glad willingness to spend and be spent for you.

"Pride of possessions." How shall I discover this sin? Whenever any thing, or any one becomes more important, or of equal importance to me than yourself, I have sinned. Time, energy, money, ability, thoughts — how are these entities used? For you? For *things*?

What personal sins do you want to confess? We *must* speak them to remove them.
Do it! *Now.* There is no one else you have sinned against more than God. Tell him so!

4. SING A PRAYER TO GOD.

O worship the King, all glorious above,
And gratefully sing His wonderful love;

Our Shield and Defender, the Ancient of days,
Pavilioned in splendor, and girded with praise.

Open your hymn book and sing the rest of the verses — or even sing another prayer song.

5. READ HIS WORD TO HIM!

His Word

34Some in the crowd shouted one thing and some another, and since the commander could not get at the truth because of the uproar, he order that Paul be taken into the barracks. 35When Paul reached the steps, the violence of the mob was so great he had to be carried by the soldiers. 36The crowd that followed kept shouting, "Away with him!"

37As the soldiers were about to take Paul into the barracks, he asked the commander, "May I say someting to you?"

"Do you speak Greek?" he replied. 38"Aren't you the Egyptian who started a revolt and led four thousand terrorists out into the desert some time ago?"

39Paul answered, "I am a Jew, from Tarsus in Cilicia, a citizen of no ordinary city. Please let me speak to the people."
— Acts 21:34-39, NIV

Read His Word to Him.

We cannot but admire the commander Claudius Lysias. He has a most difficult task. How did you view the scene unfolding before us? Does the reasonable, helpful ministry of such men go unnoticed? No, no! We can read of another army officer and know that you had a great interest in his daily conduct (Acts 10:1ff.). The two areas of your particular interest was prayer and giving, but the whole effort to be responsible was not forgotten or ignored. How good to affirm that in you, of you and before you all men live and move and have their being. How many men have come and gone on the scene of life! All the crowd, all the Roman army is gone and millions of others like them are gone, but not from your memory.

Please express your response to this beautiful text. Put your expression in your own prayer diary.

6. READ HIS WORD FOR YOURSELF.

How concerned Paul was for your name — to speak for your Son. To tell his own people the real meaning of their own scriptures, but most of all, how God had spoken to him. Do I have such an overwhelming desire to let all men know of you? Particularly, do I have such a desire to let all men know that there need not be this terrible religious confusion in which we live? Paul was looking for and sensitive to the opportunities. Men do and will misunderstand and misrepresent — no bother — the word *must* get out! I am ready to gladly give my life for this goal. Paul's body must have been crying out in pain, but his heart was crying out in love. The voice of love was louder than the voice of pain.

It is so important that you pause in his presence
and either audibly or in written form tell him what his word means to you.

7. READ HIS WORD IN THANKSGIVING.

Thank you, oh, thank you: (1) For a commander in the Roman army who wanted "the truth" on any subject. I do verily believe there are those commanders in the U.S. army who look for the same thing. (2) For the fact that the cry and desire of the crowd does not always prevail. (3) For Paul's dedicated knowledge — all he knew was dedicated to the One he knew. (4) For law and order that has overcome unnumbered terrorist attacks. (5) For Paul's citizenship — it saved his life here and hereafter. (6) For the hope that "springs eternal" in the human heart — that in spite of many futile efforts this one will succeed. (7) For the Aramaic language we can study today and read as Paul read.

Give yourself to your own expression of gratitude — write it or speak it!

8. READ HIS WORD IN MEDITATION.

". . . a citizen of no ordinary city." To Paul and the commander (although it appears the commander was not listening — or maybe he did not know) this meant Paul was a Roman citizen for this was the privilege of some cities in the Roman empire. To us it means we "are free born" too. Our city is in heaven. It has eternal foundations — its builder and planner (architect) is God. We are just strangers and sojourners in this earth. Anyone from another country talks about it to anyone who will listen to him. Everything is compared with "the old country." Should not this be our interest and attitude? Nothing here can compare with the beauty and wonder we will see and experience "over there." What excitement and anticipation wells up within us to be "at home with the Lord."

Pause — wait — think — then express yourself in thoughtful praise or thanks.

9. READ HIS WORD FOR PETITIONS.

No doubt Paul had much about which to pray — so do we: (1) Keep me listening to your voice of truth from your word. (2) In the face of the rejection of men let me read again of your acceptance of me. (3) I want to appreciate more fully Paul's willingness to suffer for you. (4) Give me the creative courage in the face of opposition I see here. (5) Open my eyes to the influence of one well placed testimony. (6) How often is mistaken identity a real problem — may men always know who you are! (7) May my heavenly citizenship be as important to me as it should.

Please, please remember these are prayers — speak them — reword them!

10. READ HIS WORD AND WAIT — LISTEN — GOD SPEAKS!

There is much you can say to me in these verses: (1) "The voices of men will always hinder the reception of the truth." (2) "Help can and does come from very unexpected sources." (3) "You will be often mistaken for someone or something other than you are."

11. INTERCESSION FOR THE LOST WORLD

Vietnam — Points for prayer: (1) *Bible translation* was in progress in 24 of the smaller language groups. By the time of the Communist takeover, 7 tribes had the New Testament and a further 17 had portions of the New Testament. Pray for the distribution and preservation of this precious treasure in the years to come. (2) *Unreached peoples in Vietnam*. It is hard to see how these people can now be reached with the Gospel. Pray that the Lord may open up a way. We mention a few: a) Cham, 50,000 — a mixed Hindu and Muslim tribe in the Mekong delta — very few believers. b) The Mountain tribes of the North — Muong 400,000, Tai 400,000, Tho 150,000 and Yao. Some refugees were evangelized in the South. Pray that these may be free to go back to their unreached fellows in the North.

12. SING PRAISES TO OUR LORD.

All people that on earth do dwell,
Sing to the Lord with cheerful voice;

Him serve with fear, His praise forth tell;
Come ye before Him and rejoice.

WEEK TWENTY-TWO — FRIDAY

1. PRAISE GOD FOR WHO HE IS.

Jah—The Independent One (Exodus 15:2; Isa. 12:2; 38:11; Psa. 46:1)—the eternal One, the self-existing One — the same as "I am that I am." How awesome a thought to know One who is totally apart from all else and everyone else. One who is sufficient unto himself. Man attempts this in attitude and action, but really never achieves it. Man must have fellowship with his fellow creatures to be complete—most of all man must have fellowship with you to find rest unto his soul. Man was not created because you had a need, but once man was created he met a need. Man *was* created for companionship and fellowship with you. It is a solace to our inward being to worship Someone who needs nothing and yet finds joy in my fellowship.

Express yourself in adoration for this quality of God.
Speak it audibly or write out your praise in your own devotional journal.

2. PRAISE GOD FOR WHAT HE MEANS TO ME.

The Independent One for me. He is an everlasting refuge and defense. "He himself is not tempted with evil for he has no need that is not already supplied. This is *only one* aspect of his nature. If such were the only quality I would find you quite foreboding and so separate from me that I could only hide in despair. Your separateness and independence is for my protection and defense. Here is One whom Satan cannot tempt—One whom the devil must fear. I rush to this Rock of Ages to hide myself in him. You love me and understand me and only long to comfort and help me.

How do you personally relate to the independence of God, and God who is Jah—The Independent One?
Speak it out or write it out. It is *so important* that you establish *your own* devotional journal.

3. CONFESSION OF SIN

It is easy to say that I have often played God and found myself woefully lacking. I am not at all sufficient unto myself. In any area of life I come up very short: (1) My intelligence is like a little child, and not a very bright little child. (2) My moral strength is as water in consistency — the track record is so spotty it beggars description. (3) My social conduct is not at all perfect. In all these areas and several others I need forgiveness and how I want to hurry into the arms of One who will make up my lack!

It is a sin to *"despise authority."* When I want my own way and insist on doing it myself, I have sinned in a serious manner. Dear God, I plead guilty and want to truly repent.

What personal sins do you want to confess? We *must* speak them to remove them.
Do it! *Now.* There is no one else you have sinned against more than God. Tell him so!

4. SING A PRAYER TO GOD.

I stand amazed in the presence
Of Jesus the Nazarene,
And wonder how He could love me,
A sinner, condemned, unclean.

How marvelous! how wonderful!
And my song shall ever be:
How marvelous! how wonderful
Is my Savior's love for me!

Open your hymn book and sing the rest of the verses—or even sing another prayer song.

5. READ HIS WORD TO HIM!

His Word

[40]Having received the commander's permission, Paul stood on the steps and motioned to the crowd. When they were all silent, he said to them in Aramaic:

"Brothers and fathers, listen now to my defense."
22 [2]When they heard him speak to them in Aramaic, they became very quiet.

Then Paul said: [3]"I am a Jew, born in Tarsus of Cilicia, but brought up in this city. Under Gamaliel I was thoroughly trained in the law of our fathers and was just as zealous for God as any of you are today. [4]I persecuted the followers of this Way to their death, arresting both men and women and throwing them into prison, [5]as also the high priest and all the council can testify. I even obtained letters from them to their brothers in Damascus, and went there to bring these people as prisoners to Jerusalem to be punished.

[6]"About noon as I came near Damascus, suddenly a bright light from heaven flashed around me. [7]I fell to the ground and heard a voice say to me, 'Saul! Saul! Why do you persecute me?'

[8]"'Who are you, Lord?' I asked.

"'I am Jesus of Nazareth, whom you are persecuting,' he replied. [9]My companions saw the light, but they did not understand the voice of him who was speaking to me.

— Acts 21:40 — 22:9, NIV

WEEK TWENTY-TWO — FRIDAY

Read His Word to Him.

I know you have no problem in understanding what to us are "foreign" languages. The commander understood Greek—we do not know that he followed the words of Paul in the Aramaic language. It was the language of the Old Testament scriptures—one that these zealous Jews so much appreciated. I want to hear him all over again—with you I want to listen: Paul is reaching out to the crowd—nay, you are reaching out through him. Paul is sincere as he addresses them as "brothers and fathers"—(your sons).

Please express your response to this beautiful text. Put your expression in your own prayer diary.

6. READ HIS WORD FOR YOURSELF.

What has changed me? It has been—and continues to be—a personal encounter with the living Christ! Such an encounter is *not* without the word—indeed all I know of you issues from what you have said through the nine writers of the New Testament, and the several more of the Old Testament. But it *is* apart from the word—for the application is apart, i.e., does not automatically happen to all who read or hear this blessed story. It is the Spirit who gives life to the letter—it is the Holy Spirit who through the word enlivens the word to bring conviction of sin—righteousness—(his righteousness and my lack of it) and judgment—there is no automatic result.

Pause in his presence and either audibly or in written form tell him all his word means to you.

7. READ HIS WORD IN THANKSGIVING.

Thank you for (1) Paul's defense—in it I see myself! (2) For the wonderful education of Paul—which both helped and hindered him. (3) Thank you for the total zeal of Paul—even to death. (4) For the use of the precious term "brothers"—to each other and to our blessed Lord. (5) Thank you for the interesting time you chose to reveal yourself at high noon—not hidden—out where all could see and know.

Give yourself to your own expression of gratitude—write it or speak it!

8. READ HIS WORD IN MEDITATION.

"... but they did not understand the voice of him who was speaking to me." It would be most instructive if we knew in what tone of voice Paul said this. Was he sad? Was he regretting this fact? Was he disappointed? To his companions something had happened but they could not define it. We could ask these men with Saul and they would tell you of the unusual light. If the light continued as long as the voice, it must have been for two or three minutes. (Please read all the words our Lord spoke to Saul as in 9:1ff.; 22:9, 10; 26:12ff.) Why did the Lord arrange it this way? So we could exercise faith in his power. Either we believe Saul as a reliable witness or we do not.

Pause—wait—think—then express yourself in thoughtful praise or thanks.

9. READ HIS WORD FOR PETITIONS.

As Paul speaks to the crowd from the steps of the tower of Antonia he moves me to pray: (1) May I be as ready to speak on any and all occasions as was Paul. (2) How I want to know the heart language of those to whom I speak. (3) Humble my spirit until I can love those who hate me. (4) Give me admiration for the capacity of dedi- cation since this is what you can use. (5) Keep me aware that it is very possible to be sincerely wrong. (6) May I see my Lord in the bright light of his power and love as I read your word. (7) I want to believe in my heart of hearts that to serve men is to serve you—to hurt men is to hurt you.

Right here add your personal requests—and his answers.

10. READ HIS WORD AND WAIT—LISTEN—GOD SPEAKS!

Having ears to hear let me hear! (1) "All men are potential 'brothers and fathers.'" (2) "The new birth is the one most important preparation for service." (3) "I am alive and sensitive in the lives and bodies of men and women."

11. INTERCESSION FOR THE LOST WORLD

Vietnam — Point for prayer: (1) *Unreached peoples in Vietnam. The Chinese*—only about 2,000 believers in 10 congregations are known among these 3,000,000 people in Vietnam.

12. SING PRAISES TO OUR LORD.

Come, Thou Fount of ev'ry blessing,
Tune my heart to sing Thy grace;
Streams of mercy, never ceasing,
Call for songs of loudest praise.

Teach me some melodious sonnet,
Sung by flaming tongues above;
Praise the mount—I'm fixed upon it—
Mount of Thy redeeming love.

WEEK TWENTY-TWO — SATURDAY

1. PRAISE GOD FOR WHO HE IS.

Jehovah — the Eternal, Ever-Loving One. This is the name most often used concerning yourself in the Old Testament. I do want to try to lift up my heart to you as the Great Eternal One! You who inhabit eternity! You have no beginning and no end — the self-existent One! How many men upon the earth realize just who you are? Less than

half — of those who do, how many know of the reality of your Being? So very few! This does not change your Being. There never will be a day or a night when you do not love all men with a love that cannot stop. For just one man, I want to fall down before you in praise and deep gratitude!

Express yourself in adoration for this quality of God.
Speak it audibly or write out your praise in your own devotional journal.

2. PRAISE GOD FOR WHAT HE MEANS TO ME.

Jehovah — Eternal — Ever-Loving One for me! I take great strength from your strength — I find everlasting value in my life because of your Eternal Life. I want to be much more loving — and much more longsuffering in my love because of the exhaustless ever-loving attitude you have toward me. There are so many times, places and

people where I acted as if there was no eternal heaven or eternal hell — as if there was no wonderfully loving God who cared enough to send His Son to die for my sins. Dear God, you did not change because I did. I came back to you and found you just as I left you. The Eternal, Ever-Loving One. Praise your name!

How do you personally relate to the eternalness of God, and God who is Jehovah?
Speak it out or write it out. It is *so important* that you establish *your own* devotional journal.

3. CONFESSION OF SIN

What I have just prayed is part of my confession of sin. How many hundreds of times have I confessed my sin to you? Does it not get monotonous? Not if my sin is fresh — not if my sin is new — not if my guilt is current! Indeed it is. Oh, eternal One I shall be so glad to one day inhabit eternity with you where I shall be removed from sin, where Satan has been taken out of the environment

of man. Right now I want to open up my heart and fully, freely confess my sin and need. Forgive me. I am so glad your forgiveness is like yourself — eternal.

"Haughty eyes" — It is almost humorous to see puny man looking down on one another, or worse yet, looking down upon what you have done or said or are. Forgive us — forgive me.

What personal sins do you want to confess? We *must* speak them to remove them.
Do it! *Now.* There is no one else you have sinned against more than God. Tell him so!

4. SING A PRAYER TO GOD.

Be not dismayed whate'er betide,
God will take care of you;
Beneath His wings of love abide,
God will take care of you.
God will take cre of you,

Thro' ev'ry day,
O'er all the way;
He will take care of you,
God will take care of you.

Open up your hymn book and sing the rest of the verses — or even sing another prayer song.

5. READ HIS WORD TO HIM!

His Word

[10]"'What shall I do, Lord?' I asked.

"'Get up,' the Lord said, 'and go into Damascus. There you will be told all that you have been assigned to do.' [11]My companions led me by the hand into Damascus, because the brilliance of the light had blinded me.

[12]"A man named Ananias came to see me. He was a devout observer of the law and highly respected by all the Jews living there. [13]He stood beside me and said 'Brother Saul, receive your sight!' And at that very moment I was able to see him.

[14]"Then he said: 'The God of our fathers has chosen you to know his will and to see the Righteous One and to hear words from his mouth. [15]You will be his witness to all men of what you have seen and heard. [16]And now what are you waiting for? Get up, be baptized and wash your sins

away, calling on his name.'

[17]"When I returned to Jerusalem and was praying at the temple, I fell into a trance [18]and saw the Lord speaking. 'Quick!' he said to me. 'Leave Jerusalem immediately, because they will not accept your testimony about me.'

[19]"'Lord,' I replied, 'these men know that I went from one synagogue to another to imprison and beat those who believe in you. [20]And when the blood of your martyr Stephen was shed, I stood there giving my approval and guarding the clothes of those who were killing him.'

[21]"Then the Lord said to me, 'Go; I will send you far away to the Gentiles.'"

[22]The crowd listened to Paul until he said this. Then they raised their voices and shouted, "Rid the earth of him! He's not fit to live!"
— *Acts 22:10-22, NIV*

Read His Word to Him.

It is good to remember what you *didn't* say to Saul as well as what you did say. Surely the most remarkable fact is that you did not tell him what to do to be saved. This wonderful task was given to a disciple—not a preacher—not an elder—not even an apostle, but to just a humble, unknown learner of our Lord. It surely seems here that

Jesus is speaking with demanding authority. "What it has been assigned for you to do." I hear you Lord! I hear you! We do know some things about the disciple who spoke to Saul: (1) He was a devout observer of the law. (2) He was highly respected by all the Jews living in Damascus.

Please express your response to this beautiful text. Put your expression in your own prayer diary.

6. READ HIS WORD FOR YOURSELF.

What a message Ananias had for Saul! Here is Saul's assignment: (1) God has chosen you to know his will. Evidently for salvation and service. (2) To see the Righteous One. I place myself—as much as possible—in the place of Saul. I have received my inward spiritual sight. I believe

you have chosen me through the good news, as you have all others who will respond to your voice through the preaching. I have seen the only one who is righteous. I am delighted that he has decided to give me his righteousness.

It is so important that you pause in his presence
and tell him all his word means to you.

7. READ HIS WORD IN THANKSGIVING.

(1) Thank you for Saul's wonderful question: "What shall I do, Lord?" (2) Thank you that we tell men what to do to be saved. (3) Thank you that each of us are in a different sense—but nonetheless real—"a chosen vessel." (4) Thank you for the wonder and meaning of Christian

baptism. (5) Thank you for Paul's prayer life—what an example and pattern for me. (6) Thank you for Stephen and his testimony—it was God's goad in Saul's heart. (7) Thank you for the courage of Paul in telling the truth even when he knew it meant rejection and imprisonment.

Give yourself to your own expression of gratitude—write it or speak it!

8. READ HIS WORD IN MEDITATION.

". . . the blood of your martyr Stephen." The term *martyr* could also be translated "witness." Our Lord told the apostles they would be his witnesses—and each one of them was called upon to give their lives for their testimony. Stephen's blood—like that of Abel, cries from the ground.

What does it say? (1) I loved the truth of salvation more than my life. We can say that and not die a violent death. We all give our lives for something. (2) I did not run from a difficult situation. I did not ask for it, but once I was in it, I did not run from it.

Pause—wait—think—then express yourself in thoughtful praise or thanks.

9. READ HIS WORD FOR PETITIONS.

What a great effort Paul put forth to reach his beloved fellow kinsmen—in what he said there are many petitions: (1) I want to remember you do not tell men what to do to be saved—I do! (2) Keep my eyes closed to this world—but open to your world. (3) May I remember that I am chosen to do a work no one else can do. (4) Thank you

that I can see your blessed "Righteous One" any time I am willing to look. (5) Make me a witness of what I have seen and heard from you. (6) I know some men will not hear your word—show me who they are. (7) Remind me of all the associations in my past that can become your goad to my conscience.

Please, please remember these are prayers—speak them—reword them!

10. READ HIS WORD AND WAIT—LISTEN—GOD SPEAKS!

In these several verses there are several messages to me: (1) "Day by day it will be told you from my word what I want you to do." (2) "You are the only witness I

have in several places." (3) "Some men will never understand, but many will."

11. INTERCESSION FOR THE LOST WORLD

Vietnam — Point for prayer: (1) *About one half million Vietnamese fled* to other lands in 1975; many are seeking the Lord in refugee camps in Asia, and also in the lands to

which they have gone—espeically in France and the U.S.A. Pray for the brethren ministering to them.

12. SING PRAISES TO OUR LORD.

Come, we that love the Lord,
And let our joys be known;

Join in a song with sweet accord,
And thus surround the throne.

1. PRAISE GOD FOR WHO HE IS.

"O come, let us worship and kneel before *Jehovah Our Maker*" (Psa. 95:6; Eph. 2:22). There is so much in this word: This is a reference to your work after creation. As Paul says in Ephesians 2:10 "We are his *workmanship*." It is common knowledge that the Greek term here is the one from whom we have the English word "poem." How wonderful to know you are at work composing poems of each life. You are in the business of making something beautiful out of each person. Poetry has such an appeal — it touches us more deeply than any other form of expression. What if man refuses to yield to you? Paul's expression has reference to all Christians not all men.

Express yourself in adoration for this quality of God.
Speak it audibly or write out your praise in your own devotional journal.

2. PRAISE GOD FOR WHAT HE MEANS TO ME.

Dear God, I want to be so pliable in your hand that you can fashion a poem in the clay that is me. This surely gives a new reason for loving poetry. "Could my heart but see Creation as God sees it, — from within: See His grace behind its beauty, see his will behind its force; see the flame of life shoot upward when the April days begin; see the wane of life rush outward from its pure eternal source" (*Edmond G. A. Holms*). What is here said so beautifully of physical creation is far more meaningfully said of the new creation. My loving, all-wise, all-powerful Potter, Artist, Poet, I yield myself gladly to you. Write another stanza of my life.

How do you personally relate to the poetry of God, and God who is "Jehovah Our Maker"?
Speak it out or write it out. It is *so important* that you establish *your own* devotional journal.

3. CONFESSION OF SIN

We have such a strong aversion to poor poetry — what is sometimes called "doggerel." Why is this true? Because such is a reflection on the Great Poet. All our efforts to wax poetic are but the yapping of a mongrel compared to the beauty of your heart expressed in life. Dear God, forgive my stupid expression! Help me to quietly yield to your use in what you want to say through me today.

What personal sins do you want to confess? We *must* speak them to remove them.
Do it! *Now.* There is no one else you have sinned against more than God. Tell him so!

4. SING A PRAYER TO GOD.

Break Thou the bread of life,
Dear Lord, to me,
As Thou didst break the loaves
Beside the sea;

Beyond the sacred page I seek Thee, Lord;
My spirit pants for Thee,
O living Word.

Open your hymn book and sing the rest of the verses — or even sing another prayer song.

5. READ HIS WORD TO HIM!

His Word

[23] As they were shouting and throwing off their cloaks and flinging dust into the air, [24] the commander ordered Paul to be taken into the barracks. He directed that he be flogged and questioned in order to find out why the people were shouting at him like this. [25] As they stretched him out to flog him, Paul said to the centurion standing there, "Is it legal for you to flog a Roman citizen who hasn't even been found guilty?"

[26] When the centurion heard this, he went to the commander and reported it. "What are you going to do?" he asked. "This man is a Roman citizen."

[27] The commander went to Paul and asked, "Tell me, are you a Roman citizen?"

"Yes, I am," he answered.

[28] Then the commander said, "I had to pay a big price for my citizenship."

"But I was born a citizen," Paul replied.

[29] Those who were about to question him withdrew immediately. The commander himself was alarmed when he realized that he had put Paul, a Roman citizen, in chains.
— *Acts 22:23-29, NIV*

Read His Word to Him.

What impact will the cries of the mob make upon you? I'm sure you can hear them yet. No doubt there have been many since who cried out equal blasphemy! How loud are some men in their blatant rejection of eternal life. Then there are the larger group represented by the army commander. He is more confused than ever. He thought Paul was an Egyptian. He turns out to be a Greek-speaking Jew. When he lets him speak he talks Aramaic. Now he finds a man of influence on his hands whom all men seem to hate. When he proceeds to do the one thing he believes will loosen his tongue, he finds he is a Roman citizen. He, like a multitude today, is confused.

Please express your response to this beautiful text. Put your expression in your own prayer diary.

6. READ HIS WORD FOR YOURSELF.

How easy this is to do: (1) When is it right—and when is it not right to "claim your rights"? How I have struggled with this principle—I'm sure that in Paul we have an example of what should be done. (2) How open and honest is Paul under any and all conditions. So must I be regardless of the price. (3) Honesty and openness always honors the one we serve and ultimately it honors all. (4) I believe there are officials in our own government who could be strongly influenced for you if there were only someone like Paul to tell them. Dear Lord, if you want me for this task, here am I.

It is so important that you pause in his presence
and either audibly or in written form tell him all his word means to you.

7. READ HIS WORD IN THANKSGIVING.

(1) Thank you for even an army barracks (the Tower of Antonia) where protection and rest can be found. (2) Thank you that Paul was willing, but not anxious, to receive a flogging—he had had several. (3) Thank you for all the rights of a Roman citizen—many of them transferred into rights as American citizens. (4) Thank you that a sense of justice does prevail in the most unlikely places. (5) Thank you that I can be a prisoner to King Jesus. (6) Thank you for all the rights of a citizen of the heavenly country. (7) Thank you that one day *all* injustice will be put into balance.

Give yourself to your own expression of gratitude—write it or speak it!

8. READ HIS WORD IN MEDITATION.

"...I was born a citizen." I was born a citizen of America. What a priceless privilege! I have also been to 28 countries and I have seen how much more Americans have of everything. Of everything but gratitude. I found many people in India or Burma who have much more appreciation of what God has given them than the average American has for the hundred-fold God has given him. All of which demonstrates in loving example the truth of our Lord's words: "A man's life (or happiness) does not consist in the abundance of what he has." At the same time, neither does a man's life consist in forgetting or ignoring what he has. A man's real happiness is found in living on this earth in whatever country we are a citizen in just the same way my Lord did who was a citizen of the eternal country called heaven. Our Lord could have said He also represented "no ordinary city"—it is called the new Jerusalem—the city four square!

Pause—wait—think—then express yourself in thoughtful praise or thanks.

9. READ HIS WORD FOR PETITIONS.

Paul had been beaten many times—but if he could avoid it he did. I find requests in his action: (1) How tame are all my efforts to serve you when compared with Paul—move me to more meaningful effort. (2) Move me to ask questions that probe motives. (3) How glad I am to claim the rights of my heavenly citizenship. (4) Etch upon my heart these words: "There is therefore *now* no condemnation to them who are in Christ Jesus" (Rom. 8:1). (5) Do I know what it means to be "born free" by the new birth? Help me! (6) My Lord said of Lazarus, and the commander must have said of Paul, "loose him and let him go"—speak these words to my heart. (7) Even though Paul was still in jail he was the most liberated man there.

Right here add your personal requests—and his answers.

10. READ HIS WORD AND WAIT—LISTEN—GOD SPEAKS!

Speak to me through these verses: (1) "Four walls and iron bars is not the only prison." (2) "Use whatever means possible to give the gospel a hearing." (3) "A very large price has been paid for your eternal citizenship."

11. INTERCESSION FOR THE LOST WORLD

Vietnam — Points for prayer: (1) Radio broadcasts from Manila are the only direct contact with the believers now. Pray for the two-hour daily broadcast in Vietnamese, one-hour daily in Cambodian and Laotian. (2) *Thousands of Vietnamese continue to flee from oppression by boat.* Only about 30%-50% ever reach a non-Communist land. The surrounding countries cannot absorb this flow of refugees, and refuse them sanctuary. Pray for these tragic people.

12. SING PRAISES TO OUR LORD.

O Worship the King, all glorious above,
And gratefully sing His wonderful love;

Our Shield and Defender, the Ancient of days,
Pavilioned in splendor, and girded with praise.

WEEK TWENTY-THREE — MONDAY

1. PRAISE GOD FOR WHO HE IS.

Jehovah-Jireh—"The Lord will provide, or the Lord will see" (Gen. 22:14). ". . . His *pre-vision* means His *pro-vision*" (Lockyer). Bless your name which includes so very, very much! How well does this name describe my relationship to you! Surely this would be my testimony for the past 62 years. You saw my need and moved to meet it. Let me try to list the ways—I shall only mention those which have as much application to others as they do to myself: (1) Parents who loved me and provided food,

shelter and clothes. They also gave me love. I want to honor my dear mother who will be 86 years old one month from today. You provided through her and my dear good father. (2) A school system—teachers who no doubt were under paid and gave unselfishly of themselves—but actually it was your pre-vision that worked through this provision. We would have no such free school system without faith moving our founding fathers.

Express yourself in adoration for this quality of God.
Speak it audibly or write out your praise in your own devotional journal.

2. PRAISE GOD FOR WHAT HE MEANS TO ME.

Jehovah-Jireh to me. I have combined the two concepts for this day and this name. How glad I am to express my praise and thanksgiving to you. (3) You provided me companions of a moral upright kind—the simple joys of childhood were surely mine. I did not mingle with thieves or drug users, or immoral people. I was not religious—I

had little or no faith in you—but your dearest prevision gave me this provision. (4) You gave me associations that led to my salvation—for which I shall never cease to thank you and shout for joy—hallelujah! You did indeed show me the lamb slain from the foundation of the world—just for me!

How do you personally relate to the provisions of God, and God who is Jehovah-Jireh for me?
Speak it out or write it out. It is so important that you establish your own devotional journal.

3. CONFESSION OF SIN

That I should ever forget or become indifferent to your wonderful provision would be—and is, the sin of all sins! Forgive me. How gloriously you have provided in the work you have given me to do! Dear God, I have taken the credit when it all belonged to you. Forgive me! I have been, and am now delighted to teach, preach, write, but most of all to evangelize and make learners of your wonderful self! Too much emphasis has been placed on physical

appearance of books—buildings—etc., forgive me! Standing and status among men has at times been my sin— forgive! Dear God, I freely confess that all I am and have is from you and that not of myself—it is your gift!

"Insult on insult." Have I ever thought injury or hurt or disappointment came from you and returned in kind? Yes. Oh, what blindness—what total selfishness. Forgive me.

What personal sins do you want to confess? We must speak them to remove them.
Do it! Now. There is no one else you have sinned against more than God. Tell him so!

4. SING A PRAYER TO GOD.

"Give me thy heart," says the Father above,
No gift so precious to Him as our love,
Softly He whispers wherever thou art,
"Gratefully trust me, and give me thy heart."
"Give me thy heart,

Give me thy heart,"
Hear the soft whisper, whever thou art;
From this dark world He would draw thee apart,
Speaking so tenderly,
"Give me thy heart."

Open your hymn book and sing the rest of the verses—or even sing another prayer song.

5. READ HIS WORD TO HIM!

His Word

³⁰The next day, since the commander wanted to find out exactly why Paul was being accused by the Jews, he released him and ordered the chief priests and all the Sanhedrin to assemble. Then he brought Paul and had him stand before them.

23 Paul looked straight at the Sanhedrin and said, "My brothers, I have fulfilled my duty to God in all good conscience to this day." ²At this the high priest Ananias ordered those standing near Paul to strike him on the

mouth. ³Then Paul said to him, "God will strike you, you whitewashed wall! You sit there to judge me according to the law, yet you yourself violate the law by commanding that I be struck!"

⁴Those who were standing near Paul said, "You dare to insult God's high priest?"

⁵Paul replied, "Brothers, I did not realize that he was the high priest; for it is written: 'Do not speak evil about the ruler of your people.'"
— *Acts 22:30 – 23:5, NIV*

Read His Word to Him.

How shall we go into the meeting of Paul with the Sanhedrin Council? You have known every man there since he was a small boy. Paul was sincere and child-like. He had indeed turned around and had become as transparent as a child in his faith. But there is another issue involved here: Paul is saying he contrasts with these men.

His conscience is clear and theirs has festered, rotted and died. They are even as our Savior described them, whitewashed tombs full of all manner of corruption. I hope I have represented the circumstance as it truly was. Forgive me where I am wrong.

Please express your response to this beautiful text. Put your expression in your own prayer diary.

6. READ HIS WORD FOR YOURSELF.

How would I react to this same type of treatment? Surely I would need the wisdom that comes down from above. But there would not be time to ask for such wisdom in such a circumstance. In many such times the wisdom we need comes from within as a spontaneous response of the Holy Spirit to the human spirit. Paul was seeking understanding and acceptance on behalf of our Lord. Was Paul struck on the mouth? The text does not say if he was or wasn't. Paul's instant reaction is as if he were struck. The command of the high priest was a slap in the face. We believe Paul. He simply did not know the man who spoke was the high priest. His words of description were accurate. Dear Lord, I do not know how I would have reacted. I am too weak and selfish.

Either audibly or in written form tell him all his word means to you.

7. READ HIS WORD IN THANKSGIVING.

I gladly do this: (1) Thank you for the sincere concern of Claudius Lysias to find out just who Paul was and what he had done. (2) Thank you for Paul's straight-forward expression of honesty and sincerity. (3) Thank you that the encounter was out in the open where the issues could be defined. (4) Thank you that both participants appealed to the law — it only points up the total inadequacy of law to settle any dispute. (5) Thank you for Paul's humility in admitting he was wrong. (6) Thank you that above it all and through it all the great judge of all men was a very interested participant. (7) Thank you for Luke's inspired account that includes all details.

Give yourself to your own expression of gratitude — write it or speak it!

8. READ HIS WORD IN MEDITATION.

"Do not speak evil about the ruler of your people." If this was a regulation of ancient Israel (and it was), how much more could it relate to a nation, a large share of which professes acceptance of our Lord? Speaking evil we take in the sense in which it is used here. No good is accomplished by accusation against leaders. A constant effort of this type of action can erode confidence and end in anarchy.

Pause — wait — think — then express yourself in thoughtful praise or thanks.

9. READ HIS WORD FOR PETITIONS.

If ever prayer was appropriate it was as Paul spoke to the Sanhedrin. (1) May I be as ready to stand before the judgment seat of my Lord. (2) How could I ever say, "I have fulfilled my duty to God"? (3) Dear Lord, I want to educate my conscience by your word. (4) Why did the high priest want Paul struck on the mouth? (5) Open my heart to be able to answer everyone as I should. (6) I know how destructive criticism can be — guard my mouth!

Please, please remember these are prayers — speak them — reword them!

10. READ HIS WORD AND WAIT — LISTEN — GOD SPEAKS!

Your word speaks to me today: (1) "Speak the truth in love, but speak the truth." (2) "Expect misunderstanding, but do not seek it." (3) "Give honor to whom honor is due."

11. INTERCESSION FOR THE LOST WORLD

Afghanistan — Population: 19,500,000. Growth rate 2.2%. 30 people per sq. km.

Point for prayer: (1) *Afghanistan is to all intents and purposes unevangelized.* Pray that this land may be opened for the preaching of the Gospel. Though there has been religious freedom since 1964, proselytization is forbidden, but all kinds of witness goes on quietly.

12. SING PRAISES TO OUR LORD.

Praise ye the Father! for His loving kindness,
Tenderly cares He for His erring children;

Praise Him, ye angels, praise Him in the heavens,
Praise ye Jehovah!

WEEK TWENTY-THREE — TUESDAY

1. PRAISE GOD FOR WHO HE IS.

Lord of hosts (Isa. 1:24). There are many hosts of whom you are Lord. All the angels are your hosts. I cannot imagine what commands are given to and carried out by these angelic beings. Surely this is indeed another whole world. May your will be done today in my life as it is done by those hosts of heaven who obey you there.

You are Lord of the hosts of demons — Satan and all his servants know that one day (in man's terms) they will all be cast into the eternal lake of fire. If we can read such a promise in your word, then such information is not unknown to our adversary and his host. How wonderfully encouraging this is to every one of your present children.

Express yourself in adoration for this quality of God.
Speak it audibly or write out your praise in your own devotional journal.

2. PRAISE GOD FOR WHAT HE MEANS TO ME.

Lord of hosts for me. Dear God, how poorly I do sometimes express my praise! Forgive me for being so terribly inadequate. At the same time I am determined to praise you. I need to, I want to, I will! You are Lord of the host of the spirits of just men made perfect. All those who have departed the body are presently under your Lordship. It must be an exhilarating experience to worship you and serve you in the world of the spirit. Abraham, Isaac and Jacob are not dead — you are *not* the God of the dead but of the living. What an immense host of individual living beings inhabit eternity with you.

You are the Lord of the host of your people alive on this earth today! How good it would be to see all of them at the same time — and to know each one as individuals.

How do you personally relate to the rulership of God, and God who is Lord of hosts?
Speak it out or write it out. It is *so important* that you establish *your own* devotional journal.

3. CONFESSION OF SIN

Are you the Lord of the host of thoughts that course through my mind in just one day? Every thought should be, can be brought under your Lordship. What of the host of choices I must make for this day? How can you be Lord of them? If my will is submitted to your will then my choices will be yours. It is so easy to say, Dear God, forgive me. I am not hiding anything from you. I do want my thoughts and decisions to be yours.

"Immodesty" — This is usually associated with women. But men can also be very immodest. In so many ways we are full of self and pride. Immodest in words — immodest in dress — immodest in not preferring others before self. Dear Lord of hosts, forgive me.

What personal sins do you want to confess? We *must* speak them to remove them.
Do it! *Now.* There is no one else you have sinned against more than God. Tell him so!

4. SING A PRAYER TO GOD.

'Tis so sweet to trust in Jesus,
Just to take Him at His Word;
Just to rest upon His promise;
Just to know, "Thus saith the Lord."

Jesus, Jesus, how I trust Him!
How I've proved Him o'er and o'er!
Jesus, Jesus, precious Jesus!
O for grace to trust Him more!

Open your hymn book and sing the rest of the verses — or even sing another prayer song.

5. READ HIS WORD TO HIM!

His Word

[6]Then Paul, knowing that some of them were Sadducees and the others Pharisees, called out in the Sanhedrin, "My brothers, I am a Pharisee, the son of a Pharisee. I stand on trial because of my hope in the resurrection of the dead." [7]When he said this, a dispute broke out between the Pharisees and the Sadducees, and the assembly was divided. [8](The Sadducees say that there is no resurrection, and that there are neither angels nor spirits, but the Pharisees acknowledge them all.)

[9]There was a great uproar, and some of the teachers of the law who were Pharisees stood up and argued vigorously. "We find nothing wrong with this man," they said. "What if a spirit or an angel has spoken to him?" [10]The dispute became so violent that the commander was afraid Paul would be torn to pieces by them. He ordered the troops to go down and take him away from them by force and bring him into the barracks.
— *Acts 23:6-10, NIV*

Read His Word to Him.

Dear Lord, what was the purpose of Paul's actions and words in this text? It is so obvious to you — so elementary — but with me — I struggle over it! Dear Lord, I know you were present when the examination took place. Was Paul using a ruse; a foil to escape what could have been at the best another beating? So it seems to me. Am I right? These men were capable of murder — as we shall see later. Did Paul know this and use this ancient controversy between Pharisees and Sadducees to protect himself from their wrath?

Please express your response to this beautiful text. Put your expression in your own prayer diary.

6. READ HIS WORD FOR YOURSELF.

I read this text for myself — as your sword to divide the thoughts and intents of my own heart! I have felt often like a Pharisee and the son of a Pharisee. I have felt this way — why? Because I have prayed more, taught more, preached more, because I have written more, traveled more or given more than other men — or especially than those I see and know about me. So what? So you Pharisee! You hypocrite! You worst of sinners! To be seen of men is to lose your eternal reward! Dear God, I love you and want to know you!

Pause in his presence and either audibly or in written form tell him all his word means to you.

7. READ HIS WORD IN THANKSGIVING.

This is a most pleasant task: (1) Thank you for Paul's daring wisdom in setting the Pharisees against the Sadducees. (2) Thank you for Paul's heritage, all of which he used for the advantage of the gospel. (3) Thank you for the wonderful hope of the resurrection of the dead. (4) Thank you that the only dead thing about me is my body — when I separate from this body it will be dead — I won't. (5) Thank you for the presence of ministering angels — present right now — right here helping me in ways best known to them and you. (6) Thank you that the spirit world is the real world — into which world I will move right on the other side of my last heart beat!

8. READ HIS WORD IN MEDITATION.

"We find nothing wrong with this man." Dear Lord, that this could always be our reputation! It was what those who examined him said of my Lord. The words of the governor of Judea are so poignant: "I find no fault in Him." The comparison between Paul's examination and that of our Savior is most striking. (1) There was nothing wrong in either's understanding of the scriptures and in perfect agreement with each other. (2) There was nothing wrong with their relationship to the fading glory of temple worship — both worship in spirit and truth. (3) There was nothing wrong with their understanding of the place of the law — one came to fulfill it and Paul proclaimed such was fulfilled.

Pause — wait — think — then express yourself in thoughtful praise or thanks.

9. READ HIS WORD FOR PETITIONS.

Paul set two groups against each other and escaped, but he needed prayer: (1) Give me the wisdom to be as wise as a serpent and harmless as a dove. (2) I want to be known as just a Christian — separate me from all party spirit. (3) Keep my hope of the resurrection burning brightly. (4) Send your ministering spirits to aid me today. (5) I want to be totally in submission to you as the Father of my spirit. (6) Deliver me from violent men.

Right here add your personal requests — and his answers.

10. READ HIS WORD AND WAIT — LISTEN — GOD SPEAKS!

I know you have much to tell me from this text: (1) "There are Pharisees and Sadducees today — beware." (2) "Let the dead bury the dead — publish the good news." (3) "There are lessons I am teaching in all opposition."

11. INTERCESSION FOR THE LOST WORLD

Afghanistan — Point for prayer: (1) *Unreached peoples* — this includes all the 40 peoples of this country. Special mention must be made of the Uzbeks, the many tribes north and east of Kabul living in the rugged mountain valleys of Nooristan, and also the nomadic peoples of the west. There are translations of the Scriptures in versions of the two official languages, but nothing is available in the minor languages.

12. SING PRAISES TO OUR LORD.

To God be the glory — great things He hath done,
So loved He the world that He gave us His Son,
Who yielded His life an atonement for sin
And opened the Life-gate that all may go in.
Praise the Lord, praise the Lord,

Let the earth hear His voice!
Praise the Lord, praise the Lord,
Let the people rejoice!
O come to the Father thro' Jesus the Son,
And give Him the glory — great things He hath done.

WEEK TWENTY-THREE — WEDNESDAY

1. PRAISE GOD FOR WHO HE IS.

My fortress (Psa. 144:2). How attractive is the thought of a large protective building of some type—a castle or some other sort of hiding place. No building can stand today against a nuclear attack. But our fortress is not a building but the divine Person of your very self! I am so glad to worship and bow before you in full recognition of those qualities of your character that match this metaphor. (1) A fortress is immediately identified by those who are in its vicinity. Oh, that all men would see you and know you for who you are and what you are! You can and want to be such a refuge and strength for all men. (2) A fortress is commodious—at least when we think of you in this regard, it is true. How many millions—yea, billions of men have found you such a place? No one has ever been disappointed in the adequacy of provisions for them in this fortress.

Express yourself in adoration for this quality of God.
Speak it audibly or write out your praise in your own devotional journal.

2. PRAISE GOD FOR WHAT HE MEANS TO ME.

My fortress—personally. Dear, dear God, I have so found you—and so I find you today! (3) A fortress reaches up high and impressive as a giant building against the sky—and yet has an immense foundation deep in the earth. This is what I have found and now find in you. All the way to the throne of heaven and yet you reach down to the deepest of human need. So strong and impressive, but fulfilling, you more than fulfill all my imagination conjures up. Higher than the highest—wider than ten million galaxies—deeper than the abyss. "A mighty fortress is my God—a bulwark never failing." (4) We think a fortress is for another age—it was meaningful for the past generations, but is only a museum reference today. Not so with you. I never felt my need more than now. In no time in human experience have we needed a shelter—a hiding place more than now. I securely rest and view the panorama of today's activities from my fortress.

How do you personally relate to the protection of God, and God who is my fortress?
Speak it out or write it out. It is *so important* that you establish *your own* devotional journal.

3. CONFESSION OF SIN

Have I always sought your protection? Have I withdrawn into my fortress and pulled up the gate? Have I rather found myself out in the open country attacked and wounded by the enemy? To ask is to answer. What was it that drew me away? "Every man is drawn away by his own desires" (Jas. 1:13-15). I need not, I do not blame you. Can I live always in a fortress? Where the fortress is in my own mind I can. It is when you dominate my mind that you become my "bulwark never failing." The walls of this building are my own will—when my will is your will, Satan cannot and will not enter. Dear God, forgive me for not being willing to do your will. My strength is in your will for me!

"Retaliation." We retaliate evil for evil when we believe that somehow our rights are being threatened. When we have no rights there is no retaliation. When all our rights are given to you then all vengeance also belongs with you. Dear God, I believe, help my unbelief.

What personal sins do you want to confess? We *must* speak them to remove them.
Do it! *Now.* There is no one else you have sinned against more than God. Tell him so!

4. SING A PRAYER TO GOD.

Walking in sunlight, all of my journey;
Over the mountains, thro' the deep vale;
Jesus has said "I'll never forsake thee,"
Promise divine that never can fail.

Heavenly sunlight, heavenly sunlight,
Flooding my soul with glory divine;
Hallelujah, I am rejoicing,
Singing His praises, Jesus is mine.

Open your hymn book and sing the rest of the verses—or even sing another prayer song.

5. READ HIS WORD TO HIM!

His Word

[11]The following night the Lord stood near Paul and said, "Take courage! As you have testified about me in Jerusalem, so you must also testify in Rome."

[12]The next morning the Jews formed a conspiracy and bound themselves with an oath not to eat or drink until they had killed Paul. [13]More than forty men were involved in this plot. [14]They went to the chief priests and elders and said, "We have taken a solemn oath not to eat anything until we have killed Paul. [15]Now then, you and the Sanhedrin petition the commander to bring him before you on the pretext of wanting more accurate information about his case. We are ready to kill him before he gets here."

[16]But when the son of Paul's sister heard of this plot, he went into the barracks and told Paul.

[17]Then Paul called one of the centurions and said, "Take this young man to the commander; he has something to tell him." [18]So he took him to the commander.

The centurion said, "Paul, the prisoner, sent for me and asked me to bring this young man to you because he has something to tell you."

— *Acts 23:11-18, NIV*

Read His Word to Him.

How remarkable you only need one small boy to overcome the power of forty men! Thank you, oh, thank you for speaking to Paul in the Jerusalem jail! Courage was to be found in your presence and promise. Your promise was not one of protection—although you provided that. It is enough to know we can speak for you. The word we speak is "a testimony." The personalness of our relationship to you can never be separated from what we speak on your behalf. A fast of death! What are you saying to me about fasting? You have a plot or plan for life and fasting is a part of it! How could the chief priests and elders of your people agree to such a plot?

Please express your response to this beautiful text. Put your expression in your own prayer diary.

6. READ HIS WORD FOR YOURSELF.

Dear Lord, I know you are always standing near me—according to your blessed promise you are with me always. The Lord is at hand! Blessed be your sweet presence. I know too, that the one word you give to me at all times and in every circumstance is to "Take courage." I also know the one thing you want most from me is a personal testimony to others of my relationship to you as saved sinner. This is not all I will tell but if I do not tell this there will be little reality to the rest of my words. From how many plots of Satan have you delivered me? How many dear loved ones have spoken a word to my great heavenly commander on my behalf and saved me from death? My Lord, you know, but I am most grateful!

It is so important that you pause in his presence and tell him all his word means to you.

7. READ HIS WORD IN THANKSGIVING.

(1) Thank you for our Lord's personal concern in Paul's outlook on life. (2) Thank you for the promise of travel mercies. (3) Thank you for the multiple ways you have of frustrating the evil plans of men. (4) Thank you for the courage and wisdom of Paul's nephew. (5) Thank you for the measure of justice, fairness found in the Roman army. (6) Thank you for Paul's willingness to be helped in whatever way you led. (7) Thank you for the believable details of this record.

Give yourself to your own expression of gratitude—write it or speak it!

8. READ HIS WORD IN MEDITATION.

"... this young man ... has something to tell you." Indeed he does! He could tell us of the respect and honor which his parents and himself had for his uncle. Evidently Paul was able to communicate his new found faith to at least a part of his family. This young man could tell us of how his faith delivered him from the confusion of the practices of the ritual and traditions of religion. The whole city of Jerusalem was full of conspiracy and unrest—this would have been so confusing to such a young man.

Pause—wait—think—then express yourself in thoughtful praise or thanks.

9. READ HIS WORD FOR PETITIONS.

Help comes from unexpected sources—it must have moved Paul to prayer—it does me: (1) Keep me aware my basic task is to be a witness for you. (2) I am aware that evil men even now plot to defeat your work—defeat their counsel. (3) Give me the dedication to the spread of your word these men had to stop it. (4) Thank you that young men are important in your work. (5) Teach me how important it is to include the whole family in your work. (6) Give me good and honest men in the government under which I live. (7) Open my mouth on all occasions to say something for you.

Please, please remember these are prayers—speak them—reword them!

10. READ HIS WORD AND WAIT—LISTEN—GOD SPEAKS!

I am listening—what do you want me to hear from this text? (1) "Take courage, I am with you as I was with Paul." (2) "Men's conspiracy cannot overcome my conspiracy of love." (3) "I have many ways of protecting you."

11. INTERCESSION FOR THE LOST WORLD

Afghanistan — Point for prayer: (1) *Missions*—there are a number of societies interested in the land. Pray for the right strategy to fulfill the Great Commission.

12. SING PRAISES TO OUR LORD.

We gather together to ask the Lord's blessing,
He chastens and hastens His will to make known;
The wicked oppressing cease them from distressing,
Sing praises to His name, He forgets not His own.

WEEK TWENTY-THREE — THURSDAY

1. PRAISE GOD FOR WHO HE IS.

"Cast your cares on the Lord and he will sustain you" (Psa. 55:22). You are the one who truly cares and can and does hold us up. How good to have one upon whom I can cast all my anxiety! What kind of a divine person are you that this is true? (1) A living sympathetic person. You listen with real understanding. You know much more about every problem than anyone else. You look into the face of every man and woman with kindly eyes of sympathetic interest. (2) You are never too busy or too occupied with "other things" to give your total interest for as long as we want to talk. (3) You say things and move things so we can get through the circumstance. You have promised to make it possible for us to solve our problems.

Express yourself in adoration for this quality of God.
Speak it audibly or write out your praise in your own devotional journal.

2. PRAISE GOD FOR WHAT HE MEANS TO ME.

For me. I do indeed gladly welcome this invitation. I do want to open my heart and share not only my mistakes but my plans and projects. Dear Lord, I have unsolved problems on the job. People make mistakes and some of them are very difficult to unravel. In ways that are only known by yourself help me to help those with whom I work. I have plans for spreading your word and helping your children to serve you. How I do need your wisdom in each and every part of these plans. Please help me to pause long enough to hear you speak. My strength and ability are all in you. Dear God, carry me through! What a wonderful quality of your character—bless you forever!

How do you personally relate to the concern of God, and God who is totally interested?
Speak it out or write it out. It is *so important* that you establish *your own* devotional journal.

3. CONFESSION OF SIN

Shall I admit that I carry my cares when your invitation is always open for me to cast them on you? Yes, this points up my blindness and insensitivity. But I am becoming more aware of your perpetual interest! If I only really knew just how much you truly care I would be much more than ready to lay down my burden at your feet. Much of my sin is a direct result of frustration, tension, anxiety. Dear Lord, if I could learn to relax in your presence and "cast all my care on you"—cast it away from me—inwardly, truly, deeply—I could live and move and decide and speak in a relaxed atmosphere and I would not sin so often. Help me! Open my willingness!

"Homosexuality." I am repulsed by this sin. I have no sexual desire whatsoever for my own kind. This is repugnant to me. But I *must* try to understand and help those who do.

What personal sins do you want to confess? We *must* speak them to remove them.
Do it! *Now.* There is no one else you have sinned against more than God. Tell him so!

4. SING A PRAYER TO GOD.

The name of Jesus is so sweet,
I love its music to repeat;
It makes my joys full and complete,
The precious name of Jesus.

"Jesus," oh, how sweet the name!
"Jesus," ev'ry day the same;
"Jesus," let all saints proclaim
Its worthy praise forever.

Open your hymn book and sing the rest of the verses—or even sing another prayer song.

5. READ HIS WORD TO HIM!

His Word

[19]The commander took the young man by the hand, drew him aside and asked, "What is it you want to tell me?"

[20]He said: "The Jews have agreed to ask you to bring Paul before the Sanhedrin tomorrow on the pretext of wanting more accurate information about him. [21]Don't give in to them, because more than forty of them are waiting in ambush for him. They have taken an oath not to eat or drink until they have killed him. They are ready now, waiting for your consent to their request."

[22]The commander dismissed the young man and cautioned him, "Don't tell anyone that you have reported this to me."

[23]Then he called two of his centurions and ordered them, "Get ready a detachment of two hundred soldiers, seventy horsemen and two hundred spearmen to go to Caesarea at nine tonight. [24]Provide mounts for Paul so that he may be taken safely to Governor Felix."

[25]He wrote a letter as follows:
[26]Claudius Lysias,
To His Excellency, Governor Felix:
Greetings.

[27]This man was seized by the Jews and they were about to kill him, but I came with my troops and rescued him, for I had learned that he is a Roman citizen. [28]I wanted to know why they were accusing him, so I brought him to their Sanhedrin. [29]I found that the accusation had to do with questions about their law, but there was no charge against him that deserved death or imprisonment. [30]When I was informed of a plot to be carried out against the man, I sent him to you at once. I also ordered his accusers to present to you their case against him.

— Acts 23:19-30, NIV

Read His Word to Him.

How good it is to identify yourself with the incident before us — since you have a particular interest in the innocency and sincerity of young people. How sad to think that such a good man as Claudius Lysias was not saved. Perhaps he was at some time not here indicated.

How did you look on the forty men? I could venture some opinions, but I do not really know. Did you place the decision in the mind of the commander to assemble such a large detachment to protect Paul? You have done this before in other cases. Is there a lie in the letter of Lysias?

Please express your response to this beautiful text. Put your expression in your own prayer diary.

6. READ HIS WORD FOR YOURSELF.

Paul had a long horseback ride to begin at nine o'clock at night. Paul must have been past fifty years old — it would not be easy for him — he had already been through so much, and now this. What was Paul's attitude? He has already told us: "I am ready not only to be bound, but also to die in Jerusalem for the name of the Lord Jesus." "I consider my life worth nothing to me, if only I may finish the race and complete the task the Lord has given me." Do you hear these words? Do you accept them for yourself? (I am speaking this to myself.)

Pause in his presence and either audibly or in written form tell him all his word means to you.

7. READ HIS WORD IN THANKSGIVING.

(1) Thank you for the respect for personal privacy on the part of the army commander. (2) Thank you for the negative response Lysias was receiving from his association with the Jews — and the positive one had had with Paul. (3) Thank you for the importance of Paul (or the Roman law) in the mind of the commander. (4) Thank you for the wide influence given to the gospel through Paul. (5) Thank you for the example of how all things are working together for good. (6) Thank you for Paul's deliverance from the center of hatred and controversy.

Give yourself to your own expression of gratitude — write it or speak it!

8. READ HIS WORD IN MEDITATION.

"... for I learned that he is a Roman citizen." The order of events is conveniently slanted so as to leave the commander in the best light. It would give him credit for rescuing a Roman citizen from death at the hands of a Jewish mob, when the facts are Lysias thought he was apprehending an Egyptian terrorist. How easy it is to arrange events on paper for our advantage.

In a Roman army officer we can understand the motives. In a Christian leader we have a much more serious problem. Pride and position become more important than truth.

Pause — wait — think — then express yourself in thoughtful praise or thanks.

9. READ HIS WORD FOR PETITIONS.

Uncle Paul was really in trouble. We wonder what requests this young man had for Paul. We can lift our hearts with him in prayer: (1) Give us young men today with the same courage and boldness. (2) Warn me, through whatever means you have, of impending danger. (3) Give me the care and courtesy of the commander. (4) Thank you for the protective escort of Paul — give me protection on my many journeys. (5) Did Claudius Lysias lie to cover up his mistakes? Deliver me from such a temptation. (6) Help me to claim my rights as a citizen of heaven.

Right here add your personal requests — and his answers.

10. READ HIS WORD AND WAIT — LISTEN — GOD SPEAKS!

Speak to me through these verses: (1) "I still have young men who will risk all to help my cause." (2) "There are good and honest men in positions of authority." (3) "Be always prepared to move to the third heaven."

11. INTERCESSION FOR THE LOST WORLD

Afghanistan — Point for prayer: (1) *There are Christians serving the Lord* from other lands as doctors, teachers, etc. Pray that their lives may recommend the Savior to those with whom they come into contact, and that they may obtain opportunities to witness and see fruit for their labors. Most of these workers are, at present, working in Kabul; pray that some may be able to work in other parts of the land. There is one Community Church that serves their ex-patriates, but no Afghan is allowed to attend any meetings.

12. SING PRAISES TO OUR LORD.

"Man of Sorrows," what a name
For the Son of God who came

Ruined sinners to reclaim!
Hallelujah! what a Savior!

WEEK TWENTY-THREE — FRIDAY

1. PRAISE GOD FOR WHO HE IS.

"His truth endureth to all generations" (Psa. 100:5). How strong is this word! All you have said—which is written truth—all you have done, which is created truth—all you are which is living truth—or the source of truth, shall never end. Every generation shall find it even as I have found it. If a generation is considered as forty years I shall live into two generations. My father and grandfather found all you said and all you created and all you are the same as I have. Two thousand generations from today truth (that which is equal with reality) will be the same! Praise your wonderful eternal self!

Express yourself in adoration for this quality of God.
Speak it audibly or write out your praise in your own devotional journal.

2. PRAISE GOD FOR WHAT HE MEANS TO ME.

Your truth endureth for me! Dear God, I have forgotten your truth—but it did not change. I have ignored your truth, but it was the same. I have substituted for your truth, but it remained the same. How comforting to move in the context of truth! How I want our children, the next generation, to know the security and solidness of such a faith. The meaning of what you have made—the description of yourself depends entirely on the written word, therefore the truth written is the most important entity we have. May I do all I can to preserve and spread your word.

How do you personally relate to the truth of God, and God who is truth?
Speak it out or write it out. It is *so important* that you establish *your own* devotional journal.

3. CONFESSION OF SIN

Since it is the responsibility of each generation to let every other generation know your truth, and since living it is the best means of showing the truth, I ask forgiveness! You desire truth (or reality) in the inward man—I do too. Why do I find myself hedging and vacillating when I know what is right? Forgive me! Dear Savior, you are living truth. How I want to follow you. Cleanse my motives! I take your gracious offer of freedom!

"Arrogance." Dear God, why should I ever entertain such an idea? But I have, I do, it will take a long time and many repetitions, but I want to kneel again with the One who washed feet. Arrogance begins and ends in the mind.

What personal sins do you want to confess? We *must* speak them to remove them.
Do it! *Now.* There is no one else you have sinned against more than God. Tell him so!

4. SING A PRAYER TO GOD.

Break Thou the bread of life,
Dear Lord, to me,
As Thou didst break the loaves
Beside the sea;

Beyond the sacred page
I seek Thee, Lord;
My spirit pants for Thee,
O living Word.

Open your hymn book and sing the rest of the verses—or even sing another prayer song.

5. READ HIS WORD TO HIM!

His Word

[31]So the soldiers, carrying out their orders, took Paul with them during the night and brought him as far as Antipatris. [32]The next day they let the cavalry go on with him, while they returned to the barracks. [33]When the cavalry arrived in Caesarea, they delivered the letter to the governor and handed Paul over to him. [34]The governor read the letter and asked what province he was from. Learning that he was from Cilicia, [35]he said, "I will hear your case when your accusers get here." Then he ordered that Paul be kept under guard in Herod's palace.

— *Acts 23:31-35, NIV*

Read His Word to Him.

How very good to relate this text to yourself! It does seem like a very large contingent of men to march most of the night in protection of one man. But then Paul was only representative of the value Rome placed on every citizen of her empire. I am sure it occurred to you (please excuse my presumption) that this is but a poor representation of the value you place on every one of your citizens.

There is a rather remarkable comparison possible here. I do believe Satan can do nothing with me or to me that you (and myself) do not permit him to. What far, far superior power we have in you and your angels and in the present person of the Holy Spirit than the forty men of Satan's force. Praise you for this assurance.

6. READ HIS WORD FOR YOURSELF.

An all-night ride—Paul must have been totally worn out when he was shown to his room in Herod's palace. Did Paul talk to the soldiers on the journey? Did he question God's strange directions in his life? He would have been less than human if he didn't. I wonder what Paul did in Herod's palace? I am sure he prayed. Did he have anything to read? Did he influence his guards here as he did in Rome? Did he write letters we do not have? Perhaps these are all idle questions, but they represent my own relationship to this text. Dear Lord, may I rejoice all over again that I have liberty of movement and choice of residence.

It is so important that you pause in his presence
and either audibly or in written form tell him all his word means to you.

7. READ HIS WORD IN THANKSGIVING.

(1) Thank you for the well developed sense of duty that direction in the right area can accomplish. (2) Thank you for Paul's humble submission to your will in his life. (3) Thank you that Paul did not understand the immediate purpose for all things—since I do not this encourages me. (4) Thank you for the influence of the gospel in high-places—even the governor. (5) Thank you for the reasonable care given to Paul. (6) Thank you for Paul's persistence in waiting out a solution to his imprisonment. (7) Thank you for your ultimate purpose which was being worked out through all man's actions for and against your servant.

Give yourself to your own expression of gratitude—write it or speak it!

8. READ HIS WORD IN MEDITATION.

". . . kept under guard in Herod's palace." What thoughts filled the mind and heart of Paul in Herod's palace? Here are a few possibilities: (1) Why is Herod so prosperous when we all know what type of life he lives? God's answer: Physical prosperity is *not* always an indication of my blessing. My dear Son had no where to lay his head. (2) How can my confinement advance the gospel? God's answer: You be faithful where you are and I'll handle the larger purposes of promoting the good news. (3) Why does truth always come out second best? God's answer: It doesn't— 2,000 years of reading Luke's record has told over and over again who was true.

Pause—wait—think—then express yourself in thoughtful praise or thanks.

9. READ HIS WORD FOR PETITIONS.

Paul's journey and arrival at Caesarea no doubt moved him to pray. We can also find here petitions: (1) I want to be as willing to carry out some inconvenient tasks as the soldiers who traveled with Paul. (2) Help me to be as uncomplaining as Paul in my service for my Lord. (3) Is there a governor in one of our states to whom we could deliver a message from you? (4) Deliver me from the great "accuser of the brethren." (5) Thank you for the treatment Paul received from civil authority. (6) How can we reach the leaders of our country with the message of your Son? (7) Grant me wisdom to interpret your answer to the two above questions—which are really requests for help.

Please, please remember these are prayers—speak them—reword them!

10. READ HIS WORD AND WAIT—LISTEN—GOD SPEAKS!

Speak to me through Paul's experience: (1) "I am able to work through all circumstances." (2) "Every one of the soldiers is spending all eternity in heaven or hell." (3) "Paul did all he could to be my witness."

11. INTERCESSION FOR THE LOST WORLD

Afghanistan — Points for prayer: (1) *Afghan believers* —pray for some who are secret believers, and have little opportunity to share with other believers. Pray that their faith may grow strong and be without compromise in a very hostile environment. (2) *Witness to Afghans in other lands.* Pray for the witness in mission hospitals in Pakistan to which many Afghans go. There they have the opportunity to hear the Gospel and take back literature and Gospel records to their homes. Afghan university students in the West have proved quite responsive to the Gospel, and a number have sought the Lord in North America and Europe. Pray for these Afghans who have believed but who find it very difficult to remain in their own land on the completion of their studies.

12. SING PRAISES TO OUR LORD.

All creatures of our God and King,
Lift up your voice and with us sing
Alleluia! Alleluia!
Thou burning sun with golden beam,

Thou silver moon with softer gleam!
O praise Him, O praise Him!
Alleluia! Alleluia! Alleluia!

WEEK TWENTY-THREE — SATURDAY

1. PRAISE GOD FOR WHO HE IS.

"His greatness is unsearchable" (Psa. 145:3). Bless your wonderful name—beyond the keenest minds of this earth are the laws of yourself. This is just one example of how your greatness is beyond man's ken. Like a search for hidden treasure, we find a large vein of gold—but the more we search the more we find. There is no end of the search, and there is no end of the discovery! Man will always be in search of the greatness of the complexities of this world in which he is physically but a small part. Man will be and is in search of the written revelation. We shall never fully appreciate the greatness of what you have said until we see you.

Express yourself in adoration for this quality of God.
Speak it audibly or write out your praise in your own devotional journal.

2. PRAISE GOD FOR WHAT HE MEANS TO ME.

Your greatness is indeed unsearchable to me! I have been in search of your mercy. I have found that indeed "it endureth forever"—it is beyond my search. Dear God, I do not want to presume on your goodness—I want to be truly yielded to your word—to obey you. I have found your "renewing of my mind" has no end—no terminus— Bless your dear self! I want to continue this search. I want to find out just how complete, how full, how rich is your power of renewal. Right now I rethink and re-evaluate my relationship to the world: (1) I am dead unto sin—I am crucified to the world—my relationship to those with whom I live and work: (2) I count them better than myself. (3) I love them as you love me. In truth your greatness is unsearchable!

How do you personally relate to the greatness of God, and God who is unsearchable?
Speak it out or write it out. It is *so important* that you establish *your own* devotional journal.

3. CONFESSION OF SIN

"Great is the Lord, and greatly to be praised; and his greatness is unsearchable!" Has this always been true for me? To whom has credit been given for projects completed? Dear God, forgive me! There is no need of saying I intended to give you the praise, but did not—the plain facts of the matter are that you did not receive the praise. You are great, not me—you are to be praised, not me. Men *are* to see our good works, but in such a way that you receive the credit. Forgive me for this terrible sin of pride.

"Disobeying parents." Surely I have been guilty of this. Surely this is rampant as a sin in our society.

What personal sins do you want to confess? We *must* speak them to remove them.
Do it! *Now.* There is no one else you have sinned against more than God. Tell him so!

4. SING A PRAYER TO GOD.

"There shall be showers of blessing":
This is the promise of love;
There shall be seasons refreshing,
Sent from the Saviour above.

Showers of blessing,
Showers of blessing we need:
Mercy drops round us are falling,
But for the showers we plead.

Open your hymn book and sing the rest of the verses—or even sing another prayer song.

5. READ HIS WORD TO HIM!

His Word

24 Five days later the high priest Ananias went down to Caesarea with some of the elders and a lawyer named Tertullus, and they brought their charges against Paul before the governor. [2]When Paul was called in, Tertullus presented his case before Felix: "We have enjoyed a long period of peace under you, and your foresight has brought about reforms in this nation. [3]Everywhere and in every way, most excellent Felix, we acknowledge this with profound gratitude. [4]But in order not to weary you further, I would request that you be kind enough to hear us briefly. *— Acts 24:1-4, NIV*

Read His Word to Him.

How pompus and ridiculous men must look to one who has all knowledge and all power (strength). Who is Ananias the high priest? You know him better than he knows himself! Who were the elders he had with him? How many were there? Dear Lord, it is good to remember that there never has been a trial held without your presence! What did you know—what do you know of Tertullus? How inadequate is his understanding of the one against whom he speaks! In your sight how incomplete is the man himself! What of this man Felix—the governor of this little province? What a sham this all must seem to you! At the same time with what infinite compassion do you view the whole proceeding. If only your servant Paul could communicate to all your love and purpose!

Please express your response to this beautiful text. Put your expression in your own prayer diary.

6. READ HIS WORD FOR YOURSELF.

Paul knew he would face trial. How did he prepare? He had no lawyer but himself! Oh, but he did! He had two advocates: (1) Your Son at your right hand to plead his innocence. (2) The blessed Holy Spirit to intercede through his prayers. Each day I awake I face the trial of the day. I must stand before men — and on some days the men are not unlike those in the text. How I need the same divine lawyers to plead my case. Paul could almost — but not quite — predict the outcome. At the same time he must give the test his best effort. Does today call for less? Most especially when I face a friendly amiable circumstance. Bless your name, you yet rule in the affairs of men!

It is so important that you pause in his presence
and either audibly or in written form tell him all his word means to you.

7. READ HIS WORD IN THANKSGIVING.

(1) Thank you for our wonderful high priest who can and does plead our case before you. (2) Thank you for elders in the "called out" body of your Son — they are such good men. (3) Thank you for my wonderful lawyer who can defend me before your throne. (4) Thank you for yourself — it is indeed because of you that I have peace and reform. (5) Thank you that I feel thankful and I know whom to thank. (6) Thank you that you never tire of hearing me. (7) Thank you for the marvelous contrast I have found in the above comparison.

Give yourself to your own expression of gratitude — write it or speak it!

8. READ HIS WORD IN MEDITATION.

". . . Tertullus presented his case before Felix." It was just another job for the lawyer Tertullus. It did pay well, and it gave him further opportunity to find out more about these strange people called "Jews." He was to be introduced to another man who undoubtedly made some impression upon him: Saul of Tarsus. Did Paul's defense impress Tertullus? Luke does not tell us. But he did hear the governor before whom he spoke. How did the lawyer estimate Felix's response to the trial? All such questions are interesting because they make us look at the participants as real people who lived before and after the incident described in the Acts record. Somehow I believe we will one day be introduced to the whole story of the lives of these men we have known so long in this text.

Pause — wait — think — then express yourself in thoughtful praise or thanks.

9. READ HIS WORD FOR PETITIONS.

As Paul faced trial before Felix he must have appeared often before your throne of grace. (1) Deliver me from the political maneuvers of selfish men. (2) How shall I reach a man like Ananias? (3) How could I possibly speak the good news to elders like those with Ananias? (3) There are lawyers today like Tertullus — how can I help them? (4) Even Felix is not immune from the power of the gospel — how can I reach him? (5) Grant me heaven's wisdom in responding to your answers to the above questions. (6) The period of peace to which Tertullus referred was a result of the slaughter of all who disagreed with Felix — deliver our land from such rulers. (7) Give me grace to be kind even to those I know are enemies.

Please, please remember these are prayers — speak them — reword them!

10. READ HIS WORD AND WAIT — LISTEN — GOD SPEAKS!

Speak to me from these verses: (1) "All will one day present their case before me." (2) "Some evil men become worse not better." (3) "Your love for me can overcome in every situation."

11. INTERCESSION FOR THE LOST WORLD

Afghanistan — Point for prayer: (1) *Many hippies and drug addicts come to Afghanistan* (150,000 per year and 3,000 at any one time) where they can obtain cheap drugs. These derelicts come from all over the world. Some Christians have been given permission to set up a Christian rehabilitation center for them. Pray for this ministry — that it may lead to some being delivered from both drugs and sin by trusting in the Lord Jesus.

12. SING PRAISES TO OUR LORD.

All hail the pow'r of Jesus' name!
Let angels prostrate fall:
Bring forth the royal diadem,
And crown Him Lord of all,
Bring forth the royal diadem,
And crown Him Lord of all!

1. PRAISE GOD FOR WHO HE IS.

"My deliverer" (Psa. 144:2). How appropriate is this name! You are the deliverer of all men—for all time in all circumstances. These words are but words until turned into reality. But such has indeed happened! (1) You have and can and do deliver from death. Man brought death upon himself—but you opened the door to life. "By man came death"—deliverance from death and the grave all from you. (2) You have delivered us from hatred and separation by uniting us in your Son. (3) Most of all you have delivered us from our own self destruction. You save us from ourselves! When we lose our lives in you we find ourselves all over again.

Express yourself in adoration for this quality of God.
Speak it audibly or write out your praise in your own devotional journal.

2. PRAISE GOD FOR WHAT HE MEANS TO ME.

My deliverer. Dear Father, I want you to be my deliverer today from the fear of not doing an adequate job of teaching. I have prepared adequately and believe deeply in what I am about to teach. Why am I fearful? Because of what man might or might not think or say. Dear God, deliver me from such an obvious sin of pride. Am I teaching to please and honor you or not? Dear God, you know I am! Deliver me from nervousness that hinders the free flow of thoughts I want to express. Give me the confidence of your presence and your approval. This is enough. Praise your name!

How do you personally relate to the deliverance of God and God who is Deliverer?
Speak it out or write it out. It is *so important* that you establish *your own* devotional journal.

3. CONFESSION OF SIN

How easy it is to confess my total inadequacy in being a true humble servant! The prayer of Watchman Nee I want to make mine: "Let me love but not be thanked. Let me serve but not be recompensed. Let me spend my strength but not be noted. Let me suffer much but not be seen. Let me pour my wine without drinking. Let me break my bread without reaping." Dear God, in all these areas I am so woefully short. Forgive me!

"Faithless." If faith is taking you at your word, then many times I have been without faith. Dear God I do want to press on in action.

What personal sins do you want to confess? We *must* speak them to remove them.
Do it! *Now.* There is no one else you have sinned against more than God. Tell him so!

4. SING A PRAYER TO GOD.

Savior, like a shepherd lead us,
Much we need Thy tender care;
In Thy pleasant pastures feed us,
For our use Thy folds prepare;

Blessed Jesus, Blessed Jesus,
Thou hast bought us, Thine we are;
Blessed Jesus, Blessed Jesus,
Thou hast bought us, Thine we are.

Open your hymn book and sing the rest of the verses—or even sing another prayer song.

5. READ HIS WORD TO HIM!

His Word

[5]"We have found this man to be a troublemaker, stirring up riots among the Jews all over the world. He is a ringleader of the Nazarene sect [6]and even tried to desecrate the temple; so we seized him. [8]By examining him yourself you will be able to learn the truth about all these charges we are bringing against him."

[9]The Jews joined in the accusation, asserting that these things were true.

[10]When the governor motioned for him to speak, Paul replied: "I know that for a number of years you have been a judge over this nation; so I gladly make my defense. [11]You can easily verify that no more than twelve days ago I went up to Jerusalem to worship. [12]My accuers did not find me arguing with anyone at the temple, or stirring up a crowd in the synagogues or anywhere else in the city. [13]And they cannot prove to you the charges they are now making against me. [14]However, I admit that I worship the God of our fathers, as a follower of the Way, which they call a sect. I believe everything that agrees with the Law and that is written in the Prophets, [15]and I have the same hope in God as these men, that there will be a resurrection of both the righteous and the wicked. [16]So I strive always to keep my conscience clear before God and man.

[17]"After an absence of several years, I came to Jerusalem to bring my people gifts for the poor and to present offerings. [18]I was ceremonially clean when they found me in the temple courts doing this. There was no crowd with me, nor was I involved in any disturbance. [19]But there are some Jews from the province of Asia, who ought to be here before you and bring charges if they have anything against me. [20]Or these who are here should state what crime they found in me when I stood before the Sanhedrin —[21]unless it was this one thing I shouted as I stood in their presence: 'It is concerning the resurrection of the dead that I am on trial before you today.'"

— *Acts 24:5-21, NIV*

Read His Word to Him.

I want to enter the court of Felix—as I know you did in that far off day. It is only removed from me—it is as if it were happening now with you. I want it to be that way with me! There were four charges laid against Paul. I want to turn each of them over and see them as you do. (1) "We have found this man a *troublemaker*." Oh, blessed trouble! That men should be startled out of their tradition and sin and made to take a fresh look on their lives.

(2) "Stirring up riots among the Jews all over the world. Yea, verily! What Tertullus calls a riot we would call a revival! It is a fulfillment of the marching orders of his commander. Oh, that men would be so stirred today! (3) "He is a ring leader of the Nazarene sect." When the Nazarene is also "Immanuel" who wouldn't want to lead men to know Him? (4) "Tried to desecrate the temple." Paul was supporting and worshipping in the temple.

Please express your response to this beautiful text. Put your expression in your own prayer diary.

6. READ HIS WORD FOR YOURSELF.

Dear Lord, I do so want to see these words through your eyes—set them on fire—let them burn and light up my heart and life! I want the same polite respect for those who rule over me as Paul had with Felix. It would seem that Paul knew of the governor's background and realized

he appreciated more than the Jews knew the teaching of the good news. This could also be true today for men in authority. One by one Paul answers the charges. I want to read more than Paul's answers; I want some answers for myself!

Either audibly or in written form tell him all his word means to you.

7. READ HIS WORD IN THANKSGIVING.

How full of possibilities is this text! (1) Thank you for such a wonderful troublemaker as Paul. We have not seen his kind before or since. (2) Thank you for the world-wide outreach of this indomitable apostle. (3) Thank you for our blessed Nazarene who died and rose again. (4) Thank

you for the monumental effort of Paul to be conciliatory toward those who hated him. (5) Thank you for the thousand promises and prophecies fulfilled in our Lord. (6) Thank you for that plain promise "that there will be a resurrection of both the righteous and the wicked."

Give yourself to your own expression of gratitude—write it or speak it!

8. READ HIS WORD IN MEDITATION.

"*. . . I shouted as I stood in their presence.*" "It is concerning the resurrection of the dead that I am on trial before you today." No wonder Paul shouted; he had something to shout about. Notice a couple of startling facts: (1) "*All* that are in the graves—or *all* that are presently dead—or will be dead when Jesus comes will hear his voice and come

forth! There will be a recreation much, much greater than the creation of Adam and Eve. At the resurrection God begins with nothing and recreates the whole human race. (2) This will be the eternal body in which we will live for eternity in heaven or in hell. No wonder Paul shouted.

9. READ HIS WORD FOR PETITIONS.

In Paul's defense before Felix there is much to prompt prayer: (1) Dear Lord, help me to be the same kind of troublemaker as Paul. (2) How little effect does our witness have on the world as compared with Paul. (3) I am glad to belong to the same so-called sect as Paul. Make me worthy of the name. (4) What a wonder to consider

my body the temple of your very self. May I be holy through my Lord. (5) May I be able to speak so clearly to those who question me. (6) I want the same clear conscience before God and man. (7) May the hope of the resurrection be ever before me.

Please, please remember these are prayers—speak them—reword them!

10. READ HIS WORD AND WAIT—LISTEN—GOD SPEAKS!

Surely there is much to be heard from you in this text: (1) "All good actions can be misconstrued to evil." (2) "There

will be indeed a resurrection of both righteous and wicked." (3) "Charges not proven will not always be dismissed."

11. INTERCESSION FOR THE LOST WORLD

Bangladesh — Population: 76,100,000. Annual Growth 2.7%. People per sq. km.—532.

Point for prayer: (1) *Bangladesh has been a hard and neglected field* but is now open for the Gospel. Receptivity

is due to national disasters, disillusionment and the good testimony of Christian aid organizations. Pray that this golden opportunity may be seized by believers. This land is reckoned to be still 80% unevangelized.

12. SING PRAISES TO OUR LORD.

Amazing grace! how sweet the sound,
That saved a wretch like me!

I once was lost, but now am found,
Was bind, but now I see.

WEEK TWENTY-FOUR — MONDAY

1. PRAISE GOD FOR WHO HE IS.

"The Lord is *my strength, and song*, and is become *my salvation*" (Psa. 118:14). Because I have discussed strength and salvation, I should like to praise you for being the song of all men.

Men do not have a song to sing if you do not give it to them. Indeed men would not sing at all without you. I am thinking of songs of hope, joy and purpose. (1) Songs of hope. How totally hopeful is life with you! There is hope for every day—each of our days are ordered by you. We can say with the psalmist, "This is the day the Lord hath made; we will rejoice and be glad in it" (Psa. 118:24). (2) Songs of joy—"Open to me the gates of righteousness; I will go into them; I will praise the Lord" (Psa. 118:19). What a song of joy every man *could* sing if he would.

Express yourself in adoration for this quality of God.
Speak it audibly or write out your praise in your own devotional journal.

2. PRAISE GOD FOR WHAT HE MEANS TO ME.

The Lord is *my song!* Amen! Out of my heart I am glad to acknowledge you as the only source of my *strength* —my *salvation* and my *song*. There are so many songs that will express my gratitude to you! John Kendricks Bangs, 1862-1922, said it so well—it is what I offer you today:

For summer rain, and winter's sun,
For autumn breezes crisp and sweet;

For labors doing, to be done,
   and labors all complete;
For April, May, and lovely June,
For bud, and bird, and berried vine;
For joys of morning, night, and noon,
My thanks, dear Lord, are Thine!

How do you personally relate to the source of song of God, and God who is our song?
Speak it out or write it out. It is *so important* that you establish *your own* devotional journal.

3. CONFESSION OF SIN

Dear Lord, that I should not always be singing your praise is a sin. "Rejoice, in the Lord always"—is not only a truism, it is a glorious fact! I know that both my mental and physical health relate to my praise or lack of it. But such being true, it is also true that cause for joy and happiness is always present! That I should even complain and gripe about anything seems totally out of character, i.e., not true or real or right. Forgive me. You are helping me in so many areas of my life. Thank you!

"*Judgment of others*." This is impuning motives, i.e., deciding why men act or speak the way they do. Dear God, I have done this. Please forgive me. How absurd that I should do this. I *know* this is your job.

What personal sins do you want to confess? We *must* speak them to remove them.
Do it! *Now*. There is no one else you have sinned against more than God. Tell him so!

4. SING A PRAYER TO GOD.

Savior, more than life to me,
I am clinging, clinging close to Thee;
Let Thy precious blood applied,
Keep me ever, ever near Thy side.

Ev'ry day, ev'ry hour,
Let me feel Thy cleansing pow'r;
Let Thy precious blood applied,
Keep me ever, ever near Thy side.

Open your hymn book and sing the rest of the verses—or even sing another prayer song.

5. READ HIS WORD TO HIM!

His Word

[22]Then Felix, who was well acquainted with the Way, adjourned the proceedings. "When Lysias the commander comes," he said, "I will decide your case." [23]He ordered the centurion to keep Paul under guard but to give him some freedom and permit his friends to take care of his needs.

[24]Several days later Felix came with his wife Drusilla, who was a Jewess. He sent for Paul and listened to him as he spoke about faith in Christ Jesus.

—*Acts 24:22-24, NIV*

Read His Word to Him.

For how long is your servant Paul going to be confined to the four walls of imprisonment? Paul could not predict the response of Felix to the message of Paul, but you could! He was "well acquainted with the Way," yet he did not want to walk in it. Why? Our Lord answered this question (Dear Lord, help me as I think your thoughts.): (1) "The deceitfulness of riches"—riches promise what they cannot fulfill—riches offer what they cannot give— riches give answers that are lies! (2) "The cares of this life"—how full of care and deceit was the life of Felix! Just to take up and be caught up in the duties of his office silenced your voice. (3) "The lust for other things"—the strong desires of sex, food, and status did it!

Please express your response to this beautiful text. Put your expression in your own prayer diary.

6. READ HIS WORD FOR YOURSELF.

I am not at all immune to temptations of Felix and Drusilla. There was something wonderfully fascinating about this new prisoner. Felix had not totally forgotten what he heard the first time, or what he had heard earlier. He wanted his Jewish wife to hear it. The scandal of his immoral life had spread over the whole countryside. How did he hear? Surely with some real interest. But how do *I* hear? Indulgence in sex—food or money dulls the hearing, paralyzes the senses, sears the conscience. I speak this not of Felix and Drusilla alone, but to my own heart. Faith does indeed come by hearing—of your word—clean out my inner ears that I might hear!

It is so important that you pause in his presence
and either audibly or in written form tell him all his word means to you.

7. READ HIS WORD IN THANKSGIVING.

How good to do this! (1) Thank you for Felix's generous attitude toward Paul. (2) Thank you for all of Paul's friends who came to see him in the prison at Caesarea—was one of them Philip and his daughters? (3) Thank you for Paul's courage and transparent sincerity in speaking before these important people. (4) Thank you for the reasons for our faith in the Lord Jesus Christ. (5) Thank you for these evidences that demand a verdict from all who hear and understand. (6) Dear Lord, I want to hear Paul—again and again—thank you that I can do so. (7) Thank you for yourself who is the ultimate judge of us all.

Give yourself to your own expression of gratitude—write it or speak it!

8. READ HIS WORD IN MEDITATION.

". . . as he spoke about faith in Christ Jesus." This would be so important—so full of purpose and meaning for both of these listeners. The evidences of our Lord's deity in his miracles. The obvious divine origin of his teaching. His wonderful death for our sins. His glorious resurrection. All such truths could be accepted by these two. Felix had for a long time known these facts. He now had someone to reinforce their meaning. How hard it is for a rich man (and woman) to allow God to rule their lives! Paul is yet speaking to me about faith in Christ Jesus my Lord! Will I allow him to rule in every area of my life? What about my personal relationship with him?

Pause—wait—think—then express yourself in thoughtful praise or thanks.

9. READ HIS WORD FOR PETITIONS.

What an opportunity Paul had to witness for you! In his actions and attitudes petitions arise: (1) Dear Lord, forgive me for not praying more consistently for men in high places. (2) I do right now lift the governor of our state before your throne—guide his decisions. (3) For the chief of police in our city I pray—protect and use him today in his work. (4) Give me opportunity to emphasize the sacredness of marriage. (5) Thank you for the wonderful freedom we enjoy in America. (6) Dear Lord, give me the courage and wisdom Paul had as he spoke to Felix and Drusilla. (7) How I need grace to speak effectively this weekend about faith in Christ Jesus.

Right here add your personal requests—and his answers.

10. READ HIS WORD AND WAIT—LISTEN—GOD SPEAKS!

(1) "When the King of kings comes he will decide all cases of all men." (2) "There are those who are curious about faith in our Lord—use such an opportunity." (3) "Be as winsome and bold as Paul."

11. INTERCESSION FOR THE LOST WORLD

Bangladesh — Points for prayer: (1) *Missions have neglected this land in the past*—the people were unresponsive, the climate difficult and most mission work was channelled into institutions and not evangelism. Many international workers are urgently needed but visas are not always easy to obtain. There is now one missionary for every 400,000 people. There is much cooperation between missions to conserve limited manpower. (2) *Christian aid* has proved a dramatic stimulus to church growth in some areas due to the impartial love and sympathy of the Christians. There has been a surge of people into the tribal churches and a large number of Hindu enquirers as well as a trickle of Muslim converts (there are now about 2,000 Muslims and Hindus converted every year).

12. SING PRAISES TO OUR LORD.

Blessed assurance, Jesus is mine!
Oh, what a foretaste of glory divine!
Heir of salvation, purchase of God,
Born of His spirit, washed in His blood.

This is my story, this is my song,
Praising my Saviour all the day long;
This is my story, this is my song,
Praising my Saviour all the day long.

WEEK TWENTY-FOUR — TUESDAY

1. PRAISE GOD FOR WHO HE IS.

"The Lord is on my side; I will not fear. What can man do unto me?" (Psa. 118:6). Oh, that all men would be able to say this! If you are defending, protecting, providing for us how rich is our relationship! If you were not on men's side, then what? What a tragedy! There seems to me to be two ways you are for man, i.e., in his defense: (1) You are always on our side in provision—physically, morally, emotionally, in you we live and move and have our being or wholeness. The only one against us in Satan and ourselves. Bless your wonderful name!

Express yourself in adoration for this quality of God.
Speak it audibly or write out your praise in your own devotional journal.

2. PRAISE GOD FOR WHAT HE MEANS TO ME.

Personally—(2) You are on our side because we are (gladly) on your side. In the face of old age—"I will not fear." In the presence of economic problems—"I will not fear." When problems loom up in domestic relationships —"I will not fear." If you are on our side what can man do to us? Man can do much to us, but nothing, not one thing he can do that defeats your purpose. The words of that blessed hymn express this thought so well:

He leadeth me, O blessed tho't!

O words with heav'nly comfort fraught!
Whate'er I do, where'er I be,
Still 'tis God's hand that leadeth me.
Lord, I would clasp thy hand in mine,
Nor ever murmur nor repine,
Content, whatever lot I see,
Since 'tis my God that leadeth me.
Joseph H. Gilmore (1834-1918)

How do you personally relate to the protection of God, and God who is our defender?
Speak it out or write it out. It is *so important* that you establish *your own* devotional journal.

3. CONFESSION OF SIN

Shall I confess that you have always been with me, but I have not at all always been with you? What a sad loss! Dear Father, I do want to practice your presence—to pause and bow my head and heart and wait for my mind to focus on you. Oh, that my mind should be so occupied with many things—so many things that I cannot —I will not—do not set it on you! Forgive me! How I wish my repentance were deeper—more wholly given to you! What does it mean to be a supplicant? To be pliable? I want to be clay in your hands. I do. Help me!

"Seared conscience"—as with a hot iron. Oh Father, I do want a tender conscience. I do not want to expose my eyes, ears, to the fire of sin. I will close my eyes, stop my ears.

What personal sins do you want to confess? We *must* speak them to remove them.
Do it! *Now.* There is no one else you have sinned against more than God. Tell him so!

4. SING A PRAYER TO GOD.

I need Thee ev'ry hour,
Most gracious Lord;
No tender voice like Thine
Can peace afford.

I need Thee, O I need Thee;
Ev'ry hour I need Thee!
O bless me now, my Savior,
I come to Thee!

Open your hymn book and sing the rest of the verses—or even sing another prayer song.

5. READ HIS WORD TO HIM!

His Word

[25] As Paul discoursed on righteousness, self-control and the judgment to come, Felix was afraid and said, "That's enough for now! You may leave. When I find it convenient, I will send for you." [26] At the same time he was hoping that Paul would offer him a bribe, so he sent for him frequently and talked with him.

[27] When two years had passed, Felix was succeeded by Porcius Festus, but because Felix wanted to grant a favor to the Jews, he left Paul in prison.

— *Acts 24:25-27, NIV*

Read His Word to Him.

Dear Lord, dear Lord, I want to hear the life-giving, burning words from the lips of Paul. I know you can hear them now as then. Just what did he say about righteousness? Felix and Drusilla surely had no righteousness. Even by man's standards they were woefully short. But in the glaring light of your perfect righteousness all of us are dressed in filthy rags! We are dirty and guilty! But, oh, he told of the *gift* of righteousness—that we can be made the righteousness of yourself in Him! Blessed be your grace! I have no real true, consistent control of myself! Except by your spirit as a fruit you give me self-control I shall have none! No man, no man is ready to be judged by the absolute standards of right and wrong found in your word! No wonder Felix was afraid!

Please express your response to this beautiful text. Put your expression in your own prayer diary.

6. READ HIS WORD FOR YOURSELF.

Just for me! How lightly did Felix treat (ultimately) the message of Paul — and Paul as a person! He was once "terrified," "trembled," was "alarmed," "took fright," was "afraid." But time has a way of putting out the fire. No it doesn't! It is not time; it is *choice*! Felix chose to desensitize his heart. Is that your choice — oh, my soul? No, no, I want to yield my heart — I want to immediately repent! I need not think about it — I already know what to do! What a calloused man was this governor! He often heard Paul and only hoped Paul would let down his guard and offer a bribe! Dear Lord, I relate to all of this — drive it deeply into my subconsciousness!

It is so important that you pause in his presence
and either audibly or in written form tell him all his word means to you.

7. READ HIS WORD IN THANKSGIVING.

Yes, yes. (1) Thank you for the total righteousness I find in you. My faith is counted for me for righteousness. In the good news of my Lord's death is your righteousness revealed and given. Thank you, oh, thank you! (2) Thank you for the fruit of the Spirit which is self-control. (3) Thank you that on judgment day I shall be just-as-if I had never sinned. (4) Thank you that I have found several, several convenient seasons to hear Paul (to hear you through him). (5) Thank you for the passing of time that always brings change — and it can be always for the better. (6) Thank you for the undaunted determination of Paul to be your prisoner — and not of Rome. (7) Thank you for Paul's example of hardships — I really haven't had any problems at all compared to him.

Give yourself to your own expression of gratitude — write it or speak it!

8. READ HIS WORD IN MEDITATION.

"*. . . he left Paul in prison.*" I wonder if Paul prayed to be released? We can't imagine he didn't. Was he then disappointed that God did not answer his prayer? Did Paul ever think about the ingratitude of Felix? After all the days he had spoken to him — after all the good news Felix heard from Paul — after all the effort to put life in perspective, and most of all, after Felix learned the whole truth about Paul's unjust imprisonment — after all that "he left Paul in prison." How did Paul relate this to the deliverance of Daniel from the lion's den? Or his own release from the jail in Philippi?

Pause — wait — think — then express yourself in thoughtful praise or thanks.

9. READ HIS WORD FOR PETITIONS.

Two years waiting in jail as an innocent man; there must have been many petitions — indeed there are today from this text: (1) Open my heart to a full appreciation of the righteousness we have in our Lord. (2) Keep us aware that there *is* a code of ethics which calls us to live a righteous life today. (3) Dear Lord, I need your motivation for self-control. (4) There *is* a judgment to come! Keep me ready if it should be today. (5) Dear Lord, there is a day when all men will be full of awe — keep me ready to welcome it not in fear but joy. (6) Guard me from the subtlety of bribing. (7) Paul and his Lord were of less importance for Felix than favor with the Jews.

Please, please remember these are prayers — speak them — reword them!

10. READ HIS WORD AND WAIT — LISTEN — GOD SPEAKS!

In these few verses I hear you speak to me: (1) "Paul's example of speaking to the conscience is good for today." (2) "Paul spoke frequently to Felix but did not convert him — he yet remained faithful." (3) "Paul was unjustly imprisoned and unjustly kept there — we hear no complaint from him."

11. INTERCESSION FOR THE LOST WORLD

Bangladesh — Point for prayer: (1) *The Church* is very small and half of the community is among the tribal peoples that make up only 2% of the population. Pray for the Bengali speaking believers as they emerge from their spiritual shallowness, introspective inferiority and dependence on missionary aid and initiative. The present opportunities have brought in a new spirit of evangelism, cooperation and expectancy of a future harvest among Hindus and Muslims. Pray for the conversion of whole families — most necessary in the close-knit Muslim and Hindu societies.

12. SING PRAISES TO OUR LORD.

Come, Thou Almighty King,
Help us Thy name to sing,
Help us to praise.
Father, all glorious,
O'er all victorious,
Come, and reign over us,
Ancient of Days.

WEEK TWENTY-FOUR — WEDNESDAY

1. PRAISE GOD FOR WHO HE IS.

"It is better to trust in the Lord than to put confidence in man" (Psalm 118:8). Praise your wonderful name our trust in you is never misplaced. There is no disappointment in you! All your promises are "yea, and amen." You have total provisions for fulfillment. All men could find all their lives completed and fulfilled in you. In the first place you understand our need better than we our-

selves. In the second place, you want to help us more than we want to ask for help. In the third place, there is nothing or no one who could stand in your way of fulfillment. How very much better it is to put our trust in you. Just for today will I be ready to say: I trust in you with all my heart and lean not on my own understanding? May it be so.

Express yourself in adoration for this quality of God.
Speak it audibly or write out your praise in your own devotional journal.

2. PRAISE GOD FOR WHAT HE MEANS TO ME.

For me. How often have I been disappointed by man! How often I have been a disappointment! How often have I found abundant satisfaction in you? Shall I say ten thousand times ten thousand? Yea, more! It is good to lean back and soak up all the meaning of these words from you: "It is better . . ."—indeed, indeed it is. So much

better to relate all my life to you than to men. "To trust in the Lord . . ." Since our trust is in your character we have no hesitancy or fear. *Trust* is a strong word. I put my whole weight upon you. I release all hold and give it to you. Oh, how much better it is!

How do you personally relate to the faithfulness of God, and God who is our trust?
Speak it out or write it out. It is *so important* that you establish *your own* devotional journal.

3. CONFESSION OF SIN

How often have I been frustrated and upset because I put my confidence in man? The first man to disappoint me is the one writing these words. The one who fails to fulfill is the one who appears before you. Dear Lord, how I do seek your forgiveness. How I long to make my promises in the context of what you have promised me and others through me. I have perhaps disappointed myself more often than I have anyone else. It is so good to look forward to a time and a place where there will be no disappointments.

Dear God, I want to so purify my heart and cleanse my hands that men can put confidence in me and find faithfulness. Help me. Forgive me. Empower me.

"Dishonor to parents." I have been guilty of this. I have sought your forgiveness earlier. But even now I know I cannot repair the harm I did. You have forgotten it; why should I remember it? I know in first honoring you I will find the resources to honor all others.

What personal sins do you want to confess? We *must* speak them to remove them.
Do it! *Now.* There is no one else you have sinned against more than God. Tell him so!

4. SING A PRAYER TO GOD.

O worship the King, all glorious above,
And gratefully sing His wonderful love;

Our Shield and Defender, the Ancient of days,
Pavilioned in splendor, and girded with praise.

Open your hymn book and sing the rest of the verses—or even sing another prayer song.

5. READ HIS WORD TO HIM!

His Word

25 Three days after arriving in the province, Festus went up from Caesarea to Jerusalem, [2]where the chief priests and Jewish leaders appeared before him and presented the charges against Paul. [3]They urgently requested Festus, as a favor to them, to have Paul transferred to Jerusalem, for they were preparing an ambush to kill him

along the way. [4]Festus answered, "Paul is being held at Caesarea, and I myself am going there soon. [5]Let some of your leaders come with me and press charges against the man there, if he has done anything wrong."

— Acts 25:1-5, NIV

Read His Word to Him.

Who was (is) this man Festus? He seems to be almost totally ignorant of yourself or your Son. He seems to know little or nothing of your law. How well he represents most of the rulers of this world! For whatever reason, he does save the life of the apostle. We know that one reason is your infinite goodness and the fulfillment of your eternal purpose. How I would have liked to ride in the chariot of the governor from Caesarea to Jerusalem! But you were

there! How did Festus view the task given to him? Just another job? He no doubt saw much that held his interest. He must have asked questions of those who did not side with the Jews or Rome and could give him some balanced view of the prisoner Paul. Did Festus know of the plot to kill Paul? The Jews were not interested in a trial or justice. Hatred and jealousy knows no rules! Dear Lord, how did you relate to the scene in Jerusalem?

6. READ HIS WORD FOR MYSELF.

For more than 40 times I have attempted to lead others to see this text—now I want to look at it as if I had never seen it before! Caesarea was where the palace of the governor was located; but everyone knew the real center of rule was Jerusalem. It was an all-day ride from the busy seaport to the crowded streets of the holy city. How radically changed are both places today! No wonder Ananias and the priests wanted to ambush Paul. They knew from at least two attempts that their charges would not stand examination. I am so glad that Jesus is my attorney at your right hand and Satan's efforts will be no more successful—"Who can lay anything to the charge of God's elect?" Can I then, like Paul, expect some unreasonable attempts of Satan to "ambush" my faith? Praise your name he will be no more successful than the high priest!

It is so important that you pause in his presence
and either audibly or in written form tell him all his word means to you.

7. READ HIS WORD IN THANKSGIVING.

(1) Thank you for the willingness of Festus to face the issues as they were, and not to lie or kill. (2) Thank you for your interest in all affairs of men—in this case to preserve the life of your servant for a few more years. (3) Thank you for the strength of Festus' refusal in the face of urging from those who could hurt him politcally. (4) Thank you for the open decision as to who was right and who was wrong. (5) Thank you for the preservation of Luke's account over all these years. It is as fresh today as when the first "lover of God" read it. (6) Thank you there is *always* a way out of every trial, every temptation. Dear Lord, I want to find it each time! (7) Thank you for history (his story) that tells us over and over again who is right and who is wrong!

Give yourself to your own expression of gratitude—write it or speak it!

8. READ HIS WORD IN MEDITATION.

"...come with me and press charges against the man..." We could indeed level several charges, but they could all be to the glory of our Lord. We could charge Paul with a love that would not let go of his kindred. He even wanted to go to hell on their behalf—if such would save them. We could charge him with a great sympathy for the poor and hungry. He obtained money from the "despised" Gentiles to help the weak and unfortunate among the Jewish population in Jerusalem and Judea. We could charge him with a deep worship commitment. Paul wanted to spend time with the Lord in prayer and praise and meditation. Dear Lord, give us men like Paul!

Pause—wait—think—then express yourself in thoughtful praise or thanks.

9. READ HIS WORD FOR PETITIONS.

Paul no doubt prayed while Festus talked to the chief priests in Jerusalem. Requests do arise from this text. (1) Lack of knowledge and lack of communication destroy so much. Deliver me from such problems. (2) Determined evil men are such a threat—give me humility and courage. (3) Thank you that some men will not be intimidated—I want to be one of them. (4) Did Festus already know of Paul's innocence? What problems politics produce! At the same time such is no problem with you. May I learn a lesson here. (5) May I appreciate more fully than ever what measure of justice we have in our courts. (6) Is there a particular purpose in Luke's inclusion of this exchange? Give me wisdom to know. (7) Paul was not afraid of death but he wanted to live—why?

Right here add your personal requests—and his answers.

10. READ HIS WORD AND WAIT—LISTEN—GOD SPEAKS!

What messages arise from this text? (1) "Change is the one consistent ingredient of life." (2) "Religion is no indication of morality." (3) "Men moved by passion will go to almost any lengths to gain their objective."

11. INTERCESSION FOR THE LOST WORLD

Bangladesh — Point for prayer: (1) *Leadership in the churches* is the biggest bottleneck to growth. There is still no major Bengali Bible School (though one is being planned), yet scores of believers are seeking to prepare for full time service. Ten groups are cooperating to launch a program but this has limited value and effect at present.

12. SING PRAISES TO OUR LORD.

Day is dying in the west,
Heav'n is touching earth with rest;
Wait and worship while the night
Sets her evening lamps alight
Thro' all the sky.

Holy, holy, holy, Lord God of Hosts!
Heav'n and earth are full of Thee!
Heav'n and earth are praising Thee,
O Lord most high!

WEEK TWENTY-FOUR — THURSDAY

1. PRAISE GOD FOR WHO HE IS.

"For Jehovah knoweth the way of the righteous, but the way of the wicked shall perish" (Psa. 1:6). Dear Lord, you are a participant in the way of the righteous — but you have no part or participation in wickedness; therefore his way shall perish.

How wonderful that you can and do participate with men in everything they do. Your knowledge of our lives is intuitive, i.e., you have an experiential knowledge of every part of life. The only reason the way of the wicked comes to nothing is because you are not in it. It is both amazing and humbling to contemplate your participation in all that I am and all you can give. I do not come to get, I come to praise and worship you. At the same time, man is such a needy creature. To worship before Someone who knows everything and is able to do everything is an awesome thought.

Express yourself in adoration for this quality of God.
Speak it audibly or write out your praise in your own devotional journal.

2. PRAISE GOD FOR WHAT HE MEANS TO ME.

He *knows* my way. Dear, dear Lord, I am trying to assimilate this truth. You are a constant participator in all I am. I know you love me, but to be present in all I think, this is shocking. I have known this before, but I haven't known it. For today: you will be, and are personally knowledgeable of all that will happen. No wonder I can claim the promises of the earlier verses of this blessed psalm: "He is like a tree planted by brooks of water, which giveth its fruit in its season, and whose leaf fadeth not; and all that he does shall prosper." Since you are in me and with me the life and energy to produce fruit are from you — you are indeed the "water of life." How delighted I am to claim that my life will never lose its color. I am almost afraid to express the next promise — and yet I am sure you said it. I'm sure you mean it — I'm sure I want it. "All that he does shall prosper." Dear Lord, how precious you are!

How do you personally relate to the omniscience of God, and God who knows all?
Speak it out or write it out. It is *so important* that you establish *your own* devotional journal.

3. CONFESSION OF SIN

"The way of the wicked shall perish." The wicked could ultimately himself perish, but *right now the way* of the wicked shall come to nothing. How many times have I found this true? Dear Lord, I have lost my way because it was not *your* way. "Little is much if God is in it." But much is nothing if he isn't. Oh Father, I want so much to give you the steering wheel of my life! I want so much to let the water of life soak through the substrata of my heart. Help me, forgive me, indwell all I am!

"Loss of first love." How better could I describe my need? I return to the intimacy I want with you and you want with me in every part of this day. I want to — help me!

What personal sins do you want to confess? We *must* speak them to remove them.
Do it! *Now.* There is no one else you have sinned against more than God. Tell him so!

4. SING A PRAYER TO GOD.

I am Thine, O Lord,
I have heard Thy voice,
And it told Thy love to me;
But I long to rise in the arms of faith,
And be closer drawn to Thee.

Draw me nearer, nearer, blessed Lord,
To the cross where Thou hast died;
Draw me nearer, nearer, nearer, blessed Lord,
To Thy precious, bleeding side.

Open your hymn book and sing the rest of the verses — or even sing another prayer song.

5. READ HIS WORD TO HIM!

His Word

[6]After spending eight or ten days with them, he went down to Caesarea, and the next day he convened the court and ordered that Paul be brought before him. [7]When Paul appeared, the Jews who had come down from Jerusalem stood around him, bringing many serious charges against him, which they could not prove. [8]Then Paul made his defense: "I have done nothing wrong against the law of the Jews or against the temple or against Caesar."

[9]Festus, wishing to do the Jews a favor, said to Paul, "Are you willing to go up to Jerusalem and stand trial before me there on these charges?"

[10]Paul answered: "I am now standing before Caesar's court, where I ought to be tried. I have not done any wrong to the Jews, as you yourself know very well. [11]If, however, I am guilty of doing anything deserving death, I do not refuse to die. But if the charges brought against me by these Jews are not true, no one has the right to hand me over to them. I appeal to Caesar!"

— *Acts 25:6-11, NIV*

Read His Word to Him.

Blessed Lord, read this again into my heart! Festus is such a poor judge before whom to stand. He is self-seeking and ignorant. But you can use anyone and everything to your own advantage. How very, very good it is to decide everything on adequate evidence! You have given me more than enough reason to accept your intervention in the affairs of men, of your present presence in every circumstance. The three areas of law-breaking are interesting—speak to me through them! (1) The law; (2) the temple; (3) Caesar.

Please express your response to this beautiful text. Put your expression in your own prayer diary.

6. READ HIS WORD FOR YOURSELF.

In the above I have tried to look at myself as you see me. In this expression I want you to speak to me in the deepest needs of my heart. It is before your court I stand to be tried! How delighted and confident I am when I remember there is nothing Satan can bring against me and support with evidence. He is indeed the great accuser, but none of his charges can be proven! Bless your holy name! At the same time I am not unwilling to receive your judgment in my life. I want to repent toward and because of yourself! How strong a word it is to say that *no one, no one* has a right to turn me over to Satan. I have the supreme judge on my side—it is to him that I appeal! No one has a right (including the devil) to hand me over to bondage and death. How gladly I appeal to you and your dear Son. How eagerly I exercise the rights of my heavenly citizenship.

Pause in his presence and tell him all his word means to you.

7. READ HIS WORD IN THANKSGIVING.

(1) Thank you for a confrontation with Satan—he cannot and will not make any of his lies stick. (2) Thank you for Paul's perception of the wiles of the devil. (3) Thank you that no trial or temptation will come my way that has not been used by Satan on man for centuries—there is always a way out. (4) Thank you for Paul's wisdom in knowing just when to exercise his rights and when to give them up. (5) Thank you that in the area of moral choice we have no rights—they are all given to you. (6) Thank you for the defeat of the evil men in religious robes.

Give yourself to your own expression of gratitude—write it or speak it!

8. READ HIS WORD IN MEDITATION.

"I appeal to Caesar"! This was the unique right of a Roman citizen. It saved the life of Paul. How much of our life do we owe to Caesar? Without the benefits of democracy we would lose many things—perhaps even our lives. At the same time we remember that democracy is a fruit of Christianity. I am glad to respect our government, but my appeal is first of all to King Jesus! I claim the right of my heavenly citizenship, to be judged by him.

Pause—wait—think—then express yourself in thoughtful praise or thanks.

9. READ HIS WORD FOR PETITIONS.

What a momentous decision it was to appeal to Caesar. In this are occasions for prayer: (1) Wasn't it sad that Paul was forced to reiterate the circumstance of his innocence? Only when it was a fruitless, useless effort did he appeal to Caesar. What does this say to me? (2) Paul's relationship with the Jewish law was one of blamelessness; I want to be that innocent with the laws of our land. (3) May I keep your temple, my body, as the sanctuary of your presence. (4) May I stand in just the place you want me for your witness today. (5) I deserve to die eternally, but my Lord took my place. Help me to tell someone else. (6) Deliver me from the plots of evil men.

Please, please remember these are prayers—speak them—reword them!

10. READ HIS WORD AND WAIT—LISTEN—GOD SPEAKS!

Give me ears to hear: (1) "You are on trial every day." (2) "You bear testimony for me every day." (3) "The right of appeal to me is always open."

11. INTERCESSION FOR THE LOST WORLD

Bangladesh — Point for prayer: (1) *Bible correspondence courses* have proved the best way to reach Muslims and Hindus. Enrollment has doubled since 1971. More is being done to personally follow up students and hold follow-up rallies. Pray for many to be saved and brought into the churches.

12. SING PRAISES TO OUR LORD.

God the Omnipotent! King, who ordainest
Thunder Thy clarion, the lightning Thy sword;

Show forth Thy pity on high where Thou reignest;
Give to us peace in our time, O Lord.

WEEK TWENTY-FOUR — FRIDAY

1. PRAISE GOD FOR WHO HE IS.

"Ask of me, and I will give thee the nations from thine inheritance, and the uttermost parts of the earth for thy possession" (Psa. 2:8). What quality of God is here seen? It is kingliness or majesty. The whole Psalm seems to be Messianic—it is our dear Lord who is addressed. God is saying to Jesus, "Ask of me, and I will give you the nations for your inheritance." Did Jesus ever ask? Oh, yes he did. On the cross he asked in blood! The nations of the world belong to him! The uttermost parts of the earth are his possession! Dear God, how can I possibly express myself in any kind of praise or wonder or worship? As I stand beneath the cross I realize that two billion people alive on this earth have never even heard they belong to you! If men just knew who you are and what your Son did, wouldn't they believe and be saved? We will never know until we tell them!

Speak or write out your praise in adoration for this quality of God.

2. PRAISE GOD FOR WHAT HE MEANS TO ME.

Read and apply to yourself! I praise you for this amazing quality! How can I sit idly by while billions have never heard? The fact of the matter is we are trying to do something about this overwhelming need. A young man in India reaches hundreds who have never heard. Our dear son, Chris, is in Santiago, Chile for this purpose. We are doing all we can to get the Pictorial Book of Acts in at least ten languages of a 100,000 copies. But all of this is so small and impersonal. Dear God, are you speaking to me? Do I have ears to hear? I have helped to prepare several hundred young people who have gone to tell this good news. Yes, yes, but still the nations of the world have really not been told! Their cry seems but a distant sorrow. Dear God, break my hard heart!

How do you personally relate to the inheritance of God, and God who is Owner of all?
Speak it out or write it out. It is *so important* that you establish *your own* devotional journal.

3. CONFESSION OF SIN

I sat in homes yesterday sharing the good news that all men belong to you by right of purchase. It seemed so very good to do this! At the same time, I want to confess how guilty I feel most of the time for not doing this. Is not the preparation of others for this task and the teaching of the saved also important? I know I cannot do it alone—but I want to feel like I should! Forgive me for my complacency!

"Evil suspicions." How easy it is to enter your sphere of action. Why should I think ill of any man? You are hurt more than I am—I turn it over to you. You decide their motives and act appropriately.

What personal sins do you want to confess? We *must* speak them to remove them.
Do it! *Now.* There is no one else you have sinned against more than God. Tell him so!

4. SING A PRAYER TO GOD.

Face to face with Christ, my Savior,
Face to face—what will it be?
When with rapture I behold Him,
Jesus Christ who died for me.

Face to face I shall behold Him,
Far beyond the starry sky;
Face to face in all His glory,
I shall see Him by and by!

Open your hymn book and sing the rest of the verses—or even sing another prayer song.

5. READ HIS WORD TO HIM!

His Word

[12]After Festus had conferred with his council, he declared: "You have appealed to Caesar. To Caesar you will go!"

[13]A few days later King Agrippa and Bernice arrived at Caesarea to pay their respects to Festus. [14]Since they were spending many days there, Festus discussed Paul's case with the king. He said: "There is a man here whom Felix left as a prisoner. [15]When I went to Jerusalem, the chief priests and elders of the Jews brought charges against him and asked that he be condemned.

[16]"I told them that it is not the Roman custom to hand over any man before he has faced his accusers and has had an opportunity to defend himself against their charges.
— *Acts 25:12-16, NIV*

Read His Word to Him.

You were present in that council that day! There is never a decision made without you. In the choices of men of state, kings and princes and potentates, you are not left out—even if they intend to do so. Most especially is this true when a decision is being made concerning one of your servants. How I do wonder what they said—but these you know. Paul's wisdom was from heaven—it was transparent; it had no shadow to cast by turning. His appeal was accepted. When the Caesar before whom he was to appear was Nero, Paul's prospects of a fair trial were not too bright. But then there were many days yet ahead. Was this a delaying action on Paul's part?

Please express your response to this beautiful text. Put your expression in your own prayer diary.

WEEK TWENTY-FOUR — FRIDAY

6. READ HIS WORD FOR YOURSELF.

I wonder how Luke obtained the very words Festus spoke to King Agrippa? Did the Holy Spirit tell him? Did Festus later become a Christian and tell him? Did Bernice or Agrippa give their decision for Christ a second thought and later tell Luke what was said? All of these could be true. The point is that they are true as they stand! These words speak to me: (1) The monotony of a prison confinement is never mentioned. (2) Frustration and griping over an unjust sentence does not once appear in one word of Luke's account. (3) No harsh criticism of the political "weasel" words of Festus or Felix are mentioned. Dear Lord, dear Lord, what have I to complain about?

*It is so important that you pause in his presence
and either audibly or in written form tell him all his word means to you.*

7. READ HIS WORD IN THANKSGIVING.

Yes, yes. (1) Thank you for the many decisions of the councils of men that were inadvertently your decisions for the eternal good of men. (2) Thank you for the means of going to Rome—whether at Paul's expense or the government's. (3) Thank you for unusual opportunities to speak on your behalf—these are by your intent and not accident. (4) Thank you for King Agrippa and for Bernice. I do not know more about them than appears in the text (except some facts (?) of history). You know them; they represent so many today! (5) Thank you for the "Roman customs"—some of them based on your jurisprudence in the Old Testament. (6) Thank you for "the customs" of our land which include so much of your law of fairness and right of trial. (7) Thank you most of all for the dear man Paul who is my constant example in a hundred ways.

Give yourself to your own expression of gratitude—write it or speak it!

8. READ HIS WORD IN MEDITATION.

"Festus discussed Paul's case with the king." Wasn't Paul known to Festus or Agrippa before they met together to talk over his case? We believe he was. This was why the subject intrigued both men. What did they say, i.e., beyond the fact that Paul was a prisoner without a charge? Did they know just why there was such hatred of just who this Jesus of Nazareth might be? Why was there such deep opposition to Paul? Did either man seriously investigate the resurrection of our Lord? Perhaps it is idle to imagine the personal interest of these men, but then you are knowledgeable of all they said. Will we all one day know when we stand before you in judgment?

Pause—wait—think—then express yourself in thoughtful praise or thanks.

9. READ HIS WORD FOR PETITIONS.

Reaction to Paul's appeal to Caesar can move us to prayer: (1) For the following qualities of character necessary to endure the tedious monotony of political confusion we pray: Godlike patience. (2) For the long view of the whole picture. (3) For understanding that all men are important to you. (4) For my Lord's kind of love that is willing to "endure all things." (5) For a willingness to sincerely pray for these men in high places. (6) For the conversation that Paul knew would take place between Festus and Agrippa. (7) For God's decision to operate through the decision of these men.

Right here add your personal requests—and his answers.

10. READ HIS WORD AND WAIT—LISTEN—GOD SPEAKS!

What do you say to me in these verses? (1) "Be careful about your choices—some of them are irreversible." (2) "You never know to whom you can speak on my behalf— be ready." (3) "It could be you will be in a place of confinement—realize that much can be done from this place that can be done in no other way."

11. INTERCESSION FOR THE LOST WORLD

Bangladesh — Points for prayer: (1) *The tribal churches* have been growing through people movements and perhaps up to 15% of these peoples are now Christian, though there is much nominalism and lack of understanding about the Gospel. Only four languages have been reduced to writing and most of these tribes have nothing of the Scriptures. Many tribes are still unreached. (2) *Literature*— unprecedented demand; reports of tenfold increase in distribution of Scripture portions, and also there is a large increase in sales of all Christian literature. Pray that this literature, and also the two new versions of the Bengali Bible (one for Hindus and one for Muslims), may lead to conversions and church growth.

12. SING PRAISES TO OUR LORD.

"Man of Sorrows," what a name
For the Son of God who came

Ruined sinners to reclaim!
Hallelujah! what a Savior!

WEEK TWENTY-FOUR — SATURDAY

1. PRAISE GOD FOR WHO HE IS.

"But thou, O Jehovah, art . . . my glory, and the lifter up of my head" (Psa. 3:3). Bless your name forever! How good it is to rejoice in your presence! I claim for all men what David claimed for himself. David said you are his *character*—we understand the word "glory" to refer to essential being. The psalmist is claiming God as a model of character. He is saying "all I want to be you already

are." God is the ultimate goal of all men in character development. Of course there are some qualities that are exclusively yours—but there are many, many qualities we all need and can share. How wonderful it would be to live in a world where all men were full of generosity! Dear God, I do want to see just how we can reflect your nature by seeing it demonstrated in your dear Son.

Express yourself in adoration for this quality of God.
Speak it audibly or write out your praise in your own devotional journal.

2. PRAISE GOD FOR WHAT HE MEANS TO ME.

You are my character model and at the same time "the lifter up of my head." This whole psalm is couched in the context of a battle scene. I have been wounded by the enemy, I have fallen on the field. The wound is deep and painful. I expect any moment to see the grimacing face of my enemy as he draws his sword to slay me. Instead I look into the dearest, kindest face I have ever seen. I feel

a support under my head. I sense the surge of healing strength throughout my body. I am raised up and in his strength I will not be afraid of ten thousand. . . ." Dear Lord, how I praise you for the daily strength you give me —for the very personal help you offer me. It is my head in your hand.

How do you personally relate to the glory of God, and God who is our example?
Speak it out or write it out. It is *so important* that you establish *your own* devotional journal.

3. CONFESSION OF SIN

Dear Lord, you have surely not been the model of my character development, i.e., in every circumstance. It is abiding in your word that produces this change. It is abiding in your Son that enables me to abide in you. Forgive me for finding a model for imitation in anyone— or anything but yourself! Why should I want anyone else? Once again the tracks of the evil one are discovered. I

can and do resist him—but my greatest victory is in my attraction to you. Forgive me for shutting myself off from the power of your love.
"Love of money." It would be so easy to say, "I do not love money"—but the love of what money can do is the love of money. I want to ask you for what I need—not money!

What personal sins do you want to confess? We *must* speak them to remove them.
Do it! *Now.* There is no one else you have sinned against more than God. Tell him so!

4. SING A PRAYER TO GOD.

Abide with me: fast falls the eventide;
The darkness deepens; Lord, with me abide:

When other helpers fail, and comforts flee,
Help of the helpless, O abide with me!

Open your hymn book and sing the rest of the verses—or even sing another prayer song.

5. READ HIS WORD TO HIM!

His Word

[17]When they came here with me, I did not delay the case, but convened the court the next day and ordered the man to be brought in. [18]When his accusers got up to speak, they did not charge him with any of the crimes I had expected. [19]Instead, they had some points of dispute with him about their own religion and about a dead man named Jesus who Paul claimed was alive. [20]I was at a loss how to investigate such matters; so I asked if he would be will-

ing to go to Jerusalem and stand trial there on these charges. [21]When Paul made his appeal to be held over for the Emperor's decision, I ordered him held until I could send him to Caesar."
[22]Then Agrippa said to Festus, "I would like to hear this man myself."
He replied, "Tomorrow you will hear him."
— *Acts 25:17-21, NIV*

Read His Word to Him.

Is Festus telling the whole of the truth? Didn't he know more of our Lord than he indicated in his "speech" to Agrippa? Wasn't he being just polite and artful in his choice of words? At least Agrippa knew Paul and our Lord for almost the total extent of his life. Agrippa's

father had killed James and imprisoned Peter. Since Paul was born almost the same time our Lord was Agrippa had been associated with Christianity all his life—in one form or another. How vastly important was the little drama about to be given!

Please express your response to this beautiful text. Put your expression in your own prayer diary.

6. READ HIS WORD FOR YOURSELF.

"Some points of dispute about a dead man named Jesus, who Paul claimed was alive." I have read the evidence of his resurrection and I am glad to affirm with Paul that it is even as he said. Festus is not telling the whole truth — his reason for sending Paul to Jersualem was to deliver him into the hands of the Jews. Am I at times any better than he? Do I always and in every place, with everyone always tell the whole truth and nothing but the truth? Dear Lord, open my eyes to see that nothing — utterly *nothing* is hidden from you. How little hidden was the governor's deception! Two thousand years have not hidden it! Dear Father, through the blood of your Son clear my record!

Pause in his presence and tell him all his word means to you.

7. READ HIS WORD IN THANKSGIVING.

(1) Thank you for the interest and a certain measure of fairness on the part of Festus. (2) Thank you that none of our Lord's accusers — nor Paul's accusers were able to establish a charge against him. Satan cannot today lay anything to the charge of "God's elect." (3) Thank you for the pleasant surprises Christians can offer those who have eyes to see. (4) Thank you for the world religion of our Lord — a Way of Life for all men. (5) Thank you we are still investigating the power of the good news. (6) Thank you for the unusual manner you took in taking Paul to Rome that he might testify there on your behalf. (7) Thank you that we can today still hear the wonderful defense of Paul before King Agrippa.

Give yourself to your own expression of gratitude — write it or speak it!

8. READ HIS WORD IN MEDITATION.

"Tomorrow you will hear him." For every tomorrow of many years I have heard him. How eloquently, poignantly, yea, personally has Paul spoken to me! There is so much he has said that I really have not heard. Paul has spoken to me, and millions like me, of his conversion. It has become a pattern for all of us, i.e., by way of the wonderful change wrought in his whole life. This revolution was caused by three truths: (1) He saw our Lord for who he really is: King of kings and Lord of glory. Once we see him "even as he is" we shall never be the same. (2) Saul heard Jesus speak to him. Our Lord called him by name — this was a very personal, intimate encounter between Saul and our Lord. Once he speaks to you you cannot hear anyone else. (3) Jesus made Saul personally responsible for either serving him or persecuting him. Such an encounter totally altered Saul from the inside.

Pause — wait — think — then express yourself in thoughtful praise or thanks.

9. READ HIS WORD FOR PETITIONS.

The problem of Festus poses some real questions for prayer: (1) How can we ever open the heart of a man like Festus? (2) King Agrippa knew much more about our Lord, yet how shall we reach him? (3) The prominence of Jesus and the resurrection is such an example for me. (4) Deliver me from pride that prompts deception. (5) Help me to listen to Paul as if I had never heard him before. (6) Some glad tomorrow I will be able to speak to Paul where there are no schedules or interruptions — help me to be ready. (7) May I prepare myself in prayer for each meeting of those who need our Lord.

Please, please remember these are prayers — speak them — reword them!

10. READ HIS WORD AND WAIT — LISTEN — GOD SPEAKS!

Speak to me words of comfort and challenge from this text: (1) "Guard your heart; it is easy to be deceived." (2) "Guard your heart; it is too easy to deceive others." (3) "Guard your heart; the deceiver is even now at work."

11. INTERCESSION FOR THE LOST WORLD

Bangladesh — Points for prayer: (1) *Other needy groups:* a) *Students* — several missions are starting a witness among them. Pray for the establishment of strong, witnessing groups in the universities. b) *The Biharis* — despised and rejected, and many living in vast and squalid refugee camps, these Muslim people are now more open to the Gospel because of their sufferings. Pray that conversions among them may lead to the evangelization of the large Muslim Bihari population in India.

12. SING PRAISES TO OUR LORD.

Glorious things of thee are spoken,
Zion, city of our God;
He, whose word cannot be broken,
Formed thee His own abode:

On the Rock of Ages founded,
What can shake thy sure repose?
With salvations' walls surrounded,
Thou mayst smile at all thy foes.

WEEK TWENTY-FIVE — SUNDAY

1. PRAISE GOD FOR WHO HE IS.

"Thou hast set me at large when I was in distress" (Psa. 4:1). How dear and kind an act is this! We all feel "hemmed in" at times. In these times you position me (us) in such a manner that we can get the larger look. How precious and thoughtful you are! Such a capacity is available to all men. There is no circumstance where this would not

be true. Shall we imagine the very worst of all possible places for this to happen: a prison. Paul is a grand example of this. Narrowness or largeness is in the mind. Bless your wonderful interest in each of us. You can give us the breath of the world from a prison cell. You can transport us into the third heaven from such a confinement!

Express yourself in adoration for this quality of God.
Speak it audibly or write out your praise in your own devotional journal.

2. PRAISE GOD FOR WHAT HE MEANS TO ME.

You have so often "set me at large" when I was "pressed on every side." Because I have lived long enough I recognize such feelings of confinement come from fatigue and boredom. A good rest for eight hours is sometimes the most holy thing I can do. It liberates me from myself! There is no way I should be bored—the best study of your word has yet to be written. The best record of how men can

be won to your Son has yet to be established.

How glad I am for the wisdom from above that opens my mind to vistas of thought and areas of service unheard of before! I believe you could do a much better job on someone else, but I praise you from the very depths for what you do through me.

How do you personally relate to the deliverance of God, and God who "sets at large"?
Speak it out or write it out. It is *so important* that you establish *your own* devotional journal.

3. CONFESSION OF SIN

I have sometimes complained and wondered—it was when I was tired or bored, or both. The sin is not resting—not opening my heart to the needs of others all around me. Dear God, forgive me! Aloneness in any relationship can cause or be the environment for selfishness—expressed in many sins. Since I know this, dear God, push me out into the main stream of life! I sin in not waiting—sometimes I sin by waiting. Oh, how I need the wisdom to know the difference! I have come to believe that failure to ask

is a sin. "I have not because I ask not." I purpose from today onward to set up an asking service. Forgive me for being so selfish.

"Impatient." Why are we impatient? Because we simply are not ready to accept your timing. I do believe your will is revealed in the midst of our best efforts to do what we think is your will. Help me to patiently accept your refusals and changes in my best efforts.

What personal sins do you want to confess? We *must* speak them to remove them.
Do it! *Now.* There is no one else you have sinned against more than God. Tell him so!

4. SING A PRAYER TO GOD.

I hear Thy welcome voice,
That calls me, Lord, to Thee
For cleansing in Thy precious blood
That flowed on Calvary.

I am coming, Lord!
Coming now to Thee!
Wash me, cleanse me in the blood
That flowed on Calvary!

Open your hymn book and sing the rest of the verses—or even sing another prayer song.

5. READ HIS WORD TO ME!

His Word

[22]Then Agrippa said to Festus, "I would like to hear this man myself."

He replied, "Tomorrow you will hear him."

[23]The next day Agrippa and Bernice came with great pomp and entered the audience room with the high ranking officers and the leading men of the city. At the command of Festus, Paul was brought in. [24]Festus said: "King Agrippa, and all who are present with us, you see this man! The whole Jewish community has petitioned me about him in Jeursalem and here in Caesarea, shouting that he ought

not to live any longer. [25]I found he had done nothing deserving of death, but because he made his appeal to the Emperor I decided to send him to Rome. [26]But I have nothing definite to write to His Majesty about him. Therefore I have brought him before all of you, and especially before you, King Agrippa, so that as a result of this investigation I may have something to write. [27]For I think it is unreasonable to send on a prisoner without specifying the charges against him."
— *Acts 25:22-27, NIV*

Read His Word to Him.

How absurd to you must appear all attempts of man to elevate himself above other men—to say nothing of

being an insult to the One to whom all praise and glory belongs. Why would Agrippa and Bernice put on such a

WEEK TWENTY-FIVE — SUNDAY

Read His Word to Him.

show when all men knew of their human frailties? It was all they had to offer. It is all any of us has to offer. We are all so very, very fallible! Dear Lord, look in kindness and love upon us and open our eyes to see things not as they appear but as they are! You were in the audience room — essentially, *you are the audience* — it is before you and in your sight that we appear before men. You have told us through the pen of Paul what you saw when you beheld the man Paul! Thank you for this fresh look at your "sent one."

Please express your response to this beautiful text. Put your expression in your own prayer diary.

6. READ HIS WORD FOR YOURSELF.

I do indeed want to sit in the audience and take a new look at Paul. Through the eyes and words of Festus, I will look at Paul. Paul has affected the whole Jewish community. Festus is saying there is not a man in all Jerusalem that has not heard of Paul. All have heard of Paul's faith in Jesus as the Messiah. What an example for me! How many in my city have heard of my Lord from me? It isn't who could have heard and didn't. The reputation of such a man ran ahead of him and prepared the heart of the king to listen with an attention he would not otherwise give.

Either audibly or in written form tell him all his word means to you.

7. READ HIS WORD IN THANKSGIVING.

Indeed, indeed. (1) Thank you for the opportunity the gospel had to influence those in high places. (2) Thank you that at times even when men oppose and lay plans to kill your servants your word is not limited or hindered. (3) Thank you for all that has been written about Paul since that day when the governor had nothing to write. (4) Thank you for the unnamed persons in the audience before Paul. (5) Thank you for the letter Festus wrote to send with Paul to the Emperor. It evidently commended Paul in such a way as to obtain his release. (6) Thank you for the patience of Paul with the injustices of men.

Give yourself to your own expression of gratitude — write it or speak it!

8. READ HIS WORD IN MEDITATION.

"I think it unreasonable to send on a prisoner without specifying the charges against him." It was not only unreasonable, it was also illegal. Festus would be in trouble with Nero. How many prisoners are condemned without proving the charges against them? Our Lord was the first one. Only those who have been falsely accused and condemned could truly identify with our Lord. Only some- one who has been confined in jail could tell what it means to be shut out of and away from the mainstream of life. If life seems monotonous or boring to those who are not in prison, what must be the depths of depression of those inside? Paul experienced imprisonment but not depression or boredom — at least we do not catch the slightest hint of such from his letters.

Pause — wait — think — then express yourself in thoughtful praise or thanks.

9. READ HIS WORD FOR PETITIONS.

It is easy to see petitions related to this text: (1) Keep me aware of how fleeting is the pomp of men. (2) Open my heart to see how eternal is your honor. (3) Move me to remember all men in the incident and all men since will appear before your judgment seat. (4) I want to follow the example of Paul — wisdom from above. (5) I want to imitate his total confidence in your presence. (6) May I remember that truth has a wonderful way of rising to the surface.

Right here add your personal requests — and his answers.

10. READ HIS WORD AND WAIT — LISTEN — GOD SPEAKS!

What can I hear from you in this text? (1) "All men deserve to die an eternal death." (2) "All men can be saved from such a fate." (3) "Paul left the example of how all men can be saved."

11. INTERCESSION FOR THE LOST WORLD

Bhutan — Population 1,200,000. Annual growth 2.3%. People per sq. km. — 25.
Point for prayer: (1) *Totally closed and without Chris-* *tian witness until 1965*, but now a small Christian witness is growing. Pray for the opening of this land for the Gospel.

12. SING PRAISES TO OUR LORD.

Jesus has loved me — wonderful Savior!
Jesus has loved me, I cannot tell why;
Came He to rescue sinners all worthless,
My heart He conquered — for Him I would die.

Glory to Jesus — wonderful Savior!
Glory to Jesus, the One I adore;
Glory to Jesus — wonderful Savior!
Glory to Jesus, and praise evermore.

WEEK TWENTY-FIVE — MONDAY

1. PRAISE GOD FOR WHO HE IS.

"Thou hast put gladness, in my heart" (Psa. 4:7). How wonderfully true this is. You are the source of all joy and happiness! The optimism and delight we often associate with the word "gladness" all comes from you. Oh, when will all men know you? To have such delight in our hearts means we have first thought your thoughts. We *think* with our heart, we *meditate* with our heart, we *reason* with our heart. To have your gladness we must discover in your word the cause of joy and meditate on it. To have your gladness means we will or accept what you have thought. We *purpose* in our hearts, we *decide* with our hearts, we *choose* with our hearts. I not only understand what joy and gladness you can bring; I *want* it!

Express yourself in adoration for this quality of God.

2. PRAISE GOD FOR WHAT HE MEANS TO ME.

Your gladness is in *my* heart; it could be and should be in every heart—but at least it is in *my* heart. I can open your word and read: "In peace will I both lay me down and sleep" (Psa. 4:8). My mind assimilates this information—that I can both lie down and I can sleep in confident hope of either tomorrow or heaven. My will accepts such a thought—indeed eagerly assents to this truth. My emotions become aroused—I feel a sense of wonder and appreciation—indeed, gladness fills my heart. My conscience approves of such a thought. Thus my whole heart is filled with your gladness. Praise your name, you have in 10,000 ways put gladness in my heart.

How do you personally relate to the happiness of God, and God who is source of gladness?
Speak it out or write it out. It is *so important* that you establish *your own* devotional journal.

3. CONFESSION OF SIN

That I am not always glad is a confession of my failure to meditate on your word day and night! I read now again just as if I never read it before these precious words from you:

May you always be joyful in your union with the Lord. I say it again: Rejoice!
Show a gentle attitude toward everyone. The Lord is coming soon. Don't worry about anything, but in all your prayers ask God for what you need, always asking him with a thankful heart.
—*Philippians 4:4, 5, Good News Bible*

Your peace and joy are always available. Bless your wonderful name! Forgive me!

"Unkindness." How people look for kindness! How I look for it. How I *need it!* How I want to give it. It is but a return of the gift you have given me. There really is no reason in the face of your goodness and my sin for me to be unkind to anyone.

There is no one else you have sinned against more than God. Tell him so!

4. SING A PRAYER TO GOD.

O worship the King, all glorious above,
And gratefully sing His wonderful love;

Our Shield and Defender, the Ancient of days,
Pavilioned in splendor, and girded with praise.

Open your hymn book and sing the rest of the verses—or even sing another prayer song.

5. READ HIS WORD TO HIM!

His Word

26 Then Agrippa said to Paul, "You have permission to speak for yourself."

So Paul motioned with his hand and began his defense: [2]"King Agrippa, I consider myself fortunate to stand before you today as I make my defense against all the accusations of the Jews, [3]and especially so because you are well acquainted with all the Jewish customs and controversies. Therefore, I beg you to listen to me patiently.

[4]"The Jews all know the way I have lived ever since I was a child, from the beginning of my life in my own country, and also in Jerusalem. [5]They have known me for a long time and can testify, if they are willing, that according to the strictest sect of our religion, I lived as a Pharisee. [6]And now it is because of my hope in what God has promised our fathers that I am on trial today. [7]This is the promise our twelve tribes are hoping to see fulfilled as they earnestly serve God day and night. O king, it is because of this hope that the Jews are accusing me. [8]Why should any of you consider it incredible that God raises the dead?

[9]"I too was convinced that I ought to do all that was possible to oppose the name of Jesus of Nazareth. [10]And that is just what I did in Jerusalem. On the authority of the chief priests I put many of the saints in prison, and when they were put to death, I cast my vote against them. have them punished, and I tried to force them to blaspheme. In my obsession against them, I even went to foreign cities to persecute them.

[12]"On one of these journeys I was going to Damascus with the authority and commission of the chief priests. [13]About noon, O king, as I was on the road, I saw a light from heaven, brighter than the sun, blazing around me and my companions. [14]We all fell to the ground, and I heard a voice saying to me in Aramaic, 'Saul, Saul, why do you persecute me? It is hard for you to kick against the goads.'
— *Acts 26:1-14, NIV*

WEEK TWENTY-FIVE — MONDAY

Read His Word to Him.

How full of meaning are these few verses! How I do read these words over and over again to catch their meaning. I know you need not read words, since what happened centuries ago is as real and alive today as it was then. The exchange between Paul and King Agrippa is still happening! Just how much of the "Jewish customs and controversies" the King knew, and just how he responded to them you alone can know. Paul had such a great desire to tell of the power and purpose of his Lord! How I admire him! The close knit society of the Jews was a very large part of Paul's life. You asked him to break away from it. Thank you for your goads in the lives of all your people.

Please express your response to this beautiful text. Put your expression in your own prayer diary.

6. READ HIS WORD FOR YOURSELF.

I tried unsuccessfully to read this text just to you and to look at it from your perspective. I kept seeing myself instead of you in it. It is because I have for such a long time identified with Paul's experience: (1) In the very midst of very religious work I hear you call, and I actually find myself hurting your body, the church. Dear Lord, forgive me. (2) I have obtained what I thought was authority from "the chief priests" to pursue a project of my own—I was wrong—you stopped me. It hurt me in my pride and selfishness, but it helped you. Praise your name!

Pause in his presence and either audibly or in written form tell him all his word means to you.

7. READ HIS WORD IN THANKSGIVING.

(1) Thank you for Paul's open, generous attitude with King Agrippa. (2) Thank you for the record of Paul's life from his youth to his manhood—in Tarsus and Jerusalem so like so many religious people today. (3) Thank you for the marvelous hope Jesus gives to life! (4) Thank you for the hundreds of prophecies and promises fulfilled in our Lord. (5) Thank you for hope—oh, how good it is to hope! How sure is our hope in him. (6) Thank you for the personal interest you took in Saul—calling him by his name in the language of his home and religion.

Give yourself to your own expression of gratitude—write it or speak it!

8. READ HIS WORD IN MEDITATION.

"It is hard for you to kick against the goads." It is hard in several ways for anyone of us to oppose our conscience. Let's notice a few of them: (1) Our conscience is our divine umpire (animals do not have a conscience). When the rules given to this umpire come from God, then to oppose him is to oppose God. (2) It is hard on us because our conscience represents our own best interests—to oppose the conscience produces depression—deep anger is one form of this depression. (3) When we reject our conscience we are stopping growth since we add to the rules from time to time. (4) We can sear our conscience and stop the whole process of spiritual sensitivity. All of this and more was experienced by Paul as he prepared for his encounter on the road to Damascus.

Pause—wait—think—then express yourself in thoughtful praise or thanks.

9. READ HIS WORD FOR PETITIONS.

Paul's defense before Agrippa moves us to pray: (1) May I have the wisdom and courage to answer each man for the faith I have in yourself and your Son. (2) Thank you that there are no accusations Satan can bring against those in Christ Jesus. (3) Deliver me from present day Phariseeism. (4) May the hope of eternal life be more real every day I live. (5) Open my eyes to see my Lord as I read your word. (6) May I examine my opposition in every area lest I be found fighting against my Lord.

Please, please remember these are prayers—speak them—reword them!

10. READ HIS WORD AND WAIT—LISTEN—GOD SPEAKS!

As you spoke to Saul, you can speak to me through these verses: (1) "Listen to my voice every day as you read my word." (2) "Living as a strict Pharisee did not save Paul." (3) "I am touched with the hurts of my people."

11. INTERCESSION FOR THE LOST WORLD

Bhutan — Point for prayer: (1) *The number of believers among the Nepalis has grown dramatically since 1970 through the work of several Nepali preachers, with regular meetings in two places. Pray for spiritual and numerical growth, and also a reaching out to the Bhotia.*

12. SING PRAISES TO OUR LORD.

God the Omnipotent King, who ordainest
Thunder Thy clarion, the lightning Thy sword;

Show forth Thy pity on high where Thou reignest;
Give to us peace in our time, O Lord.

1. PRAISE GOD FOR WHO HE IS.

"Evil shall not sojourn with Thee" (Psa. 5:4b). We must be reminded from time to time, and even twice in a time, that we cannot and will not travel with evil and also travel with you. It is more than interesting to notice evil is considered an outsider, a visitor from another country. The footnote suggests the term "evil" could be (perhaps should be) translated "evil man." Evil is not evil until someone does it. Evil is always the option or the opposite of what you have said. Evil companionship will (not might) corrupt good morals. Is it true that evil has an ally in us? i.e., in our flesh? I do *not* believe this. If we have an ally it is you — in the Spirit you have put within us — your own nature in us! What an ally!

Express yourself in adoration for this quality of God.
Speak it audibly or write out your praise in your own devotional journal.

2. PRAISE GOD FOR WHAT HE MEANS TO ME.

Evil (or evil men) shall not sojourn with me (or you). Evil men can pay us a visit in various forms and manners: (1) Through books we read. However interesting and entertaining and even informative such books are, there is a subtle question being asked in a hundred ways: "Yea, hath God said?" "Is God really and truly all in all?" To spend more time with the secular and sensual than we do with the sacred — and I am thinking of secular/sensual literature. (I know all things created and all of life can be sacred.) Such time and thought will lead into sin and worse than this, it will lead into an attitude of sin. We will begin to answer life's questions from the evil man's point of view. I want to spend hours and hours each day in what you have said! (2) When we choose the companionship of those who *never* or *very seldom* talk of you and your word, we are being influenced by evil men regardless if they are elders or preachers or professors. If you will not sojourn with evil men why should I?

How do you personally relate to the holiness of God, and God who abhors evil?
Speak it out or write it out. It is *so important* that you establish *your own* devotional journal.

3. CONFESSION OF SIN

I am rebuked in my spirit when I read again what I wrote. It sounds like I am saying I do not enjoy or seek out the company of sinners, i.e., lost sinners. Our Lord was a friend to them — how can I be so exclusive? Dear Lord, I cannot. But just how did our Lord establish friendship with publicans and sinners? Zacchaeus and Matthew would be examples of one and Mary Magdalene and the woman of Samaria would exemplify the other. What conversation was exchanged in the homes of the two tax collectors? How often did Jesus talk with Mary before she left all to follow him? Following her great discovery what did the Samaritan woman learn from our Lord? Dear God, break me away from just the "church folk." Forgive me for exclusiveness!

"Rudeness." How could a word better describe my attitude — at times — with those who need you so badly. Dear God, reduce me to the place of the Publican in the temple. I have been a Pharisee long enough!

What personal sins do you want to confess? We *must* speak them to remove them.
Do it! *Now.* There is no one else you have sinned against more than God. Tell him so!

4. SING A PRAYER TO GOD.

Must Jesus bear the cross alone,
And all the world go free?

No; there's a cross for ev'ry one,
And there's a cross for me.

Open your hymn book and sing the rest of the verses — or even sing another prayer song.

5. READ HIS WORD TO HIM!

His Word

[15]"Then I asked, 'Who are you, Lord?'

"'I am Jesus, whom you are persecuting,' the Lord replied. [16]Now get up and stand on your feet. I have appeared to you to appoint you as a servant and as a witness of what you have seen of men and what I will show you. [17]I will rescue you from your own people and from the Gentiles. I am sending you [18]to open their eyes and turn them from darkness to light, and from the power of Satan to God, so that they may receive forgiveness of sins and a place among those who are sanctified by faith in me.'

[19]"So then, King Agrippa, I was not disobedient to the vision from heaven. [20]First to those in Damascus, then to those in Jerusalem and in all Judea, and to the Gentiles also, I preached that they should repent and turn to God and prove their repentance by their deeds. [21]That is why the Jews seized me in the temple courts and tried to kill me. [22]But I have had God's help to this very day, and so I stand here and testify to small and great alike. I am saying nothing beyond what the prophets and Moses said would happen — [23]that the Christ would suffer and, as the first to rise from the dead, would proclaim light to his own people and to the Gentiles."

— Acts 26:15-23, NIV

WEEK TWENTY-FIVE — TUESDAY

Read His Word to Him.

Of all the passages we have considered together, this one does seem to relate to you in a most direct manner. You spoke from heaven — it was a vision from your presence that changed Paul! There are so many things you said to Saul. I want to ingest each word. (1) "I am Jesus" — can it be?!! the *same* One who walked the hills of Galilee and the streets of Jerusalem and slept in the house of Mary and Martha and Lazarus? The very *same* one! (2) "I have appeared to appoint!" Your appearances are not to make us feel good, but to make us *"servants"* — *slaves*. Gladly, gladly do I give myself to you. (3) You appear to enable us to witness — give our personal testimony. If you do not appear we have nothing to say! I believe the four gospels are your appearance to me and all men.

Please express your response to this beautiful text. Put your expression in your own prayer diary.

6. READ YOUR WORD FOR YOURSELF.

Dear Lord, I want to be a source of testimony to those whom you send me. I have, like Saul, an increasing testimony, not only of what I have seen and heard, but of everything I see and hear each day down the road of life. Your purpose for Paul is your purpose for me: (1) To open eyes. What a rich privilege — for today help me to do this! (2) To turn them from darkness to light! Just how terribly dark it is. Just how bright and beautiful is the light into which we step and walk! (3) From the power of Satan — to the power of God!

It is so important that you pause in his presence and either audibly or in written form tell him all his word means to you.

7. READ HIS WORD IN THANKSGIVING.

(1) Thank you for the daily, heavenly vision we can have. (2) Thank you we are the ones to be obedient or disobedient. (3) Thank you that my job is to change men's minds by the preaching of the good news about your Son. (4) Thank you for your daily help in health, travel, food, raiment. (5) Thank you that our testimony is for all men.

Give yourself to your own expression of gratitude — write it or speak it!

8. READ HIS WORD IN MEDITATION.

"But I have had God's help to this very day." Oh, dear Lord, how true this is! Your help has not all been known. Probably very little of it has been appreciated. How subtle is your help! Behind the scenes. How easy it is to attribute your help to some other source. We had "good luck" or "things" turned out well. The real truth is "every good and perfect gift comes down from above." Dear Lord, I do want to acknowledge the true source of my blessings. I have been helped inwardly as well. You provide the peace of mind and heart that are so essential to getting anything done. You have given health of body and mind. Your mercies are fresh every morning.

Pause — wait — think — then express yourself in thoughtful praise or thanks.

9. READ HIS WORD FOR PETITIONS.

How I do lift my heart in these requests as I read these verses: (1) Teach me to be sensitive to how I can hurt you by hurting your body, the church. (2) Make me your servant today in some area of need. (3) I want to open my mouth and heart to witness for you — help me. (4) Rescue me from some of my well-intentioned friends. (5) Open the eyes of some who have heard of you from me. (6) Keep your heavenly vision ever before me.

Right here add your personal requests — and his answers.

10. READ HIS WORD AND WAIT — LISTEN — GOD SPEAKS!

I believe you can speak to me through this text: (1) "Men still must repent and turn to me." (2) "Repentance is produced through preaching." (3) "You have my help today as Paul did in the long ago."

11. INTERCESSION FOR THE LOST WORLD

Bhutan — Points for prayer: (1) *Missions* have been allowed to operate several small leprosy hospitals — pray for the silent witness of the workers. These missions have been forced to promise that they would not proselytize. Pray for a relaxation of limitations on witnessing. (2) *Christians in government service* — mostly Indians and some westerners have good opportunities to witness all over the country. Pray that they may lead some to Christ.

12. SING PRAISES TO OUR LORD.

A wonderful Savior is Jesus my Lord,
A wonderful Savior to me,
He hideth my soul in the cleft of the rock,
Where rivers of pleasure I see.
He hideth my soul in the cleft of the rock

That shadows a dry, thirsty land;
He hideth my life in the depths of His love,
And covers me there with His hand,
And covers me there with His hand.

WEEK TWENTY-FIVE — WEDNESDAY

1. PRAISE GOD FOR WHO HE IS.

"Give ear to my words, O Jehovah, consider my meditation." The quality of real interest in our needs is the quality here described. It is so good, my Father, to appear before you with the full knowledge that you are truly listening. You are *not* only waiting until I am through talking to get involved in something important. You hear with the inner ear. I want to tell you how much your listening means to me: (1) You sustain attention — no fluctuating in your absorption of listening. How good to right now know you are leaning forward, looking me directly in the eyes, wholly interested in what I am saying. (2) You are intelligent and are thinking with me each thought I present. There is no distraction or lack of understanding. Even when I am unclean you read the intentions of my heart. Praise you — I love you!

Express yourself in adoration for this quality of God.
Speak it audibly or write out your praise in your own devotional journal.

2. PRAISE GOD FOR WHAT HE MEANS TO ME.

What was said above concerning myself is but representative of your interest in all men of all the nations of the world. Every day such listening is available! But for me I would like to tell you how very, very much this quality means to me: (3) You listen to help and not just to be interested. I am so glad there is a counterpart to all I say in your word. I have *no* need, no sin, no problem you have not discussed in your word. Even the fact that I so sorely need someone who will give this type of interest and I find you are this type of person when I read your word is an example. (4) You listen as the same person — you are eternally the same — you have as much interest today as you had yesterday, and you will be listening tomorrow with the same total absorption you gave me this morning. Oh, blessed be your name!

How do you personally relate to the attentiveness of God, and God who is always listening?
Speak it out or write it out. It is *so important* that you establish *your own* devotional journal.

3. CONFESSION OF SIN

Since I know you are such a good conversationalist — since I know this dialogue called prayer is such a rich help to me — how is it I do not much more often call on you? Why am I taken up with talking to men and women who do not listen or understand? Forgive this sin! But forgive another sin: selfish ego-centeredness. If I am bothered by those who only half-listen, what of yourself? I have a difficult time selling 12 copies of a pictorial version of your word to 300-400 people. Not because they do not believe it, but because they will not read it! They are not reading the copies without pictures; why read it with pictures? Some do! Some do! Thank you! Thank you! Forgive my lack of faith. I know your word will one day be heard and known by all men. It will judge them in the last day.

What personal sins do you want to confess? We *must* speak them to remove them.
Do it! *Now.* There is no one else you have sinned against more than God. Tell him so!

4. SING A PRAYER TO GOD.

There have been names that I have loved to hear,
But never has there been a name so dear
To this heart of mine, as the name divine,
The precious, precious name of Jesus.

Jesus is the sweetest name I know,
And He's just the same as His lovely name,
And that's the reason why I love Him so;
Oh, Jesus is the sweetest name I know.

Open your hymn book and sing the rest of the verses — or even sing another prayer song.

5. READ HIS WORD TO HIM!

His Word

²⁴At this point Festus interrupted Paul's defense. "You are out of your mind, Paul!" he shouted. "Your great learning is driving you insane."

²⁵"I am not insane, most excellent Festus," Paul replied. "What I am saying is true and reasonable. ²⁶The king is familiar with these things, and I can speak freely to him. I am convinced that none of this has escaped his notice, because it was not done in a corner. ²⁷King Agrippa, do you believe the prophets? I know you do."

²⁸Then Agrippa said to Paul, "Do you think that in such a short time you can persuade me to be a Christian?"

²⁹Paul replied, "Short time or long — I pray God that not only you but all who are listening to me today may become what I am, except for these chains."

³⁰The king rose, and with him the governor and Bernice and those sitting with them. ³¹They left the room, and while talking with one another, they said, "This man is not doing anything that deserves death or imprisonment."

³²Agrippa said to Festus, "This man could have been set free, if he had not appealed to Caesar."

— Acts 26:24-32, NIV

WEEK TWENTY-FIVE — WEDNESDAY

Read His Word to Him.

Oh, let me see this incident through *your* eyes! When you created man as a rational being and he fails to use his capacities for your purpose—when a recital of your interest and involvement in Paul's life sounds like the words of a mad man—what will you say? Either Festus was not listening or did not care or both! What was said was reasonable and could be understood. How near to acceptance of your Son was King Agrippa? Was he saying with just a little more persuasion Paul would have won him to yourself? Or was he saying what Paul said was not at all adequate to convince him? You know—I wish I did.

Please express your response to this beautiful text. Put your expression in your own prayer diary.

6. READ HIS WORD FOR YOURSELF.

Paul is saying what he did for a real purpose—what was it? Isn't he telling me something very personal to him that he wants to be very personal with me? I believe he is! He is saying to me: "What converted me should convert you." I saw the Lord—you through my vision can see him too. Dear Lord, I do! "I heard him call to me—accuse me, commission me." Dear Lord, dear Lord, I *do* hear you—I *do* want to respond to you. I *know* you include me in your commission. Surely I know as much as Agrippa. I can become what Paul was. Paul was a Christian first—"one sent" second. Such is the position of every one of your servants. Paul was also left in chains because of the pride of men. How disappointing are men. How eternally satisfying and fulfilling are all your ways! What Festus and Agrippa didn't know was that Paul was already set free!

Either audibly or in written form tell him all his word means to you.

7. READ HIS WORD IN THANKSGIVING.

(1) Thank you for Paul's polite response to the unreasonable outburst of the governor. (2) Thank you that Paul's abilities were recognized—even though misunderstood. (3) Thank you that Paul cared about one man named Agrippa. (4) Thank you that we like Agrippa can know and believe what the prophets wrote. (5) Thank you that Paul felt that all who heard on that wonderful day could have become Christians. (6) Thank you that Paul convinced those present of his innocence—and we believe of much, much more.

Give yourself to your own expression of gratitude—write it or speak it!

8. READ HIS WORD IN MEDITATION.

"This man could have been set free . . ." The rulers didn't know that the greatest freedom possible was already the possession of Paul. "Freedom" is an elusive word—just when we think we have it defined we discover another facet we had not considered. We receive our Lord's words with new meaning. "You shall know the truth, and the truth shall make you free" (John 8:32). The knowledge here spoken of by our Lord is experiential knowledge. He is saying, "When you experience the truth then you shall be set free." Paul had inwardly received the truth of the forgiveness of sins through grace—he then was free from the guilt of condemnation of sin.

Pause—wait—think—then express yourself in thoughtful praise or thanks.

9. READ HIS WORD FOR PETITIONS.

I wonder what requests Paul made after he left the court room? We have requests from this experience: (1) Keep me as calm as Paul when men do not understand what I say. (2) Keep my motive clear: to persuade men to become Christians. (3) I believe your prophets—increase my faith. (4) I want to indeed become the kind of a Christian I see in Paul. (5) Increase my desire to be a totally submissive slave to King Jesus.

Please, please remember these are prayers—speak them—reword them!

10. READ HIS WORD AND WAIT—LISTEN—GOD SPEAKS!

What are you saying in these verses? (1) "There are yet men who consider gospel preachers insane." (2) "There are leaders today who are near the kingdom—speak out." (3) "Politics still mean more to many than truth."

11. INTERCESSION FOR THE LOST WORLD

Bhutan — Point for prayer: (1) *Indian believers* are active in the border region in evangelism and literature distribution among visitors from Bhutan. Pray for conversions. Pray for the unreached Bhotia in their isolation.

12. SING PRAISES TO OUR LORD.

Holy, Holy, Holy, Lord God Almighty!
Early in the morning our song shall rise to Thee;

Holy, Holy, Holy! Merciful and Mighty!
God in Three Persons, blessed Trinity!

1. PRAISE GOD FOR WHO HE IS.

"But as for me, in the abundance of thy loving-kindness will I come into thy house: in thy fear will I worship toward thy holy temple" (Psa. 5:7). I am well aware that I am (along with all other Christians) your house today. We are "a holy temple" unto you, made up of living stones, i.e., the lives of your dear people (I Pet. 2:5). At the same time it is with the same attitude as Daniel that I come before you just now. It is in an awareness of the great abundance of loving-kindness that I approach you. I accept every piece of clothing, every bite of food, every hour of rest, every provision for transportation as direct expression of your loving-kindness to me. It humbles me; I bow in awe before you! I bow down in wonder! What I have said of myself should be true of all men. How sad that one day all men will see and acknowledge the source of all good, but it will be too late then.

Express yourself in adoration for this quality of God.
Speak it audibly or write out your praise in your own devotional journal.

2. PRAISE GOD FOR WHAT HE MEANS TO ME.

How infinitely good you have been this week! You have enabled us to lead a few persons to accept your dear Son and your salvation. I count it the highest of joy to teach and lead eternal people to yourself! To give me strength and health for more than 40 years of such activity is a total amazement to me! It will finally be that "in the abundance of thy loving-kindness" I will be led into your everlasting house called "your presence"—or "at home." Surely I shall never reach thee by any other means! I am keenly aware of how inadequate my conduct and thoughts have been to plead for anything but mercy! Today let me bow anew in "fear" or deep reverence toward your eternal Temple.

How do you personally relate to the loving-kindess of God, and God who is infinitely good?
Speak it out or write it out. It is *so important* that you establish *your own* devotional journal.

3. CONFESSION OF SIN

How I need this time in my worship of you. Indeed, if we were inclined most of the time could be spent in introspection of all our failures and sins. I only want to be yielded, open, honest. You see and define my sins. Not as I see and define them. I do indeed bow and "worship" before you in *fear*. If I did not believe and accept your grace, mercy, and loving-kindness as readily as your holiness I would be hopeless! Please accept me (as I know you do) in "the beloved."

"Easily angered." If you are not easily angered with me —and you surely are not—how or why should I be so with others?

What personal sins do you want to confess? We *must* speak them to remove them.
Do it! *Now.* There is no one else you have sinned against more than God. Tell him so!

4. SING A PRAYER TO GOD.

O Zion, haste, thy mission high fulfilling,
To tell to all the world that God is Light;
That He who made all nations is not willing
One soul should perish, lost in shades of night.

Publish glad tidings,
Tidings of peace;
Tidings of Jesus,
Redemption and release.

Open your hymn book and sing the rest of the verses—or even sing another prayer song.

5. READ HIS WORD TO HIM!

His Word

27 When it was decided that we would sail for Italy, Paul and some other prisoners were handed over to a centurion named Julius, who belonged to the Imperial Regiment. ²We boarded a ship from Adramyttium about to sail for ports along the coast of the province of Asia, and we put out to sea. Aristarchus, a Macedonian from Thessalonica, was with us. — *Acts 27:1, 2, NIV*

Read His Word to Him.

Dr. Luke here joins the contingent that sails for Rome. I know he knows that you too were present. Man proposes but you dispose. This voyage was to be with much danger. Why did the authorities wait until the last few days of sailing time to make such a decision? I am sure you alone really know—I would assume this decision and action is like most governmental moves—tied-up with red tape until it can hardly move at all. What a fortunate choice was Julius! But then, you know who to choose. Was the friendship that Paul established with this centurion what opened the door to the "whole Imperial Regiment in Caesar's household"? (Phil. 1:13). Only you can truly know—but it is a most intriguing thought and it fits the zealous character of your dear servant Paul (and such speaks to my heart).

Please express your response to this beautiful text. Put your expression in your own prayer diary.

6. READ HIS WORD FOR YOURSELF.

How I *do* want to stand on the dock and prepare to board the ship from Adramyttium! Luke and Aristarchus are there. Then there are also "some other prisoners." Who were they? How many? I shall gladly take the place of one of them. There is a long and uncertain voyage ahead of us. What shall we think about and do while on board the ship? Shall I introduce the subject of salvation to some of the sailors, or to the prisoners? What shall we eat? Where shall we sleep? What if I get seasick? All these questions and more must have been asked by Luke, Aristarchus and Paul. Why was Luke along? Was he too a prisoner? Perhaps Paul was sick and needed a physician. All of them needed your presence and so do I!

Pause in his presence and either audibly or in written form tell him all his word means to you.

7. READ HIS WORD IN THANKSGIVING.

As we anticipate this voyage we pause to thank you. (1) For health of body and mind that makes it possible. (2) For the record from Festus that Julius carries to the Emperor. It is probably much better than the record of some of the other prisoners. (3) For your own choice of the centurion in charge. (4) For the fond memories Paul had of all Luke had shared with him. (5) For the confidence Paul could place in you to deliver them through the unknown. (6) For Luke's willingness to serve.

Give yourself to your own expression of gratitude—write it or speak it!

8. READ HIS WORD IN MEDITATION.

". . . *and we put out to sea.* . . ." How well does this describe the whole life of the apostle Paul! He was always going somewhere or uncertain as to what would happen to him in his present location. At the same time, we have not met a man who was more confident and peaceful. The answer to why he could find such rest in unrest is in the fact that our Lord was the captain of his ship. There was someone at the helm who had already charted the course and knew every channel in the sea. So often it would seem Paul had to settle for an uncertain way. He knew not what form bonds and afflictions awaited him in Jerusalem, but He went. He knew not what to expect on the way to Rome, except that he would bear witness and he went.

Pause—wait—think—then express yourself in thoughtful praise or thanks.

9. READ HIS WORD FOR PETITIONS.

When sailing time came Luke joined Paul at Caesarea. We can see much need for prayer: (1) The needs of Paul as he sailed for Rome can also be ours: Help us to influence all on board with our attitude and words. (2) On every journey give us your traveling mercies. (3) Give us sympathy and understanding for our fellow prisoners. (4) May we never forget your word and yourself are not bound. (5) Give us listening ears for the hurts of those with us. (6) May we see your power in your handiwork of creation. (7) Keep us calm in the face of danger.

Right here add your personal requests—and his answers.

10. READ HIS WORD AND WAIT—LISTEN—GOD SPEAKS!

For preparation of today's journey speak to me: (1) "I see beyond the obvious physical needs to the needs of your heart." (2) "Speak to me often on your journey." (3) "I have an eternal port all ready with a warm welcome for you."

11. INTERCESSION FOR THE LOST WORLD

Brunei — Population: 160,000. Growth rate—3.5%. People per sq. km.—27.

Point for prayer: (1) *Unreached peoples*—There are no known Christians among the Malays and open evangelism of them is not allowed. There are few believers among the tribal Bisaya, Kedayan and Iban peoples—these are a potential mission field for the Chinese believers in Brunei (there is some outreach from one group), and Iban missionaries from Sarawak, East Malaysia. Local Christians must do the evangelism with the ban on missions. (2) *The churches are entirely led by immigrants*, mostly Chinese, and most of the believers are expatriate Westerners, Koreans or Chinese. Pray that all opportunities for witness may be fully used—such as literature, camps and visiting Asian evangelists (all being legal).

12. SING PRAISES TO OUR LORD.

Walking in sunlight, all of my journey;
Over the mountains, thro' the deep vale;
Jesus has said "I'll never forsake thee,"
Promise divine that never can fail.

Heavenly sunlight, heavenly sunlight,
Flooding my soul with glory divine:
Hallelujah, I am rejoicing,
Singing His praises, Jesus is mine.

WEEK TWENTY-FIVE — FRIDAY

1. PRAISE GOD FOR WHO HE IS.

"But let all those that take refuge in thee rejoice, let them shout for joy because thou defendest them" (Psa. 5:11). How delightful to acknowledge these two wonderful qualities: (1) You are my hiding place, my protector, my true escape. (2) You are my defender; you fight some battles for me. Bless your holy and beautiful name! I love to draw away each day and hide myself in you. Such a comfortable place is the security of your arms! To change the figure just a little: the beautiful, peaceful place I have to live—a charming house full of surprises. One lovely painting, color scheme, carpet after another—somehow the place I stay is alive; it emanates energy and strength to me. What I find all men can and should find.

How many battles have been fought and won of which I had no knowledge at all? I do believe you have "kept me from the evil one" full many a time. I believe you have told Satan, "This far and no further."

Express yourself in adoration for this quality of God.
Speak it audibly or write out your praise in your own devotional journal.

2. PRAISE GOD FOR WHAT HE MEANS TO ME.

What a refuge and defender you are! Let me cite times when I so sorely need you and seek you: (1) When the events of life just do not make sense or hold any value to me—it is then I can come and relax in your presence and peacefully reach out to eternity, to infinity, to total power, to total knowledge, to absolute love. What a calm and assurance comes over me! (2) When I have lost in the fight of temptation, when trials have really hurt me, I have no doubt whatsoever that you love me and forgive me. I will be able to overcome the same testing later. You forgive me and I can hear you say, "Try again, you are stronger now." I take refuge in you and because I do I can in the depths of my being rejoice. I shout for joy because you are defending me before your throne.

How do you personally relate to the defense of God, and God who is defender?
Speak it out or write it out. It is *so important* that you establish *your own* devotional journal.

3. CONFESSION OF SIN

Dear God, how often have I tried to find refuge in the fig leaves of my own invention! How many times have I tried to defend myself only to find I was fighting a foe much too strong and wise for me. Forgive me for my stupidity and pride! Most of all: forgive me for not remembering, for being so busy about other things that I found myself exposed to Satan, vulnerable to his attack. I have been hurt and overcome so often just because I was not willing, or ready, or hurting enough to look up, to look away, to break the schedule, to stop the drift. Dear God, here I am. I hide myself in you. Please insulate me today!

What personal sins do you want to confess? We *must* speak them to remove them.
Do it! *Now.* There is no one else you have sinned against more than God. Tell him so!

4. SING A PRAYER TO GOD.

Christ the Lord is ris'n today, Alleluia!
Sons of men and angels say: Alleluia!

Raise your joys and triumphs high, Alleluia!
Sing, ye heav'ns, and earth reply. Alleluia!

Open your hymn book and sing the rest of the verses—or even sing another prayer song.

5. READ HIS WORD TO HIM!

His Word

[3]The next day we landed at Sidon; and Julius, in kindness to Paul, allowed him to go to his friends so they might provide for his needs. [4]From there we put out to sea again and passed to the lee of Cyprus because the winds were against us. [5]When we had sailed across the open sea off the coast of Cilicia and Pamphylia, we landed at Myra in Lycia. [6]There the centurion found an Alexandrian ship sailing for Italy and put us on board. [7]We made slow headway for many days and had difficulty arriving off Cnidus. When the wind did not allow us to hold our course, we sailed to the lee of Crete, opposite Salmone. [8]We moved along the coast with difficulty and came to a place called Fair Havens, near the town of Lasea.

— *Acts 27:3-8, NIV*

Read His Word to Him.

It does become redundant to mention the obvious, i.e., you are always "on board." Paul had already gained the respect of Julius. Was it because Paul was a citizen of heaven or of Rome? For whatever reason, it was appreciated. We are sure Paul and Luke lifted their hearts to you in gratitude. What needs did Paul have? Was he seasick? Did he need traveling money? There must have been several interesting days of sailing. What accommodations were furnished? How wonderful it would be to be able to see and know this incident today as if it had only happened yesterday. This capacity is surely present with yourself! This account is in the first person. How glorious to know all your life is that way with you!

Please, please express your response to this beautiful text. Put your expression in your own prayer diary.

6. READ HIS WORD FOR YOURSELF.

How little of the physical difficulty is here discussed. What creaking and cracking and rocking of the ship is in that little phrase: "The winds were against us."! How many vessels lay at the bottom of the deep waters off the coast of Cilicia and Pamphylia? How very little emotion is a part of Luke's record! Could Paul look on the coast of Cilicia and not think of Tarsus and home? What a record of events had passed by ere he left the care of his mother and father. Did he mention such thoughts to Luke? How I do want to sail with these good men! A new ship, new people, new quarters, new responsibilities. Paul seems impervious to it all, but was he? I'm sure I would be praying! Since I would not know if these men would live beyond this voyage, I would want to share the hope of the gospel with them. Isn't this true of all men you meet on the ship of your life?

It is so important that you pause in his presence
and either audibly or in written form tell him all his word means to you.

7. READ HIS WORD IN THANKSGIVING.

Yes, yes! (1) Thank you for all kindness shown to me (as with Paul) by those who do not even recognize you — the source of all that is kind and good. (2) Thank you for the unselfish interest of so many in the apostle Paul. (3) Thank you for the nautical and geographical accuracy of the historian Luke. (4) Thank you for providing a ship sailing for Italy. There were many on board who could be influenced for our Lord. (5) Thank you for the sense of control Paul had (because of you) on every circumstance. (6) Thank you for uncertainty that can always move us toward yourself! (7) Thank you that I want to thank you.

Give yourself to your own expression of gratitude — write it or speak it!

8. READ HIS WORD IN MEDITATION.

". . . with difficulty (we) came to a place called Fair Havens, . . ." Dear Lord, it is with difficulty all of us come to such a place. It is the fair haven of your presence toward which we sail. There are no difficulties in our life with which there is not also a way of escape that we may be able to endure it. I realize this speaks of temptation (I Cor. 10:13), but temptation becomes tests and steps of maturity if we receive them as such. I am so glad the angels of God have taken up their place of service on our behalf. The greatest way out in all our trials (and sins) is the bright, eternal hope of heaven. We might add that that haven will be very commodious and will last throughout eternity.

Pause — wait — think — then express yourself in thoughtful praise or thanks.

9. READ HIS WORD FOR PETITIONS.

Thank you for the kind centurion named Julius. Thank you for Dr. Luke. In this whole circumstance we pray for: (1) An appreciation for friends who have often provided for our needs. (2) For those who sail with us and offer help. (3) For your everlasting power seen in your creation. (4) For what seems accidental that we can interpret as providential. (5) For every contrary wind which can teach us a lesson. (6) For the safety we have enjoyed time after time on our journey thus far. (7) For your total knowledge of the total picture where we can only see a small part.

Please, please remember these are prayers — speak them — reword them!

10. READ HIS WORD IN MEDITATION.

As we pause for a little while at "fair havens" we hear you speak to us through this text: (1) "I have been on every voyage of every man every day." (2) "There are no winds or waves I cannot calm." (3) "I give wisdom — but man must want it and ask for it."

11. INTERCESSION FOR THE LOST WORLD

Burma — Population: 31,200,000. Growth rate — 2.4%. People per sq. km. — 46.
Points for prayer: (1) *Pray for peace*, religious freedom and a mighty turning to God in this divided and suffering land. (2) *Missions have done a wonderful work.* So, when the government expelled all Protestant and most Roman Catholic missionaries in 1966 (400 left the land), the Church was able to speedily make the many painful adjustments and carry on the ministry. Since that time the believers have been almost completely isolated from contacts with Christians outside the country. Pray for the removal of restrictions.

12. SING PRAISES TO OUR LORD.

I love Thy Kingdom, Lord,
The house of Thine abode,

The Church our blest Redeemer saved
With His own precious blood.

WEEK TWENTY-FIVE — SATURDAY

1. PRAISE GOD FOR WHO HE IS.

"O Lord, our Lord, how excellent is Thy name in all the earth! Who hast set Thy glory above (upon) the heavens" (Psa. 8:1). The word "excellent" does well describe the quality of yourself seen in your handiwork. Man is constantly seeking "excellence" in all his work. This is but a reflection of yourself! I want to praise you for the following qualities of excellence. I see in all you have made: (1) Your work all has perfect balance, i.e., when man has not caused a malfunction. The planets and stars are far enough removed from man's bungling to be a grand example. Without your perfect balance our little planet would long ago have been dissolved. (As indeed it one day shall.) (2) Your work has a real satisfying purpose. However, small or large the purpose, it is fulfilled. Most of man's work (apart from you) has no fulfillment.

Express yourself in adoration for this quality of God.
Speak it audibly or write out your praise in your own devotional journal.

2. PRAISE GOD FOR WHAT HE MEANS TO ME.

For me alone. "O Lord, my Lord, how excellent is your name in all the earth, your real character is above the heavens." I tried in the above expression to include all men—in this section let me just speak for myself! I stand in constant amazement and wonder at the beauty and purpose I see all about me! The renewal of my physical strength is such an excellent power, blessing, gift of yourself. The ability to reason and relate is excellent beyond description. One tree in its total growth cycle is so very excellent! The explanation you have given in your word for the origin, growth and purpose of life is more than excellent! The most excellent of all your works is the work of salvation you gave us as a free gift. Indeed, all your works are gifts for us to enjoy! Blessed and wonderful is your name!

How do you personally relate to the excellence of God, and God who is excellent?
Speak it out or write it out. it is *so important* that you establish *your own* devotional journal.

3. CONFESSION OF SIN

That I should not always so praise you is a sin above all sins. I shall do so—and right gladly—in your eternal presence. Dear Lord, make it so today! Ingratitude is the fundamental sin of man. How interesting is the fact that we never truly appreciate something until we know what it is to be without it. Such as health from sickness, food out of hunger, money out of debt. Oh, that for once I would look at my hand and appreciate it and its wonderful work for me. Do I have to lose it to thank you deeply, truly for it? Oh, not so!

"Failing to discern the body." Remarkable! This is carrying the above sin of insensitivity to its ultimate end! When we fail to see you in all of life, we fail to see you at the table! Forgive me, not someone else, but *me!*

What personal sins do you want to confess? We *must* speak them to remove them.
Do it! *Now.* There is no one else you have sinned against more than God. Tell him so!

4. SING A PRAYER TO GOD.

More like the Master I would ever be,
More of His meekness, more humility;
More zeal to labor, more courage to be true,
More consecration for work He bids me do. . . .

Take Thou my heart, . . . I would be Thine alone;
Take Thou my heart . . . and make it all Thine own;
Purge me from sin, . . . O Lord, I now implore,
Wash me and keep . . . me Thine forevermore.

Open your hymn book and sing the rest of the verses—or even sing another prayer song.

5. READ HIS WORD TO HIM!

His Word

⁹Much time had been lost, and sailing had already become dangerous because by now it was after the Fast. So Paul warned them, ¹⁰"Men, I can see that our voyage is going to be disastrous and bring great loss to ship and cargo, and to our own lives also." ¹¹But the centurion, instead of listening to what Paul said, followed the advice of the pilot and of the owner of the ship. ¹²Since the harbor was unsuitable to winter in, the majority decided that we should sail on, hoping to reach Phoenix and winter there. This was a harbor in Crete, facing both southwest and northwest.

¹³When a gentle south wind began to blow, they thought they had obtained what they wanted; so they weighed anchor and sailed along the shore of Crete. ¹⁴Before very long, a wind of hurricane force, called the "Northeaster," swept down from the island. ¹⁵The ship was caught by the storm and could not head into the wind; so we gave way to it and were driven along. ¹⁶As we passed to the lee of a small island called Cauda, we were hardly able to make the lifeboat secure. ¹⁷When the men had hoisted it aboard, they passed ropes under the ship itself to hold it together. Fearing that they would run aground on the sandbars of Syrtis, they lowered the sea anchor and let the ship be driven along.

— *Acts 27:9-17, NIV*

WEEK TWENTY-FIVE — SATURDAY

Read His Word to Him.

Yes, yes. What an exciting, fearful time these verses describe! But you were there all the time. I wonder if anyone thought that to inquire of Paul was tantamount to inquiring of yourself? How good it would be to be so near to yourself and know your word so well that this would be true of us. Paul was speaking not only on your behalf, but out of all the experience he had in sailing these same waters before. To sail or not to sail, to go or stay—how often have we all faced these decisions. Paul does not here seem to be speaking out of divine illumination. Dear Father, are you saying something about the decisions of life? Man seems to be left up to his own devices, but above and beneath and ahead of us is yourself—in whom we live and move and have our being.

Please express your response to this beautiful text. Put your expression in your own prayer diary.

6. READ HIS WORD FOR YOURSELF.

In a place of crisis, in a time of indecision, in the valley of choice—dear Lord, what shall I do? You seem to say: (1) Examine the whole picture—the total subject. (2) Realize there could be, most likely will be, another time to get what you want now. (3) Do not jump at conclusions—"a south wind" can be deceptive. (4) Even if you make the wrong choice, all is not lost. God is with you in the storm as well as the calm. (5) God expects me to do all I can to solve the problem. (6) There *are* storms that *can* and *will* wreck your little ship, i.e., of finance, or job security, or of local influence. All is not lost. He has something better prepared for you.

Either audibly or in written form tell him all his word means to you.

7. READ HIS WORD IN THANKSGIVING.

(1) Thank you even for delays in timing—you can and do use it, if not arrange it. (2) Thank you for the preciseness of Luke's record (i.e., "fast"—Jewish Day of Atonement. In the year 59 A.D. it was on October 5; in 60 A.D. it would have been September 23.). (3) Thank you that you can override the foolishness of men and use it to your glory. (4) Thank you for all the winds that blow—all of them blow some good.

8. READ HIS WORD IN MEDITATION.

". . . *They tied ropes around the ship itself to hold it together.*" What desperate precautions will man take to save himself from suffering and death. However much we work at it, this old ship will come apart and we shall all stand before him with whom we have to do. Why are we so anxious to avoid death? We can understand the attitude of the men (and women?) on board this ship. But it is much more difficult to account for the fear in the hearts of Christians. Paul faced this inevitable journey with great, eager, positive anticipation. "For me to die is gain." He said, "I have a great desire to depart the body which is very far better."

Pause—wait—think—then express yourself in thoughtful praise or thanks.

9. READ HIS WORD FOR PETITIONS.

It was dangerous to sail, but more dangerous to ignore the advice of Paul. (1) As I face the storms of life may I hear the words of your servant Paul. (2) Help me not to be deceived by the "gentle south wind" of the evil one. (3) Lead me to a harbor for the winter of life. (4) Help me to make all necessary precautions in sailing a safe course in life. (5) May I expect the best and prepare for the worst. (6) Thank you for Paul's courageous attitude.

Right here add your personal requests—and his answers.

10. READ HIS WORD AND WAIT—LISTEN—GOD SPEAKS!

As we enter the storm there is much we can hear from you: (1) "I can work through a storm as well as without one." (2) "I have ways of convincing even stubborn men." (3) "A gentle south wind can be the precursor of a storm."

11. INTERCESSION FOR THE LOST WORLD

Burma — Point for prayer: (1) *The churches have continued to grow steadily* at about 3% a year. Almost the entire Church in all denominations is Bible believing and evangelistic. Church leaders have gained immensely in maturity and also in standing in the eyes of the authorities and people since the expulsion of the missionaries, for Christianity did not collapse, but proved to be truly rooted in the hearts of the people. Many Christians are well educated and to be found in positions of responsibility all over the country. Many young people are being converted and form a large proportion of many of the congregations. Pray for continued witness, spirituality and growth.

12. SING PRAISES TO OUR LORD.

Jesus shall reign where'er the sun
Does his successive journeys run;
His kingdom spread from shore to shore,
Till moons shall wax and wane no more.

WEEK TWENTY-SIX — SUNDAY

1. PRAISE GOD FOR WHO HE IS.

"But the Lord shall endure forever: he hath prepared his throne for judgment" (Psa. 9:7). It sounds like you are given a great deal of opposition. How eternally true this is! Men have opposed you out of their own selfish desires. It is a strange fact full of wonder that the very qualities that reflect yourself have been used by man to oppose you. Man can choose and he has chosen to reject and refuse. Man has the capacity and desire to worship—he

worships himself. It is not that you are in a "waiting game" to simply endure longer than man's opposition. You have done so much to awaken man to Satan's lies. You are even now opening the eyes of men to your love and forgiveness. But there will be a judgment—a time of total evaluation. It is so good to worship One who will always endure and who will balance the books.

Express yourself in adoration for this quality of God.
Speak it audibly or write out your praise in your own devotional journal.

2. PRAISE GOD FOR WHAT HE MEANS TO ME.

Just for me! I want to trust Someone who has never betrayed a confidence—I want to love Someone who never in the slightest disappoints. I want to believe Someone who has never told a lie. I want to follow Someone who knows exactly where he is going. Oh, joy unspeakable! I have found that Someone! I want to believe in

Someone who has a total record of what all men said—and exactly *why* they said it. What an unspeakable, unimaginable day it will be when you set up your judgment! Truly, truly, I cannot imagine what it will be. But that it will be, I am as sure as your promise backed by your integrity!

How do you personally relate to the judgment of God, and God who is Judge?
Speak it out or write it out. It is *so important* that you establish *your own* devotional journal.

3. CONFESSION OF SIN

Do I really and truly believe I will be judged? Is your grace and mercy an automatic bath that is turned on each time I sin and is applied without fail before I appear before you? Is there no need for true, deep, personal repentance? If some sins have held on like stubborn barnacles, shall I yet be accepted? There will needs be a cleansing—is that a part of the judgment? No sin or unrepentant sinner will enter into your presence. I know this and tremble in fear!

At the same time, I also know that my knowledge and performance are *not* the basis of acceptance. I simply do not want "to continue in sin that grace might abound"! Dear God, forgive me! Accept me! Praise your name, I know you do.

"Lukewarmness." Dear Lord, I want to feed the fire. I want to stir up the gift. Forgive me for the times I haven't.

What personal sins do you want to confess? We *must* speak them to remove them.
Do it! *Now.* There is no one else you have sinned against more than God. Tell him so!

4. SING A PRAYER TO GOD.

Lord, speak to me, that I may speak
In living echoes of Thy tone;

As Thou hast sought, so let me seek
Thy erring children lost and lone.

Open your hymn book and sing the rest of the verses—or even sing another prayer song.

5. READ HIS WORD TO HIM!

His Word

They lowered the sea anchor and let the ship be driven along. [18]We took such a violent battering from the storm that the next day they began to throw the cargo overboard. [19]On the third day, they threw the ship's tackle overboard with their own hands. [20]When neither sun nor stars appeared for many days and the storm continued raging, we finally gave up all hope of being saved.
[21]After the men had gone a long time without food, Paul stood up before them and said: "Men, you should have taken my advice not to sail from Crete; then you

would have spared yourselves this damage and loss. [22]But now I urge you to keep up your courage, because not one of you will be lost; only the ship will be destroyed. [23]Last night an angel of the God whose I am and whom I serve stood beside me [24]and said, 'Do not be afraid, Paul. You must stand trial before Caesar; and God has graciously given you the lives of all who sail with you.' [25]So keep up your courage, men, for I have faith in God that it will happen just as he told me. [26]Nevertheless, we must run aground on some island."
— *Acts 27:17c-26, NIV*

Read His Word to Him.

How little and frail is man. As compared to the quantity of water in the sea he is an infinitesimal speck! Since he *is* so small and incapable, how is it you have an interest in

him? It would be easy to say, "because you created him in your own likeness"—and so you have. How is it you placed your likeness in such a small temporary body?

If you were going to make man to rule over all the rest of your handiwork, how is it you did not give him a stronger and larger body in which to live? Why create him as subject to all the buffeting of sea and weather?

Ah, it is easy to answer part of this question: If man does not do any better with the little you have given him what would he do with more? Bless your name, you have made all things well!

Please express your response to this beautiful text. Put your expression in your own prayer diary.

6. READ HIS WORD FOR YOURSELF.

Just for me. How I can identify with the seasickness of those on board. What sad words are those of Luke: "We *finally* gave up all hope of being saved." After being without food for so many days (two weeks) there was an apathetic acceptance of the inevitable. It would seem that the last thing they needed to hear were the words of Paul when he said: "I told you so"! But in such a condition this is the one thing I need to hear. I need to be deeply, deeply reminded that you are *always right*—that if I would only listen ahead of time I need not suffer. But even now—in the midst of despair there is hope—my hope is in you and only in you.

Pause in his presence and either audibly or in written form tell him all his word means to you.

7. READ HIS WORD IN MEDITATION.

(1) Thank you dear Lord that the ship escaped the sandbars of Syrtis. (2) Thank you that your chastening does lighten our lives of all excess baggage. (3) Thank you for the immense power you manifest in the physical creation about us, only remotely comparable to your Spiritual power. (4) Thank you that when we give up hope there is always someone who does not. (5) Thank you for Paul's willingness to take advantage of every opportunity to say a word for you. (6) Thank you for the promise that even Caesar will hear from Paul (and you).

Give yourself to your own expression of gratitude—write it or speak it!

8. READ HIS WORD IN MEDITATION.

"Nevertheless we must run aground on some island." What a remarkable prophecy this was! There are so many other things that could have happened: (1) The ship could have sunk with all on board. (2) They could have weathered the storm and continued their voyage. (3) They could have made it into a harbor to spend the winter. (4) The ship could have been broken up in the waves and ultimately sunk. Not one (of 276) would be lost! How wonderfully good you were to Paul and all the people on board. This has not always been your will, but when it is it is indeed appreciated. It is a strange phenomenon that we can be so much more concerned about physical safety than we are with the real person in danger. All 276 persons (with the exception of Paul and his companions) were lost and headed for an eternal drowning in the lake of fire.

Pause—wait—think—then express yourself in thoughtful praise or thanks.

9. READ HIS WORD FOR PETITIONS.

In every desperate situation we need prayer: (1) It is so easy to be marooned in life—"Jesus Savior pilot me." (2) Open my mind to take every precaution I can take against Satan's storm. (3) May I lighten up all *excess* baggage for the voyage of every day. (4) Teach me again that what is hopeless with men is full of hope with you.

Please, please remember these are prayers—speak them—reword them!

10. READ HIS WORD AND WAIT—LISTEN—GOD SPEAKS!

Speak to me from these verses: (1) "Angels still minister to my servants." (2) "I can save men through you from a death worse than drowning." (3) "Seldom do I work through ideal circumstances."

11. INTERCESSION FOR THE LOST WORLD

Burma — Point for prayer: (1) Opposition to the Christians has been more for political reasons—links with other lands, so loyalty to state and socialist policies doubted; also nearly all Christians are among restive minority groups with a recent history of uprisings against the central government. Pray for the believers in their very difficult situation facing hostility from both the government and also the Chinese Communists who exploit the national chaos to make military incursions into Burma. In some border areas the Christians have suffered much.

12. SING PRAISES TO OUR LORD.

Wounded for me, wounded for me,
There on the cross He was wounded for me;

Gone my transgressions, and now I am free,
All because Jesus was wounded for me.

WEEK TWENTY-SIX — MONDAY

1. PRAISE GOD FOR WHO HE IS.

"And they that know thy name will put their trust in thee: for thou, Lord, hast not forsaken them that seek thee" (Psa. 9:10). Praise just for the qualities I see in this beautiful verse: (1) You are knowable, i.e., man can and should enter into this knowledge. Your qualities or characteristics are all knowledgeable. How wonderful is this thought! We need to pause long before your two great books: a) Nature and b) the Bible. (2) Assimilating facts does not give us a knowledge of yourself—we must become emotionally involved with such information before it becomes real. Such knowledge is experiential or it is nothing. (3) Our response to such knowledge is that we *will* (not *might*) put our trust in you. Only when man walks and talks with you, and you with him can man truly know you.

Express yourself in adoration for this quality of God.
Speak it audibly or write out your praise in your own devotional journal.

2. PRAISE GOD FOR WHAT HE MEANS TO ME.

Just for me. Dear Lord, I do, I do want to *know* your whole self! To know your name (which is many names) is to know you, and not to know you. I must and I do pause before you to contemplate your greatness and goodness! I look with the eyes of my heart at these words which but represent all you are: (1) Love, (2) Power, (3) Wisdom, (4) Grace, (5) Mercy, (6) Kindness, (7) Patience. All of these qualities need to be raised to the *absolute* or totality! Indeed, indeed, you have "not forsaken those who seek you." Right now I bow in wonder and amazement and joy!

How do you personally relate to the known nature of God, and God who is knowable?
Speak it out or write it out. It is *so important* that you establish *your own* devotional journal.

3. CONFESSION OF SIN

That I am not always caught up in the joy of worship is a sad confession. Such joy need not be loud or seen, but Jesus did say "my joy I leave with you, my joy I give to you, and no man shall take away my joy." Therefore for such joy to leave is the sin here confessed. Dear Lord, anger and selfish desire removes such joy. Forgive me. I do, I do forgive those who sin against me.

"Stinginess." It is only when we freely give ourselves away to you that we are ready to give generously to others. Forgive me for the miserly attitude I have had toward giving.

What personal sins do you want to confess? We *must* speak them to remove them.
Do it! *Now.* There is no one else you have sinned against more than God. Tell him so!

4. SING A PRAYER TO GOD.

I must tell Jesus all of my trials;
I cannot bear these burdens alone;
In my distress He kindly will help me;
He ever loves and cares for His own.

I must tell Jesus! I must tell Jesus!
I cannot bear my burdens alone;
I must tell Jesus! I must tell Jesus!
Jesus can help me, Jesus alone.

Open your hymn book and sing the rest of the verses—or even sing another prayer song.

5. READ HIS WORD TO HIM!

His Word

[27]On the fourteenth night we were still being driven across the Adriatic Sea, when about midnight the sailors sensed they were approaching land. [28]They took soundings and found that the water was a hundred and twenty feet deep. A short time later they took soundings again and found it was ninety feet deep. [29]Fearing that we would be dashed against the rocks, they dropped four anchors from the stern and prayed for daylight. — *Acts 27:27-29, NIV*

Read His Word to Him.

How easy it is to relate this circumstance to yourself! Only you can handle it! How many thousands of ships and sailors have come and gone on the seas of life? There has never been a despairing cry for help you have not heard. Whatever help any received came from you—recognized or not, appreciated or not, acknowledged or not. Just why thousands (millions) have drowned—just why ships have sunk is best known to you. I am sure it will be no problem at all to explain this to me and to anyone else in the light of eternity. If I am prepared to say there is a plain understanding above mine then, I can safely rest in the One who lives in that realm. From my own understanding it would seem that those who place themselves in the environment of the operation of the laws of nature or the created world will receive the consequences of those laws.

Please express your response to this beautiful text. Put your expression in your own prayer diary.

6. READ HIS WORD FOR YOURSELF.

I do want to get on board that ship. I want to stand on the reeling deck and feel the force of the wind and rain. What strange and different thoughts would I have after fourteen days with little or no food. Fourteen days of seasickness would move me to near despair. How many times I would wish I was dead. Luke evidently was right there to see and hear all that happened. One hundred and twenty feet of turbulent water in the middle of the night is an awesome thought. How would prayers hasten the day? Did all the occupants of the ship participate in these prayers? This seems to be nothing more than a fervent desire which is here described by Luke as a prayer. Dear Lord, how would I word a prayer in such conditions? Like Peter, I cry "Lord save me!"

It is so important that you pause in his presence
and either audibly or in written form tell him all his word means to you.

7. READ HIS WORD IN THANKSGIVING.

(1) Thank you for the fact that you see and know as well in the night as well as the day. (2) Thank you for your promises that all the storms of life cannot defeat. (3) Thank you for every desperate situation when I must trust in you. (4) Thank you that my sins are cast into a deeper sea than the Adriatic. (5) Thank you for the four anchors of our faith: (a) Justification; (b) Sanctification; (c) Redemption; (d) Hope. (6) Thank you for the ship of faith that shall never be broken by any rocks of this world. (7) Thank you for the captain of the ship of our life.

Give yourself to your own expession of gratitude—write it or speak it!

8. READ HIS WORD IN MEDITATION.

"*. . . they dropped four anchors from the stern and prayed for daylight.*" This must describe millions of men in the desperate darkness of a storm at sea. It could describe millions of others who found themselves in a place where danger was present and life has lost its meaning. There is a lesson in this for me—for all who have felt like the night would never end. (1) We need to do what we can. The four anchors have represented as many things as the imagination of man could manufacture. They do represent what we can do. (a) We can read your word—what an anchor! (b) We can talk with others who love us. (c) We can pray with someone else in the same plight. (d) We can take the Lord's supper and remember him who died in darkness. We need to remember *there will be another day.*

Pause—wait—think—then express yourself in thoughtful praise or thanks.

9. READ HIS WORD FOR PETITIONS.

At midnight it is hard to keep a balance—we need prayer: (1) We are all coming closer to the shore of eternity—how far is it? Lord give us a "sounding" from time to time. (2) There are four anchors we need as we sail through any storm: (a) The anchor of real personal prayer. (b) The anchor of daily meditation upon your word. (c) The anchor of a close friend in whom we can confide. (d) The anchor of a hope both sure and steadfast that reaches through the veil of death into heaven itself. (3) How I do pray for the dawning of that eternal day when all storms will be past. (4) Thank you that you know so much more about every situation than we do.

Right here add your personal requests—and his answers.

10. READ HIS WORD AND WAIT—LISTEN—GOD SPEAKS!

In this midnight hour what do you say to us? (1) "Be urgent when life is calm as well as when troubled." (2) "There are men counting on you to speak a word for their salvation." (3) "I am your guide through every dark night."

11. INTERCESSION FOR THE LOST WORLD

Burma — Point for prayer: (1) *The missionary vision* of the believers is outstanding. There is much outreach to the unevangelized all over the country. Nearly all preachers and evangelists do much evangelistic work in animist and Buddhist villages. Most churches have vigorous lay-training schemes to get believers winning souls. Young peoples' evangelistic teams are greatly used. There are more trained full time workers than churches, despite the poverty of the congregations, so many go out as missionary evangelists to plant churches in new areas. There is a growing outreach to the Burmans and all Buddhists, as well as to tribes in Thailand. Pray for these believers as they evangelize the unreached peoples of their land.

12. SING PRAISES TO OUR LORD.

All hail the pow'r of Jesus' name!
Let angels prostrate fall;
Bring forth the royal diadem,
And crown Him Lord of all.

Let us crown Him, . . . Let us crown Him, . . .
Let us crown the great Redeemer Lord of all; . . .
Let us crown Him, . . . Let us crown Him, . . .
Let us crown Him Lord of all.

WEEK TWENTY-SIX — TUESDAY

1. PRAISE GOD FOR WHO HE IS.

"Thou wilt shew me the path of life; in thy presence is fulness of joy, at thy right hand there are pleasures for evermore" (Psa. 16:11). I realize this is a Messianic Psalm fulfilled in the resurrection of my Lord. However, the beautiful promises made in it have such a general application for all men. Oh, will you not gladly show all men the path of life? Indeed you have in the life of your dear Son. But in another sense you have spoken to the fathers in the prophets. You have spoken to all men today through your apostles and prophets as they told of your Son. It is such an encouragement to know there is indeed "a path of life." Living and thinking and talking "in your presence" is indeed "the fulness of joy." These tremendous promises all fulfilled in Jesus are open to all men.

Express yourself in adoration for this quality of God.
Speak it audibly or write out your praise in your own devotional journal.

2. PRAISE GOD FOR WHAT HE MEANS TO ME.

Just for me — open for myself — *right now!* For my own life — *today*, I claim these promises: (1) You will show me the way to walk and talk — indeed you have in your word and in your Son. Am I going to memorize more of your word? Am I going to look again at the life of my Lord? (2) Only in your way is there *life* at all — death is the alternate! The life you give is like yourself — eternal, strong, constant! (2) Is your presence in the fulness of joy! This will be eternally true in heaven, but for today, just for today, I need and I want this fulness of joy. I hear my Savior say: "Hitherto have you asked nothing in my name: ask and ye shall receive, that your joy may be full" (John 16:24). I want to embrace to my heart the words of fisherman Peter: "Whom having not seen, ye love; in whom, though now ye see him not, yet believing, ye rejoice with joy unspeakable and full of glory" (I Pet. 1:8). By your authority are there pleasures for evermore. Amen!

How do you personally relate to the pleasures of God, and God who is the fulness of joy?
Speak it out or write it out. It is *so important* that you establish *your own* devotional journal.

3. CONFESSION OF SIN

Dear Lord, how is it that I am not always filled with joy? It is for the simple reason that I do not always live in your presence. I am not personally identified with the Source of the joy. It is when I meditate upon what you have said that I understand and emotionally respond. But there is a deeper satisfaction. There is a far more fundamental eternal pleasure. It is in the "living hope."

Dear God, I purpose today to make myself more keenly aware of the meaning of what you have said. Forgive me, forgive me for my sad, sick, sinful neglect of practicing your presence.

"Loving to have the preeminence." Dear God, you have a prior claim on all the preeminence — my Lord has such a position in *all things*. Take it, Lord, I do not want it!

What personal sins do you want to confess? We *must* speak them to remove them.
Do it! *Now.* There is no one else you have sinned against more than God. Tell him so!

4. SING A PRAYER TO GOD.

O perfect Love, all human thought transcending,
Lowly we kneel in prayer before Thy throne,

That theirs may be the love which knows no ending,
Whom Thou forevermore dost join in one.

Open your hymn book and sing the rest of the verses — or even sing another prayer song.

5. READ HIS WORD TO HIM!

His Word

[30]In an attempt to escape from the ship, the sailors let the lifeboat down into the sea, pretending they were going to lower some anchors from the bow. [31]Then Paul said to the centurion and the soldiers, "Unless these men stay with the ship, you cannot be saved." [32]So the soldiers cut the ropes that held the lifeboat and let it fall away.
— *Acts 27:30-32, NIV*

Read His Word to Him.

How exciting is this word! How strong is the desire for self-preservation. Somehow I want to look at this incident from *your* perspective. Who were these several sailors? You know them, you know the families left behind in some town to which they fondly hoped to return. You can see the situation that surely appears desperate to these men. I can't imagine you look on them with anything but mercy and pity. At the same time the words of your servant Paul are to be considered. You had already promised the lives of all on board, but not without the help of these sailors could the ship be run aground so all could escape. Paul's cooperation in your plan must have pleased you.

Please express your response to this beautiful text. Put your expression in your own prayer diary.

6. READ HIS WORD FOR YOURSELF.

Whose place shall I take? Could I imagine that I would be as driven by a desire to live as these men? Would I stoop to deception to preserve my life? How about the soldiers? I am sure by this time I would repect any words the apostle said. Would I respond as quickly and decisively as these men? Would I cut away the boat? Was this a wise choice? It removed any possibility of using it for a land-ing, but then it was inadequate at best. Could I imagine myself in Paul's place? It would seem that he was the only one who really knew what was happening. The expertise of these sailors was essential. Their act was selfish; it must be stopped. I cannot say just where I fit in the action here. But I am glad to try to imagine. I remember the angel of the Lord who sees all of this.

*It is so important that you pause in his presence
and either audibly or in written form tell him all his word means to you.*

7. READ HIS WORD IN THANKSGIVING.

(1) Thank you for unsuccessful attempts to escape — it has been very needful that we stay with the good ship Zion. (2) Thank you for weakness that leads to your strength. (3) Thank you for those who love us and warn us when we are wrong. (4) Thank you for those who have responded immediately to our need and helped us. We might surely have been lost if such had not happened. (5) Thank you for removing all ways of escape except in your dear self! (6) Thank you for the sharp sword of your word that can cut through all my deceit. (7) Thank you for Paul who through all the stress was your man with your message.

Give yourself to your own expression of gratitude — write it or speak it!

8. READ HIS WORD IN MEDITATION.

"... *cut the ropes that held the lifeboat and let it fall away.*" Dear Lord, I know this represents just what must happen and what has happened in my own experience. Until I am ready to cut away all "provisions for the flesh to fulfill the lusts thereof," I can never really and truly "put on the Lord Jesus." The life this boat represents to me I do not want. But until the boat is cut off it can be, it does become a provision, a temptation. I take this principle to be the same my Lord had in mind when he said, "If your right eye offend you, pluck it out"; "if your right hand offend you, cut it off"! We are in the midst of a storm; the situation is desperate — it calls for drastic measures. Cut it off and let it go!

Pause — wait — think — then express yourself in thoughtful praise or thanks.

9. READ HIS WORD FOR PETITIONS.

Desperation moves men to do strange things — it moves others to pray: (1) May I stay with the ship of life for others if not for myself. (2) Dear Lord, I know some of my complaints are a form of escape — open my eyes. (3) Help me to stop deceiving myself and do what I can to help others. (4) I want to pray as if everything depended on you and work like it all depended on me. (5) Enable me to cut away all avenues of escape into this world. (6) Lord, keep me honest about my motives when I am distressed. (7) Thank you for the ark of safety I find in Jesus.

Please, please remember these are prayers — speak them — reword them!

10. READ HIS WORD AND WAIT — LISTEN — GOD SPEAKS!

When men's hearts fail them for fear, speak to me: (1) "There are many things worse than death." (2) "To live is Christ; to die is gain." (3) "I see a way out when there is none from your viewpoint."

11. INTERCESSION FOR THE LOST WORLD

Burma — Points for prayer: (1) *Unreached peoples: a) The Burman people* are resistant. There are only 20,000 Protestants among them. It is not easy for the tribal be-lievers to witness to them because of the years of mistrust between them. Pray for the conversion of Buddhists. (2) *b) Resistant tribal peoples* include Shan, Mon and Palaung (Buddhists), Moken, also the Kayah and Arakanses peoples.

12. SING PRAISES TO OUR LORD.

I've a message from the Lord, Hallelujah!
The message unto you I'll give;
'Tis recorded in His word, Hallelujah!
It is only that you "look and live."

"Look and live," ... my brother, live,
Look to Jesus now and live;
'Tis recorded in His word, Hallelujah!
It is only that you "look and live."

WEEK TWENTY-SIX — WEDNESDAY

1. PRAISE GOD FOR WHO HE IS.

"Thou hast proved mine heart; thou hast visited me in the night; Thou has tried me, and shalt find nothing; I am purposed that my mouth shall not transgress" (Psa. 17:3). There are several marvelous qualities of yourself that I want to appreciate fully: (1) You "prove" or test, or declare genuine or faulty the hearts of men. The heart is the mind, will, emotions and conscience—essentially the soul of man. (2) You are not troubled by fatigue therefore need no rest and night is the same as day with you. But when man is tired and weak and resting you come to see if he yet trusts in you. Or is your nocturnal visit to offer strength and help? (3) Man can be and is weighed in your scales—heated in your crucible. David is speaking of consistency, not perfect obedience, when he says "and shalt find nothing," i.e., nothing lacking when David's heart was tried, it was found trusting in and faithful to you. (4) Your word is the criteria for sinning or not sinning, i.e., we either keep it and do not transgress or we fail to keep it and sin.

Express yourself in adoration for this quality of God.
Speak it audibly or write out your praise in your own devotional journal.

2. PRAISE GOD FOR WHAT HE MEANS TO ME.

I am tempted by Satan to simply give up! To *prove* my heart! But when I remember the test is only for the basic desire to love you and trust you, not to perfectly obey you, I am greatly encouraged. What happens when you visit me in the night? You will find me quite unresponsive—I am asleep. Dear God, I want to be able to openly welcome you at all times. Break through—penetrate fully my subconsciousness. Dear Lord, I do want to say with the psalmist, "Thou has tried me, and shalt find nothing." No rebellion, no resistance, no hesitancy, no unwillingness—you can find much full of fault, but you will find a heart open and willing. If *purpose* keeps me from sinning, i.e., with my mouth, then indeed I do purpose. My mouth is the opening for sin. Dear God, I do purpose; deepen it!

How do you personally relate to the testing of God, and God who is Examiner?
Speak it out or write it out. It is *so important* that you establish *your own* devotional journal.

3. CONFESSION OF SIN

Most of the above was a confession of sin. Dear Lord, I cannot even know my heart; it is too deceitful. You alone know it. However, I *can* and *do* control the input of my mind. I *can* and *do* control the decisions of my will. I *can* and *do* respond emotionally to what I understand and decide. I *can* and *do* program my conscience to react in approval or disapproval. I can therefore control the content of my heart. Right now I ask for forgiveness for terrible deficiencies in this area. I ask for the divine wisdom I need to best use the input.

"Pride in what is seen." Dear Lord, what would I do if I could not "show and tell" with people? Help me to work for you and let people see for themselves! This is a serious juvenile sin. Forgive me!

What personal sins do you want to confess? We *must* speak them to remove them.
Do it! *Now.* There is no one else you have sinned against more than God. Tell him so!

4. SING A PRAYER TO GOD.

Crown Him with many crowns,
The Lamb upon His throne;
Hark! how the heav'nly anthem drowns
All music but its own!

Awake, my soul, and sing
Of Him who died for thee;
And hail Him as thy matchless King
Thro' all eternity.

Open your hymn book and sing the rest of the verses—or even sing another prayer song.

5. READ HIS WORD TO HIM!

His Word

[33]Just before dawn Paul urged them all to eat. "For the last fourteen days," he said, "you have been in constant suspense and have gone without food—you haven't eaten anything. [34]Now I urge you to take some food. You need it to survive. Not one of you will lose a single hair from his head." [35]After he said this, he took some bread and gave thanks to God in front of them all. Then he broke it and began to eat. [36]They were all encouraged and ate some food themselves. [37]Altogether there were 276 of us on board. [38]When they had eaten as much as they wanted, they lightened the ship by throwing the grain into the sea.

[39]When daylight came, they did not recognize the land, but they saw a bay with a sandy beach, where they decided to run the ship aground if they could. [40]Cutting loose the anchors, they left them in the sea and at the same time untied the ropes that held the rudders. Then they hoisted the foresail to the wind and made for the beach.

— Acts 27:33-40, NIV

Read His Word to Him.

Paul included you in the eating of the bread. I'm sure you never left after thanksgiving. Indeed you were present at the time and after the time or Paul would never have paused to acknowledge the source of all we are and have. How confident was Paul! What a source of strength and encouragement he was. It was all because he believed you!

Luke was there as a participant in all that occurred. The grain would be of no use to anyone — it was only a burden. How totally inadequate are all our provisions unless you are in them. Simply because you promised they *would* run aground does *not* mean they need not do all they could to make it possible.

6. READ HIS WORD FOR YOURSELF.

Can I position myself alongside one of the occupants of this ship? It has been two weeks of seasickness and hunger, of wonder and despair, of prayer and brief conversation. But there is someone who has not reacted as we have — his name is Saul of Tarsus or Paul the apostle. Why is he so different? Somehow he has identified with his God. Was

Luke as confident as Paul? We believe he was. It is all working out even as Paul said it would. How wonderfully subtle are all your moves! It is always this way. A circumstance occurs which we could attribute to you. But there is *always* another explanation. If we listen we will soon hear the voice of humanism.

Either audibly or in written form tell him all his word means to you.

7. READ HIS WORD IN THANKSGIVING.

(1) Thank you for fourteen days of sharpening up our sensibilities to receive the message of our Lord. A fourteen day fast can be a great conditioner. (2) Thank you for the common sense and spiritual emphasis combined in

Paul. (3) Thank you for the reiteration of your promise. (4) Thank you for Paul's boldness in the midst of unbelievers (or were they now wondering about his God?). (5) Thank you for your direction to the island of Malta.

Give yourself to your own expression of gratitude — write it or speak it!

8. READ HIS WORD IN MEDITATION.

". . . they hoisted the foresail to the wind and made for the beach." There are indeed times in life when decisions must be made and carried out regardless of the consequences. What are the feelings of the occupants of this ship? What about the prisoners? What of the soldiers? Who made up the 276 on board? Were most of them prisoners? All of life becomes very much like this voyage to Rome: (1) We are all on this journey — like it or not.

(2) We encounter the unexpected in so many areas of living. (3) We know God's messenger has given us assurances and promises — but somehow in the storm we do not hear him. (4) There are times when we simply cut away the anchors and hoist the foresail to the wind and make for the beach. We cannot say that every time God delivered us safely without the loss of one. But we can say our voyage was (and is) constantly under his care.

Pause — wait — think — then express yourself in thoughtful praise or thanks.

9. READ HIS WORD FOR PETITIONS.

Luke reports from firsthand observation on a desperate situation. We wonder what he prayed? Perhaps he prayed: (1) Continue to give Paul the practical courage he has now. (2) Thank you for his humble boldness in the presence of this company of people. (3) We are so glad we have food

to give us the physical stamina we will need. (4) Thank you for the assurance of the angel's message of safety for us all. (5) Help me Lord, I can't swim. (6) Give us courage to do all we can and leave the rest to you.

Right here add your personal requests — and his answers.

10. READ HIS WORD AND WAIT — LISTEN — GOD SPEAKS!

In the hours of the early morning speak to us: (1) "It is always appropriate to thank me for food." (2) "The promise

of my protection does not eliminate your need for work." (3) "Men will do almost anything to save their lives."

11. INTERCESSION FOR THE LOST WORLD

Burma — Point for prayer: (1) *Unreached peoples:* c) *The Chinese and Indian communities* — some work has been done but the response has been small. Many of the

Christians among them have emigrated because of the harsh and discriminatory policies of the government.

12. SING PRAISES TO OUR LORD.

When morning gilds the skies,
My heart awakening cries:
May Jesus Christ be praised;

Alike at work and prayer . . .
To Jesus I repair: . . .
May Jesus Christ be praised.

1. PRAISE GOD FOR WHO HE IS.

"For Thou wilt light my candle: the Lord God will enlighten my darkness" (Psa. 18:28). How all men need to know this! All men are lights. How sad—more than sad—that some men, most of the world has never found the One to give them the fire of life! The new birth does just this. The renewal of the Holy Spirit (Titus 3:5) is the fulfillment of this beautiful verse. You do not want to leave one man to wander in darkness. It is your intention that every man will provide his own light, after you have given him the source of such light. The Holy Spirit has regenerated us at the time we were born of the water. He has given us his word to enlighten all the dark recesses.

Express yourself in adoration for this quality of God.
Speak it audibly or write out your praise in your own devotional journal.

2. PRAISE GOD FOR WHAT HE MEANS TO ME.

Just for me—for *my* candle, lamp, spirit, *my* darkness. Dear Lord, I do believe you are the total source of all light—my spirit has been set on fire, fused with divine power to be the light of my life. How beautiful a thought: each life is lighted by you, but no two lights shine just the same. Each offers a charming new light or appearance; each enlightens the same areas but each in a new and bright way. Others are helped when they see what you have done for others. We cannot defuse the light or shine in the darkness of this world system as someone else can. But we have a lamp or light or candle they do not have and you have asked us to shine. It is *our* light and your *light*. For my individual darkness there is no light at all apart from you. Praise your name I claim your light for every dark place in my life today!

How do you personally relate to the light of God, and God who is Light?
Speak it out or write it out. It is *so important* that you establish *your own* devotional journal.

3. CONFESSION OF SIN

Oh, wonderful Father, how is it we so often forget? I *know* why! We do not keep the switch on. It is in an open connection with heaven that your power can enlighten our lives—I refer to prayer and Bible study and to sincere repentance of seeking false lights. There is in them no light at all. Forgive me! It is in the meditation on your word, day and night, that my darkness flees away! Light is equal to the absence of darkness—turn on the light! How I do want to absorb every word you have given me! All of it is light!

What personal sins do you want to confess? We *must* speak them to remove them.
Do it! *Now.* There is no one else you have sinned against more than God. Tell him so!

4. SING A PRAYER TO GOD.

The Church's one foundation
Is Jesus Christ her Lord;
She is His new creation
By water and the word:

From Heav'n He came and sought her
To be His holy bride;
With His own blood He bought her,
And for her life He died.

Open your hymn book and sing the rest of the verses—or even sing another prayer song.

5. READ HIS WORD TO HIM!

His Word

[41]But the ship struck a sandbar and ran aground. The bow stuck fast and would not move, and the stern was broken to pieces by the pounding of the surf.
[42]The soldiers planned to kill the prisoners to prevent any of them from swimming away and escaping. [43]But the centurion wanted to spare Paul's life and kept them from carrying out their plan. He ordered those who could swim to jump overboard first and get to land. [44]The rest were to get there on planks or on pieces of the ship. In this way everyone reached land in safety.   — *Acts 27:41-44, NIV*

Read His Word to Him.

Dear Lord, how often do men run aground? How often are lives broken to pieces? But such is an analogy not at all a part of the text except in my own imagination. The surf still pounds on the shore, on the beach at Malta. How many of the 276 were saved? All of them were from the Adriatic Sea, but how many were saved from the lake of fire? Dear Lord, you know. I would like to think Paul baptized all who needed you in the Adriatic waters before they left Malta. Once again, thou Lord knowest, I do not. All the prisoners owed their very lives to Paul. Why was Paul so valuable to Julius? Was it because Paul had a spot on the agenda of Nero or had Paul so befriended this centurion that he did not want to harm him? I am so glad to acknowledge your constant presence: "In the covert of thy presence thou hidest them from the plots of men" (Psa. 31:20).

Please express your response to this beautiful text. Put your expression in your own prayer diary.

WEEK TWENTY-SIX — THURSDAY

6. READ HIS WORD FOR YOURSELF.

I owe my life to others: I owe my life to the care my dear mother and father gave me when I was a child at home. I owe my life to a stranger who saw me drowning in the pacific ocean and jumped in and saved my life. I owe my life to the carefulness of several bus drivers who delivered me to school and back home, to hundreds of pilots of planes, to the peace of our country established by those in high places. Most of all I owe my life to the preacher who first told me the good news and my dear wonderful Savior, who saved me from hell to heaven, from death to life. I confidently expect to reach that eternal shore.

It is so important that you pause in his presence
and either audibly or in written form tell him all his word means to you.

7. READ HIS WORD IN THANKSGIVING.

This text is indeed a source of gratitude: (1) Thank you for every ship of life that has run aground within the range of help by those who care. (2) Thank you that we can show those whose lives are being broken to pieces Someone who can put it back together again. (3) Thank you for every soldier who this very day is in the armed forces to protect our country from destruction—from within or without. (4) Thank you for men like Paul who love your word more than life itself. (5) Thank you for some of the strange ways you have saved us from ourselves and others. (6) Thank you for the testimony of those who were saved from the sea according to Paul's promise. (7) Thank you for the research on the island of Malta that establishes the accuracy of Luke's record.

Give yourself to your own expression of gratitude—write it or speak it!

8. READ HIS WORD IN MEDITATION.

"In this way everyone reached the land in safety." In the first century only "some" could swim. No doubt real fear gripped the hearts of many, many on board that ship. The very thing that was going to be their place of death— the ship—was going to furnish the means of saving them. The storm that all but cost them their lives was now going to break the ship up into a form that would save their lives. How mercifully good God was to every one of them. This has not been the record of ten thousand ships that have sunk at sea. We want to meditate on this account for what it is—not what it is not. The frantic efforts of these men (and women?) to reach the land reminds me of our efforts to get safely through many a trying experience. We did not get there as planned—and we lost a great deal —but we are safe and alive and there is yet another day ahead of us, and you are in it all.

Pause—wait—think—then express yourself in thoughtful praise or thanks.

9. READ HIS WORD FOR PETITIONS.

Saved at last! Were prayers prayed on the way to the shore? We can find requests in this text: (1) Extremity produces petitions: Paul: "I honor your word and praise you for your mercy." (2) Luke: "How beyond human understanding are your ways of preserving our lives." (3) Aristarchus: "Give me a deeper commitment to your love." (4) Paul: "Open the heart of Julius that he might understand just who Jesus is." (5) Luke: "Lord, help me to remember all of this for my second treatise." (6) Aristarchus: "What an example Paul is. Help me be more like him."

Please, please remember these are prayers—speak them—reword them!

10. READ HIS WORD AND WAIT—LISTEN—GOD SPEAKS!

In this life and death situation speak to me: (1) "All of life will one day break up; be sure you have Someone who can save you." (2) "I will save other men because of you." (3) "I want all men to be saved."

11. INTERCESSION FOR THE LOST WORLD

Burma — Point for prayer: (1) *Bible translation*—7 languages have the whole Bible, 9 the New Testament and 12 have portions. There is an urgent need for the completion of the Pa-O New Testament and Lahu Old Testament, as well as three important revisions. It is virtually impossible to import Christian literature and the government makes it very hard for the believers to obtain paper to print Bibles and Christian literature locally. Government censorship further complicates the production of literature. Pray for the critical lack of Bibles and literature to be supplied. A small amount of literature is entering the country. Pray also for the entry of the valuable Gospel records—records in 59 languages.

12. SING PRAISES TO OUR LORD.

Praise ye the Lord, the Almighty, the King of creation!
O my soul, praise Him, for He is thy health and salvation!
All ye who hear, Now to His temple draw near;
Join me in glad adoration!

WEEK TWENTY-SIX — FRIDAY

1. PRAISE GOD FOR WHO HE IS.

"For by thee I have run through a troop and by my God have I leaped over a wall" (Psa. 18:29). This is the response of the psalmist to your character, to your essential person. Several rather obvious thoughts present themselves to us: (1) We are in a warfare. The enemies troops are near enough to hurt us. (2) Deathless courage was given to David — perhaps this describes several battles you helped him win. (3) David did not have promised that he would split the troop — he charged and let you handle the result. (4) The situation is desperate — it calls for risk — put your life on the line (the battle line). Does all of the above describe my battle with Satan? Indeed it does! I would that all men would see the following qualities of yourself from this text: (1) Nearness — you are in the battle with us. (2) Knowledge — i.e., you *know* what is happening; you see *all* the circumstances. You *know* where the enemy is weak. (3) Power and strength not our own that you share with us!

Speak audibly or write out your praise in your own devotional journal.

2. PRAISE GOD FOR WHAT HE MEANS TO ME.

What troop shall I break through? Over which wall shall I leap? Troops and walls show up every day! There will be no problem with troops and walls *if* I relate to you in the way I want to! Dear Lord, I want to intimately identify with your nearness. You are right here, right now! Blessed be your wonderful presence. I want to trust in your perspective. You see all that occurs. Nothing, utterly nothing, is hidden from your omniscience, absolute knowledge. Oh, my Father, I cast myself upon you and rest in your knowledge. At the same time, as I see opportunity, I will take it. I will lay my life behind my decisions — break a way for me with your Almighty Power!

How do you personally relate to the empowering of God, and God who is our strength?
Speak it out or write it out. It is *so important* that you establish *your own* devotional journal.

3. CONFESSION OF SIN

What a problem I have in separating presumption from boldness or faith! Am I saying what seems presumptuous to man is faith with you? Dear Lord, I want to *know*, I want to be humble-minded, to prefer others before myself. I want the honor and praise to go to you! How often such is *not* the case — help me! I claim the wisdom I need (Jas. 1:5ff.). If I move ahead and let men see the works and not the worker, they will glorify you! Thank you!

"Disrespect." What you respect I do not want to disrespect. You respect age, little children, public law offices, law and order, per se! In all these areas I set a guard by your help.

What personal sins do you want to confess? We *must* speak them to remove them.
Do it! *Now.* There is no one else you have sinned against more than God. Tell him so!

4. SING A PRAYER TO GOD.

True-hearted, whole-hearted, faithful and loyal,
King of our lives, by Thy grace we will be;
Under the standard exalted and royal,
Strong in Thy strength we will battle for Thee.

Peal out the watchword! silence it never!
Song of our spirits, rejoicing and free;
Peal out the watchword! loyal forever,
King of our lives, by Thy grace we will be.

Open your hymn book and sing the rest of the verses — or even sing another prayer song.

5. READ HIS WORD TO HIM!

His Word

28 Once safely on shore, we found out that the island was called Malta. ²The islanders showed us unusual kindness. They built a fire and welcomed us all because it was raining and cold. ³Paul gathered a pile of brushwood and, as he put it on the fire, a viper, driven out by the heat, fastened itself on his hand. — *Acts 28:1-3, NIV*

Read His Word to Him.

How gladly do I take up this word. Dr. Luke was in the water. Those who could swim were the first on shore. Were he and Paul two of the early ones? This was not the first shipwreck of Paul — perhaps Luke was with him. "A night and a day" Paul had spent in deep waters (II Cor. 11:25b). Perhaps it was in a cave or on the open beach the islanders had built a fire. Did they also have food prepared for them? (I am trying as best I can to see this incident as you do.) Was it in November? I would like so much to visit Malta in November — 1922 years later. But with you there are no yesterdays or tomorrows — only one eternal *now*, so this is happening now as all other events of man's short sojourn.

A snake came from the brushwood as Paul tried to feed the fire. This is the only form of "taking up serpents" I find in your word. It was not taken up on purpose, but by accident. You had a purpose larger than a poisonous snake bite. It did become a sign to the unbelieving islanders.

Please express your response to this beautiful text. Put your expression in your own prayer diary.

6. READ HIS WORD FOR YOURSELF.

Just for me—yes, yes. Probably the first question asked to those who met them on the beach was, "Where are we?" How very different this whole story could have been! There are several possible alternatives that we will not postulate—the same can be said for my life. I have not just survived a shipwreck (except vicariously with Paul) but I do want to ask others, myself, and most of all the only One who really knows: "Where am I?" There are so many things that could have happened to me, perhaps *should* have happened, but they didn't. I am here; I am safe; I am saved, but right now I want to look out and see life as I have never seen it before and ask you, "Where am I?" There are several areas in which I want to make inquiry: (1) Where am I in my personal devotions. (2) Where am I in my personal knowledge of your word? (3) Where am I in real genuine evangelism. (4) Where am I as a father and grandfather? (5) Where am I as a husband? Dear Lord, I purpose to find out!

It is so important that you pause in his presence
and either audibly or in written form tell him all his word means to you.

7. READ HIS WORD IN THANKSGIVING.

(1) Thank you for the sure knowledge of your word that tells us just where we are at all times. (2) Thank you for unexpected kindness from unexpected sources. (3) Thank you for fire and water and their many uses. (4) Thank you for kindness from those we would expect the very opposite. (5) Thank you for shelter from the weather, for warmth from the cold. (6) Thank you for Paul who wanted to help anyone at anytime in anyway he could. (7) Thank you for the miracles of your record, all of which move us to believe in what you have said.

Give yourself to your own expression of gratitude—write it or speak it!

8. READ HIS WORD IN MEDITATION.

". . . a viper, driven out by the heat, fastened itself on his hand." A viper called Satan has done the same thing to us. How often has that same snake fastened its poison fangs in our heart? Even when we were trying to do good, evil is present. When we are in the act of helping others we are hurt by the devil. Why? Why? Because hidden in all our efforts to do good, deceit, selfish ambition, pride, the love of money are always at least potentially present. Snakes do not attack them who do not disturb them. It should be a comfort for us to know we have bothered the old serpent. Our response should be that of Paul. He made no show of it; he simply shook it off into the fire. Since this will be the ultimate end of the devil and his angels we can at least consign him there. We need suffer no more permanent injury than Paul—our great physician is able to heal.

Pause—wait—think—then express yourself in thoughtful praise or thanks.

9. READ HIS WORD FOR PETITIONS.

In trying to help others you yourself are hurt. How shall we pray? (1) Since your hand is upon me why should I be afraid? (2) We have all found ourselves in a similar situation. Open the eyes of those who oppose you as to just who is innocent or guilty. (3) Deliver me from the serpent hid in some very ordinary pursuits. (4) Help me to be prepared for the evil the heat of your word drives out. (5) Thank you for the promised protection of Mark 16:17. (6) Thank you for the supernatural necessary to confirm your word through Paul. (7) May I be as ready to help in the mundane matters of life as was Paul.

Right here add your personal requests—and his answers.

10. READ HIS WORD AND WAIT—LISTEN—GOD SPEAKS!

What do you say to me from these verses? (1) "There are many islanders who would gladly hear the good news if you would take it to them." (2) "There are always problems when you try to help people." (3) "There are snakes today who cannot stand the heat of truth."

11. INTERCESSION FOR THE LOST WORLD

Burma — Point for prayer: (1) *Christian Radio*—there are daily broadcasts in Burmese or Karen. The response is good, but all letters appeal for literature.
Hong Kong — Population: 4,600,000. Growth rate— 2.1%. People per sq. km.—4,300.

Point for prayer: (1) *Hong Kong* is one of the most important centers strategically for the Gospel in Asia, with its close links with Communist China, the Overseas Chinese and all Asia. Yet the threat of Communist take-over is ever there.

12. SING PRAISES TO OUR LORD.

Praise ye the Father! for His loving kindness,
Tenderly cares He for His erring children;

Praise Him, ye angels, praise Him in the heavens,
Praise ye Jehovah!

WEEK TWENTY-SIX — SATURDAY

1. PRAISE GOD FOR WHO HE IS.

"Thou hast also given me the shield of thy salvation; and thy right hand hath holden me up, and thy gentleness hath made me great" (Psa. 18:35). The qualities of our God are here set before us in a most poignant manner: (1) You have given all men (who want it) the protection of your salvation. Behind your shield we are safe from the fiery darts of the evil one. Who would not want the safety of salvation from the shaft of justice? If we stand unprotected before justice we are dead! (2) How weary we become in the long days of conflict! How good to hide beneath the protection of your strong right arm. Indeed we could easily transfer this figure to our Lord as the right arm of our God. (3) Your gentleness has made us great. This is a mother or wife-like quality. It is the softness and tender kindness in the midst of hurt that gives us strength and resources we never knew were ours.

Speak audibly or write out your praise in your own devotional journal.

2. PRAISE GOD FOR WHAT HE MEANS TO ME.

Just for today: Just for *today* I want to find in you a hiding place, a shelter of safety, a shield of salvation. I need to be saved from much more than eternal hell. You are for me right now my deliverance! You are for me *today* holding me up and renewing my strength. It is your strong right arm underneath to lift me up when I fall, to give me the strength to fight through just this one more battle! Praise your name! Most of all it is your gentleness that has made me great. I am not at all great by evaluation of talent, by power of promotion, by record of accomplishments, but "through your gentleness" all greatness has been placed within each of us by you. It is in the quietness of love and tenderness of personal care that such is released for expression.

How do you personally relate to the protective love of God, and God who is your Shield?
Speak it out or write it out. It is *so important* that you establish *your own* devotional journal.

3. CONFESSION OF SIN

Dear Lord, there are those around me who are hoping for a gentle look, touch or word. Their greatness is also released through this beautiful quality. Help me to be like you. Forgive me, I have been selfish and hurtful without much cause. I have been perverse and hard. Forgive, forgive me! My dear Lord had more than enough reason to be hard and harsh, and yet he was gentle, kind, thoughtful of others. Paul could have treated the Thessalonians in a stern and unyielding manner, but he says he was gentle as he worked among them even as a mother with her children. Dear Lord, I have less reason to behave in any way but gentle, i.e., where I compare what faces me and what Paul endured.

"Fearfulness." Is it a sin to be afraid? Yes, yes, when God has promised victory, it is a sin to be defeated. Dear Lord, I enter as a victor, not the victim!

There is no one else you have sinned against more than God. Tell him so!

4. SING A PRAYER TO GOD.

Savior, Thy dying love Thou gavest me,
Nor should I aught withhold, Dear Lord, from Thee:
In love my soul would bow,
My heart fulfill its vow,
Some off'ring bring Thee now,
Something for Thee.

Open your hymn book and sing the rest of the verses — or even sing another prayer song.

5. READ HIS WORD TO HIM!

His Word

[4]When the islanders saw the snake hanging from his hand, they said to each other, "This man must be a murderer; for though he escaped from the sea, Justice has not allowed him to live." [5]But Paul shook the snake off into the fire and suffered no ill effects. [6]The people expected him to swell up or suddenly fall over dead, but after waiting a long time and seeing nothing unusual happen to him, they changed their minds and said he was a god.

[7]There was an estate nearby that belonged to Publius, the chief official of the island. He welcomed us to his home and for three days entertained us hospitably.

— *Acts 28:4-7, NIV*

Read His Word to Him.

Dear Lord, I do so very, very much appreciate all your word is saying to me. My purpose here is to read it back again to you and attempt to share your viewpoint. What appears as a large matter and full of importance is sometimes small and insignificant to you. It is not that you ignore the serpent fastened in Paul's flesh, but your perspective turns the incident in an entirely different light. First, the person must be accepted and then his message. This will become a means to that end. Since the islanders thought Paul a god, they would listen to him. I'm sure you didn't put the snake in the brush, or did you? How unusual that Publius was so hospitable — 276 guests?!!! Or was it only Paul and the soldiers? You know and one day I will.

Please express your response to this beautiful text. Put your expression in your own prayer diary.

6. READ HIS WORD FOR YOURSELF.

Yes, yes. Dr. Luke was there to report first hand as a participator what happened. I would like to take his place or a place with him. Isn't it wonderful to see how God works? It is exciting to be a part of the moving of God's Spirit in the circumstances of life. I know how deadly is the bite of that particular snake. There are hundreds of dead victims to confirm this fact. Paul will die, but not from a snake bite. I do remember something

our Lord said about this! "These *signs* will follow them that belive: ". . . they will pick up serpents." Paul had just done it—it was a sign (and advertizement) to make the Maltese wonder—which they surely did. Their faith in you came from the words Paul spoke to them. Dear Lord, I believe, not because of the signs but because of your word. These signs confirmed my faith, but did not produce it.

Pause in his presence and either audibly or in written form tell him all his word means to you.

7. READ HIS WORD IN THANKSGIVING.

Indeed I do: (1) Thank you for the innate sense of justice that prevails in many cultures. (2) Thank you for Paul's immediate reliance upon you for your direction in his life. Did Paul know he would not die from the snake bite? It would seem to be a matter of indifference to him. (3) Thank you for the honest effort of the islanders to seek

an explanation that included the supernatural. (4) Thank you for Publius who had a wide influence for our Lord when he became a believer. (5) Thank you for the marvelous preservation of your word down through two millennia. (6) Thank you for the same Lord—the same faith and the same hope we have today as Paul had then.

Give yourself to your own expression of gratitude—write it or speak it!

8. READ HIS WORD AND WAIT—LISTEN—GOD SPEAKS!

"He welcomed us to his house and for three days entertained us hospitably." Why would this man do this? We can pose two or three possibilities: (1) It was customary and just a part of what would happen to any strangers who landed on Malta. This is not a very real possibility, and most especially if he was entertaining 276 people. (2) He did it for the tribune who was with Paul as a repre-

sentative from Rome. Since his island was under the rule of Rome, he felt it was to his distinct advantage. (3) He was told of Paul's encounter with the viper. We need to remember that Paul's life story is written by a doctor who is an eyewitness to what happened. Publius wanted help for his father who was sick. He received it.

Pause—wait—think—then express yourself in thoughtful praise or thanks.

9. READ HIS WORD FOR PETITIONS.

The men of Malta were superstitious. Dear Lord, I want to be full of faith. (1) Lord, if I received justice it would not be heaven. Thank you for your mercy. (2) Satan has fastened his fangs in me more than once. I am glad for the deliverance of Satan back into the fire. (3) What a

wonder to be delivered from death in trespasses and sins. (4) Thank you that we are sons of God, and the best is yet to come. (5) Give me the courage and contact to pray for those in high places. (6) Thank you for the kindness that fills the hearts of some who do not even know you.

Please, please remember these are prayers—speak them—reword them!

10. READ HIS WORD AND WAIT—LISTEN—GOD SPEAKS!

In these few verses speak to me: (1) "Judge not by appearances, but by truth." (2) "People are ready to accept feelings

before faith." (3) "What do ye more than some unbelievers?"

11. INTERCESSION FOR THE LOST WORLD

Hong Kong — Point for prayer: (1) *The churches* have grown in number and maturity with outstanding Christian leaders in denominations, theological training, literature and mass media. The expense of land, and overcrowded state of the country has compelled many groups to meet in homes, roof-top churches, or build high-rise multi-

purpose, church-school-hostels. Materialism is slowing church growth. Pray for the leadership and outreach of the churches to the many unreached Chinese. Pray that the believers may be well taught and well prepared for the possibility of a Communist takeover.

12. SING PRAISES TO OUR LORD.

I have a song I love to sing,
Since I have been redeemed,
Of my Redeemer, Savior, King,
Since I have been redeemed.
Since I have been redeemed,

Since I have been redeemed,
I will glory in His name;
Since I have been redeemed,
I will glory in His name.

WEEK TWENTY-SEVEN — SUNDAY

1. PRAISE GOD FOR WHO HE IS.

"The law of the Lord is perfect, converting the soul; the testimony of the Lord is sure, making wise the simple" (Psa. 19:7). Even as my words say much about my inner self, so your words describe your character. Your law, or word, is "perfect." This is true from several perspectives: (1) Perfect in the sense of being without flaw or mistake. Blessed be your wonderful name—such would be the only conclusion if you were without flaw, then your word would necessarily express the same quality. (2) Your law is perfect in the sense of maturity, i.e., it expresses the thoughts of one who has total understanding. This is a strong encouragement for us to allow it to turn our lives around and put them on the right path. If we want to be wise, we will assimilate such wisdom from him who knows all.

Express yourself in adoration for this quality of God.
Speak it audibly or write out your praise in your own devotional journal.

2. PRAISE GOD FOR WHAT HE MEANS TO ME.

Just for me. "The law of the Lord is perfect" for me! I am glad to acknowledge that I am persuaded that not one word of the 66 books of the Bible is in error in any form. The autographs were without flaw. I have no reason to think or suggest the existing copies are in any way changed from the autographs. Most of all, I want to say that the perfection or maturity I find in reading and meditating upon your word convinces me more each day that your law indeed is perfect. My life has been turned around and I am glad. I attribute it to *your word.* To yourself, but all I know about you is from your word. How simple and ignorant I am without your testimonies! How wise and mature I can become through them!

How do you personally relate to the word of God, and God who has spoken?
Speak it out or write it out. It is *so important* that you establish *your own* devotional journal.

3. CONFESSION OF SIN

How sorely I have neglected a close personal meditation on every word you have spoken. In these last days of my life, be they few or many, I want to repair this lack. Forgive me for being so late in fulfilling what is a real joy to do! Dear Lord, grant grace and strength, and heaven's wisdom in this pursuit. Forgive me for any presumption on my part.

"Fearfulness." Dear Lord, you did not give me a spirit of fearfulness, but of power and of love and discipline and a sound mind (II Tim. 1:7). When I am hesitant or afraid, be thou near. In so many areas we need courage—your courage—I claim it! Forgive my timidity.

What personal sins do you want to confess? We *must* speak them to remove them.
Do it! *Now.* There is no one else you have sinned against more than God. Tell him so!

4. SING A PRAYER TO GOD.

Saved by the blood of the Crucified One!
Now ransomed from sin and a new work begun,
Sing praise to the Father and praise to the Son,

Saved by the blood of the Crucified One!
Saved! saved! My sins are all pardoned, my guilt is all gone!
Saved! saved! I am saved by the blood of the Crucified One!

Open your hymn book and sing the rest of the verses—or even sing another prayer song.

5. READ HIS WORD TO HIM!

His Word

[8]His father was sick in bed, suffering from fever and dysentery. Paul went in to see him and, after prayer, placed his hands on him and healed him. [9]When this had happened, the rest of the sick on the island came and were cured. [10]They honored us in many ways and when we were ready to sail, they furnished us with the supplies we needed.

[11]After three months we put out to sea in a ship that had wintered in the island. It was an Alexandrian ship with the figurehead of the twin gods Castor and Pollux.

— Acts 28:8-11, NIV

Read His Word to Him.

How I do want to read these words as if I had never read them before. Why did you heal the father of Publius? Why heal all the others of the island? Luke reports it even as it happened. He does not mention the obvious: i.e., that many islanders believed and became Christians. Is it at all possible these people—at least some of them—were already Christians when Paul landed? Luke has given a record of so many others who wondered at the signs and believed the message. Paul has not altered his purpose. For reasons best known to Luke and yourself he does not record the "head count" of those who accepted you and your Son. How I wish I knew more. I am so glad for the success of your servants amid the most trying of circumstances.

Please express your response to this beautiful text. Put your expression in your own prayer diary.

6. READ HIS WORD FOR YOURSELF.

Yes, yes, I do. Apply these words to my life. When Paul visited the father of the governor, he did two things: (1) He prayed for him—how I would love to hear the voice of Paul in prayer; how I would listen so very carefully to every word he prayed. (I can read several of his prayers now in his letters.) (2) He placed his hands on him and healed him. He didn't get better, he got well! Instantaneous restoration to full health is the impression I receive. What happened to one happened to all. There is no way to explain what happened without your supernatural intervention. How I do wonder just who is included in the pronoun "us," i.e., 'They honored *us* in many ways." It would seem from the fact that all 276 people were detained on the island that the honors and provisions were for all of them. How Paul did "take charge" in this whole situation!

It is so important that you pause in his presence
and either audibly or in written form tell him all his word means to you.

7. READ HIS WORD IN THANKSGIVING.

(1) Thank you for the wonderful way you can use any and all circumstances for our good and your glory. (2) Thank you for the wonderful gift of healing used by Paul to point to yourself and your Son. (3) Thank you for the report of Luke that there were no unsuccessful attempts at healing. (4) Thank you for the provisions Paul supplied for the whole group that would not otherwise have been there. (5) Thank you for the whole three month sojourn on Malta—everyone learned much. (6) Thank you for supplying a ship going to the very place they wanted. (7) Thank you that time has a way of eliminating Castor and Pollux and retaining Jesus and yourself.

Give yourself to your own expression of gratitude—write it or speak it!

8. READ HIS WORD IN MEDITATION.

". . . an Alexandrian ship with the figurehead of the twin gods Castor and Pollux." I wonder why Luke mentioned the figurehead of this ship? It does seem incongruous that God's servants would sail aboard a ship dedicated to the mythical gods of the Greeks. Castor and Pollux are the early counterparts of Saint Christopher of today. Of *late* Saint Christopher—the saint to protect travelers has been decanonized. We can find in all such mythology a principle truth. Our Lord is indeed interested in our protection while traveling. We are glad to give him the praise and credit for every safe trip we have made.

Pause—wait—think—then express yourself in thoughtful praise or thanks.

9. READ HIS WORD FOR PETITIONS.

As Paul and his friends prepared to sail for Rome we can think of our preparations to sail for our eternal home. (1) May I help just as many people as I can to know you before I leave. (2) I know if just one is raised from death in sin many will be affected. Lord, lead me to that one. (3) Dear Lord, surely there are many I can reach with the healing love of my Lord; open my eyes. (4) How infinitely good you are to me—may your goodness lead me to repentance. (5) I know you know the day and method of my departure from this life—this is enough. (6) I am so glad I serve and worship a living heavenly Father. Thank you. (7) You have surely provided all I need for the eternal journey.

Right here add your personal requests—and his answers.

10. READ HIS WORD AND WAIT—LISTEN—GOD SPEAKS!

What do you say in these verses? (1) "I might come before you leave." (2) "Take as many with you as you can." (3) "Behold, I come quickly."

11. INTERCESSION FOR THE LOST WORLD

Hong Kong — Points for prayer: (1) *Outreach by the churches*—some older denominations are less enthusiastic in evangelism, but some younger, indigenous and mission oriented churches are vigorously evangelizing. (2) *Missions*—many agencies with over 452 Protestant missionaries—many serving in Asia-wide ministries, and the minority actually serving the Hong Kong Church in evangelism, Bible teaching and church planting. Pray for a happy relationship in humility between the expatriates and Chinese believers, and also for the most effective use of the former for the building up of the Church. Many missions work in a support capacity in literature, evangelism and church support and ministries involving Red China.

12. SING PRAISES TO OUR LORD.

Holy, Holy, Holy, Lord God Almighty!
Early in the morning our song shall rise to Thee;

Holy, Holy, Holy! Merciful and Mighty!
God in Three Persons, blessed Trinity!

WEEK TWENTY-SEVEN — MONDAY

1. PRAISE GOD FOR WHO HE IS.

"The statutes of the Lord are right, rejoicing the heart: the commandment of the Lord is pure, enlightening the eyes" (Psa. 19:8). As a man's word represents the man, so do your words express your character. Dear Lord, I am glad and delighted to affirm with the psalmist that your precepts or statutes are always and in every place with everyone exactly what should have been done. The term *right* means the law or principle or advice perfectly fits

the occasion. Life is like a jig-saw puzzle with several parts missing. We are given several offerings by Satan — each time we attempt to fit his pieces we hurt because they do not mesh and the edges rubbed are our nerves! When we get a good look at your statutes; when we turn them this way and that and see the whole and then try it in the open space, it is *right*! What a joy to our heart!

Express yourself in adoration for this quality of God.
Speak it audibly or write out your praise in your own devotional journal.

2. PRAISE GOD FOR WHAT HE MEANS TO ME.

For me, just for me—your commandments are pure, they enlighten my eyes! I have noticed again just yesterday how authoritative are the teachings of my Lord. Jesus does not offer suggestions. He gives commands. He states it like it is. Dear Savior, I hear you. Your commandments are like a good pair of glasses: they perfectly fit my eyes — the eyes of my heart. I can only see very dimly life and

its meaning (what else is there to see?). When I look at life through your commandments all is clear and sharply defined. What enlightenment your commandments have given me. I never tire of putting on your glasses. I do not enjoy the out-of-focus living I get when I forget to look through your commandments. You give me a trifocal view of all things. Bless your holy name!

How do you personally relate to the statutes of God, and God who has given them?
Speak it out or write it out. It is *so important* that you establish *your own* devotional journal.

3. CONFESSION OF SIN

It is one thing to put down on paper, or speak out in public my prayer of affirmation, of approval and commitment to your statutes and commandments; it is quite another to fulfill this in the daily routine of private living. This is a good example of what we have just said. It is altogether *"right"* to confess my sins—what *enlighten-*

ment such a command gives to the eyes of my heart! The *doing* of what you have said is a part of the expression itself. There is no life or fruit without doing.

"Disbelief." Surely this is all we can really do other than obey you! I know I have selfishly thus sinned. Please forgive me!

What personal sins do you want to confess? We *must* speak them to remove them.
Do it! *Now.* There is no one else you have sinned against more than God. Tell him so!

4. SING A PRAYER TO GOD.

Thou, my everlasting portion,
More than friend or life to me;
All along my pilgrim journey,
Savior, let me walk with Thee.

Close to Thee, close to Thee,
Close to Thee, close to Thee;
All along my pilgrim journey,
Savior, let me walk with Thee.

Open your hymn book and sing the rest of the verses—or even sing another prayer song.

5. READ HIS WORD TO HIM!

[12]We put in at Syracuse and stayed there three days. [13]From there we set sail and arrived at Rhegium. The next day the south wind came up, and on the following day we reached Puteoli. [14]There we found some brothers who invited us to spend a week with them. And so we

went to Rome. [15]The brothers there had heard that we were coming, and they traveled as far as the Forum of Appius and the Three Taverns to meet us. At the sight of these men Paul thanked God and was encouraged.
— *Acts 28:12-15, NIV*

Read His Word to Him.

How always glad I am to enter this phase of worship. When I attempt to see these verses as you do it always gives fresh and new meaning to the text. What happened during the three days at Syracuse? What evaluations are the travelers making of Paul's God and his Son? What meditation is going through the mind of Luke? We have heard nothing of Aristarchus since we left Caesarea—

what happened to him? How rapidly and fully had your word spread! In only thirty or thirty-five short years the good news was preached in the far outreaches of the empire. The devotion of the saints of Rome was an example to all (cf. Rom. 1:8). Only you can answer some of these questions, but it has done me good to ask them.

Please express your response to this beautiful text. Put your expression in your own prayer diary.

6. READ HIS WORD FOR YOURSELF.

I want to be a traveling companion of Paul. How I would like to ask him one hundred questions. One day I shall — if when I see him the answers are not already mine. Here are a few of them as related to this portion of our journey: (1) "Has your thorn in the flesh bothered you on this journey?" (2) "How did you handle this eternal sitting around?" (3) "How could you find companionship with these Gentiles who had no knowledge or appreciation of your Jewishness?" (4) How could this journey be so leisurely? i.e., spending a week with Christian brothers? (5) Didn't the centurion and almost everyone else become a Christian? I am humbled to the ground when I attempt to follow Paul's example of devotion.

It is so important that you pause in his presence
and either audibly or in written form tell him all his word means to you.

7. READ HIS WORD IN THANKSGIVING.

There is much here for which we can thank you! (1) Thank you for the safe journey all the way to Rome from Malta. (2) Thank you for what seems to be a transference of authority from the centurion to Paul. (3) Thank you for the thousands of Christians of the first 30 or 40 years of the history of our Lord's called out ones. (4) Thank you for all the mutual joy and love that must have been shared at Puteoli. (5) Thank you for the willingness of the Christians at Rome to walk over 40 miles to see Paul. (6) Thank you for Paul's spontaneous gratitude upon seeing the Christians from Rome. (7) Thank you for the completion of Paul's long time prayer and desire to be in Rome.

Give yourself to your own expression of gratitude — write it or speak it!

8. READ HIS WORD FOR MEDITATION.

"At the sight of these men Paul thanked God and was encouraged." We wonder if Paul thought the cause of our Lord had been defeated in Rome, or if he thought false reports of himself had preceded him to Rome. Why was Paul so thankful? It could be that in a sense he was full of relief — Rome at last! For how many years had he planned and longed and prayed that he might be able to visit Rome. In spite of the fact that God had repeatedly promised that "he would bear witness in Rome" Paul wanted to express his personal appreciation for answered prayer and fulfilled promises. How warm must have been the greetings! How many inquiries were made concerning this one and that one?

Pause — wait — think — then express yourself in thoughtful praise or thanks.

9. READ HIS WORD FOR PETITIONS.

Four stops on the way to Rome: what requests arise from this journey? (1) Paul seemed to be in no hurry to reach Rome — neither am I to reach heaven — I want to learn all you have for me along the way. (2) How I do wish I knew what was said in the three days at Syracuse — thank you for mutual interests in our Lord. (3) Did Paul hold a week's evangelistic crusade at Puteoli? Luke doesn't tell us. Thank you for Christians at this Italian town. (4) How good to read of Christians in almost every stop — how can we so increase your word today? (5) May I today be the source of encouragement to my fellow travelers. (6) May I find today in my brothers a reason to be encouraged. (7) More than 40 miles is a long way to walk just to greet and strengthen a brother. May I learn from this.

Please, please remember these are prayers — speak them — reword them!

10. READ HIS WORD AND WAIT — LISTEN — GOD SPEAKS!

What do you say to me as I journey through the land? (1) "I have people in places of which you never heard." (2) "You can always speak a good word for me." (3) "I went further than 40 miles to tell you I loved you."

11. INTERCESSION FOR THE LOST WORLD

Hong Kong — Point for prayer: (1) *Refugees from Communist China* continue to arrive illegally (and often with great danger) at the rate of about 30,000 a year. Some are expatriated by the government to China and an unknown future. Two out of every three in Hong Kong are refugees. These needy and despairing refugees often become embittered and disillusioned in the overcrowded and difficult conditions of Hong Kong. Some local Chinese groups and several missions have made a real effort to win these people.

12. SING PRAISES TO OUR LORD.

The Church's one foundation
Is Jesus Christ her Lord;
She is His new creation
By water and the word:

From Heav'n He came and sought her
To be His holy bride;
With His own blood He bought her,
And for her life He died.

WEEK TWENTY-SEVEN — TUESDAY

1. PRAISE GOD FOR WHO HE IS.

"The fear of the Lord is clean, enduring forever; the judgments of the Lord are true and righteous altogether" (Psa. 19:9). Once again: the qualities of yourself are seen in yourself and your actions. How can I fear you? This is to ask "how can I reverence you?" Does this reverence or "fear" carry in it the thought of punishment? Yes, but it is only one of the qualities for which I reverence you.

In what sense is my reverence or fear of you clean or pure? In two ways: (1) It should be whole or one or single. Your overpowering character should at all times be in focus and be the single most significant attitude of my heart. Dear Lord, I *want* this to be! (2) If this is true then the second meaning will be mine. I will be clean or pure or wholistic in my living and in my inner attitudes.

Express yourself in adoration for this quality of God.
Speak it audibly or write out your praise in your own devotional journal.

2. PRAISE GOD FOR WHAT HE MEANS TO ME.

Just for me. I try to praise you in the above expressions as a personal representative of principles applied to or for all men. In this area I want to apply your word as relating to yourself just to me! How I do want to hold you constantly before me as my meditation day and night!

I can only do this as I memorize and internalize your word! I will never be clean or whole until this happens! I am much closer today than last year, or ten years or twenty years ago! I take courage in the fact that my pursuit is like what is pursued—"it endureth forever."

How do you personally relate to the fear of God, and God who is holy?
Speak it out or write it out. It is *so important* that you establish *your own* devotional journal.

3. CONFESSION OF SIN

I have sinned and have fallen far short of your character. This is *not* to say I have first fallen far short of your expectations for me for this is *not* my first thought! It is yourself that is first to be disgraced by my sin. I believe with all that is within me that if I seek first your rule in my life and your acceptance among men my attitudes and actions would follow as light follows day. I fail so miserably—please forgive. Thank you for letting me see what

could be and for the Spirit-prompted desire to fulfill it.
"Praying to be seen of men." When this is our primary purpose, we are sinning, not praying. It is almost impossible to pray in public, i.e., to lead in public prayer, or to pray with the public in heart, without including them or being aware of them. Dear God, I want only and always to address you, pray to you, for you, through you.

What personal sins do you want to confess? We *must* speak them to remove them.
Do it! *Now.* There is no one else you have sinned against more than God. Tell him so!

4. SING A PRAYER TO GOD.

O worship the King, all glorious above,
And gratefully sing His wonderful love;

Our Shield and Defender, the Ancient of days,
Pavilioned in splendor, and girded with praise.

Open your hymn book and sing the rest of the verses—or even sing another prayer song.

5. READ HIS WORD TO HIM!

His Word

[16]When we got to Rome, Paul was allowed to live by himself, with a soldier to guard him.

[17]Three days later he called together the leaders of the Jews. When they had assembled, Paul said to them: "My brothers, although I have done nothing against our people or against the customs of our ancestors, I was arrested in Jerusalem and handed over to the Romans. [18]They examined me and wanted to release me, because I was not guilty of any crime deserving death. [19]But when the Jews objected, I was compelled to appeal to Caesar—not that I had any

charge to bring against my own people. [20]For this reason I have asked to see you and talk with you. It is because of the hope of Israel that I am bound with this chain."

[21]They replied, "We have not received any letters from Judea concerning you, and none of the brothers who has come from there has reported or said anything bad about you. [22]But we want to hear what your views are, for we know that people everywhere are talking against this sect."

— Acts 28:16-22, NIV

Read His Word to Him.

It would be a real experience to seek out and find the house where Paul lived in Rome and pay him a visit. I know you never left him and were indeed with him. I hope I can meet some of the soldiers who guarded Paul and get their impressions of him. What was the purpose of Paul's words to the Jews in Rome? Dear Lord, I read these words to understand the mind of Paul—which is the

mind of your dear Son. This is a defense: "I have done nothing against our people or against the customs of our ancestors." ". . . I was not guilty of any crime deserving death." ". . . not that I had any charge to bring against my own people." Paul loves his people, the Jews! I know you do too. What a tremendous influence they could be if all were your children!

Please express your response to this beautiful text. Put your expression in your own prayer diary.

6. READ HIS WORD FOR YOURSELF.

Just suppose I was Paul in Rome in 60 A.D.! How would I react to the confinement? Since I had been repeatedly treated so very badly by the Jews would I now call the leaders of them to me? What would I say to the soldiers who guarded me? Would my defense convince anyone? What would I anticipate as I appeared before Nero the emperor? What would I do day after day after day in the house when I was confined? How would I react to the use of the term "sect" as applied to my faith? I guess what I am saying is that I can learn so much from Paul by way of love and patience.

It is so important that you pause in his presence
and either audibly or in written form tell him all his word means to you.

7. READ HIS WORD IN THANKSGIVING.

Who was it who said "in everything give thanks"? Who was it who wrote later from this very place "rejoice in the Lord—again I say rejoice"? If Paul could, surely we can: (1) Thank you for the accommodations for Paul, which could have been far worse than they were. (2) Thank you for Paul's desire to clear his name and the name of our Lord with the Jews. (3) Thank you for the term "brother" applied in sincerity to both Jews and Christians. (4) Thank you for the fairness in the laws of the Romans. (5) Thank you for the saints in Rome who were beloved of God and also of Paul. (6) Thank you that the saints in Rome "belonged to Jesus Christ and we do too." (7) Thank you for the faith of the Roman Christians that was "proclaimed in all the world."

Give yourself to your own expression of gratitude—write it or speak it!

8. READ HIS WORD IN MEDITATION.

". . . people everywhere are talking against this sect." It makes one wonder just in what context this question was asked: (1) Were these Jews (at least some of them) Christians and they wanted to hear one of their own defend Christianity so as to reinforce their faith? (2) Were they interested in getting more information so they could become Christians? i.e., they had a real genuine interest in knowing about Jesus as the Christ. (3) They were "ever hearing but never understanding" and thus were only seeking to oppose our Lord. From what follows as a result of Paul's speaking we could believe there were some of each. Surely in our audience of unbelievers we find the same type of listener. May we be as faithful as Paul.

Pause—wait—think—then express yourself in thoughtful praise or thanks.

9. READ HIS WORD FOR PETITIONS.

Paul was ever and always full of concern for those with whom he associated—especially his own people. (1) Give me the same concern. (2) Dear Lord, I want to become all things to all men that I might win some of them to you. (3) I want to learn from the example of Paul's speech to the Jews: he referred to them as "brothers." (4) He was completely frank with them. (5) He considered his Lord as the only hope that the Jews or anyone else had. (6) He did all he could to give adequate time to explain his position. (7) Dear Lord, in all the above areas give me grace to be like your servant Paul.

Right here add your personal requests—and his answers.

10. READ HIS WORD AND WAIT—LISTEN—GOD SPEAKS!

What do you say to me out of this text? (1) "Paul as a prisoner had more freedom than those to whom he spoke." (2) "Paul used all means available to reach men with the good news." (3) "Men will always be curious—use this capacity for me."

11. INTERCESSION FOR THE LOST WORLD

Hong Kong — Point for prayer: (1) *Christian communications* are very developed. There are many publishing groups producing new translations of the Bible in "Mao" script, and literature—both for Asia and also for Mainland China. Pray for the entry of this literature into the closed lands of Asia. Much work is done in preparing Christian films and radio programs. This extensive ministry needs to be covered in prayer.

12. SING PRAISES TO OUR LORD.

I love Thy Kingdom, Lord,
The house of Thine abode,

The Church our blest Redeemer saved
With His own precious blood.

1. PRAISE GOD FOR WHO HE IS.

"More to be desired are they (the statutes of the Lord) than gold, yea, than much fine gold: sweeter also than honey and the honeycomb" (Psa. 19:10). I just come to praise you for the qualities of yourself I see in this beautiful verse: (1) You must be wonderfully interested in the deepest needs of man or you would never have given us your word at all. (2) There must be something intrinsically attractive about your word or man would have no desire for it. (3) Your word must be understandable or man would not be attracted to it. (4) The value is deep and lasting and permanently satisfying—this can not be said of gold. (5) Its value grows. Even much fine gold finally is gone. (6) Your word appeals to man's senses. All his sensate abilities are given full expression: (a) The more we look at it the more we see. (b) The more we hear it the more we listen. (c) The more we taste it the more we want to devour it all—over and over again.

Express yourself in adoration for this quality of God.
Speak it audibly or write out your praise in your own devotional journal.

2. PRAISE GOD FOR WHAT HE MEANS TO ME.

Just for me. To make personal application of the general principles is both painful and profitable. I know you are indeed interested in the deepest needs of my life. I want to do two things about this. (1) Read much of your word each day. (2) Be sensitive to what you will say to me. Relate your words to my personal sins, weaknesses, ignorance. Your word has more attraction to me than anything else in this whole world. My consuming desire is that all men might hear you speak to them through your Son in your word. Dear God, keep me on the track running toward the goal.

I do indeed believe your word is a revelation not a riddle. I also believe we must yield to your Lordship before we have a personal desire to know what you have said.

How do you personally relate to the word of God, and God who is speaking to you?
Speak it out or write it out. It is *so important* that you establish *your own* devotional journal.

3. CONFESSION OF SIN

My blessed Father, all my fondest expressions are read for what they truly and actually mean. As I know (and you know perfectly) they, i.e., my expressions, are mixed with desire and fulfillment. I am in a constant struggle to match my desire with my action. Forgive me, dear Lord, for the large gap that often develops between the two. I do praise you that at times I have felt the two were one (you know how easily I am deceived). Forgive me for excuses—rationalizations, justifications and just plain wilful disobedience.

What personal sins do you want to confess? We *must* speak them to remove them.
Do it! *Now.* There is no one else you have sinned against more than God. Tell him so!

4. SING A PRAYER TO GOD.

Glorious things of thee are spoken,
Zion, city of our God;
He, whose word cannot be broken,
Formed thee for His own abode:

On the Rock of Ages founded,
What can shake thy sure repose?
With salvation's walls surrounded,
Thou mayst smile at all thy foes.

Open your hymn book and sing the rest of the verses—or even sing another prayer song.

5. READ HIS WORD TO HIM!

His Word

²³They arranged to meet Paul on a certain day, and came in even larger numbers to the place where he was staying. From morning till evening he explained and declared to them the kingdom of God and tried to convince them about Jesus from the Law of Moses and from the Prophets. ²⁴Some were convinced by what he said, but others would not believe. ²⁵They disagreed among themselves and began to leave after Paul had made this final statement: "The Holy Spirit spoke the truth to your forefathers when he said through Isaiah the prophet:
²⁶"'Go to this people and say,
    "You will be ever hearing but never understanding;
    you will be ever seeing but never perceiving."
²⁷For this people's heart has become calloused;
    they hardly hear with their ears,
    and they have closed their eyes.
Otherwise they might see with their eyes,
    hear with their ears,
    understand with their hearts
    and turn and I would heal them.'
²⁸"Therefore I want you to know that God's salvation has been sent to the Gentiles, and they will listen!"
³⁰For two whole years Paul stayed there in his own rented house and welcomed all who came to see him. ³¹Boldly and without hindrance he preached the kingdom of God and taught about the Lord Jesus Christ.

— Acts 28:23-31, NIV

WEEK TWENTY-SEVEN — WEDNESDAY

Read His Word to Him.

Dear Lord, was Paul satisfied that he had fulfilled his commitment and accomplished his purpose in "seeing some"? There were "large numbers." How many? I'm so glad that only you know. Where did Paul get the energy to speak from morning till night? Oh, my Father, what is meant by "declaring" your kingdom? Your rule, your king-ship in the hearts of men. Dear Lord, how I need to see and hear this word for myself. To be convinced is something far more than being baptized or confessing that Jesus is the Messiah—although I'm sure it included such. The practical daily application of your will lived out in human relationships.

Please express your response to this beautiful text. Put your expression in your own prayer diary.

6. READ HIS WORD FOR YOURSELF.

I unavoidably include myself in the above, but here I want to apply this text as personally as at all possible: (1) If Paul could talk from morning till evening when he was past sixty years old, who am I that I should complain about the classes I have to teach? (2) I can be and want to be convinced from the Law of Moses and from the prophets that Jesus is the Messiah. (3) Dear Lord, I want never to be among those who "would not believe." (4) How easy it is for religious people to disagree among themselves—what a danger there is in this for me!

Pause in his presence and either audibly or in written form tell him all his word means to you.

7. READ HIS WORD IN THANKSGIVING.

Yes, yes, there is much gratitude here: (1) Thank you for the Holy Spirit who spoke the truth in the Old Testament scriptures. (2) Thank you for the courage of Isaiah and Paul in applying the text to life. (3) Thank you for ears that can hear and eyes that can see your wonderful truth. (4) Thank you that I can set a guard on my ears and eyes and heart lest they become calloused. (5) Thank you that I can be healed and made whole. I can see and hear and believe as you want me to. (6) Thank you for the two whole years Paul had to preach and teach.

Give yourself to your own expression of gratitude—write it or speak it!

8. READ HIS WORD IN MEDITATION.

"Boldly and without hindrance he preached the kingdom of God and taught about the Lord Jesus Christ." Here is such a meaningful verse. We have here described both the manner and the matter of Paul's work in Rome. "Boldly"—in freedom of speech—this does not refer to brashness or offensiveness—the content might have been received as brash or some because of their life or beliefs would have been offended! But the majority did not so consider the preaching of Paul. Did he only preach to the lost and teach the saved? Perhaps so—but the communicative dynamics were the same in both if the crowd was large as seems to be here indicated.

Pause—wait—think—then express yourself in thoughtful praise or thanks.

9. READ HIS WORD FOR PETITIONS.

In these last verses of Acts we can find areas for petitions: (1) Give me the same dedication to the teaching of your word. (2) Is your rule in the hearts of men my *primary* subject in teaching? Help me! (3) May I always remember that your Son is the subject or theme of all the Bible. (4) I *want* to believe—help me to find men who share this attitude. (5) As the Holy Spirit speaks through your word, give me ears to hear and a heart to receive.

Please, please remember these are prayers—speak them—reword them!

10. READ HIS WORD AND WAIT—LISTEN—GOD SPEAKS!

In these closing words speak to me: (1) "I still rule as king in the hearts of some men." (2) "Consider again the evidence of fulfilled prophecy." (3) "I want you to preach and teach to your generation what Paul did to his."

11. INTERCESSION FOR THE LOST WORLD

Hong Kong — Point for prayer: (1) *MACO* is Portugal's last remaining colony—a 15 sq. km. peninsula 30 km. from Hong Kong, with 400,000 people. The Communists virtually control the colony, yet a little Christian work continues. Pray that these believers may be well prepared for a Communist future. There are few Christian workers. More could be done by Hong Kong believers to evangelize these people—many being refugees.

12. SING PRAISES TO OUR LORD.

"Man of Sorrows," what a name
For the Son of God who came

Ruined sinners to reclaim!
Hallelujah! what a Savior!

WEEK TWENTY-SEVEN — THURSDAY

1. PRAISE GOD FOR WHO HE IS.

"Some trust in chariots, and some in horses; but we will remember the name of the Lord our God" (Psa. 20:7). What are the attributes of yourself I see in this verse? Here are some: (1) Chariots are a protection in battle. You are my strength and protection in any and every conflict. A soldier is much less vunerable in a chariot than on foot in the field. How often do we need to repair to the cover of your presence. (2) Chariots offer much more speed and maneuverability than any foot soldier could find. The psalmist is saying that the physical battle advantages of chariots and horses are nothing without your direction, but we see a parallel in what chariots and horses offer with the name or character of our God. In the realm of the spirit — where all battles are really fought — our Lord is superior to all chariots and horses can offer.

Express yourself in adoration for this quality of God.
Speak it audibly or write out your praise in your own devotional journal.

2. PRAISE GOD FOR WHAT HE MEANS TO ME.

Just for me. It was by no accident that Paul described the Christian life as a battle. I find it so! I want to "fight a good fight." Dear Lord, if we didn't have to fight every day it would be easier. I hear my commander say: "As your days are so shall thy strength be." I can climb into his chariot right now in this early morning hour and let him direct my moves through the battle of this day. Praise the Lord, I do not need to fight one battle of yesterday, nor make one move in tomorrow's conflict.

How do you personally relate to the protection of God, and God who is a protector?
Speak it out or write it out. It is *so important* that you establish *your own* devotional journal.

3. CONFESSION OF SIN

Dear Lord, as you know I have trusted in what men can do and have found it sorely, sadly lacking! "Blessed are you when you fall into manifold trials (temptation) because you know that the testing of your faith develops perseverance" (Jas. 1:2, 3). If I would turn to you automatically, if I didn't have to make a value judgment temptations would only become tests and would indeed develop perseverance. As it is, it is your grace and mercy that develops my perseverance. Temptations too often become a trap or snare — not all temptations — but "the sins that so easily ensnare us." Dear Lord, I am still in the battle and I do indeed love you. Forgive my defeats — they are also your loss.

What personal sins do you want to confess? We *must* speak them to remove them.
Do it! *Now.* There is no one else you have sinned against more than God. Tell him so!

4. SING A PRAYER TO GOD.

If you are tired of the load of your sin,
Let Jesus come into your heart;
If you desire a new life to begin,
Let Jesus come into your heart.

Just now, your doubtings give o'er;
Just now, reject Him no more;
Just now, throw open the door;
Let Jesus come into your heart.

Open your hymn book and sing the rest of the verses — or even sing another prayer song.

5. READ HIS WORD TO HIM!

His Word

[8]Therefore, although in Christ I could be bold and order you to do what you ought to do, [9]yet I appeal to you on the basis of love. I then, as Paul — an old man and now also a prisoner of Christ Jesus — [10]I appeal to you for my son Onesimus, who became my son while I was in chains. [11]Formerly he was useless to you, but now he has become useful both to you and to me.

[12]I am sending him — who is my very heart — back to you. [13]I would have liked to keep him with me so that he could take your place in helping me while I am in chains for the gospel. [14]But I did not want to do anything without your consent, so that any favor you do will be spontaneous and not forced. [15]Perhaps the reason he was separated from you for a little while was that you might have him back for good — [16]no longer as a slave, but better than a slave, as a dear brother. He is very dear to me but even dearer to you, both as a man and as a brother in the Lord.

[17]So if you consider me a partner, welcome him as you would welcome me. [18]If he has done you any wrong or owes you anything, charge it to me. [19]I, Paul, am writing this with my own hand. I will pay it back — not to mention that you owe me your very self. [20]I do wish, brother, that I may have some benefit from you in the Lord; refresh my heart in Christ. [21]Confident of your obedience, I write to you, knowing that you will do even more than I ask.

[22]And one thing more: Prepare a guest room for me, because I hope to be restored to you in answer to your prayers.
— *Philemon 8-22, NIV*

Read His Word to Him.

What a precious message I have to share with you! Am I right in seeing in this letter a strong emphasis on apostolic authority? Please help me! These are the reasons I say this: (1) "I could be bold and *order you* to do *what you ought to do."* (2) "so he could take your place *in helping me."* (3) ". . . not to mention that *you owe me your very* self." (4) "I do wish, brother, that I may *have some benefit from you* in the Lord." (5) "Confident of *your obedience."* All these phrases seem to say that Paul has a rank that should be respected. He did not want to "pull rank" but appeal out of love. Is this what you are saying to me through Paul?

Please express your response to this beautiful text. Put your expression in your own prayer diary.

6. READ HIS WORD FOR YOURSELF.

There are so many areas where I can use this text. I want to take the place of Philemon: (1) I receive the appeal of love *and* apostolic authority. There are a hundred things I *ought* to do and the love of my dear friends and brothers moves me to do them. At the same time the apostolic authority enforces it and breaks me away from my selfishness into action. (2) I believe I am almost as old as Paul was when he wrote this letter, but my body is soft and flabby compared with Paul's. How his age and imprisonment rebuke me!

Either audibly or in written form tell him all his word means to you.

7. READ HIS WORD IN THANKSGIVING.

(1) Thank you for a slave who was willing to listen and learn to be converted. He became a slave to a new Master. (2) Thank you that Paul saw the value of a person not a position. (3) Thank you for the fact that our usefulness to anyone is in you. Formerly we were useless, but now we are useful. (4) Thank you for showing me that Paul gave his heart to many people—"his *very* heart." (5) Thank you for Paul's example of welcoming and seeking others to help him in your work. (6) Thank you that Paul ever sought spontaneous service. (7) Thank you Paul referred to himself as he wrote to Philemon as "a partner."

Give yourself to your own expression of gratitude—write it or speak it!

8. READ HIS WORD IN MEDITATION.

"Confident of your obedience, I write to you, knowing that you will do even more than I ask." How good it would be if our Lord was always confident of our obedience. This quality is essentially all we have to offer our Lord. We, like our Lord, must learn obedience by the things we suffer. The lesson of obedience comes from three sources: (1) Respect for authority. If we do not have confidence in the integrity of the one who has given us the commnad, we have little reason to obey. Can we respect and honor the One who commands us? Indeed, we can! (2) The value or purpose in the command. Our Lord obeyed "for the joy that was set before him." There is no order given by our commander that does not have great reward.

Pause—wait—think—then express yourself in thoughtful praise or thanks.

9. READ HIS WORD FOR PETITIONS.

Surely in these personal requests of Paul we can find requests for prayer. (1) May my motives always be "for love's sake." (2) I want to be indeed "a prisoner of Christ Jesus." (3) How many who now enjoy new life owe their life to my teaching or preaching? Not near enough. Help me. (4) *Onesimus* is such a meaningful name, i.e., *useful* or *beneficial.* I want it for my name. (5) How I need more real empathy for those with whom I work. (6) I wonder just what type of service Onesimus gave to Paul? (7) How can I say to those about me: "Charge that to my account"?

Right here add your personal requests—and his answers.

10. READ HIS WORD AND WAIT—LISTEN—GOD SPEAKS!

There is much you can say to me in these verses: (1) "Let others refresh your heart in Christ." (2) "You can refresh others in my Son." (3) "Treat your fellow Christians as 'beloved brothers.'"

11. INTERCESSION FOR THE LOST WORLD

Hong Kong — Point for prayer: (1) *Missionary vision*—increasing through greater maturity of the Church. There are now more than 10 Chinese sending bodies or churches with over 50 missionaries serving in other lands. Pray for the increase of this vision and its better co-ordination and support.

12. SING PRAISES TO OUR LORD.

Praise ye the Father! for His loving kindness,
Tenderly cares He for His erring children;

Praise Him, ye angels, praise Him in the heaven,
Praise ye Jehovah!

WEEK TWENTY-SEVEN — FRIDAY

1. PRAISE GOD FOR WHO HE IS.

"Let the words of my mouth, and the meditation of my heart, be acceptable in thy sight, O Lord, my strength (rock), and my redeemer" (Psa. 19:14). There are three or four qualities of yourself I see in this verse: (1) You know the words I form in my mind before they come out of my mouth! This is an awesome thought! But to think less of yourself is to lack omniscience. You do know all. (2) The meditations—or evaluations—I make before action is taken is also known to you. It is in such meditations I reveal your real involvement in my life. Praise your name you do not expect or demand perfection—sincere desire to doing right is acceptable with you! This is all we can give. (3) You are indeed my total source of strength—of stability. (4) You have bought me with a great price; I belong to you.

Express yourself in adoration for these qualities of God.
Speak it audibly or write out your praise in your own devotional journal.

2. PRAISE GOD FOR WHAT HE MEANS TO ME.

Just for me—I want this text to sink down into the very depths of my being! (1) You *know*, you *hear*, you *listen* to the *words* of my mouth. By my words I am cleared or condemned! (2) The evaluations I give to any project or any choice in life—*all* choices in life are also *known, understood, shared* by you! (3) You do not expect, nor can I give perfect obedience, but you *do* expect and I *can* give consistent sincerity. Dear Lord, dear Lord, I do! (4) I have no strength at all to fulfill what I have just written, except you build this house it won't be built, but you want to live in it therefore you will help me to build it. (5) I have been bought with a price; I *want* to glorify you in my body!

How do you personally relate to the strength of God, and God who is our Rock?
Speak it out or write it out. It is *so important* that you establish *your own* devotional journal.

3. CONFESSION OF SIN

There is much confession of my missing the mark in the above worship. At the same time, I want to seek your cleansing blood. I want to claim your inward strength. I want to hide in the rock. I want openly, fully, dear God, *finally* confess all my sin, cast all my guilt over on you; free me and clear my record—I claim your promise!

"Keeping Jesus on the outside." This can apply to all my relationships. I do not want him on the outside for salvation or forgiveness of past sins—I surely do not want to go to hell. But do I really want him to eat with me, live with me every day in every relationship? Yes, yes, come in Lord Jesus and make my house your home!

What personal sins do you want to confess? We *must* speak them to remove them.
Do it! *Now.* There is no one else you have sinned against more than God. Tell him so!

4. SING A PRAYER TO GOD.

My faith looks up to Thee,
Thou Lamb of Calvary, Saviour divine!
Now hear me while I pray,

Take all my guilt away,
O let me from this day
Be wholly Thine!

Open your hymn book and sing the rest of the verses—or even sing another prayer song.

5. READ HIS WORD TO HIM!

His Word

[3]I thank God, whom I serve, as my forefathers did, with a clear conscience, as night and day I constantly remember you in my prayers. [4]Recalling your tears, I long to see you, so that I may be filled with joy.
—*II Timothy 1:3, 4, NIV*

[8]Remember Jesus Christ, raised from the dead, descended from David. This is my gospel, [9]for which I am suffering even to the point of being chained like a criminal. But God's word is not chained.
—*II Timothy 2:8, 9, NIV*

[6]For I am already being poured out like a drink offering, and the time has come for my departure. [7]I have fought the good fight, I have finished the race, I have kept the faith.
—*II Timothy 4:6, 7, NIV*

[9]Do your best to come to me quickly, [10]for Demas, be-cause he loved this world, has deserted me and has gone to Thessalonica. Crescens has gone to Galatia, and Titus to Dalmatia. [11]Only Luke is with me. Get Mark and bring him with you, because he is helpful to me in my ministry. [12]I sent Tychicus to Ephesus. —*II Timothy 4:9-12, NIV*

[16]At my first defense, no one came to my support, but everyone deserted me. May it not be held against them. [17]But the Lord stood at my side and gave me strength, so that through me the message might be fully proclaimed and all the Gentiles might hear it. And I was delivered from the lion's mouth. [18]The Lord will rescue me from every evil attack and will bring me safely to his heavenly kingdom. To him be glory for ever and ever. Amen.
—*II Timothy 4:16-18, NIV*

Read His Word to Him.

Did Paul have two times of "prayers"? You were the One to whom he lifted his voice—so I know you know and heard. I do wonder so earnestly just how he worded his prayer to you about Timothy. Paul had a clear conscience

Read His Word to Him.

because his performance was near enough to what he planned that your umpire (his conscience) approved of his actions. Am I right on this? How Paul did find happiness in the presence and work of others. Dear Lord, I want to do the same! I am woefully short here. Help me! How precious are the words of Paul in the few closing days of his life. What an outlook: (1) The word of God is not chained. (2) I have fought the good fight. (3) I have finished the race. (4) I have kept the faith. (5) Mark is helpful to me in my ministry (he could not always say that). (6) The Lord (even yourself) stood at my side and gave me strength. (7) I was delivered from the lion's mouth. (8) The Lord (even yourself) will bring me safely to his heavenly kingdom. To him be glory forever and forever!

Please express your response to this beautiful text. Put your expression in your own prayer diary.

6. READ HIS WORD FOR YOURSELF.

How gladly I take this up! What did Paul do? Where did Paul go after he was released from his first imprisonment? It is good for me to read again what I wrote several years ago in my study of his letters to Timothy and Titus. Right now I want to go into that prison with Paul and share his words: (1) How I do want to serve as my forefathers did! I can think of those who served from 1809 to 1919. I know many of them had a clear, clean, good conscience or they would never have done what they did. May I imitate their faith.

Pause in his presence and either audibly or in written form tell him all his word means to you.

7. READ HIS WORD IN THANKSGIVING.

(1) Thank you for Paul's devotion in spite of desertion. (2) Thank you for Crescens and Titus—good men who had jobs to do for you in Galatia and Dalmatia. (3) Thank you for Luke the beloved and faithful physician. (4) Thank you for Mark the profitable servant. (5) Thank you that Paul had "a ministry" even while in prison. (6) Thank you for the personal touches Paul includes in his letter to Timothy. (7) Thank you that "all the Gentiles heard the message through Paul." I do not know just how this was done, but I'm glad it was.

Give yourself to your own expression of gratitude—write it or speak it!

8. READ HIS WORD FOR MEDITATION.

"The Lord will rescue me from every evil attack and will bring me safely to his heavenly kingdom." Does the promise always hold with everyone in every situation? The "rescue" of the Lord must always be first our reaction to such evil attacks. Our Lord does not necessarily deliver us *from* such attacks. Let us listen to Paul tell us of many of those "evil attacks": (1) Many, many imprisonments (not just this last one at Rome). (2) "Countless beatings"—often near death from these beatings. (3) "Five times my back has been torn to ribbons by the lash of the Jews." (4) "Three times I have received the rods of the Romans—even when I am a Roman citizen." (5) "I have been shipwrecked three times before the latest episode—I spent all night and all day adrift in the briny deep."

Pause—wait—think—then express yourself in thoughtful praise or thanks.

9. READ HIS WORD FOR PETITIONS.

In these last words of Paul there is so much about which to pray: (1) Dear, dear Lord, I want to keep up the names and needs on my prayer list. Help me. (2) Where is the deep longing for fellow workers that filled the heart of Paul? (3) How can I better impress upon my heart the reality of my Lord's resurrection? (4) Since the word of God is not bound, release it through me. (5) May I be as ready to depart this day, this moment as was Paul.

Please, please remember these are prayers—speak them—reword them!

10. READ HIS WORD AND WAIT—LISTEN—GOD SPEAKS!

You speak real often to me in these verses: (1) "Finish the race." (2) "Keep the faith." (3) "I will stand by you even as I did with Paul."

11. INTERCESSION FOR THE LOST WORLD

India — Population: 620,700,000. Growth rate—2%. People per sq. km.—190.

Point for prayer: (1) *Pray that India may remain open for the Gospel* in the face of Communism which exploits India's social and economic woes, and militant Hinduism that bitterly opposes the advances of Christianity. Anti-conversion laws are in operation in two states and are being contemplated for three more. Much of the country is still a pioneer mission field. Pray for the Christians that they may use present opportunities to evangelize.

12. SING PRAISES TO OUR LORD.

Jesus shall reign where'er the sun
Does his successive journeys run;
His kingdom spread from shore to shore,
Till moons shall wax and wane no more.

WEEK TWENTY-SEVEN — SATURDAY

1. PRAISE GOD FOR WHO HE IS.

"The king shall joy in thy strength, O Lord; and in thy salvation how greatly shall he rejoice" (Psa. 21:1). Since I am a king—as are all Christians—I can make direct application of this text. I know of its original context and have written on it earlier. I know you want all men of every tongue and race to be able to express for themselves these beautiful words. The joy of your children is in your strength.

Our joy is not in what we have, or even in who we are, but in yourself! How full of wonder and deep happiness we are as we contemplate your strength! Endless, unlimited power! To add to such unexcelled joy at your strength is the expression of such strength—our salvation. How rich and full is the life and heart of those who know you!

Express yourself in adoration for this quality of God.
Speak it audibly or write out your praise in your own devotional journal.

2. PRAISE GOD FOR WHAT HE MEANS TO ME.

Just for me! To be a king is enough for me! A king has so much: (1) Dominion over Satan. I need not be ruled over—I can rule! He has made me a king! (2) Riches of grace—all unearned, but all *very real!* Forgiveness, eternal purpose in living—hope of the life and world to come—the presence of the blessed Holy Spirit. (3) Gifts to give to others. How wonderfully generous I can be in all you

have given me! Mercy, kindness, peace, cheer, all these from your strength or power—all these a result of my salvation, how greatly do I rejoice in you!

Dear Lord, I have found through much experience (at least in my short life) my joy is so fleeting and shallow until and unless it is in *you* and *for you!*

How do you personally relate to the salvation of God, and God who is Savior?
Speak it out or write it out. It is *so important* that you establish *your own* devotional journal.

3. CONFESSION OF SIN

It is wonderfully good to worship you, and praise you, especially to praise you for your very self—to take delight in your essential being. At the same time, I am here to confess my miserable shortcoming in the very matter. I have been attracted to this object or this project and they have totally absorbed my mind and heart—only to find how incomplete and transitory all such matters are!

How long will it be before I learn that only in you and of you can I find fulfillment! Forgive my wanderings—I come back home!

"Uncleanness." This is primarily a sin of the mind. Anything unclean is such because of a foreign matter upon it or in it. Wash my mind with the deep cleansing agent of the blood of your Son and make me clean from the inside!

What personal sins do you want to confess? We *must* speak them to remove them.
Do it! *Now.* There is no one you have sinned against more than God. Tell him so!

4. SING A PRAYER TO GOD.

O worship the King, all glorious above,
And gratefully sing His wonderful love;

Our Shield and Defender, the Ancient of days,
Pavilioned in splendor, and girded with praise

Open your hymn book and sing the rest of the verses—or even sing another prayer song.

5. READ HIS WORD TO HIM!

His Word

1 In the beginning was the Word, and the Word was with God, and the Word was God. ²He was with God in the beginning. ³Through him all things were made; without him nothing was made that has been made. ⁴In him was life, and that life was the light of men. — *John 1:1-4, NIV*

Read His Word to Him.

Dear Lord, I feel like Moses before the burning bush. I know not what to say! I want to tell you all your dear Son means to me. At the same time, I know he hears all I say and shares these words of praise! It is almost beyond human understanding to say, "In the beginning was the Word." This is saying there really never was a time when our Lord did not exist. The very expression of yourself,

so near to you as our words are near to us. This One was always with you. Today I shall take a new look at the created world: it is the creation of your Son! Not one single thing I can see, and much I cannot see, was not fashioned by his mind and brought into existence. "In him is life." Eternal life is in him and of him. Man has no light or hope without him!

Please express your response to this beautiful text. Put your expression in your own prayer diary.

WEEK TWENTY-SEVEN — SATURDAY

6. READ HIS WORD FOR YOURSELF.

Dear, dear Lord, I *need so much* to prostrate myself before you and just stay there for awhile. I am overcome by your majesty! It is delightful to contemplate the fact that there never has been a time when you did not exist and there never will be such a time. What assurance this gives to me! I see two distinct divine Beings sharing the same nature. My dear Lord was with you and at the same time shared your essential being. He was your creative agent. This truth stimulates me like a bolt of electricity! To step outside and find all I see the result of what he made! I can look through a telescope and see the immensity and indescribable greatness in reference to size of what Jesus as the Word did! I can peer through a microscope and marvel over and again of his infinite care with the smallest of his work.

It is so important that you pause in his presence
and either audibly or in written form tell him all his word means to you.

7. READ HIS WORD IN THANKSGIVING.

How gloriously good it is to approach this facet of worship. (1) Thank you for your self existence — there never has been a time when you were not. (2) Thank you for the penetrating meaning of the term "word" — the exact expression of yourself in living form. (3) Thank you for the little word "was" because even when I do not know what beginning is referred to, you *are*. (4) Thank you for the beautiful cooperative effort in all creation. (5) Thank you for *the life* — the eternal life that was in and of and through our Lord. (6) Thank you for my claim and part in the gift of eternal life he came to give to all men. (7) Thank you for the light I find in every area of thought and life because he came.

Give yourself to your own expression of gratitude — write it or speak it!

8. READ HIS WORD IN MEDITATION.

"In him was life, and that life was the light of men." Physical life is in all men as a result of creation. Is the "life" here described simply the image of God? Is this text saying that man's intellectual "enlightenment," in contrast to animals who lack intelligence, came from our Lord? When our Lord came he often said he came to bring "eternal life" to all men. We would prefer this thought. Man's real life and light in this world comes from our Lord. In him is life here and life hereafter; this life is the light for all men's lives. It is indeed my own experience to find that life abundant in him and in him alone.

Pause — wait — think — then express yourself in thoughtful praise or thanks.

9. READ HIS WORD FOR PETITIONS.

There never will be an end to the requests these verses suggest: (1) Wisdom, give me wisdom to be able to worship you as I should. (2) Humble my heart in the presence of the great Self-existent One. (3) Deepen my adoration of the One who perfectly expresses your Self. (4) Fill me with wonder as I bow before my Lord who created all things. (5) Open my eyes to see the meaning of the word "life" as here used. (6) What light have you given to all men? (7) I expect an answer to the above questions as I meditate before you. Help me.

Right here add your personal requests — and his answers.

10. READ HIS WORD AND WAIT — LISTEN — GOD SPEAKS!

In the stillness of this moment speak to me through these words: (1) "There never has been a time when I was not." (2) "You will never know what condescension it was for Jesus to come to earth." (3) "I am the light of life."

11. INTERCESSION FOR THE LOST WORLD

India — Point for prayer: (1) *The missionary force* in India has declined by 40% in the last 15 years. Entry and re-entry visas for missionaries are hard to obtain. Few new missionaries are entering the country. The entry and use of mission funds from abroad are strictly scrutinized. There are about 2,000-2,500 missionaries in India. Pray for the issuing of visas to expatriates needed for the Lord's work, and also for the most effective use of the present missionary force. Pray that these limitations may stimulate outreach by Indian Christians.

12. SING PRAISES TO OUR LORD.

Face to face with Christ, my Savior,
Face to face — what will it be?
When with rapture I behold Him,
Jesus Christ who died for me.

Face to face I shall behold Him,
Far beyond the starry sky;
Face to face in all His glory,
I shall see Him by and by!

WEEK TWENTY-EIGHT — SUNDAY

1. PRAISE GOD FOR WHO HE IS.

"The Lord is my shepherd; I shall not want" (Psa. 23:1). How very familiar are these words, and yet they never lose their meaning nor have we explored their depths. What David has said here of himself can be, or should be, said for all men. You want to be the shepherd of all men. What does this mean in the practical application to life? It means: (1) That all men are as limited in their understanding of life as sheep are to the circumstances of their pasture. Sheep are quite reluctant to go where the shepherd wants to lead them, but they can be led. (2) Sheep are not driven like hogs, but led by the shepherd. (3) Sheep become very much dependent upon the shepherd; they await his decision and seldom make one of their own. (4) The shepherd becomes very much attached to the sheep. He knows them as individuals, and gives every one a name. How well all the above relates to all men of the world can easily be appreciated.

Express yourself in adoration for this quality of God.
Speak it audibly or write out your praise in your own devotional journal.

2. PRAISE GOD FOR WHAT HE MEANS TO ME.

Just for me. How I long to identify with you as my shepherd—if ever I was given a full length portrait on the inside, it is here. (1) How I *need, need, need* a shepherd! I *want* you to lead me. At the same time, I do not want to be led. Somehow my stupid reluctance must be, and can be overcome. If only I would wait long enough to hear your voice. (2) You have wonderful ways of leading me. You do not force me against my will; you only make me willing to go. Dear Lord, your ways are pleasant and lead by green pastures and still waters. When I love you enough—deeply, personally—I will follow. When I get a good look over the edge of a precipice or two; when I pause long to look at the dead carcass of what was once a sheep like me—I will follow you. (3) My decisions have been like the sheep—made with a lack of perspective—and therefore contribute only to wandering.

How do you personally relate to the leadership of God, and God who is a shepherd?
Speak it out or write it out. It is *so important* that you establish *your own* devotional journal.

3. CONFESSION OF SIN.

There is much of confession in the above. I listen even now to hear your voice. I open up your word, and lo, you speak to me! You are doing so even now—dear good shepherd, great shepherd, my shepherd I hear you. Forgive my stupidity, my willful wandering! I feel so comfortable and secure when I pause and wait before you! How are sheep cleansed and refreshed for a new day in your pasture? However that is done, I claim it and bow before you. I know you will give your life for me—indeed you have! Why, why, then should I ever want another shepherd? All other shepherds are hirelings; they do not know me or care for me—I am "used" by them. They are Satan's servants called demons! I am afraid of them. I hasten to your side. May this day be the best ever!

What personal sins do you want to confess? We *must* speak them to remove them.
Do it! *Now.* There is no one else you have sinned against more than God. Tell him so!

4. SING A PRAYER TO GOD.

Abide with me: fast falls the eventide;
The darkness deepens; Lord with me abide:

When other helpers fail, and comforts flee,
Help of the helpless, O abide with me!

Open your hymn book and sing the rest of the verses—or even sing another prayer song.

5. READ HIS WORD TO HIM!

His Word

[5]The light shines in the darkness, but the darkness has not understood it.
[6]There came a man who was sent from God; his name was John. [7]He came as a witness to testify concerning that light, so that through him all men might believe. [8]He himself was not the light; he came only as a witness to the light. [9]The true light that gives light to every man was coming into the world.
— John 1:5-9, NIV

Read His Word to Him.

What "darkness" is here described? In the context of the verse before and the verse after I must say it refers to the darkness of the sinful indifference of this world. Am I right? Your dear Self in the Person of your Son came to walk among men and those that saw him did not at all understand who he was. How I would like to take the place of John to testify today in the dark world where I live of the light, and do it in such a manner that all men (or at least some men) might believe. Dear Lord, I want your mind in these comments. Help me. John put his whole life into his witness. Dear Father, I want to do the same! My dear Lord is the only light for any and all men. Have I represented your thoughts as they should be?

Please express your response to this beautiful text. Put your expression in your own prayer diary.

6. READ HIS WORD FOR YOURSELF.

I am sorry for the overbalance of subjective element in the above comments. Here I do want to read these words all over again until they are read into my inmost being! There is darkness in my world—into that world he shines! It do understand—I want all others to understand. How I praise you for every man you have sent my way who has, like John, testified concerning that light. Oh dear Lord, is it possible that *all men* might believe through the men you have sent into this dark world? I believe it is! Bless your name! If men only see John (or Don) they will never see him! When he is seen and recognized let this witness move on. He must (and will) increase as I decrease. Do I really believe that or is it just a pious platitude? Break my heart! I break it before you!

It is so important that you pause in his presence and either audibly or in written form tell him all his word means to you.

7. READ HIS WORD IN THANKSGIVING.

(1) Thank you for the divine energy found only in yourself! (2) Thank you for the darkness, for without it there would be no appreciation of the light. (3) Thank you for the understanding or comprehension you can give to all of life through your Son. (4) Thank you for the one hundred lessons I can learn from your man named John. (5) Thank you for the term "witness" which really means "martyr." I want to give my life in witnessing. (6) Thank you that you alone can save the world, but alone you cannot (or choose to not) save the world. We must do our part! (7) Thank you that I can be reminded often that I am not at all *the* light or "the true light." My light is a reflection of his.

Give yourself to your own expression of gratitude—write it or speak it!

8. READ HIS WORD IN MEDITATION.

"The true light that gives light to every man was coming into the world." What a glorious purpose: to give light to every man. Our dear Lord has so much light to give but as he said, "I am the light of the world." The light is his own blessed self! Men need a philosophy of life so he said, "I am the Way." Men need a propositional revelation so he said, "I am the truth." Men need the hope of purpose and energy in this world and a world to come so he said, "I am the *life.*" Men need constant nourishment and support so he said, "I am the vine"—abide in me. Man is stupid and erring like sheep so he said, "I am the good shepherd." In all these ways and many more he came as a light to all men.

Pause—wait—think—then express yourself in thoughtful praise or thanks.

9. READ HIS WORD FOR PETITIONS.

Surely these verses are the holy ground before Bethlehem's manger. (1) May your light shine in the darkness—all my life. (2) Send me, not as John, but as myself to prepare the way for your Son. (3) Give me a special testimony to someone special today. (4) How I do want men to believe and have life. How can I help? (5) When I imagine I am some kind of light—put it out! (6) How do you "enlighten every man"? (7) Give me wisdom for answering the above question.

Please, please remember these are prayers—speak them—reword them!

10. READ HIS WORD AND WAIT—LISTEN—GOD SPEAKS!

Speak through this beautiful light: (1) "My light is still shining—put it on a stand." (2) "I need a witness today." (3) "All light is not the true light."

11. INTERCESSION FOR THE LOST WORLD

India — Point for prayer: (1) *Missions* have done an immense amount of work since 1706, and many large and independent Churches are the fruit of this labor. Some missionaries are still in pioneer work and evangelism, but most work within the national churches in church planting, lay and preaching training, Christian education, rural uplift and technical ministries. Pray for missions. Pray for individual missionaries—those in sensitive areas where every action and every soul won for Jesus can be a pretext to end their ministry in the land. Pray for those who may be discouraged by lack of visible results, carnality among the Christians and the frustrating restrictions under which they work.

12. SING PRAISES TO OUR LORD.

Fairest Lord Jesus!
Ruler of all nature!
O Thou of God and man the Son!

Thee will I cherish,
Thee will I honor,
Thou, my soul's glory, joy, and crown!

WEEK TWENTY-EIGHT — MONDAY

1. PRAISE GOD FOR WHO HE IS.

"He maketh me to lie down in green pastures. He leadeth me beside the still waters" (Psa. 23:2). It would appear in this verse that the sheep really do not have much choice. The shepherd takes whatever measures are necessary to cause the sheep to lie down. Is the emphasis upon the "green pastures" or on the rest? Perhaps one must come before man can recognize the other. Man *must* rest. When our Lord is our shepherd he will arrange the circumstances of life so from time to time we will have rest. Because of our busyness most of our rests are forced. But when we look around we find it in "green pastures" and "beside still waters." It does not become apparent to us right away. It takes some long time to open our eyes to where we are and what has happened.

Express yourself in adoration for this quality of God.
Speak it audibly or write out your praise in your own devotional journal.

2. PRAISE GOD FOR WHAT HE MEANS TO ME.

Just for me. It is really only a matter of time until you will cause me to lie down. It makes much more sense to leave the crowd—to walk away from the pressing duties and seek out "a solitary place." My blessed Lord heard your voice and left the poor, the sick, the blind—the untaught and withdrew to find the green pastures of prayer and the still waters of meditation. Paul wanted to walk several miles in meditation. If these divinely led examples took time out why should I wait until I am forced to do so? The green pastures are no place of idleness. This is a place of nourishment. I find food—heaven's food—for my soul, my whole life! Thank you, gentle shepherd, for knowing this sheep better than he knows himself.

How do you personally relate to the leadership of God, and God who is Shepherd?
Speak it out or write it out. It is *so important* that you establish *your own* devotional journal.

3. CONFESSION OF SIN

Dear Lord, how stubborn I am! How taken up with a thousand pressing tasks that all seem so important—all are "God-related," but there *are* limitations to this body, to these nerves. Perhaps it takes some of us much longer than others to discover this. Dear Father, personal shepherd, I am afraid of inactivity! I do not want to be bored. How could I ever, ever think *you* would lead me into a boring situation? You are the very source of *excitement*! My fear and misunderstanding is always my biggest sin. Please forgive me. Since you are the shepherd and I am the sheep—since you are love and I am the object of your love—the pastures will be *green*.

"Forgetting our cleansing." How easy it is for sheep to get dirty! It is even easier to forget what it feels like to be clean. Dear Lord, give me a vivid rerun!

What personal sins do you want to confess? We *must* speak them to remove them.
Do it! *Now.* There is no one else you have sinned against more than God. Tell him so!

4. SING A PRAYER TO GOD.

Lead on, O King Eternal,
The day of march has come;
Henceforth in fields of conquest
Thy tents shall be our home.

Thro' days of preparation
Thy grace has made us strong,
And now, O King Eternal,
We lift our battle song.

Open your hymn book and sing the rest of the verses—or even sing another prayer song.

5. READ HIS WORD TO HIM!

His Word

[10]He was in the world, and though the world was made through him, the world did not recognize him. [11]He came to that which was his own, but his own did not receive him. [12]Yet to all who received him, to those who believed in his name, he gave the right to become children of God — [13]children born not of natural descent, nor of human decision or a husband's will, but born of God.

— John 1:10-13, NIV

Read His Word to Him.

I tremble before you in the presence of such a truth! How silently and quietly, how subtly and without pomp you came. "You were in the world." In the little world of Israel, but only representatively. I believe you are saying you could have come to any part of the world. What you did in this country and this land you could have done in any country and any land. Indeed all men in all the world need to believe you have that much interest in their little "Bethlehems" and in their "Jerusalems." But if you came all over again you would not be recognized today any more readily than before. Could it be that you are as misunderstood today by those who are your own—even the religious establishment?

Please express your response to this beautiful text. Put your expression in your own prayer diary.

6. READ HIS WORD FOR YOURSELF.

Just for me! Am I so busy with my own affairs that I cannot recognize him? Is my Lord speaking while I am speaking and I can hear no voice but my own? Am I too involved in being religious that I will not accept his authority? I do, I do want to accept, embrace, welcome your authority in my life. Even as I do so I think of areas where you are knocking for admission. Do I really and truly hear you say, "I was hungry and you gave me to eat"? There are millions of hungry people in our world — *my* world. They are hungry twice over. In prison, naked, twice over are they! They are all your potential children — fed, freed, clothed! Born of God! But do I care — do I obey beyond this worship time? Oh, blessed Lord, I do!

It is so important that you pause in his presence
and either audibly or in written form tell him all his word means to you.

7. READ HIS WORD IN THANKSGIVING.

How shall I adequately do this? I can only try: (1) Thank you that my dear Lord was once as a man "in the world." (2) Thank you for his marvelous creative ability. (3) Thank you for this dear One who was the One not appreciated (shall I ever feel slighted again?). (4) Thank you that even when the Jewish nation did not want you you did not give up on them. (6) Thank you for the authority contained in "his name"! (7) Thank you for the right to become and remain a child of God!

Give yourself to your own expression of gratitude — write it or speak it!

8. READ HIS WORD IN MEDITATION.

"... *children born not of national descent nor of human decision, or, of a husband's will, but born of God.*" There are four types of children described here. We are proud of our heritage when we can trace our lineage back to some illustrious person. What would one say if we could actually date the time when the Almighty God of all things became our Father? It was by both a human and divine decision that we were born from above. When we were born of God our blessed Lord became our bridegroom. It was with his decision and agreement and sacrifice that our new birth was a reality. Most of all, we were indeed regenerated by direct heavenly input. We respond emotionally to the facts stated in his wonderful word. Our appreciation of the new birth proceeds from: (1) The facts stated in his word; (2) my faith in these facts; (3) my emotional response.

Pause — wait — think — then express yourself in thoughtful praise or thanks.

9. READ HIS WORD FOR PETITIONS.

How can I avoid the same tragic mistake of those who did not know him? (1) Keep me always aware of who made the world I see all around me. (2) May I see him today in his world. (3) Impress upon me again how important a knowledge of your word is to all men. (4) He has come to his own people in the form of the Holy Spirit — do we know him? (5) Dear Lord, I receive you — welcome! Keep me sensitive. (6) Show me the difference between religion and yourself. (7) Thank you for everyone who does receive you — lead me to them.

Right here add your personal requests — and his answers.

10. READ HIS WORD AND WAIT — LISTEN — GOD SPEAKS!

In these two verses speak to me: (1) "I am still in my world — look for me." (2) "I am still creating in the lives of men." (3) "You are my home."

11. INTERCESSION FOR THE LOST WORLD

India — Point for prayer: (1) *Many of the larger and older denominations* are the fruit of mass movements to Christianity in the last century that were inadequately discipled. There is now much nominalism. Yet there is a growing Bible believing voice with some outstanding Christian leaders in them. The churches are generally in decline in Uttar Pradesh and Gujarat, growing by natural increase in most states, and growing through conversions in the north east. Revival is needed to rid the churches of introspection, petty squabbles, social climbing and sin, and to get the believers out to evangelize. The people are now more receptive to the Gospel, but there are too few Christians in a position to witness to them. There are too many Christians who are still bound by Hindu caste loyalties, prejudice and superstitions; court cases are common among Christians. Pray that the Church in India may soon shine brightly for the Lord.

12. SING PRAISES TO OUR LORD.

How sweet the name of Jesus sounds
In a believer's ear!

It soothes his sorrows, heals his wounds,
And drives away his fear.

WEEK TWENTY-EIGHT — TUESDAY

1. PRAISE GOD FOR WHO HE IS.

"He restoreth my soul; he leadeth me in the paths of righteousness for his name's sake" (Psa. 23:3). You are seeming to say that in being led in the paths of righteousness my soul will be restored. Is this the correct understanding? The soul is the whole man—"soul" means "life." We are a spirit and we have a body, but we are a soul. The uniting of the spirit with the body produced my soul or myself.

And so it has happened to all men of all time. Man's separate identity is his soul. How easily and surely will his soul be discouraged and depressed! How fragile is the human spirit-soul! How very, very much we need to be revived, refreshed, restored! Dear Lord, it is down the path of righteousness I find refreshment!

Express yourself in adoration for this quality of God.
Speak it audibly or write out your praise in your own devotional journal.

2. PRAISE GOD FOR WHAT HE MEANS TO ME.

Just for me! How earnestly I want to probe the depths of the word "righteousness" that I might be restored, refreshed, revived! The little phrase "his name's sake" intrigues me! It is because of my Great Shepherd's authority and power (position) that all this can happen! I see a cross lifted up on this path of righteousness. I see the scroll of

the book in which are written the blessed words of life, but they can never be more than "a law of sin and death" without the cross. Again and again I am refreshed and restored because I love your law and need your cross and open tomb!

How do you personally relate to the refreshment from God, and God who is All Authority?
Speak it out or write it out. It is *so important* that you establish *your own* devotional journal.

3. CONFESSION OF SIN

"So I find that this law is at work; when I want to do what is good, what is evil is the only choice I have. My inner being delights in the law of God. But I see a different law at work in my body—a law that fights against the law that my mind approves of. It makes me a prisoner to the law of sin which is at work in my body. What an unhappy man I am! Who will rescue me from this body that is taking

me to death? Thanks be to God, through our Lord Jesus Christ!" (He will!) (Rom. 7:21-25, TEV). I could paraphrase Paul's confession but it says exactly what I want to say, what I want to confess. What I can testify by personal experience is altogether true! Dear Lord, I accept your Son's deliverance!

What personal sins do you want to confess? We *must* speak them to remove them.
Do it! *Now.* There is no one else you have sinned against more than God. Tell him so!

4. SING A PRAYER TO GOD.

Break Thou the bread of life,
Dear Lord, to me,
As Thou didst break the loaves
Beside the sea;

Beyond the sacred page
I seek Thee, Lord;
My spirit pants for Thee,
O living Word.

Open your hymn book and sing the rest of the verses—or even sing another prayer song.

5. READ HIS WORD TO HIM!
His Word

[14]The Word became flesh and lived for a while among us. We have seen his glory, of the one and only Son, who came from the Father, full of grace and truth.

[15]John testifies concerning him. He cries out, saying, "This was he of whom I said, 'He who comes after me has surpassed me because he was before me.'" [16]From the

fullness of his grace we have all received one blessing after another. [17]For the law was given through Moses; grace and truth came through Jesus Christ. [18]No one has ever seen God, but God the only Son, who is at the Father's side, has made him known. — *John 1:14-18, NIV*

Read His Word to Him.

It seems almost redundant to read this word with you as the recipient, but this is but another form of praise and appreciation for all you are and have done and are doing. How could it be that flesh became your limitation and this world became for a little while your house? Surely I will never, never be able to appreciate this immense condescension. I love those two words "grace" you came

to express interest, love, favor, goodness to us, and for us. Oh dear Lord, how we *need* it. You came to show us reality—"*truth*": i.e. is that which equals things as they really are. Dear Father, help me to read these wonderful words with their real meaning. John said your Son was born both after and before himself. What John said of your Son I say of both yourself, your Son and the Holy Spirit.

Please express your response to this beautiful text. Put your expression in your own prayer diary.

WEEK TWENTY-EIGHT — TUESDAY

6. READ HIS WORD FOR YOURSELF.

Just for me. From the fulness of his unearned approval and love I have indeed received one blessing after another! If I received what I deserved I would be dead and in torment. My physical health is a gift I have not earned. I have often abused it and ignored it, but I have never deserved it. The length of my life is in your hands, but every day I have received of this present hour is mine out of your love and goodness. That someone came to me and told me of yourself and your salvation—what a gift that was. How beautiful were their feet! Whatever abilities I have in any area of life are all your unmerited gifts.

It is so important that you pause in his presence
and either audibly or in written form tell him all his word means to you.

7. READ HIS WORD IN THANKSGIVING.

(1) Thank you for the living, speaking representative of yourself in Jesus. (2) Thank you that you in the Person of the Other Comforter might live among us—and "in us" forever. (3) Thank you that I have seen, I am seeing, I will see his glory—the one and only Son. (4) Thank you that Jesus was "full" of grace and truth—just how full we will never fully appreciate. (5) Thank you that John was so willing to let Jesus surpass him. (6) Thank you that we do not just receive grace, we receive "fulness of grace." (7) Dear Lord, thank you that I shall never cease knowing you through your Son!

Give yourself to your own expression of gratitude—write it or speak it!

8. READ HIS WORD IN MEDITATION.

". . . *the only Son, who is at the Father's side, has made him known."* There will never be adequate words to express the meaning of this momentous event! How did Jesus give us a knowledge of God? In several ways he did it. (1) He has made known the infinite interest of God in every man and woman by his constant involvement with so many people in so many different situations. There are twenty-eight persons to whom he spoke personally to win them to himself. God our Father is just that concerned with each and all of us. (2) He made God known by his life style. God came down in the Person of his Son to show us how to do it by doing it. It took very little to satisfy the physical needs of Jesus—so it does take but little to meet the essential needs of anyone of us.

Pause—wait—think—then express yourself in thoughtful praise or thanks.

9. READ HIS WORD FOR PETITIONS.

John wrote his gospel *after* Luke wrote *Acts*—help me to read this gospel with that fact in mind. (1) "They then that received" Peter's word on Pentecost received your Son and became your children—repeat it again today. (2) Thank you for the authority or power behind my sonship. (3) Teach me more fully what it means to be born of yourself! (4) How shall I ever know just what it meant for Jesus (the Word) to "become flesh"? (5) May I look again and see yet another facet of his glory. (6) Thank you for the abundant grace received from your Son.

Please, please remember these are prayers—speak them—reword them!

10. READ HIS WORD AND WAIT—LISTEN—GOD SPEAKS!

What incredible riches are in these verses: (1) "To be born of myself is the ultimate human experience." (2) "I want to give you more grace for the needs of your life." (3) "Please look at my Son again; there is much you have not seen."

11. INTERCESSION FOR THE LOST WORLD

India — Points for prayer: (1) *Outreach by the Christians has been very poor,* but much is being done to rectify this and impart a vision to the churches. Visitation is being made to every home in India in order to leave a portion of Christian literature. Pray for conversions. Pray for the large number of Christian young people involved, and their aggressive evangelistic coverage of many of India's most poorly evangelized areas. (2) *The Bible believing witness needs prayer:* a) *In giving the Bible its rightful place* both in the theologically liberal denominations and in the Bible believing churches. In the former, dialogue and universalism have replaced evangelism and conversion. In the latter there is little solid teaching or expository preaching or application of Bible answers to real and pressing needs of India today.

12. SING PRAISES TO OUR LORD.

All praise to Him who reigns above
In majesty supreme,
Who gave His Son for man to die,
That He might man redeem!

Blessed be the name, blessed be the name,
Blessed be the name of the Lord;
Blessed be the name, blessed be the name,
Blessed be the name of the Lord.

WEEK TWENTY-EIGHT — WEDNESDAY

1. PRAISE GOD FOR WHO HE IS.

"Yea, though I walk through the valley of the shadow of death, I fear no evil; for thou art with me; thy rod and thy staff they comfort me" (Psa. 23:4). I am attempting to see in every verse some quality of yourself for which all men may praise you—and for which I can personally praise you. This verse has been associated for centuries by millions to close encounters with death—or with death for someone else. Whether we are sick or hurt or we seek to comfort others this verse speaks to our heart. Blessed be your powerful, loving presence! How all men need this assurance. How glad I am to affirm that all men can and should have this grace from you. What shall we say of those millions who have been (and are) tortured by the inhumanity of man? We say: You are there! The body and mind of man are variable, but you are present even when there is no sense of communication. You see, you know, you will receive us into eternal joy.

Express yourself in adoration for this quality of God.
Speak it audibly or write out your praise in your own devotional journal.

2. PRAISE GOD FOR WHAT HE MEANS TO ME.

Just for me. If I believe this life is but a vapor—"a tale told in the night," "like the grass of the field and the flower of the grass"—if I believe I am an eternal being that lives in a limited, temporary house called the human body—if I believe I walk *"through* the valley of death," then I can say "I fear *no* evil"! I *can* be made to suffer—I *do* hurt! I *am* unhappy with pain—but I *do not* fear it. I know if I but wait (which I surely will) it will all be over and I will awake in eternal fulfillment! You have been, you are and you shall be *with* me. Your *rod* comforts me? This seems a strange instrument for comfort. It all depends on what kind of comfort I seek. Comfort in this instance is encouragement. Your rod can be and is used by you on your enemies! There will be a day of balance. There will be final and full equity. This is a true source of encouragement to me! Bless your name!

How do you personally relate to the presence of God, and God who is always present?
Speak it out or write it out. It is *so important* that you establish *your own* devotional journal.

3. CONFESSION OF SIN

Dear Lord, I have tried to be wholly honest with you—and myself! I am *not* brave or full of courage in the face of unknown pain or suffering—or even known pain and suffering. But dear God, I do not fear it—I cast myself upon you. I need so much forgiveness for complaining! How well the sheep motif fits me. I need your staff to stop me, direct me, or even bruise me. Forgive me for crying in pity—self pity is but another form of pride, produced by the deceitful one. I do not suffer as much or as long as others. I can see much more reason for my suffering than I can for those I see about me.

"Seeking to be justified by the law." This is by *any* law, by *any* form of doing. I am just by faith or I am not just at all.

What personal sins do you want to confess? We *must* speak them to remove them.
Do it! *Now.* There is no one else you have sinned against more than God. Tell him so!

4. SING A PRAYER TO GOD.

Some day the silver cord will break,
And I no more as now shall sing;
But oh, the joy when I shall wake
Within the palace of the King!

And I shall see Him face to face,
And tell the story—Saved by grace;
And I shall see Him face to face,
And tell the story—Saved by grace.

Open your hymn book and sing the rest of the verses—or even sing another prayer song.

5. READ HIS WORD TO HIM!

His Word

1 Many have undertaken to draw up an account of the things that have been fulfilled among us, ²just as they were handed down to us by those who from the first were eyewitnesses and servants of the word. — *Luke 1:1, 2, NIV*

Read His Word to Him.

I am so glad that whereas these four men thought they were compiling the narrative of your Son it was really yourself through them. It was your own direction that prompted them to record what had happened. If this record had been neglected, or others than the ones you chose to do it, we would know nothing of yourself in the Person of your Son. I cannot thank you enough! How I do want to meet Dr. Luke (and Matthew, Mark and John). To pause here before you and see these men talking with those who were eyewitnesses to all here recorded moves me deeply! Did Luke have a list of questions he asked each one? Did he have a framework or outline he wanted to fill in from the information these "ministers of the word" told him? It does seem reasonable. Thou knowest.

Please express your response to this beautiful text. Put your expression in your own prayer diary.

6. READ HIS WORD FOR YOURSELF.

Gladly, gladly do I do it! How I need it, want it! I too am compiling a narrative (a treatise) of the life of my Lord as lived out in my own experience. Am I going to be as careful and accurate as this beloved doctor? Will I pause long before each word that tells of his life (*The* Life) and absorb it into my understanding and make it a part of my willingness? Dear God, I want to. I will earnestly try to. What was accomplished in the days of Luke (by way of those who responded to the incarnation) *must, will* be accomplished today—at least in one life. It is such a beautiful thought to know that I must—and do—minister and deliver the word (*The* Word) to others.

It is so important that you pause in his presence
and either audibly or in written form tell him all his word means to you.

7. READ HIS WORD IN THANKSGIVING.

How easily this is done! (1) Thank you for the many who took an avid personal interest in recording the momentous fact of his coming. (2) Thank you for the four whose records you preserved for us. (3) Thank you for the carefulness of Luke's account. (4) Thank you for the "finished" task of both my Lord and those who wrote of him. (5) Thank you for the early start each of these eyewitnesses had in their experience with our Lord. (6) Thank you for the selective procedure used by Luke—only those who were eyewitnesses were interviewed. (7) Thank you for the word "ministers" or "servants" of the word—all of us qualify as such today.

Give yourself to your own expression of gratitude—write it or speak it!

8. READ HIS WORD IN MEDITATION.

"*. . . ministers of the word.*" What higher position could anyone have? To be servants who dispense the word of God. There is no greater work. It would seem the primary task of the apostles was to give themselves to the ministry of the word. It was literally the increase of the word that produced the increase of the disciples. Didn't these men tire of talking about Jesus and his love? Does one tire of talking about the day he received his sight after being blind for years? Does one tire of telling how he once was a leper and now is clean and whole? Not only who Jesus was but what Jesus did for them and meant personally to them was all part of their ministry.

Pause—wait—think—then express yourself in thoughtful praise or thanks.

9. READ HIS WORD FOR PETITIONS.

In this beautiful prologue of Luke we can find petitions: (1) May the life of our Lord be lived again through his body, the church. (2) Give us the courage to be his witnesses today in our generation. (3) Make me a servant of your word. (4) Grant me the grace to investigate before I speak. (5) Thank you for the orderliness of your word—make it an example for my life. (6) I want to be Theophilus (lover of God) for my friends. (7) Give me the certainty that comes from reasonable faith.

Right here add your personal requests—and his answers.

10. READ HIS WORD AND WAIT—LISTEN—GOD SPEAKS!

In these verses speak to me: (1) "The gospel of Luke is as much needed as when it was first written." (2) "I need servants of my word for this generation." (3) "There are many men whom I could call 'Theophilus'—find them and teach them."

11. INTERCESSION FOR THE LOST WORLD

India — Points for prayer: (1) *Leadership training* is critically important. The lack of dedicated Christian workers prepared to leave for the sake of Christ is the biggest single factor limiting the growth of the Church. There is now an average of one preacher for 8 churches and 400 villages over the country, though some preachers have oversight of over 200 churches. Pray for the lay training programs. Pray also for the 40 seminaries and the students being prepared for the ministry; only a few are truly Bible believing. Pray also for the very many Bible Schools in India. (2) *The missionary vision of the Indian Church* is small, but growing. There are now about 600 Indian missionaries in cross-cultural mission work. Pray for the cultivation of missionary concern in the churches. Pray for effective missionary training programs.

12. SING PRAISES TO OUR LORD.

So precious is Jesus, my Savior, my King,
His praise all the day long with rapture I sing;
To Him in my weakness for strength I can cling,
For He is so precious to me.

For He is so precious to me,
For He is so precious to me;
'Tis Heaven below My Redeemer to know,
For He is so precious to me.

WEEK TWENTY-EIGHT — THURSDAY

1. PRAISE GOD FOR WHO HE IS.

"Thou preparest a table before me in the presence of mine enemies; thou anointest my head with oil; my cup runneth over" (Psa. 23:5). How I do want to enter fully into an appreciation of yourself as seen in this verse—please help me to do so! Our enemies are those things that oppose fulfillment of your purpose in our lives. Any and all and everyone who is far from you and does not care can yet find this promise fulfilled in their life. Oh, that men—all men would turn and live! This is the desire you have (and I have) for all men. In the midst of our greatest difficulty

there is a table spread. A table is there for refreshment and strength. Open up his book! The open Bible is the table of the Lord—we live constantly in the presence of our enemeies. There is food and drink, bread and meat upon the table spread! We hurt! All men hurt—the wounds of the battle can be healed—the oil of comfort, hope, peace are all available. He is ready to anoint you! Take a long drink of the water of life. All of this and more are found in worship before the open book! The table of the Lord!

Express yourself in adoration for this quality of God.
Speak it audibly or write out your praise in your own devotional journal.

2. PRAISE GOD FOR WHAT HE MEANS TO ME.

For me—just for me—I praise you for the fulfillment of this blessed verse in my life! Dear Lord, I know I live in a hostile environment! I feel it, see it, hear it everyday. But bless your name, anytime I want to I can spread open your word and set the table of refreshment! This morning I will go to the public table. Upon it will be the remembrance of my Lord's body and blood. I will indeed be refreshed and renewed with others as we eat and drink in remembrance of him. But there will be times of fatigue

and confusion today. It is then I need the oil and water of life. There will be times of relaxing and sleep. Help me, move me, rebuke me, remind me of your table, Lord. I see this as a portable great physician's table upon which he sets his medicine and instruments—or my dear wife or mother running out into the middle of the fray of battle to set up a table and set upon it the unexpected cool drink or nourishing food. Stop me Lord, open up my eyes!

How do you personally relate to the provisions of God, and God who is a Provider?
Speak it out or write it out. It is *so important* that you establish *your own* devotional journal.

3. CONFESSION OF SIN

The above expressions are true and have happened, but it is also true that there have been many days with no table. There have been many battles with no pause to refresh. Dear Lord, forgive me. I purpose to stop so often that it becomes a habit. As you know the thoughts and intents of my heart you know I do seek after you! Oh, help me to eat and live! Forgive my self-inflicted thirst and hunger. I am afraid of my enemies—I know from experience they can hurt me. I hear you say, "Fear me

more and all will be well"—this "fear" is holy, joyful awe! It is when I am full of this personal reverence for you that I am delivered! Bless your wonderful name!

"Lose heart." How easy it is to do this! Enthusiasm is from you—indeed it is yourself within me. I do not lose heart unless I have lost you—you have promised to be with me forever—all I need is a willingness to accept this promise!

What personal sins do you want to confess? We *must* speak them to remove them.
Do it! *Now.* There is no one else you have sinned against more than God. Tell him so!

4. SING A PRAYER TO GOD.

I would be true, for there are those who trust me;
I would be pure, for there are those who care;
I would be strong, for there is much to suffer;

I would be brave, for there is much to dare;
I would be brave, for there is much to dare.

Open your hymn book and sing the rest of the verses—or even sing another prayer song.

5. READ HIS WORD TO HIM!

His Word

[3]Therefore, since I myself have carefully investigated everything from the beginning, it seemed good also to me to write an orderly account for you, most excellent Theophilus, [4]so that you may know the certainty of the things you have been taught.

[5]In the time of Herod king of Judea there was a priest named Zechariah, who belonged to the priestly division of Abijah.
— *Luke 1:3-5a, NIV*

Read His Word to Him.

Here is your servant Luke. What a good man! He takes a deep personal interest in you and your dear Son. He felt totally positive about his task. Did he sense the presence of your Spirit working through him in what he was writing?

WEEK TWENTY-EIGHT — THURSDAY

I do not know—thou knowest! What an interest he had in all that happened! Did Luke take notes on what he heard and saw? Did this beloved doctor carry a diary of all he thought and prayed? For how long was this dear man an observer of all he wrote? Where did he train that he might write such an orderly account? When I attempt to view this text from your perspective I come up with many more questions than answers. I am so glad that one day (when there is no time) I will meet Luke and all will be clear.

Please express your response to this beautiful text. Put your expression in your own prayer diary.

6. READ HIS WORD FOR YOURSELF.

Theophilus! He had an enviable position! To receive these two documents from Luke—52 chapters of 65 years of history. An orderly account from Herod in Judea to Paul in Rome. Dear Lord, you have another lover of yourself—it is I! I purpose to absorb every word this penman of yourself wrote. I hope I can be as eager as the first Theophilus to read and reread every word you have written. How good to be given the *truth!* This treatise will perfectly match with the facts—therefore it will be the truth! Truth and reality are equal. Dear Lord, move me to so approach every word of this essay. Someone had gotten to this important man before Luke. Theophilus had already heard some things about our Lord.

Pause in his presence and either audibly or in written form tell him all his word means to you.

7. READ HIS WORD IN THANKSGIVING.

(1) Thank you for the joy of truth—the delight of eternal values. (2) Thank you for Luke who was there when it all happened. (3) Thank you for someone who is interested in detailed accuracy. (4) Thank you for preserving Luke's life long enough to follow the whole record. (5) Thank you for the easy-to-follow account Luke has given us. (6) Thank you for this important man called "most excellent Theophilus." (7) Thank you for that the only reason we know about Herod (or other so-called important men) is because they were associated with your servants.

Give yourself to your own expression of gratitude—write it or speak it!

8. READ HIS WORD IN MEDITATION.

"In the days of Herod King of Judea." How fleeting is earthly glory! All we know about this man comes from the New Testament. He did live and rule in the most enviable of times for it was in God's fullness of time. Were the days of my Lord so different from today? In so many ways they were the same: (1) There is a mayor of our city or a governor of our state who compares very well with Herod the King. (2) There are devoted religious leaders in our land. Some of them very sincere, but like those of our Lord's days sadly lacking in a living relationship with God. (3) Men and women still get up before daybreak to go to work. (4) Children are still here to remind us of the kind of faith and love we should have toward God.

Pause—wait—think—then express yourself in thoughtful praise or thanks.

9. READ HIS WORD FOR PETITIONS.

How I do want to make my requests known: (1) Give me the careful investigative attitude Luke had as he served you. (2) From the very beginning to the end of my service may I be careful in my attempt to communicate my Lord and not myself. (3) I want to teach through the written word—help me. (4) How I want to accomplish my service to you in an orderly fashion—direct my efforts. (5) Give me a real respect for those who hold authority from you. (6) Theophilus is such a lovely name—may it describe my desire toward you. (7) Give me certainty in the things of which I have been taught.

Please, please remember these are prayers—speak them—reword them!

10. READ HIS WORD AND WAIT—LISTEN—GOD SPEAKS!

In these brief words speak to me: (1) "There are many whose lives tell the story of my life through them." (2) "You can write a record of my life through your daily conduct." (3) "Love for me has no saturation point."

11. INTERCESSION FOR THE LOST WORLD

India — Point for prayer: (1) *Young people* are, unfortunately, largely neglected by many churches due to lack of manpower and interest. Pray for those who are seeking to win and disciple India's youth.

12. SING PRAISES TO OUR LORD.

God the Omnipotent! King, who ordainest
Thunder Thy clarion, the lightning Thy sword;
Show forth Thy pity on high where Thou reignest;
Give to you peace in our time, O Lord.

WEEK TWENTY-EIGHT — FRIDAY

1. PRAISE GOD FOR WHO HE IS.

"Surely goodness and mercy shall follow me all the days of my life; and I will dwell in the house of the Lord forever" (Psa. 23:6). What quality of character do I see in this beautiful verse? Goodness and mercy are two attributes that stand at the opening of the verse. Constant interest and concern are also there. A welcome home appears in the last half of the verse. I need to remember I am trying to see this verse for the benefit of all men. What you are and can be for all men. You do follow the movements of all men upon the face of the whole earth. The sun and rain and fruitful seasons are surely a part of your goodness that has followed all men since you placed the rainbow in the sky. You have a place in your bounteous house for all men. Oh, that all men would know you!

Express yourself in adoration for these qualities of God.
Speak it audibly or write out your praise in your own devotional journal.

2. PRAISE GOD FOR WHAT HE MEANS TO ME.

Just for me! This verse can be, and is, my lifetime testimony! Your goodness—far, far beyond anything that I could even ask or think has followed me all the many days of my life. Has your goodness always led me to repentance (Rom. 2:5)? I am grieved to say it has not. Dear Lord, in these latter days I long and yearn after your presence and turn my heart again and again to you and the example of your Son. Mercy is applied love. This too I have received until I am embarrassed. Bill Gothard said, *"Maturing* is discovering that the most difficult lessons that we ever learn are the ones we thought we already knew." How true I find this in my experience.

How do you personally relate to the goodness and mercy of God, and God who is Goodness and Mercy?
Speak it out or write it out. It is *so important* that you establish *your own* devotional journal.

3. CONFESSION OF SIN

Gothard said that *"Confession* is explaining how we have failed so that God will not be blamed for the consequences." I am sure this would be true of public sin, but even then there are those who would see a failure on the part of our God. But this is always true of personal sin—I am guilty—I am responsible and I do not now blame you for the results of my sin. I accept the consequences as mine not yours! I need to add: in the confession of sin we do not lose our worth before you—we increase it! Our estimate of self-worth is also enlarged. We *are not* what once we were. We are changed, we are new, we are forgiven! Praise your name!

What personal sins do you want to confess? We *must* speak them to remove them.
Do it! *Now.* There is no one else you have sinned against more than God. Tell him so!

4. SING A PRAYER TO GOD.

All the way my Savior leads me;
What have I to ask beside?
Can I doubt His tender mercy,
Who thro' life has been my Guide?
Heav'nly peace, divinest comfort,

Here by faith in Him to dwell!
For I know, whate'er befall me,
Jesus doeth all things well;
For I know whate'er befall me,
Jesus doeth all things well.

Open your hymn book and sing the rest of the verses—or even sing another prayer song.

5. READ HIS WORD TO HIM!

His Word

His wife Elizabeth was also a descendant of Aaron. [6]Both of them were upright in the sight of God, observing all the Lord's commandments and regulations blamelessly. [7]But they had no children, because Elizabeth was barren; and they were both well along in years. — *Luke 1:5b-7, NIV*

Read His Word to Him.

How delightful to go into the house of these two godly people and share with them. I know you can review the past as if it were but the activities of today. Somehow this good man had dropped into the trap of form without power, of religion without relationship. They were disciplined and obedient. Day after day, week after week, month after month, year after year these good people "walked in all the commandments and ordinances of yourself." I love them for it, I know you did. Dear Lord, are there men and women like Zechariah and Elizabeth alive on the earth today? No doubt you see many, many of them. Are you looking at me? Was Elizabeth barren on purpose? It was in your purpose. Can we say that all disappointments have a purpose? Dear Father, I want to say this! I do believe this is so. If your purpose is not made known in this life it will be fully known in the life to come!

Please express your response to this beautiful text. Put your expression in your own prayer diary.

6. READ HIS WORD FOR YOURSELF.

Just for me. You do have surprises for those "advanced in years." Whereas you do indeed want much more than form in our worship — without the discipline of form — without obedience to your law there will not be the preparation for appreciation. We can not thank you as we should without discipline and duty. Prehaps nothing really important will happen today — just as in the hundreds of days in the life of Zechariah and Elizabeth. Nothing will happen that will be widely known or long remembered. We have prayed, we have read and meditated upon your word. We have worshiped you. Perhaps nothing more important could happen but this, all of these acts are but a preparation as well as a fulfillment. I receive and expect great things from you!

It is so important that you pause in his presence
and either audibly or in written form tell him all his word means to you.

7. READ HIS WORD IN THANKSGIVING.

(1) Thank you that there have always been men and women you could use. (2) Thank you for all of the precious heritage that adds so much depth to daily living. (3) Thank you for your laws — especially the law of the Spirit of life in Christ Jesus. (4) Thank you for the desire to love you and obey you. (6) Thank you for barrenness, for only then can we appreciate fulness. (7) Thank you for every year — each one a year closer to your eternal house.

Give yourself to your own expression of gratitude — write it or speak it!

8. READ HIS WORD IN MEDITATION.

". . . and both were advanced in years." How easily many present day older people relate to this phrase. Such persons feel there are limitations imposed upon them for a reason they cannot control. Such a conclusion is false. The limitations of age are minimal compared with the advantages. It is indeed interesting that God chose an older couple to model his power in human life. Because they were advanced in years several lessons could be taught: (1) A willingness to accept God's great surprises is not limited to the young. (2) Even though advanced in years God has a special work for them. (3) They could relate to the young — indeed in their case a young man would grow up as an example for all men. (4) It was in *their* worship God spoke to them.

Pause — wait — think — then express yourself in thoughtful praise or thanks.

9. READ HIS WORD FOR PETITIONS.

As Zechariah prayed in the temple so I pray before you today: (1) I want to fulfill my priesthood today. (2) Lord, give me a true identity with those for whom I should pray. (3) Praise your name that I am in your family. I want to claim my inheritance. (4) Thank you for your grace that constitutes imperfect obedience as righteousness. (5) Keep my eyes open to the truth that by the blood of Jesus I am blameless. (6) As your bride I want to bring many children into glory. (7) For each year that I have left may I put you first.

Right here add your personal requests — and his answers.

10. READ HIS WORD AND WAIT — LISTEN — GOD SPEAKS!

In these brief verses speak to me: (1) "You are my priest today — act accordingly." (2) "Men can live uprightly today as in the days of Zechariah." (3) "I will not forgive an unrepentant heart."

11. INTERCESSION FOR THE LOST WORLD

India — Points for prayer: (1) *University students* — over 2,500,000 in 32 universities. Most universities have a group meeting regularly — pray for their witness to the many unconverted, and also pray for their purity of life, spiritual growth, and their involvement in local churches. (2) *Literature.* Pray for the distribution of scriptures and Christian literature. Pray for conversions and church growth thereby. Christian bookstores and literature agencies face major problems with importation of literature, lack of local writing talent, high costs in a poor land. (3) *Bible correspondence courses* have proved most successful. 60-70 centers send out courses.

12. SING PRAISES TO OUR LORD.

When I saw the cleansing fountain
Open wide for all my sin,
I obeyed the Spirit's wooing,
When he said, Wilt thou be clean?

I will praise Him! I will praise Him!
Praise the Lamb for sinners slain;
Give Him glory, all ye people,
For His blood can wash away each stain.

WEEK TWENTY-EIGHT — SATURDAY

1. PRAISE GOD FOR WHO HE IS.

"The earth is the Lord's and the fulness thereof; the world, and they that dwell therein" (Psa. 24:1). Praise just for yourself. What is the quality I see in this verse that commends you to all men as worthy of praise? The creator is also the owner — the earth belongs to you by right of creation. Since it belongs to you, you can and will do with it what seems best to you. What is said here of the infinitely small planet called "earth" can also be said of the immense galaxies of outer space. Blessed be your wonderful creative power. All the plant and animal creation also belong to you. It is right for man to see your creative genius in the flowers of the field or the trees of the forest.

Express yourself in adoration for this quality of God.
Speak it audibly or write out your praise in your own devotional journal.

2. PRAISE GOD FOR WHAT HE MEANS TO ME.

Just for me! Dear Lord, dear Creator, how startling, how thought provoking to address the creator of all. The whole race of mankind and the areas where they live all belong to you. Will you one day ask us to give an account of our stewardship of your property? We believe you shall. How am I using the portion of the world where I live? Dear Lord, open my eyes and mind that I might see creation and mankind as you do! I just came to praise you in wonder and love, in awe and the deepest reverence. How I do want to see the 220 nations of the world as individuals — each of them, all of them — you know them, see them, love them, want them as your children. There is much poverty, hunger, suffering. None of this is ignored. You have through your Son left us a plan to change it all. When will we hear him?

How do you personally relate to the creation of God, and God who is Creator?
Speak it out or write it out. It is *so important* that you establish *your own* devotional journal.

3. CONFESSION OF SIN

It is most difficult to think in such immense numbers. Such becomes far too impersonal. Yet the larger problem (sin) is to not think in this way. If my Lord should come this very day how would I relate to the fulfilling of the great commission? Did someone outside of salvation hear from me about my Lord? When? How many? Where? My sin is that my concern for the lost world never gets past a concern for the lost world. Dear Lord, I can help evangelize where I am. I can help others evangelize where they are. Forgive me dear Lord for failures — in each area.

"Callousness." Dear Lord, how easy it is to become hardened to your love and power, your presence and personal interest! Sensitize my heart and keep me tender.

What personal sins do you want to confess? We *must* speak them to remove them.
Do it! *Now.* There is no one else you have sinned against more than God. Tell him so!

4. SING A PRAYER TO GOD.

My hope is built on nothing less
Than Jesus' blood and righteousness;
I dare not trust the sweetest frame,
But wholly lean on Jesus' name.

On Christ, the solid Rock, I stand;
All other ground is sinking sand,
All other ground is sinking sand.

Open your hymn book and sing the rest of the verses — or even sing another prayer song.

5. READ HIS WORD TO HIM!

His Word

[8]Once when Zechariah's division was on duty and he was serving as priest before God, [9]he was chosen by lot, according to the custom of the priesthood, to go into the temple of the Lord and burn incense. — *Luke 1:8, 9, NIV*

Read His Word to Him.

Dear Lord, how many thousands of priests entered the temples — Solomon's, Nehemiah's, Zerubbabel's and now Herod's — to burn incense? Not one priest or one fire was unseen or ignored. What were the deep feelings of Zechariah when he was chosen? How I wish I could truly approximate your viewpoint. I can only imagine he was filled with gratitude and wonder. Perhaps eager antici- pation was a part of his approach to his duty. Since the incense was only representative of the prayers of the worshipers, he too was in prayer. I am sure he had a sense of true concern that he perform his duty accurately. Perhaps he remembered the two classic examples in the sons of Aaron who had not. I do want to ascend the steps with this good man and step inside your temple of worship.

Please express your response to this beautiful text. Put your expression in your own prayer diary.

6. READ HIS WORD FOR YOURSELF.

I do hope I have read aright the attitudes of Zechariah, but whether I have or haven't I can know my own heart as I come to worship you! Here are some of my thoughts offered as prayer to you: (1) "That I should be chosen among the millions who have not found you to offer praise and petition to you fills me with the joy of thanksgiving." (2) "It is a never ceasing wonder that I can come into your presence and actually believe and know you hear and answer." (3) "I come before your throne of grace, before my altar, even my wonderful sin offering, full of eagerness as to just what you have for me to do today." (4) "Most of all I am so glad this is not a once in a lifetime activity, but my priceless privilege every day." Praise you!

It is so important that you pause in his presence
and either audibly or in written form tell him all his word means to you.

7. READ HIS WORD IN THANKSGIVING.

A part of every sacrifice was the incense as a thank offering. So it is today—a part of all my expression is thanksgiving. (1) Thank you for the dear man Zechariah —so much like many of us. (2) Thank you for our priesthood—we are on service every day. (3) Thank you for the service we have to the people with whom we live and serve —in prayer and encouragement. (4) Thank you that our prayers are always heard and answered—sometimes "yes," sometimes "no," and sometimes "wait." (5) Thank you for your temple today, even our bodies. (6) Thank you for your divine presence in us in the person of the Holy Spirit. (7) Thank you for our day—the fulfillment for which all of the prophets and priests looked.

Give yourself to your own expression of gratitude—write it or speak it!

8. READ HIS WORD IN MEDITATION.

". . . to go into the temple of the Lord and burn incense." The supreme blessing: to be chosen to go into the temple and approach the Lord on behalf of the people. This must have been the thinking of the priests who served in the days of our Lord. What was then a sacred privilege for a very few has now become the joy of every believer. Each day—and several times each day—we can come into the sacred place; we can close the door of the closet our blessed Lord built us and lift our hearts to him in praise and intercession.

Pause—wait—think—then express yourself in thoughtful praise or thanks.

9. READ HIS WORD FOR PETITIONS.

As your "chosen ones" we have many needs answered only in prayer: (1) Without your presence I cannot serve you. Please stand by me. (2) Keep me aware that my duties as a priest never change. I am always on duty. (3) Choose that area where I can intercede for men today. (4) Thank you that I am your temple now. (5) Thank you for the sweet incense of prayer. (6) Thank you for our eternal high priest at your right hand. (7) Keep me humble lest I be struck dumb.

Please, please remember these are prayers—speak them—reword them!

10. READ HIS WORD AND WAIT—LISTEN—GOD SPEAKS!

In these two verses you can say something eternally important to me: (1) "You are on duty now as my priest." (2) "You live and serve every day before me." (3) "Your prayers can come up before me as lovely fragrant incense."

11. INTERCESSION FOR THE LOST WORLD

India — Points for prayer: (1) Bible translation. Of India's 800 languages, only 26 have the Bible, 48 the New Testament and a further 48 portions of the New Testament. Work is now in progress in 35 languages, but many more await translators. More Indian believers need to be raised up for this exacting ministry. (2) Gospel recordings—now with records in 187 of India's languages. This is a valuable tool together with cassettes for evangelizing and teaching the smaller or less accessible peoples of India. (3) Christian radio. There is no Christian broadcasting in India, but over 20 studios produce programs for transmission from other areas. There is an increasing audience, but pray for a greater impact and response among Hindus and Muslims.

12. SING PRAISES TO OUR LORD.

I will sing the wondrous story
Of the Christ who died for me,
How He left His home in glory
For the cross of Calvary.

Yes, I'll sing . . . the wondrous story
Of the Christ . . . who died for me,
Sing it with . . . the saints in glory,
Gathered by . . . the crystal sea.

WEEK TWENTY-NINE — SUNDAY

1. PRAISE GOD FOR WHO HE IS.

"Who is this King of glory? The Lord strong and mighty, the Lord mighty in battle . . . the Lord of hosts, he is the King of glory" (Psa. 24:8, 10). This is a Messianic psalm, full of wonderful meaning in reference to our Lord. The primary purpose is to praise you (both of you) for the wonder of meaning in these descriptive terms. You are "the King of *character*"—for so the meaning of the word "glory." It means "the essential quality or the essence." You are *the source* (and in this sense King) of all character.

You are the only one indeed THE ONE who can give meaning or character to anything. I want to set aside this one attribute and lift up my whole heart to you in praise. "Strong and mighty—mighty in battle." Bless your wonderful self—your strength and the use of such strength in the battles of life are beyond human appreciation or expression. You have a host of those who (like myself) have gladly joined ranks behind the One who has never lost a battle!

Express yourself in adoration for this quality of God.
Speak it audibly or write out your praise in your own devotional journal.

2. PRAISE GOD FOR WHAT HE MEANS TO ME.

Just for myself. I, like thousands before me, have seen my Lord returning in triumph through the gates of the eternal city to enter back into the glory he had with the Father before the foundation of the world. At the same time, I want to open the gates of my own heart and invite him to enter in a march of triumphant coronation. Take the throne of my heart oh King of all virtue, of all true

holiness, of all abundant life. Welcome home! How gladly, gladly do I acknowledge your strength—how beyond adequate expression are your exploits of battle with my enemy! I have really not answered the question, "Who is the King of glory?" I have only tried to appreciate in such a limited way the awesome qualities of One who is the captain of the hosts of heaven.

How do you personally relate to the rule of God, and God who is King?
Speak it out or write it out. It is *so important* that you establish *your own* devotional journal.

3. CONFESSION OF SIN

I am so glad that your greatness never discourages me—for I remember that you are *Love*, as well as power, indeed power in love! How is it that when I know so well that you are the King of character, i.e., leader of all virtue, that I act and think as if I were the source? How sadly do I find out that "in me dwelleth no good thing." To will is present, but the power, the ability to fulfill comes from

the King of virtue! How easy it is to admit my lack, my poor attempts, my willful stupidity! I gladly, out of my need, cast myself at your feet. Forgive me, but at the same time live through me in the strength of your might!

"Filthiness." This is of the mind, the will, the emotions, the conscience, not only of sex but of humanism, materialism, and the cares of this life. Clean me up!

What personal sins do you want to confess? We *must* speak them to remove them.
Do it! *Now.* There is no one else you have sinned against more than God. Tell him so!

4. SING A PRAYER TO GOD.

Breathe on me, Breath of God,
Fill me with life anew,

That I may love what Thou dost love,
And do what Thou wouldst do.

Open your hymn book and sing the rest of the verses—or even sing another prayer song.

5. READ HIS WORD TO HIM!

His Word

[11]Then an angel of the Lord appeared to him, standing at the right side of the altar of incense. [12]When Zechariah saw him, he was startled and was gripped with fear.
— *Luke 1:11, 12, NIV*

Read His Word to Him.

This is surely your text! I feel like an outsider. You look into the hearts of all those "assembled worshipers." How many were truly praying? How many are only going through a form they performed hundreds of times before? Dear Lord, we fit this description! But no doubt there were those who bowed their heads because it represented their hearts. Here was a man and over there another whose

uplifted hands indicate the true wonder and joy of their hearts. All you did in the appearance of the angel was to materialize a fact that happened any time anyone offered incense. Your angels are here now, today, in this place—we just cannot see them. It is startling even to attempt to live in the realm of the spirit world.

Please express your response to this beautiful text. Put your expression in your own prayer diary.

6. READ HIS WORD FOR YOURSELF.

I do identify with Zechariah in several ways. Therefore, I can sense his amazement and surprise. I can even now see it on his face. He always knew you had angels, he believed they were your ministering servants. He no doubt believed they were present in the temple as he performed his duties. But the visible presence of just one angel catapulted him into an entirely new dimension. So it would be for me! No doubt you thought Zechariah needed this miracle to establish or confirm his faith. Even after such an appearance he did not react as he should. Dear Lord, I want to learn from his mistake. I do want to accept without question this message of your angels.

It is so important that you pause in his presence and either audibly or in written form tell him all his word means to you.

7. READ HIS WORD IN THANKSGIVING.

Surely this is an appropriate circumstance for thanksgiving. (1) Thank you for a time set aside and kept for worshiping you. If we do not do this we will never have it. (2) Thank you that you appeal to man through his senses in the fragrance of incense as well as intellectually through your word. (3) Thank you for "assembled worshipers" who have been there from the beginning. (4) Thank you that you have promised your presence every time we gather for worship. (5) Thank you for our altar of your presence, even your Son. (6) Thank you for the "right side" of all experiences in life — you are always there. (7) Thank you for the strong hold on my heart. I do not want you ever to let go!

Give yourself to your own expression of gratitude — write it or speak it!

8. READ HIS WORD IN MEDITATION.

"*. . . he was startled and gripped with fear.*" We in America need to be startled out of our complacency and gripped with the fear of the loss of our freedoms. This is the constant message of some people in our nation. The real danger begins in our complacency in our worship and our lack of real personal reverence. If our eyes could be opened to the real world of the spirit our response would be very much like that of Zechariah. What an awesome thought that angels are right here with me in this room! Do they influence me in any way? If they are to serve me, as I know they do, then they *must* influence me. Since angels are spirits they would have access to my spirit, or to me as a spirit. I want to be yielded to God's will so the angels will not be hindered in their service. I am sure when I get into the spirit world after death I will be startled and gripped with holy reverence at all angels did while I was on earth.

Pause — wait — think — then express yourself in thought praise or thanks.

9. READ HIS WORD FOR PETITIONS.

In your appearance to this old man there is much for which to pray: (1) I want to know how I can help others to worship you. (2) Keep me aware that there *are* many who do sincerely worship you. (3) Sensitize my heart that I might appreciate the ministry of your angels. (4) As I allow prayer to burn out the dross of my heart, minister to my spirit. (5) Thank you for the assurance that even when I cannot see you you are at work on my behalf. (6) I want the capacity to be startled with your goodness. (7) Fill me with holy awe at the prospect of the end of all things.

Right here add your personal requests — and his answers.

10. READ HIS WORD AND WAIT — LISTEN — GOD SPEAKS!

Gabriel came to speak to this man — speak to me in these circumstances. (1) "I speak best to those who worship me in sincerity and truth." (2) "All I have said in the New Testament is my message to you — hear it." (3) "I am always standing on the right side of every issue."

11. INTERCESSION FOR THE LOST WORLD

India — Point for prayer: (1) *Christian medical work* has had to be greatly streamlined with the run-down of missionary staff. *The Christian Medical Association* has oversight over 430 institutions with both Indian and expatriate medical workers. *The Emmanuel Hospitals Association* now has responsibility for all the hospitals, etc. that were run by Bible believing missions. Pray for the witness that goes out from these hospitals to the many patients, and that this may lead to many seeking the Savior.

12. SING PRAISES TO OUR LORD.

Wounded for me, wounded for me,
There on the cross He was wounded for me;

Gone my transgressions, and now I am free,
All because Jesus was wounded for me.

WEEK TWENTY-NINE — MONDAY

1. PRAISE GOD FOR WHO HE IS.

"Show me thy ways, O Lord; teach me thy paths. Lead me in thy truth, and teach me, for thou art the God of my salvation; on thee do I wait all the day" (Psa. 25:4, 5). I am sure I shall run out of days before I run out of the beautiful qualities of your character. There are several life changing qualities in these two verses. To show me the way I should walk several things are necessary. (And what is needed for me is needed for all men.): (1) My attention must be arrested. Man is fascinated by his own interests. But you do have ways of getting our attention — some ways are wonderfully subtle and some are very blunt! (2) You must create a desire to walk in your paths or ways, i.e., once I have seen them. Such a desire is almost automatic since (sad to say) we do not look for your way until we are in need. Dear God, say it isn't so! But too often it is. (3) I must be in a "walkable" or "teachable" frame of mind — humility and trust must be present. Dear Lord, why is man so wilfully stupid?

Express yourself in adoration for these qualities of God.
Speak them audibly or write out your praise in your own devotional journal.

2. PRAISE GOD FOR WHAT HE MEANS TO ME.

Just for me! To praise you and bow before you is my joy and privilege! Bless your holy name that I have the strength to do so. I have your truth in your word, but I need to be led (as a little child) in my understanding of its application to my life and the lives of those about me. What are the qualities of a learning child? (1) Wide-eyed confidence in the teacher. Whatever he says is true. (2) A concentration with understanding on what is being said. (3) An eager uninhibited willingness to do whatever is taught. Oh my Lord! I do, I do throw out all other words. I open my whole self to your word. I want to fasten my whole attention on what you say. Blessed Savior, if you said it, I will do it.

How do you personally relate to the teaching of God, and God who is Teacher?
Speak it out or write it out. It is *so important* that you establish *your own* devotional journal.

3. CONFESSION OF SIN

My always present Lord, you know so well that such qualities as I have just expressed are indeed the deep desires of my heart, but they are not the daily practice of my life. Forgive the sad gap between desire and fulfillment. But I know that desire held often enough and deeply enough does become fulfillment. So since I have no other — and want no other — I wait before you for the change!

"Unforgiving." Since forgiveness is inseparably linked with forgetfulness can I now remember anyone who sinned against me? Do I feel in my spirit a hurt, a resentment? Am I open and full of good will toward all men? Just now I ask for the memory healing blood of your Son!

What personal sins do you want to confess? We *must* speak them to remove them.
Do it! *Now.* There is no one else you have sinned against more than God. Tell him so!

4. SING A PRAYER TO GOD.

The Lord's our Rock, in Him we hide,
A shelter in the time of storm;
Secure whatever ill betide,
A shelter in the time of storm.

Oh, Jesus is the Rock in a weary land,
A weary land, a weary land;
Oh, Jesus is a Rock in a weary land,
A shelter in the time of storm.

Open your hymn book and sing the rest of the verses — or even sing another prayer song.

5. READ HIS WORD TO HIM!

His Word

[13]But the angel said to him: "Do not be afraid, Zechariah; your prayer has been heard. Your wife Elizabeth will bear you a son, and you are to give him the name John. [14]He will be a joy and delight to you, and many will rejoice because of his birth, [15]for he will be great in the sight of the Lord. He is never to take wine or other fermented drink, and he will be filled with the Holy Spirit even from birth.
— *Luke 1:13-15, NIV*

Read His Word to Him.

What an awesome word! Had Zechariah actually been praying about the birth of a child? The answer is obvious, but we have difficulty believing he could pray and not accept your answer. But then, we too are there. How I do want to relate this text to yourself. How very specific and personal are all your words. (1) You call men by their names. (2) You know their wife's name and their relationship with each other. (3) You give the name of a boy baby. (4) You know our reaction to your gifts — because you know us. (5) You know all our neighbors and our relationship to them. (6) You know the future of our children. (7) You specify the life style of our children. Praise your name forever!

Please express your response to this beautiful text. Put your expression in your own prayer diary.

6. READ HIS WORD FOR YOURSELF.

I do wonder how many of my prayers have been heard and I did not know it! How many times have my prayers been based on my understanding of what you could or could not do. Dear Lord, open my eyes! Forgive me! Did you know of the birth of our children (and grandchildren) before we did? I'm sure you did! Could we say that your intentions for every son and daughter born was in principle the same as your purpose for John? You sent the spirit of that son or daughter into the womb of the mother so the child would be "a joy and a delight" to us. If some other reaction was present it wasn't your intention. Praise your blessed Person. I do believe you intend for every single child born to at least Christian parents, yea *all* parents, to be great in your sight. Oh, that your purpose might be fulfilled.

It is so important that you pause in his presence
and either audibly or in written form tell him all his word means to you.

7. READ HIS WORD IN THANKSGIVING.

(1) Thank you, oh thank you that you do hear and answer prayer. (2) Thank you that your answers are not circumscribed by our lack of faith or understanding. (3) Thank you that each and everyone of us are individuals to you, known by name and need. (4) Thank you for the joy and delight that has a lasting quality. (5) Thank you for the many who can and will rejoice if I rejoice. (6) Thank you for the fact that we can be filled with the Holy Spirit from the day of our new birth. (7) Thank you for the grand example of John the Baptist.

Give yourself to your own expression of gratitude—write it or speak it!

8. READ HIS WORD IN MEDITATION.

"*. . . he will be filled with the Holy Spirit even from birth.*" How wonderful it would be to be filled with the Holy Spirit from the first day of our new birth and stay filled with the Holy Spirit until we left this life. Perhaps we can learn a secret or two from John the Baptist so this can be true: (1) Have parents who are also yielded to the rule of the Holy Spirit in their hearts. We are later to read of both Zechariah and Elizabeth that they were "filled with the Holy Spirit." If we do not have Christian parents —at least your parent in the faith should be so filled. (2) Give God through his word the throne of your heart and allow him to control the demands of your body. Of John it is said, "He will never take wine or strong drink." The control of the desires of the body are directly related to the Spirit's rule in our life.

Pause—wait—think—then express yourself in thoughtful praise or thanks.

9. READ HIS WORD FOR PETITIONS.

In the beautiful promises to Zechariah is much material for prayer: (1) Quiet my fears of the unknown—they are all known to you. (2) Thank you that thou Lord hearest me! (3) Lord, I have been as faithless as this man—deepen my willingness to believe. (4) Thank you for the wonderful assurance that nothing is too hard for you. (5) You can use older people—use me. (6) Thank you that you know our names before we are born. (7) May the greatness of John impress itself more and more fully upon my heart.

Please, please remember these are prayers—speak them—reword them!

10. READ HIS WORD AND WAIT—LISTEN—GOD SPEAKS!

How easily you could speak to me through these verses: (1) "You are greater than John." (2) "Many can rejoice because of the new birth of any child of mine." (3) "It is possible to be filled with the Holy Spirit from the time of your new birth."

11. INTERCESSION FOR THE LOST WORLD

India — Point for prayer: (1) *Unreached peoples and areas: The North Indian Plains* with their teeming millions have far fewer believers than better evangelized South India. *Uttar Pradesh's* population has increased 300% in 50 years, but the number of Christians of all kinds has decreased and most of these are only nominal and rarely attend a church service. There are six small Bible Schools in the state and few Christian workers.

12. SING PRAISES TO OUR LORD.

Jesus is all the world to me,
My life, my joy, my all;
He is my strength from day to day,
Without Him I would fall.

When I am sad, to Him I go,
No other one can cheer me so;
When I am sad He makes me glad,
He's my Friend.

WEEK TWENTY-NINE — TUESDAY

1. PRAISE GOD FOR WHO HE IS.

"Remember not the sins of my youth, nor my transgression; according to thy mercy remember me for thy goodness' sake, O Lord" (Psa. 25:7). O what a joy to tell you again how I appreciate this one quality of yourself! You can and do forget—you cannot and do not and will not remember the sins of my youth. The problem is we do! But it is possible to totally forget. When we truly and deeply do not want to remember and we stay with the purpose for twenty-one days we will not remember! Praise your name. I wonder how old David was when he wrote this psalm? Was he past 50, or 60, or 70? It is my persuasion that all the qualities of character that we so admire in you we can also develop to a limited, but very real extent in us. Our Lord has been grievously sinned against and yet he treats us in mercy for the sake of his goodness; can we do less with those who sin against us?

Express yourself in adoration for this quality of God.
Speak it audibly or write out your praise in your own devotional journal.

2. PRAISE GOD FOR WHAT HE MEANS TO ME.

Just for me. I want to praise you for a clean, clear, fresh, new record. Each day I can and do begin with just such a record. I confess my sins. (I do wish I could remember them more adequately.) But then my forgiveness is *not* contingent upon my ability to remember. The inward effect of your forgiveness could be related to my ability to remember. My appearance before you today is to praise you for your mercy and goodness. Mercy is such a lovely, tender, personal quality. I have often said, mercy is love applied. Love forgives and forgets and mercy makes such love personal. This is just what you have done for me with the sins of my youth (and old age). It is more than a comfort to know that your essential being is *goodness*. How glad I am!

How do you personally relate to the goodness and mercy of God, and God who is Goodness and Mercy?
Speak it out or write it out. It is *so important* that you establish *your own* devotional journal.

3. CONFESSION OF SIN

It will also be easy to seek your cleansing (deep within) for remembering and in a sense repeating any of my sins. It is Satan's business to remember sins to accuse us with them. I reject and resist him! Forgive me for falling prey to his wiles. I do indeed cast myself upon your goodness. I have no perfect goodness of myself—all my value is in you. Do you keep a record for each day? What shall be written on today's page? Bless your name, because of my confession and your merciful forgiveness only what good is done this day will remain for tomorrow's record! How delightful to claim your forgiveness!

"Perverseness." How easily I relate to this sin. Why is it that I am so very unreasonable in my demands upon my wife—not all the time—but at times I know I am perverse. Dear God, dear wife, forgive me! I can blame it on several things—the blame is mine! So also is the forgiveness!

What personal sins do you want to confess? We *must* speak them to remove them.
Do it! *Now.* There is no one else you have sinned against more than God. Tell him so!

4. SING A PRAYER TO GOD.

What a fellowship, what a joy divine,
Leaning on the everlasting arms;
What a blessedness, what a peace is mine,
Leaning on the everlasting arms.

Leaning, leaning,
Safe and secure from all alarms;
Leaning, leaning,
Leaning on the everlasting arms.

Open your hymn book and sing the rest of the verses—or even sing another prayer song.

5. READ HIS WORD TO HIM!

His Word

[16]Many of the people of Israel will he bring back to the Lord their God. [17]And he will go on before the Lord, in the spirit and power of Elijah, to turn the hearts of the fathers to their children and the disobedient to the wisdom of the righteous—to make ready a people prepared for the Lord."

[18]Zechariah asked the angel, "How can I be sure of this? I am an old man and my wife is well along in years."

[19]The angel answered, "I am Gabriel. I stand in the presence of God, and I have been sent to speak to you and to tell you this good news. [20]And now you will be silent and not able to speak until the day this happens, because you did not believe my words, which will come true at their proper time." — *Luke 1:16-20, NIV*

Read His Word to Him.

How fine it is to read of this servant—yea, a bond servant of yours! John brought many of your people back to you because he himself was with you. We cannot bring people to where we ourselves will not go. Isn't it possible to have the same demeanor and attitude of Elijah today? I *know* we can have the same power, even your blessed Holy Spirit. Elijah and John the Baptist both turned the hearts of people to you by their words (which were actually your words) and so can we today! It is wise and good and satisfying to obey you. Oh, that today we were the people ready to receive your rule in all of our lives. I do mean for each of these words to be in agreement with your mind. Forgive me where I have erred.

Please express your response to this beautiful text. Put your expression in your own prayer diary.

6. READ HIS WORD FOR YOURSELF.

I am so very much like the priest: "How can I be sure of this?" How often have I said it? I have said it in actions and attitudes far more often than in words. Bless your name, age has nothing to do with the fulfillment of your purposes. This is a *real* comfort to me. The answer of the angel should have been, and was more than adequate: "I am Gabriel"! That could have sufficed; but he offered much more. This angel, representative of millions of angels, stood in the presence of God (yourself). He was a messenger and therefore was sent to deliver your word. What he had to say was "good news." I want to absorb every word inasmuch as such messengers are with me here.

Pause in his presence and either audibly or in written form tell him all his word means to you.

7. READ HIS WORD IN THANKSGIVING.

(1) Thank you for numbers—"many of the people of Israel"—so today you want *all* saved. (2) Thank you for a way back—even obedient repentance. (3) Thank you for our priceless privilege of going before to preach your word in preparation for your coming into the hearts of men. (4) Thank you for the lovely expression "to turn the hearts of the fathers to the children." How we all need to be like children. (5) Thank you that the disobedient can be changed—they can see the reasonableness of righteousness. (6) Thank you that we can always be ready and be your people. (7) Thank you that when you command you furnish the means with the command.

Give yourself to your own expression of gratitude—write it or speak it!

8. READ HIS WORD IN MEDITATION

"*. . . my words, which will come true at their proper time.*" Wouldn't it be wonderful if all our words came true in just the way we planned? Truth is simply that which equals reality. When Gabriel made this promise he declared a monumental quality of God's character. Whatever God has said will find fulfillment. More dependable than the laws of this universe is the One who set the laws in motion. It is a provocative thought that refusal to accept this promise resulted in muteness. The thought seems to be that all men should gladly exclaim in wonder and praise at such an ability. The very life of fulfillment is in the words of God. The principle of acceptance or rejection is based on the integrity of the speaker. If a poor man promises us a million dollars we doubt the possibilities of fulfillment. If a billionnaire promises us a million dollars we should rejoice at the good news.

Pause—wait—think—then express yourself in thoughtful praise or thanks.

9. READ HIS WORD FOR PETITIONS.

The character and mission of John move me to prayer: (1) Keep my purpose to bring men back to you. (2) Give me divine wisdom as I speak to religious people. (3) I need the discipline of John and Elijah. (4) I need the boldness of these your servants. (5) I need the spiritual awareness of these men. (6) Somehow help me to break the hearts of men as they see your love. (7) You said it—I believe it—and may this settle it without question of doubt or fear.

Right here add your personal requests—and his answers.

10. READ HIS WORD AND WAIT—LISTEN—GOD SPEAKS!

Speak to me in this example of unbelief: (1) "You do not need explanation when you have revelation." (2) "Good news is not good news unless someone believes it." (3) "Not one promise I have made will ever fail of fulfillment."

11. INTERCESSION FOR THE LOST WORLD

India — Point for prayer: (1) *Unreached peoples and areas: Bihar* is prone to droughts and famines and is very needy spiritually—the eight million Muslims and 65,000 schools have no Christian witness.

12. SING PRAISES TO OUR LORD.

When my lifework is ended, and I cross the swelling tide,
When the bright and glorious morning I shall see;
I shall know my Redeemer when I reach the other side,
And His smile will be the first to welcome me.

I shall know Him, I shall know Him,
And redeemed by His side I shall stand,
I shall know Him, I shall know Him
By the print of the nails in His hand.

WEEK TWENTY-NINE — WEDNESDAY

1. PRAISE GOD FOR WHO HE IS.

"All the paths of the Lord are steadfast love and faithfulness, for those who keep his covenant and his testimonies" (Psa. 25:10). What marvelous qualities of yourself we find in just this one verse. Oh my Father, I want to find myself traveling your paths. "Steadfast love." Love that does not give up. Love that remains constant and unchanging. Since love is giving, this is really saying you are always giving me what is best and most needful in my life. You have always kept your part of any agreement. You are there to fulfill what you have promised! Blessed be your name! In the keeping of our part of your agreement is the fulfillment of your promises. We know by experience your love and faithfulness. How I praise you for what I see here of yourself!

Express yourself in adoration for this quality of God.
Speak it audibly or write out your praise in your own devotional journal.

2. PRAISE GOD FOR WHAT HE MEANS TO ME.

Just for me. Am I walking in your paths today, if I am keeping your covenant and testimonies? What are the terms of your covenant? I believe what I read on the page of your book: *"The new covenant commonly called the New Testament of our Lord and Savior Jesus Christ."* I believe every word in these twenty-seven documents is a part (my part) of this agreement. I would be terribly discouraged and depressed beyond hope if I did not know this is a covenant of "grace through faith." This is no "cop out." I can and will never *know* (experientially) your steadfast love and faithfulness until I act upon the words of your agreement. Your steadfast love, your comforting faithfulness is never experienced except in my stumbling attempts to do your will. It is only in doing that I can "know." I love you!

How do you personally relate to the love of God, and God who is Love?
Speak it out or write it out. It is *so important* that you establish *your own* devotional journal.

3. CONFESSION OF SIN

How open I am to a free confession of my sin before you. I teach and preach and live "in your sight," and I do not sin without your presence. Why would anyone, least of all myself, *want* to sin? All sin has its motivation in the three areas of man's deepest needs: (1) flesh, (2) eyes, and (3) pride. How should we satisfy the flesh? Have you made adequate provision for this? Evidently not (or so we must think), or we would not seek fulfillment outside your covenant. Sin must be stopped at the source for its nature is to feed on itself! Have you told me what possessions will be enough? Food and shelter and clothes -- with these I can *be* content if I *want* to be. Dear God, I do! How shall we satisfy the desire to be accepted and appreciated? You have shown me in the person of your Son.

What personal sins do you want to confess? We *must* speak them to remove them.
Do it! *Now.* There is no one else you have sinned aginst more than God. Tell him so!

4. SING A PRAYER TO GOD.

Dear Lord and Father of mankind,
Forgive our foolish ways!
Reclothe us in our rightful mind;

In purer lives Thy service find,
In deeper rev'rence, praise.

Open your hymn book and sing the rest of the verses — or even sing another prayer song.

5. READ HIS WORD TO HIM!

His Word

[21]Meanwhile, the people were waiting for Zechariah and wondering why he stayed so long in the temple. [22]When he came out, he could not speak to them. They realized he had seen a vision in the temple, for he kept making signs to them but remained unable to speak. [23]When his time of service was completed, he returned home. [24]After this his wife Elizabeth became pregnant and for five months remained in seclusion. [25]"The Lord has done this for me," she said. "In these days he has shown his favor and taken away my disgrace among the people."
— Luke 1:21-25, NIV

Read His Word to Him.

The people in the temple for the public worship service were so much like people today: worried about the time or length of the public worship. Or was it their concern about how long it took the leader to fulfill his function? Only you know the hearts of those worshipers that day or today. I'm so glad this is so! Have I misread their wonder? I hope so. Bless your wonderful name, you always have a pleasant, unusual surprise ready for us! Any place where man draws aside to worship you can be a temple. Indeed, "your room" when we shut the door and look up to you becomes a temple. Have we seen a vision in our worship?

Please express your response to this beautiful text. Put your expression in your own prayer diary.

6. READ HIS WORD FOR YOURSELF.

Just for me. All over again, new and fresh and clean I want to absorb every word you have said in these verses. May I always out of my heart worship you in public. I am conscious of those present, and whatever part I have in the worship meeting, but I want to be supremely conscious of you! I do believe I communicate more eloquently by my body language, by my total attitude than I ever do by my words. Open up my inner most being to your love and power. One of these days the time for my service for you will be ended and I will go to my eternal home. What would it mean to me to not be able to speak for nine months? It would seem there was a dear good woman there who was full of humility, faith and praise — just like my dear wife. How blessed I am in her presence. Your best gift to me except salvation.

It is so important that you pause in his presence
and either audibly or in written form tell him all his word means to you.

7. READ HIS WORD IN THANKSGIVING.

It is always a blessing to approach this time of worship. (1) Thank you that there has always been a place where man can worship you. (2) Thank you for forms of worship that can be filled with your power. (3) Thank you for the discipline necessary to keep the form and enjoy the power. (4) Thank you for the deep joy and desire to meet you in worship. (5) Thank you that you have made man's mouth to praise you. (6) Thank you for the wonder of the birth of a child; our part and your part. (7) Thank you for your tender concern expressed in Elizabeth's pregnancy.

Give yourself to your own expression of gratitude — write it or speak it!

8. READ HIS WORD IN MEDITATION.

"Thus the Lord has done to me in the days when he looked on me, . . ." Children are indeed "the gifts of God." The whole person is a spirit — even as God as a whole person is spirit. We share his nature, therefore what really happened at conception is the entrance of spirit from God into the genetic combination provided by the mother (in this case Elizabeth) and the father (in this case Zechariah). The expression of the human spirit grows with the body, but the whole person is present at conception. We take all this to be included in Elizabeth's words: "Thus the Lord has done to me." The Lord sees us at all times, but there are special times (from our perspective) when he uses us in fulfillment of a larger plan than he has just for our own personal lives. A forerunner had been promised long ago. John was to be that forerunner.

Pause — wait — think — then express yourself in thoughtful praise or thanks.

9. READ HIS WORD FOR PETITIONS.

Zechariah was in the temple while the people were waiting and wondering. (1) Teach me to wait without anxiety. (2) Keep me mute if my words are not of faith. (3) What important word do you want me to speak for you today? Lead me to just the text I should use. (4) How I do long to be able to speak into the hearts of people — help me. (5) What an awesome responsibility each of us has as your priests — keep us sensitive. (6) Thank you that there are really no impossibilities with you. (7) May I say with Elizabeth — "The Lord has done this for me."

Please, please remember these are prayers — speak them — reword them!

10. READ HIS WORD AND WAIT — LISTEN — GOD SPEAKS!

In these words I hear your voice: (1) "I will not accept rejection of my word — I'll do it another way." (2) "You are my temple now; it is in you and through you I want to speak to my people today." (3) "Your repentance does not always change my plans."

11. INTERCESSION FOR THE LOST WORLD

India — Points for prayer: (1) *The 68,000,000 Muslims* are found all over India, and are more willing than ever before to listen to the Gospel, but there are only about 20 Christian workers seeking to witness to them. Pray for a greater concern for these people among the believers. (2) *The rural population* is generally poor, backward and unevangelized. Very few of the 700,000 villages of the land have any Bible believing witness. In North India there is an average of one church for every 2,000 villages.

12. SING PRAISES TO OUR LORD.

O could I speak the matchless worth,
O could I sound the glories forth
Which in my Savior shine,
I'd soar and touch the heav'nly strings,
And vie with Gabriel while he sings
In notes almost divine,
In notes almost divine.

WEEK TWENTY-NINE — THURSDAY

1. PRAISE GOD FOR WHO HE IS.

"The friendship of the Lord is for those who fear him, and he makes known to them his covenant" (Psa. 25:14). How wonderful to know the Great God of the universe wants to be my friend! Indeed, he wants to be a friend to all men. It is his essential nature to be friendly. This is almost more than I can assimilate. Friends visit about little things of personal interest, on a very local and limited scale. Could we say this of yourself? It is out of "fear" or reverence I say it is true! There are no unimportant subjects. There are subjects that do not edify—God will have little to say about our discussion of some subjects. He is interested. He does listen. But he is a true friend, and at times he will disagree with you. Most of the time there can be a warm exchange and communion in conversation, sometimes known as prayer.

Express yourself in adoration for this quality of God.
Speak it audibly or write out your praise in your own devotional journal.

2. PRAISE GOD FOR WHAT HE MEANS TO ME.

Just for me. It is in friendship and reverence his covenant is made known (experientially) to me. Dear heavenly, present Father, I do want to confide in you as with the dearest and nearest friend. I have no better or nearer friend. I want to absorb every word you have written in your book the Bible. I want to be very sensitive to the application of these words to my heart. I want to pause often and long before your other book: the world you have created and as I interrelate and intermingle your messages to me I can do what your Son asked me to to: to abide in your word and let your word abide in me. In truth you can come and enter my heart and eat and drink with me as a friend. Dear God, I love you!

How do you personally relate to the friendship of God, and God who is your Friend?
Speak it out or write it out. It is *so important* that you establish *your own* devotional journal.

3. CONFESSION OF SIN

All I have said has been (as you know) out of my heart—I hide nothing from you. At the same time, it is *not* true! So often I have ignored or slighted our friendship, for this I seek forgiveness. Truly I have communion with you. How wonderfully balanced is this concept: it is in reverent friendship that your covenant or agreement with me is made a reality! I confess sadly that your covenant could be much more fully known in my daily experience.

What personal sins do you want to confess? We *must* speak them to remove them.
Do it! *Now.* There is no one else you have sinned against more than God. Tell him so!

4. SING A PRAYER TO GOD.

Ere you left your room this morning,
Did you think to pray?
In the name of Christ our Savior,
Did you sue for loving favor,
As a shield today?

Oh, how praying rests the weary!
Prayer will change the night to day;
So in sorrow and in gladness,
Don't forget to pray.

Open your hymn book and sing the rest of the verses—or even sing another prayer song.

5. READ HIS WORD TO HIM!

His Word

1 A record of the genealogy of Jesus Christ the son of David, the son of Abraham:
²Abraham was the father of Isaac,
  Isaac the father of Jacob,
  Jacob the father of Judah and his brothers,
³Judah the father of Perez and Zerah, whose mother was Tamar,

Perez the father of Hezron,
Hezron the father of Ram,
⁴Ram the father of Amminadab,
Amminadab the father of Nahshon,
Nahshon the father of Salmon,

— Matthew 1:1-4, NIV

Read His Word to Him.

How good to think with you about the important people in the coming of your Son. Let me list each one and pause before your throne and ask for your insight of appreciation: (1) David—"he knew my heart." (2) Abraham—"he was my friend." (3) Isaac—"he obeyed even to death." (4) Jacob—"he did prevail." (5) Judah and his brothers—"he saved his brother." (6) Perez and Zerah by Tamar—"their mother was truly humble." (7) Hezron—"I know good things about him—you do not." (8) Ram—"an unknown important man." (9) Amminadab—"he was available and usable." (10) Nahshon—"he wanted to continue my covenant." (11) Salmon—"married the harlot who loved me."

Please express your response to this beautiful text. Put your expression in your own prayer diary.

6. READ HIS WORD FOR YOURSELF.

Of course the first thought is that if you can use these men and women you can use me. At the same time, I want to incorporate all the good qualities I see in their lives into my own. Dear Lord: (1) I do want to make my heart your heart. (2) How I do want to be a close constant companion of yourself. (3) How I do want to obey you from the heart — even when it hurts. (4) Change my name! I want to be your prince. (5) Joseph has won my heart, I want to keep him alive in my own heart. (6) Am I as anxious to have children in your family as Tamar was in hers? (7) Oh dear Lord, there are thousands of important people I do not know — I praise you for the larger picture. (8) What surprise do you have for me today? I know it will be good! (9) Salmon was such an unusual man — he was willing to risk ridicule and misunderstanding. I wait before you in the face of this company — what an incentive to run the race with patience!

It is so important that you pause in his presence
and either audibly or in written form tell him all his word means to you.

7. READ HIS WORD IN THANKSGIVING.

(1) Thank you for David the humble shepherd who became the humble king. (2) Thank you for Abraham the idol maker's son who became your friend. (3) Thank you for Isaac the unassuming man who honored you. (4) Thank you for Jacob who had his ultimate priorities straight. (5) Thank you for Tamar — sinned against but not bitter. (6) Thank you for Rahab, the harlot — who became the forgiven, the accepted, the honored. (7) Thank you for my dear Lord who was before all and after all.

Give yourself to your own expression of gratitude — write it or speak it!

8. READ HIS WORD IN MEDITATION.

"The book of the genealogy of Jesus Christ, the son of David, . . ." What book can really contain the record of the life of our Lord? How very carefully Matthew traces our Lord back to David the King of Israel! There are several fine lessons to learn here: (1) God in the person of his Son did want to identify with man — all men — all kinds of men. There is hardly a person alive who could not identify with one or more of the persons here mentioned. (2) Our Lord wanted us to know that women were a very real part of the record of his life. In each case the women were crucial to an answer, met a need, overcame a crisis. (3) He was indeed the Son of man and the Son of God. He was the King of the Jews and the Lord of glory. Praise him all men and angels!

Pause — wait — think — then express yourself in thoughtful praise or thanks.

9. READ HIS WORD FOR PETITIONS.

In the heritage of my Lord are requests for me: (1) My requests will be for the virtues I see in the lives of your servants. For David's humble heart. (2) For Abraham's invincible faith. (3) For Isaac's total submission. (4) For Jacob's change of character. (5) For Judah's respect for Joseph amid those who hated him. (6) For your grace in the life of Tamar. (7) For your mercy in the lives of very fallible men and women.

Right here add your personal requests — and his answers.

10. READ HIS WORD AND WAIT — LISTEN — GOD SPEAKS!

What do you say through these lists of names? (1) "I can use anyone who is willing to be my servant." (2) "I will use some who are unwilling." (3) "I will make some willing and others will never know I was at work."

11. INTERCESSION FOR THE LOST WORLD

India — Points for prayer: (1) *The upper and middle class Hindus* tend to despise the Christians for their low caste or tribal origin, and there are very few believers among them. (2) *States seeking to limit Christian evangelism* — Orissa and Madhya Pradesh have both passed laws making it very hard for anyone to change his religion. Pray that this may stimulate prayer and action by the believers, and also raise the quality of discipleship in the churches. (3) *Gujarat* — most of the Christians are of the lowest castes (road-sweepers, weavers and the tribal Bhil); 32 higher Hindu castes remain unreached, and the number of Christians (many nominal) is declining.

12. SING PRAISES TO OUR LORD.

O for a thousand tongues to sing
My great Redeemer's praise,

The glories of my God and King,
The triumphs of His grace.

WEEK TWENTY-NINE – FRIDAY

1. PRAISE GOD FOR WHO HE IS.

"The Lord is my light and my salvation; whom shall I fear? The Lord is the stronghold (or refuge) of my life, of whom shall I be afraid?" (Psa. 27:1). My dear wonderful Father, ever living Savior, ever present Holy Spirit. How I do want to enter fully into the attributes of yourself as here described! (1) You are the whole and final source of light. I have no light at all on any subject unless it comes from you. Light offers illumination and warmth. (2) You save me by a great payment of ransom. (3) You dispell all anxiety, all uncertainty. If you save me and illumine my way, what is there to fear? (4) I am so glad to run into my refuge—how very often do I need such a stronghold!

Express yourself in adoration for this quality of God.
Speak it audibly or write out your praise in your own devotional journal.

2. PRAISE GOD FOR WHAT HE MEANS TO ME.

I have selfishly thought of myself in the above expres-.sions—what is said of me can be and should be said of all men. Bless your wonderful name! Ah, there is always *much more* to say in worship and praise to yourself: (1) How beautiful to describe yourself with one word—and that word is *"light."* Light holds one's attention—most especially when there is a man in the center of that brightness. Even my blessed Lord! (2) Light blots out, removes by contrast all other interests. Dear God, how delightful to be lost to all else and just give myself wholly to yourself! But it really requires but little effort when you are brighter than the Syrian sun at noonday! (3) I am saved by light! How profoundly true this is! I walk with confidence when I have a total view of life—this you give me!

How do you personally relate to the light of God, and God who is Light?
Speak it out or write it out. It is *so important* that you establish *your own* devotional journal.

3. CONFESSION OF SIN

That I should walk in darkness or lose my way is the antithesis of all we have just offered in our worship to you. But such *does* happen. It is only when I am unwilling to confess my sin, unwilling to face and admit my stupidity and ignorance, that I walk in darkness. But, oh bless the Lord, when I confess my sin and purpose to forsake it, hate it, there is no more darkness, only light—the Light of life. Why should I hide in the dark when I can walk in the light?

What personal sins do you want to confess? We *must* speak them to remove them.
Do it! *Now.* There is no one else you have sinned against more than God. Tell him so!

4. SING A PRAYER TO GOD.

I am Thine, O Lord,
I have heard Thy voice,
And it told Thy love to me;
But I long to rise in the arms of faith,
And be closer drawn to Thee.

Draw me nearer, nearer, blessed Lord,
To the cross where Thou hast died;
Draw me nearer, nearer, nearer, blessed Lord,
To Thy precious, bleeding side.

Open your hymn book and sing the rest of the verses—or even sing another prayer song.

5. READ HIS WORD TO HIM!
His Word

[5]Salmon the father of Boaz, whose mother was Rahab,
Boaz the father of Obed, whose mother was Ruth,
Obed the father of Jesse,
[6]and Jesse the father of King David.
David was the father of Solomon,
whose mother had been Uriah's wife,

[7]Solomon the father of Rehoboam,
Rehoboam the father of Abijah,
Abijah the father of Asa,
[8]Asa the father of Jehoshaphat,
Jehoshaphat the father of Joram,
Joram the father of Uzziah,

— Matthew 1:5-8, NIV

Read His Word to Him.

I am so glad to read about some of the men and women with whom I am acquainted. I am even happier to know you know *all* about *all* of them. There is Boaz—what a good man he was. I see him in the fields of Bethlehem. You knew him from his birth, in his childhood, as a young adult. Dear Lord, he is but representative of all the men you have chosen, as these men chose you. I really know nothing about Obed, beyond the fact that he is the father of Jesse! He was David's grandfather. Did David, as a boy, visit him, talk with him? What a large family Jesse had! All of them known so well by yourself. There are no families from whom you want to be absent. How I wish I could see David's face as a shepherd boy in Jesse's home, or as the king upon his throne in Jerusalem.

Please express your response to this beautiful text. Put your expression in your own prayer diary.

6. READ HIS WORD FOR YOURSELF.

How often did Boaz discuss his mother's background? Remember, she was from the city of Ai. What did others say concerning her? And then when Boaz married Ruth from Moab tongues really began to wag! I really do not know if this is true, but if such persons were like people today it would have happened. Praise your name, you worked with and through and in spite of such unworthy people! This is a large encouragement to me for I can identify with each one of these persons. Then there is Solomon who was really not wholly Jewish—his mother was a Hittite—her name was Bathsheba! Dear Lord, you are saying over and over and over again that you can use *anyone* who is willing to be used. How I do want to be that one! What a spoiled child was Rehoboam! But he had a wonderful grandson named Asa. I do not want to forget the point of these names: it was from these persons and for these persons your Son came.

Pause in his presence and either audibly or in written form tell him all his word means to you.

7. READ HIS WORD IN THANKSGIVING.

Thank you Lord for: (1) Jehoshaphat, a wonderful king, who loved you and served you. He was not all you wanted him to be, but you loved him and taught him. (2) Thank you for Uzziah—it was in his day that you sent that wonderful prophet called Isaiah! (3) Thank you I do not need to feel responsible for the sins of anyone but myself. (4) Thank you for my place in history—for anyone's place—all known and important to you. (5) Thank you for the thousands of unrecorded lives, each of which contributed—all of them recorded in your heavenly history. (6) Thank you again for preserving the records through all these centuries. (7) Thank you for the importance of history to give depth and perspective to present life.

Give yourself to your own expression of gratitude—write it or speak it!

8. READ HIS WORD IN MEDITATION.

". . . *Abijah the father of Asa, and Asa the father of Jehoshaphat . . .*" Here are three generations from which we can learn much: (1) Abijah—he followed the evil ways of his father Rehoboam. He only reigned three years. He led in a war in which Israel lost one million men. He had fourteen wives, twenty-two sons and sixteen daughters. (2) Asa punished his own mother for idolatry. He reformed the people from their apostasy under his father. In his old age he was diseased in his feet. He was backslidden in his old age. (3) Jehoshaphat was one of the best kings of Judah. He honored the Lord, carried forward the reform of his father. He commissioned the Levites to instruct the people in the law. We give this information to remind ourselves God can and does use a wide variety of people in spite of themselves.

Pause—wait—think—then express yourself in thoughtful praise or thanks.

9. READ HIS WORD FOR PETITIONS.

Each life has many reasons for prayer: (1) For the unprejudiced love of Boaz. (2) For the courageous faith of Rahab. (3) For the selfless love of Ruth. (4) For the patience of Jesse. (5) For the early humility of Solomon. (6) For Nathan's courage with his friend David. (7) For the heavenly wisdom of Solomon.

Please, please remember these are prayers—speak them—reword them!

10. READ HIS WORD AND WAIT—LISTEN—GOD SPEAKS!

Speak to me in the lives of these men and women. (1) "There are many women like Ruth—do not be blind to their lives of service." (2) "No one is unimportant in the family of heaven." (3) "You are my only means of continuing my work in your generation."

11. INTERCESSION FOR THE LOST WORLD

India — Point for prayer: (1) *The North East* (The old Assam), now made into six states: *Assam*—there is considerable turning to the Lord among the Santal and the Oraon peoples. Most of the peoples remain unreached. Small fellowships are springing up in some centers. *Manipur*—most of the tribal people have become Christian, but the valley Meitei despise them, but are tired of Hinduism.

12. SING PRAISES TO OUR LORD.

There is a name I love to hear,
I love to sing its worth;
It sounds like music in mine ear,
The sweetest name on earth.

Oh, how I love Jesus,
Oh, how I love Jesus,
Oh, how I love Jesus,
Because He first loved me!

WEEK TWENTY-NINE — SATURDAY

1. PRAISE GOD FOR WHO HE IS.

"One thing have I asked of the Lord, that will I seek after; that I may dwell in the house of the Lord all the days of my life, to behold the beauty of the Lord, and to inquire in his temple" (Psa. 27:4). How very comforting to consider the characteristics of yourself as seen in this beautiful verse. I want to praise you that such qualities can be seen and admired by all the peoples of the world.

(1) You are a Father with a large house—full of the warm welcome of love. (2) You can provide such a house or presence with us right here and right now—so that we can prepare for eternity "all the days of my life." (3) There is a wondrous beauty in your presence—the beauty of power—of total knowledge without intimidation. (4) You want us to ask for help—in information or in personal help.

Express yourself in adoration for this quality of God.
Speak it audibly or write out your praise in your own devotional journal.

2. PRAISE GOD FOR WHAT HE MEANS TO ME.

Just for me (i.e., of myself I praise you). How harried my life becomes; how I need your relaxed atmosphere of love. How I need to feel the unqualified acceptance of your welcome! Praise your name! I do plan on seeking your presence today—I so sorely need it! I want you to express yourself through me—to live in me—I want to live in and through and of yourself. It is so good to be able to ask

questions of you and not feel less for asking (as if I should already know). You make me feel like you are thanking me for asking. I am not in the temple of David or Herod, but I am in the temple of yourself—along with all other Christians, a habitation for yourself through the Holy Spirit. How reassuring is this truth!

How do you personally relate to the fatherhood of God, and God who is Father?
Speak it out or write it out. It is *so important* that you establish *your own* devotional journal.

3. CONFESSION OF SIN

I guess the reason I ask is because I do not know or because I do not have that for which I ask. But I do purpose to seek after all the qualities we have just expressed. Dear Lord, I do not like living in the house of this world. All the attraction is an empty shame. Forgive me, forgive me for accepting Satan's invitation—it was a mistake, yea,

much more—a sin! When will I learn that this world has no answers for me, or anyone else?
"Meanness." This is what you have called elsewhere "perversity." When I am frustrated and unhappy with myself and my relationship with you, I am mean with others.

What personal sins do you want to confess? We *must* speak them to remove them.
Do it! *Now.* There is no one else you have sinned against more than God. Tell him so!

4. SING A PRAYER TO GOD.

I stand amazed in the presence
Of Jesus the Nazarene,
And wonder how He could love me,
A sinner, condemned, unclean.

How marvelous! how wonderful!
And my song shall ever be:
How marvelous! how wonderful
Is my Savior's love for me!

Open your hymn book and sing the rest of the verses—or even sing another prayer song.

5. READ HIS WORD TO HIM!
His Word

[9]Uzziah the father of Jotham,
Jotham the father of Ahaz,
Ahaz the father of Hezekiah,
[10]Hezekiah the father of Manasseh,
Manasseh the father of Amon,
Amon the father of Josiah,

[11]and Josiah the father of Jeconiah
and his brothers at the time of the exile to Babylon.
[12]After the exile to Babylon:
Jeconiah was the father of Shealtiel,
Shealtiel the father of Zerubbabel,

— Matthew 1:9-12, NIV

Read His Word to Him.

It would seem these many names offer no food for our souls. But names are people! You know what each one of them looked like. I have tried to see each of these men through the eyes of imagination. What did Jotham look like? He was 25 years old, and began to reign only after his father became a leper. What about the boy king, Josiah?

Like all young people, he could be and was influenced by those adults close to him. Only eight years old. Praise you that there was a priest who loved you and helped him. I am a priest and I can influence several eight-year-old kings today. What an influence for good is available everywhere if I only see it.

Please express your response to this beautiful text. Put your expression in your own prayer diary.

WEEK TWENTY-NINE — SATURDAY

6. READ HIS WORD FOR YOURSELF.

There is that terrible man called Ahaz! How I want to be warned. He sacrificed his own son on the altar of his personal ambition! Maybe he wasn't so bad, several men have done that in our day! God have mercy! He lived in the time of that greatest of all Old Testament preachers: Isaiah. It was to this king Isaiah made the beautiful Messianic prophecy of the virgin birth (Isa. 7:1-16). But what is a great preacher to someone who lives for sex, food and money? Then there was the son of this godless idolater—and what was his name? *Hezekiah*—one of the very finest kings in the history of Judah. Maybe he listened to the preacher Isaiah when he was a boy, instead of his father.

It is so important that you pause in his presence
and either audibly or in written form tell him all his word means to you.

7. READ HIS WORD IN THANKSGIVING.

(1) Thank you for Uzziah—it was in the year of his death Isaiah saw the Lord, high and lifted up! (2) Thank you for Jotham—he is a glaring example of what I do not want to be. (3) Thank you for Hezekiah—I have been in a tunnel he had dug in the ancient city of Jerusalem—a good man who really lived as you wanted him to. (4) Thank you for Manasseh—began reigning at twelve and reigned the longest of all kings. (5) Thank you for Amos the unknown man who had the name of a well known prophet. (6) Thank you for the boy king Josiah—he did much good by working through another. (7) Thank you for Jechoniah and his brothers—I do not know them, but you do! I will one day know so much more.

Give yourself to your own expression of gratitude—write it or speak it!

8. READ HIS WORD IN MEDITATION.

"*. . . at the time of the deportation to Babylon.*" What a time never to be forgotten that was! It would be interesting to hear all the reasons why it was nobody's fault that it happened. It happened and the Jews were at fault; but how easy it is to blame everyone else. When we are carried away captive by Satan, it is for the same reasons. A break with personal worship—all spirituality begins and ends with our own intimacy with our Lord. When we are not emotionally involved on a day-by-day basis, we are open to bondage.

Pause—wait—think—then express yourself in thoughtful praise or thanks.

9. READ HIS WORD FOR PETITIONS.

What a variety you have to work with! (1) I continue to pray for the admirable qualities I see in the lives of those you have chosen. For the energy in your service Uzziah used his rule. (2) For respect and reverence of Jotham. (3) For the lesson from Ahaz that a godly father does not necessarily produce a godly son. (4) For the devotion of Hezekiah in spite of all opposition. (5) For the genuine repentance of Manasseh. (6) For Josiah's acceptance of your word when once it was found. (7) For the warning that exile and bondage are still possible for our country.

Right here add your personal requests—and his answers.

10. READ HIS WORD AND WAIT—LISTEN—GOD SPEAKS!

Speak to me through this history: (1) "I have always had my preachers to speak to the needs of people." (2) "Each man will decide his own fate—not circumstances." (3) "My patience does finally run out."

11. INTERCESSION FOR THE LOST WORLD

India — Points for prayer: (1) *The North East: Arunachal Pradesh* on the north eastern frontier is made up of 40 different tribal peoples. The area is closed to all open Christian work. Most people are animists or Buddhists, but God is moving through children converted in mission schools in Assam and Christians from Nagaland. In spite of official persecution, there are growing churches with over 4,000 believers. (2) *Nagaland*—16 Naga tribes now 66% Christian. For years a war of independence by the Nagas has hindered the great potential for a great missionary movement from these people to the 43 million tribal peoples of all India. Revival broke out in some areas of Nagaland in 1976.

12. SING PRAISES TO OUR LORD.

Praise Him! praise Him!
Jesus, our blessed Redeemer!
Sing, O Earth, His wonderful love proclaim!
Hail Him! hail Him! highest archangels in glory;
Strength and honor give to His holy name!

Like a shepherd, Jesus will guard His children,
In His arms He carries them all day long:
Praise Him! praise Him! tell of his excellent greatness;
Praise Him! praise Him! ever in joyful song!

WEEK THIRTY — SUNDAY

1. PRAISE GOD FOR WHO HE IS.

"I believe that I shall see the goodness of the Lord in the land of the living! Wait for the Lord; be strong, and let your heart take courage; yea, wait for the Lord" (Psa. 27:13, 14)! I want to enter into the meaning of this text and fully appreciate all you are! It does help to list your qualities as seen here: (1) *Goodness*—such a complete quality! All that pleases and satisfies, all that complements and completes life is in this powerful word. There seems to be some hesitancy on the part of the psalmist. David is saying that he believes there will be a time when he shall see a perfect balance in all of life. He also says that this harmony will happen in the area of his own observation.

Express yourself in adoration for this quality of God.
Speak it audibly or write out your praise in your own devotional journal.

2. PRAISE GOD FOR WHAT HE MEANS TO ME.

Just for me. Dear Lord, the next quality of yourself is, and has been the hardest for me to assimilate, "Wait for the Lord." Wait for his time, wait for his fulfillment in me—in the world about me. It is only in time that waiting happens—there would be no waiting if there was no time. I am so glad to affirm that waiting has been better than not waiting. What you gave me after the waiting time was always better than I would have had without the wait. I have found strength and courage in this quality of yourself! Is there a process in action in the developing of my patience? Of course there is! "Let patience have its *perfect work*." Isn't that just like yourself! Why settle for less than the perfect—the mature or the fully grown?

How do you personally relate to the goodness of God, and God who is Good?
Speak it out or write it out. It is *so important* that you establish *your own* devotional journal.

3. CONFESSION OF SIN

It surely will not be difficult to confess my sin in this area! In spite of all the terrible, terrible inequities of life, I do believe you are absolute goodness and one day there will be a great day of equity! What an amazement that will be. But I have truly, often wondered why, oh why, some projects tarry? Why some plans must be delayed or laid aside. Impatience, anger, frustration, anxiety—all these are my sins. Forgive me! I do have such a constant struggle as to what is foolhardiness and what is faith.

What personal sins do you want to confess? We *must* speak them to remove them.
Do it! *Now.* There is no one else you have sinned against more than God. Tell him so!

4. SING A PRAYER TO GOD.

Crown Him with many crowns,
The Lamb upon His throne;
Hark! how the heav'nly anthem drowns
All music but its own!

Awake, my soul, and sing
Of Him who died for thee;
And hail Him as thy matchless King
Thro' all eternity.

Open your hymn book and sing the rest of the verses—or even sing another prayer song.

5. READ HIS WORD TO HIM!
His Word

¹²After the exile to Babylon:
  Jeconiah was the father of Shealtiel,
  Shealtiel the father of Zerubbabel,
¹³Zerubbabel the father of Abiud,
  Abiud the father of Eliakim,
  Eliakim the father of Azor,
¹⁴Azor the father of Zadok,
  Zadok the father of Akim,
  Akim the father of Eliud,
¹⁵Eliud the father of Eleazar,

Eleazar the father of Matthan,
  Matthan the father of Jacob,
¹⁶and Jacob the father of Joseph, the husband of Mary, of whom was born Jesus, who is called Christ.
¹⁷Thus there were fourteen generations in all from Abraham to David, fourteen from David to the exile of Babylon, and fourteen from the exile to the Christ.
— Matthew 1:12-17, NIV

Read His Word to Him.

Dear Lord, I am overwhelmed with the enormity of the task of thinking your thoughts about fourteen generations! They were all born one at a time. Each lived a life very important to him—and to you. Each of these people had relatives and friends. I want only to be able to praise you and honor your person as related to one of those fourteen: *Zerubbabel*. This man was born in Babylon. He must have loved and worshiped you with a fresh unselfishness to leave his home and go to Jerusalem to lead in rebuilding your temple.

Please express your response to this beautiful text. Put your expression in your own prayer diary.

6. READ HIS WORD FOR YOURSELF.

It is with Joseph and Mary I can relate! My father was a carpenter even as was Joseph. A dear good man he was. My father, like Joseph, lived and worked and died in obscurity. We would know utterly nothing about Joseph if it had not been for Jesus. Somehow I believe all of us will one day know all about all of us. We will have time (where there is no time) to appreciate fully "all the ways he led us to that blessed promised land." All the interesting details will be known about each of us. No one will be bored, or in a hurry or inattentive or lack real personal interest. How old was Joseph when he died and transferred to the Spirit world? My dad was 72. How many houses did Joseph build? How many yokes did he make? We know just nothing of his personal life. Is that important? It is to him!

Pause in his presence and either audibly or in written form tell him all his word means to you.

7. READ HIS WORD IN THANKSGIVING.

I want to try to thank you for carpenter Joseph—as he does remind me of my dear father: (1) Thank you for Joseph's unassuming honesty. (2) Thank you for his total willingness to assume responsibility. (3) Thank you for his spiritual sensitivity. (4) Thank you for his true and constant love for Mary. (5) Thank you for his willingness to leave his job and friends to save the baby from death. (6) Thank you for his close companionship with our Lord in his early years. (7) Thank you for his home where our Lord could find shelter and love.

Give yourself to your own expression of gratitude—write it or speak it!

8. READ HIS WORD IN MEDITATION.

"... Joseph the husband of Mary, of whom Jesus was born, who is called Christ." Let's think and pray for a few minutes about the mother of our Lord: (1) She was of the royal line of the house of David, but had no personal pride in this fact. (2) She was full of faith in God's messenger's promise, but asked a candid question as to just how God was to accomplish what he had promised. (3) She was in love with her husband Joseph, but more in love with the great God of the universe. (4) She lived in the midst of a wicked city, but was herself a virgin. (5) She lived in a busy demanding society, but she knew from study and meditation what God said in the scriptures. (6) She was totally immersed in the mundane routine of her household chores, but had a deep spiritual openness. (7) She did provide the seed, but God himself was the life of her womb.

Pause—wait—think—then express yourself in thoughtful praise or thanks.

9. READ HIS WORD FOR PETITIONS.

In these strange names (to most readers) there are nonetheless thoughts for prayer: (1) Zerubbabel: I need his divine determination to finish a task. (2) Eliakim: I want to be as faithful in bearing your message of good news. (3) Zadok: There are at least five men with this name. Am I ready to be anonymous? (4) Eliud: No record has been kept except by God. (5) Eleazar: Is it important that your name be remembered? (6) Jacob: It is enough to be the grandfather of the Messiah, even if by marriage. (7) Joseph: How I need the patient love of this man.

Please, please remember these are prayers—speak them—reword them!

10. READ HIS WORD AND WAIT—LISTEN—GOD SPEAKS!

Surely in these many generations there are words for me: (1) "I am yet at work through each family." (2) "I work through my larger family the church." (3) "I work very well through one man or one woman."

11. INTERCESSION FOR THE LOST WORLD

India — Points for prayer: (1) *The North East: Kashmir* is largely Muslim. Several missions work in the Kashmir Valley, but very few Christian groups. There are probably no more than six people converted out of Islam. A number of Indian missionaries from S. India have seen a turning to the Lord in neighboring Jammu. Ladakh, once evangelized by the Moravians, has a weak Christian community that is inter-marrying with Muslims. Pray for the conversion of nominal Christians and Muslims. (2) *Sikkim* in the sensitive mountainous border region between Bhutan and Nepal was taken over by India in 1975. Largely unevangelized and closed to mission work. The Nepali and Bhotia majority is virtually without a Bible believing witness, but there are about 1,500 believers among the minority ruling Lepcha people. (3) *The Laccadive Islands* west of India are Muslim and unevangelized.

12. SING PRAISES TO OUR LORD.

We praise Thee O God! for the Son of Thy love,
For Jesus who died, and is now gone above.
Hallelujah! Thine the glory;

Hallelujah! Amen!
Hallelujah! Thine the glory;
Revive us again.

1. PRAISE GOD FOR WHO HE IS.

"The Lord is my strength and my shield; in him my heart trusts; so I am helped, and my heart exalts, and with my song I give thanks to him" (Psa. 28:7). How good it is to examine this text for the attributes of the ruler of all. He is the sole source of strength for all men. How can men rejoice in their strength, whether physical, social or intellectual and assume it is of themselves? How all men do need protection from themselves and the enemy. We are open prey without the shield of yourself. You are the real source of trust—we can place our confidence in all you are and all you say. You have naught but good in mind for man. How important it is to know whom to thank! How vital it is to know the true source of praise and exaltation! I offer up to you these brief words to say praise you, but what I really mean is that all men should so praise you.

Express yourself in adoration for this quality of God.
Speak it audibly or write out your praise in your own devotional journal.

2. PRAISE GOD FOR WHAT HE MEANS TO ME.

Just for me. You are indeed and in truth my strength. How weak, helpless and vulnerable I am without you. When I fail to draw near I can know my strength of heart and hope are less and less. The closer I draw to you in praise and wonder the stronger I am. I do not want to face life without you. I refuse to look at the events of any one day without your protection. The longer I live, the less I trust men—at the same time, the more I trust you! In the "little things" of life I have been, I am being helped and my heart exalts; I am profoundly happy! I know not how to express my joy. How well do many songs say what I feel! Praise your name!

How do you personally relate to the strength of God, and God who is our strength?
Speak it out or write it out. It is *so important* that you establish *your own* devotional journal.

3. CONFESSION OF SIN

It is not always so! Dear Lord, you know I am more than foolish to be anything but wholly honest with you. It seems to me my largest problem is taking enough time to think your thoughts. Almost before I know it, I am trusting in my own strength or hiding behind my own fig leaves. This is not altogether true—the real problem is that you have not become such an essential part of me that my response is your response. Forgive me for this very fundamental sin.

"Always right." There are those who "justify themselves." There is always a way to shift blame. Dear God, I do not at all purpose to be in that number. I am guilty. I have sinned—I need and claim your forgiveness. I am not right at all—you are.

What personal sins do you want to confess? We *must* speak them to remove them.
Do it! *Now.* There is no one else you have sinned against more than God. Tell him so!

4. SING A PRAYER TO GOD.

Nearer, still nearer, close to Thy heart,
Draw me, my Savior, so precious Thou art;
Fold me, O fold me close to Thy breast,

Shelter me safe in that "Haven of Rest,"
Shelter me safe in that "Haven of Rest."

Open your hymn book and sing the rest of the verses—or even sing another prayer song.

5. READ HIS WORD TO HIM!

His Word

[26]In the sixth month, God sent the angel Gabriel to Nazareth, a town in Galilee, [27]to a virgin pledged to be married to a man named Joseph, a descendant of David. The virgin's name was Mary. [28]The angel went to her and said, "Greetings, you who are highly favored! The Lord is with you."

[29]Mary was greatly troubled at his words and wondered what kind of greeting this might be.   — *Luke 1:26-29, NIV*

Read His Word to Him.

I can hardly contain the excitement I feel in the presence of your word. When I try to contemplate how much is behind these words of your servant Luke, "I scarce can take it in." Luke is always so careful with details. He tells us of the progress of pregnancy with Elizabeth as related to the announcement of Gabriel to Mary. Is it at all possible to see these words as you do? Dear Lord, I want to try. What a pleasant surprise was coming for all in this little town of Nazareth! It would seem you specialize in surprises! I am surprised, as all would be who were not acquainted with the meaning of prophecy, that you would select a virgin. Couldn't you have infused an ordinary child with your power and turned him into your Son? Does he have to be your Son *literally*? It is a thousand times more exciting, and human and real this way! Praise your name!

Please express your reponse to this beautiful text. Put your expression in your own prayer diary.

WEEK THIRTY — MONDAY

6. READ HIS WORD FOR YOURSELF.

Just for me. Speak these words into my heart! Why select an engaged couple? Why not use a couple already married? It is easy to see that much more humility is required to accept what you did than any circumstance we might invent. You get honor and praise for your power and love. I gladly give this to you! I imagine the streets were dirty—the hours were long—life was one tedious monotony in Nazareth. Into this darkness shone your light! The darkness didn't understand it, but Mary did! The pots and vessels were old and broken, but Mary was new and whole! I want to see all the favor you saw in this lovely village maid.

It is so important that you pause in his presence and either audibly or in written form tell him all his word means to you.

7. READ HIS WORD IN THANKSGIVING.

This is a really fine thanksgiving passage: (1) Thank you for the interest of God in the mundane matter of pregnancy. (2) Thank you for the angel Gabriel—I do hope I can see him one day. (3) Thank you for the dear girl who kept herself for her husband—and for you. (4) Thank you for the seriousness of the marriage pledge—oh, that it were so today. (5) Thank you for the example Mary has been to the millions of girls named in her honor. (6) Thank you for the high favor you gave to Mary—may I meditate more fully upon it. (7) Thank you for the rebirth of your Son in our bodies in the person of the Holy Spirit.

Give yourself to your own expression of gratitude—write it or speak it!

8. READ HIS WORD IN MEDITATION.

"Greetings, you who are highly favored! The Lord is with you." In what sense shall we say of Mary that she was "highly favored"? "Full of unearned favor" would be another way of saying what the angel said about Mary. It was not her worthiness (although she was a very fine person)—it was the priceless privilege of being the mother of the Messiah that was prominent in this expression. She had willingness and yieldedness coupled with humility.

Pause—wait—think—then express yourself in thoughtful praise or thanks.

9. READ HIS WORD FOR PETITIONS.

Who knows, maybe our Lord was born in July. Surely there is much here about which to pray: (1) May the announcement of a "new birth" today into your family mean so much more to me. (2) Do I pay attention to the time and place of those who are "born from above"? Dear God, I want to. (3) Where is the joy of heaven repeated on earth when one sinner repents and is baptized? (4) How we need young women like Mary in your service today. (5) Thank you for the favor expressed by the angel for such a humble village maid. (6) Keep me as candid and honest as Mary. (7) Awaken me to a sense of your presence in me and with me now.

Right here add your personal requests—and his answers.

10. READ HIS WORD AND WAIT—LISTEN—GOD SPEAKS!

Speak to me through what was said to Mary: (1) "I am still sending angels on missions to help for those who will inherit salvation." (2) "If there were no domestic problems, my help would not be needed." (3) "Embarrassment can be another form of humility."

11. INTERCESSION FOR THE LOST WORLD

Indonesia — Population: 134,700,000. Growth rate— 2.1%. People per sq. km.—varies from Java's 644, to Irian Jaya's 2.

Points for prayer: (1) *One of the most significant movements* to Christianity in history is occurring in this great and diverse land with a great ingathering of souls. This is the only country in the world where significant numbers of Muslims have turned to Christ. Pray for a continued open door in the face of Communist threat and rising Muslim opposition. (2) *The great people movements* seen in Sumatra, Java and Kalimantan over the last 15 years were accelerated by the events surrounding the 1965 coup. The cruelty of the Communists and bloodthirsty Muslim reprisals caused revulsion among many, and the virtual outlawing of animism further helped to bring thousands of Muslims, ex-Communists and animists into the churches or open to the vigorous evangelistic work of many churches and missions.

12. SING PRAISES TO OUR LORD.

The great Physician now is near,
The sympathizing Jesus;
He speaks the drooping heart to cheer,
Oh, hear the voice of Jesus.

Sweetest note in seraph song,
Sweetest name on mortal tongue;
Seetest carol ever sung,
Jesus, blessed Jesus.

WEEK THIRTY — TUESDAY

1. PRAISE GOD FOR WHO HE IS.

"Ascribe to the Lord, O heavenly beings, (sons of God) ascribe to the Lord glory and strength. Ascribe to the Lord the glory of his name; worship the Lord in holy array" (Psa. 29:1, 2). If the hosts of heaven praise you, what is man that he is hesitant or unwilling to do so? The multiplied millions of angelic beings surround your throne and express their worship in adoration and praise. The particular expression of praise refers to your essential being described by the word "glory." There is no way we could ever imagine the overwhelming brightness or the stupendous beauty and endless variety of color the "sons of God" or the angels see in your presence. The impression of "strength" is such an interesting expression. This is the reaction of the angels when standing before you. I hear my Savior say: "Thy will be done on earth *as it is in heaven."* O, may my worship of you be at least a little like theirs.

Express yourself in adoration for this quality of God.
Speak it audibly or write out your praise in your own devotional journal.

2. PRAISE GOD FOR WHAT HE MEANS TO ME.

For me! O dear Lord, I do, I do want to ascribe to you your "glory and strength." I do want to express just as fully as I can the true "glory" or essential quality of your very self! I do feel like John of old—I want to face prostrate before you. My mouth is closed, I am speechless, I have no words. But a deep sense of wonder, of inexpressible joy wells up within me. How could it be that sinful man could be ushered into the presence of a holy God and sinless beings to be allowed to join in the array of billions of heavenly beings? Holy, holy, holy, Lord God Almighty!

How do you personally relate to the strength of God, and God who is our strength?
Speak it out or write it out. It is *so important* that you establish *your own* devotional journal.

3. CONFESSION OF SIN

That I do not feel this way much more often is in itself a sin! You have not changed—the angels have not left since David first sang this Psalm of praise to you. Is it a sin not to worship you? Surely this must be the capital crime! I do want to play the game of minutes today. That is I want to think of you each minute of this day. Considering the reality of the spirit world this is a reasonable response. Forgive me, forgive me! There is a wondrous beauty in your holiness. I feel as dead as the moon, but I can reflect your light. I am not dead, but alive forever more! I have a divine life and light. Dear, dear God help me to share it!

What personal sins do you want to confess? We *must* speak them to remove them.
Do it! *Now.* There is no one else you have sinned against more than God. Tell him so!

4. SING A PRAYER TO GOD.

Have you been to Jesus for the cleansing pow'r?
Are you washed in the blood of the Lamb?
Are you fully trusting in His grace this hour?
Are you washed in the blood of the Lamb?
Are you washed in the blood,

In the soul-cleansing blood of the Lamb?
Are your garments spotless?
Are they white as snow?
Are you washed in the blood of the Lamb?

Open your hymn book and sing the rest of the verses—or even sing another prayer song.

5. READ HIS WORD TO HIM!

His Word

[30]But the angel said to her, "Do not be afraid, Mary, you have found favor with God. [31]You will be with child and give birth to a son, and you are to give him the name Jesus. [32]He will be great and will be called the Son of the Most High. The Lord God will give him the throne of his father David, [33]and he will reign over the house of Jacob forever; his kingdom will never end."
[34]"How will this be," Mary asked the angel, "since I am a virgin?"
— *Luke 1:30-34, NIV*

Read His Word to Him.

How can I read these wonderful words back to you and tell you all they mean to me? More adequately I want to try to appreciate these words from your perspective. I know how woefully short I fall, but I do want to try. To give birth to a son called "the Son of the Most High." What an awesome thought! How little did *anyone* realize what was happening. Even those to whom you appeared and spoke did not know. How much did Mary understand? She seems to grasp the promise of a supernatural birth. Or did she? I feel totally inadequate to approximate a heavenly viewpoint. I do want to say I appreciate more each day the depth of these words. But I shall never know all their fulness.

Please express your response to this beautiful text. Put your expression in your own prayer diary.

6. READ HIS WORD FOR YOURSELF.

Just for me. "Do not be afraid"—"do not panic" would be the thought. It wasn't as if the name "Jesus" had never been used before—it was a very common name. The Greek form of the Hebrew, Joshua. Many women named their sons Jesus, but none of them for Mary's reason. Just how "great" would be Mary's son! Did Mary ever wonder about the throne of David? How very deeply did this village maid ponder these things in her heart? As Mary stood at the foot of his cross and read the sign "This is the King of the Jews" what did she think? Did she think about Gabriel's words? Dear Lord, I want to tarry long in the home of Mary and think deeply of all you meant when you became flesh and lived for such a little while among us. There are a couple of qualities I admire in Mary: (1) She was capable of wonder and amazement. (2) She was a virgin. Both are so tragically lacking now.

It is so important that you pause in his presence
and either audibly or in written form tell him all his word means to you.

7. READ HIS WORD IN THANKSGIVING.

What a joy to do. (1) Thank you for the understanding of angels—they know our limitations. (2) Thank you that angels also know our names. (3) Thank you that angels know our favor with God is in what we can do—not what we are. (4) Thank you for the precise detailed interest of angels such as: (a) You will become pregnant. (b) You will give birth to a child. (c) It will be a boy. (d) His name shall be "Jesus." (5) thank you for *your* definition of greatness. (6) Thank you that my Lord is on your throne in heaven. (7) Thank you that the rule of my Lord will never end.

Give yourself to your own expression of gratitude—write it or speak it!

8. READ HIS WORD IN MEDITATION.

"*. . . he will reign over the house of Jacob forever.*" Will there be a "house of Jacob" in heaven? As Jacob's name was changed to "Israel," so the tribes of Jacob have been changed to the new "Israel of God," even the body of his dear Son. The church is "the house of Jacob" now. Right now our Lord rules and reigns over each one who will receive his Lordship. One day *every* knee will bow to him. How blessed and beautiful is the thought that he rules with love and humility today to show us just how we can reign over our own house; whether it is our family, our employees or our own body. It was with a towel as he washed dirty feet that he ruled the hearts of his followers.

Pause—wait—think—then express yourself in thoughtful praise or thanks.

9. READ HIS WORD FOR PETITIONS.

In these precious familiar words there is much to lead us to prayer: (1) May I never lose the ability to be amazed at your goodness. (2) Mary's faith and love are such an example for all of us. (3) Our Lord has been formed in each of us as Christians at the new birth—how can I relate to this? (4) How glad I am to claim the meaning of the name of Jesus—or Savior for my life. (5) I want to exalt you indeed as "the Most High God" in my daily experience. (6) How can I relate to the present reign of my Lord? (7) Thank you for the promise of eternal rule on the part of my Lord.

Please, please remember these are prayers—speak them—reword them!

10. READ HIS WORD AND WAIT—LISTEN—GOD SPEAKS!

(1) "When I call a servant I also provide for the fulfillment of my purpose." (2) "This record of the birth of my Son will ever be fresh and new to those who have eyes to see." (3) "My Son now shares the glory that he had with me before be became flesh."

11. INTERCESSION FOR THE LOST WORLD

Indonesia — Point for prayer: (1) *There are acute dangers* in this rapid growth. Although God also gave revival to the churches in some areas, much of the Indonesian Church is nominal, and most do not yet understand about the new birth because earlier people movements were not well discipled due to the lack of Bible teachers. The same danger is there in the present movement. Pray for the raising up of many leaders and teachers who are able to bring these hungry souls into a living relationship with the Lord.

12. SING PRAISES TO OUR LORD.

I have found a friend in Jesus, He's everything to me,
He's the fairest of ten thousands to my soul;
The Lily of the Valley, in Him alone I see
All I need to cleanse and make me fully whole.

In sorrow He's my comfort, in trouble He's my stay,
He tells me every care on Him to roll:
He's the Lily of the Valley, the Bright and Morning Star,
He's the fairest of ten thousand to my soul.

WEEK THIRTY — WEDNESDAY

1. PRAISE GOD FOR WHO HE IS.

"The voice of the Lord is upon the waters; the God of glory thunders, the Lord, upon many waters. The voice of the Lord is powerful, the voice of the Lord is full of majesty" (Psa. 29:3, 4). In these verses the one quality of your character is that you communicate through words—"you speak." Three times over it is said: (1) Your voice is upon the waters. (2) Your voice is powerful. (3) Your voice is full of majesty. I am sure when I am ushered into your eternal presence I will hear you speak! Until that time I will with the psalmist simply make comparisons. Your voice has been compared to the roar or immense noise of a thundering water or waterfall. (cf. Rev. 19:6). I do want to enter into this comparison and appreciate all I can about you. (a) Such a noise can be and is all-consuming —the total person is overwhelmed by it. (b) It can be exhilarating by its very strangeness. (c) Man feels so small and weak in the face of this gigantic moving body of water. (d) It never ends. There seems to be no end to the volume of water. (e) The power present and that which could be transmitted is beyond human imagination.

Express yourself in adoration for this quality of God.
Speak it audibly or write out your praise in your own devotional journal.

2. PRAISE GOD FOR WHAT HE MEANS TO ME.

Just for me. Each time I try to keep my perspective objective it becomes impossible. I somehow turn it inward. I do indeed want to stand before "the voice of many waters." Is there anything, I mean *anything* more important to me than hearing your voice? Dear God, dear God, this is the type of total interest I want to give to your word! I love to sit before you and let you speak to me. May I so give myself to you that I am consumed by what you say! How often have I been filled with an exaltation and joy this world could not know or describe! It is the exhilaration of your presence—"the fullness of joy." But always as I embrace your word to my heart. I do not need to feel weak and small—I already am! I am weak, I am small. I need and want to be lost in you—my identity is in you and in your Son. At the same time, I, and all other men, are the *only* means you have for communicating your word! How humbling, how exalting!

How do you personally relate to the communication of God, and God who communicates?
Speak it out or write it out. It is *so important* that you establish *your own* devotional journal.

3. CONFESSION OF SIN

This is such a basic sin that when I have adequately confessed it I will have included all other sins in it. To confess that I have lived my life in a dry desert where just over the hill is a gigantic waterfall of the purest of water. Or to say it another way—I have stood blind before the "Voice of Many Waters" and thought it was the beating of my own heart. Dear, dear God, forgive me! How treasured a possession is your word to me. Why is it I have not memorized all of it? But behind your words is yourself. I do not worship the Bible, but the One who wrote it! May I do my worshiping all the time. Forgive my blind secular outlook!

What personal sins do you want to confess? We *must* speak them to remove them.
Do it! *Now.* There is no one else you have sinned against more than God. Tell him so!

4. SING A PRAYER TO GOD.

Sinners Jesus will receive;
Sound this word of grace to all
Who the heav'nly pathway leave,
All who linger, all who fall.

Sing it o'er. . . and o'er again;
Christ receiveth sinful men;
Make the message clear and plain:
Christ receiveth sinful men.

Open your hymn book and sing the rest of the verses—or even sing another prayer song.

5. READ HIS WORD TO HIM!

His Word

[35]The angel answered, "The Holy Spirit will come upon you, and the power of the Most High will overshadow you. So the holy one to be born will be called the Son of God. [36]Even Elizabeth your relative is going to have a child in her old age, and she who was said to be barren is in her sixth month. [37]For nothing is impossible with God.

[38]"I am the Lord's servant," Mary answered. "May it be to me as you have said." Then the angel left her.

— Luke 1:35-38, NIV

Read His Word to Him.

I shall attempt to take a new look at these words, just as if I read them in your presence for the very first time. The Holy Spirit is a person. I am convinced of this by the many intelligent capacities attributed to him. And by the constant use of the personal pronoun in reference to him. The phrase: "The Holy Spirit will come upon you," is tantamount of saying: "You will become pregnant from the Holy Spirit." The same thought is repeated in the lovely phrase: "The power of the Most High will over-shadow you." What a promise to make to this humble obscure girl. And then to go beyond the concept to the birth! What kind of a child would come out of her womb when the Holy Spirit was the father? The child to be born would be like the father: *holy* — and because God was the father he would be called "the Son of God." How many times did Mary tell this story? She no doubt told it to Luke. This is why it is so poignant, so beautiful, so full of the wonder of Mary. Praise your glorious name!

Please express your response to this beautiful text. Put your expression in your own prayer diary.

6. READ HIS WORD FOR YOURSELF.

Was it to give Mary encouragement that Gabriel de-scribed the pregnancy of Elizabeth? I believe it was. Since the impossible was accomplished with Elizabeth, it could also be with Mary. There was a vast difference in the impossibilities, but they were both by human standards, impossible. How I do revel in these words: "For with God nothing will be impossible." What would happen in our lives (in my life) if we found something in our experience that was in his will and stayed before his throne of grace until the impossible became a reality? We are like Mary, afraid! Dear God, push me beyond fear into faith. When you have said it, it *shall be* done! The blessed mother of my Lord said exactly what I want to say: "Behold, I am the hand maid (slave) of the Lord; let it be to me accord-ing to your word."

Pause in his presence and either audibly or in written form tell him all his word means to you.

7. READ HIS WORD IN THANKSGIVING.

This is a most blessed passage for this purpose: (1) Thank you for the unlimited power of the Holy Spirit. (2) Thank you for the personal interest and involvement God through the Holy Spirit has in our lives. (3) Thank you for the holy child born of Mary. (4) Thank you for the Son of God, born of Mary. (5) Thank you for the dear aged sister called Elizabeth. (6) Thank you for the call to live aware that really nothing is impossible when God is in it! (7) Thank you for the joy of being your slave!

Give yourself to your own expression of gratitude — write it or speak it!

8. READ HIS WORD IN MEDITATION.

"And the angel departed from her." Gabriel left, but other unseen angels stayed to minister to her needs. Since angels minister to those who inherit salvation we can not imagine a better candidate for the celestial realm than the mother of our Lord. Upon what other mission was Gabriel sent? In this case we could reverse the words of Peter about the desire of angels to look into the fulfill-ment of the Messianic prophecies. We would like to investigate their activities. I am glad I have the confidence that angels really never leave me or any other Christian.

Pause — wait — think — then express yourself in thoughtful praise or thanks.

9 READ HIS WORD FOR PETITIONS.

The incredible answer of a miracle birth. How I do *want* to worship you. (1) Grant that just now I may claim your promise of the Holy Spirit's presence in my body. (2) Keep me constantly aware of the power of yourself — even "the Most High." (3) Open my eyes to see your leadership in the incarnation. I believe; deepen my faith. (5) Make me more aware of your interest in people and their needs and struggles. (6) How interesting that you touch women at both ends of life — a village maid and an old woman.

Right here add your personal requests — and his answers.

10. READ HIS WORD AND WAIT — LISTEN — GOD SPEAKS!

In these words speak to me: (1) "The Holy Spirit is still conceiving for the new birth." (2) *"The Power of the Most High* has not abdicated." (3) "Nothing is impossible with me."

11. INTERCESSION FOR THE LOST WORLD

Indonesia — Point for prayer: (1) *The Muslim back-lash*, stimulated by over-enthusiastic reporting in the Christian press about the great turning of Muslims to the Lord in Java, has led to some persecution, rioting and destruction of some churches. The government has bowed to this pressure a bit. Pray that Christian leaders might know the Lord's plan for evangelizing Muslims.

12. SING PRAISES TO OUR LORD.

Holy, Holy, Holy, Lord God Almighty!
Early in the morning our song shall rise to Thee;

Holy, Holy, Holy! Merciful and Mighty!
God in Three Persons, blessed Trinity!

WEEK THIRTY – THURSDAY

1. PRAISE GOD FOR WHO HE IS.

"How abundant is thy goodness, which thou hast laid up for those who fear thee, and wrought for those who take refuge in thee, in the sight of the sons of men" (Psa. 31:19)! Let me mark the attributes of yourself I find in this beautiful verse: (1) Abundant goodness. (2) A personal interest in those who fear thee. (3) An abundance of goodness for those who take refuge in you. (4) A demonstration of your goodness in the presence of men.

I now claim these promises – not only for myself, but as a source of praise that this promise is for all who will accept its terms. You have a wonderful way of meeting all the needs of all men. Goodness in this connection is simply satisfying the longing heart. Man reaches out to find fulfillment in three areas: (1) For his flesh in sex and food. You promise here to show all men how abundant is your provision for those who worship you and hide themselves in you. (2) For possessions of life – "the desire of the eyes" – or what the eye can see and what man can claim for his own. Is there not enough in the world you have created for all men to have and to enjoy?

Express yourself in adoration for this quality of God.
Speak it audibly or write out your praise in your own devotional journal.

2. PRAISE GOD FOR WHAT HE MEANS TO ME.

For myself! Dear, dear Lord, I want to discover and claim – right here, right now – in the presence of all men your abundant provisions for the deepest needs of my life. (1) For my flesh I have indeed found, praise your name, abundant provision in the realm of sex – your provisions in my dear wife are indeed "abundant goodness." That I can control the intake of food and live in a strong body for many years is always before me. Dear Lord, I claim this promise. (2) Why, oh why, should I want more than food and clothes and only enough to cover my body and keep me warm? Dear Lord, I do want to relate all I have to yourself and your purposes – help me. (3) Indeed, indeed, have you provided abundant goodness in fulfillment of purpose – and it has been "in the sight of the sons of men."

How do you personally relate to the goodness of God, and God who is Good?
Speak it out or write it out. It is *so important* that you establish *your own* devotional journal.

3. CONFESSION OF SIN

Even as I write these words I know how woefully short I am in resting in your goodness. What a restless soul (life) I am! Why *must* I be constantly searching for a larger and fuller expression of what I consider good or valuable? When will I rest my mind and my will in your mind and your will? Your mind and your will is found in my total obedience to your word. It is when (and *only* when) I present my body as a living sacrifice – to be controlled and used as an animal was for the altar – that I will *experientially know* what your good and perfect will is for me. I like this little equation of reality: (1) presentation; (2) consecration; (3) revelation. Dear Lord, for today – forgive and help me to do it!

What personal sins do you want to confess? We *must* speak them to remove them.
Do it! *Now.* There is no one else you have sinned against more than God. Tell him so!

4. SING A PRAYER TO GOD.

From ev'ry stormy wind that blows,
From ev'ry swelling tide of woes,

There is a calm, a sure retreat:
'Tis found beneath the mercy seat.

Open your hymn book and sing the rest of the verses – or even sing another prayer song.

5. READ HIS WORD TO HIM!

His Word

³⁹ At that time Mary got ready and hurried to town in the hill country of Judah, ⁴⁰where she entered Zechariah's home and greeted Elizabeth. ⁴¹When Elizabeth heard Mary's greeting, the baby leaped in her womb, and Elizabeth was filled with the Holy Spirit. ⁴²In a loud voice she exclaimed: "Blessed are you among women, and blessed is the child you will bear! ⁴³But why am I so favored, that the mother of my Lord should come to me? ⁴⁴As soon as the sound of your greeting reached my ears, the baby in my womb leaped for joy. ⁴⁵Blessed is she who has believed that what the Lord has said to her will be accomplished!"
⁴⁶And Mary said:
"My soul praises the Lord

⁴⁷ and my spirit rejoices in God my Savior,
⁴⁸for he has been mindful of the humble state of his servant.
From now on all generations will call me blessed,
⁴⁹ for the Mighty One has done great things for me –
holy is his name.
⁵⁰His mercy extends to those who fear him,
from generation to generation.
⁵¹He has performed mighty deeds with his arm;
he has scattered those who are
proud in their inmost thoughts.
⁵²He has brought down rulers from their thrones
but has lifted up the humble.

– Luke 1:39-52, NIV

WEEK THIRTY — THURSDAY

Read His Word to Him.

I do want to walk those difficult miles from Nazareth to the hill country of Judea. I have been over these miles in an air-conditioned bus. Looking out the window of that bus I see Mary trugging along between the rocks on the rough hillside. What were her thoughts in what must have been at least a two day's walk? You went with her, you knew every thought. She must have known the location of the house of her kinswoman. Elizabeth was in another room when Mary entered. Mary called out some greeting —when Elizabeth recognized the voice of Mary there was a strong movement in the womb of the aged woman. Just how Elizabeth knew the baby leaped for joy only you could tell me.

Please express your response to this beautiful text. Put your expression in your own prayer diary.

6. READ HIS WORD FOR YOURSELF.

This I must do! This I *want* to do! How is it that Elizabeth said: "And blessed is she (Mary) who believed that there would be (or, for there will be) a fulfillment of what was spoken to her from the Lord." How did Mary's faith relate? I take this to mean: that God's word would come to pass regardless of whether man accepted it like Mary, or rejected it like Zechariah. But Mary was so much happier and full of peace and wonder when she did accept your word.

Pause in his presence and either audibly or in written form tell him all his word means to you.

7. READ HIS WORD IN THANKSGIVING.

I will confine the expression of joy and gratitude to Mary's song of praise. (1) Thank you for the totalness of Mary's praise—her soul, her spirit was involved. She wanted to enlarge upon the beauty of your character and rejoice in your presence—I do the same! (2) Thank you that you have regarded the low estate of all us sinners and have given us such a mighty salvation. (3) Thank you for every good, every great and every worthwhile thing in my life—all from you! (4) Thank you that every generation can enjoy the bounties that are ours in you.

Give yourself to your own expression of gratitude—write it or speak it!

8. READ HIS WORD IN MEDITATION.

"He has filled the hungry with good things, and the rich he has sent empty away." This is not a testimony of perverseness. The underlying principle of sowing and reaping is here. If we sow in the flesh and come to the Father of spirits to be filled we will be sent away empty. Those who come with a great hunger and thirst after righteousness will be filled with the good things of his righteousness. If we have "found" our life he has nothing to offer—but if we have "lost" our life he is ready to fill us with good things. It was the hungry maid of Nazareth who was filled with the good things of heaven. It was the rich in Herod's court who were sent empty away. May we repeat this law of the Spirit in our lives today.

Pause—wait—think—then express yourself in thoughtful praise or thanks.

9. READ HIS WORD FOR PETITIONS.

In Mary's visit and song there is so much about which to pray: (1) I want to be like Mary: "the Lord's servant." (2) I want to say out of my heart, "May it be to me as you have said." (3) Give me the sense of awe that filled the heart of Elizabeth. (4) May the impact of these words never leave me: ". . . the mother of my Lord"! (5) I want to be among the blessed who believe what you have said. (6) May my whole self praise and rejoice in you.

Please, please remember these are prayers—speak them—reword them!

10. READ HIS WORD AND WAIT—LISTEN—GOD SPEAKS!

In these lovely words speak to me: (1) "I lift up the humble." (2) "My mercy is always available to those who fear me." (3) "I will fill the hungry with good things."

11. INTERCESSION FOR THE LOST WORLD

Indonesia — Point for prayer: (1) *The churches* are strong and revived in some areas, nominal in others and virtually non-existent in yet others. *Nominalism* is rife in the islands which have been Christian for centuries.

12. SING PRAISES TO OUR LORD.

We would see Jesus, for the shadows lengthen
Across this little landscape of our life;
We would see Jesus, our weak faith to strengthen
For the last weariness, the final strife.

WEEK THIRTY — FRIDAY

1. PRAISE GOD FOR WHO HE IS.

"Yea, thou art my rock and my fortress; for thy name's sake lead me and guide me, take me out of the net which is hidden for me, for thou art my refuge" (Psa. 31:3, 4). Dear Father, there are such good, precious qualities of yourself in these two verses: (1) My rock — *the* rock of all men. (2) My fortress — a place of protection for all men. (3) You have the authority and ability to lead all men, i.e., as a group — and the same authority and ability to guide the feet of each one. (4) When I find myself trapped (as so often I do) — or when any man, every man does so find himself — you can extricate me, remove me from the net. I did not see the trap, but you did! (5) I do not want to hide from you in Satan's trap. I want to hide in you from Satan. Such you are and want to be for all men.

Express yourself in adoration for this quality of God.
Speak it audibly or write out your praise in your own devotional journal.

2. PRAISE GOD FOR WHAT HE MEANS TO ME.

Just for me. It is with strong desire I come to you this day. I do so want to personally claim all I see in these lovely verses. (1) I see a great rock, high on a hill — there is a shaded place beneath it. From this elevated position I can get a panoramic view of all the world. At the same time, I can go into the rock and it will close and Satan cannot enter; I am hidden and safe. (2) You are a great and mighty impregnable fortress. I hurry through the gates into the streets of my fortress city. There is absolutely no way Satan can reach me. It is good to know the limitations of our enemies' powers as well as the strength of our God. (3) The terms "lead" and "guide" are not synonyms. One word points out the way, the other identifies where to put your feet. How I praise you for this promise! (4) How often have I discovered Satan's snares — *too late!* Dear Lord, I believe you will point them out to me *before* I get there. (5) Rock and fortress and refuge of my soul — let me hide myself in you!

How do you personally relate to the protection of God, and God who is our Fortress?
Speak it out or write it out. It is *so important* that you establish *your own* devotional journal.

3. CONFESSION OF SIN

There is confession in my praise — for what you have said called it forth. I do want to think as carefully as I can upon the process of temptation: (1) *Doubt* — There must be a hesitancy, a lack of confidence or Satan would not have an approach to me. "Yea, hath God said?" is his insistent question. (2) *Desire* — This is exercised along with doubt — we separate them to think about temptation, but they come at the same time. (3) *Decision* — This, too, comes on the heels of doubt-desire — A decision *is* made and in that decision and by that decision, and of that decision, we *sin!* (4) *Death* follows, separation, estrangement, a deep disappointment! Dear Lord, analysis is of no value without *you* — only *you* as a divine personal presence can deliver me!

What personal sins do you want to confess? We *must* speak them to remove them.
Do it! *Now.* There is no one else you have sinned against more than God. Tell him so!

4. SING A PRAYER TO GOD.

O safe to the Rock that is higher than I,
My soul in it conflicts and sorrows would fly;
So sinful, so weary, Thine, Thine would I be;
Thou blest "Rock of Ages," I'm hiding in Thee.

Hiding in Thee,
Hiding in Thee,
Thou blest "Rock of Ages,"
I'm hiding in Thee.

Open your hymn book and sing the rest of the verses — or even sing another prayer song.

5. READ HIS WORD TO HIM!

His Word

[57] When it was time for Elizabeth to have her baby, she gave birth to a son. [58] Her neighbors and relatives heard that the Lord had shown her great mercy, and they shared her joy.
[59] On the eighth day they came to circumcise the child, and they were going to name him after his father Zechariah, [60] but his mother spoke up and said, "No! He is to be called John."
[61] They said to her, "There is no one among your relatives who has that name."
[62] Then they made signs to his father, to find out what he would like to name the child. [63] He asked for a writing tablet, and to everyone's astonishment he wrote, "His name is John." [64] Immediately his mouth was opened and and his tongue was loosed, and he began to speak, praising God. [65] The neighbors were all filled with awe, and throughout the hill country of Judea people were talking about all these things. [66] Everyone who heard this wondered about it, asking, "What then is this child going to be?" For the Lord's hand was with him.

— Luke 1:57-66, NIV

Read His Word to Him.

What a remarkable birth experience! In the house of Zechariah the midwives and the aged mother wonder together in the coming forth of that one our Lord said was the greatest born of woman. A man sent from God whose name was John. I know you are present at every birth, but in a special way were you there at this unusual blessed event. This little body was to be filled with the Holy Spirit from this day onward. How many of the neighbors and kinfolk really knew of the vast spiritual importance of this birth? Am I right in assuming that people then are like they are today: too taken up with the mundane to see the marvelous?

Please express your response to this beautiful text. Put your expression in your own prayer diary.

6. READ HIS WORD FOR YOURSELF.

Just for me. In the hill country of Judea something wonderful was happening. For four hundred years the voice of a prophet had not been heard. The voice of God's last great prophet is now raised in the cry of an infant for food. It is important that I see the significance of your naming this little one. I like to think you have something to do with the naming of each of us. After all, you will and do record our names in your own book of life! Most all of our names have a significant meaning. I have noticed you have a wonderful capacity for enabling us to live out the meaning of our names.

Pause in his presence and either audibly or in written form tell him all his word means to you.

7. READ HIS WORD IN THANKSGIVING.

(1) Thank you for your visit to us in the prophets and most of all in your Son. (2) Thank you for the power of your redeeming salvation. (3) Thank you for the hundreds of prophecies fulfilled in your Son. (4) Thank you so much for mercy or your personal expression of love. (5) Thank you for the constant assurance that you will keep your covenant and bless all the families of the earth. (6) Thank you for the daily forgiveness of sins through your tender mercy. (7) Thank you for "dayspring from on high." What refreshment I receive as I drink of him!

Give yourself to your own expression of gratitude—write it or speak it!

8. READ HIS WORD IN MEDITATION.

"And the child grew and became strong in spirit . . ." John the Baptist was in the wilderness almost all his life. The reader would imagine Luke to say that John became strong in body—which was no doubt true—but Luke mentions the inward man. We would imagine that since John was filled with the Holy Spirit from his birth that a reference to his spiritual growth would not be necessary, but it was. John was responsible for the fulfillment of God's purposes in his life in the same way we are. Just what did John do to grow "strong in spirit"? There are only three sources of growth so we know he must have cultivated all three: (1) Prayer—What type of prayer life did John have? (2) The study of God's word—Did John have access to the Old Testament scriptures through Zechariah? (3) Expression in teaching or preaching—To tell others is to grow ourselves.

Pause—wait—think—then express yourself in thoughtful praise or thanks.

9. READ HIS WORD FOR PETITIONS.

(1) May the birth of a baby never lose its wonder. (2) May I recognize your mercy in the lives of others. (3) Help me to sincerely share the joy of others. (4) May I remember the name you gave us at our new birth. (5) Teach me how important each person is.

Right here add your personal requests—and his answers.

10. READ HIS WORD AND WAIT—LISTEN—GOD SPEAKS!

What do you say to me here? (1) "Please accept the fact that every birth is so important I would die for any-one of them." (2) "Praise is one of the greatest blessings of life." (3) "I do have teachers today—listen to them."

11. INTERCESSION FOR THE LOST WORLD

Indonesia — Point for prayer: (1) *The churches: Liberal theology* is having an increasing influence. The younger preachers and the theological institutions are more affected than the older and senior leaders. Pray that the Bible may have its rightful place in the affections and teaching of the leaders.

12. SING PRAISES TO OUR LORD.

Christ has for sin atonement made,
What a wonderful Savior!
We are redeemed! the price is paid!

What a wonderful Savior!
What a wonderful Savior is Jesus, my Jesus!
What a wonderful Savior is Jesus, my Lord!

WEEK THIRTY — SATURDAY

1. PRAISE GOD FOR WHO HE IS.

"But I trust in thee, O Lord, I say, 'Thou art my God.' My times are in thy hand; . . . Let thy face shine on thy servant; save me in thy steadfast love" (Psa. 31:14, 15a, 16). It is a delight for me to express day after day another quality of yourself! (1) The use of the term "trust" here suggests Someone in whom or with whom confidence can be shared and not betrayed. How wonderful it would be if the whole world knew! David's expression: "Thou art my God" suggests true worship and a holy regard for One alto-gether worthy of adoration. (2) "My times are in your hands" — Oh, how reassurring to know that every day of man's life can be and should be ordered by yourself! I shall have no more days than those decided upon by yourself. The appointment for my death and the death of all men has already been made. (4) Look on me and all men with approval — "smile on me" is the thought of "Let thy face shine on thy servant."

Express yourself in adoration for this quality of God.
Speak it audibly or write out your praise in your own devotional journal.

2. PRAISE GOD FOR WHAT HE MEANS TO ME.

Just for me. "Save me in thy steadfast love." Steadfast love is all I need! My love is so terribly fluctuating! I am circumscribed by the limitations of the flesh — not nearly as much as I would want to imagine and excuse myself — but as compared to your steadfastness my record is indeed inadequate! It is the constancy of your love that saves me: (1) Your steadfast love saves me from losing heart and quitting. You have not given up on me — why should I give up on you? There will never, never be a time or place or circumstance when you do not love me. (2) Your steadfast love saves me from giving up on others — oh, oh, how sorely tempted I have been! There are those who to all my understanding are beyond help and hope, but then if I saw some of those whom you have saved I would take heart — a careful look at your steady love and concern and constant help are all I need to react the same way.

How do you personally relate to the love of God, and God who is Love?
Speak it out or write it out. It is *so important* that you establish *your own* devotional journal.

3. CONFESSION OF SIN

The sin of feverishness! Dear Lord, I am guilty! When will I rest in my "trust" in you? It is *not* necessary that I understand everything, or even a small part of everything, to let you be God! Forgive me for assuming your role! When I think I do not have enough time or when time is all I do have and for either reason I become anxious, dear Lord, forgive! When will I learn and accept the fact that "my times are in your hands"? I am so very glad that you can and do smile upon me. I claim the cleansing blood and with it your approval. There is approval in your eyes! Dear Lord, in thy steadfast love save me from myself. It is so good to begin anew, fresh and clean and saved!

What personal sins do you want to confess? We *must* speak them to remove them.
Do it! *Now.* There is no one else you have sinned against more than God. Tell him so!

4. SING A PRAYER TO GOD.

Praise Him! praise Him!
Jesus, our blessed Redeemer!
Sing, O Earth, His wonderful love proclaim!
Hail Him! hail Him! highest archangels in glory;
Strength and honor give to His holy name!

Like a shepherd, Jesus will guard His children,
In His arms He carries them all day long:
Praise Him! praise Him! tell of His excellent greatness;
Praise Him! praise Him! ever in joyful song!

Open your hymn book and sing the rest of the verses — or even sing another prayer song.

5. READ HIS WORD TO HIM!

His Word

[18]This is how the birth of Jesus Christ came about. His mother Mary was pledged to be married to Joseph, but before they came together, she was found to be with child through the Holy Spirit. [19]Because Joseph her husband was a righteous man and did not want to expose her to public disgrace, he had in mind to divorce her quietly.

[20]But after he had considered this, an angel of the Lord appeared to him in a dream and said, "Joseph son of David, do not be afraid to take Mary home as your wife, because what is conceived in her is from the Holy Spirit. [21]She will give birth to a son, and you are to give him the name Jesus, because he will save his people from their sins."

[22]All this took place to fulfill what the Lord had said through the prophet: [23]"The virgin will be with child and will give birth to a son, and they will call him Immanuel" — which means, "God with us."

[24]When Joseph woke up, he did what the angel of the Lord had commanded him and took Mary home as his wife. [25]But he had no union with her until she gave birth to a son. And he gave him the name Jesus.

— *Matthew 1:18-25, NIV*

Read His Word to Him.

It surely seems redundant in the extreme to read these lovely verses to you. But in the reading I will be able to praise you and wonder once again before the record of your incarnation. Speak to me, just as if these words were heard first by me: "This is how the birth of Jesus came about." I can see Mary standing with head down and eyes averted from her beloved Joseph. Mary's mother has brought her to Joseph to tell him the incredible news that she is pregnant with a child from the Holy Spirit. What a shock! Joseph could have made a public disgrace of Mary. Because he loved her, but most of all because he loved God, he chose a quiet way to solve this problem.

Please express your response to this beautiful text. Put your expression in your own prayer diary.

6. READ HIS WORD FOR YOURSELF.

I hope the above thoughts were acceptable to my dear Lord. They spoke so poignantly to my heart. Angels surely did have a large part in the birth of my Lord. This is as it would be expected. He came from the spirit world. The dream of Joseph must have been very vivid. It must have been so impressive as to leave no room for doubt. I thank you for the righteous, kind man called Joseph. I do wonder what he thought about the statement that Mary's son would "save his people from their sins." Did Joseph know enough to equate this with the promise of "the Christ"?

Pause in his presence and either audibly or in written form tell him all his word means to you.

7. READ HIS WORD IN THANKSGIVING.

We should lift one continual song of praise as we read those exquisite words: (1) Thank you for the candidness of the account — nothing hidden or ignored. (2) Thank you for Mary's humility in confronting Joseph with her problem. (3) Thank you for Joseph's desire to protect his beloved. (4) Thank you for your answer to our problem — always a surprise and always better. (5) Thank you for your constant interest in all of life — but your larger purpose that is also at work. (6) Thank you for this clear uncompromising statement of a miracle.

Give yourself to your own expression of gratitude — write it or speak it!

8. READ HIS WORD IN MEDITATION.

"But he had no union with her until she gave birth to a son." We are full of praise for both of these dear people. It would seem from Luke's narrative that Mary left very shortly after her wedding and visited for three months with Elizabeth. This was a most thoughtful thing to do. It could also have stopped some of the gossip of Nazareth. When she returned being three months pregnant she would have less to explain.

Pause — wait — think — then express yourself in thoughtful praise or thanks.

9. READ HIS WORD FOR PETITIONS.

How good it is to pray through these charming verses: (1) I want to read again just like I never read before just how your Son was born. (2) Help me to retain your estimate of the sanctity of promise for marriage. (3) May I be as honest and humble as Joseph. (4) Open my heart to the present work of the Holy Spirit in and through me. (5) Thank you for your thoughtful concern over Joseph's dilemma. (6) Fulfill the meaning of the name of your Son in my life. (7) It is possible to exercise self-control in sex relations — help me.

Please, please remember these are prayers — speak them — reword them!

10. READ HIS WORD AND WAIT — LISTEN — GOD SPEAKS!

You can and do communicate to me through these verses: (1) "Marriage is just as important today as in the day of Mary and Joseph." (2) "Fornication is still just as wrong now." (3) "Jesus is still the only Savior of the world."

11. INTERCESSION FOR THE LOST WORLD

Indonesia — Point for prayer: (1) *The churches: The training of leaders* — there is a desperate shortage of Christian workers, due to the explosive growth of the Church recently. Many preachers are ill-taught but the number and quality of the Bible seminaries and schools has grown. The great need is for the conversion of many who come for theological training, and then for the development of their walk with God and vision of the need of the lost.

12. SING PRAISES TO OUR LORD.

When morning gilds the skies,
My heart awaking cries:
May Jesus Christ be praised;

Alike at work and prayer
To Jesus I repair:
May Jesus Christ be praised.

WEEK THIRTY-ONE — SUNDAY

1. PRAISE GOD FOR WHO HE IS.

"Blessed is he whose transgression is forgiven, whose sin is covered. Blessed is the man to whom the Lord imputes no iniquity, and in whose spirit there is no deceit" (Psa. 32:1, 2). Oh, to list the qualities of yourself from this blessed text! (1) You want to make man happy. (2) You extend forgiveness, not condemnation. (3) You want to cover or remove man's sin. (4) You keep no record of sin, you rather offer "no condemnation." (5) You want total honesty and openness from us. Peace and confidence puts a smile on our face. When we know everything is right with you, we know all is right with everyone else. How delighted we are when we see a glad willingness to accept and overlook our willfulness. What a beautiful word is "forgiveness." When you cannot see our sin we can't either. Praise the Lord! Not only are we forgiven, but there is no record of wrong! Truly you have made provisions for the blessed or happy man.

Express yourself in adoration for this quality of God.
Speak it audibly or write out your praise in your own devotional journal.

2. PRAISE GOD FOR WHAT HE MEANS TO ME.

I do want to have that tranquility of spirit, that calmness of outlook, that inward joy from hope that you alone can give! Dear Lord, I do not want to need to constantly come to you for forgiveness of the same transgressions — and I am delighted, more than delighted, to say I have actually found it unnecessary; you *have* strengthened by your Spirit my inward man. Bless your name. When I do sin I know of your love and patience, but these qualities of yourself have won me to obey you! Dear Lord, my Lord, my boss, I *want* to be totally honest and open and free from all deceit! Praise your wonderful name! I love you. I yield. I obey you!

How do you personally relate to the forgiveness of God, and God who offers forgiveness?
Speak it out or write it out. It is *so important* that you establish *your own* devotional journal.

3. CONFESSION OF SIN

This is David's psalm, repeated by Paul, applied to us. David no doubt thought of his sin with Uriah's wife, i.e., since it was common knowledge in his kingdom. How is it we are more ashamed before men than we are before you? Dear Lord, I do freely and openly confess my sin, my sins to you! I come to you because I have sinned against you. I come to you to claim the forgiveness, the covering, the clear record you have promised. You have imputed something to me — it is absolute righteousness. I am more than happy to enter this place and position of "no condemnation"! Bless the Lord, O my soul! Happy is this man.

What personal sins do you want to confess? We *must* speak them to remove them.
Do it! *Now.* There is no one else you have sinned against more than God. Tell him so!

4. SING A PRAYER TO GOD.

Must Jesus bear the cross alone,
And all the world go free?

No; there's a cross for ev'ry one,
And there's a cross for me.

Open your hymn book and sing the rest of the verses — or even sing another prayer song.

5. READ HIS WORD TO HIM!

His Word

[57]When it was time for Elizabeth to have her baby, she gave birth to a son. [58]Her neighbors and relatives heard that the Lord had shown her great mercy, and they shared her joy.
[59]On the eighth day they came to circumcise the child, and they were going to name him after his father Zechariah, [60]but his mother spoke up and said, "No! He is to be called John."

[61]They said to her, "There is no one among your relatives who has that name."

[62]Then they made signs to his father, to find out what he would like to name the child. — *Luke 1:57-62, NIV*

Read His Word to Him.

How delighted I am to share with you in the joy of Elizabeth and Zechariah! It is one thing for a grandmother to rejoice in her grandchildren; it is surely something else for her to have a child in her old age. This was unheard of then, and so it has been since. What were the phrases repeated over and over in the home of Zechariah on that glad day? Were they: "It's amazing." or "How can it be?" Or perhaps: "This baby will indeed be some one great." All of these exclamations were true. All were to be surprised at his circumcision. What a strange seal or sign for your covenant! And yet it is not strange if we think more deeply. "His name shall be John." So was his name before his conception. How often must his mother have told him of the choice of his name?

Please express your response to this beautiful text. Put your expression in your own prayer diary.

6. READ HIS WORD FOR YOURSELF.

Just for me. Dear Lord, what great mercy have you shown to me. Yea, mercy upon mercy. It is a natural response to want to share our joy. I do want to tell to all my relatives and friends of the supernatural birth that has occurred in my house! Yea, the "new birth" of a child of the heavenly Father. It is not at all as easy to share this joy. My neighbors and relatives rejoice easily at physical blessings, or respond quickly to physical needs. But for spiritual blessings or hurting—they just do not know how to react. What a sad commentary on our immaturity. If we raise a prayer need it is almost always physical—if we tell of a blessing it is more money. Dear Lord, open my eyes!

It is so important that you pause in his presence
and either audibly or in written form tell him all his word means to you.

7. READ HIS WORD IN THANKSGIVING.

(1) Thank you for the love and respect shown by neighbors and relatives. (2) Thank you for the willingness of all to acknowledge the true source of praise and mercy. (3) Thank you for seven happy days of praise and rest Elizabeth had at home. (4) Thank you for the loyalty to your law seen in the lives of Elizabeth and Zechariah. (5) Thank you for the new name you gave to the child, and to all your children. (6) Thank you for the deference paid to the father. (7) Thank you for the circumcision of the heart we presently enjoy.

Give yourself to your own expression of gratitude—write it or speak it!

8. READ HIS WORD IN MEDITATION.

". . . then they made signs to his father, to find out what he would like to name the child." This was the one thing this dear priest wanted to say above everything else. Why wasn't his tongue loosed at the birth? Why wasn't his tongue freed after the pregnancy? Why wait until the circumcision? It is easy to see when we remember Zechariah knew the full meaning of the covenant. Circumcision was the seal of God's agreement with his people. It was during the sealing of the national covenant that God chose to fulfill his private covenant with Zechariah.

Pause—wait—think—then express yourself in thoughtful praise or thanks.

9. READ HIS WORD FOR PETITIONS.

What a happy and surprising occasion was the birth of John: (1) In the long annals of the birth of sons was there ever a happier mother than this dear old lady? May I appreciate your kindness. (2) Keep my heart tender toward birth and death. (3) For all the "great mercy" shown me I thank thee. (4) In the humbling mark of circumcision teach me of your intimate involvement in all of life. (5) There has never been born the son of a mother whose name you have not known—praise you for such knowledge. (6) Give me the determination of Elizabeth to do just what you have said. (7) Zechariah was clear as to your will for him and his son—may I have such a plain knowledge and full commitment.

Right here add your personal requests—and his answers.

10. READ HIS WORD AND WAIT—LISTEN—GOD SPEAKS!

In these words speak to me: (1) "As I have said before, nothing is impossible with me." (2) "No one is born that I do not rejoice." (3) "I want everyone to be born twice."

11. INTERCESSION FOR THE LOST WORLD

Indonesia — Points for prayer: (1) *The churches: Bible believing missions* have some first-class Bible schools. From these a stream of evangelistic teams have gone out all over the country and to other lands and these teams have been the cause of people movements in Irian Jaya, Kalimantan, S. Sumatra and Java, and the dramatic revival in Timor. (2) *Outreach*—the dramatic growth rate is now falling. Pray that the churches may all have a vision for outreach locally and to other unreached areas and islands. Much of Sumatra, parts of Java, Bali, Sumba, Sumbawa, Flores and E. Timor remain unreached.

12. SING PRAISES TO OUR LORD.

There is never a day so dreary,
There is never a night so long,
But the soul that is trusting Jesus
Will somewhere find a song.

Wonderful, wonderful Jesus,
In the heart He implanteth a song;
A song of deliv'rance, of courage, of strength,
In the heart He implanteth a song.

WEEK THIRTY-ONE — MONDAY

1. PRAISE GOD FOR WHO HE IS.

"I will instruct you and teach you the way you should go; I will counsel you with my eye upon you" (Psa. 32:8). Dear Lord, you are speaking to me. I hear you! I claim the promises of this verse from David. I know you want to instruct and teach me in the way I should go. There are three verbs here that tell me of your character. These are qualities of your essential being: (1) "I will instruct you." This seems to be personal teaching. There are various ways of teaching men. You use them all. Such as: *example, chastening, goodness, information.* (2) "I will teach you." This could refer to collective instruction—you do indeed have a large class to teach. Some good and some very poor students. (3) "I will counsel you." This is the promise of intimate direction for each and every man on earth.

Express yourself in adoration for this quality of God.
Speak it audibly or write out your praise in your own devotional journal.

2. PRAISE GOD FOR WHAT HE MEANS TO ME.

Just for me. I believe your word is the sum source of personal instruction I will receive. I want, therefore, to digest every word you have given me. If you give me life and strength I shall worship you and listen to you from each of the sixty-six documents of instruction. I shall, with many other disciples, sit at your feet as you teach me through the men and women you have helped write books. I am at present very profitably so engaged. Dear Lord, I know you have your eye upon me! Your intimate counsel is just for me with a purpose of love and personal concern. Dear Lord, I do not want to be stubborn or insensitive to your chastening or blessing.

How do you personally relate to the instruction and counsel of God, and God who is Instructor/Counselor?
Speak it out or write it out. It is *so important* that you establish *your own* devotional journal.

3. CONFESSION OF SIN

David's words in Psalm 32:5 are so deeply meaningful: "I acknowledged my sin to thee, and do not hide my iniquity; I said, 'I will confess my transgressions to the Lord.' then thou didst forgive the guilt of my sin."

It is honestly monotonous to confess the same basic sin. Sins of pride, flesh, selfishness—these are specific individual acts and attitudes, but only basic sins, only fundamental transgressions. The monotony is in the failure to have any permanent deliverance. Am I expecting too much? I really and truly do not want to continue in sin! It seems to me you are saying, "You will always need my forgiveness—if not I would lose you to independence and I do not want that kind of liberty."

What personal sins do you want to confess? We *must* speak them to remove them.
Do it! *Now.* There is no one else you have sinned against more than God. Tell him so!

4. SING A PRAYER TO GOD.

"Man of Sorrows," what a name
For the Son of God who came

Ruined sinners to reclaim!
Hallelujah! what a Savior!

Open your hymn book and sing the rest of the verses—or even sing another prayer song.

5. READ HIS WORD TO HIM!

His Word

[63]He asked for a writing tablet, and to everyone's astonishment he wrote, "His name is John." [64]Immediately his mouth was opened and his tongue was loosed, and he began to speak, praising God. [65]The neighbors were all filled with awe, and throughout the hill country of Judea people were talking about all these things. [66]Everyone who heard this wondered about it, asking, "What then is this child going to be?" For the Lord's hand was with him.

[67]His father Zechariah was filled with the Holy Spirit and prophesied:

[68]"Praise be to the Lord, the God of Israel,
because he has come and has redeemed his people.
[69]He has raised up a horn of salvation for us
in the house of his servant David
[70](as he said through his holy prophets of long ago),
[71]salvation from our enemies
and from the hand of all who hate us—
[72]to show mercy to our fathers
and to remember his holy covenant,
[73] the oath he swore to our father
Abraham:
[74]to rescue us from the hand of our enemies,
and to enable us to serve him without fear
[75] in holiness and righteousness
before him all our days.

— Luke 1:63-75, NIV

Read His Word to Him.

How good it is to worship through this word from you! Most of these words are a praise to you. It was no astonishment to you that Zechariah wrote: "His name is John." But it was good to see the astonishment on the faces of the

424

onlookers. It would seem you specialize in acts and words of astonishment. Our first response after a time of testing and trial should be praise. "Whom the Lord *loveth* he chastens." Dear Lord, isn't it your will today that through-out our city and country that all shall be filled with wonder? Perhaps you are saying to me: "Get it done in your town and let me take care of the country." How little do we know of the depth of the words of prophecy—help us!

Please express your response to this beautiful text. Put your expression in your own prayer diary.

6. READ HIS WORD FOR YOURSELF.

I can take the prophecy of Zechariah and learn and praise from it: (1) You have redeemed me! The price has been paid and I belong to you. (2) The power of my salvation is the good news. He was of the royal house of David —"King of the Jews." (3) What a deliverer he is! From every enemy of my life. There is not a sin that cannot be overcome through my Lord! (4) He indeed remembered his covenant with Abraham to bless every man in the seed of Abraham—the blessing through Abraham is my Lord! (5) I can serve him with fear—I am "justified by faith"— "there is therefore *now* no condemnation." I affirm all this prophecy first fulfilled in John but gladly related to my needs!

It is so important that you pause in his presence and either audibly or in written form tell him all his word means to you.

7. READ HIS WORD IN THANKSGIVING.

This is a blessed text for this purpose: (1) Thank you for an open mouth of praise—may it be mine. (2) Thank you for my Lord who is here referred to as "horn of salvation." (3) Thank you that our salvation does deliver us from all the enemies of our soul. (4) Thank you for your personal interest in my personal hurts. (5) Thank you for the power and beauty of holiness. (6) Thank you that men can be filled with awe and wonder—even today. (7) Thank you I have found the One of whom Moses and the prophets spoke!

Give yourself to your own expression of gratitude—write it or speak it!

8. READ HIS WORD IN MEDITATION.

". . . serve him without fear in holiness and righteousness before him all our days." How I do need the promises of this verse! It is so easy to fear the face of man. It is such a temptation to please man instead of yourself. What does it mean to serve you "in holiness"? The root meaning of the word is *separation*, or *apartness*. Perhaps this refers to our basic attitude: i.e., we are focusing our whole attention on you. The word is describing an absorption in worship that nothing around us can distract. Our holiness is in yourself—our total identity with you. What is said of the location of holiness is also true of our righteousness. John the Baptist is a good example of that kind of a man.

Pause—wait—think—then express yourself in thoughtful praise or thanks.

9. READ HIS WORD FOR PETITIONS.

"His name is John." Open my heart to ask of you according to your word: (1) Loose my tongue to speak your name to those who should hear it. (2) Move me to much more praise for your goodness. (3) Dear Lord, somehow help in publishing your name to my neighbors. (4) As I see children help me to see in them what you do. (5) Grant me grace to so yield myself to your Spirit's word that he might fill me. (6) What a price was paid for our redemption! Open my heart to appreciate it. (7) I do want to serve you in every way I can. Direct my opportunities.

Please, please remember these are prayers—speak them—reword them!

10. READ HIS WORD AND WAIT—LISTEN—GOD SPEAKS!

What do you say in these verses: (1) "The fulness of all time is upon us." (2) "How can I plan so well and men serve so poorly?" (3) "John is yet an example for all."

11. INTERCESSION FOR THE LOST WORLD

Indonesia — Point for prayer: (1) *Missionary vision* has resulted in the formation of Gospel teams that have spread the Gospel to other language groups. Pray for the development of this vision—Indonesia could mean much for world evangelism, especially the great unreached Muslim world.

12. SING PRAISES TO OUR LORD.

I love Thy Church, O God:
Her walls before Thee stand,

Dear as the apple of Thine eye,
And graven on Thy hand.

WEEK THIRTY-ONE — TUESDAY

1. PRAISE GOD FOR WHO HE IS.

"For the word of the Lord is upright; and all his work is done in faithfulness. He loves righteousness and justice; the earth is full of the steadfast love of the Lord" (Psa. 33:4, 5). Bless the Lord, Oh my soul, all that is in me, praise his holy name! What are the characteristics of yourself I see in these verses? They are: (1) Truthfulness so all your words stand inspection. (2) Faithfulness—you never promised to do and failed to fulfill. (3) Righteousness. (4) Justice. (5) Steadfast love. Oh that all men would praise you! How comforting it would be to be able to pray to one who was the very essence of all these qualities. All men can examine all your words as given in your book and find every one of them totally dependable. How many hundreds of promises have you made and kept? I have listed one thousand myself! I take "righteousness" to be in any given circumstance that which is appropriate and helpful. How well does this describe your actions! A beautiful balance is set for you in all of life—no question about any one of your decisions—perfect justice!

Express yourself in adoration for this quality of God.
Speak it audibly or write out your praise in your own devotional journal.

2. PRAISE GOD FOR WHAT HE MEANS TO ME.

Just for me. I am so very much comforted in doing what I recommend for all men. I do love your words, each of them and all of them. The more I examine them the more "upright" I find them. Total agreement with reality! What a long record I have of your promises fulfilled in my life! Whereas I have not kept or completed what was right I find no fault in the fact that your word is the norm and my infractions were (and are) a lens out of focus, static on the frequency of reality. I cannot and do not complain about justice in my experience. I see the regular invariable response of a perfect balance in every relationship of living—"justice" is always present. Praise your wonderful Person! Love, love, love is what I am given—the whole world of my experience with you is full of countless expressions of your love!

How do you personally relate to the uprightness of God, and God who is Upright?
Speak it out or write it out. It is *so important* that you establish *your own* devotional journal.

3. CONFESSION OF SIN

It is easy to praise you in the five areas indicated in these two verses; it is even easier to confess my sin in the same areas: (1) Your word is "upright" and stands inspection, but my words are not. I want them to be—I try —but I am a sinner here. (2) My works are started and not completed. My works turn out to be something other than I promised. (3) All my righteousness is imputed— given as a gift. I have none of myself! (4) Dear Lord, I try to be just and fair—mercy is my need! (5) How my life needs more and more expression of love!

What personal sins do you want to confess? We *must* speak them to remove them.
Do it! *Now.* There is no one else you have sinned against more than God. Tell him so!

4. SING A PRAYER TO GOD.

In the secret of His presence
  how my soul delights to hide!
Oh, how precious are the lessons
  which I learn at Jesus' side!

Earthly cares can never vex me,
  neither trials lay me low;
For when Satan comes to tempt me,
  to the secret place I go, to the secret place I go.

Open your hymn book and sing the rest of the verses—or even sing another prayer song.

5. READ HIS WORD TO HIM!
His Word

[76]And you, my child, will be called a
  prophet of the Most High;
  for you will go on before the Lord
  to prepare the way for him,
[77]to give his people the knowledge of salvation
  through the forgiveness of their sins,
[78]because of the tender mercy of our God, by which the rising sun will come to us from heaven
[79]to shine on those living in darkness
  and in the shadow of death,
  to guide our feet into the path of peace."
[80]And the child grew and became strong in spirit; and he lived in the desert until he appeared publicly to Israel.

— Luke 1:76-80, NIV

Read His Word to Him.

As I read this powerful text I think of your man Elijah as fulfilled in John the Baptist. Indeed both of them were "prophets of the Most High"—even of yourself. Elijah prepared the way in the long ago. John's preparation is much nearer your coming, but both were preparing the hearts of men to receive yourself. How I like the expression: "The knowledge of salvation." Such an experiential knowledge comes with the forgiveness of sins. Indeed real salvation is tantamount to the forgiveness of sin. We know we are saved when we know our sins are forgiven. The beautiful imagery of comparing the sun with your Son is lovely!

Please express your response to this beautiful text. Put your expression in your own prayer diary.

6. READ HIS WORD FOR YOURSELF.

This I shall gladly take up: (1) Out of your tender mercy, or your intimate interest in my daily needs, you cast a light upon my path and furnish a lamp for my feet. (2) I have been in the darkness of death—it was your tender mercy that reached me there—such was expressed in the sun of righteousness shining into my heart through the preaching of the good news. (3) You have led me into the way of "peace." Praise your name! It is so easy to be constantly embroiled in some area of controversy. I am full of joy and praise that my path has been one of peace.

Pause in his presence and either audibly or in written form tell him all his word means to you.

7. READ HIS WORD IN THANKSGIVING.

This text is full of possibilities: (1) Thank you for every one of your prophets—especially those of whom I am acquainted through their writings. (2) Thank you for the ministry of the forerunner. In a very real sense we are all forerunners of our glorious King. (3) Thank you for the sure knowledge that my sins are forgiven me for his name's sake. (4) Thank you for your daily tender mercy. (5) Thank you for the new rising Son (Sun) for every day. (6) Thank you for the beautiful phrase: "strong in spirit"—may it be said of me. (7) Thank you for all places of solitude where we could grow strong in our spirit.

Give yourself to your own expression of gratitude—write it or speak it!

8. READ HIS WORD IN MEDITATION.

". . . to guide our feet into the path of peace." What welcome words are these! There is no deeper need or more pervasive problem than peace. A calmness and tranquility of spirit is so much to be desired! But our Lord offers more! He is not only "our peace" in a personal sense, but he will guide our feet into the way of peace. Our whole life can be one of peacefulness. At the same time we hear Jesus say, "I came not to bring peace but a sword." How shall we reconcile these two thoughts? In one case he is discussing God and in the other man. His peace is like a sword to those who do not know him. The submission to the rule of the Prince of peace is strongly resisted by some people. Even those of our own household could resist such rule. Thus his peace (a yielding to his rule) becomes also a sword.

Pause—wait—think—then express yourself in thoughtful praise or thanks.

9. READ HIS WORD FOR PETITIONS.

In this beautiful description of John there is much about which we can pray: (1) I know you speak to us through your word and preachers—help me to listen. (2) May I prepare someone's heart today for your coming. (3) Salvation is "the forgiveness of sins." May I right now claim it. (4) Move me to appreciate ever more fully your tender mercy. (5) May the warmth of your Son be appreciated. (6) May the light of your Son shed his rays to the ends of the world. (7) May illumination of your Son remove all darkness from my heart.

Right here add your personal requests—and his answers.

10. READ HIS WORD AND WAIT—LISTEN—GOD SPEAKS!

In these words about John the Baptist speak to me: (1) "I still need those who will prepare hearts for my coming." (2) "Millions are still sitting in the darkness of ignorance." (3) "The shadow of death is fast approaching millions of those who will live forever in hell."

11. INTERCESSION FOR THE LOST WORLD

Indonesia — Points for prayer: (1) *The Chinese believers* are a large minority of the scattered Chinese population. There are many fine leaders and strong missionary-minded congregations in Java. There are also Chinese churches in W. Kalimantan, etc. Many Chinese believers are now being absorbed into the Indonesian churches. Over 12% of the Chinese are now Christian. (2) *Missions*—early efforts by Dutch and German missions were highly successful in the areas where they were permitted by the Dutch authorities. There are now about 1,300 missionaries. Many more are needed to do pioneer work, church planting, church support work and Bible teaching, etc.

12. SING PRAISES TO OUR LORD.

All people that on earth do dwell,
Sing to the Lord with cheerful voice;

Him serve with fear, His praise forth tell;
Come ye before Him and rejoice.

WEEK THIRTY-ONE — WEDNESDAY

1. PRAISE GOD FOR WHO HE IS.

"By the word of the Lord the heavens were made, and all their host by the breath of his mouth. "Let all the earth fear the Lord, let all the inhabitants of the world stand in awe of him! For he spoke, and it came to be; he commanded, and it stood forth" (Psa. 33:6, 8, 9). How marvelous are the qualities of yourself in these three verses: (1) You created the ten million—the ten billion galaxies by "the word" of your mouth. (2) Whereas you were the Creator, the Holy Spirit shared in such creation—for so we understand the expression: "the breath (Spirit) of your mouth." (3) There are no words to even begin to express the "holy awe" or "sacred fear" all men should have in the presence of such power and authority! The more we examine your handiwork the more amazed we are. Dear God, I bow in silence and wonder before you! How I want all men to do the same.

Express yourself in adoration for this quality of God.
Speak it audibly or write out your praise in your own devotional journal.

2. PRAISE HIM FOR WHAT HE MEANS TO ME.

I praise you for all you mean to me as described in these verses. I live in the midst of a humanist, evolutionist society. How much less faith does it take to believe your word than the speculations and vagaries of men! I see obvious and sometimes subtle evidences of your divine intelligence in your creation. Just the check-and-balance system you have built into your world is enough to indicate planning and purpose. I do honestly believe if I were Adam you would create this world all over again just for me. I want to walk in the cool of your garden of creation and hear your voice. If I will lie down on my back some clear dark night and look into your heavens, I shall be overcome with awe and praise!

How do you personally relate to the power of God, and God who is Creator?
Speak it out or write it out. It is *so important* that you establish *your own* devotional journal.

3. CONFESSION OF SIN

Surely I am confessing the parent sin of all sins. To fail to recognize and appreciate you as creator and sustainer is the essence of stupidity and selfishness. Oh, divine Father, oh Creator of all, I bow before you in wonder at my own insensitiveness—at my own blindness—forgive me! It is only in my awareness of your creative power and intelligence that I am able to proceed to an understanding of all else you have done and are doing in the history of man. Can the clay rebel against the potter? Can the wood resist the carpenter? Yet I have resisted you. Dear, dear God, forgive me. I submit, not passively but willingly, full of desire to *obey you!* Afraid and trembling within, not knowing what you might ask, but not at all afraid of you for you are Creator and Love at the same time.

What personal sins do you want to confess? We *must* speak them to remove them.
Do it! *Now.* There is no one else you have sinned against more than God. Tell him so!

4. SING A PRAYER TO GOD.

I have a Savior, He's pleading in glory,
A dear, loving Savior, tho' earth friends be few;
And now He is watching in tenderness o'er me,
But oh, that my Savior were your Savior, too.

For you I am praying,
For you I am praying,
For you I am praying,
I'm praying for you.

Open your hymn book and sing the rest of the verses—or even sing another prayer song.

5. READ HIS WORD TO HIM!

His Word

2 In those days Caesar Augustus issued a decree that a census should be taken of the entire Roman world. ²(This was the first census that took place while Quirinius was governor of Syria.) ³And everyone went to his own town to register.

⁴So Joseph also went up from the town of Nazareth in Galilee to Judea, to Bethlehem the town of David, because he belonged to the house and line of David. ⁵He went there to register with Mary, who was pledged to be married to him and was expecting a child.

— Luke 2:1-5, NIV

Read His Word to Him.

How long ago does it seem to me—a decree from a great one in his day—how soon he is gone and his decree forgotten! But it was so very important on that day when Mary and Joseph heard it. I must remind myself again that it is happening even now in your eternal presence—there is no time with you! What demands do the governments of men make upon others and themselves! I can visualize this event and I attempt to do so, but you are there all the time. To be of the royal line of David was a high honor,

428

but it did also mean a very long hard walk when it came time for the enrollment. Mary was in no condition to make such a trip. But make it she must. How almost incidental did all this seem which when viewed from our perspective was so very important. Mary must be in Bethlehem for the birth of your Son. So it is that in the ordinary affairs of men you worked out the eternal purposes of heaven. Blessed be your name forever.

Please express your response to this beautiful text. Put your expression in your own prayer diary.

6. READ HIS WORD FOR YOURSELF.

This will be easy and a pleasant task: In my day, even today, a decree has gone out from the King of all kings, and the Lord of all lords that all the world be enrolled in the Lamb's book of life. This was first given when our Lord was upon earth and was issued by him from the Mount of Olivet. All can be enrolled—in every city, village and hamlet someone can tell them of the good news and the recording angel can add their names to the eternal record. All that are thus enrolled become kings of the royal line of David's holy Son.

Pause in his presence and either audibly or in written form tell him all his word means to you.

7. READ HIS WORD IN THANKSGIVING.

(1) Thank you for your plan behind and above all the plans of men. (2) Thank you for the historical accuracy of Luke's account. (3) Thank you for every other unnamed person who also appeared at the place of enrollment— none of them unknown to our Lord. (4) Thank you for the faith and obedience seen in Mary and Joseph in the journey to Bethlehem. (5) Thank you for the example of obedience to the laws of the land, even when Caesar was the authority. (6) Thank you for the obvious love shared by Joseph and Mary.

Give yourself to your own expression of gratitude—write it or speak it!

8. READ HIS WORD IN MEDITATION.

"... Mary, his betrothed, who was with child." What were the thoughts of Joseph as he walked from Nazareth to Bethlehem? Was Joseph full of resentment against the government for making this unreasonable demand upon them? Was he worried that his livelihood was thus interrupted and he would not have enough for his family? Was Joseph adding up the grievances he had against God— and now here is one more? Was he hurt that other men could marry a virgin, but he must not unite with his wife until she delivers a baby? None of these were the thoughts of this good man. Not one word of complaint against the government is recorded. Joseph and Mary had four other sons and at least two daughters. He was able to provide.

Pause—wait—think—then express yourself in thoughtful praise or thanks.

9. READ HIS WORD FOR PETITIONS.

These verses have become so familiar we sometimes forget what they say: (1) We could reach the whole world with the good news today. Oh, how shall we do it! (2) You have ways of working through men's decrees—do it again! (3) Keep me ready to obey the laws of the land. (4) Thank you for the royal blood in the lineage of my Lord. (5) A royal carpenter! What a wonder—but then all Christians are royal priests! (6) Oh, the humility in the birth of my Lord—break my pride, dear Lord. (7) Are we as concerned about the expectation of new births as we are in physical births? I want to be.

Please, please remember these are prayers—speak them—reword them!

10. READ HIS WORD AND WAIT—LISTEN—GOD SPEAKS!

From Nazareth to Bethlehem—speak to me: (1) "Nothing in the lives of my children is unimportant." (2) "Both Mary and Joseph were subject to the same limitations you are." (3) "Leaders seldom know of the most important people under their rule."

11. INTERCESSION FOR THE LOST WORLD

Indonesia — Points for prayer: (1) Student witness—a largely neglected, but ripe harvest field. There are wonderful openings to teach the Bible in primary and secondary schools, and also to witness to the 250,000 university students in 24 universities, but the laborers are too few. (2) Christian literature—there is a colossal appetite for any evangelistic literature—pray for the many printing presses working on this, and for the distribution thereof.

12. SING PRAISES TO OUR LORD.

Bearing shame and scoffing rude,
In my place condemned He stood;

Sealed my pardon with His blood;
Hallelujah! what a Savior!

WEEK THIRTY-ONE — THURSDAY

1. PRAISE GOD FOR WHO HE IS.

"The Lord looks down from heaven, he sees all the sons of men; . . . he who fashions the hearts of them all, and observes all their deeds" (Psa. 33:13, 15). What an amazing quality of yourself is seen here! You are the silent, intelligent observer of all men. You fashioned or thoughtfully made the hearts or spirits of all men. You look on with great interest at all the deeds of all men. This is omniscience and omnipresence in action. *All* the sons of men are six billion human beings! Most of these sons of men couldn't care less if you see them or not. How wonderfully enlightening it would be to discover that the very One who created the world and the heavens and in whose image they are formed is a very, very interested observer of all they are and do! This is mind staggering! It cannot be that what you see does not move you. Your steadfast love reaches out to every single one of those 5,000,000 refugees in Africa or the millions who starve for your word and your Son around the world.

Express yourself in adoration for this quality of God.
Speak it audibly or write out your praise in your own devotional journal.

2. PRAISE GOD FOR WHAT HE MEANS TO ME.

Just for me — what is it this means to me? It is more than easy to blame you — to call you totally insensitive. It would be easy to think that whereas you see us you are actually a gigantic all-knowing Observer of a complicated machine you have made and are only waiting until it runs down. If we use the smaller model in the nation of Israel we can see you are anything but a disinterested onlooker. At the same time, there were centuries when man ignored you and went his own way. You have made more than adequate provisions for man. Any generation that wants to can spread your word to every person in every tribe in all the world. No generation today need spend its days without you. You have furnished the means; we have the responsibility to use them. I believe you are only waiting for man to act upon your command through your Son. This could be, and probably is, a monstrous oversimplification. But I do not blame you!

How do you personally relate to the omniscience of God, and God who is interested?
Speak it out or write it out. It is *so important* that you establish *your own* devotional journal.

3. CONFESSION OF SIN

I do want to open up to you and get my guilt out and forgiven. If I am not willing to speak to every man in the community where I live why should I blame anyone else? I and every Christian must go to everyone in his world before everyone in your great world will ever be reached. I am committed to forty days of calling upon everyone in our community. But I have been committed by you for many years to the same task. I have stumbled around in a feeble effort. Dear God, dear God, forgive me! You read my heart and see my deeds. Dear Lord, forgive! I do purpose not only to plan better, but to *do* better! How can you hold the poor unsaved man responsible for not hearing when it is my fault he has never heard? I take his place. I truly believe there will be less responsibility upon any one of the 5,000,000 refugees than upon 5,000,000 church members. Have mercy, O Lord!

What personal sins do you want to confess? We *must* speak them to remove them.
Do it! *Now.* There is no one else you have sinned against more than God. Tell him so!

4. SING A PRAYER TO GOD.

Abide with me: fast falls the eventide;
The darkness deepens; Lord, with me abide:

When other helpers fail, and comforts flee,
Help of the helpless, O abide with me!

Open your hymn book and sing the rest of the verses — or even sing another prayer song.

5. READ HIS WORD TO HIM!

His Word

[6]While they were there, the time came for the baby to be born, [7]and she gave birth to her firstborn, a son. She wrapped him in strips of cloth and placed him in a manger, because there was no room for them in the inn.
[8]And there were shepherds living out in the fields near-by, keeping watch over their flocks at night. [9]An angel of the Lord appeared to them, and the glory of the Lord shone around them, and they were terrified.

— *Luke 2:6-9, NIV*

Read His Word to Him.

Shall I ever be able to read this record with the meaning there ought to be in these verses? I am sure you read them in a much different way than I do. How wonderfully subtle are all your ways — or at least most of your ways. What reads like an almost incidental event is actually the culmination of millenniums of preparation! Even the casual circumstance of not having a reservation in the inn — to be shunted out to the cattle stall was all planned — "in his

430

humiliation his judgment was taken away"—not only at his trial before Pilate but in his birth we all would have failed to see who lay in the manger. Oh, dear Father, I am kneeling again with the shepherds before the birth of your Son! Forgive me and accept my praise.

Please express your response to this beautiful text. Put your expession in your own prayer diary.

6. READ HIS WORD FOR YOURSELF.

Once again I could not stay apart from the blessed scene. Joseph helped Mary in the birth of her son. Who else would even be there but Joseph? You surely gave this dear man more than recompense for his faith and patience. Did Joseph live long enough to know what really happened when he helped his beloved in the hour of her pain and joy? I would like to believe he did. I want to go out to the shepherd's fields and share the amazement and fear of these humble men. The angel (was it Gabriel?) was clearly visible—what appearance did he have? Was he smiling? Serious? I believe he was full of the wonder and importance of his mission and it was reflected in his face. The bright beauty of the light from heaven shown around them. Praise your name forever!

Pause in his presence and either audibly or in written form tell him all his word means to you.

7. READ HIS WORD IN THANKSGIVING.

It does seem altogether appropriate to offer our deepest gratitude just here: (1) Thank you for Mary's willingness to suffer that she and all the world might have joy. (2) Thank you for the stark simplicity of Luke's description of the birth. (3) Thank you that Joseph was there—no doubt to help Mary. (4) Thank you for your choice of those who were given the birth announcement. (5) Thank you for again reminding us that angels are always the unseen participants in all of life. (6) Thank you for the incarnation of yourself in the person of your Son. (7) Thank you for the incarnation of your Son in our poor selves.

Give yourself to your own expression of gratitude—write it or speak it!

8. READ HIS WORD IN MEDITATION.

"Because there was no place for them in the inn." What a contrast! There was plenty of room for him in the universe—he created it all. There was more than enough room for him in heaven—a tumultuous welcome awaited him. There was room for the rich when he was rich beyond human comparison. There was room for the powerful when he had all power in heaven and on earth. But here all men could see was a wee little baby. How differently did God look at the stable scene in Bethlehem! Perhaps God was thinking that the particular place in Bethlehem was of very little consequence since his standard of status and station was not the same as those who did not even know him. Dear Lord, we know you, I want my heart to be a warm place—a pure place for your birth. Welcome Lord Jesus!

Pause—wait—think—then express yourself in thoughtful praise or thanks.

9. READ HIS WORD FOR PETITIONS.

At the birth of our Lord surely we can find many petitions: (1) Keep me aware again of just how time began at Bethlehem. (2) What a humble birth! There was pain and poverty and little help. Why should I complain? Forgive me! (3) What did Mary see when she looked at that precious little bundle? Open my eyes. (4) I want to make room for you in my house. (5) I have the privilege of announcing his birth. May I do it. (6) Why did you choose a shepherd to whom to tell of his birth? (7) Give me a fresh understanding of all the details of his coming.

Right here add your personal requests—and his answers.

10. READ HIS WORD AND WAIT—LISTEN—GOD SPEAKS!

Speak to me in this beautiful account: (1) "It is time for my Son to be born all over again in the hearts of men." (2) "His birth teaches you many lessons—pause long before the manger." (3) "Only humble men will appreciate my coming into the world."

11. INTERCESSION FOR THE LOST WORLD

Indonesia — Point for prayer: (1) *Bible translation* is still a pressing need for the many small languages of Irian Jaya. The rapid spread of the use of Indonesian lessens the need for many more translations of the Bible, but much primary translation and also revision is still needed.

12. SING PRAISES TO OUR LORD.

Come, we that love the Lord,
And let our joys be known;

Join in a song with sweet accord,
And thus surround the throne.

WEEK THIRTY-ONE — FRIDAY

1. PRAISE GOD FOR WHO HE IS.

"Our soul waits for the Lord; he is our help and shield. Yea, our heart is glad in him, because we trust in his holy name. Let thy steadfast love, O Lord, be upon us, even as we hope in thee" (Psa. 33:20-22). It would seem to most men that most of their time is spent "waiting for the Lord." If we have our own plans which we fondly hope are his plans then we wait and wait and wait to see them find fulfillment. This is fundamentally wrong! Move right ahead in whatever plan you have (and we assume you want to please him) and God will let you know what he thinks of your project. He will either oppose it or help it. In between are many variations of opposition or help. But God is in them all. We are glad; we do trust in him. In him we live and move and have our total being or life. God works through our actions not our anxieties.

Express yourself in adoration for this quality of God.
Speak it audibly or write out your praise in your own devotional journal.

2. PRAISE GOD FOR WHAT HE MEANS TO ME.

For me: How delighted I am to worship before you! My whole life (soul) waits each day before you. This is my constant position—not one I take only in the morning. You are indeed all my help and protection. You are going to help me today in ways I cannot even now imagine. You will and do protect me from my own ignorance and selfishness, and from Satan's efforts to defeat me! My mind, will, emotions and conscience or "my heart" is glad in you. When I think your thoughts, will your will, I feel your emotions and I am unspeakably glad! Dear Lord, how, oh how I want to say "I trust totally in your essential Being." In your Holy Name or your Holy Person I put my confidence. Indeed, indeed how steadfast is your love!

How do you personally relate to the help of God, and God who is our Helper?
Speak it out or write it out. It is *so important* that you establish *your own* devotional journal.

3. CONFESSION OF SIN

Dear Father, you know how often I have violated the very truth I have just expressed! Instead of holding my confidence in your interest I have ignored you and plunged into my own ways—which in so many instances were folly. Forgive me! Help me, dear Lord, to act under your all-seeing eye! I have sought help and protection from so many other sources of my own invention. How stead- fast is your love that brought me back again and again to yourself! Dear, dear Father, I want to one day be able to say that the sum of my gladness is in my trust in your character. There *is* hope in you—the *only* hope for this otherwise hopeless life. Bless your holy name, it is so exciting to watch and see what you will do today!

What personal sins do you want to confess? We *must* speak them to remove them.
Do it! *Now.* There is no one else you have sinned against more than God. Tell him so!

4. SING A PRAYER TO GOD.

True-hearted, whole-hearted, faithful and loyal,
King of our lives by Thy grace we will be;
Under the standard exalted and royal,
Strong in Thy strength we will battle for Thee.

Peal out the watchword! silence it never!
Song of our spirits, rejoicing and free;
Peal out the watchword! loyal forever,
King of our lives, by Thy grace we will be.

Open your hymn book and sing the rest of the verses—or even sing another prayer song.

5. READ HIS WORD TO HIM!

His Word

[10]But the angel said to them, "Do not be afraid. I bring you good news of great joy that will be for all the people. [11]Today in the town of David a Savior has been born to you; he is Christ the Lord. [12]This will be a sign to you: You will find a baby wrapped in strips of cloth and lying in a manger."

[13]Suddenly a great company of the heavenly host appeared with the angel, praising God and saying,

[14]"Glory to God in the higest,
    and on earth peace to men on
        whom his favor rests."

[15]When the angels had left them and gone into heaven, the shepherds said to one another, "Let's go to Bethlehem and see this thing that has happened, which the Lord has told us about."
— Luke 2:10-15, NIV

Read His Word to Him.

The best I can do with this overwhelming text is to list all this means to all the world—and even as I write these words I know how presumptuous such a statement is. Here is all my small cup will hold: (1) I need not come groveling into your presence—there is a welcome here, a heavenly warm welcome. (2) There is amazement—indicated in the one wonderful word: *"behold"*! (3) There is the greatest, grandest good news this poor tired world has ever heard. This news carries "great joy" for the angels who announced it and sang about it. It can and does produce "great joy" for those who understand and receive it. (4) This amazing invasion from outer space has come to be told "to all the people." (5) Finally the object or purpose of this announcement is One glorious Person who is our Savior—our Lord—his name is Jesus! How poorly I have tried to represent your viewpoint.

Please express your response to this beautiful text. Put your expression in your own prayer diary.

6. READ HIS WORD FOR YOURSELF.

I find myself too often in the above expression of praise. My intention was to hold up this record into your presence and read it from above. Just here I want to stand on the rocky hillside with the shepherds. Did these humble men really hear and understand what the angels said? We doubt it. The depth of meaning in just who was born escaped them; however, the second half of the angel's words were well understood and fulfilled in their experience. He said:

"And this will be a sign for you: you will find a babe wrapped in swaddling cloths and lying in a manger." Just how far did these men have to walk to find the cattle stall and the manger? We cannot imagine it took much investigation in "the little town of Bethlehem." But before they left on their amazing mission they were to be startled by a further heavenly display.

Pause in his presence and either audibly or in written form tell him all his word means to you.

7. READ HIS WORD IN THANKSGIVING.

The angels of all ranks speak the language of men. In one great gigantic chorus they said, "Glory to God in the Highest, and on earth peace among men with whom he is pleased." Let me lift up gratitude from these words: (1) Thank you for a small revelation of your true character. (2) Thank you that even our highest praise is not enough.

(3) Thank you for coming to bring peace upon the earth. (4) Thank you that you said peace comes also from men. (5) Thank you that you can be, and are, pleased with some men. (6) Thank you that whereas heaven is the home of angels they yet serve in this earth. (7) Thank you the shepherds acted upon their faith.

Give yourself to your own expression of gratitude—write it or speak it!

8. READ HIS WORD IN MEDITATION.

"Let us go over to Bethlehem and see this thing that has happened." It is important to identify just who is involved in this amazing occurrence: they are shepherds. This means men of very ordinary means; men who are not at all given to supernatural religious activity. There are several shepherds. How many? Were there four? Six?

Eight? We must say that this is going to be told again and again by several men. The credibility of several ordinary men has made a lasting impression for almost two millenniums. God wanted these shepherds to confirm the words of the angel. The unusual birth, i.e., in a manger helped convince these men that God had visited this earth!

Pause—wait—think—then express yourself in thoughtful praise or thanks.

9. READ HIS WORD FOR PETITIONS.

We shall never be able to pray like we should until we kneel before the manger bed. (1) May the words of the angel burn upon our conscience: "good news of a great joy." (2) Oh, that I might help to spread this news to all

people. (3) The city of David became the vestibule of heaven—open my eyes! (4) I want Jesus to be the King of my life. (5) What a shocking sign it was to see the Messiah in a stable—may the wonder of it never leave.

Please, please remember these are prayers—speak them—reword them!

10. READ HIS WORD AND WAIT—LISTEN—GOD SPEAKS!

(1) "I still need humble men to tell the good news." (2) "If it is not good news to you it will not be to those who hear you." (3) "Any angel in my presence would be glad to tell the tidings I have given to you."

11. INTERCESSION FOR THE LOST WORLD

Indonesia — Point for prayer: (1) *Prayer needs of the major islands: Sumatra* 23,000,000 — The 2.4 million ardently *Muslim Atjeh* in extreme north are unevangelized. The 5 million *Menangkabau* in Centre are also strongly Muslim, and only a handful of Christians among them (one congregation in W. Java). There are some Christians in the area, but all are from other language groups. The *Toba Bataks* and people of Nias have been Christian for decades, now there is much nominalism. Pray for revival. The Toba Batak Church has one million members.

12. SING PRAISES TO OUR LORD.

O worship the King, all glorious above,
And gratefully sing His wonderful love;

Our Shield and Defender, the Ancient of days,
Pavilioned in splendor, and girded with praise.

WEEK THIRTY-ONE — SATURDAY

1. PRAISE GOD FOR WHO HE IS.

"I will bless the Lord at all times; his praise shall continually be in my mouth. My soul makes its boast in the Lord, let the afflicted hear and be glad. O magnify the Lord with me, and let us exalt his name together" (Psa. 34:1-3). Dear Father, I want to agree with the psalmist that you indeed deserve praise and adoration at all times. I want to credit you with all I have and all I ever hope to be. How can I make a practical application out of this little phrase: "his praise shall continually be in my mouth"? Indeed, how shall all men come to this realization? If we related all of life to you we would talk of you continually. If we know we are the recipient and you are the giver of every good and perfect gift our praise would ascend continually. I want to agree with your purposes in life. Men were created for your fellowship. Dear Lord, help me to contribute a little to the fulfillment of your purpose.

Express yourself in adoration for this quality of God.
Speak it audibly or write out your praise in your own devotional journal.

2. PRAISE GOD FOR WHAT HE MEANS TO ME.

For me—my whole life (soul) can make its boast in nothing but yourself. The term "soul" refers to the whole person. All I know, all I choose, all I feel, i.e., in the realm of what has benefited me, comes from you. If there are those who suffer with a feeling of inferiority or lack in any area of living, let them hear this good word! Let them lift up their heads and be glad! How refreshing and restoring is praise and wonder in the presence of our Lord! The whole purpose of worship is to gather the qualities of yourself before our consciousness and express them from our heart that we might magnify the Lord and exalt his name together!

How do you personally relate to the exaltation of God, and God who is exalted?
Speak it out or write it out. It is *so important* that you establish *your own* devotional journal.

3. CONFESSION OF SIN

Such a basic sin! A failure in motives! Do I honor and recognize you at all times? I am much more impressed with some man's position and prestige than I am yourself. Dear God, forgive me. How often do I consciously express my praise to you during a twenty-four hour period? Could you rerun a day for me and see? No, do not do it! Oh, my Father, this day shall be better! How many people have heard of the greatness and beauty of yourself from my lips? Forgive me, forgive me. There are those bowed down with trouble and care of one kind or another, who would look up if I would praise you. Days have gone by and nothing like this has happened. Today shall be different! Cleanse my motives.

What personal sins do you want to confess? We *must* speak them to remove them.
Do it! *Now.* There is no one else you have sinned against more than God. Tell him so!

4. SING A PRAYER TO GOD.

Nearer, still nearer, close to Thy heart,
Draw me, my Savior, so precious Thou art;
Fold me, O fold me close to Thy breast,

Shelter me safe in that "Haven of Rest,"
Shelter me safe in that "Haven of Rest."

Open your hymn book and sing the rest of the verses—or even sing another prayer song.

5. READ HIS WORD TO HIM!

His Word

[16]So they hurried off and found Mary and Joseph, and the baby, who was lying in the manger. [17]When they had seen him, they spread the word concerning what had been told them about this child, [18]and all who heard it were amazed at what the shepherds said to them. [19]But Mary treasured up all these things and pondered them in her heart. [20]The shepherds returned, glorifying and praising God for all the things they had heard and seen, which were just as they had been told.   — Luke 2:16-20, NIV

Read His Word to Him.

I can catch the urgency of these humble men as they left their fields and sheep (probably under the care of others) and walked down the streets of Bethlehem in search of a baby in a manger. How all of this scene must have pleased you! The expression of your love in the birth of your Son. The wonder and worship of men before the manger. The spread of your good news to others. The thoughtfulness of Mary. The praise and open expression of amazement from the shepherds. Dear Lord, how I want to treasure every word of these verses in my heart and turn every thought around in my mind.

Please express your response to this beautiful text. Put your expression in your own prayer diary.

6. READ HIS WORD FOR YOURSELF.

How eager I am to worship before the manger scene. I know so much more about what I see than the shepherds did. Or do I? I know more by way of information, but they knew more by way of confrontation. Did the shepherds ask questions of Mary and Joseph? We can't imagine they didn't. Their heads must have been swimming when they left the humble family. Did they relate the virgin birth to Isaiah the prophet? We hope so! These men could much more easily believe a virgin birth after their visit from the angels. It is more than interesting that Luke records that the one thing that impressed them was that every thing happened as God said it would.

It is so important that you pause in his presence
and either audibly or in written form tell him all his word means to you.

7. READ HIS WORD IN THANKSGIVING.

Somehow I can get much more thanksgiving into Christmas. (1) Thank you for sending your Son into the busy schedule of man—expected and unexpected. (2) Thank you that this good news is always too good to keep. (3) Thank you that the first persons who heard believed. (4) Thank you that men do always have the capacity to be amazed. (5) Thank you once again for Mary the grand example for all women. (6) Thank you that when we have pondered these things for all our life, there will be much more to ponder. (7) Thank you that you want us to see and to hear so we can believe.

Give yourself to your own expression of gratitude—write it or speak it!

8. READ HIS WORD IN MEDITATION.

"Mary treasured up all these things and pondered them in her mind." What are the factors in Mary's mind? Let us try to reconstruct what she has to ponder: (1) She was engaged to Joseph. This does not relate directly to what happened, but it became a real factor in all this drama. Without Joseph many things would not have happened. (2) She was suddenly confronted with an angel who told her she would become pregnant from the Holy Spirit. She was also told of the supernatural (but natural) pregnancy of Elizabeth. (3) She left Joseph and Nazareth and spent several months in Judea with Elizabeth. (4) She was pregnant and there was no man as the father. (5) The shocking news that in her ninth month they must make the long trip to Bethlehem. In every point there are many angles and inuendos. Could Mary discern a divine purpose in it all? How much like the ever changing circumstances of our own life.

Pause—wait—think—then express yourself in thoughtful praise or thanks.

9. READ HIS WORD FOR PETITIONS.

This is far more than just another reading of the so-called *Christmas* text: (1) I want to hurry to a position of prayer before you—to lift up praise. (2) Open my heart and my lips to tell like it was only yesterday that my Lord was born. (3) Break my hard heart that I might communicate the wonder felt by the shepherds. (4) I want the meditative capacity of Mary. (5) Open my mind that new and fresh applications might be made of this ageless truth. (6) Thank you for the simple beauty of Bethlehem. (7) Thank you for the profound depth of what I see and hear.

Right here add your personal requests—and his answers.

10. READ HIS WORD AND WAIT—LISTEN—GOD SPEAKS!

Speak to me once again: (1) "Men still need to hear of my first coming." (2) "I am coming again and when I do it will not be 'good news' to most of the world." (3) "Please ponder long over these verses."

11. INTERCESSION FOR THE LOST WORLD

Indonesia — Points for prayer: (1) *Sumatra: The Karo Bataks* are turning to the Lord in large numbers—pray for this growing church and the work of missionaries assisting it. *The 16 tribes of the South*—only one now reached with the Gospel—live in rugged country and most are Muslim. One tribe is turning from Islam to the Lord. (2) *Java 90,000,000—Unreached peoples*—the Banten and Sunda (15 million) in the West (with a few churches) and the resistant Madurese in the East (6 Madurese Christians on Madura Is.) are all Muslim. Pray for the difficult ministry among the latter. Pray also for the evangelization of the largely unreached Hindu Tennger in the mountains of E. Java.

12. SING PRAISES TO OUR LORD.

Holy, Holy, Holy, Lord God Almighty!
Early in the morning our song shall rise to Thee;

Holy, Holy, Holy! Merciful and Mighty!
God in Three Persons, blessed Trinity!

WEEK THIRTY-TWO — SUNDAY

1. PRAISE GOD FOR WHO HE IS.

"I sought the Lord, and he answered me, and delivered me from all my fears. Look to him, and be radiant; so your faces shall never be ashamed" (Psa. 34:4, 5). There are so many qualities of yourself; I shall never exhaust them. How is the word "sought" used? Are you someone who can be lost and therefore must be found? Or is this word a synonym for "inquiry"? i.e., "I *made inquiry* of the Lord and he answered me"? The term seems to be one of urgency. There is nothing casual here. Perhaps "out of focus" or "unrecognized" or "unappreciated" would be a better word than "*lost.*" I have sought you because the eyes of my heart were dim. I sought you because I have failed to practice your presence and you are therefore unrecognized and unappreciated. What is true of me is true of all. Is it only when man is afraid that he seeks you? So it would seem. The positive encouragement is that personal exchange can be established! We can get an answer! You can and do deliver us from all our fears. Blessed be your name!

Express yourself in adoration for this quality of God.
Speak it audibly or write out your praise in your own devotional journal.

2. PRAISE GOD FOR WHAT HE MEANS TO ME.

For me. How can I claim the *radiance* here promised? You can and do give radiance to men who fulfill this promise. This is an inward strength and confidence that is reflected on the face. A brightness and light begins within and manifests itself to all those who know us. What shall I see in you that will produce this effect? How shall I look in order for this to happen? How intently I must look. How totally fascinated and wholly enamored I must be—for a long time I must remain before you before this will happen! My total trust and absolute confidence must be placed in you. Out of the depths of need I refocus my whole heart on you. Only then will your light shine through me.

How do you personally relate to the radiance of God, and God who is Radiance?
Speak it out or write it out. It is *so important* that you establish *your own* devotional journal.

3. CONFESSION OF SIN

Dear Lord, the sad fact is that I have not sought you in the manner here described and I have been intimidated and overcome by my fears. Worry and anxiety are terrible masters. How wonderfully different is my outlook when I arise from a session of worship before you! Dear Lord, I rededicate myself to seeking and looking to you! It is so easy to be caught away by what is near—by what is clamoring for attention and interest. We are so much like the parents of my Lord who thought he was with them, but left him in Jerusalem. The painful fact was that he was not lost, they were. If you seem distant I know it is not because you have moved.

What personal sins do you want to confess? We *must* speak them to remove them.
Do it! *Now.* There is no one else you have sinned against more than God. Tell him so!

4. SING A PRAYER TO GOD.

Lead on, O King Eternal,
The day of march has come;
Henceforth in fields of conquest
Thy tents shall be our home.

Thro' days of preparation
Thy grace has made us strong,
And now, O King Eternal,
We lift our battle song.

Open your hymn book and sing the rest of the verses—or even sing another prayer song.

5. READ HIS WORD TO HIM!
His Word

[21]On the eighth day, when it was time to circumcise him, he was named Jesus, the name the angel had given him before he had been conceived.

[22]When the time of their purification according to the Law of Moses had been completed, Joseph and Mary took him to Jerusalem to present him to the Lord [23](as it is written in the Law of the Lord, "Every firstborn male is to be consecrated to the Lord"), [24]and to offer a sacrifice in keeping with what is said in the Law of the Lord: "a pair of doves or two young pigeons." *— Luke 2:21-24, NIV*

Read His Word to Him.

Dear Lord, I am overwhelmed in an attempt to read these words from your perspective! On the important eighth day of the birth of your Son the seal of the agreement with Abraham was performed on him! His name was "Joshua" or "Savior" or "Jesus" before the foundation of the world. His name was "Jesus" when the angel Gabriel made the announcement. His name was "Jesus" after the knife of circumcision. How indicative of your value system is the offering made by Mary and Joseph: "a pair of doves or two young pigeons." It was the desire to obey that was accepted—or made the sacrifice acceptable.

Please express your response to this beautiful text. Put your expression in your own prayer diary.

6. READ HIS WORD FOR YOURSELF.

How can I take Mary's place? Or consider what is happening here from Joseph's viewpoint? Perhaps the priest's perspective would be interesting. Just where *do* I stand as I travel from Bethlehem to Jerusalem? There is a very small baby in Mary's arms. There is an inscription in the work schedule of Joseph. There is some outlay of expense for even two young pigeons. I want to be a part of the little family on its way to the temple. Dear Lord, how unassuming are all your ways. What a lesson for me to learn in even this simple fact. How we do want men to notice what we do. How we do want men to be impressed and praise us for our accomplishments. I doubt if *anyone* — *anyone* even saw Mary and Joseph. Dear God, you did — it is enough!

It is so important that you pause in his presence
and either audibly or in written form tell him all his word means to you.

7. READ HIS WORD IN THANKSGIVING.

Blessed Lord, I can at least thank you: (1) Thank you for the parents' willingness to comply with the law even when both of them knew their child was heaven's exception. (2) Thank you again and again for the beautiful name "Jesus." (3) Thank you for angels' interest in the whole brief life of our Lord. (4) Thank you for the pureness of Mary — not only according to the law, but according to her heart. (5) Thank you that whereas we are always in your presence yet each day we can appear before you to present ourselves all over again. (6) Thank you that every male and female is now to be consecrated to the Lord. (7) Thank you for the one sacrifice that makes all we are and have possible.

Give yourself to you own expression of gratitude — write it or speak it!

8. READ HIS WORD IN MEDITATION.

"Every first-born male is to be consecrated to the Lord." God had a right to all men of every family. The text in Leviticus and Numbers is saying every first-born son is to be given to God's service. However, to allow the first-born to serve in the home a sacrifice took his place. Perhaps some of the Israelites would remember that since Egypt every first-born male or female belonged to the Lord. There would have been no first-born if the lamb had not been slain and the blood applied. How all the above information related to our Lord is easy to see. The doves or pigeons were the smallest, cheapest possible sacrifice. How humbling it was to offer only birds in the place of the Son of God! Was this one of the deep thoughts Mary pondered? If she didn't we should!

Pause — wait — think — then express yourself in thoughtful praise or thanks.

9. READ HIS WORD FOR PETITIONS.

What a humble but meaningful service it was! (1) Jesus was a true son of Abraham — thank you that I can share this distinction. (2) I want His name to be fulfilled in my experience — "my Savior." (3) If it was necessary to present Jesus to you how much more do I need to present myself! (4) Set me aside as your servant today. (5) Thank you that my Lord is my sacrifice for acceptance with you. (6) "Life for life" has been your law from the beginning — thank you that Christ died for me.

Please, please remember these are prayers — speak them — reword them!

10. READ HIS WORD AND WAIT — LISTEN — GOD SPEAKS!

How poignant are these words: (1) "Write the name of my Son upon your heart." (2) "If my Son needed ceremonial purification what do you imagine you need?" (3) "Every new-born child of mine is now holy because of Jesus."

11. INTERCESSION FOR THE LOST WORLD

Indonesia — Points for prayer: (1) *Java: The Church* (2% of population) has seen hundreds of thousands of Muslims coming into the fellowships in spite of being generally weak and immature. The Christians are not fully able to take advantage of the great openness of the 50 million Muslim Javanese to the Gospel. Pray for the missionaries, the evangelistic and church planting ministries. (2) *Bali,* a 3,000,000 tourist-infested Hindu island in great spiritual darkness, demonic oppression and witchcraft. The progress of the Gospel has been slow until recently. The great volcanic eruptions over the last decade have brought a great change because of Christian love shown to the victims, and whole communities are turning to the Lord. Pray for the work in Bali.

12. SING PRAISES TO OUR LORD.

I love Thy Kingdom, Lord,
The house of Thine abode,

The Church our blessed Redeemer saved
With His own precious blood.

WEEK THIRTY-TWO — MONDAY

1. PRAISE GOD FOR WHO HE IS.

"The angel of the Lord encamps around those who fear him, and delivers them. O taste and see that the Lord is good! Happy is the man who takes refuge in him" (Psa. 34:7, 8). Here are surprising qualities of yourself. How pleasant it is to believe angels are encamped around us at all times. "The angel of the Lord" in this psalm could have reference to our Lord before he came to this earth, or to one of the archangels. We are assured that the angelic host is pressed into service on behalf of children and Christians (Heb. 1:14, Matt. 18:10). Does our reverence and worship relate to this angelic ministry? Indeed it does! Our reverence and worship (even now) makes us sensitive to their presence. Can we say our "fear" activates their service? Just what deliverances have we received from our Lord or his messengers? I am glad I do not know. If I did, then all men would look for the same kind and would feel less if they didn't have it. How wise you are!

Express yourself in adoration for this qualtiy of God.
Speak it audibly or write out your praise in your own devotional journal.

2. PRAISE GOD FOR WHAT HE MEANS TO ME.

Just for me! I am tasting, I am eating at your banquet table—"your banner over me is love" (Song of Solomon 2:4). The food is your word (milk and meat) and yourself (bread and water). The adjective "good" has a much, much deeper meaning in its biblical setting than it has in our English vocabulary. Dear Lord, the more I eat the stronger becomes my appetite! I shall never eat or drink enough to satiate my hunger or thirst. This opens to me the meaning of those who spend all eternity praising and adoring you! I am delighted to hide in you! I need "a refuge"—a cool, peaceful place where I can relax and find rest. You are saying to me, "That place is a Person even myself!"

How do you personally relate to the goodness of God, and God who is Love?
Speak it out or write it out. It is so important that you establish your own devotional journal.

3. CONFESSION OF SIN

That there should be such bounties and I should be so hungry and poor is my sin. I realize the development of a sensitive spirit is a life-long process, but for me to make no (or very little) progress in this process is indicative of a serious lack. Forgive me. I find such delight when I am willing, I wonder that it is not always so! How fleeting and unsatisfying are the pursuits of this world. Why should I have any interest in them at all except as they relate to the necessities of life? The Lord is too good to leave! Dear Father, you know how far short I fall of a constant fulfillment of such goals. Help me! I do love you. Cleanse me deeply!

What personal sins do you want to confess? We must speak them to remove them.
Do it! Now. There is no one else you have sinned against more than God. Tell him so!

4. SING A PRAYER TO GOD.

Stand up, stand up for Jesus,
Ye soldiers of the cross,
Lift high His royal banner,
It must not suffer loss;

From vict'ry unto vict'ry,
His army shall He lead,
Till ev'ry foe in vanquished
And Christ is Lord indeed.

Open your hymn book and sing the rest of the verses—or even sing another prayer song.

5. READ HIS WORD TO HIM!

His Word

[25] Now there was a man in Jerusalem called Simeon, who was righteous and devout. He was waiting for the consolation of Israel, and the Holy Spirit was upon him. [26] It had been revealed to him by the Holy Spirit that he would not die before he had seen the Lord's Christ. [27] Moved by the Spirit, he went into the temple courts. When the parents brought in the child Jesus to do for him what the custom of the Law required,
— Luke 2:25-27, NIV

Read His Word to Him.

Oh, Father, I do so admire this old man. Open my mind that I might think and pray your thoughts about him: (1) He was "righteous and devout." I take this to mean that he lived a consistent life and loved you from the heart. I do hope this is what is meant because in a long record of trying, this is all I can offer you. I am reminded once again that this is what he was, not what he did. This is your estimate of him. (2) He was waiting for the "consolation of Israel." This is tantamount to waiting for the Messiah. (3) "The Holy Spirit was upon him." Isn't that what was said of prophets? He had been spoken to by the Holy Spirit. He had the beautiful confidence that he would not die without your consolation: he would see your anointed One! The Holy Spirit was a very large part of his life.

Please expess your response to this beautiful text. Put your expession in your own prayer diary.

6. READ HIS WORD FOR YOURSELF.

It will not be at all difficult to apply these precious points to my own life: (1) Dear Lord, I am not at all righteous—I am full of fault and weakness. At the same time, I claim your provision for my righteousness—indeed he is my consolation! (2) Am I devout? I do love you—I do enjoy worshiping you, I do love your word. But devout I am not. (3) I need not wait—he has come! Blessed be his name! (4) The Holy Spirit is in me—that he would aid me with strength in my inner man is a claim I gladly make (Ephesians 3:16). (5) I wonder just what other wondrous things I shall see before I die? You have already shown me much more than I expected or deserve!

It is so important that you pause in his presence
and either audibly or in written form tell him all his word means to you.

7. READ HIS WORD IN THANKSGIVING.

The life of Simeon seems to be one of thanksgiving. (1) Thank you for the "hidden" men and women of faith—you have them everywhere. (2) Thank you that it is possible, by your definition, to be righteous and devout. (3) Thank you that all the prophets looked for has come in the person of your Son. (4) Thank you for your revealing agent—even the Holy Spirit. (5) Thank you for your purposes that can be worked out in every life. (6) Thank you for the temple of yourself—even our bodies. (7) Thank for the babe in Mary's arms who was the son of your love.

Give yourself to your own expression of gratitude—write it or speak it!

8. READ HIS WORD IN MEDITATION.

"Moved by the Spirit, he went into the temple courts." It has always been a question in my mind as to just how such persons knew they were "moved by the Holy Spirit"? Did they know it at the time or did they conclude later that considering the circumstances such was the case? I guess what I am asking is: "Was there a definable subjective direction from the Holy Spirit?" I am glad to acknowledge the moving of the Holy Spirit—I would like to know more about this phenomenon. It was in the temple courts he met our Lord. We are the temple or sanctuary of the Holy Spirit. At the same time, we can come into the presence of the Lord anywhere, any time even as I do now. The blessed Holy Spirit has moved me through his word to come here and close the door and pray. Even as Simeon of old, I have met my Lord! Praise his name!

Pause—wait—think—then express yourself in thoughtful praise or thanks.

9. READ HIS WORD FOR PETITIONS.

In this aged man are many lessons for prayer: (1) Give me a renewed claim on the righteousness of your Son. (2) I want a devoutness that is genuine all the time. (3) How glad I am to claim what Simeon only looked for. (4) Keep me always aware of the presence of your Holy Spirit. (5) May I be prepared every day to die. (6) How I long to see what now is only by faith—keep me prepared. (7) Thank you for the lesson here that what seems casual is actually planned by yourself.

Right here add your personal requests—and his answers.

10. READ HIS WORD AND WAIT—LISTEN—GOD SPEAKS!

In these verses speak to me: (1) "How I need more men like Simeon today." (2) "The hope of Israel and the world has already come." (3) "Simeon was not aware he was led by the Spirit—but he was led nonetheless. . . ."

11. INTERCESSION FOR THE LOST WORLD

Indonesia — Points for prayer: (1) *The lesser Sunda Islands* (Lombok, Flores and Sumbawa) are virtually without a Bible believing witness. Lack of workers hinders their evangelization. There are no Protestant workers there. (2) *The Moluccas* have been Christian for three centuries, but there is little true spiritual life on these many small islands. (3) *Timor* 2,500,000—reuinited when Indonesian troops crushed a Communist takeover after the collapse of Portuguese rule in 1976. The 700,000 people of the former Portuguese E. Timor are unevangelized but for one group on tiny Atauro Island. Pray for Timorese evangelists who pray for an entrance from W. Timor. W. Timor has been nominally Christian for 300 years, but the large church was riddled with nominalism, witchcraft and sin until revival came. Batu teams helped to consolidate the work on a Biblical basis, and hundreds of witness teams went out all over the island and beyond. Pray for greater maturity, spiritual depth and growing missionary vision.

12. SING PRAISES TO OUR LORD.

We gather together to ask the Lord's blessing,
He chastens and hastens His will to make known;

The wicked oppressing cease them from distressing,
Sing praises to His name, He forgets not His own.

WEEK THIRTY-TWO — TUESDAY

1. PRAISE GOD FOR WHO HE IS.

"The eyes of the Lord are toward the righteous, and his ears toward their cry. The face of the Lord is against evildoers, to cut off the remembrance of them from the earth" (Psa. 34:15, 16). There are several not too obvious qualities of yourself in these verses. I am delighted to hold them up as praiseworthy before all men. (1) You see, i.e., you look upon all men with an awareness we will never know. Your observation includes a total view of all man is and has been and can be. How encouraging to know you are not only absolute knowledge, but absolute love. You look with more than a fatherly interest in every act of "the righteous." (2) You hear, i.e., men do not talk anywhere any time without a silent listener. When others do not listen, you do. When others do not understand, you do!

Express yourself in adoration for this quality of God.
Speak it audibly or write out your praise in your own devotional journal.

2. PRAISE GOD FOR WHAT HE MEANS TO ME.

Just for me. How great a comfort I receive in this time of praise and wonder. You are even now at work on my behalf. You do not ignore evildoers. You see them and know of their efforts to defeat your work. If for reasons best known to you you cannot (not because you are not able) defeat them here you will indeed avenge in the life and world to come. Even in this world and upon this earth millions of evil doers have come and gone and no one alive upon this earth could tell their name or their deeds. What seems so unreasonably evil today will not be remembered in a very few years from now. I praise you that you see, hear and are personally involved in all I am and do. I do not adequately represent your divine presence—but I appreciate it.

How do you personally relate to the eyes of God, and God who sees all?
Speak it out or write it out. It is *so important* that you establish *your own* devotional journal.

3. CONFESSION OF SIN

How is it I can so often vocalize my confidence in your personal presence and live as if you were nowhere near? "Thou Lord *seest* me." "When the righteous cry for help, the Lord *hears*." How can I live and speak as if this were *not* true? I must affirm your conscious living presence real often. Indeed I do this very moment! You are full of loving interest; it is not your purpose to catch me in my sin, but to remind me of the larger picture—it includes you. Forgive me for not remembering this. There are other sins I confess to you, but this is so important—help me! Cleanse me. Keep me awake!

What personal sins do you want to confess? We *must* speak them to remove them.
Do it! *Now.* There is no one else you have sinned against more than God. Tell him so!

4. SING A PRAYER TO GOD.

My soul in sad exile was out on life's sea,
So burdened with sin and distrest,
Till I heard a sweet voice saying,
"Make me your choice";
And I entered the "Haven of Rest"!

I've anchored my soul in the "Haven of Rest,"
I'll sail the wide seas no more;
The tempest may sweep o'er the wild, stormy deep,
In Jesus I'm safe evermore.

Open your hymn book and sing the rest of the verses—or even sing another prayer song.

5. READ HIS WORD TO HIM!

His Word

[27]Moved by the Spirit, he went into the temple courts. When the parents brought in the child Jesus to do for him what the custom of the Law required, [28]Simeon took him in his arms and praised God, saying:
[29]"Sovereign Lord, as you promised,
   you now dismiss your servant in peace.
[30]For my eyes have seen your salvation,
[31]   which you have prepared in the sight of all the people,
[32]a light for revelation to the Gentiles and for glory to your people Israel."
[33]The child's father and mother marveled at what was said about him. [34]Then Simeon blessed them and said to Mary, his mother: "This child is destined to cause the falling and rising of many in Israel, and to be a sign that will be spoken against, [35]so that the thoughts of many hearts will be revealed. And a sword will pierce your own soul too."
— Luke 2:27-35, NIV

Read His Word to Him.

How precious is this lovely record! How full of meaning to me, but a thousand times more meaningful to you! I must try to imagine the scene—you can see it! What a meaningful expression of praise and thanksgiving came from the heart of this old man. But then, it was the Holy Spirit who moved him. I want to lift every word up to you in wonder and praise. Just the opening expression is enough! "Sovereign Lord,"—how I bow before you in acknowledgement. Dear God, I am speechless! How solid is my hope and confidence in you in the light of all you have said and done. All you have promised has happened even as you said. Like Simeon I would gladly accept dismissal in your peace?

Please express your response to this beautiful text. Put your expression in your own prayer diary.

6. READ HIS WORD FOR YOURSELF.

I do not want to miss any part of these burning words. What prophetic promises are in these few sentences: (1) Salvation prepared in the sight of all the people. Was he anticipating Calvary where the inscription advertised the king in three languages? (2) Is this wonderful man anticipating the universal salvation of our Lord? How all of this shocks me! How full of praise this one Gentile is! (3) The real purpose and character of Israel can be seen in what our Savior did—and in who he was. No wonder Joseph and Mary marveled at what was said about their little son.

Pause in his presence and either audibly or in written form tell him all his word means to you.

7. READ HIS WORD IN THANKSGIVING.

I am like the parents of my Lord—full of wonder: (1) Thank you that sometimes in the very normal course of life the most amazing things happen. (2) Thank you for the tenderness and kindness in the words and actions of Simeon. (3) Thank you for the meaningful description of yourself given by Simeon; (a) Sovereign Lord; (b) a promise keeper; (c) One in control of death; (d) Source of salvation. (4) Thank you for this early anticipation of the whole purpose of our Lord's ministry. (5) Thank you for "the sign" even my Lord—he could not be ignored. (6) Thank you that you know my thoughts—I give them to you for correction before they are revealed. (7) Thank you for the devotion of Mary to the child of her heart.

Give yourself to your own expression of gratitude—write it or speak it!

8. READ HIS WORD IN MEDITATION.

"And a sword will pierce your own soul too." How very poignant must these words have been to Mary! Which sword did Simeon have in mind? Was it the sword of misunderstanding from those who should have known better? How often was Mary accused of fornication? But she had already felt the pain of this sword. Was it the sword of ridicule—i.e., that she, an unknown village maid, would be the mother of the Messiah? Perhaps as people observed the conduct and heard the words of her son such ridicule lessened, but perhaps it didn't. How sharp was the sword of rejection by the people of Nazareth. Her son could be appreciated every place but at home.

Pause—wait—think—then express yourself in thoughtful praise or thanks.

9. READ HIS WORD FOR PETITIONS.

How I do want to lift up the precious bundle in the infant form of my Lord: (1) Surely it is enough to be able to see him as he is indeed the Savior! (2) Open my eyes even wider to behold more and more of his beauty. (3) Dear Lord, how can the peoples of the earth be told of your Son and His love? (4) Enlighten my understanding as I bow before you. (5) I too marvel at what was said by Simeon—deepen my desire to share it. (6) I want to read again with deeper meaning the story of this child who became the Son of God and the Son of Man.

Please, please remember these are prayers—speak them—reword them!

10. READ HIS WORD AND WAIT—LISTEN—GOD SPEAKS!

How well can you speak to me from this text: (1) "There is more need for my Son today than when he came long ago." (2) "He is today what he will ever be, the light of the world." (3) "A sword has been given for the dividing of hearts today."

11. INTERCESSION FOR THE LOST WORLD

Indonesia — Point for prayer: (1) *Kalimantan* (Indonesian Borneo) 6,000,000. A vast underpopulated land of rivers and forests and very few roads. There are many nominal Christians in the south, but a great people movement is in progress among the majority Dayak tribes in the east, center and west with thousands seeking the Lord every year.

12. SING PRAISES TO OUR LORD.

Holy, Holy, Holy, Lord God Almighty!
Early in the morning our song shall rise to Thee;

Holy, Holy, Holy! Merciful and Mighty!
God in Three Persons, blessed Trinity!

WEEK THIRTY-TWO — WEDNESDAY

1. PRAISE GOD FOR WHO HE IS.

"They feast on the abundance of thy house, and thou givest them drink from the river of thy delights. for with thee is the fountain of life; in thy light do we see light" (Psa. 36:8, 9). The beautiful figures of speech here describe the even more beautiful reality behind them—even yourself! As if you were a wealthy householder, which indeed you are! The limitless expanse of eternity is your house. All that man has on this earth (and there is an abundance for all, distribution is the problem) is from your hand. Man's physical needs as poorly as they are met, are but

a means to a much more important end. Jesus said his food, his feast was in doing your will. There is a delight in teaching the lost, in educating the saved. What is "the river of your delights"? Sounds exciting to say the least. "If any man keeps on drinking of the water that I shall give him he shall never thirst, but always be satisfied" (John 4:14). I have expanded the translation but this is the meaning, and praise your name, this is "the river of delights." Oh, dear Lord, I would that all men would find in yourself and your Son such a river and such a fountain!

Express yourself in adoration for this quality of God.
Speak it audibly or write out your praise in your own devotional journal.

2. PRAISE GOD FOR WHAT HE MEANS TO ME.

Just for me. I so much need and want to come before you with praise and gladness! With you and in you is *"the fountain of life."* In your very self as opened up in your word and your Son is an experience just like jumping into a fountain of sparkling water! Every figure breaks down if we press it beyond its intended meaning. In this lovely example life comes from the fountain, but are we in the fountain or is the fountain in us? Perhaps both thoughts

are intended. We think of Jesus' reference to the artesian spring within us (John 4:15). Is it possible (I have thought of it often) to lose our identity in you? Can we become so glad and eager to know you and know more and more about you that we lose contact with our life in your life? This is so poorly expressed. Dear Lord, help me. As I come to your light, shining out of your word and your Son, I see new light—everywhere! Praise your name!

How do you personally relate to the fountain of God, and God who is the water of life?
Speak it out or write it out. It is *so important* that you establish *your own* devotional journal.

3. CONFESSION OF SIN

If there is such an abundance in your house, if drinking of the water of life is so refreshing, if the fountain of joy is bubbling near by, how is it at times I am so unsatisfied? The answer is so clear: I just do not stay long enough, or often enough at your table; I do not drink deeply enough at your well; I do not tarry long enough or often enough in your fountain! Why? Why? How easy to for-

get! Dear Lord, forgive me! I have sinned against myself as well as you. I have sinned against all who could be helped by the "newness of life" found in me through you. I confess the specific transgression of your will. I name my selfishness. Cleanse me. I do now forget so you can and will forget it! Praise your name!

What personal sins do you want to confess? We *must* speak them to remove them.
Do it! *Now.* There is no one else you have sinned against more than God. Tell him so!

4. SING A PRAYER TO GOD.

Abide with me: fast falls the eventide;
The darkness deepens;
Lord, with me abide:

When other helpers fail, and comforts flee,
Help of the helpless,
O abide with me!

Open your hymn book and sing the rest of the verses—or even sing another prayer song.

5. READ HIS WORD TO HIM!

His Word

[36]There was also a prophetess, Anna, the daughter of Phanuel, of the tribe of Asher. She was very old; she had lived with her husband seven years after her marriage, [37]and then was a widow until she was eighty-four. She never left the temple but worshiped night and day, fasting

and praying. [38]Coming up to them at that very moment, she gave thanks to God and spoke about the child to all who were looking forward to the redemption of Jerusalem.
— *Luke 2:36-38, NIV*

Read His Word to Him.

What a charming story to read in your presence! I guess all the ten tribes were not lost—here is a record of a dear woman and her heritage in the tribe of Asher is well known. What is meant by "great age"? How almost absurd it is to read this to you with whom time means nothing. I am

to think of someone 80 or 90 years old—84 to be precise. She found her new husband in you! How often did you see this dear woman in the precincts of your holy place? For many months and years she appeared before you in prayer and praise. Most of all she seems to sense her own unworthiness and expresses it in fasting. Every morning at the appointed hour she was there — every night she also was found before you in prayer. What an example! I know you appreciated Anna — and so do I!

Please express your response to this beautiful text. Put your expression in your prayer diary.

6. READ HIS WORD FOR YOURSELF.

Just for me — read this word into my heart! There was, and there is, a prophetess, Anna! I do not know how you decided who would be and who would not be a prophetess. It must have related to the need and opportunity and surely to the preparation of the heart of the one involved. So it is today for your servants — I think of myself, and of all others who want to serve you. How long shall I serve you? I have been more than 40 years preaching and teaching your word. I feel like Anna — a need for humiliation before you! I want to establish more definite times of worship — night and day — to do this is my deep desire. This is my largest, most constant need! I do wonder just what Anna said, but it serves as a good example for me. She spoke of the redemption of your people. It is enough! Can I expect or want more?

Pause in his presence and either audibly or in written form tell him all his word means to you.

7. READ HIS WORD IN THANKSGIVING.

This seems to lend itself to thanksgiving in a special way: (1) Thank you for every unnamed, unknown prophetess that loved you and labored for you in far off days and places. (2) Thank you for all loving and patient wives who have lived with their husbands from their virginity — it was not always easy. (3) Thank you for the host of widows who love you and worship you and serve you in ways no one else can. (4) Thank you for this beautiful definition of worship: a life style attitude. (5) Thank you for the power of fasting to bring our bodies under subjection. (6) Thank you for Luke's desire to contribute Anna's unassuming confirmation of our Lord's deity.

Give yourself to you own expression of gratitude — write it or speak it!

8. READ HIS WORD IN MEDITATION.

". . . to all who were looking for the redemption of Jerusalem." This is the same thing as saying: "for all who were looking for the Messiah who would deliver the holy city from the hands of the Roman oppressors." This is Luke's description of the expectations of the people of his day. How I do wonder just what Anna told these people of our Lord? It would indeed been a blessed time to have lived — or would it? Isn't it better to live on this side of "the redemption of Jerusalem"? Redemption for the whole human race occurred just outside the walls of that ancient city. Indeed this was the only redemption the Messiah came to give. How materially minded has man been!

Pause — wait — think — then express yourself in thoughtful praise or thanks.

9. READ HIS WORD FOR PETITIONS.

Anna the prophetess offers so much to all of us: (1) Keep me aware of how important prayer is to all of life. (2) Increase my desire to live always aware of your presence. (3) Teach me the real meaning of fasting. (4) Increase my life to communicate the redemptive work of your Son. (6) How I do want to learn more and more about worshiping you. (7)I do want the same sympathetic understanding of widows as found in the New Testament.

Right here add your personal requests — and his answers.

10. READ HIS WORD AND WAIT — LISTEN — GOD SPEAKS!

Speak to me in the example of Anna: (1) "The words of my prophets yet speak through my word — hear them." (2) "There are many old women who could teach you much — learn from them." (3) "Men ought to continually give thanks for my mercy and love."

11. INTERCESSION FOR THE LOST WORLD

Indonesia — Point for prayer: (1) Sulawesi (Celebes) 10,000,000. Unreached peoples — the Muslim Bugi — a few believers now among them, also many smaller tribes in the interior. Minahassa in the north has over one million Protestants, mostly nominal. The Toradja people in central Sulawesi have emerged from much Muslim persecution for their turning to the Lord some years ago as a strong Church reaching out to the unsaved.

12. SING PRAISES TO OUR LORD.

We would see Jesus, for the shadows lengthen
Across this little landscape of our life;

We would see Jesus, our weak faith to strengthen
For the last weariness, the final strife.

WEEK THIRTY-TWO — THURSDAY

1. PRAISE GOD FOR WHO HE IS.

"Trust in the Lord, and do good; so you will dwell in the land, and enjoy security. Take delight in the Lord and he will give you the desires of your heart" (Psa. 37:3, 4). How wonderfully easy it is to praise you with these words before me! I do trust you—shall I say "I trust you implicitly"? I want to—yet I am reminded that someday, perhaps today, I will be called upon to exercise such trust when I cannot explain a circumstance of stress or suffering. I trust you not because I can explain all your actions, but because of your essential character. I will surely enjoy more security if I trust in you than if I do not trust you and live for myself. Oh, dear Lord, I have no reason whatsoever not to trust you. I want all men to have the personal security that comes by trusting you!

Express yourself in adoration for this quality of God.
Speak it audibly or write out your praise in your own devotional journal.

2. PRAISE GOD FOR WHAT HE MEANS TO ME.

Just for me.—The hidden qualities of yourself are all here. Every one of more than two hundred qualities of yourself are all encompassed in the word "trust" and "delight." This is my response to all you are. "Delight" suggests excitement and wonder—so should it be—and this *is* my reaction to yourself. What is there about you that would move me to such trust and delight? Here are a few qualities: (1) absolute love; (2) total personal interest in me; (3) intelligence and power beyond the wildest imagination; (4) a plan and program you are working out in my life right now; (5) a new world and life right on the other side of my last heart beat.

How do you personally relate to the personalness of God, and God who is personal?
Speak it out or write it out. It is *so important* that you establish *your own* devotional journal.

3. CONFESSION OF SIN

So often have I run across the root sin—the ultimate transgression—so it is here. If I do not trust you, if I find no enjoyment in your presence then all else falls apart. Dear Lord, I do not want to wait for some emergency—some stressful moment—but just for today, just now I want to trust you and rejoice in your presence. That I have not always done so is a sad admission—a terrible sin. I have trusted someone or something—I have found pleasure in the lust of the flesh, the lust of the eyes or the pride of life. Dear, dear Lord, it was terribly disappointing and the desires of my heart were not satisfied. Forgive me.

What personal sins do you want to confess? We *must* speak them to remove them.
Do it! *Now.* There is no one else you have sinned against more than God. Tell him so!

4. SING A PRAYER TO GOD.

Dear Lord and Father of mankind,
Forgive our foolish ways!
Reclothe us in our rightful mind;

In purer lives Thy service find,
In deeper rev'rence, praise.

Open your hymn book and sing the rest of the verses—or even sing another prayer song.

5. READ HIS WORD TO HIM!

His Word

2 After Jesus was born in Bethlehem in Judea, during the time of King Herod, Magi from the east came to Jerusalem ²and asked, "Where is the one who has been born king of the Jews? We saw his star in the east and have come to worship him."

³When King Herod heard this he was disturbed, and all Jerusalem with him. ⁴When he had called together all the people's chief priests and teachers of the law, he asked them where the Christ was to be born. ⁵"In Bethlehem in Judea," they replied, "for this is what the prophet has written:
⁶"'But you, Bethlehem, in the land of Judah,
   are by no means least among the rulers of Judah;
for out of you will come a ruler
   who will be the shepherd of my people Israel.'"
— *Matthew 2:1-6, NIV*

Read His Word to Him.

I am sometimes quite hesitant to read these words as if you were listening—as if I were looking at them from heaven's perspective. How presumptuous beyond human reason is such a thought! But, as you well know it is only a means of seeing more deeply into the meaning of what you are saying to me and all men. Only your servant Levi tells us of this amazing visit. Dear Lord, I have not come from the east, but I have indeed come to worship him! How did you prepare these "wise men" for this visit? How I do want to meet them and have a long visit with them. The arrival of these wealthy important men caused no small stir in the courts of Herod and the city of Jerusalem. How almost amused you must have been at their concern.

Please express your response to this beautiful text. Put your expression in your own prayer diary.

6. READ HIS WORD FOR YOURSELF.

I await eagerly this time with you! I believe the actual historical account—we can look upon the face of "Herod the King" in the representations men have left us—but he lived and acted as described by Matthew I believe because of historical evidence. Bless your name for the dependability of your record. How amazing that you would bring the lowest and the highest to the birth of your Son. This speaks sharply to me! If you brought the lowest and the highest—you want me to accept such as worshipers of yourself and your Son. I love the imagination behind the star! It is so real, so unusual, so beyond all man would do! This happened 2,000 years ago! Thank you! What an amazement! The chief priests and scribes knew the scriptures! They could turn to the right references. Did they believe your word? Not for themselves. Can I be living in their place today? Dear Lord, deliver me!

Pause in his presence and either audibly or in written form tell him all his word means to you.

7. READ HIS WORD IN THANKSGIVING.

How awesome it is to pause before *"the child* with Mary his mother": (1) Thank you for Bethlehem of Judea, a real town and a real province. (2) Thank you for these unnamed and unnumbered men of wisdom. (3) Thank you that these men knew from the very beginning that he was a king. (4) Thank you for the wondrous ways you have in leading men to yourself. (5) Thank you that men cannot be neutral when they are confronted with your Son. (6) Thank you Jesus is a ruler—my ruler. (7) Thank you for the "Israel of God" today, even his "called out ones." Govern us, dear Lord!

Give yourself to your own expression of gratitude—write it or speak it!

8. READ HIS WORD IN MEDITATION.

". . . from you shall come a ruler who will govern my people Israel." How very much came from "the little town of Bethlehem"! Let's notice: (1) A ruler came—and O what a ruler! One who had ruled the heaven of the heavens before he emptied himself and took the form of flesh. A ruler of his own body while upon this earth. Tempted in all points like us and yet without sin. A ruler of the world about him—he walked on water, cursed a fig tree, created food. A ruler of the men with whom he associated. He needed not for man to teach him—for he himself knew what was in man. (2) A governor came from Bethlehem. Whereas we know this term is almost a synonym for "ruler" we yet want to make a fresh application of it. He was governor of the new Jerusalem that only awaited his return. He was governor of ten million angels who eagerly anticipated his return and followed his every word and action.

Pause—wait—think—then express yourself in thoughtful praise or thanks.

9. READ HIS WORD FOR PETITIONS.

I indeed, like the wise men of old, have come to worship him: (1) Rule in my life as King. (2) Give me the wisdom that comes down from above. (3) Bow my total inward being before your throne. (4) Trouble my heart with the possibility that my Lord has a rival king—even myself. (5) Thank you that many men today know where your Son was born. (6) There are also more who do not know he came—move me to help.

Please, please remember these are prayers—speak them—reword them!

10. READ HIS WORD AND WAIT—LISTEN—GOD SPEAKS!

In these familiar verses say a new thing: (1) "Men will see him from all points of the compass when he comes again." (2) "Men still are wondering why no one has told them of my coming." (3) "Israel has yet to recognize her ruler."

11. INTERCESSION FOR THE LOST WORLD

Indonesia — Point for prayer: (1) *Irian Jaya* (West New Guinea) 1,000,000. A wild, undeveloped land with many small tribes emerging from the stone age. Yet God has moved in a remarkable way through the sacrificial work of many missions, and now 70% of the population is Christian. Pray for the continuing work in evangelism, church planting, Bible teaching and Bible translation. The *Church* needs more trained leaders, but many of the tribespeople are illiterate. The large people movements need to be well disciplined to avoid error, heathen practices and nationalistic splits within the churches. Pray for the growing number of missionaries going out to unevangelized tribes from these tribal churches.

12. SING PRAISES TO OUR LORD.

All hail the pow'r of Jesus' name!
Let angels prostrate fall:
Bring forth the royal diadem,
And crown Him Lord of all,
Bring forth the royal diadem,
And crown Him Lord of all!

WEEK THIRTY-TWO — FRIDAY

1. PRAISE GOD FOR WHO HE IS.

"Commit your way to the Lord; trust in him, and he will act. He will bring forth your vindication as the light, and your right as the noonday" (Psa. 37:5, 6). Dear Father, it would seem here that you are making some very definite promises. The conditions are clear, but so are the promises. The covenant concept seems to be so very prominent in all your word. If I commit my life and all I plan and do into your hands; and I trust you with what I have com-mitted you will act! I would expect you to act through the daily routine. Can this happen today? Praise your name, I *know* it can. I do not want to simply seek your benediction on what I have already planned. I want to yield up all I have planned for your inspection and judgment. This is an invariable principle for all men in every situation. Oh, that all men practiced it!

Express yourself in adoration for this quality of God.
Speak it audibly or write out your praise in your own devotional journal.

2. PRAISE GOD FOR WHAT HE MEANS TO ME.

For me. In a practical application of this principle I think of the practice of George Muller. He said: "To ascertain the will of God: (1) I seek at the beginning to get my heart into such a state that it has no will of its own in regard to a given matter. Nine-tenths of the trouble with people generally is just here. Nine-tenths of the difficulties are overcome when our hearts are ready to do the Lord's will, whatever it may be. When one is truly in this state, it is usually but a little way to the knowledge of what His will is. (2) Having done this, I do not leave the result to feeling or simple impression. If so, I make myself liable to great delusions. (3) I seek the Will of the Spirit of God through, or in connection with, the Word of God. The Spirit and the Word must be combined. If I look to the Spirit alone without the Word, I lay myself open to great delusions also. If the Holy Ghost guides us at all, He will do it according to the Scriptures and never contrary to them. (4) Next I take into account providential circumstances. These often plainly indicate God's Will in connection with His Word and Spirit. (5) I ask God in prayer to reveal His Will to me aright. (6) Thus, through prayer to God, the study of the Word, and reflection, I come to a deliberate judgment according to the best of my ability and knowledge, and if my mind is thus at peace, and continues so after two or three more petitions, I proceed accordingly. In trivial matters, and in transactions involving most important issues, I have found this method always effective."

How do you personally relate to the direction of God, and God who directs your way?
Speak it out or write it out. It is *so important* that you establish *your own* devotional journal.

3. CONFESSION OF SIN

I want to confess freely how far short I fall in the very areas where I could be blessed. (1) It is very, very difficult for me to have no will in any given matter. Dear Lord, I do, I do want to say not my will be done. I give it up to you! (2) I have acted on mere feeling or impressions. This is a sin. I confess it as another form of pure selfishness. (3) I have *not* meditated on your word enough—I need to be in your word during the day. I need also to be far more sensitive to your Spirit's presence. (4) I must have the wisdom from above to evaluate providential circumstances. I claim it! I want to wait before I leap. Help me. Forgive me. (5) Dear God, that I would ask specifically. Forgive me for the sin of not specifically asking.

What personal sins do you want to confess? We *must* speak them to remove them.
Do it! *Now.* There is no one else you have sinned against more than God. Tell him so!

4. SING A PRAYER TO GOD.

O tell of His might, and sing of His grace,
Whose robe is the light, whose canopy space;

His chariots of wrath the deep thunder-clouds form,
And dark is His path on the wings of the storm.

Open your hymn book and sing the rest of the verses—or even sing another prayer song.

5. READ HIS WORD TO HIM!
His Word

[7]Then Herod called the Magi secretly and found out from them the exact time the star appeared. [8]He sent them to Bethlehem and said, "Go and make a careful search for the child. As soon as you find him, report to me, so that I too may go and worship him." [9]After they had heard the king, they went on their way, and the star they had seen in the east went ahead of them until it stopped over the place where the child was. [10]When they saw the star, they were overjoyed. [11]On coming to the house, they saw the child with his mother Mary, and they bowed down and worshiped him. Then they opened their treasures and presented him with gifts of gold and of incense and of myrrh. [12]And having been warned in a dream not to go back to Herod, they returned to their country by another route.   — *Matthew 2:7-12, NIV*

WEEK THIRTY-TWO — FRIDAY

Read His Word to Him.

A delight! To now look back upon these events as an accomplished fact—at the same time to view them as happening in the present—to know that they shall always be in the future is much more than my poor mind can encompass, and yet this must be a small part of your per-spective. What words were exchanged between Herod and the wisemen as they met in secret? I ask you because I know it was no secret to you. Man's secret meetings must appear ludicrous to you! Herod should have worshiped him. One day he will worship him—as will everyone.

Please express your response to this beautiful text. Put your expression in your own prayer diary.

6. READ HIS WORD FOR YOURSELF.

I wonder what there was about the appearance of the star that produced such an immediate response in the wise men? "When they saw the star, they *rejoiced exceedingly with great joy.*" Had the star disappeared momentarily? Did the star become brighter or nearer? There *was* something about it to obtain such happiness. Before them was a new born king—the king of the whole nation of Israel —a king in a spiritual, supernatural sense. After all, what king has ever had such an unusual announcement for his coming? There must be some significance to the gifts offered: (1) Gold—precious and pure like the nature of the One before them. (2) Frankincense—a lovely fragrance like the character of this dear One—a continual expression of praise was the conduct of our Lord. (3) Myrrh— used in burial, in part of the anointing of the body. How full of meaning are these gifts.

Pause in his presence and either audibly or in written form tell him all his word means to you.

7. READ HIS WORD IN THANKSGIVING.

How abundant are our sources for gratitude: (1) Thank you that Herod did not himself or his men accompany the wise men. (2) Thank you that worship was such an important pursuit for the men from the east. (3) Thank you for your timing and direction of the celestial body. (4) Thank you for the provision of a "house"—who provided it? (5) Thank you for every day Mary gave in the care of our blessed Lord. (6) Thank you for the strange unusual scene that must have greeted Mary's eyes as she met those men and received their gifts.

8. READ HIS WORD IN MEDITATION.

"And being warned in a dream not to return to Herod, they departed to their own country by another way." How very kind of you to take a personal interest in the safety of these men. We are not going to meet them again this side of the world to come. I imagine this incident became the largest event in their lives, or the lives of those from whom they came. Do you speak to people in dreams today? Your word *does* say that in these last days "old men shall dream dreams." Indeed, I have! I have dreamed of the evangelization of so many who have never once heard our Lord. I have dreamed of every Christian being a student of your word.

Pause—wait—think—then express yourself in praise or thanks.

9. READ HIS WORD FOR PETITIONS.

The worship of the wise men leads me to prayer: (1) Since you control the galaxies of space I know you can meet every need of every man—praise your name! (2) I also know you will not meet human needs apart from our cooperation. (3) Deliver me from deceit—what a sore temptation! (4) Thank you for the leadership of your word for my life today.

10. READ HIS WORD AND WAIT—LISTEN—GOD SPEAKS!

As I bow with these men speak to me: (1) "There *are* men in the world today who want to destroy my Son." (2) "My presence is always seen in the worship of my Son." (3) "My gift is enough and no gift is too small to offer to my Son."

11. INTERCESSION FOR THE LOST WORLD

Japan — Population: 112,300,000. Growth rate—1.2%. People per sq. km.—302.

Point for prayer: (1) *This talented people* are materialistic, unresponsive and hidden in a centuries-old cocoon of culture and bondage to demonic powers and multiplied varieties of Buddhism. Few are willing to make the decisive break with the past despite many being sympathetic to the claims of the Gospel. Pray for a mighty work of the Holy Spirit to break down these barriers and liberate these people through the Gospel.

12. SING PRAISES TO OUR LORD.

Amazing grace! how sweet the sound,
That saved a wretch like me!

I once was lost, but now am found,
Was blind, but now I see.

WEEK THIRTY-TWO — SATURDAY

1. PRAISE GOD FOR WHO HE IS.

"The steps of a man are from the Lord, and he establishes him in the way he delights; though he fall, he shall not be cast headlong, for the Lord is the stay of his hand" (Psa. 37:23, 24). Praise your name, I'm gald to come before you and claim your promises. You are saying here in words that cannot be misunderstood that you will direct my steps, indeed so carefully will you guide me that you will be walking in my shoes! If such is true — and I know it is — then you must be in me to give such directions. If such is true it is because I want you inside of me. Not only so, I want you to have total control. "It is no longer I that live, but Christ who liveth in me." By this simple but profound relationship this blessed quality of yourself can be a reality for any man.

Express yourself in adoration for this quality of God.
Speak it audibly or write out your praise in your own devotional journal.

2. PRAISE GOD FOR WHAT HE MEANS TO ME.

Just for me. The second verse (24) speaks especially to me. "Though he fall," has been true so often. It has been my experience to walk in your way, and to walk in my own way. The little phrase "he (God) establishes him (you and me) in whose way he (you and I) delights." If we delight in our way we will walk in it, if we delight in your way we will walk in that. I agree whole heartedly with George Muller that it is not all that different to discover your way in every matter if we are truly serious about prayer and the study of your word. There have been no decisions in my life unknown or unnoticed by you. The principles of your word are altogether adequate.

How do you personally relate to the leadership of God, and God who leads?
Speak it out or write it out. It is *so important* that you establish *your own* devotional journal.

3. CONFESSION OF SIN

I am so glad I have not been "cast head long" — although I thought at times it had surely happened. In your infinite mercy my hand was held from striking the blow that would have severed the cord of love. By your grace I was restrained from the last decision that would have removed me from contact with those who love you and me. That I found myself in such a pigpen was my fault — my choice — my stupidity. Forgive me, I will arise and go home. Dear Lord, I purpose to delight myself in your words — in your ways — in yourself in your Son.

What personal sins do you want to confess? We *must* speak them to remove them.
Do it! *Now.* There is no one else you have sinned against more than God. Tell him so!

4. SING A PRAYER TO GOD.

O Rock divine, O Refuge dear,
A shelter in the time of storm;
Be Thou our helper ever near,
A shelter in the time of storm.

Oh, Jesus is a Rock in a weary land,
A weary land, a weary land;
Oh, Jesus is a Rock in a weary land,
A shelter in the time of storm.

Open your hymn book and sing the rest of the verses — or even sing another prayer song.

5. READ HIS WORD TO HIM!

His Word

[13]When they had gone, an angel of the Lord appeared to Joseph in a dream. "Get up," he said, "take the child and his mother and escape to Egypt. Stay there until I tell you, for Herod is going to search for the child to kill him."

[14]So he got up, took the child and his mother during the night and left for Egypt, [15]where he stayed until the death of Herod. And so was fulfilled what the Lord had said through the prophet: "Out of Egypt I called my son."

[16]When Herod realized that he had been outwitted by the Magi, he was furious, and he gave orders to kill all the boys in Bethlehem and its vicinity who were two years old and under, in accordance with the time he had learned from the Magi.   — Matthew 2:13-16, NIV

Read His Word to Him.

There is so much of yourself in these few verses! I want to tell you how very much they mean to me. Joseph was not mentioned in the visit of the wisemen but it does not mean he was not there. It could have been because he was away or working, or both. He is very much alive. He is also very much aware of the danger present. The name of the angel is not given, only his instruction. The murderous intentions of Herod were known by heaven before anyone else knew. Joseph doesn't even wait until morning — no sooner had the dream registered than he acted! What an unusual fulfillment of prophecy! Dear Lord, I want to say how very much your concern and personal interest mean to me. I believe you are at work in our lives today.

Please express your response to this beautiful text. Put your expression in your own prayer diary.

6. READ HIS WORD FOR YOURSELF.

Amen! Help me to be as ready to adapt my life and schedule to your will for me. Did Joseph use some of the gold given by the wisemen for the trip to Egypt? At least I believe you never give a command without the means to carry it out. Praise your name for this confidence. Praise you that you are in the business of helping man to see his limitations—even when he is a "big" man like Herod. This text lets me see your Son as a dear little boy of two years old. What was the look on his face as he looked up at the stars on the way to Egypt? What thoughts were in the minds of the soldiers as they went to protect the ruler against boys of two years old? Dear Father, how wondrous are your ways!

It is so important that you pause in his presence
and either audibly or in written form tell him all his word means to you.

7. READ HIS WORD IN THANKSGIVING.

From Mary and Joseph's viewpoint this is surely a text of thanksgiving: (1) They could thank you that angels were always beholding the face of the Father and the needs of his children. (2) They could be thankful they were willing to obey and not to rationalize. (3) They could be thankful for the open travel routes. (4) They could be thankful there was a place to stay in Egypt when they got there. (5) They could be thankful for the money to live on while they stayed in Egypt. (6) They could be thankful your goodness can always overcome man's wrath, either in this world or the next. (7) They could be thankful that God provided a shelter in a foreign land where once there was no shelter.

Give yourself to your own expression of gratitude—write it or speak it!

8. READ HIS WORD IN MEDITATION.

". . . in accordance with the time he learned from the Magi." Why did Herod react so irrationally? He could have investigated and found Jesus no threat to his rule. (1) He could have learned that God does indeed have his own time, i.e., God has a scheduled sequence of events —it was "the fulness of time." The completion of the promises and prophecies made to the Fathers. (2) He could have learned that time is only a relative term, i.e., created by man to give him a sense of progress. The importance of time is measured by the event. The birth of the Messiah was *the event*. That it happened during the reign of Herod or the life of the wisemen was almost parenthetical.

Pause—wait—think—then express yourself in thoughtful praise or thanks.

9. READ HIS WORD FOR PETITIONS.

What a privilege it is to pray—especially as guided by this text: (1) Give me an increasing awareness of your constant involvement in my life. (2) Open my understanding to include your interest in all of my life in every relationship. (3) What an encouragement to know you know Satan's moves before he makes them. (4) Give me the total willing obedience I see in Joseph. (5) How kind you were to supply gold and other gifts to help them make the journey to Egypt. (6) Keep me aware that if I know it or not your word is being fulfilled. (7) Defeat Satan's strategy in my own experience.

Please, please remember these are prayers—speak them—reword them!

10. READ HIS WORD AND WAIT—LISTEN—GOD SPEAKS!

Speak to me in these verses: (1) "I can deliver my children from any efforts of men to defeat my purpose." (2) "I am still at work in the lives of my children." (3) "The deceiver is not dead—he is still at work."

11. INTERCESSION FOR THE LOST WORLD

Japan — Points for prayer: (1) *The Church in Japan* needs our prayers. We mention some points: *The United Church of Christ*, the largest Church, is basically a government imposed union of Presbyterian, Reformed, etc., churches of nearly 40 years ago. The Church is crippled by liberalism and violent controversy stirred up by leftist young preachers over social action. The Church, and other larger liberal denominations, are in serious decline, and only kept going by a few faithful believers who carry on in spite of the leaders. Pray for a moving of the Spirit and a return to Biblical theology. (2) *The smaller and younger Bible believing Churches* are growing both in numbers, evangelistic zeal and missionary vision. There is a new surge of evangelism in progress which is being ably led by some of Japan's finest Christian leaders and evangelists. Pray for a great harvest of souls to be both won and retained in the churches.

12. SING PRAISES TO OUR LORD.

My Jesus, I love Thee, I know Thou art mine,
For Thee all the follies of sin I resign;
My gracious Redeemer, my Savior art Thou;
If ever I loved Thee, my Jesus, 'tis now.

1. PRAISE GOD FOR WHO HE IS.

"He put a new song in my mouth, a song of praise to our God. Many will see and fear, and put their trust in the Lord" (Psa. 40:3). I am so glad you are a God of song. You have originated so many songs. You appreciate singing. I like new things—all men are interested in innovation. You are the original source of all that is new and interesting! Dear Lord, whereas I do praise you and rejoice that my life can be one succession of new and interesting blessings, this is not true of most of the human population. We can "walk in newness of life," i.e., all of life is new and fresh and interesting. But not so with so much of your world. I do want to help. How I long for the last half of this verse to be true: "Many will see and fear (wonder in adoration) and put their trust in the Lord."

Express yourself in adoration for this quality of God.
Speak it audibly or write out your praise in your own devotional journal.

2. PRAISE GOD FOR WHAT HE MEANS TO ME.

What is *new* about the new song you have given to me? (1) A *new purpose* for singing. Sex, food and money are the themes of the songs of this world. Peace, hope and love are the themes of the new song. The restlessness, the unsatisfied feeling, the elusive desire has been replaced by a fulfillment we never found anywhere else. (2) A *new response* to the song we sing. When we truly communicate the reality of your presence men do wonder. There is a genuine deep interest. How soon are the songs of our day forgotten! There is something hauntingly real and lasting to your song. Even when men do not believe they cannot ignore the joy of the new song! What a promise! "Many will see (hear) and fear, and put their trust in the Lord."

How do you personally relate to the song of the Lord, and God who produces song?
Speak it out or write it out. It is *so important* that you establish *your own* devotional journal.

3. CONFESSION OF SIN

It is just as true that we too often sing the songs of time and not eternity; of earth and not heaven; of the flesh and not of the spirit. Dear Lord, forgive. Stealing is yet stealing after we have what we have stolen. Lying is yet lying after we have lied. Adultery is yet adultery after the act is completed. There is no song in sin. Dear Lord, open my mouth to you in the song of deliverance; in the song of freedom. If I pause and attempt an analysis of my sin I only end up in frustration. Dear God, I admit the fact of sin and accept gladly the fact of forgiveness!

What personal sins do you want to confess? We *must* speak them to remove them.
Do it! *Now.* There is no one else you have sinned against more than God. Tell him so!

4. SING A PRAYER TO GOD.

A mighty fortress is our God,
A bulwark never failing;
Our helper He, amid the flood
Of mortal ills prevailing.
For still our ancient foe
Doth seek to work us woe;
His craft and pow'r are great,
And, armed with cruel hate,
On earth is not his equal.

Open your hymn book and sing the rest of the verses—or even sing another prayer song.

5. READ HIS WORD TO HIM!

His Word

[17]Then what was said through the prophet Jeremiah was fulfilled:
[18]"A voice is heard in Ramah,
weeping and great mourning,
Rachel weeping for her children
and refusing to be comforted.
because they are no more."
[19]After Herod died, an angel of the Lord appeared in a dream to Joseph in Egypt [20]and said, "Get up, take the child and his mother and go to the land of Israel, for those who were trying to take the child's life are dead."
[21]So he got up, took the child and his mother and went to the land of Israel. [22]But when he heard that Archelaus was reigning in Judea in place of his father Herod, he was afraid to go there. Having been warned in a dream, he withdrew to the district of Galilee, [23]and he went and lived in a town called Nazareth. So was fulfilled what was said through the prophets: "He will be called a Nazarene."
— *Matthew 2:17-23, NIV*

Read His Word to Him.

I do so want to tell you all this text means to me, but first of all I want to praise you for your active, up-front concern in the lives of all. For every mother in Bethlehem; they are as near and dear to you as was Jacob's beloved wife Rachel. As her first-born was sold into Egypt and presumed dead by Jacob—and even though Rachel herself was dead—yet she somehow shared the grief. It was as if this ancient mother arose from her tomb to weep also with the bereft mothers of the little town. (We are well aware of Jeremiah's reference to the Babylon captivity, but I want to relate all of this as closely as at all possible to your dear Son and my Savior!) (2) You got the message of Herod's death to Joseph faster than the couriers of the king could get it out to the provinces. Your warning and protection is such an encouragement for today!

Please express your response to this beautiful text. Put your expression in your own prayer diary.

6. READ HIS WORD FOR YOURSELF.

There never are enough or adequate words to tell you all your eternal word means to me. But it is always a joy to try. (1) If you were touched by the weeping of the mother of the murdered, I know you are concerned every time a mother weeps today. (2) If you knew ahead of the latest news just what was happening in the political maneuvers of Israel surely you know what is happening in America today! (3) Even when we make a move in what seems to be the right direction—if it is not, you have ways of letting us know. It may not be a dream as in Joseph's experience, but you will direct us, i.e., if we are sensitive to your leading. Dear Lord, I do want to be!

Pause in his presence and either audibly or in written form tell him all his word means to you.

7. READ HIS WORD IN THANKSGIVING.

Gratitude seems a very prominent part of these words: (1) Thank you for Matthew's ability to show the Old Testament fulfillment in so many events. (2) Thank you for each of Joseph's dreams—you said so much in each of them. (3) Thank you that there is an end to all human opposition. (4) Thank you that our Lord lived in a town where men thought it would be impossible to live a pure life. (5) Thank you that our Lord had brothers and sisters that his beautiful life might be an example for all (cf. Matthew 3:55, 56). (6) Thank you for the whole Herodian family—what an example of rejection! (7) Thank you for the beautiful innocent child Jesus.

Give yourself to your own expression of gratitude—write it or speak it!

8. READ HIS WORD IN MEDITATION.

"He shall be called a Nazarene." Matthew says that several, or even all the Old Testament prophets agree to this designation. We believe it refers to his being despised and rejected of men. The slanderous ridicule of the Messiah coming from this insignificant town was behind the name. Let's consider just how he was despised: (1) As to his education—he had no credentials from the schools at Jerusalem. And yet this is the one quality that enhances him in our eyes. His wisdom was far beyond men. (2) As to his possessions—he had to depend on others to feed and cloth him (Luke 8:1ff.). "He who was rich became poor, that we through his poverty might become rich."

Pause—wait—think—then express yourself in thoughtful praise or thanks.

9. READ HIS WORD FOR PETITIONS.

How meaningful prayer is when directed by your word: (1) There are many who weep today because they have lost their children—open my heart to them. (2) Keep me open to the possibility that you will use very unusual circumstances to teach me. (3) Remind me again that even the greatest of men die—your work is dependent upon yourself not men. (4) I want to remember the death of Pharaoh and Herod—opposition removed in one day. (5) I claim your protection for my life today. (6) Open my mind to your direction: When shall I decide and when shall I let you decide? (7) I do ask your definite direction in the rule of our men in high places.

Right here add your personal requests—and his answers.

10. READ HIS WORD AND WAIT—LISTEN—GOD SPEAKS!

What can I hear from you through these verses? (1) "My service will not make you immune from sufferings." (2) "Death is at times a great blessing." (3) "It is just as important for you to decide as it is for myself."

11. INTERCESSION FOR THE LOST WORLD

Japan — Point for prayer: (1) *The needs and problems of the churches*—it is reckoned that around 90% of all those who seek the Lord later backslide through the pressures of family, society, unequal marriages and the pervasive influence of the spiritual darkness of Japan. Revival is the great need—to bring Christians to a point of total abandonment to the Lord Jesus, and rid them of the cloying power of their background.

12. SING PRAISES TO OUR LORD.

"Man of Sorrows," what a name
For the Son of God who came

Ruined sinners to reclaim!
Hallelujah! what a Savior!

WEEK THIRTY-THREE — MONDAY

1. PRAISE THE LORD FOR WHO HE IS.

"I have not hid thy saving help within my heart, I have spoken of thy faithfulness and thy salvation; I have not concealed thy steadfast love and thy faithfulness from the great congregation" (Psa. 40:10). There are four characteristics of yourself in this one verse. Each of these qualities are to be made known "to the great congregation." In David's day it was the nation of Israel. Today each man has a "great congregation" he meets during his lifetime. All the people who have touched my life and I theirs. How many of these people will hear and know of: (1) your saving help? (2) your faithfulness? (3) your salvation? (4) your steadfast love? I cannot say for all the world, I *can* say, I do say for my own life.

Express yourself in adoration for this quality of God.
Speak it audibly or write out your praise in your own devotional journal.

2. PRAISE GOD FOR WHAT HE MEANS TO ME.

Just for me. Indeed, indeed, you have given me "saving help" in all of my life! (1) Your help saved me from the bondage of drugs—I believe I could easily have been enslaved. I am so glad you gave me a reason to live so I did not need this escape. (2) Your help saved me from deep bondage—hatred for other people—I could easily have harbored resentment for others. You have been so merciful to me. I have seen such total forgiveness in my Lord. You have had much more reason to be perpetually unhappy with men—but you are not. (3) Your help saved me from chronic complaint, i.e., complaining about everything. (I sound like the Pharisee in the temple.) Dear Lord, I am *not* saying these thing to be compared with others. These are temptations to me—from which you have saved me. Praise your name!

How do you personally relate to this saving by God, and God who is Savior?
Speak it out or write it out. It is *so important* that you establish *your own* devotional journal.

3. CONFESSION OF SIN

It is easy to see very clearly that I yet need all four of these qualities of yourself yet operative in my life! There are several, several areas in my life where I need your saving help! (1) Save me from the praise of men. (2) Save me from the lust of the flesh. (3) Save me from the pride of possessions. (4) Save me from comfortable living. I freely confess that whereas you abide faithful I have oft times been faithless—I have had but little faith in the power of the good news to change some men and women. Forgive me! I have been faithless in believing you have ways of changing all men.

What personal sins do you want to confess? We *must* speak them to remove them.
Do it! *Now.* There is no one else you have sinned against more than God. Tell him so!

4. SING A PRAYER TO GOD.

Thro' this changing world below,
Lead me gently, gently as I go;
Trusting Thee, I cannot stray,
I can never, never lose my way.

Ev'ry day, ev'ry hour,
Let me feel Thy cleansing pow'r;
Trusting Thee, I cannot stray,
I can never, never lose my way.

Open your hymn book and sing the rest of the verses—or even sing another prayer song.

5. READ HIS WORD TO HIM!

His Word

[39]When Joseph and Mary had done everything required by the Law of the Lord, they returned to Galilee to their own town of Nazareth. [40]And the child grew and became strong; he was filled with wisdom, and the grace of God was upon him.

[41]Every year his parents went to Jerusalem for the Feast of the Passover. [42]When he was twelve years old, they went up to the Feast, according to the custom.
— Luke 2:39-42, NIV

Read His Word to Him.

How precious is this word! As Joseph and Mary and the boy Jesus passed through the city gates and down the streets of Nazareth to their home I wonder what the residents of the town thought? Perhaps nothing; they were too occupied with their own affairs. I'm sure you thought of many things! I would not at all presume to be your counselor or read your mind, but I am sure you saw the scene in an entirely different light. What poignant words "he was (as a child) filled with wisdom, and the grace of God was upon him." How good it would be to hear from Mary and Joseph some of the words of wisdom spoken by Jesus at this early age. Did any of his brothers or sisters remember? I do want to hear all about those so-called "silent years" when we all get to your house!

Please express your response to this beautiful text. Put your expression in your own prayer diary.

WEEK THIRTY-THREE — MONDAY

6. READ HIS WORD FOR YOURSELF.

I am so glad I never tire of praising you and worshiping you through what you say to me in these beautiful words! Dear Lord, I do want to be obedient, obedient in every relationship of life. I am not, but I do want to — to obey the state and government; to obey my obligations of employment; to obey in my family relationship. Forgive me and help me! In what sense was your grace upon our Lord in his childhood? In the little carpenter shop in Nazareth, how did you express your favor with Jesus? Was it with his answers to the customers who came into the shop? Was it in his answers to his brothers and sisters in the home? Was it while working with Joseph? In all of these relationships I'm sure Jesus wanted to represent you perfectly, because of this desire, and out of your love he did perfectly mirror all a boy of that age should be. Thank you!

It is so important that you pause in his presence
and either audibly or in written form tell him all his word means to you.

7. READ HIS WORD IN THANKSGIVING.

A charming area for this expression! (1) Thank you for the unresisting willingness to keep the law as seen in the conduct of Joseph and Mary. (2) Thank you for their meekness in taking up residence in a very difficult town. (3) Thank you for the beautiful example of the natural homelife of our Lord. (4) Thank you for every meal Jesus ate at the table in Nazareth. He can eat with me again today. (5) Thank you for all the Passover meant to Jesus — did he know then that he would be God's Passover Lamb? (6) Thank you for the joy of the journey — and all the conversations along the way. (7) Thank you for the emphasis upon family unity.

Give yourself to your own expression of gratitude — write it or speak it!

8. READ HIS WORD IN MEDITATION.

". . . according to the custom." So many, many things are done "according to the custom"; some customs are good and some have lost their meaning. It was customary for every male Jew to go to Jerusalem three times a year to observe the feasts of Passover, Pentecost and Tabernacles. It was the custom to bring your child to the temple for worship when twelve years old. These customs, and no doubt others, were observed by Joseph and Mary. What meaning did all of this have to our Lord? We wish we knew just how God lived in human form, i.e., how much influence the body had on the spirit. What were the thoughts of Jesus as he walked the seventy miles from Nazareth to Jerusalem?

Pause — wait — think — then express yourself in thoughtful praise or thanks.

9. READ HIS WORD FOR PETITIONS.

This is such a charming story I can find many places in it for prayer: (1) May I have the same humble willingness to obey your law as I see in Joseph and Mary. (2) If our Lord could grow in wisdom surely I have even a greater need to do so. (3) Give me your grace for this day and its cares. (4) May I establish good habits that become customs in my family. (5) Thank you that we can remember our Passover Lamb each day. (6) Increase my wisdom. (7) Deepen my appreciation of your grace.

Please, please remember these are prayers — speak them — reword them!

10. READ HIS WORD AND WAIT — LISTEN — GOD SPEAKS!

How meaningful are your words to me through this text: (1) "The body of my Son is yet growing in wisdom and grace." (2) "Custom can be a very meaningful expression of your love for me." (3) "Custom can be dead and dull — you decide."

11. INTERCESSION FOR THE LOST WORLD

Japan — Points for prayer: (1) *The training of leaders* is being ably done through many Seminaries. There are also some fine Bible Schools that emphasize the spiritual life of the students. Pray for the calling of dedicated young people into the ministry and also for missionary service. (2) *Missionary vision* is growing. There are now about 140 Japanese missionaries serving the Lord in 24 countries. Pray for the sending of more students with a call to the mission field.

12. SING PRAISES TO OUR LORD.

Day is dying in the west,
Heav'n is touching earth with rest;
Wait and worship while the night
Sets her evening lamps alight
Thro' all the sky.

Holy, holy, holy, Lord God of Hosts!
Heav'n and earth are full of Thee!
Heav'n and earth are praising Thee,
O Lord most high!

453

WEEK THIRTY-THREE — TUESDAY

1. PRAISE GOD FOR WHO HE IS.

"As a hart longs for flowing streams, so longs my soul for thee, O God. My soul thirsts for God, for the living God. When shall I come and behold the face of God?" (Psa. 42:1, 2). You are alive, responsive and present. You can and do bring refreshment to the whole life of man. You have created a deep longing in us that can only be satisfied in our praise and worship before you. We are uncomfortable until we give ourselves to you. All of these qualities and more are found in those two verses. The deer was created for the flowing stream—man is created for you. The whole of man: (1) his mind; (2) will; (3) emotions; (4) conscience reaches out to you. It is so good to know you are alive and eager to satisfy the deepest needs of all men. We surely can answer the psalmist's question: we behold your face in the face of your Son!

Express yourself in adoration for this quality of God.
Speak it audibly or write out your praise in your own devotional journal.

2. PRAISE GOD FOR WHAT HE MEANS TO ME.

Just for me. I like the preciseness of the text. A deer prefers the "flowing stream," not the still pool. So it is you are perfectly matched with me. More accurately, I was created to complement yourself! I like also the thought of refreshment and contentment here suggested. Peacefulness and serenity are only mine in you! Bless your name forever! I am so glad that there will never be a time when I cannot fully satisfy my intellectual pursuits in an examination of your word. There are no choices in my life that cannot find definite direction from what you have said. There are no emotions that cannot find total expression within your will. My conscience can always be good and clear and clean as I obey your word. Praise your name!

How do you personally relate to the desire for God, and God who longs for you?
Speak it out or write it out. It is *so important* that you establish *your own* devotional journal.

3. CONFESSION OF SIN

How easily I say the above words—too easily. To will indeed is present. But to do that which is good and right—ah, here is where I need another One to work in me both to will and to work. I have been deceived! I have been trapped! Someone has lied to me! How weak I am! How open to error! Satan is the deceiver, the trapper, the liar. Dear God, oh, flowing stream of clear water! oh, fountain of refreshment and cleansing I come to you! When shall I ever learn that "in me, that is in my present body, dwells no good thing"? When? When? Now! I learn it now. But to remember at all times, with all people and in all circumstances! I must, I will meditate on your word day and night. I *want* to lose myself in you.

What personal sins do you want to confess? We *must* speak them to remove them.
Do it! *Now.* There is no one else you have sinned against more than God. Tell him so!

4. SING A PRAYER TO GOD.

Holy, Holy, Holy! Tho' the darkness hide Thee,
Casting down their golden crowns around the glassy sea;
Cherubim and seraphim falling down before Thee,
Which wert, and art, and evermore shalt be.

Open your hymn book and sing the rest of the verses—or even sing another prayer song.

5. READ HIS WORD TO HIM!

His Word

[43] After the Feast was over, while his parents were returning home, the boy Jesus stayed behind in Jerusalem, but they were unaware of it. [44] Thinking he was in their company, they traveled on for a day. Then they began looking for him among their relatives and friends.

— Luke 2:43,44, NIV

Read His Word to Him.

What a meaningful time it must have been for Jesus to enter into the observance of the Passover feast for the first time. When we pause to consider we know he was present at the first passover in Egypt. Dear Lord, I have a difficult time each time with this attempt to reach above my perspective to yours. I know it is good, and I want to do it, I am greatly blessed by it, but I need your help, your wisdom. As an example: "Why did your Son stay in Jerusalem while he knew his parents had left him?" Was it to call attention to his mission for you? It was such a typical human thing to do. Our own children have done so many similar things. So are all the subtleties of your actions among men. Blessed be your name!

Please express your response to this beautiful text. Put your expression in your own prayer diary.

WEEK THIRTY-THREE — TUESDAY

6. READ HIS WORD FOR YOURSELF.

Indeed, indeed, I gladly enter into it! How I would like to have been there to recline at the Passover table with my Lord. I would not want to say anything, or to even be observed, just a silent invisible guest to watch Joseph and Jesus as they ate together.

I am shocked to remember I do indeed share with him in another feast which is but the fulfillment of the Pass-over. I hear him say again to me: "I shall not drink again of this fruit of the vine until that day when I drink it new with you in my Father's kingdom" (Matthew 26:29). I believe one expression of the Father's kingdom is the church of our Lord. Every Lord's day I can expect him to keep his appointment. Will I see him there?

It is so important that you pause in his presence
and either audibly or in written form tell him all his word means to you.

7. READ HIS WORD IN THANKSGIVING.

Dear Lord, I shall center most of my expression of worship in 2:44 — (I really do not know why I write such introductory words.) (1) Thank you for the boy Jesus so much like every boy — and yet so unlike every boy. (2) Thank you for this clear glimpse of the frailties of Mary and Joseph. (3) Thank you for the attraction of the temple and its worship that kept my Lord in Jerusalem. (4) Thank you for the trust Mary and Joseph placed in Jesus, i.e., that he was able to take care of himself. (5) Thank you for the strong family relationships — in that they looked first among their relatives. (6) Thank you for the concern his parents had that it was no more than a day's journey before they began inquiry. (7) Thank you for the reminder that we can never take your presence for granted.

Give yourself to your own expression of gratitude — write it or speak it!

8. READ HIS WORD IN MEDITATION.

"Thinking he was in their company, they traveled on for a day." In the close mutual fellowship of the Hebrew family this would be easy to do. Most especially when there were large crowds in the temple, and even on the road home. How many things there were to discuss about the Passover feast or the events of life with persons Mary and Joseph had not seen in several years. Since Jesus was the oldest of at least seven children (Matthew 13:55, 56) it could be that Mary was a little preoccupied with the other children — (or were they left at home?). There are as many rationalizations and justifications then as there are now.

The only way we will know Jesus is with us is for us to take time to see him, to hear him, to speak to him. How sad and inadequate is that day when we have gone through all twenty-four hours and we have not looked into his blessed face, nor heard his dear voice or spoken to him about the events of the journey. Dear God, forgive!

Pause — wait — think — then express yourself in thoughtful praise or thanks.

9. READ HIS WORD FOR PETITIONS.

What a loss there is in assuming Jesus is with us. (1) May I remember Jesus has never left his point of interest. (2) Keep me aware that Jesus is in his temple — even my body in the Person of the Holy Spirit. (3) Teach me over again that I *must not* assume anything in spiritual development. (4) I am so glad I know where to look for my Lord — all I will ever know of him is found in the gospels. (5) I want to make direct contact with Jesus by reading his life as recorded by his biographer — he will not be found among his relatives. (6) If Jesus seems distant or not present, I know who has been lost. (7) Thank you that Jesus is alive for evermore.

Right here add your personal requests — and his answers.

10. READ HIS WORD AND WAIT — LISTEN — GOD SPEAKS!

In these two verses speak to me: (1) "My Son is still at work in My House." (2) "Jesus is at work through his body the church." (3) "Make sure you are with him."

11. INTERCESSION FOR THE LOST WORLD

Japan — Point for prayer: (1) *Missions* — There is complete freedom for the entry of missionaries, but adaptation to the culture and learning what is reputed to be the world's hardest language is a barrier to effective service that takes years to cross. Pray for first term missionaries as they seek to prepare themselves for future usefulness, and pray that they may not be discouraged, but filled with faith and power for their difficult task. There are many opportunities for both career and short-term missionaries, the latter in teaching English and using this as a door for evangelism; many missions use this method to great profit.

12. SING PRAISES TO OUR LORD.

I love Thy Kingdom, Lord,
The house of Thine abode,

The Church our blessed Redeemer saved
With His own precious blood.

WEEK THIRTY-THREE — WEDNESDAY

1. PRAISE GOD FOR WHO HE IS.

"By day the Lord commands his steadfast love; and at night his song is with me, a prayer to the God of my life" (Psa. 42:8). Bless the Lord, oh, my soul—my whole self! There is such encouragement in each of these words: (1) All day long you will look upon me like a loving parent with eyes and heart full of steadfast love. (2) When I retire I have a song to sing—it is a prayer song of praise and gratitude. (3) The One to whom I lift up my praise is vitally, personally interested in all of my life every day of my life. This is the model of his interest in every man and woman upon this earth.

Express yourself in adoration for this quality of God.
Speak it audibly or write out your praise in your own devotional journal.

2. PRAISE GOD FOR WHAT HE MEANS TO ME!

Just for me. There is a "command" in your steadfast love. What does this mean? I take this to mean that whatever thought of interest and concern you have for me it is accompanied with adequate energy to carry it out, or to find its completion! Praise your wonderful name! It is exciting to contemplate just how your steadfast love will be fulfilled in my life today! I shall watch for it!

I have not always had a song of prayer and praise to close out the day. Why is this? Isn't it because I want to be the god of my life? If I run the decisions of the day, I have no song of praise to you at night.

How do you personally relate to the steadfast love of God, and God who is Love?
Speak it out or write it out. It is *so important* that you establish *your own* devotional journal.

3. CONFESSION OF SIN

The above expression of praise has much of the element of confession in it. I am trying to be open and honest. How easy it is to hide behind words. Dear Lord, forgive me! If for just today I can hold this one steadfast conviction: all that happens in this day is under your control of steadfast love. I need not understand it. I need not explain it. I need not in any way resent it. How exceedingly far short I fall in fulfililng this intention—forgive me! I do not purpose to *do* better—I purpose to *be* better. It is my *life* you want.

What personal sins do you want to confess? We *must* speak them to remove them.
Do it! *Now.* There is no one else you have sinned against more than God. Tell him so!

4. SING A PRAYER TO GOD.

There is a place of comfort sweet,
Near to the heart of God,
A place where we our Savior meet,
Near to the heart of God.

O Jesus, blest Redeemer,
Sent from the heart of God,
Hold us, who wait before Thee,
Near to the heart of God.

Open your hymn book and sing the rest of the verses—or even sing another prayer song.

5. READ HIS WORD TO HIM!

His Word

[45]When they did not find him, they went back to Jerusalem to look for him. [46]After three days they found him in the temple courts, sitting among the teachers, listening to them and asking them questions. [47]Everyone who heard him was amazed at his understanding and his answers. [48]When his parents saw him, they were astonished. His mother said to him, "Son, why have you treated us like this? Your father and I have been anxiously searching for you."
[49]"Why were you searching for me?" he asked. "Didn't you know I had to be in my Father's house?" [50]But they did not understand what he was saying to them.

— Luke 2:45-50, NIV

Read His Word to Him.

How could I find six verses with more poignancy? It is my purpose here just to rehearse what beauty, power, meaning, purpose I see in these words, and lift my heart to you in adoration. There was a real love attachment to Jesus on the part of Mary and Joseph—of course, this would be natural as parents. (Joseph no doubt loved Jesus no less because he was not the father.) But there must have been some other deep yearnings in their hearts. To lose Jesus was indeed to lose the most important member of their family. They traveled a day before they discovered their loss—they walked another day back—and spent almost the whole third day looking for him. It would seem the temple was the last place they looked—at least in the worship area frequented by the teachers. Luke has questioned those who could tell him of the exchange between our Lord and the wisemen of the temple.

Please express your response to this beautiful text. Put your expression in your own prayer diary.

6. READ HIS WORD FOR YOURSELF.

I open my conscience—write these words upon it! (1) Jesus is found right where you left him. Go back, go back to your first love, to the place where you stopped walking and talking with him. (2) Look inside for him. He is in the temple. Your temple, your body is the dwelling place. He is there to sit with you and teach you! Hear him! Open up his word, digest it, hear it, ask him to repeat it! (3) He has two basic things to give *me*. (a) Understanding of the meaning and purpose of life. If life is going to make sense at all, it will be because Jesus has explained it to me. (b) He has answers to my questions. But even my Lord cannot answer the questions I do not ask. Quit hiding. Stop procrastinating. *Ask* him! When Mary and Jospeh found him they chided him. How like myself. It is *never* my Lord's fault that I cannot find him—he has been in the same place all the time. He hasn't left—I have. Forgive me!

Pause in his presence and either audibly or in written form tell him all his word means to you.

7. READ HIS WORD IN THANKSGIVING.

How glad and grateful were Mary and Joseph when they found Jesus and so with me: (1) Thank you that we all know where Jesus is if we have lost him. (2) Thank you that Jesus was listening as well as talking—so today. (3) Thank you that he can ask questions I cannot answer—but he has given also the answer. (4) Thank you for the continued amazement I can have in the presence of his wisdom. (5) Thank you that Jesus said we really need not seek him since we already know where we can find him! (6) Thank you that my body is the Father's house, i.e., he lives in me by the Holy Spirit and he has fashioned this body. (7) Thank you that we know more than Mary and Joseph—we know him of whom Moses and the prophets spoke.

Give yourself to your own expression of gratitude—write it or speak it!

8. READ HIS WORD IN MEDITATION.

"And they did not understand the saying which he spoke to them." How easily we can relate to his parents. There are many words of our dear children that we miss. We do not hear what they say. The more serious fact is we fail to understand them. Do we understand his saying any better? There are several meanings (or applications) in these words. What is our Lord saying? (1) "I must worship my Father and here is a special place set aside for this purpose. I have been here ere you left it. If you had come first to the temple you would have never lost me." How true it is that we will find him in worship. We shall never lose him if we seek him there. (2) Perhaps he said: "This is why I came to earth, i.e., to make my Father known—this is but the first expression of what will become my consuming passion. My mission has been announced to you and this is but the beginning."

Pause—wait—think—then express yourself in thoughtful praise or thanks.

9. READ HIS WORD FOR PETITIONS.

Prayers from "the Father's house": (1) May I look for my Lord just where I lost him. (2) Forgive me for the wasted days I spent looking for you. (3) Your dear Son never left the temple courts—I claim his presence and intercession at your right hand. (4) How glad I am Jesus listens to me now. (5) Guard me from misunderstanding my Lord's motives. (6) I want to be among those who hear him with amazement. (7) By faith I claim the wisdom that comes down from above.

Please, please remember these are prayers—speak them—reword them!

10. READ HIS WORD AND WAIT—LISTEN—GOD SPEAKS!

May I hear you speak to me: (1) "Keep your ears open to my questions for today." (2) "I will be found in the presence of my Son." (3) "Association is not the same as companionship."

11. INTERCESSION FOR THE LOST WORLD

Japan — Point for prayer: (1) *Student witness* is a strategic ministry — Japan has 933 colleges with two million students. The greatest hindrances are apathy and Marxism (90% of students claim to be atheists, though most express themselves more favorable to Christianity than to any other religion). Young people, generally speaking, are unwilling to fully commit themselves to the Lord. There is a need for a witness to be started in the secondary schools.

12. SING PRAISES TO OUR LORD.

Guilty, vile and helpless we;
Spotless Lamb of God was He;

"Full atonement!" can it be?
Hallelujah! what a Savior!

WEEK THIRTY-THREE — THURSDAY

1. PRAISE GOD FOR WHO HE IS.

"Your divine throne endures for ever and ever. Your royal scepter is a scepter of equity; you love righteousness and hate wickedness. Therefore God, your God, has anointed you with the oil of gladness above your fellows; your robes are all fragrant with myrrh and aloes and cassia. From ivory palaces stringed instruments make you glad; . . ." (Psa. 45:6-8a). I realize this is a Messianic Psalm and I am to see my Lord in these verses. Such a beautiful vision of both divine beings—inspired by the Holy Spirit. Let me mark out the several attributes of yourself and your Son: (1) You (and he) are king! How gladly I acknowledge this! (2) You are eternal! No change in rulership—no wonder as to who will reign! Bless your name! (3) Your rule is one of total fairness—a perfect balance of mercy and law. (4) You reign in a clear-cut well-known, black and white distinction—all you do is right, all against you is wrong. (5) Our blessed Lord came to exemplify in his own person each of these qualities.

Express yourself in adoration for this quality of God.
Speak it audibly or write out your praise in your own devotional journal.

2. PRAISE GOD FOR WHAT HE MEANS TO ME.

Just for me. How I relish this time with you. Nothing lifts my heart more than to lift it up to you! Was my Lord the happiest man in all the world? I believe he was! His joy came from the confidence that he knew he was right! My Lord walked in the fulfillment of your will. There was no shadow of turning in his conduct. To know you are totally right could bring a satisfaction above that of anyone now walking on this earth. Since Jesus hated sin of all kinds and did not in any form participate, he had no pride in his righteousness. He fulfilled righteousness with no exalting of self. The deep gladness we do not want to brag about when we have done your will could be a faint comparison. The description of your garments suggests the king's wardrobe, but we remember it is the fragrance caught by the disciples in the upper room when you came forth from the tomb!

How do you personally relate to the throne of God, and God who is King?
Speak it out or write it out. It is *so important* that you establish *your own* devotional journal.

3. CONFESSION OF SIN

How can you be my king if I am an unwilling subject? How can you rule from my mind if I will not think your thoughts? Dear sovereign, it is *not* because I do not acknowledge you as king—indeed I do—but I am caught between two powerful rulers, yourself and the great deceiver. I freely confess my decision to sin was my own. I was given, or originated, excuses both before I sinned and afterward. But the decision was mine. How could I have made it? I do take courage that my total track record is improving—(or is this another excuse?). Away with such thoughts! I simply cast myself at your feet and ask and receive forgiveness and a clean, clear record. May I write on it my praise and love for you.

What personal sins do you want to confess? We *must* speak them to remove them.
Do it! *Now.* There is no one else you have sinned against more than God. Tell him so!

4. SING A PRAYER TO GOD.

I will sing the wondrous story
Of the Christ who died for me,
How He left His home in glory
For the cross of Calvary.

Yes, I'll sing . . . the wondrous story
Of the Christ . . . who died for me, . . .
Sing it with . . . the saints in glory,
Gathered by . . . the crystal sea.

Open your hymn book and sing the rest of the verses—or even sing another prayer song.

5. READ HIS WORD TO HIM!

His Word

[50]But they did not understand what he was saying to them. [51]Then he went down to Nazareth with them and was obedient to them. But his mother treasured all these things in her heart.
— *Luke 2:50, 51, NIV*

Read His Word to Him.

My dear heavenly Father, as you know I am but attempting to read these words as if indeed they are: alive, fresh, new—help me! I see my dear Lord walking alongside Mary and Joseph on his way to Nazareth "and (he) was obedient to them." Did this require any humbling of his spirit? I'm sure there were countless times when our Lord could have told Mary or Joseph that there was a better way to do whatever it was they asked of him—but he didn't. How often could Jesus see the inadequacies of his parents? Did Mary and Joseph argue? Did Jesus hear the argument? Was there any sibling rivalry among the children in the house of the carpenter?

Please express your response to this beautiful text. Put your expression in your own prayer diary.

6. READ HIS WORD FOR YOURSELF.

I feel very, very much like Mary —"his mother kept all these things in her heart!" As she watched the process of which Luke speaks, i.e., "Jesus increased in wisdom and stature and in favor with God and man." What did she think? Jesus, as always, was the embodiment of all he said. He said, "Let your light *so* shine before men that they may see your good works (but) and glorify your Father in heaven." Our Lord's good works in character and action were of just this kind. How beautifully did this flower of God's planting grow! How the mother's heart swelled with pride! But *praise* would be a better word. How unobtrusive are all the works of God. Somehow he is hidden behind his actions —men can even attribute such works to themselves and miss the point altogether. Mary (and Joseph?) were not going to do this, and neither am I! Bless your dear self!

Pause in his presence and either audibly or in written form tell him all his word means to you.

7. READ HIS WORD IN THANKSGIVING.

(1) Thank you for the unspeakable condescension of my dear Lord as he took the form of man. (2) Thank you for the incredible moral force in the little phrase "was obedient to them." (3) Thank you for Mary and Joseph, who themselves were obedient to you. (4) Thank you for the dear mother of my Lord, thoughtful and full of love. (5) Thank you for the natural growth process found in my dear Lord —not at all understood —but appreciated. (6) Thank you that even Jesus increased in wisdom, i.e., the application of truth to life —should I not do likewise? (7) Thank you that men —all men in Nazareth could see something admirable in Jesus.

Give yourself to your own expression of gratitude —write it or speak it!

8. READ HIS WORD IN MEDITATION.

"And Jesus increased in wisdom and stature (years), and in favor with God and man." It would seem that our increase is only in one direction: in stature or years. Of course this is a reference to the fact that as my Lord developed physically he also developed spiritually. Jesus was able to apply to life, and in an increasing measure, your truth. Wisdom is the very best use of knowledge. In the natural maturation process Jesus applied everything he knew to his daily conduct. This became a "showcase" of how to live the ideal life. All that a young man from 18 to 30 should know and do was here on exhibit. Who saw it? Who knew about it? There were those in Nazareth who knew something amazing was being lived out before their very eyes. Was there anyone in that little town who discussed it among themselves? Surely there must have been sincere women who had enough spiritual perception to know what was happening. Amazing obscurity!

Pause —wait —think —then express yourself in thoughtful praise or thanks.

9. READ HIS WORD FOR PETITIONS.

In the attitude of Jesus as a young man there is so much to learn: (1) Keep me sensitive to your willingness to be in our company. (2) Give me the kind of yieldedness I see in Jesus. (3) Grant me a meditative capacity far beyond what I now have. (4) May I try to think over the thoughts of Mary's heart. (5) Since wisdom is the best use of knowledge I come to you and ask: "Give me wisdom." (6) Continue your blessing of good health —may I recognize its source. (7) How I want to increase the popularity of your Son —help me!

Right here add your personal requests —and his answers.

10. READ HIS WORD AND WAIT —LISTEN —GOD SPEAKS!

In these two verses there is much you can say to me: (1) "If my Son yielded himself to humble parents what do you have to complain about "in human relationships"? (2) "Quietness sometimes teaches more than many words." (3) "The threefold growth of my Son is yet today's example: (1) wisdom, (2) stature, (3) social.

11. INTERCESSION FOR THE LOST WORLD

Japan — Points for prayer: *Unreached peoples:* (1) *Okinawa and all the Ryukyu Islands* need pioneer evangelism and there are very few Christians among the Ryukyu people. (2) The majority of the people in the *cities,* have never really had a chance to understand the Gospel. 65% of the *towns* and 85% of the *villages* have no witness for the Lord. (3) *The 700,000 Koreans* form an unpopular and dispersed minority. About 60% are Communist and there are only 6 Korean churches in Japan (all in Tokyo). They are not welcome in Japanese churches.

12. SING PRAISES TO OUR LORD.

When my life-work is ended, and I cross the swelling tide,
When the bright and glorious morning I shall see;
I shall know my Redeemer when I reach the other side,
And His smile will be the first to welcome me.

I shall know . . . Him, I shall know Him
And redeemed by His side I shall stand,
I shall know . . . Him, I shall know Him
By the print of the nails in His hand.

WEEK THIRTY-THREE — FRIDAY

1. PRAISE GOD FOR WHO HE IS.

"God is our refuge and strength, a very present help (or a well proved help) in trouble" (Psa. 46:1). Bless and praise your holy name! Your character is here described as: (1) "our refuge"; (2) our strength; (3) a very present or always present help in trouble; (4) a well proven help in trouble. I want to pause and lift you up before all men, before the whole world (how I wish I could) as altogether worthy of our praise and wonder. How very often do we all need a place to rest and recuperate? A quiet place of reflection and peace. You are just that place—in you I find all this and more. How soon our strength is gone! How soon our energy has been dissipated! What power or energy would it take to hold one star in its orbit? But there is moral strength of which we have even less. Live in me—and you want to live in all men—be my strength! It would seem man is always in trouble and therefore always needs you.

Express yourself in adoration for this quality of God.
Speak it audibly or write out your praise in your own devotional journal.

2. PRAISE GOD FOR WHAT HE MEANS TO ME.

Just for me. Dear Lord, I want to tell you all over again how much I appreciate your always being present when I need help! I have never found you too busy or absent. Indeed I have proved you over and over again! I want to name the kind of help you have been to me—(not that you do not know—this is but another form of praise as you also know). You have been right there to help me in discouragement—I have started a song of praise and love for you and my depression was gone! You have helped me so much when I have had an argument with someone—forgiveness from you led me to forgive them from my heart. At the time of death—what a bright confident hope I found only in you! Thank you. Praise you for such a proven helper! The only help!

How do you personally relate to the refuge of God, and God who is our strength?
Speak it out or write it out. It is *so important* that you establish *your own* devotional journal.

3. CONFESSION OF SIN

Have there been days when I did not look for or want a refuge? Have there been times when I was "the strong man"? Could it be that I got into trouble and worked out my own solution? Dear Lord, you know this has been tragically true! Forgive me! That I should act so independently when I am so totally dependent is beyond explanation. Sin is *nonsense*. The worship and fellowship I enjoy with you makes sense. There is a person—a powerful person who wants to throw confusion and chaos into every situation. His name is Satan. I resist him, hate him and reject and refuse his suggestions. At the same time, I freely admit I must find a refuge in you.

What personal sins do you want to confess? We *must* speak them to remove them.
Do it! *Now.* There is no one else you have sinned against more than God. Tell him so!

4. SING A PRAYER TO GOD.

Bless Thou the truth, dear Lord
To me—to me—
As Thou didst bless the bread
By Galilee;

Then shall all bondage cease,
All fetters fall;
And I shall find my peace,
My All in All.

Open your hymn book and sing the rest of the verses—or even sing another prayer song.

5. READ HIS WORD TO HIM!

His Word

3 In the fifteenth year of the reign of Tiberius Caesar— when Pontius Pilate was governor of Judea, Herod tetrarch of Galilee, his brother Philip tetrarch of Iturea and Trachonitis, and Lysanias tetrarch of Abilene—²during the high priesthood of Annas and Caiaphas, the word of God came to John son of Zechariah in the desert.
— *Luke 3:1, 2, NIV*

Read His Word to Him.

How fleeting and empty is all the pomp of men. Here are seven men of whom we would know almost nothing if it were not for two other men who in their day seemed to be almost nothing. If it were not for John the Baptist and your dear Son no one would know about Pilate, Herod, Philip, Lysanias or Annas and Caiaphas. Even Tiberius Caesar gains prominence by his association with the King of kings. Dear, dear Lord, I want to hide myself in your greatness. I, like John, want to decrease until it is no longer I who live. I want my dear Lord to increase, more and more until we see no one, but only Jesus! It must be almost ludicrous or humorous to you in retrospect (i.e., from man's perspective) to review the balance sheet of life.

Please express your response to this beautiful text. Put your expression in your own prayer diary.

WEEK THIRTY-THREE — FRIDAY

6. READ HIS WORD FOR YOURSELF.

I want to learn and apply every single word of this text to myself. Let me look again at each of these men and see myself: (1) It was in the 15th year of Tiberius Caesar—amid all the multitude of important things he must now be interrupted with news of a weird man in the desert. Does your word get any better hearing with me? (2) Pilate had a tough job. Now to add one more pressure someone came to tell him of a man many people said was a prophet with God's word. I have a tough job— I am pressed on every side. Can I pause long enough to hear you speak to me? (3) Annas and Caiaphas were "born and bred" on religion—we don't need another fresh look at God's word—we are leaders—we know what God says. Dear, dear Lord, how dangerously close do I come to reproducing their sin! Forgive me!

It is so important that you pause in his presence and either audibly or in written form tell him all his word means to you.

7. READ HIS WORD IN THANKSGIVING.

I do want to open my heart in gratitude! (1) Thank you for the clear fulfillment of your word "he that sows to the flesh reaps corruption." (2) Thank you that your honor does not disappear. (3) Thank you for the governor of Judea—he did say, "I find no fault in him." (4) Thank you for the little kingdoms and little kings who are all forgotten in the eternal presence of the King of kings. (5) Thank you that religion will ultimately all be gone with Caiaphas and Annas, but Christianity abideth forever. (6) Thank you for your great desire to communicate with man. (7) Thank you for the son of Zechariah who was ready to hear and speak your word.

Give yourself to your own expression of gratitude—write it or speak it!

8. READ HIS WORD IN MEDITATION.

"... the word of God came to John ... in the desert." Of course this is the direct input of the Holy Spirit as related to the prophetic office, but it does offer a number of parallels to us. If anyone was ever in a desert of society our generation is there. There is a dryness and a sameness about all of life. Boredom is one of the largest problems we have in our day. How startling it would be to have someone like John appear on the scene. How we need to wake up! The word of the Lord has come into this wilderness experience! We have it in permanent form. What it needs is "a voice." John said he was glad to be just a voice. But a voice must be heard to produce any results. Someone may cry out long enough and loud enough to be heard. If all of us wait for someone else to say something—nothing will be said. We all have the word of God—it has come from God to each of us saints. May we let it be heard.

Pause—wait—think—then express yourself in thoughtful praise or thanks.

9. READ HIS WORD FOR PETITIONS.

In the names and offices of long dead rulers there are points for prayer? (1) May I remember you remember who is ruler in each country—I do ask your grace in the life of our president. (2) How can I pray for a governor who has been caught in bribery? In the same way Timothy prayed for Pilate. (3) Could any good come of praying for a son of Herod the Great? We are sure many prayers went up on his behalf. Can I do less for today's men in high places?

Please, please remember these are prayers—speak them—reword them!

10. READ HIS WORD AND WAIT—LISTEN—GOD SPEAKS!

Speak to me again in these verses: (1) "Men in authority are all known to me." (2) "My word has come to the world in the form of my Son." (3) My word is needed today for the same purposes as in the days of John—that men may repent."

11. INTERCESSION FOR THE LOST WORLD

Japan — Points for prayer: (1) *Literature* is widely used and increasing in quality and range of coverage in subject matter. 70% of converted students attribute their conversion to Christian literature. There are 70 Christian bookstores, 90 publishers and 25 printing presses. (2) *Ministry in hospitals* has proved an especially fruitful field—there are many long-term patients in the large number of T.B. hospitals among whom many have come to the Lord.

12. SING PRAISES TO OUR LORD.

Jesus has loved me—wonderful Savior!
Jesus has loved me, I cannot tell why;
Came He to rescue sinners all worthless,
My heart He conquered—for Him I would die.

Glory to Jesus—wonderful Savior!
Glory to Jesus, the One I adore;
Glory to Jesus—wonderful Savior!
Glory to Jesus, and praise evermore.

461

WEEK THIRTY-THREE — SATURDAY

1. PRAISE GOD FOR WHO HE IS.

"There is a river whose streams make glad the city of God, the holy habitation of the Most High. God is in the midst of her, she shall not be moved" (Psa. 46:4, 5). This sounds like a description of an ideal city made beautiful by a river flowing through it. God lives and reigns in this city. Since God through the Holy Spirit lives in us and we are compared to a city elsewhere in his word we want to relate these lovely verses to man as a habitation for God in the Spirit. Notice: (1) The river is the Holy Spirit in his various expressions. When we keep on drinking at the Spring of living water which is his Son revealed in his blessed word—an artesian well springs up and flows out to all in several directions. (2) What an awesome privilege to be "the habitation of the Most High"! This is almost more than we can assimilate. We are impregnable through him!

Express yourself in adoration for this quality of God.
Speak it audibly or write out your praise in your own devotional journal.

2. PRAISE GOD FOR WHAT HE MEANS TO ME.

Just for me. Dear Lord, my total gladness comes from you! It is when I spend time before your throne, time in your word, time in public teaching and worship that I am glad. There is no gladness apart from you. I want to welcome you as the occupant of my house, indeed I want you to make my house your home. I cannot understand how the Most High God could live in me! If I do not believe you can or will, the whole response of wonder and beauty is lost. I *do* believe my strength is your strength, your help is a constant need, but also constantly present.

How do you personally relate to the presence of God, and God who lives in us?
Speak it out or write it out. It is *so important* that you establish *your own* devotional journal.

3. CONFESSION OF SIN

It will not be difficult to confess my shortcomings as they relate to this relationship! My sins have been—and are—the following: (1) My mind is so dull through overuse in mundane matters. I cannot think your thoughts as I should. (2) My schedule excludes you from my conscious mind or at least I have not learned how to include you "up front" in my consciousness. (3) Too many times I simply do not want to think your thoughts—forgive, forgive me—perhaps this contrast is too great. I do believe I can "bring every thought into captivity" and I purpose to do that today. I want your transformation by the renewing of my mind!

What personal sins do you want to confess? We *must* speak them to remove them.
Do it! *Now.* There is no one else you have sinned against more than God. Tell him so!

4. SING A PRAYER TO GOD.

Though Satan should buffet, tho' trials should come,
Let this blest assurance control,
That Christ has regarded my helpless estate,
And hath shed His own blood for my soul.
It is well . . . with my soul, . . .
It is well, it is well with my soul.

Open your hymn book and sing the rest of the verses—or even sing another prayer song.

5. READ HIS WORD TO HIM!

His Word

³He went into all the country around the Jordan, preaching a baptism of repentance for the forgiveness of sins. ⁴As is written in the book of the words of Isaiah the prophet:
  "A voice of one calling in the desert,
  'Prepare the way for the Lord,
    make straight paths for him.
⁵Every valley shall be filled in,
    every mountain and hill made low.
  The crooked roads shall become
    straight,
    the rough ways smooth.
⁶And all mankind will see God's
    salvation.'"

— Luke 3:3-6, NIV

Read His Word to Him.

What an amazing man was your servant and prophet John the Baptist! Dear Lord, I want to go with the crowd and see and hear this wonderful man. At the same time, I want to go with you to hear him, for you were in attendance on that day. How I wish I could hear him speak to me about my sins. What was it in the preaching of this prophet that produced repentance in the hearts of those who heard him? A sorrow for sin against yourself is the answer. On second thought, do I *really* want to hear John preach? If I want the course of my life altered—"the valleys filled in and the hills and mountains leveled off." Then the answer is "yes," but not until and only when this is true am I ready to repent.

Please express your response to this beautiful text. Put your expression in your own prayer diary.

6. READ HIS WORD FOR YOURSELF.

Speak into the deep needs of my life. I have too many valleys and hills on the way that should be a highway for the King. Level off my heart! Am I truly ready to receive an answer to my own prayer? How about some of those mountains of pride? What do you say of the valleys of selfishness? Do you honestly want them torn down and filled in? Are these words more than pious platitudes?

Dear Lord, straighten me out! At the same time, I sorrow and cry over my sins. I yet look into the Jordan — there I can find the purpose of my repentance: "a baptism of repentance *for* the forgiveness of sins." In my situation I can look back to that time and place where such was once accomplished. Oh, how I need to renew this relationship!

It is so important that you pause in his presence
and either audibly or in written form tell him all his word means to you.

7. READ HIS WORD IN THANKSGIVING.

The one immediate response to forgiveness is thanksgiving: (1) Thank you for John's preaching — how I want to be able to preach like him. (2) Thank you for repentance — how much we need it *daily.* (3) Thank you for the confident assurance of the forgiveness of sins. (4) Thank you for the beautiful book of Isaiah and every word in it about

your Son. (5) Thank you for the privilege of being a highway for my Lord. (6) Thank you that I can be in the constant action of keeping my heart straight that he might travel through it to others. (7) Thank you for the promise that "all mankind shall see God's salvation."

Give yourself to your own expression of gratitude — write it or speak it!

8. READ HIS WORD IN MEDITATION.

"And all mankind shall see God's salvation." In a way unknown in John's day God's salvation can be spread to all mankind via satellites. However, Colossians 1:23 does say the gospel "which has been preached to every creature under heaven." The first century Christians took seriously the great commission. It could seem to be the only generation who did.

One day every knee shall bow and every tongue confess that Jesus is Lord to the glory of God the Father. But such

a forced obedience is hardly what the prophet had in mind.

I am as guilty as the next person in the terrible disobedience we practice as related to all mankind being told of God's salvation. The answer is as profound as it is simple: let mankind in your part of the world see his salvation. When every Christian today shares as the Christian of the first century, we will see the fulfillment of these beautiful words.

Pause — wait — think — then express yourself in thoughtful praise or thanks.

9. READ HIS WORD FOR PETITIONS.

In the mission of John the Baptist we can find areas for prayer: (1) Dear Lord, I want to learn how to preach repentance. (2) Enlighten my heart from your word as to how to obtain the remission of sins today. (3) I want to be a voice in my desert. (4) The repentant heart is the

only preparation we can make for your coming — keep me open to change. (5) Fill in the valleys of my life. (6) Cut down my mountains to your measurements. (7) Dear Lord, straighten me out — I do so want my heart to be your highway.

Right here add your personal requests — and his answers.

10. READ HIS WORD AND WAIT — LISTEN — GOD SPEAKS!

Speak to me in these verses: (1) "Baptism for the remission of sins is still correct — preach it." (2) "The One of whom John was a forerunner is now King-of-kings." (3)

"Open your eyes — unstop your ears, I want all mankind to see my salvation."

11. INTERCESSION FOR THE LOST WORLD

Japan — Point for prayer: (1) *Christian radio* has had a great impact. The Pacific Broadcasting Association prepares 4 weekly and 3 daily programs transmitted over 92 Japanese stations. The average Japanese spends 6 hours a day watching television; brief 3 minute T.V. advertise-

ments on commercial stations have proved very profitable for reaching needy people. Pray for all follow up work, personal visitation and linking contacts with a local church.

12. SING PRAISES TO OUR LORD.

Great God of wonders! all Thy ways
Are matchless, Godlike, and divine;
But the fair glories of Thy grace
More Godlike and unrivaled shine,

More Godlike and unrivaled shine.
Who is a pard'ning God like Thee?
Or who has grace so rich and free?
Or who has grace so rich and free?

WEEK THIRTY-FOUR — SUNDAY

1. PRAISE GOD FOR WHO HE IS.

"Great is the Lord and greatly to be praised in the city of our God! His holy mountain, beautiful in elevation, is the joy of all the earth, Mount Zion, in the far north, the city of the great King" (Psa. 48:1, 2). Two or three lovely qualities of our God: (1) He is great. (2) He is greatly to be praised. (3) He rules from his beautiful capital or city. Indeed, indeed *great* is our Lord! In every way we want to express it, he is great! (1) Great in desire to give us a purposeful life. (2) Great in communicative

ability through his two books: (a) the Bible and (b) the world about us. He is to be greatly praised in his place of rulership. Where is that? In David's day it was Jerusalem. Today it is your body and mine. What a life-changing thought! If out of our bodies he was to receive the praise he so richly deserves such could become the joy of all the earth. I want it to start with me in my little part of the world.

Express yourself in adoration for this quality of God.
Speak it audibly or write out your praise in your own devotional journal.

2. PRAISE GOD FOR WHAT HE MEANS TO ME.

Just for me! Dear Lord, you are great in my eyes. You deserve all the praise I can give and much more. To try to contemplate the meaning of being the place of your rulership is mind boggling! I realize the whole church is "Mount Zion," but what is true of the whole is also true of the part. I am your place of rulership on this earth. My body is "His holy mountain"—my body is "beautiful for ele-

vation"—because my body is a habitation for yourself in the Spirit it can become a source of "joy for the whole earth." I have no desire to press a metaphor beyond its meaning. At the same time such thoughts lift my heart to you in wonder and praise! That I could be a part of "the city of the great King" moves me deeply!

How do you personally relate to the greatness of God, and God who is Great?
Speak it out or write it out. It is *so important* that you establish *your own* devotional journal.

3. CONFESSION OF SIN

That you should be so great and be so greatly ignored is an amazement to demons and angels. It seems but an idle thing to most men. Oh, sin of all sins! How can I change my mind about including your praise in my daily routine? Surely there are areas where I can call attention to yourself—I know there are—if I really want to praise you I will! Forgive me for this terrible sin. If I do not

express praise, it is because I do not know you as I should and could. I am only holy because I am your abiding place. I do respond to the purifying thought of your presence in me! It is because I want to honor you and not in any way cast reflection on your person that I act and react. Forgive me! Cleanse me!

What personal sins do you want to confess? We *must* speak them to remove them.
Do it! *Now.* There is no one else you have sinned against more than God. Tell him so!

4. SING A PRAYER TO GOD.

O happy bond, that seals my vows
To Him who merits all my love!
Let cheerful anthems fill His house,
While to that sacred shrine I move.
Happy day, happy day,

When Jesus washed my sins away!
He taught me how to watch and pray,
And live rejoicing ev'ry day;
Happy day, happy day,
When Jesus washed my sins away!

Open your hymn book and sing the rest of the verses—or even sing another prayer song.

5. READ HIS WORD TO HIM!

His Word

[5]People went out to him from Jerusalem and all Judea and the whole region of the Jordan. [6]Confessing their sins, they were baptized by him in the Jordan River.
[7]But when he saw many of the Pharisees and Sadducees coming to where he was baptizing, he said to them: "You brood of vipers! Who warned you to flee from the coming wrath? [8]Produce fruit in keeping with repentance. [9]And

do not think you can say to yourselves, 'We have Abraham as our father.' I tell you that out of these stones God can raise up children for Abraham. [10]The ax is already at the root of the trees, and every tree that does not produce good fruit will be cut down and thrown into the fire.
— *Matthew 3:5-10, NIV*

Read His Word to Him.

Oh, to be able to stand on the banks of the Jordan—or in its waters, and hear John preach! I know his words are as contemporary to you as are our words today. In their

meaning they speak today as they spoke then. You see everyone present on that eventful day—you know who were chaff and who were wheat. Did any of the vipers change their nature as a result of John's preaching? I would surely like to believe they did. Who was it? Who was saying, "We have Abraham for our Father"? You know them every one! What a fearful word to hear: ". . . *every tree* that does not produce good fruit will be cut down and thrown into the fire."

Please express your response to this beautiful text. Put your expression in your own prayer diary.

6. READ HIS WORD FOR YOURSELF.

Dear Lord, I am glad to confess my sins before you, and in the presence of men, if that is necessary. Nothing is hidden from men that will not ultimately be revealed. Why were these people baptized by John? Mark says plainly that it was for the forgiveness of their sins. We conclude this must mean that where they were truly repentant that in the act of burial there was the death and burial of the former selves and in the act of emergence from the water a new person—clean, whole, forgiven came forth. Dear Lord, I have expressed these thoughts because they represent just what I want to be my testimony! I do want to be raised up a child of yourself, a true son of Abraham.

Pause in his presence and either audibly or in written form tell him all his word means to you.

7. READ HIS WORD IN THANKSGIVING.

"Glad" is too small a word to express my joy. (1) Thank you for the response to John's message—I believe people are still listening for a voice from heaven. (2) Thank you that people will and do repent—even today. (3) Thank you for John's holy boldness—he spoke to the conscience! May *I* hear him! (4) Thank you that I cannot and must not trust in position or title—only in you. (5) Thank you that you will never lack for true children—even from stones. (6) Thank you for the sharp, heavy ax of your word—cut! strike! I want to be clean! (7) Thank you we can produce fruit that indicates genuine repentance.

Give yourself to your own expression of gratitude—write it or speak it!

8. READ HIS WORD IN MEDITATION.

"We have Abraham as our Father." What a jarring revelation! To have someone tell you—and convince you that your religion was false! Such was the response of the Pharisees to John's preaching. At the same time, the deep satisfaction with worship by the law must have been present in their hearts. The sense of guilt and unfulfill-ment was calling for something better. We are not told, but there must have been some sincere men among these leaders who welcomed the opportunity to repent and change. There were others who were blinded and when they recovered from the shock fell back into the bondage of legalism.

Pause—wait—think—then express yourself in thoughtful praise or thanks.

9. READ HIS WORD FOR PETITIONS.

In the baptizing and preaching of John I find real motivation for prayer: (1) Give me a much larger audience to hear your word. (2) Grant the convicting power of your Holy Spirit as I speak your word. (3) Dear Lord, how I do want to baptize someone into the body of your Son. (4) Speak to my heart that I might speak to the hearts of those who hear me. (5) How I do want my conduct and attitude to be a true evidence of my surrender to your will.

Please, please remember these are prayers—speak them—reword them!

10. READ HIS WORD AND WAIT—LISTEN—GOD SPEAKS!

How I do want to hear you speak to me through these verses: (1) "You cannot continue in sin with my approval." (2) "Only a yielded heart can house my Son." (3) "Every tree that does not produce good fruit will be cut down and thrown into the fire."

11. INTERCESSION FOR THE LOST WORLD

Korea (South) — Population: 34,800,000. Growth rate —2%. People per sq. km.—353.

Point for prayer: (1) *The receptivity of the Korean people* for the Gospel has been unmatched in this century, with rapid growth, dramatic revivals and strong indigenous churches that have shown great faithfulness in years of persecution under the Japanese and later the Communist invaders. Communism remains a serious threat. Pray that this uncertainty may be used of God to keep the believers praying and the people hungry for spiritual things.

12. SING PRAISES TO OUR LORD.

Dying for me, dying for me.
There on the cross He was dying for me;

Now in His death my redemption I see,
All because Jesus was dying for me.

WEEK THIRTY-FOUR — MONDAY

1. PRAISE GOD FOR WHO HE IS.

"Have mercy on me, O God, according to thy steadfast love; according to thy abundant mercy blot out my transgressions" (Psa. 51:1). There are three qualities of yourself mentioned in this verse: (1) mercy; (2) steadfast love; (3) abundant mercy. David needed and wanted all of these attributes of yourself applied to his need. Mercy is non-reciprocal goodness or kindess. David wanted you to be kind to him even though he deserved punishment. David wanted to sense and enter into your steadfast love. David needed abundant mercy, i.e., considering the enormity of his sin. The need of the king is the need of the whole world. What a lovely portrait appears from this psalm. It is of yourself as a father who loves his willful, ignorant lustful son with an everlasting kindness. "You looked beyond his fault and saw his need." Praise your glorious person!

Express yourself in adoration for this quality of God.
Speak it audibly or write out your praise in your own devotional journal.

2. PRAISE GOD FOR WHAT HE MEANS TO ME.

Just for me—praise you for what you mean to me! I, like millions of others, can immediately identify with David. Why is my call for mercy always "after the fact"? Dear Lord, here is one time when it isn't! I acknowledge to you that I live and move and have my total being in your mercy! I am the living object lesson of your mercy! How strong is the expression: *"steadfast love."* It is this quality that makes possible the abundant mercy we are given in blotting out our transgressions. I understand that the expression "blot out" as related to clay or wax meant to rub out or smooth over until the record disappeared. Bless your wonderful love—blot out my sin!

How do you personally relate to the forgiveness of God, and God who is Mercy?
Speak it out or write it out. It is *so important* that you establish *your own* devotional journal.

3. CONFESSION OF SIN

Such is the whole purpose of this psalm. This is the fresh expression of guilt and sorrow. This is the cry of the wounded—the anguish of the one who has been pierced in his heart by the arrow of truth. Nathan the prophet has just relaxed the bow of God's judgment. Dear Lord, this is my cry! I do want to do more than cry over my sin. I want to go much further than guilt for my transgressions. I want to so fully appreciate your loving kindness, so truly accept your forgiveness that the motivations for daily living will be totally altered. Dear Lord, I want this to be much more than pious platitudes! Write your words upon my heart! True humility is my greatest need!

What personal sins do you want to confess? We *must* speak them to remove them.
Do it! *Now.* There is no one else you have sinned against more than God. Tell him so!

4. SING A PRAYER TO GOD.

A wonderful Savior is Jesus my Lord,
A wonderful Savior to me,
He hideth my soul in the cleft of the rock,
Where rivers of pleasure I see.
He hideth my soul in the cleft of the rock

That shadows a dry, thirsty land;
He hideth my life in the depths of His love,
And covers me there with His hand,
And covers me there with His hand.

Open your hymn book and sing the rest of the verses—or even sing another prayer song.

5. READ HIS WORD TO HIM!

His Word

[11]"I baptize you with water for repentance. But after me will come one who is more powerful than I, whose sandals I am not fit to carry. He will baptize you with the Holy Spirit and with fire. [12]His winnowing fork is in his hand, and he will clear his threshing floor, gathering the wheat into his barn and burning up the chaff with unquenchable fire." — *Matthew 3:11, 12, NIV*

Read His Word to Him.

Speak the words of John into my heart of hearts! John says every day I live: "After me will come one who is more powerful than I, whose sandals I am not fit to carry." Our Lord was before John (even as John said)—our Lord came after John and our Lord is now with John. We could say that Jesus was also above John in every sense. What John said and felt about your Son I want to also say. After I have long gone from this earthly scene my blessed Lord will be here in all his power and beauty. John was a prophet and could claim some divine distinction and comparison with your Son. I have no such position— I feel there is nothing but contrast in my relationship with him. If John, the greatest born of woman, felt he could not even carry his sandals, where does that put me?

Please express your response to this beautiful text. Put your expression in your own prayer diary.

WEEK THIRTY-FOUR — MONDAY

6. READ HIS WORD FOR YOURSELF.

This I have been doing, but as I have said so often, I do so with the thought that I stand where all men stand. Just here I want to stand in my own place! My place is in the water! Before I go down into the water I want to allow his winnowing fork to thoroughly cleanse my heart. May the wind of the Spirit blow out all chaff. May I stay long enough before you in repentance — in fasting and prayer — until I am ready to let go of all that is chaff in my experience. Dear Lord, take what wheat there is in my heart into your garner. I feel like Peter when our Lord said to him — "when you are converted (after the cleaning period) strengthen your brothers." Until I am cleansed I cannot. I am so glad my strength is in you, I have none of myself!

It is so important that you pause in his presence
and either audibly or in written form tell him all his word means to you.

7. READ HIS WORD IN THANKSGIVING.

In the midst of true repentance there is thanksgiving: (1) Thank you for the baptism John preached — it prepared all of us for the baptism our Lord commanded. (2) Thank you for the perception of John — he knew his relationship to our Lord. (3) Thank you for power and purpose of our Lord. (4) Thank you for the privilege of falling at his feet in worship. (5) Thank you that Jesus is administrator of both baptism in the Holy Spirit and baptism in fire. (6) Thank you that we all can be either wheat or chaff — it is up to us. (7) Thank you that Jesus is as much alive now as he was with John in the Jordan.

Give yourself to your own expression of gratitude — write it or speak it!

8. READ HIS WORD IN MEDITATION.

"He will baptize you with the Holy Spirit and with fire." Such an expression probably meant very little if anything to the multitude who first heard it. Perhaps a connection was made between the chaff and the wheat and the Holy Spirit and the fire. The wheat would be baptized in the Holy Spirit and the chaff would be baptized in fire. Our Lord would be the administrator of both baptisms. We need to be reminded that the twelve apostles were present in the crowd for part of the qualifications for the apostleship was to be with Jesus from his baptism until his ascension (Acts 1:21, 22). It would be three years later that our Lord would take these general words and make them specific in reference to his apostles (Acts 1:1-5). The understanding of the promises must be read in the light of the historic fulfillment on Pentecost and the house of Cornelius (Acts 2 & 10).

Pause — wait — think — then express yourself in thoughtful praise or thanks.

9. READ HIS WORD FOR PETITIONS.

For what can I ask you as I read these verses? (1) Teach me over and over again the true meaning of repentance. (2) Break my heart that I might bow before you in worship. (3) Give me real wisdom in the searching out of the fulfillment of this promise of Holy Spirit baptism. (4) What is the baptism in fire administered by my Lord? Is it the lake of fire (Matt. 25:41, 46)? (5) Dear Lord, purify my motives until all dross is gone.

Right here add your personal requests — and his answers.

10. READ HIS WORD AND WAIT — LISTEN — GOD SPEAKS!

In these two verses speak to me: (1) "My Son will indeed baptize many in fire." (2) "Let him remove the chaff from your heart." (3) "There is an eternal barn called heaven."

11. INTERCESSION FOR THE LOST WORLD

Korea (South) — Points for prayer: (1) *Christianity has made a vital impact on Korea.* There are 2,000 churches in Seoul alone. One third of all parliamentarians are Christian. Revival in the 600,000 strong army had raised the number of believers to 51% in 1977. (2)*The Protestant Church,* founded on sound indigenous principles, blessed with many periods of revival, and refined by years of suffering has emerged as a mighty praying, evangelizing army of believers. Early morning prayer meetings attended by hundreds are still the pattern in many denominations. Pray that materialism and present ease of being a Christian may not blunt their earnestness and outreach.

12. SING PRAISES TO OUR LORD.

In the bright sunlight, ever rejoicing,
Pressing my way to mansions above;
Singing His praises gladly I'm walking,
Walking in sunlight, sunlight of love.

Heavenly sunlight, heavenly sunlight,
Flooding my soul with glory divine:
Hallelujah, I am rejoicing,
Singing His praises, Jesus is mine.

WEEK THIRTY-FOUR — TUESDAY

1. PRAISE GOD FOR WHO HE IS.

"Behold, thou desirest truth in the inward being; therefore teach me wisdom in my secret heart. Purge me with hyssop, and I shall be clean; wash me, and I shall be whiter than snow" (Psa. 51:6, 7). I do want to lift the qualities of yourself from these two beautiful verses and praise you for each of them. (1) You have personal preferences and strong desires. This speaks of One who thinks and cares. How good to have One who is so real. (2) You want reality in the deepest desires of man. You want his words and his actions to match. You want my prayers and my conduct to be equal. (3) You are a teacher—you can make the best use of the knowledge I already have. This teaching is for my "secret heart." As David cried this prayer out of the anguish of his own need, so do I. As he expected an answer so I expect an answer. What I have said of David and myself can be and should be said for all men. Blessed be your name!

Express yourself in adoration for this quality of God.
Speak it audibly or write out your praise in your own devotional journal.

2. PRAISE GOD FOR WHAT HE MEANS TO ME.

"Purge me with hyssop" seems to refer to the action of applying the blood of the passover lamb. Such a plant was used with my Lord while he was on the cross. Dear Lord, there is nothing I want more than "truth in my inward being"; "wisdom in my secret heart"—to be clean before you. The deep, consuming desire of my heart is to be washed! That I could be "whiter than snow" is almost more than I can take in. All of these expressions are related to several qualities of your nature: (1) You know me. (2) You love me—and personally care. (3) You have provided for my sin in forgiveness. My largest response to all we have shared together is to accept all you offer in the attitude of wonder and joy! *"Praise"* is such a weak word to express my exhilaration!

How do you personally relate to the truth of God, and God who is Truth?
Speak it out or write it out. It is *so important* that you establish *your own* devotional journal.

3. CONFESSION OF SIN

This whole psalm is devoted to this subject. At the same time I need to say there is no praise like the praise of a forgiven sinner. I do want to enter into the deeper reasons for my sin. I want "truth in the inward being." It seems to me that the simple fact that I do not like to be uncomfortable becomes an occasion for Satan. I do not want to "endure" temptation. I want to overcome temptation and be done with it! But it never, or very seldom happens that way. The offer of Satan is made. If it is immediately rejected he leaves. But he comes back, and with the same offer. It is in a consistent rejection I fail. It is also in the "inward being" and "secret heart" that I settle for a lie—a rationalization for the sin. Dear God, dear God, wash me and I shall be whiter than snow!

What personal sins do you want to confess? We *must* speak them to remove them.
Do it! *Now.* There is no one else you have sinned against more than God. Tell him so!

4. SING A PRAYER TO GOD.

Fear not, I am with thee, O be not dismayed,
For I am thy God, and will still give thee aid;

I'll strengthen thee, help thee, and cause thee to stand,
Upheld by My gracious, omnipotent hand.

Open your hymn book and sing the rest of the verses—or even sing another prayer song.

5. READ HIS WORD TO HIM!

His Word

[13]Then Jesus came from Galilee to the Jordan to be baptized by John. [14]But John tried to deter him, saying, "I need to be baptized by you, and do you come to me?"

[15]Jesus replied, "Let it be so now; it is proper for us to do this to fulfill all righteousness." Then John consented.
— *Matthew 3:13-15, NIV*

Read His Word to Him.

It was one long walk from Nazareth to the banks of the Jordan. It took my Lord more than one day to travel this far. What did he think as he walked? Did he stop to visit with anyone on the way? What were his thoughts as he lay down at night? Did he sleep out in the open or did he find those who gave him a place to lay his head? Of course I must leave all these questions to you. Since you live in the eternal *"now."* Jesus is still making that journey. He did find John. What flashes of divine recognition passed between the eyes of John and Jesus? John did know him and in a sense that moved him to say: "I have need to be baptized by you." John is saying essentially: "Why come to me?" I am here to preach repentance; you have no sin of which to repent. I am here to baptize those who do repent so as to obtain forgiveness. You have no need of either." Dear Lord, I stand with John!

Please express your response to this beautiful text. Put your expression in your own prayer diary.

6. READ HIS WORD FOR YOURSELF.

I must pause long before these words: Jesus was baptized not because he was a sinner, but *as a sinner* for me." It is in his baptism I find righteousness. My baptism is only effective because of his. Jesus began his ministry by taking the sinner's place and he ended his ministry in the same way. It was in the water and on the cross he filled up righteousness and handed it to all mankind. Oh, dear Lord, I say these words just to remind myself once again how much I owe to your dear Son. I owe him all—he has provided all. Open the eyes of my heart that I might see with illuminated understanding his baptism. Matthew's description is from John's viewpoint—the heavens were opened to the vision of John—*he* saw the Spirit of God descending as a dove, and alighting upon him—and remaining on him. And then that never, never to be forgotten announcement! "My beloved Son"! "The One with whom I am well pleased!"

It is so important that you pause in his presence
and either audibly or in written form tell him all his word means to you.

7. READ HIS WORD IN THANKSGIVING.

Yes yes. (1) Thank you that my Lord demonstrated my need to be baptized. (2) Thank you for the sensitive Spirit of John the Baptist. (3) Thank you for the genuine humility of John. (4) Thank you for the only righteousness I have—that given me by Jesus. (5) Thank you that accepting his righteousness shuts out continuing in sin. (6) Thank you for the clear example as to how to be baptized. (7) Thank you for the announcement eternal. May I hear it every day. "This is my beloved Son, in whom I am well pleased." Oh, how I agree with you!

Give yourself to your own expression of gratitude—write it or speak it!

8. READ HIS WORD IN MEDITATION.

"... I need to be baptized by you, and do you come to me?" We can surely appreciate John's dilemma. Jesus had no need that could be satisfied by John. Most of all, for Jesus to come to a sinner's baptism was unthinkable. The baptism of John was a public testimony of sin and repentance. The righteousness our Lord came to fill up was accomplished by his association with sinners here and Calvary. Here he associated himself with sin and sinners; on Calvary he identified himself with sin and the sinful. In this way he provided for our righteous standing with God.

Pause—wait—think—then express yourself in thoughtful praise or thanks.

9. READ HIS WORD FOR PETITIONS.

Surely at the baptism of our Lord we should pause to pray: (1) Jesus walked seventy miles to be baptized—may I always remember the importance of my baptism. (2) What a privilege to see my Lord's baptism as an example of obedience. (3) I want to share the humility of John. (4) Thank you for righteousness fulfilled in my Lord's baptism. (5) Give me a firmer grasp on the righteousness I have in Jesus. (6) Deepen my gladness as I participate in the meaning of being baptized into his body. (7) I am so glad John consented to the words of my Lord—even when he could not understand—a grand example for me.

Please, please remember these are prayers—speak them—reword them!

10. READ HIS WORD AND WAIT—LISTEN—GOD SPEAKS!

Jesus is saying something to me at his baptism: (1) "You have died and have been buried to be raised to walk in newness of life." (2) "Think again of the meaning of your baptism—you will never exhaust its meaning." (3) "Because I fulfilled righteousness you are counted as righteous before me."

11. INTERCESSION FOR THE LOST WORLD

Korea (South) — Point for prayer: (1) *Division* has sadly caused major splits in every large denomination—over earlier compromise under Japanese rule, liberal theology and ecumenism. The bitter divisions have led to authoritarianism among preachers and an emphasis on right doctrine at the expense of fellowship with the Lord and His Word. Pray for a spirit of love and reconciliation among all true believers.

12. SING PRAISES TO OUR LORD.

Holy, Holy, Holy, Lord God Almighty!
All Thy works shall praise Thy name,
  in earth, and sky, and sea;

Holy, Holy, Holy! Merciful and Mighty!
God in Three Persons, blessed Trinity!

1. PRAISE GOD FOR WHO HE IS.

"Cast your burden (what he has given you) *on the Lord, and he will sustain you; he will never permit the righteous to be moved"* (Psa. 55:22). I am finding so many lovely qualities of yourself in the songs of David. This charming expression is such an encouragement to me! There are many days (and nights) when I want to give up and throw in the towel. I am ashamed of my weakness and failure. How could I be so stupid? How could I repeat what I know is fruitless? I can blame it on irritability or fatigue or three or four other excuses and then I hear you say: "Cast all you cares on me." "I care for you." "I have been there all the time." In one sense I have given such burdens to you, give them to me. What a weight lifted! I am stronger because of this experience. I am more intent than ever to walk and live in your way.

Express yourself in adoration for this quality of God.
Speak it audibly or write out your praise in your own devotional journal.

2. PRAISE GOD FOR WHAT HE MEANS TO ME.

Just for me. What I have said above is a pattern for all men, i.e., it is the common experience of temptation and sin and forgiveness and renewed strength. Right here I want to apply this to my own heart. My biggest problem, or at least one of the biggest, is to read or hear of some brother or sister who overcame a burden and then to try and fail to follow the pattern they set. In one sense all temptations and sins are alike; in another sense all are individual and the *only* one who can help is the Lord himself! Attempting to cast off my burdens by following someone else's example has frustrated me. Casting my burdens on others has been less than adequate—only when I cast the whole load on you and leave it there do I find the relief of a burden let go! Since you have been with me from the beginning you know how to forgive and sustain. Bless your name, I am on the rock to stay!

How do you personally relate to the security of God, and God who sustains you?
Speak it out or write it out. It is *so important* that you establish *your own* devotional journal.

3. CONFESSION OF SIN

It would seem all my worship so far today has been one long confession of sins. Let me spend some time with you on your response to my confession. Have you not bound yourself by your own law that if I confess my sins to you, which I do, however inadequately, you are faithful and righteous to forgive me of the same sins I have confessed? Further, you will cleanse me, and forget what I have done? How I do need this assurance! My being "sustained" and "not moved" has so much to do with my acceptance of your kind of forgiveness. A "fresh start" or "clean page" would not describe the new beginning I have right now! Bless your love and forgiveness forever!

What personal sins do you want to confess? We *must* speak them to remove them.
Do it! *Now.* There is no one else you have sinned against more than God. Tell him so!

4. SING A PRAYER TO GOD.

When you met with great temptation,
Did you think to pray?
By His dying love and merit,
Did you claim the Holy Spirit
As your guide and stay?

Oh how praying rests the weary!
Prayer will change the night to day;
So in sorrow and in gladness,
Don't forget to pray.

Open your hymn book and sing the rest of the verses—or even sing another prayer song.

5. READ HIS WORD TO HIM!

His Word

4 Then Jesus was led by the Spirit into the desert to be tempted by the devil. [2]After fasting forty days and forty nights, he was hungry. [3]The tempter came to him and said, "If you are the Son of God, tell these stones to become bread."

[4]Jesus answered, "It is written: 'Man does not live by bread alone, but on every word that comes from the mouth of God.'"

[5]Then the devil took him to the holy city and had him stand on the highest point of the temple. [6]"If you are the Son of God," he said, "throw yourself down. For it is written:

'He will command his angels
    concerning you,
  and they will lift you up in their
    hands,
so that you will not strike your foot
    against a stone.'"

[7]Jesus answered him, "It is also written: 'Do not put the Lord your God to the test.'" — *Matthew 4:1-7, NIV*

Read His Word to Him.

Surely, dear Lord, you need to read these words to me! At the same time, it is renewing to try (and that is all I do) to relate these beautiful words to yourself. I am so glad the Holy Spirit had such a vital part in these temptations.

WEEK THIRTY-FOUR — WEDNESDAY

What has become an occasion of sin for me was a time of growing for my Lord. I am sure it was his relationship with you that made the difference. My blessed Lord entered the arena of conflict in the only three realms of desire available to man: (1) appetite, (2) audacity, (3) and ambition (*H. Fowler*). How glad I am Jesus met Satan on his own ground and overcame him. It is only as I find refuge in Jesus that I find any victory over temptation.

Please express your response to this beautiful text. Put your expression in your own prayer diary.

6. READ HIS WORD FOR YOURSELF.

I am delighted to affirm the Holy Spirit's constant ministry in me and for me. He is my encourager and the strengthener of my inner man. I, by acceptance of your promises, claim his strength. Here is a list of the desires through which Satan works: (1) *Self-preservation:* Satisfying body needs for food, clothing, shelter, self-defense. (2) *Mating desires:* Sex, care of family, children's appeal to us. (3) *Social desires:* Gregariousness, companionship, approval, self-assertion, pride, ambition, competition. (4) *Desires to submit:* Tendency to imitate heroes, conform to law, to regard higher powers with respect. (5) *Acquisitive desires:* Joy of ownership. (6) *Creative desires:* Pleasure of being a power or a cause capable of creating or destroying. (7) *Aesthetic desires:* Enjoyment of the beautiful. (*H. Fowler*) Dear Lord, I look so carefully at each one of these and want to find them in you not in the world.

Pause in his presence and either audibly or in written form tell him all his word means to you.

7. READ HIS WORD IN THANKSGIVING.

(1) Thank you for the personalness of this encounter — it is just how Satan tempts me. (2) Thank you for the wilderness setting — how like my temptations. (3) Thank you for the wild animals (Mk. 1:13a). This is all men mean to me when tempted. (4) Thank you for the assurance of the presence of the Holy Spirit — oh, how I need him! (5) Thank you for the example of fasting — to supplement the desires of the body.

Give yourself to your own expression of gratitude — write it or speak it!

8. READ HIS WORD IN MEDITATION.

"Do not put the Lord your God to the test." Why not put God to the test? Didn't he say, "prove me" or "test me" in Malachi 3:10-11? Why then is this text or trial wrong? It is because it is based on an apriori assumption that God does not (sometimes) mean what he says and therefore needs to prove to us that he does before we will believe him. It is the same root sin involved in our Lord's words: "A wicked and adulterous generation seeks after a sign." It was by and through signs our Lord confirmed his deity. For those who do not want to believe, no signs are enough. For those who do not want to believe in God's essential character there will never be enough proof.

Pause — wait — think — then express yourself in thoughtful praise or thanks.

9. READ HIS WORD AND WAIT — LISTEN — GOD SPEAKS!

What a wonderful text for prayer requests: (1) Lead me by your Spirit to be tested and made strong. (2) Teach me how to use discipline. (3) Reinforce my conviction that all of life should be and can be directed by your word. (4) Give me the courage and humility to reject Satan's suggestions of doubt. (5) Guard me from self pity — Satan's deception. (6) Give me a deeper understanding of angels' ministry for me. (7) Give me a full acceptance of your total sovereignty.

Right here add your personal requests — and his answers.

10. READ HIS WORD AND WAIT — LISTEN — GOD SPEAKS!

In these verses you do indeed speak to me: (1) "The devil is bound but not dead." (2) "You can live a complete, full and totally satisfied life apart from Satan." (3) "My Son did not seek the praise and approval of men."

11. INTERCESSION FOR THE LOST WORLD

Korea (South) — Point for prayer: (1) *There is a growing missionary vision* which Christian leaders are seeking to foster and co-ordinate. There is a need for more to be done to train workers for the mission field. Pray that all the churches may become enthusiastic for missions. There are now about 280 Korean missionaries in many lands of the world and there are plans to send out many more.

12. SING PRAISES TO OUR LORD.

My Jesus, I love Thee, I know Thou art mine,
For Thee all the follies of sin I resign;

My gracious Redeemer, my Savior art Thou;
If ever I loved Thee, my Jesus, 'tis now.

WEEK THIRTY-FOUR — THURSDAY

1. PRAISE GOD FOR WHO HE IS.

"The sacrifice acceptable to God (my sacrifice, O God) is a broken spirit; a broken and contrite heart, O God, thou wilt not despise" (Psa. 51:17). Such a blessed verse! So much is said of you and of all men in this one verse! Let me mark out the attributes of yourself. I see in these burning words: (1) You do want to be appeased, i.e., you have been offended and you expect some type of expiation. (2) If proper action is taken you will be satisfied, i.e., you are ready to accept man's efforts to be forgiven, or reconciled to yourself. (3) Man should feel very, very deeply his need of communion of spirit intimacy with you. Indeed this was true of David—it is true of myself, and I am persuaded of all men. (4) The inner man must be totally yielded or "broken." (5) There must be, and will be grief over sin against you. (6) You could blame us for our ignorance and wilfullness, but you will not, you will love us and accept us.

Express yourself in adoration for this quality of God.
Speak it audibly or write out your praise in your own devotional journal.

2. PRAISE GOD FOR WHAT HE MEANS TO ME.

For me—I want to shout "glory, hallelujah!" There is nothing I need or any other man needs more than such reconciliation. Essentially you are saying to me: "It is *not* what you *do* that I accept, but what you *are*." Do I now have a broken spirit? Do I now offer you a broken and contrite heart? If tears and loud cries indicate the presence of such a heart I must say "no." At times "with strong cries and tears" I *have* tried to learn yieldedness or obedience. But on this day I am silent and still before you. I am like Job on the dust heap. I consider my willfulness and your greatness and I am mute. Dear Father, as you know my stupid, rebellious spirit you know I want nothing more than to let you break it with your goodness, your holiness, your promises. I want to offer it up as my sacrifice to you. I do it through my body (Rom. 2:1).

How do you personally relate to the forgiveness of God, and God who is Forgiver?
Speak it out or write it out. It is *so important* that you establish *your own* devotional journal.

3. CONFESSION OF SIN

Psalm 51 will move me like no other to an open confession of my sins. I want to let verse 17 percolate through my spirit one more time: (1) A broken spirit or heart is one that for some reason will not function as it should. Surely this is what I have found of myself! My thoughts, my choices, my affections, my conscience have all malfunctioned. It is in presenting this mess to you with a humble willingness to give you control of my mind, will, emotions and conscience that I will find help and you will receive an acceptable sacrifice. (2) A contrite heart is one that is much more than sorry. There is a sorrow that leads to death and not life! David is the good example of the broken spirit—the contrite heart. Repentance is a change of mind, brought about by a godly sorrow for sin, that results in a complete change of conduct. It is only in the changed conduct that God's purpose for sorrow is seen. Dear God, I am assimilating all of this, I want it to be my life before you!

What personal sins do you want to confess? We *must* speak them to remove them.
Do it! *Now.* There is no one else you have sinned against more than God. Tell him so!

4. SING A PRAYER TO GOD.

Consecrate me now to Thy service, Lord,
By the pow'r of grace divine;
Let my soul look up with a steadfast hope,
And my will be lost in Thine.

Draw me nearer, nearer, blessed Lord,
To the cross where Thou hast died;
Draw me nearer, nearer, nearer, blessed Lord,
To Thy precious, bleeding side.

Open your hymn book and sing the rest of the verses—or even sing another prayer song.

5. READ HIS WORD TO HIM!

His Word

[8]Again, the devil took him to a very high mountain and showed him all the kingdoms of the world and their splendor. [9]"All this I will give you," he said, "if you will bow down and worship me."

[10]Jesus said to him, "Away from me, Satan! For it is written: 'Worship the Lord your God, and serve him only.'"
[11]Then the devil left him, and angels came and attended him.
— *Matthew 4:8-11, NIV*

Read His Word to Him.

How shall I ever really and truly empathize with you in this record concerning your Son? I want to, but I am so alloyed with ignorance and failure. Even as I say this I know in this text is the answer to my needs from your Son! What little promises has Satan made to me, or any man as compared to what he offered Jesus! Could Satan have kept his promise? Did he actually own the kingdoms of this world? It would make little difference if we believed he did. This is part of Satan's deception: that we should believe him. He is a liar and the father of lies—we should assume that nothing he says is true and reject him out of hand. Jesus' answer is the answer I want to give: *worship* is the crucial issue—not if he could fulfill his promise. Service is implicit in worship—how easily we are deceived.

Please express your response to this beautiful text. Put your expression in your own prayer diary.

6. READ HIS WORD FOR YOURSELF.

I must not forget that this offer of the devil was in the very area of our Lord's interest. He came to establish his kingdom. It is at the beginning of his ministry and there stretches before him all the difficult times—all the ignorance of weak disciples—and ultimately the cross! Here is a way out—here is a shortcut! How often have I accepted the shortcut! Dear Lord, forgive! Satan does not leave out the stipulation—"*if* you will bow down and worship me." Jesus was a man—Satan is an arch-angel—our Lord is flesh and blood; Satan is spirit. There is a real strong temptation here. I can only praise you and bow down before you in gratitude that Satan was overcome!

Pause in his presence and either audibly or in written form tell him all his word means to you.

7. READ HIS WORD IN THANKSGIVING.

(1) Thank you that Jesus was tempted and overcome in all the basic temptations of my life. (2) Thank you that I know how fleeting and unsatisfying are the splendors of this world. (3) Thank you that Solomon accepted the offers and found them empty! (4) Thank you that I can tell Satan to his face that he is a liar and I want the truth— even my Lord. (5) Thank you that Satan does leave. (6) Thank you that angels are the silent observers of all this conflict and do minister or attend to us. (7) Thank you that I have been warned once again in praying and worshiping in connection with these temptations.

Give yourself to your own expression of gratitude—write it or speak it!

8. READ HIS WORD IN MEDITATION.

"*. . . he left him until an opportune time.*" When would be an opportune time to return and tempt our Lord? This question is easy to answer since he was tempted in all ways just as we are. Satan must have returned when our Lord was worn out from emotional physical effort. When emotion is depleted it is easy to allow our view to become distorted. In such a time we are glad Jesus' view of the scriptures were just as clear as when he was rested. At the same time we believe our Lord sought and found adequate rest. If we must have rest in order to think clearly, our Lord must (as a life style) have set this example. Satan must have come to him again when those of his home town rejected him. Jesus was disappointed; he was hurt by their blindness. At the same time, he knew the record of the prophets before him.

Pause—wait—think—then express yourself in thoughtful praise or thanks.

9. READ HIS WORD FOR PETITIONS.

In this final effort of Satan I find real need for prayer: (1) Draw me nearer to yourself that Satan might flee. (2) Keep me more and more aware just how powerful is our enemy. (3) Thank you that my Lord knew what he missed when he chose what you can give. (4) How wonderful to know Jesus overcame Satan to become the perfect sacrifice for my sin. (5) How I want to learn more of how to follow my Lord's example in overcoming the evil one. (6) Teach me to worship you only. (7) Purify and enlighten my service for you.

Please, please remember these are prayers—speak them—reword them!

10. READ HIS WORD AND WAIT—LISTEN—GOD SPEAKS!

My Lord addressed Satan to enable me to hear you speak: (1) "This offer of Satan has never been withdrawn —it must be refused." (2) "You will bow down and worship someone." (3) "You *must* command Satan to leave— he will not if you do not."

11. INTERCESSION FOR THE LOST WORLD

Korea (South) — Point for prayer: (1) *Missions* have placed a healthy emphasis on Korean leadership and initiative. Most missions today are involved in leadership training programs or in specialist ministries. Missionaries who go as servants of the Korean Church are both needed and welcome.

12. SING PRAISES TO OUR LORD.

How sweet the name of Jesus sounds
In a believer's ear!

It soothes his sorrows, heals his wounds,
And drives away his fear.

WEEK THIRTY-FOUR — FRIDAY

1. PRAISE GOD FOR WHO HE IS.

"Lead thou me to the rock that is higher than I; for thou art my refuge, a strong tower against the enemy" (Psa. 61:2b, 3). It is my truest, greatest joy to come before you in praise. These verses offer such an attractive picture of yourself! You are a high eminence up to which I can climb and not only find protection but solitude and perspective for life. I think of Alice Springs in the outback of Australia and the incredibly large rock that rises from the desert floor. Each person will envision something similar, or dissimilar that will represent you as such a "Rock." The blessing of praise is in you we can find the rest and peace that comes from total security. How I seek and find this place, which is actually a Person. I need to begin the day "in perspective." Without my journey to "the Rock" I would not even want to look at life.

Express yourself in adoration for this quality of God.
Speak it audibly or write out your praise in your own devotional journal.

2. PRAISE GOD FOR WHAT HE MEANS TO ME.

Just for me. I have tried in the above praise to be objective and speak for all men. How very poorly I have done it you know. In this time of praise I lift my own heart up—I pour out my personal joy and happiness that I have such a refuge, such a strong tower against my enemy. There are steps up to the top of this tower—if I am going to be removed from the enemy, if I am going to see life as you do, I must and gladly take them. They are: (1) Concentration on what you have said—each word. (2) A humble attitude toward what you say. (3) A deep willingness to receive your word—read it as a child reading a love letter from his parent. (4) A confidence that each time I read it there is something wonderfully good for me. (5) A strong desire to thank you for all you show me.

I have only one enemy—I am no match for him. The further I can get from him the better I will be. In you I have no fear—in you I have all your strength. How I do need you!

How do you personally relate to the refuge of God, and God who is our Rock?
Speak it out or write it out. It is *so important* that you establish *your own* devotional journal.

3. CONFESSION OF SIN

As with all other attributes of yourself I must and do confess to terrible blindness and dullness of hearing. Why is it that at times I do not want such a rock or refuge? Why is it that at times I actually prefer to encounter the enemy and lose? There is something terribly independent about me. There are periods when I do not care what anyone thinks about what I do. I am slain like the horses in the plain of battle. Indeed, I act like the dumb animals. But I praise you over and over again that these times have been less and less frequent. Indeed, I have an almost constant desire to climb to the rock that is higher than I. Oh, Rock, move in my experience until wherever I look, I see you. Forgive me, I am tired, I need your peace and protection. I gladly accept them. Hide thou me!

What personal sins do you want to confess? We *must* speak them to remove them.
Do it! *Now.* There is no one else you have sinned against more than God. Tell him so!

4. SING A PRAYER TO GOD.

From ev'ry stormy wind that blows,
From ev'ry swelling tide of woes,

There is a calm, a sure retreat:
'Tis found beneath the mercy seat.

Open your hymn book and sing the rest of the verses—or even sing another prayer song.

5. READ HIS WORD TO HIM!

His Word

[23]Now Jesus himself was about thirty years old when he began his ministry. He was the son, so it was thought, of Joseph,
the son of Heli, [24]the son of Matthat,
the son of Levi, the son of Melki,
the son of Jannai, the son of Joseph,
[25]the son of Mattathias, the son of Amos,
the son of Nahum, the son of Esli,
the son of Naggai, [26]the son of Maath,
the son of Mattathias, the son of Semein,
the son of Josech, the son of Joda,
[27]the son of Joanan, the son of Rhesa,
the son of Zerubbabel, the son of Shealtiel,
the son of Neri, [28]the son of Melki,
the son of Addi, the son of Cosam,
the son of Elmadam, the son of Er,
[29]the son of Joshua, the son of Eliezer,
the son of Jorim, the son of Matthat,
the son of Levi, [30]the son of Simeon,
the son of Judah, the son of Joseph,
the son of Jonam, the son of Eliakim,
[31]the son of Melea, the son of Menna,
the son of Mattatha, the son of Nathan,
the son of David, [32]the son of Jesse,
the son of Obed, the son of Boaz,
the son of Salmon, the son of Nahshon,
[33]the son of Amminadab, the son of Ram,
the son of Hezron, the son of Perez,
the son of Judah.

— Luke 3:23-33, NIV

WEEK THIRTY-FOUR — FRIDAY

Read His Word to Him.

When our Lord stepped out of his home in Nazareth for the last time and set his face toward the Jordan and John the Baptist, what were the thoughts of his heart? Yea, what were the thoughts of his beloved mother? How did his four brothers feel? Were his sisters married? Did they discuss his departure with their husbands? I can know what you thought by reading your record. This is enough. O my dear Lord, how I love him.

Please express your response to this beautiful text. Put your expression in your own prayer diary.

6. READ HIS WORD FOR YOURSELF.

All the list of names found in the genealogy of my Lord are a tremendous challenge to me. I want to examine every one and become friends with them all. I did this in the list of Matthew, but time and space just does not permit here (it will in other studies and worship). Just now I want to express my joy and praise for two of the interesting people who preceded my Lord's ministry and in a small sense made it possible! (1) Jesus was "the son of Isaac." He has always appealed to me as a meaningful example. We could conjure up all kinds of pictures as to just what he did when his father Abraham told him he was to be the sacrifice on the altar they had just built. But the text does not tell us. Perhaps he was as meek as the lamb he typified! (2) I like the father of Isaac too. He left his home and walked "by faith" which meant he moved when you spoke.

Pause in his presence and either audibly or in written form tell him all his word means to you.

7. READ HIS WORD IN THANKSGIVING.

Gladly do I review five men for whom I can truly be thankful: (1) First of all and most of all my Lord in all the strength of manhood, pure and holy and undefiled — separated and yet identified with us sinners. (2) Thank you for Heli, the father of Joseph — he must have been a good father to rear such a fine son. (3) For Nathan, whose name was like the prophet who moved David to repentance. (4) Thank you for Jesse the father of David — such a patient, good man. (5) For Boaz who let love and respect overrule prejudice and bigotry.

Give yourself to your own expression of gratitude — write it or speak it!

8. READ HIS WORD IN MEDITATION.

"The son of Seth, the son of Adam." What would it mean to be "the son of Adam"? Seth was surely a commendable example. From Seth we have the "sons of God." In a real sense we are indeed all "sons of Adam." As a result of our heritage we shall all die. It is a much greater fact that we can be sons of the second Adam. "The life giving spirit." "As in Adam all die so in Christ shall all be made alive" (I Cor. 15:22). This is only in reference to our physical escape from the grave — such an escape is promised to all men. But when our Lord is also our elder brother we shall escape everlasting punishment. This is the "much more" of "the free gift" (Rom. 5:19ff.).

Pause — wait — think — then express yourself in thoughtful praise or thanks.

9. READ HIS WORD FOR PETITIONS.

There are many in this list who can teach me much: (1) I claim my inheritance through my being a son of yourself through Jesus. (2) I claim also my royal priesthood through my heritage in my Lord. (3) I want the transparent sincerity I see in Joseph. (4) I want a heart like David.

Right here add your personal requests — and his answers.

10. READ HIS WORD AND WAIT — LISTEN — GOD SPEAKS!

What are you saying to me through this genealogy table? (1) "I have been wise and faithful over many, many years." (2) "No one or nothing will ever stop my plan to save man. (3) "The second Adam, the life-giving spirit has come."

11. INTERCESSION FOR THE LOST WORLD

Korea (South) — Point for prayer: (1) *Student work* in the 97 colleges and universities and among the 190,000 students has made great progress. Emphasis has been on Bible study and personal evangelism, and now workers have gone out to the USA, Germany, Switzerland and other lands to witness among students. There are many Christian schools all over the country in which the Gospel is preached.

12. SING PRAISES TO OUR LORD.

O worship the King, all glorious above,
And gratefully sing His wonderful love;
Our Shield and Defender, the Ancient of days,
Pavilioned in splendor, and girded with praise.

475

WEEK THIRTY-FOUR — SATURDAY

1. PRAISE GOD FOR WHO HE IS.

"So I have looked upon thee in the sanctuary, beholding thy power and glory. Because thy steadfast love is better than life, my lips will praise thee. So I will bless thee as long as I live; I will lift up my hands and call on thy name" (Psa. 63:2-4). This is a little more text than we ordinarily use in praising you, but there were so many beautiful expressions of adoration I just could not leave one out. I will just mention them as I lift my heart to you in praise: (1) In the tabernacle and the temple your She-kinah glory or brightness appeared. It was a great source of encouragement to know in this physical way you were present. It wasn't the smoke or fire or effulgent brightness that left a lasting impression—it was *the power* and *character* or *glory* of the person behind such manifestations. We have the same One present in us as his sanctuary! —even our bodies.

Express yourself in adoration for this quality of God.
Speak it audibly or write out your praise in your own devotional journal.

2. PRAISE GOD FOR WHAT HE MEANS TO ME.

Just for me—(2) "Because thy steadfast love is better than life my lips will praise thee." There is nothing in my life to be preferred above your steadfast love. Your love is like a light that never goes out that follows me wherever I go. This light only awakens me when I am responsive. You are always there—not to bother but to enlighten. (3) "I will bless thee (or praise thee) as long as I live." You merit our continual praise. There is really nothing I do in life of more importance than pausing often during the day to contemplate your goodness and continually allow such praise to change my attitude toward all of life. (4) "I will lift up my hands and call on thy name," but another form of praise and adoration. This surely seems a spontaneous act of worship—no one asked David to raise his hands.

How do you personally relate to the power of God, and God who is steadfast Love?
Speak it out or write it out. It is *so important* that you establish *your own* devotional journal.

3. CONFESSION OF SIN

The lack of praise can be one of my worst sins. The causes are easy to discern. (1) I have not tarried long enough before your word in prayer to see your power and glory. (2) I have been too tired to be able to see clearly—my spirit has been insensitive because of fatigue. (3) I have been unwilling to face up to disobedience in some areas of my living. Dear Lord, I want to rearrange my schedule. I want to rest long and be refreshed. I want you to cleanse my heart and purify my hands.

What personal sins do you want to confess? We *must* speak them to remove them.
Do it! *Now.* There is no one else you have sinned against more than God. Tell him so!

4. SING A PRAYER TO GOD.

Guide me, O thou great Jehovah,
Pilgrim thro' this barren land;
I am weak, but Thou art mighty,
Hold me with Thy pow'rful hand:

Bread of Heaven,
Feed me till I want no more;
Bread of Heaven,
Feed me till I want no more.

Open your hymn book and sing the rest of the verses—or even sing another prayer song.

5. READ HIS WORD TO HIM!

His Word

[29] The next day John saw Jesus coming toward him and said, "Look, the Lamb of God, who takes away the sin of the world! [30] This is the one I meant when I said, 'A man who comes after me has surpassed me because he was before me.' [31] I myself did not know him, but the reason I came baptizing with water was that he might be revealed to Israel."

[32] Then John gave this testimony: "I saw the Spirit come down from heaven as a dove and remain on him. [33] I would not have known him, except that the one who sent me to baptize with water told me, 'The man on whom you see the Spirit come down and remain is he who will baptize with the Holy Spirit.' [34] I have seen and I testify that this is the Son of God."
— John 1:29-34, NIV

Read His Word to Him.

How shall I ever read these words with the meaning they deserve? Perhaps all I can do is to take any place with one of the spectators at the feet of John. This announcement meant more to you than to anyone else except our Lord. "The Lamb of God, who takes away the sin of the world"! I see the quizzical look on the faces of those about me. They understand the Levitical system of offerings but a lamb to remove the sins of the whole world? How can it be? John said something else just as startling. He said that the whole purpose of his ministry was now complete—

his purpose was to reveal to Israel God's Lamb—the Messiah! Dear Lord, have I at all represented your thoughts in the above expression! I have tried—forgive my ignorance!

Please express your response to this beautiful text. Put your expression in your own prayer diary.

6. READ HIS WORD FOR YOURSELF.

This will be easier and at the same time more difficult. I am mute before you as I try to assimilate the meaning of these momentous words: "The Lamb of God." Indeed, I do want to "look" and look again, and again. I shall never be able to look enough or to catch the wonder of your love or the fulness of your plan for man. I shall be looking when I fall down before you in heaven and shout with the angels "Worthy is the Lamb!" How much did John know of your Son's pre-existence when he said of him "He was before me."? Did he even know a one-hundredth part of what the other John meant when he said, "In the beginning was the word"? All four biographers said Jesus would baptize in the Holy Spirit—it must be very important for four of them to say it?

Pause in his presence and either audibly or in written form tell him all his word means to you.

7. READ HIS WORD IN THANKSGIVING.

I shall run out of space before I run out of thanksgiving from this text: (1) Thank you for that wonderful day of all days when John identified my Lord and his mission. (2) Thank you that he has taken my sin, I need not feel guilty at all! (3) Thank you that Jesus is always ahead of each of us—oh, I want to follow you, dear Lord! (4) Thank you for the eternal existence of my Lord, he has always been alive and well. (5) Thank you for the bold humility of John the Baptist. (6) Thank you for the dove which identified all three divine persons—the dove was the embodiment of the Holy Spirit—it came from yourself—it identified your Son. (7) Thank you for the powerful promise of Holy Spirit baptism.

Give yourself to your own expression of gratitude—write it or speak it!

8. READ HIS WORD IN MEDITATION.

"I have seen and I testify that this is the Son of God." Did John know Jesus was his relative? Had John seen Jesus before he met him on the banks of the Jordan? We do not know the answers to these questions. John was in the wilderness until the day of his message to Israel. John was certain when he gave his testimony. There was a positive strong assertion in his voice when he said: "This is the Son of God." We have much more reason than John had to give the same testimony. We have the four books of the eyewitness biographers. The apostle John wrote the purpose of all four gospels when he said, ". . . These are written that you might believe that Jesus is the Christ, the Son of God, and that believing you may have life in his name" (John 20:31). We have seen and we do believe and we do claim the eternal life he promised!

Pause—wait—think—then express yourself in thoughtful praise or thanks.

9. READ HIS WORD FOR PETITIONS.

(1) I want to see your Son as my sacrifice for every day. (2) Give me a deeper awareness of the fact that my sins are taken away as far as the east is from the west. (3) Let me appreciate the universal salvation provided by my Lord. (4) Deepen my understanding of the rank of Jesus as Lord of lords. (5) How I want to follow John's example in making my mission to make my Lord known. (6) Grant wisdom in understanding the anointing with the Holy Spirit of my Lord at his baptism. (7) Open my heart to see him as truly the Son of God.

Please, please remember these are prayers—speak them—reword them!

10. READ HIS WORD AND WAIT—LISTEN—GOD SPEAKS!

(1) "Your ministry offers something John could never offer." (2) "The presence of the Holy Spirit in you identifies you as a Christian." (3) "So many men have yet to know that my Son came to save."

11. INTERCESION FOR THE LOST WORLD

Korea (South) — Point for prayer: (1) *Christian broadcasting* has a strong base with two missionary stations in the country broadcasting to both the Koreas and the closed lands of China and Russia. Pray for these key installations, their staff and the impact of these programs in the target areas.

12. SING PRAISES TO OUR LORD.

We would see Jesus, the great rock foundation,
Whereon our feet were set by sov'reign grace;

Not life, nor death, with all their agitation,
Can thence remove us, if we see His face.

WEEK THIRTY-FIVE — SUNDAY

1. PRAISE GOD FOR WHO HE IS.

"My soul is feasted as with marrow and fat, and my mouth praises thee with joyful lips, when I think of thee upon my bed, and meditate on thee in the watches of the night; . . ." (Psa. 63:5, 6). How I do want to hold you up as the One worthy of praise and adoration. Before all men I do want to so exalt you. The reasons for such exaltation are found in this text: (1) You satisfy the total and deepest needs of the human heart, or soul. Indeed, you offer the fulness of satisfaction. (2) You alone can give abundant reasons for songs of joy.

Express yourself in adoration for this quality of God.
Speak it audibly or write out your praise in your own devotional journal.

2. PRAISE GOD FOR WHAT HE MEANS TO ME.

Just for me. Surely what is true for all men is more than true for this one man. In all these many days I have found a thousand qualities or reasons for adoration of yourself. My mind, affections, will and conscience have found more than enough reasons for joyful praise. I want to remember some descriptive verse of yourself just before I drop off to sleep. My subconscious mind will integrate this quality into my spirit and when I awaken you will be more precious than ever before! The basic reason for such meditation on your nature or character is because I need to. Either I meditate on your divine goodness or Satan will offer me his options. I much prefer yourself!

How do you personally relate to the joy of the Lord, and God who is Joy?
Speak it out or write it out. It is *so important* that you establish *your own* devotional journal.

3. CONFESSION OF SIN

It has not always been so! i.e., I have not always wanted to meditate on your goodness. Neither is it always true now, i.e., as you know, my mind is taken up with "other things" and the weeds choke out the word, and when this happens something else is choked out: True praise is stifled when I do not open up your word and think through the words upon that page. "Thy word have I hid in my heart that I might not sin against you." At the same time, the opposite result is also present. When I hide your word in my heart it tells me of your greatness and goodness and songs of joy leap to my lips! The tragic truth is this does not happen as often as it should. Forgive me for preferring to be poor when I could be so rich—for preferring hunger to being filled.

What personal sins do you want to confess? We *must* speak them to remove them.
Do it! *Now.* There is no one else you have sinned against more than God. Tell him so!

4. SING A PRAYER TO GOD.

All that I am and have,
Thy gifts so free,
In joy, in grief, thro' life,
Dear Lord, for Thee!

And when Thy face I see,
My ransomed soul shall be,
Thro' all eternity,
Something for Thee.

Open your hymn book and sing the rest of the verses—or even sing another prayer song.

5. READ HIS WORD TO HIM!

His Word

[35]The next day John was there again with two of his disciples. [36]When the saw Jesus passing by, he said, "Look, the Lamb of God!"

[37]When the two disciples heard him say this, they followed Jesus. [38]Turning around, Jesus saw them following and asked, "What do you want?"

They said, "Rabbi" (which means Teacher), "where are you staying?"

[39]"Come," he replied, "and you will see."

So they went and saw where he was staying, and spent that day with him. It was about the tenth hour.

[40]Andrew, Simon Peter's brother, was one of the two who heard what John had said and who had followed Jesus. [41]The first thing Andrew did was to find his brother Simon and tell him, "We have found the Messiah" (that is, the Christ).

[42]Then he brought Simon to Jesus, who looked at him and said, "You are Simon son of John. You will be called Cephas" (which, when translated, is Peter).

—John 1:35-42, NIV

Read His Word to Him.

I am always full of trembling wonder that I can not truly represent the meaning of the text as it relates to yourself. But I am also always ready to try. I am blessed and helped so much by the effort. No wonder you said what you did of John—it took one of deep humility and one of a clear eyed vision to turn his own disciples from himself to your Son. And John *really* meant it! There were no "sour grapes" in John's choices.

Please express your response to this beautiful text. Put your expression in your own prayer diary.

6. READ HIS WORD FOR YOURSELF.

How anxious I am to relate every word of these verses to my own heart! What would it be to spend a whole day in the presence of my Lord? How would I react as I looked into the face of the Son of God and heard him speak directly and personally? Since one of the disciples is unnamed I can opt to use my name. It is most interesting to observe the natural tendencies of men are not thwarted or hindered in their reponse to Jesus. The natural response of Andrew was to tell his brother. But it wasn't the natural response of the "other disciple"—(we believe the disciple was John the apostle—the writer of the gospel). What did John do? We are reading what he did. I want to let Jesus look into me and tell me who I am. And when he does I will believe him!

Pause in his presence and either audibly or in written form tell him all his word means to you.

7. READ HIS WORD IN THANKSGIVING.

I am sure Andrew and John thanked you for all their lives and are presently thanking you in your presence for that glad day: (1) Thank you for the repeated emphasis John gave to the identification of Jesus. (2) Thank you for the wonderful naturalness of all the action of the text. (3) Thank you that even today you are at work in the very ordinary affairs of our coming and going. (4) Oh, dear Lord, I hear you say to me, "What do you want?" Thank you that it is you I want! (5) Thank you that there are several days in my schedule when I could begin listening and learning. (6) Thank you that all of us know someone who needs to hear about the Messiah. (7) Thank you that Jesus knows me better than I know myself.

Give yourself to your own expression of gratitude—write it or speak it!

8. READ HIS WORD IN MEDITATION.

"You will be called Cephas (which, when translated, is Peter.") How very much was in these few words! Our Lord could give each of us a name that would exactly describe our character. I wonder what name he would give me? What name would he give you? Cephas or Peter meant "a stone" or "a rock." Our Lord was speaking in a dimensional form, i.e., he was telling Peter what he could become, what he should become, what our Lord would help him become. So it is with us. I am not what I should be nor what I want to be, but thank you dear Lord, neither am I what I used to be. When our Lord believes we can attain a certain goal and then lives in us in the person of the Holy Spirit to help us, we can do all things through him who thus strengthens us!

Pause—wait—think—then express yourself in thoughtful praise or thanks.

9. READ HIS WORD FOR PETITIONS.

(1) Give me the repetitious urgency of John. (2) May any who follow me be pointed to my Lord. (3) I want to appreciate all over again the meaning of the words: "The lamb of God." (4) Speak your words: "What do you seek?" deep into my heart. (5) Dear Lord, I do indeed wonder where you are staying today. (6) How glad I am for my Lord's open invitation to "come and see." (7) Andrew has such wonderful concern for others—I want to be like him.

Right here add your personal requests—and his answers.

10. READ HIS WORD AND WAIT—LISTEN—GOD SPEAKS!

(1) "You too have found the Messiah—what will you do about it?" (2) "Does the centuries of fulfilled prophesies mean anything to you?" (3) "What word or name could I give you to describe your true potential?"

11. INTERCESSION FOR THE LOST WORLD

Malaysia — Population: 12,400,000. Growth rate — 2.9%. People per sq. km. — 94 in P.M., 10 in E.M.

Points for prayer: (1) *Pray for interracial peace and harmony* and freedom for the Gospel in the face of increasing unrest and creeping limitations on Christian activities by Malay rulers. (2) *The Malay Muslims* cannot be evangelized by normal means. The few who have trusted the Lord have suffered severely and generally leave the country. Pray for the Christians who have contacts with Malays that they may have opportunities to tactfully tell them of Jesus and pass on literature in spite of the hindrances. It is only possible to openly evangelize Malays in S. Thailand and also in Singapore.

12. SING PRAISES TO OUR LORD.

Life is offered unto you, Hallelujah!
Eternal life thy soul shall have,
If you'll only look to Him, Hallelujah!
Look to Jesus who alone can save.

"Look and live," . . . my brother, live,
Look to Jesus now and live;
'Tis recorded in His word, Hallelujah!
It is only that you "look and live."

WEEK THIRTY-FIVE — MONDAY

1. PRAISE GOD FOR WHO HE IS.

"Let the righteous rejoice in the Lord, and take refuge in him! Let all the upright in heart glory!" (Psa. 64:10). David's definition of "the righteous" would be somewhat different than ours. David would relate righteousness to the law. Our Lord had not yet come as "our righteousness." At the same time, we believe David was honest enough to know he and all others failed to obey perfectly the law under which they lived. So the elements of mercy

and grace had to be a part of the rejoicing of the righteous even in David's day. The only universal offer we can make of righteousness is in our Lord. My heart is not upright. I am *not* proud of my track record of obedient righteousness. But our Lord can be and is the one in whom I take refuge—in him I glory. "He who knew no sin was made to be sin for me that I (and all men) might be made the righteousness of God in him."

Express yourself in adoration to this quality of God.
Speak it out or write it out. It is *so important* that you establish *your own* devotional journal.

2. PRAISE GOD FOR WHAT HE MEANS TO ME.

For me. A great deal of what I have said in the above relates to me. I want to lift my heart in praise—at the same time, I want to think of you and praise you from an international perspective. Oh, that all men would take refuge in you and rejoice! I want to affirm every day of

my life that you are worthy of all praise of all men. Just now I want to gladly enter the closet of praise. I have found my righteousness and my uprightness *in you*, and not in myself.

How do you personally relate to the righteousness of God, and God who is Righteous?
Speak it out or write it out. It is *so important* that you establish *your own* devotional journal.

3. CONFESSION OF SIN

It is easy to confess how far short I am of being totally righteous, or upright in heart. It actually becomes very discouraging even to think about it. How shall I improve my conduct? It seems to me the more I worship you out of my entire self the more I want to do what you have

commanded. The whole law is fulfilled in love. I feely, fully admit and name my sins before you. It is not that you do not know them, you do—but to get rid of them I must spit them out.

What personal sins do you want to confess? We *must* speak them to remove them.
Do it! *Now.* There is no one you have sinned against more than God. Tell him so!

4. SING A PRAYER TO GOD.

I hear Thy welcome voice,
That calls me, Lord, to Thee
For cleansing in Thy precious blood
That flowed on Calvary.

I am coming, Lord!
Coming now to Thee!
Wash me, cleanse me in the blood
That flowed on Calvary!

Open your hymn book and sing the rest of the verses—or even sing another prayer song.

5. READ HIS WORD TO HIM!

His Word

[43]The next day Jesus decided to leave for Galilee. Finding Philip, he said to him, "Follow me."
[44]Philip, like Andrew and Peter, was from the town of Bethsaida. [45]Philip found Nathanael and told him, "We have found the one Moses wrote about in the Law, and about whom the prophets also wrote—Jesus of Nazareth, the son of Joseph."
[46]"Nazareth! Can anything good come from there?" Nathanael asked.
"Come and see," said Philip.
[47]When Jesus saw Nathanael approaching, he said of him,

"There is a true Israelite, in whom there is nothing false."
[48]"How do you know me?" Nathanael asked.
Jesus answered, "I saw you while you were still under the fig tree before Philip called you."
[49]Then Nathanael declared, "Rabbi, you are the Son of God; you are the King of Israel."
[50]Jesus said, "You believe because I told you I saw you under the fig tree. You shall see greater things than that." [51]He then added, "I tell you the truth, you shall see heaven open, and the angels of God ascending and descending on the Son of Man." — *John 1:43-51, NIV*

Read His Word to Him.

How very good it is to travel from place to place with my Lord in his ministry. I can become the very first one to join him—I can be the very last one to watch him return to heaven. Oh, bless your name! Since Philip and both

Andrew and Peter were from Bethsaida we could imagine the three men were talking together about the Messiah when Jesus approached and called Philip. Our Lord knew what was in the hearts of men—hence his words went like an arrow to the heart of Philip. Was there something also in the face and eyes of your dear Son that reached for the heart of Philip? Whatever it was he was reached for he reached out to others. Philip — and Nathanael both knew your word — believed what they knew. Dear Lord, you know me — how do I compare to these men? Not at all! I am myself and you call me — am I as ready to follow?

Please express your response to this beautiful text. Put your expression in your own prayer diary.

6. READ HIS WORD FOR YOURSELF.

Since I have in the last several years studied Moses and the prophets I receive the command of my Lord just as did Philip on that far off day. "Finding Philip" — (Oh, Lord, you have found me, thou Lord seest me.) he said to him, "Follow me." I wish I knew the tone of voice — but I know you are speaking to me right now — for this day — "Follow me." This means leaving all that would hinder such following. If I am motivated to tell others like Philip then I have truly responded to my Lord's call. Dear Lord, I have been so motivated for more than forty years, not like I want to, but I have found a good number to whom I said, "We have found the Son of God." In every case each one of them had to come and see for themselves. I didn't win them — Jesus did.

Pause in his presence and either audibly or in written form tell him all his word means to you.

7. READ HIS WORD IN THANKSGIVING.

It is easy to see so many areas of gratitude here: (1) Thank you for the searching Savior — he has found me! (2) Thank you for friends with whom we can share our faith and excitement. (3) Thank you for men in whom there is no guile — I want to be one of them. (4) Thank you for all of the hundreds of prophecies fulfilled in my Lord. (5) Thank you for the good and honest heart of Nathanael who needed personal proof. (6) Thank you for the only answer to skepticism, "come and see." (7) Thank you for my Lord's total knowledge of every man.

Give yourself to your own expression of gratitude — write it or speak it!

8. READ HIS WORD IN MEDITATION.

". . . you shall see heaven open, and the angels of God ascending and descending on the Son of man." It would seem that from the first contact our Lord had with Nathanael he compared him to Jacob. Yea, even before he met him. It is a redundancy but our Lord is saying of Nathanael: "Behold an Israelite in whom there is no Jacob." Now Jesus again compares Nathanael's experience and attitude with Jacob. What a startling promise it was! As this transparently sincere man followed Jesus throughout his ministry when did he see the heaven opened and the angels of God ascending and descending upon our Lord? Isn't Jesus saying that Nathanael would find Jesus to be the ladder to heaven?

Pause — wait — think — then express yourself in thoughtful praise or thanks.

9. READ HIS WORD FOR PETITIONS.

(1) I want to hear your Son say to me as he did to Philip, "Follow me." (2) Help me to make the great discovery all over again. (3) I want to see *your good* coming out of many Nazareths. (4) How I do want to be a Christian in whom there is no guile. (5) Lord, find me under my fig tree — you know me better than I know myself.

Please, please remember these are prayers — speak them — reword them!

10. READ HIS WORD AND WAIT — LISTEN — GOD SPEAKS!

(1) "Jesus is still calling: 'Follow Me.'"! (2) "We have found him of whom Moses in the law and also the prophets wrote, . . ." (3) "Truly, truly . . . you will see heaven opened, and the messengers of God ascending through your prayers and descending through my word all through my Son."

11. INTERCESSION FOR THE LOST WORLD

Malaysia — Point for prayer: (1) *The state-aided Muslim missionary outreach* to the tribal peoples has had some success — through bribery and subtle coercion — among the interior tribes of Malaya and also in Sabah and Sarawak. Pray that Christians may not give way to imtimidation but rather be strong and alert to forestall this effort by winning the uncommitted to Christ.

12. SING PRAISES TO OUR LORD.

Does sadness fill my mind,
A solace here I find:
May Jesus Christ be praised;

Or fades my earthly bliss, . . .
My comfort still is this: . . .
May Jesus Christ be praised.

WEEK THIRTY-FIVE — TUESDAY

1. PRAISE GOD FOR WHO HE IS.

"Make a joyful noise to God, all the earth, sing the glory of his name; give to him glorious praise!" (Psa. 66:1, 2). This is indeed a true expression of what should happen. If rocks and trees and the physical world had a voice it would be raised in adoration to your glorious person. The stars would shout for joy and all the trees would clap their hands. To describe all the "glory" or "character" that belongs to your name would result in an endless chorus of praise throughout eternity. We are not suggesting unintelligent noise—the "noise" produced from an understanding of your essential being will have more meaning than anything else we will ever express. Oh, that all men as well as nature would praise you!

Express yourself in adoration for this quality of God.
Speak it audibly or write out your praise in your own devotional journal.

2. PRAISE GOD FOR WHAT HE MEANS TO ME.

Just for me. There is one infinitesimal speck in your great creation who will gladly lift up his voice and total being in praise. I want to sing of your glory and to your glory for the rest of my life. It is good to know someone—*the* Someone is listening when such "noise" is made. If all we did was to impress man it would become tedious and old. But when absolute love and knowledge is listening it draws the very best from us every time. I like the term "glorious praise." We could as well say "praise that describes the character of the One to whom we lift our voices. This refers to *character describing* praise. This is my attempt each day—I shall run out of days but not praise.

How do you personally relate to praising God, and God who is worthy of praise?
Speak it out or write it out. It is *so important* that you establish *your own* devotional journal.

3. CONFESSION OF SIN

That I should for whatever reason not want to praise you would of itself be a very fundamental sin. There are various contributing sins to this one basic sin: (1) A failure to spend time in your word to acquire a knowledge of all your attributes. (2) Caught away by other tasks that seem important at the time but are robbing me of my time with you. (3) Allowing my mind to be bombarded by the imagery of T.V. which is a diet of sex, food and money. (4) Ill will and resentment toward others in the family. All these and others dampen and quench my desire to glorify your name. Forgive me—discipline my priorities!

What personal sins do you want to confess? We *must* speak them to remove them.
Do it! *Now.* There is no one else you have sinned against more than God. Tell him so!

4. SING A PRAYER TO GOD.

I am trusting Thee, Lord Jesus!
Trusting only Thee!

Trusting Thee for full salvation,
Great and free.

Open your hymn book and sing the rest of the verses—or even sing another prayer song.

5. READ HIS WORD TO HIM!

His Word

2 On the third day a wedding took place at Cana in Galilee. Jesus' mother was there, [2]and Jesus and his disciples had also been invited to the wedding. [3]When the wine was gone, Jesus' mother said to him, "They have no more wine."

[4]"Dear woman, why do you involve me?" Jesus replied, "My time has not yet come."

[5]His mother said to the servants, "Do whatever he tells you."

[6]Nearby stood six stone water jars, the kind used by the Jews for ceremonial washing, each holding from twenty to thirty gallons.

[7]Jesus said to the servants, "Fill the jars with water"; so they filled them to the brim.

[8]Then he told them, "Now draw some out and take it to the master of the banquet."

They did so, [9]and the master of the banquet tasted the water that had been turned into wine. He did not realize where it had come from, though the servants who had drawn the water knew. Then he called the bridegroom aside [10]and said, "Everyone brings out the choice wine first and then the cheaper wine after the guests have had too much to drink; but you have saved the best till now."

[11]This, the first of his miraculous signs, Jesus performed in Cana of Galilee. He thus revealed his glory, and his disciples put their faith in him.   *— John 2:1-11, NIV*

Read His Word to Him.

Of all the texts to read in your presence this seems most appropriate! The beginning of the miracles and ministry of my Lord! Three days after Jesus decided to leave Galilee he arrived in Cana for a wedding feast. I want to attend

WEEK THIRTY-FIVE — TUESDAY

this wedding, but my eyes will be on Jesus and not the bride or the groom. I want to watch him as I know you must have. I will not see as you do, or even what you do, but I have the greatest of interest. Jesus and Peter and John and Andrew and Philip and Nathanael had all been invited.

Please express your response to this beautiful text. Put your expression in your own prayer diary.

6. READ HIS WORD FOR YOURSELF.

Just for me. Why did Mary ask our Lord about the wine? How kind and thoughtful was our Lord with the interruption and demands of those who really did not understand. Dear Lord, I am not so kind. Forgive me! That dear woman Mary! How thoughtful she was! I wonder what she thought when she heard our Lord's words: "My time is not yet come"? She was perfectly willing to leave the decision in our Lord's hands. If he says anything, do it! If he says nothing, there is nothing to do. I need to be as patient as Mary and as obedient as the servants.

Pause in his presence and either audibly or in written form tell him all his word means to you.

7. READ HIS WORD IN THANKSGIVING.

Yea, verily: (1) Thank you for our Lord's mother, always so interested and thoughtful. (2) Thank you for the learners. I want to count myself among them. (3) Thank you that your time did come and I have beheld your glory. (4) Thank you for the clear miracle of creation. (5) Thank you that there were many who saw it. (6) Thank you that there were many who tasted it. (7) Thank you that there never was a doubt about the signs of my Lord.

Give yourself to your own expression of gratitude—write it or speak it!

8. READ HIS WORD IN MEDITATION.

"*. . . his disciples put their faith in him.*" Jesus revealed in his miracles his true nature. Something of the majesty of deity was seen in each one of them. In this particular miracle it was the creative power of God seen in changing the chemical component of water into wine. None of the chemical elements of wine were in the water—it was truly a miracle of creation. The characteristics of our Lord's signs are such that there is no question as to the total supernatural character of what was done. Notice: (1) It was done in daylight so what was done could be clearly observed. (2) It was done with what was present — he didn't bring in a "rigged" prop. The jars and water were the most common of items. (3) It was observed by several who could not possibly have had knowledge beforehand. (4) It was tested by a large crowd. "These things are written that we might believe," and indeed I do!

Pause—wait—think—then express yourself in praise or thanks.

9. READ HIS WORD FOR PETITIONS.

(1) I want to be as interested and disinterested in the affairs of this life as my Lord. (2) Help me to learn as much as I can from the mother of my Lord. (3) I want to relate to eating and drinking just as my Lord did. (4) How I want to appreciate "the hour" of my Lord. (5) Whatever he says to me I do indeed want to do it. (6) Open my heart to see the quantity and quality of this miracle. (7) May I be as unobtrusive in my work as my Lord was in his.

Right here add your personal requests—and his answers.

10. READ HIS WORD AND WAIT—LISTEN—GOD SPEAKS!

(1) "I still save the best till the last." (2) "I am still in the business of turning water into wine." (3) "My glory is ever manifest that men may believe in me."

11. INTERCESSION FOR THE LOST WORLD

Malaysia — Point for prayer: (1) *There are increasing limitations* on mission work, and the number of missionaries is dropping rapidly. There are still 60 missionaries in P.M., but it is now impossible for any missionary to remain in the country for more than 10 years. Pray that needed missionaries may be allowed to enter and that the national believers may be able to take over and maintain the evangelistic, teaching and missionary impetus.

12. SING PRAISES TO OUR LORD.

Praise ye the Lord,
who o'er all things so wondrously reigneth,
Shelters thee under His wings, yea, so gently sustaineth!

Hast thou not seen
How thy desires e'er have been
Granted in what He ordaineth?

WEEK THIRTY-FIVE — WEDNESDAY

1. PRAISE GOD FOR WHO HE IS.

"May God be gracious to us and bless us and make his face to shine upon us; that thy way be known upon the earth, thy saving power among all nations" (Psa. 67:1, 2). What a beautiful description of your very self is in this reference! Consider: (1) You are God! Elohim. The all powerful, all knowing One. (2) You are gracious, i.e., full of concern for the needs of man and ready to meet those needs. (3) You are ready to grant gifts to men — to reach out with good things. (4) You are like a father or grandfather who leans over the family as he puts his arms around them and looks longingly into their faces — there is a smile of approval and happiness upon his face. (5) Such a beautiful picture! It is the deep desire of your heart (and of mine) that such a way of life be known in all the earth.

Express yourself in adoration for this quality of God.
Speak it audibly or write out your praise in your own devotional journal.

2. PRAISE GOD FOR WHAT HE MEANS TO ME.

Just for me. I have tried to hold up your blessed qualities in the above words. In this time I want to hold up my heart and ask you to speak to me: to paraphrase these verses: "May you be gracious to me and bless me, and make your face to shine upon me, that your way may be known in every area of my life. I want your saving power for my life today." This is a selfish request — but nonetheless needed. I am just as concerned that you may be known throughout the earth and your saving power among all nations. Dear Lord, I want to be shown just how I can help. Just how can I do my little part in fulfilling these blessed words? Even in a song over 2,900 years old I see your heart interest in all men of all nations. There are surely many more men alive upon the earth today than were alive when David wrote this song!

How do you personally relate to the saving power of God, and God who is our Savior?
Speak it out or write it out. It is *so important* that you establish *your own* devotional journal.

3. CONFESSION OF SIN

It does seem horribly selfish to be constantly heaping upon myself your benefits! Such as: "be gracious to *me*" — "bless *me*" — "make your face to shine on *me*." — "That *I* might know your way." You are the Lord of all! — of all men in every nation. Break me out of my little selfish mold! However, if I am not ready to talk to the man across the street or next door I am not ready for the fulfillment of your international concern. Work a work of grace in my own life that you might fulfill it in the lives of all.

What personal sins do you want to confess? We *must* speak them to remove them.
Do it! *Now.* There is no one else you have sinned against more than God. Tell him so!

4. SING A PRAYER TO GOD.

Lead on, O King Eternal,
Till sin's fierce war shall cease,
And holiness shall whisper
The sweet Amen of peace;

For not with swords loud clashing,
Nor roll of stirring drums;
With deeds of love and mercy,
The heav'nly kingdom comes.

Open your hymn book and sing the rest of the verses — or even sing another prayer song.

5. READ HIS WORD TO HIM!

His Word

[12]After this he went down to Capernaum with his mother and brothers and his disciples. There they stayed for a few days.
[13]When it was almost time for the Jewish Passover, Jesus went up to Jerusalem. [14]In the temple courts he found men selling cattle, sheep and doves, and others sitting at tables exchanging money. [15]So he made a whip out of cords, and drove all from the temple area, both sheep and cattle; he scattered the coins of the money changers and overturned their tables. [16]To those who sold doves he said, "Get these out of here! How dare you turn my Father's house into a market!"

[17]His disciples remembered that it is written: "Zeal for your house will consume me."
[18]Then the Jews demanded of him, "What miraculous sign can you show us to prove your authority to do all this?"
[19]Jesus answered them, "Destroy this temple, and I will raise it again in three days."
[20]The Jews replied, "It has taken forty-six years to build this temple, and you are going to raise it in three days?" [21]But the temple he had spoken of was his body. [22]After he was raised from the dead, his disciples recalled what he had said.
— *John 2:12-22, NIV*

WEEK THIRTY-FIVE — WEDNESDAY

Read His Word to Him.

I do hesitate to read this word and relate it to your perspective. I have such a limited capacity of seeing events as you see them. Most especially is this true of such an event as cleansing the temple! It all happened at the time of a feast that should have reminded everyone of your power and goodness. As our Lord walked into the bedlam of noise, confusion and stench he was ignited like a fire-brand from your presence. I see so many indications of your presence in these verses: (1) This cleansing probably occurred in the Gentile quarter—non-Jews could not worship you in this chaos! Neither can this non-Jew when my mind is cluttered with the sights and sounds and smell of this world. (2) Money means little to you when it is a competitor to yourself. Overturn it! Lose it! Out with it!

Please express your response to this beautiful text. Put your expression in your own prayer diary.

6. READ HIS WORD FOR YOURSELF.

I try to enter with my Lord into the temple precincts. If there were only half as many people as Josephus says were present there would be 1½ million people in Jerusalem on that day. Hundreds of thousands in and around the temple. If every family present needed a sacrificial animal or at the least a dove—how many thousand upon thousands would have greeted the gaze of our Lord and his disciples? Who could pray in a place like this?

Pause in his presence and either audibly or in written form tell him all his word means to you.

7. READ HIS WORD IN THANKSGIVING.

(1) Thank you that my Lord does not excuse, apologize or rationalize sin—he rebukes and cleanses. (2) Thank you that God's house—even our bodies, are never to be used as a marketplace, i.e., a means of getting and buying, but as a place of worship. (3) Thank you that the disciples related all events of life to your word. (4) Thank you that Jesus was not impressed with men's demands for authority. (5) Thank you that he did raise up the destroyed temple—even as he said. (6) Thank you that our Lord did credential his words with many miracles. (7) Thank you that my Lord, even today, knows what is in the mind and heart of every man (beginning with the writer!).

Give yourself to your own expression of gratitude—write it or speak it!

8. READ HIS WORD IN MEDITATION.

"But Jesus would not entrust himself to them, for he knew all men." Was this an absolute kind of knowledge? i.e., could our Lord read the purposes and intents of the minds of all men? From what we know of his nature and what we read of his record we would have to say "yes." These were those to whom he did entrust himself. Consider the very close association of Jesus and the twelve. In just the next chapter Nicodemus seems to be an exception —or the woman at the well, although his ability to know what was in this poor woman was surely evident.

Pause—wait—think—then express yourself in thoughtful praise or thanks.

9. READ HIS WORD FOR PETITIONS.

(1) I want to be as disturbed as my Lord with the defiling of his temple today—even our bodies. (2) How can I balance the overturning of the money tables with the loss of personal property? (3) Against what was the anger of my Lord directed? (I do expect answers to these questions as I study your word.) (4) How I do want much more zeal for your work. (5) If our Lord told them who gave him the authority to cleanse the temple would they have believed him? (6) I want the resurrection to ever be fresh and real to me.

Please, please remember these are prayers—speak them—reword them!

10. READ HIS WORD AND WAIT—LISTEN—GOD SPEAKS!

(1) "I am still choosing the men to whom I will trust myself." (2) "I still see and know what men think and do."

(3) "Love me more than money."

11. INTERCESSION FOR THE LOST WORLD

Peninsular Malaya — Point for prayer: (1) *The churches* are almost entirely Chinese and Indian in composition. Growth is slow, and rate of backsliding high, due to the hostile environment for all races with many social and family pressures on young Christians. Revival is needed and a greater willingness to suffer shame for Jesus and to witness to the unsaved. There is a lack of well trained church leaders and good Bible teaching, so many congregations are weak and spiritually shallow.

12. SING PRAISES TO OUR LORD

Amazing grace! how sweet the sound,
That saved a wretch like me!

I once was lost, but now am found,
Was blind, but now I see.

WEEK THIRTY-FIVE — THURSDAY

1. PRAISE GOD FOR WHO HE IS.

"Blessed be the Lord, who daily bears us up; God is our salvation. Our God is a God of salvation; and to God, the Lord, belongs escape from death" (Psa. 68:19, 20). To turn my heart and voice up to you in adoration seems a natural consequence of a recognition of yourself! It is always good for me to list the qualities of your dear self I see in your word: (1) You are Lord—total, absolute ruler—I accept you as such for the whole earth and for myself. (2) Every day you lift me up out of myself and the ordinary pursuits of life. (3) You are salvation—in every situation for every man. (4) You offer the only escape from death. To list these four qualities of yourself is enough to keep me before you much longer than this little time of worship. My heart does long to see you accepted by all men—even as I say it I know many, many men are only awaiting the goodness to accept it. How the very thought of your power and love as seen in your Son does bear me up above the limitations of this body.

Express yourself in adoration for this quality of God.
Speak it audibly or write out your praise in your own devotional journal.

2. PRAISE GOD FOR WHAT HE MEANS TO ME.

For me. I am sorry to mix my approach to you in this time of worship. I started out to praise you just for yourself as related to all men, but I was soon relating all of my words to just myself. I want to praise you for just one wonderful blessing. Without "escape from death" there would be no hope in life. I want to express the details of this escape: (1) You are the escape from the uncertainty of death. I will one day lose consciousness here with the total confidence that I will regain it in the world to come which is called "at home" with you. (2) You are the escape from the finality of death. Death is a door—not the end but the beginning. Praise your glorious name!

How do you personally relate to the salvation of God, and God who is Savior?
Speak it out or write it out. It is *so important* that you establish *your own* devotional journal.

3. CONFESSION OF SIN

How is it you offer to bear me up and I prefer to be down? Can it be that you are salvation and I want to be lost? When I know death is certain how can I ignore it so often? I am not habitual in these sins, but they are my sins. I want complete deliverance from them. Give me the calm assurance that you are at work holding me up by the word of your power even as you do the physical universe. Dear Lord, I do want to be saved—I am saved and I will be saved. I do not believe I have ever totally forgotten that you alone are the escape from the "pangs" or "powers" of death. At the same time I have not rejoiced nearly as much or as often as I should in "the resurrection and the life." Forgive me.

What personal sins do you want to confess? We *must* speak them to remove them.
Do it! *Now.* There is no one else you have sinned against more than God. Tell him so!

4. SING A PRAYER TO GOD.

Jesus, the very thought of Thee
With sweetness fills my breast;

But sweeter far Thy face to see,
And in Thy presence rest.

5. READ HIS WORD TO HIM!

His Word

3 Now there was a man of the Pharisees named Nicodemus, a member of the Jewish ruling council. [2]He came to Jesus at night and said, "Rabbi, we know you are a teacher who has come from God. For no one could perform the miraculous signs you are doing if God were not with him."

[3]In reply Jesus declared, "I tell you the truth, unless a man is born again, he cannot see the kingdom of God."

[4]"How can a man be born when he is old?" Nicodemus asked. "Surely he cannot enter a second time into his mother's womb to be born!"

[5]Jesus answered, "I tell you the truth, unless a man is born of water and the Spirit, he cannot enter the kingdom of God. [6]Flesh gives birth to flesh, but the Spirit gives birth to spirit. [7]You should not be surprised at my saying, 'You must be born again.' [8]The wind blows wherever it pleases. You hear its sound, but you cannot tell where it comes from or where it is going. So it is with everyone born of the Spirit."

[9]"How can this be?" Nicodemus asked.

[10]"You are Israel's teacher," said Jesus, "and do you not understand these things? [11]I tell you the truth, we speak of what we know, and we testify to what we have seen, but still you people do not accept our testimony. [12]I have spoken to you of earthly things and you do not believe; how then will you believe if I speak of heavenly things? [13]No one has ever gone into heaven except the one who came from heaven—the Son of Man. [14]Just as Moses lifted up the snake in the desert, so the Son of Man must be lifted up, [15]that everyone who believes in him may have eternal life.

[16]"For God so loved the world that he gave his one and only Son, that whoever believes in him shall not perish but have eternal life.
— *John 3:1-16, NIV*

Read His Word to Him.

I do feel like I am walking on holy ground as I approach these blessed eternal words. Oh, so often I have identified with Nicodemus. I too have accepted the evident purpose of your miracles—such power and wisdom and control is not from man. The words of my Lord burn like fire in my mind and conscience: ". . . unless a man is born again, he cannot see the kingdom of God." I take the "Kingdom of God" to refer to your rule in my life. Your control of my heart is therefore contingent on my being "born again."

Please express your response to this beautiful text. Put your expression in your own prayer diary.

6. READ HIS WORD FOR YOURSELF.

I am trying: The supernatural nature of this transaction called the new birth is evident again and again. It has become among so many of us an argument over words until the birth of the Spirit is eclipsed. If the *water* in our Lord's words does not refer to the water used on Pentecost then I am at a total loss to what he does mean. The sad, sorry fact is that multitudes have gone through the form —with and without water and have never been born again. My dear Lord just meant only one thing and therefore conclusions drawn from his words *must* be based on the one thing meant by him.

Pause in his presence and either audibly or in written form tell him all his word means to you.

7. READ HIS WORD IN THANKSGIVING.

Oh, what a privilege to thank you for the new birth: (1) Thank you for the quiet personal time our Lord spent with Nicodemus. (2) Thank you for the honesty and interest this ruler had as he talked with our Lord. (3) Thank you for the soul-penetrating words of Jesus—". . . a man *must* be born again." (4) Thank you for the willingness of Nicodemus to admit the limitations of humanism. (5) Thank you for the clear explanation of the new birth, i.e., in light of its fulfillment on Pentecost. (6) Thank you for the miraculous nature of the new birth. (7) Thank you that no teacher in the New Israel need be ignorant of this wonderful truth.

Give yourself to your own expression of gratitude—write it or speak it!

8. READ HIS WORD IN MEDITATION.

". . . that everyone who believes in him may have eternal life." This is one verse so old it has become new all over again. We do need to remember the gospel of John was written after the book of Acts. John was present at Pentecost, he was in Jerusalem in the spread of the word. John knew what men and women did to be saved and have the promise of eternal life. What I am saying in a somewhat extended manner is that John knew just what was involved in the word "believers."

Pause—wait—think—then express yourself in thoughtful praise or thanks.

9. READ HIS WORD FOR PETITIONS.

Jesus moves all us religious people to new requests in prayer: (1) Cut across my tradition to speak to my heart need. (2) Dear Lord, be indeed my "Rabbi" or "teacher." (3) I want to read all over again the record of the signs you did—may I see in them what you want me to see. (4) How I do want your rule in my life—I want to reaffirm my new birth each day. (5) Somehow sensitize my heart to be able to respond to the new Spirit within my body. (6) May my new birth be as evident as the effect of wind—its sound and its work.

Right here add your personal requests—and his answers.

10. READ HIS WORD AND WAIT—LISTEN—GOD SPEAKS!

How clearly you do speak to me in these verses: (1) "My Son must be 'lifted up' in preaching to save those who believe." (2) "Eternal life is either received or rejected." (3) "Please think again! Do you know the meaning of the word 'perish'?"

11. INTERCESSION FOR THE LOST WORLD

Peninsula Malaysia — Point for prayer: (1) *Unreached peoples*—not only have many of the Chinese and Indians never heard the Gospel, but great sections of the population are untouched—especially the poorer and older people. The *Malays* are totally unreached. The *13 small tribes* are considered to be Muslim, but are actually animists and open to the Gospel.

12. SING PRAISES TO OUR LORD.

We gather together to ask the Lord's blessing,
He chastens and hastens His will to make known;
The wicked oppressing cease them from distressing,
Sing praises to His name, He forgets not His own.

WEEK THIRTY-FIVE — FRIDAY

1. PRAISE GOD FOR WHO HE IS.

"Answer me, O Lord, for thy steadfast love is good; according to thy abundant mercy, turn to me. Hide not thy face from thy servant; for I am in distress, make haste to answer me" (Psa. 69:16, 17). How wonderfully good it is to come before you on this day! I am so glad to lift up my praise for the lovely qualities I see in these verses of yourself! (1) You are listening to me. That I have a conscious intelligent, all-wise and all-powerful God to hear me as I pray is one gigantic *a priori* in all my praying. Amen! (2) I can say with the psalmist "Thy steadfast love is good," i.e., I have found you to be more than good in your gifts and directions in my life. Good is too weak a word as related to all you constantly do for me! (3) I must ask even as David: "answer according to thy abundant mercy" for if you should answer according to justice I would not even be heard.

Express yourself in adoration for this quality of God.
Speak it audibly or write out your praise in your own devotional journal.

2. PRAISE GOD FOR WHAT HE MEANS TO ME.

Just for me. How often do I imagine that something has gone wrong in heaven. Your face seems to be turned away from me and my prayers are not getting through. Such stupidity! If I cannot see your face it is not because you have turned away! How very frequent must my cry come up before you? Each day I could say, and do say, "Make haste to answer me, for I am in distress"! My distress is so often of my own making.

How do you personally relate to the mercy of God, and God who is Mercy?
Speak it out or write it out. It is *so important* that you establish *your own* devotional journal.

3. CONFESSION OF SIN

In contrast to all your qualities are mine: (1) Whereas you are ready to answer me I am not at all ready to ask — forgive me. (2) When your love is steadfast and good my love is terribly fluctuating and weak — have mercy. (3) Your mercy is abundant and constant, mine is small and soon runs out — cleanse me. (4) Your face is always toward me — you are always ready to smile upon me — (not my sins). There are times when I simply do not want to look up to you — increasingly less are such times as you know, but there *are* times — forgive me. What I am saying in essence is, "I am in distress, make haste to answer me." I thank you from my whole heart for your mercy!

What personal sins do you want to confess? We *must* speak them to remove them.
Do it! *Now.* There is no one else you have sinned against more than God. Tell him so!

4. SING A PRAYER TO GOD.

So precious is Jesus, my Savior, my King,
His praise all the day long with rapture I sing;
To Him in my weakness for strength I can cling,
For He is so precious to me.

For He is so precious to me, . . .
For He is so precious to me; . . .
'Tis Heaven below my Redeemer to know,
For He is so precious to me.

Open your hymn book and sing the rest of the verses — or even sing another prayer song.

5. READ HIS WORD TO HIM!

His Word

²²After this, Jesus and his disciples went out into the Judean countryside, where he spent some time with them, and baptized. ²³Now John also was baptizing at Aenon near Salim, because there was plenty of water, and people were constantly coming to be baptized. ²⁴(This was before John was put in prison.) ²⁵An argument developed between some of John's disciples and a certain Jew over the matter of ceremonial washing. ²⁶They came to John and said to him, "Rabbi, that man who was with you on the other side of the Jordan — the one you testified about — well, he is baptizing, and everyone is going to him."

²⁷To this John replied, "A man can receive only what is given him from heaven. ²⁸You yourselves can testify that I said, 'I am not the Christ but am sent ahead of him.' ²⁹The bride belongs to the bridegroom. The friend who attends the bridegroom waits and listens for him, and is full of joy when he hears the bridegroom's voice. That joy is mine, and it is now complete. ³⁰He must become greater; I must become less.

³¹"The one who comes from above is above all; the one who is from the earth belongs to the earth, and speaks as one from the earth. The one who comes from heaven is above all. ³²He testifies to what he has seen and heard, but no one accepts his testimony. ³³The man has accepted it has certified that God is truthful. ³⁴For the one whom God has sent speaks the words of God; to him God gives the Spirit without limit. ³⁵The Father loves the Son and has placed everything in his hands. ³⁶Whoever believes in the Son has eternal life, but whoever rejects the Son will not see life, for God's wrath remains on him."

— *John 3:22-36, NIV*

Read His Word to Him.

In this section of scripture I find so much for which I can express joy, sorrow, hope, and wonder. I know from reading John 4:2 that Jesus himself baptized no one. The baptism was one of repentance and for the same purpose as John's baptism—indeed it was a repeating of the baptism of John. It is rather obvious that this whole section is a discussion of how John and our Lord handled the problem of jealousy among their followers. I am moved to exclaim with your Son: "That of those born of woman there has not arisen a greater than John the Baptist"!

Please express your response to this beautiful text. Put your expression in your own prayer diary.

6. READ HIS WORD FOR YOURSELF.

How very easy it is to be caught up in the vortex of jealousy. Even when leaders are not jealous of each other their followers are! We all have followers if we are leaders. The only solution to envy and jealousy is to let our Lord became all and in all.

John was delighted to tell what he had received from heaven—and he was just as glad to allow anyone else the same privilege. If God wanted to eclipse his ministry by that of Jesus John was ready to receive such a message. It was God in heaven who was calling the shots not the preachers. For me this means I must be constantly meditating upon your word, day and night.

Pause in his presence and either audibly or in written form tell him all his word means to you.

7. READ HIS WORD IN THANKSGIVING.

(1) Thank you for being so clear about who is important. (2) Thank you for the obvious fact that baptism was done with "much water." (3) Thank you for the bridegroom, my glorious Lord. (4) Thank you that we are his bride! (5) Thank you that we can help the bridegroom and the bride to get ready for the marriage supper in heaven. (6) Thank you for the "one above all." (7) Thank you that we can read in the words of the gospels what you told your Son in the chambers of heaven!

Give yourself to your own expression of gratitude—write it or speak it!

8. READ HIS WORD IN MEDITATION.

"The Father loves the Son and has placed everything in his hands." Just how inclusive is this charming statement. Are we to conclude that the human family is a small replica of heaven? Even as an earthly father loves his child and is glad to turn all he has over to the son, so the heavenly parent loves the Son and has placed everything in his hands. God just had one plan and all of it centered in his Son. All the Father hopes to accomplish on this earth begins and ends with his Son and the body of his Son, the church.

Pause—wait—think—then express yourself in thoughtful praise or thanks.

9. READ HIS WORD FOR PETITIONS.

What a wonderful witness was John. His example leads me to prayer: (1) How important baptism was to these men! I want the baptism Jesus commanded to be important to me. (2) Why was it necessary to have "plenty of water" in order to baptize? (3) Teach me again that influence is inseparably associated with character. (4) There was no jealousy in John—keep me as humble. (5) Become greater and greater that I might be less and less. (6) May my highest joy be in listening for the bridegroom's voice. (6) I want to set your Son above all in my life. (7) I want to hear and obey your Son in the "little things" of my life today.

Please, please remember these are prayers—speak them—reword them!

10. READ HIS WORD AND WAIT—LISTEN—GOD SPEAKS!

I do want to heed what you say to me from this text: (1) "The Father loves the Son and has placed everything in his hands." (2) "Who ever believes in the Son has eternal life." (3) "Who ever rejects the Son will not see life."

11. INTERCESSION FOR THE LOST WORLD

Sarawak (East Malaysia) — Point for prayer: (1) *Sarawak* has been the scene of one of the most wonderful people movements this century. The movement began in the 1930s among the Murut people and has spread over much of Sarawak. Pray for the continued maturing of these believers as they come more and more into contact with the outside world—many of these believers are from primitive and illiterate backgrounds.

12. SING PRAISES TO OUR LORD.

Then let our songs abound,
And every tear be dry;

We're marching thro' Emmanuel's ground
To fairer worlds on high.

1. PRAISE GOD FOR WHO HE IS.

"I will praise the name of God with a song; I will magnify him with thanksgiving. This will please the Lord more than an ox or a bull with horns and hoofs" (Psa. 69:30, 31). These are encouraging words. Several rather obvious things appear as I come before you: (1) That man should want to praise you. Oh, how true this is, but only because I know you and have reasons for my praise. So the knowledge of yourself is essential to praise. (2) That you want men to praise you. This is a completion of your nature. A fulfillment of man's purpose for being. (3) That your whole being — represented by the term *"name"* should be the object of our praise. (4) That a song is an appropriate vehicle for our expression of praise. Having said these things, how utterly natural does it seem to lift our voice to you in a song of joy and wonder about yourself!

Express yourself in adoration for this quality of God.
Speak it audibly or write out your praise in your own devotional journal.

2. PRAISE GOD FOR WHAT HE MEANS TO ME.

Just for me. The little phrase "magnify him" is most interesting to me. God becomes God by thanksgiving. The more we thank him the greater he becomes! This I have found to be so wondrously true. I like the time of thanksgiving because it separates me from myself and lifts me up to see the Giver of all I have, to consider the value of what was given and the love of the Giver.

I am totally amazed that you would find pleasure in our praise and thanksgiving. But I do believe I can bring happiness to you! You do seek our adoration and gratitude even as we reach out for your love and greatness. How fulfilling! Praise your wonderful name!

How do you personally relate to the praise of God, and God who is worthy of praise?
Speak it out or write it out. It is *so important* that you establish *your own* devotional journal.

3. CONFESSION OF SIN

Why is there always the dark side of life? I have not found a real satisfying answer. I know it is sin and Satan — but why man has a continuing interest is my problem. I say this most especially in the face of these beautiful verses. Forgive me for not praising you! Forgive me for my utter selfishness. Oh, lift me up into the realm of reality that I might see your purpose of goodness for all men. I have a strong tendency to minimize or ignore my sin. Show me just how important is your law of life. To transgress the law of life is to ask for death — or separation.

What personal sins do you want to confess? We *must* speak them to remove them.
Do it! *Now.* There is no one else you have sinned against more than God. Tell him so!

4. SING A PRAYER TO GOD.

Thou art the bread of life,
O Lord, to me,
Thy holy Word the truth that saveth me;

Give me to eat and live
With Thee above;
Teach me to love Thy truth, for Thou art love.

Open your hymn book and sing the rest of the verses — or even sing another prayer song.

5. READ HIS WORD TO HIM!

His Word

4 The Pharisees heard that Jesus was gaining and baptizing more disciples than John, [2]although in fact it was not Jesus who baptized, but his disciples. [3]When the Lord learned of this, he left Judea and went back once more to Galilee.

[4]Now he had to go through Samaria. [5]So he came to a town in Samaria called Sychar, near the plot of ground Jacob had given to his son Joseph. [6]Jacob's well was there, and Jesus, tired as he was from the journey, sat down by the well. It was about the sixth hour.

[7]When a Samaritan woman came to draw water, Jesus said to her, "Will you give me a drink?" [8](His disciples had gone into the town to buy food.)

[9]The Samaritan woman said to him, "You are a Jew and I am a Samaritan woman. How can you ask me for a drink?" (For Jews do not associate with Samaritans.)

[10]Jesus answered her, "If you knew the gift of God and who it is that asks you for a drink, you would have asked him and he would have given you living water."

[11]"Sir," the woman said, "you have nothing to draw with and the well is deep? Where can you get this living water? [12]Are you greater than our father Jacob, who gave us the well and drank from it himself, as did also his sons and his flocks and herds?"

[13]Jesus answered, "Everyone who drinks this water will be thirsty again, [14]but whoever drinks the water I give him will never thirst. Indeed, the water I give him will become in him a spring of water welling up to eternal life."

[15]The woman said to him, "Sir, give me this water so that I won't get thirsty and have to keep coming here to draw water."

— John 4:1-15, NIV

Read His Word to Him.

What a blessed encounter! How representative! How all men and women can relate to these blessed words. Just briefly I want to list them. Dear Lord, all of us can identify. (1) We are all thirsty; deep within us we are thirsty. (2) We know people are not talkative nor do they communicate well when they are hungry and tired—our Lord did—blessed be his name. (3) Jacob (or Israel) cannot give us an answer—it is Jacob's son by the Spirit who does. (4) We meet a need in the life of our Lord—how can it be? —but we do. (5) Jesus came to give us the gift of God.

Please express your response to this beautiful text. Put your expression in your own prayer diary.

6. READ HIS WORD FOR YOURSELF.

Dear Lord, how eager I am to do this! (1) Deep down within me is a thirst that I have quenched from time to time at the well of living water! But I know my Lord was using a continuing action verb when he said: "he that drinketh"—he meant I must continue to drink if I want to continue to be satisfied. My own experience would teach me this if I knew nothing about the Greek verb tense. (2) Must not my Lord be very tired of my feeble efforts? Have I not left my Lord unfulfilled from the standpoint of communion with me? And yet I see him reaching out to me—and saying ever so tenderly, "Will you give me a drink?"

Pause in his presence and either audibly or in written form tell him all his word means to you.

7. READ HIS WORD IN THANKSGIVING.

How appropriate is thanksgiving to this text: (1) Thank you for Jesus' unwillingness to contribute to jealousy. (2) Thank you Jesus was willing to go through Samaria. (3) Thank you for the human limitations of my Lord— an example of how to deal with those same limitations in me. (4) Thank you Jesus was ready to make the first move. (5) Thank you for the honesty of the woman as to prejudice and bigotry. (6) Thank you that Jesus is still in the living water business. (7) Thank you that we need never thirst again!

Give yourself to your own expression of gratitude—write it or speak it!

8. READ HIS WORD IN MEDITATION.

"Indeed, the water I give him will become in him a spring of water welling up to eternal life." We are much like the woman: "Sir, give me this water . . ." I do hope we have a little more perception. Our Lord didn't promise H_2O. The promise of a spring of water or what we would think of as an artesian well, is based on the condition that we keep on drinking. I have surely found the promise to be true.

Pause—wait—think—then express yourself in thoughtful praise or thanks.

9. READ HIS WORD FOR PETITIONS.

(1) Our Lord avoided prideful popularity—give me the same courage. (2) May I be willing to go through the Samarias that arise today in my experience. (3) I want to remember that being tired in your work is so different than being tired of it. (4) Open my heart and my mouth to communicate to those who would seemingly be not interested. (5) Break down *any* barrier of race or sex I might have as related to other people. (6) I do want to know better than ever "the gift of God." (7) Lord, I purpose right now to keep on drinking of the living water.

Right here add your personal requests—and his answers.

10. READ HIS WORD AND WAIT—LISTEN—GOD SPEAKS!

How poignantly you can speak to me out of this text: (1) "I am still giving 'living water.'" (2) "Whoever keeps on drinking will never thirst." (3) "You can be my own source of living water for others."

11. INTERCESSION FOR THE LOST WORLD

Sarawak (East Malaysia) — Point for prayer: (1) *Missionary work seems to be drawing to a close* but, praise God, the churches are rapidly reaching the position of being able to manage. Pray for the missionaries that they may use their time strategically. Bible translation and evangelistic outreach in 10 unreached peoples. Bible translation work is in progress in 7 languages. Pray for this ministry.

12. SING PRAISES TO OUR LORD.

The Church's one foundation
Is Jesus Christ her Lord;
She is His new creation
By water and the word:

From Heav'n He came and sought her
To be His holy bride;
With His own blood He bought her,
And for her life He died.

WEEK THIRTY-SIX — SUNDAY

1. PRAISE GOD FOR WHO HE IS.

"May all who seek thee rejoice and be glad in thee! May those who love thy salvation say evermore, 'God is great!'" (Psa. 70:4). How I do enjoy this fellowship with you! It is a real privilege to praise you for all the attributes of yourself I see in each of these verses. (1) Praise you for being someone we (all men) can want to seek. All who know you have a strong desire to be with you. There is no hesitancy in being with you. I *want* to seek your presence. Love and sacred respect combine to draw me to yourself. (2) When once we understand your essential nature of love and power there arises a great expression of praise and gladness that cannot be found anywhere else or from anyone else. (3) Who would not love to be saved? There are those who do not know they are lost. Once we catch just a glimpse of the greatness of your interest in man we shall all exclaim from the depth of our hearts "God is great!"

Express yourself in adoration for this quality of God.
Speak it audibly or write out your praise in your own devotional journal.

2. PRAISE GOD FOR WHAT HE MEANS TO ME.

Just for me. Dear Lord, I do seek you! Just what is involved in this little word *"seek"*? You are not lost that I should find you to lead me out of my confusion. For every day, and several times during the day, I want to seek your face for direction and approval. When I open up the guide book and look up to the guide I find joy.

How do you relate to the gladness of God, and God who is Salvation?
Speak it out or write it out. It is *so important* that you establish *your own* devotional journal.

3. CONFESSION OF SIN

As David said just after this verse of praise: "But I am poor and needy; hasten to me, O God! Thou art my help and my deliverer; O Lord, do not tarry." (Psa. 70:5). How can we hold both of these verses in the same heart? But we can, and do. I am poor and needy even in my expression of praise. My total sufficiency is in you.

What personal sins do you want to confess? We *must* speak them to remove them.
Do it! *Now.* There is no one else you have sinned against more than God. Tell him so!

4. SING A PRAYER TO GOD.

For the wonder of each hour
Of the day and of the night,
Hill and vale and tree and flower,

Sun and moon and stars of light:
Christ our God, to Thee we raise
This our hymn of grateful praise.

Open your hymn book and sing the rest of the verses — or even sing another prayer song.

5. READ HIS WORD TO HIM!

His Word

[16]He told her, "Go, call your husband and come back." [17]"I have no husband," she replied.

Jesus said to her, "You are right when you say you have no husband. [18]The fact is, you have had five husbands, and the man you now have is not your husband. What you have just said is quite true."

[19]"Sir," the woman said, "I can see that you are a prophet. [20]Our fathers worshiped on this mountain, but you Jews claim that the place where we must worship is in Jerusalem."

[21]Jesus declared, "Believe me, woman, a time is coming when you will worship the Father neither on this mountain nor in Jerusalem. [22]You Samaritans worship what you do not know; we worship what we do know, for salvation is from the Jews. [23]Yet a time is coming and has now come when the true worshipers will worship the Father in spirit and truth, for they are the kind of worshipers the Father seeks. [24]God is spirit, and his worshipers must worship in spirit and in truth."

[25]The woman said, "I know that Messiah" (called Christ) "is coming. When he comes, he will explain everything to us."

[26]Then Jesus declared, "I who speak to you am he."

[27]Just then his disciples returned and were surprised to find him talking with a woman. But no one asked, "What do you want?" or "Why are you talking with her?"

[28]Then, leaving her water jar, the woman went back to the town and said to the people, [29]"Come, see a man who told me everything I ever did. Could this be the Christ?" [30]They came out of the town and made their way toward him.
— *John 4:16-30, NIV*

Read His Word to Him.

It is always good to participate in a grand discovery. Surely this is the grandest! To this one woman our Lord opened up his heart. It would seem almost like an accident. Why was she at the well at noon? Why was Jesus alone? Dear Lord, we know the answer to these questions. Such an encounter was planned by you. As many times as I have read these words they always embarrass me. I am always the sinner — and Jesus knows I am.

Please express your response to this beautiful text. Put your expression in your own prayer diary.

WEEK THIRTY-SIX — SUNDAY

6. READ HIS WORD FOR YOURSELF.

Dear Father, I want to take the place of the woman. (1) I know I am a sinner. (2) I have made the wonderful discovery that Jesus is the Messiah. (3) I want to be able to express my worship in confidence that I am doing it in the right place and manner. (4) I now see real worship is of the total inward being. (5) How delighted I am to learn God is "seeking" men and women to worship him.

(6) Even when men come and could interrupt my relationship with you I can be—(and I am)—so absorbed in my discovery of your Son that I do not even notice it. (7) I want to tell everyone! "Come and see." Here is One who knows me better than I will ever know myself. Wonder of all wonder I have found the Savior of the world!

Pause in his presence and either audibly or in written form tell him all his word means to you.

7. READ HIS WORD IN THANKSGIVING.

I am sure the woman of Samaria never ceased thanking you. (1) Thank you for the deep conviction of personal sin. (2) Thank you that I want to repent of such sin—even as the woman. (3) Thank you for my Lord who sees and knows and meets my deepest needs. (4) Thank you for the desire of all men to be right in their worship of you.

(5) Thank you for my Lord's words that let me know my heart is the place for worship and my spirit is the means of worship. (6) Thank you that even now God yearns for me to lift my spirit in worship to him. (7) Thank you I can leave all and tell others of the One I have found.

Give yourself to your own expression of gratitude—write it or speak it!

8. READ HIS WORD IN MEDITATION.

"Come, see a man who told me everything I ever did." Let us go at the woman's bidding and see the one who has produced such excitement in her heart. When we do we will find one who speaks as no other man ever spoke. He seems to anticipate our questions before we ask them, he seems to know just how we hurt and has words to not only explain but to heal. We will find one who seems to know the scriptures and their meaning like no other teacher we have ever heard. But the quality that most attracts us is that we meet a man who lives as no other man. His whole attitude is different than anyone else. He has a softer manner, or perhaps we could say more compassionate. At the same time, there is a pureness of speech and thought that fills us with wonder. We agree with the woman, we wouldn't be at all surprised if he told us just what we were thinking or just what we had been doing.

Pause—wait—think—then express yourself in thoughtful praise or thanks.

9. READ HIS WORD FOR PETITIONS.

(1) How I do need the bold humility to confront people in their sin. (2) Open my heart to the suffering of those who continue in adultery. (3) How I do long to worship you everywhere every day. (4) Thank you for the present of knowledge of salvation through my Lord. (5) I want to lift my heart up to you as directed by the example of my Lord. (6) Give me the perception and humility necessary to accept Jesus as my King. (7) I want to "leave my water jar" and tell of him.

Please, please remember these are prayers—speak them—reword them!

10. READ HIS WORD AND WAIT—LISTEN—GOD SPEAKS!

What a powerful example in this woman—you can speak to me through her: (1) "I am still seeking men to worship me." (2) "Men will never be saved until they find out they are lost." (3) "You have more to tell and more reason to tell it."

11. INTERCESSION FOR THE LOST WORLD

Sarawak (East Malaysia) — Point for prayer: (1) *Unreached peoples*—many of the smaller and more inaccessible groups must still be contacted and evangelized. Pray that missionaries may be successful in this. Pray for a growing missionary vision among believers for these people. Also the larger Iban and Bidayuh tribes have proved unresponsive. Pray for their evangelization.

12. SING PRAISES TO OUR LORD.

The name of Jesus is so sweet,
I love its music to repeat;
It makes my joys full and complete,
The precious name of Jesus.

"Jesus," oh, how sweet the name!
"Jesus," ev'ry day the same;
"Jesus," let all saints proclaim
Its worthy praise forever.

WEEK THIRTY-SIX — MONDAY

1. PRAISE GOD FOR WHO HE IS.

"Blessed be the Lord, the God of Israel, who alone does wondrous things. Blessed be his glorious name forever; may his glory fill the whole earth! Amen and Amen" (Psa. 72:18, 19). What the psalmist sang and prayed to you in the long ago I want to repeat today: (1) I want to set you apart and admire your greatness and goodness.

Who, oh Lord, is like you? No one! (2) You alone have done those things worthy of praise — accomplishments of eternal value. There is nothing done in this whole world that will outlast the world in which it exists if it does not have your nature in it. (3) May your very self be the object of my adoration throughout eternity.

Express yourself in adoration for this quality of God.
Speak it audibly or write out your praise in your own devotional journal.

2. PRAISE GOD FOR WHAT HE MEANS TO ME.

I have tried to hold an objective view in the above praise — just now I want to relate all my words to the desires of my own heart. Words indeed fail me to tell of the "blessedness" of your name! When I attempt to praise man I am always reminded of some human quality that indicates he is much less than perfect. But such will never be found in you. Such has never been found in you. No one at anytime in any place has found one flaw in your character. If you alone do "wondrous things" then what praise is left for man?

How do you personally relate to the works of God, and God who is at work?
Speak it out or write it out. It is *so important* that you establish *your own* devotional journal.

3. CONFESSION OF SIN

It is so easy to be carried away in adoration and praise and forget, at least momentarily, how terribly far short I fall in fulfilling this concept on a daily basis. It is one thing to praise you in private devotion or worship — and I am delighted to do it — but it is another thing to raise that praise in the marketplace. To tell of your goodness in the office. If I want all the earth to be filled with your glory, it is up to me to fill my little earth with it.

What personal sins do you want to confess? We *must* speak them to remove them.
Do it! *Now.* There is no one else you have sinned against more than God. Tell him so!

4. SING A PRAYER TO GOD.

Lord Jesus, for this I most humbly entreat,
I wait, blessed Lord, at Thy crucified feet;
By faith, for my cleansing, I see Thy blood flow,

Now wash me, and I shall be whiter than snow.
Whiter than snow, yes, whiter than snow;
Now wash me, and I shall be whiter than snow.

Open your hymn book and sing the rest of the verses — or even sing another prayer song.

5. READ HIS WORD TO HIM!

His Word

[31] Meanwhile his disciples urged him, "Rabbi, eat something."

[32] But he said to them, "I have food to eat that you know nothing about."

[33] Then his disciples said to each other, "Could someone have brought him food?"

[34] "My food," said Jesus, "is to do the will of him who sent me and to finish his work. [35] Do you not say, 'Four months more and then the harvest'? I tell you, open your eyes and look at the fields! They are ripe for harvest. [36] Even now the reaper draws his wages, even now he harvests the crop for eternal life, so that the sower and the reaper may be glad together. [37] Thus the saying 'One sows and another reaps' is true. [38] I sent you to reap what you have not worked for. Others have done the hard work, and you have reaped the benefits of their labor."

[39] Many of the Samaritans from that town believed in him because of the woman's testimony, "He told me everything I ever did." [40] So when the Samaritans came to him, they urged him to stay with them, and he stayed two days. [41] And because of his words many more became believers.

[42] They said to the woman, "We no longer believe just because of what you said; now we have heard for ourselves, and we know that this man really is the Savior of the world."

— *John 4:31-42, NIV*

Read His Word to Him.

What a blessed wonderful section of your word! I gladly worship before you in praise and thanksgiving. Your Son's attitude toward his work is such an example for me! Seldom have I ever been so caught up in what I have been doing I have forgotten to eat — if I have there have always been those around like the disciples of my Lord to remind me. Dear Lord, even if I have not lost my appetite for physical food I do purpose to fulfill your Son's words in my experience: to do the will of yourself and finish the work you have given me to do.

Please express your response to this beautiful text. Put your expression in your own prayer diary.

6. READ HIS WORD FOR YOURSELF.

Dear Lord, I want to hear more clearly than I ever have the words of your Son . . . "The sower and reaper may be glad together." Right here in this town I am entering into the labors of others. For more than 100 years someone has been telling the good news of my Lord in this place. I rejoice they have planted and I can water, or that I can plant. The teaching of your word, the announcement of the good news. What a joy it is to all who do it! If I had to wait for some man or group of men to send me I guess I would never be sent (and I do not minimize their part in evangelism), but Jesus said: "I sent you to reap . . ." Dear Lord, I hear you! If the disciples could win the Samaritans to the acceptance of a Jewish Messiah then there is hope for all our efforts.

Pause in his presence and either audibly or in written form tell him all his word means to you.

7. READ HIS WORD IN THANKSGIVING.

Indeed I will. (1) Thank you for the patience of my Lord with the non-spiritual attitude of the disciples. (2) Thank you that Jesus kept right on teaching—he knew they would understand by and by. (3) Thank you that Jesus finished his work and I enter into his labors. (4) Thank you that today is harvest day. (5) Thank you there need be no jealousy at all in your work. (6) Thank you that some believed the woman—believed her new lifestyle. (7) Thank you that many more believed because they had heard personally. Their faith also came from hearing, but from hearing our Lord.

Give yourself to your own expression of gratitude—write it or speak it!

8. READ HIS WORD IN MEDITATION.

"*. . . Now we have heard for ourselves, and we know that this man really is the Savior of the world.*" Ultimately this is what *must* happen to all who discover the Savior. How eternally true it is that saving faith comes by hearing. The hearing of the inner ear must be involved. Hearing with a real personal understanding. We cannot imagine that there were not questions asked by the Samaritans and answered by our Lord. It must also have been true that Jesus repeated with emphasis some of the points he wanted remembered. The examples of his teachings in other parts of the word will bear this out. How unlike some of our efforts to make converts! How refreshing it would be to assemble today interested persons who had not found the Savior and let him speak to them through his word.

Pause—wait—think—then express yourself in thoughtful praise or thanks.

9. READ HIS WORD FOR PETITIONS.

(1) How I do want my Savior's hunger and thirst for your will in my life. (2) Give me also my Lord's patience with those who do not share my concern. (3) Help me my Lord, to indeed complete the work you have given me to do. (4) Open my eyes to see the harvest fields—*now.* (5) Praise your name for every person won to you. I want to truly rejoice with the reaper and the sower. (6) I want to be like the Samaritans who believed *because* of his words. (7) Keep on saving me from all that loses your presence.

Right here add your personal requests—and his answers.

10. READ HIS WORD AND WAIT—LISTEN—GOD SPEAKS!

How clearly you speak to me in these verses! (1) "You have two men to feed—" (2) "The harvest is still for 'eternal life.'" (3) "I can tell you everything you ever did or said or thought, but I have forgotten all your sins!"

11. INTERCESSION FOR THE LOST WORLD

Sarawak (East Malaysia) — Point for prayer: (1) *The coastal churches* are predominantly Chinese, with some indigenous believers as well. Revival is needed among these Christians, for outreach is not their strong point. There are growing churches also in the towns on the coast.

12. SING PRAISES TO OUR LORD.

His name above all names shall stand,
Exalted more and more,
At God the Father's own right hand,
Where angel hosts adore.

Blessed be the name, blessed be the name,
Blessed be the name of the Lord;
Blessed be the name, blessed be the name,
Blessed be the name of the Lord.

WEEK THIRTY-SIX — TUESDAY

1. PRAISE GOD FOR WHO HE IS.

"But as for me it is good to be near God; I have made the Lord God my refuge, that I may tell of all thy works" (Psa. 73:28). Indeed it is good that I draw near to you, that you might draw near to me. There are several beautiful qualities of yourself found in this verse: (1) We are of the same nature, i.e., spirit that we can draw near to each other. I have no fellowship with beasts or even with other fellow creatures as I do with you. You are the original source of myself. (2) I have needs that cannot be satisfied by anyone else, but this is true of all men; only in you can these deepest of needs be satisfied. Bless your glorious name!

Express yourself in adoration for this quality of God.
Speak it audibly or write out your praise in your own devotional journal.

2. PRAISE GOD FOR WHAT HE MEANS TO ME.

Just for me. Too much of the above has me in it. I always intend to praise you just for yourself as you relate to all men, but I am such a part of all men I forget. It is when I draw near to you and lift up my heart to you that I want to tell of all your works. How very good it is to recite just a few of your "works" in my life: (1) You sent a proclaimer of the good news to tell me of your love and my need. (2) You moved me to commit my life to your service. (3) You gave me a wife of price far above rubies. (4) You gave us three dear children. (5) Most of all you saved me from hell to heaven. Oh, blessed be your name forever!

How do you personally relate to the protection of God, and God who is our refuge?
Speak it out or write it out. It is *so important* that you establish *your own* devotional journal.

3. CONFESSION OF SIN

How I would like to always feel the way I do at this time of worship. But I do not. There are times, as you well know, when I must make a real effort to draw near to you. I always *want to* but there are barriers to be removed. Why? It is my own predisposition to setting my mind upon the things of the flesh, and not upon the things of the Spirit—forgive me! I am sincerely sorry, but there are times when I run away from my refuge and seek to find fulfillment in the broad expanse of my own way. It never works! What a fool! I am learning.

What personal sins do you want to confess? We *must* speak them to remove them.
Do it! *Now.* There is no one else you have sinned against more than God. Tell him so!

4. SING A PRAYER TO GOD.

My heart has no desire to stay
Where doubts arise and fears dismay;
Tho' some may dwell where these abound,
My prayer, my aim, is higher ground.

Lord, lift me up and let me stand,
By faith, on Heaven's tableland,
A higher plane than I have found;
Lord, plant my feet on higher ground.

Open your hymn book and sing the rest of the verses—or even sing another prayer song.

5. READ HIS WORD TO HIM!

His Word

[43] After the two days he left for Galilee. [44] (Now Jesus himself had pointed out that a prophet has no honor in his own country.) [45] When he arrived in Galilee, the Galileans welcomed him. They had seen all that he had done in Jerusalem at the Passover Feast, for they also had been there.

[46] Once more he visited Cana in Galilee, where he had turned the water into wine. And there was a certain royal official whose son lay sick at Capernaum. [47] When this man heard that Jesus had arrived in Galilee from Judea, he went to him and begged him to come and heal his son, who was close to death.

[48] "Unless you people see miraculous signs and wonders," Jesus told him, "you will never believe."

[49] The royal official said, "Sir come down before my child dies."

[50] Jesus replied, "You may go. Your son will live."

The man took Jesus at his word and departed. [51] While he was still on the way, his servants met him with the news that his boy was living. [52] When he inquired as to the time when his son got better, they said to him, "The fever left him yesterday at the seventh hour."

[53] Then the father realized that this was the exact time at which Jesus had said to him, "Your son will live." So he and all his household believed. —*John 4:43-53, NIV*

Read His Word to Him.

Dear Lord, I do so want to express my appreciation of each verse in your book! I can identify with your Son as he prepared to return to an area where those who knew him lived. But of late they had been to Jerusalem and had watched his miracles at the passover feast. Am I right in assuming they were far more interested in the miracle than in its meaning. What a tragedy to be more interested in the advertising than the product. But I meet people like this every day. There have been times when I saw one in the mirror. Dear Lord, forgive! How I want to be like the noble man from Capernaum!

Please express your response to this beautiful text. Put your expression in your own prayer diary.

6. READ HIS WORD FOR YOURSELF.

Oh, there is so much I can say in the application of this living word to my heart! (1) The nobleman had come to a full realization of his own helplessness. He had run out of all resources. Not only so—he must *act* upon his need. (2) Perhaps he had been to Jerusalem to see our Lord's miracles—or someone in his household had been there. (3) He did not allow pride or position to hinder him. In all these areas I want to relate myself! (4) How surprised he must have been at our Lord's response to his request. Jesus was testing the nobleman's faith. Even as he does mine.

Pause in his presence and either audibly or in written form tell him how much his word means to you.

7. READ HIS WORD IN THANKSGIVING.

There was one man who never could thank you enough for your Son and his love and power. (1) Thank you for the friends Jesus had in Cana that made his visit pleasant. (2) Thank you that the nobleman was willing to walk eight hours to reach Jesus, i.e., from Capernaum to Cana. (3) Thank you that our Lord knows our hearts better than we know ourselves. (4) Thank you that Jesus motivates us to act on our faith. (5) Thank you Jesus always gives us an option—we can chose to disbelieve if we want to. (6) Thank you that no word of our Lord ever failed. (7) Thank you that faith, real faith, is contagious!

Give yourself to your own expression of gratitude—write it or speak it!

8. READ HIS WORD IN MEDITATION.

"This was the second miraculous sign that Jesus performed." This sign, like the "certain royal official" has convinced me. It is most important that we notice the official believed *before* the sign. The miracle only confirmed what he believed. There are several other important aspects of this healing to consider: (1) As near as we know there was no faith exercised by the sick child. (2) The miracle was accomplished over a space of miles that separated the healed from the healer. (3) It was instantaneous and permanent. The little son did not improve, he was well. We never read of a retrogression in the healings of Jesus. (4) The time element was important to the father —when our Lord said it, it happened.

Pause—wait—think—then express yourself in thoughtful praise or thanks.

9. READ HIS WORD FOR PETITIONS.

Such a beautiful compact account of my Lord's concern. (1) Keep me as undisappointed as my Lord was with those who refused to believe. (2) There are those even among disbelievers who will believe; help me to find them. (3) There are so many qualities in the life of the royal official—I want the total confidence in the miraculous nature of your Son. (4) Give me the beseeching humility of this man. (5) Give me the urgency that breaks through barriers to life. (6) How I do want to "take you at your word" on all subjects.

Please, please remember these are prayers—speak them—reword them!

10. READ HIS WORD AND WAIT—LISTEN—GOD SPEAKS!

How penetrating will be your words out of the experience of this man: (1) "There are men today who want to believe—find them and tell them." (2) "Every hour there are those who are sick unto death—it could be the hour of their healing." (3) "Review again all the signs of my Son as written here by John."

11. INTERCESSION FOR THE LOST WORLD

Nepal — Population: 12,900,000. Growth rate—2.3%. People per sq. km.—92.

Point for prayer: (1) *This long-closed land* opened up a little for the Gospel in 1951, but the conversion of people is illegal and those seeking the conversion of others are liable to punishment. Some workers were expelled from the land in 1976, probably from complaints about infringing this law. Pray for complete freedom of religion.

12. SING PRAISES TO OUR LORD.

We would see Jesus, for the shadows lengthen
Across this little landscape of our life;

We would see Jesus, our weak faith to strengthen
For the last weariness, the final strife.

1. PRAISE GOD FOR WHO HE IS.

"How lovely is thy dwelling place, O Lord of hosts! My soul longs, yea, faints for the courts of the Lord; my heart and flesh sing for joy to the living God" (Psa. 84:1, 2). This no doubt first referred to the temple of Solomon. Today your dwelling place is the body of man. To consider man as a body apart from your purpose and your Son he is not lovely at all. To contemplate the complexity and precision with which man is made does call forth expressions of wonder. Man as a machine or an animal, quite apart from your own image is amazing! However it is the assembly inside your temple for which the heart of the psalmist yearns. There *is* something about the expanse of the pillared ceiling—a view of the long collonades of the temple that impressed the worshiper. The environment was surely conducive to worship, but it was in the meaning of the words of the songs that worship arose.

Express yourself in adoration for this quality of God.
Speak it audibly or write out your praise in your own devotional journal.

2. PRAISE GOD FOR WHAT HE MEANS TO ME.

Just for me. I want to review again each word in these beautiful verses: (1) Make the place of worship as beautiful and meaningful as the worship itself. Such should be our bodies. The lovely dwelling place of yourself in the Spirit. (2) You are Lord of the whole host of heaven. All the angels are at this moment bowing before you in wonder and admiration. Can I do less? (3) My total inmost being, my life reaches out for you. A great void and emptiness that no one else and nothing else can fill is within me! (4) If I do not find completion in my praise and thanksgiving I will become very, very discouraged. (5) In contrast I can find the power of new life in my worship of you.

How do you personally relate to the dwelling place of God, and God who lives in us?
Speak it out or write it out. It is *so important* that you establish *your own* devotional journal.

3. CONFESSION OF SIN

There is nothing hidden from you and we only deceive ourselves if we attempt to deceive you. Dear Lord, my body is my largest problem. I want it to be a lovely dwelling place for you, but I find it a burden instead of a joy. I would indeed enjoy the Old Testament concept of a habitation for yourself—transfer the responsibility to a building! But I live in this day when I know your house is my house—my body! I can identify with the psalmist as he reaches out for the beauty of Solomon's temple. I reach out—my soul longs, yea faints for a house under constant control and prepared as a lovely place for you to live.

What personal sins do you want to confess? We *must* speak them to remove them.
Do it! *Now.* There is no one else you have sinned against more than God. Tell him so!

4. SING A PRAYER TO GOD.

Jesus is all the world to me,
And true to Him I'll be;
Oh, how could I this Friend deny,
When He's so true to me?

Following Him I know I'm right,
He watches o'er me day and night;
Following Him, by day and night,
He's my Friend.

Open your hymn book and sing the rest of the verses—or even sing another prayer song.

5. READ HIS WORD TO HIM!

His Word

[12]When Jesus heard that John had been put in prison, he returned to Galilee. [13]Leaving Nazareth, he went and lived in Capernaum, which was by the lake in the area of Zebulun and Naphtali—[14]to fulfill what was said through the prophet Isaiah:
[15]"Land of Zebulun and land of
      Naphtali,
   the way to the sea, along the
      Jordan,
   Galilee of the Gentiles—
[16]the people living in darkness
   have seen a great light;
   on those living in the land of the
   shadow of death
   a light has dawned."
[17]From that time on Jesus began to preach, "Repent, for the kingdom of heaven is near."   — Matt. 4:12-17, NIV

[14]After John was put in prison, Jesus went into Galilee, proclaiming the good news of God. [15]"The time has come," he said. "The kingdom of God is near. Repent and believe the good news!"   — Mk. 1:14, 15, NIV

[19]But when John rebuked Herod the tetrarch because of Herodias, his brother's wife, and all the other evil things he had done, [20]Herod added this to them all: He locked John up in prison.   — Lk. 3:19, 20, NIV

Read His Word to Him.

It is with genuine joy I take up a most careful word-by-word reading of these verses. In each of these sections or periods of worship I want to praise you, thank you, repent, make requests. All of such expressions come as a natural expression of my response to what you have written. It would seem there was a close relationship between John and your Son. Did our Lord want to call John's disciples from Judea to Galilee? Nazareth was left behind—what a poignant thought: if we like those of his home reject and refuse he will move on and we will be left in our self-imposed darkness.

Please express your response to this beautiful text. Put your expression in your own prayer diary.

6. READ HIS WORD FOR YOURSELF.

I have been to the location of where Capernaum used to be. It is a lovely spot. This was to be the headquarters for our Lord's campaign of Galilee—he would be here for sixteen months. I want to say that I believe my town, my community, yea, my home can be his headquarters today for the evangelizing of every man and woman. Oh, how full of meaning are the words of my Lord: "the people living in darkness have seen a great light; on those living in the land of the shadow of death a light has dawned." How many in the population of Galilee heard the good news? We believe everyone was given an opportunity. There is no community today in which Christians live that could not be given the same opportunity.

Pause in his presence and either audibly or in written form tell him all his word means to you.

7. READ HIS WORD IN THANKSGIVING.

(1) Thank you for John's courage in rebuking those who sin in high-places. (2) Thank you for my Lord's deep sympathy for John the Baptist. (3) Thank you for the beautiful fulfillment of prophecy in the life of our Lord. (4) Thank you that the "great light" is still shining in the darkness of this world. (5) Thank you for the preaching of Jesus—what an example! (6) Thank you that there is a whole way of life offered by Jesus to which I can conform. (7) Thank you that I can presently be a citizen of the kingdom of heaven.

Give yourself to your own expression of gratitude—write it or speak it!

8. READ HIS WORD IN MEDITATION.

"The kingdom of heaven (of God) is near. Repent and believe the good news." This statement by Mark is in itself good news. The rule and reign of God in our lives is indeed good news. The change of mind (repentance) necessary was simply that the Messiah had come and it was now possible to see him and hear him. Life *can* take on new meanings. Light and hope and peace have come in the person of God's Son. Our voluntary submission to his words and rule can now become a reality. There is *nothing quite so important as allowing him to dominate each day.*

Pause—wait—think—then express yourself in thoughtful praise or thanks.

9. READ HIS WORD FOR PETITIONS.

Move me to love and good works—but first to prayer: (1) Keep me aware that evil men are as free to choose as are your children. (2) Lift my heart to always know we have *"good news."* (3) Embolden my faith to believe your rule in my heart is as near as my own choice. (4) Use all the means necessary to move me to repentance. (5) Tune my inner ear to hear you say again and again: "Come, follow me." (6) Make of me a fisher of men.

Right here add your personal requests—and his answers.

10. READ HIS WORD AND WAIT—LISTEN—GOD SPEAKS!

Speak Lord, thy servant heareth: (1) "People still live in darkness and need 'the great light.'" (2) "There are those dead in trespasses and sins who could be raised if they could but hear." (3) "My kingdom is here and here-after—lead men into it."

11. INTERCESSION FOR THE LOST WORLD

Nepal — Point for prayer: (1) *Missions* in Nepal need great tact and wisdom in their very delicate relationship with the Government, which carefully watches their activities. Pray that these brethren may be a vital witness in their limiting circumstances, and also a real strength to the national brethren as they fellowship in the little congregations around the country.

12. SING PRAISES TO OUR LORD.

Holy, Holy, Holy! Tho' the darkness hide Thee,
Tho' the eye of sinful man Thy glory may not see,

Only Thou art holy; there is none beside Thee
Perfect in pow'r, in love, and purity.

WEEK THIRTY-SIX — THURSDAY

1. PRAISE GOD FOR WHO HE IS.

"Blessed are the men whose strength is in thee, in whose heart are the highways to Zion. As they go through the valley of Baca they make it a place of springs; the early rain also covers it with pools. They go from strength to strength; the God of gods will be seen in Zion" (Psa. 84:5-7). Bless the Lord, oh my soul! What beautiful expressions of yourself are seen in what you can do in man.

Let us notice: (1) You are my total source of strength. How disappointing and frustrating are the men who trust in their own strength—it fails—runs out and does not produce. (2) You make known your ways through the hearts of men. If the way to heaven is in our heart it will also come from our mouth. It is good to know the way; it is better to share it.

Express yourself in adoration for this quality of God.
Speak it audibly or write out your praise in your own devotional journal.

2. PRAISE GOD FOR WHAT HE MEANS TO ME.

Praise for what you mean to me! I want to be that man whose strength is in you, and not in myself. I have found how very weak and inadequate is all my strength. My meditation on your word, my time of prayer with you, my teaching and preaching of your word—in all these I find my strength. Most of all, it is in *you* and *you* alone—expression of strength is one thing, the *source* of strength

is another—it is in my intimacy with you, it is in oneness or abiding! Men must travel through my heart to you! It could be painful. I can lead men through the dark, tough places of life; such can be places of refreshment and not defeat, a place of beauty and not of hurt. ". . . from strength to strength" is such a beautiful description—open my heart to its meaning!

How do you personally relate to the strength of God, and God who is our strength?
Speak it out or write it out. It is *so important* that you establish *your own* devotional journal.

3. CONFESSION OF SIN

I want to be specific in the confession of my sins—I know the more specific I am in confession the more specific will be my forgiveness and cleansing. (1) I have tried to find strength in human companionship. It is not there—my heart is still lonesome and sad. In you I find true fellowship and in you I find joy! (2) I have tried to find strength in entertainment—there is nothing there—it runs

out with the action. My fulfillment, my relaxation is only in you. Why do I go to the broken cisterns when the everlasting fountain is so near? (3) Forgive me for expecting strength from education on a human level. I am bored and frustrated. In your word and the pursuit of your truth I can and do go "from strength to strength."

What personal sins do you want to confess? We *must* speak them to remove them.
Speak it audibly or write out your praise in your own devotional journal.

4. SING A PRAYER TO GOD.

What have I to dread, what have I to fear,
Leaning on the everlasting arms?
I have blessed peace with my Lord so near,
Leaning on the everlasting arms.

Leaning, leaning,
Safe and secure from all alarms;
Leaning, leaning,
Leaning on the everlasting arms.

Open your hymn book and sing the rest of the verses—or even sing another prayer song.

5. READ HIS WORD TO HIM!

His Word

[14]Jesus returned to Galilee in the power of the Spirit, and news about him spread through the whole countryside. [15]He taught in their synagogues, and everyone praised him.

[16]He went to Nazareth, where he had been brought up, and on the Sabbath day he went into the synagogue, as was his custom. And he stood up to read. [17]The scroll of the prophet Isaiah was handed to him. Unrolling it, he found the place where it is written:

[18]"The Spirit of the Lord is on me,

because he has anointed me
    to preach good news to the poor.
He has sent me to proclaim freedom
    for the prisoners
    and recovery of sight for the blind,
to release the oppressed,
[19]   to proclaim the year of the Lord's
        favor."

— Luke 4:14-19, NIV

500

WEEK THIRTY-SIX — THURSDAY

Read His Word to Him.

Dear Lord, there could be no more appropriate text than this for my need today! It would seem that Luke is showing a contrast in the response my Lord received in the synagogues of Galilee and the response those of Nazareth gave him. Did it "just so happen" that the text for that particular Sabbath was this beautiful Messianic prophecy? It is wonderfully remarkable how many beautiful things "just happen" when we want your will to be fulfilled in our lives. I do want to attend the synagogue service and hear your Son read the word of the "gospel prophet."

Please express your response to this beautiful text. Put your expression in your own prayer diary.

6. READ HIS WORD FOR YOURSELF.

It is easy to listen to "the words of grace" that fall from his lips. The good tidings are for me for I am poor—the freedom is mine for I am the prisoner! The new sight is mine for I have been blind. The release is mine for I have been the oppressed. All of this could be but another reading of the scripture, or just an interesting message if we do not *truly* identify with him!

Pause in his presence and either audibly or in written form tell him all his word means to you.

7. READ HIS WORD IN THANKSGIVING.

(1) Thank you for the wonderful power of the Holy Spirit in the life of our Lord. (2) Thank you for the praise worthiness of my Lord. I want to praise him too. (3) Thank you for a routine that carries meaning and purpose. (4) Thank you for your word—the same today as when my Lord read from it. (5) Thank you for the presence of the Holy Spirit in us right now. (6) Thank you for the wonder of being poor in spirit and rich in mercy. (7) Thank you that I am free from sin but a prisoner of my Lord.

Give yourself to your own expression of gratitude—write it or speak it!

8. READ HIS WORD IN MEDITATION.

"... *recovery of sight to the blind.*" This expression has so much to offer us as description of our Lord's work in all our lives: A blind man must live from his own imagination as to how the world about him really looks. He must listen to others describe it—he can exercise the marvelous sense of touch, but at the best he really never knows how the world looks until or unless he sees it. We can say we see things as they really are, but until we have the eyes of our heart and understanding opened by our Lord we have at best a distorted concept of reality.

Pause—wait—think—then express yourself in thoughtful praise or thanks.

9. READ HIS WORD FOR PETITIONS.

How the message of our Lord should move us to prayer: (1) How I need the power of your Holy Spirit to help me spread your word! (2) Grant me the wisdom I so much need in teaching your word. (3) Thank you for all the good customs related to worship—may I use them even as my Lord did. (4) I want to praise my Lord as my King. (5) May his message of good news be found on my lips today. (6) Deliver me that I might deliver others.

Please, please remember these are prayers—speak them—reword them!

10. READ HIS WORD AND WAIT—LISTEN—GOD SPEAKS!

How I want these words to be fulfilled in my experience: (1) "I want to release the oppressed today as in the days of my Son." (2) "This is the year of the Lord's favor." (3) "The poor you still have with you and they await the good news."

11. INTERCESSION FOR THE LOST WORLD

Nepal — Point for prayer: (1) *The Church is small*, but steadily growing. Nepali Christian workers itinerate much, and every Christian home is used as a point of contact with the people around. Pray for these believers who have suffered many difficulties and inconveniences for their faith, and some have even been imprisoned for infringing the conversion law. Pray for the growth in grace of the few believers and their witness under difficult circumstances.

12. SING PRAISES TO OUR LORD.

What rejoicing in His presence,
When are banished grief and pain;
When the crooked ways are straightened,
And the dark things shall be plain.

Face to face I shall behold Him,
Far beyond the starry sky;
Face to face in all His glory,
I shall see Him by and by!

WEEK THIRTY-SIX — FRIDAY

1. PRAISE GOD FOR WHO HE IS.

"For the Lord God is a sun and shield; he bestows favor and honor. No good thing does the Lord withhold from those who walk uprightly. O Lord of hosts, blessed is the man who trusts in thee" (Psa. 84:11, 12). Blessed be your name! I gladly list the qualities of yourself found in this lovely text: (1) You are a sun. I want to hold this quality up and admire it. It is even yourself in powerful perspective! The sun is this world's total source of light.

Oh, that men would acknowledge you as the sum source of all understanding of all kinds. The sun offers the essential warmth for all plant and animal life. Indeed, man himself would die without the warmth of the sun. The application is obvious.

At the same time, there is the contrasting quality — you are a shield. Because there is another power or person present in this world we sorely need such protection.

Express yourself in adoration for this quality of God.
Speak it audibly or write out your praise in your own devotional journal.

2. PRAISE GOD FOR WHAT HE MEANS TO ME.

Just for me. I want to enter into the other qualities in this text from a personal viewpoint: (1) You do indeed bestow favor — not earned or many times not deserved — but nonetheless freely given. It is a wonder as well as a favor that we should be called your children. Favor of all favors — it does not yet appear what we shall be! The favor of fellowship with those who love you and love us is such a blessing! (2) Honor is given to man by right of creation. He is the sole intelligent creation from the hand of yourself. The high honor of reasoning capacity is the supreme privilege of man. Of course, we can prostitute this honor, but honor it is! (3) What a promise is mine! I plan on claiming it today! "No good thing will you withhold to those who walk uprightly." Of course, I do not imagine I will turn in a flawless performance, but I will attempt to work without stooping.

How do you personally relate to the light of God, and God who is our Sun?
Speak it out or write it out. It is *so important* that you establish *your own* devotional journal.

3. CONFESSION OF SIN

If you are a sun, how is it that I am so content to live in the darkness of the cave of complacency? If you are a shield, why do I expose myself to the fiery darts of the evil one? If you are ready to give favors, why do I turn my back upon you and busy myself about things that do not matter at all? If you want to honor me, how is it I raise a clenched fist in your face? Walk — do I walk like an animal when I was created to walk upright? Dear God, it is because in all these ways and more I sin against you and myself! How will you ever forgive such ignorance? I know you will — I claim your blessed, needed promise!

What personal sins do I want to confess? We *must* speak them to remove them.
Do it! *Now.* There is no one else you have sinned against more than God. Tell him so!

4. SING A PRAYER TO GOD.

Consecrate me now to Thy service, Lord,
By the pow'r of grace divine;
Let my soul look up with a steadfast hope,
And my will be lost in Thine.

Draw me nearer, nearer, blessed Lord,
To the cross where Thou hast died;
Draw me nearer, nearer, nearer, blessed Lord,
To Thy precious, bleeding side.

Open your hymn book and sing the rest of the verses — or even sing another prayer song.

5. READ HIS WORD TO HIM!

His Word

[20]Then he rolled up the scroll, gave it back to the attendant and sat down. The eyes of everyone in the synagogue were fastened on him, [21]and he said to them, "Today this scripture is fulfilled in your hearing."

[22]All spoke well of him and were amazed at the gracious words that came from his lips. "Isn't this Joseph's son?" they asked.

[23]Jesus said to them, "Surely you will quote this proverb to me: 'Physician, heal yourself! Do here in your home town what we have heard that you did in Capernaum.'"

[24]"I tell you the truth," he continued, "no prophet is accepted in his home town. [25]I assure you that there were many widows in Israel in Elijah's time, when the sky was shut for three and a half years and there was a severe famine throughout the land. [26]Yet Elijah was not sent to any of them, but to a widow in Zarephath in the region of Sidon. [27]And there were many in Israel with leprosy in the time of Elisha the prophet, yet not one of them was cleansed — only Naaman the Syrian."
— Luke 4:20-27, NIV

Read His Word to Him.

How I do want to enter the synagogue at Nazareth and listen to my Lord speak. How I would much prefer my Lord's explanation of just how he freed the captives and gave sight to the blind. Luke says his words were

WEEK THIRTY-SIX — FRIDAY

full of grace. His words produced amazement. I know he was much more than "Joseph's son"—indeed he was not Joseph's son at all. Except in the loving care our Lord received from Joseph. Dear Lord, teach me the power of

the point Jesus was making in his reference to the widow of Zarephath and Naaman the leper. How could it be that those who knew him best appreciated him the least? This is a shocking revelation!

Please express your response to this beautiful text. Put your expression in your own prayer diary.

6. READ HIS WORD FOR YOURSELF.

It is not that our Lord could not perform a miracle, or several of them in Nazareth, he simply refused to do so. In the two examples cited by our Lord faith was present before the miracle was performed—the miracle confirmed what was already present—miracles did not produce faith —that comes by the hearing of the word—miracles deepened what was already there. Why did Nazarenes fail to believe in him? There are several possibilities and all of

them my own possibility—dear Lord give me eyes to see and ears to hear: (1) He had not gone to their schools or studied from their teachers—do I treat any members of his body like they treated our Lord, like the Nazarenes treated our Lord? (2) Those who were his blood brothers —Joseph, Simon, James and Judus did not believe him. Have I followed the dull, dead example of those who are supposed to know him and do not?

Pause in his presence and either audibly or in written form tell him all his word means to you.

7. READ HIS WORD IN THANKSGIVING.

(1) Thank you for the powerful reality of Isaiah's prophecy in my own ears. (2) Thank you that Jesus set the example of explaining the scripture and applying it to life. (3) Thank you for the clear humanness of this

incident—we all can relate it to someone who has been made a new creation in our community—will we accept the greater works? (4) Thank you for the clear teaching here on the purpose of miracles.

Give yourself to your own expression of gratitude—write it or speak it!

8. READ HIS WORD IN MEDITATION.

"... *not one of them was cleansed—only Naaman the Syrian.*" We have such a strong tendency to emphasize the physical that it would seem we could imagine our Lord's purpose in coming into the world was to bring good health. If he did come for this purpose he was a colossal failure in his own land. The prophets also healed,

but that was not their purpose. Even in the use of miracles to establish the truthfulness of their mission both our Lord and the prophets had problems. Jesus gave voice to it, he said: "A wicked and an adulterous generation seeks after a sign," i.e., when the sign becomes the end instead of the means it is clear evidence your heart is not right.

Pause—wait—think—then express yourself in thoughtful praise or thanks.

9. READ HIS WORD FOR PETITIONS.

What an awful indictment our Lord gave to the people of Nazareth! It should indeed move us to prayer: (1) Fasten the eyes of my heart forever on your Son! (2) I know that my Lord could say all over again "Today has this scripture been fulfilled in your ears"—make it so with me! (3) Give

me heaven's humility that I might look beneath the familiar and obvious and see *yourself!* (4) Deliver me from any desire to see the bizarre or sensational in order to confirm my faith which should be based on your word.

Right here add your personal requests—and his answers.

10. READ HIS WORD AND WAIT—LISTEN—GOD SPEAKS!

The messages you have for me could be a shock! (1) "Men still mock and misunderstand—what I said to Nazareth I say to them." (2) "There are many Gentiles in other lands

who will hear me gladly." (3) "Men's failure to see is their fault, not mine."

11. INTERCESSION FOR THE LOST WORLD

Nepal — Point for prayer: (1) *Unreached peoples*— very few of the peoples of this land have any believers among them. The large investment of Wycliffe Bible Translators with 100 workers in 21 languages was suddenly

terminated, and it is hard to see how this Bible translation program can be continued. Pray for these many peoples without a witness or the Scriptures.

12. SING PRAISES TO OUR LORD.

Beautiful Savior!
Lord of all the nations!
Son of God and Son of Man!

Glory and honor,
Praise, adoration,
Now and forevermore be Thine!

503

WEEK THIRTY-SIX — SATURDAY

1. PRAISE GOD FOR WHO HE IS.

"For thou art great and doest wondrous things, thou alone art God. Teach me thy way, O Lord, that I may walk in thy truth; unite my heart to fear thy name" (Psa. 86:10, 11). There is such comfort and security in praise and adoration. These words can easily lift me—and all men up into your presence. (1) You are great, i.e., in the sense of power or majesty. Far above all that we see about us is your presence above us. (2) Your greatness is expressed in action. The physical world in which we live is a constant testimony to your greatness. The record of your greatness is in your book. At the same time, if any one of our lives could be written from the inside, i.e., from your perspective I am persuaded we would exclaim with the psalmist "you do wondrous things, you alone are God." (3) You can and do teach man. It is good to know you have that much personal interest. Bless your holy powerful name!

Express yourself in adoration for this quality of God.
Speak it audibly or write out your praise in your own devotional journal.

2. PRAISE GOD FOR WHAT HE MEANS TO ME.

Just for me. How will you teach me your way? I can think of several methods—I want all of them to be operative in me: (1) You can chasten me and get my attention through my dependence upon you. Essentially chastening makes me more willing to understand your word. (2) You humble me through your goodness, and I am led to a re-evaluation of life. Once again it is a conditioning of my senses to respond to what you are saying to me in your word. (3) You do teach me through your servants—I have come to walk more closely to thy truth because men have enlightened my mind in the teaching of your word. In all of this I praise you for leading me. (4) In answers to prayer you have "united my heart to fear your name." In definite answer to prayer I have seen the fulfillment of your plan for my life.

How do you personally relate to the greatness of God, and God who alone is great?
Speak it out or write it out. It is *so important* that you establish *your own* devotional journal.

3. CONFESSION OF SIN

It is equally easy to see my shortcomings in the light of this beautiful text: (1) Your greatness needs to be far more impressive and prominent with me. (2) I need to pause again and again to acknowledge the true source of all the wondrous things I see and hear. In the physical world and the world of my own experience. (3) I am so unwilling to be taught, i.e., by anyone but myself—forgive me! (4) Dear Lord, how I do need to activate your truth in my life. There are a number of areas where I *must do and not say!* (5) Oh, Father, I want my heart to be united with your heart—as seen in the life of your Son! Forgive me, help me!

What personal sins do you want to confess? We *must* speak them to remove them.
Do it! *Now.* There is no one else you have sinned against more than God. Tell him so!

4. SING A PRAYER TO GOD.

Jesus, Savior, pilot me
Over life's tempestuous sea;
Unknown waves before me roll,
Hiding rock and treacherous shoal;
Chart and compass came from Thee:
Jesus, Savior, pilot me.

Open your hymn book and sing the rest of the verses—or even sing another prayer song.

5. READ HIS WORD TO HIM!

His Word

[28] All the people in the synagogue were furious when they heard this. [29] They got up, drove him out of town, and took him to the brow of the hill on which the town was built, in order to throw him down the cliff. [30] But he walked right through the crowd and went on his way.
— Lk. 4:28-30, NIV

Read His Word to Him.

How, oh, how could it be that those who knew him hated him? Or was it hatred for yourself? As I see it (and I want to bring this concept to you in prayer), the worshipers that sabbath day in Nazareth were saying: They could not see the scriptures of the Messiah fulfilled in a local-town boy! This was blasphemy. When was our Lord conscious that he was the Messiah? It is not a question that needs an answer. A much larger question is: "When will he declare his Messiahship?" He chose the synagogue in his home town! Of course there was the declaration of God to John the Baptist and earlier indications of his deity, but here in words that could not be ignored he declared himself! Our Lord wants action, response, decision. Dear Lord, I believe.

Please express your response to this beautiful text. Put your expression in your own prayer diary.

WEEK THIRTY-SIX — SATURDAY

6. READ HIS WORD FOR YOURSELF.

Oh, how I want to listen to him again, and again! What a wonderful teacher and preacher was my Lord. Those who heard him could not and did not escape the direct personal application of what he said. "They were furious when they heard this." But there was something else in the hearts of these same people. On the way to the brow of the hill did some of them have second thoughts? When they were ready to push him over and he turned around and faced them—there *was* something strange, different, about this carpenter's son. Jesus shook free of those who were pushing and shoving him and began to walk toward them—they parted, they paused, he walked right through the crowd! No one laid a hand on him. My dear Lord, walk right into my heart and rule there! I love you, I worship you!

It is so important that you pause in his presence
and either audibly or in written form tell him all his word means to you.

7. READ HIS WORD IN THANKSGIVING.

(1) Thank you for the fact that all men can see the meaning of your word. (2) Thank you that we cannot be neutral with your Son. (3) Thank you that Jesus let men think for themselves. (4) Thank you for his non-resistance to violence. (5) Thank you for the beautiful, powerful poise of my Lord. (6) Thank you for his patience with those of Nazareth. (7) Thank you for his priority of interest in these stubborn people—he gave them the first chance.

Give yourself to your own expression of gratitude—write it or speak it!

8. READ HIS WORD IN MEDITATION.

". . . he walked right through the crowd and went on his way." What supernatural powers did he use to accomplish this amazing feat? One moment the furious mob is about to overpower him and push him over the cliff, the next he has overpowered the mob and they fall back and let him escape. It reminds us of the soldiers who came out to arrest him. Not once but twice they fell back and were unable to capture him. The gospel writers really do not tell us why. There is a definite hint of something much more than they are able to explain. To stay in the presence of Jesus for long one would know there was an awesomeness and heavenly strangeness about him that really defied description. How I do love to try to imagine all he was and is! Bless his holy name!

Pause—wait—think—then express yourself in thoughtful praise or thanks.

9. READ HIS WORD FOR PETITIONS.

What a wealth of meaning in these three verses: (1) How I need the same calmness in facing the fury of men. (2) I wonder what my Lord heard from these men as they drove him through the streets?—none of it true or deserved—what an example for me! (3) Jesus let them lead him so far and no more—give me wisdom to know how far. (4) How did Jesus separate the crowd for his escape? I need his wisdom here. (5) How sad that "his way" was not that of those who knew him—how is it with me? (6) Where were our Lord's brothers in this mob scene? Where are his brothers today? (7) What a sword for his mother's heart.

Please, please remember these are prayers—speak them—reword them!

10. READ HIS WORD AND WAIT—LISTEN—GOD SPEAKS!

Without a word Jesus spoke to these men: (1) "Anger or not what I said is true." (2) "You can drive me out of town, but not out of your life." (3) "The wrath of men never has worked the righteousness of God."

11. INTERCESSION FOR THE LOST WORLD

Nepal — Points for prayer: (1) *Pray for the radio broadcasts* in Nepali. Pray that this may lead to conversions and the building up of the Church. (2) *Literature* has been much used of God—through books sold in the several little bookstores. Bible correspondence courses to Nepalis inside Nepal and in surrounding lands. Pray also for wide distribution of the Scriptures.

12. SING PRAISES TO OUR LORD.

I am so wondrously saved from sin,
Jesus so sweetly abides within,
There at the cross where He took me in;
Glory to His name.

Glory to His name, . . .
Glory to His name; . . .
There to my heart was the blood applied;
Glory to His name.

WEEK THIRTY-SEVEN — SUNDAY

1. PRAISE GOD FOR WHO HE IS.

"Lord, thou hast been our dwelling place in all generations. Before the mountains were brought forth, or ever thou hast formed the earth and the world, from everlasting to everlasting thou art God" (Psalm 90:1, 2). How wonderfully good it is to come again and find our refuge or dwelling place in you! I want to just now attempt to relate these beautiful concepts to every part of life. You want man to live in you. Not only have you made us in your likeness, but you want to be the center and circumference of our living.

Express yourself in adoration for this quality of God.
Speak it audibly or write out your praise in your own devotional journal.

2. PRAISE GOD FOR WHAT HE MEANS TO ME.

Just for me. These verses are saying to me that from the beginning of creation it has been your desire for us to live in you and for you to live in us. Your creative genius and everlasting power are the source of this truth. Dear Lord, I do accept this relationship. I am learning every day how better to apply it. Just for today I want to look around this house in which I find myself, i.e., the four-walled domicile in which I live — and remember that all of my inward being, all of my thought processes, all of my energy for moving, all of my purpose for existence are in and of you.

How do you personally relate to the eternalness of God, and God who is Eternal?
Speak it out or write it out. It is *so important* that you establish *your own* devotional journal.

3. CONFESSION OF SIN

Dear Lord, it has been most difficult to express in even a small way the greatness and goodness of yourself. I feel I have so tragically neglected you. Like those who move into a house and do nothing to indicate their responsibility to the place where they live. A "dwelling place" offers protection and I have lived outside until I was forced in. Forgive me! A "dwelling place" is prepared especially for man's enjoyment. You are the original proto-type for all men — and I choose to live in a shack of my own invention — how stupid! Forgive me. A "dwelling place" will be there long after I have come and gone — how absurd that I should not come in and make yourself my home!

What personal sins do you want to confess? We *must* speak them to remove them.
Speak it out or write it out. It is *so important* that you establish *your own* devotional journal.

4. SING A PRAYER TO GOD.

When sore trials came upon you,
Did you think to pray?
When your soul was bowed in sorrow,
Balm of Gilead did you borrow,
At the gates of day?

Oh, how praying rests the weary!
Prayer will change the night to day;
So in sorrow and in gladness,
Don't forget to pray.

Open your hymn book and sing the rest of the verses — or even sing another prayer song.

5. READ HIS WORD TO HIM!

His Word

[18] As Jesus was walking beside the Sea of Galilee, he saw two brothers, Simon called Peter and his brother Andrew. They were casting a net into the lake, for they were fishermen. [19]"Come, follow me," Jesus said, "and I will make you fishers of men." [20]At once they left their nets and followed him.
— Matt. 4:18-20, NIV

[16] As Jesus walked beside the Sea of Galilee, he saw Simon and his brother Andrew casting a net into the lake, for they were fishermen. [17]"Come, follow me," Jesus said, "and I will make you fishers of men." [18]At once they left their nets and followed him.
— Mk. 1:16-18, NIV

Read His Word to Him.

I am trying to absorb the meaning of every one of these burning words, but I feel so very inadequate! I realize our Lord had been known by these brothers for at least 8 months — they had heard him and doubtless saw some of his miracles in Capernaum. It could have been that the miraculous draught of fish occurred before this call. But all of that being so, it is one amazing record. What did Jesus see in Peter and John? They were mature men with families, or at least with wives. They were unlearned by the standards of men. They were very much occupied in a business they had pursued all their lives. But there was something in the invitation: to be with him, to follow him, to worship him. I have very poorly described the content of these verses from your viewpoint. Forgive me!

Please express your response to this beautiful text. Put your expression in your own prayer diary.

6. READ HIS WORD FOR YOURSELF.

Just for me! It is like hearing all over again the call of the Lord to leave all and follow him. I am so glad for three facts in this encounter — (for it is indeed just that): (1) That you, Lord, *see me*. I know from sad, sorry experiences just how fallible I am. But then you knew (and know) before you called me just who it was to whom you spoke. (2) That you called me to *follow you*. I really and truly do not know where I am going — I *must* have a guide. Since you have left me an imperishable full account of just where and when and how you want me to follow you I am ready to answer the call. (3) Most of all I am glad you have said, "I will *make you* fishers of men." I could never, never do it on my own. You can and you will! With fresh expectancy I arise to follow you this day.

It is so important that you pause in his presence
and either audibly or in written form tell him all his word means to you.

7. READ HIS WORD IN THANKSGIVING.

(1) Thank you that my dear Lord yet walks by the sea of my life. (2) Thank you that Jesus sees me even now with compassion and concern. (3) Thank you that Jesus calls each of us to salvation and service. (4) Thank you that in following him we will learn all we need to know. (5) Thank you that in his own wonderful way he is making me a fisher of men. (6) Thank you for those who have been willing all down through the centuries to leave all and follow you. (7) Thank you that nets have lost their appeal in the presence of the call of my Lord.

Give yourself to your own expression of gratitude — write it or speak it!

8. READ HIS WORD IN MEDITATION.

"At once they left their nets and followed him." Commentators are divided over just how much association these men had with our Lord before they reached this decision. The facts of the matter are that they did at this time immediately act upon the call of our Lord. We would like to attempt a reconstruction of their decision: (1) They followed him because they were disciples of John and believed what John had said about him. (2) They followed him because they were either in Jerusalem or Capernaum and saw the signs he did — they were convinced that no mere man could do these things. (3) They followed him because they had just participated in the miraculous draught of fish (i.e., if we reverse the time sequence). (4) Most of all they followed him just to be with this One who had such a "presence" and "poise" about him. They wanted to see if they could not imbibe a part of his personality. Dear Lord, we have all these reasons and more to leave all and follow you.

Pause — wait — think — then express yourself in thoughtful praise or thanks.

9. READ HIS WORD FOR PETITIONS.

In the calling of Peter and Andrew there is also a call to prayer: (1) Walk beside my place of work today — may I be looking and listening. (2) Jesus called both men, but each man — speak to my heart! (3) Jesus didn't call some of them, but all of each one — I want to so respond. (4) I am so glad I am first, last and always a "follower" of yourself — keep me aware. (5) Make me, break me, educate me, use me, as your fisherman. (6) Fishing is a smelly, dirty business — does this relate? (7) How I need that impulsive total response I see in Peter and Andrew!

Right here add your personal requests — and his answers.

10. READ HIS WORD AND WAIT — LISTEN — GOD SPEAKS!

Somehow I know you are speaking and calling again: (1) "Leave your nets and follow me." (2) "Leave yourself and follow me." (3) "Leave others and follow me."

11. INTERCESSION FOR THE LOST WORLD

Nepal — Point for prayer: (1) *Nepalis outside Nepal* number about 8,000,000. A number of Indian and Western Christians have prayed and worked for a harvest among these people, and now there are many Nepali Christian Fellowships all over N. India, and some in Sikkim and Bhutan. There is a Bible School in Darjeeling in India where Nepali believers are trained for pastoral work. Pray for this ministry and for the men who go out from it to evangelize the Nepali people.

12. SING PRAISES TO OUR LORD.

He stood at my heart's door 'mid sunshine and rain,
And patiently waited an entrance to gain;
What shame that so long He entreated in vain,
For He is so precious to me.

For He is so precious to me, . . .
For He is so precious to me; . . .
'Tis Heaven below My Redeemer to know,
For He is so precious to me.

WEEK THIRTY-SEVEN — MONDAY

1. PRAISE GOD FOR WHO HE IS.

"For a thousand years in thy sight are but as yesterday when it is past, or a watch in the night" (Psalm 90:4). Oh, bless your name throughout eternity! What a joy to lift before you my adoration for several attributes of yourself in this verse: (1) The passing of men and events is all known to you, but do not impress you as it does man. (2) We can remember a few things about yesterday; you can remember all. (3) We cannot relive the events of yesterday, but you have total instant recall. (4) Most especially is our feebleness and your greatness compared and contrasted by what we can remember about "a watch in the night." That we had a watch that we kept is all we remember, but you are on watch with eternal vigilance and total knowledge! O dear Lord, how great thou art!

Express yourself in adoration for this quality of God.
Speak it audibly or write out your praise in your own devotional journal.

2. PRAISE GOD FOR WHAT HE MEANS TO ME.

I have praised you for yourself, and as much apart from myself as possible. Now I want to absorb these words and your attributes into my inmost being! What is so important to you is sometimes not appreciated by me, but there is nothing important to me that is not appreciated by you. All that I say and am and do are important to you. Every event of every day for a thousand years can be replayed by you. However, this is not to be considered so important; it is only one of your many capacities. Yesterday happened —the watch is over and gone, so are the events of a thousand years, and another thousand years. Time is no factor with you! Dear Lord, I am overwhelmed with the immensity of such a thought! Such understanding (as limited as it is) gives me great calmness and assurance. Bless your holy name!

How do you personally relate to the timelessness of God, and God who is timeless?
Speak it out or write it out. It is *so important* that you establish *your own* devotional journal.

3. CONFESSION OF SIN

The words of the one who lived in the light of eternity strike me with a jarring blow! *"Be not anxious about your life. . . ."* In the perspective of eternity the source of our anxiety will be put in balance; it will appear absurd. As absurd as a bird meditating all night over whether it could find adequate food for the morrow. What I need is more concentration on your power and goodness — of your interest in every little event — but also a long look at life as you see it.

What personal sins do you want to confess? We *must* speak them to remove them.
Do it! *Now.* There is no one else you have sinned against more than God. Tell him so!

4. SING A PRAYER TO GOD.

All the way my Savior leads me;
Cheers each winding path I tread,
Gives me grace for ev'ry trial,
Feeds me with the living bread.
Though my weary steps may falter,
And my soul athirst may be,
Gushing from the Rock before me,
Lo! a spring of joy I see;
Gushing from the Rock before me,
Lo! a spring of joy I see.

Open your hymn book and sing the rest of the verses — or even sing another prayer song.

5. READ HIS WORD TO HIM!

His Word

[21]Going on from there, he saw two other brothers, James son of Zebedee and his brother John. They were in a boat with their father Zebedee, preparing their nets. Jesus called them, [22]and immediately they left the boat and their father and followed him.   — Matt. 4:21, 22, NIV

[19]When he had gone a little farther, he saw James son of Zebedee and his brother John in a boat, preparing their nets. [20]Without delay he called them, and they left their father Zebedee in the boat with the hired men and followed him.   — Mk. 1:19, 20, NIV

Read His Word to Him.

Perhaps I am to read Luke 5:1-11 in connection with this incident. Perhaps I am not. At whatever juncture I want to read these precious verses just for themselves. How I want to know James and John, and their father Zebedee. They are all fishermen, but each of them is a different type of fisherman — Zebedee will tell anyone who wants to listen just how different James is from John or visa versa. But I need not mention this to you. You know the smallest detail in the lives of each of these men. Such knowledge was shared to some extent by my Lord when he so casually (?) walked by their boat and called them. Perhaps they had been ready for days and only awaited his word. Dear Lord, I want to be so prepared.

Please express your response to this beautiful text. Put your expression in your own prayer diary.

6. READ HIS WORD FOR YOURSELF.

In a very real sense my Lord only calls me as he called James and John: (1) Jesus called them from where they were. There was no convenient time or place. In the midst of a busy day of work he said: "Leave all and follow me." It must be this way; there is no other way. (2) He called them in the presence of others. Their lives touched the lives of their father, the servants who worked for them and all others who were soon to hear about their decision. There is no avoiding or ignoring the fact that our example speaks to many others. (3) Jesus called them to do just *one thing*: to follow him. This meant listening to his words, watching his life, eating with him, living all day with him. It wasn't what James and John had to give to Jesus; it was what they would receive from following him.

It is so important that you pause in his presence
and either audibly or in written form tell him what his word means to you.

7. READ HIS WORD IN THANKSGIVING.

(1) Thank you for the definite choices of my Lord—he knows who he wants for what. (2) Thank you that Jesus doesn't wait for a convenient time to call us. (3) Thank you that my Lord put worship into the fishing boat. (4) Thank you that work clothes and the smell of the fish didn't hinder our Lord. (5) Thank you for James and John who were ready to keep their priorities straight. (6) Thank you for Zebedee who offered no objection. (7) Thank you for the excitement of expectation that must have filled their heads as they made the break and followed him.

Give yourself to your own expression of gratitude—write it or speak it!

8. READ HIS WORD IN MEDITATION.

"Without delay he called them." There seems to be an urgency about all the gospel record. The disciples immediately leave all and follow him. Our Lord is intent on fulfilling the task his father gave him. We know that nothing our Savior did was out of haste nor was it ill-planned. The record tells us he spent all night in prayer before he selected his apostles. We are to learn that he got up a great while before day and went to a solitary place where he prayed. Did a season of prayer precede the calling of these four men? We are sure that it did. The account here is just the conclusion of that preparation. Because he had prayed and because his father had answered his prayer, "without delay he called them." Dear Lord, may such an example burn its way into my subconsciousness.

Pause—wait—think—then express yourself in thoughtful praise or thanks.

9. READ HIS WORD FOR PETITIONS.

Our Lord was interested in family units—he called two sets of brothers to be his first disciples—what interpersonal needs for prayer: (1) Keep me aware I could be interrupted by you in the midst of any work to hear your call to follow you. (2) These men were prepared for your call —prepare me. (3) Just when should I leave close family ties to follow you? (4) How can I relate personal responsibility to yourself? (5) How did Zebedee and the servants relate to your work? (6) Did James and John ever have second thoughts about their decision? (7) Did Jesus thank these men for making their decision?

Please, please remember these are prayers—speak them—reword them!

10. READ HIS WORD AND WAIT LISTEN—GOD SPEAKS.

Ever and always there will be the calling of our Lord: (1) "Follow me only after you trust me." (2) "Follow me because you love me." (3) "Follow me because you do not know your way."

11. INTERCESSION FOR THE LOST WORLD

Pakistan — Population: 72,500,000. Growth rate— 2.9%. People per sq. km.—90.

Points for prayer: (1) *This needy Muslim land is no longer wide open for evangelism* and the entry of missionaries. Pray for God's direction despite pressures from the Islamic World Conference in 1976 recommending the ending of all Christian missions. Pray that Asian and Western churches may use these opportunities to send in more workers.

12. SING PRAISES TO OUR LORD.

Glory, glory to the Father!
Glory, glory to the Son!
Glory, glory to the Spirit!
Glory to the Three in One!

I will praise Him! I will praise Him!
Praise the Lamb for sinners slain;
Give Him glory, all ye people,
For His blood can wash away each stain.

WEEK THIRTY-SEVEN — TUESDAY

1. PRAISE GOD FOR WHO HE IS.

"It is good to give thanks to the Lord, to sing praises to thy name, O Most High; to declare thy steadfast love in the morning, and thy faithfulness by night, to the music of the lute and the harp, to the melody of the lyre. For thou, O Lord, hast made me glad by thy works; at the works of thy hands. I sing for joy" (Psalm 92:1-4). There are several beautiful attributes of yourself in these divine words. (1) It is a genuine benefit to man to acknowledge your goodness and express it in gratitude. It is natural and right to honor the One from whom all goodness comes. (2) There could never be enough songs of praise and adoration — throughout all eternity all men and angels will praise you and never exhaust the superlatives! As I begin the day it is more than good to lift up my heart and voice in songs of prayer and praise!

Express yourself in adoration for this quality of God.
Speak it audibly or write out your praise in your own devotional journal.

2. PRAISE GOD FOR WHAT HE MEANS TO ME.

Just for me. Whereas the above is written or expressed in the first person it but represents what I believe should come from the hearts of all men. It is at night when we most need to lift our praises to you. Perhaps the work schedule of men has been different in other times and places. I'm sure it has, but for us the night is the time of relaxation and too often this means a lack of the discipline necessary to spend time before you in worship. In this we ask your forgiveness. It is a lack of the integration of yourself into all of life, all the time. I want to do much better in declaring your steadfast love and thy faithfulness at night.

How much help I can get for this expression of worship from the lute and the harp and the lyre. Dear Lord, I lift my heart with the words accompanied with the music. I praise you and love you.

All the above expression of joy and praise arises because of your work for me, through me, and much of it in spite of me! Oh, bless your name!

How do you personally relate to the goodness of God, and God who is praiseworthy?
Speak it out or write it out. It is *so important* that you establish *your own* devotional journal.

3. CONFESSION OF SIN

It is good to give thanks to yourself; indeed, it makes sense to do so. There are times when I do not, will not, and forget. Why? Why? Forgive me. It is my unfathomable selfishness! To sing praises to your name is indeed the most natural expression of a soul set free. But there are times when my heart is cold and my lips are mute! When I am tired I can understand — when I am not I do not.

I am a sinner — forgive me. There have been many mornings when my voice was not raised, when no words appeared on paper to declare your steadfast love — dear, dear Lord, I was the loser. Your love will remain steadfast for a million mornings after I am gone (if Jesus should tarry). Forgive me! I do not plan to miss one more morning!

What personal sins do you want to confess? We *must* speak them to remove them.
Do it! *Now.* There is no one else you have sinned against more than God. Tell him so!

4. SING A PRAYER TO GOD.

All to Jesus I surrender,
Humbly at His feet I bow,
Worldly pleasures all forsaken,
Take me, Jesus, take me now.

I surrender all,
I surrender all.
All to Thee, my blessed Savior,
I surrender all.

Open your hymn book and sing the rest of the verses — or even sing another prayer song.

5. READ HIS WORD TO HIM!

His Word

5 One day as Jesus was standing by the Lake of Gennesaret, with the people crowding around him and listening to the word of God, ²he saw at the water's edge two boats, left there by the fishermen, who were washing their nets. ³He got into one of the boats, the one belonging to Simon, and asked him to put out a little from shore. Then he sat down and taught the people from the boat. ⁴When he had finished speaking, he said to Simon, "Put out into deep water, and let down the nets for a catch."

⁵Simon answered, "Master, we've worked hard all night and haven't caught anything. But because you say so, I will let down the nets."

⁶When they had done so, they caught such a large number of fish that their nets began to break.

— Luke 5:1-6, NIV

Read His Word to Him.

I am always at a loss to know just how to read this word in such a manner as to honor you and express my wonder and appreciation for all it means. What a glad day it was in the experience of Peter and John — James and

510

Andrew when our Lord appeared on the shore of the lake and began to teach. These few men had been up all night working hard at the job of fishing. How well could Simon and Andrew concentrate on the teaching of Jesus? I have been up all night and I have also tried to listen to someone teach—I could with effort keep my eyes open, but not my mind—it drifted off to sleep. But then I was not listening to your Son.

Please express your response to this beautiful text. Put your expression in your own prayer diary.

6. READ HIS WORD FOR YOURSELF.

I try to put myself in the crowd by the lake on the day of teaching by my Lord. I know I have some of his teaching in the records of his four biographers. I can read and reread all he said, but even so I so easily forget. How long did the crowd remember? There is a young man listening to Jesus—beside him is an old man—how many of his words remained in their mind? I know they must have been impressed, and to summarize, they could say "never a man so spake," but just specifically what did he say? Dear Lord, how glad I am that I have the imperishable specific record I can memorize and integrate into my life.

Pause in his presence and either audibly or in written form tell him all his word means to you.

7. READ HIS WORD IN THANKSGIVING.

(1) Thank you for the lovely specific report of Luke. (2) Thank you that every day of the year Jesus can walk again by the Lake of Gennesaret and teach me! (3) Thank you for Luke's definition of Jesus' words: "the word of God." (4) Thank you for the perfectly naturalness of my Lord's manner among men—he used what was near at hand—did not ignore the need to speak to all—asked for help. (5) Thank you for the example of teaching given by Jesus—my Lord was a teacher! (6) Thank you that Jesus was full of surprises to open the eyes of the heart.

Give yourself to your own expression of gratitude—write it or speak it!

8. READ HIS WORD IN MEDITATION.

"When they had done so, they caught such a large number of fish that their nets began to break." It is more than curious that Peter and John were to have this experience twice: here at the beginning of their experience with our Lord, and then after he was raised from the dead, at the very close of their relationship. There was something wonderfully impressive about this miracle. It was first of all related to the work of these men. If anyone knew the habits of fish, they did. At the same time, the control of the laws of nature presupposed far more than the miracle itself. Jesus was in charge of the movement and number of fish.

Pause—wait—think—then express yourself in thoughtful praise or thanks.

9. READ HIS WORD FOR PETITIONS.

My dear Lord, I am captive to your charm! How beyond poignancy is the scene on the shore of the Lake of Galilee! (1) How I want to hear him speak to my heart now as he spoke to Peter in that far off day. (2) Jesus never asked Simon Peter if he could use his boat—why should I think he needs to ask me if he wants to use anything related to me to teach others—dear Lord, this could be dangerous. (3) Thank you for your impossible demands on my faith. (4) How I want the kind of unqualified obedience found in Peter.

Right here add your personal requests—and his answers.

10. READ HIS WORD AND WAIT—LISTEN—GOD SPEAKS!

He has much to teach me here—I *want* to listen: (1) "My words are still 'the word of God.'" (2) "Put out into the deep water of your own unprofitableness and let down my net." (3) "I helped Simon catch the fish and also to pull them in—I am interested in *all* that relates to your work for me."

11. INTERCESSION FOR THE LOST WORLD

Pakistan — Point for prayer: (1) *Response among Muslims* is slow, but growing markedly. Few are prepared to take the costly step of open discipleship and associate with the Christians, who are usually socially poorer and basically of low-caste Hindu origin. Possibly only one tenth of the missionary force give much time to this 97% of the population. Pray for more missionaries well equipped for Muslim work, and for the winning of Muslims.

12. SING PRAISES TO OUR LORD.

I was lost, but Jesus found me,
Found the sheep that went astray,
Threw His loving arms around me,
Drew me back into His way.

Yes, I'll sing . . . the wondrous story
Of the Christ . . . who died for me, . . .
Sing it with . . . the saints in glory,
Gathered by . . . the crystal sea.

WEEK THIRTY-SEVEN — WEDNESDAY

1. PRASE GOD FOR WHO HE IS.

"O come, let us worship and bow down, let us kneel before the Lord, our Maker! For he is our God, and we are the people of his pasture, and the sheep of his hand" (Psalm 95:6, 7). Bless and praise the Lord O my soul; let all that is in me praise his holy name! How very good it is to come before you and worship. What comfort and strength is mine—in my inmost being! The attributes I see in these beautiful words are the following: (1) You are one before whom we instinctively kneel or bow down.

If we have not prostituted our nature it will be natural for us to kneel, even prostrate ourselves before you. This presupposes a knowledge of your person. (2) Your holiness and purity rebuke our sinfulness and we seek forgiveness in our worship before you. (3) You have *made* us! What a statement! As a man would fashion any product of his mind and hand so you have made us. We gladly acknowledge your ownership!

Express yourself in adoration for this quality of God.
Speak it audibly or write out your praise in your own devotional journal.

2. PRAISE GOD FOR WHAT HE MEANS TO ME.

Just for me. Indeed, indeed, you are my God! In the broad pasture of this world I am your person! I belong to you. There are only two shepherds. Since you know me better than I know myself I gladly recognize your ownership. As extensive as is your pasture yet you know me by name and need. I am directed personally by your hand. Bless and praise to you for the personal interest you take in this one dumb sheep. I know from sad experience that

if you let me be exposed to the full power of Satan I would have long ago been in torment (here and hereafter). You have indeed directed the affairs of my life so I could have your goodness and mercy to follow me all of my days. I do not know what there is in store for me today, but I know Someone who loves me and knows me and will arrange the circumstances of life in the lovely subtle manner he has.

How do you personally relate to the creative power of God, and God who is our Maker?
Speak it out or write it out. It is *so important* that you establish *your own* devotional journal.

3. CONFESSION OF SIN

There surely is no problem in confessing my sin in the light of these two beautiful verses: (1) I have felt so very independent at times (and not long ago) that I would not bow down to anyone! Dear, dear God, when will I yield my inner being? (2) I am so busy making my own way, my own plans, my own projects that I forget that all my powers are a gift to be used for as long as the owner deems

best. Dear Lord, forgive. (3) If you are God, then you are God and I should let you be God in my life—not some of it, but all of it! What ungodly presumption I have often expressed! Dear Lord, forgive me. (4) My self image should be one of a sheep under the constant care and direction of an all-wise shepherd. Dear Lord, I have been anything but meek. Forgive me.

What personal sins do you want to confess? We *must* speak them to remove them.
Do it! *Now.* There is no one else you have sinned against more than God. Tell him so!

4. SING A PRAYER TO GOD.

My Jesus, I love Thee,
I know Thou art mine,
For Thee all the follies of sin I resign;

My gracious Redeemer, my Savior art Thou;
If ever I loved Thee, my Jesus, 'tis now.

Open your hymn book and sing the rest of the verses—or even sing another prayer song.

5. READ HIS WORD TO HIM!

His Word

⁷So they signaled their partners in the other boat to come and help them, and they came and filled both boats so full that they began to sink.

⁸When Simon Peter saw this, he fell at Jesus' knees and said, "Go away from me, Lord; I am a sinful man!" ⁹For he and all his companions were astonished at the catch

of fish they had taken, ¹⁰and so were James and John, the sons of Zebedee, Simon's partners.

Then Jesus said to Simon, "Don't be afraid; from now on you will catch men." ¹¹So they pulled their boats up on shore, left everything and followed him.

— Luke 5:7-11, NIV

Read His Word to Him.

What shall I say dear Lord that has not been said ten thousand times before? But, on second thought, I have not

said any one of such expressions. It is *my* praise, *my* confession, *my* thanksgiving you wait to hear. It would seem these fishermen were so busy fishing that they had no time to think of you. But such was not the case. As their hands were busy with the net and fish their minds and hearts were busy with wonder and praise. What Peter knew of your holiness and his sinfulness created a deep sense of unworthiness—even abject fear in the presence of such a one who could control creation. I am free to say I feel the same way! The words of your dear Son speak peace to the troubled waters of my heart!

Please express your response to this beautiful text. Put your expression in your own prayer diary.

6. READ HIS WORD FOR YOURSELF.

What a poignant lesson is in this text for me! It opens my mind as to just how someone can be employed eight hours per day and yet meditate upon your word and yourself. There are millions of jobs that do not require more than physical concentration and even as the fishermen were thinking about our Lord and his power so men today while doing a good job are yet worshiping you. The mind of man is such an amazing intrument it can perform at a capacity of which we have not even dreamed! I am glad to honor and praise you for this fact. May I so allow you to use me! Most of all I want to fall at your feet—even as Peter.

Pause in his presence and either audibly or in written form tell him all his word means to you.

7. READ HIS WORD IN THANKSGIVING.

(1) Thank you for the overpowering nature of this miracle. No one could doubt it. (2) Thank you for the wisdom in it—only the men you wanted to follow you were in it. (3) Thank you that anyone could see the families of Peter and Andrew would have provisions for sometime to come from the miracle as the breadwinners left all to follow him. (4) Thank you that no doubt someone thought that if he could provide once, he could provide always. (5) Thank you for astonishment—a form of worship—it is such a blessed quality. (6) Thank you for my Lord's desire to be with me. (7) Thank you for my desire to follow him.

Give yourself to your own expression of gratitude—write it or speak it!

8. READ HIS WORD IN MEDITATION.

"So they pulled their boats up on the shore, left everything and followed him." Over how many years have these blessed words of Luke spoken to our hearts. We like to remind ourselves that Luke was written before Acts. The reason should be obvious: The conversions in the Acts account would not mean much to Theophilus unless he knew the one to whom the persons were converted. In a most practical personal sense I want to say that some of us have been converted (?) and have really never absorbed the message of the gospels. When will we "pull our boats" up on the shore of time and leave all and follow him?

Pause—wait—think—then express yourself in thoughtful praise or thanks.

9. READ HIS WORD FOR PETITIONS.

What an exciting text as a basis for prayer: (1) I really cannot do near as much by myself as I could while working with others—lead me to just the ones with whom I should work. (2) Impress me anew with your control of all the world in which we live. (3) I want to remain aware of the super abundance you use in all you create. (4) To be so close to God incarnate should impress us with our unworthiness, even as Peter. (5) It would seem all four fishermen worked together and worshiped together— what a good example.

Please, please remember these are prayers—speak them—reword them!

10. READ HIS WORD AND WAIT—LISTEN—GOD SPEAKS!

In so many ways you can speak to me: (1) "You are partners with me in the man-fishing business." (2) "You *are* a sinful man—but forgiven." (3) "Depart with me—not from me."

11. INTERCESSION FOR THE WHOLE WORLD

Pakistan — Point for prayer: (1) *The greatest response in the land now is among the scheduled caste Hindu tribes of the Sindh where there has been a considerable turning to the Lord of late. There are about 30 tribes, each with its own dialect, and most are semi-nomadic. Pray especially for the Mawaris, Kohlis, etc. More national and missionary workers are urgently needed. Pray for the development of a strong, well-led Church.

12. SING PRAISES TO OUR LORD.

I love Thy Kingdom, Lord,
The house of Thine abode,

The Church our blest Redeemer saved
With His own precious blood.

WEEK THIRTY-SEVEN — THURSDAY

1. PRAISE GOD FOR WHO HE IS.

"O sing to the Lord a new song; sing to the Lord, all the earth! Sing to the Lord, bless his name; tell of his salvation from day to day. Declare his glory among the nations, his marvelous works among all the peoples!" (Psalm 96:1-3). Dear Lord, I am so glad to express my joy and delight before you! I need each day "a new song." All men need a new song each day. I want to go on record as saying you can and do give me a new song each day.

How many thousands of days have come and gone in my life and not one in which there could not have been a new song of praise and joy before you. Every inhabitant of this little cosmic speck could say the same thing, i.e., if they loved you. Gladly, gladly do I lift my heart with the psalmist. I am embarrassed with the multitude of reasons for which to praise you! Most of all it is for your salvation! Bless your name forever!

Express yourself in adoration for this quality of God.
Speak it audibly or write out your praise in your own devotional journal.

2. PRAISE GOD FOR WHAT HE MEANS TO ME.

For me: Most of the above has been subjective, but I hope I only represent a multitude who will sing before your eternal throne. I want to enlarge on the concept of a *new song.* How deeply grateful I am to begin a new day with you! (1) I have a *new page for today*—new, clean, clear. I claim the cleansing of every sin on every page of the past. All the pages preceding this one contain only the gold and silver of what you have done. I have

such a lovely new start! Bless your name! (2) A new opportunity full of fresh and interesting people and events and thoughts. Dear Lord, may I so approach it. You are all and in all so why should I see anything or anyone in any other light? When I am able to enter into such an attitude it seems but one step into your eternal presence! How joyous and good is all of life!

How do you personally relate to the song of God, and God who causes us to sing?
Speak it out or write it out. It is *so important* that you establish *your own* devotional journal.

3. CONFESSION OF SIN

It would be easy to be remorseful and depressed most of the time, i.e., if one believed the lie of Satan—"damn you, Satan!" But I do not believe him. I know the truth and he (who is the truth) has set me free from all sense of condemnation. This does not mean that I am ignoring my sins—my tragic failures. I am ashamed of them and

I do not hide even one of them. I lay them all out before you—having done so I claim their total disappearance! Dear Lord, you know if I did not have such an assurance I would not make it. I could not live! But I do claim your cleansing. I am washed in the blood—"There is power, wonder working power in the blood of your Lamb!"

What personal sins do you want to confess? We *must* speak them to remove them.
Do it! *Now.* There is no one else you have sinned against more than God. Tell him so!

4. SING A PRAYER TO GOD.

Christ, the blessed One, gives to all,
Wonderful words of Life;
Sinner, list to the loving call,
Wonderful words of Life.
All so freely given,

Wooing us to Heaven:
Beautiful words, wonderful words,
Wonderful words of Life.
Beautiful words, wonderful words,
Wonderful words of Life.

Open your hymn book and sing the rest of the verses—or even sing another prayer song.

5. READ HIS WORD TO HIM!

His Word

[21] They went to Capernaum, and when the Sabbath came, Jesus went into the synagogue and began to teach. [22] The people were amazed at his teaching, because he taught them as one who had authority, not as the teachers of the law. [23] Just then a man in their synagogue who was possessed by an evil spirit cried out, [24] "What do you want with us, Jesus of Nazareth? Have you come to destroy us? I know who you are—the Holy One of God!"

[25] "Be quiet!" said Jesus sternly. "Come out of him!" [26] The evil spirit shook the man violently and came out of him with a shriek.

[27] The people were all so amazed that they asked each other, "What is this? A new teaching—and with authority! He even gives orders to evil spirits and they obey him." [28] News about him spread quickly over the whole region of Galilee. *— Mark 1:21-28, NIV*

Read His Word to Him.

It is a blessed experience to read your word back to the One who caused it to be written. I always wish I could express my joy more adequately. So many wonder-

ful things happened at Capernaum—I want to be present for each one of them. Even while some were thinking of the meaning your Son gave to your word there was one

514

who was sorely hindered in his hearing. However, the same authority by which my Lord explained and applied your word was going to be used to open this man's mind that he might receive your word. But this was accomplished by the action of the command to the evil or unclean spirit to come out of this man.

Please express your response to this beautiful text. Put your expression in your own prayer diary.

6. READ HIS WORD FOR YOURSELF.

Dear Lord, I want your word to enter my heart with all authority in heaven and on earth. In a very real sense I want you to teach me. I have read many books of men, but in opening your book I want to face directly what you are saying in each verse and let you speak to me with all authority. If I will allow you to make as personal an application as I know you want to, I too will be "astonished." It is such a powerful consolation to read: "Greater is he who is in you than he who is in the world" (I John 4:4). Was John present that day in the synagogue of Capernaum? When our Lord commands demons *must* obey — men can choose — demons cannot choose when our Lord speaks.

Pause in his presence and either audibly or in written form tell him all his word means to you.

7. READ HIS WORD IN THANKSGIVING.

(1) Thank you for the living Christ who is yet teaching with the same authority today. (2) Thank you we can over and over again be delightedly astonished at the meaning and power of his word. (3) Thank you that all that is evil and unclean can be removed by his authority. (4) Thank you that I can *know* demons do not live in me. (5) Thank you that right now Satan can be bound and have no power.

Give yourself to your own expression of gratitude — write it or speak it!

8. READ HIS WORD IN MEDITATION.

Indeed this incident teaches us several powerful lessons. Dear Lord, I want to learn them! (1) Only my Lord has power and authority over demons. It would seem people are almost the pawns of demons without our Lord. We cannot say as to why demons possessed certain men and did not possess others. In the attack of demons today only Jesus has the power to defeat them. (2) It was with his word he took authority over Satan. If Jesus is going to exert his power over men today it will be by his word. I am so glad he is alive and his word is with us.

Pause — wait — think — then express yourself in thoughtful praise or thanks.

9. READ HIS WORD FOR PETITIONS.

How good it is to pray through Someone who has power of the evil one: (1) Since our Lord was a teacher I want to be the very best student possible. (2) Grant me the wisdom to follow his example in teaching. (3) Open my conscience to receive the full impact of his authority. (4) Are we blind today to the work of demons? (5) Do we have definitions for maladies now that are really demon's work? (6) How I do need heaven's wisdom in answering the above two questions. (7) How I need his authority over evil spirits *right now!*

Right here add your personal requests — and his answers.

10. READ HIS WORD AND WAIT — LISTEN — GOD SPEAKS!

(1) "I am still teaching through those who love me." (2) "I have not lost any of my authority." (3) "I can destroy the works of Satan in your life."

11. INTERCESSION FOR THE LOST WORLD

Pakistan — Point for prayer: (1) *Unevangelized areas* and peoples abound. Pray for Baluchistan with its very small Church, and the many warlike Muslim tribes of the North West Frontier with Afghanistan. Pray also for the many peoples living in the isolated valleys of the north that have begun now to open up for the Gospel. Several national evangelists and the Afghan Border Crusade have made occasional visits to these northern regions, but there is no permanent work and the people remain in darkness. Medical work may provide the key to these areas.

12. SING PRAISES TO OUR LORD.

All praise to Him who reigns above
In majesty supreme,
Who gave His Son for man to die,
That He might man redeem!

Blessed be the name, blessed be the name,
Blessed be the name of the Lord;
Blessed be the name, blessed be the name,
Blessed be the name of the Lord.

WEEK THIRTY-SEVEN — FRIDAY

1. PRAISE GOD FOR WHO HE IS.

"For great is the Lord, and greatly to be praised; he is to be feared above all gods. For all the gods of the peoples are idols; but the Lord made the heavens. Honor and majesty are before him; strength and beauty are in his sanctuary" (Psalm 96:4-6). Dear Lord, how refreshing it is to worship in your presence. I know I am in your presence at all times. This indeed is a part of your greatness, but just now I come to praise you and remind my-self once again. As I contemplate the many attributes found in yourself, I feel as all men should feel — overcome with amazement! Like a giant ocean wave that sweeps all in its path so does your greatness and goodness sweep over me. In such a simile there is no thought of harm in the figure; joyous refreshment is man's response! You are to be feared only in the sense of wonder, i.e., if we love you.

Express yourself in adoration for this quality of God.
Speak it audibly or write out your praise in your own devotional journal.

2. PRAISE GOD FOR WHAT HE MEANS TO ME.

Just for me. I know there is indeed a "hell to be feared," and I do, but I adore and praise and rejoice before you and have no dread of that place of torment. I know sin will be punished and I do not at all in any sense propose to continue in any sin — so I simply am full of delight and happiness not guilt and fear. How beautifully good it is to separate just one quality of yourself and hold it up for worship! You have made "the heavens" — when I look at man's photographs of the expanse of your creation, I am dumb with amazement. As far as man's exploration has indicated, this little speck of terrafirma is the only planet around our star (sun) on which you have placed life.

How do you personally relate to the greatness of God, and God who is above all?
Speak it out or write it out. It is *so important* that you establish *your own* devotional journal.

3. CONFESSION OF SIN

If there is one basic sin, one fundamental flaw in man, it must be that he forgets. We forget who we are and why we are and most of all we forget who you are! How easily I am caught up in the maelstrom of life. Dear God, as you know such comments can be but a smoke screen for my willful sin! Indeed sometimes this is true. Forgive me! At the same time, it does represent my dilemma. Since I know what it is to hurt, I do fear pain. Since I know what it is to be lonesome, I fear eternal isolation. Since I know what it is to be able to see nothing but what my imagination will envision, I fear the eternal darkness. At the same time, I know what unalloyed joy is in your presence.

What personal sins do you want to confess? We *must* speak them to remove them.
Do it! *Now.* There is no one else you have sinned against more than God. Tell him so!

4. SING A PRAYER TO GOD.

"Almost persuaded," come, come today;
"Almost persuaded," turn not away;
Jesus invites you here,

Angels are ling'ring near,
Prayers rise from hearts so dear,
O wand'rer, come.

Open your hymn book and sing the rest of the verses — or even sing another prayer song.

5. READ HIS WORD TO HIM!

His Word

14 When Jesus came into Peter's house, he saw Peter's mother-in-law lying in bed with a fever.
— *Matthew 8:14, NIV*

29 As soon as they left the synagogue, they went with James and John to the home of Simon and Andrew. 30 Simon's mother-in-law was in bed with a fever, and they told Jesus about her.
— *Mark 1:29, 30, NIV*

38 Jesus left the synagogue and went to the home of Simon. Now Simon's mother-in-law was suffering from a high fever, and they asked Jesus to help her.
— *Luke 4:38, NIV*

Read His Word to Him.

Simon Peter had a house, a wife and a mother-in-law. Did he have any children? Of course, we do not know, but you do! How I want to step inside his house there at Capernaum and see his wife and his wife's mother. Matthew and Mark say she had fever, but Dr. Luke says it was *a high fever.* My blessed Lord was asked to come to Simon's house to help his mother-in-law. Just what help they expected is not told. It would seem all three accounts are guarded at just what help was expected — it was our Lord's decision. And so it is in every need we have.

Please express your response to this beautiful text. Put your expression in your own prayer diary.

WEEK THIRTY-SEVEN — FRIDAY

6. READ HIS WORD FOR YOURSELF.

Dear Savior, come into my house. My dear mother-in-law lay sick for some long time and died and is with you. If human virtues would command healing, she would have been healed. I have only met one woman who could exceed her in unselfish service—her daughter! If prayers lifted in love and faith would have healed her she would be with us today. Praise your name, dear Lord, it was enough to invite you into our house—and to know that you came.

There are so many ways of helping us—we have so many areas of need. From your record we learn that your help usually comes as a wonderful surprise. Dear Savior, we only await the time when we can unwrap your next gift of love!

It is so important that you pause in his presence
and either audibly or in written form tell him all his word means to you.

7. READ HIS WORD IN THANKSGIVING.

(1) Thank you that worship came first in order of need. (2) Thank you that worship leads to meeting human needs. (3) Thank you that the family is such a real part of all our Savior's work with man. (4) Thank you that marriage is assumed to be the life style of your followers. (5) Thank you for friends who care and will share our burdens. (6) Thank you that Jesus always had time to meet individual human needs. (7) Thank you for a professional, personal observation on a physical healing.

Give yourself to your own expression of gratitude—write it or speak it!

8. READ HIS WORD IN MEDITATION.

"*. . . and they asked Jesus to help her.*" It should be noted that the disciples, Peter, John, James and Andrew, never made any demands on our Lord. In every situation they knew Jesus could help—that was enough. Of course his healing of many, both in Capernaum and Jerusalem, could not be forgotten and perhaps this would be just the help he would offer them. But it could have been that he would not have healed Peter's mother. There were many sick he did not heal—there was a whole cemetery full of dead bodies he did not raise. The miracles were signs—the sign is always a means not an end. The point here seems to be that regardless of the need, Jesus can help—indeed he can! To bring our Savior into any situation is to bring God's answer.

Pause—wait—think—then express yourself in thoughtful praise or thanks.

9. READ HIS WORD FOR PETITIONS.

In the healing of Peter's mother-in-law there is much I can learn for prayer: (1) I want to be as concerned with human need as my Lord. (2) May I be as involved with families as Jesus. (3) Even though we know nothing of Peter's wife Peter must have loved her much or he wouldn't have been so concerned about her mother—what a good example for me. (4) Help me to remember that good people also get sick. (5) I want to look at people and their needs through the eyes of Jesus. (6) Open my mind to know that Jesus never considered helping as an interruption.

Please, please remember these are prayers—speak them—reword them!

10. READ HIS WORD AND WAIT—LISTEN—GOD SPEAKS!

Speak to me in these few verses: (1) "I see all who are sick—but Jesus did not heal every sick person." (2) "Public worship that does not lead you to meet human need is of no value." (3) "Jesus would not have gone to Peter's home if he was not asked."

11. INTERCESSION FOR THE LOST WORLD

Pakistan — Points for prayer: (1) *The Protestant Church* has some outstanding leaders and fine congregations but, generally, there is a dead orthodoxy in most of the older churches. Pray for: *A greater openness and concern* for the evangelization of Muslims and their reception in the churches. The cultural and social barriers are high and make it hard for the believers to be bold with their low social standing. (2) *Illiteracy* is higher among the Christians than the national average. Hence the churches are often weak and spiritually immature. (3) *Nominalism* is the greatest hindrance to growth, due to the large people movements of the last century and succeeding generations remaining unconverted. Much of the Christian work is aimed at evangelizing "Christians" and building them up through the various means of literature, teaching and discipleship training. The greatest need is for revival that liberates, emboldens and mobilizes the Church.

12. SING PRAISES TO OUR LORD.

Amazing grace! how sweet the sound,
That saved a wretch like me!

I once was lost, but now am found,
Was blind, but now I see.

WEEK THIRTY-SEVEN — SATURDAY

1. PRAISE GOD FOR WHO HE IS.

"Ascribe to the Lord, O families of the peoples, ascribe to the Lord glory and strength! Ascribe to the Lord the glory due his name; bring an offering, and come into his courts! Worship the Lord in holy array; tremble before him, all the earth!" (Psalm 96:7-9). I do want to follow the psalmist's directions! I, with all the families of the earth, want to ascribe or offer up my recognition of your glory and strength. I take the term "glory" to refer to your essential nature—to your effulgent brightness as represented in the Shekinah presence. To describe your strength is beyond my poor capacity of words. At the same time, I am greatly encouraged at the attempt. I want to tell you all I can of my response to your majesty and beauty. It would be much easier (and more natural?) to fall down before you in silence.

Express yourself in adoration for this quality of God.
Speak it audibly or write out your praise in your own devotional journal.

2. PRAISE GOD FOR WHAT HE MEANS TO ME.

Just for me. Dear Father, I do want to say something in this time of praise that will represent my deepest feelings before you. There are separate areas here involved. (1) I believe all the families of the earth should right now recognize your glory and strength and come before you in open free worship. (2) I believe all men (beginning with myself) should describe each and every attribute of yourself represented in the true "name"—each quality of yourself should be held up and admired and praised. (3) All the peoples of the earth should, and one day will, appear before you in trembling wonder! If all of this is true, and I surely believe it is, then I want to be the first to ascribe such praise to yourself.

How do you personally relate to the strength of God, and God who is all power?
Speak it out or write it out. It is *so important* that you establish *your own* devotional journal.

3. CONFESSION OF SIN

A strain of confession runs all through my attempts to praise you. Dear Lord, how could it be otherwise? I have not (and do not) credit you with the qualities you obviously deserve. How easy it is to accept the praise of men when I know, I know it belongs to you! Dear Lord, forgive! What offering shall I bring to you? With what sacrifice shall I appear before you today? To ask is to answer "Present your bodies a living sacrifice"; "Come before me with a renewed mind." Dear Father, as you know my intentions do not at all match my practice. That I still retain my intention is my only hope. I do now accept your cleansing and clear new record. Such forgiveness deepens my desire to please you.

What personal sins do you want to confess? We *must* speak them to remove them.
Do it! *Now.* There is no one else you have sinned against more than God. Tell him so!

4. SING A PRAYER TO GOD.

O to grace how great a debtor
Daily I'm constrained to be!
Let Thy goodness, like a fetter,
Bind my wand'ring heart to Thee:

Prone to wander, Lord, I feel it,
Prone to leave the God I love;
Here's my heart, O take and seal it;
Seal it for Thy courts above.

Open your hymn book and sing the rest of the verses—or even sing another prayer song.

5. READ HIS WORD TO HIM!

His Word

[15]He touched her hand and the fever left her, and she got up and began to wait on him. — *Matthew 8:15, NIV*
[31]So he went to her, took her hand and helped her up. The fever left her and she began to wait on them.
  — *Mark 1:31, NIV*

[39]So he bent over her and rebuked the fever, and it left her. She got up at once and began to wait on them.
[40]When the sun was setting, the people brought to Jesus all who had various kinds of sickness.
  — *Luke 4:39, 40a, NIV*

Read His Word to Him.

Oh, what wonderful words! I feel awkward in an attempt to assume anything like your viewpoint. At the same time I am eager to try. The biographers of your Son were surely careful (though independent) observers. "He touched her hand" or "took her hand and helped her up." What happened in the body and mind of this dear woman? It is obvious that she felt responsible for this house full of guests. Her joy simply shined out of her face and eyes. No doubt there were exclamations of joy and astonishment but they are not recorded. The immediacy of this healing is a strong evidence of its supernatural character.

Please express your response to this beautiful text. Put your expression in your own prayer diary.

6. READ HIS WORD FOR YOURSELF.

Jesus could have spoken to Peter's mother-in-law and she would have been healed. He could have spoken to the large crowd enmass and they would have been healed. But he touched her and he laid his hands upon each one of the others who were sick to make them well. How wonderfully personal and interested is my Lord in every need of every man. But of course I am not every man; I am only one man, and like Peter's wife's mother he sees me in my sickness and lays his hand upon me! The service in the home that day was easier, more full of meaning and joy than it had ever been! Could I not remember that in to-day's tasks?

It is so important that you pause in his presence
and either audibly or in written form tell him all his word means to you.

7. READ HIS WORD IN THANKSGIVING.

(1) Thank you for the living personal Savior and Lord. (2) Thank you that he is touching me in every need of life right now! (3) Thank you that you heal me of sin, of any infirmity for the purpose of serving. (4) Thank you that even in healing Jesus supplies help for my weakness. (5) Thank you that Jesus can rebuke wind and wave and sickness and there is calm and sunlight! (6) Thank you that we have the record of a whole day in the life of our Lord. (7) Thank you that Jesus healed people when he knew some of them would forget.

Give yourself to your own expression of gratitude — write it or speak it!

8. READ HIS WORD IN MEDITATION.

"... the people brought to Jesus all who had various kinds of sickness." the pressing physical needs of people led them to someone who could meet those needs. How many of them stayed to become his devoted disciples? No doubt some of them did. But even as today there are many who come to either be entertained or helped in some physical way. Even when our Lord was the teacher there were some who did not want to learn. Why, then did he heal them? The simple answer is that he had compassion upon them. He loved them and reached out to help them in every way he could. The same Saviour is alive right now and wants to help us. Jesus came as a teacher — if we miss his words we miss his purpose. Of course, his primary purpose was to die for our sins, but even his death must be understood by what he taught. Dear Lord, speak, I am listening.

Pause — wait — think — then express yourself in thoughtful praise or thanks.

9. READ HIS WORD FOR PETITIONS.

Luke's account of this miracle is full of points for prayer: (1) Come into my home Lord Jesus. (2) Look on and into the needs of my loved ones. (3) Help me in ways I do not know but gladly accept — I attribute every good thing to you. (4) Lean over me and my need just now. (5) Through ways better known to you than to me, rebuke the fever of my desires to do wrong. (6) I want to remember that I am healed to help. (7) Give me the commitment to your service I see in Jesus.

Right here add your personal requests — and his answers.

10. READ HIS WORD AND WAIT — LISTEN — GOD SPEAKS!

In this personal healing speak to me: (1) "I am waiting for someone to ask for my help." (2) "My patience with human suffering is one of my most static attributes." (3) "Peter's mother-in-law is a grand example of the response all should give to my goodness."

11. INTERCESSION FOR THE LOST WORLD

Pakistan — Points for prayer: (1) *Leadership training* — both at preacher and lay-worker level is vital. Pray for the developing program into which a number of missions have entered. This is a valuable tool for leadership training in the context of Pakistan's many small, scattered groups of Christians. The development is hindered by lack of personnel and time to prepare the teaching materials in local scripts. (2) *The potential of the Pakistani Church* for world evangelization is great. Large numbers of Pakistanis (including many Christians) now work in lands right across the Middle East, some totally closed to the Gospel, such as Qatar, Saudi Arabia, Libya, etc. Pray that they may truly be tent-maker missionaries.

12. SING PRAISES TO OUR LORD.

Thro' the gates to the city in a robe of spotless white,
He will lead me where no tears will ever fall;
In the glad song of ages I shall mingle with delight;
But I long to meet my Savior first of all.

I shall know . . . Him, I shall know Him,
And redeemed by His side I shall stand,
I shall know . . . Him, I shall know Him
By the print of the nails in His hand.

WEEK THIRTY-EIGHT — SUNDAY

1. PRAISE GOD FOR WHO HE IS.

"O sing to the Lord a new song, for he has done marvelous things! His right hand and his holy arm have gotten him victory" (Psalm 98:1). Blessed Father, I can indeed sing with the psalmist "a new song." It is so good to know you enjoy singing. In reality this is but another form of praise, at the same time such expression does indicate your involvement with the feelings of man. Each day should produce a new song from our hearts to you. Each day there is some marvelous thing for which we should thank you. The motif of battle and all that is associated are very prominent in these psalms. All men can relate inasmuch as they are competitors in this warfare called "life." I am so glad to serve under a commander who has never lost a battle. "Victory" is the word to describe your record!

Express yourself in adoration for this quality of God.
Speak it audibly or write out your praise in your own devotional journal.

2. PRAISE GOD FOR WHAT HE MEANS TO ME.

Just for me. What a blessed "new song" I have to sing! I want to sing three new songs just now: (1) A new song of victory over pain. It is *not* necessary to allow pain to dominate your whole mind—in the midst of it you can lift your heart to the presence of the Father—I know I just did it! (2) A new song of victory over debts. Obligations for which we are responsible and cannot pay. It is possible to ask for your provisions to pay such debts, and leave them in your hands. I know—I just did it! (3) A new song of victory over a humanly impossible sickness, i.e., one that has no cure. When I give this burden to you, you care for me—this is enough. I know I just did it! Bless your powerful right hand and holy arm. When I know you get the credit and the praise, then I know the victory is yours—it is enough!

How do you personally relate to the conquests of God, and God who is our victory?
Speak it out or write it out. It is *so important* that you establish *your own* devotional journal.

3. CONFESSION OF SIN

Dear Lord, you know I do not always sing in the midst of the problems of life. Sometimes I complain and most of the time I forget and simply endure. Bless you for your wonderful mercy and patience. At the same time, I am so much in need just here. Forgive me and remind me of my total dependence upon you. If you do not obtain victory in the hearts of your people, there really is no victory at all. My dear Father, I do openly lay before you the sins of my heart and life. Wash me, and I shall be whiter than snow! Singing is not always done because of joy and gladness—sometimes I sing because it is the very best way to express the deep needs of my heart. Some of my songs are surely in a minor note.

"Light dawns for the righteous, and joy for the upright in heart" (Psalm 97:11)
Forgive me that I might sing this song!

What personal sins do you want to confess? We *must* speak them to remove them.
Do it! *Now.* There is no one else you have sinned against more than God. Tell him so!

4. SING A PRAYER TO GOD.

'Tis Jesus calls me on
To perfect faith and love,
To perfect hope, and peace, and trust,
For earth and heav'n above.

I am coming, Lord!
Coming now to Thee!
Wash me, cleanse me in the blood
That flowed on Calvary!

Open your hymn book and sing the rest of the verses—or even sing another prayer song.

5. READ HIS WORD TO HIM!

His Word

[16] When evening came, many who were demon-possessed were brought to him, and he drove out the spirits with a word and healed all the sick. [17] This was to fulfill what was spoken through the prophet Isaiah:

"He took up our infirmities
and carried our diseases." — *Matthew 8:16, 17, NIV*

[32] That evening after sunset the people brought to Jesus all the sick and demon-possessed. [33] The whole town gathered at the door.
— *Mark 1:32, 33, NIV*

and laying his hands on each one, he healed them. [41] Moreover, demons came out of many people, shouting, "You are the Son of God!" But he rebuked them and would not allow them to speak, because they knew he was the Christ.
— *Luke 4:40b, 41, NIV*

Read His Word to Him.

It is so good to be able to enter into the house of Peter and Andrew and watch our Lord as he heals the sick and casts out demons. It surely must have been a time of amazement for Peter, his wife and his mother-in-law.

What did James and John think of what they saw that night? Luke is so careful in all his expressions — "laying his hands on *each one*." Matthew adds that "he drove out the spirits with a word." What shouts of joy and of distress — one from the healed and the other from the demons. How I would like to hear the testimony of both. Perhaps one day I shall. Did our Lord intersperse his healing with teaching — or was it teaching and healing?

Please express your response to this beautiful text. Put your expression in your own prayer diary.

6. READ HIS WORD FOR YOURSELF.

It had been a long and a very tiring day for my Lord, and yet he found time to minister to the sick and possessed. The multitudes had waited until the Sabbath was over to bring their sick and possessed to him. How many, many times have I wanted to be left alone so I could rest. And if I was disturbed from this purpose I was not at all happy about it. What was the difference in the fatigue of my Lord and my own? Could it be that he was tired *in* his work and I was tired *of* it! His work was his life and my life is somewhat apart from my work. Frustration is a result of interrupted purpose. If my purpose is to serve, to help, to heal, then I am not interrupted when opportunity is given to do it.

Pause in his presence and either audibly or in written form tell him all his word means to you.

7. READ HIS WORD IN THANKSGIVING.

(1) Thank you for the individual treatment given by the great physician. (2) Thank you for his 100% success. (3) Thank you for his power over demons. (4) Thank you that all the spirit world knows who he is even if we do not. (5) Thank you for the "whole town" interest in my Lord. (6) Thank you for Matthew's careful observation of Isaiah's prophecy and fulfillment. (7) Thank you that one day all men will be delivered from all sickness, demons and death — his death and resurrection made it so.

Give yourself to your own expression of gratitude — write it or speak it!

8. READ HIS WORD IN MEDITATION.

"... he took up our infirmities and carried our diseases." This text has caused or is the source of no end of discussion. It is truly a shame that what was given to show the Savior's identification with human need has become the center of argument. The point is: do we have the healing of our bodies in the same act that healed our souls? (I Peter 2:24 needs to be read in this connection.) The forgiveness of our sins is accomplished by our faith (which is far more than a mere mental assent) in what our Lord did on Calvary. Can we also have the healing of our sickness, infirmities, diseases by trusting in what he did at Calvary?

Pause — wait — think — then express yourself in thoughtful praise or thanks.

9. READ HIS WORD FOR PEITIONS.

What a remarkable account of the power or authority of our Lord. How shall I learn to pray from this text? (1) I want to bring the sin-sick to my Lord — help me! (2) I want to know far more about how to deal with demons today. (3) May my house be the door of his house. (4) Teach me more and more of the power and purpose in the healings of my Lord. (5) How is it demons know him and men do not? (6) Give me an answer to the above question. (7) Dear Lord, I do believe and know you are the Son of God.

Please, please remember these are prayers — speak them — reword them!

10. READ HIS WORD AND WAIT — LISTEN — GOD SPEAKS!

Impress upon my conscience the meaning of these words (1) "I am yet touched and sympathetic with the infirmities of men." (2) "The diseases of men of body and spirit are a real concern to me." (3) "I healed so I could help the spirit and heart not just the body."

11. INTERCESSION FOR THE LOST WORLD

Pakistan — Point for prayer: (1) *Christian literature* — much excellent material of all kinds is produced in Lahore — problems are: a dearth of good national writers, distribution and the high level of illiteracy among the Christians. Pray for the ministry of occasional Gospel advertisements in the secular press — which has led to an unusual response.

12. SING PRAISES TO OUR LORD.

There is never a day so dreary,
There is never a night so long,
But the soul that is trusting Jesus
Will somewhere find a song.

Wonderful, wonderful Jesus,
In the heart He implanteth a song:
A song of deliv'rance, of courage, of strength,
In the heart He implanteth a song.

WEEK THIRTY-EIGHT — MONDAY

1. PRAISE GOD FOR WHO HE IS.

"Enter his gates with thanksgiving, and his courts with praise! Give thanks to him, bless his name" (Psalm 100:4). How blessed and refreshed I am as I come before you in worship. I enter the gates of praise with the most meaningful thanksgiving I can give you. There are so many peoples who live in a country where there is not enough to eat. You have given us an abundance of daily bread. Dear Lord, thank you! There are so many right in our land who have no appetite for the bread available. They are sick and I am well. Not because I am better than any-

one else—I could truly say there are many, many sick people who are closer to you than I am. For good health—I thank you! There are thousands and thousands who do not have the right use of their mind. This is such a tragic loss. I can use the mental faculties you have given—I thank you. Most of all: there are millions who have never one time had opportunity to hear of my dear Lord and his salvation. How could I ever say thank you adequately? I thank you and bless your holy name. I want this to be representative of all men.

Express yourself in adoration for this quality of God.
Speak it audibly or write out your praise in your own devotional journal.

2. PRAISE GOD FOR WHAT HE MEANS TO ME.

Just for me. It is indeed a joy to apply again this verse to my heart and lift my words before you in thanksgiving. Through what gates should I pass to express my gratitude? As I enter the gate of justification (that I am judged not guilty), I do so with praise so deep and continual I cannot stop! As I walk through the blood-marked gate of redemption, I do so with a shout of joy and gratitude.

There is a gate that sets me apart from all men who are not saved—the gate of *sanctification.* All these are entrances into but one place: *"the courts of praise."* I could speak of other gates all of which open into your presence and into the sanctuary of praise. We enter the gates of: salvation, adoption, hope. Bless your holy name! We have found the temple of thanksgiving!

How do you personally relate to the generosity of God, and God who is worthy of thanksgiving?
Speak it out or write it out. It is *so important* that you establish *your own* devotional journal.

3. CONFESSION OF SIN

Dear Lord, as you know I am not at all always grateful. I have every reason to be—I repent! I confess my sin. If I am not thankful I shut out ten thousand other blessings. I remember my grandfather who came to America from Europe—he remained so humbly grateful for this land throughout all his life. I have left Egypt for Canaan—am

I grateful? Dear Father, forgive my selfish, hard heart! What was the one largest and dominant expression of the prodigal when he sat down at the table of his father? What was the constant thought of the merchant with the pearl of great price? What filled the heart and the mouth of the man who bought the field with the treasure in it?

What personal sins do you want to confess? We *must* speak them to remove them.
Do it! *Now.* There is no one else you have sinned against more than God. Tell him so!

4. SING A PRAYER TO GOD.

With numberless blessings each moment He crowns,
And filled with His fullness divine,
I sing in my rapture, oh, glory to God
For such a Redeemer as mine!
He hideth my soul in the cleft of the rock

That shadows a dry, thirsty land;
He hideth my life in the depths of His love,
And covers me there with His hand,
And covers me there with His hand.

Open your hymn book and sing the rest of the verses—or even sing another prayer song.

5. READ HIS WORD TO HIM!

His Word

[35]Very early in the morning, while it was still dark, Jesus got up, left the house and went off to a solitary place, where he prayed. [36]Simon and his companions went to look for him, [37]and when they found him, they exclaimed: "Everyone is looking for you!"
[38]Jesus replied, "Let us go somewhere else—to the nearby villages—so I can preach there also. That is why I have

come."   *—Mark 1:35-38, NIV*
[42]At daybreak Jesus went out to a solitary place. The people were looking for him and when they came to where he was, they tried to keep him from leaving them. [43]But he said, "I must preach the good news of the kingdom of God to the other towns also, because that is why I was sent."   *—Luke 4:42, 43, NIV*

Read His Word to Him.

These verses could be the proof text for this whole blessed endeavor. This was very early on Sunday morning!

I leave with him. Indeed, I want to try to imagine why he arose so early when he had had such an exhausting day on Saturday. I can imagine several possibilities: (1) He was concerned about all those who had just come to him to be healed; he could see their faces and look into their lives and see their deep needs. (2) He wanted to be ready to preach to the villages of Galilee — there were so many with so much to learn. (3) He wanted to pray for Peter, John, James, and Andrew. Oh, how much these men needed to understand! (4) Most of all it was because it was his habit to prepare for every day and its needs with prayer.

Please express your response to this beautiful text. Put your expression in your own prayer diary.

6. READ HIS WORD FOR YOURSELF.

In these few verses there are volumes of truth for me! As my Lord found the press of the day would catch him up and carry along on the tide of the day, so with me. If I do not get up (sometimes when necessary a great while before sunrise), I do not find time for the closet of prayer. I also must find a solitary, separate place, where I cannot be disturbed. Praise God, there is always such a place in the early morning. The place is solitary because only men are not there. It is alive with yourself! Over an extended period of time and experience I have not been in a circumstance where I could not find a solitary place.

Pause in his presence and either audibly or in written form tell him all his word means to you.

7. READ HIS WORD IN THANKSGIVING.

(1) Thank you for the wonderful example of prayer in my Lord. (2) Thank you for the need our Lord felt for prayer — if he needed it what about me? (3) Thank you that Jesus did not let any circumstance hinder him in fulfilling the time of prayer. (4) Thank you that there always is a solitary place for prayer. (5) Thank you that Jesus was not worried about the concern of people for his safety. (6) Thank you for our Lord's firmly established purpose that was not side tracked by men's ideas. (7) Thank you Jesus came to preach.

Give yourself to your own expression of gratitude — write it or speak it!

8. READ HIS WORD IN MEDITATION.

". . . so I can preach there also. That is why I have come." If my Lord came for the express purpose of being a preacher then it ill behooves me to minimize in any way this highest of all efforts. It would appear from what we can read right on the surface of the text that Jesus attracted people by his preaching and then held their interest by his teaching. We must not in any way discount his miracles. How we do wish we had a sermon recorded on video tape, so we could see and hear his delivery. It is in the delivery of the sermon we succeed or fail in communication. We do have what has been called his "sermon on the mount."

Pause — wait — think — then express yourself in thoughtful praise or thanks.

9. READ HIS WORD FOR PETITIONS.

If I cannot learn about prayer — and how to pray from my Lord's example I will never learn: (1) Keep me committed to never begin a day without you. (2) Give me a loneliness for yourself that cannot be satisfied except in prayer. (3) Deepen my understanding of the prayer-life of my Lord. (4) Keep me away from distracting interruptions — i.e. those sent by Satan. (5) Keep me open to your interrupting distractions. (6) If Jesus needed prayer before he preached, how much more do I need it!

Right here add your personal requests — and his answers.

10. READ HIS WORD AND WAIT — LISTEN — GOD SPEAKS!

In the prayer time of my Lord what do you say to me? (1) "There is nothing you need more than prayer." (2) "If you do not *take* time for prayer you will never find it." (3) "Jesus, my Son was a preacher — is there anything better or more important than preaching?

11. INTERCESSION FOR THE LOST WORLD

Pakistan — Point for prayer: (1) *Missions have been working in the land since 1833.* There are many opportunities in evangelism, church planting, Bible teaching and in various service ministries such as literature, health services, etc. Pray much for more laborers — especially from Britain and Canada, for these nations need no visas. Pray also for a more concerted, prayer-covered assault on the need of the Muslim majority, and the unevangelized majority, and the unevangelized Muslim peoples.

12. SING PRAISES TO OUR LORD.

Amazing grace! how sweet the sound,
That saved a wretch like me!

I once was lost, but now am found,
Was blind, but now I see.

WEEK THIRTY-EIGHT — TUESDAY

1. PRAISE GOD FOR WHO HE IS.

"I will sing of loyalty and of justice; to thee, O Lord, I will sing. I will give heed to the way that is blameless. Oh when wilt thou come to me? I will walk with integrity of heart within my house; I will not set before my eyes anything that is base" (Psalm 101:1-3). It is a real joy to me to set aside this time just to focus my whole attention on yourself. To lift my heart in adoration for the characteristics of yourself I see in your word. In these three verses there are several qualities: (1) You have been loyal to me (do you expect reciprocal action?). (2) You are just in every transaction. (3) You are blameless in all your ways. (4) You want to have a close personal relationship with man (me).

It would seem the psalmist, so representative of all of us, has an identity problem—he cannot establish a closeness and intimacy with you. I believe he reveals the source of the estrangement in his words, "I will not set before my eyes anything that is base."

Express yourself in adoration for this quality of God.
Speak it audibly or write out your praise in your own devotional journal.

2. PRAISE GOD FOR WHAT HE MEANS TO ME.

Just for me. Turn on the TV and it is almost certain you will set something base before your eyes! Continue to look at it, or switch the channel to something equally base and look at it and the following spiritual estrangement will take place: (1) A sense of your loyalty to the Holy God is broken. (2) It seems justice has been violated, i.e., on your part; you are not treating God in a fair manner. (3) You blame yourself for not rejecting immediately what is base. (4) Most of all, the nearness and fellowship with our Lord has left you.

As any reader could easily see I am talking about myself! If we want the song of loyalty and justice—if we want the way of blamelessness then we must mean what we say about our promise: "I will not set before my eyes anything that is base." Dear God, I praise you that such can and will happen in my home!

How do you personally relate to the loyalty of God, and God who is loyal?
Speak it out or write it out. It is *so important* that you establish *your own* devotional journal.

3. CONFESSION OF SIN

I have in the above areas of praise allowed confession to become a large part of the expression. It is due to the nature of the word you have spoken to me. At the same time, I have not at all confessed all of my willfulness. On second thought, I have been through this before! Introspection from a negative viewpoint only results in depression. It becomes apparent to us that somehow we do not have power to do much more than describe the details of our sin. To do that which is good is not present in confession. To accept cleansing and begin to praise you develops the motivation for "that which is good." How true it is that: "The joy of the Lord is our strength." It is on the other side of open confession of our sin we find the strength and joy of forgiveness!

What personal sins do you want to confess? We *must* speak them to remove them.
Do it! *Now.* There is no one else you have sinned against more than God. Tell him so!

4. SING A PRAYER TO GOD.

Savior, more than life to me,
I am clinging, clinging close to Thee;
Let Thy precious blood applied,
Keep me ever, ever near Thy side.

Ev'ry day, ev'ry hour,
Let me feel Thy cleansing pow'r;
Let Thy precious blood applied,
Keep me ever, ever near Thy side.

Open your hymn book and sing the rest of the verses—or even sing another prayer song.

5. READ HIS WORD TO HIM!

His Word

8 When he came down from the mountainside, large crowds followed him. ²A man with leprosy came and knelt before him and said, "Lord, if you are willing, you can make me clean."

³Jesus reached out his hand and touched the man. "I am willing," he said. "Be clean!" Immediately he was cured of his leprosy. ⁴Then Jesus said to him, "See that you don't tell anyone. But go, show yourself to the priest and offer the gift Moses commanded, as a testimony to them."
— *Matthew 8:1-4, NIV*

Read His Word to Him.

Dear Lord, how all of us can identify with the leper! I believe that was the purpose in the minds of Matthew and Luke when they recorded this blessed event. We are daily pressed with our need of cleansing. The deity of our Lord is so fully demonstrated here. The whole incident seems to be out of order: (1) The leper should not have been in the city. (2) He should not fall down and worship a man. (3) Jesus should not touch a leper lest he be defiled. (4) Jesus must have known the leper would not, could not, be quiet. But in these very exceptions we see the glory of our Lord!

Please express your response to this beautiful text. Put your expression in your own prayer diary.

6. READ HIS WORD FOR YOURSELF.

As an unclean person I surely have no right to appear before you. But my need presses upon me to such an extent that any word of help pushes me beyond hesitancy and human regulation. I fall down before you, because you are not a man—in Jesus I see the whole fullness of God. He who took charge of your temple in Jerusalem and cleansed it can surely cleanse me of my uncleanness. The one who needed no sacrifices offered for his sin has become the sacrifice for my sin and can make me clean. Jesus can but speak the word and the problem will be solved. When the hand of our Lord reached the head (or whatever portion of his body he touched) the leprosy was gone. Jesus touched a man cleaner than any who looked on the scene. Bless the Lord, I claim and advertise my cleansing!

Pause in his presence and either audibly or in written form tell him all his word means to you.

7. READ HIS WORD FOR THANKSGIVING.

(1) Thank you for the three records to let me know Jesus has compassion on all us lepers. (2) Thank you that it is my privilege to daily bow before you and worship. (3) Thank you that you are always able and are always willing to make me whole. (4) Thank you that the hand of my Lord is always stretched out toward me and my need. (5) Thank you that I can tell it today—men need to hear of your power to heal the human heart. (6) Thank you that I can and must obey your laws today—for others if not for myself. (7) Thank you for the privilege of testimony to all who need to hear it.

Give yourself to your own expression of gratitude—write it or speak it!

8. READ HIS WORD AND WAIT—LISTEN—GOD SPEAKS!

"Don't tell anyone, . . . See that you don't tell this to anyone." The gospel writers are quite clear that our Lord did not want a premature announcement of his Messiahship to hinder his work. We can excuse the enthusiasm of this man, but his action nonetheless was disobedience and it did pose a real problem for our Lord.

Our Lord was just as plain in his instruction of what he wanted the leper to do. "Go show yourself to the priests." It was one long walk to Jerusalem. Did he go? We do not know. If he did it was sometime later. There was a real purpose in everything Jesus commanded. Zeal without knowledge seldom accomplishes as much good as harm. At times it can be altogether negative. We are full of admiration for the compassion and power present. We only wish the healed would have respected such compassion and power by obeying him.

Pause—wait—think—then express yourself in thoughtful praise or thanks.

9. READ HIS WORD FOR PETITIONS.

What does this man and our Lord's healing say to me? (1) This man seemed like a hopeless case—but he had hope in our Lord's power—he is much like all of us at one time or another. (2) Teach me from this leper true obeisance. (3) I see in this man a definition of the sovereignty of Jesus—teach me well. (4) Jesus dared to touch the leper—or was he well when Jesus said: "I am willing"? (5) I want to be willing to obey you even when it appears contradictory. (6) Give me a testimony to the religious leaders of my day.

Please, please remember these are prayers - speak them—reword them!

10. READ HIS WORD AND WAIT—LISTEN—GOD SPEAKS!

Speak to me through this man: (1) "If you will I can make you clean." (2) "Your only cleanliness is from me." (3) "What offering do you make to me as a testimony for your cleansing?"

11. INTERCESSION FOR THE LOST WORLD

Pakistan — Point for prayer: (1) *Bible correspondence courses* are very useful for the evangelization of Muslims and nominal Christians and building up converts. Pray especially for the follow-up of students.

12. SING PRAISES TO OUR LORD.

Guilty, vile and helpless we;
Spotless Lamb of God was He;

"Full atonement!" can it be?
Hallelujah! what a Savior!

WEEK THIRTY-EIGHT — WEDNESDAY

1. PRAISE GOD FOR WHO HE IS.

"Bless the Lord, O my soul; and all that is within me, bless his holy name! Bless the Lord, O my soul and forget not all his benefits, who forgiveth all your iniquity, who heals all your diseases, . . ." (Psalm 103:1-3). I take this word "bless" to mean "praise" or "adoration"—give expression to your admiration. Indeed I do! The word "soul" in reference to the whole person, intellect, will, emotions and conscience is such an encouragement to me! It is easy for me to allow this to become my expression of praise. What you want, and what *I* want is for *all men* to thus lift their whole being up to you in wonder and praise. Most men have not forgotten your benefits. They do not even know you have given them. Our Lord's ministry could be well described as forgiving and healing. The one great benefit from whom all others flow was offered to all men on the cross and in the open tomb!

Express yourself in adoration for this quality of God.
Speak it audibly or write out your praise in your own devotional journal.

2. PRAISE GOD FOR WHAT HE MEANS TO ME.

Just for me. These verses can become the paean of praise —the epitome of adoration in description of my whole desire to praise you! Dear Lord, I want to think your thoughts after you—to do this I will need to memorize your word. I want to will to do your will as revealed in your word. If I think your thoughts and will your will I know I will feel your emotions! My conscience will strongly approve of all such relationship. Dear Lord, I do not have a greater need than this! How easy it is to forget! How fleeting all the feelings and joys of men! Right now I want to practice these verses: (1) I will right here list some of your benefits as seen in your word. (2) I will open my willingness to receive them. (3) I will express my happiness in such possession. (4) My conscience will give a strong affirmation! Bless the Lord O, my soul!

How do you personally relate to the benefits of God, and God who is the Giver?
Speak it out or write it out. It is *so important* that you establish *your own* devotional journal.

3. CONFESSION OF SIN

Dear Lord, you know better than I do that there are so many times I *do* forget your benefits. How glad I am to be reminded every day of my standing in the Beloved! I would surely faint and fall out if I did not have this blessed time of prayer. What a joy to come and lay all my cares and burdens and sins down and claim your promise of forgiveness! I take the term "diseases" to refer in context to the sickness and infirmity of the soul. I know you can heal man's body in answer to prayer. But of what benefit is that if his life is lost? If we are not redeemed from the pit it will be of no benefit to be physically well. Dear Lord, forgive my sin—my transgression of your law. Bless the Lord, I *do* claim your promise of release from condemnation!

What personal sins do you want to confess? We *must* speak them to remove them.
Do it! *Now.* There is no one else you have sinned against more than God. Tell him so!

4. SING A PRAYER TO GOD.

I've found a friend who is all to me, . . .
His love is ever true; . . .
I love to tell how He lifted me . . .
And what His grace can do for you. . . .

Saved . . . by His pow'r divine,
Saved . . . to new life sublime!
Life now is sweet and my joy is complete,
For I'm Saved, saved, saved!

Open your hymn book and sing the rest of the verses—or even sing another prayer song.

5. READ HIS WORD TO HIM!

His Word

[23]Jesus went throughout Galilee, teaching in their synagogues, preaching the good news of the kingdom, and healing every disease and sickness among the people. [24]News about him spread all over Syria, and people brought to him all who were ill with various diseases, those suffering severe pain, the demon-possessed, the epileptics and the paralytics, and he healed them. [25]Large crowds from Galilee, the Decapolis, Jerusalem, Judea and the region across the Jordan followed him.

—Matthew 4:23-25, NIV

Read His Word to Him.

The wonder and beauty of the healing ministry of my Lord impresses upon me as never before! At the same time, I want to assimilate the true purpose of my Lord's ministry —it was not to heal that he came! He came to preach the good news of the rule of God in the hearts of men. Our Lord chose the synagogue as the best beginning place to accomplish his purpose. The extent and influence of my Lord's preaching is here summarized by Matthew. How many synagogues were there in Galilee? What was the population of this whole province? How many people are included in the expression "large crowds from Galilee"? We do not know the answer to such questions, but our estimate of his influences grows by the minute.

Please express your response to this beautiful text. Put your expression in your own prayer diary.

6. READ HIS WORD FOR YOURSELF.

How shall I relate to this tremendous summary of my Lord's work? Jesus is always a surprise and wonder to me: (1) I wonder at his energy in being able to travel so far and expend so much of his "virtue" in healing and teaching. (2) I wonder at his mercy in healing many "nobodies" who really didn't know what happened, i.e., as to eternal meaning. (3) I wonder at the variety of healings performed: (a) various diseases (what diseases were current in the first century Palestine?); (b) severe pain; (c) paralytics — and then the many who were demon possessed. The simple all-inclusive word of Matthew is that "he healed them." Instantaneous, permanent, no failures. No waiting and no regrets! Oh, dear Lord, it simply staggers my imagination!

Pause in his presence and either audibly or in written form tell him all his word means to you.

7. READ HIS WORD IN THANKSGIVING.

(1) Thank you for the preparation Jesus made for this tremendous tour — he prayed. (2) Thank you that during the tour he prayed (Luke 5:15, 16). (3) Thank you that my Lord's power over evil (demons) is very prominent. (4) Thank you Jesus chose a human institution (the synagogue) to accomplish his divine purpose. (5) Thank you that Jesus always had, does always have and will always have "good news." (6) Thank you it is possible to have your rule in my heart. (7) Thank you that crowds did not impress Jesus — may your purpose be my purpose too.

Give yourself to your own expression of gratitude — write it or speak it!

8. READ HIS WORD IN MEDITATION.

"Large crowds from Galilee, the Decapolis, Jerusalem, Judea and the region across the Jordan followed him." Large crowds followed him when he healed them. At the same time, it was to the same crowd he preached. It was our Lord who told us of the expected response to his preaching — we refer to the parable of the soils. How did Jesus relate to the large crowds? We could say several things about this: (1) When a large crowd gathered in the synagogue in Capernaum he retired to a solitary place and prayed. Jesus was not impressed with the crowd. (2) He saw them as no man could see them — as a sheep without a shepherd — scattered, harassed.

Pause — wait — think — then express yourself in thoughtful praise or thanks.

9. READ HIS WORD FOR PETITIONS.

Surely the miracles of my Lord can lead me to prayer: (1) I want to learn more and more about the teaching methods of my Lord. (2) If my Lord was a preacher — and we know he was — then I too want to be most like him. (3) Jesus healed *every* disease and *every* infirmity — how unlike present day efforts — why? (4) Gentiles from Syria came to him — he did not turn them away — keep me open to everyone's need. (5) Once again I am forced to face demoniacs — I know there is more to learn here than I know — teach me!

Right here add your personal requests — and his answers.

10. READ HIS WORD AND WAIT — LISTEN — GOD SPEAKS!

Jesus taught and preached to others — I want to hear him speak to me: (1) "I speak to men again every time you preach my word." (2) "I teach again every time you teach my word." (3) "The 'greater works' of spiritual healing is yours because I have gone to my Father."

11. INTERCESSION FOR THE LOST WORLD

Pakistan — Points for prayer: (1) *Bible translation* — most of the major languages have the Bible or New Testament, but many languages have yet to be reduced to writing and translation work begun. Work has been initiated in four languages — pray for those involved. (2) *Christian Radio* has not had a great impact due to the lack of short wave receivers in the country. Pray for the recording studios in Rawalpindi, and also the stations transmitting to Pakistan.

12. SING PRAISES TO OUR LORD.

Living for me, living for me,
Up in the skies He is living for me;

Daily He's pleading and praying for me,
All because Jesus is living for me.

WEEK THIRTY-EIGHT — THURSDAY

1. PRAISE GOD FOR WHO HE IS.

". . . as far as the east is from the west, so far does he remove our transgressions from us. As a father pities his children, so the Lord pities those who fear him. For he knows our frame; he remembers that we are dust" (Psalm 103:12-14). How delightfully good it is to lift my heart to you in praise. Let me mark out the qualities in the verses of your wonderful character: (1) Total forgiveness, which includes forgetfulness. How good to be able to look into your face and know you do not even remember my sin.

If I have been forgiven (and I have) then to remind you of my sin is actually an embarrassment to you! You cannot and do not remember any of my sins, or the sins of any of your repentant children. You look with pity, or mercy, or understanding and love upon the stumbling efforts of your children. This does *not* mean you are encouraging their mistakes—any more than a loving father would with his children. He remembers we are limited and forgives us. Bless your holy name forever!

Express yourself in adoration for this quality of God.
Speak it audibly or write out your praise in your own devotional journal.

2. PRAISE GOD FOR WHAT HE MEANS TO ME.

Just for me. Whereas all the above is true and I gladly embrace it to my heart, I am troubled by the little phrase in Hebrews 5:12: "For though by this time you ought to be teachers, you need someone to teach you." For how long are we to be taught? For how long are we to be children? Is the answer as long as God is our Father we are children and in need of pity and care? As long as God

is our teacher we are his disciples and need to be taught by him. As related to others we do not remain children long; we grow up and have our own children. We do not remain disciples with others; we learn and teach others. But with God we are his forever children and disciples. Bless your eternal self! He will not need to look far to remember that I am dust!

How do you personally relate to the forgiveness of God, and God who forgets?
Speak it out or write it out. It is *so important* that you establish *your own* devotional journal.

3. CONFESSION OF SIN

I am in a constant dilemma, i.e., how do I know when I am using your grace as a license to sin? Does the very fact that I am worried about it negate the thought that I am doing it? When will it be that I simply will not entertain the thought that if I sin I can obtain forgiveness, *therefore,* I will go ahead and sin. Grace in this circumstance becomes an ally to sin. Such was never the purpose

of your mercy or goodness. If I knew that if I committed a sin one more time I would never be forgiven and would end up in eternal torment, would I commit that sin? Why is the fear motivation stronger than the love motivation? Or is it? I need to see the disappointment on your face when I sin. I won't do it because it hurts you; it hurts me too.

What personal sins do you want to confess? We *must* speak them to remove them.
Do it! *Now.* There is no one else you have sinned against more than God. Tell him so!

4. SING A PRAYER TO GOD.

May Thy rich grace impart
Strength to my fainting heart,
My zeal inspire;

As Thou hast died for me
O may my love to Thee
Pure, warm, and changeless be, a living fire!

Open your hymn book and sing the rest of the verses—or even sing another prayer song.

5. READ HIS WORD TO HIM!

His Word

Because of the importance of this text we want to pray about it twice.

[45] Instead he went out and began to talk freely, spreading the news. As a result, Jesus could no longer enter a town openly but stayed outside in lonely places. Yet the people still came to him from everywhere.
— *Mark 1:45, NIV*

[15] Yet the news about him spread all the more, so that crowds of people came to hear him and to be healed of their sicknesses. [16] But Jesus often withdrew to lonely places and prayed.
— *Luke 5:15, 16, NIV*

Read His Word to Him.

My dear Father, you know how difficult I find this effort; it is not that I do not want to read this word (your word) to you, but I know not how. I want to walk amid the crowd—I want to kneel before your Son. I want to personally examine each healing! I want the wonder and

tingling excitement of every miracle to fill my heart. Most of all, dear Father, I want to withdraw with my Lord to the wilderness, to a solitary place, to a quiet place and watch him pray today!

Please express your response to this beautiful text. Put your expression in your own prayer diary.

6. READ HIS WORD FOR YOURSELF.

My loving Father, you know how very feeble I feel these efforts are, but I gladly lift them to you. Why did Jesus pray? (1) Because without he could not maintain a balance between the demands of the daily routine and his communion with you. If ever I have found any reason for prayer this is it! (2) Because he was lonesome to talk to someone who cared and understood and who could help. Even in the action of pronouncing words to others, I cry out to you—the nearest and dearest cannot help like you. (3) Because he needed instruction or directions for the day just ahead of him. Of course, I know my dear Lord received direct intuitive direction. I find mine in your all-sufficient word. Praise your name you have never failed one day to speak to my deepest need!

It is so important that you pause in his presence
and either audibly or in written form tell him all his word means to you.

7. READ HIS WORD IN THANKSGIVING.

(1) Thank you for a good report concerning my Lord (however alloyed with selfishness). (2) Thank you for those who came to hear. (3) Thank you for those who came to be healed—no doubt this spoke to some of them too. (4) Thank you that you are always "touched with the feeling of our infirmities." (5) Thank you for our Lord's choice to withdraw and pray. (6) Thank you for Jesus' willingness to "put up" with the disobedience of the leper who was healed. (7) Thank you that my Lord is patient and kind with my failures—"He looked beyond my fault and saw my need."

Give yourself to your own expression of gratitude—write it or speak it!

8. READ HIS WORD IN MEDITATION.

". . . so that Jesus could no longer openly enter a town, but was out in the country; and people came to him from every quarter." The popularity of Jesus was an advantage: (a) More people could hear him when he preached to them. (b) More people could be healed and thus help their physical needs. (c) More people would accept him as their Messiah—they would be prepared hopefully for the time when he would publicly declare his purpose. Disadvantages: (a) Even while the multitude listened they were restless. They had come to be healed and they simply put up with "the commercial." (b) Many who were healed soon forgot. Their physical infirmity hindered what they wanted to do and it wasn't to worship God.

Pause—wait—think—then express yourself in thoughtful praise or thanks.

9. READ HIS WORD FOR PETITIONS.

We can understand the exuberance of this man, but we cannot excuse his disobedience. How shall we pray about this? (1) If my Lord says "wait" it is wrong to move—how can I know the difference? (2) When our Lord cannot fulfill his purpose in the lives of people perhaps it is because I have moved when I should have waited. (3) It is easy to get in my own way—or in his way—give me wisdom. (4) Help me to take the larger opportunity—the one Jesus directs. (5) Something good did work out from this—may I believe that about mistakes in my life.

Please, please remember these are prayers—speak them—reword them!

10. READ HIS WORD AND WAIT—LISTEN—GOD SPEAKS!

You have been speaking to me out of this incident: (1) "Some joys are better kept to yourself." (2) "There is a right time for all things—ask me about it." (3) "More can always be done in planned effort—i.e. when I direct the plan."

11. INTERCESSION FOR THE LOST WORLD

Philippines — Population: 45,000,000. Growth rate—3%. People per sq. km.—150.

Points for prayer: (1) *The Philippines* is now one of the most open and also receptive countries in Asia. Pray that this opportunity may be fully used by nationals and missionaries. (2) *Roman Catholics* are more tolerant, desirous of reading and studying the Bible and open to the Gospel than ever before. Pray that believers may be open to help these seeking people to know the Lord Jesus.

12. SING PRAISES TO OUR LORD.

There is a name I love to hear,
I love to sing its worth;
It sounds like music in mine ear,
The sweetest name on earth.

Oh, how I love Jesus,
Oh, how I love Jesus,
Oh, how I love Jesus,
Because He first loved me!

WEEK THIRTY-EIGHT — FRIDAY

1. PRAISE GOD FOR WHO HE IS.

"The Lord has established his throne in the heavens, and his kingdom rules over all. Bless the Lord, O you his angels, you mighty ones who do his word, hearkening to the voice of his word" (Psalm 103: 19, 20). I am full of wonder and curiosity! Just where in the heavens is your throne? I know that Paul went into "the third heaven" (II Cor. 12:2ff.), but just where is that? I am acquainted with the explanation of the heaven where the clouds are and the heaven of the stars. Just to contemplate the grandeur and immensity of the Milky Way galaxy of which our earth is an infinitesimal speck overwhelms my thinking! I know you rule and reign over all the ten million galaxies but this does not describe your greatness at all! The physical facts of your creative power carry me away into amazement! The nearest star to our star called the sun is so far away it would take 80,000 years to arrive if we traveled at the fastest speed known to man!

Express yourself in adoration for this quality of God.
Speak it audibly or write out your praise in your own devotional journal.

2. PRAISE GOD FOR WHAT HE MEANS TO ME.

If only all men knew who created all we have. If only all men could say with the psalmist, "You made them all." I want to add my little voice to that of the angels and the mighty ones (probably the same as angels). What missions will you fulfill today? What project has the Creator-Father whose name is power and wisdom sent you on today? To speak presupposes intelligence and purpose. What a record it would make for an angel to tell us of just one of the smaller (?) works he had been sent to do. I know I am fantasizing, but it is based upon real possibility. Bless and praise your holy name. O, my soul!

How do you personally relate to the rule of God, and God who is Ruler?
Speak it out or write it out. It is *so important* that you establish *your own* devotional journal.

3. CONFESSION OF SIN

Why is it I do not always have such an exalted attitude, or word to express my estimate of your greatness? Of course the answer is sin, but it is the particular sin of dullness and blindness, of insensitivity that comes from too close exposure to the stupidity of this world and the one who runs it. Dear God, I want to hide in you. I want to escape into the heaven of the heavens and be forever in your presence. At the same time I say this, I know your answer. The example of man and for man is the "Son of man," who lived and hurt and gave to save. In the quietness of a summer night did your Son ever feel lonesome for you? Dear Lord, I'm truly glad I only have a few more years to give before I can enter into the life that will be life indeed. While I'm here I do renew my commitment to being the light of my little world! Forgive me for complaining!

What personal sins do you want to confess? We *must* speak them to remove them.
Do it! *Now.* There is no one else you have sinned against more than God. Tell him so!

4. SING A PRAYER TO GOD.

I know not how this saving faith
To me He did impart,
Nor how believing in His Word
Wrought peace within my heart.

But "I know whom I have believed,
  and am persuaded that He is able
To keep that which I've committed
Unto Him against that day."

Open your hymn book and sing the rest of the verses—or even sing another prayer song.

5. READ HIS WORD TO HIM!

His Word

Once again we examine this text in prayer.

[45]Instead he went out and began to talk freely, spreading the news. As a result, Jesus could no longer enter a town openly but stayed outside in lonely places. Yet the people still came to him from everywhere. — *Mark 1:45, NIV*

[15]Yet the news about him spread all the more, so that crowds of people came to hear him and to be healed of their sicknesses. [16]But Jesus often withdrew to lonely places and prayed. — *Luke 5:15, 16, NIV*

Read His Word to Him.

How excusable and inexcusable are the actions and attitudes of the leper who was healed. He was going to bring in the reign of the Messiah whether Jesus wanted such an action or not. How like him we are! We act in such presumptuous ways so often. We are going to have it our way come what may! No doubt the leper thought Jesus was just being modest—Jesus really wanted him to tell the good news of the Messiah, but was just using reverse psychology on him. Dear Lord, how man tries to second guess your desires!

Please express your response to this beautiful text. Put your expression in your own prayer diary.

WEEK THIRTY-EIGHT — FRIDAY

6. READ HIS WORD FOR YOURSELF.

I want to find direct application of these three verses to my life. (1) How presumptuous I am in assuming the way you deal with me is the way you deal with everyone. I can testify that you healed me, but to assume you are going to act in exactly the same way with everyone is a sad presumption. How I need to let you work *in* people instead of my working *on* them. (2) How presumptuous I am in making my methods your methods in calling on the lost and teaching the saved. I decided you wanted me to call on every house in this town. I decided that I knew the time you wanted it done. You gave me a tumor on my foot that made it impossible, or at least permitted me to have such a tumor. I have been calling, but as a much wiser servant.

It is so important that you pause in his presence
and either audibly or in written form tell him all his word means to you.

7. READ HIS WORD IN THANKSGIVING.

(1) Thank you for the opportunity to speak freely; help me to do it wisely. (2) Thank you for the attitude of my Lord; he didn't complain about his restrictions. (3) Thank you for the divine interest in people which will hurtle all barriers. (4) Thank you for the unlimited power of Jesus to heal. (5) Thank you for the lovely place for prayer. (6) Thank you for the need of Jesus for prayer — what an example. (7) Thank you for the example of priority for prayer seen in my Lord.

Give yourself to your own expression of gratitude — write it or speak it!

8. READ HIS WORD IN MEDITATION.

"But Jesus often withdrew to lonely places and prayed." I want to underline the words *often* and *withdrew*. Just how "often" is "often"? Was this once a day? If so it must have been at a time when no one knew about it. If others followed him it would not be a lonely place. Perhaps the reference to a "great while before day" was typical of my dear Lord. In the routine of my life there just is no other time for prayer. As I begin a new day I do want to start it with you. At the close of the day I need you for the kind of rest my body needs.

How is it that Jesus *often withdrew*? It was unobtrusive — he did not call attention to it. But he did pull out of the stream of life for a quiet place near to the heart of God. Dear Lord, there is *nothing* I need more!

Pause — wait — think — then express yourself in thoughtful praise or thanks.

9. READ HIS WORD FOR PETITIONS.

In the presumptuous zeal of this man we can see ourselves and our need for prayer: (1) How easy it is to speak when I should be quiet — shut my mouth! (2) How silent I am when I should speak — open my mouth! (3) How often has the work of my Lord been hindered by my hasty words? (4) Forgive me Lord for not spending more time in prayer — I would know better what to say. (5) Keep me aware that crowds alone are not an indication of success. (6) Thank you for the example of my Lord as he found a solitary place to pray — I want to follow him.

Right here add your personal requests — and his answers.

10. READ HIS WORD AND WAIT — LISTEN — GOD SPEAKS!

When men did not understand and would not follow your words your Son sought your face in prayer. What can you say to me through this example? (1) "I can work around people if I can't work through them." (2) "Some good can come out of this unfortunate situation." (3) "If Jesus *often* withdrew to lonely places to pray — how is it you do not do so?"

11. INTERCESSION FOR THE LOST WORLD

Philippines — Points for prayer: (1) *Unreached peoples* — the Philippines has been patchily covered with the Gospel, pray for the needy Muslims, many unreached little tribes and large lowland areas that have little Bible believing witness. (2) *The Protestant Church* is emerging as a significant force in the life of the country: a) *Growth through evangelism* has been stimulated by various conferences on evangelism. The younger Bible believing groups started since World War II are increasingly important. b) *Some of the older and larger denominations* have stagnated through an overemphasis on institutions and dialogue with Roman Catholics, rather than on evangelism, though many of the congregations are unhappy about these developments. Revival is needed.

12. SING PRAISES TO OUR LORD.

We praise Thee, O God! for Thy Spirit of light,
Who has shown us our Savior, and scattered our night.
Hallelujah! Thine the glory;

Hallelujah! Amen!
Hallelujah! Thine the glory;
Revive us again.

531

WEEK THIRTY-EIGHT — SATURDAY

1. PRAISE GOD FOR WHO HE IS.

"Bless the Lord, O my soul! O Lord my God, thou art very great! Thou art clothed with honor and majesty, who coverest thyself with light as with a garment, who stretched out the heavens like a tent, . . ." (Psalm 104:1-2). The word "bless" means to offer praise and presupposes a focus of attention. In this little expression I am saying I want to fasten my whole attention on you! The term "soul" refers to the total man. My whole being is involved in this form of praise. You have not only my attention and praise but my service. The word "great" seems weak inasmuch as we apply it to so many things and people. The rest of this psalm will tell of your greatness which will lift you out of the area of comparison. How wonderful it is to worship you in this form of adoration!

Express yourself in adoration for this quality of God.
Speak it audibly or write out your praise in your own devotional journal.

2. PRAISE GOD FOR WHAT HE MEANS TO ME.

Just for me. I want to turn over every word of the psalmist and make it mine in praise to you. You are "clothed with honor and majesty" as I see a garment upon a king or some great ruler so I am to see honor covering you! Indeed such is not at all difficult! I can begin in the garden of creation and see honor covering you — to create a being in your own likeness and then set him free! Honor is a result of an adequate cause. There could be no more adequate cause than your creative act in fashioning man and woman. I could never, never thank you or honor you enough! You clothed yourself in honor when you kept your word and removed man from the garden. Your creative genius and your total integrity clothe you in honor to me! Bless your holy name!

How do you personally relate to the honor of God, and God who is clothed with honor?
Speak it out or write it out. It is *so important* that you establish *your own* devotional journal.

3. CONFESSION OF SIN

I really am at a loss to know all that is meant in the little expression: "who coverest thyself with light as with a garment." But what I do know lets me know that standing before your pure white light I feel anything but comfortable. I know some of my sins, your light reveals *all of them!* Somehow they are magnified in your presence. It must be the contrast! And then I remember! O, bless the Lord, I remember your light is not only revealing, it is purifying. As I stand before you hiding nothing I can and do claim your forgiveness — I can and do stand then as pure as you are pure. I too can be covered with light (your light) as with a garment! O wonder of all wonders! Thank you! praise you! bless the Lord O my soul!

What personal sins do you want to confess! We *must* speak them to remove them.
Do it! *Now.* There is no one else you have sinned against more than God. Tell him so!

4. SING A PRAYER TO GOD.

I have a Father; to me He has given
A hope for eternity, blessed and true;
And soon He will call me to meet Him in heaven,
But oh, that He'd let me bring you with me, too!

For you I am praying,
For you I am praying,
For you I am praying,
I'm praying for you.

Open your hymn book and sing the rest of the verses — or even sing another prayer song.

5. READ HIS WORD TO HIM!

His Word

2 A few days later, when Jesus again entered Capernaum, the people heard that he had come home. ²So many gathered that there was no room left, not even outside the door, and he preached the word to them.
— *Mark 2:1, 2, NIV*

Read His Word to Him.

It is a joyous experience I have in reading these beautiful verses in your presence. How much we all want to know what happened in the days that lapsed from the healing of the leper to the incident before us. We know at least that several times Jesus withdrew to a lonely place and prayed. But now he has returned "home." When we pause and think we are shocked to realize Jesus really never owned a house in Capernaum — he did not have money for rent. He lived as a guest in someone's home. "Dear Lord, you can live with me!" Wait a moment! *He is doing that right now!* In the person of "the Other Comforter" he is living in me! and also with me. Is he teaching me? Do I hear his words as a preacher?

Please express your response to this beautiful text. Put your expression in your own prayer diary.

WEEK THIRTY-EIGHT — SATURDAY

6. READ HIS WORD FOR YOURSELF.

As always, I have a difficult time separating these two concepts. My blessed Savior, I want you to feel at home in my body. As we do all we can to anticipate the desires and needs of a very important guest in our home I do want to be constantly conscious of your presence in me. What was your task while upon this earth? To teach, to preach, to save. Am I solicitous only for physical comforts? These can soon be satisfied. They are only a means to an end. You want to teach me; preach to me. In every way I have a need you want to save me. "He preached the word to them." What did he say? Whatever it was it did not disagree with what I can read in the gospel accounts. You are speaking to me now in these words—having ears I want to hear.

It is so important that you pause in his presence
and either audibly or in written form tell him all his word means to you.

7. READ HIS WORD IN THANKSGIVING.

(1) Thank you for the abundance of work you did in Capernaum; somehow I feel America is much like this town. (2) Thank you for Jesus' ability to make his "home" in this unworthy place. (3) Thank you that the report of my Lord's work is spreading today. (4) Thank you for every one who crowded around his door in that far off day. How I do want to talk to some of them. (5) Thank you for the patient love of my Lord. He knew many who came did not understand him, but he preached nonetheless. (6) Thank you for the infinite goodness of Jesus. He knew most of these people came to be healed, but he preached to them nonetheless. (7) Thank you that just the presence of your dear Son did so much for everyone.

Give yourself to your own expression of gratitude—write it or speak it!

8. READ HIS WORD IN MEDITATION.

"... and he was preaching the word to them." It does seem strange to read this expression concerning our Lord. We hear Paul tell Timothy to "preach the word," but here is Mark telling us that Jesus "preached the word." This expression has an ancient antecedent in the prophets. We hear Baruch ask Jeremiah: "Is there *any word* from the Lord?" Jesus who himself was God's word made flesh now speaks the message he himself represented. This should teach us a tremendous lesson: Our Lord was the word and he preached the word. So, we are what we preach, but this is no substitution for preaching. The word must be incarnate, but it must also be spoken! Dear Lord, may it find its dual fulfillment in my life and the lives of all those who are preachers of your word.

Pause—wait—think—then express yourself in thoughtful praise or thanks.

9. READ HIS WORD FOR PETITIONS.

Could there be two more charming verses? (1) How brief were the days of my Lord—help me to so number my days. (2) Capernaum is gone but the memory of his presence is with us—will we learn any better than they did? (3) Dear Lord, welcome home to my heart! (4) I want to crowd close to you as I read again every word you said—open my conscience! (5) I know there is always room at the cross and at the throne of grace—how I claim both. (6) Somehow help me to follow my Lord in preaching the word.

Please, please remember these are prayers—speak them—reword them!

10. READ HIS WORD AND WAIT—LISTEN—GOD SPEAKS!

In the visit of my Lord to Capernaum speak to me: (1) "I come again to your town every time you see a person in need." (2) "I am preaching the word again through your lips." (3) "You can be as concerned about your heart as these people were about their bodies."

11. INTERCESSION FOR THE LOST WORLD

Philippines — Points for prayer: (1) *The Protestant Church: Problems to be prayed over*—Bible believing churches and leaders are often too dependent on funds and initiative from the U.S.A. Although there are some outstanding preachers and leaders in the ministry, there are too few to meet the need, especially in the rural areas. The rapidly growing cities are inadequately covered with the Gospel. A greater spiritual depth is needed in the congregations for more effective outreach. (2) *Leadership training*—over 71 Seminaries and Bible Schools, most being Bible believing. Number of graduates for all levels of the preaching ministry is very inadequate.

12. SING PRAISES TO OUR LORD.

Your many sins are all forgiv'n,
Oh, hear the voice of Jesus;
Go on your way in peace to heav'n,
And wear a crown with Jesus.

Sweetest note in seraph song,
Sweetest name on mortal tongue;
Sweetest carol every sung,
Jesus, blessed Jesus.

WEEK THIRTY-NINE — SUNDAY

1. PRAISE GOD FOR WHO HE IS.

"Thou dost cause the grass to grow for the cattle, and plants for man to cultivate, that he may bring forth food from the earth, and wine to gladden the heart of man, oil to make his face shine, and bread to strengthen man's heart" (Psalm 104:14, 15). Blessed Lord I want to enter into the description of your creative power and identify the personal interest you have in the world you have made: (1) You not only made the cattle with an appetite but with an altogether adequate means of satisfying their desire. This is but representative of all your work. (2) There is no desire in man that is not met in your provision. If this is true in the physical world how very much more would it be true in the spiritual world! There is no mental or psychological need that cannot find abundant completion in yourself!

Express yourself in adoration for this quality of God.
Speak it audibly or write out your praise in your own devotional journal.

2. PRAISE GOD FOR WHAT HE MEANS TO ME.

Just for me. What is generally true I have found to be personally true! The fact that millions are starving this very moment is not your fault. There is abundant provision of food. It is the heart-breaking fact that man has so utterly failed in the use of what you have provided. We can blame each other and ourselves, and we should, the truth still stands that your provision is adequate. Dear Lord, I refuse to be bogged down in human argument and speculation. I want to simply apply your word to my life. For today, am I willing to appropriate your provisions in my sex life? Or will I look somewhere else? In my domestic life? Are my eyes and ears and heart hungry for the bread of life here? In the economics of today—am I aware of what you have said? Dear Lord, strengthen my heart!

How do you personally relate to the provisions of God, and God who is adequate?
Speak it out or write it out. It is *so important* that you establish *your own* devotional journal.

3. CONFESSION OF SIN

I have been shocked several times with the statistics of starvation. I have been rebuked in my spirit that I seem to do almost nothing about it. The words of my Lord haunt me: "I was hungry and you gave no food, I was thirsty and you gave me no drink, I was a stranger and you did not welcome me, naked and you did not clothe me, sick and in prison and you did not visit me" (Matthew 25:42, 43). And I *know* whom he had in mind; it is the hungry, thirsty, lonesome, naked, sick and prisoners of our day, of any day. Dear Lord, I want to do something — maudlin sentiment will not get it done! Genuine repentance is what I want and need! I can't do everything, but I can do something! I will.

What personal sins do you want to confess? We *must* speak them to remove them.

4. SING A PRAYER TO GOD.

Sweet hour of prayer! sweet hour of prayer!
Thy wings shall my petition bear
To Him whose truth and faithfulness
Engage the waiting soul to bless;
And since He bids me seek His face,
Believe His word and trust His grace,
I'll cast on Him my ev'ry care,
And wait for thee, sweet hour of prayer.

Open your hymn book and sing the rest of the verses — or even sing another prayer song.

5. READ HIS WORD TO HIM!

His Word

[3]Some men came, bringing to him a paralytic, carried by four of them. [4]Since they could not get him to Jesus because of the crowd, they made an opening in the roof above Jesus and, after digging through it, lowered the mat the paralyzed man was lying on.   *— Mark 2:3, 4, NIV*

Read His Word to Him.

This incident must have been important: it was recorded by all three of the biographers you chose to record the life of your Son. In so many ways this example speaks to me of your concern. (1) Here is a man who cannot at all help himself. If this man is to be healed it will be from you. How often do we find ourselves just like him! (2) He did have friends who would do what they could. They couldn't heal him but they could make it possible. (3) Someone knew about your dear Son; someone knew where he lived. (4) Someone had adventuresome creative ideas as to how to help their friend. (5) They must have known Jesus would not interpret their actions as "out of order." Jesus read their intentions.

Please express your response to this beautiful text. Put your expression in your own prayer diary.

WEEK THIRTY-NINE — SUNDAY

6. READ HIS WORD FOR YOURSELF.

Indeed I do! I share the paralytic's condition: (1) Unless you help me I shall not be helped. This is true in several areas of my life. It is because you have healed me and raised me up that I am able to stand at all. (2) I owe more than I could ever repay to dear friends who have "carried" me in a good number of situations. I wish I had the space to detail a number of them. I would begin with the dearest of all to me—my wife. (3) A preacher long ago knew your Son and led me to him. I want to be that "someone" for the important men and women all about me. (4) It is such a challenge to me to be able to be creative and different in my approach to helping men to know my Lord. There is always a new fresh way of letting others know him. (5) Men are critical, men delight in cutting and slashing other men. My dear Lord has no such attitude! Praise his name forever!

It is so important that you pause in his presence
and either audibly or in written form tell him all his word means to you.

7. READ HIS WORD IN THANKSGIVING.

(1) Thank you for men who care about the needs of others. (2) Thank you for disease and sickness—without such there would be no healing. (3) Thank you for the classic examples of healing—so unlike others. (3) Thank you for those who do not let "the crowd" hinder them. (4) Thank you for the daring faith of these four men. (5) Thank you for the paralytic who was willing to venture with his friends. (6) Thank you for the man who owned the house—he did not object. (7) Thank you most of all for One who can deliver the impossible.

Give yourself to your own expression of gratitude—write it or speak it!

8. READ HIS WORD IN MEDITATION.

". . . they let down the pallet on which the paralytic lay." There must have been a total suspension of teaching while the roof was taken apart and the dust settled on the inside of the room. Our Lord saw a lesson in faith in the presumptuous actions of these men. Someone else would have objected, but our Lord looked beyond the interruption and saw their faith! How we would like to know just who the four men were who held the ropes while they lowered the paralytic. Stubborn love that would not take no for an answer was back of the bold action. What happened to the man who was healed when once he left the house? We could well imagine, but that really is all we can do. It sounds almost saccharine to say that something more wonderful has happened to every Christian, but it has!

Pause—wait—think—then express yourself in thoughtful praise or thanks.

9. READ HIS WORD FOR PETITIONS.

In this familiar story, just beneath the surface, are requests we can make in prayer: (1) Give me as much concern about the spiritual impotence of my friends as these men were with this man's physical need. (2) How I want such a determination in meeting my Lord in his word. (3) Keep me aware that unless I bring men to you they will never be healed. (4) Make me innovative and creative in my attempts to bring men to you. (5) How I need the boldness of these men in meeting human needs. (6) Any way I can get into the presence of your Son I want to do it. (7) How good to learn that cooperation is needed to heal men. Help me with my part.

Right here add your personal requests—and his answers.

10. READ HIS WORD AND WAIT—LISTEN—GOD SPEAKS!

As Jesus spoke to this man speak to me: (1) "So many men do not care if the sick live or die—how about you?" (2) "Some things will have to be broken up to get through to me." (3) "I am still waiting to forgive sins if someone will only ask."

11. INTERCESSION FOR THE LOST WORLD

Philippines — Points for prayer: (1) Missionary vision of the Filipino Church is growing—now with 13 sending agencies and 170 missionaries serving in other lands or areas. (2) Missions—many new groups and missionaries have entered the land of late, and now there are around 1,500. There are more opportunities than there are laborers to use them—in evangelism, church planting, pioneer work, as well as in teaching and helping in the churches. There are many needs in Bible translation work, student outreach and in technical ministries such as radio.

12. SING PRAISES TO OUR LORD.

He all my griefs has taken, and all my sorrows borne;
In temptation He's my strong and mighty tower;
I have all for Him forsaken, and all my idols torn
From my heart, and now He keeps me by His power.

Though all the world forsake me, and Satan tempt me sore,
Through Jesus I shall safely reach the goal:
He's the Lily of the Valley, the Bright and Morning Star,
He's the fairest of ten thousand to my soul.

1. PRAISE GOD FOR WHO HE IS.

"O give thanks to the Lord, call on his name; make known his deeds among the peoples! Sing to him, sing praises to him, tell of all his wonderful works!" (Psalm 105:1, 2). These verses seem to explain just what I want to do each time I come before you in personal worship. The one quality of yourself that stands out so prominently is that you are worthy of all gratitude. The reasons for such an expression are in what you have done for each man upon this earth. How I would love to stand on a promontory somewhere and make known your deeds among all the peoples of the earth. I am sure every missionary has also felt the same way. At least I can tell you in deepest of feeling how much I appreciate all the uncounted, and sometimes unknown, blessings you have sent into my life. Songs do seem to express more adequately the thanks we have to give you.

Express yourself in adoration for this quality of God.
Speak it audibly or write out your praise in your own devotional journal.

2. PRAISE GOD FOR WHAT HE MEANS TO ME.

Just for me. There is no effort here. This seems to be so naturally spontaneous. Let me express thanks for several of your benefits and associate each one with a quality of yourself! (1) Thank you for creating me with your own capacities. What infinite love is in this. (2) Thank you for chastening me when I think and act by Satan's direction. What care and concern is in this. (3) Thank you for forgiveness each time I sin and each time I repent. I can hardly comprehend such mercy! (4) Thank you for your direction in my service for you — how well you know me and just where I could best serve. (5) Thank you for the means of communication now available to us. What an open door you have given us that your deeds might be made known to all peoples!

How do you personally relate to the deeds of God, and God who is a worker?
Speak it out or write it out. It is *so important* that you establish *your own* devotional journal.

3. CONFESSION OF SIN

It seems to me there is constantly someone who is ready to deceive me. In every move I make toward you, he offers an option of deception. As an example: (1) If I praise you for creating me, he is ready to explain such on a natural level. He is a liar and speaks nonsense. (2) If I thank you for chastening me, he says I do not deserve it, or there is no hope for such a sinner — both are lies. I am not ignorant of his devices, that liar! (3) If I praise you for forgiveness the deceiver says: "Have you really repented adequately?" — that liar! I could never repent with total knowledge — it is in my Lord's knowledge and willingness to accept my willingness that I have hope. (4) If I thank you for direction in service he is there to point out that it would all have happened in the same way anyway — just a coincidence. Satan, I rebuke you and resist you! I have read his word who is truth. You can call answers to prayer a coincidence if you want to, you know you are wrong — and so do I!

What personal sins do you want to confess? We *must* speak them to remove them.
Do it! *Now.* There is no one else you have sinned against more than God. Tell him so!

4. SING A PRAYER TO GOD.

Praise Him! praise Him!
Jesus, our blessed Redeemer!
Sing, O Earth, His wonderful love proclaim!

Hail Him! hail Him! highest archangels in glory;
Strength and honor give to His holy name!

Open your hymn book and sing the rest of the verses — or even sing another prayer song.

5. READ HIS WORD TO HIM!

His Word

[5]When Jesus saw their faith, he said to the paralytic, "Son, your sins are forgiven."

[6]Now some teachers of the law were sitting there, thinking to themselves, [7]"Why does this fellow talk like that? He's blaspheming! Who can forgive sins but God alone?"

[8]Immediately Jesus knew in his spirit that this was what they were thinking in their heart, and he said to them, "Why are you thinking these things? [9]Which is easier: to say to the paralytic, 'Your sins are forgiven,' or to say, 'Get up, take your mat and walk'? [10]But that you may know that the Son of Man has authority on earth to fogive sins . . ." He said to the paralytic, [11]"I tell you, get up, take your mat and go home."   — *Mark 2:5-11, NIV*

Read His Word to Him.

The words of our Lord seem so strange. "My son, your sins are forgiven." What does the forgiveness of sins have to do with palsy? How are the two related? Or are they related? If they were not related before, they are now. Jesus came to forgive sins — he uses any and all occasions to teach this blessed truth. There were two impossibilities happening before their eyes. Only God can forgive sins, and only God can suspend or change his laws and heal.

Both are being done in their presence. There could be only one conclusion: *God is in their midst!* What a beautiful condescension and indentification to call himself "the son of man." Jesus is saying: "You can see one prerogative of God—healing—you can accept the other by faith—the forgiveness of sins." What wonderful credentials were the miracles.

Please express your response to this beautiful text. Put your expression in your own prayer diary.

6. READ HIS WORD FOR YOURSELF.

What a strong encouragement is this text for me! When Jesus saw they accepted his deity he immediately could and did forgive the paralytic. Dear Lord, I know you respond to me in the same way. I do sorely need forgiveness. It is my confidence in your Son as yourself in bodily form that commends me as a candidate for forgiveness. The scribes were students (scholars) of your law. They were right. Only God can forgive sins. But look again dear brother—Jesus *is God!* I believe you see and read the questioning of my heart.

Pause in his presence and either audibly or in written form tell him all his word means to you.

7. READ HIS WORD FOR YOURSELF.

(1) Thank you for my Lord's definition of faith. (2) Thank you for the tender words, "My Son"—(although Jesus could easily have been younger than the paralytic). (2) Thank you that Jesus knows all men feel guilty and he wants to remove such guilt. (3) Thank you for people who think—even as the scribes. (4) Thank you for the omniscient perception of my Lord—even today—even of me. (5) Thank you for our Lord's definition of the function of the heart, i.e., to question, or reason.

Give yourself to your own expression of gratitude—write it or speak it!

8. READ HIS WORD IN MEDITATION.

"I say to you, rise, take up your pallet and go home." It would surely seem that anyone our Lord so restored to health would be his best witness for the rest of his life. But we have been raised from death in trespasses and sins—how do we relate? Can we visualize what happened when this man who had been so sick for so long walked into his house? Two reactions would be expected: (1) *Surprise!* The incongruity that one who had been so weak, so unable, was new, well and walking. How could it be? (2) *Disbelief.* Man minus an acceptance of the supernatural is going to work out an explanation that fits his naturalistic presuppositions.

Pause—wait—think—then express yourself in thoughtful praise or thanks.

9. READ HIS WORD FOR PETITIONS.

What a wonderful transaction occurs in these verses. It is our desire to enter fully into their meaning through prayer: (1) Open my mouth to sometimes say the totally unexpected—but needed thing. (2) My Lord saw beneath the surface the deep need of this man. I want that capacity. (3) May I receive the obvious conclusion that Jesus was indeed divine. (4) How can I be as sensitive to the thoughts and motives of men as my Lord? (5) Deepen my worship of this One who is obviously worthy. (6) I want to be as obedient, even in impossible situations, as was this man.

Please, please remember these are prayers—speak them—reword them!

10. READ HIS WORD AND WAIT—LISTEN—GOD SPEAKS!

The paralytic never forgot the words of your Son. Impress these words on my heart: (1) "How I would like to speak forgiveness to every son of Adam." (2) "I still know the contents of the hearts of all men." (3) "Take home the evidence of the healing of your heart."

11. INTERCESSION FOR THE LOST WORLD

Philippines — Points for prayer: (1) *Literature* is extensively used and is largely run by Filipino Christians. Pray for the publishing and distribution ministries. There are severe difficulties with the distribution of Bibles, and there is a great lack of Scriptures. Pray for the speedy removal of these difficulties. Government censorship also delays publication of needed literature. (2) *Bible translation* is being undertaken in 54 languages. Most of these languages are fairly small.

12. SING PRAISES TO OUR LORD.

That name I fondly love to hear,
It never fails my heart to cheer,
Its music dries the falling tear;
Exalt the name of Jesus.

"Jesus," oh, how sweet the name!
"Jesus," ev'ry day the same;
"Jesus," let all saints proclaim
Its worthy praise forever.

WEEK THIRTY-NINE — TUESDAY

1. PRAISE GOD FOR WHO HE IS.

"Glory in his holy name; let the hearts of those who seek the Lord rejoice! Seek the Lord and his strength, seek his presence continually!" (Psalm 105:3, 4). This is just what I try to do each day. How I do want to characterize yourself. I want to hold up each attribute and shout it for joy! As much as in me is I want to honor and magnify your name in my mind and heart and life. I seek you in so many ways: I know my feverish efforts to prepare an adequate lesson or sermon is but a reaching out after you. Trying to find fulfillment in those with whom I live and work is another form of seeking (in the wrong place) for the only one who can satisfy. It is your strength, your presence and I need and want. Where shall we find your strength? To where shall we go to find your presence?

Express yourself in adoration for this quality of God.
Speak it audibly or write out your praise in your own devotional journal.

2. PRAISE GOD FOR WHAT HE MEANS TO ME.

Just for me. It is good to answer personally the two questions asked in the above time of praise. I find your strength so well described in the experience of others: Peter was so often without strength. He ran out of all resources several times. In his cry, "Lord, save me," we are hearing a man seeking you. I wonder why our Lord asked Peter to walk on the water? I wonder why Peter wanted to walk on the water? If such a miracle was to happen it would be by our Lord's strength and presence. In Peter's curses and denials we see the total loss of his courage and hope. How could the same man a few weeks later stand before the Sanhedrin and amaze them with his boldness? It was Peter's practicing the presence of the Lord. It was not that he *had* been with the Lord; the Lord was with him at the time. It is those who seek his presence continually that have the joy and strength of the Lord!

How do you personally relate to the presence of God, and God who is present?
Speak it out or write it out. It is *so important* that you establish *your own* devotional journal.

3. CONFESSION OF SIN

There *are* 365 sins to confess this year! Our sin is related to our praise—strange! Even as we lift our hearts in adoration we face a need. A need to more adequately and openly praise your name. Much confession is an inverted form of praise. I want to clear away anything that hinders my expression from being totally genuine. Forgive my unwillingness to seek you. I know right where you can be found. There are very definable steps in finding you: (1) You are found first right on the other side of the sin that lost your presence. Right on the other side of the confession and repentance of that sin is yourself! Bless your holy name! (2) You then appear on every page of your book, the Bible. I couldn't find you anywhere I read, but now you look out from behind every verse. (3) I see you in all the world around me. The colors are brighter, the sun is warm, the water is refreshing, my heart does rejoice!

What personal sins do you want to confess? We *must* speak them to remove them.
Do it! *Now.* There is no one else you have sinned against more than God. Tell him so!

4. SING A PRAYER TO GOD.

I stand on the mountain of blessing at last,
No cloud in the heavens a shadow to cast;
His smile is upon me, the valley is past,
For He is so precious to me.

For He is so precious to me, . . .
For He is so precious to me; . . .
'Tis Heaven below My Redeemer to know,
For He is so precious to me.

Open your hymn book and sing the rest of the verses—or even sing another prayer song.

5. READ HIS WORD TO HIM!

His Word

9 Jesus stepped into a boat, crossed over and came to his own town. ²Some men brought to him a paralytic, lying on a mat. When Jesus saw their faith, he said to the paralytic, "Take heart, son; your sins are forgiven."

³At this, some of the teachers of the law said to themselves, "This fellow is blaspheming!"

⁴Knowing their thoughts, Jesus said "Why do you entertain evil thoughts in your hearts? ⁵Which is easier: to say, 'Your sins are forgiven,' or to say, 'Get up and walk'? ⁶But so that you may know that the Son of Man has authority on earth to forgive sins. . . ." Then he said to the paralytic, "Get up, take your mat and go home." ⁷And the man got up and went home. ⁸When the crowd saw this, they were filled with awe; and they praised God, who had given such authority to men.
— *Matthew 9:1-8, NIV*

¹²He got up, took his mat and walked out in full view of them all. This amazed everyone and they praised God, saying, "We have never seen anything like this!"
— *Mark 2:12, NIV*

(Cf. Luke 5:17-26).

Read His Word to Him.

If it were not for my joy and desire to worship you and to honor your word as the very expression of yourself, I would have ceased these words long ago. But it is a privilege to pause here before you and absorb the meaning of every word from your book. It is more than interesting that all the records speak of the faith of the four men who brought the man and not of the faith of the sick man.

Please express your response to this beautiful text. Put your expression in your own prayer diary.

6. READ HIS WORD FOR YOURSELF.

I have applied the general principle to myself in the above section at the same time I have hoped to be representative of all men. I believe what you do for me you can do for all. Just now I want to see what he is doing for me: (1) The healing of Jesus — and thus a display of his divine credentials was presented in the presence of "Pharisees and teachers of the law sitting by, who had come from every village of Galilee and Judea and from Jerusalem" (Luke 5:17a). What was their response to what they saw and heard? "And amazement seized them all, and they glorified God and were filled with awe, saying, 'We have seen strange things today.'"

Pause in his presence and either audibly or in written form tell him all his word means to you.

7. READ HIS WORD IN THANKSGIVING.

(1) Thank you for the power, or authority that was so wonderfully present to heal. (2) Thank you that when we have faith nothing, or no one can hinder us from encountering yourself and your Son. (3) Thank you for the presence of my Lord today — I can accept him *now*! (4) Thank you for innovation and the unusual that focus attention on my Lord. (5) Thank you for the willingness of Jesus to challenge those who questioned him. (6) Thank you that my Lord has not lost his capacity to read my thoughts. (7) Thank you for the praise and thanksgiving expression of the man who was healed.

Give yourself to your own expression of gratitude — write it or speak it!

8. READ HIS WORD IN MEDITATION.

"And amazement seized them all, and they glorified God and were filled with awe, saying, 'We have seen strange things today.'" How wonderfully good are these words — they give us a very close insight to the reaction of the persons who were "up close" to our Lord and his miracles. Luke's expression: *"amazement seized them"* is such a strong description. Such amazement didn't happen to just a few it "seized them all." How careful our Lord was to transfer the praise from himself to God. At the same time, it soon became apparent to the perceptive observer that Jesus and God were one in the same person. People were not just respectful, they were *"filled with awe."* How I do rejoice in these expressions — they say just what I want to about my Lord!

Pause — wait — think — then express yourself in thoughtful praise or thanks.

9. READ HIS WORD FOR PETITIONS.

In these alternate accounts of this wonderful miracle there are points for prayer: (1) How I want to be a part of the unusual that calls attention to the deity of my Lord. (2) How interesting that the forgiveness of the sins of this sick man was contingent on the faith of his friends — so it is today. (3) Since the mind is equated here by our Lord with the heart — how I do need to guard my thoughts. (4) The example of the response of the crowd says much to me — all men are not opposed to our Lord. (5) How widespread was the influence of my Lord — how complete was his answer to those who came. How I long for him to have such influence today.

Right here add your personal requests — and his answers.

10. READ HIS WORD AND WAIT — LISTEN — GOD SPEAKS!

Speak to me in my need as you did to this man in his need: (1) "My power to heal the needs of men is still present." (2) "You can find a way to reach the needs of men if you will." (3) "Your sins are forgiven on my merit and authority today as then."

11. INTERCESSION FOR THE LOST WORLD

Philippines — Point for prayer: (1) *Student ministry* among the 1,500,000 students in the many universities has developed well despite the strong leftist element. Pray for the development of strong witnessing groups in the universities.

12. SING PRAISES TO OUR LORD.

Amazing grace! how sweet the sound,
That saved a wretch like me!

I once was lost, but now am found,
Was blind, but now I see.

1. PRAISE GOD FOR WHO HE IS.

"Praise the Lord! O give thanks to the Lord, for he is good; for his steadfast love endures for ever! Who can utter the mighty doings of the Lord, or show forth all his praise?" (Psalm 106:1, 2). What an appropriate scripture to express adoration to your holy name! I will indeed give thanks to you and acknowledge your goodness to me. Thank you for matching my needs, and the needs of all men with just those attributes of your character which satisfy our needs. As example: We have an insatiable appetite for discovery. We are like the Athenians; we have a desire to be "always telling or hearing something new." In the magnificent complex world you have created there is something new and exciting for our discovery every day we live. However, an investigation of the creation without a recognition of the Creator becomes a meaningless pursuit! I see your goodness, wisdom and power in all you have made—praise and thanks be to you.

Express yourself in adoration for this quality of God.
Speak it audibly or write out your praise in your own devotional journal.

2. PRAISE GOD FOR WHAT HE MEANS TO ME.

I do want to put into words some of your "mighty doings" and tell you just how much I appreciate and praise you: (1) You have created me and all men with the capacity to put into words the deepest thoughts of both our hearts and your heart. Language is an expression and extension of your very self. No animal you have created can express itself in words. Language is the gift of your very nature. It is an expression of intelligence, the essence of your nature. I am just overwhelmed in wonder at such a gift. (2) You have created me with the capacity of enjoyment of the beautiful. Animals have no aesthetic appreciation. And oh how you have satisfied this capacity! The intricate detail, the lovely colors, the satisfying fragrances, the expanse and perspective of all your handiwork is a joy to my heart! Praise you forever.

How do you personally relate to the goodness of God, and God who is Good?
Speak it out or write it out. It is *so important* that you establish *your own* devotional journal.

3. CONFESSION OF SIN

How is it that I do not always feel so glad, so full of joy of the Lord? It is because I believe Satan's lie that I am some type of an educated, sophisticated animal! Animals have no conscience. I try to live at times as if I had no conscience. I know that man has given this heavenly umpire a wrong set of rules, and like all good umpires he "calls 'em like he sees 'em." If he doesn't have your rules he can't call an infraction of your rules. But I *do* have your rules. I do believe your rules. My conscience reminds me I have violated all that is good and holy and right. I agree; I want to repent! I want to change, and praise your name, I can look back over a record of years and see that I have changed! But I am always in need of adjustment —a daily adjustment—it is no burden to ask for forgiveness; it is a necessity gladly received!

What personal sins do you want to confess? We *must* speak them to remove them.
Do it! *Now.* There is no one else you have sinned against more than God. Tell him so!

4. SING A PRAYER TO GOD.

Sweet are the promises,
Kind is the word,
Dearer far than any message man ever heard;
Pure was the mind of Christ,
Sinless I see;

He the great example is, and pattern for me.
Where . . . He leads I'll follow,
Follow all the way.
Where . . . He leads I'll follow,
Follow Jesus ev'ry day.

Open your hymn book and sing the rest of the verses—or even sing another prayer song.

5. READ HIS WORD TO HIM!
His Word

[9] As Jesus went on from there, he saw a man named Matthew sitting at the tax collector's booth. "Follow me," he told him, and Matthew got up and followed him.
— *Matthew 9:9, NIV*

[13] Once again Jesus went out beside the lake. A large crowd came to him, and he began to teach them. [14] As he walked along, he saw Levi son of Alphaeus sitting at the tax collector's booth. "Follow me," Jesus told him, and Levi got up and followed him.
— *Mark 2:13, 14, NIV*

[27] After this, Jesus went out and saw a tax collector by the name of Levi sitting at his tax booth. "Follow me," Jesus said to him, [28] and Levi got up, left everything and followed him.
— *Luke 5:27, 28, NIV*

Read His Word to Him.

Dear Lord, how pointed and full of meaning is your calling of Matthew Levi. There could hardly be a more Jewish man than this one. We could think with the commentators of all the possible associations Levi had with you before you confronted him at his place of business. Perhaps all of them are right, or none of them are right. The facts are: Matthew got up, left everything and followed you. Even more important: he continued to follow you. Sometime later our Lord chose him with eleven others to be one of his apostles. The longer Levi followed, the more sure he was he had made the right choice.

Please express your response to this beautiful text. Put your expression in your own prayer diary.

6. READ HIS WORD FOR YOURSELF.

How true it is that we never know who it is that sits behind a desk in any place of business. Matthew was an exceptional student of the Old Testament. He referred to the Old Testament more than ninety times in his gospel. Dear Lord, help me to be your instrument in calling someone today from a place of business to leave all and follow you. There are thousands of men and women who are sick and tired of the useless routine of their job—they are hoping—perhaps only subconciously, for someone to come and call them out. Could it be that leaving all could also mean leaving all the wrong attitudes that hinder our following him right in the place where we work?

Pause in his presence and either audibly or in written form tell him all his word means to you.

7. READ HIS WORD IN THANKSGIVING.

(1) Thank you for Jesus' penetrating look—he looks into the heart. (2) Thank you Jesus does not quibble about what kind of a job we have. (3) Thank you for those all encompassing two words: "Follow me"! (4) Thank you for daring courageous men who will get up and go. (5) Thank you for careful precise students who will get up and go. (6) Thank you for older men who have been in business for several years who will leave all and follow him. (7) Thank you that all these men are the same man—his name is Matthew Levi.

Give yourself to your own expression of gratitude—write it or speak it!

8. READ HIS WORD IN MEDITATION.

"... *Matthew got up and followed him.*" This is recorded by the man who did it. Matthew tries to be as objective as he can. It is the other writers, Mark and Luke, who call him Matthew *Levi*. Was there something in his life that caused him to withhold the name of the father of the Jewish priesthood? When our Lord spoke, Matthew was ready. The tax collector was a man of decision and resolve. When he committed himself he did not look back. We could pose several possible reasons: (1) Here was an opportunity to clear his conscience once and for all. (2) He had followed the activities of this Nazarene and with Matthew's knowledge of the Old Testament he was convinced Jesus was the Christ. (3) Pressures were so high in his job he was glad for a way out. Perhaps none of these relate to the real reason but they do speak to our own hearts.

Pause—wait—think—then express yourself in thoughtful praise or thanks.

9. READ HIS WORD FOR PETITIONS.

Oh, for the joy of decision seen in the example of Levi! (1) Keep me aware of your involvement in my life long before you called me. (2) Keep my heart sensitive enough that I can answer when you call. (3) Break me away from the love of money. (4) May I always remember that the whole Christian life is summed up in following Jesus. (5) Open my heart to these words: "... left everything and followed him." (6) Give me the wisdom I need to apply the scriptures I have learned to following your Son. (7) May the example of Matthew never leave me.

Please, please remember these are prayers—speak them—reword them!

10. READ HIS WORD AND WAIT—LISTEN—GOD SPEAKS!

Call me again through these verses: (1) "All men have 'a booth' from which I call them—understand them as my Son did and I will call them through you." (2) "My calling is as continual as the need." (3) "Many are called but only a few hear my voice."

11. INTERCESSION FOR THE LOST WORLD

Philippines — Point for prayer: (1) *Minority groups: The Chinese* number 500,000 but only 3% are Christian. There are over 40 Chinese churches in the Manila area that are strong and with a missionary vision, but many are still in darkness.

12. SING PRAISES TO OUR LORD.

Does sadness fill my mind,
A solace here I find:
May Jesus Christ be praised;

Or fades my earthly bliss,
My comfort still is this;
May Jesus Christ be praised.

WEEK THIRTY-NINE — THURSDAY

1. PRAISE GOD FOR WHO HE IS.

"My heart is steadfast, O God, my heart is steadfast! I will sing and make melody! Awake my soul! Awake, O harp and lyre! I will awake the dawn!" (Psalm 108:1, 2) How often have I felt even as the psalmist—how more often I have not—you know and you understand better than I. Confidence, assurance and trust; all of these are qualities

I want to find in my heart, in my attitude toward you. Steadfastness or confident trust is a result of accepting the full weight of evidence. These words of the psalmist describe the attitude all men should have. Considering all you are and have done, this is but a personable expression of our joy and praise.

Express yourself in adoration for this quality of God.
Speak it audibly or write out your praise in your own devotional journal.

2. PRAISE GOD FOR WHAT HE MEANS TO ME.

Just for me. Praise you for all you mean to me. The weight of some responsibility holds us down. Why? Is not your greatness and goodness more important than any task we have to perform? Indeed! "Awake thy soul." Songs and expressions of joy are a natural response to your goodness and mercy! All men and women can be musicians in imagination and lift the harp and lyre to express their melody of adoration. How shall I respond to that beautiful little phrase: "I will awake the dawn"? I could read

ten books or more and see what others have said, but I want this to be a personal expression of my praise to you. Is this the dawn of my true awareness of your greatness? Surely this is a dawn that needs awakening. Is this the dawn of that eternal day and my confidence in its appearance? Is this the dawn that even now breaks in the eastern sky to tell me of your faithfulness for the ten thousand days I have enjoyed from your hand? Yea, it is all this, and more!

How do you personally relate to the joy of the Lord, and God who is Joy?
Speak it out or write it out. It is *so important* that you establish *your own* devotional journal.

3. CONFESSION OF SIN

In the presence of praise I am silent. When I should be shouting for joy, I am sad. Why? Selfishness—a real conflict of interest! Turn me, oh turn me from the absorbing attraction of this world, in whatever form. Praise and wonder not only represent a right attitude—all other attitudes are involved. Is it a sin not to be delighted when someone has died to give you life? Is it wrong to remain aloof when all the riches of heaven have been poured at

your feet? It is not wrong; it is monstrously sinful! Of this sin I am guilty! I am *not* discussing emotion; I *am* discussing a fundamental attitude expressed in emotion. If I do not from time to time "make melody and sing," if I seldom or ever want to "awake the dawn" am I not in the "bond of iniquity," the worst of sin: ingratitude! Forgive, forgive me! Awake the dawn of unending joy in your presence!

What personal sins do you want to confess? We *must* speak them to remove them.
Do it! *Now.* It is *so important* that you establish *your own* devotional journal.

4. SING A PRAYER TO GOD.

I yielded myself to His tender embrace,
And faith taking hold of the Word,
My fetters fell off, and I anchored my soul;
The "Haven of Rest" is my Lord.

I've anchored my soul in the "Haven of Rest,"
I'll sail the wide seas no more;
The tempest may sweep o'er the wild, stormy deep,
In Jesus I'm safe evermore.

Open your hymn book and sing the rest of the verses—or even sing another prayer song.

5. READ HIS WORD TO HIM!

His Word

[10]While Jesus was having dinner at Matthew's house, many tax collectors and "sinners" came and ate with him and his disciples.
— *Matthew 9:10, NIV*

[15]While Jesus was having dinner at Levi's house, many tax collectors and "sinners" were eating with him and his

disciples, for there were many who followed him.
— *Mark 2:15, NIV*

[29]Then Levi held a great banquet for Jesus at his house, and a large crowd of tax collectors and others were eating with them.
— *Luke 5:29, NIV*

Read His Word to Him.

I imagine you were most pleased when Matthew decided to celebrate his decision to follow your Son. It must have been a real joy to your heart to find this man who wanted to share his discovery and decision with his fellow tax collectors. Jesus did indeed become a friend of the poorest

people: prostitutes, lepers, tax-collectors, and other sinners not mentioned by profession. Dear Lord, how is it we do not follow him in this practice? Are we just religious—like some others who associated with Jesus? Dear Lord, deliver me! Jesus attended the feast Matthew gave.

Please express your response to this beautiful text. Put your expression in your own prayer diary.

WEEK THIRTY-NINE — THURSDAY

6. READ HIS WORD FOR YOURSELF.

In answer to the above question: I believe I would indeed go! For today—if one of the Mafia was called to follow our Lord and he gave a great feast in his house and there was a large company of other Mafia members and other sinners seated at the table and also mingling in the rooms of his house, would I go? What was the attraction at Matthew's feast? It was Jesus. It was the possibility of meeting the Messiah. Most, if not all, who attended Matthew's feast were Jews. What would be the attraction at the Mafia feast? Of course, it is easy to say that Jesus would be the attraction, but how can we present him in the same attractive manner that Matthew did? Dear Lord, you know I am reading these verses into my own experience—help me!

Pause in his presence and either audibly or in written form tell him what his word means to you.

7. READ HIS WORD IN THANKSGIVING.

(1) Thank you for Levi who entered a new priesthood. (2) Thank you for the joy that filled Matthew's heart. (3) Thank you this man wanted, indeed he *must* share his joy with others. (4) Thank you his decision included his money. (5) Thank you that he had not talked first to the Pharisees about his decision to give a feast. (6) Thank you that food was a part of fellowship with Jesus. (7) Thank you for our Lord's openness and freedom in making choices—may his choices be mine and I know such openness and freedom will also be mine.

Give yourself to your own expression of gratitude—write it or speak it!

8. READ HIS WORD IN MEDITATION.

". . . and there was a large company of tax collectors and others sitting at the table with them." What a celebration it was! Matthew had found the Messiah and he wanted everyone to know about it! There are several interesting factors in this celebration: (1) He was willing to spend a good deal of money to let people know about Jesus. We can only estimate the financial outlay involved in the feast. (2) He wanted to "go public" in his expression of discovery. He did just what our Lord recommended: he wanted to shout it from the housetops. (3) He knew the social risks involved. The criticism of the Pharisees was not unexpected. This was just a part of being willing to let every one know that he was leaving all and following him. (4) Perhaps he knew there were other tax collectors who were as frustrated as he was—they too could make such a decision; he wanted to help them with it.

Pause—wait—think—then express yourself in thoughtful praise or thanks.

9. READ HIS WORD FOR PETITIONS.

Did Levi pray before he called the feast for Jesus? What were his requests? (1) I want to invite Jesus again and again to dine with me. (2) Help me to have ears to hear his every word. (3) Open the hearts of the friends I have invited to this feast. (4) May the disciples not misunderstand my motives. (5) May my former sin not hinder my testimony. (6) May many more accept him as Messiah because of what happens tonight. (7) Deepen my commitment to him as a result of what I see and hear at this feast.

Right here add your personal requests—and his answers.

10. READ HIS WORD AND WAIT—LISTEN—GOD SPEAKS!

Speak to me—as you doubtless did to Levi: (1) "Knife and fork evangelism will work today if Jesus is at the dinner." (2) "Spare no expense—eternal people are more important than money." (3) "Sinners are attracted to someone who spends his money on them."

11. INTERCESSION FOR THE LOST WORLD

Philippines — Points for prayer: (1) *Minority groups: The Muslims*—there has been work among them but with little response, though praise God that there are five or so congregations made up almost entirely of converted Muslims. Much of the thrust has been among the pagan and Roman Catholic people in the area. Work among Muslims has been greatly hindered by the continuing guerrilla war in which the Muslims seek to secede. Pray for peace and open hearts among these Muslim people. Pray also for the new outreach of missionaries to Muslims in Mindanao—there are several translation teams among them.

12. SING PRAISES TO OUR LORD.

There is never a cross so heavy,
There is never a weight of woe,
But that Jesus will help to carry
Because He loveth so.

Wonderful, wonderful Jesus,
In the heart He implanteth a song:
A song of deliv'rance, of courage, of strength,
In the heart He implanteth a song.

1. PRAISE GOD FOR WHO HE IS.

"Be exalted, O God, above the heavens! Let thy glory be over all the earth! That thy beloved may be delivered, give help by thy right hand, and answer me!" (Psalm 108:5, 6). Such beautiful qualities of yourself are seen! Your power and greatness call forth praise and wonder. There is no way we could express your immense greatness; your exaltation could never be put into words. ". . . above the heavens" is much more meaningful now (or is it?) than when written. Did the psalmist know just how extensive that word "heavens" was? We could say, and do say, today "be exalted above ten million galaxies." In my estimation you are indeed so exalted! When the psalmist asks that "your glory be over the earth," I want to shout amen! I do so fully agree with him. When the term glory is used to describe "character," I agree even more!

Express yourself in adoration for this quality of God.
Speak it audibly or write out your praise in your own devotional journal.

2. PRAISE GOD FOR WHAT HE MEANS TO ME.

Just for me. To continue my praise: This is one tremendous thought: that all the attributes of yourself would be seen and appreciated over all the earth. When we remember that you are fully shown to man in the person of your son, we can more fully agree with the psalmist.

The purpose of the above praise was: "that thy beloved may be delivered, give help by thy right hand, and answer me!" This is no doubt David's request as he flees from Saul. At the same time there is so much in the expression full of meaning for me. You loved David. David felt free to use this endearing term. David knew he was loved. There is nothing for which I could more fully praise you. That you love me! Time after time you have let me know I am loved.

How do you personally relate to the exaltation of God, and God who is exalted?
Speak it out or write it out. It is *so important* that you establish *your own* devotional journal.

3. CONFESSION OF SIN

Somehow I fail to remember or I have lost my sight, or I am surely dull of hearing! I am cultivating the habit of seeing your exalted position in this world and in the heaven of heavens. But my perception does need sharpening, my habit needs to go deeper. I want to integrate a God-view, i.e., your view of everything and everyone. As you know I am so far short of this now. Please forgive me! How easy it is to exalt man, or man's accomplishments. I cry and pray with David, "That thy beloved may be delivered, give help by thy right hand, and answer me!" I am pursued by someone far worse than King Saul. How close Satan has come to overcoming me! Dear God, only you can deliver. Only your might can prevail.

What personal sins do you want to confess? We *must* speak them to remove them.
Do it! *Now.* There is no one else you have sinned against more than God. Tell him so!

4. SING A PRAYER TO GOD.

Open my eyes, that I may see
Glimpses of truth Thou hast for me;
Place in my hands the wonderful key
That shall unclasp, and set me free.

Silently now I wait for Thee,
Ready, my God, Thy will to see;
Open my eyes, illumine me, Spirit divine!

Open your hymn book and sing the rest of the verses—or even sing another prayer song.

5. READ HIS WORD TO HIM!

His Word

[11]When the Pharisees saw this, they asked his disciples, "Why does your teacher eat with tax collectors and 'sinners'?"

[12]On hearing this, Jesus said, "It is not the healthy who need a doctor, but the sick. [13]But go and learn what this means: 'I desire mercy, not sacrifice.' For I have not come to call the righteous, but sinners." — *Matthew 9:11-13, NIV*

[16]When the teachers of the law who were Pharisees saw him eating with the "sinners" and tax collectors, they asked his disciples: "Why does he eat with tax collectors and 'sinners'?"

[17]On hearing this, Jesus said to them, "It is not the healthy who need a doctor, but the sick. I have not come to call the righteous, but sinners." — *Mark 2:16, 17, NIV*

[30]But the Pharisees and the teachers of the law who belonged to their sect complained to his disciples, "Why do you eat and drink with tax collectors and 'sinners'?"

[31]Jesus answered them, "It is not the healthy who need a doctor, but the sick. [32]I have not come to call the righteous, but sinners to repentance." — *Luke 5:30-32, NIV*

Read His Word to Him.

It is a real honor to read this word as if, and indeed it is true, you were the silent listener to all I read. Since I am the sinner Jesus came to forgive and I am the sick he came to heal I can read this with real enthusiasm. The

Pharisees and their scribes are saying that association is contamination. My Lord says he comes as a doctor to the sick. He comes as a teacher to the ignorant and un-enlightened. There could be no healing without a doctor. There could be no learning without a teacher.

Please express your response to this beautiful text. Put your expression in your own prayer diary.

6. READ HIS WORD FOR YOURSELF.

How I want to learn in all its depth of significance the meaning of these words: "I desire mercy, and not sacrifice." Are you saying: "I want you to be more interested in the application of my law than repeating the words of it over and over again?" You are more interested in the meaning of the sacrifice than the sacrifice itself; why did men need to offer the millions of animals upon the thousands of altars? — because they needed mercy — the animal took the place of the worshiper; he was there at the altar to obtain mercy. You want to give man mercy and not to only move him to kill another animal.

Pause in his presence and either audibly or in written form tell him all his word means to you.

7. READ HIS WORD IN THANKSGIVING.

(1) Thank you that there was a conflict — we can learn by this experience. (2) Thank you the tax collectors and other sinners thought enough of Matthew to accept his invitation. (3) Thank you for the kindness that filled the heart of Jesus toward the house full of sinners. (4) Thank you for our Lord's characterization of himself as a physician. (5) Thank you that Jesus called himself a teacher who could change minds (the meaning of the word "repentance"). (6) Thank you my dear Lord is even now calling me to leave all that hinders my following him.

Give yourself to your own expression of gratitude — write it or speak it!

8. READ HIS WORD IN MEDITATION.

"For I came not to call the righteous, but sinners." Such a welcome word! Evidently there were men in the day of our Lord who considered themselves righteous, i.e., they believed their conduct was so exemplary that God had to give them heaven. For those who are honest with themselves no such claim would ever be made. In what way did our Savior "call" men? We can think of at least three ways: (1) He called men to himself by his teachings. In his words there was such light and hope that men wanted to leave all and hear more and more and more. So today, he calls us through what he says to us in Matthew, Mark, Luke and John. (2) He called men by his life or his conduct. There was something marvelously magnetic about his presence. (3) He called men by what he did. His miracles attracted a multitude. His death for all us sinners calls us to himself like no other one thing!

Pause — wait — think — then express yourself in thoughtful praise or thanks.

9. READ HIS WORD FOR PETITIONS.

Dear Lord, I am the sick, I am the sinner — I want to attend Matthew's banquet and petition you for my needs: (1) I have real hearing problems — open my inner ear. (2) How can I make every meal one with you? (3) It is so good to read here of the social relationships of my Lord, I want to imitate him — help me. (4) Heal the wounds of my heart — yea, give me a new heart. (5) Guard me from the infection of the spirit of this world. (6) I am so glad to claim your mercy in my stupid sinfulness. (7) Thank you for the sacrifice that makes me righteous.

Please, please remember these are prayers — speak them — reword them!

10. READ HIS WORD AND WAIT — LISTEN — GOD SPEAKS!

Speak to me through the words of your Son to the Pharisees: (1) "I am still able to heal the worst of sickness in the soul." (2) "I am still calling sinners — listen — you can hear me!" (3) "There are men just like Matthew waiting in their booth — yea, we are all so much like him — look up, I am passing by!"

11. INTERCESSION FOR THE LOST WORLD

Philippines — Point for prayer: (1) *Minority groups: The animist tribes* — pray for the work in Palawan and Luzon, in the Mangyan tribes of Mindoro and in various tribes in Mindanao. Pray about reaching out to the un-evangelized Manobo and Subanen in Mindanao, and also the Kalinga in N. Luzon. Pray for the tribal churches and their spiritual growth and raising up of mature leaders able to teach their people and prepare them for their ever increasing involvement in national life — many are primitive, timid and exploited by the lowland Filipinos.

12. SING PRAISES TO OUR LORD.

Holy, Holy, Holy, Lord God Almighty!
Early in the morning our song shall rise to Thee;

Holy, Holy, Holy! Merciful and Mighty!
God in Three Persons, blessed Trinity!

WEEK THIRTY-NINE — SATURDAY

1. PRAISE GOD FOR WHO HE IS.

"With my mouth I will give great thanks to the Lord; I will praise him in the midst of the throng. For he stands at the right hand of the needy, to save him from those who condemn him to death" (Psalm 109:30, 31). With all my heart I praise you for the following: (1) That I can even put into words the poor expression of praise I lift up to you. (2) That I have a great desire to thank you — over and over again. (3) That I am not at all ashamed to express my joy and love for you in the midst of a crowd, or in the presence of those who do not know you. (4) That I can remember so many times when you have helped the needy — not only myself. (5) When all men were condemned to eternal death you stepped in to die in our place — oh, blessed be forever your wonderful name.

Express yourself in adoration for this quality of God.
Speak it audibly or write out your praise in your own devotional journal.

2. PRAISE GOD FOR WHAT HE MEANS TO ME.

Just for me. I want to review each of these five points from a purely personal view: (1) There is no point in emphasizing what is more than obvious to you. I have a real problem expressing the true expression of praise due to yourself. Such will it ever be until I awake in his likeness. (2) As you know my heart — and I'm sure you are the only one who does — there is a continual urgency of thanksgiving within me. Not as pure and whole as I would want it, but there nonetheless. (3) I have given a word of praise and recognition of you before strangers to your name — I want to do it so much more effectively. (4) Dear Lord, how many times have you lifted me up and restored my soul! Bless your name. (5) I know I have been under the sentence of eternal death and you saved me from the guilt and power of my own sin! "With my mouth will I give great thanks to you, my Lord!"

How do you personally relate to the deliverance of God, and God who is our Salvation?
Speak it out or write it out. It is *so important* that you establish *your own* devotional journal.

3. CONFESSION OF SIN

It would be easy to review each of the above five points and know how none of them are true, i.e., in any absolute sense: (1) I do not thank you as I should. (2) The urgency of thanksgiving is not as great as you deserve. (3) I have been silent amid some who needed a word of praise about you. (4) My neediness has been because of my own selfishness. (5) I deserve to die the eternal death of hell. In the midst of this sad confession of sins comes the bright truth that you already know it and have sent your Son to forgive me. I hide nothing from you. There is no sin that cannot be removed and forgotten. Bless your wonderful name. I am so glad you are willing to accept me for my intentions and fill in the blank spaces with your mercy. Joy of all joys — I am loved and forgiven.

What personal sins do you want to confess? We *must* speak them to remove them.
Do it! *Now.* There is no one else you have sinned against more than God. Tell him so!

4. SING A PRAYER TO GOD.

Tempted and tried I need a great Savior,
One who can help my burdens to bear;
I must tell Jesus, I must tell Jesus;
He all my cares and sorrows will share.

I must tell Jesus! I must tell Jesus!
I cannot bear my burdens alone;
I must tell Jesus! I must tell Jesus!
Jesus can help me, Jesus alone.

Open your hymn book and sing the rest of the verses — or even sing another prayer song.

5. READ HIS WORD TO HIM!

His Word

[14]Then John's disciples came and asked him, "How is it that we and the Pharisees fast, but your disciples do not fast?"

[15]Jesus answered, "How can the guests of the bridegroom mourn while he is with them? The time will come when the bridegroom will be taken from them; then they will fast.

[16]"No one sews a patch of unshrunk cloth on an old garment, for the patch will pull away from the garment, making the tear worse. [17]Neither do men pour new wine into old wineskins. If they do, the skins will burst, the wine will run out and the wineskins will be ruined. No, they pour new wine into new wineskins, and both are preserved."
— *Matthew 9:14-17, NIV*
(Cf. Mark 2:18-22; Luke 5:33-39.)

Read His Word to Him.

Dear Lord, there is so much in this text I hardly know where to begin. I know you saw every one of the men who approached our Lord. Was Jesus still at the feast in Matthew's house? Had John's disciples heard about the feast and come to see if the report was true? If John's disciples had adopted the fast days of the Pharisees and the feast of Levi was held on one of those days it would indeed be a cause of concern for these conscientious disciples. Your Son always has the right, and totally convincing answer. The Pharisees fasted by law; they were motivated to fast not by need but by rule. Jesus said both feasting and fasting are a result not a cause — a means not an end. Is your Son saying: "We are as happy as the bridegroom and his guests; how can we fast?"

Please express your response to this beautiful text. Put your expression in your own prayer diary.

6. READ HIS WORD FOR YOURSELF.

My Lord says to me he came to give me a totally new garment. He came to give me new wine and a new wineskin. He came as the bridegroom. He also said that at appropriate times when he is away we will have reason to fast. Fasting is spontaneous as a result of need. But there *are* needs that move us to fast. At the same time, the joy of the new garment of undeserved righteousness and the new wine of the Holy Spirit's presence in our lives while living in our bodies is such that most of the "time" or "day" will be spent in righteousness and joy. I want to enter fully into the appreciation of this *"newness of life."* Bless your name!

Pause in his presence and either audibly or in written form tell him all his word means to you.

7. READ HIS WORD IN THANKSGIVING.

(1) Thank you for the dear sincere followers of John the Baptist. (2) Thank you they came to the one who caused the problem in their heart. (3) Thank you for the mercifully kind manner in which our Lord dealt with them. (4) Thank you for my wonderful bridegroom — most especially since all Christians are the bride. (5) Thank you for the ominous word that we are living in the day when there will be and are occasions for fasting. (6) Thank you for the best robe in my Father's house — the new garment of acceptance. (7) Thank you for the new wine of joy and righteousness in the Holy Spirit.

Give yourself to your own expression of gratitude — write it or speak it!

8. READ HIS WORD IN MEDITATION.

". . . they pour new wine into new wineskins, and both are preserved." Dear Father, how can I be a new wineskin? Both the new wine and the new wineskin are important. This is saying that both the gospel and those who contain it or carry it must be considered. If I am not fresh and elastic the new wine will cause me no end of problems. It might be appropriate to also meditate upon the little phrase ". . . no one after drinking old wine wants the new, for he says, 'The old is better.'" This is saying that it is almost impossible to break some people away from the old traditional forms.

Pause — wait — think — then express yourself in thoughtful praise or thanks.

9. READ HIS WORD FOR PETITIONS.

In the questioning of my Lord about fasting I too have some questions. I will put them in the form of petitions: (1) Open my heart that I might see the practical use of fasting in my life. (2) I do want to learn from the disciples of John the Baptist — such devout good men — teach me. (3) Speak to my heart as the bride awaiting the coming of the bridegroom — I do have areas for fasting. (4) Your Son is indeed taken away from us — does fasting relate to his return? (5) How can I relate my own personal life to the old and new garments?

Right here add your personal requests — and his answers.

10. READ HIS WORD AND WAIT — LISTEN — GOD SPEAKS!

I know you have much to say to me about fasting: (1) "Fasting has never been an end in itself — please do not make it one now." (2) "Fasting can help like nothing else in reaching some goals." (3) "Fasting can relate directly to the humbling of your heart and whole life."

11. INTERCESSION FOR THE LOST WORLD

Philippines — Point for prayer: (1) *Christian Radio* — extensive use has been made of both the radio and T.V. media by denominations and interdenominational groups. The largest work has headquarters in Manila, with a staff of over 200 in radio, printing, programming and follow-up ministries. Pray for these brethren that they may know the blessing of the Lord on their lives as they serve — often behind the scenes. Pray for the smooth running of equipment, the supply of funds and programs, for the spiritual impact in the Philippines and also in the closed lands of Asia.

12. SING PRAISES TO OUR LORD.

O worship the King, all glorious above,
And gratefully sing His wonderful love;
Our Shield and Defender, the Ancient of days,
Pavilioned in splendor, and girded with praise.

WEEK FORTY — SUNDAY

1. PRAISE GOD FOR WHO HE IS.

"Praise the Lord, I will give thanks to the Lord with my whole heart, in the company of the upright in the congregation. Great are the works of the Lord, studied by all who have pleasure in them" (Psalm 111:1, 2). Each day there are new attributes for which I can praise you. For the privilege of praise in the "company of the upright." I am glad you are a gregarious Person, i.e., one who enjoys being with people. You live in us privately, but at the same time you mix and move among the assembly as we sing your praise or read your word, or lift our hearts in prayer. Most especially as we break the loaf and drink the cup. I realize the text hints at the temple or tabernacle, but you haven't changed since the places of worship have. Another quality of yourself for which I praise you with my whole heart is that the more I study you the more I love you. You wear so well!

Express yourself in adoration for this quality of God.
Speak it audibly or write out your praise in your own devotional journal.

2. PRAISE GOD FOR WHAT HE MEANS TO ME.

Just for myself—I mix the emphasis and get more of the subjective element in the above than I really intend to. Just now I want to fasten on each of the lovely phrases of these two verses: (1) Thanks with the whole heart. My whole understanding—my whole desire to do what I understand—my whole capacity for affection—my whole sense of evaluation and admiration for what is excellent; with my whole heart I thank you. (2) I want to offer this gratitude in the presence of others. May I find occasion for doing this today. (3) I want to study in as much detail as possible your works in this world. I can begin with the creation all about me. I can look beyond to your new creation in the lives of the saved. What a wonder of praise arises even as I begin this investigation.

How do you personally relate to the works of God, and God who is the worker?
Speak it out or write it out. It is *so important* that you establish *your own* devotional journal.

3. CONFESSION OF SIN

How often should thanksgiving arise from my heart to you? I know there can be no specified number given. It does, however, seem to me that all of my life should be lived in the fundamental attitude of thanksgiving. Every day is thanksgiving. How calm and poised and cheerful would I be if I was conscious of your goodness moment by moment. Dear Lord, the above description is almost an absurdity—as you know. "For him who knows to do right and does not do it" (James 4:17). It is sin—but a sin of loss—the loss of good. The emphasis is not on the guilt, but the missed blessing. "The saddest words of tongue or pen are these words: It might have been." This is my confession as related to living a life of gratitude. Dear Lord, forgive me, but move me to change.

What personal sins do you want to confess? We *must* speak them to remove them.
Do it! *Now.* There is no one else you have sinned against more than God. Tell him so!

4. SING A PRAYER TO GOD.

"Give me thy heart," says the Father above,
No gift so precious to Him as our love,
Softly He whispers wherever thou art,
"Gratefully trust me, and give me thy heart."
"Give me thy heart,

Give me thy heart,"
Hear the soft whisper, wherever thou art;
From this dark world He would draw thee apart,
Speaking so tenderly, "Give me thy heart."

Open your hymn book and sing the rest of the verses—or even sing another prayer song.

5. READ HIS WORD TO HIM!

His Word

5 Some time later, Jesus went up to Jerusalem for a feast of the Jews. ²Now there is in Jerusalem near the Sheep Gate a pool, which in Aramaic is called Bethesda and which is surrounded by five covered colonnades. ³Here a great number of disabled people used to lie—the blind, the lame, the paralyzed. ⁵One who was there had been an invalid for thirty-eight years. ⁶When Jesus saw him lying there and learned that he had been in this condition for a long time, he asked him, "Do you want to get well?"

⁷"Sir," the invalid replied, "I have no one to help me into the pool when the water is stirred. While I am trying to get in, someone else goes down ahead of me."

⁸Then Jesus said to him, "Get up! Pick up your mat and walk." ⁹At once the man was cured; he picked up his mat and walked.
— *John 5:1-9a, NIV*

Read His Word to Him.

How delighted I am to read this word in your presence! It is the essence of your Son's work: to make men whole! How well does the pool of Bethesda represent all men. Always so near to help and yet so far away! It is my dear

Lord who walks among the disabled, the blind, the lame and the paralyzed.

What would it be to have been an invalid for thirty-eight years? Jesus wanted to find out. He didn't need to ask, but he did. When natural means would supply the answer he obtained the answer by natural means.

Please express your response to this beautiful text. Put your expression in your own prayer diary.

6. READ HIS WORD FOR YOURSELF.

How good to know Jesus is alive today! He yet mingles among men on the five porches of life. In my life he meets me in the following places: (1) The porch of the morning — I am glad to meet him here. His healing wholeness is ever fresh and ever needed. It is easy to see him and hear him in this porch of prayer. (2) The porch of the 10 a.m. break — there is always a pause in mid-morning. It is easier to miss him here, but how good it is when I meet him. (3) The porch of noon — I want always to have lunch with my Lord. (4) The porch of the 3 p.m. break time — when I am tired, and sometimes sleepy, it is such a blessing to hear him say: "Do you *still* want to be whole?" (5) The porch of the close of the day — to close out the day with him fulfills his words, "I will give you rest for your soul."

Pause in his presence and either audibly or in written form tell him all his word means to you.

7. READ HIS WORD IN THANKSGIVING.

(1) Thank you that Jesus sought out the place of need. (2) Thank you my Lord spiritually opens blind eyes. (3) Thank you there are no crippled people in the presence of Jesus in heaven. (4) Thank you Jesus cares enough to want to know all about our needs (and we can openly tell him). (5) Thank you Jesus still asks all men: "Do you want to get well?"

Give yourself to your own expression of gratitude — write it or speak it!

8. READ HIS WORD IN MEDITATION.

"At once the man was cured; he picked up his mat and walked." The qualities of yourself are seen in your action: (1) You act "at once"; there is no hesitancy or indecision. With one exception, all the healings of my Lord were instantaneous. (The exception is in another class and has its own reasons.) (2) The illness of the man was entirely removed. He did not have faith so he had no lapse of faith and a return to the sickness. Praise your wonderful name when you remove something, it is gone! (3) Your works all carry with them the ability to do what is commanded. Jesus asked the man to walk.

Pause — wait — think — then express yourself in thoughtful praise or thanks.

9. READ HIS WORD FOR PETITIONS.

Surely there is much to learn in the area of prayer in this text: (1) Jesus saw human need in the midst of public worship — open my eyes! (2) How much like the whole world is the porch upon which a great many disabled people lie. Open my eyes to their needs. (3) I can't help everyone, but I can help someone — lead me to him. (4) Give me the grace that filled my Lord's heart as he made inquiry about the man's condition — may I do likewise. (5) Help me to ask the same kind of penetrating question my Lord asked — to those who hurt.

Please, please remember these are prayers — speak them — reword them!

10. READ HIS WORD AND WAIT — LISTEN — GOD SPEAKS!

In the midst of this incident we can yet hear the voice of Jesus speak to us: (1) "Do you really want to be made whole or only to complain about your problems?" (2) "I see everyone but I only speak to those who will hear me." (3) "I will never give a false hope to anyone who wants to be made whole."

11. INTERCESSION FOR THE LOST WORLD

Singapore — Population 2,400,000. Growth rate — 1.6%. People per sq. km. — 4,200.

Point for prayer: (1) *Singapore* has, proportionately, one of the largest Christian communities in Asia today, with many young people seeking the Lord. Most of the Protestant Churches are Bible believing and evangelistic and now number around 250. House churches are multiplying rapidly to cater for the nearly 60% of the population living in high rise flats. Pray for a continuing harvest among people of many races who are being uprooted and thrust into the modern materialistic age.

12. SING PRAISES TO OUR LORD.

My Jesus, I love Thee, I know Thou art mine,
For Thee all the follies of sin I resign;

My gracious Redeemer, my Savior art Thou;
If ever I loved Thee, my Jesus, 'tis now.

WEEK FORTY — MONDAY

1. PRAISE GOD FOR WHO HE IS.

"The fear of the Lord is the beginning of wisdom; a good understanding have all those who preach it. His praise endures forever" (Psalm 111:10). This has been a favorite verse for a multitude of people for many years. I do want to enter into a deeper appreciation of yourself through this open door. Perhaps I can reason from the result back to the cause. The result of the fear of yourself is that I shall have the best use of the knowledge I possess.

I believe wisdom is the best use of knowledge. I am defining the term "fear" as *reverence* or *awe*. When I fall before you in amazement, as indeed I do, then I shall better be able to evaluate all I know of life. My reverence toward you is something I practice — it becomes a life-style. Such a concept produces a humblemindedness I surely need. The result in my own life is "good" in the sense that I cannot find such goodness anywhere else!

Express yourself in adoration for this quality of God.
Speak it audibly or write out your praise in your own devotional journal.

2. PRAISE GOD FOR WHAT HE MEANS TO ME.

Just for me. Dear Lord, I do fear you in the sense of holy reverence and amazement. I could say I fear you in the sense of being afraid if I did not know you love me with an everlasting love, or as the psalmist has said so often, "his love endures forever." Your power and majesty are not used to impress me. I am impressed because of them. Your incredible wisdom (the application of your knowledge) is not there to show me how little I know —

you have shown me and all men what you are as a fact. Our response is a result of our relationship with you. In my case I want to understand all of the characteristics or attributes of yourself I can. I shall really never be able to appreciate you as fully as I want until I arrive in the world to come. While here I want to honor and worship you. Bless your holy name.

How do you personally relate to the majesty of God, and God who is worthy of awe?
Speak it out or write it out. It is *so important* that you establish *your own* devotional journal.

3. CONFESSION OF SIN

Of course, I could say that I do not reverence you as I should, and that would by itself be a vast understatement. But it would at the same time be superficial. Somehow my reverence and respect toward you has not been integrated into my inmost being deeply enough to influence my basic attitude toward all of life. I want to practice my "fear" of yourself far more often and in many more relationships

than I have in times past. Please forgive me for what must be one of the most serious of my sins. If reverence and respect for you is the beginning of understanding then not to practice it is stupidity personified! In the eons of eternity all men and angels will praise you — I want to add my voice to them. Cleanse me and open my understanding!

What personal sins do you want to confess? We *must* speak them to remove them.
Do it! *Now.* There is no one else you have sinned against more than God. Tell him so!

4. SING A PRAYER TO GOD.

Oh, the pure delight of a single hour
That before Thy throne I spend,
When I kneel in prayer, and with Thee, my God,
I commune as friend with friend!

Draw me nearer, nearer, blessed Lord,
To the cross where Thou hast died;
Draw me nearer, nearer, nearer, blessed Lord,
To Thy precious, bleeding side.

Open your hymn book and sing the rest of the verses — or even sing another prayer song.

5. READ HIS WORD TO HIM!

His Word

The day on which this took place was a Sabbath, ¹⁰and so the Jews said to the man who had been healed, "It is the Sabbath; the law forbids you to carry your mat."

¹¹But he replied, "The man who made me well said to me, 'Pick up your mat and walk.'"

¹²So they asked him, "Who is this fellow who told you to pick up and walk?"

¹³The man who was healed had no idea who it was, for Jesus had slipped away into the crowd that was there.

¹⁴Later Jesus found him at the temple and said to him, "See, you are well again. Stop sinning or something worse may happen to you." ¹⁵The man went away and told the Jews that it was Jesus who had made him well.

— *John 5:9b-15, NIV*

Read His Word to Him.

Whereas I look back upon this incident as I read it in John's record you do not. It just happened in your frame of reference. Since there is no time with you there is no past,

present or future. When I think as you do (how poorly I do it), I do see this sign as a contemporary record for my learning. Only you can know the motives behind the words

550

of the Jews who said: "it is the Sabbath; the law forbids you to carry your mat." Their total silence about the fact that the man healed does indicate something about their hearts. Dear Lord, focus my heart on the needs of people and not on outward form. Your purpose in telling this story through John is to shock all us religious people as to the value of man above the law.

Please express your response to this beautiful text. Put your expression in your own prayer diary.

6. READ HIS WORD FOR YOURSELF.

The primary purpose of this miracle was to point away from the sign to the sign maker—even my wonderful Lord! Why did Jesus choose to walk into the area of the five porches on the Sabbath? It was only one of seven days —he could have waited one more day—the man had been there thirty-eight years already. I want to see it for what it really was: a deliberate choice on my Lord's part to teach me something. What is it? (1) The day of worship can become more important than what you do on the day. (2) The Lordship and deity of Jesus supercedes any consideration of any day. (3) Conduct has a direct bearing on our response to what Jesus has done for us: "Stop sinning or something worse may happen to you."

Pause in his presence and either audibly or in written form tell him all his word means to you.

7. READ HIS WORD IN THANKSGIVING.

(1) Thank you for the wonderful "day of rest" when we were raised up to walk in newness of life. (2) Thank you for the bold candid answer of the man who was healed. (3) Thank you that he is not named so all of us can supply our name. (4) Thank you for the obvious supernatural nature of this act. (5) Thank you that Jesus found him—he always does. (6) Thank you that Jesus connected gratitude and living with healing. (7) Thank you the lame man was ready to endanger himself to tell about Jesus.

Give yourself to your own expression of gratitude—write it or speak it!

8. READ HIS WORD IN MEDITATION.

"The man went away and told the Jews that it was Jesus who had made him well." This man felt a responsibility in two directions. He was full of joy at this healing and was drawn to the one who had made him well. At the same time, he knew the Jews had the power to make it very difficult for him socially so he felt he must tell them who it was who healed him. The man had something in his life to which our Lord pointed when he said, "stop sinning." Perhaps in this man's early life he sinned in such a manner that he found himself a cripple for life. Evidently this man sustained his wrong attitude all during those long more than thirty-eight years. Jesus is saying, "Give it up; forget about it."

Pause—wait—think—then express yourself in thoughtful praise or thanks.

9. READ HIS WORD FOR PETITIONS.

The encounter and testimony of the man made whole contains much to help us to pray: (1) Keep me in the center of spiritual need when I consider the questions of tradition. (2) How often have I emphasized the law and forgotten the purpose of the law? Remind me, dear Lord! (3) Keep me aware that the command of my Lord supersedes all other commands. (4) How could these men totally ignore this obvious miracle? There are lessons in this for me! (5) Jesus linked sin and health—I wish I knew much more about this—help me. (6) "Something worse" has happened to many who have continued in sin—keep me sensitive to this great eternal transaction.

Right here add your personal requests—and his answers.

10. READ HIS WORD AND WAIT—LISTEN—GOD SPEAKS!

There seems no way that the persons in his record can ignore your Son. I too want to confront him: (1) "I am in the crowd, but I know where you are, and I love you." (2) "Remember sin can be progressive." (3) "Your healing makes you responsible to the healer."

11. INTERCESSION FOR THE LOST WORLD

Singapore — Point for prayer: (1) *The Church in Singapore* is largely divided along ethnic lines, but an increasing number of people are using English. There is a need for more full time workers who are able to minister to the many house churches (church buildings are too expensive due to the lack of land) and really give Bible teaching. Some feel that the foreign influence in the churches is still too great and initiative is stifled.

12. SING PRAISES TO OUR LORD.

"Man of Sorrows," what a name
For the Son of God who came

Ruined sinners to reclaim!
Hallelujah! what a Savior!

WEEK FORTY — TUESDAY

1. PRAISE GOD FOR WHO HE IS.

"Blessed be the name of the Lord from this time forth and for evermore! From the rising of the sun to its setting the name of the Lord is to be praised!" (Psalm 113:2, 3).

In each of these expressions I want to find a new expression or facet of praise. I want each day to lift up a fresh quality of your value and praise you! I understand the use of the word "blessed" to refer to this very practice. I feel foolish telling all this to you, but it does me good to put it down in words. Your greatness and goodness are such that man need never exhaust the qualities of praise. As the sun begins to rise in the east we can begin our praise; as it sets in the west we are yet expressing our wonder over your divine nature. Man is constantly talking—from the rising of the sun to the setting thereof—what is he saying? He speaks what is in his heart!

Express yourself in adoration for this quality of God.
Speak it audibly or write out your praise in your own devotional journal.

2. PRAISE GOD FOR WHAT HE MEANS TO ME.

Dear Lord, such was said to you because I feel so strongly about it. I want on this day to list a few qualities that arise from my heart to you. I am poorly equipped to continue this throughout the day, but I want to develop a basic attitude of praise that could prompt pause several times through the hours of this day. (1) I bless your name for your eternal nature. It is such a strength to worship Someone who never changes! (2) Praise you for the balanced arrangement of day and night. The beauty of change in your creation is a lovely contrast to the unchangeableness of yourself. (3) Praise you that we are only living in the vestibule of your eternal temple. Somehow I believe the veil of death will open from this vestibule into the life we could never in our wildest imagination ever conceive! Keep me open and sensitive to you today.

How do you personally relate to the eternalness of God, and God who is eternal?
Speak it out or write it out. It is *so important* that you establish *your own* devotional journal.

3. CONFESSION OF SIN

So often do I confess my oft repeated sin of being taken captive. As I pause here before your throne I know (as I should have known earlier) it was my thoughts that were captivated. How I praise you that I read in your word that "every thought can be taken captive for King Jesus," or *by* my Lord. It is in the thought life the battle is won or lost. Upon what shall I meditate today? I know what you have said—I agree to it, but *how* shall I do it? This prayer time is a tremendous help, but I want to carry worship into all of life. Help me! At the opening of such a pursuit I need forgiveness and cleansing. I cannot and do not pretend with you. I name and admit each sin. I am lifted up by forgiveness. I want to remember that most growth is imperceptible—most of all by the one who is growing.

What personal sins do you want to confess? We *must* speak them to remove them.
Do it! *Now.* There is no one else you have sinned against more than God. Tell him so!

4. SING A PRAYER TO GOD.

Standing on the promises of Christ my King,
Thro' eternal ages let His praises ring;
Glory in the highest, I will shout and sing,
Standing on the promises of God.

Standing, standing,
Standing on the promises of God my Savior;
Standing, standing,
I'm standing on the promises of God.

Open your hymn book and sing the rest of the verses—or even sing another prayer song.

5. READ HIS WORD TO HIM!

[16]So, because Jesus was doing these things on the Sabbath, the Jews persecuted him. [17]Jesus said to them, "My Father is always at his work to this very day, and I, too, am working." [18]For this reason the Jews tried all the harder to kill him; not only was he breaking the Sabbath, but he was even calling God his own Father, making himself equal with God.

[19]Jesus gave them this answer: "I tell you the truth, the Son can do nothing by himself; he can do only what he sees his Father doing, because whatever the Father does the Son also does. [20]For the Father loves the Son and shows him all he does. Yes, to your amazement he will show him even greater things than these. [21]For just as the Father raises the dead and gives them life, even so the Son gives life to whom he is pleased to give it. [22]Moreover, the Father judges no one, but has entrusted all judgment to the Son, [23]that all may honor the Son just as they honor the Father. He who does not honor the Son does not honor the Father, who sent him.

[24]"I tell you the truth, whoever hears my word and believes him who sent me has eternal life and will not be condemned; he has crossed over from death to life. [25]I tell you the truth, a time is coming and has now come when the dead will hear the voice of the Son of God and those who hear will live.
— *John 5:16-25, NIV*

Read His Word to Him.

I am overcome by the power and meaning of these words! The best I can do is to read them over again three times audibly and allow them to become to me what they really are: your Son and yourself speaking to me!

Please express your response to this beautiful text. Put your expression in your own prayer diary.

6. READ HIS WORD FOR YOURSELF.

How shocking is all this section! I want to absorb all the claims of my Lord in these verses: (1) Jesus ignored human claims to authority in divine decisions. (2) Jesus opens their minds to a thought never entertained—"God works on Saturday"! Since God does and he is my Father, I will too. (3) Jesus clearly claimed equality to God. (4) Jesus said he and God were co-equal partners in all Jesus did—at the same time, all the Father did he cleared with the Son. (5) There are much greater works coming than the one you have just seen. (6) God raises the dead and so will the Son. (7) The Father has turned all judgment over to the Son (the amazement was that the Judge of every man who would ever live was standing before them!). (8) Equal honor was to be given to God and Jesus. How wonderful it is to worship you!

Pause in his presence and either audibly or in written form tell him all his word means to you.

7. READ HIS WORD IN THANKSGIVING.

(1) Thank you that right now I have eternal life—my name is already recorded in the roll call of heaven. (2) Thank you that I have passed over from eternal death to eternal life. (3) Thank you that even now the dead in trespasses are hearing his voice and being resurrected. (4) Thank you that Jesus is the judge. I am glad to commit myself to him. (5) Thank you for the promise of the resurrection of all who are in their tombs. (6) Thank you for the total confidence Jesus had in himself—all he said and all he did.

Give yourself to your own expression of gratitude—write it or speak it!

8. READ HIS WORD IN MEDITATION.

"I can do nothing on my own authority; as I hear, I judge; and my judgment is just, because I seek not my own but the will of him who sent me." It seems too bad that we have such a little time and space to consider this tremendous text. My dear Lord spoke such wonderful words. Truly, never man so spoke! I want to separate a few of the jewels here. (1) Jesus did utterly nothing on his own authority. He was in constant contact with you and acted and spoke under your direction. (2) My Lord was "tuned in" on the frequency of heaven and heard from you on every matter of judgment. (3) He was totally submissive to you in all areas of life. In word and in deed it was not his will but yours he sought throughout his life.

Pause—wait—think—then express yourself in thoughtful praise or thanks.

9. READ HIS WORD FOR PETITIONS.

Requests I find in these words of my Lord: (1) I want to share with you in the work you have for this day. (2) Open my heart to receive the demands of the deity of Jesus. (3) I want to be able to identify your work in the hearts of people. (4) Keep me aware of the tremendous authority entrusted to your Son. (5) I want to judge myself that I will not be condemned with the world. (6) I claim my possession of eternal life—open the eyes of my heart as I read your word. (7) Prepare me for the hour of resurrection.

Please, please remember these are prayers—speak them—reword them!

10. READ HIS WORD AND WAIT—LISTEN—GOD SPEAKS!

My Lord surely reaches my heart in these words: (1) "My Father is always at his work. . . ." (2) "He who does not honor the Son does not honor the Father who sent him." (3) ". . . a time is coming when all who are in their graves will hear his voice and come out."

11. INTERCESSION FOR THE LOST WORLD

Singapore — Point for prayer: (1) *Bible training* is given in seven Seminaries and Bible Schools. Many young people have gone out to serve the Lord in Singapore Churches and also to the mission field.

12. SING PRAISES TO OUR LORD.

Risen for me, risen for me,
Up from the grave He has risen for me;

Now evermore from death's sting I am free,
All because Jesus was risen for me.

WEEK FORTY — WEDNESDAY

1. PRAISE GOD FOR WHO HE IS.

"I love the Lord, because he has heard my voice and my supplication. Because he inclined his ear to me, therefore I will call on him as long as I live" (Psalm 116:1, 2). This seems an almost selfish reason for prayer. If I look behind these words to the One to whom they are directed all selfishness disappears. We lift our most personal and intimate requests to you because we know you understand as no one else ever could! Not only do your sheep know *your voice* — you know ours. Supplications are the deep needs of our lives. You are never too busy or too involved with your own thoughts to listen to our ignorant cries. There is a sympathetic personal interest in every need. You are always alertly interested in all we say.

Express yourself in adoration for this quality of God.
Speak it audibly or write out your praise in your own devotional journal.

2. PRAISE GOD FOR WHAT HE MEANS TO ME.

Just for me. There are times, many times when our requests are full of ignorance and selfishness. But you listen and do not chide us for asking. There are times when I should have been much bolder and kept on asking and kept on knocking. But regardless of how well or how poorly I prayed you always were (and are) ready to give your individual attention to what I say. This quality of yourself — along with the fact that you are able to do all things — moves me to exclaim with the psalmist "I will call on him as long as I live." I believe you are interested in all I do — the largest help I can have is to keep the communication lines up and in use every day of my life — and many times during each day.

How do you personally relate to the alertness of God, and God who is always listening?
Speak it out or write it out. It is *so important* that you establish *your own* devotional journal.

3. CONFESSION OF SIN

How often can we use the words of Romans 8:26: ". . . We know not how to pray as we ought. . . ." How I do wish I knew how to pray for all the financial transactions in my experience. The sin of it is I do not, many times, pray at all! Must I be pushed into a crisis before I pray? I want to mix prayer with my check writing — help me! How I do wish I knew how to pray about family conversation. The fact is we can talk with each other for hours and never get you into the scene. Dear God, forgive me! Somehow help me to lift my heart to you and to encourage others to lift their hearts to you in the midst of our talking to each other. Perhaps I am about to discover the meaning of the little phrase "pray without ceasing." Praise you. Cleanse me!

What personal sins do you want to confess? We *must* speak them to remove them.
Do it! *Now.* There is no one else you have sinned against more than God. Tell him so!

4. SING A PRAYER TO GOD.

Bless Thou the truth, dear Lord
To me — to me —
As Thou didst bless the bread
By Galilee;

Then shall all bondage cease,
All fetters fall;
And I shall find my peace,
My All in All.

Open your hymn book and sing the rest of the verses — or even sing another prayer song.

5. READ HIS WORD TO HIM!
His Word

[31]"If I testify about myself, my testimony is not valid. [32]There is another who testifies in my favor, and I know that his testimony about me is valid.

[33]"You have sent to John and he has testified to the truth. [34]Not that I accept human testimony; but I mention it that you may be saved. [35]John was a lamp that burned and gave light, and you chose for a time to enjoy his light.

[36]"I have testimony weightier than that of John. For the very work that the Father has given me to finish, and which I am doing, testifies that the Father has sent me. [37]And the Father who sent me has himself testified concerning me. You have never heard his voice nor seen his form, [38]nor does his word dwell in you, for you do not believe the one he sent. [39]You diligently study the Scriptures that testify about me, [40]yet you refuse to come to me to have life.

[41]"I do not accept praise from men, [42]but I know you. I know you do not have the love of God in your hearts. [43]I have come in my Father's name, and you do not accept me; but if someone else comes in his own name, you will accept him. [44]How can you believe if you accept praise from one another, yet make no effort to obtain the praise that comes from the only God?

[45]"But do not think I will accuse you before the Father. Your accuser is Moses, on whom your hopes are set. [46]If you believed Moses, you would believe me, for he wrote about me. [47]But since you do not believe what he wrote, how are you going to believe what I say?"

— John 5:31-47, NIV

Read His Word to Him.

There is so much in this text, I want to do with it what we did with yesterday's word: to read it audibly three times in your presence. To read it with real thought before your throne of grace.

Please express your response to this beautiful text. Put your expression in your own prayer diary.

6. READ HIS WORD FOR YOURSELF.

There are 16 verses in this beautiful text. There are 16 blessed truths for which I want to praise you: (1) Jesus was true because God said so. (2) Jesus agreed with God's estimate of himself. (3) John bore witness to Jesus as truth. (4) If we do not accept such testimony we will be lost. (5) We can rejoice in the light John gave concerning Jesus. (6) Jesus has a greater word or light than John — our Lord's works confirm this. (7) The Father spoke to and through the One he sent. (8) We must believe the words of our Lord to have God in us. (9) The Scriptures are full of testimony for our Lord. (10) To refuse Jesus is to refuse eternal life. (11) Jesus refused men's glory of himself. (12) We can fail to have the love of God in us. (13) Jesus came to be received as from the Father. (14) To seek one another's glory is to refuse the glory from God. (15) Moses is clear on who Jesus is. (16) If we believe Moses, we will believe Jesus.

Pause in his presence and either audibly or in written form tell him all his word means to you.

7. READ HIS WORD IN THANKSGIVING.

(1) Thank you for the convincing testimony of the deity of Jesus. (2) Thank you for the burning and shining lamp of John the Baptist. (3) Thank you for the great works of my Lord which can convince all he is your Son. (4) Thank you we have heard the voice of God and have seen the form of God in Jesus. (5) Thank you that we can have God's word living in our minds and hearts. (6) Thank you for the wonderful witness of the Scriptures concerning your Son. (7) Thank you we have been warned of the deadly danger of receiving glory from men.

Give yourself to your own expression of gratitude — write it or speak it!

8. READ HIS WORD IN MEDITATION.

"How can you believe, who receive glory from one another and do not seek the glory that comes from the only God?" Here is a *real* hindrance to faith! Indeed we could say this is the fundamental barrier to faith. It is easy to relate this to the Pharisees involved and forget the principle applies to all of us. Our trust and worship of our Lord is in the exact proportion to our pride. If we want praise for ourselves and offer the same kind of praise to those with whom we associate it will be impossible to believe One who claims total authority.

Pause — wait — think — then express yourself in thoughtful praise or thanks.

9. READ HIS WORD FOR PETITIONS.

In the testimonies about your Son I find real areas for petitions: (1) May I be willing to read and read again your testimony about your Son — and believe it! (2) How I would like to be like John — "a lamp" for you. (3) Open my mind to a deeper, fuller understanding of the works of your Son. (4) May your word dwell in me richly. (5) Enlarge my appreciation of every word of your Scriptures. (6) For every day of my life I come to you for guidance — and believe you give it. (7) Guard me from the flattery of men.

Right here add your personal requests — and his answers.

10. READ HIS WORD AND WAIT — LISTEN — GOD SPEAKS!

How I do want to hear with the inner ear your testimony: (1) "Your identity is also in my hands." (2) "Enjoy all the light I have given you." (3) "Diligently study the Scriptures — because they are your only source of faith and eternal life."

11. INTERCESSION FOR THE LOST WORLD

Singapore — Point for prayer: (1) *Young people* are open to the Gospel. It is reckoned that 30% of all university students claim to be Christian. Pray that converted young people may make a powerful impression on church and national life when their education is over — many fall away.

12. SING PRAISES TO OUR LORD.

All creatures of our God and King,
Lift up your voice and with us sing
Alleluia! Alleluia!
Thou burning sun with golden beam,

Thou silver moon with softer gleam!
O praise Him, O praise Him!
Alleluia! Alleluia! Alleluia!

WEEK FORTY — THURSDAY

1. PRAISE GOD FOR WHO HE IS.

"The Lord preserves the simple; when I was brought low, he saved me. Return, O my soul, to your rest; for the Lord has dealt bountifully with you" (Psalm 116:6, 7).

Thank you for these precious words! I realize the use of the word "simple" in this context refers to the helpless, the ignorant or the guileless. This is a general statement for encouragement as we consider your essential character, but at the same time, all men can at one time or another relate to this circumstance. Our ignorance could easily have destroyed us. We have found ourselves in a helpless circumstance — out of such you have delivered us. This kindness, this thoughtfulness, nay this *love* is the quality so much appreciated. Like David, we have felt like a willow branch hanging down. In your infinite grace you kept us from despair and saved us!

Express yourself in adoration for this quality of God.
Speak it audibly or write out your praise in your own devotional journal.

2. PRAISE GOD FOR WHAT HE MEANS TO ME.

Just for me — I am so glad to "return to my rest." The words of my Lord are speaking to my soul: "Come unto me all you who are weary and heavy laden and I will give you rest." It is only under his yoke and in his school that I can find rest. Perhaps *"restlessness"* is the best one word to describe the bondage of sin. It is good that we run out of all resources; if we didn't we might never run home. There is another motivation: we remember just who gave us the "good life" we are enjoying. "The Lord has dealt bountifully with you." Once again your goodness leads us to repentance.

How do you personally relate to the restfulness of God, and God who is rest?
Speak it out or write it out. It is *so important* that you establish *your own* devotional journal.

3. CONFESSION OF SIN

How shall I confess more or less than I have already expressed? Essentially this is a confession of my ability to forget. This is an open admission of my willingness to be deceived. Sin is offered as an escape or a diversion from the dull routine of the daily round. The bait to this trap is the strong desires already in man. I do believe worship itself could be the wonderful alternative to sin. Worship is more than prayer — it is meditation on all you offer to man in your word. Worship is spending time with you. Once time is taken, once your word is opened, once contact and communication begin all the desires of my heart are taken up in the enjoyment of worship.

What personal sins do you want to confess? We *must* speak them to remove them.
Do it! *Now.* There is no one you have sinned against more than God. Tell him so!

4. SING A PRAYER TO GOD.

Holy, Holy, Holy! Tho' the darkness hide Thee,
Tho' the eye of sinful man Thy glory may not see,

Only Thou art holy; there is none beside Thee
Perfect in pow'r, in love, and purity.

Open your hymn book and sing the rest of the verses — or even sing another prayer song.

5. READ HIS WORD TO HIM!

His Word

12 At that time Jesus went through the grainfields on the Sabbath. His disciples were hungry and began to pick some heads of grain and eat them. ²When the Pharisees saw this, they said to him, "Look! Your disciples are doing what is unlawful on the Sabbath."
— *Matthew 12:1, 2, NIV*

²³One Sabbath Jesus was going through the grainfields, and as his disciples walked along, they began to pick some heads of grain. ²⁴The Pharisees said to him, "Look, why are they doing what is unlawful on the Sabbath?"
— *Mark 2:23, 24, NIV*

Read His Word to Him.

It is no problem for you to replay this incident. I want to share as much as possible with such a recreation of what happened in that grainfield of Galilee. How is it that Peter, James, John and Andrew did not know the law well enough that their conscience would prevent them from plucking the heads of grain? How is it that once they plucked them and began eating Jesus did not say something to them? The answer is obvious: the Pharisees have made an application of your law that was not intended. Dear Lord, this is the one large problem of religious men from that day till this day. It is more than good that your Son is there to make the proper application of your law.

Please express your response to this beautiful text. Put your expression in your own prayer diary.

6. READ HIS WORD FOR YOURSELF.

Dear Lord, your disciples are still hungry and are still passing through the grainfields of life! How sorely pressed I am in the application of your word to the hungers of life! How easy it is to judge in the sense of condemnation, the actions of others in their infraction of your law. In particular is this true of special days and special religious activities. Dear Lord, I need so much the love and wisdom that so characterized your dear Son! Form without worship and purpose is an empty shell. How many times have I found this true in my own personal experience. May I listen with my heart to the words of your Son and follow with my heart his example!

It is so important that you pause in his presence
and either audibly or in written form tell him all his word means to you.

7. READ HIS WORD IN THANKSGIVING.

(1) Thank you for every day of worship—particularly the resurrection morning. (2) Thank you for the patience of my Lord in his explanation of what should have been common knowledge. (3) Thank you for the Lord of the Sabbath. (4) Thank you for hunger that can only be satisfied in your will. (5) Thank you for the humanness of this incident. I would be plucking the grain myself. (6) Thank you for the Pharisees—some of them became Christians— like Saul of Tarsus. (7) Thank you for the privilege of following Jesus today.

Give yourself to your own expression of gratitude—write it or speak it!

8. READ HIS WORD IN MEDITATION.

"Why are you doing what is not lawful to do on the Sabbath?" What *was* lawful to do on the Sabbath? The law of the Sabbath was a law of rest. What these men meant was that the disciples of Jesus were not doing on the Sabbath what they expected them to do. The disciples of Jesus were breaking the laws the fathers and grandfathers of these Pharisees had fastened on to God's Sabbath law. Jesus was to remind them that the spirit of the law was far more important than the petty regulations men had attached to it. There is so much application to this principle in my own experience. What has our Lord asked us to do on the first day of the week? The example of the early church is to meet together to break bread and to hear the word taught and preached. But where is the spirit of joy and wonder that our Lord arose on this day? Have we lost the significance of the resurrection—we could be repeating the sin of the Pharisees.

Pause—wait—think—then express yourself in thoughtful praise or thanks.

9. READ HIS WORD FOR PETITIONS.

Open my heart to the difference between religion and following my Lord: (1) I want to walk with Jesus through the very ordinary pursuits of life. (2) Worship was a way of life with my Lord—as well as public and private—I want this too. (3) I want to walk with my Lord every day—not only in the bright spring of April as here, but in the dark days of December. (4) I do want to satisfy my hunger as directed and blessed by Jesus. (5) Rest my mind and heart sufficiently that I might serve you better. (6) Check me from expecting a supernatural answer when a natural one is at hand. (7) Hold me from condemning in others what I do myself.

Please, please remember these are prayers—speak them—reword them!

10. READ HIS WORD AND WAIT—LISTEN—GOD SPEAKS!

In the actions and attitudes of these disciples speak to me: (1) "I have set you free from legalism in all its forms." (2) "If I approve of you, you need not fear what men will say." (3) "Some men will never hear or see—this must never prevent you from following me."

11. INTERCESSION FOR THE LOST WORLD

Singapore — Points for prayer: (1) *Singapore* has become one of the most strategic centers for the evangelization of Asia. A number of missionaries have gone out to other lands. The Singapore churches have the means to support them too. There are now about 50 Singaporean missionaries serving in other lands. (2) *Missions*—There are now about 188 missionaries. It is not easy to obtain visas for new missionaries if the intended work is able to be done by a Singaporean. (3) *Unreached peoples: The Muslim Malays* are not responsive and too little is done in prayer and evangelism to win them, but there have been some saved.

12. SING PRAISES TO OUR LORD.

Let ev'ry kindred, ev'ry tribe
On this terrestrial ball,
To Him all majesty ascribe,

And crown Him Lord of all,
To Him all majesty ascribe,
And crown Him Lord of all!

WEEK FORTY – FRIDAY

1. PRAISE GOD FOR WHO HE IS.

"For thou hast delivered my soul from death, my eyes from tears, my feet from stumbling; I walk before the Lord in the land of the living" (Psalm 116:8, 9). In these precious verses several characteristics of yourself appear: (1) You are interested in the personal life of every man — but in particular your children. The term "soul" refers to the whole being of the whole man. (2) You have pledged yourself to oppose our enemy and give us deliverance.

(3) You have power over death — indeed I hear your Son say: "He that liveth and believeth in me shall never die"! (4) You are touched with our feelings — our weaknesses and hurts are a concern to you. (5) You have a deliverance from tears — perhaps there are many ways you can dry our tears. (6) In this very day I can expect my feet will escape many a treacherous place because of your love.

Express yourself in adoration for this quality of God.
Speak it audibly or write out your praise in your own devotional journal.

2. PRAISE GOD FOR WHAT HE MEANS TO ME.

Just for me. With the above qualities of yourself before me how much more does the little phrase "before the Lord" mean! I live and move and have my being before you, but it is before One who: (1) has a deeper, more intimate concern than could anyone else. (2) You understand the evil one — I do not. I know I am deceived and accused, but only you can deliver me from him. I even now cast

myself upon your interest. (3) Death could be an option of this day. I do not know the day of my death, but *you* do. (4) I have cried just yesterday, and before this day is over tears could come. I know Someone who understands and cares — even yourself! (5) Keep my feet in your way. As I walk in the land of men I want to do so full of praise! I have every reason for joy!

How do you personally relate to the deliverance of God, and God who is our Deliverer?
Speak it out or write it out. It is *so important* that you establish *your own* devotional journal.

3. CONFESSION OF SIN

It would be easy to offer the antithesis of the qualities just described as a list of my sins. Such as: (1) I believed Satan's lie that "no one cares or understands" — such self-pity, such sin! (2) "There is no use, sin and Satan are too strong for me." As I express it I see over and over again the problem is selfishness. No wonder I sin when I am,

instead of you, the center of concern. (3) Do I fear death? Is there a dread that makes death something to ignore? What faithlessness! What a denial of the fundamental attraction of salvation! (4) "Don't bother me!" Let me wallow in my own hurt — another expression of ego centered worship.

What personal sins do you want to confess? We *must* speak them to remove them.
Do it! *Now.* There is no one else you have sinned against more than God. Tell him so!

4. SING A PRAYER TO GOD.

Guide me, O Thou great Jehovah
Pilgrim thro' this barren land;
I am weak, but Thou art mighty,
Hold me with Thy pow'rful hand:

Bread of Heaven,
Feed me till I want no more;
Bread of Heaven,
Feed me till I want no more.

Open your hymn book and sing the rest of the verses — or even sing another prayer song.

5. READ HIS WORD TO HIM!

His Word

[3]He answered, "Haven't you read what David did when he and his companions were hungry? [4]He entered the house of God, and he and his companions ate the consecrated bread — which was not lawful for them to do, but only for the priests. [5]Or haven't you read in the Law that on the Sabbath the priests in the temple desecrate the day and yet are innocent? [6]I tell you that one greater than the temple is here. [7]If you had known what these words mean, 'I desire mercy, not sacrifice,' you would not have condemned the innocent. [8]For the Son of Man is Lord of the Sabbath."
— *Matthew 12:3-8, NIV*

[25]He answered, "Have you never read what David did when he and his companions were hungry and in need? [26]In the days of Abiathar the high priest, he entered the

house of God and ate the consecrated bread, which is lawful only for priests to eat. And he also gave some to his companions."
[27]Then he said to them, "The Sabbath was made for man, not man for the Sabbath. [28]So the Son of Man is Lord even of the Sabbath."
— *Mark 2:25-28, NIV*

[3]Jesus answered them, "Have you never read what David did when he and his companions were hungry? [4]He entered the house of God, and taking the consecrated bread, he ate what is lawful only for priests. And he also gave some to his companions." [5]Then Jesus said to them, "The Son of Man is Lord of the Sabbath."
— *Luke 6:3-5, NIV*

Read His Word to Him.

Dear Father, I want to read these words as if you were reading them to me and we were sharing them together, which is indeed what is happening! Your Son is letting me know, and all men know what relationship we all have to the law principle. Essentially you are saying: man is more important than the law which regulates him. David's needs and the need of the priests superseded the law. Hunger, and how it is satisfied is the subject being considered. Jesus' disciples satisfied their hunger in a way that *seemed* to violate the law, but they did not violate the law. David and the temple priests did the same thing! Finally: the words of Jesus are to be accepted as authoritative since he is Lord — of the Sabbath (subject) and all other subjects. Have I spoken truly? Dear Lord, I have tried.

Please express your response to this beautiful text. Put your expression in your own prayer diary.

6. READ HIS WORD FOR YOURSELF.

The grandest lesson in this text for me is the little phrase "the Son of man is Lord . . ." He has become man to live among us; at the same time he is Lord! I want to honor him as my Lord — the Lord of all subjects under my consideration. He is also Lord of my mouth, my feet, my hands, my eyes — and the rest of my body. He is Lord in the morning, noon, afternoon and evening. He is Lord especially in my relationshps, with my wife, my fellow-workers, with strangers who meet me too. Most of all, he is Lord in satisfying my hunger (or hungers). How I want to learn what the little phrase means: "I desire mercy, not sacrifice," i.e., as related to appetite.

Pause in his presence and either audibly or in written form tell him what his word means to you.

7. READ HIS WORD IN THANKSGIVING.

(1) Thank you that I can read what David did. (2) Thank you that Jesus used your word as authoritative. (3) Thank you for the good example of David. (4) Thank you for the failure of David; inasmuch as you forgive him there is hope for me. (5) Thank you that I can be your temple today. (6) Thank you for the Sabbath rest awaiting us in heaven. (7) Thank you for my Lord, Lord of all!

Give yourself to your own expression of gratitude — write it or speak it!

8. READ HIS WORD IN MEDITATION.

"The Son of Man is Lord of the Sabbath." Whereas we believe the reference to "the Son of Man" refers to our Lord, there is a sense in which every son of man is Lord of the Sabbath law — or indeed any other law, i.e., he can decide how he will relate to the law. Man can decide to obey the law or not, but he can also decide just how his obedience will be carried out. However, we believe that in this context Jesus is saying: "I am in charge here. I'll not allow my disciples to do anything that will violate God's law. I am living by the great principle which you have not yet learned: "I desire mercy not sacrifice." How easy it is to fall into the trap of legalism!

Pause — wait — think — then express yourself in thoughtful praise or thanks.

9. READ HIS WORD FOR PETITIONS.

How I do want to learn from the principles given by my Lord. (1) Keep me aware of the superiority of human need. (2) Things are never as important as people — how I need to remember this. (3) Give me the courage and wisdom to look behind actions to attitudes. (4) May the greatness of your Son be an increasing awareness of mine. (5) How I want to know the real meaning of mercy as compared with sacrifice. (6) How I want Jesus as Lord of every day.

Right here add your personal requests — and his answers.

10. READ HIS WORD AND WAIT — LISTEN — GOD SPEAKS!

I want to hear him speak to me from this confict: (1) "Be careful to put my values on acts of worship." (2) "Be very careful you do not condemn the innocent." (3) "Let me be Lord of all."

11. INTERCESSION FOR THE LOST WORLD

Singapore — Point for prayer: (1) *Unreached peoples: The older Chinese* who speak over six different non-Mandarin dialects are largely by-passed by most evangelistic efforts.

12. SING PRAISES TO OUR LORD.

Thro' many dangers, toils and snares,
I have already come;

'Tis grace hath bro't me safe thus far,
And grace will lead me home.

WEEK FORTY – SATURDAY

1. PRAISE GOD FOR WHO HE IS.

"It is better to take refuge in the Lord than to put confidence in man. It is better to take refuge in the Lord than to put confidence in princes" (Psalm 118:8, 9). What a charming thought! "To take refuge in the Lord!" You are a refuge for the whole man, i.e., we can find protection for our mind in you. To think your thoughts is to bring a calmness of thought we cannot find anywhere else. We can find a bulwark of strength for our family in you. As we read together what you have said to each of us we sense a strength with each other and a love for each other we just do not have until we find it in you! What a refuge you are for the emotional chaos that fills our land! Man offers a refuge—indeed this seems to be his strongest emphasis—we could better label it "escapism."

Express yourself in adoration for this quality of God.
Speak it audibly or write out your praise in your own devotional journal.

2. PRAISE GOD FOR WHAT HE MEANS TO ME.

Praise you for what you mean to me in this very quality! "Rock of ages, let me hide myself in you." These words do indeed describe my desire and pursuit. All my confidence in what man can offer has ended in disappointment. It is just that it is not in man to direct his own steps, to say nothing of anyone else. My acknowledgement of need is not the same as the satisfaction of that need. Dear Lord, I do want to spend much more time in my refuge. I am so glad my refuge is not a place but a person, and an omnipresent, omnipotent Person!

How do you personally relate to the protection of God, and God who is our refuge?
Speak it out or write it out. It is *so important* that you establish *your own* devotional journal.

3. CONFESSION OF SIN

All the above has been an expression of my spirit. At the same time, I can just as truly confess I have time after time put confidence in men and yes, princes. I am learning, but it is a slow process. I am glad you not only understand me, but associated with the example of One who "did not trust himself to man for he knew what was in man" (John 2:24, 25). My Lord found his daily refuge in you. How wonderful to be able to say we have never been disappointed in Jesus! In a very real sense confession becomes a means of strength since it propels me back into my only refuge—your dear self! I hide nothing, I want to repent deeply enough to change. Cleanse me of all my unwillingness!

What personal sins do you want to confess? We *must* speak them to remove them.
Do it! *Now.* There is no one else you have sinned against more than God. Tell him so!

4. SING A PRAYER TO GOD.

Rock of Ages, cleft for me,
Let me hide myself in Thee;
Let the water and the blood,

From Thy riven side which flowed,
Be of sin the double cure,
Save me from its guilt and pow'r.

Open your hymn book and sing the rest of the verses—or even sing another prayer song.

5. READ HIS WORD TO HIM!

His Word

⁹Going on from that place, he went into their synagogue, ¹⁰and a man with a shriveled hand was there. Looking for a reason to accuse Jesus, they asked him, "Is it lawful to heal on the Sabbath?"

¹¹He said to them, "If any of you has a sheep and it falls into a pit on the Sabbath, will you not take hold of it and lift it out? ¹²How much more valuable is a man than a sheep! Therefore it is lawful to do good on the Sabbath."
— *Matthew 12:9-12, NIV*

3 Another time he went into the synagogue, and a man with a shriveled hand was there. ²Some of them were looking for a reason to accuse Jesus, so they watched him closely to see if he would heal him on the Sabbath. ³Jesus said to the man with the shriveled hand, "Stand up in front of everyone."

⁴Then Jesus asked them, "Which is lawful on the Sabbath: to do good or to do evil, to save life or to kill?" But they remained silent.
— *Mark 3:1-4, NIV*

Read His Word to Him.

My Father, why did your Son go into the synagogue? He knew this was the very arena of conflict with the wild beasts who came only to wait for an occasion to devour him. He went there because that is where your word was read and where some men worshiped you. Indeed, Jesus went there to worship you in public as he worshiped you in private. Was the man with the withered hand "planted" there by these Pharisees? He seems to be very well known. His physical problem was easily seen. How wonderfully complete and full of life is your Son's answer to the accusing

560

question: (1) *As to morality:* Is it lawful to do good on the Sabbath? Is healing good? Is it lawful to save life? Is healing saving life? (2) *As to value:* Would you help a sheep on the Sabbath? Is man worth as much as a sheep — then shall I help this man? Thank you for such a courageous all-wise Savior!

Please express your response to this beautiful text. Put your expression in your own prayer diary.

6. READ HIS WORD FOR YOURSELF.

"They were silent." Dear Lord, how often I have found myself here! I have been answered but I do not translate the answer into my life! Forgive, forgive me! Long held traditions are not easily given up, but we *can* change, we *must* change if Jesus is to be Lord. I can be *so* much like the scholars of the law. God wants me above and beyond *everything* else to show mercy and *meet* the needs of man. Open my heart through the words of my Lord:

"How much more valuable is a man than a sheep?" I want to answer that question: (1) Only man is conscious of himself and will carry that consciousness throughout eternity. (2) Only man can sin — an animal cannot — therefore only man can be lost and only man can be, and must be saved. (3) Only man will live eternally and therefore only the salvation of man has eternal value — this could not be said of a sheep.

Pause in his presence and either audibly or in written form tell him all his word means to you.

7. READ HIS WORD IN THANKSGIVING.

(1) Thank you for my Lord's example of the need for public worship. (2) Thank you Jesus was ready to face his accusers on their own ground. (3) Thank you that the closer we watch Jesus the better he looks. (4) Thank you for the eternal good Jesus came to give. (5) Thank you that my owner saved his sheep. (6) Thank you Jesus never did any of his miracles in such a way they could be doubted.

Give yourself to your own expression of gratitude — write it or speak it!

8. READ HIS WORD IN MEDITATION.

"Is it lawful to heal on the Sabbath?" Our Lord had already plainly indicated that it was not a matter of law; it was the question of mercy. The question should read: "Is it merciful to heal on the Sabbath?" The need of man seems to be eclipsed by the question of law. Is it lawful to plot against an innocent man's life on the Sabbath? Is it right to hate and criticize on the Sabbath? These are all questions much more to the point. The seriousness of the situation is increased by the fact that Jesus knew their motives. The application of law is the whole point at issue. Our Lord's answer is "we shall apply it in mercy and love, with a desire to meet human need." Dear Lord, may we accept your word.

Pause — wait — think — then express yourself in thoughtful praise or thanks.

9. READ HIS WORD FOR PETITIONS.

How much like the man here described do we all feel from time to time. (1) I want to bring all my needs to you in worship. (2) I know I operate far below the level you want me to — heal my withered efforts. (3) As this man looked with expectation and then joy upon your Son, help me to so see him. (4) Make me deaf to all but the words of your Son as they relate to my need. (5) I want to remember who has the answers to the tough questions of life.

Please, please remember these are prayers — speak them — reword them!

10. READ HIS WORD AND WAIT — LISTEN — GOD SPEAKS!

As the man with the withered hand listened to your Son, so do I: (1) "It is always lawful to help in the limitations of life." (2) "I can make you whole — stretch out your hand." (3) "How very valuable is one person."

11. INTERCESSION FOR THE LOST WORLD

Sri Lanka (Ceylon) — Population: 14,000,000. Growth rate — 2%. People per sq. km. — 216.

Point for prayer: (1) *The land is very poorly evangelized* and much prejudice and misunderstanding about the Gospel must be broken down. The colonial powers suppressed national culture and language and imposed national forms of Christianity in the past. Independence has brought in a backlash against Christianity and a "revival" of Buddhism. Pray for the evangelizing of this needy land.

12. SING PRAISES TO OUR LORD.

Perfect submission, perfect delight,
Visions of rapture now burst on my sight;
Angels descending, bring from above
Echoes of mercy, whispers of love.

This is my story, this is my song,
Praising my Saviour all the day long;
This is my story, this is my song,
Praising my Saviour all the day long.

1. PRAISE GOD FOR WHO HE IS.

"The Lord is my strength and my song; he has become my salvation. Hark, glad songs of victory in the tents of the righteous: 'The right hand of the Lord does valiantly, . . .'" (Psalm 118:14, 15). What was sung so long ago—possibly in the Temple has now become the expression of every Christian heart. At least such expressions of confidence and praise should arise from every one who is your son or daughter. It is my purpose to lift from these verses those qualities of yourself for which all men can praise you. (1) In you all men can find strength—indeed if any strength is to be found for the heart, it is in you. (2) There are so many qualities in yourself that exactly meet man's needs we spontaneously burst into songs of praise. (3) We can all enjoy personal salvation—deliverance from all our enemies.

Express yourself in adoration for this quality of God.
Speak it audibly or write out your praise in your own devotional journal.

2. PRAISE GOD FOR WHAT HE MEANS TO ME.

Just for me. Dear Lord, I have no strength at all without you. I have no intellectual strength without your thoughts. Indeed, I would not even have the capacity of thought itself without sharing your likeness. The thoughts of man are like garbage compared with your knowledge. There is much good in the thoughts of men and all such good comes either directly or indirectly from you. I am neither unwilling nor unable to read and assim-ilate the thoughts of men—I have just lost interest. The grandeur of your mind and its expressions have taken me captive! I have no moral strength without you—to will is present but *to do* that which is good, right or moral is just not there. Only as you move me, or I am willing to be moved by you, do I fulfill one of my least desires to do good! Praise your strength, you have indeed become my song!

How do you personally relate to the strength of God, and God who is our strength?
Speak it out or write it out. It is *so important* that you establish *your own* devotional journal.

3. CONFESSION OF SIN

It will be easy to confess my sin in this realm. Whereas "the Lord is my strength" I at the same time find myself often turning to man or myself for resources. I praise you that I am learning—very often I can sing with the song writer: "My strength indeed is small." That I should lean upon this broken staff at all is one of the mysteries of my iniquity. Forgive me! Out of this tattered tent should arise the glad song of victory. Instead too often are heard the laments of selfishness. Dear Lord, forgive me! To repeat my sins in prayer after I have confessed them is no value whatsoever. I am glad to cast them at your feet, or to cast them into the fountain filled with blood—to forget them; I know you do. Praise your wonderful grace!

What personal sins do you want to confess? We *must* speak them to remove them.
Do it! *Now.* There is no one else you have sinned against more than God. Tell him so!

4. SING A PRAYER TO GOD.

I need Thee ev'ry hour,
Stay Thou near by;
Temptations lose their pow'r
When Thou art nigh.

I need Thee, O I need Thee;
Ev'ry hour I need Thee!
O bless me now, my Savior, I come to Thee!

Open your hymn book and sing the rest of the verses—or even sing another prayer song.

5. READ HIS WORD TO HIM!

His Word

[13]Then he said to the man, "Stretch out your hand." So he stretched it out and it was completely restored, just as sound as the other. [14]But the Pharisees went out and plotted how they might kill Jesus.
— *Matthew 12:13, 14, NIV*

[5]He looked around at them in anger and, deeply distressed at their stubborn hearts, said to the man, "Stretch out your hand." He stretched it out, and his hand was com-pletely restored. [6]Then the Pharisees went out and began to plot with the Herodians how they might kill Jesus.
— *Mark 3:5, 6, NIV*

[10]He looked around at them all, and then said to the man, "Stretch out your hand." He did so, and his hand was completely restored. [11]But they were furious and began to discuss with one another what they might do to Jesus.
— *Luke 6:10, 11, NIV*

Read His Word to Him.

Dear Father, I hesitate to express myself on your behalf. Indeed such is presumption of the worst sort. I only want to tell you how much your word means to me as I try to read it from your perspective. Was it really necessary to confront these religious leaders head on? I know it was; I am only trying to think through this circumstance. Talk about minimal human effort! The healing by your Son was just that. What "work" was there in pronouncing four words "stretch out your hand"? This was not the first encounter with these men. I need to remember this as I respond to their rejection of my Lord: (1) He had exposed their greed and love of money in cleansing the temple. (2) He had plainly said he was the Messiah in the Nazareth synagogue. (3) He forgave sins. (4) He ate with tax collectors and other sinners. (5) He did not keep their fast days. (6) He ignored their rules for Sabbath observance. (7) He claimed equality with God. They had had it! They had abundant evidence pointing to just one conclusion.

Please express your response to this beautiful text. Put your expression in your own prayer diary.

6. READ HIS WORD FOR YOURSELF.

How do I really respond to him? I want to read the account of Mark for myself. It is in his words I best see myself. Does my Lord ever look at me in "anger and deeply distressed"? I'm very sure he does. I look at my own attitudes and actions with the same response. However, right there the comparison becomes a contrast. I do leave my confrontation with you not to plot how I might further grieve you, but how I might "put to death" the thoughts of my heart and the deeds of my body. I want to more and more count myself crucified with your Son—I want to affirm "it is no longer I who live, but Christ lives in me."

Pause in his presence and either audibly or in written form tell him all his word means to you.

7. READ HIS WORD IN THANKSGIVING.

(1) Thank you for the direct unassuming manner our Lord used in healing this man. (2) Thank you for the wonderful clear evidence of deity in this healing. (3) Thank you for the joy that must have flooded the heart of the healed. (4) Thank you for my Lord's concern for everyone present in the synagogue. (5) Thank you my Lord is always clear and pure in his call for acceptance or rejection. (6) Thank you for the completeness and permanence of the healing. (7) Thank you I can reverse the response of these religious leaders in my response to this miracle.

Give yourself to your own expression of gratitude—write it or speak it!

8. READ HIS WORD IN MEDITATION.

"He looked around at them in anger and, deeply distressed at their stubborn hearts, . . ." What was it that so deeply distressed my Lord? It was their stubbornness, but in what areas? (1) They were stubborn about mercy—Jesus healed the man to show mercy. These men hardened their heart at his joy of being healed. (2) They stubbornly rejected this clear evidence of the supernatural. They are about to decide Jesus is in league with Satan. (3) They stubbornly refused to admit the human authority for their traditions.

Pause—wait—think—then express yourself in thoughtful praise or thanks.

9. READ HIS WORD FOR PETITIONS.

In the heart and words of your Son I find reasons to pray: (1) I want to become angry with my stubbornness before you do. (2) Melt my resistance—all resistance to you. (3) Open my inner ear to every word you speak. (4) Keep me always aware that you will not do what you expect me to do. (5) Keep me expecting complete answers to all my prayers. (6) May I expect negative responses to those who do not understand. (7) Remember, oh my soul, that no one can destroy Jesus!

Right here add your personal requests—and his answers.

10. READ HIS WORD AND WAIT—LISTEN—GOD SPEAKS!

Speak Lord, thy servant heareth: (1) "Fear not the wrath of men—I didn't." (2) "No man can do more than I permit." (3) "All the plans of man are under my control."

11. INTERCESSION FOR THE LOST WORLD

Sri Lanka (Ceylon) — Point for prayer: (1) *A greater openness to the Gospel* has been evident in the last three years. The lessening of resentments against the West and the growing economic privations of the land have made people more ready to listen to the Good News. Literature is in great demand and people are being won thereby.

12. SING PRAISES TO OUR LORD.

Come, Thou Incarnate Word,
Gird on Thy mighty sword,
Our prayer attend:
Come, and Thy people bless,

And give Thy word success:
Spirit of holiness,
On us descend.

WEEK FORTY-ONE — MONDAY

1. PRAISE GOD FOR WHO HE IS.

"The stone which the builders rejected has become the head of the corner. This is marvelous in our eyes. This is the day which the Lord has made; let us rejoice and be glad in it" (Psalm 118:22-24). This is a messianic psalm and full of meaning and for that reason I want to hold up the qualities of these three verses and praise you for each one: (1) Your dear Son has become the cornerstone of all of life. I remember that measurements for the whole build-ing were taken for the cornerstone. The whole building was right because the cornerstone was right. However, (2) the stone was rejected by the builders. Dear Lord, there are various ways of rejecting you. When we do not know the measurements as related to the cornerstone, we cannot and will not build our house as you want it. I do not want to repeat the sin of those who first rejected him.

Express yourself in adoration for this quality of God.
Speak it audibly or write out your praise in your own devotional journal.

2. PRAISE GOD FOR WHAT HE MEANS TO ME.

Just for me. My basic problem is that I want to design and build the house, but when that happens who gets the credit? It is only when we are willing to let you build the house that we can say, "This is the Lord's doing; it is mar-velous in our eyes." I want to praise you that you have such a vital interest in every life that you want to be the architect. I believe the blueprint for every life is in your word. I also believe that a meditation on your word, both day and night is an essential prerequisite to applying in life what we learn in our meditation. I am confident that the construction of life preceded by those two steps be-comes the house the Lord has made. Such building is done one day at a time. Let me say and mean — "This is the day the Lord has made; let us rejoice and be glad in it."

How do you personally relate to the house of God, and God who is the builder?
Speak it out or write it out. It is *so important* that you establish *your own* devotional journal.

3. CONFESSION OF SIN

How altogether too obvious is our sin as related to these beautiful verses: (1) Every day is a test as to whether I will accept or reject the Cornerstone for that day. If I rush into the day without meditation and prayer, how could it be anything but a disaster? (2) If my admiration and love for my Lord is not fresh and new for each day I cannot use the term "marvelous" with any meaning at all. (3) If I am not thoughtful in the major choices of this day how could I possibly say "This is the day the Lord has made"? I want to so condition my heart that my response is automatic. However, such conditioning is a daily, even hourly, practice. Forgive me, dear Lord, for not enjoying your fellowship.

What personal sins do you want to confess? We *must* speak them to remove them.
Do it! *Now.* There is no one else you have sinned against more than God. Tell him so!

4. SING A PRAYER TO GOD.

Dear Lord and Father of mankind,
Forgive our foolish ways!
Reclothe us in our rightful mind;

In purer lives Thy service find,
In deeper rev'rence, praise.

Open your hymn book and sing the rest of the verses — or even sing another prayer song.

5. READ HIS WORD TO HIM!

His Word

[12]One of those days Jesus went out into the hills to pray, and spent the night praying to God. [13]When morning came, he called his disciples to him and chose twelve of them, whom he also designated apostles: [14]Simon (whom he named Peter), his brother Andrew, James, John, Philip, Bartholomew, [15]Matthew, Thomas, James son of Alphaeus, Simon who was called the Zealot, [16]Judas son of James, and Judas Iscariot, who became a traitor.

— Luke 6:12-16, NIV

Read also Matthew 10:1-6 and Mark 3:13-19.

Read His Word to Him.

Since your Son spent all night in prayer over his choice of the twelve it behooves us to spend at least a few minutes in as careful an understanding as we can. My primary purpose is praise and adoration. Why would Jesus spend all night praying to you? How we want to hear him pray — how we wish we knew what he said. But if we did, would we understand? Probably not. He must have re-viewed all the disciples by name and need. The twelve were chosen the next morning because they were already chosen the night before. Jesus knew how poorly prepared they were; he must equip them. He gave them power and direction. His purpose in calling the twelve was not just to send them out but that they might first be with him.

Please express your response to this beautiful text. Put your expression in your own prayer diary.

6. READ HIS WORD FOR YOURSELF.

Just for me. I can identify with each of these men. (1) *Peter or Simon who is called Peter.* I identify so closely because I, like Peter, say too many things I need to retract. (2) *Andrew his brother.* I *do* have a deep desire to bring men to my Lord, and I thank you for it. (3) *James the son of Zebedee.* Here is one of the "sons of thunder." Energy and vigor have been mine ever since I can remember. May I be as willing a martyr, or witness as James. (4) *John his brother.* How I want the same vigorous love and commitment I see in John. (5) *Philip of Bethsaida.* I like the beautiful challenge of our Lord's appeal to Philip in John 6:6 "to prove him." Dear Lord, I want to be like him. (6) *Bartholomew* or possibly Nathanael. "The Israelite in whom there was no guile." (7) *Thomas Didymus*—I want his proven faith expressed in the words: "My Lord and my God." (8) *Matthew the publican.* This man never ceased to wonder what God's grace could do with a tax collector. (9) *James, the son of Alphaeus.* Possibly the cousin of our Lord, one who shared his personal fellowship often. (10) *Thaddaeus or Judas.* Jesus had two apostles named Judas. (11) *Simon the Zealot.* Here is a super patriot in company with a tax collector. (12) *Judas Iscariot*, who also betrayed him.

Pause in his presence and either audibly or in written form tell him all his word means to you.

7. READ HIS WORD IN THANKSGIVING.

(1) Thank you for Peter the first to open the door of salvation. (2) Thank you for Andrew who was first to tell his brother of our Lord. (3) Thank you for James who gave his life away for Jesus. (4) Thank you for the fisherman who became the apostle of love. (5) Thank you for Philip who brought others to Jesus. (6) Thank you for Nathanael of transparent sincerity. (7) Thank you for the publican who was called to tell others.

Give yourself to your own expression of gratitude—write it or speak it!

8. READ HIS WORD IN MEDITATION.

". . . and spent the night praying to God." Unless there was some overwhelming burden upon our heart it would seem an impossibility to actually spend a whole night in prayer. What would we say that would fill up six or eight hours? It was no problem for our Lord. If he prayed for each of the twelve in detail he would only spend 40 minutes each in an eight hour prayer vigil. When these men were going to be the foundation upon which his whole work was to be built 40 minutes apiece would not be unusual. Considering the enormity of the need, all night hardly seems long enough.

Pause—wait—think—then express yourself in thoughtful praise or thanks.

9. READ HIS WORD FOR PETITIONS.

If your dear Son could spend all night in prayer, surely there must be much in this record about which I can pray: (1) How I do want to learn more and more about the prayer-life of my Lord—help me. (2) Give me the engery of communion with you. (3) How I want the power of intercessory prayer—enlighten me. (4) Give me boldness like Peter. (5) How I need the love as taught by John. (6) The practical lessons in obedience as written by James are a real need in my life. (7) What a need there is in my life for the guilelessness of Philip. (8) Oh that I might know your word as Matthew did.

Please, please remember these are prayers—speak them—reword them!

10. READ HIS WORD AND WAIT—LISTEN—GOD SPEAKS!

In the lives of these twelve men you can say so much to me: (1) "I can use the temperaments and talents of all men—if they are willing." (2) "Not all men named Judas were bad." (3) "Do you pray for those who learn from you?"

11. INTERCESSION FOR THE LOST WORLD

Sri Lanka (Ceylon) — Point for prayer: (1) *Missions*—entry is very difficult. Only 50 missionaries remain. Pray that they may have a fruitful and strategic influence in this needy land.

12. SING PRAISES TO OUR LORD.

Amazing grace! how sweet the sound,
That saved a wretch like me!

I once was lost, but now am found,
Was blind, but now I see.

1. PRAISE GOD FOR WHO HE IS.

"With my whole heart I seek thee; let me not wander from thy commandments! I have laid up thy word in my heart, that I might not sin against thee" (Psalm 119:10, 11). The attributes of yourself are not at all explicit in these verses, but there are several implicit qualities for me, and all men to extol before your throne: (1) You want us to worship you. We were created to worship you, and eagerly do I respond to this quality. (2) You deserve an undivided attention from man. The whole total being of man should focus on you. How gladly do I take up such a practice—I *want* to give you all my heart. (3) Man has lost you, i.e., in the sense of awareness, we must *seek* you to find you—you are not lost; we are. Our Lord described you as the waiting father. Praise your name!

Express yourself in adoration for this quality of God.
Speak it audibly or write out your praise in your own devotional journal.

2. PRAISE GOD FOR WHAT HE MEANS TO ME.

Just for me. You and your word are inseparable. There is no way I can seek you apart from your commandments. When I wander from a careful meditation upon your word I wander from you. The "laying up of your word in my heart" includes several relationships: (1) I know my heart refers to my inward being—my mind, will, emotions and conscience. To "lay up" your word would include memory work—which is a wonderful form of meditation. (2) This is a decision before it is anything—I *must* decide to give a time, a place, energy, concentration to this practice. I shall never do it without a priority decision. (3) Sinning is directly related to your word. Sin is indeed "the transgression of your law" (I John 3:4). I want to so saturate my whole being with your word that my brain is washed, my will is overcome, my emotions are tuned and my conscience is educated. I do want to seek you with my whole heart.

How do you personally relate to the law of God, and God who is the law giver?
Speak it out or write it out. It is *so important* that you establish *your own* devotional journal.

3. CONFESSION OF SIN

If you do, why is it you fail to do it? I refer in soliloquy to my strong desire to overcome sin and not being overcome by it. Dear Lord, I shall never be anything but a sinner, but I am not discouraged. To be anything else but a sinner I would need to know everything and do it. If I reached that place you would have another job. I say this in tragic jest. Forgive me. But you do expect improvement, or growth, and so do I. As I read verse twelve of this blessed 119th Psalm I find a beautiful answer to my deep need: "Blessed be thou, O Lord; teach me thy statutes." Man (including myself) has been very unsuccessful in teaching me. You can do it! I want to pause before the author of your word and let him implant it in my heart.

What sins do you want to confess? We *must* speak them to remove them.
Do it! *Now.* There is no one else you have sinned against more than God. Tell him so!

4. SING A PRAYER TO GOD.

His banner over us is love,
Our sword the Word of God;
We tread the road the saints above
With shouts of triumph trod.
By faith, they like a whirlwind's breath,
Swept on ov'er ev'ry field;

The faith by which they conquered Death
Is still our shining shield.
Faith is the victory!
Faith is the victory!
Oh, glorious victory,
That overcomes the world.

Open your hymn book and sing the rest of the verses—or even sing another prayer song.

5. READ HIS WORD TO HIM!

His Word

[7]Jesus withdrew with his disciples to the lake, and a large crowd from Galilee followed. [8]When they heard all he was doing, many people came to him from Judea, Jerusalem, Idumea, and the regions across the Jordan and around Tyre and Sidon. [9]Because of the crowd he told his disciples to have a small boat ready for him, to keep the people from crowding him. [10]For he had healed many, so that those with diseases were pushing forward to touch him. [11]Whenever the evil spirits saw him, they fell down before him and cried out, "You are the Son of God." [12]But he gave them strict orders not to tell who he was.

— Mark 3:7-12, NIV

Read His Word to Him.

As you observed the popularity of your Son what did you think? How empty was the praise some gave to him! The healer was forgotten almost as soon as the healing was completed. How incredibly sad this was. Why did he

566

heal them when he knew they would soon forget him? He knew—as you did—that some would not forget. That some would have a delayed reaction to what happened. The real answer is twofold: He healed the multitude because he had compassion upon them; he was touched with the feeling of their infirmities. He healed because in these miracles they could see his deity. How delighted I am to see yourself moving among that vast multitude reaching out to heal and help everyone.

Please express your response to this beautiful text. Put your expression in your own prayer diary.

6. READ HIS WORD FOR YOURSELF.

It will not be difficult to identify with several who followed him, from Galilee or with some of those from Judea or Jerusalem. Like those from the lovely countryside of Galilee I have heard him and seen him before. But there is something about him—I just cannot stay away; I want to hear more, I want to see him again and again. As many times as I have read the gospels (and I could not count them) I yet read them this morning with new eyes—eyes he opened, as if I had never read them before. Some who came to him from Judea or Jerusalem came home skeptical to see if indeed it was all true, i.e., what they had heard. I want to go back and tell everyone the half has never yet been told.

Pause in his presence and either audibly or in written form tell him all his word means to you.

7. READ HIS WORD IN THANKSGIVING.

(1) Thank you for the planned work of my Lord; it helps me plan my work. (2) Thank you for the *learners* who followed him; may I be one of them. (3) Thank you for everyone in that multitude; each of them known and important to you. (4) Thank you for the service his disciples could be to him then; he needs us today. (5) Thank you there was no one who could not be healed. (6) Thank you for the constant consistent response of demons; they always fell down and worshiped him. What does this say to us? (7) Thank you that I can right here and right now fall down and praise and worship him.

Give yourself to your own expression of gratitude—write it or speak it!

8. READ HIS WORD IN MEDITATION.

". . . he gave them strict orders not to tell who he was." Instructions to demons! Who would hear the news of his Messiahship from demons? Perhaps it was at the occasion of the large crowd that he wanted the demons silent. Could it be that demons would publish abroad in the spirit world his fame? There was one obvious reason he wanted the demons not to speak of who he was: It came from the wrong source—the message is inseparably associated with the messenger. This was also true with the demon-possessed girl in Philippi (Acts 16:16-18).

Pause—wait—think—then express yourself in thoughtful praise or thanks.

9. READ HIS WORD FOR PETITIONS.

Even my Lord had problems with crowds and those who did not understand. I want to ask help as I read of his work: (1) I do need wisdom in knowing when it is best to say "no" and move on. (2) When shall I cease to help?— there were times when Jesus did and times when he didn't. (3) Help me to fulfill Isaiah's prophecy that your Son would be preached to the Gentiles. (4) Give me the meek and lowly attitude of my Lord. (5) May all my speeches have my Lord's purposes behind them. (6) How I need the grace to cultivate faith through your word in the hearts of hearers. (7) Keep me aware that Jesus alone is the hope of the world.

Right here add your personal requests—and his answers.

10. READ HIS WORD AND WAIT—LISTEN—GOD SPEAKS!

In these verses speak to me: (1) "My Lord had no unsuccessful attempts at healing." (2) "Demons know who Jesus is." (3) "There is a time for preaching and there is a time to not preach."

11. INTERCESSION FOR THE LOST WORLD

Sri Lanka (Ceylon) — Point for prayer: (1) *The Protestant Church* is one of the weakest and most nominal in Asia. Few know about the new birth. Non-Bible believing theological colleges and literature have not produced committed Christians or soul-winning evangelists. Church union is seen as a better solution than a vital personal union of individuals with the Lord.

12. SING PRAISES TO OUR LORD.

Holy, Holy, Holy! All the saints adore Thee,
Casting down their golden crowns around the glassy sea;
Cherubim and seraphim falling down before Thee,
Which wert, and art, and evermore shalt be.

WEEK FORTY-ONE — WEDNESDAY

1. PRAISE GOD FOR WHO HE IS.

"In the way of thy testimonies I delight as much as in all riches. I will meditate on thy precepts, and fix my eyes on thy ways. I will delight in thy statutes; I will not forget thy word" (Psalm 119:14-16). I realize this whole psalm is devoted to the meaning and beauty of your law—or your word. But since a man's word is but the outward expression of the man himself, to appreciate one is to appreciate the other. It will be my delight for the next several weeks to hold up one quality after another of yourself as related to your word and praise you: (1) The meaning and purpose and value of your word is much better than the meaning, value and purpose of *all riches.* One life saved here to usefulness and unselfish service and then to the eternal joys of heaven is a clear testimony of the truth of the statement.

Express yourself in adoration for this quality of God.
Speak it audibly or write out your praise in your own devotional journal.

2. PRAISE GOD FOR WHAT HE MEANS TO ME.

Just for me. (In these expressions of praise the generic and specific merge.) (2) Praise you that your precepts are such that they merit meditation. Praise you that they are written in such a manner that all men can meditate upon them. After a thousand attempts to probe the depths of what you have written there is yet much more to explore. (3) I am so very, very thankful for eyesight, but more than that for the ability to understand—for what men call intelligence—which is in truth your own image in man. It would do but little good to fix my eyes on your ways if I could not discern them. (4) Praise your name that I do have a deep excitement about investigating every word of your statutes. I have been so wonderfully helped in the efforts I have given to this blessed pursuit!

How do you personally relate to the testimonies of God, and God who speaks to man?
Speak it out or write it out. It is *so important* that you establish *your own* devotional journal.

3. CONFESSION OF SIN

The last little phrase of these verses "stabs me awake"! "I will not forget thy word." How is it I have such a lapse of memory? i.e., I only remember your word *sometimes,* but not all the time? The answer is obvious enough: memory is programmed. We precondition our memory to function under specific conditions at specified times. My sin is that I have not programmed my memory and conscience via my will to include your word. Your word is left in my subconsciousness and is not brought forward to the self-consciousness thus I forget your word. Meditation upon the meaning of your word both day and night will solve this problem—called sin!

What personal sins do you want to confess? We *must* speak them to remove them.
Do it! *Now.* There is no one else you have sinned against more than God. Tell him so!

4. SING A PRAYER TO GOD.

Thro' days of toil when heart doth fail,
God will take care of you;
When dangers fierce your path assail,
God will take care of you.
God will take care of you,

Thro' every day,
O'er all the way;
He will take care of you,
God will take care of you. . . .

Open your hymn book and sing the rest of the verses—or even sing another prayer song.

5. READ HIS WORD TO HIM!

His Word

[15]Aware of this, Jesus withdrew from that place. Many followed him, and he healed all their sick, [16]warning them not to tell who he was. [17]This was to fulfill what was spoken through the prophet Isaiah:
[18]"Here is my servant whom I have chosen,
the one I love, in whom I delight;
I will put my Spirit on him,
and he will proclaim justice to the nations.
[19]He will not quarrel or cry out;

no one will hear his voice in the streets.
[20]A bruised reed he will not break,
and a smoldering wick he will not snuff out,
till he leads justice to victory.
[21] In his name the nations will put their hope."

— Matthew 12:15-21, NIV

Read also Luke 6:17-19.

Read His Word to Him.

It is with our Lord's use of Isaiah 42:1-4 I want to particularly praise you. Indeed, my Lord, I want to observe what kind of servant you have chosen for yourself. What is affirmed of this servant of yourself goes infinitely beyond anything to which the prophet was ever called, or of which man was ever capable. He is indeed and in a unique sense "your beloved." He pleased you well. He pleases me beyond all words! You put your Spirit upon him in the sense of anointing him (Acts 10:38). From beginning to end the Holy Spirit empowered his ministry. Dear Father, how I love to read of the direction and inspiration your Spirit gave to the ministry of your Son.

Please express your response to this beautiful text. Put your expression in your own prayer diary.

6. READ HIS WORD FOR YOURSELF.

Whereas I tried in the above words to identify your perspective I want in these brief words to identify with him and love him to the extent that I can be like him: (1) He will not argue and shout. My dear Lord did so much without fanfare and rabble-rousing. "He does not seek his own, therefore denies himself; he brings what commends itself; therefore requires no trumpeting." How unlike some of our efforts! (2) He will never crush the weak nor destroy the smallest amount of faith. (3) He will not stop until he has won the victory, making justice to triumph. He will indeed be (and is) the hope of the world!

Pause in his presence and either audibly or in written form tell him all his word means to you.

7. READ HIS WORD IN THANKSGIVING.

(1) Thank you for the poignant name "Servant" — how well does this describe him. (2) Thank you for the assurance that servanthood is your choice. (3) Thank you for the fulness of your Spirit who was present in my Lord. (4) Thank you that his ministry has reached to this one needy Gentile. (5) Thank you for the example of silent success seen in my Savior.

Give yourself to your own expression of gratitude — write it or speak it!

8. READ HIS WORD IN MEDITATION.

"And in his name shall the Gentiles hope." Just one Gentile can say that without him there is no hope. I would find no hope for our family because without my Lord's instructions for interpersonal relationships we would be at one another's throats. Without Jesus' words about the life to come "in my father's house" there would be no hope for those who have lived to the three score and ten and beyond. Without my Lord and his presence in me and with me any job would be meaningless. The hope of our neighborhood is in my Lord. How easy it is to find fault with others. Only Jesus can show me how to live alongside others in peace and love.

Pause — wait — think — then express yourself in thoughtful praise or thanks.

9. READ HIS WORD FOR PETITIONS.

This remarkable statement of the healing ministry of Jesus moves me to pray: (1) How I want to stand day by day with him and hear his words. (2) Make me a fisher of men. (3) Open my inner ear that you might truly be my teacher. (4) Heal me of the disease of blindness and deafness as related to your word. (5) I am indeed troubled by demons — I want my Lord to rebuke them. (6) How I want to draw near enough to touch you and be touched by you.

Please, please remember these are prayers — speak them — reword them!

10. READ HIS WORD AND WAIT — LISTEN — GOD SPEAKS.

There are so many things you could teach me: (1) "Not everyone really ever heard all I spoke and taught — you have much more than any one of them did." (2) "Let not your heart be troubled, neither let it be afraid." (3) "I can heal all hearts who come to me."

11. INTERCESSION FOR THE LOST WORLD

Sri Lanka (Ceylon) — Point for prayer: (1) *Evangelistic outreach* is, however, more noticeable now than for many years. Bible believing groups inside and outside the churches are now more aggressively reaching out. Efforts are now being made to win the university students. Since the nationalism of all schools, Christian teachers have been making an impact in government schools. Yet all these are but small beginnings.

12. SING PRAISES TO OUR LORD.

Beyond my highest joy
I prize her heavenly ways,

Her sweet communion, solemn vows,
Her hymns of love and praise.

WEEK FORTY-ONE — THURSDAY

1. PRAISE GOD FOR WHO HE IS.

"Deal bountifully with thy servant, that I may live and observe thy word. Open my eyes, that I may behold wondrous things out of thy law. I am a sojourner on earth; hide not thy commandments from me!" (Psalm 119:17-19). Such blessed attributes of yourself for which I can praise you! (1) Your desire to supply all my needs, all the needs of all men. We should lift our hearts in deep gratitude every morning we open our eyes. (2) We are your voluntary slaves—we are "your servants." In a most practical factual sense we are all your servants, whether we acknowledge it or not. You have created the entire environment—personal and public in which we live. (3) Indeed, you have given us "life and breath."

Express yourself in adoration for this quality of God.
Speak it audibly or write out your praise in your own devotional journal.

2. PRAISE GOD FOR WHAT HE MEANS TO ME.

Just for me. The psalmist is to say over and over again that our whole purpose in living is to "observe" your word. Indeed it is! What point or purpose is there in life without your word? (4) You can and will give us wisdom as we read your will. Applications and meanings that escaped us before will now appear as if by divine intention—which is exactly what is happening. Bless your holy name! Thank you! (5) You are aware of the brevity of our life—of the fact that we are but pilgrims and we need news from home. How wondrously good you are!

How do you personally relate to the bountifulness of God, and God who is the Giver?
Speak it out or write it out. It is *so important* that you establish *your own* devotional journal.

3. CONFESSION OF SIN

There is no point to my repeated confession of failure unless there is with it a repeated sincere desire to repent. Such I offer you! How I *do* want to change. In the daily routine I can inject meditation and memorization of your word. You have already dealt very bountifully with your servant—to what purpose? "That I might live and observe your word." There is nothing monotonous in reading your word again *if* I *want to*—and I do! If my eyes were opened (i.e., the eyes of my heart) and I did not have before me your law what would be the purpose of seeing?—life means nothing without your explanation. Dear Lord, I affirm this because of my need! Forgive my attachments to this city which has no foundation—to this country that will not abide.

What personal sins do you want to confess? We *must* speak them to remove them.
Do it! *Now.* There is no one else you have sinned against more than God. Tell him so!

4. SING A PRAYER TO GOD.

Sweetly echo the gospel call,
Wonderful words of Life;
Offer pardon and peace to all,
Wonderful words of Life.
Jesus, only Savior,

Sanctify forever:
Beautiful words, wonderful words,
Wonderful words of Life.
Beautiful words, wonderful words,
Wonderful words of Life.

Open your hymn book and sing the rest of the verses—or even sing another prayer song.

5. READ HIS WORD TO HIM!

His Word

Now when he saw the crowds, he went up on a
5   mountainside and sat down. His disciples came to him,
²and he began to teach them, saying:
³"Blessed are the poor in spirit,
for theirs is the kingdom of heaven.
⁴Blessed are those who mourn,
for they will be comforted.
⁵Blessed are the meek,
for they will inherit the earth.
⁶Blessed are those who hunger and
thirst for righteousness,
for they will be filled.
⁷Blessed are the merciful,
for they will be shown mercy.

⁸Blessed are the pure in heart,
for they will see God.
⁹Blessed are the peacemakers,
for they will be called sons of God.
¹⁰Blessed are those who are persecuted
because of righteousness,
for theirs is the kingdom of heaven.
¹¹"Blessed are you when people insult you, persecute you and falsely say all kinds of evil against you because of me. ¹²Rejoice and be glad, because great is your reward in heaven, for in the same way they persecuted the prophets who were before you.
— Matthew 5:1-12, NIV

Read also Luke 6:20-26.

Read His Word to Him.

The best I can do in reading these beautiful words to you is to read with prayerful thought a paragraph of the first seven verses into which is written the meaning: "How well off are you who know that you are poor in Spiritual things, as well as materially (Luke 6:20): the kingdom of God is yours! How blest are those who know what sorrow means, because they are in a position to receive consolation and courage! Happy are those of a gentle spirit, who claim nothing of their own rights, for the whole earth will belong to them! Blessed are you who are hungering and thirsting for that character which is God's own righteousness: you shall be fully satisfied!"

Please express your response to this beautiful text. Put your expression in your own prayer diary.

6. READ HIS WORD FOR YOURSELF.

Happy are those whose hearts are pure, those who are completely sincere, for they shall see God. Happy are those who work to produce peace in human society, peace between God and man and peace with man himself; these will be known as God's sons. How blest are they who have suffered persecution for the cause of righteousness! The kingdom of God belongs to such as they. Indeed what happiness will be yours when men hate you and turn you out of their company, when you suffer insults and persecution, when they slander you and despise all you stand for, because you are loyal to the Son of Man.

Pause in his presence and either audibly or in written form tell him all his word means to you.

7. READ HIS WORD IN THANKSGIVING.

(1) Thank you for the assurance that I can be blessed or happy. (2) Thank you for the promise of your concern in my dependence upon others for my support. (3) Thank you for the privilege of repentance—of real godly sorrow. (4) Thank you for the solid assurance you will and do strengthen my weaknesses through my sorrow.

Give yourself to your own expression of gratitude—write it or speak it!

8. READ HIS WORD IN MEDITATION.

"But alas for you who are rich, for you are in little position to receive further comfort" (Luke 6:24). It seems incongruous to bemoan the fate of the rich. It would seem this is the whole pursuit of the whole world. But then our Lord looks at things as they are and *not* as they seem. The comfort riches afford are all the rich will receive. Many rich find no consolation in their possessions. Others seem to enjoy their luxury. But if this life is but the smallest infinitesimal fraction of the life to come, i.e., by comparison of time to eternity, and riches do not count at all in the world to come, then the comfort found here is small indeed.

Pause—wait—think—then express yourself in thoughtful praise or thanks.

9. READ HIS WORD FOR PETITIONS.

Here is the "blessed life"—how I need to pray about it: (1) Poverty of spirit is what I want and need. (2) Break my spirit that I might let you rule. (3) Convict my heart of the reality of sin that I might seek and find your forgiveness. (4) How I want a yielded attitude in every relationship of life. (5) I do want to enter the full inheritance of meekness. (6) Deepen my hunger—increase my thirst for your righteousness. (7) Lead me to some one who hurts that I may show mercy.

Right here add your personal requests—and his answers.

10. READ HIS WORD AND WAIT—LISTEN—GOD SPEAKS!

How these words can penetrate my heart if I will let them: (1) "The pure in heart will see me—no one else." (2) "My sons make peace and pursue peace." (3) "It can be a good thing to be persecuted."

11. INTERCESSION FOR THE LOST WORLD

Republic of the Maldives — Population: 130,000. 220 small coral islands 600 km. east of Sri Lanka.

Point for prayer: (1) *There are no Maldivian Christians* —the only totally unevangelized nation in Asia. No Christian propaganda is permitted, for Christianity is abhorred by the people. Pray for these people in their sin and need —it would appear that their major hobby is immorality.

12. SING PRAISES TO OUR LORD.

Amazing grace! how sweet the sound,
That saved a wretch like me!

I once was lost, but now am found,
Was blind, but now I see.

WEEK FORTY-ONE — FRIDAY

1. PRAISE GOD FOR WHO HE IS.

"Teach me, O Lord, the way set out in thy statutes, and in keeping them I shall find my reward. Give me the insight to obey thy law and to keep it with all my heart; make me walk in the path of thy commandments, for that is my desire" (Psalm 119:33-35). Dear Lord, in these brief verses are all the cooperative principles of the fulfillment of your will in the lives of your servants. How marvelous are your ways! The one quality of yourself I

see in these verses is "great wisdom." I immediately think of Paul's words: "You must work out your own salvation with fear and trembling; for it is God who works in you, inspiring both the will and the deed, for his own chosen purpose" (Philippians 2:12, 13). Together we will get it done. What is your part; what is my part? They are so much a part of each other we cannot separate them. Praise you for such unexcelled wisdom!

Express yourself in adoration for this quality of God.
Speak it audibly or write out your praise in your own devotional journal.

2. PRAISE GOD FOR WHAT HE MEANS TO ME.

Just for me. It surely would seem that all these verses were especially written for me! Let me mark out my part and your part and marvel at the merging. *My part:* (1) Keeping your statutes. (2) Enjoying the reward of my obedience. (3) To obey thy law. (4) To keep it with all my heart. (5) To walk in the path of your commandments. (6) To fulfill my desire to walk in your path. *Your part:* (1) Teach me the way set out in your statutes. (2) Give me insight to obey thy law and to obey it with all my

heart. (3) To make me walk in the path of thy commandments. How I do rejoice in the merging of my will in your will—in the "working in" as I "work out." *The results are:* (1) I shall be taught by you through your word. (2) I shall keep or live out your word in my life. (3) I will have a subjective response of joy in this fulfillment. (4) I shall have insight needed to obey your word. (5) Your word will find expression in all of my heart. (6) My desire to obey your commandments will find an answer.

How do you personally relate to the wisdom of God, and God who is the giver of wisdom?
Speak it out or write it out. It is *so important* that you establish *your own* devotional journal.

3. CONFESSION OF SIN

All of the above sounds so wonderful—and it is! How then is it so infrequently fulfilled in my life? It would be easy to say that I have not cooperated as I should. This is true but it is a superficial answer. The well-spring of motivation is in my love—my deep desire to do your will, and with it my strong love for your word. When I am ready to cultivate these qualities I will have all your power

and strength flowing through me—*and not until and only when!* Dear Lord, I want to confess this basic sin. I have not taken the time and thought to give myself in love for your will as expressed in your word. This is a love for you, since it is impossible to separate what One says from the Person who says it. Forgive me and move me into a love relationship with you and your word.

What personal sins do you want to confess? We *must* speak them to remove them.
Do it! *Now.* There is no one else you have sinned against more than God. Tell him so!

4. SING A PRAYER TO GOD.

When sore trials came upon you,
Did you think to pray?
When your soul was bowed in sorrow,
Balm of Gilead did you borrow,
At the gates of day?

Oh, how praying rests the weary!
Prayer will change the night to day;
So in sorrow and in gladness,
Don't forget to pray.

Open your hymn book and sing the rest of the verses—or even sing another prayer song.

5. READ HIS WORD TO HIM!

His Word

[13]"You are the salt of the earth. But if the salt loses its saltiness, how can it be made salty again? It is no longer good for anything, except to be thrown out and trampled by men.
[14]"You are the light of the world. A city on a hill cannot

be hidden. [15]Neither do people light a lamp and put it under a bowl. Instead they put it on its stand, and it gives light to everyone in the house. [16]In the same way, let your light shine before men, that they may see your good deeds and praise your Father in heaven.   —*Matthew 5:13-16, NIV*

Read His Word to Him.

I have read these blessed words hundreds of times. But never have I read them with more meaning than just now. Never have I approached you in just the way I do

this morning to try to think and pray through each word in your presence. Your dear Son selects such common and ordinary things to give meaning to his words. "Salt,"

"Light," "a bushel"; "a lamp." And now the transfer! I am the salt; I am the light. I have a stand and a bushel. Speak to me, dear Lord! I am listening; my heart is open to you! I hear him say to me, "You are the world's salt! You stand in the same relation to the world as does salt to meat which is decomposing. But if the salt (*you and I*) becomes insipid or tasteless, how is its saltiness to be restored or the meat to be preserved? That is, if you lose your power to preserve from moral corruption, how could you restore that lost power?"

Please express your response to this beautiful text. Put your expression in your own prayer diary.

6. READ HIS WORD FOR YOURSELF.

Just for me. Just here I want to apply every word I can from this passage to my own heart cry. Jesus tells me that I am a lamp lit by his fire to burn as a light in this dark world—the particular dark world in which I live. There is a real problem in this responsibility. ". . . The museum of human history is quite cluttered with the wrecked lives of men and institutions who could not resist the temptation of self-glory." What motives will save us from this peril? When once we see how truly *lost* the world is we will have "that courageous humility that makes us truly helpful to men without seeking our own glory."

Pause in his presence and either audibly or in written form tell him all his word means to you.

7. READ HIS WORD IN THANKSGIVING.

(1) Thank you it is my privilege to do what I can through living and preaching your word to preserve this rotten world from destruction. (2) Thank you that much is being done right here in our world even if there is very little "furious fanfare." (3) Thank you I can be "a walking conscience" to bring your Son right into the evil society in which I live. (4) Thank you I am reminded over and again that "salt retains its value only if it maintains its distinctive character." (5) Thank you that I can truly believe that if I lose my saltiness the world will lose all hope.

Give yourself to your own expression of gratitude—write it or speak it!

8. READ HIS WORD IN MEDITATION.

". . . *that men may see your good works and glorify your Father who is in heaven.*" There are two sides to this coin: (1) That men would glorify us and not our Father. Isn't it almost unavoidable? Men glorified Peter and John—men praised and worshiped Paul and Barnabas—not all men immediately thought of God following their healing from our Lord. Some men will refuse to transfer their praise even when they know better. (2) We can allow this problem to be used as an excuse for false modesty and never give ourselves to any "good works." Men *must* see our good works if they are going to glorify yourself. The answer is not only in the source of the good works, but also in the manner in which they are done. Egocentric action is detectable.

Pause—wait—think—then express yourself in thoughtful praise or thanks.

9. READ HIS WORD FOR PETITIONS.

In these sometimes too familiar words I find real reasons for prayer: (1) I can give life and favor to the part of the earth I affect—help me. (2) O thou, the source of all saltiness, keep me salty. (3) Show me today the good for which I was created. (4) Light my candle. (5) Put me on a hill. (6) Set me on a stand in your house. (7) Show men your good works through me.

Please, please remember these are prayers—speak them—reword them!

10. READ HIS WORD AND WAIT—LISTEN—GOD SPEAKS!

How powerful will be your words in these verses. (1) "Keep near me—I'll make you salty." (2) "Keep near me—I'll turn on your light." (3) "I am the hill and I am the stand for your light."

11. INTERCESSION FOR THE LOST WORLD

Taiwan — Population: 16,500,000. Growth rate—1.9%. People per sq. km.—460.

Point for prayer: (1) *The outstanding Christian testimony* in the will of the late Pres. Chiang Kai-Shek in 1975 gave fresh impetus to believers to evangelize among a more responsive people. Pray that this land may be fully evangelized while there is time. The growing power of Communist China may be used to occupy Taiwan.

12. SING PRAISES TO OUR LORD.

"Man of Sorrows," what a name
For the Son of God who came

Ruined sinners to reclaim!
Hallelujah! what a Savior!

1. PRAISE GOD FOR WHO HE IS.

"I walk in freedom wherever I will, because I have studied thy precepts. I will speak of thy instructions before kings and will not be ashamed; in thy commandments I find continuing delight. I love them with all my heart" (Psalm 119:45-47). What a profound statement of truth is in the promise of freedom! The words of your dear Son come immediately to mind. "You shall know the truth and the truth shall make you free." In every situation of life we can move confidently—in every changing circumstance of life we can walk with a sure step. Praise your name for the liberating experience we find in studying your word! I have tested this concept enough to know how true it is. Dear Father, how we long to have your word honored and accepted by the heads of countries. If there is anyway at all I can cause this to happen I am ready.

Express yourself in adoration for this quality of God.
Speak it audibly or write out your praise in your own devotional journal.

2. PRAISE GOD FOR WHAT HE MEANS TO ME.

I am not worshiping your book; I am worshiping you. I am not in love with ink on paper; I am in love with the meaning of yourself as seen in what you have said. Having said this I at the same time can enter into the expression of the psalmist with the most exuberance possible! "In thy commandments I find continuing delight"; indeed, indeed I do! If you give me enough days I purpose to examine every word of your book in the closet of prayer. I have no greater need or delight! I have thought through the words of the Old Testament in more than thirty years of classes, but dear Lord, such was but a preparation of meditation on your commandments.

How do you personally relate to the truthfulness of God, and God who is Truth?
Speak it out or write it out. It is *so important* that you establish *your own* devotional journal.

3. CONFESSION OF SIN

A paraphrase in the negative could easily say what I want to in confession of my sin. I walk in bondage in every relationship of life because I have neglected the study of thy precepts. I mean that my bondage is a result of my neglect of daily study on your precepts. I am ashamed to mention my interest in the Bible to almost anyone. I am intimidated by those in high places and somehow my mouth and heart are closed. I know why: it is because I am not current in my meditation on yourself and your Son as found in your word. Forgive me! I already know what the Bible says and I am bored! It is because I have been deceived—I shall never exhaust the precious treasure of your word! Break the apathy of indifference and open my heart to receive with meekness your life-changing word! Forgive me and renew my mind!

What personal sins do you want to confess? We *must* speak them to remove them.
Do it! *Now.* There is no one else you have sinned against more than God. Tell him so!

4. SING A PRAYER TO GOD.

The Lord is my Shepherd, no want shall I know;
I feed in green pastures, safe-folded I rest;
He leadeth my soul where the still waters flow,
Restores me when wand'ring, redeems when oppressed;
Restores me when wand'ring, redeems when oppressed.

Open your hymn book and sing the rest of the verses—or even sing another prayer song.

5. READ HIS WORD TO HIM!

His Word

[17]"Do not think that I have come to abolish the Law or the Prophets; I have not come to abolish them but to fulfill them. [18]I tell you the truth, until heaven and earth disappear, not the smallest letter, not the least stroke of a pen, will by any means disappear from the Law until everything is accomplished. [19]Anyone who breaks one of the least of these commandments and teaches others to do the same will be called least in the kingdom of heaven, but whoever practices and teaches these commands will be called great in the kingdom of heaven. [20]For I tell you that unless your righteousness surpasses that of the Pharisees and the teachers of the law, you will certainly not enter the kingdom of heaven.

[21]"You have heard that it was said to the people long ago, 'Do not murder, and anyone who murders will be subject to judgment.' [22]But I tell you that anyone who is angry with his brother will be subject to judgment. Again, anyone who says to his brother, 'Raca,' is answerable to the Sanhedrin. But anyone who says, 'You fool!' will be in danger of the fire of hell.

[23]"Therefore, if you are offering your gift at the altar and there remember that your brother has something against you, [24]leave your gift there in front of the altar. First go and be reconciled to your brother; then come and offer your gift.

— *Matthew 5:17-24, NIV*

Read His Word to Him.

It does seem redundant to read the words of your blessed Son back to yourself. But as you know it is a means of praise and wonder. I surely am on holy ground as I read the words of his sermon on the mount. Jesus did not come to repeal or ruin the law but to fulfill it. The law must remain in effect so it can be the standard against which those will be judged who will not accept your leniency through faith in your Son.

Please express your response to this beautiful text. Put your expression in your own prayer diary.

6. READ HIS WORD FOR YOURSELF.

Just for me. I do not have the time or space to worship you through all these verses. I do praise you for the un-alloyed joy I find in my Lord's fulfillment of the law for me. (1) My Lord fulfilled the law's purpose to demonstrate the standard of righteousness by showing himself to be the perfect man and all that you had in mind when you gave the law. Once the law was kept and we can identify with the one who kept it, the law can also be fulfilled in me. Praise your name! (2) My Lord fulfilled the law's purpose to declare the exceeding sinfulness of sin by living as a man above sin, thus condemning all sin that men commit and dissolving all the rationalizations they (we) offer to justify their (our) sinning.

Pause in his presence and either audibly or in written form tell him all his word means to you.

7. READ HIS WORD IN THANKSGIVING.

(1) Thank you that the law has been fulfilled in him — since I am *in him* it is also fulfilled in me! (2) Thank you that all things necessary for my salvation have been accompanied by my Lord. (3) Thank you that there is no escape from the guilt of disobedience — such guilt can drive us to yourself. (4) Thank you for One who was himself all he taught others. (5) Thank you for the *exceeding* righteousness I find in my Lord.

Give yourself to your own expression of gratitude — write it or speak it!

8. READ HIS WORD IN MEDITATION.

". . . leave there your gift before the altar, and go thy way, first be reconciled to thy brother, and then come and offer thy gift." Does our Lord expect us to have a friendly good will toward all with whom we associate? This is exactly what our Lord expects. There are persons who for several reasons become a source of irritation to us. What shall we do with them? These are the very ones of whom we are speaking. There need be no ill will in our heart. Hopefully there will be none in the heart of our brother, but at least in our heart we have freely forgiven him. My Lord is saying to me that resentment and grudges cannot be present if I am truly to worship you. We must give up our hatred or resentment of our brother or our attempted worship.

Pause — wait — think — then express yourself in thoughtful praise or thanks.

9. READ HIS WORD FOR PETITIONS.

How can I receive the fulfillment of the law and the prophets? (1) Relate me to the meaning of the law's fulfillment. (2) I want to see with my heart the One of whom all the prophets spoke. (3) Has all been accomplished in your Son? (4) I want to be taught by Jesus to keep your law. (5) Show me the true motives behind my service for you and others. (6) I do want to right now let heaven rule in my life. (7) Rule from the throne of my heart.

Right here add your personal requests — and his answers.

10. READ HIS WORD AND WAIT — LISTEN — GOD SPEAKS!

Deliver me from being just religious — speak to my conscience! (1) "Claim your citizen's rights in my kingdom." (2) "Your rights are found in me and my words." (3) "Teach men my words and be called by myself great in the kingdom.'"

11. INTERCESSION FOR THE LOST WORLD

Taiwan — Point for prayer: (1) *Missions* — There are now about 770 missionaries in the land. There are many openings for new missionaries in evangelism, church planting, and inspiring of believers to action, but national believers are increasingly shouldering the leadership, administration and burden of the work.

12. SING PRAISES TO OUR LORD.

I love Thy Kingdom, Lord,
The house of Thine abode,

The Church our blessed Redeemer saved
With His own precious blood.

WEEK FORTY-TWO — SUNDAY

1. PRAISE GOD FOR WHO HE IS.

"I have thought much about the course of my life and always turned back to thy instructions. I have never delayed but always made haste to keep thy commandments. . . . At midnight I rise to give thee thanks for the justice of thy decrees" (Psalm 119:59, 62). How full of meaning are these words of the song writer of long ago. How many thousands upon thousands of men and women can say: "I have thought much about the course of my life"? What shall it be that directs my paths? Where shall I find point and purpose to my living? If we cannot find a reason for life in your word we shall not find it! How I want to testify that in the "dead ends of life" I have never delayed but always made haste to keep thy commandments. There really is no option that makes sense. Thank you for your wonderful Son revealed in your word.

Express yourself in adoration for this quality of God.
Speak it audibly or write out your praise in your own devotional journal.

2. PRAISE GOD FOR WHAT HE MEANS TO ME.

Just for me. I have now lived past the "three score" and I am living out the "ten." In these years—and even now—I consider the direction and reason for my life. I find no meaning at all apart from your word! Can we find value in our children—indeed we can if they find life in you and your Son. They are indeed an extension of ourselves, separate and valuable for themselves, but what is there for them without your precepts? What shall we leave in the lives of others that lives after we have moved to another life? The more I think on these matters, the more I want to praise you for your truth that abides forever! An investment with eternal dividends! Praise your name as revealed in your word.

How do you personally relate to the justice of God, and God who is Justice?
Speak it out or write it out. It is *so important* that you establish *your own* devotional journal.

3. CONFESSION OF SIN

Perhaps the first confession would be that verse 62 of this psalm does not apply to me. When has it been that I awoke at midnight and arose to thank you for your self-revelation found in the Bible? If I did it, I can't remember it. What would produce such a nocturnal response? If I was meditating upon the words and meaning of your book just before I retired, such a response might be expected. What we do in our leisure hours does indicate what is in our heart. Dear Lord, forgive me! I could right now choose to change my leisure habits. Is there nothing in your book to fascinate me? Is there nothing I could read that would hold my interest? Dear Lord, I am trying to be as honest with you as I can. (I already know you see the intents of my heart.) Forgive me, I repent!

What personal sins do you want to confess? We *must* speak them to remove them.
Do it! *Now.* There is no one else you have sinned against more than God. Tell him so!

4. SING A PRAYER TO GOD.

A shade by day, defence by night,
A shelter in the time of storm;
No fears alarm, no foes affright,
A shelter in the time of storm.

Oh, Jesus is the Rock in a weary land,
A weary land, a weary land;
Oh, Jesus is a Rock in a weary land,
A shelter in the time of storm.

Open your hymn book and sing the rest of the verses—or even sing another prayer song.

5. READ HIS WORD TO HIM!

His Word

27"You have heard that it was said, 'Do not commit adultery.' 28But I tell you that anyone who looks at a woman lustfully has already committed adultery with her in his heart. 29If your right eye causes you to sin, gouge it out and throw it away. It is better for you to lose one part of your body than for your whole body to be thrown into hell. 30And if your right hand causes you to sin, cut it off and throw it away. It is better for you to lose one part of your body than for your whole body to go into hell.

31"It has been said, 'Anyone who divorces his wife must give her a certificate of divorce.' 32But I tell you that anyone who divorces his wife, except for marital unfaithfulness, causes her to commit adultery, and anyone who marries a woman so divorced commits adultery.

33"Again, you have heard that it was said to the people long ago, 'Do not break your oath, but keep the oaths you have made to the Lord.' 34But I tell you, Do not swear at all: either by heaven, for it is God's throne; 35or by the earth, for it is his footstool; or by Jerusalem, for it is the city of the Great King. 36And do not swear by your head, for you cannot make even one hair white or black. 37Simply let your 'Yes' be 'Yes,' and your 'No,' 'No'; anything beyond this comes from the evil one.

— Matthew 5:27-37, NIV

5. READ HIS WORD TO HIM.

Of all the sections of your word this is the one where it would be so easy to leave the real purpose of these words and launch into a commentary comment on the meaning. My purpose here is to read your word to you in an expression of praise and attempt as much as at all possible to receive with meekness your engrafted word that is able to save my whole life. The problem of adultery has been with society from the beginning of Satan's work. To stop it in the individual heart is to stop it in society. Dear Lord, I am that individual! I want to receive the censure and purifying your son brings to me.

Please express your response to this beautiful text. Put your expression in your own prayer diary.

6. READ HIS WORD FOR YOURSELF.

Just for me. What can save me from the all-pervasive sexuality of this day? Here are the commitments I make to receive this salvation: (1) I want to read all over again and again what you have said about this subject. I Cor. 6:9-20; 10:1-13; chapters 5 and 7 of I Corinthians; I Thess. 4:3-8; Heb. 13:4. I want these words to sink into my conscience. I claim the promise of II Peter 1:3, 4. (2) I want to be so constantly in love with you that I cannot, I do not love the world. I believe this is exactly what I John 2:15, 16 says to me. "The intelligent choice to love all of the opposite sex even as God loves them destroys the power of lust." (3) I want to get a good look at hell and realize that no lustful desire is worth the price attached. I John 3:3 tells me the hope of heaven makes me pure.

Pause in his presence and either audibly or in written form tell him all his word means to you.

7. READ HIS WORD IN THANKSGIVING.

(1) Thank you for your clear unambiguous statement: you shall not commit adultery. (2) Thank you for the opportunity of stopping adultery where it begins. (3) Thank you for the drastic measures my Lord spelled out in stopping lust. (4) Thank you that what seem severe and unusual measures by men are not considered so by you. (5) Thank you for your clear teaching on divorce. (6) Thank you you are just as severe with divorce as with lust. (7) Thank you for the wonderful motivation you have given for telling the truth.

Give yourself to your own expression of gratitude — write it or speak it!

8. READ HIS WORD IN MEDITATION.

"Let your yes be yes and your no, no; anything beyond this comes from the evil one." Man is such a strange creature; when he wants to impress one of his fellow creatures he adds emphasis to his affirmations or denials, when all the while there is a strange possibility that he is not telling the truth. If the heart is basically false, dishonest or unjust the mouth cannot but reveal that condition. Such a man must resort to oaths to guarantee his affirmations, for how else can he make up for his generally-known lack of integrity?

Pause — wait — think — then express yourself in thoughtful praise or thanks.

9. READ HIS WORD FOR PETITIONS.

These revisions of the ten commandments move me to ask for help: (1) How can I prevent the lustful look? (2) I want to see every woman as a precious person not a sex symbol. (3) My look need not enter my imagination — keep me aware of this. (4) Give me the courage to perform the drastic mental surgery here suggested. (5) I know you want my whole self — I want to give it. (6) I am so glad for the wife you gave me — I want to give my whole self to her. (7) It is so easy for me to over emphasize — deliver me — I want my "yes to be a simple 'yes.'"

Please, please remember these are prayers.

10. READ HIS WORD AND WAIT — LISTEN — GOD SPEAKS!

Emphasize all over again the depth of these words: (1) "Bring every thought into my captivity." (2) "Bring your mate often to me in prayer." (3) "Hold your emotions up to me that I might heal them."

11. INTERCESSION FOR THE LOST WORLD

Taiwan — Point for prayer: (1) *Literature work is now extensive.* There are plans to penetrate the secular book market with Christian books as well as publishing new books translated from other languages and encouraging local writers.

12. SING PRAISE TO OUR LORD.

O worship the King, all glorious above,
And gratefully sing His wonderful love;
Our Shield and Defender, the Ancient of days,
Pavilioned in splendor, and girded with praise.

WEEK FORTY-TWO – MONDAY

1. PRAISE GOD FOR WHO HE IS.

"Thy statutes are the theme of my song (or wonderful to me) wherever I make my home. In the night I remember thy name, O Lord, and dwell upon thy law. . . . With all my heart I have tried to please thee; fulfill thy promise and be gracious to me" (Psalm 119:54, 55, 58). What marvelous qualities of yourself are found in these verses! (1) Your word (which is but an expression of yourself) is such that it makes me want to sing, i.e., there is happi-ness in the meaning of your word. (2) Your word is of such substance it produces a theme—your word has continuing meaning in it. (3) No environment need hinder my song. Your word produces my environment. (4) If I meditate upon your word for a period of the day you will bring it to mind at night. In all these ways and more you are active in my life. Praise your name!

Express yourself in adoration for this quality of God.
Speak it audibly or write out your praise in your own devotional journal.

2. PRAISE GOD FOR WHAT HE MEANS TO ME.

Just for me. I have related the above praise to myself— only because what is true for me can be, and should be true of all men. I continue the attributes of yourself I see in this text. (5) At night I can quietly absorb the meaning of what you have said, i.e., "meditate upon your word," or "dwell upon your law." I am not reading rules and regulations; I am reveling in revelation that has life and hope and peace for my troubled heart. (6) You prompt a desire in me to please you. I would not do it only out of fear; if I did I would not be so happy about it. The text says it exactly as I do it: *"I have tried* to please you." I'm delighted to include the last quality. (7) "Fulfill thy promise *and be gracious to me."* I claim your unearned favor!

How do you personally relate to the song of God, and God who is the source of our song?
Speak it out or write it out. It is *so important* that you establish *your own* devotional journal.

3. CONFESSION OF SIN

Much of my praise has been admixed with confession. At the same time, it will be good to delineate the specifics of my failures to be forgiven and be reminded again how totally dependent I am upon you. (1) Whereas I could sing your praises everyday, I fail to do so because I simply do not spend adequate thought on your word. (2) The theme of my life is yourself, but I feel like I am just learning how to make them true. (3) I have been (or allowed myself to be) overcome with the environment. Forgive me. (4) Night time is a period of real need—I am tired and vulnerable—thank you for speaking to this need. (5) I have not meditated on your word at night—not at all as I could—I am glad to respond to what you are saying here. (6) I am not always filled with a desire to please you, but I want to be. (7) I do indeed claim your grace. Thank you for your mercy!

What personal sins do you want to confess? We *must* speak them to remove them.
Do it! *Now.* There is no one else you have sinned against more than God. Tell him so!

4. SING A PRAYER TO GOD.

Take the world, but give me Jesus,
All its joys are but a name;
But His love abideth ever,
Thro' eternal years the same.

Oh, the height and depth of mercy!
Oh, the length and breadth of love!
Oh, the fullness of redemption,
Pledge of endless life above!

Open your hymn book and sing the rest of the verses—or even sing another prayer song.

5. READ HIS WORD TO HIM!

His Word

[38]"You have heard that it was said, 'Eye for eye, and tooth for tooth.' [39]But I tell you, Do not resist an evil person. If someone strikes you on the right cheek, turn to him the other also. [40]And if someone wants to sue you and take your tunic, let him have your cloak as well. [41]If someone forces you to go one mile, go with him two miles. [42]Give to the one who asks you, and do not turn away from the one who wants to borrow from you.

[43]"You have heard that it was said, 'Love your neighbor and hate your enemy.' [44]But I tell you: Love your enemies and pray for those who persecute you, [45]that you may be sons of your Father in heaven. He causes his sun to rise on the evil and the good, and sends rain on the righteous and the unrighteous. [46]If you love those who love you, what reward will you get? Are not even the tax collectors doing that? [47]And if you greet only your brothers, what are you doing more than others? Do not even pagans do that? [48]Be perfect, therefore, as your heavenly Father is perfect.
— *Matthew 5:38-48, NIV*

Read His Word to Him.

Dear Lord, who is sufficient to receive the application of your Son's words to his interpersonal relationships?

Non-resistance in personal problems. You are speaking to me in the four examples of my Lord: (1) In personal insults of a physical or verbal nature: "Whosoever smiteth thee on thy right cheek, turn to him the other also." (2) In litigation over trifles (which includes personal property): "If any man would go to law with thee, and take away thy coat, let him have thy cloak also." Considering how valuable the coat and cloak were in my Lord's day such would include equally valuable items with me. (3) When I am pressed into service I do not want to give I must hear my Lord speak to me: ". . . Whosoever shall compel thee to go one mile, go with him two." (4) Most of all, when asked for a gift or a loan "return good for evil by intelligent liberality."

Please express your response to this beautiful text. Put your expression in your own prayer diary.

6. READ HIS WORD FOR YOURSELF.

These words speak so powerfully to my heart. *On verse 44:* ". . . this word *enemy* covers the whole realm of those who oppose: personal antagonists, business competitors, political opponents, social rivals." *On verse 45:* "The honest man, whose conscience has been stabbed by Christ's message and who feels keenly his own imperfection, will be reminded that God did truly bless him even in his sinfulness. Such a disciple will be motivated to bless and help men, especially his enemies, loving them as God first loved him." Dear Lord, this is my desire and prayer.

Pause in his presence and either audibly or in written form tell him all his word means to you.

7. READ HIS WORD IN THANKSGIVING.

(1) Thank you there is a way to remove the desire for personal retaliation. (2) Thank you that I now know love and good will are more important than personal property. (3) Thank you that it is not necessary to determine if a person deserves the gift before I give it. (4) Thank you I can actually return good for evil—Lord, help me to *do it!*

Give yourself to your own expression of gratitude—write it or speak it!

8. READ HIS WORD IN MEDITATION.

"Be perfect, therefore, as your heavenly Father is perfect." If our Lord knew we could not keep the law of Moses, and he did, then what *does* he mean by asking us to "be perfect"? "He who loves like the heavenly Father loves, is thoroughly equipped to grow into absolute perfection. He who loves, needs no other rules or standards, for he will always act in the best interest of his neighbor, friend or enemy. To love consistently is to be perfect." One translation of I John 2:5 is: "Whoever practices obedience to his message really has a perfect love of God in his heart." We are indebted to Harold Fowler for the thoughts in the above. "Laws are but the muscles of love, given to punish those who are unable or unwilling to be governed directly by love" (*ibid*).

Pause—wait—think—then express yourself in thoughtful praise or thanks.

9. READ HIS WORD FOR PETITIONS.

These words of my Lord on non-resistance and love call for the following requests: (1) What real spiritual value is there in non-resistance? (2) I want to make real practical application of these words—lead me into a situation where this can happen. (3) When am I being taken advantage of? I really need heaven's wisdom in answering this question. (4) Who are the enemies for whom I shall pray? (5) How can I express my love for those who hate me? (6) I want the perfection my Lord asked of me. (7) In all the above areas I do expect your answer as I am willing to perceive it and receive it.

Right here add your personal requests—and his answers.

10. READ HIS WORD AND WAIT—LISTEN—GOD SPEAKS!

You surely have much to say to me in these verses: (1) "Do not resist an evil person." (2) "Love your enemies." (3) "Pray for those who persecute you."

11. INTERCESSION FOR THE LOST WORLD

Taiwan — Point for prayer: (1) *Between 1945 and 1960* there was great growth in the Church—both due to the influx of Christians and many experienced Christian workers at the fall of the Mainland, and also a remarkable people movement among the mountain tribes. Growth has slowed due to increasing materialism, the overdependence of many of the smaller churches on overseas funds and failure to teach and mobilize the church members for outreach and personal evangelism. The need of the Church today is for systematic Bible teaching and revival to bring unity and zeal for outreach.

12. SING PRAISES TO OUR LORD.

Come, we that love the Lord,
And let our joys be known;

Join in a song with sweet accord,
And thus surround the throne.

WEEK FORTY-TWO — TUESDAY

1. PRAISE GOD FOR WHO HE IS.

"Thou, Lord, art all I have; I have promised to keep thy word . . . Thou hast shown thy servant much kindness, fulfilling the word, O Lord. Give me insight, give me knowledge, for I put my trust in thy commandments" (Psalm 119:57, 65, 66). All praise is a form of testimony when it comes from the heart. What did the psalmist mean when he said, you were all he had? Dear Lord, this is so literally true in the lives of all men. All we have in the capacity to understand is from you. Our intelligence is from you. All we have in the use of this marvellous capacity capacity is found in your word. Life would make no sense without your word—there would be no point to intelligence without your word.

Express yourself in adoration for this quality of God.
Speak it audibly or write out your praise in your own devotional journal.

2. PRAISE GOD FOR WHAT HE MEANS TO ME.

Just for me. I am "thy servant" of verse 65. You have been so kind to me that I am simply overcome. You have promised over and over again to be kind to me, and yet when your promise is fulfilled I am surprised, delighted all over again! Because of my guilt I do not expect kindness. I so easily forget my guilt is only a hedge to lead me to you. How I rejoice to read the promise in verse 66 that you promise me insight if I only ask, and O how I do ask! Insight I receive as equal to wisdom. I read and claim your promise in James 1:5, 6 as well as in this verse.

How do you personally relate to the kindness of God, and God who is Sufficient?
Speak it out or write it out. It is *so important* that you establish *your own* devotional journal.

3. CONFESSION OF SIN

My desires and dreams are not matched with reality. But more and more I see one merged with the other. At the same time, it would be easy to be despondent over the difference. A replay of the activities of one day, or one week, would give lie to the claim that: "Thou art all I have"—or would it? "Man looketh on the outward appearance, but God looketh on the heart." Dear Lord, at the best, with the most one could say for attitude and performance I am miserably short. Forgive me. Sin is like the refuse of daily living—we surely have a large amount of it to get rid of.

What personal sins do you want to confess? We *must* speak them to remove them.
Do it! *Now.* There is no one else you have sinned against more than God. Tell him so!

4. SING A PRAYER TO GOD.

"Give me thy heart," says the Savior of men,
Calling in mercy again and again;
"Turn now from sin, and from evil depart,
Have I not died for thee? give me thy heart."

"Give me thy heart, Give me thy heart,"
Hear the soft whisper, wherever thou art;
From this dark world He would draw thee apart,
Speaking so tenderly, "Give me thy heart."

Open your hymn book and sing the rest of the verses—or even sing another prayer song.

5. READ HIS WORD TO HIM!

His Word

6 "Be careful not to do your 'acts of righteousness' before men, to be seen by them. If you do, you will have no reward from your Father in heaven.

2"So when you give to the needy, do not announce it with trumpets, as the hypocrites do in the synagogues and on the streets, to be honored by men. I tell you the truth, they have received their reward in full. 3But when you give to the needy, do not let your left hand know what your right hand is doing, 4so that your giving may be in secret. Then your Father, who sees what is done in secret, will reward you.

5"But when you pray, do not be like the hypocrites, for they love to pray standing in the synagogues and on the street corners to be seen by men. I tell you the truth, they have received their reward in full. 6When you pray, go into your room, close the door and pray to your Father, who is unseen. Then your Father, who sees what is done in secret, will reward you. 7And when you pray, do not keep on babbling like pagans, for they think they will be heard because of their many words. 8Do not be like them, for your Father knows what you need before you ask him.

9"This is how you should pray:
"'Our Father in heaven,
hallowed be your name,
10your kingdom come,
your will be done
on earth as it is in heaven.
11Give us today our daily bread.
12Forgive us our debts,
as we also have forgiven our debtors.
13And lead us not into temptation,
but deliver us from the evil one.'
14For if you forgive men when they sin against you, your heavenly Father will also forgive you.

—Matthew 6:1-14, NIV

Read His Word to Him.

Dear Lord, there could be no passage of scripture that strikes closer to my heart than this one. What a struggle I have with my motives! If I worry about what men say or think about this righteous act or that one then I know I am wrong. It is with your good pleasure and approval I must concern myself. Dear Lord, as you know my motives so you judge me. It is a small matter to be judged of man. It is good to be able to give to the needs of men with no fanfare or recognition. Praise you that such is possible today. I have wondered *much* and *often* about the publication of these prayers I am even now writing. I know just two things about them: (1) Without either writing or speaking audibly there is no way I can keep my mind on what I am doing. (2) My desire is to help others in the one most important area of need which is prayer. If I can be of help in the development of personal worship I want to do it. We all learn better by a model. If those reading these lines have been able to see how you have led me and directed my wayward mind to your throne I shall be glad, very glad.

Please express your response to this beautiful text. Put your expression in your own prayer diary.

6. READ HIS WORD FOR YOURSELF.

Just for me. It does occur to me that writing or speaking in prayer would eliminate vain repetitions, i.e., if we are sincere. My particular concern just here is to pray the prayer my Lord here taught his disciples. Just as if I had never before prayed these lovely words let me say them again with all the meaning I can put into them.

Pause in his presence and either audibly or in written form tell him all his word means to you.

7. READ HIS WORD IN THANKSGIVING.

(1) Thank you that there is a wonderful exciting reward reserved in heaven for me. (2) Thank you for the privilege and joy of giving especially to those who do not know who gave. (3) Thank you for the "recompense" from yourself promised to those who give. (4) Thank you for the life-changing experience of praying to you "in secret," i.e., with total sincerity. (5) Thank you that you know my needs and meet many of them without my request.

Give yourself to your own expression of gratitude—write it or speak it!

8. READ HIS WORD IN MEDITATION.

"Lead us not into temptation, but deliver us from evil." Back of all action is God. He either directly or ultimately controls everything. This request is based squarely upon such a truth. James tells us not to attribute temptation to God (James 1:13-15). I Corinthians 10:13 tells us that no temptation will appear in our experience without a way out or through. This is a prayer to not lead us into an overbearing situation where instead of growing stronger we are overcome. What a blessed request this is! God knows we are not match for the evil one, our Lord reminds us we can ask him to so arrange the circumstances of our daily life that we will be delivered from the power of Satan. This is no insurance against chastening—"whom the Lord loveth he chasteneth" (Heb. 12:6-8), but it is a promise that if we ask he will rescue all of us from what could be an impossible situation.

Pause—wait—think—then express yourself in thoughtful praise or thanks.

9. READ HIS WORD FOR PETITIONS.

I have good reasons to pray over my acts of righteousness: (1) Keep my expressions of worship hidden from men. (2) Increase my desire and capacity to give to the needy. (3) Open my eyes to see your rewards for me. (4) Deliver me from praying in any way to be seen of men. (5) Wherever I go give me a prayer room. (6) "Hallowed by your name." (7) May your will be done by my willingness this day in my eating and speaking.

Please, please remember these are prayers—speak them—reword them!

10. READ HIS WORD AND WAIT—LISTEN—GOD SPEAKS!

I can think of no more important words from you to me than these: (1) "I will give you your daily bread." (2) "Forgive as you want to be forgiven." (3) "If you ask I will deliver you from the evil one."

11. INTERCESSION FOR THE LOST WORLD

Taiwan — Point for prayer: (1) *The witness to Students* —the 300,000 university students are probably the most open section of the community now. Many churches have student centers that are well used.

12. SING PRAISES TO OUR LORD.

Wounded for me, wounded for me,
There on the cross He was wounded for me;
Gone my transgressions, and now I am free,
All because Jesus was wounded for me.

WEEK FORTY-TWO — WEDNESDAY

1. PRAISE GOD FOR WHO HE IS.

"The law thou hast ordained means more to me than a fortune in gold and silver. Thy hands moulded me and made me what I am; show me how I may learn thy commandments" (Psalm 119:72, 73). If Solomon wrote this psalm he could speak from experience — to him we could refer for a real example of one who had a fortune in gold and silver. We could even relate this to David as an example. But for us who have never had anything close to a fortune in gold and silver, and have never been all that taken up in the value and beauty of your word, how could we offer anything but an inexperienced opinion? Dear Lord, we do have more than opinion! We have Jesus' own words. He who was rich beyond our wildest imagination said: "A man's happiness, satisfaction, or 'life' does not consist in gold and silver (or the abundance of the things he can buy)."

Express yourself in adoration for this quality of God.
Speak it audibly or write out your praise in your own devotional journal.

2. PRAISE GOD FOR WHAT HE MEANS TO ME.

Just for me. If I had to make a choice between one or the other, I do not believe there would be a problem. It is trying to have both that causes no end of problems. We like to think that a fortune in gold and silver would be the means of advancing your cause. If we are not in love with our Lord and his word now we will not be in love with him and his word when we have the gold and silver. The basic problem is how do I use what I have to honor your rule in my life? Dear Lord, I want to impress these words upon my deepest consciousness: *"Thy hands moulded me and made me what I am."* This happened historically in Adam — it happened spiritually thru the second Adam and my acceptance of his free gift. Dear Lord, it is happening *personally* by my learning from you as you teach me from your commandments.

How do you personally relate to the molding of God, and God who is the Potter?
Speak it out or write it out. It is *so important* that you establish *your own* devotional journal.

3. CONFESSION OF SIN

In the realm of law it is not difficult to feel very, very guilty. We can fill up the page or the air with rationalizations, or justification, or excuses, but when it has all been said the guilt remains.

It seems there is more in this one psalm than I had ever imagined. But without your grace and mercy there is nothing here — nothing but guilt. It is only when I regard your work in me as a continuing, never ending, process that I can enter the reality of the values here discerned. I try (I only try) to be as open and honest with you as I possibly can; my sin is a true embarrassment to me. I have marked this in two or three areas just yesterday. Dear God, if you are not in the process of teaching me your commandments (even through my failures), I have no hope at all. But I know you are! Praise your name! My admiration for your law grows every day!

What personal sins do you want to confess? We *must* speak them to remove them.
Do it! *Now.* There is no one else you have sinned against more than God. Tell him so!

4. SING A PRAYER TO GOD.

My Jesus, I love Thee, I know Thou art mine,
For Thee all the follies of sin I resign;

My gracious Redeemer, my Savior art Thou;
If ever I loved Thee, my Jesus, 'tis now.

Open your hymn book and sing the rest of the verses — or even sing another prayer song.

5. READ HIS WORD TO HIM!

His Word

[16]"When you fast, do not look somber as the hypocrites do, for they disfigure their faces to show men they are fasting. I tell you the truth, they have received their reward in full. [17]But when you fast, put oil on your head and wash your face, [18]so that it will not be obvious to men that you are fasting, but only to your Father, who is unseen; and your Father, who sees what is done in secret, will reward you.

[19]"Do not store up for yourselves treasures on earth, where moth and rust destroy, and where thieves break in and steal. [20]But store up for yourselves treasures in heaven, where moth and rust do not destroy, and where thieves do not break in and steal. [21]For where your treasure is, there your heart will be also.

[22]"The eye is the lamp of the body. If your eyes are good, your whole body will be full of light. [23]But if your eyes are bad, your whole body will be full of darkness. If then the light within you is darkness, how great is that darkness!
— *Matthew 6:16-23, NIV*

WEEK FORTY-TWO — WEDNESDAY

Read His Word to Him.

Dear Lord, there is so much to assimilate in these verses I am embarrassed to give only a superficial consideration to them. As I see them there are three areas in which you are speaking to my heart: (1) *Fasting* (vss. 16-18). (2) *Treasures* (vss. 19-21). (3) *Personal dedication* (vss. 22-24). How I do want to open my ears and eyes to hear and see all you have for me. It is my deepest desire to be open to receive with meekness your word.

Please express your response to this beautiful text. Put your expression in your own prayer diary.

6. READ HIS WORD FOR YOURSELF.

Just for me. I receive to my whole self these words: "Put your trust in God alone! Put your whole confidence in things eternal, for only they are permanent. Concentrate your attention and service upon God and his promises, since double-mindedness is a really impossible course. It brings on unnecessary worries and draws the attention away from God. Real faith is able to concentrate upon God's rule and provisions and accept life as a matter of course, living one day at a time" (*Fowler*).

Pause in his presence and either audibly or in written form tell him all his word means to you.

7. READ HIS WORD IN THANKSGIVING.

(1) Thank you for the provision of fasting—I know I need it. (2) Thank you for all three of these provisions for worship: (a) alms, (b) prayer and (c) fasting. I want and need them all. (3) Thank you that you are ever vigilant to see and meet my need. (4) Thank you for the identity of real treasure. (5) Thank you for the clear statement that focus of attention and interest produces either light or darkness.

Give yourself to your own expression of gratitude—write it or speak it!

8. READ HIS WORD IN MEDITATION.

"You cannot serve God and Mammon." Our Lord is not talking about God *or* money, he is talking about God *and* money. He is saying we cannot serve both of them at the same time. We can serve money or we can serve God, but it is impossible to give adequate service to both at the same time. The service suggested here is that of a slave—it is the giving of one's self to a master. There are several reasons besides the one basic reason just cited. (1) Money and God have different goals—one is selfless service; the other is selfishness. (2) Money and God have motivations; one asks to walk by sight the other by faith. (3) They have different fulfillment; one is of this earth earthy and the other is eternal. (4) They have different effect on those who serve; one produces contentment and the other anxiety.

Pause—wait—think—then express yourself in thoughtful praise or thanks.

9. READ HIS WORD FOR PETITIONS.

I find no passage of scripture more full of potential for petitions: (1) Enable me to forgive as I want to be forgiven. (2) Give me the courage to claim the forgiveness you promise. (3) Lead me into a practical use of the instructions on fasting. (4) Open my eyes as to the real reward from fasting. (5) How I do want to know how to store up treasures in heaven. (6) Enlarge my understanding of the real value of heaven's treasures. (7) Having my whole body full of light is such an attractive thought—develop my point of view that this might happen.

Right here add your personal requests—and his answers.

10. READ HIS WORD AND WAIT—LISTEN—GOD SPEAKS!

What do you say to me in these words? (1) "Forgiveness of others from the heart is much more than a good idea—it is essential!" (2) "I assume that my disciples will fast." (3) "You can and should accumulate treasures in the eternal world."

11. INTERCESSION FOR THE LOST WORLD

Taiwan — Point for prayer: (1) *The Protestant Church* today is stronger among the Mandarin speakers, but weaker among the Hoklo, and very weak among the Hakka. There are fine national leaders of maturity and many Bible Schools and Seminaries training workers for the churches. Greatest growth is seen among the two larger indigenous Chinese Churches because of a high degree of loyalty to the Lord and their fellowship and the involvement of the whole membership in outreach.

12. SING PRAISES TO OUR LORD.

We gather together to ask the Lord's blessing,
He chastens and hastens His will to make known;
The wicked oppressing cease them from distressing,
Sing praises to His name, He forgets not His own.

WEEK FORTY-TWO — THURSDAY

1. PRAISE GOD FOR WHO HE IS.

"Those who fear thee shall see me and rejoice, because I have hoped in thy word. I know, O Lord, that thy judgments are right, and that in faithfulness thou hast afflicted me" (Psalm 119:74, 75). As I appear before your throne of grace and affirm the statement of the psalmist, I at the same time must remember that: "Thou Lord, seest me." Dear Lord, I have hoped in your word—I do hope in your word—but you know how woefully short all my best efforts are. What quality of yourself do I see in these two verses? There are two attributes for which I praise you and all men can praise you: (1) *Hope.* Only in you as revealed in your word is there hope. How empty and meaningless is life without this quality. (2) *Chastening.* Because you love me, and all men, you interrupt our selfishness to let us know there is something more in life than sex, food and money.

Express yourself in adoration for this quality of God.
Speak it audibly or write out your praise in your own devotional journal.

2. PRAISE GOD FOR WHAT HE MEANS TO ME.

Just for me. It is both good and frightening that our lives are observed by others. It is good because we have opportunity to give life to all the lessons and sermons we have taught and preached. It is frightening because the *credibility gap* is sometimes rather large. Dear Lord, I do want to be my own best convert, my own best student. Even as I praise you for this privilege there are those who observe us and who also love us. They are as willing to accept us with our imperfections as you are. I take this to refer to the interpersonal living of the family and close friends. But even here, dear Father, I want to "hope" or "trust" in your word.

Could it be that I accept affliction as coming from you? You permit it if you do not immediately send it. You use it whatever its source. Praise your wonderful grace.

How do you personally relate to the chastening of God, and God who is our Father?
Speak it out or write it out. It is *so important* that you establish *your own* devotional journal.

3. CONFESSION OF SIN

It is very easy to fall into the trap of self-pity, or morbid introspection. I have recognized such qualities as from the evil one. I reject them and ask for your help. In the same principle of accepting affliction in self-pity is the possibility of recognizing it as an expression of your love. In the option to self-loathing is the possibility of inward cleansing. Dear Lord, I ask for humility and freedom— praise your name—I find them both in my response to Calvary. Help me dear Lord, to be so busy meditating upon your word that there will be no time to wonder or worry about what men will see or say. In your personal interest in my needs you have afflicted me. I refer to whatever it is that hinders my plans.

What personal sins do you want to confess? We *must* speak them to remove them.
Do it! *Now.* There is no one else you have sinned against more than God. Tell him so!

4. SING A PRAYER TO GOD.

Not a shadow can rise,
Not a cloud in the skies,
But His smile quickly drives it away;
Not a doubt or a fear,
Not a sigh nor a tear,

Can abide while we trust and obey.
Trust and obey, for there's no other way
To be happy in Jesus,
But to trust and obey.

Open your hymn book and sing the rest of the verses—or even sing another prayer song.

5. READ HIS WORD TO HIM!
His Word

[25]"Therefore I tell you, do not worry about your life, what you will eat or drink; or about your body, what you will wear. Is not life more important than food, and the body more important than clothes? [26]Look at the birds of the air; they do not sow or reap or store away in barns, and yet your heavenly Father feeds them. Are you not much more valuable than they? [27]Who of you by worrying can add a single hour to his life?

[28]"And why do you worry about clothes? See how the lilies of the field grow. They do not labor or spin. [29]Yet I tell you that not even Solomon in all his splendor was dressed like one of these. [30]If that is how God clothes the grass of the field, which is here today and tomorrow is thrown into the fire, will he not much more clothe you, O you of little faith? [31]So do not worry, saying, 'What shall we eat?' or 'What shall we drink?' or 'What shall we wear?' [32]For the pagans run after all these things, and your heavenly Father knows that you need them. [33]But seek first his kingdom and his righteousness, and all these things will be given to you as well. [34]Therefore do not worry about tomorrow, for tomorrow will worry about itself. Each day has enough trouble of its own.
—Matthew 6:25-34, NIV

(Cf. Luke 12:22-48)

WEEK FORTY-TWO — THURSDAY

Read His Word to Him.

It is a rare opportunity we have to look every day at part of your word with a fresh perspective — just as if we had never seen it before. What a startling statement this verse appears! Do not worry! Do not be anxious; quit fretting! Ah, it is all well enough to say, but a man must eat! That is the very point — life is not the pursuit of food. A man has to have clothes — no, he doesn't; if life is one constant effort to acquire clothes, life is not worth the living.

Please express your response to this beautiful text. Put your expression in your own prayer diary.

6. READ HIS WORD FOR YOURSELF.

Dear Lord, it would be easy for me to "bow out" on this text. I could say quite plainly, "I do not worry" and to some extent this is true. But as you know my heart, there are several areas where such is not true. Do I give much more anxious thought than I should to what men think of what I said, wrote or did? Dear Lord, I'm guilty. Have I asked far too many times about how this or that project will eventuate? My Lord, how wrong I have been here! When will I take a good look at the track record of all my concern? What have I added by all my inquiries?

Pause in his presence and either audibly or in written form tell him all his word means to you.

7. READ HIS WORD IN THANKSGIVING.

(1) Thank you for the example of your care and interest in birds — such an example for me! (2) Thank you for the beauty of the lilies teaching me of your law and your mercy. (3) Thank you for the promise of clothes and food from my unanxious response to what you have given me. (4) Thank you that you make these promises to your children — to those who trust you. (5) Thank you, thank you for the *One* principle that solves anxieties: "Seek first your rule in my life."

Give yourself to your own expression of gratitude — write it or speak it!

8. READ HIS WORD IN MEDITATION.

"Let the day's own trouble be sufficient for the day." This is my Lord's way of saying, "Live one day at a time." How wonderfully good to know he is also promising sufficient grace to cope with the trouble of that day. To borrow tomorrow's cares is real presumption — we do not know we will have tomorrow. When we learn to live one day at a time we can stop our worrying. Tomorrow really never exists — when it dawns, lo, it is today! If we anticipate problems for tomorrow along with the troubles of today we will have more than we are able to handle. How beautiful is the promise of Deuteronomy, "As thy days are so shall thy strength be" (Deuteronomy 23:23).

Pause — wait — think — then express yourself in thoughtful praise or thanks.

9. READ HIS WORD FOR PETITIONS.

Here is a gold mine of prayer requests: (1) Deliver me from the demands of anxiety — give me *your* peace. (2) Enlarge my understanding of the importance of being alive. (3) Open my eyes to see the birds of the air as you do. (4) I want to stand again beneath the cross of your Son and remember how much any one of us is worth to you. (5) I want wisdom to know the difference between trusting and fatalism.

Please, please remember these are prayers — speak them — reword them!

10. READ HIS WORD AND WAIT — LISTEN — GOD SPEAKS!

Speak to me in these beautiful words: (1) "Who has given you all you have to this present moment? Is it not even myself?" (2) "I know what you need and I will give it." (3) "Seek first my rule in your heart and my direction in your conduct."

11. INTERCESSION FOR THE LOST WORLD

Taiwan — Point for prayer: (1) *The Tribal Church* now claims 80% of the people and nearly half the Christians. In recent years there has been spiritual decline due to poverty, inadequate Bible teaching and ensuring of a personal relationship with the Lord for each Christian. The breakdown of tribal life has been speeded up by the drift of many to the cities and increasing education among the young people. Immorality among the youth, and inability of parents to control their children in a changing society have led to the loss of many young people.

12. SING PRAISES TO OUR LORD.

My gracious Master and my God,
Assist me to proclaim,
To spread thro' all the earth abroad,
The honors of Thy name.

WEEK FORTY-TWO — FRIDAY

1. PRAISE GOD FOR WHO HE IS.

"Let me give my whole heart to thy statutes, so that I am not put to shame. I long with all my heart for thy deliverance, hoping for the fulfillment of thy word" (Psalm 119:80, 81). Right here and right now I want to give my whole heart to you in praise for the qualities I see of yourself in these verses. (1) You care about my embarrassment. Indeed you do not want any man anywhere at anytime to be "put to shame." (2) This verse is really discussing a positive action for man. You want man to be constantly fulfilled. (3) You are very much concerned that we be the victor instead of the victim—the overcomer instead of the overcome. Praise your name for such a promise! (4) Most of all you are immutable, i.e., you never change—your word is *always* fulfilled! This can be both joy and grief—unspeakable joy and grief beyond words.

Express yourself in adoration for this quality of God.
Speak it audibly or write out your praise in your own devotional journal.

2. PRAISE GOD FOR WHAT HE MEANS TO ME.

Just for me. It seems so often that the words of the text were written just for me alone. My shame and embarrassment are all associated with one lack: the translation of your word into daily conduct. What I want above all is a consistency in conduct that will enable me to be the same at all times in all places with everyone. I am really asking for a fulfillment of your own nature in me! Somehow, dear Lord, I believe if I give my whole heart to you the whole time it will happen. Even as I say this I want to read again the verse that speaks of giving my whole heart to your statutes.

How do you personally relate to the love of God, and God who loves us?
Speak it out or write it out. It is *so important* that you establish *your own* devotional journal.

3. CONFESSION OF SIN

I can identify with the nation of Israel (or at least with the minority) who looked and longed for the coming of the Messiah. As they expected the Christ to deliver them—as their sight grew dim with looking for the promise so does my heart long after the forming of Christ within me. This is my basic sin and greatest need. There seem to be two worlds: (1) The world of worship and meditation—of rejoicing in your presence. (2) The world of the daily routine duties of the day. Somehow my dear Lord was able to merge these two worlds until his life and attitudes were worship. It is for the forming of this one in my heart that I yearn.

What personal sins do you want to confess? We *must* speak them to remove them.
Do it! *Now.* There is no one else you have sinned against more than God. Tell him so!

4. SING A PRAYER TO GOD.

He stood at my heart's door 'mid sunshine and rain,
And patiently waited an entrance to gain;
What shame that so long He entreated in vain,
For He is so precious to me.

For He is so precious to me,
For He is so precious to me;
'Tis Heaven below My Redeemer to know,
For He is so precious to me.

Open your hymn book and sing the rest of the verses—or even sing another prayer song.

5. READ HIS WORD TO HIM!

His Word

7 "Do not judge, or you too will be judged. ²For in the same way you judge others, you will be judged, and with the measure you use, it will be measured to you. ³"Why do you look at the speck of sawdust in your brother's eye and pay no attention to the plank in your own eye? ⁴How can you say to your brother, 'Let me take the speck out of your eye,' when all the time there is a plank in your own eye? ⁵You hypocrite, first take the plank out of your own eye, and then you will see clearly to remove the speck from your brother's eye.

⁶"Do not give dogs what is sacred; do not throw your pearls to pigs. If you do, they may trample them under their feet, and then turn and tear you to pieces.

⁷"Ask and it will be given to you; seek and you will find; knock and the door will be opened to you. ⁸For everyone who asks receives; he who seeks finds; and to him who knocks, the door will be opened.

⁹"Which of you, if his son asks for bread, will give him a stone? ¹⁰Or if he asks for a fish, will give him a snake? ¹¹If you, then, though you are evil, know how to give good gifts to your children, how much more will your Father in heaven give good gifts to those who ask him! ¹²In everything, do to others what you would have them do to you, for this sums up the Law and the Prophets.

— *Matthew 7:1-12, NIV*

Read also Luke 6:37-42.

Read His Word to Him.

Dear Lord, how often I feel totally inadequate and full of presumption to attempt to read these words back to you and yet, once I begin I find in this an experience of purifying and enlightenment I could find nowhere else.

In this passage I want to know just who is included in these words. I believe he is talking to me. When I am unmerciful in my criticism of others he speaks to me. When I condemn on the basis of suspicion and surmises, I am guilty of judging as my Lord here describes it. When my motive for criticism has no help to offer the one criticized I am guilty. How easy it is to fall into the trap of smug self-righteousness!

Please express your response to this beautiful text. Put your expression in your own prayer diary.

6. READ HIS WORD FOR YOURSELF.

Whereas I spoke about myself (and meant every word) it was the principle applicable to all I had in mind. Here, dear Lord, speak just to my heart!

Fault finding is the sad admission of a sinful heart. Do I have some secret joy in finding a failure in someone else I imagine is not found in me? Why am I ready to presume my brother or sister guilty before proper investigation? Isn't this the terrible sin my Lord is here condemning?

Harold Fowler has said it so well:
"To judge or criticize another is to put oneself in a position superior to, and removed from, the one he criticizes. But as long as we are men, we do not enjoy that privileged position. A critical spirit makes us hard, cruel and vindictive and, worse yet, quite convinced that we are indeed superior men."
Dear Lord, forgive! My goodness is in you not myself!

Pause in his presence and either audibly or in written form tell him all his word means to you.

7. READ HIS WORD IN THANKSGIVING.

(1) Thank you that judgment has been taken out of my hands when it relates to motives. (2) Thank you for the lovely oil of gladness we have in these verses as related to interpersonal relationships. (3) Thank you for the promise that men will reciprocate in kind. (4) Thank you that we need not be blind men, nor follow blind men.

Give yourself to your own expression of gratitude—write it or speak it!

8. READ HIS WORD IN MEDITATION.

"... *for out of the abundance of the heart his mouth speaks.*" It would seem our Lord is saying that when the heart gets full enough it will spill over into the mouth. Not everything that comes into our mind is expressed with our mouth. It is only when the mind understands it, the will identifies or agrees with it, and the emotions are aroused by it that what has thus filled our heart comes out of our mouth. We are not suggesting that any long period of time is involved. If the subject is of such a nature that we are immediately made responsible for what we say, then more time is necessary.

Pause—wait—think—then express yourself in thoughtful praise or thanks.

9. READ HIS WORD FOR PETITIONS.

What a privilege to allow you to help me pray from these verses: (1) Guard my heart against criticism of my brother. (2) I do *not* know men's motives—keep me full of love. (3) Show me my own hypocrisy. (4) I do want to get the planks out of my own eye—help me. (5) Please enlighten my understanding as to just when I am casting pearls to pigs. (6) I am asking for heaven's wisdom in my praying. (7) How I want to apply the golden rule in my house to those I know the best.

Right here add your personal requests—and his answers.

10. READ HIS WORD AND WAIT—LISTEN—GOD SPEAKS!

(1) "What you condemn in others may not be sin—please be careful." (2) "Do you know how long your brother resisted temptation before he fell? Where is your spirit of gentleness?" (3) "Do not judge your brother by your own growth."

11. INTERCESSION FOR THE LOST WORLD

Taiwan — Needy areas and peoples: The 2 million Hakka speaking people need to be evangelized in their own language despite increasing use of Mandarin. They have no Bible and there are only about six missionaries.

12. SING PRAISES TO OUR LORD.

Praise ye the Lord! O let all that is in me adore Him!
All that hath life and breath,
Come now with praises before Him!

Let the Amen sound from His people again:
Gladly for aye we adore Him.

WEEK FORTY-TWO — SATURDAY

1. PRAISE GOD FOR WHO HE IS.

"For ever, O Lord, thy word is firmly fixed in the heavens. Thy faithfulness endures to all generations; thou hast established the earth, and it stands fast. By thy appointments they stand this day; for all things are thy servants" (Psalm 119:89-91). The qualities associated with your creative power are often mentioned in this beautiful psalm. As permanent as heaven so permanent is your word. What a source of confidence and strength for all men is this promise! The heavens we can see and the heavens we can- not see will sooner dissolve and disappear before one word you have spoken will fail to be fulfilled. How many generations had lived upon earth before the Psalmist wrote these words? How many generations have lived since the day when the words were penned? How many generations will live upon this earth before Jesus comes again? In not one generation has one word of yourself failed of fulfillment. Praise your name!

Express yourself in adoration for this quality of God.
Speak it audibly or write out your praise in your own devotional journal.

2. PRAISE GOD FOR WHAT HE MEANS TO ME.

Just for me. Since you through the psalmist spoke these words, we know much more about the relationship of this little planet to the galaxy in which it is a very small part. Our estimate of you increases upon each exploration of space. The laws you set in operation are sustaining all we see in space. What the psalmist said 900 years before your Son came we can say this day 2,000 years since he came. If he should remain with you another 5,000 years we could repeat these words and find every one of them true! Glory to your name and power! How glad I am to acknowledge ". . . all things are thy servants"! Since you do not live in *time* it is very easy to agree with this truth. Ultimately all men and angels will agree with this statement. This servant wants to express it now!

How do you personally relate to the greatness of God, and God who is above all?
Speak it out or write it out. It is *so important* that you establish *your own* devotional journal.

3. CONFESSION OF SIN

If your word is so firmly fixed in heaven, how is it that it is not much more firmly fixed in my heart? There is someone who is intent on disrupting your word, i.e., defeating your purposes. He is only a created being and his power is related to man and other angels. I am simply delighted to say that his influence relates *not at all* to your essential being. Satan has not carried out one single act without your permission. The evil one's actions relate to man. Of course, this involves me. More and more I am becoming aware of reality. Man does *not* live by the sensate responses of this life. Man really has life only when he is directed by your word. The more I can relate your word to every hour of every day the more full of peace and joy I will be.

What personal sins do you want to confess? We *must* speak them to remove them.
Do it! *Now.* There is no one else you have sinned against more than God. Tell him so!

4. SING A PRAYER TO GOD.

My hope is built on nothing less
Than Jesus' blood and righteousness;
I dare not trust the sweetest frame,
But wholly lean on Jesus' name.

On Christ, the solid Rock, I stand;
All other ground is sinking sand,
All other ground is sinking sand.

Open your hymn book and sing the rest of the verses—or even sing another prayer song.

5. READ HIS WORD TO HIM!

His Word

[12]In everything, do to others what you would have them do to you, for this sums up the Law and the Prophets.
[13]"Enter through the narrow gate. For wide is the gate and broad is the road that leads to destruction, and many enter through it. [14]But small is the gate and narrow the road that leads to life, and only a few find it."
— Matthew 7:12-14, NIV

Read also Luke 6:37-49.

Read His Word to Him.

If I waited until I was ready to say all I want to say in the most meaningful manner possible I would be waiting when you called me home. It is somewhat easy to understand your meaning, i.e., I am to put myself in my neighbor's place and do to him just what I would want him to do to me. The problem is I am not my neighbor. To compound the problem, I do not want to be my neighbor. What I am saying so poorly is that my overpowering selfishness shuts me out from this kind of identity. Could I be so bold as to refer to such an attitude as the "narrow gate"? There are two cities toward which all men move: *Destruction* or *Life.* The choice is made at the gate.

Please express your response to this beautiful text. Put your expression in your own prayer diary.

6. READ HIS WORD FOR YOURSELF.

Dear Lord, for today and its opportunities and relationships help me to be interested enough in all men to try to take their place and respond accordingly. Most of all may I adopt in every relationship the mind of Christ. Every decision of life is a gate — my mind-set will determine how I shall enter that opportunity, and just how I will travel that road. It would seem my Lord intended to say to me that I will need to look, and even to at times search for his way before I can find it. Dear Lord, keep me aware that I will be lonesome for companions on the narrow way. I will act many times against custom and convention.

Keep me aware of the end of the easy way; destruction! One day many men will discover to their eternal sorrow that "all they spent their lives for was nothing but dust and ashes." My Lord, I plan on finding your way for each choice today!

It is so important that you pause in his presence
and either audibly or in written form tell him all his word means to you.

7. READ HIS WORD IN THANKSGIVING.

(1) Thank you for the wonderful complete application of the golden rule. (2) Thank you for the summation of the principle of the law and prophets in one verse. (3) Thank you that I do want to find your way for each choice. (4) Dear Lord, thank you that I can leave the many and walk with you. (5) Thank you that I feel no smugness about my need for your way. (6) Thank you for the way of life here and hereafter. (7) Thank you that I really do not mind being different.

Give yourself to your own expression of gratitude — write it or speak it!

8. READ HIS WORD IN MEDITATION.

". . . and few are they that find it." Jesus knew so well just how *few* there would be in his own ministry who would find the narrow gate and stay on the narrow way. In our day and time narrowness has become a *bad* word. But only in relationship to God and his word is this true. Narrowness in other fields is called *specialization*. If there are no banks to the river there is no force to the water's flow. If there are no limitations on a work project, no work is done. Considering the ultimate end of *life* or *destruction* a search for the narrow gate and the narrow way seems altogether reasonable. A careful consideration of the lives of those who have found the gate and way is a good recommendation for the continued search.

Pause — wait — think — then express yourself in thoughtful praise or thanks.

9. READ HIS WORD FOR PETITIONS.

I do want to pray about my entrance into the narrow gate: (1) How often shall I enter? Shall it not be every day? (2) Teach me just how narrow is narrow? (3) If I follow your Son as I read his biographers I know I shall be on the narrow way — give me wisdom. (4) How shall I identify the broad way? (5) Is the "Broadway" of today the broad way of which my Lord spoke? (6) Is Jesus describing the outcome of evangelization? (7) To the above questions I know you have answers — I do expect to receive them.

Please, please remember these are prayers — speak them — reword them!

10. READ HIS WORD AND WAIT — LISTEN — GOD SPEAKS!

Speak to me. (1) "You must be prepared to go against custom and the crowd if you follow me." (2) "You cannot learn my way from others — it *must* come from me." (3) "Fear of destruction is no enemy to love but its true guardian."

11. INTERCESSION FOR THE LOST WORLD

Taiwan — Points for prayer: (1) *Needy areas and peoples:* There are still about *500 small towns and larger villages* without a resident Bible believing witness. (2) *Factory workers* of the lower income group are relatively unreached — most believers coming from a middle class background. Pray for the factory evangelism. (3) *The fishing villages* are poor, and the people work long hours and few have ever witnessed to these needy and superstitious people.

12. SING PRAISES TO OUR LORD.

I have a Christ that satisfies,
Since I have been redeemed,
To do His will my highest prize,
Since I have been redeemed.
Since I have been redeemed,

Since I have been redeemed,
I will glory in His name;
Since I have been redeemed,
I will glory in my Savior's name.

WEEK FORTY-THREE — SUNDAY

1. PRAISE GOD FOR WHO HE IS.

"If thy law had not been my delight, I should have perished in my affliction. I shall never forget thy precepts; for by them thou hast given me life" (Psalm 119:92, 93). What poignant attributes of yourself are in these words: (1) You speak to man in precept and promise he can understand. (2) The content of your word (law) is such as to prompt delight in the heart of the hearer or reader. Praise you for these qualities—there are others—but I want to pause in the joy of praise. (3) Your law is of such a nature as to overcome and explain affliction. Some of your answers amount to a simple confidence in your essential character, but it *is* an answer! (4) Your precepts are so beautiful and valuable that we want never to forget them. (5) In your word, and from your word, we have life.

Express yourself in adoration for this quality of God.
Speak it audibly or write out your praise in your own devotional journal.

2. PRAISE GOD FOR WHAT HE MEANS TO ME.

In praise I read this word for myself. This is a privilege. (1) I do believe you have communicated to man in words that can be understood. Indeed to believe less would be to attribute less ability to yourself than to a newspaper editor. (2) Your word's primary message to me is one of delight. Indeed, I have found it so! From Genesis to Revelation I come away with the total impression that you have such a deep interest in man's happiness that you would die to give it. The "joy that was set before him" as he endured the cross was also for us! (3) There are times of depression for all of us, but it is not a continuing attitude. Your word, through your Son lifts us out. Our memory turns back to the blessed beautiful promises and depression disappears. (4) I really lose interest in other things when I compare them with the everlasting quality of your word.

How do you personally relate to the delight from God, and God who is Delight?
Speak it out or write it out. It is *so important* that you establish *your own* devotional journal.

3. CONFESSION OF SIN

The predictable nature of your laws is both encouraging and discouraging. The law of forgiveness presupposes sin and repentance. The law of light presupposes darkness. The law of life anticipates or at least includes death. We need not continue in disobedience but we will continue to need forgiveness. Such as: (1) I understand your law, but I do not obey it, i.e., perfectly—or even in a way that pleases me. (2) I do delight in your law, but I am sometimes carried away by pleasure instead of joy. (3) I *know* all things are working together under your direction for my good, but I gripe about it. (4) Of all things I want to remember, it is your law that I do forget! (5) When I have life from your word I sometimes choose death by ignoring your will. I need and claim forgiveness. I want these ideals to become my life-style. I gladly accept your cleansing.

What personal sins do you want to confess? We *must* speak them to remove them.
Do it! *Now.* There is no one else you have sinned against more than God. Tell him so!

4. SING A PRAYER TO GOD.

Nearer, still nearer, close to Thy heart,
Draw me, my Savior, so precious Thou art;
Fold me, O fold me close to Thy breast,

Shelter me safe in that "Haven of Rest,"
Shelter me safe in that "Haven of Rest."

Open your hymn book and sing the rest of the verses—or even sing another prayer song.

5. READ HIS WORD TO HIM!

His Word

[15]"Watch out for false prophets. They come to you in sheep's clothing, but inwardly they are ferocious wolves. [16]By their fruit you will recognize them. Do people pick grapes from thornbushes, or figs from thistles? [17]Likewise every good tree bears good fruit, but a bad tree bears bad fruit. [18]A good tree cannot bear bad fruit, and a bad tree cannot bear good fruit. [19]Every tree that does not bear good fruit is cut down and thrown into the fire. [20]Thus, by their fruit you will recognize them..

— *Matthew 7:15-20, NIV*

Read also Luke 6:43-45.

Read His Word to Him.

My dear Father, I will attempt to paraphrase the words of your Son as an expression of my relationship to you. You are saying to me through these words from your Son: Look out for phony teachers and preachers. They say all the right things and present credentials that recommend them. At one time perhaps they were all they seem to be now. But today they are hungry with money madness. These very innocent looking men are promoters of

590

a variety of evil. You can only tell this if you observe them long enough and close enough, but observe it you will! It is as easy to expect a life of purity and sincerity from these men as it would be to get grapes from thorn bushes or figs from a thistle bush.

Please express your response to this beautiful text. Put your expression in your own prayer diary.

6. READ HIS WORD FOR YOURSELF.

Just for me. How pungently does the above relate to me! How deceptively easy it is to be a phony preacher! Dear Lord, I do not in any way want to be that kind of a man! By following Paul's manner of life Timothy became well acquainted with the fruit of his whole being. Dear Lord, I want anyone to be able to follow my habits, conversations and attitudes and say your fruit has been growing from this tree! How well do I know that orthodoxy is no criteria for inward evaluation! Respectability might be the covering for a rotten heart. Dear Lord, I am also glad to read these blessed words: "A good tree *cannot* bring forth evil fruit." I could be frightened out of all trying by this terribly severe condemnation of the false. At long last the fruit of the whole life will identify the real and separate it from the false.

Pause in his presence and either audibly or in written form tell him all his word means to you.

7. READ HIS WORD IN THANKSGIVING.

(1) Thank you for this shocking warning. (2) Thank you that your Son can look beneath all covering and see the real person. (3) Thank you that this is said in such a manner that each of us asks "Lord, is it I?" (4) Thank you that each of us knows what kind of fruit our life has produced in the last 20 years. (5) Thank you that we are not called upon to do *anything* with the tree, just examine the fruit. (6) Thank you that the running sands of time leave a clear picture of what they have uncovered. (7) Thank you that you do the cutting and burning.

Give yourself to your own expression of gratitude — write it or speak it!

8. READ HIS WORD IN MEDITATION.

"Therefore by their fruits you shall know them." By the mature development of their whole lives we shall know them. Not by some individual act that we would consider "out of character." "Two trees of the same species may be identical in every respect but the maturing of the fruit reveals their true nature." It is more than unfortunate to judge a man or a woman on the basis of a single incident. This is done all the time, but it is totally contrary to the principle our Lord here gives to us.

Pause — wait — think — then express yourself in thoughtful praise or thanks.

9. READ HIS WORD FOR PETITIONS.

Here is a text to move us to your throne of grace to ask for help: (1) Keep my convictions strong in the objective nature of truth. (2) Teach me real fear in regard to false teachers. (3) Keep my eyes open for those who look like sheep, but are really wolves. (4) May my evaluations be on the outcome of a life not on appearances. (5) A man be morally sound but doctrinally wrong — give me wisdom to help such a one. (6) Keep me in a good humor or no one will be helped.

Right here add your personal requests — and his answers.

10. READ HIS WORD AND WAIT — LISTEN — GOD SPEAKS!

Speak to me. (1) "A man's words, especially when he is unconscious of them is a fairly good indication of his heart." (2) "Every tree — i.e. *all trees* that do not bring forth good fruit will be hewn down." (3) "Rejoice that I alone will judge the fruit of the lives of men."

11. INTERCESSION FOR THE LOST WORLD

Taiwan — Point for prayer: (1) *The missionary vision* of the national Church is only seen in a few groups and congregations. There are stirrings of greater things — such as through recent conferences on evangelism, but this burden is not seen to be part of the life of the Church. Some tribal preachers have gone as missionaries to Sarawak, Malaysia, other denominational workers have gone to minister to Chinese congregations in other lands (but this is hardly mission work!).

12. SING PRAISES TO OUR LORD.

Amazing grace! how sweet the sound,
That saved a wretch like me!

I once was lost, but now am found,
Was blind, but now I see.

WEEK FORTY-THREE — MONDAY

1. PRAISE GOD FOR WHO HE IS.

"I have seen a limit to all perfection, but thy commandment is exceedingly broad. Oh, how I love thy law! It is my meditation all the day." (Psalm 119:96, 97). What a rare opportunity is mine that I can pause every day and hold up another facet of your character and praise you for it! In these two verses there is one quality that speaks very personally to me. (I try to think of myself as a rather poor representation of all men.) (1) There are no mistakes in your work—or yourself. I do admire quality work in any field. I have found out that there is always someone around who can and will point out its limitations. But when you have commissioned a task your efforts include *all* contingencies—there are no areas where someone can point out a mistake. Thank you! I can say with no hesitancy "O how I love thy law," but I have yet to find a way to meditate upon it all the day.

Express yourself in adoration for this quality of God.
Speak it audibly or write out your praise in your own devotional journal.

2. PRAISE GOD FOR WHAT HE MEANS TO ME.

Just for me. I do advance the above as an example for all or as representative of what I consider for all men. Just here I do want to be as personal as possible. The limitations of human efforts at perfection are many: (1) Nothing is static, i.e., there is always a better way to do it. (2) It does not fit every circumstance; so much of our work is provincial. (3) Some men cannot understand it. (4) Some of our efforts are not practical. (5) Not everyone has even heard of it.

In stark contrast your work is: Eternal—never needs an improvement. Such as the smallest flower, or the largest tree. Or we could consider any part of the human body. Has man improved on the human eye? Any photographer will tell you his best camera is a clumsy copy.

How do you personally relate to the perfection of God, and God who is Perfect?
Speak it out or write it out. It is *so important* that you establish *your own* devotional journal.

3. CONFESSION OF SIN

Sorrow—real genuine God-prompted sorrow must precede repentance. Repentance must precede confession. Confession must be totally open and honest, a full admission of my sin. The one sin that includes many others is the sin of failure to meditate upon your word "all the day." I am guilty, I am wrong, I feel very guilty about this. You have ways of changing this. If I am going to meditate upon your word every day throughout the day your word in some form must be with me. I have memorized some of your word, but it does me little good unless I call it from my subconsciousness to my consciousness and slowly turn over the phrases of what you have said.

What personal sins do you want to confess? We *must* speak them to remove them.
Do it! *Now.* There is no one else you have sinned against more than God. Tell him so!

4. SING A PRAYER TO GOD.

Must Jesus bear the cross alone,
And all the world go free?

No; there's a cross for ev'ry one,
And there's a cross for me.

Open your hymn book and sing the rest of the verses—or even sing another prayer song.

5. READ HIS WORD TO HIM!

His Word

[21]"Not everyone who says to me, 'Lord, Lord,' will enter the kingdom of heaven, but only he who does the will of my Father who is in heaven. [22]Many will say to me on that day, 'Lord, Lord, did we not prophesy in your name, and in your name drive out demons and perform many miracles?' [23]Then I will tell them plainly, 'I never knew you. Away from me, you evildoers!'
[24]"Therefore everyone who hears these words of mine and puts them into practice is like a wise man who built his house on the rock. [25]The rain came down, the streams rose, and the winds blew and beat against that house; yet it did not fall, because it had its foundation on the rock. [26]But everyone who hears these words of mine and does not put them into practice is like a foolish man who built his house on sand. [27]The rain came down, the streams rose, and the winds blew and beat against that house, and it fell with a great crash."

— Matthew 7:21-27, NIV

Read His Word to Him.

Of all the texts we have considered this is one of the few with such conclusive words as to stand by itself. Here is the great eternal moral principle upon which all my life, or the lives of all men are built. I will attempt to paraphrase these precious words: "Everyone who opens his heart to receive with meekness what you say and does not hesitate or procrastinate but obeys your word shall be like a man building a house upon a solid foundation of bedrock. There are many floods or crises in life. When such a rain, flood and wind hit our lives *then* we shall discover upon what we have built our lives."

Please express your response to this beautiful text. Put your expression in your own prayer diary.

6. READ HIS WORD FOR YOURSELF.

Just for me. Dear Lord, to some extent I am always failing to obey your word as I would want to—let alone fulfill it as you would want it. At the same time, I recognize my Lord—and even yourself—is asking "What will you do in a crisis?" Let me ask myself what I would do in the following floods of life? (1) If I were suddenly struck blind? (2) If our house burned down and all that is in it were turned to ashes? (3) If all three of our children were taken in death—or with an incurable disease. (4) If my wife were taken in death or with a long lingering illness. (5) If I was involved in a conspiracy of lies and lost my job? Is my dwelling place in you? Is my security in yourself? Is my whole being lost in your Son and his word?

It is so important that you pause in his presence
and either audibly or in written form tell him all his word means to you.

7. READ HIS WORD IN THANKSGIVING.

(1) Thank you that I still have ears to hear your word. (2) I thank you I still have your word to hear. (3) Thank you I can obey you. (4) Thank you that I *want* to obey you. (5) Thank you for the invariable promises or consequences of obedience or lack of it. (6) Thank you for your definition of who is wise and foolish. (7) Thank you for your eternal security.

Give yourself to your own expression of gratitude—write it or speak it!

8. READ HIS WORD IN MEDITATION.

". . . and great was the fall thereof." Indeed, indeed! In so many ways the collapse of a life is a tragedy. (1) A great deal of effort has come to naught. Think of how very much work, time, energy and money have all been lost as a result of a faulty foundation! How many wonderful friends and loved ones have been estranged and lost because they could not trust the person whom they knew. When our life is built on the pursuit of money we at the best can only get what money can give—and it has a way of slipping through your fingers like sand. The same result comes in the pursuit of pleasure. Our Lord is speaking of the lasting value of what he taught. The above thoughts read like cliches. Dear Lord, they are not! They are the eternal sober facts of sand or rock!

Pause—wait—think—then express yourself in thoughtful praise or thanks.

9. READ HIS WORD FOR PETITIONS.

This is much more than a sermon—these powerful words lead me to prayer: (1) In so many relationships I want to know your will so I can do it—open my heart as I read your word. (2) I do want an intimacy with you that gives meaning to my service. (3) Day by day I want to build upon yourself in the words of my mouth and the meditations of my heart. (4) I want to remember Judas Iscariot—he called you Lord, and did many mighty works—holy company does not make us holy. Probe my conscience! (5) Open my eyes and ears to hear and see the meanings you have given to us in your own life-style.

Please, please remember these are prayers—speak them—reword them!

10. READ HIS WORD AND WAIT—LISTEN—GOD SPEAKS!

Speak to me. (1) "Remember: the principle of 'faith that works' is the only faith I accept." (2) "Rains will come, floods are on their way—check your foundation." (3) "It is possible to be the wise man—now is the time to start."

11. INTERCESSION FOR THE LOST WORLD

Thailand — Population: 43,300,000. Growth rate—2.5%. People per sq. km.—84.

Points for prayer: (1) *A very marked increase in interest in the Gospel* since 1968 after 150 years of very discouraging and hard mission work. This interest has been caused by a number of factors working together—the grave Communist threat, the excellent witness of Christian medical mission work, and also a breath of revival and spiritual deepening among the few Thai believers. (2) *Pray for the breaking of the demonic powers behind the entrenched Buddhism* and widespread fear of the spirits among both Thai and tribal peoples. (3) *Needy areas*—the whole of the country is still a pioneer mission field, but more needy is rural central Thailand and also the poor north east where the density of Christians is one tenth of the low national average.

12. SING PRAISES TO OUR LORD.

The Church's one foundation
Is Jesus Christ her Lord;
She is His new creation
By water and the word:

From Heav'n He came and sought her
To be His holy bride;
With His own blood He bought her,
And for her life He died.

WEEK FORTY-THREE — TUESDAY

1. PRAISE GOD FOR WHO HE IS.

"I have more understanding than all my teachers, for thy testimonies are my meditation. I understand more than the aged, for I keep thy precepts. I hold back my feet from every evil way, in order to keep thy word" (Psalm 119:99-101). The purpose of recording these verses is to hold up before our hearts an attribute of yourself for all men's admiration and praise. Not that all men praise you, but they should. Here is reason for praise.

(1) You recognize the need of man for a rational explanation of the world in which we live. The explanation you offer in your word gives a depth of understanding that cannot be found from anyone else. At the same time it honors yourself as the Source. (2) You understand how terribly futile even a long life can be without an explanation from heaven. (3) Evil is overcome by admiration of good and you are Good!

Express yourself in adoration for this quality of God.
Speak it audibly or write out your praise in your own devotional journal.

2. PRAISE GOD FOR WHAT HE MEANS TO ME.

I cannot think of anything I need more than these precious words: If I am unwilling to meditate upon your word all such promises fall to the ground. Meditation is a rethinking—a reevaluation—a checking and double checking—and then checking again. Such a practice is carried out today in a thousand jobs. There are three obvious practical applications of this principle: (1) Carry your word in printed form of a testament or even the whole Bible—open it and meditate upon it. If someone offered me an opportunity to obtain $100,000, i.e., if I understood what he said, I would turn over his words in my mind regardless of what else I did. (2) Listen to an audio cassette and meditate. Play and replay—listen and listen again. (3) Memorize his word—this is what I want to do. Thank you for helping me in the practical application of these verses to my life.

How do you personally relate to the understanding of God, and God who understands?
Speak it out or write it out. It is *so important* that you establish *your own* devotional journal.

3. CONFESSION OF SIN

It would seem the sins here are sins against the light. (1) Why am I so ignorant and stupid when I could be full of your understanding? It is easy to answer and in doing so confess my sin. "The desire for other things choked out the word." Forgive me! I am glad I can every day renew my mind and be transformed. (2) How is it that instead of growing older and wiser, I only grow older? There is a teacher teaching—Satan has teachers. He has translated his lies into printed form—into audio and video form. We are being taught. The older we get under such instructions, the sadder we become. Stop! Stop! Turn it off! I flee to your word for shelter and protection—to say nothing of light and warmth. (3) I love verse 101 in this psalm: "I hold back my feet from every evil way in order to keep thy word." My respect and love for you is what keeps me in your way.

What personal sins do you want to confess? We *must* speak them to remove them.
Do it! *Now.* There is no one else you have sinned against more than God. Tell him so!

4. SING A PRAYER TO GOD.

I must tell Jesus all of my troubles;
He is a kind, compassionate Friend;
If I but ask Him, He will deliver,
Make of my troubles quickly an end.

I must tell Jesus! I must tell Jesus!
I cannot bear my burdens alone;
I must tell Jesus! I must tell Jesus!
Jesus can help me, Jesus alone.

Open your hymn book and sing the rest of the verses—or even sing another prayer song.

5. READ HIS WORD TO HIM!

His Word

[28]When Jesus had finished saying these things, the crowds were amazed at his teaching, [29]because he taught as one who had authority, and not as their teachers of the law.

8 When he came down from the mountainside, large crowds followed him. — *Matthew 7:28 — 8:1, NIV*
Read also Luke 6:43-49.

Read His Word to Him.

How wonderful it would have been to be seated in that crowd long ago and hear your Son! I am astonished now—what would have been my reaction then? I do not know that my astonishment is for the same reason. I am more amazed at the meaning of what he has said than his authority. I have accepted your Son's supreme position—it is the impact of what his words could mean for all mankind that astonish me!

Please express your response to this beautiful text. Put your expression in your own prayer diary.

6. READ HIS WORD FOR YOURSELF.

My Father, I do not want to be a fool. The scribes are yet with us! Could I be considered as one of them? Dear Lord, strike from my hand the pen with which I write if any one of these words is to be considered as having any authority whatsoever. I respect the scribes—many are as sincere as yours truly. But I do not at all respect any scribe who suggests that just because he said it or wrote it that it has any authority. All of us are on an equal level. We sit at Jesus' feet and learn from him. If we gain something to share, its value is in what he said and we communicate. May we move from place to place as we follow him and listen with all our hearts to *what he says!*

Pause in his presence and either audibly or in written form tell him all his word means to you.

7. READ HIS WORD IN THANKSGIVING.

(1) Thank you for the words of his sermon preserved and with us today! (2) Thank you that his word will never lose its power. (3) Thank you that in eternity all scribes will know the answers to questions they cannot now answer. (4) Thank you that the answers are in his knowledge and not ours. (5) Thank you for the ability to be astonished. (6) Thank you that I can identify for myself and others who has the authority. (7) Thank you that today I can follow him!

Give yourself to your own expression of gratitude—write it or speak it!

8. READ HIS WORD IN MEDITATION.

"*. . . great multitudes followed him.*" How I do want to join the crowd and stay with him. To be in the company of God in human flesh. "The wonder of it all" would not describe the reaction. We are sure some who followed him knew who he was, but even then the impact of walking in the presence of God was not what we who live 2,000 years later would expect. If he were here today just *why* would I want to follow him? (1) To hear his teaching? How much time do I spend each day reading what his eye-witnesses wrote? (2) To be amazed again and again at his miracles? Have I spent adequate time meditating over the miracles recorded by those who saw him?

Pause—wait—think—then express yourself in thoughtful praise or thanks.

9. READ HIS WORD FOR PETITIONS.

As I reflect on his whole discourse I want to pause in prayer: (1) May my amazement issue in obedience. (2) Give me a sharp accurate remembrance of what he said. (3) If he has all authority—and he does—why do I spend time with anyone else? (4) How closely have I followed you today? Dear Lord, I ask these questions as petitions—give me *your* answer. (5) How could so many people afford to miss work as they followed my Lord? Probably the answer is in the abject poverty—they didn't have a job—forgive my excuses.

Right here add your personal requests—and his answers.

10. READ HIS WORD AND WAIT—LISTEN—GOD SPEAKS!

Speak to me in these two verses: (1) "I can only teach those who want to be taught." (2) "Amazement doesn't of itself mean anything." (3) "Acceptance in your heart of my authority is the key."

11. INTERCESSION FOR THE LOST WORLD

Thailand — Points for prayer: (1) *The churches* have not grown as fast as the population for decades, until the last several years. The rather nominal and older congregations were in decline, but there is a new surge of life with some spiritual Bible believing church leaders emerging that have been stimulated by revival in northern Thai congregations. The younger churches (the fruit of the newer Bible believing missions) are showing steady growth —especially among the tribal people. Pray that the believers may become strong and effective witnesses for the Lord. (2) *The problems faced by the churches*—lack of mature preachers, most believers only semi-literate or illiterate and many are converts from among "outcast" leprosy patients at mission hospitals and clinics. Thus many are open to aggressive propaganda by sects and not able to really form an effective evangelistic force.

12. SING PRAISES TO OUR LORD.

All praise to Him who reigns above
In majesty supreme,
Who gave His Son for man to die,
That He might man redeem!

Blessed be the name, blessed be the name,
Blessed be the name of the Lord;
Blessed be the name, blessed be the name,
Blessed be the name of the Lord.

WEEK FORTY-THREE — WEDNESDAY

1. PRAISE GOD FOR WHO HE IS.

"I have not departed from your laws, for you yourself have taught me. How sweet are your promises to my taste, sweeter than honey to my mouth" (Psalm 119:102, 103). Dear Lord, here is real motivation for keeping your word! If you are the teacher I am going to be on the front row with both my ears open. I am going to truly learn if my instruction comes from you! If somehow I can make the transference from the printed page to yourself

I will listen and learn. It is easy for me to relate the words in the letters from my dear wife to herself—it is as if she were there talking to me. So it is this morning! I bow before you and listen with my inner ear.

I can only testify to the sweetness of your promises as I have claimed them in my experience. But such as I have ingested are even as your word "sweeter than honey."

Express yourself in adoration for this quality of God.
Speak it audibly or write out your praise in your own devotional journal.

2. PRAISE GOD FOR WHAT HE MEANS TO ME.

I feel so strongly about this quality of yourself! You can and do personally instruct me from your word. Perhaps I am so involved in this concept because I know the principle is true: if once I can make the transference from the words on the page to yourself I will not depart from your laws. I praise you that I can even now

close my eyes and visualize your reality in the person I read about in the gospels. He was a teacher, indeed, *the* teacher. The Holy Spirit is the author of your word—may he give life to the letter! Praise your name, I even now claim your presence!

How do you personally relate to the teaching of God, and God who is the Teacher?
Speak it out or write it out. It is *so important* that you establish *your own* devotional journal.

3. CONFESSION OF SIN

There have been many times when you were separated from your law and it became a cold, hard set of legal regulations that I hated with a passion. You were not at fault—it was my stupidity and willfulness. As you know, it took me a long time to hear your voice behind the voice of the preacher. I delight in the experience of opening

your word and letting *you* teach me. Forgive me for every time I did not look behind the book and see who was really speaking. Forgive me for every time I listened critically to another brother or sister whom you really wanted to use to tell me something, but I wasn't hearing you. Forgive me.

What personal sins do you want to confess? We *must* speak them to remove them.
Do it! *Now.* There is no one else you have sinned against more than God. Tell him so!

4. SING A PRAYER TO GOD.

In loving kindness Jesus came
My soul in mercy to reclaim,
And from the depths of sin and shame
Thro' grace He lifted me.

From sinking sand He lifted me,
With tender hand He lifted me,
From shades of night to plains of light,
Oh, praise His name, He lifted me!

Open your hymn book and sing the rest of the verses—or even sing another prayer song.

5. READ HIS WORD TO HIM!

His Word

7 When Jesus had finished saying all this in the hearing of the people, he entered Capernaum. ²There a centurion's servant, whom his master valued highly, was sick and about to die. ³The centurion heard of Jesus and sent some elders of the Jews to him, asking him to come and heal his servant. ⁴When they came to Jesus, they pleaded earnestly with him, "This man deserves to have you do this, ⁵because he loves our nation and has built our synagogue." ⁶So Jesus went with them.   *— Luke 7:1-6a, NIV*
Read Matthew 8:2-13. (We print here the text of Luke but we read the account of Matthew.)

Read His Word to Him.

I see myself and all men twice over in these accounts. Dear Lord, I am the leper! (1) The disease of sin has infected my being until all hope of being clean is gone. (2) I have heard of your Son and what he can do. I believe he can do all I have heard and more! (3) I feel totally unworthy to be healed. I find nothing in myself to recom-

mend my healing. (4) I must cast myself upon his mercy. (5) My need forces a confession from my lips. (6) A shocking unexpected development! He didn't need to touch me —he could have spoken the word of healing. But he did touch me! (7) In this I am so greatly comforted—and healed. My uncleanness and sickness are gone! I am well!

Please express your response to this beautiful text. Put your expression in your own prayer diary.

6. READ HIS WORD FOR YOURSELF.

Just for me. I can also identify with the centurion. In a very real personal sense I take his place: (1) I am a Gentile outsider. I have no birthright claims for your favor. (2) I am in the army of the enemy. I wear the obvious uniform of opposition. I cannot hide my sin and the fact that I have sinned. (3) My need is so overpowering that it breaks all conventional barriers down. Dear Lord, I *must* have some help! (4) There are many who are precious to me who lie "paralyzed" in the power of Satan. (5) It is only from the word of my Lord that these dear ones can be made well. (6) My blessed Lord, I want right *now* to trust you for the healing of those so dear to me!

Pause in his presence and either audibly or in written form tell him all his word means to you.

7. READ HIS WORD IN THANKSGIVING.

(1) Thank you Jesus was willing to touch the untouchables. (2) Thank you Jesus was careful about obedience to the law. (3) Thank you Jesus was so approachable—to lepers and soldiers. (3) Thank you that Jesus never turned either of them away. (4) Thank you for the beautiful word "clean"—it means so much to this leper! (4) Thank you for the centurion's confidence in our Lord's authority. (5) Thank you for the wonderful quality of submission seen here. (6) Thank you for my Lord's rebuke for us religious people. (7) Thank you for the promised feast in heaven.

Give yourself to your own expression of gratitude—write it or speak it!

8. READ HIS WORD IN MEDITATION.

"Go; be it done for you as you have believed." The wonderful law of faith is here stated and finds fulfillment in the life of the centurion. It is first enunciated at creation when God spoke and it was done. Faith from our point of view always comes by hearing. The centurion believed the words of our Lord and it was done. So many wonderful things could happen in our lives if we would listen to our Lord and believe him. But there must be the whole-hearted confidence we see in this soldier. This army captain considered it done when our Lord spoke. His faith was in the authority of our Lord. Our faith is in the nature of the one speaking. The more we learn of the essential being of our Lord the more confidence we can place in his words.

Pause—wait—think—then express yourself in thoughtful praise or thanks.

9. READ HIS WORD FOR PETITIONS.

In these two incidents there are many points for prayer: (1) Am I as ready to reach out and touch the moral lepers of our day? (2) Lead me to someone in deep need who wants help. (3) Guard me from hasty premature announcements of success. (4) Keep me aware that you have men who will believe in places and jobs to which I do not relate. (5) How I want the humble faith of the centurion. (6) Deepen my understanding of the word "authority." (7) Enlarge my understanding of the expression: "kingdom of heaven."

Please, please remember these are prayers—speak them—reword them!

10. READ HIS WORD AND WAIT—LISTEN—COD SPEAKS!

Speak to me through the leper and the centurion: (1) "There is something worse than leprosy—you have been healed and there are no restrictions on telling about it." (2) "If an army captain can care so much about his servant how is it you are so indifferent to greater needs?" (3) "Wake up!"

11. INTERCESSION FOR THE LOST WORLD

Thailand — Points for prayer: (1) *Leadership training* —there are a number of good denominational and inter-denominational Bible Schools. There are a number of talented young men coming into the Lord's work. Pray for the much used cassette ministry for the training of local leaders. This is vital with the poor communications and widely scattered Christian community. (2) *Missions*—a rapid post-war increase from two groups to 35. There are now over 800 missionaries, mostly with the newer Bible believing groups and the majority in evangelism and church planting ministries among both the Thai and minority groups. There is a pressing need for more to use the present receptivity of the people and build them up into strong churches. Communist and Malay insurgency has limited missionary activity in some areas.

12. SING PRAISES TO OUR LORD.

All praise to Him who reigns above
In majesty supreme,
Who gave His Son for man to die,
That He might man redeem!

Blessed be the name, blessed be the name,
Blessed be the name of the Lord;
Blessed be the name, blessed be the name,
Blessed be the name of the Lord.

WEEK FORTY-THREE — THURSDAY

1. PRAISE GOD FOR WHO HE IS.

"Thy word is a lamp to my feet and a light to my path. I hold my life in my hand continually, but I do not forget thy law" (Psalm 119:105, 109). For many years I have loved verse 105 of this blessed psalm. Dear Father, I claim your promise and praise your name. Your word illumines each day, "a lamp to my feet" and lightens the distinct future, "a light to my path." The attribute of yourself in this verse is your personal interest in today and every tomorrow. I want to praise you that you have such a capacity to exercise in the life experience of every man and woman upon the face of the earth. In contrast to verse 105 is verse 109. My life and the lives of all men are not only in your hand and the concern of your heart but all men hold their own lives in their hands. How eternally important it is that we forget not your law.

Express yourself in adoration for this quality of God.
Speak it audibly or write out your praise in your own devotional journal.

2. PRAISE GOD FOR WHAT HE MEANS TO ME.

Just for me. Dear Lord, I want more and more of your word for every day. How I want to in a most practical way relate what you say to what I am and what I do. Open my mind so I might find very real ways of making this true. Two or three occur to me now: (1) I could decide to memorize one verse before I ate each meal. And to talk about that verse's application to my life. (Dear Lord, I am praising you for your word as a lamp and trying to accept it as such.) (2) To print three verses on 3" x 5" cards and fasten them in places I would see them several times each day. (3) Make a covenant with some dear friend who would agree to say at least three verses to me and I to him each day.

How do you personally relate to the lamp and light of God, and God who is Light?
Speak it out or write it out. It is *so important* that you establish *your own* devotional journal.

3. CONFESSION OF SIN

In all my words you read my heart behind them. You know amid my desire to integrate your word into my life there is an admission of failure to do so. My life is in my hand—my responsibility—how fleeting and elusive is life! How soon forgotten are all the important plans and accomplishments of man. That I should be caught up in the "illusive dream" of sex, food and money is sad, sad! *"But I do not forget thy law."* How solid and sure is this word! How glad I am to be forgiven and to be able to start all over again each day I live. While my life is in my hand, I do not forget your law! Your law is fulfilled in your Son and your Son made full the law for me! Praise your name!

What personal sins do you want to confess? We *must* speak them to remove them.
Do it! *Now.* There is no one else you have sinned against more than God. Tell him so!

4. SING A PRAYER TO GOD.

Amazing grace! how sweet the sound,
That saved a wretch like me!

I once was lost, but now am found,
Was blind, but now I see.

Open your hymn book and sing the rest of the verses—or even sing another prayer song.

5. READ HIS WORD TO HIM!

His Word

He was not far from the house when the centurion sent friends to say to him: "Lord, don't trouble yourself, for I do not deserve to have you come under my roof. [7]That is why I did not even consider myself worthy to come to you. But say the word, and my servant will be healed. [8]For I myself am a man under authority, with soldiers under me. I tell this one, 'Go,' and he goes; and that one, 'Come,' and he comes. I say to my servant, 'Do this,' and he does it."

[9]When Jesus heard this, he was amazed at him, and turning to the crowd following him, he said, "I tell you, I have not found such great faith even in Israel."
— *Luke 7:6b-9, NIV*

Read His Word to Him.

What a delight it will be to journey with my Lord to the house of the centurion. We are stopped on the way. The centurion demonstrates the meaning of his words in the persons of his friends. He said to them "Go," and they went with the message for our Lord! We wonder just who these friends were—how many were there? What effect did the words of our Lord have on them? More importantly: What effect do his words have on me? I want to open my heart as I look to my Lord and hear him speak. (1) "Jesus marveled at him." I could think of nothing I would like to do more than to bring the surprise of delight to my Lord.

Please express your response to this beautiful text. Put your expression in your own prayer diary.

6. READ HIS WORD FOR YOURSELF.

(2) My Lord now addresses the multitude: "I tell you, not even in Israel have I found such faith." I want to take a very careful look at this faith: (1) Jesus is addressed as "Lord"—as a man under authority he acknowledges my Lord's position. (2) He recognizes our Lord has more important things to do than to answer his request, but he does want an answer. (3) He honestly feels he is un- worthy to be in the same room with our Lord—or he feels his house is such an unworthy place for the presence of God in human form. (4) He could not bear the thought of looking at Jesus face to face. (5) "Say the word, and let my servant be healed." For this man all that was necessary was for my Lord to say it and it would be done!

Pause in his presence and either audibly or in written form tell him all his word means to you.

7. READ HIS WORD IN THANKSGIVING.

(1) Thank you that there were no interruptions in my Lord's life—the needs of people were always in his schedule. (2) Thank you for the obedience of the servants. (3) Thank you for the encouragement that culture barriers can be overcome. (4) Thank you for the outstanding example of humility seen in the centurion. (5) Thank you that my Lord defined faith in the action of this man. (6) Thank you that I can expectantly listen for the "go" or "come" of my Lord. (7) Thank you that my Lord separates religion, "Israel" from real "faith"—the centurion.

Give yourself to your own expression of gratitude—write it or speak it!

8. READ HIS WORD IN MEDITATION.

"When Jesus heard this he marveled at him, . . ." Men marveled at Jesus, but here our Lord marveled at a man. An unlikely man he was! There had no doubt been other army captains who had servants who had become sick. A servant would be a real loss to one who needed his service. But this man *loved* his servant. It wasn't his service but the servant that was the concern of the centurion. This unusual man had no doubt heard of Jesus earlier. Had he stood in a crowd and watched Jesus heal someone? Had he listened to our Lord as he taught? By whatever means this good man had acquired a total trust in the power or authority of our Lord over sickness. No doubt he believed Jesus could do anything else he chose. At this quality of faith our Lord marveled.

Pause—wait—think—then express yourself in thoughtful praise or thanks.

9. READ HIS WORD FOR PETITIONS.

In Luke's account of the centurion I can learn much: (1) If this good man did not deserve your presence in his house how much less myself—may I never forget the privilege it is to have you living in me. (2) Over so many of my friends I want you to "say the word" and make them well—dear Lord, say it through me. (3) Send your ministering angels to help me in needs you alone can see. (4) Teach me from this text the real meaning of faith. (5) Deepen my meditation on the power in the words of your Son.

Right here add your personal requests—and his answers.

10. READ HIS WORD AND WAIT—LISTEN—GOD SPEAKS!

Speak to me again: (1) "It is still true today that my real servants respond to my call to "go" and "come." (2) "The example of faith presupposes my authority." (3) "Is this text so many words or do you really believe it?"

11. INTERCESSION FOR THE LOST WORLD

Thailand — Points for prayer: (1) *Medical work* has proved a valuable key and many owe their conversion to the loving witness in these institutions. There are about 30 Protestant hospitals. Pray for the witness to the many non-Christian nurses (some are seeking the Lord), and for the raising up of Christian Thai medical workers. Leprosy control and treatment among the 400,000 sufferers of this disease has resulted in the planting of many small churches among the Thai, and one even among the Malays. (2) *Student witness* is yet small, but growing. (3) *Literature*—a number of publishers are producing more and more Thai books and much is distributed through the ten Christian bookstores. Several groups plan massive Bible and literature distribution programs in the light of Thailand's exposure to Communist aggression.

12. SING PRAISES TO OUR LORD.

Guilty, vile and helpless, we;
Spotless Lamb of God was He;

"Full atonement!" can it be?
Hallelujah! what a Savior!

WEEK FORTY-THREE — FRIDAY

1. PRAISE GOD FOR WHO HE IS.

"Thy testimonies are my heritage for ever; yea, they are the joy of my heart. Thou art my hiding place and my shield; I hope in thy word" (Psalm 119:111, 114). I do want my opening praise to be generic, i.e., I want everyone to be able to relate to what I say about you. If any man anywhere has any heritage—we call it today "roots"—it is your word. If any of us wanted to be remembered beyond our own generation we need to relate our life to your testimonies. It would be interesting to

list the one hundred men who are most remembered in America and see how many are related to your word. At the same time if no public remembrance is involved yet throughout an endless eternity it will be true: "Thy testimonies are my heritage."

All men need a "hiding place." The song writer spoke for all of us: "There is a place of quiet rest near to the heart of God." Bless your name! Our hope is in you and your word.

Express yourself in adoration for this quality of God.
Speak it audibly or write out your praise in your own devotional journal.

2. PRAISE GOD FOR WHAT HE MEANS TO ME.

There is no other verse to which I can relate quite like this one. If I am going to leave anything at all to my children and grandchildren—and their children, it will be my attempts to teach your word. My importance is in you—not at all in myself. I know how limited I am in expression and thought. The closer I relate to what you say in your word the more meaning and value there is in my stumbling attempts at teaching. I can say with increasing fervor

"they (your words) are the *joy* of my heart." The more I meditate and pray the happier I am in the study of your book. Having said the above I want to agree with the psalmist that my "hiding place"—my "shield" is not a book but a person—even yourself! In times of stress and strain and misunderstanding I go to the One behind the words on the page even your own precious self!

How do you personally relate to the heritage from God, and God who gives us roots?
Speak it out or write it out. It is *so important* that you establish *your own* devotional journal.

3. CONFESSION OF SIN

It is no problem to admit I have been lured away from your word and yourself by Satan. Dear Lord, forgive me for trying to find identity and importance in what I know is plastic. I need to go far far more often into my "hiding place" and be quiet I want to wait before you until I can get life into focus. Forgive me for facing life without a

shield. It has hurt me—and you. I list here my personal sins against you and myself—forgive me. I claim your beautiful promise of cleanness. Dear Lord, I want to resist all effort to fake any expression of joy—if I do not mean it, i.e., with a clear conscience, I will not say it! Praise you for helping me! You have 10,000 reasons for joy.

What personal sins do you want to confess? We *must* speak them to remove them.
Do it! *Now.* There is no one else you have sinned against more than God. Tell him so!

4. SING A PRAYER TO GOD.

Anywhere with Jesus I can safely go;
Anywhere He leads me in this world below;
Anywhere without Him dearest joys would fade;

Anywhere with Jesus I am not afraid.
Anywhere! anywhere! Fear I cannot know;
Anywhere with Jesus I can safely go.

Open your hymn book and sing the rest of the verses—or even sing another prayer song.

5. READ HIS WORD TO HIM!

His Word

[11]Soon afterward, Jesus went to a town called Nain, and his disciples and a large crowd went along with him. [12]As he approached the town gate, a dead person was being carried out—the only son of his mother, and she

was a widow. And a large crowd from the town was with her. [13]When the Lord saw her, his heart went out to her and he said, "Don't cry."

– Luke 7:11-13, NIV

Read His Word to Him.

I am just one more person in that "great crowd" who went with your Son as he approached the city of Nain. He is talking with his disciples. Or is he quiet and thoughtful as he draws near to the gate of the city? Out of the city gate four men walk carrying a coffin. In it is the dead body of "the only son" of the weeping mother who follows

as close to the pallbearers as she can. This woman is a widow and all her hopes are in that casket! Dear Lord, I am trying as best I can to identify with this poignant record. Our Lord has eyes only for the widow. He walks directly to her. There is an expression of pathos such as I have never seen on the face of any man!

Please express your response to this beautiful text. Put your expression in your own prayer diary.

6. READ HIS WORD FOR YOURSELF.

I became so involved in the reading of this beautiful record to you that it was read into my own heart. But even here I want to tell you what these precious words mean to me. (1) They are only representative of many incidents the gospel writers could have chosen to tell me of the many wonderful acts of compassion my Lord did. (2) My Lord was looking for a need he might meet and help. He is alive *now* and looks for the same thing in my life.

(3) Jesus did his miracles in the presence of many witnesses in the broad daylight with no fanfare. The fanfare followed his miracles—it did not precede them. (4) Jesus considered the need of the widow more important than bringing life back to her son. (5) There was no question at all in the mind of that woman that Jesus loved her and helped her. In all these ways and many more you speak to my heart.

It is so important that you pause in his presence
and either audibly or in written form tell him all his word means to you.

7. READ HIS WORD IN THANKSGIVING.

(1) Thank you for the tangible circumstances of this miracle. (2) Thank you that we are still one of the learners in this incident. (3) Thank you that one day we shall meet the son and the mother personally. (4) Thank you for my Lord's compassion that is just as real today as then. (5)

Thank you for the precious words my Lord speaks to every tear-stained face: "Weep not." (6) Thank you that Jesus has an answer to every heartbreak. (7) Thank you for those eyewitnesses who told this story to Luke.

Give yourself to your own expression of gratitude—write it or speak it!

8. READ HIS WORD IN MEDITATION.

"*. . . and said to her, 'Do not weep.'*" From the woman's perspective such words could have been almost an insult. She had every reason in human experience to weep. She had just lost the dearest in her life. Her only child had been taken from her. She had no other means of support. Her days ahead looked bleak indeed. She had just lost her only family identity and companionship.

From our Savior's perspective he had many reasons for saying what he did. He offered to her the hope of the world and life to come where there would be no death or separation. He was offering to her a trust in a heavenly Father who has a special interest in widows. He is about to restore all she had before this loss along with the hope for the future.

Pause—wait—think—then express yourself in thoughtful praise or thanks.

9. READ HIS WORD FOR PETITIONS.

It is good to relate our requests to these encouraging words: (1) What a testimony of the deity of Jesus to these servants—how can I communicate this good news to such men today? (2) Dr. Luke can tell us more about sickness and death than any of the other gospel writers—how I

want to relate better to such persons and their loved ones. (3) Jesus did his miracles in the presence of a large crowd in the broad daylight—give me deeper and deeper understanding of the purpose and power of his mighty acts. (4) Break my heart with those whose hearts are breaking.

Please, please remember these are prayers—speak them—reword them!

10. READ HIS WORD AND WAIT—LISTEN—GOD SPEAKS!

Speak to me in this poignant story: (1) "My heart yet goes out to every grieving mother." (2) "No word of mine shall ever be void of power." (3) "My word has been pre-

served so it can live again and again in the hearts of those who need hope."

11. INTERCESSION FOR THE LOST WORLD

Thailand — Points for prayer: (1) *Minority groups:* The Chinese number around 3 million, but fewer have put their trust in the Lord than in other overseas communities of Chinese such as Singapore, etc. There are about 17 churches with 3,500 believers only, i.e., 0.1% of the people. (2) *The Malays* (1,000,000) live in the 5 provinces adjoining Malaysia. There is much political tension and

unrest. This is the only Malay community open to evangelism in Asia, thus is strategic—especially for the Malays in Malaysia who are legally not allowed to be evangelized. After years of work by missionaries a little Malay Church of 20 believers and 30 almost committed believers has been born. Many others have heard the Gospel and believe, but hold back because of fear.

12. SING PRAISES TO OUR LORD.

Crown Him with many crowns,
The Lamb upon His throne;
Hark! how the heav'nly anthem drowns
All music but its own!

Awake, my soul, and sing
Of Him who died for thee;
And hail Him as thy matchless King
Thro' all eternity.

WEEK FORTY-THREE — SATURDAY

1. PRAISE GOD FOR WHO HE IS.

"Depart from me, you evildoers, that I may keep the commandments of my God. Uphold me according to the promise, that I may live, and let me not be put to shame in my hope!" (Psalm 119:115, 116). There is a certain exclusiveness in your nature. You abhor evil and love righteousness. All plants must have room to grow. Our Lord came "separated from sinners." Jesus withdrew from the crowd to allow time for the fulfillment of your will in his heart. When evildoers stifle and hinder the keeping of your will in our lives we must do something—either withdraw or cause them to leave. Such has been the record of your conduct from Genesis through the Old Testament. At the same time, if *you* yourself do not uphold us no amount of separation will give us life or hope. I believe the "promise" of verse 116 is generic, i.e., your promise to meet our needs. Dear Lord, I want to allow you also to *define* my needs.

Express yourself in adoration for this quality of God.
Speak it audibly or write out your praise in your own devotional journal.

2. PRAISE GOD FOR WHAT HE MEANS TO ME.

Just for me. "Evildoers" do not always force themselves upon me. Sometimes, too many times they came by invitation. I am speaking this to my own conscience. To spend time before the TV set is too often to invite evildoers who will defeat the fulfillment of your word in my life. To spend time talking about other people soon can turn negative and sour and become gossip and lo your word has been set aside! Dear Lord, I say these things to remind myself of my tremendous need of you! I *must* withdraw and spend time before you. I *must* memorize your word that you might uphold me according to your promise and I shall not be put to shame in my hope. Thank you for opening my heart to this deeper appreciation of your very self.

How do you personally relate to the exclusiveness of God, and God who is Love?
Speak it out or write it our. It is *so important* that you establish *your own* devotional journal.

3. CONFESSION OF SIN

It is so good to be able to clear my record every day. I am glad because I know as if never before that, "a little leaven leaveneth the whole lump," i.e., an association with evildoers, unless it is to be a friend to sinners in order to teach them, as my Lord did, will corrupt my conduct! I say from my heart with the psalmist, "Depart from me, you evildoers, that I may keep thy commandments." At the same time, I am confessing my failure to say this often enough or with enough conviction to prevent such corruption. I am not lost by failure—I am lost by continuing in failure. Dear Lord, I will come each day and be transformed by the continual renewing of my mind.

What personal sins do you want to confess? We *must* speak them to remove them.
Do it! *Now.* There is no one else you have sinned against more than God. Tell him so!

4. SING A PRAYER TO GOD.

Love divine, all loves excelling,
Joy of heaven, to earth come down;
Fix in us Thy humble dwelling;
All Thy faithful mercies crown.

Jesus, Thou art all compassion,
Pure, unbounded love Thou art;
Visit us with Thy salvation;
Enter ev'ry trembling heart.

Open your hymn book and sing the rest of the verses—or even sing another prayer song.

5. READ HIS WORD TO HIM!

His Word

[14]Then he went up and touched the coffin, and those carrying it stood still. He said, "Young man, I say to you, get up!" [15]The dead man sat up and began to talk, and Jesus gave him back to his mother.
[16]They were all filled with awe and praised God. "A great prophet has appeared among us," they said. "God has come to help his people." [17]This news about Jesus spread throughout Judea and the surrounding country.
— Luke 7:14-17, NIV

Read His Word to Him.

I could never in ten thousand worlds ever tell you what these words mean to me! I want to look—and then look again—to hear and then hear again the actions and words of your dear Son. Jesus touched the coffin. My dear Lord will touch every coffin that was ever lowered into a grave! And with the same results! One day, "I tell you the truth . . . the dead will hear the voice of the Son of God and those who hear will live. For as the Father has life in himself, so he has granted the Son to have life in himself" (John 5:25, 26).

Please express your response to this beautiful text. Put your expression in your own prayer diary.

6. READ HIS WORD FOR YOURSELF.

Just for me. As soon as the dead body became the living son he began to talk. What did he say? Was it a recital of what he had experienced since he died? We cannot imagine the gospel writers would have omitted this if such was the topic of his conversation. It is far more in keeping with what we know of the circumstances that he discussed topics both he and his dear mother could share. It was in his words his mother realized he was alive again. The whole point of this glorious resurrection is in the little word "awe." A great hush and amazement must have swept over the crowd that assembled for the funeral. Oh, dear Lord, I want to kneel before you in the same reverent spirit. I want to say with even more meaning than those present "God has come to help his people."

Pause in his presence and either audibly or in written form tell him all his word means to you.

7. READ HIS WORD IN THANKSGIVING.

(1) Thank you for the personalness of my Lord—he touched men and their needs. (2) Thank you that my Lord used the words "young man" because I can identify and so can all men. (3) Thank you for the direct brevity of my Lord's words—so unlike some of us. (4) Thank you for the dual purpose of this magnificent miracle—"he gave him back to his mother." (5) Thank you that no one present could escape (at least for a little while) the wonder of the occasion. (6) Thank you that these people praised the right One: "They praised God." (7) Thank you that this spread the testimony of my Lord's deity like wildfire across Judea and surrounding country.

Give yourself to your own expression of gratitude—write it or speak it!

8. READ HIS WORD IN MEDITATION.

"God has come to help his people." How beautifully descriptive of the whole mission of the Messiah. It was God in human form who raised the dead that day outside the city of Nain. God came to help his people to see that man lives in this body and also lives without his body. The son had to return to the inert form ere it could leave the coffin. God came to help his people see how much he cared about human relationships. Jesus moved immediately to help the widow in her grief. There would be a day, perhaps, when the son would follow the coffin of his mother. And there would indeed be a day when the burial of this son would be completed. But for today our Lord could dissolve their grief in joy—so he would do it! Most of all God came to help his people to see himself in the person of his Son.

Pause—wait—think—then express yourself in thoughtful praise or thanks.

9. READ HIS WORD FOR PETITIONS.

How often I have prayed at a funeral—here I can pray at a resurrection: (1) Help me to reach out and touch even when there doesn't seem to be any way to help. (2) It would be such a joy to be able to stop pall-bearers and tell the dead body to come to life. Keep me aware that one day there will be no more funerals—when my Lord returns— "Maranatha"—even so come Lord Jesus. (3) How glad I will be when my Lord gives all who have gone on before back to those who meet them in the air—I want to be ready if he should come today!

Right here add your personal requests—and his answers.

10. READ HIS WORD AND WAIT—LISTEN—GOD SPEAKS!

Speak to me in these brief verses: (1) "I am your prophet today—hear me!" (2) "I have indeed come to help my people this day." (3) "Spread the word around today that I am the resurrection and the life."

11. INTERCESSION FOR THE LOST WORLD

Thailand — Point for prayer: (1) *The tribal peoples* are generally very poor (unless they illegally grow opium), illiterate and under terrible domination of the spirit world. Many missions have labored and wept for a harvest which is now beginning to appear. Among the Meo, Lisu and Lahu strong, well led churches are emerging, but the Yao, Pwo Karen, Akha and Shan and the Kui and Khmu and also the Lawa, etc., the work is slow and hard, with believers lacking work and the encouraging of potential leaders are the great needs. Conditions are hard for the missionaries and now worsened by Communist infiltration.

12. SING PRAISES TO OUR LORD.

Face to face with Christ, my Savior,
Face to face—what will it be?
When with rapture I behold Him,
Jesus Christ who died for me.

Face to face I shall behold Him,
Far beyond the starry sky;
Face to face in all His glory,
I shall see Him by and by!

1. PRAISE GOD FOR WHO HE IS.

"With open mouth I pant, because I long for thy commandments. Turn to me and be gracious to me, as is thy wont toward those who love thy name" (Psalm 119:131, 132). The purpose of this portion of my worship to you is to separate from these verses the qualities of your character for which I praise you. Dear Lord, I never attempt this without a deep feeling of inadequacy. Here is what I see in this text: (1) Man becomes like a deer or some other animal about to die of thirst when he tries to live apart from you. The reverse is also true that when we are listening to you and walking in your will we are alert and strong and satisfied. Praise your name. (2) Your word is created for us and we are created for your word. The depths of man's thirst is satisfied in you. How wonderful! (3) It is your habit to turn to man and meet his needs. How beautiful are these qualities.

Express yourself in adoration for this quality of God.
Speak it audibly or write out your praise in your own devotional journal.

2. PRAISE GOD FOR WHAT HE MEANS TO ME.

Just for me. It is one thing to find such attributes for others — it is just as important to find them for myself. Which I am very glad to do. I have been both empty of your word — and full of your word — so I know from experience what a difference there is! Satan is so clever that there have been times when I did not know what was wrong. I was thirsty inside — a great emptiness held me.

And then I opened my mouth at the fountain of living water — indeed I felt like jumping in! How refreshing, how exhilarating is the meaning of every word of your book! I have no greater joy than the eternal value — the life changing application of your word!

How I love you for your very nature is love. It is your habit to be gracious to me!

How do you personally relate to our thirst for God, and God who satisfies?
Speak it out or write it out. It is *so important* that you establish *your own* devotional journal.

3. CONFESSION OF SIN

There is no hesitancy on my part to admit my sin — embarrassment — and I am ashamed — but I *want* to come to you for cleansing. I *want* to be clean. I *want* to be whole. I am glad to see indications that I am losing interest in what once attracted me. At the same time, I simply do not "long for your commandments" as deeply and as often as I need to. It is much too easy to be deceived into thinking that you will *always* be gracious unto me. I need to read again this verse: "My flesh trembles for fear of thee, and I am afraid of thy judgments" (Psalm 119:120). Indeed I am! I read this "beneath the cross of Jesus," but I do not want to continue in any sin. Forgive me and make me whole!

What personal sins do you want to confess? We *must* speak them to remove them.
Do it! *Now.* There is no one else you have sinned against more than God. Tell him so!

4. SING A PRAYER TO GOD.

When all my labors and trials are o'er,
And I am safe on that beautiful shore,
Just to be near the dear Lord I adore,
Will thro' the ages be glory for me.

O that will be glory for me,
Glory for me, glory for me;
When by His grace I shall look on His face,
That will be glory, be glory for me.

Open your hymn book and sing the rest of the verses — or even sing another prayer song.

5. READ HIS WORD TO HIM!

His Word

[2]When John heard in prison what Christ was doing, he sent his disciples [3]to ask him, "Are you the one who was to come, or should we expect someone else?"

[4]Jesus replied, "Go back and report to John what you hear and see: [5]The blind receive sight, the lame walk, those who have leprosy are cured, the deaf hear, the dead are raised, and the good news is preached to the poor. [6]Blessed is the man who does not fall away on account of me."

[7]As John's disciples were leaving, Jesus began to speak to the crowd about John: "What did you go out into the desert to see? A reed swayed by the wind? [8]If not, what did you go out to see? A man dressed in fine clothes? No, those who wear fine clothes are in kings' palaces. [9]Then what did you go out to see? A prophet? Yes, I tell you, and more than a prophet. [10]This is the one about whom it is written:

"'I will send my messenger ahead of you,
who will prepare your way before you.'
— *Matthew 11:2-10, NIV*

Read also Luke 7:18-27.

Read His Word to Him.

How well do all of us relate to the discouragement and bewilderment of John in prison! How often have we all had second thoughts — and they were not all good. Am I right in paraphrasing your Son's words to John (and to myself and all others) "John, I am engaged in the very work you know confirms my Messiahship: (1) Many blind have their sight. (2) The lame walk. (3) The lepers are cured. (4) The deaf now hear. (5) The dead are now alive. (6) The good news of my Messiahship is preached to the poor. You will be a happy man if you just trust me implicitly." Did John trust Jesus? Whether he did or didn't we do not know; we do know Jesus eulogized John as the greatest man who ever lived.

Please express your response to this beautiful text. Put your expression in your own prayer diary.

6. READ HIS WORD FOR YOURSELF.

The discouragements of imprisonment cannot even be imagined by those who have never been there. We can read of the dismal despondency that takes a hold of the whole being of those thus incarcerated. We all have asked the question: "Are you the one? Or should we look for someone else?" Maybe this too is just one more dead-end street! Dear Lord, speak again into my heart the new life you gave to John in his prison. "I have power over all of this life. No one has ever come even close to performing the obvious acts of divinity seen in my miracles. Poor imprisoned humanity will never have such good news preached to them as I bring. I am the One; there is no other!" Dear Lord, I do believe. Forgive me for doubting!

Pause in his presence and either audibly or in written form tell him all his word means to you.

7. READ HIS WORD IN THANKSGIVING.

(1) Thank you for the humanness of this account — John was the greatest — but not perfect. (2) Thank you that some of John's disciples were not perfect either; they were yet followers of John, not Jesus. (3) Thank you that we are not perfect — only forgiven. (4) Thank you for the wonderful credentials our Lord presented to John and all of his deity. (5) Thank you that Jesus knew of the weakness of the flesh and offered strength in himself. (6) Thank you for Jesus' estimate of John. (7) Thank you that the last prophet was more than a prophet.

Give yourself to your own expression of gratitude — write it or speak it!

8. READ HIS WORD IN MEDITATION.

"I will send my messenger ahead of you, who will prepare your way before you." How wonderfully true this was of John. It is the real task of every Christian. It seems incongruous that the creator of the world would need preparations for his coming. If he was a military hero or a political leader he would have included all such preparations in his budget. But when his highway is the human heart a much different preparation is needed. The one word that described those who were ready for him was *"repentance."* It is only when our minds are altered to match his view of life that we are ready for him.

Pause — wait — think — then express yourself in thoughtful praise or thanks.

9. READ HIS WORD FOR PETITIONS.

No doubt some of both our Lord's disciples and John's disciples prayed for this great man. There are requests in this text for our life: (1) The evident signs of deity need to be repeated often from my encouragement. (2) My Lord can and does open the eyes of our hearts to see as never before — may it happen this day. (3) How lame we all are in areas of our life — dear Lord, make me whole! (4) Only your Anointed One can open my ears to hear your word — do it today! (5) Happy is the man who finds no occasion of falling in my Lord — I want to be that man! (6) He must increase, I must decrease. (7) I do want to prepare the hearts of men for your coming — help me.

Please, please remember these are prayers — speak them — reword them!

10. READ HIS WORD AND WAIT — LISTEN — GOD SPEAKS!

Speak to me in these verses: (1) "My report to John has much more in it — look for it." (2) "Your estimate of John should agree with mine." (3) "The newest member of my body is greater than John."

11. INTERCESSION FOR THE LOST WORLD

Thailand — Point for prayer: (1) *Refugees from Laos and Cambodia* have proved a very receptive field of labor for missionaries with thousands seeking the Lord from both lands. Many of these new believers have moved on to other lands such as the U.S.A., France, etc. Pray for continuing evangelistic and relief ministries.

12. SING PRAISES TO OUR LORD.

Fairest Lord Jesus!
Ruler of all nature!
O Thou of God and man the Son!

Thee will I cherish,
Thee will I honor,
Thou, my soul's glory, joy, and crown!

WEEK FORTY-FOUR — MONDAY

1. PRAISE GOD FOR WHO HE IS.

"Thy testimonies are wonderful; therefore my soul keeps them. Keep steady my steps according to thy promise, and let no iniquity get dominion over me" (Psalm 119:129, 133). In these words are serveral beautiful attributes of yourself: (1) You have given us a word that is of its very nature a reflection of yourself, i.e., your word constantly fills us with wonder. What the ancient psalmist said about your testimonies in times past is true of all your revelation since that day. (2) All the qualities I see in yourself motivate me to want to keep your will for my life. I am drawn to worship you by your essential nature. The same is true of your word. I want to keep your testimonies because of their beauty—both in content and purpose.

Express yourself in adoration for this qualtiy of God.
Speak it audibly or write out your praise in your own devotional journal.

2. PRAISE GOD FOR WHAT HE MEANS TO ME.

Just for me. If all of the above is true—and it is, how could my steps ever falter? Once again we are reminded that there another power present. How very, very much I need the next quality of yourself alive and active in my daily experience: (3) You are at work steadying my steps. Indeed, this is the promise you have made to me and even now you are in the process of keeping. (4) What a beauti-ful combination: you have told me what to do and you give me the strength to do it! It isn't that there will never be temptation and failures—there will be, but they will not be of such a nature that they have "dominion over me." I praise you for such altogether adequate provisions for every day of every year.

How do you personally relate to the promise of God, and God who is faithful?
Speak it out or write it out. It is *so important* that you establish *your own* devotional journal.

3. CONFESSION OF SIN

I can see immediately what my need is in confession. My sin is in not spending more time with your testimonies. Not only more time, but more meditation that the wonder and beauty of your word might be increasingly apparent. My sin is that I have not put my *whole soul* into this pur-suit. It will take real thought—a total willingness—unre-strained love and a clean conscience before I can say "my soul," i.e., my whole inner person is given to keeping your will. Iniquity is never static—it never stands still. Either I have dominion over it, or it is over me. Dear Lord, I have sinned by treating sin and Satan so lightly. How I do want to develop your Son's attitude toward sin—he hated it with deep constant hatred! Forgive me and help me to do the same.

What personal sins do you want to confess? We *must* speak them to remove them.
Do it! *Now.* There is no one else you have sinned against more than God. Tell him so!

4. SING A PRAYER TO GOD.

I need Thee ev'ry hour,
Most gracious Lord;
No tender voice like Thine
Can peace afford.

I need Thee, O I need Thee;
Ev'ry hour I need Thee!
O bless me now, my Savior,
I come to Thee!

Open your hymn book and sing the rest of the verses—or even sing another prayer song.

5. READ HIS WORD TO HIM!

His Word

[11]I tell you the truth: Among those born of women there has not risen anyone greater than John the Baptist; yet he who is least in the kingdom of heaven is greater than he. [12]From the days of John the Baptist until now, the kingdom of heaven has been forcefully advancing, and forceful men lay hold of it. [13]For all the Prophets and the Law prophesied until John. [14]And if you are willing to accept it, he is the Elijah who was to come. [15]He who has ears, let him hear.

[16]"To what can I compare this generation? They are like children sitting in the marketplaces and calling out to others:

[17]"'We played the flute for you,
    and you did not dance;
  we sang a dirge,
    and you did not mourn.'
[18]For John came neither eating nor drinking, and they say, 'He has a demon.' [19]The Son of Man came eating and drinking, and they say, 'Here is a glutton and a drunkard, a friend of tax collectors and "sinners."' But wisdom is proved right by her actions."   — *Matthew 11:11-19, NIV*
Read also Luke 7:28-35.

Read His Word to Him.

Dear Lord, in these few words and this little space I could never say one hundredth of what could be said of these beautiful words from your Son. His estimate of John the Baptist has always interested me. How different is your estimate of man's greatness! John was greater than Abraham? Greater than Moses? Greater than David? In what sense greater? He did have a unique function, i.e., of being the immediate forerunner of our Lord. Greater than all other prophets in that he could see and point out the One of whom others could only foretell. But it was his personal character also that formed a part of your estimate of John. Full of the Holy Spirit since his birth. Full of humility, self-denial and courage.

Please express your response to this beautiful text. Put your expression in your own prayer diary.

6. READ HIS WORD FOR YOURSELF.

Just for me. The "bewildering amendment" attached to the foregoing estimate of John speaks so deeply to my heart! *"Yet he that is but little in the kingdom of heaven is greater than he."* To say it in a few words: John was not a Christian and therefore lacked all that we have. A Christian is one who has been forgiven by the shed blood of our Lord. John could anticipate his death, and when our Lord died his sacrifice for sin was retroactive and included John and all others before the cross who died in faith. At the same time, we can presently claim what John could only promise. "The least born of the Holy Spirit is greater than the greatest born of woman." Glory to his name!

Pause in his presence and either audibly or in written form tell him all his word means to you.

7. READ HIS WORD IN THANKSGIVING.

(1) Thank you that my Lord estimated the whole record of John's life in his commendation. (2) Thank you for the present grand example John is for us yet today. (3) Thank you that we have what John promised. (Dear Lord, give me grace to receive it.) (4) Thank you that zeal and force are commendable when used in the right attitude for the right purpose. (5) Thank you for the Elijah to come that I see in John.

Give yourself to your own expression of gratitude—write it or speak it!

8. READ HIS WORD IN MEDITATION.

"They are like children sitting in the market places and calling on others . . ." In a very real sense our Lord could have said: "We are all like children sitting in the market places and calling out to others . . ." But what are we saying? Our Lord called out the very will of yourself. We could hardly compare Jesus to children—although he once was a child. We are the juveniles. How immature we are! Nothing pleases us. It is because we have found no satisfying purpose. It is also because we are looking for a deliverer but we have never taken the time or thought to discover just what he looks like.

Pause—wait—think—then express yourself in thoughtful praise or thanks.

9. READ HIS WORD FOR PETITIONS.

How important are these verses to life each day: (1) How great an influence was Zachariah and Elizabeth in the life of this good man? Give me such influence in the lives of others. (2) May the joys and values of the Christian life be clearer than ever to me. (3) Keep me aware that there is nothing easy about your rule in the lives of men. (4) Elijah was a bold yet humble man—how I want to be like him. (5) As I read your word—I do have ears—may I hear what you are saying. (6) Petulant childlessness is such a sin—deliver me! (7) Make me a friend to sinners—just like my Lord.

Right here add your personal requests—and his answers.

10. READ HIS WORD AND WAIT—LISTEN—GOD SPEAKS!

In these verses speak to me: (1) "There are great men in rough dress today." (2) "It still takes force and determination to allow me to rule your heart." (3) "Some men will never respond."

11. INTERCESSION FOR THE LOST WORLD

The Middle East — Population: 221,000,000. Growth rate—2%. People per sq. km.—14.
Point for prayer: (1) *The Challenge of Islam.* The home of the First Century Church is now the most needy mission field in the world. The Muslim conquests virtually wiped out the decadent Christianity prevailing in these lands, leaving a despised and harassed remnant of a great variety of ancient churches that did not succumb to Islam. Islam reigns supreme where once the Gospel was preached.

12. SING PRAISES TO OUR LORD.

Wounded for me, wounded for me,
There on the cross He was wounded for me;
Gone my transgressions, and now I am free,
All because Jesus was wounded for me.

WEEK FORTY-FOUR — TUESDAY

1. PRAISE GOD FOR WHO HE IS.

"Thy righteousness is righteous for ever, and thy law is true. Trouble and anguish have come upon me, but thy commandments are my delight" (Psalm 119:142, 143). It is so good to know Someone who amid change changes not. You are always right and always will be right. There is no smugness in your claim to righteousness. You do not consider us less then because we know less or fail to fulfill. What a comforting and amazing fact it is that all your qualities are absolute. No wonder that your commandments are my delight. Your law perfectly matches man's need; it is true in the sense of perfectly stating reality. This life is full of trouble and anguish—some of it from my own willfulness and some by the nature of the environment in which we live, but always and ever there is something to delight my heart!

Express yourself in adoration for this quality of God.
Speak it audibly or write out your praise in your own devotional journal.

2. PRAISE GOD FOR WHAT HE MEANS TO ME.

Just for me. In my first expression of praise I have tried unsuccessfully to speak for all men. Just here I can speak wholeheartedly for myself. It will be a joy for me to finally arrive in that land of endless day—or of pure delight, and rejoice with all others in the completion of what now is a blessed promise: "Thy righteousness is righteous for ever." It will be good to review all the subjects of man's interest one after another and find what you have said in your book the Bible was right in every instance. I can rejoice in tribulation since I know it is but a necessary corollary to the enjoyment of heaven. If there was no darkness, how could I possibly appreciate the light? Praise your name!

How do you personally relate to the righteousness of God, and God who is Righteous?
Speak it out or write it out. It is *so important* that you establish *your own* devotional journal.

3. CONFESSION OF SIN

There is much repetition in this psalm as relating to your law, testimonies, or commandments. There is also much repetition in my sinning. If it were not for your eternal nature of love I am sure my sin and confession would become exceedingly dull. In all of my admission of failure I am only confessing my total dependence upon you—my desperate need of you. I am glad it is not my responsibility to mark out my moral practice or progress. I would either quit or become vain. I am ready to admit failure but never defeat. If you are on my side, and I know you are, who can successfully be against me?

What personal sins do you want to confess? We *must* speak them to remove them.
Do it! *Now.* There is no one else you have sinned against more than God. Tell him so!

4. SING A PRAYER TO GOD.

Savior, more than life to me,
I am clinging, clinging close to Thee;
Let Thy precious blood applied,
Keep me ever, ever near Thy side.

Ev'ry day, ev'ry hour,
Let me feel Thy cleansing pow'r;
Let Thy precious blood applied,
Keep me ever, ever near Thy side.

Open your hymn book and sing the rest of the verses—or even sing another prayer song.

5. READ HIS WORD TO HIM!

His Word

[20]Then Jesus began to denounce the cities in which most of his miracles had been performed, because they did not repent. [21]"Woe to you, Korazin! Woe to you, Bethsaida! If the miracles that were performed in you had been performed in Tyre and Sidon, they would have repented long ago in sackcloth and ashes. [22]But I tell you, it will be more bearable for Tyre and Sidon on the day of judgment than for you. [23]And you, Capernaum, will you be lifted up to the skies? No, you will go down to the depths. If the miracles that were performed in you had been performed in Sodom, it would have remained to this day. [24]But I tell you that it will be more bearable for Sodom on the day of judgment than for you."

— *Matthew 11:20-24, NIV*

Read His Word to Him.

Dear Lord, I am often at a loss for words to enter an appreciation of the words from the lips of your dear Son and my king. I wonder what words he used in his condemnation of these cities. It is a judgment pronounced upon *people. Repentance* is *such* an important response to all he did and said. I want to in deed and in truth *repent!* It is a total change of the total mind. Repentance is neither sorrow nor change; it stands between both. It is preceded by sorrow and is followed by change. A change of mind that lasts indicates true repentance.

Please express your response to this beautiful text. Put your response in your own prayer diary.

WEEK FORTY-FOUR — TUESDAY

6. READ HIS WORD FOR YOURSELF.

Is there an admission of failure in the words of my Lord? There is as to the response of these people. That my Lord should do so many, many miracles in these cities and yet fail to get the response expected says something very clearly to me: Not everyone with eyes sees; not everyone with ears hears; not everyone with brains thinks! These words shock me! Jesus *will* condemn to hell some people. The people here described as under his judgment were nice religious people who would not harm a hair of his head. Just an acquaintance with Jesus does not produce faith. Faith is doing what he says. Goodness is not repentance. A submission of the will and intellect to his Lordship is repentance. An education in what he did or said is not necessarily faith. Dear Lord, do I even now hear you?

It is so important that you pause in his presence
and either audibly or in written form tell him all his word means to you.

7. READ HIS WORD IN THANKSGIVING.

(1) Thank you for the revelation of the "other side of the coin" of my Lord's deity. (2) Thank you that at least someone can accept the message of his miracles. (3) Thank you for the quantity and quality of my Lord's signs. (4) Thank you for the omniscience of Jesus in his knowledge of the past. (5) Thank you for his omniscience seen in a knowledge of the judgment and just where all would stand. (6) Thank you for the fairness and even mercy of the judgment. (7) Thank you that one day all will know who Jesus is.

Give yourself to your own expression of gratitude — write it or speak it!

8. READ HIS WORD IN MEDITATION.

"But I tell you that it will be more bearable for Sodom on the day of judgment than for you." Such a strong word! But just as in all our Lord's words there is more than adequate reason behind this assertion. Let's examine several possible reasons for such condemnation: (1) Whereas Sodom had a righteous man in its gates "who vexed his righteous soul from day to day with their ungodly deeds," they had no one like the very Son of God to walk their streets and visit their homes. (2) The only miracle of Sodom was its destruction. How many hundreds, even thousands of people were healed in Korazin, Bethsaida and Capernaum? (3) Sodom was a heathen city — the towns of Galilee were all inhabited by the children of Israel.

Pause — wait — think — then express yourself in thoughtful praise or thanks.

9. READ HIS WORD FOR PETITIONS.

Surely in the judgments of Jesus there are reasons for requests: (1) How utterly insensitive some people can be! Lord, is it I? (2) My largest need each day is to repent — I seek your motivation. (3) Since I can see, as I read, more miracles than were performed in these towns I shall have less reason not to accept his Lordship. I am asking for a willingness. (4) Opportunity spells responsibility — how overwhelming is the responsibility of our nation — and most especially her teachers! Forgive me! (5) There is a hell ahead of some people — am I associated with such persons? Speak through me to them.

Please, please remember these are prayers — speak them — reword them!

10. READ HIS WORD IN MEDITATION.

In these sharp words you can reach my conscience — speak to me: (1) "How many more miracles of redeeming grace do you need before you obey Me?" (2) "He that exalts himself will be humbled." (3) "He that humbles himself will be exalted."

11. INTERCESSION FOR THE LOST WORLD

The Middle East — Point for prayer: (1) *Missions.* Early Protestant Missions in the last century frequently turned from the difficult Muslim majority to evangelizing the more receptive nominal Christians. Few of the present Protestants are from a Muslim background. Yet the sacrificial labors and tears of many missionaries among Muslims will surely yield the longed-for harvest. Missionaries need much prayer, for this is Satan's territory; discouragements, lack of visible fruit and hostility of many can cause some to give up the struggle. Pray for adaptability to new cultures, acceptability among the people.

12. SING PRAISES TO OUR LORD.

So precious is Jesus, my Savior, my King,
His praise all the day long with rapture I sing;
To Him in my weakness for strength I can cling,
For He is so precious to me.
For He is so precious to me,

For He is so precious to me;
'Tis Heaven below
My Redeemer to know,
For He is so precious to me.

WEEK FORTY-FOUR — WEDNESDAY

1. PRAISE GOD FOR WHO HE IS.

"I rise before dawn and cry for help; I hope in thy words. My eyes are awake before the watches of the night, that I may meditate upon thy promise" (Psalm 119:147,148). How I do wonder at the circumstances that prompted such words. What was it that moved the psalmist to rise before dawn to cry for help? What problem would keep him awake most of the night? Regardless of the environment out of which these words come they express qualities of yourself for which we lift our hearts in praise. There is no stress in life for which we cannot seek your help. If something presses down upon us and sleep will not come we can cry to you and you will indeed help us! The source of help is in your words. How eternally important it is that we keep your word ever before us.

Express yourself in adoration for this quality of God.
Speak it audibly or write out your praise in your own devotional journal.

2. PRAISE GOD FOR WHAT HE MEANS TO ME.

There have been times when sleep escaped me—not many times—but I want to confess that my meditation was on some solution and not upon your word or upon your promise. Perhaps there will be other nights when I can make direct application of these blessed words. I want to learn how to so meditate upon your word that all the hope in life is found there. Your essential promise is to enable me and forgive me. I purpose to give myself to you in the examination of every word in your book every day of my life, i.e., some portion of it every day! I need to improve on my meditation—help me!

How do you personally relate to the hope from God, and God who is our Hope?
Speak it out or write it out. It is *so important* that you establish *your own* devotional journal.

3. CONFESSION OF SIN

For all the days when I called upon someone else or something else for help forgive me! When my hope has been in things and not in your words forgive me. For all the times when I forgot or neglected your wonderful promise to be with me—forgive! I am so glad that I want to ask you for cleansing. It is good to be inwardly moved to want to seek your approval. I sense that just on the other side of this present circumstance is a really bright tomorrow. There is a time really close when I will find more and more hope in your words. There is a day really near when I will be able to meditate upon your promise in such a manner that I will be filled with peace and joy! In the face of hope I ask for forgiveness of my present sins.

What personal sins do you want to confess? We *must* speak them to remove them.
Do it! *Now.* There is no one else you have sinned against more than God. Tell him so!

4. SING A PRAYER TO GOD.

Sweetly, Lord, have we heard Thee calling,
Come, follow Me!
And we see where Thy footprints falling
Lead us to Thee.
Footprints of Jesus, that make the pathway glow;
We will follow the steps of Jesus where'er they go.

Open your hymn book and sing the rest of the verses—or even sing another prayer song.

5. READ HIS WORD TO HIM!

His Word

[25]At that time Jesus said, "I praise you, Father, Lord of heaven and earth, because you have hidden these things from the wise and learned, and revealed them to little children. [26]Yes, Father, for this was your good pleasure. [27]"All things have been committed to me by my Father. No one knows the Son except the Father, and no one knows the Father except the Son and those to whom the Son chooses to reveal him.
[28]"Come to me, all you who are weary and burdened, and I will give you rest. [29]Take my yoke upon you and learn from me, for I am gentle and humble in heart, and you will find rest for your souls. [30]For my yoke is easy and my burden is light." — *Matthew 11:25-30, NIV*

Read His Word to Him.

Of all times when our Lord should be full of praise and thanksgiving we would hardly expect it here. Jesus had failed to communicate to those who should have appreciated him most. What profound purpose we can find in this for our reasons for praising you! Here are some reasons for our Lord's praise: (1) His Father, the Lord of heaven and earth was in control; the universal Sovereign had not lost his position. (2) The separation of those who wanted to hear and those who did not want to hear was clearly drawn. (3) For the obvious autonomous nature of salvation. Salvation is of God. (4) That God the ruler of heaven and earth stoops to bless the nobodies and rankest beginners—the babes!

Please express your response to this beautiful text. Put your expression in your own prayer diary.

WEEK FORTY-FOUR — WEDNESDAY

6. READ HIS WORD FOR YOURSELF.

I have hoped (sometimes unsuccessfully) that my expression of worship in the above section has generic application. In this area I want to be just as personal as possible. How hauntingly poignant is the invitation of my Lord to: "Come unto me." And yet, I *must* read just as carefully his pre-conditions for approaching him. I cannot, I will not, come until I am as humble as a child. I cannot learn from him until I am transparently sincere in my desire to know. If I feel I am wise and learned I just as well not come for I will not listen—if I do I will not hear—if I do I will not submit. It is only when I am truly weary and burdened that I can find his rest. Dear Lord, I must think and pray before I come. I believe my Lord has fashioned a yoke that just fits my stubborn neck. Dear Lord, I *do want* your rest for my life.

Give yourself to your own expression of gratitude—write it or speak it!

7. READ HIS WORD IN THANKSGIVING.

(1) Thank you for the example of my Lord in praising and thanking you. (2) Thank you that I can with him praise you as "Lord of heaven and earth." (3) Thank you for the marvelous prerequisites to learning: ignorance, wonder, faith. (4) Thank you that you (my Father) take pleasure in such an attitude on our part. (5) Thank you for the plain claim of omniscience made by my Lord in these verses. (6) Dear Lord, I want to be that one to whom your Son chooses to reveal your will. (7) Thank you for the privilege of bowing my head and receiving your yoke.

Give yourself to your own expression of gratitude—write it or speak it.

8. READ HIS WORD IN MEDITATION.

"For my yoke is easy and my burden is light." Our Lord must have made and helped make a good number of yokes while he worked in the carpenter's shop. The fit of the yoke to the neck of the ox was so very important. If the yoke was not "easy" or did not fit it could cause great discomfort to the poor beast and could result in the loss of the animal as of any use to the owner. We are sure that Joseph and Jesus made the best yokes in all of Nazareth. This says so much to us. Everyone wears a yoke. We are all in someone's service—even if we just serve ourselves—we serve. Who could know better how to help us find peace and purpose than the One who created us? Isn't it better to serve a gentle humble master under a light burden with a yoke that fits?

Pause—wait—think—then express yourself in thoughtful praise or thanks.

9. READ HIS WORD FOR PETITIONS.

Here is an example of praying from my Lord—surely I can learn from him. (1) I praise you Father because you are Lord of heaven and earth. I want this to be a reality in my understanding. (2) Please reveal to this babe the deeper meaning of your words. (3) That you take pleasure in revealing your will to us becomes a great motive for study—help me. (4) I accept at face value the words of your Son: "No one knows the Son except the Father"—how much more there is to learn of him! I do so want to know more. (5) I am delighted for the modifying clause concerning yourself—Jesus has made you known to us. Open my heart!

Right here add your personal requests—and his answers.

10. READ HIS WORD AND WAIT—LISTEN—GOD SPEAKS!

In the gracious invitation of your Son I hear you speak to me: (1) "I specialize in helping the weary and burdened —bow your heart to receive my yoke." (2) "Rest in your soul is much different than rest for your body." (3) "If you are not gentle and humble you are not like me."

11. INTERCESSION FOR THE LOST WORLD

The Middle East — Point for prayer: (1) *Missions*—There are encouraging signs of a growing concern in Western lands for the evangelization of the Muslim world. a) The number of missionaries in the Middle East has risen to over 1,300. b) The increasing numbers of Christians in secular employment in the Middle East, who give up good prospects in their homelands to witness in this way. These need much prayer. c) The growing army of permanent and short term workers witnessing among immigrant Muslims in Europe. There are 3,000,000 Muslims from the Middle East now working in Western Europe. There are now more Turkish and North African Christians in Europe than in their own countries.

12. SING PRAISES TO OUR LORD.

There is a name I love to hear,
I love to sing its worth;
It sounds like music in mine ear,
The sweetest name on earth.

Oh, how I love Jesus,
Oh, how I love Jesus,
Oh, how I love Jesus,
Because He first loved me!

WEEK FORTY-FOUR — THURSDAY

1. PRAISE GOD FOR WHO HE IS.

"But thou art near, O Lord, and all thy commandments are true. Long have I known from thy testimonies that thou hast founded them forever" (Psalm 119:151, 152). My purpose is always the same: to raise an attribute of yourself before the throne of grace in adoration and praise. In these two beautiful verses I can gladly do this. Praise to your glorious name because: (1) You are near. Nearer indeed than the very air I breathe. Present above me, within me, around me, ahead of me, behind me. So near that I can speak to you as my most intimate friend. At the same time, I am moved to fall before you in wonder — the Creator and Sustainer of all things. (2) All that you have said in your word — and I equate this with the Bible — is in total agreement with reality. In every examination your "comandments" conform perfectly with what we know in every branch of science. (3) Long have I demonstrated subjectively that your word is true. I have proved it time and again to meet every need of my heart and life.

Express yourself in adoration for this quality of God.
Speak it audibly or write out your praise in your own devotional journal.

2. PRAISE GOD FOR WHAT HE MEANS TO ME.

Just for me. Dear Lord, I would that what I have just said were said by all men. Surely all men could come to the same conclusion if given the same evidence. You are not far from anyone of us. Just now I want to acknowledge the lovely thought that "Long have I known from thy testimonies that thou hast founded them forever." I am a few years from the alloted three score and ten but the more I meditate upon your words the more deeply am I convinced of their eternal nature. Someone beyond time and space has caused them to be written. To look beneath the surface of your word is to find yourself. I have been greatly impressed all over again at the record of "fisherman" John. Given the set of circumstances out of which this man came there could be no other explanation to the profundity of his thought. Praise your name.

How do you personally relate to the everlastingness of God, and God who is Eternal?
Speak it out or write it out. It is *so important* that you establish *your own* devotional journal.

3. CONFESSION OF SIN

It is the whole-soul purpose of Satan to cast doubt upon your word. From his first expression in the garden: *"Yea, hath God said?"* to the present so-called "liberal" theologian he has not stopped his efforts to overturn your testimony. How sad it is that I must confess my sin in listening to his doubts. I listen to his lies and the doubt is mine. I do not minimize the need for a thorough examination of all the evidence. But even after such a pursuit "How can you believe, who receive glory from one another and do not seek the glory that comes from the only God?"

What personal sins do you want to confess? We *must* speak them to remove them.
Do it! *Now.* There is no one else you have sinned against more than God. Tell him so!

4. SING A PRAYER TO GOD.

Alas, and did my Savior bleed?
And did my Sov'reign die?
Would He devote that sacred head
For such a worm as I?

At the cross, at the cross where I first saw the light,
And the burden of my heart rolled away,
It was there by faith I received my sight,
And now I am happy all the day!

Open your hymn book and sing the rest of the verses — or even sing another prayer song.

5. READ HIS WORD TO HIM!
His Word

[36]Now one of the Pharisees invited Jesus to have dinner with him, so he went to the Pharisee's house and reclined at the table. [37]When a woman who had lived a sinful life in that town learned that Jesus was eating at the Pharisee's house, she brought an alabaster jar of perfume.
— *Luke 7:36, 37, NIV*

[20]Then Jesus entered a house, and again a crowd gathered, so that he and his disciples were not even able to eat. [21]When his family heard about this, they went to take charge of him, for they said, "He is out of his mind."
— *Mark 3:20, 21, NIV*

Read His Word to Him.

There is always so much to see and hear for my own heart in every word I read from the life of my Lord. I do want to read this from your perspective. I do not know who the Pharisee was who invited my Lord to his home,

WEEK FORTY-FOUR — THURSDAY

but I am sure he did not know who it was who reclined with him at the table. How far away was my Lord when they were ready to eat? Since the crowd was so great Jesus probably was only a few inches away. How I would like to have been a guest at that meal.

How easy it would be to misunderstand our Lord's work. What a contrast this feverish activity was to the quiet life he had lived in Nazareth! But then our Lord has always been misunderstood by us who should know him best.

Please express your response to this beautiful text. Put your expression in your own prayer diary.

6. READ HIS WORD FOR YOURSELF.

It has been a constant source of wonder to me as to how James, Joseph, Simon and Judus could live for years and years in the same house with Jesus and really never know him. I believe James wrote the epistle that bears his name. Is this why he is so insistent on a faith that works? He had faith—and he had *no* faith. Lest I am too critical of James or Judus or Joseph, I need to remember that the "Other Jesus" or the "Other Comforter" has taken up residence in my house—or my body, and I really "know him not." Jesus came to his own—and those who were his own in the nearest of human relationships knew him not. The one we would least expect to know him came with a gift of perfume.

Pause in his presence and either audibly or in written form tell him all his word means to you.

7. READ HIS WORD IN THANKSGIVING.

(1) Thank you that there was at least one Pharisee who wanted to offer hospitality to our Lord. (2) Thank you that Jesus integrated his teaching with eating. (3) Thank you for the popularity of our Lord, at least he could speak to many who would have otherwise never heard. (4) Thank you for the concern of his mother and brothers—even if misplaced, it was concern. (5) Thank you that what seems insanity to some is the work of my Lord.

Give yourself to your own expression of gratitude—write it or speak it!

8. READ HIS WORD IN MEDITATION.

". . . she brought an alabaster jar of perfume." Why did she bring this expensive ointment? What she did with it will of course answer our question. The real reason is found in her love for our Lord. She must have known Jesus before he went to the Pharisee's house. It was a bold act of faith to enter this house uninvited. It was even more courageous to anoint our Savior's feet. Who was this woman? All attempts to identify her seem to me to be inadequate. It is enough to know she can represent only one of us. She was a sinner who loved much.

Pause—wait—think—then express yourself in thoughtful praise or thanks.

9. READ HIS WORD FOR PETITIONS.

What an encouragement to pray is the encounter of human need: (1) I wonder how many houses my Lord entered during his ministry—I do want, Lord, for you to make my house your house. (2) My Lord was not distracted or disturbed with the interruption by men—how I want to be like him. (3) Those who were the closest to my Lord seemed to understand him the least—if such happens with me help me to remember him. (4) Jesus went to a Pharisee's house to eat—wouldn't this decision upset some people? How I want your wisdom in my associations! (5) Why did this sinful woman want to be with Jesus? There was something wonderfully approachable about Jesus. How I want to be like him!

Please, please remember these are prayers—speak them—reword them!

10. READ HIS WORD AND WAIT—LISTEN—GOD SPEAKS!

In these precious verses speak to me: (1) "Crowded can be both good and bad depending upon your motives." (2) "If people think you strange or unbalanced they thought that of me." (3) "Men are not guilty by association."

11. INTERCESSION FOR THE LOST WORLD

The Middle East — Point for prayer: (1) *The National Believers* — They are few and scattered, and much in need of prayer as they live in very difficult circumstances. It is easier for them to emigrate to lands with greater religious freedom—as many have done. Probably the majority of converts out of Islam have left their homelands for this reason, for they face extreme pressures. There is a great need for the planting and growth of vigorous churches.

12. SING PRAISES TO OUR LORD.

I will sing the wondrous story
Of the Christ who died for me,
How He left His home in glory
For the cross of Calvary.

Yes, I'll sing . . . the wondrous story
Of the Christ . . . who died for me,
Sing it with . . . the saints in glory,
Gathered by . . . the crystal sea.

613

WEEK FORTY-FOUR – FRIDAY

1. PRAISE GOD FOR WHO HE IS.

"The sum of thy word is truth; and every one of thy righteous ordinances endures forever" (Psalm 119:160). What a marvel to find hidden here in the 119th Psalm this lovely verse! I agree with the conclusion here related and apply it to your whole revelation as found in the sixty-six books of your book. (I am not at all unaware of the opinions to the contrary.) I have never found one word of your book in disagreement with fact. How com-forting to know that the sum total of what you have said is the whole truth! Dear Lord, I believe that when this earth has melted with fervent heat not one word of your righteous ordinances will have failed of fulfillment. There could hardly be a greater characteristic for which I praise you. The wonderful compatibility seen in what I read in your word and what I see in life moves me to exclamation of praise.

Express yourself in adoration for this quality of God.
Speak it audibly or write out your praise in your own devotional journal.

2. PRAISE GOD FOR WHAT HE MEANS TO ME.

For myself.—I want to honor and praise you in some specific areas of life where I have found this verse to be so eternally true: (1) "The sum of thy word is truth" on the subject of *love.* To pursue the references found in *Monser's Topical study* on this one subject is to be increasingly amazed. The example of love seen in my Lord and reflected in the life of Paul is so far above anything anyone else has said from any other source that there is no comparison. (2) "The sum of thy word is truth" on the subject of *disagreement.* This is such an important area. How shall we handle this sticky problem in human relationships? It is easy to trace from Genesis to revelation the subject and agree with the psalmist.

How do you personally relate to the revelation of God, and God who is the Revelator?
Speak it out or write it out. It is *so important* that you establish *your own* devotional journal.

3. CONFESSION OF SIN

Dear Lord, how shall I know the truth on any theme until I have digested all you have said? To be ignorant and in the dark—and even to curse it, is one thing—to be *willfully* in such a place is quite another. I have never been moved so deeply before with the need for constant meditation on your word. I confess my tragic lack in this pursuit. I have run a little way, but in so many subjects I have lived in the dark—and sometimes I complained bitterly. Forgive, forgive me! There are other areas of sin—of my personal violations of your law. But in everyone of my personal sins I see a lack of a knowledge of the sum total of your word on the subject. I know that knowledge has a tendency to puff up. I know that only a personal relationship with you avails anything, but the light of your word shows me your face! I love you, forgive me.

What personal sins do you want to confess? We *must* speak them to remove them.
Do it! *Now.* There is no one else you have sinned against more than God. Tell him so!

4. SING A PRAYER TO GOD.

Must I be carried to the skies
On flow'ry beds of ease,

While others fought to win the prize,
And sailed thro' bloody seas?

Open your hymn book and sing the rest of the verses—or even sing another prayer song.

5. READ HIS WORD TO HIM!

His Word

38and as she stood behind him at his feet weeping, she began to wet his feet with her tears. Then she wiped them with her hair, kissed them and poured perfume on them. 39When the Pharisee who had invited him saw this, he said to himself, "If this man were a prophet, he would know who is touching him and what kind of woman she is—that she is a sinner." 40Jesus answered him, "Simon, I have something to tell you."

"Tell me, teacher," he said.

41"Two men owed money to a certain moneylender. One owed him five hundred denarii, and the other fifty. 42Neither of them had the money to pay him back, so he canceled the debts of both. Now which of them will love him more?"

43Simon replied, "I suppose the one who had the bigger debt canceled."

"You have judged correctly," Jesus said.

44Then he turned toward the woman and said to Simon, "Do you see this woman? I came into your house. You did not give me any water for my feet, but she wet my feet with her tears and wiped them with her hair. 45You did not give me a kiss, but this woman, from the time I entered has not stopped kissing my feet. 46You did not put oil on my head, but she has poured perfume on my feet. 47Therefore, I tell you, her many sins have been forgiven—for she loved much. But he who has been forgiven little loves little."
— *Luke 7:38-47, NIV*

WEEK FORTY-FOUR — FRIDAY

Read His Word to Him.

Since I have been in your service so long, and since I know my own sins, to at least some extent, I hardly know how to identify. I can relate to *both* of these participants. Simon who did not love as he should, and with the woman the forgiven sinner. Dear Lord, I want to learn from both of them.

Please express your response to this beautiful text. Put your expression in your own prayer diary.

6. READ HIS WORD FOR YOURSELF.

I know that prayer has five expressions: (1) petitions; (2) intercessions; (3) thanksgiving; (4) praise; (5) confession. I want to relate myself to Simon and the woman in each of these expressions of prayer: (A) *Simon:* (1) Break my hard heart. (2) For every prostitute in my town I pray someone — even myself will communicate your forgiveness. (3) Thank you that you open my eyes to see much more than form. (4) Praise your name that you open my eyes to my need. (5) I am a self-righteous hypocrite in some areas of my life — I repent. I *want* to change. (B) *As the woman:* (1) Dear God, I could never express my gratitude for your love. (2) Open the eyes of the hearts of religious people that they may see as you do. (3) Thank you for the deep peace in my heart. (4) Praise is my whole expression of the whole day. (5) My sin is forgiven — help me to forget it as you have.

Pause in his presence and either audibly or in written form tell him all his word means to you.

7. READ HIS WORD IN THANKSGIVING.

(1) Thank you for the wonderful tears of repentance. (2) Thank you that our Lord did not resist being touched. (3) Thank you for the value the woman placed on her love for her Lord. (4) Thank you that Jesus lets none of us off as "the good guys." (5) Thank you that the debt of sin can be, and is, forgiven!

Give yourself to your own expression of gratitude — write it or speak it!

8. READ HIS WORD IN MEDITATION.

"Which of them therefore will love him more." Loving is the involvement of the whole person. Our Lord is essentially asking: Which of them will give himself to the One who forgave? To whom much is given — by way or form of forgiveness, much is expected. What would be expected? (1) A deep continual sense of thanksgiving. When he thought what could have happened to him; when he considered what happened to others who could not pay and were not forgiven he was so full of thanksgiving. (2) A very high estimate of the character of the one who forgave him. If he admired him before, he now had something very personal about his admiration. All of this speaks so near our own hearts.

Pause — wait — think — then express yourself in thoughtful praise or thanks.

9. READ HIS WORD FOR PETITIONS.

I see so much in this incident that moves me to pray: (1) How can I help those so deeply involved in illicit sex in my day? (2) Teach me ways I can use in bringing such people to Jesus. (3) My Lord was not offended by this effusive expression of affection — how much can I associate with custom — how much with character? (4) How deeply indebted I am to you — I do want my debt canceled! Will I love you for it? (5) Give me your view of the awfulness of sin's bondage that I might appreciate my liberty.

Right here add your personal requests — and his answers.

10. READ HIS WORD AND WAIT — LISTEN — GOD SPEAKS!

As a guest with my Lord in the Pharisee's house I want you to speak to me: (1) "Tears are welcome when. they wash my feet and cleanse your heart." (2) "Only real faith can save you." (3) "Only the one who has been forgiven much can love much."

11. INTERCESSION FOR THE LOST WORLD

The Middle East — Points for prayer: (1) *Converts out of Islam* — for a close walk with the Lord, deliverance from all the erroneous Muslim thought patterns, a desire and opportunities for helpful fellowship with believers, acceptability by other Christians who are often suspicious of such converts, and boldness in the face of threats, ostracism, physical danger, etc. (2) *The witness of the believers* — deliverance from fear of witnessing, life style that recommends the Gospel, tactful winning of Muslims where the law forbids such a witness.

12. SING PRAISES TO OUR LORD.

Bearing shame and scoffing rude,
In my place condemned He stood;

Sealed my pardon with His blood;
Hallelujah! what a Savior!

WEEK FORTY-FOUR — SATURDAY

1. PRAISE GOD FOR WHO HE IS.

"I rejoice at thy word like one who finds great spoil. Seven times a day I praise thee for thy righteous ordinances" (Psalm 119:162, 164). Dear Lord, how blessedly good it is to be rested and able to come into your presence with great eager anticipation! Even as our Lord said "the rule of yourself is like treasure hidden in a field, which a man found and covered up; there in his joy he goes and sells all he has and buys that field" (Matthew 13:44). How shall I know of any part of the treasure's value without your word? If Matthew, Mark, Luke and John had not written down what they saw and heard I would have no treasure. If the writers of the Old Testament had been too busy to write I would never know of all you have for me. Seven times a day will I praise you for your word.

Express yourself in adoration for this quality of God.
Speak it audibly or write out your praise in your own devotional journal.

2. PRAISE GOD FOR WHAT HE MEANS TO ME.

Just for me. How I want to examine and appreciate the value of every word you have given to me. I stand back in wonder and amazement at the beauty I see just at first look, but the more I look the more beautiful detail I see in each verse. As the man with the treasure I do not plan on keeping this treasure for my own enjoyment alone, I am going to see it and allow it to circulate in the marketplace of mankind. Even now I am engaged in a project to get your word out to at least six foreign countries.

Dear Lord, direct me! There are so many comparisons I can make to a treasure and your word. I want to lift just two up for praise to you: (1) A treasure represents much thought, energy and time—your word has your mind, your life and eternity in it! Praise and glory to your name! (2) A treasure is full not only of beauty but value. A perfect combination. Indeed, indeed your word is full of beauty and value!

How do you personally relate to the beauty of God, and God who is Beautiful?
Speak it out or write it out. It is *so important* that you establish *your own* devotional journal.

3. CONFESSION OF SIN

How sorry I am that I do not always feel as I do just now. I know that your equation of reality is: (1) Your word or your facts; (2) my faith; (3) my feelings—but there is such a difference in the attitude I have at times when I approach your word. I can be defensive because of my sin; I can be introverted because I am ashamed; I can be dull and insensitive because I do not wish to face your facts about my sin. Ah, but when I come eager to confess my sins and rid myself of anything that hinders the free course of your will in my life, what a joy is mine! Such is my desire just now, dear Lord.

What personal sins do you want to confess? We *must* speak them to remove them.
Do it! *Now.* There is no one else you have sinned against more than God. Tell him so!

4. SING A PRAYER TO GOD.

All the way my Savior leads me;
What have I to ask beside?
Can I doubt His tender mercy,
Who thro' life has been my Guide?
Heav'nly peace, divinest comfort,
Here by faith in Him to dwell!
For I know, whate'er befall me,
Jesus doeth all things well;
For I know, whate'er befall me,
Jesus doeth all things well.

Open your hymn book and sing the rest of the verses—or even sing another prayer song.

5. READ HIS WORD TO HIM!

His Word

[47]Therefore, I tell you, her many sins have been forgiven —for she loved much. But he who has been forgiven little loves little."
[48]Then Jesus said to her, "Your sins are forgiven."

[49]The other guests began to say among themselves, "Who is this who even forgives sins?"
[50]Jesus said to the woman, "Your faith has saved you; go in peace."
— *Luke 7:47-50, NIV*

Read His Word to Him.

Gladly, gladly do I do this! Sometime, somewhere before this incident our Lord had encountered this dear woman. She had confessed freely, fully, tearfully her sins. Jesus had assured her that her sins were forgiven. Indeed, she came to him as the Messiah to receive such forgiveness. But there was more to her forgiveness than relief. She was overwhelmingly in love with the One who had forgiven her. This one who had much sex and no love now was consumed with a desire to express her love.

Please express your response to this beautiful text. Put your expression in your own prayer diary.

6. READ HIS WORD FOR YOURSELF.

What they said *was* important, but it was on another subject. Related but not the subject of the love of a forgiven sinner. *Method* so often trips us up. We are so often involved in *how* something shall be done that nothing is accomplished. Jesus was God—only God can forgive sins. The words of forgiveness were given intentionally to point to his deity. I hear him! I see him! Dear Lord, I am the sinner to receive his words. The closing words are so full of meaning. "Your faith has saved you; go in peace." Faith comes by accepting or trusting what our Lord has said. Jesus forgave her; she believed he could and did. She emotionally—totally related to his words. This is real faith—this produces real peace!

It is so important that you pause in his presence
and either audibly or in written form tell him all his word means to you.

7. READ HIS WORD IN THANKSGIVING.

(1) Thank you for the clear plain eternal offer of sins forgiven. (2) Thank you that no sins are too numerous or too bad to be forgiven. (3) Thank you that Jesus is as much alive today as then and speaks the same words to me. (4) Thank you that I can respond just like the unnamed woman. (5) Thank you that I am taught that forgiveness can be the wellspring of gratitude. (6) Thank you that I can also see some men will never be forgiven until they know they are sinners. (7) Thank you for the sharp and clear picture of my Lord as God among men.

Give yourself to your expression of gratitude—write it or speak it!

8. READ HIS WORD IN MEDITATION.

"Your faith has saved you; go in peace." What beautiful words from the only one who can forgive sins! From how much had this woman's faith saved her! (1) From the humiliation of being a commodity instead of a person. Sex is like food—it will be a part of life because of its nature. When men buy food no problem occurs that affects the food. Men do misuse food the same as sex. But when men buy other persons and use them to satisfy their own desires it is a tragic loss to the person. (2) Saved from the deep estrangement she felt within her own self. Prostitutes tell us that a deeper loneliness takes hold of their heart than can be described in human language. (3) Most of all she was saved from the awful frustration and constant agitation associated with this relationship. She had peace!

Pause—wait—think—then express yourself in thought praise or thanks.

9. READ HIS WORD FOR PETITIONS.

How many requests are there in the context of the forgiveness of sins? (1) Remind me all over again that my sins are always viewed as under the blood. (2) Thank you that repentance is an attitude—I claim the result of such an attitude—I hear my Lord say: "Your sins are forgiven." (3) I can answer the guest's question: "It is God incarnate in human form who forgives sins." Deepen my appreciation of the deity of my Lord. (4) How much fuller is the meaning of the term "saved" as used here by Jesus. Her whole life was saved. I need and claim such a salvation for myself. (5) I cannot imagine this woman continued in her former manner of life—she had enough of the chaos of sin. I need your peace to guard my heart and thoughts.

Please, please remember these are prayers—speak them—reword them!

10. READ HIS WORD AND WAIT—LISTEN—GOD SPEAKS!

In these three verses speak to me: (1) "Your past sins have all been forgiven—do you doubt my present ability?" (2) "Trust in my willingness to forgive is the basic need of all life." (3) "Accept my peace."

11. INTERCESSION FOR THE LOST WORLD

The Middle East — Points for prayer: (1) *The need for Christian homes*—these are very few. Unequal marriages between Christians and Muslims are the major cause of backsliding. The Muslim world needs to see the beauty of a Christian home. (2) *The cultivation of a missionary vision.* Arab missionaries would be more acceptable than Westerners in many lands. There are now about 230 Middle Eastern missionaries—largely from Egypt, Jordan and Syria, who are serving the Lord in other Middle Eastern countries. Many other Christians also work in lands closed to normal mission work—in Libya, Arabia, etc.

12. SING PRAISES TO OUR LORD.

Jesus is all the world to me,
My Friend in trials sore;
I go to Him for blessings, and He gives them o'er and o'er.
He sends the sunshine and the rain,

He sends the harvest's golden grain;
Sunshine and rain, harvest of grain,
He's my Friend.

WEEK FORTY-FIVE — SUNDAY

1. PRAISE GOD FOR WHO HE IS.

"Great peace have those who love thy law; nothing can make them stumble. My soul keeps thy testimonies; I love them exceedingly" (Psalm 119:165, 167). In these two precious verses are two characteristics of yourself. As out of the abundance of the heart our mouths form the words—so your words are the expression—the extension of yourself. (1) You have given us a word that properly received will produce a great unassailable personal peace.

The quality of character reflected here would be a complete understanding of the deepest inner needs of man. (2) You have given us a revelation in the form of what we call the Bible with the capacity to bring peace and tranquility to every relationship of man: with himself, with others and with you. The 167th verse gives us the key to open this quality in our experience: "my *soul* (total self) keeps thy testimonies."

Express yourself in adoration for this quality of God.
Speak it audibly or write out your praise in your own devotional journal.

2. PRAISE GOD FOR WHAT HE MEANS TO ME.

Just for me. There are not many things that make me stumble—just one thing: the loss of peace. There are not many things that destroy my peace, just one thing: failure to love you (as revealed in your word) with my whole self! Somehow there must be an integration, a transfer, an assimilation of the words on the pages of your book into the wellsprings of action in my life. *Love* is the answer. Read again these words: "Those who *love* thy law"; "I *love* them exceedingly." How about an applica-

tion of the characteristics of love as found in I Cor. 13:4-7. (1) My love for your word is patient and kind in the application of it in every relationship. (2) My love for what you have said is not jealous or boastful as I compare my acceptance with others. (3) My love for what I read in your word is never arrogant or rude. Dear Lord, it is easy to say I love your word and your Son—it is something else to live it. Forgive me.

How do you personally relate to the peace of God, and God who is Peace?
Speak it out or write it out. It is *so important* that you establish *your own* devotional journal.

3. CONFESSION OF SIN

Do I need to spell out just how far short I fall in the above qualities? I know I do and I openly and in detail confess my miserable failures to you, Lord, how can I be more patient—more humble? Love *is* the answer—love is meeting the need—in my own life—in the lives of others, but the attitude accompanying such an effort—ah, it is there I am so short. (4) In my receiving your word

in my relationship with others I am never overbearing in an insistence of my own way. Such a statement is a "pious platitude"—it is not true. Forgive me. I want to change. (5) I am never irritable or resentful in the daily living of your word. What a joke! I am blood guilty, but I want to repent. Forgive me!

What personal sins do you want to confess? We *must* speak them to remove them.
Do it! *Now.* There is no one else you have sinned against more than God. Tell him so!

4. SING A PRAYER TO GOD.

Joy to the world! the Lord is come;
Let earth receive her King;
Let ev'ry heart prepare Him room,

And heav'n and nature sing,
And heav'n and nature sing,
And heav'n and heav'n and nature sing.

Open your hymn book and sing the rest of the verses—or even sing another prayer song.

5. READ HIS WORD TO HIM!

His Word

[22]Then they brought him a demon-possessed man who was blind and mute, and Jesus healed him, so that he could both talk and see. [23]All the people were astonished and said, "Could this be the Son of David?"

[24]But when the Pharisees heard this, they said, "It is only by Beelzebub, the prince of demons, that this fellow drives out demons." — *Matthew 12:22-24, NIV*
Read also Mark 3:22.

Read His Word to Him.

Each time I approach this section of my worship I pause—for two reasons I pause: because I really never know just how to express myself—and second, because I am reminded once against how sharp and penetrating is your word. As I look in the face of this poor man I see myself!

I do not believe any Christian is demon possessed—at least I find none in your word, but I do know since Satan is not an omnipresent being we are attacked by demons. I, indeed am under constant attack like all other Christians.

Please express your response to this beautiful text. Put your expression in your own prayer diary.

6. READ HIS WORD FOR YOURSELF.

I see myself and indeed all men in the exchange of my Lord with this unnamed man. (1) If we are going to have any help it will be because our friends have brought us to Jesus. How could I ever thank you enough — or those dear friends who first came so long ago and brought me to my Lord? (2) Of the evil influence at work in our lives we can really never know. The depth and power of Satan's influence are known only to you. (3) We do know that whereas we were blind now we see! Oh, the startled wonder of being able to look at life through your eyes! (4) We were once mute or dumb to the words of praise and eternal value; now we can speak as you speak — we can lay your word up in our hearts to come out of our mouth.

It is so important that you pause in his presence
and either audibly or in written form tell him all his word means to you.

7. READ HIS WORD IN THANKSGIVING.

(1) Thank you that the disciples had learned that no case was hopeless. (2) Thank you that the disciples did not argue among themselves as to what should be done. (3) Thank you that Jesus is our One and only deliverer. (4) Thank you for the completeness of our salvation. (5) Thank you that the wonder and power of your miracles will never leave us. (6) Thank you for the clear cut choice: either God or Satan. (7) Thank you for one who knew beyond all controversy who healed him.

Give yourself to your own expression of gratitude — write it or speak it!

8. READ HIS WORD IN MEDITATION.

"It is only by Beelzebub, the prince of demons, that this fellow drives out demons." This was a deadly dangerous statement. Since our Lord knew the hearts of these men he knew this was a calculated conclusion. These men meant it! These Pharisees had been moving toward this statement for weeks and months. "There *was* something supernatural about Jesus" they said, "and now we know who it is — it is Satan." What a totally illogical assumption. What an impossible conclusion and yet they made it. It was the unpardonable sin! It was the blasphemy of the Holy Spirit. At the base of these words is the rejection of his deity. They had heard him and seen him in his miraculous ministry — to now decide that all his work was directed and empowered by Satan was the ultimate of rejection. This was rejection with no recourse. How dangerous it is to be religious but not Christian.

Pause — wait — think — then express yourself in thoughtful praise or thanks.

9. READ HIS WORD FOR PETITIONS.

In this confrontation I find much about which I want to pray: (1) The poor possessed man is almost forgotten in the midst of the argument. How easy it is to forget human need in the heat of a theological discussion — deliver me from this. (2) Guard my thoughts that I might recognize Satan's efforts to deceive. (3) I am glad to acknowledge that Jesus has the ability to free me from Satan's power — dear Lord, I want to claim such supremacy. (4) Jesus said that His power over demons was a demonstration of your kingdom — an example of your rule in the heart of man — how I do want to learn from this thought — give me wisdom!

Right here add your personal requests — and his answers.

10. READ HIS WORD AND WAIT — LISTEN — GOD SPEAKS.

I can hear your voice in these verses if my ears are open: (1) "I have entered and bound Satan — this does not mean he is dead." (2) "You *cannot* be passive with my word and serve me." (3) "Fragmentation of personality is a result of not staying near to me."

11. INTERCESSION FOR THE LOST WORLD

The Middle East — Points for prayer: (1) *The Most Effective Means of Reaching Muslims:* a) *Medical work* — this opens up countries and hearts to the Gospel. This is the only way in which missionary work can be done in Yemen, some Gulf States and Afghanistan. Pray for this ministry — that it may create opportunities for a witness to Muslims. There is continual cry for more medical workers. b) *Personal witness* by nationals and missionaries is the most effective way — but this needs a high degree of self-giving, much love and patience and a great faith.

12. SING PRAISES TO OUR LORD.

I will sing of my Redeemer,
And His wondrous love to me;
On the cruel cross He suffered,
From the curse to set me free.

Sing, oh, sing . . . of my Redeemer,
With His blood . . . He purchased me,
On the cross . . . He sealed my pardon,
Paid the debt, . . . and made me free.

WEEK FORTY-FIVE — MONDAY

1. PRAISE GOD FOR WHO HE IS.

"I keep thy precepts and testimonies, for all my ways are before thee. . . . Let thy hand be ready to help me, for I have chosen thy precepts" (Psalm 119:168, 173). Such a blessed statement of comfort is the last phrase of verse 168: "for all my ways are before thee." There are no days without you. I may not care but you do! You indeed are the "silent observer"—in another sense you have spoken very eloquently for your precepts and testimonies are given for that purpose. I want to lift up this quality of yourself and praise you for your total involvement in all I am and all I do. My emotions are not always involved in my appreciation of this quality of yourself, but it is nonetheless true. Your hand is ever ready to lend assistance and chastening as needed. I review any week of my life and acknowledge the truth of these blessed words. What I say of myself I say of all men who love you and have made you their Father.

Express yourself in adoration for this quality of God.
Speak it audibly or write out your praise in your own devotional journal.

2. PRAISE GOD FOR WHAT HE MEANS TO ME.

Just for me. There is such a vital and essential connection between "keeping your precepts" or "choosing your precepts" and your direction in all the ways of my life or the moving of your hand to help me. I would not say the only way you take an interest in my life is in my willingness to follow the rule book you have left for mankind. This is far too cold and objective. At the same time if I am not ready to read and obey how can you help me at all? I am your child, you have given me instructions for life in your word—indeed, you have furnished to me all things for social and spiritual relationships. However, you are personally concerned in just how I carry out your instructions. If I falter you forgive, if I stumble you explain more closely. I believe the "wisdom" promised by yourself in James 1:5-7 is the best use of your instructions. I claim your presence and your help.

How do you personally relate to the guidance of God, and God who is our Guide?
Speak it out or write it out. It is *so important* that you establish *your own* devotional journal.

3. CONFESSION OF SIN

It is sad to have such a clear view of what can be done and fail to do it. In all my ways are instructions and directions from your precepts—it is up to me to ask for wisdom in the application of your word to a particular circumstance. This I have not done—dear God, I am the poorer. Your hand is ever ready to help me but I have not always chosen your precepts—how can you do your part if I will not do mine? You can't, i.e., you are limited by your own word not to. Forgive me! I purpose to spend much more time meditating upon your word.

What personal sins do you want to confess? We *must* speak them to remove them.
Do it! *Now.* There is no one else you have sinned against more than God. Tell him so!

4. SING A PRAYER TO GOD.

Here, O my Lord, I see Thee face to face;
Here would I touch and handle things unseen;

Here grasp with firmer hand th' eternal grace,
And all my weariness upon Thee lean.

Open your hymn book and sing the rest of the verses—or even sing another prayer song.

5. READ HIS WORD TO HIM!

His Word

23So Jesus called them and spoke to them in parables: "How can Satan drive out Satan? 24If a kingdom is divided against itself, that kingdom cannot stand. 25If a house is divided against itself, that house cannot stand. 26And if Satan opposes himself and is divided, he cannot stand; his end has come. 27In fact, no one can enter a strong man's house and carry off his possessions unless he first ties up the strong man. Then he can rob his house. 28I tell you the truth, all the sins and blasphemies of men will be forgiven them. 29But whoever blasphemes against the Holy Spirit will never be forgiven; he is guilty of an eternal sin."

30He said this because they were saying, "He has an evil spirit." — *Mark 3:23-30, NIV*
Read also Matthew 12:25-37.

Read His Word to Him.

I want to do the very best I can in each of these expressions of worship, but not especially in this area. Your Son seems here to confront opposition in the most basic form. Either he is who he said he was or he is controlled by the evil one. There is no neutral ground. The tree is good or bad. There is either gathering or scattering. The lines are drawn and the decision is at hand. Speak to all our hearts that we might guard well our choice!

Please express your response to this beautiful text. Put your expression in your own prayer diary.

6. READ HIS WORD FOR YOURSELF.

Just for me. To say lightly, "Lord I believe you are the Son of God and then not produce in our lives the results of that decision is a form of blasphemy. How wonderfully strengthening it is to identify all the figures of speech. (1) The king who is stronger that the great king of darkness: Our King, your dear Son, who has a kingdom and citizens. How tragic that Satan's subjects are so much more responsive to him—even if by terrible coercions— than ourselves as subjects of the King of kings and Lord of lords. (2) The strong man and the stronger man. Our bodies are the house for these strong men. How wonderful to read and accept that Jesus can bind and cast out Satan—or demons. This house and the throne in it can be made "good" or clean and Jesus can and will reign within. Even so come Lord Jesus! Welcome to the throne of my life!

It is so important that you pause in his presence
and either audibly or in written form tell him all his word means to you.

7. READ HIS WORD IN THANKSGIVING.

(1) Thank you for the ability of my Lord to know the thoughts of the hearts of all men. (2) Thank you that I know that Satan is an intelligent being and rules as sovereign over a kingdom of darkness. (3) Thank you that Jesus clearly confronts Satan's servants and makes all see—who have eyes—just who he is. (4) Thank you for the knowl- edge that I am no match for Satan and he can run and rule and ruin my house. (5) Thank you so much for the stronger man! (6) Thank you I can make the whole tree good. (7) Thank you that I am now ready to confess and do confess my Lord as your Son and my only Savior.

Give yourself to your own expression of gratitude—write it or speak it!

8. READ HIS WORD IN MEDITATION.

"*. . . men will have to give account on the day of judgment for every careless word they have spoken.*" How often have these words haunted me! And then I remember to whom they were spoken. At the same time the point is not lost on anyone of us. We would like to think that the idle or careless word could be easily overlooked as not the real measure of the speaker. It is just here our Lord points out to us that it is out of the abundance of the heart the mouth speaks. It is with the condition of the heart our Lord has special concern. The Pharisees had been cultivating the soil of their heart. They *were* responsible for what grew there.

Pause—wait—think—then express yourself in thoughtful praise or thanks.

9. READ HIS WORD FOR PETITIONS.

Here are my requests from these verses: (1) Help me to give Satan no advantage in anything. (2) Divided loyalties kill incentive—how I like being whole! (3) Rule the whole of my life. (4) I am glad there is an end to Satan's rule—in some area of my life may his end be today! (5) Dear Lord, enter my house and tie up the strong man within me. (6) I am glad to speak for the blessed Holy Spirit—may He have free course in my heart. (7) Guard me from an insensitive attitude.

Please, please remember these are prayers—speak them—reword them!

10. READ HIS WORD AND WAIT—LISTEN—GOD SPEAKS!

Speak to me in these verses: (1) "I can indeed bind the strong man—you cannot do it." (2) "All sins and blasphemies of men will be forgiven—except one." (3) "My mercy and goodness should be as apparent here as the exception—of Holy Spirit blasphemy."

11. INTERCESSION FOR THE LOST WORLD

The Middle East — Points for prayer: (1) *Literature*— more and more good literature for Muslims, and Arabic teaching literature for Christians is now being produced. Pray for ex-Muslims engaged in writing these materials, for publishers and bookstores, etc., who seek to get this literature into the hands of those who need it. Much literature has been distrubuted all over the Middle East in recent years. Pray for fruit. (2) *Radio*—the most effective means of witnessing to Muslims in many areas. There are studios for the production of programs in Spain, France, Lebanon for broadcasting by Trans World Radio in Monaco and Cyprus, in Liberia, and in Seychelles. The response has been good, and very effective when able to be followed up by Bible correspondence courses and personal contacts.

12. SING PRAISES TO OUR LORD.

When my life work is ended, and I cross the swelling tide,
When the bright and glorious morning I will see;
I shall know my Redeemer when I reach the other side,
And His smile will be the first to welcome me.

I shall know . . . Him, I shall know Him,
And redeemed by His side I shall stand,
I shall know . . . Him, I shall know Him
By the print of the nails in His hand.

WEEK FORTY-FIVE — TUESDAY

1. PRAISE GOD FOR WHO HE IS.

"He will not let your foot be moved, he who keeps you will not slumber. Behold, he who keeps Israel will neither slumber nor sleep" (Psalm 121:3, 4). In each of these verses from the psalms we are seeking attributes of yourself for which we can praise you. The imagery in these verses is of battle. As the enemy approaches we need not be full of fear. We can be confident that we shall not lose ground.

What is the source of our confidence? It is the alert omnipresence or intimate personal interest of yourself. This is a promise made to the whole "Israel of God," or to the whole army of the Lord. Praise your name! We are no match for Satan, but you not only fight with us—you fight in us and through us. You never tire or lose your vigilance. Thank you for this blessed assurance.

Express yourself in adoration for this quality of God.
Speak it audibly or write out your praise in your own devotional journal.

2. PRAISE GOD FOR WHAT HE MEANS TO ME.

Just for me. If ever I needed such a promise it is now! There are days, and times in each day when it is easy to relax our guard. Dear Lord, remind me of Satan's battle strategy. I do not want to be ignorant of his devices. Without your help I shall indeed be thrown to the ground and moved from my position of victory. Right now, for today, I claim your constant interest in the conflict. From time

to time in this day may I catch a suggestion of just how you have helped me escape his awful thrust? Could I be helped to understand that my position was not won but by your help? Thank you for the desire to put on all your armor that I might be thus enabled to stand and not be moved. Praise you!

How do you personally relate to the vigilance of God, and God who is always vigilant?
Speak it out or write it out. It is *so important* that you establish *your own* devotional journal.

3. CONFESSION OF SIN

Ephesians 6:10-20 could well be a commentary on Psalm 121:3, 4. I have the promise of your vigilance while *I* take up the whole armor you have provided. I approach this passage in confession and repentance. How easy it is to forget my insensitivity to these burning words: ". . . against the *principalities*, against the *powers*, against *the world rulers of this present darkness*, against *the spiritual*

hosts of wickedness in the heavenly places." This is almost too much for me to assimilate. How I need truth on a gut level. How I need righteousness integrated into my emotions. How I need to *go* with the good news. Unless my faith is active in the battle of life I am losing ground. Help me, dear Lord, I am one needy man.

What personal sins do you want to confess? We *must* speak them to remove them.
Do it! *Now.* There is no one else you have sinned against more than God. Tell him so!

4. SING A PRAYER TO GOD.

Sweetly, Lord, have we heard Thee calling,
Come, follow Me!
And we see where Thy footprints falling

Lead us to Thee.
Footprints of Jesus, that make the pathway glow;
We will follow the steps of Jesus where'er they go.

Open your hymn book and sing the rest of the verses—or even sing another prayer song.

5. READ HIS WORD TO HIM!

His Word

[38]Then some of the Pharisees and teachers of the law said to him, "Teacher, we want to see a miraculous sign from you."

— Matthew 12:38, NIV

Read His Word to Him.

It is with the purpose of asking we are concerned. Why did these Pharisees make this request? The next verse will tell us why they asked: They were evil and adulterous and only wished to trap our Lord by these words. We need to be very careful that we not condemn the desire for divine credentials. Our Lord did "many signs" and each of them was an evidence of his deity. These men had

testimony, eye-witness testimony of hundreds of signs our Lord had already given. Perhaps many of these teachers of the law had been present themselves. Jesus is going to say that there is a barrier that short-circuits the purpose of signs: it is sin! Moral failure shuts the eyes of faith.

Please express your response to this beautiful text. Put your expression in your own prayer diary.

WEEK FORTY-FIVE — TUESDAY

6. READ HIS WORD FOR YOURSELF.

How often have we heard someone say: "I would believe if . . ."? Just suppose our Lord would have said: "All right, what sign do you want to see?" And then he had performed according to request, what would have changed in the hearts of these men? They could have easily argued among themselves that the request was somehow not what they wanted. The point is that if we (myself) do not *want* to believe we will not. It is with my unwillingness to submit to your moral code I find my problem of faith. It is in your life and teaching I find the substance for faith. Signs will *confirm* what I already believe. Dear Lord, I *do* believe. I want to listen and learn more and more!

It is so important that you pause in his presence
and either audibly or in written form tell him all his word means to you.

7. READ HIS WORD IN THANKSGIVING.

(1) Thank you our Lord is first of all and last of all a teacher. (2) Thank you that I can sit at his feet as a learner. (3) Thank you that Jesus knew we needed our faith confirmed and he therefore gave us many miracles to do it. (4) Thank you that Jesus can and does read the thoughts and intents of our hearts. (5) Thank you that my goal in life need not be: *"one more miracle"* — I have the greatest miracle in my Lord. (6) Thank you for the sign of Jonah — the resurrection of my Lord. (7) Thank you that the case is closed on his deity — all the evidence is in and a verdict is given — "He is declared to be the Son of God with power by the resurrection from the dead" (Rom. 1:3).

Give yourself to your own expression of gratitude — write it or speak it!

8. READ HIS WORD IN MEDITATION.

". . . *we want to see a miraculous sign from you.*" What would the sign prove? If Jesus was the Sovereign God in human form or their Messiah, he would not act and react according to the beck and call of man. If he was not the Messiah a sign would only serve to deceive them. In either case, the request was out of order. Even if these men had not seen the many signs he had already performed they could talk to eyewitnesses who had. The number and variety of signs he had already performed was more than adequate to convince anyone who was truly serious about evidence. How careful we must be in our motives as related to the miraculous!

Pause — wait — think — then express yourself in thoughtful praise or thanks.

9. READ HIS WORD FOR PETITIONS.

How this one verse calls forth requests in prayer! (1) The Pharisees were blind — open my eyes. (2) These men could not hear — open my ears. (3) These men must have had short memories — I do want to remember your power and love for me. (4) I want to see your signs as given by your biographers — that I might reinforce the faith I already have. (5) Read the motives of my heart and forgive me and purify my desires. (6) I need to be taught of you before I teach others. (7) I am so glad I have the product — even His deity — that all his signs advertised. Help me to appreciate him — even yourself — more and more.

Right here add your personal requests — and his answers.

10. READ HIS WORD AND WAIT — LISTEN — GOD SPEAKS.

In this one verse you can say several things I need to hear: (1) "Faith comes by hearing not seeing." (2) "Faith comes through the mind not the emotions." (3) "Faith that acts must affect the emotions."

11. INTERCESSION FOR THE LOST WORLD

The Middle East — Points for prayer: (1) *Bible correspondence courses* have been used of the Lord to win more Muslims to Christ than any other means. This is especially true of North Africa, Turkey and Iran. Pray for missions involved in this ministry. This witness is subject to much opposition by Muslim authorities — postal censorship plus harrassment of students. Pray for these students, that they may be won for Christ and brought into living fellowships of believers. (2) *Gospel Recordings and Cassette Tapes* are proving a splendid tool of evangelism and Christian teaching in regions that can never be visited by missionaries. (3) *Muslims in other lands* are more accessible — pray for all involved in ministry to students and workers in Europe and North America. Pray that converts from this ministry may become effective evangelists when they return home.

12. SING PRAISES TO OUR LORD.

O could I speak the matchless worth,
O could I sound the glories forth
Which in my Savior shine,
I'd soar and touch the heav'nly strings,
And vie with Gabriel while he sings
In notes almost divine,
In notes almost divine.

1. PRAISE GOD FOR WHO HE IS.

"As the mountains are round about Jerusalem, so the Lord is round about his people from henceforth even forever" (Psalm 125:2). This has always been a favorite verse as it describes the geographical advantage of the city of Jersualem, and compares such with the advantages of your children. The more we look at the verse the more it becomes apparent to us. This speaks of your protection. Jerusalem did have a good natural advantage against the enemy but it was often conquered. You have offered us your protection—that we have been overcome is not due to the failure of our Protector. It was usually internal strife that overcame the city. Bless and praise your name we need never lose your strong defense. This is a collective figure, i.e., it speaks of protection for a city. Each person is as complex as a city; you offer a bulwark for all our many needs. What you do for one, you do for all, and so in a sense this is generic as well as specific.

Express yourself in adoration for this quality of God.
Speak it audibly or write out your praise in your own devotional journal.

2. PRAISE GOD FOR WHAT HE MEANS TO ME.

Just for me. I like the fact that Jerusalem was (and is) a fine place for a view of the countryside. Not only are the mountains round about it—Jerusalem is itself on mountains. What a beautiful perspective you give to life! Everything viewed from the holy city looked different: (1) Praise you for the view of the nations of the world I have as I see them from your perspective. If Jerusalem (in this figurative sense) was to be the capital of the world how different is our attitude toward all the nations? You love them all—you want to protect and bless them all. (2) Calvary can be seen from Jerusalem. Just outside the wall was the place of the death of your Son. Here I can see the power and strength of your protection. Here I see the means of fulfilling your desire for the nations of the world. I want to sustain a universal view of your presence and power.

How do you personally relate to the protection of God, and God who is our Protector?
Speak it out or write it out. It is *so important* that you establish *your own* devotional journal.

3. CONFESSION OF SIN

To leave Jerusalem is to leave my protection. Why should I ever want to step outside? Why leave the care and goodness of your love? It is because such love has become so common that we fail to appreciate what we have until it is gone. The history of Jerusalem is the history of forgetting. Dear Lord, I do not want to forget. How easy it is to relax in a knowledge that you care and all is well. All is only well when there is a watchman on the wall! Dear Lord, I want to set up a watchman for my time of prayer. I am so glad for the inward protection I find in this time with you. Forgive me for my failure to set a watch on my lips. The citadel of my heart must be guarded by your very presence lest I begin fighting inside the city. Deliver me, forgive me!

What personal sins do you want to confess? We *must* speak them to remove them.
Do it! *Now.* There is no one else you have sinned against more than God. Tell him so!

4. SING A PRAYER TO GOD.

Jesus, the very thought of Thee
With sweetness fills my breast;

But sweeter far Thy face to see,
And in Thy presence rest.

Open your hymn book and sing the rest of the verses—or even sing another prayer song.

5. READ HIS WORD TO HIM!

His Word

[39]He answered, "A wicked and adulterous generation asks for a miraculous sign! But none will be given it except the sign of the prophet Jonah. [40]For as Jonah was three days and three nights in the belly of a huge fish, so the Son of Man will be three days and three nights in the heart of the earth. [41]The men of Nineveh will stand up at the judgment with this generation and condemn it; for they repented at the preaching of Jonah, and now one greater than Jonah is here. [42]The Queen of the South will rise at the judgment with this generation and condemn it; for she came from the ends of the earth to listen to Solomon's wisdom, and now one greater than Solomon is here.

[43]"When an evil spirit comes out of a man, it goes through arid places seeking rest and does not find it. [44]Then it says, 'I will return to the house I left.' When it arrives, it finds the house unoccupied, swept clean and put in order. [45]Then it goes and takes with it seven other spirits more wicked than itself, and they go in and live there. And the final condition of that man is worse that the first. That is how it will be with this wicked generation."

—Matthew 12:39-45, NIV

WEEK FORTY-FIVE — WEDNESDAY

Read His Word to Him.

It will be enough just here if I read and reread—and then read again the words of your Son. Whereas he applied them to the generation of which these Pharisees were a part I see so many, many evidences of the same qualities in my generation. Speak to me, dear Lord!

Please express your response to this beautiful text. Put your expression in your own prayer diary.

6. READ HIS WORD FOR YOURSELF.

My Lord is saying that a different type of sign will be given—a sign to which all other signs will relate. *"The sign of the prophet Jonah"*! How wonderfully merciful was our Lord. He did not grant the request of these sign seekers and yet he did! He gave them promise of a sign that would convince all. At the same time, he warned that there was a deadly disease spreading in the hearts of men. And so it is today! My heart is not immune to this contagion. It is the terrible sin of *disbelief* not unbelief—he could deal with that—but blunt rejection of evidence—a stubborn refusal to accept the obvious. What a heartbreak! The men of Nineveh did not do this, and Jonah did no miracles. This the queen of Sheba did not do and Solomon offered no sensate signs to convince her.

Pause in his presence and either audibly or in written form tell him all his word means to you.

7. READ HIS WORD IN THANKSGIVING.

(1) Thank you for our Lord's acceptance of the historical incident of Jonah and the great fish. (2) Thank you for the wonderful promise of the resurrection. (3) Thank you for the clear word of life after death found in our Lord's words here. (4) Thank you for the sober fact that men are morally responsible before you.

Give yourself to your own expression of gratitude—write it or speak it!

8. READ HIS WORD IN MEDITATION.

"And the final condition of that man is worse than the first." This is the tragic conclusion of an uncommitted life. Jesus came to cast Satan out of the land—indeed out of his generation of Israel. If Israel would have accepted him the evil one could have been permanently removed. The miracles and teaching of Jesus *did indeed* make an impression, but most of the Jewish population were not ready to commit themselves. The deadly danger of an uncommitted life is in the fact that demons are not dead. It *is* possible to apostatize. How eternally important it is that we commit our lives to him. The commitment our Lord wants and deserves is in worship. All service begins from personal worship. Personal devotion is the foundation upon which all other relationships are built. I commit myself to prayer and the ministry of the word in fear of hell.

Pause—wait—think—then express yourself in thoughtful praise or thanks.

9. READ HIS WORD FOR PETITIONS.

In our Lord's words to an adulterous generation there is much about which we can pray: (1) The reason for sign seeking was based in disbelief—guard my heart! (2) How I thank you for the sign of Jonah. I want to appreciate it more. (3) Thank you for my Lord's stamp of approval on the story of Jonah. May I be willing to listen to him first. (4) How I do want to change my thinking to conform with that of your Son. (5) Open my heart to the wisdom of yourself found in the words of your Son. (6) Fill up my life with your worship and work. (7) I claim your overcoming power in any efforts of demons.

Please, please remember these are prayers—speak them—reword them!

10. READ HIS WORD AND WAIT—LISTEN—GOD SPEAKS!

In my Lord's message to this generation he also speaks to me: (1) "You need to repent each day—this is an attitude." (2) "I yet need men who will preach repentance." (3) "There can be no vacuum in deliverance from sin."

11. INTERCESSION FOR THE LOST WORLD

The Middle East — Points for prayer: (1) *Unreached peoples*—many! Countless villages and towns have never welcomed a preacher of the Gospel; Muslim women in many lands are virtually inaccessible in their prison-like seclusion; the nomadic tribes of the deserts of North Africa, Arabia and Iran; the expanding student population; the expatriate Asian and Western communities, etc. (2) *Closed lands*——Mauretania, Libya, Saudi Arabia, Qatar, South Yemen.

12. SING PRAISES TO OUR LORD.

My gracious Master and my God,
Assist me to proclaim,

To spread thro' all the earth abroad,
The honors of Thy name.

WEEK FORTY-FIVE — THURSDAY

1. PRAISE GOD FOR WHO HE IS.

"Unless the Lord builds the house, those who build labor in vain. Unless the Lord watches over the city, the watchman stays awake in vain" (Psalm 127:1). I love the blessed promise in this verse. Here is plain, clear assurance that when we work you work with us, in us, and through us. I need to remember there is no sacred or secular work in your sight. You were with your Son as he made yokes for farmers, or houses for the residents of Nazareth as much as you were with him in his teaching on the hills of Galilee or the precincts of the temple. Unless you are made the superintendent of any and all our jobs we labor in vain. I go to work today with the calm assurance that I am a workman together with you in the task before me.

Express yourself in adoration for this quality of God.
Speak it audibly or write out your praise in your own devotional journal.

2. PRAISE GOD FOR WHAT HE MEANS TO ME.

Just for me. However well planned is a project, I will wait in vain for its fulfillment if you are not in it and through it from the beginning. "How can I find the will of the Lord?" is a question so often asked when all the time God's will is being worked out in what we are and what we do. If we ask his presence—read his word, sense his presence in what we do his will is at work in and through us. We think we build the house—*wrong*—he built it through us. We thought we protected an investment, *wrong*—he protected it *through* us. I want to see again the twofold task of your will in this blessed verse: ". . . work out your own salvation with fear and trembling, for God is at work in you, both to will and to work for his good pleasure" (Philippians 2:12b, 13). Praise your name!

How do you personally relate to the will of God, and God who is at work?
Speak it out or write it out. It is *so important* that you establish *your own* devotional journal.

3. CONFESSION OF SIN

My confession is so obvious. I have built many a house out of pure stubborness. I could have cared less what anyone thought including God! No wonder I was depressed when I finished. I have thrown up defenses and become very negligent in my protection of some treasured city of my heart. Only to have the walls broken and the city destroyed. Dear Lord, I want to do nothing without you. I *can* do nothing without you. Forgive me for the times I have forgotten. Too many times it has been a willfull lapse of memory. Forgive me! Ideals that are not given substance become nothing but idle dreams. I want tangible, nitty gritty, practical application of your presence in all I am and do.

What personal sins do you want to confess? We *must* speak them to remove them.
Do it! *Now.* There is no one else you have sinned against more than God. Tell him so!

4. SING A PRAYER TO GOD.

Break Thou the bread of life,
Dear Lord, to me,
As Thou didst break the loaves
Beside the sea;

Beyond the sacred page I seek Thee, Lord;
My spirit pants for Thee,
O living Word.

Open your hymn book and sing the rest of the verses—or even sing another prayer song.

5. READ HIS WORD TO HIM!

His Word

[46]While Jesus was still talking to the crowd, his mother and brothers stood outside, wanting to speak to him. [47]Someone told him, "Your mother and brothers are standing outside, wanting to speak to you." [48]He replied, "Who is my mother, and who are my brothers?" [49]Pointing to his disciples, he said, "Here are my mother and my brothers. [50]For whoever does the will of my Father in heaven is my brother and sister and mother."
— Matthew 12:46-50, NIV
Read also Mark 3:31-35.

Read His Word to Him.

How very appropriate are these words! How often do we misunderstand our Lord and his purpose. We who are related to him and claim him as our Savior—and at the same time as our elder brother. He is the only begotten Son (i.e., in the unique sense of his birth), but we too are supernaturally born into the same family. We can so easily decide there is something unbalanced in the service he gives us to do. We are the body of our Lord, and he *does* work through us today. Here are some false rationalizations I have made: (1) He is making too much demand upon my time. He wants to dominate all my time. Does this make sense? (2) How is it that I am attacked more now by Satan than when I never served him?

Please express your response to this beautiful text. Put your expression in your own prayer diary.

WEEK FORTY-FIVE — THURSDAY

6. READ HIS WORD FOR YOURSELF.

It is one thing to claim kinship with Jesus, and I do; it is another thing to realize that such kinship is conditioned by his words: "For whosoever shall *do* the will of my Father who is in heaven, he is my brother, and sister and mother." There are always well meaning friends and relatives who can tell us just what the Father's will is for us. If we do not get our instructions from our Lord we can be sure it is not your will. How I *do* need to hear the word "whosoever" and apply it to someone besides my own little group. In the whole wide world whosoever shall do the will of the Father is my brother and sister.

Pause in his presence and either audibly or in written form tell him all his word means to you.

7. READ HIS WORD IN THANKSGIVING.

(1) Thank you for the respectful patient attitude of the brothers and mother of our Lord. (2) Thank you for our Lord's willingness to cut earthly ties when they interfered with your will. (3) Thank you that Jesus knew ahead of time the purpose in the coming of his family. (4) Thank you that we can be the mother of Jesus—i.e., "Christ can be formed in us." (5) Thank you that we can be a brother to Jesus and live in the same house. (6) Thank you that we can know your will and do it.

Give yourself to your own expression of gratitude—write it or speak it!

8. READ HIS WORD IN MEDITATION.

"... he is my brother, and sister, and mother." How beautiful is the thought that we can be as close to our Lord as his brothers and sisters were in Nazareth. Yea, we can be closer! What does Jesus mean by his expression: "... whosoever *does the will* of my Father in heaven"? He is saying his life ambition, his whole purpose was to fulfill his Father's will in his life—all who have the same purpose are in his family. However, it will be also easy to become as apathetic in this relationship as were his earthly brothers and sisters. They did not believe on him because of their familiarity. May we never lose the freshness and wonder of being his blood relatives!

Pause—wait—think—then express yourself in thoughtful praise or thanks.

9. READ HIS WORD FOR PETITIONS.

Our Lord's relation to his family teaches me about prayer: (1) Was Jesus insensitive to the needs of his family? —of course not!—give me his balance. (2) How could his family be so insensitive to Jesus?—am I in this class? (3) What an exalted value my Lord placed on our relationship with him. I do want to appreciate it. (4) How can I really *know* I am doing your will in my life? (5) Thank you for your imperishable word which contains all you want done in my life. How I need your wisdom in applying it to my life. (6) Give me the love that answers all problems of interpersonal relationship.

Right here add your personal requests—and his answers.

10. READ HIS WORD AND WAIT—LISTEN—GOD SPEAKS!

Did Jesus reach the hearts of his family? You can reach my heart: (1) "There are those who fulfill my will in their lives—seek them out and learn from them." (2) "You must want me before we can be one in our purpose." (3) "You are as precious to me as any son has ever been to his father."

11. INTERCESSION FOR THE LOST WORLD

The Middle East — Point for prayer: (1) *Lands with no fellowships of national believers*—Mauretania, Saudi Arabia, Qatar, Libya, Yemen (though in each are communities of expatriate believers). 15 of the 22 lands have less than 500 national believers. There are probably less than 5,000 Christians in the Middle East converted out of Islam. There is a great lack of Christian workers to use present opportunities to the full. The Middle East has the lowest missionary/people ratio of any major region of the world, yet it is the area most needing pioneer work. These lands continue to defy our Lord Jesus and we cannot remain complacent about this state of affairs.

12. SING PRAISES TO OUR LORD.

All praise to Him who reigns above
In majesty supreme,
Who gave His Son for man to die,
That He might man redeem!

Blessed be the name, blessed be the name,
Blessed be the name of the Lord;
Blessed be the name, blessed be the name,
Blessed be the name of the Lord.

WEEK FORTY-FIVE — FRIDAY

1. PRAISE GOD FOR WHO HE IS.

"The Lord has done great things for us; we are glad. May those who sow in tears reap with shouts of joy! He that goes forth weeping, bearing the seed for sowing, shall come home with shouts of joy, bringing his sheaves with him" (Psalm 126:3, 5, 6). What powerful qualities of yourself are found in these beautiful verses! (1) You are interested in the success of your people. Success has become a bad word of late. When applied to what you do in your children, it is a delightful word. (2) If we sow your word in deep humility and sorrow (as we see the need of those with whom we work), we shall reap with shouts of joy! (3) To repeat the promise with enlargement: blessed are the poor in spirit, the meek in attitude as they plant your eternal truth in the hearts of men. They shall with no doubt come home with shouts of joy bringing their sheaves with them. The blessed harvest of eternal lives — people.

Express yourself in adoration for this quality of God.
Speak it audibly or write out your praise in your own devotional journal.

2. PRAISE GOD FOR WHAT HE MEANS TO ME.

Just for me. It happened just last night; I could see a wonderful harvest in the lives of those who listened to your word. I can make the psalmist words my words, "The Lord has done great things for us; we are glad." How I need to read again the conditions prerequisite to reaping! *"Those who sow in tears* reap with shouts of joy." I do weep within for the obvious needs of men. But somehow I must identify much more closely with you as you see men. I rejoiced in the acceptance of your Son by a dear woman; I was happy as she was "baptized into Christ," but not as I should have rejoiced — there were no shouts of joy (inside or out). Dear Lord, I am so glad to find these blessed verses again and bow before you and allow them to find lodgement and growth in my heart!

How do you personally relate to the harvest of God, and God who is Lord of the harvest?
Speak it out or write it out. It is *so important* that you establish *your own* devotional journal.

3. CONFESSION OF SIN

How shall I respond to the following? (1) You have indeed done so many great things in my experience. My sin is one of blindness and ingratitude. I really do not see all you have done — some of the most important have escaped my view altogether. I do not have the depth of appreciation I could have or should have for those I do see. (2) My sowing of your seed has not been with tears — humility and meekness simply do not characterize much of my work. Dear Lord, forgive me. (3) My happiness at the salvation of men and women is not nearly as full of joy as it should be. I forget to see people as the eternal residents of heaven or hell.

What personal sins do you want to confess? We *must* speak them to remove them.
Do it! *Now.* There is no one else you have sinned against more than God. Tell him so!

4. SING A PRAYER TO GOD.

More about Jesus would I know,
More of His grace to others show;
More of His saving fullness see,
More of His love who died for me.

More, more about Jesus,
More, more about Jesus;
More of His saving fullness see,
More of His love who died for me.

Open your hymn book and sing the rest of the verses — or even sing another prayer song.

5. READ HIS WORD TO HIM!

His Word

8 After this, Jesus traveled about from one town and village to another, proclaiming the good news of the kingdom of God. The Twelve were with him, [2]and also some women who had been cured of evil spirits and diseases: Mary (called Magdalene) from whom seven demons had come out; [3]Joanna the wife of Cuza, the manager of Herod's household; Susanna; and many others. These women were helping to support them out of their own means.
— *Luke 8:1-3, NIV*

Read His Word to Him.

What a precious passage I find in these three verses! It says *so much* about my dear Lord: (1) He was involved in a very strenuous effort. To walk from one city and village to another and to keep this up for days and weeks — even months, was no little task. (2) He neglected no city or village. What an example for all us so-called preachers. (3) Jesus was a proclaimer — a preacher! He gathered all who would listen and spoke loud enough to be heard by all. What a communicator he must have been! (4) It was *good news* he brought: that God can rule in the hearts of men. Such is not many times communicated by us as "good news."

Please express your response to this beautiful text. Put your expression in your own prayer diary.

6. READ HIS WORD FOR YOURSELF.

Just for me. How I do hope I have represented your Son in the true light of what you have said through Luke. In this time I want to let you speak to me about these women who followed my Lord: (1) These women (only three are named) followed him for two reasons: (a) They were so grateful for what he had done for them. They had been cured of evil spirits and disease. (b) They followed him because they had means out of which they could help him and his disciples. Does this say anything about women in your service today? Indeed it does! Women today are many times more grateful for salvation than men. Not one woman denied him—or left him. Women of means—and many who have but little have helped our Lord and his disciples when no one else did or could.

It is so important that you pause in his presence
and either audibly or in written form tell him all his word means to you.

7. READ HIS WORD IN THANKSGIVING.

(1) Thank you for the example of energy expended in your service. (2) Thank you for elevating preaching to a place of prominence and importance. (3) Thank you for the systematic manner in which our Lord worked. (4) Thank you for the emphasis upon your rule in the hearts of men. (5) Thank you for the example of how to make preachers. (6) Thank you for the selfless devotion of these women. (7) Thank you specifically that Joanna and Susanna loved him and followed him. What a testimony to the power of my Lord to change all human relationships.

Give yourself to your own expression of gratitude—write it or speak it!

8. READ HIS WORD IN MEDITATION.

"These women were helping to support them out of their own means." It cost these women much more than money to follow our Lord. Such traveling interrupted whatever other schedule they might have had. Were the wives of the apostles represented in the little phrase "and many others"? The text does not specify. Women were with Jesus throughout his whole ministry. Indeed, they were a very important part of all his life. The picture of devotion and love shown by the women is one we need to see again today. When Herod's household was opposed to our Lord's work it is amazing to read that the wife of the manager of the household has left all to follow him.

Pause—wait—think—then express yourself in thoughtful praise or thanks.

9. READ HIS WORD FOR PETITIONS.

This is a remarkable passage—it can teach us much. (1) There are villages in many nations of the world where the gospel would be good news—open my heart to know how I can help. (2) I do wonder how the apostles reacted to the preaching of Jesus—it is an example I want to follow. (3) Why did these women follow Jesus? It must have been out of gratitude and love. What an example they are to me! (4) Why were there seven demons in Mary Magdalene? Deliver me, protect me from demon attack today. (5) Joanna is such an unlikely disciple of our Lord. How I would like to know what led her to him. Deepen my humility and gratitude. (6) How could Jesus accept charity? Or did he? It took a degree of humility we will never know. How I love him for it.

Please, please remember these are prayers—speak them—reword them!

10. READ HIS WORD AND WAIT—LISTEN—GOD SPEAKS!

Dear Lord, speak to me through these touching verses: (1) "The goodness of the news my Son preached has not lost its power." (2) "Demons are real today and attack people now. They cannot possess Christians." (3) "You can still support my service out of your means."

11. INTERCESSION FOR THE LOST WORLD

Algeria — Population: 17,300,000. Growth rate—3.2%. People per sq. km.—8.
Point for prayer: (1) *The Government stopped renewing residence permits for missionaries in 1977.* Most of the missionaries have had to find secular employment in order to remain in the country. Both missionaries and unbelievers need wisdom in this tense situation. Much of the ministry of missionaries is in encouraging believers in personal contacts, little Bible Study groups and camps. Pray that they may have wisdom in their ministry so as not to offend unnecessarily, yet to use all possible openings to the full. Servants of God have wept for the yet unseen harvest of souls in this land. Pray for it!

12. SING PRAISES TO OUR LORD.

There is a name I love to hear,
I love to sing its worth;
It sounds like music in mine ear,
The sweetest name on earth.

Oh, how I love Jesus,
Oh, how I love Jesus,
Oh, how I love Jesus,
Because He first loved me!

WEEK FORTY-FIVE — SATURDAY

1. PRAISE GOD FOR WHO HE IS.

"I wait for the Lord, my soul waits, and in his word I hope; my soul waits for the Lord more than watchmen for the morning, more than watchmen for the morning" (Psalm 130:5, 6). Dear Lord all of us can relate to these words; it would seem that most of our activity is in the inactivity of waiting. The context of these verses is the early morning—sometime before sunrise. We think it a most appropriate figure since the keeping of your word is just as dependable as sunrise. It could be an allusion to the sentinals on the wall who were awaiting the sunrise for the changing of shifts. In your creative power to speak it is to have it. "God said, 'Let there be light and there was light.'" When we know what you have said we can eagerly expect the fulfillment. All of the above is true, but is this the real thrust of the text? I believe there is more here for which we can praise you.

Express yourself in adoration for this quality of God.
Speak it audibly or write out your praise in your own devotional journal.

2. PRAISE GOD FOR WHAT HE MEANS TO ME.

Just for me. It is one thing to wait "on" the Lord, it is an entirely different thing to wait *for* the Lord. To wait *on* the Lord is to look for a completion of some agreement he has made with us, but to wait *for* the Lord is to wait for *himself.* Ah, there is indeed a vast difference in these two little words. The enjoyment of a promise is one thing; the enjoyment of a person is something else. My whole being reaches out for yourself. You have promised your presence and your very self in us. We have come through a dark night of waiting—the dawn cannot be far away. Dear Lord, I *know* you keep your promise to come to me in the person of yourself. I read again the words of your son and hold them to my heart: "If a man loves me, he will keep my word, and my Father will love him, and we will come to him and make our home (in) with him" (John 14:23b, 24).

How do you personally relate to the presence of God, and God who is Present?
Speak it out or write it out. It is *so important* that you establish *your own* devotional journal.

3. CONFESSION OF SIN

Once again, it is not difficult to confess my sin in this regard. I can freely confess that my whole soul does long for you. I do reach out to you in the darkness of my need—like the watchman for the morning. At the same time, my Lord's words are like a sharp two-edged sword. "He who does not love me does not keep my words; and the word which you hear is not mine but the Father's who sent me" (John 14:24). How shoddy is my love! "Love is not irritable or resentful." In my subconsciousness I resent your telling me what to do. Because of this I am irritable. Oh, to yield my whole self (soul) to your dear Son—to yourself. I am not what I want to be, but praise your name, I am not what I used to be! Forgive me, Lord, and keep on motivating me to love you totally.

What personal sins do you want to confess? We *must* speak them to remove them.
Do it! *Now.* There is no one else you have sinned against more than God. Tell him so!

4. SING A PRAYER TO GOD.

All the way my Savior leads me;
Cheers each winding path I tread,
Gives me grace for ev'ry trial,
Feeds me with the living bread.
Though my weary steps may falter,

And my soul athirst may be,
Gushing from the Rock before me,
Lo! a spring of joy I see;
Gushing from the Rock before me,
Lo! a spring of joy I see.

Open your hymn book and sing the rest of the verses—or even sing another prayer song.

5. READ HIS WORD TO HIM!
His Word

13 That same day Jesus went out of the house and sat by the lake. ²Such large crowds gathered around him that he got into a boat and sat in it, while all the people stood on the shore. ³Then he told them many things in parables, saying: "A farmer went out to sow his seed.
— *Matthew 13:1-3, NIV*

Read His Word to Him.

This was on the same day that your Son was interrupted by the visit of his family. Jesus did go out of the house, but it was not to visit with his mother and brothers. He left the house to be able to speak to a larger crowd. Indeed the crowd was so large he had to get into a boat and teach them from the surface of the lake. How wonderfully well your Son did communicate! How I do want to follow his example in teaching. We are not told all he taught; there were many more things said than those here recorded. The form of teaching is just as important as the subject matter: ". . . he told them many things in parables." How I do need to develop this capacity.

Please express your response to this beautiful text. Put your expression in your own prayer diary.

6. READ HIS WORD FOR YOURSELF.

It requires more time and thought to create a story in which the point can be made than to describe your point in abstract form. How often have I been content with the latter and neglected the former? Dear Lord, I am not like your Son when this happens. I want to so carefully examine every word he said that I can use the same devices of communication as I attempt to teach the same truths he taught. How wonderfully good it will be to discover that the power here described is the Son of man, my Lord himself. When I follow in his steps in sowing the seed of the word of yourself in the hearts of men it is really my Lord sowing all over again the seed of the kingdom.

It is so important that you pause in his presence and either audibly or in written form tell him all his word means to you.

7. READ HIS WORD IN THANKSGIVING.

(1) Thank you for the spontaneous popularity of my Lord. (2) Thank you for his willingness to give himself to his teaching. (3) Thank you for Jesus' adaptation to the circumstances to meet a need. (4) Thank you for the power of parables — then and now. (5) Thank you for the unlimited number of familiar things out of which parables can be formed. (6) Thank you for my Lord seen in the farmer and his seed. (7) Thank you my heart can be his field.

Give yourself to your own expression of gratitude — write it or speak it!

8. READ HIS WORD IN MEDITATION.

"A farmer went out to sow his seed." Mark uses the word, *"Behold,"* the farmer went out to sow his seed. It is possible that Jesus could have pointed to a farmer doing the very thing he described. Our Lord described himself as this farmer. Since he set an example for us how eternally important it is that we constantly make disciples. We must be reminded again and again that the seed is the word of yourself. Until and unless we plant your word in the minds and conscience of people we are not following our Lord's example. We think of the literacy rate in the days of our Lord and we remember that most of the seed planting was verbal. In the wide expanse of our world such also would be true.

Pause — wait — think — then express yourself in thoughtful praise or thanks.

9. READ HIS WORD FOR PETITIONS.

What a privilege it is to lift our hearts in prayer as we listen to him teach. (1) What wonder must have been on the faces of many who heard him. May his words fall with fresh impact on my heart. (2) Since my Lord taught so much by parable how is it we so sorely neglect this form of teaching? Increase my desire to imitate him. (3) Jesus used the most common of everyday activities. I want to do the same. (4) How good to know who the farmer represents — even my Lord — I do want him to sow his seed in my heart each day. (5) Since the seed is your word may I receive it with a good and honest heart.

Right here add your personal requests — and his answers.

10. READ HIS WORD AND WAIT — LISTEN — GOD SPEAKS!

In this beautiful setting by the sea I want to hear you speak to me: (1) "All my Son taught necessary for life and godliness is found in the four gospels and in the divine interpretation of it by the rest of the New Testament." (2) "The sower is still sowing his seed." (3) "The harvest of this planting is unto eternal life."

11. INTERCESSION FOR THE LOST WORLD

Algeria — Point for prayer: (1) *The believers are generally younger* and the little groups less strong than in Morocco. Many of the believers are young people, largely girls. There are therefore many pressure on these young people — early arranged marriages for the girls to Muslims, and hostility in schools and at work for the young men. There are many backsliders. Pray for the establishment of many strong, witnessing fellowships of believers all over the country. Many of those who seek the Lord are unable to have fellowship with other believers due to the hostility of relatives or husbands — pray for such. Pray that there may be a more courageous witness from among these believers despite the problems.

12. SING PRAISES TO OUR LORD.

Praise Him! praise Him!
Jesus, our blessed Redeemer!
For our sins He suffered, and bled, and died;
He our Rock, our hope of eternal salvation,
Hail Him! hail Him! Jesus the Crucified.

Sound His Praises! Jesus who bore our sorrows,
Love unbounded, wonderful, deep and strong:
Praise Him! praise Him! tell of His excellent greatness;
Praise Him! praise Him! ever in joyful song!

1. PRAISE GOD FOR WHO HE IS.

"O Lord, my heart is not lifted up, my eyes are not raised too high; I do not occupy myself with things too great and too marvelous for me. But I have calmed and quieted my soul, like a child quieted at its mother's breast; like a child that is quieted is my soul" (Psalm 131:1, 2). Dear Father, I shall never be equal to the task of expressing the meaning of these two precious verses. This is an expression of a soul in humiliation. David has been chastened and he speaks out of his sense of lowliness. The quality of Fatherhood, i.e., of being able to help a child see where he was wrong — how he hurt himself and others — and most of all his Father, is the attribute for which we praise you here. How often have we all been occupied "with things too great and marvelous" for our feeble fumbling efforts. But you have such a wonderful way of quieting our souls. The effort is ours but the quiet is of yourself.

Express yourself in adoration for this quality of God.
Speak it audibly or write out your praise in your own devotional journal.

2. PRAISE GOD FOR WHAT HE MEANS TO ME.

Just for me. One wonders how often you will need to teach this lesson. Of course you want us to attempt great and marvelous things for you, but you want the praise. When our motives are wrong you have various ways of upsetting our house of cards. To take the credit for any accomplishment is an asburdity. From whom did we receive our very self? i.e., our spirit? From "the father of spirits" (Num. 16:22). Who gave us the abilities resident in our spirit? Who gave us the opportunity to do what we have done? Who gave us the wealth necessary to carry it out? The answers are obvious — where then is the room (or sense) in boasting? A child upon the mother's breast would be much more appropriate than a mighty conquering hero. May such genuine humility be mine!

How do you personally relate to the eyes of God, and God who sees all?
Speak it out or write it out. It is *so important* that you establish *your own* devotional journal.

3. CONFESSION OF SIN

I do not confess something of which I am not guilty to satisfy those who feel I am. In every single endeavor in which I have been engaged my heart has been "lifted up" too high, i.e., I have not been as conscious of your purposes and presence as I should have been. At the same time, I did not enter these enterprises to seek my own glory. Dear Lord, you know I do not know my heart as you do, but I am attempting an honest confession. I lifted my eyes to see the multiplied thousands (millions) of people who need your word and your Son. All of these efforts were too great and too marvelous for me. There were several of them through which you taught me more humility than I had and I needed.

What personal sins do you want to confess? We *must* speak them to remove them.
Do it! *Now.* There is no one else you have sinned against more than God. Tell him so!

4. SING A PRAYER TO GOD.

In simple trust like theirs who heard,
Beside the Syrian sea
The gracious calling of the Lord,

Let us like them, without a word,
Rise up and follow Thee.

Open your hymn book and sing the rest of the verses — or even sing another prayer song.

5. READ HIS WORD TO HIM!

His Word

[4]As he was scattering the seed, some fell along the path, and the birds came and ate it up. [5]Some fell on rocky places, where it did not have much soil. It sprang up quickly, because the soil was shallow. [6]But when the sun came up, the plants were scorched, and they withered because they had no root. [7]Other seed fell among thorns, which grew up and choked the plants. [8]Still other seed fell on good soil, where it produced a crop — a hundred, sixty or thirty times what was sown. [9]He who has ears, let him hear."
— *Matthew 13:4-9, NIV*
Read also Matthew 13:10-23; Mark 4:1-20; Luke 8:4-15.

Read His Word to Him.

Indeed! I want to listen to these words just as if I were in the crowd and could hear each syllable that fell from the lips of your Son. I want also to hear his explanation to what he was said. My Lord is not here identified as the sower, but considering who is doing the teaching such is a fair if not obvious conclusion. I want to mark *every thing* he said about the different soils: (1) The same seed was sown in each place. *The first was "along the path."* This is described as "trampled on," as the place where birds feed.

Please express your response to this beautiful text. Put your expression in your prayer diary.

6. READ HIS WORD FOR YOURSELF.

Just for me. I am trying, dear Lord, to absorb each of your words as here related. When I have been a long time occupied with "other things" my ears are heavy and my eyes are dull. I neither hear nor see—I become *the path!* (2) *Some fell on rocky places, where it did not have much soil.* This one receives the word with joy. The results are not good: trouble and persecution—*because of the word* he quickly falls away. In the time of testing they fall away. These persons last only a short time. Dear Lord, I have been there—the price of discipline was too high—how many unfinished tasks or projects testify to this? (3) What was sown among thorns, or fell among thorns. The thorns represent: (a) the worries of this life, (b) the deceitfulness of wealth, and (c) present pleasures or the desires for other things. Luke says of these persons: "As they go on their way" such thorns develop. Dear Lord, if I do not chop out these thorns I will never mature.

Pause in his presence and either audibly or in written form tell him all his word means to you.

7. READ HIS WORD IN THANKSGIVING.

(1) I thank you I am wholly responsible for the condition of my heart. (2) Thank you for the wonderful fertile seed—even your word. (3) Thank you that I can hear your word every day. (4) Thank you that my acceptance is related to my hearing. (5) Thank you I can be of your nobility. (6) Thank you for the ability to retain your word. (7) Thank you I know that only through perseverence can I produce a crop of thirty, sixty or a hundredfold.

Give yourself to your own expression of gratitude—write it or speak it!

8. READ HIS WORD IN MEDITATION.

"Many prophets and righteous men longed to see what you see but did not see it, and to hear what you hear but did not hear it." Surely we are living in the fulness of time. How we need to keep our eyes open and our hearts atuned to all you are saying to us in these days. We see man being able to stand before you just-as-if he had never sinned—this no prophet could ever claim. We are always on service as your priests. This no righteous man could even imagine. We hear you say: "You have redemption through the blood of my Son." To be bought and paid for by yourself is such a position angels would long to have. It is better to live today than even to walk with our Lord over the fields of Galilee—we have what he there promised. How blessed above all people we are!

Pause—wait—think—then express yourself in thoughtful praise or thanks.

9. READ HIS WORD FOR PETITIONS.

How important it is that we link prayer with the sowing of the seed: (1) It would seem that sowing the seed is the one most essential factor in this whole story. Why haven't we sown more? (2) Help me to be able to identify the birds of Satan. (3) Am I responsible for removing rocks from some hearts? (4) I do believe I could help in hoeing out some thorns—help me! (5) Thank you for the promise of at least 25% of the sowing is on good soil. Once again how I need help in sowing bountifully. (6) I have ears—increase my hearing capacity. (7) Who are those who produce a hundredfold? As compared with what or whom?

Please, please remember these are prayers—speak them—reword them!

10. READ HIS WORD AND WAIT—LISTEN—GOD SPEAKS!

There is so much to hear in these verses: (1) "Seed, however good does nothing unless planted." (2) "I sow with you, but you must throw out the seed." (3) "Do you really believe this parable or only read it?"

11. INTERCESSION FOR THE LOST WORLD

Algeria — Points for prayer: (1) *There is a critical lack of leaders* among the Algerian believers. Pray for the few and also for the calling of North African or other Arab Christians willing to minister there (possibly from among those in France). (2) *There is a reading room and student center in Algiers.* This provides useful contacts with non-Christians and a haven for believers. Pray for the growth of the student witness among one of the most enquiring and open sections of the nation. (3) *Literature work* has been greatly hindered by the government closure of the one remaining Christian bookshop because it was offering Kabyle New Testament for sale. Pray for its re-opening. Pray that the increasing demand for literature may be met, and that the right literature may be allowed to enter the country.

12. SING PRAISES TO OUR LORD.

More holiness give me,
More striving within;
More patience in suff'ring,
More sorrow for sin;

More faith in my Savior,
More sense of His care;
More joy in His service,
More purpose in prayer.

1. PRAISE GOD FOR WHO HE IS.

"Behold, how good and pleasant it is when brothers dwell in unity!" (Psalm 133:1). You have made altogether adequate provisions for all believers to live together as brothers. To hold the same love and esteem you hold for your Son and your Son does for you is your provision. It is not right or necessary for brothers to divide and distrust one another. I want to lift my heart up in joyful wonder that it is clearly your will that all who believe on your name be one. If this is your will then surely you have made provision. It would be easy to say your provision is your word—and it is, but there must be something tragically lacking in my approach to what you have said. Humility and love are the unifying human factors. Dear Lord, help me, chasten me. I do want to see the unity for which your Son prayed.

Express yourself in adoration for this quality of God.
Speak it audibly or write out your praise in your own devotional journal.

2. PRAISE GOD FOR WHAT HE MEANS TO ME.

Just for me. You have promised that when we are ready to accept your desire for our unity it will be as fragrant as the anointing oil and as refreshing as the dew of Hermon. This should be a strong motivation. But more than this my dear Lord said that when we dwell together as one the world will believe you sent him—we shall have a turning to you like we have never seen! Dear Lord, for one I want to pledge myself to do all I can to make this true. No longer will I equate my understanding of the scriptures as equal with the scriptures themselves. How I hope I can persuade all my brothers to do the same. Bless your altogether adequate provision—may I be humble enough to receive it.

How do you personally relate to the oneness of God, and God who provides for our unity?
Speak it out or write it out. It is *so important* that you establish *your own* devotional journal.

3. CONFESSION OF SIN

Dear Lord, how terribly short of your will are we in this area. The *we* is editorial—I am talking about *myself!* Has there ever been a person who studied your word as diligently as myself? Of course there has! Hundreds, thousands of persons have had the same concern—many of them have exceeded me in diligence. Has there ever been anyone who attempted to separate himself from all the creeds and dogmas of man and to approach every word of your book directly without bias? Yes, yes, there are multiplied thousands of them doing it this very minute! I want to confess my pride and bigotry in my estimate of my relation to you as compared with any other brother who loves you and your Son and your word with the same intensity that I do. How shall we ever be one if I do not repent. Forgive me!

What personal sins do you want to confess? We *must* speak them to remove them.
Do it! *Now.* There is no one else you have sinned against more than God. Tell him so!

4. SING A PRAYER TO GOD.

"There shall be showers of blessing":
This is the promise of love;
There shall be seasons refreshing,
Sent from the Savior above.

Showers of blessing,
Showers of blessing we need:
Mercy drops round us are falling,
But for the showers we plead.

Open your hymn book and sing the rest of the verses—or even sing another prayer song.

5. READ HIS WORD TO HIM!
His Word

[21]He said to them, "Do you bring in a lamp to put it under a bowl or a bed? Instead, don't you put it on its stand? [22]For whatever is hidden is meant to be disclosed, and whatever is concealed is meant to be brought out into the open. [23]If anyone has ears to hear, let him hear."

[24]"Consider carefully what you hear," he continued. "With the measure you use, it will be measured to you—and even more. [25]Whoever has will be given more; whoever does not have, even what he has will be taken from him."

[26]He also said, "This is what the kingdom of God is like. A man scatters seed on the ground. [27]Night and day, whether he sleeps or gets up, the seed sprouts and grows, though he does not know how. [28]All by itself the soil produces grain—first the stalk, then the head, then the full kernel in the head. [29]As soon as the grain is ripe, he puts the sickle to it, because the harvest has come."

[30]Again he said, "What shall we say the kingdom of God is like, or what parable shall we use to describe it? [31]It is like a mustard seed, which is the smallest seed you plant in the ground. [32]Yet when planted, it grows and becomes the largest of all garden plants, with such big branches that the birds of the air can perch in its shade."

[33]With many similar parables Jesus spoke the word to them, as much as they could understand. [34]He did not say anything to them without using a parable. But when he was alone with his own disciples, he explained everything.

— Mark 4:21-34, NIV
Read also Matthew 13:24-35; Luke 8:16-18.

Read His Word to Him.

How good it would be to be alone with our Lord and listen while he explained everything to his disciples, Dear

Lord, the best I can do here is to read these blessed verses several times out loud before your presence.

Please express your response to this beautiful text. Put your expression in your own prayer diary.

6. READ HIS WORD FOR YOURSELF.

Do I have a lamp to be set on a stand? Indeed I do! What lamp stands have you given us today? We could immediately think of the mass media, but to a large extent this light does not shine where it is most needed. I believe literature is by far the most effective of the mass media. But is not the same lamp stand our Lord used available to us? I refer to the life of one person. When we set the light in the heart of one man or woman we have found the very best lamp stand.

How eternally important it is to hear with the inner ear. It is equally important that we be selective in what we hear. For today and its many voices may I choose to hear your voice and may I listen really well. Thank you for the silent but inevitable growth of your word.

Pause in his presence and either audibly or in written form tell him all his word means to you.

7. READ HIS WORD IN THANKSGIVING.

(1) Thank you for the lamp stand. (2) Thank you that I want to open my ears to what you say. (3) Thank you that I can hear with such an attitude that others will be blessed. (4) Thank you for the promise that if we will be and plant the seed it will grow. (5) Thank you for the description of growth — it is gradual and perfectly in keeping with your laws of harvest. (6) Thank you for the mustard seed parable — what an encouragement!

Give yourself to your own expression of gratitude — write it or speak it!

8. READ HIS WORD IN MEDITATION.

"He did not say anything to them without using a parable." There was at least a twofold purpose in this: (1) To prevent the Pharisees from trapping him in his words, "That seeing they should not see, and hearing they should not hear." (2) To attract the attention and interest of all. There is nothing quite so interesting as a story. *What an* *example our Lord is for us:* (1) There are persons who will not understand even if they hear again and again. Make the message attractive and interesting, but beyond that you need not go. (2) Never, never make a major point without an illustration. (3) Explain personally everything to those who want to know.

Pause — wait — think — then express yourself in thoughtful praise or thanks.

9. READ HIS WORD FOR PETITIONS.

We hardly know where to begin in the many requests we see in these verses: (1) If I am the light for my world set me on a stand. (2) Perhaps it is my task to get on the stand and shine. Give me wisdom. (3) The law of increase is operating. May I be ready. (4) Thank you for this need- ful reminder that the growth of the kingdom is sometimes imperceptible. (5) Keep my eyes open as to just where to put the sickle into the grain. (6) With only twelve members my Lord began his universal kingdom that now numbers millions. May this encourage my lack of faith.

Right here add your personal requests — and his answers.

10. READ HIS WORD AND WAIT — LISTEN — GOD SPEAKS!

I do want to hear for eternity from these verses: (1) "Consider carefully what you hear." (2) "Whoever has will be given more; whoever does not have, even what he has will be taken from him." (3) "Parables are best understood by meditation and prayer."

11. INTERCESSION FOR THE LOST WORLD

Algeria — Point for prayer: (1) *Unreached peoples* — some specific groups ought to be mentioned: a) *The Kabyle* — these people number nearly 2 million. In the past a number believed, but most later emigrated to France. There are a number of independent missionaries working among these resistant people. There are increasing diffi- culties in the use of their language due to government pressures to Arabise them — pray that even this may cause some to turn to Christianity, which their forebears followed. b) *The Oasis dwellers* in the Sahara — many different Berber tribes still unreached. c) *The Tuareg* — these nomadic people are very difficult to reach.

12. SING PRAISES TO OUR LORD.

Coming for me, coming for me,
One day to earth He is coming for me;

Then with what joy His dear face I shall see,
Oh, how I praise Him! He's coming for me.

WEEK FORTY-SIX — TUESDAY

1. PRAISE GOD FOR WHO HE IS.

"Praise the Lord, for the Lord is good; sing to his name, for he is gracious! For the Lord has chosen Jacob for himself, Israel as his own possession" (Psalm 135:3, 4). How good and pleasant it is to praise you each day at this time; and to praise you often throughout the day. The term "good" would seem to be overworked as much as we use it. But it is *your* word. Having created the world and all that is in it you said, "It is good." What did you mean? You meant it was complete or fulfilled. Wholeness is a part of the word *good*.

Express yourself in adoration for this quality of God.
Speak it audibly or write out your praise in your own devotional journal.

2. PRAISE GOD FOR WHAT HE MEANS TO ME.

Just for me. The New Testament application of these beautiful verses should be evident to each of us. We are his chosen people, the new "Israel of God" (Gal. 6:6). As a groom chooses his bride so you have chosen us. The little phrase *"for himself"* is so full of meaning. If there were no compatability there would have been no choice. I know you created me for yourself because you shared your nature with me. But in a beautiful sense you also bought me for yourself. My highest joy and purpose is fellowship with you. As a groom owns certain things to complete his life so you possess each of us to complement and complete yourself. We are "your own possession." To say I am glad to accept this relationship is a vast understatement, I am delighted!

How do you personally relate to the choice of God, and God who has chosen us?
Speak it out or write it out. It is *so important* that you establish *your own* devotional journal.

3. CONFESSION OF SIN

To praise you for your goodness or for my acceptance of your total completeness and then to read my track record is to admit there must be a third factor, or Satan. My greatest sin is lovelessness. More songs of praise and grace would help so much as I attempt to acknowledge and repent of my sin. Sin is not *good*—why? Because it lacks the quality of completeness—it misses the mark of fulfillment. There is nothing of grace in sin; it seeks its own and cares not for your desires or the needs of others. Too often these words describe my attitude. Dear Lord, forgive me. I have not lost my relationship as your chosen or your possession, but just now I want to confess my lack of response to these two lovely relationships and be in truth your chosen and your possession.

What personal sins do you want to confess? We *must* speak them to remove them.
Do it! *Now.* There is no one else you have sinned against more than God. Tell him so!

4. SING A PRAYER TO GOD.

Standing on the promises of Christ my King,
Thro' eternal ages let His praises ring;
Glory in the highest, I will shout and sing,
Standing on the promises of God.

Standing, standing,
Standing on the promises of God my Savior;
Standing, standing,
I'm standing on the promises of God.

Open your hymn book and sing the rest of the verses—or even sing another prayer song.

5. READ HIS WORD TO HIM!

His Word

[24]Jesus told them another parable: "The kingdom of heaven is like a man who sowed good seed in his field. [25]But while everyone was sleeping, his enemy came and sowed weeds among the wheat, and went away. [26]When the wheat sprouted and formed heads, then the weeds also appeared.

[27]"The owner's servants came to him and said, 'Sir, didn't you sow good seed in your field? Where then did the weeds come from?'

[28]"'An enemy did this,' he replied.

"The servants asked him, 'Do you want us to go and pull them up?'

[29]"'No,' he answered, 'because while you are pulling the weeds, you may root up the wheat with them. [30]Let both grow together until the harvest. At that time I will tell the harvesters: First collect the weeds and tie them in bundles to be burned, then gather the wheat and bring it into my barn.'"   — Matthew 13:24-30, NIV

Read His Word to Him.

We have your Son's own explanation of this parable (vss. 36-43) and I want to read it several times. How I want to carefully identify each part of this parable: (1) Your Son is the sower—he sows through us today. (2) The field is the world in which we live. The hearts of men are the field. (3) The seed is the message of our Lord. (4) The enemy is the devil who also has seed to sow. (5) There will be a harvest and an eternal separation.

Please express your response to this beautiful text. Put your expression in your own prayer diary.

6. READ HIS WORD FOR YOURSELF.

Just for me. Am I really prepared to receive the meaning of this parable? I am not at all sure that I am. Do I really believe there will be an end to this age? An end to this whole world? Am I prepared to see the angels separate the weeds from the wheat? The weeds are described as "all who cause sin and all evildoers." If I do not plant the good seed — or my Lord does not plant the good seed through me, what will happen? I already *know* what will happen. The enemy has many who plant his seed — they are demons who are his servants. The whole field of the world is growing an abundant harvest of weeds to be gathered and burned. But these weeds are people and when they are thrown into the fire there will be weeping and gnashing of teeth. Dear God, dear God, do I believe this? I am trying before your throne to assimilate the impact of these words — help me! Forgive me!

It is so important that you pause in his presence
and either audibly or in written form tell him all his word means to you.

7. READ HIS WORD IN MEDITATION.

(1) Thank you that we have such good seed to sow. (2) Thank you for the assurance that your Son will work through us as we sow. (3) Thank you for the wonderful liberty we have in sowing the seed. (4) Thank you for the warning that there is indeed an evil one hard at work. (5) Thank you for a description of the nature of his work, i.e., "at night." (6) Thank you for the plain statement that we should concern ourselves with planting and not hoeing. (7) Thank you for the wonderful promise of shining like the sun in your eternal kingdom.

Give yourself to your own expression of gratitude — write it or speak it!

8. READ HIS WORD IN MEDITATION.

"Let them both grow together until the harvest." Our Lord is not here recommending inaction. He suggests that the wheat is to grow as well as the weeds. Why is it that weeds grow more rapidly and profusely? We could easily answer that there are more of them, but this is not *necessarily* so. How much wheat is planted is our decision. We could say that it is easier for weeds to grow, i.e., they are sturdier by nature. I do not accept that as a valid answer. Wheat seed has been cultivated until it is much more hardy than weeds. The simple answer is that weeds grow because we do not care as much about the wheat as Satan does about the weeds. The awful tragedy is that there *will be* a harvest!

Pause — wait — think — then express yourself in thoughtful praise or thanks.

9. READ HIS WORD FOR PETITIONS.

In this parable I find real areas for requests: (1) Thank you for the good seed — may I sow it today in the hearts of men. (2) Keep me aware that there always is an enemy. Keep me from the evil one. (3) It was while people slept the enemy worked. Keep me awake. (4) Good and evil grow together until the eternal harvest. Guard me from a premature harvesting. (5) How I want to be wiser than the worried servants. (6) I have tried pulling up some weeds. Forgive me. (7) Thank you for showing me who will be first to be removed at the end of the world.

Please, please remember these are prayers — speak them — reword them!

10. READ HIS WORD AND WAIT — LISTEN — GOD SPEAKS!

Before the end comes speak to me: (1) "My harvest is growing — take heart." (2) "Satan's harvest is also growing — be patient." (3) "I have the angel harvesters already for the last day."

11. INTERCESSION FOR THE LOST WORLD

Algeria — Points for prayer: (1) *The Algerians in Europe* — at any one time there are nearly 2,000,000 working in France, Belgium, Holland, etc. Pray that many may turn to the Lord who will, in turn, become missionaries to their own people. (2) *Radio and Bible correspondence courses* with careful follow-up of those so contacted by visits from believers is still the most effective means of outreach. Pray that literature may not be intercepted in the post and that those receiving Bible correspondence courses may be free from harassment.

12. SING PRAISES TO OUR LORD.

I have found a friend in Jesus,
He's everything to me,
He's the fairest of ten thousands to my soul;
The Lily of the Valley, in Him alone I see
All I need to cleanse and make me fully whole.

In sorrow He's my comfort, in trouble He's my stay,
He tells me every care on Him to roll:
He's the Lilly of the Valley, the Bright and Morning Star,
He's the fairest of ten thousand to my soul.

WEEK FORTY-SIX — WEDNESDAY

1. PRAISE GOD FOR WHO HE IS.

"O give thanks to the Lord of lords, for his steadfast love endures for ever; to him who alone does great wonders, for his steadfast love endures for ever" (Psalm 136:3, 4). The names of yourself are given so clearly in this psalm that I want to lift them up again to you as an expression of my own praise to you. (1) *"Lord"* or *"Jehovah—the Eternal, he who was, and is, and is to come."* In the use here it tells us of your agreement with us as your redeemed ones. I hesitate even to write these words—so great is the meaning behind this expression! (2) *God of gods or Elohim* —in reference to your creation of the world and all that is in it. Keep my eyes open to see beyond your creation to the Creator. (3) In the verse before us is the beautiful name *"the Lord of lords."* The sovereign One who rules all—the ruler of all rulers. (4) *The God of heaven*—the Almighty One. A reference to your strength and power. Amen and amen!

Express yourself in adoration for this quality of God.
Speak it audibly or write out your praise in your own devotional journal.

2. PRAISE GOD FOR WHAT HE MEANS TO ME.

Just for me. This lovely psalm is one of thanksgiving— and oh, how I want to make it my thanksgiving to you! The *wonders* you have wrought are outlined in the whole psalm: (1) *Creation*—You called into being the heavens. As we consider now what we know of the galaxies we fall back in amazement! What we have learned of the moon and the sun and the planets only serves to increase our praise for the One who set them in their place. (2) *Deliver-ance*—In the experience of your children in history we can see ourselves today. We were all in Egypt—we have all escaped the eternal death sentence upon our sin. We have all come through the Red Sea of Christian baptism into the Canaan of the new life. (I use the editorial "we" be-cause I do not want to write "I" over and over again, but, dear Lord, you know I am the one of whom I speak.)

How do you personally relate to the wonders of God, and God who is Lord of lords?
Speak it out or write it out. It is *so important* that you establish *your own* devotional journal.

3. CONFESSION OF SIN

To approach you in confession all seems so natural. I am in need, so I come to the only One who can meet my need. All men can identify with the experiences of your people Israel in the wilderness. I have complained— (even yesterday) when all the while I have so much more than any one in Egypt. Dear Lord, forgive me! The daily —even hourly provision of manna (your beloved word and your Son)—is overlooked and misunderstood. Dear Lord, what a sin! Forgive me. Has there been any tempta-tion or trial you could not handle? To ask is to answer— of course not! But I have acted and thought in such a manner that even I interpret my conduct as a contra-diction—open my eyes, break my heart, forgive me. Dear Lord, *"remember my low estate."*

What personal sins do you want to confess? We *must* speak them to remove them.
Do it! *Now.* There is no one else you have sinned against more than God. Tell him so!

4. SING A PRAYER TO GOD.

Ere you left your room this morning,
Did you think to pray?
In the name of Christ our Savior,
Did you sue for loving favor,
As a shield today?

Oh, how praying rests the weary!
Prayer will change the night to day;
So in sorrow and in gladness,
Don't forget to pray.

Open your hymn book and sing the rest of the verses—or even sing another prayer song.

5. READ HIS WORD TO HIM!

His Word

[36]Then he left the crowd and went into the house. His disciples came to him and said, "Explain to us the parable of the weeds in the field."
[37]He answered, "The one who sowed the good seed is the Son of Man. [38]The field is the world, and the good seed stands for the sons of the kingdom. The weeds are the sons of the evil one, [39]and the enemy who sows them is the devil. The harvest is the end of the age, and the har-vesters are angels.

[40]"As the weeds are pulled up and burned in the fire, so it will be at the end of the age. [41]The Son of Man will send out his angels, and they will weed out of his kingdom everything that causes sin and all who do evil. [42]They will throw them into the fiery furnace, where there will be weeping and gnashing of teeth. [43]Then the righteous will shine like the sun in the kingdom of their Father. He who has ears, let him hear. — Matthew 13:36-43, NIV

WEEK FORTY-SIX — WEDNESDAY

Read His Word to Him.

Dear Lord, give me ears to hear! I review again just what and who is involved: (1) The sower is your Son. (2) The field is this wide world. (3) The good seed is your word. (4) The bad seed is the word of Satan. (5) The enemy is Satan who sows. (6) The harvest is the end of the world. (7) The harvesters are angels. (8) The rewards and punishment are heaven and hell.

Please express your response to this beautiful text. Put your expression in your own prayer diary.

6. READ HIS WORD FOR YOURSELF.

What a sobering experience this will be! In every class standing behind me — or above me — is your dear Son co-planting the word. (2) How — oh, how I need to remember that the field is not the assembly of the saints. It is the wide expanse of all men in every nation. (3) It is not my cleverness or commentary that will produce sons of the kingdom, but *only* your word. (4) Satan works until now — God works until now *through me* and all others who sow — but *only when and not until.* (5) There will be a general judgment — *everything and all* are involved. What a shock it will be! (6) Angels already have a tremendous task assigned. (7) Heaven and hell are described: "fiery furnace" — "shine like the sun." Dear God, this is too much for my dull heart!

Pause in his presence and either audibly or in written form tell him all his word means to you.

7. READ HIS WORD IN MEDITATION.

(1) Thank you that Jesus gave us the meaning of this parable. (2) Thank you for the assurance that the good seed is fertile and able to overcome all weeds. (3) Thank you that his life is our life — we are his seed and his Son's. (4) Thank you that we are not ignorant of Satan's work. (5) Thank you there *is* going to be an eternal harvest of all wheat and weeds. (6) Thank you that the Son of man will make the separation.

Give yourself to your own expression of gratitude — write it or speak it!

8. READ HIS WORD IN MEDITATION.

"He who has ears, let him hear." If we were to say "He who has an interest, let him listen" we would be saying the same thing — or would we? There is something deeper involved than mere listening. Our Lord is talking about the inner ear. Jesus is speaking about a heart condition; does the man inside really want to change? If he does I have a wonderful answer. But hearing in this context is equated with doing. It is like our Lord's continual use of faith. To believe is to do. How dangerous it is to hear without doing!

Pause — wait — think — then express yourself in thoughtful praise or thanks.

9. READ HIS WORD FOR PETITIONS.

As your Son explains the parable of the weeds I find place after place for prayer requests: (1) What a powerful thought — as I sow you plant — keep me full of reverence. (2) The field is the world — all the world — every part of the world — open my concern. (3) Your seed produces sons — what a miracle of birth and growth. (4) Satan's seed also produces sons — of the evil one. In both instances keep me awake! (4) The harvest is the end of the world. How can it be? But it is! When shall it be? Today? How I want to be ready! (5) Men will be burned as chaff — awesome, terrible! Teach me! (6) Men will cry and suffer in the fire. How mind boggling! (7) I have ears; I want to hear. What a joy to be a son of the kingdom!

Right here add your personal requests — and his answers.

10. READ HIS WORD AND WAIT — LISTEN — GOD SPEAKS!

You have been speaking to me in these verses: (1) "My angels are ministering to you now. They will minister to the lost later." (2) "There is a bright eternal day ahead for you." (3) "If you really have ears, hear now and for eternity."

11. INTERCESSION FOR THE LOST WORLD

Egypt — Population: 38,100,000. Growth rate — 2.3%. People per sq. km. — in fertile areas — 1,000.

Point for prayer: (1) *Pray that the promise of Isaiah 19:19-22 for Egypt may be fulfilled.* There are encouraging signs of a turning to God from among Muslims, despite legal barriers. Several hundred Muslims are turning to Christ every year. Pray that Egypt's troubles, and Islam's emptiness may turn many to the Lord Jesus.

12. SING PRAISES TO OUR LORD.

How sweet the name of Jesus sounds
In a believer's ear!
It soothes his sorrows, heals his wounds,
And drives away his fear.

639

WEEK FORTY-SIX — THURSDAY

1. PRAISE GOD FOR WHO HE IS.

"By the waters of Babylon, there we sat down and wept, when we remembered Zion" (Psalm 137:1). The capacity of memory is surely a part of your own image or nature. It is my constant purpose and joy to each day praise you for one more quality of yourself. I am sure I shall never exhaust the number. I want to say that I consider this time of praise representative of what all men should (and one day will) do. Not that all men will express themselves like I do — far from it — but all men of all time should join with the innumerable angels in adoration and wonder before you. I weep when I remember the joys and associations of childhood — how much more should I weep at my remembrances of all my Lord did for me as recorded in the good news.

Express yourself in adoration for this quality of God.
Speak it audibly or write out your praise in your own devotional journal.

2. PRAISE GOD FOR WHAT HE MEANS TO ME.

Just for me. Unless my relationship with a person has touched my conscience and has become a part of my inner being there are going to be no tears at remembrance. Even when the above is true I shall only weep if the memory is linked to some personal tangible object or subject. Tears came at the mention of Zion. Tears flowed when a song was requested. Poetry and music are wonderful catalysts for tears. I said all this, dear Lord, because I want to spell it out for myself. I want to keep my heart tender and open to you — I want to pause and read again how he died for me! I want to sing again: "Did ere such love and sorrow meet and thorns compose so rich a crown?" Will I weep when I lift the bread and the cup to my lips? "I too remember Zion!"

How do you personally relate to the personal interest of God, and God who is Personal?
Do it! *Now*. It is *so important* that you establish *your own* devotional journal.

3. CONFESSION OF SIN

I wonder at my dry-eyed performance! Dear Lord, forgive. At times I am emotionally drained and there are no tears to shed. But lest deceit and hypocrisy take over — I ask myself — "Why am I so lacking in emotion?" Is it not that I have dissipated my emotion on some lesser thing or person? How much I need to guard my heart and hold for you my shouts of joy and my tears of remembrance! Dear, dear Lord, I repent, I ask for your cleansing. The blunting of my sensibility seems to me to be a terrible sin. Dear Lord, deliver me from overbearing temptations.

What personal sins do you want to confess? We *must* speak them to remove them.
Do it! *Now*. There is no one else you have sinned against more than God. Tell him so!

4. SING A PRAYER TO GOD.

The Lord's our Rock, in Him we hide,
A shelter in the time of storm;
Secure whatever ill betide,
A shelter in the time of storm.

Oh, Jesus is a Rock in a weary land,
A weary land, a weary land;
Oh, Jesus is a Rock in a weary land,
A shelter in the time of storm.

Open your hymn book and sing the rest of the verses — or even sing another prayer song.

5. READ HIS WORD TO HIM!

His Word

[44]"The kingdom of heaven is like treasure hidden in a field. When a man found it, he hid it again, and then in his joy went and sold all he had and bought that field. [45]"Again, the kingdom of heaven is like a merchant looking for fine pearls. [46]When he found one of great value, he went away and sold everything he had and bought it.
— *Matthew 13:44-46, NIV*

Read His Word to Him.

My dear Father, over the years I have loved every word of these three verses. I have loved more the One who said them. How I do want to express my joy and praise — my confession and thanksgiving to you through these words of your Son. "The kingdom of heaven" is simply your rule in the hearts and lives of men. Such a rule began long ago and will find eternal fulfillment in heaven. The most obvious expression of such rule should be in the body of your Son or his church. There are so many beautiful comparisons we can make: (1) The sudden surprise of finding a treasure hidden in the field. What was the man doing when he found the treasure? It was just an ordinary day with the usual routine when suddenly all heaven broke through!

Please express your response to this beautiful text. Put your expression in your own prayer diary.

6. READ HIS WORD FOR YOURSELF.

I have assumed in the above expression that I do represent all men who encounter my Lord. What other comparison can I see here? (2) He had to sell all that he had to possess this treasure. Oh, how eternally true this is! Our Lord's treasures cost "everything," or "all he had." The total focus of interest and commitment is what is meant. (3) There are two types of persons who find salvation: those who are found by it and those who are searching for it. Dear Lord, I have been in both positions. Or is my Lord saying that within every man there is an indefinable longing or search and it is so hidden that when he finds it it appears as a sudden treasure?

It is so important that you pause in his presence
and either audibly or in written form tell him all his word means to you.

7. READ HIS WORD IN THANKSGIVING.

(1) Thank you for the wonderful possibilities of heaven ruling our hearts. (2) Thank you that your rule is the rule of a king. (3) Thank you that in any field — in every field (or life) the treasure can be found. (4) Thank you for the incalulable value of your treasure. (5) Thank you for the strong fact that unless I sell all, I have nothing. (6) Thank you for the joy expressed throughout these discoveries. (7) Thank you for the beauty of the treasure and the pearl — both representative of my Lord.

Give yourself to your own expression of gratitude — write it or speak it!

8. READ HIS WORD IN MEDITATION.

". . . *he went away and sold everything he had and bought it."* Even when we know this is true we wonder if we have done it. Have we sold all to buy the field? Have we really sold *everything* to obtain the pearl? I guess we would be in a constant flux and frustration if there was not another way of approaching this subject. The simple question is: "Do you have the treasure; do you have the pearl?" At times we could exclaim with a loud "yes." At other times we are not sure. Here is the secret of a victorious happy Christian life! We must sell out every day. Every morning is a "go for broke" day. Of course, there was that glad day when we first sold out to him, but unless we sustain such an attitude and commitment we have lost "the pearl of great price."

Pause — wait — think — then express yourself in thoughtful praise or thanks.

9. READ HIS WORD FOR PETITIONS.

Hidden in these verses are wonderful petitions: (1) How good it is to know your rule in my heart is as common and near as my backyard. (2) I do want to search for the real meaning of your rule in my life — this treasure is hidden. (3) Just for today let me find another facet of how I can let you have your way with me. (4) Enlarge the deep joy I feel in giving you the throne of my heart. (5) I know I must sell all of my selfish interests to obtain your treasure — purify my understanding. (6) All of us are looking for the beautiful in life — open the eyes of my understanding to see my Lord! (7) Twice over you have told me I must sell all to have your Son. I want to hear him.

Please, please remember these are prayers — speak them — reword them!

10. READ HIS WORD AND WAIT — LISTEN — GOD SPEAKS!

How pointedly you speak to me here: (1) "The fields of life are full of treasure for those who are looking." (2) "Mark it again: You must "go for broke." (3) "How beautiful and valuable is Jesus."

11. INTERCESSION FOR THE LOST WORLD

Egypt — Points for prayer: (1) *Unreached peoples.* Few Muslims have ever heard a Christian testify. Pray that the Christians may win opportunities to speak through their Christlikeness. The Desert Bedouin and Berber peoples remain unreached. (2) *The Nubian people* are now more receptive to the Gospel than ever before. Most are Muslim, but many are Coptic Christians. The great need is for more Christian workers to learn their language and to live and witness among them. (3) *Pray for the evangelization of the cities* — many rural people are being compelled by poverty to go to the cities. Pray that these uprooted people may be evangelized somehow. (4) *The Coptic Church* is largely nominal, but an extraordinary revival within it since 1930 has gained momentum and the present leadership is highly educated, articulate and Bible based. The present Patriarch gives weekly Bible studies to 7,000 people. These 5,000,000 Coptic Christians, if revived, could have a decisive impact on the Middle East.

12. SING PRAISES TO OUR LORD.

Christ has for sin atonement made,
What a wonderful Savior!
We are redeemed! the price is paid!

What a wonderful Savior!
What a wonderful Savior is Jesus, my Jesus!
What a wonderful Savior is Jesus, my Lord!

WEEK FORTY-SIX — FRIDAY

1. PRAISE GOD FOR WHO HE IS.

"I give thee thanks, O Lord, with my whole heart; before the gods I sing thy praise; I bow down towards thy holy temple and give thanks to thy name for thy steadfast love and thy faithfulness; for thou hast exalted above everything thy name and thy word" (Psalm 138:1, 2). You have provided more than adequate reason for me to give my whole being to you in gratitude. It is a supreme joy to lift my mind through your word and present it before you as yours. I want to yield my whole desire and hold it up before your throne. My emotions, giving color and emphasis to all I say, are yours. How strong is the approval of my conscience as I thus praise you! I want to do this gladly in the presence of all men. If you have such a high estimate of yourself and your word (richly deserved and altogether appropriate) who am I to hesitate or be ashamed?

Express yourself in adoration for this quality of God.
Speak it audibly or write out your praise in your own devotional journal.

2. PRAISE GOD FOR WHAT HE MEANS TO ME.

Just for me. I try to speak on behalf of all who come to you in praise, i.e., in the above expression, but here I review again these blessed words and make them altogether mine. As David had two basic reasons for this spontaneous expression of thanks so do I: (1) For your mercy, or as expressed in this translation "thy steadfast love." Dear Lord, without this quality there would indeed be for me no hope at all! But in your daily goodness I take great courage. Mercy is undeserved and non-reciprocal goodness. How often does my heart stray from a worship and recognition of yourself in my daily life. I believe it is possible to integrate your presence and your love into every day. I try but I need your mercy. How gladly do I acknowledge this gift! (2) For your *truth*—not only your propositional truth as seen in your word, but for the ring of reality in all my associations with you and your Son!

How do you personally relate to the faithfulness of God, and God who is Love?
Speak it out or write it out. It is *so important* that you establish *your own* devotional journal.

3. CONFESSION OF SIN

How do I sin against your mercy and truth? By not showing your quality of mercy to others. When someone lashes out at me for what seems to be no reason at all, how do I react? Have you deserved all the stupid outbursts of my selfish heart?—and yet you were kind and patient with me. May this time of joy and praise remain with me to remind me that only he who receives mercy can give it. Am I ready to exalt your truth—your word, in the presence of other gods? Dear Lord, I ask forgiveness for any and all hesitancy to speak up for what you have said. Men are so ready to tell what others have said or to advance their own opinions. Give me a voice for your word! Forgive me for my silence!

What personal sins do you want to confess? We *must* speak them to remove them.
Do it! *Now.* There is no one else you have sinned against more than God. Tell him so!

4. SING A PRAYER TO GOD.

Jesus, I my cross have taken,
All to leave, and follow Thee;
Destitute, despised, forsaken,
Thou, from hence, my all shalt be:

Perish ev'ry fond ambition,
All I've sought, and hoped, and known;
Yet how rich is my condition,
God and heav'n are still my own!

Open your hymn book and sing the rest of the verses—or even sing another prayer song.

5. READ HIS WORD TO HIM!
His Word

[47]"Once again, the kingdom of heaven is like a net that was let down into the lake and caught all kinds of fish. [48]When it was full, the fishermen pulled it up on the shore. Then they sat down and collected the good fish in baskets, but threw the bad away. [49]This is how it will be at the end of the age. The angels will come and separate the wicked from the righteous [50]and throw them into the fiery furnace, where there will be weeping and gnashing of teeth."

[51]"Have you understood all these things?" Jesus asked. "Yes," they replied.
[52]He said to them, "Therefore every teacher of the law who has been instructed about the kingdom of heaven is like the owner of a house who brings out of his storeroom new treasures as well as old."
[53]When Jesus had finished these parables, he moved on from there.
— Matthew 13:47-53, NIV

Read His Word to Him.

How well do I relate to these verses! My father and grandfather were commercial fishermen on the Columbia River of Oregon as the disicples of my Lord were on the Sea of Galilee. Dear Lord, speak these words into my heart.

I read them with the deepest thought and meditation. Is the net the gospel message? Is the sea the world? Are the fish by nature good or bad?—we decide our nature by our choices. The separation *is* the end of the world!

Please express your response to this beautiful text. Put your expression in your own prayer diary.

6. READ HIS WORD FOR YOURSELF.

Just for me. Dear Lord, I read these words like I never read them before! Underneath all men are not only "the everlasting arms" but the net of God! One day we will be taken up and appear before him in judgment. It is more than interesting to notice what my Lord *did not* say about the judgment. (1) He *did not* describe the size and weight of the fish—although this is man's constant interest. (2) He *did not* describe the beauty or appearance of the fish. (3) He *did not* make any exception—there were *no* borderline fish. Dear Lord, all these words burn my heart! How I do want to awake before I am pulled up out of the water! Thank you for the confidence I find in the change of my nature! The emphasis of my Lord was on the *bad fish*.

Pause in his presence and either audibly or in written form tell him all his word means to you.

7. READ HIS WORD IN THANKSGIVING.

(1) Thank you that you have called all your disciples to be fishers of men. (2) Thank you for the wonderful net we have to use. (3) Thank you that you intend for the whole lake to be involved in the catch. (4) Thank you that there will be an end—there will be a shore where the fish are separated. (5) Thank you for those who do the separating—it is not us preachers. (6) Thank you for this clear word that it is the *nature* of the fish that determines its destiny. (7) Thank you for the new and old applications we see in this parable.

Give yourself to your own expression of gratitude—write it or speak it!

8. READ HIS WORD IN MEDITATION.

"*. . . the owner of a house who brings out of his storeroom new treasures as well as old.*" Was Jesus describing himself. Surely no one else could better qualify under this description. He alone is the owner of the whole house of this world and the world to come. What a storeroom he has! In him are hidden all the treasures of wisdom and knowledge. Only our Lord knows everything and knows how to use such knowledge. How often did Jesus refer to the "old things" found in the history of his people?

Pause—wait—think—then express yourself in thoughtful praise or thanks.

9. READ HIS WORD FOR PETITIONS.

How familiar were these words of Jesus to the four commercial fishermen he had called to be his apostles. What lessons in prayer are here: (1) There is a net in which we all shall be taken. How glad I am I can claim the new nature you offer. Somehow I want to express my gratitude. (2) Open my mind to a fuller understanding of the events at the end of the world. (3) How shall I determine I am righteous? Is his righteousness mine? Praise your name I *know* it is. (4) What a fearful thought: ". . . throw them into the fiery furnace where there will be weeping and gnashing of teeth." May I have pity on these poor fish. They are eternal people! (5) If my Lord were to ask me: "Have you understood all these things?" I would have to answer "no, help me."

Right here add your personal requests—and his answers.

10. READ HIS WORD AND WAIT—LISTEN—GOD SPEAKS!

Speak Lord, thy servant heareth: (1) "My net is still down, but it might not be for long." (2) "You are responsible for the nature of the fish." (3) "Ask for wisdom."

11. INTERCESSION FOR THE LOST WORLD

Egypt — Point for prayer: (1) *The Protestant Churches* have not grown much for many years. There is some nominalism in the older churches and a considerable drift back to the Coptic Church from where the original converts came. Pray for a deepening of the spiritual life and a more consistent life-testimony before the Muslims. There are many young people now coming into the churches. There are several interdenominational groups who seek to stimulate Bible Study and outreach among the young people. Pray that, despite the difficulties, Muslims may be reached and welcomed into the churches. One church actually gained 100 converts out of Isalm in 1975.

12. SING PRAISES TO OUR LORD.

Fairest Lord Jesus!
Ruler of all nature!
O Thou of God and man the Son!

Thee will I cherish,
Thee will I honor,
Thou, my soul's glory, joy, and crown!

WEEK FORTY-SIX — SATURDAY

1. PRAISE GOD FOR WHO HE IS.

"The Lord will fulfill his purpose for me; thy steadfast love, O Lord, endures forever. Do not forsake the work of thy hands" (Psalm 138:8). What an assurance! "Being confident of this very thing that he who has begun a good work in you will bring it to completion at the day of Jesus Christ" (Philippians 1:6). This is one of the most encouraging qualities we have considered. Our Lord specializes in "follow through." Very simply expressed: his purpose for me is to bring honor to his Son and himself. This can be done in personal conduct. It can also be done through teaching others. I believe God is at work fulfilling a purpose for every life. We cannot always see just how this life or that one brought honor to him, but if it is our sincere intent to do so he will see to it such is accomplished. "None will ever be able to say of our Lord, 'He was not able to finish.'"

Express yourself in adoration for this quality of God.
Speak it audibly or write out your praise in your own devotional journal.

2. PRAISE GOD FOR WHAT HE MEANS TO ME.

Just for me. This beautiful little poem appears in Graham Scroggie's book, *Psalms.*

"The work which His goodness began,
The arm of His strength will complete.
His promise is yea and amen,
And never was forfeited yet." (p. 37)

Praise your name! How I rejoice to affirm this of your purpose in my life. My earnest desire has been — and is more so today: to teach and preach your word — most of all to *communicate* by teaching your own love and eternal goodness. I want to hold before all men the beauty of my wonderful Lord.

How do you personally relate to the follow through of God, and God who completes all he began?
Speak it out or write it out. It is *so important* that you establish *your own* devotional journal.

3. CONFESSION OF SIN

As I consider all the chaff amid a little wheat the words of *J. W. Burgon* — quoted by *Graham Scroggie* — surely speak to my heart. He said: "His creating hands formed our souls at the beginning; His nail-pierced hands redeemed them at Calvary; His glorified hands will hold our souls fast and not let them go for ever. Unto His hands let us commend our spirits, sure that even though the works of our hands have made void the works of His hands, yet His hands will again make perfect all that our hands have made."

It is a rare joy to be able to speak to many people over many years. Only you can know how much wood, hay and stubble are mixed with the gold and silver. I can see more of dross than I care to admit to anyone but yourself. Dear Lord, forgive.

What personal sins do you want to confess? We *must* speak them to remove them.
Do it! *Now.* There is no one else you have sinned against more than God. Tell him so!

4. SING A PRAYER TO GOD.

Only faintly now I see Him,
With the darkling veil between,
But a blessed day is coming,
When His glory shall be seen.

Face to face I shall behold Him,
Far beyond the starry sky;
Face to face in all His glory,
I shall see Him by and by!

Open your hymn book and sing the rest of the verses — or even sing another prayer song.

5. READ HIS WORD TO HIM!
His Word

[35]That day when evening came, he said to his disciples, "Let us go over to the other side." [36]Leaving the crowd behind, they took him along, just as he was, in the boat. There were also other boats with him. [37]A furious squall came up, and the waves broke over the boat, so that it was nearly swamped. [38]Jesus was in the stern, sleeping on a cushion. The disciples woke him and said to him. "Teacher, don't you care if we drown?"

— *Mark 4:35-38a, NIV*

Read also Matthew 8:18, 23, 24; Luke 8:22-23.

Read His Word to Him.

What a privilege it is to take up your word and expect you to be looking over my shoulder as I read it. A better figure would be for me to kneel before your throne of grace and spread out these precious words before you and ask you to open my heart as I meditate upon each word. What a long strenuous day your Son had! But perhaps no longer or more strenuous than many other days — we would not know from him as no complaint was registered. He left the crowd behind. All of us must ultimately do this. In the midst of a very busy schedule he "left the crowd behind." Does this say anything to me? Indeed it does.

Please express your response to this beautiful text. Put your expression in your own prayer diary.

6. READ HIS WORD FOR YOURSELF.

I really never succeed in separating these two expressions. What I read to you I read to myself and what I read to myself I know I read to you. At the same time, I am glad for the two approaches to you in prayer. Jesus was in the same boat from which he taught the parables. I have been in several fishing boats — they all had the strong smell of fish. What a place to sleep! But when one is tired — as our Lord was, one sleeps. The Sea of Galilee is 60-70- 80 feet deep in the area where they were. The squall was indeed furious. Swells twenty or thirty feet high would not be uncommon. With the wind lashing the water the plight of the disciples was desperate. How well does this describe my own need. It is not always that we are so in need, but it *does* happen. The storm did and did not affect Jesus.

Pause in his presence and either audibly or in written form tell him all his word means to you.

7. READ HIS WORD IN THANKSGIVING.

(1) Thank you for the wonderful evidence of the humanity of my Lord. (2) Thank you that it was Jesus' choice to "go over to the other side." (3) Thank you for the example of retirement as well as involvement set by my Lord. (4) Thank you that Jesus made use of the very common items of life for his eternal purposes. (5) Thank you for the lesson that neither Jesus nor the disciples were immune from the storm. (6) Thank you for the reality and severity of the danger. (7) Thank you for the calm of my Lord in the midst of the storm.

Give yourself to your own expression of gratitude — write it or speak it!

8. READ HIS WORD IN MEDITATION.

"Jesus was in the stern, sleeping on a cushion." How remarkably casual and natural are all the miracles of our Lord! Did Jesus know there would be a storm when he requested that they sail to the other side of the lake? Did he also know that he would be tired and would fall asleep? Was he actually anticipating the marvelous miracle he was to perform? This account could be read as a very ordinary narrative with a sequence of events not at all unlike what would have happened to anyone. Even the sleeping would have occurred to someone who was totally exhausted. The point is that God is at work in our lives amid the very ordinary routine of day by day living. God is not excited, nor seeking for the sensational. But at the same time he is not unaware or unprepared to save us either in or out of our peril.

Pause — wait — think — then express yourself in thoughtful praise or thanks.

9. READ HIS WORD FOR PETITIONS.

The holy awe that filled the hearts of the disciples should be ours as we attempt to pray from this text: (1) When the evening of my life comes I want to hear his words: "Let us go over to the other side." (2) "On this sea of life I do want to be sure you are with me in the boat, even now I call upon you. (3) Even when Jesus was in the boat a furious squall yet fell upon them. May I not be surprised if such happens to me. (4) All seems so natural in this incident and yet it was all in the plan of your Son. I believe all of my life is so planned by you. Increase my faith. (5) How I do want to hear the voice of your Son in every troubled circumstance: "Peace, be still." (6) Thank you for this powerful example — teach me from it just who Jesus is.

Please, please remember these are prayers — speak them — reword them!

10. READ HIS WORD AND WAIT — LISTEN — GOD SPEAKS!

(1) "I am never indifferent to your need." (2) "I can handle any situation." (3) "All things are now being held together by the word of my power."

11. INTERCESSION FOR THE LOST WORLD

Egypt — Point for prayer: (1) *The Christian witness among university students* is encouraging. There is now a group in every faculty of Egypt's four big university complexes; even in the Al Azhar Muslim University where Muslim missionaries are trained. Pray that these believers may find open hearts among the 250,000 students and win them in the relative freedom found there. Pray for the building up of these believers in the Lord for future usefulness in service.

12. SING PRAISES TO OUR LORD.

There is never a cross so heavy,
There is never a weight of woe,
But that Jesus will help to carry
Because He loveth so.

Wonderful, wonderful Jesus,
In the heart He implanteth a song:
A song of deliv'rance, courage, of strength,
In the heart He implanteth a song.

1. PRAISE GOD FOR WHO HE IS.

"O Lord, thou hast searched me and known me! Thou knowest when I sit down and when I rise up; thou discernest my thoughts from afar" (Psalm 139:1, 2). How true is the beautiful statement from the heart of David. You *know* all men in a deeper more personal manner than they know themselves. David is no doubt referring to all the experiences of his early life. Dear Lord, how closely did you follow the rise and fall of King David! But I believe you have searched the lives of *all* men and see every one when they sit down and when they rise up. There is not a thought that enters the mind of one man anywhere without your knowledge. Even though the enormity of this concept has just struck me it has been your capacity from eternity!

Express yourself in adoration for this quality of God.
Speak it audibly or write out your praise in your own devotional journal.

2. PRAISE GOD FOR WHAT HE MEANS TO ME.

Just for me. I know I shall be in this psalm for several days in an attempt to praise you adequately. Ah, I shall never succeed in such a pursuit! But it is with genuine delight I attempt such an expression. It is so comforting and reassuring to know you have made and are making a detailed search of my deceptive heart. I am so glad you now have your findings and are relating them to my conduct during this day. Praise you for such an interest! Since you know me so much better than I know myself I am glad to turn over the throne of my heart to you. I believe if I meditate upon your word you will speak to me about the areas of my need that you see as you search my heart. Praise your glorious name for such personal help!

How do you personally relate to the search of God, and God who knows all?
Speak it out or write it out. It is *so important* that you establish *your own* devotional journal.

3. CONFESSION OF SIN

Why should I ever want to hide from you, or ignore you, or deny you? It is always because I am afraid. I am afraid of my guilt so I hide. I am afraid of my willful ignorance, therefore, I ignore you. I am afraid of the consequence of disobedience, therefore, I deny your presence. I now know I need not be afraid—you are love! (not indulgent nothingness). I do not fear to show you my sin for you want to bind up the hurt and pour on the oil of healing. I need not feel awkward in the presence of all knowledge—you teach me with no condescension—with deep personal interest in my growth. Most of all, I need not be intimidated by my disobedience—you gladly forgive with the very real motivation that I sin no more! Praise your wonderful grace!

What personal sins do you want to confess? We *must* speak them to remove them.
Do it! *Now.* There is no one else you have sinned against more than God. Tell him so!

4. SING A PRAYER TO GOD.

O noblest Brow and dearest,
In other days the world
All feared when Thou appearedest;
What shame on Thee is hurled!

How art Thou pale with anguish,
With sore abuse and scorn;
How does that visage languish
Which once was bright as morn!

Open your hymn book and sing the rest of the verses—or even sing another prayer song.

5. READ HIS WORD TO HIM!

His Word

[24]The disciples went and woke him, saying, "Master, Master, we're going to drown!"

He got up and rebuked the wind and the raging waters; the storm subsided, and all was calm. [25]"Where is your faith?" he asked his disciples.

In fear and amazement they asked one another, "Who is this? He commands even the winds and the water, and they obey him."
— Luke 8:24, 25, NIV
Read also Matthew 8:25-27; Mark 4:38b-41.

Read His Word to Him.

Oh dear Father, I am full of hesitancy as I attempt to read this text from heaven's perspective. Many of the men in the boats were seasoned fishermen. I am so glad you included more than one boat so there would be many who could testify as to this marvelous evidence of his deity. How typical this whole circumstance is. Did the disciples imagine the ship would sink and they would drown when the commander of heaven and earth was on board? The question is really out of place—in that desperate hour they were not thinking, they were acting. And yet our Lord expected them to think. He expected them to exercise their faith.

Please express your response to this beautiful text. Put your expression in your own prayer diary.

6. READ HIS WORD FOR YOURSELF.

Just for me. I want to ask (and answer) with the disciples: "Who is this?" or "What kind of man is this?"—"even the winds and the water obey him." Jesus is asking me how long my faith will last. He is not asking about the quantity of my faith—as if I could have some faith but not enough. He asks me where my faith has gone? "How is it your faith has disappeared?" In this circumstance it would have been a trusting reliance upon the One asleep in the boat. He knew what he was doing even if we didn't. He knew also what he was doing when he spoke those strange words "Quiet! Be still." As many, many times as I have read this I really never will understand fully the power and majesty of your dear Son and my Lord.

It is so important that you pause in his presence
and either audibly or in written form tell him all his words mean to you.

7. READ HIS WORDS IN THANKSGIVING.

(1) Thank you for the very real danger present. (2) Thank you for the confidence of the disciples in Jesus—that he could do something. (3) Thank you for the rebuke of my Lord—it reaches me. (4) Thank you for the incredible power seen in the action of Jesus. (5) Thank you for the response of the disciples to his miracle—may I sustain such an attitude. (6) Thank you that even today Jesus has "all authority." (7) Thank you for his patience.

Give yourself to your own expression of gratitude—write it or speak it!

8. READ HIS WORD IN MEDITATION.

"He commands even the winds and the water, and they obey him." How revealing is this statement of the disciples: (1) It reveals their participation in a miracle. There were three boats with several men in each boat. These men were many of them fishermen who had been on this same water many times. (2) It reveals our Lord's dual interest: his compassion and his deity. Deity without compassion would not help man. It is only in One who is personally concerned about man's plight we can find hope. (3) Most of all it reveals the authority of Jesus. When he was to say later "all authority has been given to me" (Matt. 28:18) it is to such occurrences as this he could refer for confirmation. We are glad to bow before him in acceptance of such Lordship.

Pause—wait—think—then express yourself in thoughtful praise or thanks.

9. READ HIS WORD FOR PETITIONS.

As our Lord awoke to the request of the disciples we want to awaken to the prayer possibilities in this text: (1) Keep me aware you are always aware of my needs. (2) I want to relate to the name "Master" in my relationship with you. (3) Rebuke the forces of the evil one in my life. (4) I must trust totally in you—I have no other help. (5) Where is my faith today? Is it in things and people or in him? (6) I need the capacity of fear and amazement in relation to the Person of my Lord. (7) I am glad for the promise that one day all the storms of life will be over and he will be Lord of all. May this thought calm today's squall.

Right here add your personal requests—and his answers.

10. READ HIS WORD AND WAIT—LISTEN—GOD SPEAKS!

In the midst of the storm speak to me: (1) "I am always ready to help you—you need but ask in faith." (2) "My rebuke can often be a blessing." (3) "The One who commands the elements is Lord of them—and of all men."

11. INTERCESSION FOR THE LOST WORLD

Egypt — Points for prayer: (1) *Missions*—there are only about 20 agencies with 80 missionaries serving in the land. There are now more opportunities for the entry of expatriate Christians for service than for many years. Pray for workers. Pray also for the growth of the missionary vision of the Christians in Egypt. Missionaries from Egypt would be more acceptable than Western missionaries in many Muslim lands. The greatest limitation is not the willingness of believers, but the difficulty of supporting them financially when they go. (2) *Christian literature* is freely printed and sold. Many Christian groups have moved their literature ministries from war-torn Lebanon to Egypt. There are many Christian Bookstores (10 in Cairo). Pray for the effective use of this literature, and also for the raising up of more local believers who are able to write suitable evangelistic and teaching materials.

12. SING PRAISES TO OUR LORD.

Amazing grace! how sweet the sound,
That saved a wretch like me!

I once was lost, but now am found,
Was blind, but now I see.

WEEK FORTY-SEVEN — MONDAY

1. PRAISE GOD FOR WHO HE IS.

"Thou searchest out my path and my lying down, and art acquainted with all my ways" (Psalm 139:3). It is my constant purpose to look beneath these words of your book for yourself. How more than marvelous are the qualities. I see in this one verse: (1) You are a seeking, searching God. This presupposes a strong desire for and a personal interest in the one being sought. You never tire or fail in your search. Praise your name. (2) You have a plan for me—and all men—after you find us. If we are only conscious of being found then all will be well—dear Lord, open my eyes! (3) You really are only trying to get my attention. I was only lost from myself—you knew all my ways before the search began.

Express yourself in adoration for this quality of God.
Speak it audibly or write out your praise in your own devotional journal.

2. PRAISE GOD FOR WHAT HE MEANS TO ME.

Just for me. Praise you for your wonderful interest in my life, in my person. During the day as I travel along the track of my waking hours, you are there to watch my feet and read my thoughts. You are there to take a closer and greater interest in all I do and think than anyone else. Nay, you have a greater interest in my performance than I do. And at night when I give myself to rest you are there. Oh, that I might further develop the capacity to sense your presence! I know the more I think your thoughts as found in your word the more real or tangible is my relationship with you. Keep me always aware that nothing is of little interest to you. You are concerned about "all my ways."

How do you personally relate to the searching God, and God who has found us?
Speak it out or write it out. It is *so important* that you establish *your own* devotional journal.

3. CONFESSION OF SIN.

Dear Lord, as I write my praise for you and to you I sometimes have a sense of separation of the ideal from the real. I freely confess that my high goals are missed by a country mile. But dear Lord, I know you do not want me to alter my desire. The more I give myself to your ideals the closer I will be to fulfillment. I am not what you want me to be, and not what I want to be, but praise your name I am not what I used to be. Since you are acquainted with all my ways you know what the graph looks like if my path were marked out on a chart. In this time with you I want to lay at your feet all my failures—and they are many. I am glad, glad to get rid of them! Take them—forgive them—forget them.

What personal sins do you want to confess? We *must* speak them to remove them.
Do it! *Now.* There is no one else you have sinned against more than God. Tell him so!

4. SING A PRAYER TO GOD.

O tell of His might, and sing of His grace,
Whose robe is the light, whose canopy space;

His chariots of wrath the deep thunder-clouds form,
And dark is His path on the wings of the storm.

Open your hymn book and sing the rest of the verses—or even sing another prayer song.

5. READ HIS WORD TO HIM!

His Word

[28]When he arrived at the other side in the region of the Gadarenes, two demon-possessed men coming from the tombs met him. They were so violent that no one could pass that way. [29]"What do you want with us, Son of God?" they shouted. "Have you come here to torture us before the appointed time?"

[30]Some distance from them a large herd of pigs was feeding. [31]The demons begged Jesus, "If you drive us out, send us into the herd of pigs."

[32]He said to them, "Go!" So they came out and went into the pigs, and the whole herd rushed down the steep bank into the lake and died in the water.

— *Matthew 8:28-32, NIV*

Read also Mark 5:1-13 and Luke 8:26-33.

Read His Word to Him.

What a desperate situation met our Lord when He stepped out of the boat. It would seem he moves from one crisis to another. Praise his dear name he is well able to handle any and all of them. There is so much in this incident I want to learn. Most of all just now I want to praise you—confess my need of you and seek to worship you. Demon possession is such a sad and serious influence of the evil one. I am impressed over and over again how appropriate are all your ways. The demon possessed lived in the place of death and decay. There was no hesitancy on the part of demons to worship our Lord. They called him: "Son of the Most High God"—and indeed he is!

Please express your response to this beautiful text. Put your expression in your own prayer diary.

6. READ HIS WORD FOR YOURSELF.

In so many ways you speak to me in these words! In so many ways I want to express my praise and worship to you. (1) I know I am attacked by demons—I know I am not possessed by them. I know you alone can protect me and give me deliverance. (2) The efforts of men will not avail. So many men have tried so many things to alleviate the ills of humanity. We have with us the record of such unsuccessful efforts. (3) Pigs are good companions for Satan's servants. Living on an animal level is all that is left this side of the bottomless pit. Dear Lord, keep my eyes open to the option.

It is so important that you pause in his presence
and either audibly or in written form tell him all his word means to you.

7. READ HIS WORD IN THANKSGIVING.

(1) Thank you for the willingness of our Lord to face Satan in his most violent form. (2) Thank you that "greater is he who is in me than he who is in the world" (I John 4:4). (3) Thank you for the clear lesson that men under Satan's control are not at all happy. (4) Thank you that we can live among life and light and hope. (5) Thank you that I know Someone who can command sin and evil to depart. (6) Thank you that Jesus considered one man worth more than many pigs. (7) Thank you for the wonderful results from this encounter.

Give yourself to your own expression of gratitude—write it or speak it!

8. READ HIS WORD IN MEDITATION.

"What is your name?" "Legion," he replied, "because many demons had gone into him." The first question about demon possession is "How did the demons get into this man?" It could be expressed in other words: "What did he do or become that he opened himself up to these evil spirits?" It would be easy to say that he was so willing to give himself to the lust of the flesh, the lust of the eyes— to the pride of life that finally Satan had total possession of such a one. However both sin and man are much more complex than such an explanation. It is more than interesting to notice that our Lord never rebukes man (or women) for their sinfulness. It is always the demon or demons who are addressed and condemned. We are not trying to exonerate the possessed, but we are trying to understand as much as we can about the circumstance. In no instance do we have Christians possessed by demons.

Pause—wait—think—then express yourself in thoughtful praise or thanks.

9. READ HIS WORD FOR PETITIONS.

What wonderful lessons of prayer are in this unusual incident: (1) I wonder if I meet any demon possessed men today? Not having the ability to discern spirits I cannot say. (2) Why were these men near the tombs? (3) I do fully expect an answer to these questions one day. (4) In the spirit world there was no question as to who Jesus was. Why are men so unwilling today? (5) Evidently demons are limited in their understanding—at least they did not know the result of entering the swine. (6) In these realms of the spirit teach me the truth. (7) How dull of hearing were the people of the city—open my ears to truly hear what you are saying to me.

Please, please remember these are prayers—speak them—reword them!

10. READ HIS WORD AND WAIT—LISTEN—GOD SPEAKS!

(1) "There are yet men who think more of money than people." (2) "There is a wonderful deliverance for all who will accept Jesus as Lord." (3) "There were two men who would look back on this day as their greatest gain."

11. INTERCESSION FOR THE LOST WORLD

Arabian (Persian) Gulf States — Population: 2,520,000.
Points for prayer: (1) *This area is a strategic bridgehead for the Gospel*—pray for a continued open door for Christian work. A strong Arab Church here could affect the whole Middle East, for few countries in the area do not have some of their nationals working here. (2) *There are several lands that do not permit Christian work* at all or among the local people. Pray that expatriate workers in these lands may shine for Jesus.

12. SING PRAISES TO OUR LORD.

Here I raise mine Ebenezer;
Hither by Thy help I'm come;
And I hope, by Thy good pleasure,
Safely to arrive at home.

Jesus sought me when a stranger,
Wand'ring from the fold of God;
He, to rescue me from danger,
Interposed His precious blood.

WEEK FORTY-SEVEN — TUESDAY

1. PRAISE GOD FOR WHO HE IS.

"Even before a word is on my tongue, lo, O Lord, thou knowest it altogether. Thou dost beset me behind and before, and layest thy hand upon me" (Psalm 139:4, 5). How delightfully good it is to come before you this day in praise of these lovely qualities of yourself! You are reading my mind and the minds of all men. The most sophisticated computer would not compare at all with such a capacity. Even as I write this—even now as I form these words in my mind before they appear on the paper you know them. Before the tongue pronounces them you have recorded them. When I remain aware of your nature I do not react to this quality as spying on mankind—rather as the total interest of a living loving heavenly father.

Express yourself in adoration for this quality of God.
Speak it audibly or write out your praise in your own devotional journal.

2. PRAISE GOD FOR WHAT HE MEANS TO ME.

Just for me. What a verse beyond description is Psalm 139:5! You are ahead of me searching out the hard places and smoothing them out for my feet. You are behind me gathering up the loose ends to weave a pattern of meaning out of what has happened. You are at present giving me immediate direction for my life. "Such knowledge is too wonderful for me." The words of Henry Ward Beecher are so full of meaning: "Before men we stand as opaque beehives. They see the thoughts go in and out of us, but what work they do inside of a man they cannot tell. Before God we are as glass beehives, and all that our thoughts are doing within us he perfectly sees and understands." Dear Lord, it is an awesome but true comparison!

How do you personally relate to God's total knowledge of each one of us?
Speak it out or write it out. It is *so important* that you establish *your own* devotional journal.

3. CONFESSION OF SIN

It is easy to pretend, but with you there is no pretense! You know my thoughts in the split second before they are transferred from my mind to the pen. You say the words before my tongue can form them. The unexpressed thoughts are also known by you. Such knowledge is surely beyond my grasp, but you are teaching me so much by your Omniscience and your Omnipresence. You are teaching me *honesty!* I do not at all want to record on this page the thoughts that have formed in my mind—but then I need not—for you read them before they are expressed. At the same time, I also know to find forgiveness I *must* pronounce them. I *must* take full responsibility for my sin. Indeed I do! I also claim your cleansing freedom.

What personal sins do you want to confess? We *must* speak them to remove them.
Do it! *Now.* There is no one else you have sinned against more than God. Tell him so!

4. SING A PRAYER TO GOD.

The consecrated cross I'll bear,
Till death shall set me free,

And then go home my crown to wear,
For there's a crown for me.

Open your hymn book and sing the rest of the verses—or even sing another prayer song.

5. READ HIS WORD TO HIM!

His Word

[34]When those tending the pigs saw what had happened, they ran off and reported this in the town and countryside, [35]and the people went out to see what had happened. When they came to Jesus, they found the man from whom the demons had gone out, sitting at Jesus' feet, dressed and in his right mind; and they were afraid. [36]Those who had seen it told the people how the demon-possessed man had been cured. [37]Then all the people of the region of the Gerasenes asked Jesus to leave them, because they were overcome with fear. So he got into the boat and left. [38]The man from whom the demons had gone out begged to go with him, but Jesus sent him away, saying, [39]"Return home and tell how much God has done for you." So the man went away and told all over town how much Jesus had done for him.
— *Luke 8:34-39, NIV*
Read also Mark 5:14-20; Matthew 8:33, 34.

Read His Word to Him.

Each time I approach you and your word and attempt to relate this to you I am stopped at the enormity of the work. At the same time, I am drawn irresistibly to attempt it. The herdsmen became spontaneous evangelists! How I wonder what portion of this incident they emphasized? Was it Jesus' power? Was it the man who was demon possessed? Was it the loss of their hogs? Whatever it was it was told in such a manner that the people of the town had to come and see for themselves. How much there is in this for each of us.

Please express your response to this beautiful text. Put your expression in your own prayer diary.

6. READ HIS WORD FOR YOURSELF.

Just for me. The people of the country of the Gerasenes saw and didn't see: (1) They saw a man seated at Jesus' feet clothed and in his right mind. (2) They perhaps saw the dead bodies of 2,000 hogs floating in the lake. (3) They saw the amazement on the faces of the herdsmen. But then they really didn't see: (1) The man behind the miracle, i.e., the real purpose for which the miracle was performed. (2) They didn't see the value of the one man as compared with 2,000 pigs. (3) They couldn't see the conflict of emotions that struggled in the hearts of the herdsmen. Perhaps some of them ultimately became Christians. At least we know some of the earliest churches were in this area.

It is so important that you pause in his presence
and either audibly or in written form tell him all his word means to you.

7. READ HIS WORD IN THANKSGIVING.

(1) Thank you for the obvious supernatural nature of the incident. (2) Thank you that no one can really be neutral in the presence of my Lord. (3) Thank you for the influence the healed man had on many. (4) Thank you for the fact that clothing and sanity are associated here with being whole. (5) Thank you for the fear or awe that took hold of the hearts of these people—it no doubt led some of them to an acceptance of our Lord's deity. (6) Thank you that the power of Jesus was so obviously supernatural that it left no room for doubt. (7) Thank you for the wonderful word of our Lord to the man who was healed: "Return home and tell how much God has done for you."

Give yourself to your own expression of gratitude—write it or speak it!

8. READ HIS WORD IN MEDITATION.

"So the man went away and told all over town how much Jesus had done for him." What a precious example this man is! Our Lord actually felt this man would serve him better by *not* following him. This man was so well known in his town as the wild man of the region that his deliverance would have a real effect on so many people. Evidently this deliverance was more than just the removal of evil. There was *much* our Lord had done for him. We want to try to enlarge on his words and mention several things our Lord did for him (and us): (1) Our Lord delivered this man from terrible loneliness. He had made his home among the tombs. We can hardly consider a more separated cut-off existence. (2) Jesus delivered him from rejection by God and men. He was delivering him into the warmth of others who also would accept our Lord. (3) He delivered him from hopelessness and a purposeless existence into a life of everlasting meaning. No wonder he he got all excited and told everyone that Jesus Christ is King!

Pause—wait—think—then express yourself in thoughtful praise or thanks.

9. READ HIS WORD FOR PETITIONS.

Suppose I was in the crowd of that day—I came out to see and returned home to pray: (1) It was more than remarkable to see the wild man well. I want to know the One who made him well. (2) What are the owners of the pigs worried about? Are not men of more value than many pigs? (3) I do not blame the man who was delivered—he wanted to go with Jesus—I would too. Send him my way again. (4) I am going to leave this place and follow him—I must hear what he says—I must be with him—direct my steps. (5) Does my family really know what great things you have done for me?

Right here add your personal requests—and his answers.

10. READ HIS WORD AND WAIT—LISTEN—GOD SPEAKS!

Thank you for what you have already said to me in this record—speak to me again: (1) "You have been delivered from eternal punishment—what does this mean to you?" (2) "My Son did not send the demons into the pigs—it was by his permission—but their choice." (3) "Superstition and reverence are not the same."

11. INTERCESSION FOR THE LOST WORLD

Arabian (Persian) Gulf States — Point for prayer: (1) *Unreached peoples*—specific mention must be made of the following: *Local Arabs*—very few have been clearly presented with the claims of the Gospel. *Baluchis* from Pakistan are many, but there are no Christian workers available to witness to these Muslim people in their own language. *Iranians*—very few of these Muslim people are Christian and little is done to win them for the Lord.

12. SING PRAISES TO OUR LORD.

Jesus is all the world to me,
My Friend in trials sore;
I go to Him for blessings, and He gives them o'er and o'er.
He sends the sunshine and the rain,
He sends the harvest's golden grain;
Sunshine and rain, harvest of grain,
He's my Friend.

WEEK FORTY-SEVEN — WEDNESDAY

1. PRAISE GOD FOR WHO HE IS.

"Whither shall I go from thy Spirit? Whither shall I flee from thy presence?" (Psalm 139:7). Here I am before you again full of amazement at this single attribute of yourself! *Your omnipresence!* There are surely mixed emotions clamoring for expresson as I contemplate this quality. (1) I am full of wonder that you have such a capacity. There is utterly nowhere that is apart from your presence. (2) We feel unclean and unworthy since we know you are holy and altogether worthy. (3) We feel exposed because we know you are seeing us as spirit beings and read our inmost thoughts. (4) We cry for forgiveness and cleansing for we want to remain before you in worship. (5) I am totally fascinated and want to stay here to learn all I can of your essential being.

Express yourself in adoration for this quality of God.
Speak it audibly or write out your praise in your own devotional journal.

2. PRAISE GOD FOR WHAT HE MEANS TO ME.

Just for me. The more I consider myself as standing in your presence the worse I feel. It is only as I turn the eyes of my heart to you that my sorrow turns to joy. Let me respond personally to the burning words of this verse: (1) I do indeed feel like the psalmist David! David ran from Saul and really could never find a hiding place without your help. So it is with me. Unless you hide me in cross of your dear Son—unless I find protection in his blood and righteousness I will be running frantically for cover all my life. (2) I am glad you have startled me out of my comfortable home and made me aware of yourself as the eternal king of all. This was the experience of David. He would never have appreciated the throne of Israel without the realization that Saul was seeking his life. You have sought my life to make me a king and a priest with you!

How do you personally relate to the pursuit of God, and God who wants to make us a king?
Speak it out or write it out. It is *so important* that you establish *your own* devotional journal.

3. CONFESSION OF SIN

Confession can be self-defeating if all that happens is an admission of my own failures and inabilities. Renewal along with the acceptance of forgiveness *must* be a part of my confession. Dear Lord, I am expressing the deepest thoughts of my heart in this prayer (it is redundant to say so). David had to look beyond his fleeing and beyond the fact he could not escape. David hid in the midst of a battle against his enemies. It is in the midst of the battle I shall find fulfillment. I have not changed the fact of your omnipresence, or of my weakness and vulnerability, but I have found release from the terrible tension of introspection. At the same time, I freely confess my hourly need of forgiveness. I claim your interest and investment in me! Make me all over new just now!

What personal sins do you want to confess? We *must* speak them to remove them.
Do it! *Now.* There is no one else you have sinned against more than God. Tell him so!

4. SING A PRAYER TO GOD.

Joy to the world! the Savior reigns;
Let men their songs employ;
While fields and floods, rocks, hills and plains

Repeat the sounding joy,
Repeat the sounding joy,
Repeat, repeat the sounding joy.

Open your hymn book and sing the rest of the verses—or even sing another prayer song.

5. READ HIS WORD TO HIM!

His Word

[21]When Jesus had again crossed over by boat to the other side of the lake, a large crowd gathered around him. While he was by the lake, [22]one of the synagogue rulers, named Jairus, came there. Seeing Jesus, he fell at his feet [23]and pleaded earnestly with him, "My little daughter is dying. Please come and put your hands on her so that she will be healed and live."
— Mark 5:21-23, NIV

Read His Word to Him.

What a beautiful scene greets our eyes as we read this text. Jesus is back in the district of Capernaum. Was there a conversation in the boat as they sailed the several miles? The progress across the lake was slower than now. I have had several conversations on the waters of this lovely Sea of Galilee. Is it possible to travel with him today and talk with him on the way? To ask is to answer. How I do want to open your word often today. I see the large crowd assemble on the shore even before he arrives. When Jesus steps on shore and begins to walk up from the lake a large crowd moves in around him. Dear Lord, I am in that crowd! While my Lord is still close to the shore a prominent man is pushing his way toward Jesus. Perhaps when several noticed who he was a way was opened for him that he might fall at Jesus' feet.

Please express your response to this beautiful text. Put your expression in your own prayer diary.

6. READ HIS WORD FOR YOURSELF.

Just for me. I see the earnestness and longing on his face as he says: "My little daughter is dying!" It *was* for their physical needs the crowds came. Even this wealthy prominent man came for this purpose. The needs of men and women are for the whole person. Dear Lord, how easy it is in this culture of plenty to forget this. Somehow, dear Lord, help me to relate as my Saviour did to these needs. Hear Jairus again: "Please come and put your hands on her so that she will be healed and live." The presence, the touch of Jesus was so much needed. How tragic that I want to operate by remote control. Send me to people to touch them to share their burdens and thus fulfill the example of my Lord.

It is so important that you pause in his presence
and either audibly or in written form tell him all his word means to you.

7. READ HIS WORD IN THANKSGIVING.

(1) Thank you for the popularity of my Lord—then and now. (2) Thank you that he is setting an example of ministering to man's whole need. (3) Thank you for the urgency found in paternal love. (4) Thank you that priorities become really clear in the face of life or death. (5) Thank you that Jesus is always ready and responsive. (6) Thank you that Jesus was so approachable. (7) Thank you for reminding me all over again of the real needs of real people.

Give yourself to your own expression of gratitude—write it or speak it!

8. READ HIS WORD IN MEDITATION.

"Please come and put your hands on her so that she will be healed and live." This could be the cry of every father in all the world who loves his daughter. Only our Lord has the answer for the sickness unto death. Jesus has no hands but our hands to do his work today. He has no feet, but our feet to walk in his way. He has no help, but our help to bring men to his side. He has no voice but ours to tell men that he died. The whole world is to be won, one family at a time. It is friend to friend, father to daughter, husband to wife relationship or it will never happen. Dear Lord, may the need of the daughters of men and your love constrain us to allow you to express your love through us.

Pause—wait—think—then express yourself in thoughtful praise or thanks.

9. READ HIS WORD FOR PETITIONS.

In this tender scene surely we can find areas for prayer: (1) Teach me that I might have the sensitive compassion Jesus gave to this synagogue ruler. (2) How is it that physical need always seems to take precedent? Perhaps because the needs of men are all homogenized. May I look on men through such a perspective. (3) It is good to fall at Jesus' feet with this ruler. I hope I can be as urgent as this one in my needs—help me. (4) We all either have a "little daughter" or had "a little daughter"—or know one—so we share with this man the urgency of his request. Will we learn the same lesson he did? I want to. (4) Jairus thought it was necessary for Jesus to touch his daughter to make her well. Only when we relate to Jesus in our conscience can he help us. I do want to so relate.

Please, please remember these are prayers—speak them—reword them!

10. READ HIS WORD AND WAIT—LISTEN—GOD SPEAKS!

As I read of the ruler's prayer I want to hear you speak to me: (1) "There is no little child I do not know and love." (2) "Kneel before me, I love you." (3) "I go with all who come to me in need.'"

11. INTERCESSION FOR THE LOST WORLD

Arabian (Persian) Gulf States — Point for prayer: (1) *The churches are growing* and a considerable number of Indians and Pakistanis are being won to the Lord. There are strong churches in Kuwait, Bahrain, Oman and U.A.E. Most of the churches are composed of some local Arab believers and many of the immigrant minorities—Indian, European, Jordanian, etc. Pray that the unity of the Spirit may be maintained in all this diversity. Pray that these believers may have a clear testimony to the non-Christians around them.

12. SING PRAISES TO OUR LORD.

O perfect redemption, the purchase of blood!
To ev'ry believer the promise of God;
The vilest offender who truly believes,
That moment from Jesus a pardon receives.
Praise the Lord, praise the Lord,
Let the earth hear His voice!
Praise the Lord, praise the Lord,
Let the people rejoice!
O come to the Father thro' Jesus the Son,
And give Him the glory—great things He hath done.

WEEK FORTY-SEVEN — THURSDAY

1. PRAISE GOD FOR WHO HE IS.

"If I ascend to heaven, thou art there. If I make my bed in Sheol, thou art there!" (Psalm 139:8). Such a lovely verse. There are several things said about you and all mankind in this one verse. (1) Heaven is apart from and different from this earth. Heaven is above for ascent is suggested. (2) Man can be separated from his body and yet retain his consciousness and identity. Sheol is the world of spirits or the unseen world after death. The psalmist is not suggesting an escape from God, he is only saying in poetic language that if he did want to escape he could not. Dear Lord, our escape is in you not apart from you! True freedom as well as unlimited understanding is in yourself—blessed be your name!

Express yourself in adoration for this quality of God.
Speak it audibly or write out your praise in your own devotional journal.

2. PRAISE GOD FOR WHAT HE MEANS TO ME.

Just for me. My Father, it is a pleasure to appear before you—or to address you as the all pervasive One—you are everywhere at the same time. Your total Being is present right here right now. Such an awesome thought! I cannot run from you without running into you. For how many years have I loved the beautiful words of Francis Thompson:

I fled Him, down the nights and down the day;
  I fled Him, down arches of the years;
I fled Him, down the labyrinthine ways
  Of my own mind; and in the midst of tears
I hid from Him, and under running laughter

Up vistaed hopes I sped;
  And shot, precipitated;
Adown Titanic glooms of chasmed fears,
From those strong Feet that followed, followed afar,
  But with unhurrying chase,
  And unperturbed pace,
Deliberate speed, majestic instancy,
  They beat, and a voice beat
  More instant than the Feet—
"All things betray thee, who betrayest Me."

How do you personally relate to the persistence of God, and to the pursuit of God?
Speak it out or write it out. It is *so important* that you establish *your own* devotional journal.

3. CONFESSION OF SIN

To suggest that I am not full of a deep sense of unworthiness as I consider your omnipresence—to say nothing of your omnipotence, would indeed be an absurdity! I fall before you like the four and twenty elders and cry "Holy, holy, holy, Lord God Almighty." Most of all and first of all I cry "Woe is me for I am undone." "I am a sinful man O Lord!" I name my particular transgressions of your law. But my sin is one of my life style—sin has become a contagion—a cancer. I am glad to be this moment forgiven and declared "just as if I had never sinned," but your forgiveness *must* include the next moment too. You must look upon me in grace at all times or there is no hope for me at all. I am glad you do! More than glad you do! Dear Lord, accept my poor stumbling words.

What personal sins do you want to confess? We *must* speak them to remove them.
Do it! *Now.* There is no one else you have sinned against more than God. Tell him so!

4. SING A PRAYER TO GOD.

Christ the Lord is ris'n today, Alleluia!
Sons of men and angels say: Alleluia!

Raise your joys and triumphs high, Alleluia!
Sing, ye heav'ns, and earth reply. Allelulia!

Open your hymn book and sing the rest of the verses—or even sing another prayer song.

5. READ HIS WORD TO HIM!

His Word

[24]So Jesus went with him.

A large crowd followed and pressed around him. [25]And a woman was there who had been subject to bleeding for twelve years. [26]She had suffered a great deal under the care of many doctors and had spent all she had, yet instead of getting better she grew worse. [27]When she heard about Jesus, she came up behind him in the crowd and touched his cloak, [28]because she thought, "If I just touch his clothes, I will be healed." [29]Immediately her bleeding stopped and she felt in her body that she was freed from her suffering.

[30]At once Jesus realized that power had gone out from him. He turned around in the crowd and asked, "Who touched my clothes?"

[31]"You see the people crowding against you," his disciples answered, "and yet you can ask, 'Who touched me?'"

[32]But Jesus kept looking around to see who had done it. [33]Then the woman, knowing what had happened to her, came and fell at his feet and, trembling with fear, told him the whole truth. [34]He said to her, "Daughter, your faith has healed you. Go in peace and be freed from your suffering."

— *Mark 5:24-34, NIV*

WEEK FORTY-SEVEN — THURSDAY

Read His Word to Him.

Because of the length of this text it will be well enough for me to read it several times to you with thought for every word. Dear Lord, I do want all you say here to become a part of me.

Please express your response to this beautiful text. Put your expression in your own prayer diary.

6. READ HIS WORD FOR YOURSELF.

Indeed, indeed! How beautifully typical is the experience of this woman. (1) Her request and contact with Jesus was parenthetical. It would seem that everyone is in a rush to go somewhere without us. How we can take heart that Jesus is never too busy to meet our need. (2) She had a problem that defied solution. For years she had tried unsuccessfully to solve it. This does so well describe our inward bleeding. (3) All men do is to make our problem worse and deplete our resources in their efforts to help. (4) The need will not decrease; it will increase. We shall and do grow worse and worse. (5) Someone told us about Jesus — nothing anyone could say could adequately describe his wondrous power. (6) She felt she *must* make some kind of *personal* contact with Jesus.

Pause in his presence and either audibly or in written form tell him all his word means to you.

7. READ HIS WORD IN THANKSGIVING.

(1) Thank you that a large crowd is no problem with Jesus. (2) Thank you there are no impossible cases with Jesus. (3) Thank you for the ministry of suffering. (4) Thank you for the seriousness of the need — it moves me to act. (5) Thank you that we need not be conventional in our approach to our Lord.

Give yourself to your own expession of gratitude — write it or speak it!

8. READ HIS WORD IN MEDITATION.

"Daughter, your faith has healed you. Go in peace, and be freed from your suffering." It was the healing power of Jesus that freed her from her suffering. It was the miracle of healing accompanied through her contact with our Lord. But it was also her faith in what our Lord could do, and in particular just who he was that set her free. Jesus was unable to heal in Nazareth (at least to the extent that he wanted to) because there were so few in his hometown who would accept his Messiahship. It is important to see that persons believed in him *before* the healing and the healing only became a visible evidence or confirmation of what they already believed. This dear woman believed Jesus was the Christ long before she touched him. Her healing settled her conviction for the rest of her life.

Pause — wait — think — then express yourself in thoughtful praise or thanks.

9. READ HIS WORD FOR PETITIONS.

It would seem the gospel accounts are almost a running commentary on how my Lord met human needs. This is such an encouragement to prayer: (1) This dear woman is only typical of all women who have some such physical need — not one lives and hurts without my Lord's knowledge. How I do want to encourage such to talk to my Lord. (2) Whereas we all appreciate doctors and their help to us we also recognize their limitations. Help me to encourage doctors in their good work. (3) For the wonderful daring faith of this woman I come to you. (4) Feelings are *not* everything but they *are* something. I want to feel in my body the healing of my whole being by Jesus. (5) Jesus responded to a feeling in his body — he identified it with human need. He is presently also "touched" with our needs. How encouraging this is to me. I pause in wonder!

Right here add your personal requests — and his answers.

10. READ HIS WORD AND WAIT — LISTEN — GOD SPEAKS!

As you found and spoke to the woman so I want to fall at your feet and hear you speak to me: (1) "I yet need to be told 'the whole truth' to make you whole." (2) "Freedom is acceptance of my Lordship." (3) "My eyes yet run to and fro over the whole earth to find someone like this woman."

11. INTERCESSION FOR THE LOST WORLD

Arabian (Persian) Gulf States — Point for prayer: (1) *Pray for new programs of outreach* being started for more effective evangelism. Pray for the effective use of house visitation, literature and personal work to win Muslims. There is now considerable interest in Christianity among educated Arab young people.

12. SING PRAISES TO OUR LORD.

We would see Jesus, the great rock foundation,
Whereon our feet were set by sov'reign grace;

Not life, nor death, with all their agitation,
Can thence remove us, if we see His face.

WEEK FORTY-SEVEN — FRIDAY

1. PRAISE GOD FOR WHO HE IS.

"If I take the wings of the morning and dwell in the uttermost parts of the sea, even there thy hand shall hold me" (Psalm 139:9, 10). Once again I stand back amazed. In this beautiful figure of speech the psalmist is sweeping up the expanse of the morning sunrise and like a bird he disappears in the burst of light on the horizon. He disappears from human sight, but when he arrives at that distant point in "the uttermost parts of the sea" there you are! It has been your presence that has charted his flight. Like a frightened bird in the hand of the owner so man finds himself. Here the figure must be left and the facts revealed: You hold us as intelligent beings capable of knowing how much you love us. You have found us to set us free!

Express yourself in adoration for this quality of God.
Speak it audibly or write out your praise in your own devotional journal.

2. PRAISE GOD FOR WHAT HE MEANS TO ME.

Just for me. I want always to remember my purpose in coming before you. It is to praise you for one or more of your characteristics. Just here I praise you for your omnipresence and omnipotence. Your omniscience is also a part of my adoration. Such qualities are related to two needs of my life: (1) My need for guidance, "thy hand shall lead me." Dear Lord, I hear you say to me that as I fly from your presence — aware or not, you are directing my flight. The unerring instincts you have created in birds is here a comparison of your constant interest and involvement in my life. (2) My need for comfort and protection, "thy right hand shall hold me." In whatever circumstances — even *now* I can look up and know you are encircling me with your loving personal interest! Praise your name.

How do you personally relate to the guidance of God, and God who is Protector?
Speak it out or write it out. It is *so important* that you establish *your own* devotional journal.

3. CONFESSION OF SIN

Surely it is not difficult to see who loses if I lose this sense of your presence. I have often taken the wings of the morning (or night) and have sought to dwell in the uttermost parts of someplace — anywhere but the place where I found myself. It wouldn't have been at all necessary if I had just awakened before I took flight. But how infinitely good you have been to me! Through all the wonderful means of grace, best known to you, you found me and awakened my heart to your love and concern. What a confession I must make! I have sinned — it was my sin I wanted to be lost! Forgive me. Tell me again of your love and acceptance. I love you.

What personal sins do you want to confess? We *must* speak them to remove them.
Do it! *Now.* There is no one else you have sinned against more than God. Tell him so!

4. SING A PRAYER TO GOD.

Nearer, still nearer, nothing I bring,
Naught as an off'ring to Jesus my King;
Only my sinful, now contrite heart,

Grant me the cleansing Thy blood doth impart,
Grant me the cleansing Thy blood doth impart.

Open your hymn book and sing the rest of the verses — or even sing another prayer song.

5. READ HIS WORD TO HIM!

His Word

[35]While Jesus was still speaking, some men came from the house of Jairus, the synagogue ruler. "Your daughter is dead," they said. "Why bother the teacher any more?"
[36]Ignoring what they said, Jesus told the synagogue ruler, "Don't be afraid; just believe."

[37]He did not let anyone follow him except Peter, James and John the brother of James. [38]When they came to the home of the synagogue ruler, Jesus saw a commotion, with people crying and wailing loudly.

— Mark 5:35-38, NIV

Read His Word to Him.

It is so good to read this text in your presence. I can know several realities in this lovely passage: (1) We are reminded that this tragedy happened to "a synagogue ruler." We are sure he must have asked himself many times "Why me?" — of all people surely God would be especially merciful to such a leading servant of worship. (2) We are introduced to the blunt hard fact of death. This sentence is never easy to write or hear: "Your daughter (or mother, or father, or wife, or husband) is dead." (3) We are told that even Jesus can do nothing about this desperate situation. (How often have we felt the same way?) (4) We are shocked and amazed as we see the attitude and hear the words of our Lord. Jesus ignored the words of death and said: "Don't be afraid; just believe." Have I represented the whole situation as it is? I want to.

Please express your response to this beautiful text. Put your expression in your own prayer diary.

WEEK FORTY-SEVEN — FRIDAY

6. READ HIS WORD FOR YOURSELF.

There *will be* a time when I must ask "Why me?" and I have an answer: "death came to all men." There are no exceptions. It is only in the choice of time that we have any variables. Whenever you decide my appointment has arrived I will be ready for the news. Indeed, from my viewpoint I have a great desire to depart the body and be at home with yourself. (2) I am so glad to know what death is: "To be absent from the body is to be at home with my Lord." (3) I want to be as blunt with those who came with the report of death as they were with the ruler. "Only Jesus — my teacher can do anything about this situation." I do believe — and even more than Jairus I believe. I *know* you will deliver all men from death even to die no more! Praise your wonderful name!

It is so important that you pause in his presence
and either audibly or in written form tell him all his word means to you.

7. READ HIS WORD IN THANKSGIVING.

(1) Thank you for the multiple testimony of the death of the daughter — it adds depth to the actions of my Lord. (2) Thank you for the note of finality and hopelessness we hear in the words: "Why bother the teacher any more?" It is just the contrast we need to appreciate the resurrection. (3) Thank you that our Lord ignores the pessimism of men. (4) Thank you for the assurance of Jesus that we need not fear death. (5) Thank you for the confidence Jesus placed in Peter, James and John — or was this the reason he asked them to accompany him? (6) Thank you for the obvious respect in which the ruler was held. (7) Thank you for the power of my Lord to turn tears to joy.

Give yourself to your own expression of gratitude — write it or speak it!

8. READ HIS WORD FOR MEDITATION.

"Don't be afraid; just believe." How full of application these words are for any and all situations! When our Saviour speaks we listen and when he addresses our particular need we give him our total attention. However in this situation it was not at all easy to turn the heart of the father from this scene of sorrow and death. He did have confidence in our Lord's power or he would never have left home to get him. While his daughter was sick, he felt there was hope, but now after she is dead what can be done? And yet there are the words of Jesus. How he does give us hope where there is no hope.

There are so many situations where we are afraid. When we open up his word and read what he has said we can hear our Lord say again to us: "Don't be afraid; just believe."

Pause — wait — think — then express yourself in thoughtful praise or thanks.

9. READ HIS WORD FOR PETITIONS.

Despair turns to hope and hope to life. How full of prayer possibilities. (1) My Lord was constantly interrupted — it didn't bother him — how I want to be like him. (2) Jesus had to ignore what seemed the obvious and the impossible. Show me where I should do the same. (3) In so many situations his words: "Don't be afraid; just believe" are sorely needed. When I face the death of a loved one; when there is a sharp disagreement with those near and dear; when a cherished plan has fallen through. (4) Why did Jesus want Peter, James and John with him? Perhaps they needed this reassurance. I am like them, I want to find strength from this experience.

Please, please remember these are prayers — speak them — reword them!

10. READ HIS WORD AND WAIT — LISTEN — GOD SPEAKS!

As you spoke to the ruler, to your followers and even to the dead, speak to me through this text: (1) "What seems dead is only awaiting my coming for life." (2) "Fear not; only believe." (3) "I see and hear all the commotion of life."

11. INTERCESSION FOR THE LOST WORLD

Arabian (Persian) Gulf States — Point for prayer: (1) *Pray for the Christians* who have gone to witness for Christ in a secular job. There are unlimited opportunities in this line for Western Christians where Western skills are so needed to develop these countries.

12. SING PRAISES TO OUR LORD.

Blessed assurance, Jesus is mine!
Oh, what a foretaste of glory divine!
Heir of salvation, purchase of God,
Born of His Spirit, washed in His blood.

This is my story, this is my song,
Praising my Saviour all the day long;
This is my story, this is my song,
Praising my Saviour all the day long.

WEEK FORTY-SEVEN — SATURDAY

1. PRAISE GOD FOR WHO HE IS.

"If I say, 'Let only darkness cover me, and the light about me be night,' even the darkness is not dark to thee, the night is bright as the day; for darkness is as light with thee" (Psalm 139:11, 12). How often indeed have I said these words of the psalmist. How often have all men wanted to "crawl in a hole and pull it in after them"? "Let me go somewhere and get lost, disappear." In marriage this is called "desertion"—in personal life it is called "escape." You let us know in these two verses that there really is no hiding from you—and we might add—from ourselves. You are saying something even more important: *"There is no darkness with you"*! Praise your name forever!

Express yourself in adoration for this quality of God.
Speak it audibly or write out your praise in your own devotional journal.

2. PRAISE GOD FOR WHAT HE MEANS TO ME.

Just for me. Dear Lord, if all I received from these verses was a knowledge of omniscience and omnipresence apart from a knowledge that you are love and goodness, I would cry out against you and curse you to your face! You are only telling me this to help me not to hide from myself. I cannot hide from you, but I *can* hide from men and from myself. You want me to work and worship in the night and the light. Oh, praise your lovely name and your eternal all-present person! Even when my senses tell me nothing of your presence, you are present. "Could my heart but see Creation (and all of life) as God sees it—from within: See his grace behind its beauty; see his will behind its force; see the flame of life shoot upward when the April days begin; see the wave of life rush outward from its pure eternal source"—I would no longer have a desire to hide. *(Edmond G. A. Holmes)*

How do you relate personally to the omnipesence of God, and God who sees everything?
Speak it out or write it out. It is *so important* that you establish *your own* devotional journal.

3. CONFESSION OF SIN

The reasons for hiding are guilt and fear. Your perfect love casts out my fear. It is not my perfect love, for I do not have it. It is also your perfect love that removes my guilt! Oh, wonder of all wonders, I need not hide! I can freely and openly show you all the sores of my leprous heart. You are not repulsed—you do not say, "Too bad, how sorry I am for you." You alone can do something for me. My Savior is known for touching lepers! My Lord reaches out to touch blind eyes and deaf ears. Even my sin, my blindness, my dull hearing. Somehow, beyond my poor understanding in the touch of forgiveness is also the touch of wholeness.

What personal sins do you want to confess? We *must* speak them to remove them.
Do it! *Now.* There is no one else you have sinned against more than God. Tell him so!

4. SING A PRAYER TO GOD.

Some day the silver cord will break,
And I no more as now shall sing;
But oh, the joy when I shall wake
Within the palace of the King!

And I shall see Him face to face,
And tell the story—Saved by grace;
And I shall see Him face to face,
And tell the story—Saved by grace.

Open your hymn book and sing the rest of the verses—or even sing another prayer song.

5. READ HIS WORD TO HIM!

His Word

[39]He went in and said to them, "Why all this commotion and wailing? The child is not dead but asleep." [40]But they laughed at him.

After he put them all out, he took the child's father and mother and the disciples who were with him, and went in where the child was. [41]He took her by the hand and said to her, "*Talitha koum!*" (which means, "Little girl, I say to you, get up!"). [42]Immediately the girl stood up and walked around (she was twelve years old). At this they were completely astonished. [43]He gave strict orders not to let anyone know about this, and told them to give her something to eat.

— Mark 5:39-43, NIV

Read His Word to Him.

What a wondrous record is this! How unusual are the words and actions of our Lord. He first confronts everyone with the fact of death of the daughter. Not all the mourners were of the family of the ruler; some of them were paid for mourning. Their pay depended on the child being dead—no wonder they laughed at the words of Jesus: "The child is not dead but asleep." They misunderstood his words. He said Lazarus was asleep but meant he was dead. Why did Jesus use such an expression? Was it because in death a person does indeed look as if someone could come and awaken them from their sleep?

Please express your response to this beautiful text. Put your expression in your own prayer diary.

6. READ HIS WORD FOR YOURSELF.

How tender and thoughtful are the actions and words of Jesus. All those who were not personally involved were put out. Jesus wanted Peter, James and John to learn of his deity and humanity from what he was about to do. Dear Lord, how I want to be a silent observer of all that is happening inside the home of Jairus. Let me look as closely as I can so as to catch every blessed message there is here: (1) They moved into the room where the dead body had been laid out. I do believe there has never been a gathering around the body of a loved one who has died in our Lord but that our Lord was also present. (2) He took her by the hand—and a cold dead hand it was—or was it? Not when Jesus touched it. (3) He spoke to her in a most loving manner—"Little girl, get up"! How beautifully poignant is all of this to me.

Pause in his presence and either audibly or in written form tell him all his word means to you.

7. READ HIS WORD IN THANKSGIVING.

(1) Thank you for Jesus' rebuke of those who grieve when he is present. (2) Thank you for the totally believable situation described by all three writers. (3) Thank you that with Jesus there is no death. (4) Thank you that Jesus does not want those present who will not understand. (5) Thank you that we can be present to understand and worship him. (6) Thank you for the personal interest in each of us given us by our Lord. (7) Thank you for the food taken by the little girl—evidence that she was completely restored.

Give yourself to your own expression of gratitude—write it or speak it!

8. READ HIS WORD IN MEDITATION.

"Then Jesus told them to give her something to eat." Eating, sleeping, walking, talking—all the very common pursuits of life were a real part of our Lord's concern. The humanness of the One who came as God is such an attractive quality. Several things were accomplished in this little gesture: (1) The completeness of the healing would be apparent. She was not weak and sick but well and strong. (2) It would give the parents and loved ones something they could do for their daughter. They all must have felt so very helpless in the presence of death. (3) It would place the little girl back in the mainstream of life and would remove some of the embarrassment that must have been a part of so much attention. How very thoughtful and kind was our Lord.

Pause—wait—think—then express yourself in thoughtful praise or thanks.

9. READ HIS WORD FOR PETITIONS.

In this astonishing miracle I can find much reason for prayer: (1) My Lord was full of wonderful surprises. I want to receive from him today. (2) Jesus, the Lord of life steps into the presence of death—how typical of his presence in us today. In the above statements I ask your perception. (3) What a kind, tender gesture it was for my Lord to take the mother and father with him into the presence of the dead. What they saw and heard they never forgot. Etch this scene upon my heart! (4) I wonder why Jesus did not call her by name? Is it not because he wanted all girls of this age to relate? (5) The miracles of Jesus were always so totally believable—she didn't get better; "she stood up and walked around." Lord, I believe. (6) Mark recorded this miracle that I might learn and believe—and teach it to others—fulfill your purpose in me.

Right here add your personal requests—and his answers.

10. READ HIS WORD AND WAIT—LISTEN GOD SPEAKS!

Speak to me: (1) "Many will never believe—some will never doubt." (2) "Perhaps you fit neither category." (3) "These things are written that you might believe."

11. INTERCESSION FOR THE LOST WORLD

Arabian (Persian) Gulf States — Point for prayer: (1) *Christian missions*—long years of pioneering work by the U.S. through medical and educational work has opened the lands for other missions. There are now about 80 Protestant missionaries serving the Lord. Most are using medical evangelism to reach the hearts of the people. There are now about 9 medical centers run by missions, and in all there is complete freedom to evangelize the patients. There is a critical need for dedicated Christian workers (especially men) to use the many opportunities. This is a wonderful opening for Arab missionaries. Pray for the health of missionaries working in this very hot and often humid climate. Pray for eternal fruit in a field that is unusually hard and discouraging.

12. SING PRAISES TO OUR LORD.

Let ev'ry kindred, ev'ry tribe
On this terrestrial ball,
To Him all majesty ascribe,
And crown Him Lord of all,
To Him all majesty ascribe,
And crown Him Lord of all!

WEEK FORTY-EIGHT — SUNDAY

1. PRAISE GOD FOR WHO HE IS.

"For thou didst form my inward parts, thou didst knit me together in my mother's womb. I praise thee, for thou art fearful and wonderful. Wonderful are thy works! Thou knowest me right well; . . ." (Psalm 139:13, 14). These precious words have been available for man's reading for more than 2,500 years. You set the laws of growth in operation and such laws carry out your will whether you are around or not. Like a machine on an assembly line. No, no, no! This is *not* the meaning of this text. You are in the act of creation all over again each time a child is formed in the womb of its mother. Like a weaver at a loom, like an artisan in his shop, like a doctor at work on the most delicate of an operation, so you are involved in the creation of every unborn child.

Express yourself in adoration for this quality of God.
Speak it audibly or write out your praise in your own devotional journal.

2. PRAISE GOD FOR WHAT HE MEANS TO ME.

Just for me. The qualities of yourself for which I praise you relate to your creative abilities. I have found some lovely words from one who worshiped you long ago. I want to make these words of *Andrew Fuller* mine. In your creation of man I am full of awe and wonder: "Man: how poor, yet how rich, how abject yet how august. Man: how complicated, how wonderful in your highest creation. How passing all wonder is the One who made him such. You have mingled such strange extremes of different natures, all marvelously mixed. How helpless, yet immortal, how like an insect yet infinite, as humble as a worm, yet a god — I tremble to consider your creation. Our life contains a thousand springs, and dies if one be gone: strange that a harp of a thousand strings should keep in tune so long."

How do you personally relate to the creation of God, and God who is our Creator?
Speak it out or write it out. It is *so important* that you establish *your own* devotional journal.

3. CONFESSION OF SIN

Dear Lord, I believe you have not left one man since you began your marvelous creation in the womb of his mother. It is not only the body that receives your concern, but the man himself. You are "the Father of the spirits of all men" (Num. 16:22; Heb. 12:5-8). Since this is true I claim your concern in the struggles of my every day. I am indeed full of fear or awe and wonder, but I also believe you know me so much better than I know myself. It is a relatively simple thing for me to confess my stupid mistakes. I hide nothing from you.

What personal sins do you want to confess? We *must* speak them to remove them.
Do it! *Now.* There is no one else you have sinned against more than God. Tell him so!

4. SING A PRAYER TO GOD.

Christ, the blessed One, gives to all,
Wonderful words of Life;
Sinner, list to the loving call,
Wonderful words of Life.
All so freely given,

Wooing us to Heaven:
Beautiful words, wonderful words,
Wonderful words of Life.
Beautiful words, wonderful words,
Wonderful words of Life.

Open your hymn book and sing the rest of the verses — or even sing another prayer song.

5. READ HIS WORD TO HIM!

His Word

[27] As Jesus went on from there, two blind men followed him, calling out, "Have mercy on us, Son of David!"

[28] When he had gone indoors, the blind men came to him, and he asked them, "Do you believe that I am able to do this?"

"Yes, Lord," they replied.

[29] Then he touched their eyes and said, "According to your faith will it be done to you"; [30] and their sight was restored. Jesus warned them sternly, "See that no one knows about this." [31] But they went out and spread the news about him all over that region.

— *Matthew 9:27-31, NIV*

Read His Word to Him.

How well these two men represent all of us today! The blind men had to depend on what others saw of the miraculous work of your Son. They were indeed those who not having seen yet believed. How abundant then must have been the evidence for their faith! They reached the obvious conclusion that even a blind man could see: Jesus was the Christ or "the Son of David." Our Lord apparently ignores these men and goes indoors. Why? Is it because such a proclamation was dangerous? This was Galilee where opposition to Romans was strong! Why did Jesus ask these men such an obvious question? i.e., wasn't it evident that they already had faith? Was it because he wanted them to examine their own heart? Jesus didn't want them to only repeat a popular opinion.

Please express your reponse to this beautiful text. Put your expression in your own prayer diary.

WEEK FORTY-EIGHT — SUNDAY

6. READ HIS WORD FOR YOURSELF.

Just for me. Ultimately each of us must meet Jesus all by himself. Our Lord wants to know from our own heart: "Do *you* believe that I am able to do this?" It is one thing to accept him in public; it is quite another to probe our own conscience and confess our personal faith in him. My dear Lord is ever asking me each day: "Do *you* believe I am able to help you teach this class?" "Do you believe I am able to solve the problem you have with this man or that woman?" "Do you believe I can supply the means of meeting this obligation or that?" Over the years it has indeed been done "according to my faith"—at the same time, more often it has been according to his mercy. Dear Lord, today I feel like asking you to again open my eyes to all you have for me.

It is so important that you pause in his presence
and either audibly or in written form tell him all his word means to you.

7. READ HIS WORD IN THANKSGIVING.

(1) Thank you for those who did not see yet believed. (2) Thank you for their persistence and boldness of faith. (3) Thank you for the personal encounter arranged by our Lord. (4) Thank you that Jesus will not let our faith stand on what others believe. (5) Thank you for the wonderful personal touch of my Lord in the blind areas of my life. (6) Thank you for the power of faith. (7) Thank you that my Lord always knew what he was doing and when it should be done.

Give yourself to your own expression of gratitude—write it or speak it! ·

8. READ HIS WORD IN MEDITATION.

"See that no one knows about this." When Jesus had just told the demoniac that he was to tell all he had done for him these words could sound strange. It obviously had to do with the region. In Gadara there was no danger of making him king, but in Galilee it was a different matter. Galilee was a hotbed of revolt against the Roman rule. In the mind of the patriotic Jew in Galilee the appearance of the Messiah was the appearance of deliverance from the Roman occupation. It would appear that even these blind men had a twisted view of his Lordship. When Jesus warned them sternly they should have heeded him. Their direct disobedience says something about their attitude. Their own predisposition toward the kind of rule the Messiah would bring was so strong they could not hear the words of Jesus.

Pause—wait—think—then express yourself in thoughtful praise or thanks.

9. READ HIS WORD FOR PETITIONS.

In these two blind men we can represent the whole human race: (1) All men must follow him in order to see—I am one of them. (2) It is indeed mercy that we need. (3) An acknowledgement of his deity is so important. How gladly I give it! (4) A personal encounter must be present to give us our sight! I bow before you—I open my ears. (5) A total confidence in his willingness and ability is essential—I have no question here. (6) "According to your faith will it be done to you." Faith comes by hearing and believing your word. What an opportunity we have for faith—may I take it! (7) Why was Jesus so stern in his command that no one know of what was done? I do want to know when to be silent.

Please, please remember these are prayers—speak them—reword them!

10. READ HIS WORD AND WAIT—LISTEN—GOD SPEAKS!

I am in constant need of healing for the eyes of my heart: (1) "In following me you will not walk in darkness but will have the light of life." (2) "Total trust opens your eyes." (3) "It is time to tell everyone about the One who healed you."

11. INTERCESSION FOR THE LOST WORLD

Arabian (Persian) Gulf States — Points for prayer: (1) *Christian Radio*—reception from Seychelles is now quite good. Pray that the daily Arabic broadcasts may bear fruit in the hearts of many. (2) *Christian literature*—there are little Christian bookstores in Kuwait, Oman, Bahrain and Abu Dhabi that are performing valuable service.

Israel — Population: 4,500,000. Points for prayer: (1) *The Jews in Israel* are more resistant to the Gospel than those of the Dispersion. Pray for this hardness to be removed. Pray for the removal of social and legal barriers to their conversion. (2) *Pray for the peace of Israel* and for all Arab and Israeli leaders in this critical time that there may be an equitable peace with justice for all peoples.

12. SING PRAISES TO OUR LORD.

'Twas grace that taught my heart to fear,
And grace my fears relieved;
How precious did that grace appear
The hour I first believed!

WEEK FORTY-EIGHT — MONDAY

1. PRAISE GOD FOR WHO HE IS.

"Thou knowest me right well; my frame was not hidden from thee, when I was being made in secret intricately wrought in the depths of the earth" (Psalm 139:14b, 15). It is with real happiness I come to praise you this day. The various facets of your omniscience are here under constant consideration. I can truly never exhaust the possibilities of relationship. I do open my heart in praise for your knowledge of my deepest needs. To say "thou

knowest me right well," seems a real understatement. When we remember it is your knowledge we know "right well" means every and all relationships of life. The term "frame" is a poetic description of the whole person. Even when to men's eyes all was hidden and too intricate to be defined and far away in the depths of the earth it was to you known "right well." Praise your name. It is comforting to rest in your absolute knowledge of my deepest needs.

Express yourself in adoration for this quality of God.
Speak it audibly or write out your praise in your own devotional journal.

2. PRAISE GOD FOR WHAT HE MEANS TO ME.

Just for me. What a marvel is the human body! What a marvel is *my* human body. Just the thought of what keeps me a resident in this house is worthy of praise and meditation. I know when you want me to separate from this tabernacle I shall leave. But while I am here what is it that keeps me here? We know that the body is dead when we leave it, but why do we remain? It would be easy to

say that the health of the body insures occupancy, but we all know persons whose health has fled but they remain. The house in which we live is so intricate that the most complicated of human machinery seem monstrously awkward in comparison. Just the movements and capabilities of the human eye is a testimony to your creative genius a million miles beyond human achievement.

How do you personally relate to the knowledge of God, and God who knows our frame?
Speak it out or write it out. It is *so important* that you establish *your own* devotional journal.

3. CONFESSION OF SIN

If I am so important to you that such thought and care is devoted to my creation, how is it that you are not *much* more important to me? How sad beyond words is our preoccupation with the house in which we live. We are so concerned about the place that we have forgotten the person—to not even mention the Creator. Dear Lord, forgive me! Even worse it is to proceed in my life as if I was

responsible for the creation of myself and all about me. The basic sin of man is to "play God." We all know what we think when one of our children begins to play daddy or mother. It can be a source of amusement as long as they are not teenagers or older. My dear Father Creator, I want to read your rules and accept your personal help in implementing them.

What personal sins do you want to confess? We *must* speak them to remove them.
Do it! *Now.* There is no one else you have sinned against more than God. Tell him so!

4. SING A PRAYER TO GOD.

Lord Jesus, look down from Thy throne in the skies,
And help me to make a complete sacrifice;
I give up myself, and whatever I know,

Now wash me, and I shall be whiter than snow.
Whiter than snow, yes, whiter than snow;
Now wash me, and I shall be whiter than snow.

Open your hymn book and sing the rest of the verses—or even sing another prayer song.

5. READ HIS WORD TO HIM!

His Word

[32]While they were going out, a man who was demon-possessed and could not talk was brought to Jesus. [33]And when the demon was driven out, the man who had been dumb spoke. The crowd was amazed and said, "Nothing

like this has ever been seen in Israel."
[34]But the Pharisees said, "It is by the prince of demons that he drives out demons."   — Matthew 9:32-34, NIV

Read His Word to Him.

It would seem that right after leaving the house of Jairus this incident occurred. Was this a response to the testimony of the two blind men? Did the multitude know of this hard case and bring him to Jesus as a test? Dear Lord, I wish I knew. There is something wonderfully intriguing about this man: (1) He was not insane—the whole multitude and all who knew him could say this. But there *was* something other than madness that troubled him. *It was a demon.*

(2) He was not physically unable to speak, i.e., his vocal chords were present and operative. There was something else that hindered him. *It was a demon.* (3) The whole crowd knew he was demon-possessed—the Pharisees agreed to this. Most of all, our Lord so identified his problem. I do want to try as much as possible to project myself into the circumstances of this text.

Please express your response to this beautiful text. Put your expression in your own prayer diary.

6. READ HIS WORD FOR YOURSELF.

Just for me. This encounter in the spirit world has serious lessons for me. It is so easy to not hear and to become dull of hearing. How I need to be reminded over and over again that Satan is real today. There are demons abroad in the land *now.* Real genuine spirit beings under the control of Satan do even *now* attack us and vie for our attention and interest. We *are not* saying that men are today possessed and held under demon power. At least demons have no such influence in the the lives of Christians. The important emphasis must not be with our association with demons but with our Lord. Do we feel our personal need of him? If we do we will come to him often and in the same attitude as this poor man who could not speak.

It is so important that you pause in his presence
and either audibly or in written form tell him all his word means to you.

7. READ HIS WORD IN THANKSGIVING.

(1) Thank you for the compassion of someone for the poor possessed man. (2) Thank you that the miracles of Jesus did accomplish their purpose in some lives. (3) Thank you for my Lord's present power over Satan today. (4) Thank you for the character of the miracle—it could not be denied by anyone. (5) Thank you for the superior quality of this miracle—better than anything anyone had seen. (6) Thank you for the cumulative effect the continuous miracles of Jesus was having. (7) Thank you that even the Pharisees associated our Lord's work with the spirit world.

Give yourself to your own expression of gratitude—write it or speak it!

8. READ HIS WORD IN MEDITATION.

"Nothing like this has ever been seen in Israel." We might add: or in any place else. Let's get a few things straight about who Jesus really is. He is, in human form, the visible image of the invisible Father. He is high above everything in creation, and, as a matter of fact, he made everything in the whole universe. The whole spirit world as well as the material world was made by him for his own use. He existed before everything he made and he still keeps it together. He's also the head of his spiritual body, the family. He created physical life; he created the new forever life—from death—and as we share that life with him, the whole universe will see that he is the true "Supreme Commander." In that human body was all the nature and power of the living God. The Father then took all that perfection and crucified him for every being in the dying universe to live in him. And we who were his enemies and in our minds hated him and were going our own way have been welcomed into his own family.

Pause—wait—think—then express yourself in thoughtful praise or thanks.

9. READ HIS WORD FOR PETITIONS.

Casting out a demon evokes thoughts for prayer: (1) Why are the organs of sense affected by demons? Deliver me from demonic attack even now. (2) It is good to see the disciples relating men beyond human help to my Lord. I carry one of these same kind to you now in prayer. (3) I wonder what were the first words of this man? The power of speech is such a blessing—may I use it to praise you! (4) The crowd was amazed—did it go any further? It does with me—deepen my awareness. (5) How is it that the greatest of great events is somehow overlooked? Lest I become only one of the crowd may I take the place of the man who was delivered.

Right here add your personal requests—and his answers.

10. READ HIS WORD AND WAIT—LISTEN—GOD SPEAKS!

Speak to me through these verses that I might speak for you. (1) "Until men are brought to me Satan has hindered their speech." (2) "The crowd is still waiting to praise me for my power through my Son." (3) "Do you really care that men are attacked by Satanic powers? Then show your concern."

11. INTERCESSION FOR THE LOST WORLD

Israel — Point for prayer: (1) *The legal position* is not helpful to believers or missions among the Jews. It is not allowed to seek the conversion of a young person without the written permission of the parents. The legal position of a Jew who becomes a Christian is very difficult. It is hard for the Protestant Churches to gain government recognition.

12. SING PRAISES TO OUR LORD.

Blessed assurance, Jesus is mine!
Oh, what a foretaste of glory divine!
Heir of salvation, purchase of God,
Born of His Spirit, washed in His blood.

This is my story, this is my song,
Praising my Saviour all the day long;
This is my story, this is my song,
Praising my Saviour all the day long.

WEEK FORTY-EIGHT — TUESDAY

1. PRAISE GOD FOR WHO HE IS.

"Thy eyes beheld my unformed substance; in thy book were written, every one of them, the days that were formed for me, when as yet there was none of them" (Psalm 139:16). Your creative genius and omnipotence are beautifully seen in this unusual verse. You see me as no one else ever has or could. Intent and intentional is your observation. It is easy for man to define the elements out of which our bodies are made—these are the same as those in the soil beneath our feet. "Dust thou art" is a scientific fact. But before there was a sculpture in the hand of the artist there was a picture in his mind, there was a desire in his heart. All the elements of man's whole being were recorded as well as every day he would live upon this earth. (This is not an easy verse for translation—dear Lord, is this what you are saying?)

Express yourself in adoration for this quality of God.
Speak it audibly or write out your praise in your own devotional journal.

2. PRAISE GOD FOR WHAT HE MEANS TO ME.

Just for me. Your wonderful intimate personal interests in me are most clearly stated. How I rejoice in your involvement in my life while I was still in the womb of my mother. When you sent spirit into the embryo of the unformed fetus you knew the reaction or response of the union of spirit and that genetic combination. In your book was written a full description of myself before I was ever born. The number of days for my life were also there recorded. All of this is a total amazement to me; I stand back with my head and heart bowed before you in praise and wonder.

How do you personally relate to the foreknowledge of God, and God who knew us before we were born?
Speak it out or write it out. It is *so important* that you establish *your own* devotional journal.

3. CONFESSION OF SIN

How often do I think these thoughts? Dear Lord, you know it is not as often as it should be! How aware am I that all of my life is in your hands? How fragile and temporary is my life. In the same breath I can say my life is full of your very self! That I should spend so much time and thought on the house and neglect both the occupant and the Maker is one of the mysteries of the evil one. Dear Lord, deliver me! Open the eyes of my heart! Since my days are numbered and limited, give me the grace and chastening to use them as one who knows at least from whence they came!

What personal sins do you want to confess? We *must* speak them to remove them.
Do it! *Now.* There is no one else you have sinned against more than God. Tell him so!

4. SING A PRAYER TO GOD.

Jesus is all the world to me,
My Friend in trials sore;
I go to Him for blessings,
And He gives them o'er and o'er.

He sends the sunshine and the rain,
He sends the harvest's golden grain;
Sunshine and rain, harvest of grain,
He's my Friend.

Open your hymn book and sing the rest of the verses—or even sing another prayer song.

5. READ HIS WORD TO HIM!

His Word

6 Jesus left there and went to his home town, accompanied by his disciples. ²When the Sabbath came, he began to teach in the synagogue, and many who heard him were amazed.
— Mark 6:1, 2a, NIV

⁵⁴Coming to his home town, he began teaching the people in their synagogue, and they were amazed. "Where did this man get this wisdom and these miraculous powers?"
— Matthew 13:54, NIV

Read His Word to Him.

Amazement of all amazements! The young boy who grew up in the carpenter's shop and lived with us for years is now become a popular teacher and miracle worker! When our Lord returned, followed by his twelve apostles and possibly other disciples, what a commotion must have occurred in Nazareth. His brothers and sisters no doubt crowded around him and were full of questions. What poignancy must have filled the heart of his mother. He must have stayed a day or two before the Sabbath day arrived and then he went to the synagogue service. What a rare privilege it was to hear him teach. What profound thoughts were presented that Sabbath day in the little synagogue in Nazareth!

Please express your response to this beautiful text. Put your expression in your own prayer diary.

WEEK FORTY-EIGHT – TUESDAY

6. READ HIS WORD FOR YOURSELF.

Just for me. Have I become so familiar with Jesus that I like those in his hometown really do not know him? It *is* possible. Dear Lord, forgive me. Why did Jesus return to his home? Was it to give his friends and relatives and all the townsfolk one last chance? I believe it was. How easy it is to allow unrelated matters to deafen our ears and close our eyes! There was no question as to the amaz-ing wisdom by which he taught. There was no denying the multiplied miracles he had performed throughout Galilee. No one said a word about sinless conduct. And yet—he was only the carpenter's son; we know his mother, brothers and sisters. They knew him and they did not know him. How is it with me?

It is so important that you pause in his presence
and either audibly or in written form tell him all his word means to you.

7. READ HIS WORD IN THANKSGIVING.

(1) Thank you for the popularity of our Lord that followed him even to Nazareth. (2) Thank you for his devoted followers who came with him. (3) Thank you for all of the tender associations that must have crowded his mind as he again walked the streets of the city. (4) Thank you for the unknown renewal of acquaintances that must have occurred before the Sabbath. (5) Thank you for Jesus' wisdom in placing his two visits to Nazareth nine months apart. (6) Thank you for my Lord's custom of attending the public services. (7) Thank you that I can be amazed all over again at the wisdom of my Lord.

Give yourself to your own expression of gratitude—write it or speak it!

8. READ HIS WORD IN MEDITATION.

"*. . . and many who heard him were amazed.*" This is on a home town level. We wonder if Joseph or his brothers were present. Somehow they could not overcome the familiarity of previous association. Even their amazement was superficial. Is it at all possible that we have become so familiar with the records of his life that we too are only mildly amazed? Were the men in the synagogue in Nazareth really listening when he spoke? Did they *really* know him? The very thing they claimed is what they did not have. They knew his family, i.e., by name and where they lived, but they had not taken the time to really get acquainted with our Lord. It takes time and undivided attention to learn from him or about him. Surely he merits a priority of time and thought.

Pause—wait—think—then express yourself in thoughtful praise or thanks.

9. READ HIS WORD FOR PETITIONS.

I want to be a silent observer in that synagogue and be led to prayer: (1) Dear Lord, I would like to make all my associates a welcome committee for you. (2) How can I better make you feel "at home" in me? (3) Isn't it too bad we do not have what he taught that day in the synagogue? —perhaps we do in the rest of the record. (4) I want the amazement that filled the hearts of these people. (5) I ask in faith for the wisdom I so sorely need in teaching your word today. (6) I want to examine the miracles of my Lord again that I might learn all there is of his deity. (7) Did those who asked about the source of his wisdom and power ever get an answer?

Please, please remember these are prayers—speak them—reword them!

10. READ HIS WORD AND WAIT—LISTEN—GOD SPEAKS!

Speak to me through your Son: (1) "I am still teaching those who will listen." (2) "You now know the answer to their question." (3) "Accept in your conscience what I am saying to you."

11. INTERCESSION FOR THE LOST WORLD

Israel — Point for prayer: (1) *The Hebrew Christians* are considered almost traitors to their nation, and suffer ostracism and some discrimination from other Jews. There are about four Hebrew assemblies that meet on an inter-denominational basis, and some other believers that fellow-ship with some of the many small mission groups. Some of the latter are all too ready to "sponsor" promising believers—often not for the best motives. Pray for the planting of strong independent churches all over the country.

12. SING PRAISES TO OUR LORD.

Come, Thou Almighty King,
Help us Thy name to sing,
Help us to praise.
Father, all glorious,

O'er all victorious,
Come, and reign over us,
Ancient of Days.

WEEK FORTY-EIGHT — WEDNESDAY

1. PRAISE GOD FOR WHO HE IS.

"How precious to me are thy thoughts, O God! How vast is the sum of them! If I would count them, they are more than the sand. When I awake, I am still with thee. (Were I to come to the end I would still be with thee.) (Psalm 139:17, 18). It is with eager anticipation I enter your presence. I am so glad to be able to express praise for all you have said in your word. And yet such words are only the smallest fraction of your thoughts. When we take time and thought to concentrate on any branch of your creative genius we are startled at the intelligence behind such design and purpose. But when we refer to your thoughts concerning our lives it is then we must prostrate ourselves before you in silent amazement!

Express yourself in adoration for this quality of God.
Speak it audibly or write out your praise in your own devotional journal.

2. PRAISE GOD FOR WHAT HE MEANS TO ME.

Just for me. It would seem David was in a dream, or he thought of himself as dreaming and in the dream he was capable of counting your thoughts. Even if somehow he succeeded in this impossible endeavor when he awoke he would yet be in the presence of the source of an equal number. To remember that God expends immeasurable energy is one incredible concept! The whole galaxy and millions like the one of which we are a part are all for man's enjoyment. The vast complexity of the earth is here to exercise and expand the spirit of man. How costly and how valuable are your thoughts; how precious is your perpetual attention.

How do you personally relate to the mind of God, and God who is total knowledge?
Speak it out or write it out. It is *so important* that you establish *your own* devotional journal.

3. CONFESSION OF SIN

That you should think of me so often and I should think of you so seldom is a sin of giant magnitude! It would be impossible to convince my dear wife that I loved her if my thoughts were never upon her welfare or were never expressed in deeds or words. Dear Lord, in this one area I find the solution for all my needs! To return the concern you have for me is to relate you to all of my life all the time. How powerful are your words: ". . . his delight is in the law of the Lord, and on his law (and the Lawmaker) he meditates day and night.

What personal sins do you want to confess? We *must* speak them to remove them.
Do it! *Now.* There is no one else you have sinned against more than God. Tell him so!

4. SING A PRAYER TO GOD.

No more let sins and sorrows grow,
Nor thorns infest the ground;
He comes to make His blessings flow

Far as the curse is found,
Far as the curse is found,
Far as, far as the curse is found.

Open your hymn book and sing the rest of the verses — or sing another prayer song.

5. READ HIS WORD TO HIM!

His Word

[54]Coming to his home town, he began teaching the people in their synagogue, and they were amazed. "Where did this man get this wisdom and these miraculous powers?" they asked. [55]"Isn't this the carpenter's son? Isn't his mother's name Mary, and aren't his brothers James, Joseph, Simon and Judas? [56]Aren't all his sisters with us? Where then did this man get all these things?" [57]And they took offense at him.

But Jesus said to them, "Only in his home town and in his own house is a prophet without honor."
[58]And he did not do many miracles there because of their lack of faith.
— *Matthew 13:54-58, NIV*

"Where did this man get these things?" they asked. "What's this wisdom that has been given him, that he even does miracles! [3]Isn't this the carpenter? Isn't this Mary's son and the brother of James, Joses, Judas and Simon? Aren't his sisters here with us?" and they took offense at him.

[4]Jesus said to them, "Only in his home town, among his relatives and in his own house is a prophet without honor." [5]He could not do any miracles there, except lay his hands on a few sick people and heal them. [6]And he was amazed at their lack of faith.
— *Mark 6:2b-6a, NIV*

Read His Word to Him.

What a privilege beyond all privileges to read these words in your presence. Here I see and sense the response men gave to your dear Son. If this passage touches my heart I know you are even more involved. Wasn't the answer to their question obvious? Our Lord's wisdom was so superior to anything they had heard before that heaven must be its source. The mighty miracles were of such a nature and were so numerous that no one could miss their origin—or could they? Perhaps it was your Son's insist-ence that they accept or reject—honor or refuse to honor him. Dear Lord, you are speaking to me in these words. Give me the faith to accept his Lordship.

Please express your response to this beautiful text. Put your expression in your own prayer diary.

6. READ HIS WORD FOR YOURSELF.

Just for me. It *is* a strange circumstance: Those who should have known him best—and even thought they did—did not. Did Jesus discuss his mighty works? There were thousands to testify to the truthfulness of his words. At least they should have seen God behind the words he spoke. The teachings of my Lord are so superior to all the words of men that only a contrast appears as we relate them. It strikes me again and again how very common were the names used here. How many men were called James in the days of our Lord? We have four such persons in the New Testament accounts. Joseph and Simon and Judas are also very ordinary names. Perhaps we lose him as they did in the humbleness of the package for God's gift.

Pause in his presence and either audibly or in written form tell him all his word means to you.

7. READ HIS WORD IN THANKSGIVING.

(1) Thank you for heaven's wisdom in the life and words of my Lord. (2) Thank you for the fact that Jesus was indeed the adopted son of a carpenter. (3) Thank you for the patient consistent example of Mary. (4) Thank you for the epistle of James that teaches me that faith that does not act—even as James had when he lived with Jesus—is of no value. (5) Thank you for the epistle of Jude that teaches me to "contend for the faith"—which is hardly what Jude did until after the resurrection. (6) Thank you for the un-named sisters of my Lord—I would like to believe they accepted him as so many do today. (7) Thank you that your prophet can have today the honor he did not have in Nazareth.

Give yourself to your own expression of gratitude—write it or speak it.

8. READ HIS WORD IN MEDITATION.

"And he did not do many mighty works there, because of their unbelief." What a sad commentary on human nature! Until or unless someone fits into our presupposition we will not accept him. It needs to be emphasized here that our Lord expected the Nazarenes to believe on him before and without the miracles. "Faith comes by hearing and hearing of the *words* of Christ." It does cause us to wonder why he did *any* mighty works in his home town if such unbelief prevailed. There are always a few who will believe. Praise God for those few persons who had the courage to believe against popular opinion.

Pause—wait—think—then express yourself in thoughtful praise or thanks.

9. READ HIS WORD FOR PETITIONS.

How could those who were "his own" take offense at him? (1) How humble an estimate: "the carpenter's son." He was and he wasn't—help me to understand both con-cepts. (2) My Lord was one of the crowd—an ordinary citizen of Nazareth. Dear Lord, I want to be like him. (3) How I wish I could have shared a meal or two in the home of Mary and Joseph. It is wonderful to consider that Jesus can share every meal with me! (4) I want to read again the words of James and Jude (Judas) the half-brothers of my Lord. I want to get behind the words of the writers. (5) I would like to know the names of the sisters of Jesus. I believe I have met some. Keep me aware of his definition of just who are his relatives.

Right here add your personal requests—and his answers.

10. READ HIS WORD AND WAIT—LISTEN—GOD SPEAKS!

You did not have the ears or the hearts of those in Nazareth—but you have mine—speak to me: (1) "Faith both precedes and succeeds signs." (2) "The principle still holds for some teachers and preachers today."

11. INTERCESSION FOR THE LOST WORLD

Israel — Point for prayer: (1) *The Arab believers* have some fine, lively fellowships in Jerusalem and Galilee with a considerable outreach. Pray for their witness in the present difficult political situation. Pray for a greater outreach to the less evangelized West Bank, and especi-ally the 350,000 Palestinians in the Gaza Strip. Pray for closer links between the Hebrew and Arab believers.

12. SING PRAISES TO OUR LORD.

I love Thy Kingdom, Lord,
The house of Thine abode,

The Church our blest Redeemer saved
With His own precious blood.

WEEK FORTY-EIGHT — THURSDAY

1. PRAISE GOD FOR WHO HE IS.

"Search me, O God, and know my heart! Try me and know my thoughts! And see if there be any wicked (hurtful) way in me, and lead me in the way everlasting" (Psalm 139:23, 24). Dear Lord, I make the words of the poet *James Montgomery* my prayer to you:

Searcher of hearts, to thee are known
The inmost secrets of my breast;

At home, abroad, in crowds, alone,
Thou mark'st my rising and my rest,
My thoughts far off, through every maze,
Source, stream, and issue — all my ways.

What I say of myself I say for all. It is one awesome thought to invite you to so search me! Requested or not such is your power and prerogative.

Expresss yourself in adoration for this quality of God.
Speak it audibly or write out your praise in your own devotional journal.

2. PRAISE GOD FOR WHAT HE MEANS TO ME.

Just for me. Only you can know my heart. When I feel I have discovered the last room in my heart I suddenly stumble on a door that opens into a whole undiscovered area. I *want* you to search me. I do not want one hurtful thing in my heart. There are three I can hurt — yourself, others or myself. David was so concerned that there be no rebellion in his heart against you as his king. This too is my concern. This is offered as a praise to the quality of your nature that immediately makes us introspective, i.e., your omniscience. Because of the great deceiver it is essential that we often refer to this quality of yourself.

How do you personally relate to the searching of God, and God who knows your heart?
Speak it out or write it out. It is *so important* that you establish *your own* devotional journal.

3. CONFESSION OF SIN

To praise you for your ability to know us even better than we know ourselves is to confess our sins. I want to remember that unless there was something of value there would be no search. It was a *son* who was lost. It was a *Son* who was sent to save. Both were precious to the Father — and the Father was the same in both examples.

When you do find wickedness or hurtfulness in me, what will you do with it? It is as if you had found the spot under the yoke that had hurt for so long — you now apply the healing balm and remove the hurt.

What personal sins do you want to confess? We *must* speak them to remove them.
Do it! *Now.* There is no one else you have sinned against more than God. Tell him so!

4. SING A PRAYER TO GOD.

Christ, the blessed One, gives to all,
Wonderful words of Life;
Sinner, list the loving call,
Wonderful words of Life.
All so freely given,

Wooing us to Heaven:
Beautiful words, wonderful words,
Wonderful words of Life.
Beautiful words, wonderful words,
Wonderful words of Life.

Open your hymn book and sing the rest of the verses — or even sing another prayer song.

5. READ HIS WORD TO HIM!

His Word

[35]Jesus went through all the towns and villages, teaching in their synagogues, praching the good news of the kingdom and healing every disease and sickness. [36]When he saw the crowds, he had compassion on them, because they were harassed and helpless, like sheep without a shepherd. [37]Then he said to his disciples, "The harvest is plentiful but the workers are few. [38]Ask the Lord of the harvest, therefore, to send out workers into his harvest field."
— *Matthew 9:35-38, NIV*

Read His Word to Him.

How delighted I am to read this word to you. I want to see your dear Son as he tramped up the incline of this town or walked down the hill to another village in Galilee. How many synagogues did he enter? I know not one is missing in your knowledge. Not one lesson was taught that has not been recorded in heaven. The good news of your rule in the lives of men was the message of your Son. How I want to receive such rule as *good news*. It is more than startling to read these words . . . "healing *every* disease and *every* infirmity." There were no impossible cases with him. Since Jesus is alive at your right hand and sees not the few people of the hills of Galilee but the whole wide teeming multitude of this world — and *he sees each one* — how *much more* do his words mean today, "sheep without a shepherd — harassed and helpless." Dear Lord, open my eyes!

Please express your response to this beautiful text. Put your expression in your own prayer diary.

6. READ HIS WORD FOR YOURSELF.

Just for me. I hesitate to read these words! I cannot bear to open my heart and receive them, but I must. Dear Lord, you have no one else today but each of us who love you: "The harvest is plentiful, but the laborers are few." I am so glad Jesus described you as "the Lord of the harvest." It would seem from the way we act and think that we fancy ourselves the harvest Lord. You also described us with that powerful word: *"laborers."* Until we have taught someone we have not worked for you. Yes, yes, there are various ways of teaching, but teaching we *must* do. Unless we have watered what we have taught (planted) we are not your laborers. There are times when we do indeed need to "dig around" the soil of the heart of those who have been planted and watered. Dear Father, I want to hear it again: "He that soweth bountifully shall reap bountifully." There are such wide needy fields. Open my heart and mouth!

Pause in his presence and either audibly or in written form tell him all his word means to you.

7. READ HIS WORD IN THANKSGIVING.

(1) Thank you for the general and specific interest my Lord has in men. (2) Thank you that Jesus was a preacher. (3) Thank you that Jesus used the synagogue as a place of worship even when it was not "a house you built." (4) Thank you my Lord was also a teacher. (5) Thank you for the unlimited power of healing present in your Son. (6) Thank you that I can be a citizen of the kingdom he described. (7) Thank you I can be that laborer for which he asked us to pray.

Give yourself to your own expression of gratitude—write it or speak it!

8. READ HIS WORD IN MEDITATION.

"Pray therefore the Lord of the harvest . . ." How beautifully unique are all the words of my Lord! Wouldn't it be much more natural to say: "Enter into the harvest field"? Why pray? Because our heavenly Father is the only one we know who knows all about the total process of harvest. Another very large reason has to do with the harvester: If we put our labor with people on a divine level, i.e., we truly pray about it, the possibilities of our continuing and being fruitful are so much higher. Is the harvest still plentiful and are the laborers yet few? To ask is to answer. Both the harvest and the laborers are enlarged immeasurably and in both directions: we have four billion people on earth and so very few laborers. At the same time, the means of harvesting are so much more manageable. We now can reach every person on earth so much easier. There is also an equally greater need for prayer.

Pause—wait—think—then express yourself in thoughtful praise or thanks.

9. READ HIS WORD FOR PETITIONS.

This is indeed an all encompassing statement of his work. There is much to pray about in it: (1) Dear Lord, I do not believe it is your will that even one village in this world be without the teaching of your Son. How, oh how, can I help? (2) Keep me always aware that what I have to offer is "good news of the kingdom." (3) How amazing that Jesus healed *every disease and sickness."* This really says something about his compassion and power—open my heart to receive it. (4) Sheep are stupid animals—how like us—Gentle Shepherd lead us, chasten us. (5) Dear Lord, I want to take up your solution for workers for your harvest. Teach me to really pray this prayer.

Please, please remember these are prayers—speak them—reword them!

10. READ HIS WORD AND WAIT—LISTEN—GOD SPEAKS!

Since the workers are still so few I need to hear you in meeting this need: (1) "My compassion comes to men through you." (2) "If you pray I will send." (3) "The harvest is greater and whiter than it has ever been."

11. INTERCESSION FOR THE LOST WORLD

Israel — Points for prayer: (1) *The hostile environment for both Arab and Hebrew believers with limited opportunities for the future tempts many to leave the country.* Many young people emigrate and the witness they could bear is lost. (2) *A large proportion of the Israelis have immigrated* from countries all over the world. Each group comes to Israel with its own language and culture and each must be reached with the Gospel in a meaningful way. Especially needy are the over 120,000 (often atheistic) Jews now coming from Russia, where they are suffering considerable persecution. Pray for the reaching of these *Immigrant Jews.*

12. SING PRAISES TO OUR LORD.

Come, we that love the Lord,
And let our joys be known;

Join in a song with sweet accord,
And thus surround the throne.

WEEK FORTY-EIGHT – FRIDAY

1. PRAISE GOD FOR WHO HE IS.

"O Lord, my Lord, my strong deliverer, thou hast covered my head in the day of battle" (Psalm 140:7). Every day is indeed a battle to be fought. The hand-to-hand combat of David's day presents a very good metaphor in our fight with Satan and his forces. There is so much in this one verse descriptive of all you are and do for each of us each day: (1) The movements of our forces are under your control. We pause just now to ask for your strategy.

We ask in confidence of your interest in our fight. We ask aware that the movement will seem to be our choice and our effort, but aware all the while that *you are the deliverer.* (2) You are our armor-bearer. It was the task of David's armor-bearer to do this, i.e., to cover his king's head in the battle. You can and do guard our thoughts and move both the will and the choice—praise your name —I claim such help for today's battle.

Express yourself in adoration for this quality of God.
Speak it audibly or write out your praise in your own devotional journal.

2. PRAISE GOD FOR WHAT HE MEANS TO ME.

Just for me. As in the above expression I have become a large part of it. Even so there is so much more I want to say in praise of your presence in the thick of every encounter. (3) You make yourself responsible for a knowledge of the enemy's moves. Surely I am no match for Satan. If even Michael the archangel did not want to personally encounter him (Jude 9, 10) who am I to engage him in

hand-to-hand combat? (4) You ask me to do all I can in the fight but recognize you are there deflecting Satan's blows and covering me with your love and personal concern. Dear Lord, how I do hide behind this shield of faith! (5) What a mutual respect and love grows between the warrior and his armor-bearer. Yea, when I know who he is I gladly give him all the credit for every victory.

How do you personally relate to the deliverance of God, and God who is our Deliverer?
Speak it out or write it out. It is *so important* that you establish *your own* devotional journal.

3. CONFESSION OF SIN

It surely seems incongruous that in the midst of the promises of conquest we admit defeat! But such is the record of our life. We do not really lose *any* battle in which you are accepted as a companion in the fight! The only battles I have lost have been those I engaged in the loneliness of my own selfishness. The strategy of triumph is as clear as I could ever want it. (1) Admit I cannot win

by myself. (2) Ask for your presence—claim and identify your presence when once I ask. (3) Confess my sin and failure. (4) Ask your forgiveness—essentially I am asking forgiveness for trying to fight alone. (5) Take up the sword of the Spirit and the shield of faith—fully aware of who fashioned the sword, and in whom my faith is placed. Help me, dear Lord.

What personal sins do you want to confess? We *must* speak them to remove them.
Do it! *Now.* There is no one else you have sinned against more than God. Tell him so!

4. SING A PRAYER TO GOD.

A mighty fortress is our God,
A bulwark never failing;
Our helper He, amid the flood
Of mortal ills prevailing.
For still our ancient foe

Doth seek to work us woe;
His craft and pow'r are great,
And, armed with cruel hate,
On earth is not his equal.

Open your hymn book and sing the rest of the verses—or even sing another prayer song.

5. READ HIS WORD TO HIM!
His Word

[35]While Jesus was still speaking, some men came from the house of Jairus, the synagogue ruler. "Your daughter is dead," they said. "Why bother the teacher any more?"
[36]Ignoring what they said, Jesus told the synagogue ruler, "Don't be afraid; just believe."

[37]He did not let anyone follow him except Peter, James and John the brother of James. [38]When they came to the home of the synagogue ruler, Jesus saw a commotion, with people crying and wailing loudly.

— Mark 5:35-38, NIV

Read His Word to Him.

How wonderfully touching are all these words! Gladly do I walk with your Son to the house of Jairus. I see the disappointed anxiety on the face of those who say, "Your daughter is dead. Why trouble the Teacher any further?" I see also the stricken ruler as he bows his head. And

then the penetrating quiet words of Jesus—spoken directly to Jairus—"Do not fear, only believe." He is asking for the ruler to believe him against what he sees all about him.

Please express your response to this beautiful text. Put your expression in your own prayer diary.

WEEK FORTY-EIGHT — FRIDAY

6. READ HIS WORD FOR YOURSELF.

Just for me. How I do hope I represented just what happened, and somewhat from your perspective. I want to go again to the house of mourning. Dear Lord, it seems more than a coincidence that this weekend I have stood by the bed of a twelve-year-old girl who had just died. How I longed to be able to take her by the hand and say "Talitha cumi" or "Little girl, I say to you arise." But I stood as silent and sad as the mother and father. Praise your name there will be a day when our Lord will say to all little girls and boys—"Arise"—and to all old men and women: "Arise"—and to all that who have died, "Arise." Immediately on that glad resurrection morning all will get up and those who are his will be given something wonderful to eat at the marriage supper for the bride of Christ. Praise your name forever.

It is so important that you pause in his presence
and either audibly or in written form tell him all his word means to you.

7. READ HIS WORD IN THANKSGIVING.

(1) Thank you for facing the reality and finality of death. (2) Thank you that Jesus can ignore any and all discouraging words of men. (3) Thank you my dear Lord removes all fear and doubt. (4) Thank you for the thoughtfulness of Jesus in meeting the needs of Peter, James and John. (5) Thank you that even Jesus wept at the loss of loved ones. (6) Thank you that Jesus can always change weeping to rejoicing. (7) Thank you for the One who said "I am the resurrection and the life, he who believes in me, though he die, yet shall he live."

Give yourself to your own expression of gratitude—write it or speak it!

8. READ HIS WORD IN MEDITATION.

"The child is not dead but sleeping." What a beautifully kind description of the death of the body. How glad we are for the clear definition of death by our Lord's brother James: "For as *the body apart from the spirit is dead, . . ."* (James 2:26). When the spirit of the young girl left her body then the body was dead. The appearance of the body in death is so much like the appearance of the body in sleep. Our Lord knew that this likeness had other similarities: (1) Her death was but a brief time of refreshment. When the daughter was awakened by our Lord it would be to full health. (2) She would be awakened and not know that she had been dead. As near as we know none of those our Lord raised from the dead reported any dreams.

Pause—wait—think—then express yourself in thoughtful praise or thanks.

9. READ HIS WORD FOR PETITIONS.

In the questions and answers of this text there is much for which we can pray: (1) I have often been in a remote place and found it was late. I have not always appealed to you—how I want this to be my first response. (2) The disciples awaited the command of Jesus before they did anything with anyone. How I need this same attitude! (3) The words of Jesus shocked the disciples: "You give them something to eat." Is he saying that again to me? (4) There was a real concern as to expenses—Jesus did not ignore this, but took measures to meet the need. I want to bring all such problems to him. (5) "How many loaves do you have?" is still my Lord's question to me. Help me to look again.

Right here add your personal requests—and his answers.

10. READ HIS WORD AND WAIT—LISTEN—GOD SPEAKS!

Before I answer him may I hear him speak to me: (1) "There are other ways than you know for meeting human need." (2) "If you bring me what you have I can change it and use it." (3) "I can still meet impossible emergencies."

11. INTERCESSION FOR THE LOST WORLD

Israel — Point for prayer: (1) *Israel needs more men and women who humbly and simply live for Jesus* and witness personally to the very many who have not responded to the Gospel. Pray for all groups seeking to help and encourage the national believers in this ministry of personal evangelism and distribution of literature. There are surprisingly few Christians doing this and the opportunities for this ministry are many.

12. SING PRAISES TO OUR LORD.

A wonderful Savior is Jesus my Lord,
A wonderful Savior to me,
He hideth my soul in the cleft of the rock,
Where rivers of pleasure I see.
He hideth my soul in the cleft of the rock

That shadows a dry, thirsty land;
He hideth my life in the depths of His love,
And covers me there with His hand,
And covers me there with His hand.

WEEK FORTY-EIGHT — SATURDAY

1. PRAISE GOD FOR WHO HE IS.

"May my prayer be counted (fixed) as incense before thee; the lifting up of my hands as the evening offering" (Psalm 141:2). Here are the personal prayer needs of David. He comes to you with confidence that you can and will meet his needs. I want to consider the requests, but I want also to look behind the requests to the One who answers: (1) David wants his prayers to be established, to be made firm—as a receptacle fastened to receive the incense. How this does speak to all our hearts. You alone can crystalize our commitments to prayer. (2) Our prayer is compared to incense—so does John in Revelation so symbolize our prayers (Rev. 5:8; 8:3, 4). Incense was made of a mixture of several spices. Incense must be consumed or it is of no value—it must be burned.

Express yourself in adoration for this quality of God.
Speak it audibly or write out your praise in your own devotional journal.

2. PRAISE GOD FOR WHAT HE MEANS TO ME.

Just for me. Dear Lord, there is much in this for me: (1) I want to establish my time of prayer so firmly that I expect it even as a permanent fixture in my house of service to you. (2) I want to combine the elements of prayer in their proper order—praise, confession, thanksgiving, intercession, petition. (3) Most of all I want to ignite the incense. I want to give my energy and life to this wonderful experience. Indeed, I want to be consumed with this fragment act of worship. (4) The whole ceremony of worship is here described in a single verse. Following the incense is the sacrifice. David lifts his hands up to you, and in the gesture he is offering his whole self to you as a living sacrifice. Such sacrifices were offered at least twice *every day*. Dear Lord, oh my Lord, I do want to lift up my whole self to you—and I do it every day. All of these pious pretty words will be as meaningless as the sacrifices of the Old Testament without you!

How do you personally relate to the sacrifice for God, and God who asks for our body?
Speak it out or write it out. It is *so important* that you establish *your own* devotional journal.

3. CONFESSION OF SIN

How easy it is to admit my missing your target here! How is it that I have been a worshiper of you for all these years and have not *fixed* or *established* my prayer as incense before you? And even now I know that without your presence and power I will not continue. But, oh my Lord, I do so want to! Forgive my vacillation. The elements of the incense were beaten before they were burned. Until I am ready to allow my praise, thanksgiving and intercession to be purified by your discipline I cannot pray as I should. As you know my heart you know this is my sincere desire. When will I daily hold up my body as a living sacrifice to you? My sin is that I believe this is an unreasonable, impossible request. I am wrong! Paul used the strongest appeal possible to affirm such a request. When will you hear it, oh my soul? (Romans 12:1, 2) I repent—forgive me!

What personal sins do you want to confess? We *must* speak them to remove them.
Do it! *Now.* There is no one else you have sinned against more than God. Tell him so!

4. SING A PRAYER TO GOD.

"Give me thy heart," says the Father above,
No gift so precious to Him as our love,
Softly He whispers wherever thou art,
"Gratefully trust me, and give me thy heart."

"Give me thy heart, Give me thy heart,"
Hear the soft whisper, wherever thou art;
From this dark world He would draw thee apart,
Speaking to tenderly, "Give me thy heart."

Open your hymn book and sing the rest of the verses—or even sing another prayer song.

5. READ HIS WORD TO HIM!

His Word

[6]And he was amazed at their lack of faith.
Then Jesus went around teaching from village to village. [7]Calling the Twelve to him, he sent them out two by two and gave them authority over evil spirits.
[8]These were his instructions: "Take nothing for the journey except a staff—no bread, no bag, no money in your belts. [9]Wear sandals but not an extra tunic. [10]Whenever you enter a house, stay there until you leave that town. [11]And if any place will not welcome you or listen to you, shake the dust off your feet when you leave, as a testimony against them."   — *Mark 6:6-11, NIV*
Read also Matthew 10:1-25.

Read His Word to Him.

Talk about the "great commission"! Here is a commission fraught with such warnings it would stop the stoutest heart. How I do want to gather around with the apostles as they listen to the words of your Son. Jesus commissioned them, but He also equipped them. "He gave them authority to drive out evil spirits and to cure every kind of disease and sickness." I want to follow carefully his words as found by those who went or talked to those who heard him. (1) They were divided into teams of two. (2) "Do not go to the Gentiles or Samaritans" — go rather to "the lost sheep of Israel." (3) This was a preaching mission — the message was "the kingdom of heaven is near." (4) Their message was to be confirmed by the signs that followed. Such signs were to be done freely.

Please express your response to this beautiful text. Put your expression in your own prayer diary.

6. READ HIS WORD FOR YOURSELF.

Just for me. I am going to continue my journey with these twelve men. (5) The twelve were to depend upon the hospitality extended by strangers. Such hospitality was considerable: (a) No money was needed. (b) No lunch bag was needed, i.e., no meals would be missed. (c) No one will need to sleep out in the open — so no extra tunic is needed. (d) One pair of sandals and one staff will be adequate. (6) Such hospitality would not be immediately available, but if they looked they could find someone to treat them as described. (7) The reception given to these men would be very important. The peace of yourself or your judgment would be the result. (8) The whole demeanor of your servants is described: (a) As shrewd as snakes, as harmless as doves. (b) Wary of men who could and would hand them over to local counsels for a flogging in the synagogues. All this and much more. How easy is our service in comparison.

Pause in his presence and either audibly or in written form tell him all his word means to you.

7. READ HIS WORD IN THANKSGIVING.

(1) Thank you for the preparation Jesus gave these men before he sent them out. (2) Thank you for the supernatural equipment our Lord gave these men. (3) Thank you for our Lord's priority concern for the lost sheep of Israel. (4) Thank you for the degree of faith it took to even go as the Lord had commanded. (5) Thank you for the wisdom of serpents and the innocence of doves granted to his servants. (6) Thank you for the promise of "the Spirit of your Father" speaking through them.

Give yourself to your own expression of gratitude — write it or speak it!

8. READ HIS WORD IN MEDITATION.

". . . shake the dust off your feet when you leave, as a testimony against them." It is altogether remarkable that our Lord had such compassion on everyone and now makes this statement of what seems to be the rejection of some men. Jesus does not recommend a casual indifference. It would seem he wants a positive reaction to every situation. Why such an attitude? We need to first of all recognize just what it is our Lord recommends. In the first place, he is not rejecting men — he is simply accepting their rejection of him. In particular he is registering his disapproval of their refusal to understand his message. He wants those who disbelieve to know how serious their decision is.

Pause — wait — think — then express yourself in thoughtful praise or thanks.

9. READ HIS WORD FOR PETITIONS.

Dear Lord, send me out into my world — yea, you already have! I now ask for your grace in these requests: (1) Develop my perception in accepting your word — the source of my faith. (2) Jesus still walks the streets of many villages today, i.e., in the person of his servants — teach your word through me. (3) I have no authority of my own — how I do want to let your authority be known. (4) Who is the one with whom you will send me out? Give me wisdom in choosing a partner. (5) Even in the hospitable culture of my Lord's day it took real faith to start out in total dependence on others. Forgive me for my little faith. (6) I do need the courage to rebuke in the spirit of love those who need it.

Please, please remember these are prayers — speak them — reword them!

10. READ HIS WORD AND WAIT — LISTEN — GOD SPEAKS!

In these verses speak to my heart: (1) "I speak to you through my word before you can speak to anyone else." (2) "You can usually get more done by working with others than doing it on your own." (3) "People accept me or reject me — not you."

11. INTERCESSION FOR THE LOST WORLD

Israel — Point for prayer: (1) *The missionary force* is variously estimated to be 120-250. Pray for the Lord's servants who labor among the Jews where there is so little encouragement that they may not succumb to discouragement, and that they might know the Lord's will as to how best to minister.

12. SING PRAISES TO OUR LORD.

Holy, Holy, Holy! All the saints adore Thee,
Casting down their golden crowns around the glassy sea;
Cherubim and seraphim falling down before Thee,
Which wert, and art, and evermore shalt be.

WEEK FORTY-NINE — SUNDAY

1. PRAISE GOD FOR WHO HE IS.

"Set a guard over my mouth, O Lord, keep watch over the door of my lips" (Psalm 141:3). There could hardly be a quality of yourself more needed by man, at least by *this* man. If you could somehow provide a protection against the many words we wish could be retracted—oh, that we could but return them. "The watch does not stand with his back to the mouth, to challenge what would

come out." There is a profound thought in this statement from *Graham Scroggie*. Dear Lord, you know how vulnerable we are to evil thoughts. In the midst of verbal exchange between men so many thoughts form in our mind. But if they never get out of the mouth then at least no sin in word has occurred. Why do some words never escape the mouth? Because of your guard, because of your protection!

Express yourself in adoration for this quality of God.
Speak it audibly or write out your praise in your own devotional journal.

2. PRAISE GOD FOR WHAT HE MEANS TO ME.

Just for me. I am constantly embarrassed at the hasty words that stream from my mouth. I need a clutch between my thoughts and my lips. It is this *guard*, it is this *watch*, it is this *clutch* provided by yourself! In what form or guise will this powerful ally appear? Dear Lord, I can think of several. (1) *Personal loss*—when it is a great loss, it produces a thoughtfulness—at least for a time—to set a guard on our lips. Whom you love you chasten—and this is part of the fruit of such chastening. (2) *The*

rebukes of men and women. The exact opposite might occur at the moment of rebuke, but afterward it does yield this peaceable fruit. (3) *Memorizing your word*—and a constant review of it. Somehow it becomes easier to pause and wait before I answer when I have been thinking and repeating your thoughts. (4) Most of all, there is the promise of the presence of the blessed Holy Spirit who guards my heart and my thoughts in ways best known to him. Praise your dear Self.

How do you personally relate to the guard of God, and God who can guard our lips?
Speak it out or write it out. It is *so important* that you establish *your own* devotional journal.

3. CONFESSION OF SIN

In the nature of the praise there is confession. Is it with what men think or with what you think I am concerned in my words? Even as I write these words I want as much as possible with my deceitful heart to be totally honest with myself and yourself. "I do not know" is the answer to such a question. It really matters not at all to the real

need just here—the need for forgiveness. In hasty words there is such a need for forgiveness! How well do I relate to these words of *Amos N. Wilder:*

"Speak quiet words—the constellations wait,
The mountains watch; the hour for man is late
Likewise to still his heart and supplicate."

What personal sins do you want to confess? We *must* speak them to remove them.
Do it! *Now.* There is no one else you have sinned against more than God. Tell him so!

4. SING A PRAYER TO GOD.

Oh, the pure delight of a single hour
That before Thy throne I spend,
When I kneel in prayer, and with Thee, my God,
I commune as friend with friend!

Draw me nearer, nearer, blessed Lord,
To the cross where Thou hast died;
Draw me nearer, nearer, nearer, blessed Lord,
To Thy precious, bleeding side.

Open your hymn book and sing the rest of the verses—or even sing another prayer song.

5. READ HIS WORD TO HIM!

His Word

[26]"So do not be afraid of them. There is nothing concealed that will not be disclosed, or hidden that will not be made known. [27]What I tell you in the dark, speak in the daylight; what is whispered in your ear, proclaim from the housetops. [28]Do not be afraid of those who kill the body but cannot kill the soul. Rather be afraid of the one who can destroy both soul and body in hell. [29]Are not two sparrows sold for a penny? Yet not one of them will

fall to the ground apart from the will of your Father. [30]And even the very hairs of your head are all numbered. [31]So don't be afraid; you are worth more than many sparrows.

[32]"Whoever acknowledges me before men, I will also acknowledge him before my Father in heaven. [33]But whoever disowns me before men, I will disown him before my Father in heaven. — *Matthew 10:26-33, NIV*

Read His Word to Him.

Shall I ever lose my hesitancy as I approach this monumental task of reading the words of your Son back to you? This would indeed be the height of folly were it not for the purpose behind it. I am only telling you how very

much these words mean to me—or I want them to mean to me. How often men have died in despair thinking that truth died with them. How comforting are his words! "There is nothing concealed that will not be disclosed, or

674

hidden that will not be made known." The deep convictions of your heart — "get out in the sunlight before everyone and tell it!" How I do need to hear these words! Jesus here promises that men will violently oppose us (at least if we approximate the circumstances here described). What a power promise: "Do not be afraid . . ." They cannot kill the real you!

Please express your response to this beautiful text. Put your expression in your own prayer diary.

6. READ HIS WORD FOR YOURSELF.

Just for me. I do receive these words just for me. There will be a spiritual body in which men will live. How awful it will be to enter that body and be cast into hell! Love and kindness and personal concern are here, but the mind-jarring thought of everlasting punishment is also here. Wake up! *There is a hell to fear!*

If there ever was a verse I treasured to my heart it is Matthew 10:29: "Are not two sparrows sold for a penny? Yet not one of them will fall to the ground apart from the will of your Father . . .You are worth more than many sparrows." The kind of intimate interest indicated here is just marvelous! I have seen some tragic things happen to sparrows. But God has a way of balancing out their population. Sparrows will not live forever — we will!

Pause in his presence and either audibly or in written form tell him all his word means to you.

7. READ HIS WORD IN THANKSGIVING.

(1) Thank you for the constant assurance given by our Lord that there will be justice and equity in the total perspective of life. (2) Thank you for the urging of our Lord to speak out and not to hold back in declaring the good news. (3) Thank you that all fear of physical punishment can be removed by a more significant fear. (4) Thank you for the plain statement of the separation of the person from his body.

Give yourself to your own expression of gratitude — write it or speak it!

8. READ HIS WORD IN MEDITATION.

"I did not come to bring peace, but a sword." You also defined the sword you came to bring — or at least the consequences of your sword: *"For* I have come to turn a man against his father, a daughter against her mother . . . a man's enemies will be members of his own household." How sharp a sword is this! We all know just how heated a disagreement can become among members of the family. In attempting to project ourselves back to that day and time, we wonder just how the conversation went in the homes up and down the length of Canaan. It must have been over two basic points: (1) That his teachings were revolutionary and demanded much more than some were willing to give. (2) His humble station in life as a Nazarene was a barrier in the minds of many to his Messiahship. It hasn't changed from that day to this.

Pause — wait — think — then express yourself in thoughtful praise or thanks.

9. READ HIS WORD FOR PETITIONS.

Surely these strong words of warning and encouragement lead us to prayer: (1) May I believe with my Lord that truth will ultimately triumph in *every* situation. (2) How I need to remember that there are really no secrets not known to you. (3) The courage of my Lord in the face of opposition is amazing — what excuse do we have for not proclaiming his word from the housetops? (4) My Lord expected opposition *and* triumph. How I want to adopt his attitude! (5) I really do not know how I would react to physical torture for your cause — I thank you I have not had to find out. (6) I am glad there is no death for the man inside — keep this truth ever bright!

Right here add your personal requests — and his answers.

10. READ HIS WORD AND WAIT — LISTEN — GOD SPEAKS!

Speak to me in these words: (1) "Fear is an ever present threat." (2) "I know you better than Satan." (3) "Trust — not fear is the answer to your problems."

11. INTERCESSION FOR THE LOST WORLD

Israel — Point for prayer: (1) *Missionary work among Jews* could be legally stopped. Unwise methods and tactlessness by certain more extremist groups has stimulated Jewish demands for the ending of all Protestant mission work. Pray for humility and tact for all serving the Lord from other lands.

12. SING PRAISES TO OUR LORD.

Holy, Holy, Holy, Lord God Almighty!
Early in the morning our song shall rise to Thee;

Holy, Holy, Holy! Merciful and Mighty!
God in Three Persons, blessed Trinity!

WEEK FORTY-NINE — MONDAY

1. PRAISE GOD FOR WHO HE IS.

"Incline not my heart to any evil, to busy myself with wicked deeds in the company with men who work iniquity; and let me not eat of their dainties" (Psalm 141:4).

This is such a good verse to describe both your work and my work, both your involvement and mine in the development of character. This is a prayer to you but I am very much a part of the action. How do you incline my heart? How do you prevent inclination of heart? I am the active agent in busying myself with wicked deeds or seeking the company of men who work iniquity. Dear Lord, I have found through careful observation that I find circumstances being altered and environment changed because I prayed. It is *not* only my attitude that has changed. I praise you for being the Lord of circumstances!

Express yourself in adoration for this quality of God.
Speak it audibly or write out your praise in your own devotional journal.

2. PRAISE GOD FOR WHAT HE MEANS TO ME.

Just for me. In this time I want to spend it all on praise and very little on philosophy. For today and its needs: guard my heart and my desires. Arrange the circumstances of my life in such a manner that even now all my events are planned and arranged by yourself. May I be taught by trials and not overcome by them. Keep me busy about your interests. Deliver me this day from busy work, i.e. from the deadly danger in meaningless activity. Even if I am attracted to men who gather to talk and waste time make it possible for me to choose not to be there. In the fulfillment of the desires of my body give me your direction — you already have — but in the immediate application of what you have said I lean heavily upon the promises made in this verse.

How do you personally relate to the business of God, and God who is busy?
Speak it out or write it out. It is *so important* that you establish *your own* devotional journal.

3. CONFESSION OF SIN

I think again of that blessed verse in Romans 13:14: "But put on the Lord Jesus Christ, and *make no provision for the flesh,* to gratify its desires." It is in the provisions made ahead of the circumstance we find our greatest problem. Nay, more than a problem — *our greatest sin!* Do we really *want* deliverance from the inclination to sin? We have been such a long time in the world that we easily become a part of it. It is in the capitulation to the presence of evil that we sin. *It is not inevitable that evil shall conquer!* I can not and will not eradicate the desire to sin but I can decide to "put on the Lord Jesus Christ" ahead of the temptation instead of deciding that I will enjoy the pleasures of sin. It is in this last decision I have sinned. Forgive me. I am repenting — help my continuing repentance.

What personal sins do you want to confess? We *must* speak them to remove them.
Do it! *Now.* There is no one else you have sinned against more than God. Tell him so!

4. SING A PRAYER TO GOD.

Here, O my Lord, I see Thee face to face;
Here would I touch and handle things unseen;

Here grasp with firmer hand th' eternal grace,
And all my weariness upon Thee lean.

Open your hymn book and sing the rest of the verses — or even sing another prayer song.

5. READ HIS WORD TO HIM!

His Word

[12]They went out and preached that people should repent. [13]They drove out many demons and anointed many sick people with oil and healed them. — *Mark 6:12, 13, NIV*

[6]So they set out and went from village to village, preaching the gospel and healing people everywhere. — *Luke 9:6, NIV*

Read His Word to Him.

Here we read of the fulfillment of the commission. It is so good to see a plan carried out. Our Lord planned his work and worked his plan. This is the first commission accomplished. What we refer to as "the great commission" was also accomplished. Colossians 1:23 says: ". . . *the gospel which . . . has been preached to every creature under heaven. . . ."* Not since these days has any generation taken our Lord seriously enough to do it again. Dear Lord, I want to do what I can to tell the world of your love. I notice the apostles were quite systematic in their efforts: they "went from village to village." If Jesus was a preacher, i.e. a public proclaimer — and his apostles were also preachers — then it ill behooves us to say a disparaging word about this means of communicating. Indeed it is your ordained manner of getting the job done.

Please express your response to this beautiful text. Put your expression in your own prayer diary.

WEEK FORTY-NINE — MONDAY

6. READ HIS WORD FOR YOURSELF.

Healing was as much a part of the apostolic preaching as the preaching itself. I can see how it was essential to the confirmation of what was said. Dear Lord, there are several wonderful truths here I want to embrace to my heart: (1) No restrictions were placed on either the preaching or the healing. All needed both, either for their physical needs or their spiritual needs. (2) The message is described as "good news"—how I do want that one basic attitude to pervade all I say on your behalf. (3) The message's purpose is described in the one word "repent." How very far short I fall in this area you know. Teach me, dear Lord, how to so speak that men will change their minds about you. (4) I am so glad for this plain all inclusive statement that demons could not stand before the authority of your "sent ones."

It is so important that you pause in his presence
and either audibly or in written form tell him all his word means to you.

7. READ HIS WORD IN THANKSGIVING.

(1) Thank you for the moral courage of the twelve. (2) Thank you they made no exceptions—"they went from village to village." (3) Thank you they made no distinction as to who would be healed. No mention is here made of faith or lack of it. (4) Thank you these men were telling glad tidings. (5) Thank you for the one word message that covers the whole spectrum of revelation: "repent." (6) Thank you for the power of the good news over demons. (7) Thank you for the oil, representative of the presence of the Holy Spirit in the healing of the sick.

Give yourself to your own expression of gratitude—write it or speak it!

8. READ HIS WORD IN MEDITATION.

". . . and anointed many sick people with oil and healed them." We do not believe the oil was used to accomplish the healing but rather to offer comfort after the healing. The oil could have been symbolic in representation of the presence of the Holy Spirit. The three static characteristics of the healings of the New Testament are present here also: (1) Instantaneous. No progressive healings here. (We will comment on the one progressive healing in the ministry of our Lord when we come to it in our prayer time.) In the nature of the healer even Jesus, who has all authority, we preclude any other type healing. (2) Permanent. We do not read of those who lost their faith and therefore their healing. No faith is mentioned here. (3) No failures, or unsuccessful attempts. Since our Lord gave them authority to perform such miracles their confidence in his power prevented any failures.

Pause—wait—think—then express yourself in thoughtful praise or thanks.

9. READ HIS WORD FOR PETITIONS.

I want to be a participant in the healing ministry of my Lord: (1) Is it easier or more difficult today to tell the story of his power and love? No matter—it must be told. (2) Teach me how to preach repentance. (3) How did these twelve men get the attention and interest of the people? How can I move men to hear? (4) I am glad we serve One who can defeat every effort of the evil one—give me the boldness I need. (5) Increase my compassion for the sick. (6) Deepen my awareness of the Holy Spirit's presence in all I do. (7) May I never lose the wonder of the goodness we have to tell.

Please, please remember these are prayers—speak them—reword them!

10. READ HIS WORD AND WAIT—LISTEN—GOD SPEAKS!

Speak to me in these few words as you send me out to preach and teach: (1) "My message is still goodness—it just hasn't been told." (2) "There were just as many disbelievers in our Lord's day—he didn't stop." (3) "I am now omnipresently alive to give you the same commission to preach."

11. INTERCESSION FOR THE LOST WORLD

Israel — Point for prayer: (1) The Jews of the Dispersion. There are about 16,000,000 Jews living in other lands. These people are more receptive to the Gospel than those in Israel. Many societies work specifically among the Jewish people in the U.S.A. and Britain, but little work is done in Argentina and France. Pray for this ministry— usually more in personal witness and patient caring for individuals—that it may bear fruit in the conversion of Jews to their Messiah. There are reports of many Jews now seeking the Lord in the U.S.A. and in the U.S.S.R., especially young people.

12. SING PRAISES TO OUR LORD.

Amazing grace, how sweet the sound,
That saved a wretch like me!

I once was lost but now am found,
Was blind, but now I see.

WEEK FORTY-NINE — TUESDAY

1. PRAISE GOD FOR WHO HE IS.

"I cry to thee, O Lord; I say, Thou art my refuge, my portion in the land of the living. Give heed to my cry; for I am brought very low!" (Psalm 142:5, 6a).

How very, very often I need a refuge—it seems the longer I live the more I need a refuge. There are so many distracting and unsettling circumstances in life. But there has never been a man born of woman that did not need a hiding place for an escape. David thinks of the dividing of the land of Canaan under Joshua and the portions given to the separate tribes. Each man is given an allotment in life, a *portion* of life in the land of the living.

Express yourself in adoration for this quality of God.
Speak it audibly or write out your praise in your own devotional journal.

2. PRAISE GOD FOR WHAT HE MEANS TO ME.

Just for me. The last portion of this verse does indeed describe my response to life in the land of the living: ". . . I am brought very low." Am I ready to say with the psalmist or the song writer "other refuge have I none"? What a solace it is to come to One who never changes! You are like a great rock in a weary land. I think of you also as a Father who offers the warmth and understanding of his love as my refuge. When my father was alive there never was a problem greater than his love. What I found in my earthly parent I can find multiplied a thousand-fold in you! Praise your name! "Christ is our life"—i.e. all of life—"For me to live is Christ"—Thou art my portion in the living of this day.

How do you personally relate to the provisions of God, and God who is our portion?
Speak it out or write it out. It is *so important* that you establish *your own* devotional journal.

3. CONFESSION OF SIN

It is always good to enter this area of worship as I am forced (at least at times) to think of how I have failed to fulfill what I have just affirmed. I have fled here and there for an escape. I found I was more exposed to the battering of life than if I had stayed where I was. Indeed, I can agree with the song writer: *"other refuge have I none."* My sin is in forgetting and yielding to the pressure about me to "try this" or "try that." How always disappointing they have been. Forgive me! How easy it is to be caught up in the flow of life "in the land of the living" and actually find very little time or place for yourself in my experience. "*A portion*" of the land of Canaan was where the person lived. I want to live in you! Just for today this shall be true!

What personal sins do you want to confess? We *must* speak them to remove them.
Do it! *Now.* There is no one else you have sinned against more than God. Tell him so!

4. SING A PRAYER TO GOD.

Sweetly, Lord, have we heard Thee calling,
Come, follow me!
And we see where Thy footprints falling
Lead us to Thee.
Footprints of Jesus, that make the pathway glow;
We will follow the steps of Jesus where'er they go.

Open your hymn book and sing the rest of the verses—or even sing another prayer song.

5. READ HIS WORD TO HIM!

His Word

[14] King Herod heard about this, for Jesus' name had become well-known. Some were saying, "John the Baptist has been raised from the dead, and that is why miraculous powers are at work in him."
[15] Others said, "He is Elijah."
And still others claimed, "He is a prophet, like one of the prophets of long ago."
[16] But when Herod heard this, he said, "John, the man I beheaded, has been raised from the dead!"
[17] for Herod himself had given orders to have John arrested and put in prison. He did this because of Herodias, his brother Philip's wife, whom he had married. [18] For John had been saying to Herod, "It is not lawful for you to have your brother's wife." [19] So Herodias nursed a grudge against John and wanted to kill him. But she was not able to, [20] because Herod feared John and protected him, knowing him to be a righteous and holy man. When Herod heard John, he was greatly puzzled; yet he liked to listen to him.
— Mark 6:14-20, NIV
Read also Matthew 14:1-5.

Read His Word to Him.

How poignantly does this text speak to me. I do want to attempt an approach that lifts these words into your presence. How slow and ignorant are men! Such would seem to be a reasonable reaction to the words of men about your Son. How is it some men knew more of John the Baptist than they did your Messiah? I cannot answer; I can only ask. Even in this mistaken view John did no miracles (John 10:40) so why imagine he is doing so now? It would seem men are intent on misunderstanding. Satan's efforts are to get us to choose any option but yours! How is it Herod would not come face to face with the issue of your Son?

Please express your response to this beautiful text. Put your expression in your own prayer diary.

6. READ HIS WORD FOR YOURSELF.

Our estimate of John only increases the more we know of him. How courageous he was! Even in high places he did not hesitate to identify and condemn sin. Didn't John know that Herodias was a very dangerous woman? Did John know the depth of her evil designs? If he did it did not change his message. Dear Lord, how I want this courage today in every relationship of my daily living. I do believe there are evil men in my town who have a conscience much like Herod. Dear Lord, open my heart and mouth to them. Men and women on all sides live in a state of fornication or adultery without any thought of marriage—legal or otherwise. What would John say about the society of our day? We already know! Dear Lord, keep me from insensitivity!

It is so important that you pause in his presence
and either audibly or in written form tell him all his word means to you.

7. READ HIS WORD IN THANKSGIVING.

(1) Thank you for the willingness of Herod to believe with others in life after death. (2) Thank you for the tacit admission of the miraculous nature of our Lord's works. (3) Thank you for the anticipation of the coming of Elijah —however distorted. (4) Thank you for the courage of John even while in prison to preach to Herod. (5) Thank you for the rebuke to the heart of Herodias. (6) Thank you for the clear lesson here that until men and women know they are sinners they can never be saved. (7) Thank you for the attraction of the truth for all men.

Give yourself to your own expression of gratitude—write it or speak it!

8. READ HIS WORD IN MEDITATION.

". . . he was greatly puzzled; yet he liked to listen to him." There was something strongly attractive about John the Baptist. When we remember Elizabeth and Zechariah —it all seems so long ago. We wonder if they are still alive; we would not imagine they were. What of all of John's disciples? We know how deeply our Lord felt about John. Herod had had contact with the life of our Lord and his work from the beginning. The puzzlement of Herod was not as to who John was or what he represented. He was non-plussed over someone who did not fear the consequences of opposing Rome. How we would all have liked to listen to John. When one is totally full of the subject and the subject is the message from heaven he becomes a very interesting speaker. How sad to remember that Herod died in his sins and was lost!

Pause—wait—think—then express yourself in thoughtful praise or thanks.

9. READ HIS WORD FOR PETITIONS.

What a section for prayer requests in our own life: (1) People in our Lord's day believed in life after death and the resurrection—our Lord taught the same—can I believe less? (2) Thank you for the large place the supernatural had in the record of his life—this is truth—this reality—keep me tuned in. (3) There are so many fine lessons from the life Elijah—help me to learn at least one for today. (4) It is so good to agree with Peter that my Lord was indeed "the prophet" like Moses—open my ears to hear him! (5) What strange tricks a guilty conscience can play! Cleanse my conscience that I might look at all of life without fear. (6) John did no miracles (John 10:41), his life was his miracle—how I want to be like him. (7) There was something wonderfully strange about John— even for a man like Herod—it was John's courage and faith and wisdom—how such men are needed now!

Right here add your personal requests—and his answers.

10. READ HIS WORD AND WAIT—LISTEN—GOD SPEAKS!

In this vortex of conflict speak to me: (1) "He that is the newest member in the body of Christ is greater than John the Baptist." (2) "A burning message will attract attention anywhere." (3) "My laws of adultery have not changed."

11. INTERCESSION FOR THE LOST WORLD

Iran — Population: 34,100,000. Annual Growth 3%. People per sq. km.—21.

Point for prayer: (1) The needy Muslim land is wide open for the Gospel and Muslims have never been so receptive to the Gospel message. There can still be considerable and violent opposition to any attempts at converting Muslims at a local level and converts can suffer much for their faith. Pray for a great turning to the Lord among Muslims—especially among the young people.

12. SING PRAISES TO OUR LORD.

"Man of Sorrows!" what a name
For the Son of God who came

Ruined sinners to reclaim!
Hallelujah! what a Savior!

WEEK FORTY-NINE — WEDNESDAY

1. PRAISE GOD FOR WHO HE IS.

"Hear my prayer, O Lord; give ear to my supplications. In thy faithfulness answer me, in thy righteousness! Enter not into judgment with thy servant, for no man living is righteous before thee" (Psalm 143:1, 2).

The attributes of yourself seen in these two verses are so strong and helpful to me—and to all men. They are most of all just a source of praise and wonder. Just for yourself we praise you! Here is how I see you in these words: (1) You are listening to all our general requests in our *prayers*. (2) You take a personal interest in our personal needs as expressed in our *supplications*. (3) You have already pledged yourself to answer us. It is not at all because we deserve an answer—other than a blunt, "No"! (4) Your righteousness includes a means of declaring us righteous. Praise and exaltation to your glorious self!

Express yourself in adoration for this qualtiy of God.
Speak it audibly or write out your praise in your own devotional journal.

2. PRAISE GOD FOR WHAT HE MEANS TO ME.

Just for me. Dear Lord, I know you hear all our prayers—however poorly or selfishly expressed. But in my personal intimate needs I ask your particular attentiveness. I know what a presumption this is, but I am emboldened to thus speak since I know of your character in the person of your Son. "It was in thy righteousness that thou didst make all your promises, but it is thy faithfulness that will keep each one." Since I know what you have promised I know also what you will fulfill. Dear Lord, I do have such sore needs—I bring them to you and claim your interest and love.

At the same time, I do not at all want justice—"no man living (beginning with me) is righteous before thee." Give me mercy, O Lord!

How do you personally relate to the righteousness of God, and God who is merciful?
Speak it out or write it out. It is *so important* that you establish *your own* devotional journal.

3. CONFESSION OF SIN

What a true term to describe myself, *"thy servant."* Not "thy good servant" or even "profitable servant." But just and only "thy servant." You have already entered into judgment with your Son, your good and profitable *Servant!* Only because of your judgment with him can I at all take courage to even appear before you. I want to enter into judgment with myself that I be not condemned before you. How futile do all my efforts to reform become! It is only in your goodness that I find hope and motivation to repent. May this never, never become a license for disobedience. May my repentance be of yourself that it will produce the fruit of service.

What personal sins do you want to confess? We *must* speak them to remove them.
Do it! *Now.* There is no one else you have sinned against more than God. Tell him so!

4. SING A PRAYER TO GOD.

When Jesus as Lord I had crowned,
My heart with this peace did abound;
In Him the rich blessing I found,
Sweet peace, the gift of God's love.

Peace, peace, sweet peace!
Wonderful gift from above!
Oh, wonderful, wonderful peace!
Sweet peace, the gift of God's love!

Open your hymn book and sing the rest of the verses—or even sing another prayer song.

5. READ HIS WORD TO HIM!

His Word

[21] Finally the opportune time came. On his birthday Herod gave a banquet for his high officials and military commanders and the leading men of Galilee. [22] When the daughter of Herodias came in and danced, she pleased Herod and his dinner guests.   — Mark 6:21, 22a, NIV

Read His Word to Him.

How strange it seems to read these two verses in your presence—i.e. just for your benefit. On second thought, isn't this what happens every time we read your word? How tragically pathetic all the efforts of these men must appear to you! We wonder just which birthday Herod was remembering. You were there for every one of them from the first day until now. Herod, or no man, will have one more birthday than you decide. Here is a celebration of the brevity of life and the certainty of death—i.e. from eternity's perspective. What important persons were in attendance that day? We are sure you know them all by name. What was in the mind of the girl as she danced? Whatever it was you read it. Herodias was really responsible as the source of this whole fiasco. And so it is that you watch the absurdities of men in high places.

Please express your response to this beautiful text. Put your expression in your own prayer diary.

6. READ HIS WORD FOR YOURSELF.

Just for me. Such sensualism is more than prevalent in our day. To watch such a performance one need but flip the dial of the TV set or step into the Cinema. Such prostitution of your purpose for the appetites of men and women! There is such a pervasive attitude of hedonism in our day we are sorely tempted to say in exasperation: "If you want to go to hell, go to hell!" But this is *not at* all the way you see man. Your satisfaction for the strange desires of man is so much more meaningful. We do not know the daughter's name; she is just "the girl in the narrative—a "sex symbol"—"a thing." But you know her name. How much more you had for her than she found at Herod's party. How much more you have for all men than they can find at any of the parties of life.

It is so important that you pause in his presence
and either audibly or in written form tell him all his word means to you.

7. READ HIS WORD IN THANKSGIVING.

(1) Thank you for this plain example of the contemporary value of all we see here. (2) Thank you for the warning of the serious consequences of living by the desires of the body. (3) Thank you for the futility seen in the efforts of man to please himself. (4) Thank you that this word has been kept until this day to say over and over again to us happiness is not in pleasure. (5) Thank you for your enjoyments that do not leave a residue of regret. (6) Thank you for the deliverance of John. He had a good conscience.

Give yourself to your own expression of gratitude—write it or speak it!

8. READ HIS WORD IN MEDITATION.

". . . *Herod on his birthday gave a banquet for his courtiers and officers and the leading men of Galilee.*" This "stag" party was so very, very typical. (1) It gave no thought to the value of anyone present. It was "every man for himself." (2) It was based on pride and would easily explode into argument upon argument. (3) It was only an excuse for sex, food and other expressions of greed. The birthday of Herod was wholly incidental to their purpose. Probably most of the men present hated Herod and wished "*no* happy returns of the day of his birth." (4) It was over too soon and left the regret that they had ever attended.

Pause—wait—think—then express yourself in thoughtful praise or thanks.

9. READ HIS WORD FOR PETITIONS.

In Satan's opportunity there is a great need for prayer: (1) Guard me today that I might detect the evil one's devices. (2) Give me the wisdom to not give place to the devil in any area of life. (3) Satan gets much more credit than he deserves—I resist him. I need your grace to overcome. (4) I am no match for Satan—but with you and in you I am "more than a conqueror"—make this a reality today. (5) The lust of the flesh is multiple in its appeals—I want to be vigilant on all fronts. (6) Pride and ego can lead us into death-traps—deliver me! (7) I know my task in temptation is to get up and leave the dinner party and the sensual entertainment—I decide now so I will fulfill my commitment when the time comes.

Please, please remember these are prayers—speak them—reword them!

10. READ HIS WORD AND WAIT—LISTEN—GOD SPEAKS!

Speak to me: (1) "Temptation is not sin—only your wrong choice is sin." (2) "Sitting in the seat of the scornful is an open door for Satan." (3) "Even evil men do not respect weakness."

11. INTERCESSION FOR THE LOST WORLD

Iran — Point for prayer: (1) *Unreached areas and peoples:* a) Of the land's 55,000 villages, only half a dozen have a Gospel witness. b) Many sections of the population are unreached—the nomadic people, the middle class, university students, women and children, etc. c) The linguistic minorities—the 200,000 Muslim Baluchi and Brahui are more open now, but no one is working full time among them. Many other minority peoples have never been evangelized and have nothing of the Word of God.

12. SING PRAISES TO OUR LORD.

Blessed assurance Jesus is mine,
Oh, what a foretaste of glory divine.
Heir of salvation, purchase of God,
Born of His spirit, washed in His blood.

This is my story, this is my song,
Praising my Savior all the day long.
This is my story, this is my song,
Praising my Savior all the day long.

1. PRAISE GOD FOR WHO HE IS.

"Let me hear in the morning of thy steadfast love, for in thee I put my trust. Teach me the way I should go, for to thee I lift up my soul" (Psalm 143:8).

In this beautiful verse I see you from several perspectives: (1) You speak to us through your word—as I meet with you this morning I can confidently expect to hear you speak to me. I am never disappointed! Praise your name.

Each of the varied expressions I receive from you (and I am but a poor representative of all men who love you) is an expression of your steadfast love. (2) It is more than just *good* to put my trust in you—it is *glorious*. My trust is placed in your total person and this is more wonderful than I am able to express.

Express yourself in adoration for this quality of God.
Speak it audibly or write out your praise in your own devotional journal.

2. PRAISE GOD FOR WHAT HE MEANS TO ME.

Just for me. Once again the objective and the subjective aspects of my worship before you have overlapped. Morning seems to be a favorite time for David—and for David's illustrious son. It is surely *the* very best time of the day for me. When I am rested and fresh and all the world is new and bright with prospect. None of this would be true if I did not arise with the purpose of hearing your voice as I open your word. How blessedly true is the next phrase: "Teach me the way I should go, for to thee I lift up my soul." It would be a simple matter if I would pause before your throne and you would give me my instructions for the day—to some extent this is what happens—but in the larger sense I am given but the small part of the larger lesson.

How do you personally relate to the steadfastness of God, and God who is love?
Speak it out or write it out. It is *so important* that you establish *your own* devotional journal.

3. CONFESSION OF SIN

Why is it so easy some mornings and so difficult other mornings to come to hear of your steadfast love? I know it is the fluctuation of my spirit and not of yourself. You have not changed or moved—I have! But I am glad to acknowledge that there has never been a time when I did not hear your voice as I read your word, if I acted on conviction and commitment and not only on the joyous feelings I have at times. It is my sincere desire to repair the changing moods of my heart so that at all times I can lift up my whole inner being before your throne of grace.

What personal sins do you want to confess? We *must* speak them to remove them.
Do it! *Now.* There is no one else you have sinned against more than God. Tell him so!

4. SING A PRAYER TO GOD.

Come, Thou Almighty King,
Help us Thy name to sing,
Help us to praise:
Father, all glorious,

O'er all victorious,
Come, and reign over us,
Ancient of Days.

Open your hymn book and sing the rest of the verses—or even sing another prayer song.

5. READ HIS WORD TO HIM!

His Word

The king said to the girl, "Ask me for anything you want, and I'll give it to you." [23] And he promised her with an oath, "Whatever you ask I will give you, up to half my kingdom."

[24] She went out and said to her mother, "What shall I ask for?"

"The head of John the Baptist," she answered.

[25] At once the girl hurried in to the king with the request: "I want you to give me right now the head of John the Baptist on a platter."

[26] The king was greatly distressed, but because of his oath and his dinner guests, he did not want to refuse her. [27] So he immediately sent an executioner with orders to bring John's head.   — Mark 6:22b-27a, NIV

Read His Word to Him.

There could hardly be a more tragic place in the events of men. When life is in the balance all heaven pauses to see the outcome. How many millions of times such a decision has been made! No life is unimportant. No life is expendable like so much chaff. How much more was this true when the life of your prophet John was in the balance. There was no love involved in this whole transaction. Lust is not love—there is indeed "strong desire" (or lust) in love—but strong desire directed toward our own selfish ends cannot be described as love. Love is giving to others. Love is doing for others what is best for them. Lust is wholly selfish. All present were selfish: (1) the daughter was a pawn, but selfish. (2) Herodias was the essence of selfishness. (3) Herod was there to do nothing else but satisfy his lust.

Please express your response to this beautiful text. Put your expression in your own prayer diary.

6. READ HIS WORD FOR YOURSELF.

How easy it is to condemn someone else—and forget how very much we are also involved! This little senario could be repeated in one form or another in many a life. Dare I say it? in *my* life? in *your* life? Dear Lord, thou knowest! Forgive me. Does lust always result in embarrassment and regret? When it gets out of hand and goes public it can indeed repeat the embarrassment of Herod— but even if we find no regret in this life there is all eternity ahead. The total consequence of our utter selfishness can be played back to us. Dear Lord, I want you to permanently erase ten thousand of my tapes! I am glad for the promise that you already have. I find it increasingly easy to not remember. Praise your name!

It is so important that you pause in his presence
and either audibly or in written form tell him all his word means to you.

7. READ HIS WORD IN THANKSGIVING.

(1) Thank you for the impulsiveness of Herod—in it we see ourselves and our weakness. (2) Thank you for the hateful scheming of Herodias—it tells us that there have always been such people, but they were no happier then than now. (3) Thank you for John's release from this life—he was glad to enter your presence. (4) Thank you for the shock given to Herod—maybe somebody spoke to him about our Lord while his conscience was tender. (5) Thank you for the man who wielded the sword or ax in cutting off John's head—how I hope he too began to evaluate the whole circumstance. (6) Thank you for Herodias—she could have remembered ere too late the enormity of her sin. (7) Thank you for the daughter— perhaps she learned from this episode and decided to serve someone better than her mother.

Give yourself to your own expression of gratitude—write it or speak it!

8. READ HIS WORD IN MEDITATION.

"Then the king was sorry, but he was embarrassed to break his oath in front of his guests." Mark seems to suggest that if it were only a matter of breaking his oath with the daughter of Herodias or with God he would not have hesitated. Peer pressure is an awesome power! Was it wine that prompted the oath at the beginning? Was it the enflamed power of lust that put him in this embarrassment? It was all of this, but beneath it all it was Herod's weak character that did it. How often have we found ourselves in almost the same position? Just as often as we allow what "everyone" else thinks to mean more to us than what our Lord has said.

Pause—wait—think—then express yourself in thoughtful praise or thanks.

9. READ HIS WORD FOR PETITIONS.

Herod must have been very drunk to open his mouth with such a rash promise—there are various ways of being intoxicated—set a watch on my lips: (1) How easy it is to boast in the presence of our peers—humble my heart. (2) What a pawn was this daughter of Herodias!—but no more than some of us under different conditions—open the eyes of my conscience. (3) Why did Herod make such a foolish promise?—pride?—lust?—glory of men? Today the evil one will tempt me in these same areas—I want to be "slow to speak." (4) How totally unexpected was the request—how it hurt Herod—*sin does have wages!*

Right here add your personal requests—and his answers.

10. READ HIS WORD AND WAIT—LISTEN—GOD SPEAKS!

Speak to me in a very personal way: (1) "Resentment demands a terrible price." (2) "Mothers carry a heavy responsibility." (3) "Wake up—sin is here."

11. INTERCESSION FOR THE LOST WORLD

Iran — Point for prayer: (1) *The "Christians" of the ancient churches* are all too often living lives that cause Muslims to despise Christianity. Yet it is from these groups that most of the conversions have come. Very few of the believers have been converted out of a Muslim background, so are not really equipped to evangelize Muslims, nor are they always welcoming to converts out of Islam. Very rarely does a Muslim meet a true believer who is willing to witness to him.

12. SING PRAISES TO OUR LORD.

Holy, holy, holy! Lord God almighty!
Early in the morning our song shall rise to Thee;

Holy, holy, holy! Merciful and Mighty,
God in three persons, blessed Trinity!

WEEK FORTY-NINE — FRIDAY

1. PRAISE GOD FOR WHO HE IS.

"Teach me to do thy will, for thou art my God! Let thy good spirit lead me on a level path" (Psalm 143:10).

I praise your name this morning! Such important qualities of yourself are suggested in this verse—you are a teacher—your Son came to teach and preach. Implicit in this designation are other attributes: (1) You have a great store of knowledge to share with men. (2) That you *want* to communicate with us is so important. (3) You have direction and instruction especially suited to our needs. (4) You have the right by reason of your nature—we would expect you to so instruct us. (5) It is by your spirit you lead men on a level path.

Express yourself in adoration for this quality of God.
Speak it audibly or write out your praise in your own devotional journal.

2. PRAISE GOD FOR WHAT HE MEANS TO ME.

Just for me. I cast myself upon you in thanksgiving and praise and expectation. I want to relate each of the above qualities of yourself to me: (1) *Indeed, indeed* you do have a great store of knowledge you want to share just with me (and I am only representative). You have two books out of which to teach me: (a) your Word; (b) my experience. (2) I believe, like most teachers, you are far more interested in communicating than we as students are in learning—I want to be that eager student on the front row. (3) The lessons you will teach me each day are especially prepared for my needs—praise you for such interest. (4) You are my God—and therefore you have my total respect and interest as a student.

How do you personally relate to the knowledge of God, and God who is a teacher?
Speak it out or write it out. It is so important that you establish your own devotional journal.

3. CONFESSION OF SIN

How like the poorest students I have had I do appear to you! There are several kinds of poor students—and I see myself before you in every one: (1) There is that student who comes because his parents insist that he must. A sense of duty brings him to the classroom, but many times it is an unwilling sense of duty. (2) There is that student who already knows what he wants to do, and does not come to be taught but to teach. (3) The student who sits in class because that is where he has sat ever since he can remember. When one graduates from high school one enrolls in college and sits in another class. Dear Lord, dear teacher, forgive me! I am glad that these same students can suddenly (at times) become the open, willing learners we all want to be. Some loving words directed by your Spirit can lead us on your "level path." Speak to me; I want to learn!

What personal sins do you want to confess? We must speak them to remove them.
Do it! Now. There is no one else you have sinned against more than God. Tell him so!

4. SING A PRAYER TO GOD.

Break Thou the bread of life,
Dear Lord, to me,
As Thou didst break the loaves
Beside the sea;

Beyond the sacred page
I seek Thee Lord;
My spirit pants for Thee,
O living Word.

Open your hymn book and sing the rest of the verses—or even sing another prayer song.

5. READ HIS WORD TO HIM!

His Word

[6]On Herod's birthday the daughter of Herodias danced for them and pleased Herod so much [7]that he promised with an oath to give her whatever she asked. [8]Prompted by her mother, she said, "Give me here on a platter the head of John the Baptist." [9]The king was distressed, but because of his oaths and his dinner guests, he ordered that her request be granted [10]and had John beheaded in the prison. [11]His head was brought in on a platter and given to the girl, who carried it to her mother. [12]John's disciples came and took his body and buried it. Then they went and told Jesus.

[13]When Jesus heard what had happened, he withdrew by boat privately to a solitary place. Hearing of this, the crowds followed him on foot from the towns. [14]When Jesus landed and saw a large crowd, he had compassion on them and healed their sick.   — *Matt. 14:6-14, NIV*
Read also Mark 6:27b-29; Luke 9:7-9.

Read His Word to Him.

Here is the whole sad incident again before us. Dear Lord, I want only to read it several times and make a few expressions of praise and wonder as related to the closing words. I do wonder what the guards thought as they went to perform their grisly job. What did they think of John? of Herod? of Herodias? of her daughter? of themselves and their task? Will we ever know? How sad must have been our Lord when he received the news, but was it really news to him? All such questions serve to open my heart to you.

Please express your response to this beautiful text. Put your expression in your own prayer diary.

6. READ HIS WORD FOR YOURSELF

Just for me. From a purely personal view I want to try and answer some of these questions: (1) What did the guards think of John? If they were in his audience as unrepentant sinners they probably thought "It's good to get rid of him and his message against my sin." If they believed John they must have thought: "How sad, Herod is the one who should lose his head—as a matter of fact, it is because he lost his head that we are on our sorry mission." (2) What did the guards think of Herodias and her daughter? If some women could only know what some men think of them it would shock them to see how far removed these thoughts are from what these women thought these men were thinking. The physical attraction was not ignored but the character of those involved was much removed from the lust of the moment.

It is so important that you pause in his presence
and either audibly or in written form tell him all his word means to you.

7. READ HIS WORD IN THANKSGIVING.

(1) Thank you for your promises that are never made in haste. (2) Thank you I can be warned by this incident of the tragic consequences of selfish lustful decisions. (3) Thank you for reminding me again that there are men and women who will lie and cheat and steal regardless of the consequences. (4) Thank you for the beautiful record of John's life. (5) Thank you for the tender love John's disciples had for their teacher. (6) Thank you for the message John's disciples carried to Jesus. (7) Thank you for the hope mingled with grief in the death of John.

Give yourself to your own expression of gratitude—write it or speak it!

8. READ HIS WORD IN MEDITATION.

"And his disciples came and took the body and buried it; and went and told Jesus." What fond memories must have flooded the hearts of the men who came to take the body of John! People will make an evaluation of all of us shortly after our death. Will they remember us for some of the same qualities we see in John? (1) He was disciplined. From his birth he lived as a Nazarite—i.e. he lived apart from the ordinary lifestyle. He did have a different wardrobe and diet, but his distinction consisted most of all in his attitude. Do we care or dare to be different? (2) He was clear in his ethical code. There was never any doubt about what John believed about right and wrong.

Pause—wait—think—then express yourself in thoughtful praise or thanks.

9. READ HIS WORD FOR PETITIONS.

What a sad day it was for the disciples of John and for our Lord. It should indeed lead us to prayer: (1) Help me to be as ready to buy up the opportunity for good as Herodias was for evil. (2) What did the guests think of Herod? Deliver me from the need of the approval of men. (3) What did Herodias think of her offering on the platter? Such revenge really never satisfies—do I really believe all vengeance belongs to you? (4) What thoughts were in the hearts of John's disciples as they prepared his body for burial? A good life provides a good death. (5) Our Lord himself delivered the eulogy for John—may I be as ready to give credit where credit is due.

Please, please remember these are prayers—speak them—reword them!

10. READ HIS WORD AND WAIT—LISTEN—GOD SPEAKS!

In this sad incident there is much I can hear for my own heart: (1) "You can expect daughters to be very much like their mother—for good or evil." (2) "My Lord needed prayer as he thought of his dear friend John—can you do less in the loss of loved ones?"

11. INTERCESSION FOR THE LOST WORLD

Iran — Point for prayer: (1) *The Protestant Church* is very small and weak. Many of the little churches suffer from personality clashes, divisions and problems. Many are second and third generation Protestants and nominal. There are only about 500 believers in the whole country that meet together with any regularity. Pray for believers and churches to be revived, become Bible based, and to be mobilized for winning the lost. What a tragedy that the Church is such a hindrance to the Gospel in a time like this.

12. SING PRAISES TO OUR LORD.

O worship the King all glorious above,
O gratefully sing His pow'r and His love.

Our Shield and Defender, the Ancient of days,
Pavilioned in splendor and girded with praise.

1. PRAISE GOD FOR WHO HE IS.

"Great is the Lord, and greatly to be praised, and his greatness is unsearchable. One generation shall laud thy works to another, and shall declare thy mighty acts" (Psalm 145:3, 4).

In this generation I want to lift up my voice and heart in adoration. Your greatness is so manifold it will be difficult to express. Yet this is my purpose. You are great in the care and love you supply to all men. There are primi-tive people whose life appears to us as most difficult. Upon a careful investigation you have somehow given them the ability to cope. It isn't that we should not attempt to help, but I want to acknowledge your provision of courage and survival. In this land of plenty how easy it is to be selfish and forgetful. I want to return praise for every good gift of this day.

Express yourself in adoration for this quality of God.
Speak it audibly or write out your praise in your own devotional journal.

2. PRAISE GOD FOR WHAT HE MEANS TO ME.

Just for me. You are great in so many ways, in each of them I want to praise you: (1) Great in love: how very kind and longsuffering you have been to me; bless your name forever. (2) Great in mercy: ten thousand times ten thousand you have given me good things undeserved. (3) Great in protection: over the millions of miles I have traveled I have not been injured. It is not because of my superior position or person; it is because of your good-ness. (4) Great in hope: for each day my hope is in you. For all the days ahead and for eternity my hope is in you. (5) Great in purpose: if I could not open your Word and find my reason for living and dying life would be useless. Surely, "great and greatly to be praised" describes yourself.

How do you personally relate to the greatness of God, and God who is to be praised?
Speak it out or write it out. It is so important that you establish your own devotional journal.

3. CONFESSION OF SIN

Dear Lord, why do I find it sometimes difficult to praise you? It is because my capacity for praise is prostituted on myself or someone or something else. Dear Lord, forgive me! It is also because complaining or finding fault is so much a part of my interest. Dear Lord, forgive me. Awaken me to the terrible need to laud your works to the next generation. We are always just one generation from pagan-ism. How I do want to delight myself in your word—in your Son. Forgive me for apathy and business that absorbs the time that should be and could be given to developing the motivation for praise. Ungratefulness is a serious sin. Keep me aware of this.

What personal sins do you want to confess? We must speak them to remove them.
Do it! Now. There is no one else you have sinned against more than God. Tell him so!

4. SING A PRAYER TO GOD.

The whole world was lost in the darkness of sin;
The Light of the world is Jesus;
Like sunshine at noonday His glory shone in,
The Light of the world is Jesus.

Come to the Light, 'tis shining for thee;
Sweetly the Light has dawned upon me;
Once I was blind, but now I can see;
The Light of the world is Jesus.

Open your hymn book and sing the rest of the verses—or even sing another prayer song.

5. READ HIS WORD TO HIM!

His Word

[30] The apostles gathered around Jesus and reported to him all they had done and taught. [31] Then, because so many people were coming and going that they did not even have a chance to eat, he said to them, "Come with me by yourselves to a quiet place and get some rest." [32] So they went away by themselves in a boat to a soli-tary place. [33] But many who saw them leaving recognized them and ran on foot from all the towns and got there ahead of them. [34] When Jesus landed and saw a large crowd, he had compassion on them, because they were like sheep without a shepherd. So he began teaching them many things. *— Mark 6:30-34, NIV*
Read also Matthew 14:14, 13; Luke 9:10, 11; John 6:1, 2.

Read His Word to Him.

How beautifully thoughtful was our Lord! Jesus had been just as busy as his apostles, but when they returned he suggested they go to a quiet place and get some rest. The apostles had been busy—they reported to our Lord all they had done and taught. How I would like to hear their words! How long did it take for this report? We do not know the length of time, but we do know that during it there was such a press of people with so many to be healed and taught that there was not even time enough to eat. Luke tells us the apostles and our Lord decided that Bethsaida would be a good place for rest.

Please express your response to this beautiful text. Put your expression in your own prayer diary.

WEEK FORTY-NINE — SATURDAY

6. READ HIS WORD FOR YOURSELF.

Just for me. There was no escaping the crowd and their needs. Indeed, Jesus really did not want to avoid the crowd. Our Lord struggled with the same problem every busy preacher or teacher has: how shall we find enough energy to meet all the needs? How shall we avoid a collapse? Jesus managed it. We are sure our Lord was calling on his Father for strength and grace equal to the task. But we are also sure Jesus was not calling on any resources of strength that are not available to us in overcoming the weaknesses of the flesh. Jesus was relaxed in the midst of his work. It is a clear conscience that gives us the needed confidence and through this the strength to do what needs to be done.

It is so important that you pause in his presence
and either audibly or in written form tell him all his word means to you.

7. READ HIS WORD IN THANKSGIVING.

(1) Thank you for the spontaneous joy in the hearts of the apostles that prompted them to share with our Lord. (2) Thank you that Jesus did not ignore anyone, but he did decide who would get his attention. (3) Thank you for my Lord's plain statement that rest is necessary. (4) Thank you for the ability of Jesus and the apostles to decide a course of action in the middle of constant demands upon their time. (5) Thank you for the persistence of the crowd —without it they would not have been helped. (6) Thank you for the continual compassion of my Lord. (7) Thank you for the healing ministry of Jesus —so full and complete and satisfying to all.

Give yourself to your own expression of gratitude —write it or speak it!

8. READ HIS WORD IN MEDITATION.

"He welcomed them and spoke to them about the kingdom of God, and healed those who needed healing." What an incredible example of unselfishness is our Lord! It was because of the fatigue and lack of rest he and his apostles had started on this journey. When their plans were frustrated Jesus remained calm and allowed the need of the crowd to overcome his need for rest. Fatigue is very largely mental, most especially in the kind of work in which our Lord and his apostles were engaged. The rule of God in the hearts and lives of men was more important than personal comfort. The little phrase ". . . those who needed healing" is most interesting. Jesus did not heal those who deserved healing or those who expected healing, but *all* those who needed it. What a wonderful Savior is Jesus my Lord!

Pause —wait —think —then express yourself in thoughtful praise or thanks.

9. READ HIS WORD FOR PETITIONS.

How soon after the death of John did the demands of life crowd in upon our Lord —how like our own life —he needed prayer —so do we: (1) It was important for the disciples to tell Jesus of what they said and did —dear Lord I am glad for this example. (2) The "coming and going" of people was such a drain on the energies of my Lord he needed rest —so do I! Help me to recognize this need. (3) How glad I am to find each day a quiet place where I can talk with you and my Lord —I want to guard it closely. (4) They were not able to find the "solitary place" —but there was a little rest in the boat with him and it was enough. (5) The needs of people took precedence in the life of my Lord —give me grace to follow him.

Right here add your personal requests —and his answers.

10. READ HIS WORD AND WAIT —LISTEN —GOD SPEAKS!

Speak to me from these busy days of Jesus: (1) "Deepen —oh, deepen your compassion for the sheep without a shepherd." (2) "Teaching —not only food and healing will meet their needs." (3) "Variety in teaching is *so* important —remember to give it!"

11. INTERCESSION FOR THE LOST WORLD.

Iran — Point for prayer: (1) *Leadership training* is virtually non-existent. There is a small program that has now been launched. Pray for the raising up of strong, spiritual men of God to lead the churches into a new era of growth.

12. SING PRAISES TO OUR LORD.

Holy, Holy, Holy, Lord God Almighty!
Early in the morning our song shall rise to Thee;

Holy, Holy, Holy! Merciful and Mighty!
God in Three Persons, blessed Trinity!

1. PRAISE GOD FOR WHO HE IS.

"Blessed be the Lord, my rock, who trains my hands for war, and my fingers for battle; my rock and my fortress, my stronghold and my deliverer, my shield and he in whom I take refuge, who subdues the people under him" (Psalm 144:1, 2). In this psalm of David he is thinking of physical combat. With us we think of the battle of life. We are in a war, we are fighting the good fight of faith.

You are described in these two verses as: (1) my rock; (2) the one who trains us for war; (3) the one who prepares our fingers for battle; (4) my fortress; (5) my stronghold; (6) my deliverer; (7) my shield; (8) in whom I take refuge; (9) the one who subdues the people under him. In each of these relationships I lift up my heart in praise!

Express yourself in adoration for this quality of God.

2. PRAISE GOD FOR WHAT HE MEANS TO ME.

Just for me. I should begin with the full acknowledgement that you are *Lord* — and then follow each of the nine relationships. I have praised you before in each of these qualities, but since those days you have not changed — praise your name! You are the One solid, unchanging Person I find in this life. I believe that even now, right now you are training me to put to rout the enemy of my soul. In a particular sense you are refining my preparation so I will be able to overcome in the personal encounter I have with the evil one. I must admit often that the battle is too much for me — I *must* have a resting place — I must find a fortress of meditation and quiet.

How do you personally relate to the war, and God who prepares us for it?
Speak it out or write it out. It is *so important* that you establish *your own* devotional journal.

3. CONFESSION OF SIN

All of the above is true — yea, more than true. But none of the above is as full and complete as it should be, and can be. You are my rock, but I have been lost in many a swamp. You can train me for war, but I have been late to class or absent without excuse. You can prepare me for the hand-to-hand combat, but I wasn't listening when you spoke. You are my fortress and stronghold, but I would prefer to lay out in the field and complain that I had nowhere to go and it was not my fault if I was overcome. You are my deliverer and shield but I would rather do it myself. Dear, dear Lord, what a terrible admission of my sin. Thank you for opening my eyes. Turn repentance to joy!

What personal sins do you want to confess? We *must* speak them to remove them.
Do it! *Now.* There is no one else you have sinned against more than God. Tell him so!

4. SING A PRAYER TO GOD.

The whole world was lost in the darkness of sin;
The Light of the world is Jesus!
Like sunshine at noonday His glory shone in,
The Light of the world is Jesus.

Come to the Light, 'tis shining for thee;
Sweetly the Light has dawned upon me;
Once I was blind, but now I can see;
The Light of the world is Jesus.

Open your hymn book and sing the rest of the verses — or even sing another prayer song.

5. READ HIS WORD TO HIM!

His Word

[15] As evening approached, the disciples came to him and said, "This is a remote place, and it's already getting late. Send the crowds away, so they can go to the villages and buy themselves some food."
[16] Jesus replied, "They do not need to go away. You give them something to eat."
[17] "We have here only five loaves of bread and two fish," they answered.

[18] "Bring them here to me," he said. [19] And he directed the people to sit down on the grass. Taking the five loaves and the two fish and looking up to heaven, he gave thanks and broke the loaves. Then he gave them to the disciples, and the disciples gave them to the people.
— *Matthew 14:15-19, NIV*

Read also Mark 6:35-42.

Read His Word to Him.

I am truly hesitant to take up this narrative in your presence! Even your Son used this incident as the basis of a lesson on the bread of life. Truly evening has come and we all are in a remote place! For how many hours had my Lord taught them before supper time? It was a crucial hour — if the crowds were not now sent away they could not get to a village before sundown or in time to eat. What a total shock it was to hear the words of your Son: *"They do not need to go away. You give them something to eat"*! We are sure Jesus did this to open their eyes to their insufficiency and his sufficiency.

Please express your response to this beautiful text. Put your expression in your own prayer diary.

6. READ HIS WORD FOR YOURSELF.

How we would like to have been the little boy on that day! Perhaps we can. As our Lord continued to break the loaves and fish they continued to appear in his hands. Ah, but *before* he did it he prayed. Jesus looked up to heaven. What did he see? The same white clouds and blue sky, but it was all so different to him. He saw also the canopy of space he and his Father had created for these people — and all others who lived under it. Now the same Father and Son were about to create food to feed this hungry multitude. This creation was to be just as subtle as the present one on which and under which these people lived. If those who ate did not look very closely they would hardly know from whence it came. Indeed, some never did! But one little boy did!

It is so important that you pause in his presence
and either audibly or in written form tell him all his word means to you.

7. READ HIS WORD IN THANKSGIVING.

(1) Thank you for the obvious extremity which became your opportunity. (2) Thank you for the practical interest of the disciples in the welfare of the people. (3) Thank you that Jesus opened the eyes of the disciples as to just how all needs are met: by himself. (4) Thank you that Jesus asks us to feed the multitude — through him. (5) Thank you that Jesus alone can feed the world, but he cannot feed the world alone. (6) Thank you for the little boy and his lunch — so like all of us. (7) Thank you for the orderliness of this whole incident — so like God!

Give yourself to your own expression of gratitude — write it or speak it!

8. READ HIS WORD IN MEDITATION.

"Then Jesus directed them to have all the people to sit down in groups on the green grass." Our Lord knew what he was doing at all times. His total confidence amid every circumstance is an evidence of his deity. It is also good to see how Jesus did not himself do everything; he gave instructions to others and trusted them with the task. The orderliness of the feeding of this multitude is not the least of its features. Mark indicates they were separated into groups of fifties and hundreds. It must have been a beautiful sight. With the variety of colors in the robes of the people as they were seated in groups they would look much like so many flower beds spread across the hills in the green grass. How beautiful are all his ways!

Pause — wait — think — then express yourself in thoughtful praise or thanks.

9. READ HIS WORD FOR PETITIONS.

In the preparations for this miracle of creation there is much about which to pray: (1) The disciples were concerned about the needs of the crowd — even as I want to be — but I want to look beyond the physical. (2) Indeed, "it is already getting late" — for me and the generation of which I am a part — if ever they are to have the bread of heaven it must be now! (3) Jesus never sent anyone away empty — Lord make me such a teacher! (4) My Lord asked the disciples to feed the crowd, even when he knew and they knew they could not do it — ". . . apart from me you can do nothing." (5) Five loaves and two fish in the hands of Jesus are more than enough for a multitude. (6) Love is doing what my Lord says — even when I do not understand.

Please, please remember these are prayers — speak them — reword them!

10. READ HIS WORD AND WAIT — LISTEN — GOD SPEAKS!

Speak to my heart again: (1) "Even Jesus pleased not himself — but those who did not appreciate what he gave." (2) "Giving of thanks is always in order." (3) "One of the disciples — yea, *two* of the disciples who distributed the loaves gave their eyewitness account."

11. INTERCESSION FOR THE LOST WORLD.

Iran — Point for prayer: (1) *Missions* — There are now about 130 missionaries and a further 150 Christians from other lands who seek to evangelize through their secular employment. Pray for a great increase in the number of the Lord's servants in this land, and also for the issuing of visas — these are not too easy to obtain. Much of the work of missions is in literature production and distribution and also in medical work (there are three Christian mission hospitals in the country).

12. SING PRAISES TO OUR LORD.

Come, Thou Almighty King,
Help us Thy name to sing,
Help us to praise.
Father, all glorious,
O'er all victorious,
Come, and reign over us,
Ancient of Days.

WEEK FIFTY — MONDAY

1. PRAISE GOD FOR WHO HE IS.

"I will extol thee, my God and King, and bless thy name for ever and ever. Every day I will bless thee, and praise thy name for ever and ever" (Psalm 145:1, 2).

What are the characteristics of yourself in these verses for which I can praise you? (1) The fact that it is possible to find qualities of yourself for which I can lift words of praise is in itself an attribute of yourself. (2) You are my God, the one before whom I bow and to whom I gladly give obeisance. (3) My king — the ruler of all. The present reigning monarch — the One who shall reign eternally. (4) It will be possible in eternity to continue our praise — throughout the endless life of heaven we shall have no problem finding reasons to lift our voices in wonder and adoration. (5) Each day I am alive on this earth I can extol your goodness.

Express yourself in adoration for this quality of God.
Speak it audibly or write out your praise in your own devotional journal.

2. PRAISE GOD FOR WHAT HE MEANS TO ME.

Just for me. In this song of praise David is setting an example of continual praise the qualities I see in your word for praise shall never fail. Should I live to the advanced age of one hundred I shall never exhaust the reasons for adoration of your very self. I am growing in my understanding of all it means to worship you as my God. In you I live and move and have my being, but totally outside of myself are the worlds you have made. (1) You have created such a lovely world of plants and trees. To know the one who has created the leaf I hold in my hand is a true source of wonder. (2) You have created the animal world. Our little dog is a curious and interesting example. As Creator I bow in amazement before you.

How do you personally relate to praising God, and God who is praiseworthy?
Speak it out or write it out. It is *so important* that you establish *your own* devotional journal.

3. CONFESSION OF SIN

In eternity — in the world and life to come I will indeed extol thee forever and forever. It is also very possible to praise you several times during this day. Will I do it? If the yesterdays are any example it could be that I will not. But yesterdays *are not* the examples. It is in David and in the lives of many others who worshiped you daily I have an example. The attitude of praise and gratitude is such a wonderful way to live. Forgive me for living below the plane of joy.

What personal sins do you want to confess? We *must* speak them to remove them.
Do it! *Now.* There is no one else you have sinned against more than God. Tell him so!

4. SING A PRAYER TO GOD.

Fairest Lord Jesus!
Ruler of all nature!
O Thou of God and man the Son!

Thee will I cherish,
Thee will I honor,
Thou, my soul's glory, joy, and crown!

Open your hymn book and sing the rest of the verses — or even sing another prayer song.

5. READ HIS WORD TO HIM!

His Word

[12]Late in the afternoon the Twelve came to him and said, "Send the crowd away so they can go to the surrounding villages and countryside and find food and lodging, because we are in a remote place here."
[13]He replied, "You give them something to eat."
They answered, "We have only five loaves of bread and two fish — unless we go and buy food for all this crowd." [14](About five thousand men were there.)

But he said to his disciples, "Have them sit down in groups of about fifty each." [15]The disciples did so, and everybody sat down. [16]Taking the five loaves and the two fish and looking up to heaven, he gave thanks and broke them. Then he gave them to the disciples to set before the people. — *Luke 9:12-16, NIV*
Read also John 6:3-12.

Read His Word to Him.

This is surely one of the most impressive of all the miracles your Son did during his whole ministry. I do want to allow each of these blessed words to enter my heart. The twelve came to Jesus to give him an order *"Send the crowd away. . . ."* Were they a little impatient with the interruption of their proposed rest? It was Andrew who found the boy with the five loaves and two fish. Andrew brought the lad to Jesus. This seems typical of this man: he brought his brother Peter to Jesus, he brought some Greeks to Jesus and now here a little boy. I am sure we shall never be able to appreciate the total impact of this miracle, but we can praise you and thank you for it.

Please express your response to this beautiful text. Put your expression in your own prayer diary.

WEEK FIFTY — MONDAY

6. READ HIS WORD FOR YOURSELF.

John says all who were there that day ate all they wanted — or ate until they were filled. Did anyone but our Lord thank the creator of all for what they were eating? The attitude of the crowd in throwing the fragments on the ground would indicate something of their carelessness. We wonder if when the apostles came to collect the partially eaten pieces did they have any help from the crowd. It must have taken some time to walk over the hills where each of the groups had been gathered and search out the broken pieces. Dear Lord, had I been there would I have helped them? I would like to think I would have. At least I want to do so now.

It is so important that you pause in his presence
and either audibly or in written form tell him all his word means to you.

7. READ HIS WORD IN THANKSGIVING.

(1) Thank you for the countermand of Jesus in his words, "You give them something to eat." (2) Thank you for the little lad — he never forgot that day. (3) Thank you for every single group — how I want to take my place in this picnic! (4) Thank you that all four biographers recorded this miracle. (5) Thank you that with my Lord nothing is wasted. (6) Thank you that nobody argued with my Lord. (7) Thank you that this miracle was so prominent no one ever thought of doubting it.

Give yourself to your own expression of gratitude — write it or speak it!

8. READ HIS WORD IN MEDITATION.

"They all ate and were satisfied." How beautifully typical is the feeding of these people and our Lord's response to the needs of the whole world. I believe there is not only more than enough food to feed the whole world, there is an abundance! There is more than enough to serve bread to the men and women of the earth. If the several million followers of our Lord would unite in their efforts to meet the needs of mankind we would soon have all eating and satisfied. How abundantly our Lord would satisfy the hearts of all men! When Jesus created the physical world he did so in a most lavish manner. Consider just the leaves for one tree — or the stars in one galaxy! It is the tragedy of all tragedies that the bread of life is held to the pantry while the world starves to death.

Pause — wait — think — then express yourself in thoughtful praise or thanks.

9. READ HIS WORD FOR PETITIONS.

We shall look through the eyes and hearts of Luke and John at this same miracle: (1) John says the Passover was near — indeed it was part of the Passover crowd he fed — am I as blind and preoccupied with my own affairs as were some of these religious folk? (2) Test my understanding and faith today — may I learn as well as Philip. (3) Andrew was "Mr. Nobody" — but it was Andrew who became very important by finding the boy with his lunch — may I learn this lesson. (4) There is something wonderfully orderly about all the actions of Jesus. Can I learn something here?

Right here add your personal requests — and his answers.

10. READ HIS WORD AND WAIT — LISTEN — GOD SPEAKS!

Speak to me out of this miracle: (1) "Jesus blessed *both* the loaves and the fish — so must everything be brought to me." (2) "Jesus gave more than enough — how do you give?"

11. INTERCESSION FOR THE LOST WORLD

Iran — Point for prayer: (1) *The Kurdish people* in the north west need to be evangelized. Their number has greatly increased with a large influx of Iraqai Kurds fleeing their land since the Iraqi government crushed their uprising with great ferocity in 1975. There are just a few seeking to reach these unfortunate people — pray for the planting of churches.

12. SING PRAISES TO OUR LORD.

Jesus is all the world to me,
My life, my joy, my all;
He is my strength from day to day,
Without Him I would fall.

When I am sad, to Him I go,
No other one can cheer me so;
When I am sad He makes me glad,
He's my Friend.

WEEK FIFTY — TUESDAY

1. PRAISE GOD FOR WHO HE IS.

"They shall speak of the glory of thy kingdom, and tell of thy power, to make known to the sons of men thy mighty deeds, and the glorious splendor of thy kingdom" (Psalm 145:11, 12).

If ever there was a fulfillment of these verses it is today! Of all men we can tell of the character of your kingdom. Your Son came announcing the soon coming of your kingdom. Since the beginning your rule in the hearts of men is your one glorious purpose. The fulness of this kingdom is found in the acceptance of the Lordship of Jesus. Your dear Son described your kingdom as a treasure hid in the field — a pearl of great price — like a mustard seed. Your "mighty deeds" as seen in the ministry of your Son are surely a source of good news. How men today need to hear of "the glorious splendor of thy kingdom." What a privilege to tell of such a king and of such a rule.

Express yourself in adoration for this quality of God.
Speak it audibly or write out your praise in your own devotional journal.

2. PRAISE GOD FOR WHAT HE MEANS TO ME.

Just for me. How shall I tell of the glory or essence of the body of your Son? — even his church. All of the kingdom is not seen in the church but the ultimate is here. I want to say that your kingdom is like a wedding feast. All who participate should be happy, but also related to what is happening. We can be happily engaged in our own interests and not be prepared when the bridegroom comes. I want to say your kingdom is like the return of a wealthy landholder to ask for a reckoning with his servants. Those who used what the master gave them to the master's advantage were rewarded — those who didn't were thrown out as unprofitable servants. The kingdom is like a gathering of all before the throne of the king of the universe. He will then tell us that when we served others we served him!

How do you personally relate to the kingdom of God, and God who is King?
Speak it out or write it out. It is *so important* that you establish *your own* devotional journal.

3. CONFESSION OF SIN

In all these familiar relationships I rejoice — and I also am moved to repentance. In each of the above areas I do want to change my mind: (1) I want to discover anew today the beauty and value of the forgiveness of sin and the eternal home. (2) I do purpose to sell all I have that I might have the one pearl of great price! (3) How I do want to this day fill up my vessel with the oil of gladness — may I be that kind of a light to someone. (4) Use whatever you have given me to your own advantage. Give me thoughtful decisions in the use of all your goods. (5) I do want to see your Son in the person of those with whom I live today. Most of all, forgive me for not telling those who need to hear of the glorious splendor of thy kingdom.

What personal sins do you want to confess? We *must* speak them to remove them.
Do it! *Now.* There is no one else you have sinned against more than God. Tell him so!

4. SING A PRAYER TO GOD.

Thou, my everlasting portion,
More than friend or life to me;
All along my pilgrim journey,
Savior, let me walk with Thee.
All along my pilgrim journey,
Savior, let me walk with Thee.

Open your hymn book and sing the rest of the verses — or even sing another prayer song.

5. READ HIS WORD TO HIM!

His Word

[13]So they gathered them and filled twelve baskets with the pieces of the five barley loaves left over by those who had eaten.

[14]After the people saw the miraculous sign that Jesus did, they began to say, "Surely this is the Prophet who is to come into the world." [15]Jesus, knowing that they intended to come and make him king by force, withdrew again into the hills by himself.   — *John 6:13-15, NIV*
Read also Matthew 14:20, 21; Mark 6:43, 44; Luke 9:17.

Read His Word to Him.

It is in the recovery of the fragments that Matthew and Mark indicate how many were fed. Counting the women and children along with the men there must have been not less than 15,000 fed that wonderful day. I am sure no one ever ate a better barley loaf or tasted a better piece of fish than the ones created by my Lord. The baskets used for the gathering — small baskets would not have permitted the rapid distribution of that day. Dear Lord, I am trying to enter the scene and sit with the crowd. I want to move over the hills and help the apostles gather up the leftovers.

Please express your response to this beautiful text. Put your expression in your own prayer diary.

6. READ HIS WORD FOR YOURSELF.

Just for me. The people who followed him did so because of his miracles. When they had shared in this miracle some of them were ready to take him by force and carry him to Jerusalem at the Passover as their king! Dear Lord, you *are* my king. I need to ask myself just *why* I want you to be my king. Do I follow you for the bread and the fish? Supposing I were suddenly placed in the harsh environment of one of the several third world countries I have seen — would I then serve you? My Lord had to retire for eight or nine hours of prayer just after this clamor to make him king. My dear Lord, I do want to serve you just for your own dear self and my love for you — deepen and purify my motives.

It is so important that you pause in his presence
and either audibly or in written form tell him all his word means to you.

7. READ HIS WORD IN THANKSGIVING.

(1) Thank you for the insistence of the writers that there were at least 15,000 fed. (2) Thank you for the tangible evidence of such a great miracle in the pieces left over. (3) Thank you for some who looked beyond the food to the One who had given it to them. (4) Thank you for my Lord who was indeed a Prophet — but much more than a prophet. (5) Thank you for the power of the personality of my Lord that he was able to dismiss the crowd who wanted to make him king. (6) Thank you that even Jesus felt his need to be alone and separated even from his disciples. (7) Thank you for the clear strong purpose by which my Lord walked all the way to Calvary.

Give yourself to your own expression of gratitude — write it or speak it!

8. READ HIS WORD IN MEDITATION.

"Jesus, knowing that they intended to come and make him king by force, withdrew again into the hills by himself." We do wonder just how often our Lord needed to find this solitude with God? There are many of us who do not have the pre-conditioning that would make such a withdrawal beneficial. A vacation or a temporary "break" in the routine can be very boring. It was only because Jesus had established contact with the Father in the usual daily living that a visit to the mountains became a real source of strength to him. If we have not established a prayer habit we are quite uncomfortable both when we are by ourselves in prayer or when we are called upon to lead in public devotion. These people did not want his personal rule in their lives, hence Jesus withdrew.

Pause — wait — think — then express yourself in thoughtful praise or thanks.

9. READ HIS WORD FOR PETITIONS.

In this record of gathering up the broken pieces that nothing should be lost there is much pause for prayer: (1) Jesus was against waste and loss — I want to be like him — but with the same attitude! (2) What immense crowd must have been present to have left such a quantity of fragments — impress on me again the wonder of this sign. (3) At least some of the people caught the supernatural aspects of what was happening — guard me against jumping at conclusions that are only partially thought out. (4) Deliver me from the inordinate praise of men. (5) Deliver me from any desire to seek such praise.

Please, please remember these are prayers — speak them — reword them!

10. READ HIS WORD AND WAIT — LISTEN — GOD SPEAKS!

You have spoken to me so many times in the record of this miracle — do it again: (1) "Surely I was *the Prophet* — but I must also decide what is to be done." (2) "Jesus needed to be by himself to pray when men wanted to acclaim him — go thou and do likewise." (3) "The fresh bread from heaven is available every day to give you new life."

11. INTERCESSION FOR THE LOST WORLD

Iran — Point for prayer: (1) *The university students* are neglected — pray for the raising up of a witness to them. Pray also for the conversion of Iranian students studying in other lands.

12. SING PRAISES TO OUR LORD.

My Jesus, I love Thee,
I know Thou art mine,
For Thee all the follies of sin I resign;

My gracious Redeemer, my Savior art Thou;
If ever I loved Thee, my Jesus, 'tis now.

WEEK FIFTY — WEDNESDAY

1. PRAISE GOD FOR WHO HE IS.

"The Lord upholds all who are falling, and raises up all who are bowed down" (Psalm 145:14). I like this lovely verse because it refers to me. But I know I am no different than millions of other persons who have this problem. In these words we find such strength and encouragement. For one reason or another man becomes weak and begins to stumble. He is like a man sick or drunk, he cannot walk. There is no word here as to why he falls—it is describ-ing the help of the helpless not the sin of the sinful. I am so glad for the frequent use of that little word *"all."* It is the very nature of yourself to reach out to help those who stumble. The second part of the sentence is in some ways even more of a source of praise—"The Lord . . . raises up all who are bowed down." Even if we have not stumbled there are times when we carry an intolerable burden.

Express yourself in adoration for this quality of God.
Speak it audibly or write out your praise in your own devotional journal.

2. PRAISE GOD FOR WHAT HE MEANS TO ME.

Just for me. In a most personal practical way I want to tell you how you have fulfilled this verse in my life and praise you for it. (1) I have been falling away from your desire to save the lost world in which I live. You have so many ways of lifting me and protecting me from this deception of Satan. You lead me to a magazine that describes the successful evangelistic efforts of people just like me. You give me a class to teach—I cannot teach what I do not do. (2) I have a sore temptation to mistake a part for the whole in the development of human charac-ter. It is so easy to condemn a whole class because of two or three poor students; to write-off a whole congregation because of a few unconverted leaders. Thank you *so* much for opening my eyes and heart to your value system.

How do you personally relate to the strength of God, and God who is our strength?
Speak it out or write it out. It is *so important* that you establish *your own* devotional journal.

3. CONFESSION OF SIN

How sad it is to admit that the divine help was available but I did not want it! I was falling and did not want to be stopped. I was bowed down but refused help. Why? Why? It is because there was a perverse sense of enjoy-ment in falling—or at least I was deceived into believing there would be. Satan's lie has been: "Isn't it easier to let the world go to hell? They are going there anyway—they don't care, or want salvation." It has *not* been easier. Men *can be* saved if we will teach them. What an easy mark we have become for our enemies' fiery darts of pride! Somehow we imagine someone's failure in class is a reflec-tion on our integrity. What a mistake! Somehow we decide we are "the pastor" or leader or head of the church and those who will not learn or lead are a reflection on us. Dear God, forgive me!

What personal sins do you want to confess? We *must* speak them to remove them.
Do it! *Now.* There is no one else you have sinned against more than God. Tell him so!

4. SING A PRAYER TO GOD.

Abide with me, fast falls the even tide,
The darkness deepens, Lord, with me abide.

When other helpers fail and comforts flee,
Help of the helpless, O abide with me.

Open your hymn book and sing the rest of the verses—or even sing another prayer song.

5. READ HIS WORD TO HIM!

His Word

[45]Immediately Jesus made his disciples get into the boat and go on ahead of him to Bethsaida, while he dismissed the crowd. [46]After leaving them, he went into the hills to pray.
[47]When evening came, the boat was in the middle of the lake, and he was alone on land. [48]He saw the disciples straining at the oars, because the wind was against them. About the fourth watch of the night he went out to them, walking on the lake. He was about to pass by them.

— *Mark 6:45-48, NIV*

Read also John 6:16-18.

Read His Word to Him.

Dear Lord, will I ever be able to say anything adequate to express my constant amazement at actions of your Son? How I wonder if the disciples asked him what he was going to do or if they wanted to know where he was go-ing. It would seem there was an irrestible urgency in our Lord. Both the crowds and the disciples responded to it. How I would like to know what he said in his prayer. Did Jesus know he was going to defy the laws of gravity and walk on the surface of the lake? Did he know the heart needs of his disciples—we know he did—was this the content of his prayer?

Please express your response to this beautiful text. Put your expression in your own prayer diary.

6. READ HIS WORD FOR YOURSELF.

How was it possible for Jesus to see the disciples in the middle of the night two or three miles from the shore as they struggled in the raging waters? Our Lord walked several miles on the surface of the lake to reach the boat. I want to get into the boat with the disciples. Indeed, I have been there many a time, i.e., the ship of my life has often been "making headway painfully." There are such poignant touches in the different accounts of his appearance: (1) *Matthew* says: ". . . they were terrified, saying, 'It is a ghost!' 'And they cried out in fear.'" (2) *Mark* says: "He meant to pass by them." (3) *John* says: ". . . they saw Jesus walking on the sea and drawing near to the boat." Such an amazing miracle! Dear Lord, I believe!

It is so important that you pause in his presence
and either audibly or in written form tell him all his word means to you.

7. READ HIS WORD INTHANKSGIVING.

(1) Thank you for the three accounts which all contribute something different. (2) Thank you for his blessed words: "It is I; do not be afraid." (3) Thank you for Mark's account: "Take heart, it is I; have no fear." (4) Thank you for the credibility of this miracle — several men were involved and the distance was great. (5) Thank you for the wonderful way our Lord combined meeting the needs of the disciples and demonstrating his deity. (6) Thank you for the time our Lord chose for this miracle — the most unlikely possible. (7) Thank you for the cumulative effect of his miracles.

Give yourself to your own expression of gratitude — write it or speak it!

8. READ HIS WORD IN MEDITATION.

"Take heart, it is I; have no fear." How often we do need to hear these words! It would seem our ship is caught in a storm most of the time. We need these powerful words each day. Our courage comes from our relationship with our Lord. Only when we recognize who he is does a calm possess our hearts. Jesus wanted the disciples to see him — this is indicated in Mark's comment that he appeared to want to walk past them. How he does have ways of attracting our attention so we will look through the storm and see him. How much more meaningful it was for Jesus to walk on the water at night in the midst of a storm rather than in the broad daylight on a calm lake. This calls attention to the need of the disciples as well as his deity. A daylight performance would have been just a performance.

Pause — wait — think — then express yourself in thoughtful praise or thanks.

9. READ HIS WORD FOR PETITIONS.

Our Lord is full of unexpected words and actions — as he retired to pray so I want to pause before those verses to pray: (1) Jesus did not even want his disciples to stay around for gossip about the miracle — he wanted to "call the shots" — it is so today! (2) I do wonder what he said to dismiss and disperse the crowd? He needs to break up some of our assemblies — give us ears to hear him. (3) Since Jesus put them in the boat and sent them out on the water didn't the disciples wonder when such a terrible storm broke on them? It happens now in my own life — let me learn. (4) Jesus looked through the dark night and saw the disciples at a distance of several miles — can I doubt that he sees me even now?

Right here add your personal requests — and his answers.

10. READ HIS WORD AND WAIT — LISTEN — GOD SPEAKS!

What wonderful encouragement is in this incident for me: (1) "I see your strain and confusion." (2) "I will test your faith to secure my response." (3) "Trust me — I know — I see — I care."

11. INTERCESSION FOR THE LOST WORLD

Iran — Point for prayer: (1) Literature has been widely distributed all over the country, and there has been an encouraging response from areas that have no Christian witness. Pray for this hard ministry and also for the work of these pieces of literature in the hearts of the readers.

12. SING PRAISES TO OUR LORD.

We praise Thee, O God,
For the Son of Thy love,
For Jesus who died
And is now gone above.
Hallelujah! Thine the glory, Hallelujah! Amen;
Hallelujah! Thine the glory, revive us again.

WEEK FIFTY — THURSDAY

1. PRAISE GOD FOR WHO HE IS.

"The Lord is just in all his ways, and kind in all his doings. The Lord is near to all who call upon him, to all who call upon him in truth" (Psalm 145:17, 18).

How easy it is when the sun is shining and every prospect pleases to agree with the palmist. But let the clouds gather in the sky and we begin to wonder — if the thunder rolls and the lightning strikes, we are sure some mistake has been made by the One who controls such activities. Dear Lord, I want to affirm my faith in your justice. I believe that whereas I cannot understand here it will not take you longer than a few years to explain it all when I awake in your likeness. Justice is easier to accept for all conditions than *kindness*, and yet I know full well such is indeed true of yourself.

Express yourself in adoration for this quality of God.
Speak it audibly or write out your praise in your own devotional journal.

2. PRAISE GOD FOR WHAT HE MEANS TO ME.

I claim just now the promise of the eighteenth verse: *"The Lord is near to all who call upon him. . . ."* As I lift my heart to you in praise and adoration I sense your presence and power. There is a deep awareness of peace in my heart; thank you for your grace! I must add the little phrase which is the key to this door of blessings: *"To all who call upon him in truth."* It is only when my heart is in agreement with what you have written that I have a claim upon this promise. Sin has a way of desensitizing our inner being. I do not come to persuade you to accommodate your word to my understanding or desires. I come to call upon you as a Father who can forgive and help His child. I *want* to do your will, O God!

How do you personally relate to the kindness of God, and God who is kind?
Speak it out or write it out. It is *so important* that you establish *your own* devotional journal.

3. CONFESSION OF SIN

How profoundly interesting is this time of worship. In this time before you I discover the depths of your truth and of the deception of my heart. How terribly destructive is the decision that in any circumstance you are not just or kind! How utterly divisive to the human personality it is to call upon you out of falsehood! May I relax just now, and as a child who trusts the love and wisdom of his parents say out of faith: "You are just in all your ways and kind in all your doings." I will never call upon you until I have repented of my sin and have brought my conduct in line with your word. How essential then is a daily confession of my sin and a whole hearted acceptance of your forgiveness!

What personal sins do you want to confess? We *must* speak them to remove them.
Do it! *Now.* There is no one else you have sinned against more than God. Tell him so!

4. SING A PRAYER TO GOD.

I will sing the wondrous story
Of the Christ who died for me,
How He left His home in glory
For the cross of Calvary.

Yes, I'll sing . . . the wondrous story
Of the Christ . . . who died for me, . . .
Sing it with . . . the saints in glory,
Gathered by . . . the crystal sea.

Open your hymn book and sing the rest of the verses — or even sing another prayer song.

5. READ HIS WORD TO HIM!

His Word

[25]During the fourth watch of the night Jesus went out to them, walking on the lake. [26]When the disciples saw him walking on the lake, they were terrified. "It's a ghost," they said, and cried out in fear.
[27]But Jesus immediately said to them: "Take courage! It is I. Don't be afraid."   — Matthew 14:25-27, NIV
About the fourth watch of the night he went out to them, walking on the lake. He was about to pass by them, [49]but when they saw him walking on the lake, they thought he was a ghost. They cried out, [50]because they all saw him and were terrified.   — Mark 6:48b-50, NIV
[16]When evening came, his disciples went down to the lake, [17]where they got into a boat and set off across the lake for Capernaum. By now it was dark, and Jesus had not yet joined them. [18]A strong wind was blowing and the waters grew rough. [19]When they had rowed three and a half miles, they saw Jesus approaching the boat, walking on the water; and they were terrified. [20]But he said to them, "It is I; don't be afraid."   — John 6:16-20, NIV

Read His Word to Him.

The disciples evidently believed in the presence of ghosts. We would understand this to be tantamount to the presence of demons. It must have been an accepted tradition that demons would at times appear in such a form. There was *indeed* something strange and frightening out there on the surface of the lake. I want to see this situation as much like the disciples as at all possible. Matthew (who was present in the boat) says they actually recognized Jesus, but because no one can walk on the water they simply would not accept what their eyes told them. The cries of fear and dread can be heard in my imagination even now.

Please express your response to this beautiful text. Put your expression in your own prayer diary.

6. READ HIS WORD FOR YOURSELF.

Jesus wasted no time calling attention to the sensational aspects of this miracle. He *"immediately"* spoke to them. The disciples could think of no reason for a ghost appearing to them, unless to strike terror into their hearts as they went into death through drowning. In another 30 seconds the emotions of the disciples would be out of control and panic would have taken over. It must have been with a loud firm voice my Lord said, *"Take heart, it is I; have no fear"*! Dear Lord, how I want to hear you speak to me in every situation! In the midst of a financial storm—"Take heart; it is I." While the waves of personal family problems roll: "Take heart; it is I." In all of such storms I hear him say: "Have no fear."

It is so important that you pause in his presence and either audibly or in written form tell him all his word means to you.

7. READ HIS WORD IN THANKSGIVING.

(1) Thank you for the small details of this account that make it so very credible. (2) Thank you that two who were there (Matthew and John) told the story. (3) Thank you for Mark who was so glad to report from these eye-witnesses. (4) Thank you that these men acted in such an expected manner. I relate wholly with them. (5) Thank you for the planning of my Lord evident in this incident. (6) Thank you for this demonstration of my Lord's power over the laws he himself originated. (7) Thank you for the multiplied thousands who have found assurance in these beautiful words.

Give yourself to your own expression of gratitude—write it or speak it!

8. READ HIS WORD IN MEDITATION.

"When they had rowed about three or four miles, they saw Jesus walking on the sea and drawing near to the boat." Three or four miles of rowing under the heavy weather here described would take several hours. It would seem the sea was not so dangerous that they were to be drowned—perhaps they were close to their destination when Jesus appeared upon the water. It would also seem that they saw him from some distance and became increasingly frightened as he approached them. We wonder at the guarded remarks of John (6:19), but then we remember he was a fisherman. Matthew and Mark were not fishermen and their accounts are full of terror.

Pause—wait—think—then express yourself in thoughtful praise or thanks.

9. READ HIS WORD FOR PETITIONS.

In the early hours of the morning—while it was still dark Jesus came to them "walking on the lake." In such a circumstance prayer is indeed appropriate: (1) Jesus does come at the strangest times and ways—but just when we need him most—thank you! (2) The disciples had no explanation but your supernatural power—this is enough. (3) I am terrified at the wrong person or thing; why should I be terrified at all? Help me. (4) The disciples believed in the spirit world—help me to share their faith. (5) Our Lord is immediate in his response to need—I want to remember for this day and its needs. (6) Why did he direct his steps as if he would pass them by? So it does seem full many a time in our own experience? He didn't—and he will not today.

Please, please remember these are prayers—speak them—reword them!

10. READ HIS WORD AND WAIT—LISTEN—GOD SPEAKS!

As he spoke to them in the dark storm of the early morning—speak to me: (1) "I am never far away—you are." (2) "I see you now as I did with them then." (3) "Take courage! It is I. Don't be afraid."

11. INTERCESSION FOR THE LOST WORLD

Iran — Point for prayer: (1) *Bible correspondence courses* have a very fruitful ministry among Muslims. The largest has handled over 45,000 applications and applicants come from every religious background.

12. SING PRAISES TO OUR LORD.

My Jesus, I love Thee, I know Thou art mine,
For Thee all the follies of sin I resign;

My gracious Redeemer, my Savior art Thou;
If ever I loved Thee, my Jesus 'tis now.

WEEK FIFTY — FRIDAY

1. PRAISE GOD FOR WHO HE IS.

"The Lord sets the prisoners free; the Lord opens the eyes of the blind. The Lord lifts up those who are bowed down; the Lord loves the righteous" (Psalm 146:7b, 8).

We are reminded of the words of your Son in Nazareth's synagogue. The psalmist found the same promise fulfilled in yourself. What more obvious evidence that you and your Son are one in nature? It is your purpose to set all the prisoners free! Praise your wonderful name! How all men can relate to this blessed good news. We could easily describe this whole planet as held captive. We have been taken captive and are held as hostage by the Evil One. Wonder of wonders the ransom has been paid and the hostages are set free! There is an infection that has blinded the eyes of the hearts of all men. Praise your name, the Great Physician has come! Those who are lifted up and whom you love are those once blind prisoners!

Express yourself in adoration for this quality of God.
Speak it audibly or write out your praise in your own devotional journal.

2. PRAISE GOD FOR WHAT HE MEANS TO ME.

Unless and until I can be specific the above description is but one of the millions of pious platitudes written and spoken over the years for the amusement of man's ego! What are the areas where I have been set free? What have I seen since I have become a Christian that indicates that once I was blind? Dear Lord, I am glad to answer these probing questions: (1) *I am free from every sin back of the last one I confessed!* (I feel like cramming such a testimony down Satan's throat!) (2) *I am free of hopelessness* — I have the highest possible hope for all I do in this life and the hope of heaven is an excitement beyond words. (3) *I am free of anxiety.* I believe my whole life is in the hands of — not of my employer — but my Father. In my liberty, I find my sight!

How do you personally relate to the liberating power of God, and God who sets us free?
Speak it out or write it out. It is *so important* that you establish *your own* devotional journal.

3. CONFESSION OF SIN

It is good that every day I can be reminded of the dichotomy operative in my experience. I am the prisoner set free, yet at times I am hindered and bound. I am the blind man who was given his sight and yet there are glorious vistas to which I have been blind. I am the one who was raised up and yet even today I am "down" in my spirit. Why? Why? The answer is threefold: (1) *The process is continuous.* There will be new freedoms and new vistas and new burdens lifted every day. (2) *The process is growing.* What I did not know was bondage yesterday I discovered today. What we never looked for yesterday we revel in today. An inward burden that we did not see was lifted. (3) *Satan is a liar.* We have imagined with the devil's help many shackles and eye problems and burdens that never existed! Praise your name, I am fine!

What personal sins do you want to confess? We *must* speak them to remove them.
Do it! *Now.* There is no one else you have sinned against more than God. Tell him so!

4. SING A PRAYER TO GOD.

Take time to be holy,
Speak oft with thy Lord;
Abide in Him always,
And feed on His Word.

Make friends of God's children;
Help those who are weak;
Forgetting in nothing His blessing to seek.

Open your hymn book and sing the rest of the verses — or even sing another prayer song.

5. READ HIS WORD TO HIM!

His Word

[28]"Lord, if it's you," Peter replied, "tell me to come to you on the water."

[29]"Come," he said.

Then Peter got down out of the boat and walked on the water to Jesus. [30]But when he saw the wind, he was afraid and, beginning to sink, cried out, "Lord, save me!"

[31]Immediately Jesus reached out his hand and caught him. "You of little faith," he said, "why did you doubt?"

[32]And when they climbed into the boat, the wind died down. [33]Then those who were in the boat worshiped him, saying, "Truly you are the Son of God."

— *Matthew 14:28-33, NIV*
Read also Mark 6:51, 52; John 6:21.

Read His Word to Him.

The daring of Peter has been a challenge to men over the centuries. There are many good things about Peter's request: (1) He wanted to confirm his faith in our Lord. (2) He accepted the supernatural nature of our Lord—it was almost more than he could understand but he did believe. (3) He believed Jesus even in this supernatural position would take an interest in Peter. (4) He believed that whatever Jesus said it would happen. There were also several hasty ill-judged aspects of Peter's request. (1) It would seem he wanted to do something no one else did—or could—but from the wrong motive. (2) Attention to himself would have resulted if he completed his walk.

Please express your response to this beautiful text. Put your expression in your own prayer diary.

6. READ HIS WORD FOR YOURSELF.

Dear Lord, perhaps I have misjudged Peter and he had no such motives. It does seem that the other apostles would soon make the same request and all would be walking on the water. Forgive me if I have not understood this correctly. It was the command of Jesus that got Peter out of the boat and controlled gravity. It was also the living faith of Peter that made it possible. It would seem that when his focus of attention was broken by the winds and the waves the control of our Lord was also broken and he began to sink. How full of meaning this is for me.

Pause in his presence and either audibly or in written form tell him all his word means to you.

7. READ HIS WORD IN THANKSGIVING.

(1) Thank you for our Lord's patient love for Peter. (2) Thank you that Jesus was willing to honor Peter's faith. (3) Thank you that Jesus never took his eyes off Peter. (4) Thank you for the all-inclusive request of Peter: "Lord, save me." (5) Thank you for the immediate response of my Lord to his need. (6) Thank you for the clear definition of faith and doubt in this text. (7) Thank you for the unqualified expression of worship directed toward our Lord: "Truly you are the Son of God!"

Give yourself to your own expression of gratitude—write it or speak it!

8. READ HIS WORD IN MEDITATION.

"And when they got into the boat the wind ceased." Even this storm had an end. Is there something analogous about this action? We could find a comparison or two. (1) In both incidents of the storm on the lake it was when they were aware of who was with them in the boat that the storm subsided. When we become aware of just who is in the same boat with us the wind will cease. We are so prone to living our life as if Jesus was somewhere in the middle of the lake. (2) Our Lord is interested in every trip of every disciple. He sees us in our distress, he shares our efforts to overcome. He marks our location and is there to help.

Pause—wait—think—then express yourself in thoughtful praise or thanks.

9. READ HIS WORD FOR PETITIONS.

In impetuous Peter we see ourselves over and over—he needed prayer—so do we: (1) Why did Peter need assurance? Jesus was willing to give it—thank you. (2) Walking on the water supports his deity—not our greatness—please let me remember. (3) In just that wonderful one-word answer: "Come," we have such encouragement! In how many situations will it fit today? (4) Peter did it! But for what purpose? Lord, examine my motives! (5) It was only the wind—but it made him afraid and he began to sink! Keep my eyes on your Son! (6) Here is a clear definition of faith—trust me—look to me—obey me.

Right here add yours personal request—and his answers.

10. READ HIS WORD AND WAIT—LISTEN—GOD SPEAKS!

There is much to hear and learn in this text: (1) "There is no time or place for doubt in your relationship with me!" (2) "I uphold all things by the word of my power." (3) "Signs are not the product—I would have been the Son of God if I never did one miracle."

11. INTERCESSION FOR THE LOST WORLD

Iran — Point for prayer: (1) *Christian radio broadcasts* have had an encouraging response. Pray for the preparation and broadcasting of these programs.

12. SING PRAISES TO OUR LORD.

All hail the pow'r of Jesus' name!
Let angels prostrate fall:
Bring forth the royal diadem,
And crown Him Lord of all,
Bring forth the royal diadem,
And crown Him Lord of all!

WEEK FIFTY — SATURDAY

1. PRAISE GOD FOR WHO HE IS.

"He heals the brokenhearted, and binds up their wounds. He determines the number of the stars, he gives to all of them their names. Great is our Lord, and abundant in power: his understanding is beyond measure" (Psalm 147: 3-5). How wide is the expanse of qualities here ascribed to yourself! (1) You take a personal interest in the emotional and physical life of every man. (2) You know when we hurt and if we will come to you you can bind up our wounds and they will heal. (3) You also have an interest in the stars. You have created them all and you have named them all. (4) We must say with the ancient singer — "Great is our Lord, and abundant in power; his understanding is beyond measure." Praise your name!

Express yourself in adoration for this quality of God.
Speak it audibly or write out your praise in your own devotional journal.

2. PRAISE GOD FOR WHAT HE MEANS TO ME.

How I do want to appropriate each of these attributes to my own life! Dear Lord, how much I do need you! I am so glad to come to Someone who can put together the pieces of the puzzle called my life. It would seem it needs repair quite often. I have had thoughts or intellectual schemes that seem to fall apart. In areas when I have been determined to go or stay I have done neither. My emotions have *not* been compatible with reality. In all of these ways my heart has been broken. I come to you and what a peace and wholeness I find! Your thoughts hold together—your determination is backed with your power to perform. My emotional response to what you have said and done is solid and true. The more I see of the large world outside the atmosphere of this earth the larger becomes the meaning of the expression: "his understanding is beyond measure."

How do you personally relate to the understanding of God, and God who is omniscient?
Speak it out or write it out. It is *so important* that you establish *your own* devotional journal.

3. CONFESSION OF SIN

Because of who you are and who I am the element of confession is surely a necessary part of my praise. At the same time I do *want* to confess my sin. I am glad to come to the One in whom I have unqualified confidence —to One who I know does not resent my coming—indeed I believe you are glad and warmly welcome me each time I turn my thoughts toward you. I am delighted to hold up my broken heart and ask you to make it whole. How many stars are there? Even man's computers would have a problem with such a figure. To create and sustain each one is enough—but to know them in detail and give them a name! You will have no problem with my little life— what seems complex to me is so simple for you. Thank you for forgiveness!

What personal sins do you want to confess? We *must* speak them to remove them.

4. SING A PRAYER TO GOD.

I can hear my Savior calling,
I can hear my Savior calling,

I can hear my Savior calling,
"Take thy cross and follow, follow Me."

Open your hymn book and sing the rest of the verses—or even sing another prayer song.

5. READ HIS WORD TO HIM!

His Word

[53]When they had crossed over, they landed at Gennesaret and anchored there. [54]As soon as they got out of the boat, people recognized Jesus. [55]They ran throughout that whole region and carried the sick on mats to wherever they heard he was. [56]And everywhere he went—into villages, towns or countryside—they placed the sick in the marketplaces. They begged him to let them touch even the edge of his cloak, and all who touched him were healed.

— *Mark 6:53-56, NIV*

Read also Matthew 14:33-36.

Read His Word to Him.

How rewarding it is to read again and again this interesting passage. I wonder what the disciples thought as they stepped out of the boat and saw all the people? The disciples were so full of wonder and amazement at what had just happened. They were hardly ready for the rushing about of the people to get their sick healed. The impact of the divinity of their Lord was still with them. This frenzied effort to use the Lord as a free source of physical help must have hit these disciples with a solid blow. Dear Lord, am I reading this aright? How I do want to!

Please express your response to this beautiful text. Put your expression in your own prayer diary.

6. READ HIS WORD FOR YOURSELF.

If there ever was an example of wholesale healing it is described here. I wonder just how many people were involved? There must have been hundreds if not thousands. There seems to be no resistance on the part of our Lord. Jesus knew what he was about. His mission was teaching. The healing was done and was not ignored or shunted to the side, but neither did it become first place. It was indeed first place in the lives of those who were sick. How could these people appreciate a lesson while they remained lame or palsied or nauseous? But there were more who were not sick and they needed healing of another sort. How many of the healed became consistent converts? It is remarkable to read: "All who touched him were healed."

It is so important that you pause in his presence
and either audibly or in written form tell him all his word means to you.

7. READ HIS WORD IN THANKSGIVING.

(1) Thank you for the wonderful popularity of my Lord. (2) Thank you that Jesus used his popularity to teach that many more people. (3) Thank you for the record of those who were there when it happened. (4) Thank you for the instantaneous, permanent healings of my Lord. (5) Thank you that there were none who were not healed who came to be healed. (6) Thank you that none who come to him today for the healing of their hearts are turned away disappointed. (7) Thank you we now have the purpose of his healing, i.e. his own deity.

Give yourself to your own expression of gratitude—write it or speak it!

8. READ HIS WORD IN MEDITATION.

"They begged him to let them touch even the edge of his cloak, and all who touched him were healed." It would seem that there was almost superstitious devotion directed toward our Lord. Jesus did not encourage such an attitude; at the same time he did not attempt to reprove these people. The remarkable fact is that "all who touched him were healed." Was it their faith that made them well? Of course it was, but of course it was our Lord's own power or "virtue" that healed these people. He never approved or disapproved of such action. His primary purpose was to teach. If these same persons stayed to listen they would have received something more valuable than their healing. We would like to believe many of them did.

Pause—wait—think—then express yourself in thoughtful praise or thanks.

9. READ HIS WORD FOR PETITIONS.

Surely our Lord is at the height of his popularity. I want to relate to this in prayer for wisdom: (1) If the hearts of those who served the bread and the fish were confused and burdened, what hope is there for me? The same as there was for them; open up my eyes! (2) It would seem the multitude related to Jesus on a very physical, selfish manner—but he did not rebuke them. Lord, I want to learn from this—help me. (3) Did Jesus teach them while he healed them? Or was there too much confusion? The healing was a form of teaching—meeting needs teaches so much—may I not forget. (4) All who touched him—and all he touched were healed—no failures. It is my heart that I want him to touch. It is my eyes I want him to open.

Please, please remember these are prayers—speak them—reword them!

10. READ HIS WORD AND WAIT—LISTEN—GOD SPEAKS!

Nothing is said in these verses—but they do have a voice for me: (1) "I did pile up miracle upon miracle for a purpose—have you accepted it?" (2) "I can touch you— you can touch me in a more meaningful way today than then." (3) ". . . and all who touched him were healed."

11. INTERCESSION FOR THE LOST WORLD

Iraq — Population: 11,400,000. Growth rate—3.3%. Average people per sq. km.—26.
Point for prayer: (1) *This land is now closed* for mission work and no open preaching of the Gospel is allowed, yet only a very small proportion of this Muslim country has ever had a chance to hear the Gospel. Pray for the barriers against the Word of God to be broken down.

12. SING PRAISES TO OUR LORD.

There is a name I love to hear,
I love to sing its worth;
It sounds like music in mine ear,
The sweetest name on earth.

Oh, how I love Jesus,
Oh, how I love Jesus,
Oh, how I love Jesus,
Because He first loved me!

WEEK FIFTY-ONE — SUNDAY

1. PRAISE GOD FOR WHO HE IS.

"His delight is not in the strength of the horse, nor his pleasure in the legs of a man; but the Lord takes pleasure in those who fear him, in those who hope in his steadfast love" (Psalm 147:10, 11). In David's day the above reference was probably to the cavalry and the infantry of the army of that day. The strength and defense of a nation is not in their military build-up but in his steadfast love. God is not impressed with man's brains any more than his legs. Dear Father, I am glad to be reminded of the real priorities of value in personal and national defense. Our hope is in you or we have no hope.

Express yourself in adoration for this quality of God.
Speak it audibly or write out your praise in your own devotional journal.

2. PRAISE GOD FOR WHAT HE MEANS TO ME.

I am simply delighted to acknowledge the fact that you can and do "take pleasure" in my fear and hope in you. What beautiful contrasts are fear (or reverence) and hope! Like the net of a fisherman hope is the cork and fear is the lead. In this manner the net is held in the water to catch all the benefits of life. Such a net is actually held against your "steadfast love" and what a draught is taken! If I am willing to accept without question some circumstances that plunge to the bottom my plans and pleasures; if at the same time I hold buoyantly to your steadfast love and hope in your character I am sure I will catch the greatest possible benefits of this life. Praise your name!

How do you personally relate to the strength of God, and God who is our strength?
Speak it out or write it out. It is *so important* that you establish *your own* devotional journal.

3. CONFESSION OF SIN

How easy it is to fall into Satan's trap of pride. It has been made by the evil one to seem natural to trust in man's ability. How easily we congratulate ourselves for our buildings or rockets! How obvious it all seems that we should take pride in the products of our brains. Dear Lord, the editorial "we" must be dropped. I stand blood-guilty before you! Forgive *me* not *them*. I am afraid of hell. I cringe and recoil at the thought of prolonged pain. I do fear you in this sense, but I am much more impressed with your greatness and steadfast love. I do indeed admit your justice and your mercy. In all of this attempt at confession I do want to sincerely commit myself to you. I embrace your forgiveness! How much I need it!

What personal sins do you want to confess? We *must* speak them to remove them.
Do it! *Now.* There is no one else you have sinned against more than God. Tell him so!

4. SING A PRAYER TO GOD.

I hear the Savior say,
"Thy strength indeed is small,
Child of weakness, watch and pray,
Find in Me thine all in all."

Jesus paid it all,
All to Him I owe;
Sin had left a crimson stain,
He washed it white as snow.

Open your hymn book and sing the rest of the verses—or even sing another prayer song.

5. READ HIS WORD TO HIM!

His Word

15 Then some Pharisees and teachers of the law came to Jesus from Jerusalem and asked, [2]"Why do your disciples break the tradition of the elders? They don't wash their hands before they eat!"

[3]Jesus replied, "And why do you break the command of God for the sake of your tradition? [4]For God said, 'Honor your father and mother' and 'Anyone who curses his father or mother must be put to death.' [5]But you say that if a man says to his father or mother, 'Whatever help you might otherwise have received from me is a gift devoted to God,' [6]he is not to 'honor his father' with it. Thus you nullify the word of God for the sake of your tradition.
— *Matthew 15:1-6, NIV*

Read also Mark 7:1-5.

Read His Word to Him.

What was once a good idea when repeated becomes a custom—when repeated long enough becomes a tradition. Soon the tradition has become a law with moral overtones. It is now no longer a good idea—it is right or wrong. Dear Lord, how may such things have happened with me? It was not necessary to wash in just the way the elders prescribed. The disciples of my Lord were not eating with dirty hands, they had just not gone through the ceremony. Their hands might not have been any cleaner when they finished washing than when they first began—but wash they must or be "unclean." Our Lord looked into the hearts of these men and saw nothing but the shell of form. All meaning has long since left. Greed and selfishness filled their lives.

Please express your response to this beautiful text. Put your expression in your own prayer diary.

6. READ HIS WORD FOR YOURSELF.

Our Savior confronts these men as he does me. "Which is the most important? breaking the traditions of men or the laws of God?" Indeed in the very act of keeping tradition we can and do violate the laws of God. It is traditional to substitute public worship and study for personal worship and meditation. We know vaguely that you have said we should have a personal relationship with you and that we should learn your word so as to apply it to our lives. But tradition has subtly substituted *Bible School* for personal study and *Worship Service* for personal devotion. We have not only exchanged one for the other we have broken the commandment of God! Dear Lord, forgive us. Our traditions have cancelled out your will in our lives — forgive us!

It is so important that you pause in his presence
and either audibly or in written form tell him all his word means to you.

7. READ HIS WORD IN THANKSGIVING.

(1) Thank you for the close examination our Lord received from the teachers at Jerusalem — he improved by this procedure. (2) Thank you for the blunt direct answer our Lord gave these men. (3) Thank you for reminding me again of how important it is to honor our parents. (4) Thank you for this incisive reminder that one law cannot cancel out another one. (5) Thank you for the very distinction made here between the laws of men and your law. (6) Thank you for the value system implicit in these verses. (7) Thank you for the wonderful courage of my Lord in the face of the authorities from Jerusalem.

Give yourself to your own expression of gratitude — write it or speak it!

8. READ HIS WORD IN MEDITATION.

"Thus you nullify the word of God for the sake of your tradition." Dear Lord, how blood guilty we are in this area. It is not traditional for church members to be involved in evangelism. One elder said recently "it is not natural." What he really meant is that it is not traditional. It is traditional to talk about it, to teach about it, to preach about it, but to do it on a one-to-one basis by the members of the body — that just does not get done. The word of God is as clear as can be that the members of the body in the first century spoke to every creature under heaven (Col. 1:23). The fundamental problem is that evangelism disturbs our comfortableness and interrupts our schedule. Dear Lord, forgive us, change us!

Pause — wait — think — then express yourself in thoughtful praise or thanks.

9. READ HIS WORD FOR PETITIONS.

Religious leaders are always full of questions — this can be both good and bad. How I need to prayerfully learn from this text: (1) Give me your wisdom in examining my motives. (2) Do I know what is tradition and what is truth? I want to. (3) "Thy word is truth" — all else is tradition — what can this mean to me in my life? (4) I do want to honor my parents — open my heart to learn how. (5) I know we have set aside your word by our traditions — how I do want your holy honesty to know just how I have done this. (6) Lord, where I have pretense and fear of men shine your light of truth.

Right here add your personal requests — and his answers.

10. READ HIS WORD AND WAIT — LISTEN — GOD SPEAKS!

How difficult it is to receive rebuke — speak to me: (1) "Honor from the heart is easily known." (2) "Men's rules for worship are nothing." (3) "Tradition has never been equal with truth and never will be."

11. INTERCESSION FOR THE LOST WORLD

Iraq — Points for prayer: (1) *Muslims are very hard to evangelize* — just a handful are known to have believed and this more often through hearing the Gospel while studying in other lands. For a Muslim to believe, it could mean certain death. (2) *The tragic Kurdish people*, now in the despair of defeat and oppression, have had little chance to hear of the Prince of Peace. There are virtually no believers among this 9,000,000 people scattered over Turkey, Iraq, Iran and the U.S.S.R., and there is only one group of believers known — in N.W. Iran, where a few Christian teams are seeking to give material aid and the Gospel to them. There have been some who have sought the Lord.

12. SING PRAISES TO OUR LORD.

We praise Thee, O God! for the Son of Thy love,
For Jesus who died, and is now gone above.
Hallelujah! Thine the glory;

Hallelujah! Amen!
Hallelujah! Thine the glory;
Revive us again.

WEEK FIFTY-ONE — MONDAY

1. PRAISE GOD FOR WHO HE IS.

"Praise the Lord! Praise the Lord from the heavens, praise him in the heights! Praise him, all his angels, praise him, all his host!" (Psalm 148:1, 2). We could never find an expression more appropriate to exemplify praise. In these verses we have entered into heaven itself and with the angels we lift our hearts in adoration. It is the expected response of all his creation. The sun, moon and stars are enlisted in one grand chorus of praise. How much more can he expect the hosts of his presence to lift up their voices in joyous songs of praise? From heaven and in heaven does praise come. It would be most enlightening to suddenly become spirit in substance and be a spectator and listener in the courts of heaven.

Express yourself in adoration for the quality of God.
Speak it audibly or write out your praise in your devotional journal.

2. PRAISE GOD FOR WHAT HE MEANS TO ME.

Perhaps the most amazing aspect of these verses is that you accept our praise. How full of our own ignorance and other limitations are our best efforts. But I am gloriously encouraged by these words — you *want* me to praise you and even in the attempt my expression grows. I am sure angels have ten thousand more reasons to praise you than I do. Angels can praise you with the kind of humility, reverence and purity that we could never approximate. Before the worlds were made angels were exulting in your presence. You sent them to express what all the earth should say, "Glory to God in the highest." Three times in one verse we are exhorted to lift our hearts in praise. Indeed at least this one man does!

How do you personally relate to the praise of God, and God who wants our praise?
Speak it out or write it out. It is *so important* that you establish *your own* devotional journal.

3. CONFESSION OF SIN

If living intelligences in your presence praise you, if not one bright spirit is exempted from this consecrated service what is my excuse for not praising you? My excuse is that I have not been motivated to do so. If the instrument of praise is worn out in the service of self-exaltation there is indeed little motivation for heaven's praise. There *are* times — as you know better than I — when I exult in your greatness and goodness, but there are more times when I am involved in many "other things" and have no energy or interest left to express my praise. Dear Lord, what a sad sin! It is wonderfully encouraging however to know that you do not change. There is as much reason to praise you after such selfishness as there was before. Thank you for opening my eyes. Thank you for the cleansing of my record. I lift my song of gladness to you.

What personal sins do you want to confess? We *must* speak them to remove them.
Do it! *Now.* There is no one else you have sinned against more than God. Tell him so!

4. SING A PRAYER TO GOD.

Dear Lord and Father of mankind,
Forgive our foolish ways!
Reclothe us in our rightful mind;

In purer lives Thy service find,
In deeper rev'rence, praise.

Open your hymn book and sing the rest of the verses — or even sing another prayer song.

5. READ HIS WORD TO HIM!

[7]You hypocrites! Isaiah was right when he prophesied about you:
[8]"'These people honor me with their lips,
　but their hearts are far from me.
[9]They worship me in vain;
　their teachings are but rules taught by men.'"

[10]Jesus called the crowd to him and said, "Listen and understand. [11]What goes into a man's mouth does not make him 'unclean,' but what comes out of his mouth, that is what makes him 'unclean.'"

— *Matthew 15:7-11, NIV*

Read His Word to Him.

I want to listen as the disciples — and also as the Pharisees. Were the disciples shocked at these burning words: *"You hypocrites!"* What was the reaction of those to whom these words were spoken? I gladly ask you, dear Lord, to search my heart and tell me that I do not at all measure up to the standard I profess. I say one thing and do another in several areas of my life. Dear Lord, my heart *is not* far from you, but my conduct does so surely need improvement. More and more I want my heart and life to match the words of my mouth. Could my worship be in vain? When directed by pride I know it is!

Please express yourself to this beautiful text. Put your expression in your own prayer diary.

6. READ HIS WORD FOR YOURSELF.

I do take as seriously as I can this effort to let your word have free course in my heart. How many of my teachings are made by man and are taught as if they came from you? How interested am I in the eternals as compared with the condition of the heart? How much of what I say is said to be seen and heard by men and not of yourself?

These are hard words—who can hear them? Dear Lord, I can! The Pharisees were offended when first these words were spoken; do they offend me? No, no! I *want* to hear them—I *need* them. It is what comes out of my mouth that makes me clean or unclean. But the mouth is but the spigot of the heart. How I do want to guard my heart.

It is so important that you pause in his presence
and either audibly or in written form tell him all his word means to you.

7. READ HIS WORD IN THANKSGIVING.

(1) Thank you for Isaiah's prophecy—it has found more than one fulfillment. (2) Thank you for the wonderful courage and humility of my Lord. (3) Thank you that none of us need think of someone else to whom these words apply. (4) Thank you that I can honor you with both my lips and my heart. (5) Thank you that my worship can be genuine or a fake—dear Lord, *I* make the choice. (6) Thank you that Jesus addressed his words to "the crowd"; I can be one of them. (7) Thank you I can and do understand.

Give yourself to your own expression of gratitude—write it or speak it!

8. READ HIS WORD IN MEDITATION.

"What goes into a man's mouth does not make him 'unclean,' but what comes out of his mouth that is what makes him unclean." The uncleanness must be defined. Strange to say in both cases it is the same. It is moral uncleanness that is under consideration. Our Lord wants to identify the contaminant. It definitely is not food eaten with hands that are not washed in a particular manner. What we put into the heart is what defiles as it comes out of the mouth. Our Lord *does* say that a man can be defiled. Jesus said, "Here are the things that defile: (1) evil ideas, (2) murder, (3) adultery, (4) sexual immorality, (5) theft, (6) lying, (7) slander." We need to examine each of these carefully. If we do not put the motivations for such actions in our hearts they will not come out of our lives.

Pause—wait—think—then express yourself in thoughtful praise or thanks.

9. READ HIS WORD FOR PETITIONS.

What a negative section we have under consideration in these words! There are many negative experiences in life—they should lead us to prayer: (1) Give me the wisdom to be able to apply scripture to life—even as my Lord. (2) How deceptively easy it is to say one thing and do another—deliver me. (3) "The heart" is the mind, will, emotions and conscience—these all must honor our Lord.

(4) Vain worship consists of teaching as well as other expressions—I am glad to so consider my teaching. (5) Physical defilement and heart defilement are here separated by our Lord—help me to keep my priorities straight here. (6) Jesus was not worried about the truth offending religious leaders. How I need his help here.

Please, please remember these are prayers—speak them—reword them!

10. READ HIS WORD AND WAIT—LISTEN—GOD SPEAKS!

Speak as directly to my heart as you did to these Pharisees: (1) "You *can* honor me with both your heart and your lips." (2) "You *can* teach my word and worship me in truth." (3) "You *can* keep your heart clean."

11. INTERCESSION FOR THE LOST WORLD

Iraq — Point for prayer: (1) *The national believers are very few.* They are mostly from a nominal Christian background. There are a few church fellowships in Baghdad and Basra but there is little witness elsewhere. Quite a few believers are not linked with any fellowship. New converts are being added to the Church despite the harsh and repressive conditions in the country. Pray that the believers may have courage to stand for the Lord and continue to witness. Many believers emigrate to other lands.

12. SING PRAISES TO OUR LORD.

Standing, standing,
Standing on the promises of God my Saviour;

Standing, standing,
I'm standing on the promises of God.

WEEK FIFTY-ONE — TUESDAY

1. PRAISE GOD FOR WHO HE IS.

"Praise the Lord! Sing to the Lord a new song, his praise in the assembly of the faithful!" (Psalm 149:1). In this one beautiful verse I want to lift my heart with the psalmist in praise to you just for yourself. In the past several months we have read through every verse of every psalm. In each verse we looked for qualities of yourself for which we could lift our minds in praise. In this verse it is enough to begin our praise just because this is our first response to your presence. What a wonderful "new song" we could sing every day to you! There has never been a day just like this one. There will be so many new and different blessings that you have prepared just for today! Were the whole family to gather in one place we could unitedly and individually lift our hearts in praise to you.

Express yourself in adoration for this quality of God.
Speak it audibly or write out your praise in your own devotional journal.

2. PRAISE GOD FOR WHAT HE MEANS TO ME.

What a source of refreshment is your presence! It is natural to praise your name. The more I know of you as I read your word the more I want to lift my voice in adoration. It will be my joy to sing a new song each day of my life. Just for today I want to sing a new song of your subtle interest and love in my life. How true it is that we "live by faith." All of your blessings (or at least most of them) are given in such a manner that if we want to we could call them "good luck." Right here I want to sing the new song of recognition of the source of every good and perfect gift. What a fresh new meaning do the songs in the public assembly have because of this personal praise.

How do you personally relate to the new song of God, and God who gives us a new song?
Speak it out or write it out. It is so important that you establish your own devotional journal.

3. CONFESSION OF SIN

How often am I blind! How often am I deaf! How often have I looked at life as a dull dead routine with no change of meaning? When I live for myself such is the inevitable result. If I am not expecting something new and different, if I am already convinced there is nothing new I shall never find it. I need to wake up! No blade of grass is today what it was yesterday. No need of my loved ones is today just what it was yesterday. I have not been forgiven before of the sins for which I now ask forgiveness. It is in being like your dear Son I find the newest of all new songs! "He came not to be ministered unto." It was in serving he found meaningful variety. Forgive me for being bored when I know the cause of it — *pure selfishness!*

What personal sins do you want to confess? We must speak them to remove them.
Do it! Now. There is no one else you have sinned against more than God. Tell him so!

4. SING A PRAYER TO GOD.

I am Thine, O Lord,
I have heard Thy voice,
And it told Thy love to me;
But I long to rise in the arms of faith,
And be closer drawn to Thee.

Draw me nearer, nearer, blessed Lord,
To the cross where Thou hast died;
Draw me nearer, nearer, nearer blessed Lord,
To Thy precious, bleeding side.

Open your hymn book and sing the rest of the verses — or even sing another prayer song.

5. READ HIS WORD TO HIM!

His Word

[12]Then the disciples came to him and asked, "Do you know that the Pharisees were offended when they heard this?"
[13]He replied, "Every plant that my heavenly Father has not planted will be pulled up by the roots. [14]Leave them; they are blind guides. If a blind man leads a blind man, both will fall into a pit." — *Matthew 15:12-14, NIV*
Read also Mark 7:9-13.

Read His Word to Him.

It is very helpful to me to approximate your position as I read these words. The disciples were worried about their master. It would seem they were concerned that He be discredited in the halls of scholarship. They were also worried that he would lose entirely the support of these very influential men. It could be they themselves were shocked by our Lord's blunt words. If they were bothered by his rejection of Jewish tradition they are going to be totally nonplused by these words of condemnation. Is Jesus talking about the teachings or the teachers when he talks about the tree that is to be rooted up? No matter — to lose one is to lose both. Is Jesus saying there are some people who are incurably blind? So it would seem — what an awful thing to contemplate!

Please express your response to this beautiful text. Put your expression in your own prayer diary.

6. READ HIS WORD FOR YOURSELF.

"They are blind guides. If a blind man leads a blind man, both will fall into a pit." *What a warning!* Those who follow false teaching are also responsible. Since the tree discussed is the teaching of our Lord versus the teaching of the Pharisees, so the sight or blindness relates to the light or darkness obtained by true and false teaching. How careful I want to be to treasure to my heart the very words of my Lord. How earnestly I want to study all you have said and be sure my students are confronted with what you have said—and not what I or anyone else has said. Only when we read and understand for ourselves what you have said can we trust the words of anyone else.

It is so important that you pause in his presence
and either audibly or in written form tell him all his word means to you.

7. READ HIS WORD IN THANKSGIVING.

(1) Thank you for the self-confidence of my Lord—he knew who he was and what he believed. (2) Thank you that Jesus was not worried about what religious leaders thought about him. (3) Thank you for the concern of the disciples for their master—even though misplaced it was concern. (4) Thank you that you *are* planting in the field of this world. (5) Thank you that we can be your plants. (6) Thank you for the warning that some men are wilfully blind. (7) Thank you for the sober warning that there is a pit at the end of some paths.

Give yourself to your own expression of gratitude—write it or speak it!

8. READ HIS WORD IN MEDITATION.

"If a blind man leads a blind man, both will fall into a pit." This assumes that both men are responsible for their blindness. In the case cited it would be easy to define responsibility—at least with the Pharisees. These men had been following Jesus for at least two years, perhaps more. They had listened to his teaching, had watched his miracles. If they could not accept his messiahship it was because they were wilfully blind. Such a statement says *so much* as to the expectations of our Lord as related to students or followers. Jesus expected these persons to evaluate the life and teachings of the Pharisees and reject them as blind guides.

Pause—wait—think—then express yourself in thoughtful praise or thanks.

9. READ HIS WORD FOR PETITIONS.

Our Lord was severe with hypocrites—he used such terms as "blind"—and "weeds." Lord, is it I? (1) In each decision of service may I examine my motive and honestly answer who is served—your word or the traditions of men? (2) Have I tried to avoid the application of your word to my life that I might satisfy my greed? Seach my heart! (3) There are times when we should leave people alone and move to someone who will listen—give me your grace in knowing when this is true. (4) How terrible to consider the possibility of being spiritually blind—even worse to lead others to destruction—direct my praying and watching. (5) Jesus wanted the crowd to learn this lesson—he surely intends that I understand—give me your wisdom.

Right here add your personal requests—and his answers.

10. READ HIS WORD AND WAIT—LISTEN—GOD SPEAKS!

Since we are religious leaders today we expect you to speak very personally to us in these verses: (1) "You can be my plant." (2) "You can have your eyes open." (3) "You can lead others to heaven not hell."

11. INTERCESSION FOR THE LOST WORLD

Iraq — Point for prayer: (1) The believers are constantly under pressure from the authorities and it is dangerous for them to have contacts with foreigners. Pray that their testimony before the Muslim authorities may recommend the Gospel of Christ.

12. SING PRAISES TO OUR LORD.

To God be the glory—great things He hath done,
So loved He the world that He gave us His Son,
Who yielded His life an atonement for sin
And opened the Lifegate that all may go in.
Praise the Lord, praise the Lord,

Let the earth hear His voice!
Praise the Lord, praise the Lord,
Let the people rejoice!
O come to the Father thro' Jesus the Son,
And give Him the glory—great things He hath done.

WEEK FIFTY-ONE — WEDNESDAY

1. PRAISE GOD FOR WHO HE IS.

"Let Israel be glad in his Maker, let the sons of Zion rejoice in their King! Let them praise His name with dancing, let them sing praises to Him with timbrel and lyre" (Psalm 149:2, 3). What interesting qualities of yourself I see in these two verses: (1) You are the *Maker of Israel*. Israel should be happy over this fact. It was out of Jacob that Israel was made. Such unworthy material from which to make a great nation. A large degree of humility—even tears of gratitude must mingle with the joy of Israel. (2) The "sons of Zion" are to rejoice in their King! *Maker* and *King* what wondrous qualities! (3) The exuberance and delight we have in you can be and should be expressed in dancing and musical instruments. The Hebrew culture is a real part of this expression, but back of it is the total joy of man in you.

Express yourself in adoration for this quality of God.
Speak it audibly or write out your praise in your own prayer diary.

2. PRAISE GOD FOR WHAT HE MEANS TO ME.

You have made my body with all its desires for yourself. You have left me totally free as to whether I will respond to your purpose. I know that once I am willing to respond to you as Maker and King I will have no problem with false motives for joy. How I do want to pause long enough and often enough before your throne and word to encompass the meaning of your creative power and interest. The potter has a purpose or design in mind before he approaches the clay. The king does not take the throne for no reason. In both relationships it is for our highest good. If I could only look behind what you have made and understand the purpose of your rule I am sure I would be so glad and full of joy I would dance and share in the timbrel and lyre. Praise your holy name!

How do you personally relate to God as Creator, and God who is King?
Speak it out or write it out. It is *so important* that you establish *your own* devotional journal.

3. CONFESSION OF SIN

It does not even occur to us that there could be or should be such joy in your purpose for our lives. But there is! Man has a tremendous capacity for the expression of emotion—he is going to use it somewhere. The excess of praise and music before the altars of Baal can only be guessed at. The total abandonment of immense crowds to music or sports need not be imagined—we can view it on our TV screens. If we understand what we are doing in public because we have spent time with you in private our joy and praise and music would be a beautiful expression of worship. It is in this that we sin. Oh, that I might open my whole self to you in this closet of prayer. I want to meditate on your word. I want to absorb the eternal truth that you are love and you want me to be supremely happy in my service to you.

What personal sins do you want to confess? We *must* speak them to remove them.
Do it! *Now.* There is no one else you have sinned against more than God. Tell him so!

4. SING A PRAYER TO GOD.

Faith is the victory!
Faith is the victory!

Oh, glorious victory,
That overcomes the world.

Open your hymn book and sing the rest of the verses—or even sing another prayer song.

5. READ HIS WORD TO HIM!

His Word

[9]And he said to them: "You have a fine way of setting aside the commands of God in order to observe your own traditions! [10]For Moses said, 'Honor your father and mother,' and, 'Anyone who curses his father or mother must be put to death.' [11]But you say that if a man says to his father or mother: 'Whatever help you might otherwise have received from me is Corban' (that is, a gift devoted to God), [12]then you no longer let him do anything for his father or mother. [13]Thus you nullify the word of God by your tradition that you have handed down. And you do many things like that.   — *Mark 7:9-13, NIV*

Read His Word to Him.

I do so want to digest the real indepth meaning of these verses. The irony of my Lord is particularly biting here. Jesus called their efforts to evade responsibility as "clever," or "ingenious," or "how well," or "wonderful to see" or "full well." What seemed such an accomplishment to man was only a transparent facade to our Lord. How does he see some of my efforts to evade what he has said? Jesus knew the lie behind their pious words. When they said they had given their money to God and his service what they really meant was that they had put their money into the temple treasury which was under their control. They could get interest on their investment if it was "Corban," i.e. "given to God." If they gave the same money to help their parents it would be lost to the service of God.

Please express your response to this beautiful text. Put your expression in your own prayer diary.

6. READ HIS WORD FOR YOURSELF.

There is no need to attempt to justify ourselves and pull our holy robes about us as if this were for the hypocrites of Jesus' day. What indeed could have *otherwise been given* to help the poor? I can't help everyone who is hungry but I could send one package of food through those who have made the opportunity available to me. Why don't I?

Is it because I prattle some expression of excuse in my part of Christian work? I can't win everyone but I can talk to and teach those who live in the same city block as I do. Why don't I? I am too busy with "other things" that the One thing that needs to be done is not done. How indeed refined is our hypocrisy! Dear Lord, forgive us!

It is so important that you pause in his presence
and either audibly or in written form tell him all his word means to you.

7. READ HIS WORD IN THANKSGIVING.

(1) Thank you for the clear priority of your commandments over *anything* that interferes. (2) Thank you for reminding me that it is very possible today to repeat the sin of these men. (3) Thank you that Moses said and meant to "honor your father and mother." (4) Thank you we can fulfill this command gladly *right now.* (5) Thank you for the severe penalty attached to disobedience. (6) Thank you that we can give something to you — even ourselves. (7) Thank you that we are here alerted to be always careful that we allow your word to have free course in our lives and not be nullified by our traditions.

Give yourself to your own expression of gratitude — write it or speak it!

8. READ HIS WORD IN MEDITATION.

"Thus you nullify the word of God by your traditions that you have handed down." How often do we do the very same thing! In one area we are particularly guilty: Personal devotion. It is not the custom of the average middle-class (or any other class) American to have a particular time set aside for personal worship. Perhaps this custom was more prevalent a generation ago. Today it is non-existent. I am staying with very faithful church members, but they like so many more of the people with whom I stay have *no* time of personal devotion. Does the word of God teach this or not? Is the example of my Lord and the apostle Paul clear? We have nullified the word of God with the habitual practices of those who have handed them down to us by example. God forgive us!

Pause — wait — think — then express yourself in thoughtful praise or thanks.

9. READ HIS WORD FOR PETITIONS.

We can almost hear the irony in these words of our Lord. If we have it in our heart they can lead us to prayer: (1) Jesus is aroused to point of condemnation — why? I can expect the same attitude for the same sin — guard my heart. (2) Honoring our parents includes spending our money — i.e., according to Jesus — am I doing this? (3) Bad-mouthing our parents could end us up in hell! Does Jesus say this law applied only to the parents who deserved praise? Open my eyes! (4) A gift to you could be the care we give to our parents — I want to give it! (5) Jesus *did not* recognize the writings and thoughts of men as authoritative — deliver me from the temptation to do so.

Please, please remember these are prayers — speak them — reword them!

10. READ HIS WORD AND WAIT — LISTEN — GOD SPEAKS!

You have surely spoken to me in these verses — speak to me again: (1) "You *can* give to support your parents." (2) "You *can* praise your parents to other people." (3) "You *can* respect and accept only my words as authoritative.

11. INTERCESSION FOR THE LOST WORLD

Iraq — Points for prayer: (1) *Pray that the way may be opened for Jordanian and Lebanese believers* to enter for witness into this land, for they would be less under suspicion. (2) *The entry of literature* has been difficult, but since the Lebanese Civil War much more literature has been entering the country legally from Jordan. Pray for the wise and careful distribution of this literature. There are still several Christian bookrooms operating in the country.

12. SING PRAISES TO OUR LORD.

Christ has for sin atonement made,
What a wonderful Savior!
We are redeemed! the price is paid!

What a wonderful Savior!
What a wonderful Savior is Jesus, my Jesus!
What a wonderful Savior is Jesus, my Lord!

WEEK FIFTY-ONE — THURSDAY

1. PRAISE GOD FOR WHO HE IS.

"For the Lord takes pleasure in his people; he adorns the humble with victory" (Psalm 149:4). It is in praise and worship before your throne I find my highest joy and deepest satisfaction. The two attributes of yourself seen here are so much needed. (1) You have a personal interest in all of our lives; what pleases us is a source of pleasure for you, i.e. as we chose within your will. As a father sees with pleasure the maturing and service of his children so you do with us. It is so good to talk with Someone who has a real personal interest in all of our life. (2) What a charming expression are these words: "He adorns the humble with victory." When shall we remember the conditions of triumph? Humility is not something we put on — it is something we are.

Express yourself in adoration for this quality of God.
Speak it audibly or write out your praise in your own devotional journal.

2. PRAISE GOD FOR WHAT HE MEANS TO ME.

In the very attitude of humility is true beauty. Dear Lord, I believe; help thou my unbelief. In lowliness of mind there is exaltation by yourself. In service to others is the highest position. In willingness to suffer without complaint is an example that will be admired by angels — if not by men. If we are genuinely humble all such victory will come as a surprise. I am not humble *in order to be exalted* — this is but another form of pride and self-interest. I can and do choose to be humble minded and claim your promise of victory, but allow you to choose just how it shall be done. How I do praise you for the means you have to accomplish your purposes in my life!

How do you personally relate to the pleasure of God, and God who takes an interest in us?
Speak it out or write it out. It is *so important* that you establish *your own* devotional journal.

3. CONFESSION OF SIN

If there is *one* area where I feel less prepared to serve you or worship you it is in humility. I *know* you take great pleasure in a meek and quiet spirit — I am anything but meek or quiet. There are times when I am surely the very opposite. At the same time I am glad to know you have ways of producing this lacking quality. This is part of your *pleasure* in your people. This indeed must be your largest joy. However, if when you set up the conditions out of which humility could come and I rebel and refuse to respond your whole effort of love was for naught. Forgive me.

What personal sins do you want to confess? We *must* speak them to remove them.
Do it! *Now.* There is no one else you have sinned against more than God. Tell him so!

4. SING A PRAYER TO GOD.

I'm pressing on the upward way,
New heights I'm gaining ev'ry day;

Still praying as I'm onward bound,
"Lord, plant my feet on higher ground."

Open your hymn book and sing the rest of the verses — or even sing another prayer song.

5. READ HIS WORD TO HIM!

His Word

[22]The next day the crowd that had stayed on the opposite shore of the lake realized that only one boat had been there, and that Jesus had not entered it with his disciples, but that they had gone away alone. [23]Then some boats from Tiberias landed near the place where the people had eaten the bread after the Lord had given thanks. [24]Once the crowd realized that neither Jesus nor his disciples were there, they got into the boats and went to Capernaum in search of Jesus.

[25]When they found him on the other side of the lake, they asked him, "Rabbi, when did you get here?"

[26]Jesus answered, "I tell you the truth, you are looking for me, not because you saw miraculous signs but because you ate the loaves and had your fill. [27]Do not work for food that spoils, but for food that endures to eternal life, which the Son of Man will give you. On him God the Father has placed his seal of approval."

[28]Then they asked him, "What must we do to do the works God requires?"

[29]Jesus answered, "The work of God is this: to believe in the one he has sent."

[30]So they asked him, "What miraculous sign then will you give that we may see it and believe you? What will you do? [31]Our forefathers ate the manna in the desert; as it is written: 'He gave them bread from heaven to eat.'"

[32]Jesus said to them, "I tell you the truth, it is not Moses who has given you the bread from heaven, but it is my Father who gives you the true bread from heaven. [33]For the bread of God is he who comes down from heaven and gives life to the world."

[34]"Sir," they said, "from now on give us this bread."

— *John 6:22-34, NIV*

Read His Word to Him.

There surely is much to learn and apply in these verses. I want first of all to understand them. I have read and reread them in your presence. Dear Lord, open my understanding! John tells us of the crowds' knowledge of the appearance of Jesus on the other side of the lake without having used a boat. He does not say just what their reaction was to this amazing fact. Meanwhile on the other side of the lake the crowds were waking up to the fact that Jesus was not there, nor his disciples. Since they evidently knew Jesus had not sailed away with his disciples when they arrived on the other side of the lake they were very curious as to just how Jesus got there. Jesus *did not* tell them. He did speak to their heart need of real faith.

Please express your response to this beautiful text. Put your expression in your own prayer diary.

6. READ HIS WORD FOR YOURSELF.

How much of my faith relates to the temporal blessings of life? How small was the faith of this crowd! There is such a lesson in this record for today! *"Faith comes by hearing"—not by seeing*—however sensational the sight might be. Faith comes by hearing *from* or *of the Word of the Lord."* Only when we accept the authority or truthfulness of the one speaking will we have faith. Faith formed by miracles passes with the sensation of the miracle performed. When the mind is not informed and enlightened the reason for belief is just not there.

Pause in his presence and either audibly or in written form tell him all his word means to you.

7. READ HIS WORD IN THANKSGIVING.

(1) Thank you for the obvious evidence of the supernatural in the life of our Lord. (2) Thank you that Jesus did not emphasize such evidence. (3) Thank you our Lord was not hesitant about speaking to the needs of the people. (4) Thank you for the eternal life I can enjoy from the Son of Man. (5) Thank you for the most convincing seal of approval placed upon my Lord from yourself. (6) Thank you for the "work of God" which amounts to doing what God has said. (7) Thank you for the true bread from heaven from which I have life.

Give yourself to your own expression of gratitude—write it or speak it!

8. READ HIS WORD IN MEDITATION.

"For the bread of God is he who comes down from heaven and gives life to the world." Amen! He surely gives life to *my* world. How wonderful to be able to pause amid the busy rush of life and recognize that all the life we have is from him! This bread from God could be as easily misunderstood or neglected as the manna in the wilderness. (1) That manna only lasted one day. If Jesus is to give me life it will be for one day at a time. (2) I must gather it for myself—it is my own effort that appropriates what is on the ground into the energy I need. (3) It seems significant that those who gathered must kneel to do so.

Pause—wait—think—then express yourself in thoughtful praise or thanks.

9. READ HIS WORD FOR PETITIONS.

There is so much here of intense interest we will have a problem deciding what to emphasize in our praying: (1) The crowd was in search of Jesus—not for worship but for their own interests. What is my real purpose in seeking him? (2) Jesus never answered their question as to how he crossed the lake—I wonder why he didn't? Some questions do not deserve an answer—give me grace to know which are which. (3) Jesus read their motives—he knows mine too—speak to me through these words that I might be totally sincere. (4) Oh, Son of Man—give me yourself that I might eat and live forever! (5) I want to hear and read again your "seal of approval" you gave to your Son.

Right here add your personal requests—and his answers.

10. READ HIS WORD AND WAIT—LISTEN—GOD SPEAKS!

Burn these words into my inmost being! (1) "The work of God is this: to believe in the One he has sent." (2) ". . . the bread of God is he who comes down from heaven and gives life to the world."

11. INTERCESSION FOR THE LOST WORLD

Iraq — Point for prayer: (1) *Christian radio broadcasts and follow-up correspondence courses* remain virtually the only avenue for getting the Gospel to these needy people. Pray for the Arabic broadcasts.

12. SING PRAISES TO OUR LORD.

Wounded for me, wounded for me,
There on the cross He was wounded for me;
Gone my transgression, and now I am free,
All because Jesus was wounded for me.

WEEK FIFTY-ONE — FRIDAY

1. PRAISE GOD FOR WHO HE IS.

"Let the faithful exult in glory; let them sing for joy on their couches" (Psalm 149:5). My purpose is to hold up before you a quality of yourself for which I can praise you. I take the word "glory" to refer to your essential essence or being. To exult in glory is to adore or praise your total character. David is saying that the faithful should reiterate all the attributes of yourself and lift their voices in praise. It would be most instructive to review all the qualities of yourself I have considered throughout this whole year. I want to multiply these tenfold.

Speak audibly or write out your praise in your own devotional journal.

2. PRAISE GOD FOR WHAT HE MEANS TO ME.

Since the Hebrews were accustomed to reclining when eating as well as when sleeping it is a little difficult to tell if I am to think of the meal or the bed. I shall think of both. Dear Lord, enlarge my vocabulary and thought as I sit down to the table and attempt to thank you for the food. I want my expressions to be full of thought as well as praise. Give me wisdom in fulfilling this desire. At the same time it is when I retire and relax at night I need a fulfillment of these words. It is such a blessing to retire in a song of praise or in reading from your word. Sleep is so much sweeter and refreshing when you are in it.

How do you personally relate to the praise of God, and God who wants our praise?
Speak it out or write it out. It is *so important* that you establish *your own* devotional journal.

3. CONFESSION OF SIN

As you know my heart it is no problem for me to lift my heart in adoration for the qualities of yourself I see in your word. I can easily join with the faithful in exalting your divine Person. It is in the application of this capacity beyond this closet of prayer that I confess my sin and need. It is on the couch of eating and sleeping I need your help. I truly purpose to remedy this need! I plan on writing out some much more meaningful prayers at meals—some words of exulting praise for the bounties of your goodness. I shall also prepare some songs of praise I can sing just before I retire. Dear Lord, reinforce these commitments and confession of need.

What personal sins do you want to confess? We *must* speak them to remove them.
Do it! *Now.* There is no one else you have sinned against more than God. Tell him so!

4. SING A PRAYER TO GOD.

I was lost, but Jesus found me,
Found the sheep that went astray,
Threw His loving arms around me,
Drew me back into His way.

Yes, I'll sing . . . the wondrous story
Of the Christ . . . who died for me, . . .
Sing it with . . . the saints in glory,
Gathered by . . . the crystal sea.

Open your hymn book and sing the rest of the verses—or even sing another prayer song.

5. READ HIS WORD TO HIM!

His Word

[34]"Sir," they said, "from now on give us this bread." [35]Then Jesus declared, "I am the bread of life. He who comes to me will never go hungry, and he who believes in me will never be thirsty. [36]But as I told you, you have seen me and still you do not believe. [37]All that the Father gives me will come to me, and whoever comes to me I will never drive away. [38]For I have come down from heaven not to do my will but to do the will of him who sent me. [39]And this is the will of him who sent me, that I shall lose none of all that he has given me, but raise them up in the last day. [40]For my Father's will is that everyone who looks to the Son and believes in him shall have eternal life, and I will raise him up at the last day." — *John 6:34-40, NIV*

Read His Word to Him.

How typical is the reaction of these men to all men who come into superficial contact with our Lord. The crowd asks for a rain of bread from heaven. Jesus offers himself! Not only are they asking for a repeat performance of the manna from heaven, they want it to keep raining such bread. Is Jesus' offer really practical? Can he really satisfy as bread and water meet the needs of the body? Unless we are prepared to say that the needs of the heart are not that important we must say indeed he does become our bread and water. The key to making such provisions ours is in the little words: "come" and "believe." When we come truly hungry and thirsty to him and believe (which necessarily includes obedience) we are indeed filled!

Please express your response to this beautiful text. Put your expression in your own prayer diary.

6. READ HIS WORD FOR YOURSELF.

I believe the marvelous means of coming to you is my own willingness. I believe also that this is true for all who come to you. How hesitantly and fearfully we often come to you — but the sweet words of my Lord calm my fears and charm my heart: "Whoever comes to me I will never drive away." Was there a conflict in the heart of my Lord? i.e. did he have a struggle with "his will" as versus "the will" of the Father? *Of course* he did or he would be no example for me. How are we given to the Father? We all can answer this question — it was in a set of circumstances in which we were very much a part that we decided to commit ourselves to his love. What gave us to the Father keeps us in the Father's care — our willingness. Bless your wonderful name!

It is so important that you pause in his presence
and either audibly or in written form tell him all his word means to you.

7. READ HIS WORD IN THANKSGIVING.

(1) Thank you for the plain powerful promise of the resurrection on the last day. (2) Thank you for a promise I will enjoy forever — "eternal life." (3) Thank you that you will lose none who want to stay saved. (4) Thank you that my Lord "learned obedience" so well — I can too! (5) Thank you for the plain statement of my Lord's origin — "I am come down from heaven." (6) Thank you that my Lord does not consider my worthiness as a reason for accepting me. (7) Thank you that I need not go through this day as hungry or thirsty.

Give yourself to your own expression of gratitude — write it or speak it!

8. READ HIS WORD IN MEDITATION.

". . . *Everyone who looks upon the Son and puts his faith in him shall possess eternal life; and I will raise him up on the last day*" (NEB). What an audacious statement to make! Jesus was very much conscious of who he was. To include the whole human race in a promise is an incredible claim. But to include *eternal life* in the promise is beyond human comprehension. To top off these words is the assertion that he has control of death and the grave! We need to reread the conditions imposed for the fulfillment of these promises. "He who looks upon the Son and puts his trust in him." What do we see as we look? Just what is included in the term "trust"? Faith and obedience are the two words that describe our response. What an amazing Savior is Jesus our Lord!

Pause — wait — think — then express yourself in thoughtful praise or thanks.

9. READ HIS WORD FOR PETITIONS.

In these beautiful words on the bread of life we can find many requests for prayer: (1) I know for what I am asking and I say like the crowd by the lake: "Lord . . . from now on give me this bread." (2) I know also the verb tense in "coming" to my Lord is continuing action — I do indeed want to do this. (3) What a wonderful promise is here: ". . . will never go hungry." I claim the conditions and the promise. (4) I also know just what is involved in believing: *obedience*. This is much better than the thirst. I believe, help my unbelief. (5) I see in my Lord such an example of faith and obedience — strengthen my stumbling steps!

Please, please remember these are prayers — speak them — reword them!

10. READ HIS WORD AND WAIT — LISTEN — GOD SPEAKS!

I do want to hear and believe: (1) "All that the Father gives me will come to me. This means you." (2) ". . . whoever comes to me I will never drive away." (3) ". . . I shall lose none of all that he has given me."

11. INTERCESSION FOR THE LOST WORLD

Jordan — Population: 2,800,000. Growth rate — 3.3%.
Points for prayer: (1) *The long-lasting Middle East Crisis* has brought many years of suffering to Jordan. This has made many nominal Christian and Muslims more open to the Gospel. Pray for a great harvest to be reaped for God in this land. (2) *Many areas are inadequately evangelized* — to mention several: the south of the country, the nomadic Bedouin and the refugee camps.

12. SING PRAISES TO OUR LORD.

Come, we that love the Lord,
And let our joys be known,
Join in a song with sweet accord,
Join in a song with sweet accord,
And thus surround the throne,
And thus surround the throne.
We're marching to Zion,
Beautiful, beautiful Zion;
We're marching upward to Zion,
The beautiful city of God.

WEEK FIFTY-ONE — SATURDAY

1. PRAISE GOD FOR WHO HE IS.

"Let the high praises of God be in their throats and two-edged swords in their hands" (Psalm 149:6). I realize this has reference to the conquests of David as he extended his kingdom. However, there is a sense in which we can see ourselves in this verse: for every Christian we can think of no better approach to the conquest of life: praise in our mouths and the word of God in our hands. The very best praise we can give must be directed toward the One for whom it is due. Our praises are also high as to purpose inasmuch as all the wonders and beauties of heaven are our goal. How meaningful is the description of your word. The whole instrument is an edge. Such a weapon however is of no value until it is taken into the conflict and used.

Express yourself in adoration for this quality of God.
Speak it audibly or write out your praise in your own devotional journal.

2. PRAISE GOD FOR WHAT HE MEANS TO ME.

Dear Lord, this verse does describe my purpose in life. My praise will really never be high enough for all you are. However, I am going to try. I am not referring to volume. All I see in your Son—all that he says to me in his word—all of your glory I see reflected in the lives of your children will be the source of my praises to you. Most of all I want my own life to be an expression of praise. Your sword is only a decoration on the shelf until it is thrust into the battle of life. How sharp and effective do I find it in every conflict. I purpose even now to use your sword where I have been fighting with the crooked sticks of men.

How do you personally relate to the conquests of God, and God who gives us a sword?
Speak it out or write it out. It is so important that you establish your own devotional journal.

3. CONFESSION OF SIN

How often in the midst of the battle has the cry of high praise been heard? Not nearly often enough! How can I make very practical personal application of this lovely verse? I think of the relationships of my life I know will face me for this day. How shall I come to them? "Let the high praises of God be in my mouth and your two-edged sword in my hand." I do not speak of carrying a copy of the Bible. I want your word in my heart so I can use it in the conflict. Such are my goals—such have been my goals for sometime. Forgive me for not reaching them. But I do press on. Even as I do I trust in your forgiveness. I bow my head in defeat when I should lift it in praise. Forgive me.

What personal sins do you want to confess? We must speak them to remove them.
Do it! Now. There is no one else you have sinned against more than God. Tell him so!

4. SING A PRAYER TO GOD.

Shall we gather at the river,
Where bright angel feet have trod;
With its crystal tide forever
Flowing by the throne of God?

Yes, we'll gather at the river,
The beautiful, beautiful river,
Gather with the saints at the river
That flows by the throne of God.

Open your hymn book and sing the rest of the verses—or even sing another prayer song.

5. READ HIS WORD TO HIM!

His Word

⁴¹At this the Jews began to grumble about him because he said, "I am the bread that came down from heaven." ⁴²They said, "Is this not Jesus, the son of Joseph, whose father and mother we know? How can he now say, 'I came down from heaven'?" ⁴³"Stop grumbling among yourselves," Jesus answered. ⁴⁴"No one can come to me unless the Father who sent me draws him, and I will raise him up at the last day. ⁴⁵It is written in the Prophets: 'They will all be taught by God.' Everyone who listens to the Father and learns from him comes to me. ⁴⁶No one has seen the Father except the one who is from God; only he has seen the Father. ⁴⁷I tell you the truth, he who believes has everlasting life. ⁴⁸I am the bread of life. ⁴⁹Your forefathers ate the manna in the desert, yet they died. ⁵⁰But here is the bread that comes down from heaven, which a man may eat and not die. ⁵¹I am the living bread that came down from heaven. If a man eats of this bread, he will live forever. This bread is my flesh, which I will give for the life of the world."

—John 6:41-51, NIV

Read His Word to Him.

Shall we be like the religious leaders who first heard these words? The muttering and murmuring among these men was not because they did not understand but because they would not believe! Had anyone of these men really bothered to investigate just what kind of a life this Jesus of Nazareth lived at home in Nazareth? We doubt it. Had even one of them asked his mother or his so-called *"father"* Joseph what kind of a person he was? Maybe they had and had already rejected out of hand the claim of his virgin birth. We are face to face with the same decision today!

Please express yourself in response to this beautiful text. Put your expression in your own prayer diary.

6. READ HIS WORD FOR YOURSELF.

The rebuke of our Lord is well deserved! He is saying, "If you do not want to believe you will not believe." There is something about belief beyond human effort. We believe the Father supplies all the evidence in the life and miracles of his Son and through these means draws men to himself, but after all the evidence is in it is *still the decision of man to accept or reject.* If we do not want to be drawn to the Father through the Son no amount of reason will avail. It was so with these men and it is so today. Dear Lord, I want to come to you—I *want* to believe—I am *glad* to accept you. I am like one of the poorest of those you healed and helped. Glory to God in the highest!

It is so important that you pause in his presence and either audibly or in written form tell him all his word means to you.

7. READ HIS WORD IN THANKSGIVING.

(1) Thank you that we all can be indeed "taught of God." (2) Thank you that I confidently can expect Jesus to get me out of the grave. (3) Thank you I can listen to you through your word and come to your Son. (4) Thank you that one day we shall all see him even as he is! (5) Thank you I can believe and right now claim "everlasting life." (6) Thank you that I can keep on eating of the bread come down from heaven and can keep on having life. (7) Thank you for the flesh of my Lord offered on the cross for the life of the world.

Give yourself to your own expression of gratitude—write it or speak it!

8. READ HIS WORD IN MEDITATION.

"This bread is my flesh, which I will give for the life of the world." Isn't it amazing that this whole beautiful discourse on "the bread from heaven" came out of a chance remark about the miracle of manna in the days of Moses. Of course it really wasn't just "a chance" remark, it was like all the work and teaching of our Lord: He came to show that always in the midst of the "hustle bustle" of life you are at work. Nothing happens by accident, all happens by intent. Our Lord's offering on the cross is the real "bread come down from heaven to give life for the whole world!" As the grain is broken and refined for use as flour so was the body of our Lord. As bread is essential and available to all men so is his offering on Calvary.

Pause—wait—think—then express yourself in thoughtful praise or thanks.

9. READ HIS WORD FOR PETITIONS.

Grumbling is such a common trait—when related to our Lord we can be sure it comes from the evil one—guard my heart: (1) How slow to believe were those who should have known him best! By his definition of faith am I any better? (2) "Stop your grumbling among yourselves." These are the words of my Lord—help me to hear them. (3) We won't believe unless we want to—such "want to" comes from us *and* yourself. I praise you for so drawing me to yourself. (4) May I abide in your word and your word abide in me that my "want to" will be strong. (5) Jesus repeatedly promised eternal life—to raise our bodies on the last day. Considering his life teaching and works and his death in my place I have good reasons for saying: "Amen."

Right here add your personal requests—and his answers.

10. READ HIS WORD AND WAIT—LISTEN—GOD SPEAKS!

Open my heart to receive your word! (1) "No one can come to me unless the Father who sent me draws him." (2) "Everyone who listens to the Father and learns from him comes to me." (3) "I tell you the truth, he who believes has everlasting life."

11. INTERCESSION FOR THE LOST WORLD

Jordan — Point for prayer: (1) *There has been much Christian work* on the West Bank among the Arabs. Some of this work continues under the Israeli occupation. Pray that there may be fruit for the Lord there despite the tense political situation and the rising influence of the Communists among the Arabs.

12. SING PRAISES TO OUR LORD.

Amazing grace! how sweet the sound,
That saved a wretch like me!

I once was lost, but now am found,
Was blind, but now I see.

WEEK FIFTY-TWO — SUNDAY

1. PRAISE GOD FOR WHO HE IS.

"Praise the Lord! Praise God in his sanctuary; praise him in his mighty firmament!" (Psalm 150:1). It would be easy to say "Praise the Lord" inside, i.e. when we assemble to worship, and praise the Lord when we are outside looking up into the heavens he has created. Man himself is your sanctuary. No room in which we gather is properly called a sanctuary. We are your house; our bodies are the dwelling place of yourself in the Spirit. In a sense the words of Paul apply to us. "Do you not know that you are God's temple and that God's Spirit dwells in you? If any one destroys God's temple, God will destroy him. For God's temple is holy, and that temple you are." Collectively as here in I Cor. 3:16, 17 and individually as in I Cor. 6:19, 20 we praise you in your sanctuary.

Express yourself in adoration for this quality of God.
Speak it audibly or write out your praise in your own devotional journal.

2. PRAISE GOD FOR WHAT HE MEANS TO ME.

I want to step outside and look up into the canopy of space. Your everlasting power and great wisdom will immediately be seen. In our day like no other we can relate to the words of the psalmist. As we look at the pictures returned from the Voyager II showing us close-up shots of the planets let us not forget that we are not looking at stars but just the closest and smallest of your creation in the firmament. How totally amazing is the power and majesty in the expanse of the heavens! Praise leaps to our lips as an almost involuntary response of what we see. "Praise the Lord! Praise God in his sanctuary; praise him in his *mighty* firmament."

How do you personally relate to the praise of God, and God who is worthy to be praised?
Speak it out or write it out. It is *so important* that you establish *your own* devotional journal.

3. CONFESSION OF SIN

When I assemble with others and thus make up your sanctuary is praise the first and last thought that fills my mind? Such could be and should be. I have so much for which I can praise you. However, I am free to confess there are many other things that take precedence. We are so occupied with greeting one another and visiting about this and that that we sometimes even sing the songs with thoughts of other matters filling our minds while the words fill our mouths. I can go out into your beautiful world with my head down and really never look up to see your mighty firmament.

What personal sins do you want to confess? We *must* speak them to remove them.
Do it! *Now.* There is no one else you have sinned against more than God. Tell him so!

4. SING A PRAYER TO GOD.

Abide with me: fast falls the eventide;
The darkness deepens; Lord, with me abide:

When other helpers fail, and comforts flee,
Help of the helpless, O abide with me!

Open your hymn book and sing the rest of the verses — or even sing another prayer song.

5. READ HIS WORD TO HIM!

His Word

[52]Then the Jews began to argue sharply among themselves, "How can this man give us his flesh to eat?"

[53]Jesus said to them, "I tell you the truth, unless you eat the flesh of the Son of Man and drink his blood, you have no life in you. [54]Whoever eats my flesh and drinks my blood has eternal life, and I will raise him up at the last day. [55]For my flesh is real food and my blood is real drink. [56]Whoever eats my flesh and drinks my blood remains in me, and I in him. [57]Just as the living Father sent me and I live because of the Father, so the one who feeds on me will live because of me. [58]This is the bread that came down from heaven. Our forefathers ate manna and died, but he who feeds on this bread will live forever." [59]He said this while teaching in the synagogue in Capernaum.

[60]On hearing it, many of the disciples said, "This is a hard teaching. Who can accept it?"

[61]Aware that his disciples were grumbling about this, Jesus said to them, "Does this offend you? [62]What if you see the Son of Man ascend to where he was before! [63]The Spirit gives life; the flesh counts for nothing. The words I have spoken to you are spirit and they are life. [64]Yet there are some of you who do not believe." For Jesus had known from the beginning which of them did not believe and who would betray him. [65]He went on to say, "This is why I told you that no one can come to me unless the Father has enabled him."

[66]From this time many of his disciples turned back and no longer followed him.

[67]"You do not want to leave too, do you?" Jesus asked the Twelve.

[68]Simon Peter answered him, "Lord, to whom shall we go? You have the words of eternal life. [69]We believe and know that you are the Holy One of God."

[70]Then Jesus replied, "Have I not chosen you, the Twelve? Yet one of you is a devil!" [71](He meant Judas, the son of Simon Iscariot, who, though one of the Twelve, was later to betray him.)

— John 6:52-71, NIV

Read His Word to Him.

It would seem it was very important for our Lord to emphasize his body as bread and his blood as drink. He said it six times from verse 53 to 58. Your Son knew these men did not understand, more than that he knew they did not want to understand. How very important it is that we understand his death.

Please express your response to this beautiful text. Put your expression in your own prayer diary.

6. READ HIS WORD FOR YOURSELF.

I want to answer the Jews' question "How can this man give us his flesh to eat." I only ask them to stand beneath the cross and contemplate what is happening there. We need to read again and again the words the Holy Spirit gave to the apostles and prophets who wrote of his death. It is only in a daily meditation on his death and suffering that we "eat his flesh and drink his blood." We can do this each week as we gather around his table.

Pause in his presence and either audibly or in written form tell him all his word means to you.

7. READ HIS WORD IN THANKSGIVING.

(1) Thank you for the exclusive blunt words: "Except you eat the flesh and drink the blood you have no life." (2) Thank you we understand how to eat and drink of him. (3) Thank you for the wonderful satisfaction we find in eating his flesh and drinking of his blood. (4) Thank you that he abides in us as we eat — this is a continual practice and presence. (5) Thank you that Jesus said so clearly that our only source of life is himself. (6) Thank you that Jesus did not accommodate himself or his teaching to the unbelief or ignorance of men. (7) Thank you for the wonderful words of Peter: "You have the words of eternal life."

Give yourself to your own expression of gratitude — write it or speak it!

8. READ HIS WORD IN MEDITATION.

"Have I not chosen you, the Twelve? yet one of you is a devil!" What did Jesus mean by this enigmatic statement? John gives us the meaning. Did Jesus know Judas would betray him even before he chose him? A better question would be "Why did Judas betray him even if Jesus did know it?" Our Lord's knowledge of Judas' actions had nothing to do with the moral responsibility of the betrayer. We as parents can predicate some of the actions of our children, but our foreknowledge does not lessen their responsibility. Judas is representative of the first angel who sinned and the first man who sinned. Why? Why? In the wonder and purity of heaven and Eden why would they sin? In the presence of the Son of God why betray him? The answer is as simple as it is profound: because they could! Dear Lord, I want to choose not to!

Pause — wait — think — then express yourself in thoughtful praise or thanks.

9. READ HIS WORD FOR PETITIONS.

In this teaching of my Lord on the bread of life I find prayer needs I *must* bring to you: (1) I do want to eat and live forever — teach me just how I can do it. (2) I see my Savior's broken body as "the bread" from which my spirit must find nourishment for eternal life. (3) Jesus speaks to me in this figure of speech in such a sharp manner. My appreciation of what he did for me on Calvary must be as real as food and drink — make it so! (4) Since my eternal life depends on "eating and drinking" what happened on the cross, I better spend much more time beneath the cross of Jesus. (5) These words separated many of his disciples from him. I want them to draw me to you.

Please, please remember these are prayers — speak them — reword them!

10. READ HIS WORD AND WAIT — LISTEN — GOD SPEAKS!

I want to hear you speak to me in my inner ear: (1) "The Spirit gives life; the flesh counts for nothing." (2) "The words I have spoken to you are Spirit and they are life." (3) "Eat and drink and live forever."

11. INTERCESSION FOR THE LOST WORLD

Jordan — Point for prayer: (1) *The Palestinian Refugees* are embittered by their years of fruitless struggle to regain their lands in Israel. Some have been absorbed into the economic life of Jordan, but others live in refugee camps financed by the United Nations. Jordanian Christians are free to distribute literature and witness in these camps, and some do, but this can be dangerous.

12. SING PRAISES TO OUR LORD.

Fairest Lord Jesus! Ruler of all nature!
O Thou of God and man the Son!

Thee will I cherish, Thee will I honor,
Thou, my soul's glory, joy, and crown!

WEEK FIFTY-TWO — MONDAY

1. PRAISE GOD FOR WHO HE IS.

"Praise him for his mighty deeds; praise him according to his exceeding greatness" (Psalm 150:2). How easy it will be to fulfill this blessed verse! I do want to hold up your involvement in human affairs and praise you for this. In just the first book of your revelation to man I can praise you: (1) For your decision to flood the earth and at the same time save Noah and his family. This was a deed almost beyond human comprehension. (2) Your confusing the tongues of men at the tower of Babel tells me of your constant interest in the affairs of men. Praise your name. (3) I wonder just how your voice sounded when you called Abram from the Ur of Chaldees? (4) The wonderful land promise you repeatedly made to Abraham expresses your interest in the physical needs of man.

Express yourself in adoration for this quality of God.
Speak it audibly or write out your praise in your own devotional journal.

2. PRAISE HIM FOR WHAT HE MEANS TO ME.

You have already decided to again destroy the earth and all who are in it (II Peter 3:9ff.). I thank you for the beautiful rainbow that promises you will never again destroy the earth with water. But I want to just as fully thank you that I have been warned you *will* destroy this earth with fire. (2) You have a tremendous interest in the tongue of man, i.e. in languages. It would seem your largest interest is in some written form of language. How glad I am to share this interest. (3) I do believe in ways we do not always understand you are calling men (and women) out of their own country into a land you have prepared for them.

How do you personally relate to the deeds of God, and God who is mighty?
Speak it out or write it out. It is *so important* that you establish *your own* devotional journal.

3. CONFESSION OF SIN

It isn't that I fail to praise you for your mighty deeds, it is only that I am so much more occupied with my own activities that I fail to relate them to what you have done and are doing in my life. Somehow I want to live in a constant biblical context. A meditation on your word night and day would be essentially a meditation on your mighty deeds. To take the time to hear your voice through the pages of your book is to see again and again your exceeding greatness. For failure in this very important area of life I ask your forgiveness. It is good to label or name other sins which I gladly do, but it is better to work on the cause. Meditation on your mighty deeds and exceeding greatness will deliver me from my own feeble efforts and smallness.

What personal sins do you want to confess? We *must* speak them to remove them.
Do it! *Now.* There is no one else you have sinned against more than God. Tell him so!

4. SING A PRAYER TO GOD.

I stand amazed in the presence
Of Jesus the Nazarene,
And wonder how He could love me,
A sinner, condemned, unclean.

How marvelous! how wonderful!
And my song shall ever be:
How marvelous! how wonderful
Is my Savior's love for me!

Open your hymn book and sing the rest of the verses — or even sing another prayer song.

5. READ HIS WORD TO HIM!

His Word

[21]Leaving that place, Jesus withdrew to the region of Tyre and Sidon. [22]A Canaanite woman from that vicinity came to him, crying out, "Lord, Son of David, have mercy on me! My daughter is suffering terribly from demon-possession."
— *Matthew 15:21, 22, NIV*

[24]Jesus left that place and went to the vicinity of Tyre. He entered a house and did not want anyone to know it; yet he could not keep his presence secret. [25]In fact, as soon as she heard about him, a woman whose little daughter was possessed by an evil spirit came and fell at his feet. [26]The woman was a Greek, born in Syrian Phoenicia. She begged Jesus to drive the demon out of her daughter.
— *Mark 7:24-26, NIV*

Read His Word to Him.

It was quite a journey to walk from the sea of Galilee up to the region of Tyre and Sidon. Why did Jesus go here? It seems clear that he and the apostles were seeking rest and seclusion. Mark says ". . . he went into a house and did not want anyone to know he was there. . . ." My Lord needed a time and place for reorientation. Such being so it should come as no surprise that I need such a time even more often than my Lord. It should also come as no surprise that he could not find such a place — not even outside the borders of Israel! There was someone present who had such a pressing need that it could not be hidden any more than our Lord.

Please express your response to this beautiful text. Put your expression in your own prayer diary.

WEEK FIFTY-TWO — MONDAY

6. READ HIS WORD FOR YOURSELF.

When I feel taxed and pressed—when I imagine that I could not teach one more lesson or prepare one more sermon, dear Lord, may I remember your Son who came not to be ministered unto but to give his life. Indeed he did! He gave himself in healing (and there was a real loss of energy in this), in teaching—I know what loss there is in such effort—in reading the hearts of people and relating their needs to his Father in prayer. I can only imagine how this must have taxed him. Why have I come to the service of my Lord? Is it not to follow him? I am not prepared to identify the presence of demons in people—but I can see very plainly the tragic effects of Satan in the lives of people all about me. Will I hear their cry? Will I answer their need?

It is so important that you pause in his presence
and either audibly or in written form tell him all his word means to you.

7. READ HIS WORD IN THANKSGIVING.

(1) Thank you for the humanness of your Son—he needed to rest. (2) Thank you for the fact that crowds were not the whole purpose of my Lord's work. (3) Thank you that Jesus teaches us very plainly here that his primary work was discipling, not healing. (4) Thank you for this unusual woman—full of daring faith. (5) Thank you for this clear statement of the objective presence of demons. (6) Thank you that we can learn that sin and evil *are not* necessarily associated as a cause for the presence of demons. (7) Thank you for the worship and prayer of the woman in the presence of our Lord—I want to kneel with her!

Give yourself to your own expression of gratitude—write it or speak it!

8. READ HIS WORD IN MEDITATION.

"She begged Jesus to drive the demon out of her daughter." Where did this woman obtain such faith in our Lord? *"Faith comes by hearing"*—she no doubt had been told by some of those who had seen and heard him. The report of our Lord's miracles must have been very common knowledge. But there was something special about this woman. Her persistence and humility are evident. But it was her daughter's desperate condition that consumed her whole person. She must have known enough not only of the miracles of Jesus but also of his character to know that Jesus would listen to her need. Both she and the daughter seemed to be powerless in the presence of the demon. What an example this dear woman has become for a multitude of people down through the centuries.

Pause—wait—think—then express yourself in thoughtful praise or thanks.

9. READ HIS WORD FOR PETITIONS.

In the entreaties of this Canaanite woman we can learn how to pray: (1) My Lord wanted and needed a place to rest and pray—help me to find such a place. (2) It would seem to all too many your presence is a secret—I want you to be the most conspicuous person in my life. (3) May my inner spirit-needs be as urgent as was the physical/ spiritual need of this woman. (4) May I in truth—not just word—fall at your feet in worship and prayer. (5) Lord, you know how unworthy any one of us is to appear before you—have mercy upon me. (6) Deliver me from the evil one.

Right here add your personal requests—and his answers.

10. READ HIS WORD AND WAIT—LISTEN—GOD SPEAKS!

Since my Lord saw such an example in this woman, I know you can speak to me in these verses: (1) "Neither I nor demons have died since this incident." (2) "My mercy endures forever." (3) "I honor faith and love today as then."

11. INTERCESSION FOR THE LOST WORLD

Jordan — Point for prayer: (1) *The Protestant Church.* There is much nominalism among the second and third generation Christians. Yet among the Bible believing groups there is revival in some congregations and many people are being converted—especially Muslims. The most common source of new converts is from the many home fellowships where the unsaved feel more at ease. Pray that the believers may be sensitive, open and loving to those converted out of a Muslim background, for many of these converts find it hard to settle in a church fellowship.

12. SING PRAISES TO OUR LORD.

Come, we that love the Lord,
And let our joys be known;

Join in a song with sweet accord,
And thus surround the throne.

WEEK FIFTY-TWO — TUESDAY

1. PRAISE GOD FOR WHO HE IS.

"Praise him with trumpet sound; praise him with lute and harp" (Psalm 150:3). It will be a blessing to try to contemplate just how we shall praise you as indicated in this verse. The trumpets were used on ocassions to call the congregation of Israel together. How we do need to lift up our voices like trumpets and let the whole world know that you are King and worthy of our worship. At times trumpets were used to sound an alarm. If ever there was a time when such a blast needs to be given it is now. The lute and harp were used in the worship in the temple. Perhaps we could say that if we are occupied with singing the songs of Zion we will be prepared when Gabriel sounds the trumpet call for the King. There are so many beautiful songs of praise and I enjoy singing every one.

Express yourself in adoration for this quality of God.
Speak it audibly or write out your praise in your own devotional journal.

2. PRAISE GOD FOR WHAT HE MEANS TO ME.

The variety involved appeals to me as expressive of the praise I can bring to you. The trumpet is for the public announcement. I do indeed want all men to know of your greatness and goodness. The lute and harp were used for smaller groups or even for private use. How glad I am to share with classes your mercy and love, and to lift my heart even now in personal praise. The variety involved in using these instruments is meaningful to me: some of them are sounded by blowing wind into them, some by touching the strings, some by beating on them. All of the instruments give the certain sound of praise to your holy name! How I do enjoy being innovative in my expression of praise to you.

How do you personally relate to the beauty of God, and God who is beauty itself?
Speak it out or write it out. It is *so important* that you establish *your own* devotional journal.

3. CONFESSION OF SIN

The trumpet lies unused; the lute and the harp gather dust. So is at times the condition of my heart. I am glad to say that such is less and less frequent. At the same time I need to lift up the trumpet far more often; the joyful music of the lute and harp need to be heard every day in praise to your name. I could blame fatigue for my lack of urgency but I hear Paul say to me "Be urgent in season and out of season." My expressions might not always be as bright and clear as other times but I want to lift up praise to you in the out of season days as well as in the days when it is easy to do. I want to examine my heart and see if my fatigue is sin related. Forgive me and revive me again!

What personal sins do you want to confess? We *must* speak them to remove them.
Do it! *Now.* There is no one else you have sinned against more than God. Tell him so!

4. SING A PRAYER TO GOD.

Come, ev'ry soul by sin oppressed,
There's mercy with the Lord,
And He will surely give you rest
By trusting in His word.

Only trust Him, only trust Him,
Only trust him now.
He will save you, He will save you,
He will save you now.

Open your hymn book and sing the rest of the verses — or even sing another prayer song.

5. READ HIS WORD TO HIM!

His Word

[23]Jesus did not answer a word. So his disciples came to him and urged him, "Send her away, for she keeps crying out after us."
[24]He answered, "I was sent only to the lost sheep of Israel."
[25]The woman came and knelt before him. "Lord, help me!" she said.
[26]He replied, "It is not right to take the children's bread and toss it to their dogs."
[27]"Yes, Lord," she said, "but even the dogs eat the crumbs that fall from their masters' table."
[28]Then Jesus answered, "Woman, you have great faith! Your request is granted." And her daughter was healed from that very hour.   — *Matthew 15:23-28, NIV*
[27]"First let the children eat all they want," he told her, "for it is not right to take the children's bread and toss it to their dogs."
[28]"Yes, Lord" she replied, "but even the dogs under the table eat the children's crumbs."
[29]Then he told her, "For such a reply, you may go; the demon has left your daughter."
[30]She went home and found her child lying on the bed, and the demon gone.   — *Mark 7:27-30, NIV*

Read His Word to Him.

I want this whole record before me so I can as much as possible absorb every word. This is a strange response from your Son. Knowing the character of our Lord we wonder all over again if he had not planned all of this. Is he trying to say something to the nation of Israel? He treats this urgent woman with the indifference the Jews gave the Gentiles to help them to see how much confidence one, who had but little opportunity, placed in him. The disciples, as usual, misread our Lord's intentions and wanted to send her away. Jesus said all the right words as he typified the Jewish attitude: "lost sheep of the house of Israel"; "dogs." The woman had an immediate appropriate answer. Dear Father, I do hope I have read this aright!

Please express your response to this beautiful text. Put your expression in your own prayer diary.

6. READ HIS WORD FOR YOURSELF.

Is there something in my life that will call out such urgency as found in this woman? Do I have a need that can not be handled by myself? These questions are all *wrong*, or at least 90% wrong. The woman's concern was *not* for herself, but for someone else. Am I as ready to receive rebuff from men — and apparently, even from my Lord, that the need of someone else might be met? To ask is to answer — I do not like the price. The problem is that I have not yet empathized with others as my Lord did — and as this pagan woman did. Dear Lord, forgive!

Pause in his presence and either audibly or in written form tell him all his word means to you.

7. READ HIS WORD IN THANKSGIVING.

Thank you for the strange silence of Jesus — it says so much. (2) Thank you for the urgent persistence of this woman — how I need her consuming concern. (3) Thank you for the ironic rebuke in the statement: "I was sent only to the lost sheep of Israel." (4) Thank you for One lost sheep — not even in Israel that wanted to be found. (5) Thank you for the test my Lord gave the woman in his words about the bread.

Give yourself to your own expression of gratitude — write it or speak it!

8. READ HIS WORD IN MEDITATION.

"And her daughter was healed from that very hour." *"She went home and found her child lying on the bed and the demon gone."* Would that mother ever forget that hour? She would always remember the help given to her daughter, but there was something about the man who healed her she would never forget. The physical presence of our Lord was something with which to be reckoned. The eyes of Jesus must have been wonderfully impressive. When he spoke how did his voice sound? Men and women crowd around a famous man to shake his hand. What would it have been like to shake hands with God in human form?

Pause — wait — think — then express yourself in thoughtful praise or thanks.

9. READ HIS WORD FOR PETITIONS.

What a blessed example of devotion — commitment and faith this woman surely leads me to prayer: (1) When others are quick to say no and turn away, help me to pause and hear behind the words and see beneath the obvious. (2) This woman would not be disuaded even when Jesus defined the limitations of his ministry. She heard more than others did — she caught his attitude — I want to be like her. (3) I kneel before you even now with the same request of the woman: "Lord, help me" (— in the deep needs you know I have). (4) Is Jesus asking the woman to be classified as "a dog"? If so, she was ready. I am too — but I still need your help.

Please, please remember these are prayers — speak them — reword them!

10. READ HIS WORD AND WAIT — LISTEN — GOD SPEAKS!

I am as unworthy as this woman — but speak to me, end my need: (1) "There are no needs that cannot be met with your faith and my word." (2) "I have a whole banquet of food for your whole life." (3) "When you ask on behalf of others you help yourself first."

11. INTERCESSION FOR THE LOST WORLD

Jordan — Point for prayer: (1) *Outreach by believers* has increased recently. More and more young people have been enthused and involved in door-to-door visitation and tract distribution. Pray for the right Christian leaders to be raised up who can continue to teach young believers how to reach out to others with the Gospel.

12. SING PRAISES TO OUR LORD.

Face to face I shall behold Him,
Far beyond the starry sky;

Face to face in all His glory,
I shall see Him by and by!

WEEK FIFTY-TWO — WEDNESDAY

1. PRAISE GOD FOR WHO HE IS.

"Praise him with timbrel and dance; praise him with strings and pipe! (Psalm 150:4). In this time of worship my whole purpose is to lift an attribute of yourself up as a means of praise and adoration. I want to be as objective as at all possible. It would appear that there is something in yourself that creates a joy that is best expressed in music and dancing. Why were the people of David's day so happy? Was it because they lived in a land of freedom and plenty?

Was their joy and exuberance from the forgiveness promised in the sacrifices? In all of these ways and many more we have reason to be full of joy and gladness. We sometimes become so full of happiness that physical expression seems the only natural expression. We want the music to be our voice of joy and praise. The dancing is an individual expression. We are not dancing for each other but for you.

Express yourself in adoration for this quality of God.
Speak it audibly or write out your praise in your own devotional journal.

2. PRAISE GOD FOR WHAT HE MEANS TO ME.

Dear Lord, I do want to enter into this expression of praise. Do I honestly have reason to be so exceedingly happy? Indeed I do! Let me list just a few reasons for such joy: (1) All my sins are forgiven and forgotten and cannot in any way be held against me — I am totally, wholly free from guilt! I should be dancing for joy! (2) I can just as freely and fully forgive from the heart others who have sinned against me. I can and do forget what others have

said or done against me. I can and do sustain the "no condemnation" attitude toward all men. Oh what a relief! What a lightness fills my heart! (3) I have a whole new life and world prepared for me when I lay aside this worn out garment called my body. The wonder and anticipation of this adventure is surely enough to get out the timbrel or pipe!

How do you personally relate to the joy of God, and God who wants us happy?
Speak it out or write it out. It is *so important* that you establish *your own* devotional journal.

3. CONFESSION OF SIN

How sad it is when there are so many reasons for praise and happiness we are complaining and griping about matters that really do not matter. Dear Lord, forgive me! Forgive me for thinking of sins when you have forgotten them. It is Satan's delight to torment us with that which is only imaginary. If the evil one has a sense of humor this must be an expression of it. Remind me again and

again that "as the Lord forgave you, so you are to forgive each other." I really have no rights at all. I gave them up to my Lord when he bought me on Calvary. Dear Lord, keep my eyes off of that which is so near. When I fasten my attention on the problems and complexities of this life I surely do forget the life to come. I want that wonderful present transformation by the renewing of my mind!

What personal sins do you want to confess? We *must* speak them to remove them.
Do it! *Now.* There is no one else you have sinned against more than God. Tell him so!

4. SING A PRAYER TO GOD.

"Man of Sorrows," what a name
For the Son of God who came

Ruined sinners to reclaim!
Hallelujah! what a Savior!

Open your hymn book and sing the rest of the verses — or even sing another prayer song.

5. READ HIS WORD TO HIM!

His Word

31 Then Jesus left the vicinity of Tyre and went through Sidon, down to the Sea of Galilee and into the region of Decapolis. 32 There some people brought a man to him who was deaf and could hardly talk, and they begged him to place his hand on the man. 33 After he took him aside, away from the crowd, Jesus put his fingers into the man's ears. Then he spit and touched the man's tongue. 34 He looked up to heaven and with a deep sigh said to him, *"Ephphatha!"* (which means, "Be opened!"). 35 At this, the man's ears were opened, his tongue was loosened and he began to speak plainly.

36 Jesus commanded them not to tell anyone. But the more he did so, the more they kept talking about it.
— *Mark 7:31-36, NIV*

29 Jesus left there and went along the Sea of Galilee. Then he went up into the hills and sat down. 30 Great crowds came to him, bringing the lame, the blind, the crippled, the dumb and many others, and laid them at his feet; and he healed them. 31 The people were amazed when they saw the dumb speaking, the crippled made well, the lame walking and the blind seeing. And they praised the God of Israel. — *Matthew 15:29-31, NIV*

WEEK FIFTY-TWO — WEDNESDAY

Read His Word to Him.

I do want to walk with his disciples on the long trip from Tyre through Sidon down to the mountain near the sea of Galilee. There were several miles and days involved in this whole episode. What did he teach them on the way? We shall really never know this side of seeing him and asking those who were with him. We are sure they will be able to remember much, i.e. considering the wonderful details both Matthew and Mark give us here. Among the many who were healed we are told of a deaf man who had an impediment in his speech. How kindly and thoughtfully does our Lord work with this man!

Please express your response to this beautiful text. Put your expression in your own prayer diary.

6. READ HIS WORD FOR YOURSELF.

Why did Jesus separate this man from the multitude? Because there was a need in the man's heart that would be met by doing this. How helpful our Lord was: He gave the man a visual aid in placing his fingers in his own ears and moistening his fingers with his own saliva; and then lifting his face toward heaven in a gesture of adoration. How intently the deaf man was watching Jesus we can only imagine. Did the deaf man hear that wonderful word, "Ephphatha"? We would like to think he did—for it was his ears that were opened—it was his tongue that was loosed!

Pause in his presence and either audibly or in written form tell him all his word means to you.

7. READ HIS WORD IN THANKSGIVING.

(1) Thank you for the great crowds who came—they could hear and be healed. (2) Thank you for the variety of sickness healed: (a) blind; (b) crippled; (c) dumb—no exceptions—*all* were healed. (3) Thank you for the spontaneous amazement of the people. (4) Thank you that we can do greater works and praise you for it. (5) Thank you that Jesus manipulated no one—all his work was spontaneous. (6) Thank you for the constant personal concern Jesus had in his ministry of healing and teaching. (7) Thank you for the overwhelming amazement of the people.

Give yourself to your own expression of gratitude—write it or speak it!

8. READ HIS WORD IN MEDITATION.

"He has done everything well." What was meant here was that the miracles of Jesus were so very satisfying to everyone. There were no questions not answered, no failure to meet the needs of those present. It could have indeed applied to his whole life. He has done everthing with no loose ends! How easy it is to neglect some area of our experience—but not so with Jesus! "He has done everything well" in the teaching realm. His writings through his penman have been under scrutiny for over 1900 years and this is indeed the concensus. "He has done everything well" in the real purpose of his coming—i.e. to provide salvation for all men.

Pause—wait—think—then express yourself in thoughtful praise or thanks.

9. READ HIS WORD FOR PETITIONS.

As Jesus meets the needs of these multitudes of people I want him to meet my needs. I ask him: (1) As you looked into the heart of each man and each woman and gave them just what they needed, I believe you are doing the same today for me and all others. (2) How lame I am in areas of service—heal me—make me strong. (3) I have been so blind in several places—you have opened my eyes—but they need to be opened again and again. (4) How feeble are our best efforts—heal this cripple in teaching and preaching and writing.

Right here add your personal requests—and his answers.

10. READ HIS WORD AND WAIT—LISTEN—GOD SPEAKS!

How I do want you to open my ears and my mouth! Speak to me: (1) "I have you as much on my heart—as a separate person as I did the man in this text." (2) "I have greater works for you and through you than you read about in these texts." (3) "I can and do heal the whole person."

11. INTERCESSION FOR THE LOST WORLD

Jordan — Point for prayer: (1) *Christian leadership*— mature Christian leaders are urgently needed for the many opportunities for ministry that there now are. Unfortunately too many of the best men tend to go to America.

12. SING PRAISES TO OUR LORD.

Fairest Lord Jesus! Ruler of all nature!
O Thou of God and man the Son!

Thee will I cherish, Thee will I honor,
Thou, my soul's glory, joy, and crown!

WEEK FIFTY-TWO — THURSDAY

1. PRAISE GOD FOR WHO HE IS.

"Praise him with sounding cymbals; praise him with loud clashing cymbals!" (Psalm 150:5). Why are cymbals mentioned twice if the same instrument is intended? Dear Lord, you are the only one who truly knows what is meant. But I believe David is talking of two types of cymbals. Perhaps the first were finely tuned smaller instruments and the second were the larger ones used by both hands. There is one meaning that comes across with no hesitancy:

as you want all nature to recognize its creator in its praise so you want man to employ all means available to him to praise you. It would seem here that you are saying that there are times when loud exclamations are in order. There is a time to shout for joy. There is a place for a crescendo of joy! Dear Lord, I want to sound my cymbals in your presence this very morning.

Speak audibly or write out your praise in your own devotional journal.

2. PRAISE GOD FOR WHAT HE MEANS TO ME.

How limited and confined to say nothing of hindered we are by convention. It is just not the thing to do, so we do not do it. We have been reading the wrong book for conduct. Your word in describing our expressions of praise plainly recommends the use of "sounding cymbals" and "loud clashing cymbals." Whereas this was a part of the worship in the Old Testament I see it as a good example of how we could express our joy today when our joy is

commensurate to the use of these instruments. My problem is that I do not feel as exuberant as the use of these instruments would suggest. There is however a reciprocal action involved here. Perhaps if I decided to use such means of praise I could soon suit my praise to the cymbals. It is always good for me to act on my convictions and let my feelings follow.

How do you personally relate to the music of God, and God who wants our praise?
Speak it out or write it out. It is *so important* that you establish *your own* devotional journal.

3. CONFESSION OF SIN

How shall I confess my failure to praise you? Is it even necessary to make such a confession? Indeed it is! It is in this area I find both my greatest blessing and my greatest sin. If I read what you have given to us aright the intelligent beings in your presence are occupied with little else than praise and adoration. This says much to me. There must be something constantly and increasingly wonderful before them or they would not so respond. No one is

forcing such angels and men to praise you. Their praise is a response to the wonder and excitement that meets their eyes and ears and mind. I have a beautiful choice today: I can expose myself to your word and there find reason piled upon reason to praise you; or I can pick up a magazine or turn on the TV and turn my heart away from you. Forgive me; help me.

What personal sins do you want to confess? We *must* speak them to remove them.
Do it! *Now.* There is no one else you have sinned against more than God. Tell him so!

4. SING A PRAYER TO GOD.

Come, Thou Fount of ev'ry blessing,
Tune my heart to sing Thy grace;
Streams of mercy, never ceasing,
Call for songs of loudest praise.

Teach me some melodious sonnet,
Sung by flaming tongues above;
Praise the mount — I'm fixed upon it —
Mount of Thy redeeming love.

Open your hymn book and sing the rest of the verses — or even sing another prayer song.

5. READ HIS WORD TO HIM!

His Word

[32]Jesus called his disciples to him and said, "I have compassion for these people; they have already been with me three days and have nothing to eat. I do not want to send them away hungry, or they may collapse on the way."

[33]His disciples answered, "Where could we get enough bread in this remote place to feed such a crowd?"

[34]"How many loaves do you have?" Jesus asked.

"Seven," they replied, "and a few small fish."

[35]He told the crowd to sit down on the ground. [36]Then he

took the seven loaves and the fish, and when he had given thanks, he broke them and gave them to the disciples, and they in turn to the people. [37]They all ate and were satisfied. Afterward the disciples picked up seven basketfuls of broken pieces that were left over. [38]The number of those who ate was four thousand, besides women and children.
— *Matthew 15:32-38, NIV*

Read also Mark 8:1-9a.

Read His Word to Him.

These two accounts are so very similar that I want to consider them as one. At the same time I want to read

them just as if I had never read them before. This is a crowd in which a majority could be Gentiles. It is the dry season because they are going to sit not on the grass as in the feeding of the 5,000, but on the "ground." There do indeed seem to be several reasons why my Lord repeated the astounding miracle of the creation of food: (1) It deals with the basic element of deity—*creation*. There is little point in saying the seven loaves and a few fish were increased in number—the *increase* was *something out of nothing!* (2) It reinforced the conviction of the apostles that he was indeed and in truth "Emmanuel."

Please express your response to this beautiful text. Put your expression in your own prayer diary.

6. READ HIS WORD FOR YOURSELF.

As I with the disciples begin to gather the leftovers would I not be very, very thoughtful? What would I think? Perhaps: "He is always so modest and humble about all he does! He could have really made a sensation out of this meal, but now it is over—I wonder how many men in the four thousand even knew what happened? Perhaps just as many as He wanted to know, i.e. those who had eyes to see and ears to hear." We could say that 1900 years this side of the incident many more than 4,000 have understood what happened. Praise your name.

Pause in his presence and either audibly or in written form tell him all his word means to you.

7. READ HIS WORD IN THANKSGIVING.

(1) Thank you for the unfailing compassion of my Lord. (2) Thank you that my heart hunger can always be satisfied by him. (3) Thank you for the challenge of no provisions—out of this can glory come to our Lord. (4) Thank you that Jesus always thanked you before he ate—what an example! (5) Thank you that in thanksgiving there is creation. (6) Thank you that we are always in the distribution business in your program of feeding this hungry world. (7) Thank you that nothing is wasted or lost when you create it.

Give yourself to your own expression of gratitude—write it or speak it!

8. READ HIS WORD IN MEDITATION.

"They all ate and were satisfied." How beautifully does this phrase describe all those who will eat of the bread come down from heaven. What lessons we can learn here: (1) Our Lord alone can give us this bread. The exclusiveness of Jesus is apparent on the surface. He brooks no competitors—indeed he has none! (2) He expects us to look beyond the bread to the One who gave it—indeed we do! (3) This bread, like all bread, must be eaten every day. Yesterday's supply was only adequate for yesterday. It is for today—for right now that I must eat.

Pause—wait—think—then express yourself in thoughtful praise or thanks.

9. READ HIS WORD FOR PETITIONS.

Why did our Lord twice feed in a miraculous act thousands of people? There is in the answer many areas for prayer: (1) It was because of your compassion for these people that he fed them. Is feeding the multitude an indication of my compassion or a satisfaction of my ego? Examine my heart, dear Lord. (2) These people were so interested in what Jesus taught they went without food for three days. How total is my interest in his words? (3) Jesus knew the depth of interest as well as need—oh, dear Lord, deepen both qualities in me. (4) Jesus fed people with what *they* had and *he* had—not one without the other. Teach me from this.

Please, please remember these are prayers—speak them—reword them!

10. READ HIS WORD AND WAIT—LISTEN—GOD SPEAKS!

How well you feed us when we come to you with our hunger. Speak to me: (1) "Creating eternal food for the hungry from my word is your job today." (2) "Satisfaction is guaranteed when you eat of the bread from heaven." (3) "Thank me for the living bread."

11. INTERCESSION FOR THE LOST WORLD

Jordan — Point for prayer: (1) *Missionary work* is still needed and is a great encouragement to the national believers. Great tact and a low profile is needed in these times when a foreigner is under suspicion and often far less free to minister than the nationals. Several missionaries have recently been expelled. There are now about 14 mission agencies and 60 missionaries in the country. This number is increasing since many literature, radio and other ministries could no longer carry on in strife-torn Lebanon.

12. SING PRAISES TO OUR LORD.

"Man of Sorrows," what a name
For the Son of God who came
Ruined sinners to reclaim!
Hallelujah! what a Savior!

WEEK FIFTY-TWO — FRIDAY

1. PRAISE GOD FOR WHO HE IS.

"Let everything that breathes praise the Lord! Praise the Lord!" (Psalm 150:6). What shall we say of yourself in this closing verse of these beautiful songs? You have created every intelligent creature in such a manner that it seems altogether right to lift our hearts to you in expression of praise and adoration. How beyond human expression will be the world to come when all angels and men lift their voices in one incredible chorus of praise! But this is no more than what should be done. It is good to contemplate the use of instruments of music enlisted to express praise to you. It is better to see man forming the words of praise in his mind and lifting them through his voice before yourself.

Express yourself in adoration for this quality of God.
Speak it audibly or write out your praise in your own devotional journal.

2. PRAISE GOD FOR WHAT HE MEANS TO ME.

In all of the above words I have tried to express what I consider the most obvious response man could and should make to your greatness and goodness, but just now I want to praise you for the reasons I have to lift my voice in praise: (1) The intricate and beautiful design and purpose I see all about me in the world in which I live. The more I contemplate the plant life — the shape and color of flowers the more impressed I am with the One who made them all. (2) The marvelous subtleties of your work in my life — and I can extend such work to every life. In a thousand ways you have prepared my life for this very hour.

How do you personally relate to the absoluteness of God, and God who is All?
Speak it out or write it out. It is *so important* that you establish *your own* devotional journal.

3. CONFESSION OF SIN

Dear Lord, the above being true why should I not spend most of my time meditating upon the meaning of your word? I am glad, *delighted* for the time you have given me — and for the wonderful opportunities you have given to share with others — but how much better could my track record be if only I would have it so. Somehow I want to find more time to memorize your word. I have committed some to memory but there is so much more I could do. Forgive me for this sin against the development of your praise in my heart.

What personal sins do you want to confess? We *must* speak them to remove them.
Do it! *Now.* There is no one else you have sinned against more than God. Tell him so!

4. SING A PRAYER TO GOD.

Thou, my everlasting portion,
More than friend or life to me;
All along my pilgrim journey,
Savior, let me walk with Thee.

Close to Thee, close to Thee,
Close to Thee, close to Thee;
All along my pilgrim journey,
Savior, let me walk with Thee.

Open your hymn book and sing the rest of the verses — or even sing another prayer song.

5. READ HIS WORD TO HIM!

His Word

16 The Pharisees and Sadducees came to Jesus and tested him by asking him to show them a sign from heaven.

²He replied, "When evening comes, you say, 'It will be fair weather, for the sky is red,' ³and in the morning, 'Today it will be stormy, for the sky is red and overcast.' You know how to interpret the appearance of the sky, but you cannot interpret the signs of the times. ⁴A wicked and adulterous generation looks for a miraculous sign, but none will be given it except the sign of Jonah." Jesus then left them and went away.   — *Matthew 16:1-4, NIV*

And having sent them away, ¹⁰he got into the boat with his disciples and went to the region of Dalmanutha.

¹¹The Pharisees came and began to question Jesus. To test him, they asked him for a sign from heaven. ¹²He sighed deeply and said, "Why does this generation ask for a miraculous sign? I tell you the truth, no sign will be given to it."
     — *Mark 8:9b-12, NIV*

Read His Word to Him.

I am shocked! How did the Pharisees and the Sadducees get together? Surely this is an indication of the power and influence of the ministry of our Lord. The Sadducees did not even believe in such supernatural occurrences. Had any of these men been present when he performed one of the several thousand signs in his healing ministry? Had these men bothered to interview any who were either eye witnesses or actual participants in the signs he had already given? To ask is to answer. The real answer is: They did not want a sign; they wanted to discredit the signmaker. The answer our Lord gave indicates he knew their motives. Dear Lord, deliver me from this same syndrome.

Please express your response to this beautiful text. Put your expression in your own prayer diary.

6. READ HIS WORD FOR YOURSELF.

I do want to hear with my heart the answer of my Lord. What was common knowledge concerning weather conditions in Palestine was used as an analogy by Jesus. The logic is devastating! He is saying you can read cause and effect in an area where you are not experts, i.e. the weather —but in the realm where you have had training you cannot put cause and effect together! Essentially Jesus is saying to these men what he says to me and to all: "I have presented my credentials. How many copies do you need?" If you won't belive the first copy why would you believe the three thousandth copy? I am not on trial—*you are!*" He reminds them (and us) that the "sign of Jonah" will convince or you will not be convinced. Praise your name, I am convinced!

It is so important that you pause in his presence
and either audibly or in written form tell him all his word means to you.

7. READ HIS WORD IN THANKSGIVING.

(1) Thank you that Jesus shocks the modernist and the fundamentalist—we must *hear him!* (2) Thank you that Jesus was not on trial—these men were. (3) Thank you we can all be weathermen—we *know* what the signs say. (4) Thank you that his signs are for *all time!* (5) Thank you that Jesus has no hesitancy in pronouncing a generation evil and adulterous. (6) Thank you that Jesus separated disbelief and unbelief—we *can* believe *if* we *want* to. (7) Thank you that Jesus did leave and walked away from some people—(I need to be careful in following this example.)

Give yourself to your own expression of gratitude—write it or speak it!

8. READ HIS WORD IN MEDITATION.

"Jesus then left them and went away." "Then he left them, got into the boat and crossed to the other side." Jesus did leave the scene of action. He left more sick than he healed; he left more who did not believe than those who accepted him. Several thoughts are suggested by this fact: (1) His primary purpose was not to empty hospitals or graveyards. (He will do that when he comes again.) He came to let us know who he was not what he could do. (2) He expects us to carry on where he left off. After all, we are the body of himself. He has sent his Spirit into us that we might have the life necessary for this tremendous task. (3) He left because remaining did no good. For those who disbelieve—for those who refuse this becomes the only recourse. How do we stand before him?

Pause—wait—think—then express yourself in thoughtful praise or thanks.

9. READ HIS WORD FOR PETITIONS.

Seekers after signs! Is this different than those who seek the miraculous? There are surely lessons for prayer here: (1) The Pharisees and Sadducees could not agree— how could they agree on a sign? Help me never to come with the request that I "call the shots" on any subject. (2) There was a fatal flaw in the evaluating capacity of these men. May I see it ever so clearly and avoid it! (3) I am so glad that there could be a generation that was not "wicked and adulterous"—I want to be a part of it. (4) Just what is it I seek from you? Your Lordship or my own vanity? Examine my heart! (5) What a wonder is "the sign of Jonah"! How I want to fully learn from it.

Right here add your personal requests—and his answers.

10. READ HIS WORD AND WAIT—LISTEN—GOD SPEAKS!

I am constantly aware that I could be "just religious" like these men who came to Jesus. Speak to me: (1) "Seek me, not my signs and you will find all you need." (2) "Faith is a decision of the will—not the emotions." (3) "My resurrection will answer all the questions as to my deity."

11. INTERCESSION FOR THE LOST WORLD

Jordan — Point for prayer: (1) *Many Lebanese took refuge in Jordan* in 1975-6. Pray that many may be brought to the Lord through their insecurity and sorrow. Many of these people are nominally Christian. Pray that the true believers among them may have courage to testify.

12. SING PRAISES TO OUR LORD.

When I saw the cleansing fountain
Open wide for all my sin,
I obeyed the Spirit's wooing,
When He said, Wilt thou be clean?

I will praise Him! I will praise Him!
Praise the Lamb for sinners slain;
Give Him glory, all ye people,
For His blood can wash away each stain.

WEEK FIFTY-TWO — SATURDAY

1. PRAISE GOD FOR WHO HE IS.

"But whoso hearkeneth unto me shall dwell securely, and shall be quiet without fear of evil" (Proverbs 1:33). In this comforting verse is the wonderful fact that you are concerned about man's conduct. This is such a basic assumption that we often forget it. I take great courage in your interest in my life—and the lives of all men. Another equally meaningful fact is that we can understand what you say. In this *a priori* assumption is the important truth that you expect man to form in his mind from your words just what was in your mind. Moreover you are going to hold man responsible for responding properly to what you have said. Security and quietness can be ours when we open our ears and heart and receive your word.

Express yourself in adoration for this quality of God.
Speak it audibly or write out your praise in your own devotional journal.

2. PRAISE GOD FOR WHAT HE MEANS TO ME.

Over this entire year I have each day tried to do just what the wiseman Solomon here recommends. I have surely not always hearkened as well as I should, but I have been eager to read most carefully what you have written. How I praise you for the fulfillment of your promise—a deep sense of security and quietness has pervaded my life. I do not fear evil; I do fear the Evil One. I fear you much more. In both uses of the term "fear" a source of awe is meant. I have a sense of dread in relation to Satan—a sense of wonder in your presence. But I do not fear evil because I know it is under your control and I am hiding in you. Praise is my natural response to such a relationship.

How do you personally relate to the fear of God, and God who is our security?
Speak it out or write it out. It is *so important* that you establish *your own* devotional journal.

3. CONFESSION OF SIN

I am so glad to observe some improvement in my response to stressful circumstances. (I just had one yesterday.) I believe it is a direct result of each day opening my mind and heart to your word. Whatever security and quietness I have comes from you by this means. At the same time, I am a long way from where I want to be and you want me to be in my daily awareness of the application of your counsel in my life. Forgive me for wilful selfishness. I am sometimes selfish and do not know it until it is pointed out to me—but when I can choose and the choice is for self—dear Lord, forgive! My security and quietness are upset. Thank you for helping me to see the cause and effect in such a situation.

What personal sins do you want to confess? We *must* speak them to remove them.
Do it! *Now.* There is no one else you have sinned against more than God. Tell him so!

4. SING A PRAYER TO GOD.

Under His wings I am safely abiding;
Tho' the night deepens and tempests are wild,
Still I can trust Him; I know He will keep me;
He has redeemed me, and I am His child.

Under His wings, under His wings,
Who from His love can sever?
Under His wings my soul shall abide,
Safely abide forever.

Open your hymn book and sing the rest of the verses—or even sing another prayer song.

5. READ HIS WORD TO HIM!

His Word

⁵When they went across the lake, the disciples forgot to take bread. ⁶"Be careful," Jesus said to them. "Be on your guard against the yeast of the Pharisees and Sadducees."

⁷They discussed this among themselves and said, "It is because we didn't bring any bread."

⁸Aware of their discussion, Jesus asked, "You of little faith, why are you talking among yourselves about having no bread? ⁹Do you still not understand? Don't you remember the five loaves for the five thousand, and how many basketfuls you gathered? ¹⁰Or the seven loaves for the four thousand, and how many basketfuls you gathered? ¹¹How is it you don't understand that I was not talking to you about bread? But be on your guard against the yeast of the Pharisees and Sadducees." ¹²Then they understood that he was not telling them to guard against the yeast used in bread, but against the teaching of the Pharisees and Sadducees. — *Matthew 16:5-12, NIV*

Read His Word to Him.

How dull of hearing were these disciples! As learners they were slow indeed! How synchronized were all the words of Jesus to the thinking and conversation of those with whom he sailed! His words seemed so appropriate — and yet they missed the point. How very much like many present disciples. Our Lord is so infinitely kind in his rebuke! He reminds them that if he could feed 5,000 with five loaves and 4,000 with seven loaves he could feed those in the boat with one loaf. At the same time he wants them to understand he is talking about the evil influence in the teaching of these men under the figure of bread and leaven. How I do need both lessons!

Please express your response to this beautiful text. Put your expression in your own prayer diary.

6. READ HIS WORD FOR YOURSELF.

Dear Lord, I do indeed want to *beware* of the strong, rapidly spreading influence of false teaching. I wonder just what the danger was in the warning of my Lord? I can think of several possibilities: (1) Their position and influence would lend prestige to what they said and more people to accept it regardless of how strange it sounded. If history is a teacher then she would say that those in authority are usually wrong when acting as theologians. (2) When three opposing sides unite against one person jealousy and envy are behind it. The leaven of envy has cut off the head of more than John the Baptist.

It is so important that you pause in his presence
and either audibly or in written form tell him all his word means to you.

7. READ HIS WORD IN THANKSGIVING.

(1) Thank you for extremities which can always become your opportunities. (2) Thank you for the beautiful figure of *bread* used so often. (3) Thank you for the sharp clear warning of my Lord that there *are* false teachers. (4) Thank you for the patience of Jesus in teaching the disciples — how we need his patience today! (5) Thank you that we can indeed remember what happened with the 5,000 and the 4,000! (6) Thank you that Jesus pointed to himself as the object of their faith. (7) Thank you that the disciples finally did understand.

Give yourself to your own expression of gratitude — write it or speak it!

8. READ HIS WORD IN MEDITATION.

". . . *guard against the teachings of the Pharisees and Sadducees.*" This strong statement presupposes several things: (1) That the disciples would be able to discern the difference. This is indeed a compliment to the effectiveness of our Lord's teaching. (2) The man himself is judged with his teaching — or we could say his teaching decides his fate. This is one awesome thought. (3) This presupposes that these men were such effective teachers that they would be given consideration. Perhaps their political position added to their acceptance.

Pause — wait — think — then express yourself in thoughtful praise or thanks.

9. READ HIS WORD FOR PETITIONS.

After the feeding of the four thousand one would think that bread would be "up front" in the thinking of these men — but it wasn't — there are obvious points for prayer here: (1) I know at times I am as dense as these men to the real meaning of your words — I claim by faith the wisdom you promised. (2) They forgot bread and didn't understand the bread of which our Lord spoke. Do I really know the deadly danger of humanism and headoism? Open my eyes! (3) Thank you for the time we have (all of us have the same amount) we can use in meditating upon the truth — your word as a guard against error.

Please, please remember these are prayers — speak them — reword them!

10. READ HIS WORD AND WAIT — LISTEN GOD SPEAKS!

In a world full of false teaching I need to hear your voice through your word: (1) "You can know truth from error or I would never have given you truth." (2) "Evil men will and do get worse and worse." (3) "My truth is the mandate of liberty."

11. INTERCESSION FOR THE LOST WORLD

Jordan — Point for prayer: (1) *Literature* — Jordan could become the new literature base for the whole Arab World. Jordanian believers have lately been taking Christian literature into such closed lands as Iraq and Saudi Arabia.

12. SING PRAISES TO OUR LORD.

Sing, oh, sing . . . of my Redeemer,
With His blood . . . He purchased me, . . .
On the cross . . . He sealed my pardon,
Paid the debt, . . . and made me free. . . .